PSYCHOLOGY

John G. Seamon
Wesleyan University

Douglas T. Kenrick
Arizona State University

Prentice Hall, Englewood Cliffs, New Jersey 07632

Library of Congress Cataloging-in-Publication Data

Seamon, John G., (date)
    Psychology / John G. Seamon, Douglas T. Kenrick.
      p.   cm.
    Includes bibliographical references and index.
    ISBN 0-13-735051-1
    1. Psychology. I. Kenrick, Douglas T. II. Title.
BF121.S398 1992
150—dc20   91-28886
                           CIP

Editor-in-Chief/Acquisitions Editor: Charlyce Jones Owen
Development Editor: Leslie Carr
Production Editor: Barbara Reilly
Marketing Manager: Tracey Masella McPeake
Copy Editor: Joanne Palmer
Design Director: Florence Dara Silverman
Designers: Lydia Gershey/Anne T. Bonanno
Cover Designer: CIRCA 86
Page Layout: Karen Noferi
Prepress Buyers: Debra Kesar/Kelly Behr
Manufacturing Buyer: Mary Ann Gloriande
Supplements Editor: Sharon Chambliss
Editorial Assistant: Marion Gottlieb
Cover and Title Page Art: © 1955 M. C. Escher/Cordon Art-Baarn-Holland.
Photo Researcher: Alice Lundoff
Line Art Studio: Network Graphics
Medical Illustrator: Alan Landau

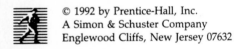

© 1992 by Prentice-Hall, Inc.
A Simon & Schuster Company
Englewood Cliffs, New Jersey 07632

Printed in the United States of America

10 9 8 7 6 5 4 3 2 1

ISBN 0-13-735051-1

Prentice-Hall International (UK) Limited, *London*
Prentice-Hall of Australia Pty. Limited, *Sydney*
Prentice-Hall Canada Inc., *Toronto*
Prentice-Hall Hispanoamericana, S. A., *Mexico*
Prentice-Hall of India Private Limited, *New Delhi*
Prentice-Hall of Japan, Inc., *Tokyo*
Simon & Schuster Asia Pte. Ltd., *Singapore*
Editora Prentice-Hall do Brasil, Ltda., *Rio de Janeiro*

To Our Sons

Eric and Mark

David

A dragon lives forever, but not so little boys.
Painted wings and giant rings make way for other toys.
(from *Puff, the Magic Dragon*
by Peter Yarrow and Leonard Lipton)

ABOUT THE AUTHORS

John Seamon is Professor of Psychology at Wesleyan University. After graduating from Columbia University, he received his Ph.D. in Cognitive Processes from the University of Massachusetts, Amherst, in 1971. The following year he completed a post-doctoral fellowship at New York University and then joined the faculty at Wesleyan. Since 1972, John Seamon has spent sabbaticals at Rockefeller University and Yale University, and he has served as chair of the psychology department at Wesleyan for many years. He has published widely in the field of memory in such journals as the *Journal of Experimental Psychology: Learning, Memory, and Cognition; Memory and Cognition;* and *Perception and Psychophysics.* His current research publications focus on working memory, olfactory memory, and the effects of mere exposure on preference and memory judgments. As an outgrowth of his teaching at Wesleyan, John Seamon has authored *Memory and Cognition: An Introduction* and edited *Human Memory: Contemporary Readings.*

Douglas T. Kenrick is Professor in the Environmental and Social Psychology programs at Arizona State University. He received his B.A. from Dowling College and his Ph.D. from Arizona State University. He taught at Montana State University for four years before returning to Arizona State. He has published research on personality and social behavior in such journals as *Psychological Review, Behavioral and Brain Sciences, American Psychologist, Journal of Personality and Social Psychology,* and the *Journal of Experimental Social Psychology.* Much of his current research focuses on gender differences in mating behavior and social cognition, and on person–environment interactions. His theoretical work involves the integration of evolutionary, social learning, and social cognition models into an interactionist framework (which provides a basis for one of the organizing themes in this text). General psychology is his favorite course, and he currently instructs a graduate course on teaching psychology.

CONTENTS

CHAPTER

3

Sensation   77

CHAPTER

6

Learning   195

CHAPTER

9

Intelligence 305

CHAPTER

10

Motivation and Emotion   341

CHAPTER

11

Infant and Child
Development   377

CHAPTER

12

Adolescent and Adult Development   413

CHAPTER

13

Personality   449

CHAPTER

14

Stress, Coping,
and Health   487

CHAPTER

15

Psychological Disorders   519

APPENDIX

The Use of Statistics in Psychology   681

PREFACE

In many ways William James's *Principles of Psychology* (1890) has been the inspiration for this book. James believed that high-level complex concepts could be taught using concrete and interesting examples that even nonexperts could appreciate. At the time, John Dewey predicted that James's book would break down the "superstition" that "every scientific book ought to be a good corpse."

WILLIAM JAMES AND THE THEMES OF MODERN PSYCHOLOGY

The spirit of William James is honored in several ways throughout this book. In Chapter 1, we use the story of James and his brilliant and troubled family to introduce the student to psychology's basic issues. Describing how his brother Henry was also a brilliant author, and how William and his sister Alice shared problems with anxiety and depression, for instance, provides a concrete way to frame the *nature/nurture* issue. We go on to show how James's training in physiology and philosophy, like Wundt's, had an influence on the modern shape of the field, and how his pragmatic philosophy fits with the modern *interplay between basic and applied psychological research.* James was also intellectual grandfather to several themes that have lately generated increasing excitement. The *cognitive and neuropsychological revolutions,* and the increasing number of *attempts to bridge psychology and evolutionary biology,* for instance, both have roots in James's work. In this book, we take an explicitly *interactionist perspective* that connects the major theoretical perspectives. Rather than adopting one perspective, or pitting different perspectives against one another, we try to show how different perspectives are complementary and how together they provide a complete and comprehensive picture of psychological processes.

William James epitomized the breadth of human curiosity. He studied art, medicine, zoology, philosophy, and literature. He was a part of the great intellectual stream that encompassed Newton, Darwin, and Helmholtz, and that had its headwaters in Plato's Academy at Athens in 387 B.C. Since the beginning, humans have puzzled over questions about human nature, about our place in the universe, and about how the human mind is connected to the outside world. Each of the students in a general psychology class, including the biology student interested in the genetics of intelligence, the literature student interested in the eccentricities of James Joyce, the philosophy student interested in what is real and what is not, and the business student interested in personnel placement, shares some of the curiosity that motivated great thinkers from Plato to James.

A COMMON CORE OF INTELLECTUAL CURIOSITY

We wanted to *tap into this common core of intellectual curiosity* that connects our students with the great thinkers. We also wanted to *show where psychology fits into the stream of human knowledge,* and *give the beginning psychology student a solid foundation* to support the wealth of empirical findings that comprises the modern discipline. Finally, we wanted to *show how the field of psychology itself fits together into an integrated whole.*

USING PSYCHOLOGY TO TEACH PSYCHOLOGY

Two general principles from research on memory guided our writing. First, and in line with William James's intuitions, modern research indicates that new material is learned and remembered best when it is connected to existing memory structures with **concrete, vivid, and sensible examples.** We have tried to avoid fictional vignettes like "Jane often wonders why she is very different from her roommate Dick." We have tried instead to use real-world examples that might stimulate other interests of the student. The personality chapter, for instance, introduces the central issues in that area by discussing the similarities and differences between Vincent van Gogh and Paul Gauguin, and the chapter on child development introduces that area by contrasting the family backgrounds of the prodigy John Stuart Mill and the psychopath Charles Manson.

The second principle that guided us is that new material is learned and remembered best when it is presented within *clear and explicit organizational schemas.*

OFFERING STUDENTS A CONCEPTUAL MAP

Students in introductory psychology are often swamped by the mass of specific research findings and mini-explanations and miss the general themes of the field. The student who must make his or her own map of the field from such connections would be in a predicament analogous to that of a foreign visitor asked to draw a map of the United States after being permitted to listen to a number of phone calls between Tucson, Jersey City, Tuscaloosa, and Anchorage. Two special features of this text are designed to give the students conceptual maps that connect the different findings, theories, and levels of analysis:

In Context. Chapter 1 shows how particular research findings are nested within a general set of methods, which are in turn nested within more general theoretical perspectives. By showing finally how the theories are themselves nested within a historical background, we again connect psychology with the wider context of ideas. *In later chapters, instead of simply listing ideas at the end of each chapter, we use this organizing scheme for each summary.*

Interactions. After presenting the major theoretical perspectives in Chapter 1, we show how these perspectives interact to integrate psychology's diverse theoretical perspectives and empirical findings:

1. *Microscopic/Macroscopic:* Students often wonder what the structures of the brain could possibly have to do with behavioral phenomena like depression, or with the even more complex interactions involved in love between two different people or prejudice between two nations. We try to show how the part processes discussed in the separate chapters are connected into a whole organism. For instance, Chapter 2 discusses how hormones and brain structures interact to influence sexual behavior. Chapter 19 discusses how social problems such as overpopulation and environmental destruction involve a level of analysis that moves us beyond the intra-individual focus of psychology and into the domain of sociology.

2. *Organism/Environment:* The experience of seeing yellow can be produced by looking at a field of buttercups or by ingesting a drug that changes the chemistry of the brain. Not only do internal processes such as sensation and perception interact with one another, they do so in the context of continual interaction between the person and his or her environment. For instance, Chapters 10 and 17 both consider how emotional states are reciprocally linked to the social environment: other people not only elicit our emotions, our emotions also influence the reactions of other people.

3. *Proximate/Ultimate:* Why do certain kinds of thoughts and experiences lead reliably to stress or depression? Why are some individuals more prone to the influences of such thoughts and experiences? Why do humans have the capacity for incapacitating depression in the first place? Cognitions and behaviors occur in the present, but are influenced by past learning experiences,

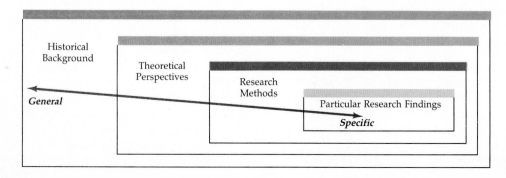

which are themselves influenced by genetically based differences between people. In turn, the range of individual differences between humans has been constrained by the evolutionary history of our particular species. We try to emphasize the interrelationship between these different time frames. In Chapter 15, for instance, we consider how disordered behaviors like depression and psychopathy might be linked not only to early learning experiences, but also to an evolutionary history that would have made less extreme versions of such behaviors pay off for our ancestors under certain circumstances. In this way, our book includes a Jamesian evolutionary perspective, integrated with different topics and theories of the field, rather than segregated in the chapter on biological processes.

FEATURES THAT FLOW FROM THE TEXT NARRATIVE

In keeping with our goal of presenting psychology as a seamless whole, all of the *special features are incorporated into the flow of the text,* rather than interjected as boxed distractions.

Historical Background. Most books relegate all the history of psychology to the first chapter, unwittingly implying that modern psychology is distinct from its historical roots. We include a historical background section in every chapter. In these sections, students will encounter Theophrastus and his descriptions of the "character" types in ancient Athens, Pierre Janet and his discovery that hypnosis could cure a "devil possession," Charles Darwin and his studies of his own child's development, and turn of the century sociologist E.O. Ross and his speculations about mobs and crowds. We use this feature to bring alive the questions asked by the pioneers of each area, and to show how they framed the important issues that we are still grappling with today.

Two other features are designed, in the Jamesian pragmatic tradition, to connect practical problems with basic research. They, too, are part of the text narrative.

Dysfunction. Psychology students are fascinated with disorders. Rather than relegating all of this inherently intriguing material to the clinical chapters, we show how an understanding of the range of psychological processes can help elucidate problems of thought and behavior. In the chapter on

interpersonal relations, for instance, we describe the phenomenon of suicide imitation, and in the chapter on intelligence, we discuss gifted retardates.

Research and Application. This feature provides an in-depth focus on the connection between research and real world problems, and simultaneously exposes students to the critical thinking processes of actual researchers. In the chapter on treatment, for instance, we cover research that raises questions about the popular "self-help" therapies that many students accept uncritically. In the chapter on language and thought, we discuss artificial intelligence.

CURRENT RESEARCH AND AN EMPHASIS ON HUMAN DIVERSITY

In addition to the main themes and integrative features, we focus on a number of current issues that bridge specific areas. For example, *connectionism* is a hot topic in cognitive psychology. We show in Chapter 4 how current work on connectionism provides an up-to-date model of how we recognize pattern and form. In Chapter 7 we show how a connectionist model can help us understand everyday memory phenomena. *Cognitive approaches to the self and social cognition* link basic experimental research in Chapters 4, 5, 7, and 8 with research on motivation and personality (Chapters 10 and 13), disorder and treatment (Chapters 15 and 16) and social behaviors such as prejudice and group conflict (Chapters 17 and 19). In the same way, we discuss *gender differences* across a variety of chapters. In Chapter 2 we discuss possible gender differences in cerebral laterality and brain damage. In Chapter 9 we review gender differences in cognitive ability and suggest that the differences are actually quite small. In Chapters 10, 11, 12, 13, and 18 we discuss gender differences in sexuality, socialization, moral development, marital conflict, personality, aggression, and attraction. *Cultural differences and similarities* in behavior are discussed in Chapter 9 (cross-cultural differences in defining intelligence), Chapter 11 (child-rearing practices), Chapter 13 (personality traits), and Chapter 19 (ethnocentrism and prejudice). Other facets of the nature/nurture issue show up in the discussions of the burgeoning new research on *behavior genetics* (Chapters 1, 9, 11, 13, 15) and *evolutionary psychology* (Chapters 1, 10, 13, 15, 17, 18, and 19).

TELLING THE STORY OF PSYCHOLOGY

In keeping with our emphasis on the deeper organization of psychology, we wanted this book to tell a story. Chapter 1 begins with a quote in which William James puzzles over physiology and inner experience; the final chapter closes with a quote from William McDougall, one of James's functionalist successors at Harvard, who argued that psychology is the essential basis of all the other social sciences. In parallel, the story in this textbook begins with microscopic inner processes and builds block by block towards the macroscopic level of global behavioral problems. Our highest hope is that the student who reads this book will experience the science of psychology as a vital organic whole, rather than as a dissected "corpse."

Finally, there is a general principle we tried to keep in mind while writing this text. It relates to an insight one of us had while reading Mark Twain's *Huckleberry Finn* to his seven-year-old son. Twain's classic tells a story that is fascinating to a young child, while running hand in hand with a level of social commentary that captivates the mature reader. We have tried to emulate Twain in telling a story designed not only to entice the novice, but also to reveal a deep texture that will please the trained eye.

SUPPLEMENTS

Our text is the center of a complete learning and teaching package.

FOR THE INSTRUCTOR

Instructor's Resource Manual A detailed description of the supplements available for each chapter, chapter outlines, learning objectives, activities, questions for writing and discussion, visual/software/audio resources, and in-class demonstrations.

The Integrator A computerized version of the *Instructor's Resource Manual*. The program allows instructors to coordinate chapter resources by computer. *For IBM PCs.*

Teaching Psychology: A Guide for the New Instructor Covers many of the issues and questions related to teaching. Includes an annotated bibliography on teaching and on the various subfields of the discipline, plus articles on current trends in teaching psychology.

Atlas Testing Program Written and reviewed by testing experts, this 2000-item test bank contains multiple-choice and true-false questions keyed by text page reference, learning objective, type of question, and correct answer.

Core Test Item File An additional test bank of approximately 1000 *class-tested* items is organized by major topics and accompanied by item analysis and percentage of responses to each alternative.

TestManager This computerized test bank contains the items from the *Test Item File* and the *Core Test Item File*. It allows full editing of all questions and answers and the addition of instructor-generated items. Other special features include: creating tests by item number or randomly, previewing tests before printing, scrambling question order, and providing content-specific help screens. *For IBM PCs and Macintosh.*

Telephone Testing Service Prentice Hall offers a telephone test preparation service through which instructors call a special toll-free number and select up to 200 questions from the printed test item files available with the text. The test and an alternate version (if requested) are mailed within 48 hours, ready for duplication.

Transparencies/Slides—Series II A set of 120 one-, two-, and four-color illustrations are available in either transparency or slide format.

Handout and Transparency Masters II Over 30 visual resources—reproduceable as handouts, transparencies, or both—emphasize application of key topics discussed in the text.

Laserdisk for Introductory Psychology The two-sided disk contains approximately 500 illustrations and 60 minutes of video material supporting the concepts in the text. An accompanying manual provides bar codes for accessing the visuals and information for integrating the visuals into lectures and classroom activities.

Video Library for Psychology (ABC News/Prentice Hall) Video is the most dynamic supplement you can use to enhance a class. But the quality of the video material and how well it relates to your course still makes all the difference. Prentice Hall and ABC News are now working together to bring you the best and most comprehensive video ancillaries available in the college market.

Through its wide variety of award-winning programs—*Nightline, Business World, 20/20, This Week with David Brinkley, World News Tonight,* and *The Health Show*—ABC offers a resource for feature and documentary-style videos related to the chapters in *Psychology*. The programs have extremely high production quality, present substantial content, and are hosted by well-versed, well-known anchors.

Prentice Hall Video Library In addition to the special segments included in the customized ABC News videos, Prentice Hall is pleased to offer a wide selection of commercial videos to reinforce the textual material.

Custom Reader Program (Prentice Hall/Ginn Press) Searching for a reader that is right on target—a reader that can expose your students to actual research findings and applications of psychology? Why not create your own? Now you can with the *Prentice Hall/Ginn Press Custom Reader Program*. The program offers you the flexibility to choose supplementary readings from a list of 100 or more popular journal and newspaper articles. Choose as many or as few articles as you would like. We'll provide you with a reader that is specifically geared to your course and students' needs, in a textbook format. *Contact your local Prentice Hall sales representative for further information.*

FOR THE STUDENT

Student Resource Manual This manual begins with an overview of reading/study techniques and critical thinking skills. Providing a solid foundation for studying content, each chapter features learning objectives, chapter overviews, pre- and post-tests, a critical thinking project based on the ABC News Video Library segments, and a key term review. There is also a unique chapter on writing research papers in psychology—focusing on the different types of papers, note taking, library research, and documentation. A brief sample paper is included to illustrate the APA documentation style.

A Guide to the Brain: A Graphic Workbook, Second Edition The Second Edition offers more review exercises, expanded figures, and brief concept summaries to help students review the locations of structures and understand their functions and effects on behavior. Answers to exercises are included.

Forty Studies That Changed Psychology: Explorations Into the History of Psychological Research (Roger Hock, New England College) Featuring 40 pivotal and influential studies in psychology, this supplementary text provides an overview of each study, its findings, and the impact these findings have had on current thinking in the discipline.

The Prentice Hall Critical Thinking Audio Study Cassette This 60-minute tape offers helpful tips on studying, note taking, reading, listening, writing, test performance, job preparation, and job performance.

StudyManager: Interactive Study Guide A computerized study guide, the *StudyManager* generates random quizzes, provides text page references for review, and prints the corrected quiz for further study and/or submission to the instructor. It also allows questions to be added, edited, or deleted. All objective questions correspond with the material featured in the *Student Resource Manual. For IBM PCs.*

The Contemporary View Program (Prentice Hall/ The New York Times) *The New York Times* and Prentice Hall are sponsoring *A Contemporary View*, a program designed to enhance student access to current information of relevance in the classroom.

Through this program, the core subject matter provided in the text is supplemented by a collection of time-sensitive articles from one of the world's most distinguished newspapers, *The New York Times*. These articles demonstrate the vital, ongoing connection between what is learned in the classroom and what is happening in the world around us.

To enjoy the wealth of information of *The New York Times* daily, a reduced subscription rate is available. For information, call toll-free: 1-800-631-1222.

Prentice Hall and *The New York Times* are proud to co-sponsor *A Contemporary View*. We hope it will make the reading of both textbooks and newspapers a more dynamic, involving process.

Psychology on a Disk Activities Software Offering brief and entertaining interactive experiments and activities in which students themselves are the subjects, these two programs demonstrate how psychology works and teach viewers about their own behavior. *For IBM PCs and Apple/Macintosh.*

ACKNOWLEDGMENTS

Our final task in completing this book is a pleasant one: thanking all of the people who helped us. First, we thank our colleagues who served as reviewers and provided us with the benefit of their wisdom and expertise. For all their time and effort, they have our sincerest appreciation.

Barbara H. Basden, *California State University–Fresno*

Roy F. Baumeister, *Case Western Reserve University*

J. Jay Braun, *Arizona State University*

Charles L. Brewer, *Furman University*

Nathan Brody, *Wesleyan University*

Karen Bush, *Washington Jefferson College*

David L.Carpenter, *Saint Bonaventure University*

Robert B. Cialdini, *Arizona State University*

John J. Colby, *Providence College*

Katherine Covell, *University of Toronto (Canada)*

Stephen F. Davis, *Emporia State University*

Richard B. Day, *McMaster University (Hamilton, Canada)*

Susan Dutch, *Westfield State College*

Steven Friedlander, *University of California–San Francisco*

David C. Funder, *University of California–Berkeley*

Matthias Giessler, *Arizona State University*

James A. Green, *University of Connecticut–Storrs*

Richard A. Griggs, *University of Florida–Gainesville*

Edward S. Halas, *University of North Dakota*

Christopher A. Hoffman, *University of Nevada–Reno*

Robert Hogan, *University of Tulsa*

Janet Shibley Hyde, *University of Wisconsin–Madison*

James J. Johnson, *Illinois State University*

John P. Keating, *University of Washington–Seattle*

Richard C. Keefe, *Scottsdale College*

Melanie Killen, *Wesleyan University*

John MacKinnon, *Connecticut College*

Dale McAdam, *University of Rochester*

Ralph R. Miller, *State University of New York–Binghamton*

Daniel Montello, *North Dakota State University*

Daniel D. Moriarty, *University of San Diego*

Carol Nemeroff, *Arizona State University*

Steve Neuberg, *Arizona State University*

Matthew Olson, *Hamline University*

Harold Pashler, *University of California–San Diego*

James L. Pate, *Georgia State University*

Peter H. Platenius, *Queen's University (Kingston, Canada)*

Deborah Prentice, *Princeton University*

Sharon Presley, *California State University–Fullerton*

John Reich, *Arizona State University*

Michael J. Ross, *Saint Louis University*

Marc M. Sebrechts, *The Catholic University of America*

Steven J. Sherman, *Indiana University*

Steven M. Smith, *Texas A & M University*

Walter C. Swap, *Tufts University*

Dianne M. Tice, *Case Western Reserve University*

Melanie R. Trost, *Arizona State University*

Ann Weber, *University of North Carolina–Asheville*

Matisyohu Weisenberg, *Bar-ilan University (Israel)*

Robert B. Welch, *University of Kansas*

Arno F. Wittig, *Ball State University*

Jeremy Wolfe, *Massachusetts Institute of Technology*

Diana S. Woodruff-Pak, *Temple University*

Second, we thank the fine professional staff at Prentice Hall for their many contributions:

Charlyce Jones Owen, *Editor-in-Chief, Social Sciences*

Will Ethridge, *Editorial Director, College Division*

Leslie Carr, *Senior Editor*

Barbara Reilly, *Production Editor*

Florence Silverman, *Art Director*

Anne T. Bonanno, *Design Coordinator*

Tracey Masella McPeake, *Marketing Manager*

Third, we extend our appreciation to several people who have a very special place in the history of this book:

Marcus Boggs for encouraging the book in the beginning,

James Anker for being matchmaker, counselor, and friend,

Leslie Carr for being steadfast in enthusiasm and support,

Charlyce Jones Owen, most important of all, for believing that our book had something new to say about the field of psychology.

Finally, we owe much to our wives and families. Diane Seamon provided love, encouragement and social support; Melanie Trost provided love, updated references, and a keen editorial eye; and our sons Eric and Mark Seamon and David Kenrick provided love and inspiration.

John G. Seamon
Douglas T. Kenrick

THE SCIENCE OF PSYCHOLOGY

Nature has many methods of producing the same effect. She may make a "born" draughtsman or singer by tipping in a certain direction at an opportune moment the molecules of some human ovum; or she may bring forth a child ungifted and make him spend laborious but successful years at school. She may make our ears ring by the sound of a bell, or by a dose of quinine; make us see yellow by spreading a field of buttercups before our eyes, or by mixing a little santonine powder with our food; fill us with terror of certain surroundings by making them really dangerous, or by a blow which produces a pathological alteration of our brain.

(William James, 1890)

Chapter Outline

At its extremes, the range of human behavior includes the spirit and adventurousness of Amelia Earhart, the humanity and brilliance of Albert Einstein, the tireless devotion of Mother Teresa, and the cold-blooded murderousness of Charles Manson. It includes the purposeful thought of a student studying for an exam and the mindless contributions of whole nations to global overpopulation and environmental deterioration. Within the same family, one sibling may become a hardened criminal while another becomes a public servant. Even the same person's behavior can vary from thoughtfulness to callous indifference and from loving kindness to angry cruelty. The sheer variety of behavior has inspired psychologists since William James first wrote the lines that we use above to open our text.

The quotation is taken from James's *Principles of Psychology*, a landmark textbook in American psychology. James taught the first American course in psychology at Harvard University just over 100 years ago. As you can see in the quote, he was fascinated by people's mental experiences, and how those experiences connected to their inner

William James. This self-portrait was sketched in pencil during 1866, a year during which James described himself as "on the continual verge of suicide," and during which his sister was undergoing treatment for an anxiety disorder. A brilliant man, trained in art, philosophy, and medicine, James went on to teach the first psychology course offered in America, to set up a psychology laboratory at Harvard, and to write *Principles of Psychology* (1890), the definitive textbook in the new field.

physiology and to the events going on in their environments. He asked such questions as:

- How are conscious thoughts and feelings influenced by changes in the body's physiology—as in the case of hallucinations caused by drugs such as quinine and santonine?

- How are conscious thoughts and bodily reactions connected to events in the outside world—such as dangerous surroundings or fields of buttercups?

As we will see throughout this book, psychologists have learned a great deal about these kinds of questions in the century since James published his great book.

William James's own life history provides an ideal point of entry to the field of psychology, for he is a case study in both intellectual achievement and psychological disorder (Allen, 1967; Perry, 1935). William's father, Henry James, Sr., never held a conventional job, but lived off an inheri-

tance, writing books on philosophy and supervising his children's development. To provide his children with a wide range of life experiences, Henry moved them back and forth across the Atlantic, and in and out of different schools.

William's childhood was divided between places as widely separated as New York City, Geneva, Albany, Paris, and London. His career plans, like his home life, were scattered. As a teenager, he studied art, but quit after a few years to study science and philosophy in Europe. He later returned to the United States to study chemistry at Harvard, but transferred into medical school, and then dropped his medical studies to collect biological specimens in South America. Following the South American adventure, James spent some time in Europe in a state that he described to a friend as "on the continual verge of suicide." He did finally complete his medical degree, but retreated to his father's home for a year afterwards. During that year he was incapacitated with headaches, mood shifts, and backaches, as well as fears of the dark and of losing control of his sanity. Psychologist Erik Erikson observed:

> William James was preoccupied all his life with what was then called "morbid psychology." He himself suffered in his youth and into his manhood under severe emotional strain for which he vainly sought the help of a variety of nerve cures. His letters also attest to the fact that he was interested in his friends' crises and that he offered them a kind of passionate advice which betrayed his own struggle for sanity.
>
> *(Erikson, 1968)*

In his problems with depression and anxiety, James was not alone in his family. His sister, though also noted for her brilliant intellect, was institutionalized for some time with similar symptoms, and James used his father as a case example of an acute panic reaction in one of his books. His brothers also had emotional problems, including depression and alcoholism (Allen, 1967).

Although James suffered emotional difficulties for years, he did not succumb to his troubles. He went on to become not only one of the founders of the field of psychology, but also a towering figure in twentieth century philosophy. When he died, philosopher Bertrand Russell described him as "the most eminent, and probably the most widely known of contemporary philosophers." In his book *Pragmatism* (1907), James helped establish what may be the most important American school of philosophy (which held that theoretical ideas should be judged by their practical payoff). In his accomplishments, as in his psychological troubles, he was not alone in his family. His father's own writings were also internationally known, and his sister Alice's personal journals are included in anthologies of English literature (McQuade et al., 1987). His brother, Henry James, is considered among the great modern novelists.

William James and his family raise several questions we will address again throughout this text: What are the roots of emotional disorder? What are the roots of creative genius? Was it the experience of growing up in that special family that led to James's accomplishments and his emotional disorders? Or did his father simply pass on genetic tendencies toward genius and emotional disturbance? These questions offer a glimpse of the topics covered by the field of psychology, but it is time to define the field more precisely.

WHAT IS PSYCHOLOGY?

In 1890, James himself defined it as "the science of mental life," and he included "feelings, desires, cognitions, reasonings, decisions, and the like" in his definition of mental life. Today, most psychologists would expand that definition to say that **psychology** is *the science of behavior and mental processes.* By behavior, psychologists mean any activity of a person or animal that can be observed and measured. Behaviors can be simple or complex, and could include any measurable action from nodding your head to giving a speech about drug addiction. Mental processes are those phenomena that James included in his definition, such as thoughts, feelings, and memories.

Thus, psychology is concerned not only with what goes on inside the head, but with the connections between those mental processes and actual behaviors. Without behavior, we have no way of inferring what is going on inside someone's mind. We cannot know your attitudes towards smoking, for example, without observing your behavior. Do you buy cigarettes, for instance, or grimace when someone else lights up a cigarette?

When we say psychology is a science, we mean that psychologists gather information using systematic empirical methods. Early Greek philosophers pondered some of the same questions as do modern psychologists (Stumpf, 1966), but they did not systematically test their speculations by collecting evidence about people's behavior. As we will

Alice James, William's troubled sister. Psychologists since James have been interested in the interaction between a person's heredity and environment. (James indicates this interest in the chapter's opening quote.) Why did William James share a psychological disturbance with his sister (and with other family members), and a genius for writing with his brother, Henry? Was it because of shared genes, a shared family environment, or a combination of the two?

see below, the first psychologists were originally trained in philosophy, but they decided to rigorously test their armchair speculations against the hard evidence. In fact, we can think of all sciences as data-gathering branches of philosophy. Astronomers, for instance, collect data about the heavenly bodies, botanists collect data about plants, and psychologists collect data about behavior and mental processes.

Note that psychologists would be interested not only in the emotionally troubled side of William James, but in his creativity and intelligence as well. It is a common misconception that psychology deals only with disordered behavior. In fact, a glance through this book will reveal that psychologists study the complete spectrum of human behavior, normal as well as abnormal. If you take a few minutes to page through the text, you will see that psychology deals with topics ranging from neural chemistry to societal problems, from inner consciousness to outer facial expressions, from normal attachment in infancy to problems in adult love relationships, and from acts of kindness to intentions of malice. In studying these topics, psychologists use a variety of methods, from laboratory experiments to field surveys, with subjects as diverse as chimpanzees, earthworms, newborn babies, and college sophomores.

SURVEYING THE FIELD: IT HELPS TO HAVE A MAP

In covering such a broad intellectual terrain, it helps to have a map such as the one we provide in Figure 1.1 to assist the introductory student in exploring the terrain of psychology. We will use this general map to organize the information in each of the chapters that follows. As shown in the "In Context" map, there are four categories of information presented throughout this book, ranging from the specific to the general.

RESEARCH FINDINGS

At the most specific level, you will read the details of many particular research studies (the centermost box). These are the basic substance of the science of psychology and provide the evidence psychologists use to corroborate their ideas. For instance, in Chapter 15 we will describe research that documents the fact that some people become depressed and begin to crave carbohydrates during the winter, and in Chapter 16 we will report on work that finds that this form of depression can be treated by sitting in front of a bright light for several hours a day (Wurtman and Wurtman, 1989).

RESEARCH METHODS

The particulars of the studies you will read about are often interesting and important in themselves, but there are more essential general lessons to take away from an introductory psychology course. Beyond particular findings, it is important to understand a few general methods that psychologists use to answer questions about thought and behavior. Psychological methods include case studies of individuals, surveys of large groups of people, observations of people in their natural surroundings, and controlled laboratory experiments. We will describe each of these methods in a later section of this chapter, and show how each method both provides useful information and has certain limitations. Understanding what you can and cannot conclude from different methods is one of the most important lessons of this course, since the mass media often present psychological research findings uncritically.

Scientific findings and research methods go hand in hand. A researcher may need to create a new method to study a particular problem that no one has yet investigated. As one example, researchers in France around the turn of the century were interested in studying mental retardation. Before addressing that particular research question, they needed to invent a psychological test to measure school performance, and determine which children were falling behind (Binet and Simon, 1905). The modern IQ test derives directly from that work. The new testing methods were later used to address other research questions, such as "How does a child's family background affect his or her school performance?"

THEORETICAL PERSPECTIVES

Why would a psychologist choose to study a problem like the effects of weather on depression, and why might he or she choose to use a survey as

FIGURE 1.1   A schematic representation of the terrain we will be covering in this text. As indicated in the innermost box, psychology examines a number of *particular research questions* about issues ranging from brain neurochemistry to urban crowding. The next box indicates that psychologists address those questions using a set of *research methods* (for example, surveys and experiments) that encompass the different specific questions. The particular questions that a psychologist asks, and the choice of a method to investigate those questions, are influenced by a general set of *theoretical perspectives* that encompass the various domains of research in the field. In turn, the outer box indicates how the theoretical perspectives are encompassed by the more general *historical background* of developments in science and philosophy.

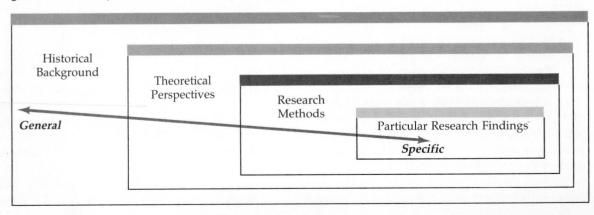

opposed to a laboratory experiment? We can better understand the significance of psychological research by moving to a still more general level, and considering the different theoretical perspectives that psychologists have adopted to guide their search. A psychologist's theoretical perspective influences which topic he or she opts to study, and which method he or she will use to study the chosen topic. Theoretical perspectives also influence how a psychologist will interpret research findings. For instance, we will later discuss findings that women have a higher reported level of depression (Nolen-Hoeksma, 1987). Depending on his or her theoretical perspective, one psychologist might interpret these findings as evidence that many women in our society are trained to play a helpless role; another might view the findings as evidence of a basic physiological difference between women and men.

HISTORICAL BACKGROUND

Finally, a psychologist's theoretical perspective is itself influenced by the general historical and philosophical context in which he or she is working. (See the outermost box in Figure 1.1.) As we will see, psychological theories have been influenced by historical developments as diverse as Darwin's evolutionary theory, the discovery of medical symptoms that could be treated with hypnotism, the invention of computers, and the feminist and environmentalist movements.

To understand why some psychologists study certain problems with certain methods and within certain theoretical frameworks, then, it helps to know something about the historical roots of the different psychological perspectives. Let us begin with the general—the historical foundations of psychology—and move to the specific—the particular research questions asked by psychologists.

HISTORICAL BACKGROUND:
The Roots of Scientific Psychology

Modern psychology has its roots in the revolutionary scientific and philosophical developments of the second half of the nineteenth century. At that time, scientists were making radical new discoveries in such fields as physics, geology, microbiology and chemistry. These developments encouraged philosophers to extend the scientific method to the study of human thought and behavior. In 1867, during his troubled years of identity crisis, William James visited Germany, and wrote to a friend:

It seems to me that perhaps the time has come for psychology to be a Science. Some measurements have already been made in the region lying between the physical changes in the nerves and the appearance of consciousness . . . I am going to study what is already known, and perhaps may be able to do some work on it. Helmholtz and a man named Wundt at Heidelberg are working at it and I hope, if I live through this winter, to go to them in the summer.

(William James, 1867; cited in Hothersall, 1984)

The two men of whom James spoke, Helmholtz and Wundt, are monumental figures in the field of psychology. Hermann von Helmholtz was a brilliant physiologist, interested in the relationship between physical energy and psychological experience. How, for instance, do we convert vibrations in the air into the sound of a symphony? His theories of color vision and hearing are still influential today. Helmholtz's protegé Wilhelm Wundt is often regarded as the official founder of the new

Historical developments and psychology.
Psychological research is the product of diverse influences including Darwinian theory, the invention of computers, and even political developments like the environmental movement (which focuses on global ecology).

Wilhelm Wundt. Wundt is often considered the first modern psychologist. A shy boy who originally did poorly in school, he went on to study medicine and physiology, and later to become a professor of philosophy. He taught a course in social psychology in 1859, but his most outstanding achievement was opening the first psychology laboratory in 1879, where he and his assistants studied the relationships between physiology, sensory impressions, and mental experiences. (See the illusion in Figure 1.2.)

discipline of psychology. That credit owes partly to his publication of the *Principles of Physiological Psychology* in 1873. He described the book as "an attempt to work out a new domain of science," and argued that the new science of psychology should be based "upon anatomical and physiological foundations" (Wundt, 1873).

Like James, Wundt was no stranger to personal difficulty. He had a very strict mother, and in school he was a shy daydreamer with few friends. He overcame his early difficulties, though, and went on to become Helmholtz's assistant at the University of Heidelberg, where he stayed for seventeen years. Wundt became involved in leftist politics at Heidelberg, and this political interest led him to develop a college course on the relationship between culture and psychology (Hilgard, 1987). In 1875 he joined the philosophy department at the University of Leipzig, and set up a psychological laboratory there. There Wundt and his assistants conducted research on consciousness, perception,

and memory, asking such questions as "How do we perceive color?" and "What causes optical illusions?", topics we will discuss in Chapters 3 and 4. (Figure 1.2.)

The scientific psychology of Wundt and Helmholtz had a profound effect on the young William James. After returning to America, James took a position at Harvard teaching courses in physiology. Three years after accepting that position, in 1875, he opened a psychology laboratory at Harvard. James jokingly observed that the first psychology lecture he ever heard was the one he himself gave (Watson, 1978). James offered his course not in the medical school but in the philosophy department, where he had taken a permanent position. For most of the next decade and a half, he worked on his classic two-volume text, *Principles of Psychology* (1890), which became required reading for generations of students. In addition to a thorough grounding in philosophy, he was influenced by the evolutionary theory of Charles Darwin. James believed that human consciousness and thinking were biological adaptations that helped our ancestors survive. As you will see, some of his ideas about emotion and consciousness are still influential today.

By 1896, when the Third International Congress of Psychology met in Munich, Wundt and James had molded the shape of the new discipline. At that time, a Berlin newspaper described Wundt and James as the "psychological Popes" of the Old and New Worlds, respectively. There were many similarities between the two men. Both were trained in medicine and therefore predisposed to look at the physiology of behavior. Though neither practiced medicine, each remained committed to the importance of using careful observation and empirical evidence. Both taught psychology from within the philosophy department, and both were influenced by evolutionary theory (Hilgard, 1987).

Thus, psychology's founders shared several common themes in their intellectual development. The most important of these include

1. an interest in using scientific methods to answer philosophical questions about the human mind,

2. a background in medicine, which emphasizes the treatment of disorder, and

3. an interest in evolutionary theory, which emphasizes how animals (and humans) adapt to their environments.

In the next section, we will see how those common themes are still alive in the major theoretical perspectives in modern psychology. ■

FIGURE 1.2   A variation of the Munsterberg illusion, in which white squares are perceived (incorrectly) as converging to the right or left. The horizontal lines are actually perfectly parallel. This type of illusion was studied in Wilhelm Wundt's Leipzig laboratory by his student Hugo Munsterberg, who was later recruited to Harvard by William James.

MAJOR THEORETICAL PERSPECTIVES

Throughout this book, we will be discussing numerous bits of evidence about behavior and thinking, gathered with many diverse methods. Without theory, all this information would be overwhelming. Theoretical perspectives connect the many findings, linking them into a larger historical context of ideas. In addition to organizing evidence, theoretical perspectives tell psychologists which evidence to weigh more heavily, and where and how to look for new evidence. Consider the problem of a psychologist interested in learning about anxiety. What causes people to feel anxious? Without a general theory, that psychologist would have no idea where to look for an answer. Perhaps anxiety comes from wearing one's shoes too tight. Perhaps it comes from eating too many vegetables. Perhaps anxious people become that way because of the number of comic books they read as children, or the failure of their roofs to deflect harmful moonbeams. Actually, any of these explanations is possible, but most psychologists look elsewhere for the causes of anxiety. As we will see in a later chapter, modern theories of anxiety focus on people's genetic predispositions, their learning experiences, the stressors in their current lives, and on the ways they interpret those stressful events. This is because there are good theoretical reasons to look at genes rather than shoe fit, learning rather than vegetables, and stressful events rather than moonbeams.

A **theory** is a set of assumptions that helps us organize a complicated set of findings, and that helps a scientist decide where to look for new evidence. Some theories are narrow in scope, explaining only specific phenomena, such as visual illusions or the relationship between heat and aggression. Other theories are broader, and attempt to explain how different psychological processes fit together; connecting phenomena as diverse as adult social relationships, early childhood learning experiences, and ongoing thought processes. We use the term "theoretical perspective" to refer to wide-range theories, those that encompass many smaller-range theories, research methods, and empirical findings. By understanding some of the important wide-range theories in the field, you should be better able to understand the roots of the many specific findings discussed in the chapters to come.

As you read about the different theoretical perspectives below, keep in mind that although some of the theories are very different from one another, each may be valid. In 1939, psychologist Robert Woodworth compared different scientific perspectives to different maps of the same area. One map of a city might focus on the individual streets; another might focus on topography, plotting hills, valleys, and rivers; and a third might show only a schematic diagram of the subway system. Each map shows different features, yet each is useful for some purposes. The same can be said of the different perspectives taken by different scientists. An anatomist and a chemist both look at the same human body, but come away with a different view of that body. Likewise, psychologists' different theoretical perspectives focus on different features, but each helps us understand part of psychology's terrain.

In the remainder of this section, we discuss several of the major wide-range theoretical perspectives in psychology, and how they apply to one specific phenomenon—remembering. We consider remembering from six perspectives: evolutionary, behavioral, cognitive, humanistic-phenomenological, psychoanalytic, and neuropsychological. For now, we will consider only how these approaches apply to remembering. However, each approach could be applied to many of the phenomena studied by psychologists, including depression, mother/infant bonding, and visual perception. At the end of this section, we will look at how these perspectives interact. Sometimes called the **interactionist perspective,** this modern view emphasizes the themes that link these perspectives rather than their differences.

THE EVOLUTIONARY PERSPECTIVE

During the 1860s, when William James was touring Europe in search of intellectual stimulation, Charles Darwin's theory of evolution was the talk of the continent. In *The Origin of Species* (1859), Darwin presented evidence that animal species have evolved into different forms because those animals that are better adapted to their environments are more likely to survive and bear offspring than are less well-adapted animals. For instance, giraffes with slightly longer necks can eat leaves high on trees that are inaccessible to their shorter cousins. Darwin's idea of natural selection applied not only to physical features (such as a carnivorous cat's sharp teeth), but also to behaviors (such as a cat's hiss when it is threatened) (Darwin, 1872). In his *Principles of Psychology*, William James applied the same logic to human thinking and memory, arguing that these processes evolved to help our ancestors survive. Following Darwin and James, modern evolutionary theorists assume that the human brain has its particular structure and its special functions (like language and memory) because it helped our ancestors win the fierce struggle for survival and successful reproduction (for example, Alcock, 1989; Lumsden and Wilson, 1981).

During the last century, the **evolutionary perspective** has been carried on by **comparative psychologists,** who study differences and similarities in behavior across different animal species (for ex-

Kalahari bushmen. For most of the evolutionary history of our species, humans lived the harsh existence of hunting and gathering shown by this Kalahari bushman. Evolutionary theorists believe that human memory is an adaptation to this lifestyle. An ability to remember the details of when and where they met dangerous predators and edible prey could have meant the difference between survival and extinction for our hunter/gatherer ancestors.

ample, Denny, 1980; Wallace, 1978). Comparative psychologists consider how human memory and thinking compares with that of other animals. What are the similarities and differences in psychological processes between humans and chimpanzees? Between primates (like us) and other social mammals (like dogs)? By looking at where we fit into the animal kingdom, these psychologists hope to understand the ultimate roots of our own behavior. For example, a comparative psychologist might ask, "Why do humans have special areas of the brain for language, whereas chimpanzees do not?"

Harvard psychologists Roger Brown and James Kulik used an evolutionary perspective to help explain why people store "flashbulb memories"— seemingly vivid mental pictures of emotionally significant events. Many people have flashbulb memories of the day the shuttle Challenger exploded. People with flashbulb memories commonly remember where they were when they heard the news, what they were doing, who told them, and how that person seemed to feel at the time. Using the evolutionary theoretical perspective to help them interpret the findings of this specific study, Brown and Kulik speculate on a biological mechanism for such memories that helped our ancestors survive over the past million years:

> To survive and leave progeny, the individual human had to keep his expectations of significant events up to date and close to reality. . . . Where was the primitive man when he saw the new carnivore or the baboon troop on the march?
>
> *(Brown and Kulik, 1977)*

As we will discuss at several points throughout this text, evolutionary models are increasingly being used to help understand thinking and memory processes (for example, Sherry and Schacter, 1987; Tooby and Cosmides, 1989).

How is the evolutionary past connected with what is going on in our brains at this moment? Past environmental pressures and present reactions are linked by genes, the cellular blueprints for building and operating our physical bodies. Many modern psychologists study **behavior genetics,** a field that poses questions about the extent to which the differences between people are affected by the genes they inherit from their parents (Plomin, De-Fries, and McClearn, 1990; Rowe, 1991, among others). Although William James accepted the evolutionary significance of human behavior, social scientists a century ago knew virtually nothing of

genetics, and next to nothing about the behaviors of our primate cousins. As we will see throughout this book, psychologists are only beginning to understand what genetics and evolutionary biology can tell us about our own thoughts, emotions, and behaviors, and there are many exciting controversies about how far these perspectives can take us.

THE BEHAVIORAL PERSPECTIVE

The father of behaviorism was John B. Watson, a professor at Johns Hopkins University in the 1910s, who argued that environmental pressures, not genetic blueprints, could explain adult human behaviors from criminality to genius. Attacks on James's evolutionary approach began during the early part of this century, led by the early proponents of *behaviorism.* Adherents to the **behavioral perspective** believe that psychology should focus only on observable behaviors and their relationship to events that can be objectively measured. By the extreme behavioral definition, a psychologist should be concerned with neither the biochemical actions of genes, nor the invisible stream of an individual's conscious memories.

According to this perspective, inner events have no more place in a scientific psychology than do such phenomena as astral projection or visits to previous lives. Since a psychologist cannot see what is going on inside a person's head any more than he or she can see whether your soul leaves your body during astral projection, behaviorists argue that your personal memories are not admissible scientific data. B. F. Skinner, one of the most influential modern behaviorists, argued that mental events have the scientific status of "fictions," like evil spirits and leprechauns. Skinner argued that we often invent invisible mental causes when we do not know the true causes of someone's behavior:

> When a professor turns up in the wrong classroom or gives the wrong lecture, it is because his *mind* is, at least for the moment, absent. If he forgets to give a reading assignment, it is because it has slipped his *mind.* . . . In all this it is obvious that the mind and the ideas . . . are being invented on the spot to provide spurious explanations. A science of behavior can hope to gain very little from so cavalier a practice. Since mental or psychic events . . . lack the dimensions of physical science, we have an additional reason for rejecting them.
>
> *(Skinner, 1953)*

If "mental or psychic events" are out, what are psychologists to study? Skinner argued that psychology should focus instead on the prediction of overt behaviors—head nods, handshakes, and showing up for work—and the environments in which those behaviors take place. In particular, behaviorists have been interested in the relationship of *learning history* to behavior: how what you do today is influenced by earlier rewards and punishments from your parents and teachers, for instance. As one example, we describe in Chapter 6 how a behaviorist traced a child's temper tantrums to the reward he received—attention from his parents (Williams, 1959). This perspective has been quite useful in allowing parents, teachers, and psychologists to predict and control problematic behaviors. However, some psychologists believe that a psychology without "inner events" is more appropriate to the study of animals like rats and dogs than to the study of humans. According to opponents of behaviorism, humans are different from other animals precisely because we can describe our inner experiences. Like William James, many modern psychologists are interested in what is going on inside people's heads, and these psychologists disagree with the strict form of behaviorism (Bandura, 1986).

THE COGNITIVE PERSPECTIVE

As philosophers, William James and Wilhelm Wundt were curious about processes occurring "in the mind." Psychologists who utilize the **cognitive perspective** follow in this tradition, studying mental processes such as perceiving, remembering, and thinking.

Cognitive psychologists often use the computer as a metaphor for psychological processes, viewing people as information processors. A cognitive psychologist might ask: "How can a person convert the ink marks on this page into meaningful words and sentences?" or "How can a person recognize the difference between a friend's face and the face of a stranger?"

To study the mental processes involved in remembering, cognitive psychologists conduct experiments to see which factors lead us to distort our recollections, and which factors lead us to remember things accurately. One important factor in remembering is the context in which an event occurs. If you are asked to remember something, you will do better if you are in the same place, or the same inner state, as you were when you formed the memory. Cognitive psychologist Gordon Bower described the conditions under which Senator Robert Kennedy's assassin, Sirhan Sirhan, could remember the events of the murder:

> Interestingly, Sirhan had absolutely no recollection of the actual murder. . . . Sirhan carried out the deed in a greatly agitated state and was completely amnesic with regard to the event. Diamond [a forensic psychiatrist] . . . hypnotized Sirhan and helped him to reconstruct from memory the events of that fateful day. Under hypnosis, as Sirhan became more worked up and excited, he recalled progressively more, the memories tumbling out while his excitement built to a crescendo leading up to the shooting. At that point Sirhan would scream out the death curses, "fire" the shots, and then choke as he reexperienced the Secret Service bodyguard nearly throttling him after he was caught. On different occasions, while in a trance, Sirhan was able to recall the crucial events . . . always accompanied by great excitement.

(Bower, 1981)

The influence of learning on behavior.
Psychologists who adopt a behavioral perspective emphasize the importance of the learning environment in shaping a person's behavior. For instance, behaviorists have emphasized the way that a child's behavior is affected by the rewards and attention the child receives from his or her parents.

To a cognitive psychologist, remembering is a process of active reconstruction, which takes into account what we pay attention to, how we store the information that we do pay attention to, and what is going on at the time that we try to retrieve a memory. For instance, if you were not paying attention to a conversation at the table behind you in the cafeteria, or if you interpreted the information incorrectly (perhaps thinking incorrectly that the conversation was about you), or if you never came across any reminders of the information (you never saw the conversants again), you are not likely to remember it accurately.

THE HUMANISTIC–PHENOMENOLOGICAL PERSPECTIVE

The evolutionary, behavioral, and cognitive perspectives share a commitment to an *objective* science of psychology. The objective approach assumes that with appropriate research methods, different observers of the same behavior could agree about exactly what they were observing. Behaviorists take this objective approach to the extreme, arguing that psychologists should only study observable behaviors. Evolutionary theorists and cognitive theorists are willing to make inferences about unobservable entities such as genes and thoughts, but they often assume that future scientists could develop methods (improved gene-mapping techniques, perhaps, and fool-proof lie detectors) that would make those unobservables public. The **phenomenological perspective** focuses instead on a person's subjective, conscious experience. Imagine, for example, a man who believes that his friend's comment that she liked his shoes was meant sarcastically, as an insult. A phenomenologist would argue that this subjective interpretation is crucially important to understanding the man's behavior, whether or not it is objectively correct.

Phenomenological studies of remembering have provided fascinating descriptions of conscious experience. Given the closeness of this approach to the humanities, it is not surprising that the most famous description of the experience of remembering was made by a writer instead of a psychologist. In his book, *Remembrance of Things Past*, French novelist Marcel Proust recalled his childhood in the city of Combrey:

The triggering of memory. Each of us has had the experience of remembering a seemingly forgotten event in the presence of some stimulus that serves as a link with the past. On one occasion, a smell triggered one of the authors to recall an event that had not been on his mind in years: "While walking on a nature trail one morning with my sons, I stopped suddenly and realized that I had smelled a particular fragrance before. Lost in thought for a moment, I was completely taken back. No longer was I an adult walking with my sons: I was a boy of nine or ten once again, walking with my friends at Camp Wonposet" (Seamon, 1980).

Many years had elapsed during which nothing of Combrey . . . had any existence for me, when one day in winter, as I came home, my mother offered me some tea. . . . She sent out for one of those short plump little cakes called "petites madelaines," . . . I raised to my lips a spoonful of the tea in which I had soaked a morsel of the cake. No sooner had the warm liquid, and the crumbs with it, touched my palate than a shudder ran through my whole body. . . . An exquisite pleasure had invaded my senses. . . . And suddenly the memory returns. The taste was that of the little crumb of madeleine which at Sunday mornings at Combrey . . . when I went to say good day to her in her bedroom my aunt Leonie used to give me, dipping it first in her own cup of tea.

And once I had recognized the taste of the crumb of madeleine . . . immediately the old grey house upon the street, where her room was, rose up like the scenery of a theatre to attach itself to the little pavilion, opening on to the garden, which had been built out behind it for my parents, and with the house the town . . . the Square . . . the streets . . . the whole of Combrey and its surroundings, taking their proper shapes and growing solid, sprang into being, town and gardens alike, from my cup of tea.

(Proust, 1934)

From the phenomenological perspective, we remember parts of the past that are still meaningful and psychologically important to us (Pollio, 1982). For the phenomenological psychologist, the importance of a remembrance is not in its accuracy in describing the past, but in the interpretation we give it in the present. Personally significant events, which define us and make us unique, are normally hidden away. But, as in the case of Proust's petites madelaines, those memories can intrude into our consciousness when they are triggered by some link to the past. The study of phenomenology is an important part of the *humanistic* approach to psychology, which emphasizes humanity's special characteristics (for example, our ability to think about our own experiences), the inherently positive aspects of human nature (including altruism and love), the individuality of each person's experience, and each person's potential for psychological growth (Maslow, 1954; Rogers, 1964). We shall see that this perspective has had an influence on theories of personality and the treatment of psychological disorder.

THE PSYCHOANALYTIC PERSPECTIVE

As we just saw, the phenomenological perspective focuses on people's conscious memories. In contrast, psychologists who adopt the **psychoanalytic perspective** assume that much of what we think and do is motivated by thoughts that may exist completely outside of our conscious awareness. According to the psychoanalytic perspective, you have emotional memories that influence what you do in the present, but you are unable to talk about them, even to yourself. This perspective was made popular by Sigmund Freud.

Like James, Freud was influenced by the work of Charles Darwin. Freud believed that our ancestors were naturally selected to have selfish biological drives that helped them reproduce and compete with others. However, those selfish biological impulses, usually associated with sex and aggression, are incompatible with living in polite society, and parents try to suppress them in their children. Freud held that people are taught to push sexual and aggressive thoughts out of consciousness.

Freud was similar to James in another way, having also been trained in medicine. Unlike James, however, Freud actually made a living from seeing patients. In fact, Freud's theory derived from his efforts to develop a treatment for emotionally dis-

Sigmund Freud. The founder of psychoanalysis, Freud was a Viennese physician who treated patients with psychological problems. On the basis of his observations, Freud believed that people forget things that relate to unconscious emotional conflicts. By analyzing a person's dreams, slips of tongue, jokes, and nonverbal mannerisms, Freud attempted to reveal the unconscious processes that he thought were responsible for much of behavior.

turbed people. The treatment, along with the theory associated with it, is called **psychoanalysis.** It involves methods designed to uncover the repressed impulses and memories that Freud believed caused neurotic symptoms in adults. Freud thought he could uncover these unconscious impulses by having his patients talk openly and candidly with him. In his 1901 book, *The Psychopathology of Everyday Life,* Freud described an incident in which a young man wanted to use a particular quote—*Exoriar(e) aliquis nostris ex ossibus ultor* (Let someone arise from my bones as an avenger). The young man became embarrassed when he forgot the word "aliquis" that Freud was able to provide.

YOUNG MAN (YM):	How stupid of me to forget a word like that! By the way, you claim that one never forgets a thing without some reason. I should be very curious to learn how I came to forget . . . in this case.
SIGMUND FREUD (SF):	. . . I must first ask you to tell me, candidly and uncritically, whatever comes into your mind if you direct your attention to the forgotten word. . . .
Y.M.:	Good. There springs to my mind, then, the ridiculous notion of dividing the word like this: *a* and *liquis.* What does that mean?
S.F.:	I don't know. And what occurs to you next? . . .
Y.M.:	Now it's St. Januarius and the miracle of his blood that comes into my mind.
S.F.:	. . . St. Januarius and St. Augustine both have to do with the calendar. But won't you remind me about the miracle of the blood?
Y.M.:	. . . They keep the blood of St. Januarius in a phial inside a church at Naples, and on a particular holy day it miraculously liquifies. . . .
S.F.:	Well, go on. Why do you pause?
Y.M.:	Well, something has come into my mind . . . but it's too intimate to pass on. . . . Besides, I don't see any connection, or any necessity of saying it.
S.F.:	. . . I can't force you to talk about something you find distasteful; but then you mustn't insist on learning from me how you came to forget *aliquis.*
Y.M.:	Really? . . . Well then, I've suddenly thought of a lady from whom I might easily hear a piece of news that would be very awkward for both of us.
S.F.:	That her periods have stopped?
Y.M.:	How could you guess that?
S.F.:	That's not difficult any longer; you've prepared the way sufficiently. Think of the calendar saints, the blood that starts to flow on a particular day, . . .

In fact you've made use of the miracle of St. Januarius to manufacture a brilliant allusion to women's periods.

(Freud, 1901)

Although Freud has been dead since 1939, his views remain important, just as they remain controversial. Many contemporary psychologists reject his sharp division between conscious and unconscious mental processes, and think instead in terms of different degrees of awareness. Moreover, many of Freud's own followers rejected the idea that most adult behaviors are rooted in suppressed sexual and aggressive motives. As we will see in later chapters, however, his ideas about topics such as inner conflict and personality development continue to be influential.

THE NEUROPSYCHOLOGICAL PERSPECTIVE

Psychologists who adopt the **neuropsychological perspective** examine how behavior and mental processes relate to changes in the brain and nervous system. They ask such questions as: Are there chemical changes in brain cells that occur when a person remembers something? Are there particular patterns of electrical activity in the brain that correspond to particular memories? Are there specific structures in the brain for remembering faces, and others for remembering words?

Neuropsychologists sometimes study clinical cases in which a person's brain has been inadvertently altered by accidents, gunshot wounds, or medical surgery. For example, Donald Hebb, one of the pioneers of this perspective, describes the *retrograde amnesia* (memory loss for prior events) produced by a severe blow to the head:

Suppose a car driver on his own side of the highway is hit by a car from the other direction—one that has gone out of control and has crossed into his lane. He is knocked out briefly, then gradually comes back to full consciousness. It is not surprising that his memory is impaired for events following the accident, his brain being more or less addled for the time being, but it is very signficant that he cannot remember what happened just *before* the accident, when his brain was functioning normally. If he had not been hit on the head—if at the last instant the other car had managed to avoid him—he certainly would have remembered seeing the car headed straight for him. . . . So the concussion wiped out learning that we know must have occurred. But it does not wipe out all learning, only recent learning; old, well-established memories are unimpaired, and the longer the interval between acquisition and concussion, the less the impairment. In that interval, therefore, something is happening to make memory less vulnerable to disruption. That something is what is known as consolidation.

(Hebb, 1972)

These findings suggest that memories are initially fragile, but harden or "consolidate" over a period of time. Only after this physiological consolidation is complete can memories survive a trauma to the brain (Wickelgren, 1979).

As we will see in later chapters, new theories have begun to piece together findings on human memory, brain structure, and computer-simulated "intelligence." However, our knowledge of neuropsychology is still rather incomplete. For instance, neuropsychologists have not yet determined the physical basis for memory consolidation. Unraveling the mysteries of the human brain, one of the most complex structures in our universe, will occupy neuropsychologists for a long time to come.

INTERACTIONS:
Connecting Different Perspectives

Throughout its history, there have been many attempts to reduce psychology to only one of the perspectives we have discussed thus far. Some have argued that it is pointless for psychologists to study anything but overt behaviors, others have suggested that psychology will eventually be engulfed by evolutionary biology, and still others have made the case that inner psychological experience can never be reduced to biology or learned responses. Modern psychologists, however, are more likely to take an *interactionist perspective,* which attempts to combine elements of the various perspectives to understand the whole human being. There are three general principles that underlie the interactionist approach:

1. *It is important to consider how different psychological processes fit together into a whole.* The perspectives we discussed often focus on different processes; behaviorists focus on learning, cognitive theorists focus on information processing, and neuropsychologists focus on brain structures and biochemical reactions in microscopic nerve cells. These processes are by no means separate from one another. As William James noted in the chapter's opening quote, biochemical changes in the brain can make us "see" yellow, or "hear" bells ringing. Biochemical events in the brain also form the basis for complex cognitive information processing, and information processing influences what we remember and learn, which in turn lead to biochemical changes in the brain. Thus, it makes little sense to assume that one psychological process is most important. We need to consider how the different processes function together.

2. *Psychological processes within a person always interact with events in his or her environment.* Some perspectives, like behaviorism, have focused on how the outside environment affects behavior. Others, like the phenomenological and neuropsychological approaches, have focused on events inside the person. The different parts that make up an individual person not only interact with one another, however, but with whatever is going on in the outside world. William James noted that the experience of seeing yellow could be produced by internal physiological changes brought on by drugs, but it could also be produced by coming upon a field of buttercups. Under normal circumstances, of course, our inner experience of seeing colors is more related to outside events, like seeing a field of flowers, than to strange biochemical events that alter our nervous systems. However, for people with certain behavioral disorders, their biochemistry may cause them to see things that others do not see. People's behaviors also change their environments—someone who claims to be receiving messages from outer space will be treated differently than a person whose experiences match those of others.

3. *The psychological present can only be fully understood in light of previous history.* Your reaction to what is going on at the present moment depends not only on your current circumstances, but also on your past experience and heritage. The same field of buttercups may remind one person of her first love and another of a time he was stung by a bee. A third person, who inherited a genetic predisposition for color-blindness, might not even realize that he is in a field of pretty yellow flowers. Finally, the fact that most people are likely to seek out fields of flowers, but to avoid the yellow and black striped bees, may tell us something about the conditions under which our ancestors evolved.

Psychological experiences depend on an interaction of internal processes and environmental events. As William James noted in the chapter's opening quote, the experience of seeing yellow could be caused by viewing a field of flowers (external) or by a drug that affected the sensory mechanisms responsible for color perception (internal). Most animals do not see "colors" in the environment because they lack the appropriate internal mechanisms.

Explanations that focus on the short-term or immediate causes of behavior (such as ongoing brain biochemistry or the colors in front of your eyes right now) are called *proximate* explanations. Explanations that take the long-range view, focussing on previous learning history, genes, or the evolutionary history of the human species, are called *ultimate* explanations. Figure 1.3 graphically depicts the continuum from ultimate to proximate explanations.

Consider how the interactionist perspective relates to remembering. What you bring to memory at any given moment is partly influenced by the limits on the kind and amount of information your brain can process. You cannot remember much of a speech if it is disorganized, rambling, or in a language that you barely understand, for instance. But what you can process now is also influenced by past learning: you could remember a lot more of a speech in Spanish if you had spent more time on

FIGURE 1.3 Theoretical perspective and time frame. Different theoretical perspectives can be arranged according to the time frame adopted by their proponents. Some explanations focus on the present causes of behavior, and are called proximate explanations. At the most immediate level, neuropsychologists focus on split-second biochemical changes that underlie single behaviors. Other explanations focus on the long-term historical causes of a behavior, and are called ultimate explanations. At the extreme, evolutionary theorists consider how such common human behaviors as smiling might have had significance for our ancestors.

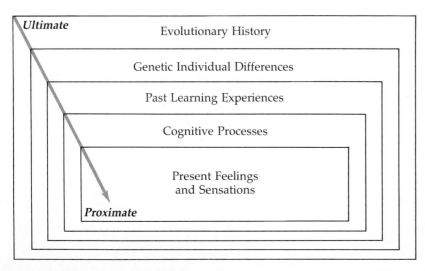

your Spanish lessons. In turn, how much you can process and learn is influenced by genetic programs that hark back to a time before you were even born. In rare cases, some people inherit a brain that cannot recognize the normal sounds of spoken words. Finally, our genetic programs have evolved to fit the environments that our ancestors had to deal with. Humans cannot even process some sounds, smells, and sights that are very vivid for other species (Alcock, 1989), and some experiences that we find deeply memorable hold little fascination for our pet dogs.

The interactionist perspective is still evolving as psychologists consider the links between the different perspectives on behavior. However, the perspective holds the promise of helping us understand the links among the many different phenomena we will discuss throughout this book, from biochemical events within single nerve cells to complex relationships between groups of people. ▪

SUMMARIZING AND ORGANIZING THE THEORETICAL PERSPECTIVES

The main assumptions of each theoretical perspective are outlined in Table 1.1. In the chapters that follow, we will begin by dissecting human behavior and experience into its component parts. We will start at the simplest and most microscopic

level, studying simple biochemical and electrical reactions in the nervous system. We will then move to a more complex level, describing such psychological processes as learning, memory, thinking, and emotion. In discussing these basic processes, it is helpful to keep scalpel in hand, cleanly separating each into its own area of the operating table. In many cases, a simple theoretical perspective may provide a satisfactory explanation for one or more of these simple processes. As we move to more complex processes, however, it will be necessary to rebuild a complete human organism. In building towards progressively more complex phenomena, from normal and abnormal personality development through simple social relationships and on to the complexities of global problems, there will be increasing need to see how these perspectives interact. By the end of this book we hope you will see psychology not as an ill-sewn patchwork quilt, but as an intricate and tightly woven tapestry.

RESEARCH METHODS

The different theoretical perspectives represent, in a sense, the philosophical ideas on which psychological research is based. What distinguishes scientific psychology from philosophy? The answer is that psychologists systematically test their ideas against external reality. Although all of us observe

TABLE 1.1 **Summary of Theoretical Perspectives**

Evolutionary	Human behavior is influenced by the interaction of genes and features of the environment that were relevant to our ancestor's survival and reproduction.
Behavioral	Psychologists should study only observable behaviors, and their relationship to observable features of the environment.
Cognitive	People are active information processors who organize, rearrange, and transform information about the environment and their own internal states.
Humanistic-Phenomenological	A person's subjective experience of him/herself and the events in the world are more important than the objective reality.
Psychoanalytic	Unconscious sexual and aggressive urges influence behavior and thinking processes.
Neuropsychological	Behavior and mental processes are related to biochemical changes in the nervous system, and to hormones in the endocrine system.
Interactionist	Different perspectives can be linked through three themes: ▪ Microscopic biological structures and part processes like cognition and learning fit together into an integrated whole person. ▪ The person is continually affected by, and having a reciprocal influence on, his or her environment. ▪ Present experiences interact with our own past experiences and the genes we inherited from our ancestors.

behavior every day, normal biases can lead us to erroneous conclusions. For instance, college students in one study were exposed to research evidence on both sides of the capital punishment issue. They read about some findings indicating that murder rates were unaffected by the death penalty, but they also read about other findings suggesting just the opposite. What was interesting was that even though they heard evidence on *both* sides of the issue, both opponents and advocates of capital punishment alike came away convinced that the evidence was squarely on their side (Lord, Ross, and Lepper, 1979). The biases of each group led them to favor evidence supporting their position. Research methods are tools designed to help eliminate these biases of everyday information processing. Without those methods, the conclusions of a psychologist are worth no more than the opinions of anyone else.

If you understand some of the difficulties of collecting scientific evidence, you should be better able to evaluate the claims of people who claim to be "experts." Go into the "psychology" section of any bookstore, or turn on a talk show, and you will find a great deal of so-called expert advice. The experts will confidently tell you how to get along with your co-workers, how to deal with a divorce in the family, or how to deal with your sister's alcohol abuse. Where did this expert advice come from? Can it be trusted? One important thing you can learn from a course in scientific psychology is to be a more skeptical consumer of this sort of popular counsel. Too often that guidance is based on faulty or incomplete evidence.

We will discuss two general types of methods commonly used by psychologists, *descriptive* and *experimental* techniques. Each of the specific methods we discuss has particular strengths, but each, by itself, also has particular limitations. Therefore, we need to scrutinize the method by which the evidence was gathered before we can come to any conclusions about a psychological question. Descriptive techniques are useful for developing precise descriptions of behavior and the circumstances under which a certain behavior might occur. Experimental techniques can be useful in determining which factors may actually cause which behaviors.

DESCRIPTIVE TECHNIQUES

Naturalistic observations, case studies, and surveys can be clustered together as *descriptive* techniques. These methods provide different ways to describe behavior, without any attempt to interfere with the behavior under study. As we discuss in more detail below, descriptive techniques can provide useful information about how different events and behaviors are related to each other. However, descriptive methods do not allow us to say for certain which events caused which behaviors. Only in experiments do researchers purposefully manipulate events to find out how they cause changes in behavior. As you will see, this distinction influences the kinds of conclusions we can make from experiments in comparison with other techniques.

NATURALISTIC OBSERVATION

If you are interested in understanding children's aggression, you might begin by going to a playground and observing what happens before and after one little tyke hits another with a block, or pushes him into a mud puddle. In the early stages of any scientific investigation, it is often most informative to observe a phenomenon as it actually happens in an everyday setting. This method—observing animals and people behaving in their natural environments—is called **naturalistic observation.**

One team of researchers used naturalistic observation to study how social dominance was related to the distance between people (Dean, Willis, and Hewitt, 1975). Based on findings that dominant animals are often granted more space by submissive ones, the researchers hypothesized that high ranking naval officers would be given a wider berth by their subordinates. To examine the dominance–space hypothesis, three uniformed sailors sat in inconspicuous locations around a naval base, such as a cafeteria and a recreation center. The observers recorded 281 interactions between naval personnel ranging across twelve ranks, from Seaman up to Captain. Every time they observed two standing men talking to one another, they recorded three things: (1) the ranks of the two men; (2) which man began the interaction; and (3) the distance between them, measured in standard 22.86 cm. floor tiles. Their results supported the prediction—more dominant men were granted more space. (See Figure 1.4.)

Another team of researchers had student bartenders and waitresses record the comings and goings of patrons in a bar noted for liaisons between married men and single women (Roebuck and Spray, 1967). Pooling across many such observations, the researchers found a general pattern of initiating heterosexual relations in the bar. Typically, a man began the interaction by sending a drink to the woman's table, which the woman

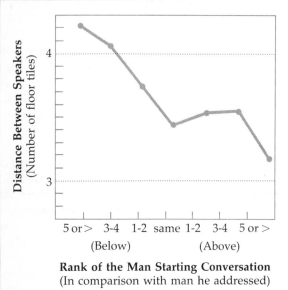

FIGURE 1.4 Results of a naturalistic observation of distance and social dominance in sailors. If a man addressed a superior, he chose a distance that was further away than if he addressed an equal or a subordinate. To read this graph, find the point on the x-axis (horizontal line) indicating five or more ranks below, and you can see that men who addressed their distant superiors stood 4.2 tiles away. (You can find this by reading the y-, or vertical, axis.) On the other hand, find the point on the x-axis indicating five or more ranks above, and you will see that men who addressed their distant inferiors stood closer (3.2 tiles, in this case, or about a foot less). Those whose rank differences were intermediate stood at intermediate distances in comparison with the very dominant and very subordinate men. (Dean, Willis, and Hewitt, 1975).

scription of what actually went on. Naturalistic observation can be used to describe the behavior of any person or group—college students, Hell's Angels, or hospitalized schizophrenics.

Advantages and Disadvantages of Naturalistic Observation. As a research method, naturalistic observation has its drawbacks. *Some interesting behaviors do not occur frequently under natural circumstances.* Using naturalistic observation to study the effects of heat on violence, for instance, would require waiting around not only for a hot day, but also for an act of violence. Another problem is that *people may change their behavior if they know that they are being observed.* Even if someone were hot under the collar, she might restrain her violent tendencies if a researcher were observing. Researchers who use naturalistic observation try to avoid this problem by watching from a concealed location or by trying to blend naturally into the background (as did the uniformed observers in the Navy cafeteria). A third problem is that naturalistic observation *does not allow cause–effect statements.* Since so many complex factors co-occur in the real world, it is difficult to make confident causal statements from naturalistic observation. For example, even if researchers observed two fights in a parking lot during a particularly hot spell in the summer, they could not be sure that other factors besides the heat did not provoke the incidents (for example, a recent layoff at the local factory).

Nevertheless, the method has important advantages. For one, it provides a *rich source of information about spontaneous behavior in natural environments.* If you are interested in dominance and spatial behavior, interactions between seamen and naval officers are an example of the "real thing." As we will see, other methods have problems of artificiality. A second advantage is that naturalistic observation provides a *rich source of hypotheses.* An **hypothesis** is a tentative and testable assumption (an "educated guess"). Naturalistic observations can lead to guesses that are more educated, and those can then be tested with other methods. Darwin's careful use of naturalistic observation, reported in his *Voyage of the Beagle* (1839), provided the ideas for his theory of evolution (Ray and Ravizza, 1985). As we noted, that theory had a great influence on psychology's founders.

CASE STUDY

A **case study** is an in-depth examination of a particular person. It differs from naturalistic observation in that it usually focuses on only one individual, and is not usually done in a natural setting. In

would accept only if she wished to pursue further contact. Instead of relying on a single client's memory or an investigator's preconceived beliefs, this method provided an accurate, objective de-fact, case studies may not involve any direct observation of behavior, but may be based on interviews with an individual and/or those close to him or her.

In medicine, the case study is used to describe a person's symptoms and response to treatment. In psychology, the case study has sometimes been used in the same way. For instance, psychologists who take a neuropsychological perspective may use case studies to determine how people's behaviors change after they suffer brain damage from accidents or surgery. A case study can also offer insights about how abnormal behavior might be linked to stressful events in a person's life. Consider the following case of a boy whose occasional blindness seemed to have no medical basis:

> At the age of 18, a young man was struck in the eye by a snowball. He was experiencing general unpopularity among his classmates when this happened. He now found that he could not see, and therefore could not study or remain in school. Whenever he sought work, over a period of four years, he would become functionally blind. He mixed well with his friends who were working and, although jobless himself, he seemed contented with his lot. As long as he did not try to work or to study his vision remained normal.
>
> (Cameron, 1963)

Freud developed his psychoanalytic theory based on cases like this one—medical problems that seemed to be caused by psychological rather than physical damage.

Advantages and Disadvantages of the Case Study Method. As a method for psychological research, the case study also has its limitations. A major problem is that *it depends on the accuracy of a person's memory*. People do not remember everything that ever happened to them, and as we have seen, do not recall everything accurately. They may not tell the researcher everything that they do remember for fear that what they remember may be irrelevant or embarassing. In addition, *case studies lack generality*. It is difficult to determine if one case study applies to others since no case ever exactly duplicates another. Like naturalistic observations, *case studies do not allow causal inferences*. There are often several incidents in a person's past that may have caused a particular problem. In Chapter 13, we will describe how different researchers studying the case of Vincent Van Gogh developed over

a dozen explanations for why he cut off his ear (Runyan, 1981).

Despite its problems, the case study has some advantages. First, *a case study involves a real person with a real problem*. Like naturalistic observation, it is not artifical or contrived. In addition, *a case study can be used to observe a rare phenomenon that would otherwise be difficult or impossible to study*. For instance, psychologists could not study hysterical blindness with naturalistic observation of a group of normal people in normal environments because the malady occurs only in rare individuals under unusual circumstances. Like naturalistic observation, the case study is an invaluable *method for generating hypotheses* that can later be tested with other research techniques.

SURVEYS

Imagine that you wanted to know what percentage of high school students have had sexual relations. You would not study an unusual clinical case, and you could probably not make a truly naturalistic observation. (A researcher with a notebook and a flashlight at a drive-in movie would disrupt the very behaviors she wanted to study.) A psychologist interested in such behavior might instead conduct a *survey*. A survey is a questionnaire or interview study in which people are asked to describe their behaviors, feelings, or thoughts about a particular topic. Survey results conveniently summarize the opinions, beliefs, or behaviors of large groups of people. For instance, a recent survey of 1,300 students in 16 United States high schools found that 57 percent of them had lost their virginity, and that the average age for first sexual intercourse was 16.9 years old (Van-Biema, 1987).

Advantages and Disadvantages of Surveys. A crucial problem with surveys is that *it is difficult to obtain an unbiased sample*. For instance, many high schools refused to participate in the study of sex among high school students. In fact, the researchers approached 148 schools, and fully 132 of them were unwilling to have the survey conducted in their schools (VanBiema, 1987). If the 16 schools that did agree to participate were in more sexually liberal areas, the estimates of teenage sexuality would be inflated. Another problem is that *people's responses to surveys may be biased*. People may not remember accurately, or they may be embarassed, and therefore answer dishonestly. Consider the problems in getting high school students to recollect accurately and tell about their sexual histories. Someone who recently has had sex might tend to overestimate the frequency of his or her sexual activity, while someone who has broken up with his or her steady partner might underestimate. Then, too, a student who is worried that his or her answers might be made public may not tell the unadulterated truth.

Despite these problems, surveys have some important advantages. They *allow researchers to examine phenomena that would be difficult or impossible to study with other methods.* For instance, naturalistic observation of students would reveal little about their sexual lives, since most of them would go to some lengths to avoid being observed during a sexual act. Surveys also allow *easy access to data describing large populations.* Surveys require no special equipment or laboratory conditions, and can be easily administered in homes, shopping malls, and high school classrooms.

THE DISTINCTION BETWEEN CORRELATIONAL AND EXPERIMENTAL RESEARCH

The descriptive findings provided by surveys, case studies, and naturalistic observations can be analyzed to determine the relationship between different **variables.** Variables are changes or differences that researchers use to make comparisons across time, across people, or across environmental conditions. Gender, IQ, blood alcohol level, and political party affiliation are examples of variables that

have been studied in psychological research. Each of these variables can be measured, and different people will obtain different scores on the different measures. For instance, three different people might obtain IQ scores of 60, 100, and 145. As we will discuss in the chapter on intelligence, those scores correspond to retarded, average, and gifted intelligence, respectively.

Research that looks for a relationship between two observed variables is said to use the **correlational method** because it examines the extent to which the variables co-relate, or occur together. This relationship is expressed by a statistic called the **correlation coefficient.** Psychologists use this statistic to determine the relationship between such variables as high school grades and IQ test performance, or social class and rate of sexual intercourse. The correlation coefficient is discussed more fully in the Appendix. Since a basic understanding of correlation findings is essential to psychological research, however, we will now discuss how it is used in research.

A correlation can range in value from +1.0 through 0 to –1.0. A correlation indicates two things; the sign (+ or –) indicates whether two variables change together in the same direction, (+), or if one goes up in frequency as the other goes down, (–). The magnitude (from 0 to 1.0) indicates how strongly the two variables are related to one another. For example, students who get high grades on college entrance exams tend to get high grades in their college courses, while

Behaviors likely to be correlated with college grades. It is likely that college grades are *positively* correlated with the amount of time spent studying, and *negatively correlated* with the amount of time spent on such distractions as watching television. A positive correlation indicates that as one variable (such as number of hours spent in the library studying) increases, the other variable (grades, in this case) also increases. A negative correlation indicates that as one variable (such as number of hours of television watched) increases, the other decreases.

those who get low scores on the entrance exams tend also to get low grades in college courses. Thus, the correlation between entrance exams and college grades is positive (higher scores on one are associated with higher scores on the other). A perfect positive correlation would be indicated by a +1.0, which would tell us that the score on one variable is perfectly predicted by the other variable. Fortunately for those who do not score well on college entrance exams, the correlation between entrance scores and grades is only moderate (about +.3 to +.4). This moderate positive correlation means that, although good entrance scores are somewhat related to good grades, some people who score poorly on entrance exams go on to attain good grades, while conversely, some who attain high entrance scores go on to fail in college. A negative correlation indicates that two variables change in opposite directions. For instance, there may be a negative relationship between the number of hours a college student watches television and his or her grade point average. Finally, a zero correlation indicates that two variables are unrelated. The relationship between college grades and preference for pea soup is probably zero. Whether you like or dislike pea soup has no bearing on your grades, and your earning good grades has no bearing on your taste for pea soup. Examples of these different correlations are provided in Figure 1.5.

Table 1.2 gives examples of actual correlations. As you can see there, there is a strong positive

relationship between one twin's IQ score and that of his or her identical twin (Bouchard and McGue, 1981). That means that if you know the IQ of one twin, you can make a pretty good (but not perfect) guess about what the second identical twin's score will be. There is a moderately positive relationship between stressful life events and depression (Barrera, 1981). A correlation of +.39 tells us that people who experience many stressful events (such as losing a job) are generally more depressed than those who have less stress in their lives. But +.39 is far from a perfect relationship, meaning that many people who experience stress do not become depressed. The .00 correlation between a mother's IQ and her boy's aggression means that knowing a woman's IQ tells us nothing about her son's level of hostility (Renken, Egeland, Marvinney, Manglesdorf, and Sroufe, 1989). Finally, the negative correlation between economic conditions and lynchings of blacks in the south indicates that when the economy went *down* during the first half of this century, lynchings went *up*, and vice versa (Hepworth and West, 1989).

Correlations help us see whether there is or is not a relationship between two variables, but they cannot explain how and why the variables are related. Consider the fact that monthly ice cream sales and monthly drowning deaths in Atlantic City are positively correlated. One could speculate that the drowning deaths are caused by the ice cream sales (children who go swimming too soon after eating ice cream get cramps and drown), or

FIGURE 1.5 Hypothetical examples of different correlations.   The points in each graph represent students according to their college grades (*x*-axis) and three other variables (different *y*-axes). The letter next to each point stands for a particular student; A = Ann, B = Bob, and so on. As indicated by the different graphs, a correlation can range in value from −1.00 (the lower the amount of TV watching, the higher the college grades) to zero (no relationship between pea-soup preference and college grades) to +1.00 (the higher the number of hours spent studying, the higher the college grades).

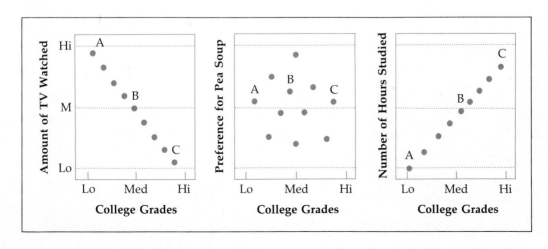

TABLE 1.2 Examples of Actual Correlations from Psychological Research

Variables Measured	Correlation	Interpretation
IQ test scores of identical twins	+.86	One twin's IQ is usually very similar to the other's IQ.
Stressful life events and depression	+.39	Stressful life events are slightly related to depression, but not strongly.
Mother's IQ score and boy's aggression	.00	A woman's IQ score is completely unrelated to her son's aggressiveness.
Economic conditions and lynchings of blacks	−.43	Lynchings and economic conditions were inversely related; when the economy was up, lynchings were down.

that ice cream sales are caused by drowning deaths (mourning friends buy ice cream to overcome their feelings of grief). However, the most plausible explanation is that the two variables are not directly related at all, but are linked by a third variable, daily temperatures—when it's hot, people swim, and they buy ice cream; when it's cold, they do less of both.

An important distinction in research involves the issue of whether the researcher manipulates the phenomenon of interest, or simply records it. Data from surveys and observational studies are simply recorded, and the researcher does not manipulate the presumed causal variable. Thus, the methods we have discussed thus far (case studies, naturalistic observations, and surveys), in which the researcher looks for relationships between variables, but does not manipulate any variable, are correlational methods; they allow researchers to compute correlations between variables. On the other hand, studies in which the researcher controls, or manipulates, one or more variables utilize the **experimental method,** and hence are called *experimental studies.* This distinction is an important one. To determine cause and effect relationships

between variables, researchers generally rely on the method of experimentation.

EXPERIMENTATION

In using the **experimental method,** the researcher systematically manipulates one or more variables to determine how those variables affect behavior. Researchers conduct experiments primarily to establish cause and effect relationships. For instance, a researcher who wanted to know whether high-sugar diets contribute to children's hyperactivity might begin by finding two similar groups of hyperactive children. The researcher would then divide the children into an experimental group and a control group. The **experimental group** is a group for whom the experimenter alters some feature of the environment. In this case, an experimental group could be a group of hyperactive children put on a low sugar diet. A **control group** is a comparison group that is treated identically, except that it is not exposed to the crucial experimental manipulation. In this case, a control group might consist of a group of hyperactive children left on a normal diet. To determine whether sugar indeed played a causal role in hyperactivity, the activity levels of children in the experimental group would be compared to those of the control group.

In an experiment, the variable that is manipulated is called the **independent variable** (sugar in this example), while the behavior that is measured is called the **dependent variable** (here, hyperactive behavior). Independent variables are manipulated, dependent variables are measured.

Let us consider one actual experiment. Psychologists Robin Damrad-Frye and James Laird (1989) were interested in the causes of a psychological state that plagues many students: boredom. The researchers speculated that we sometimes become bored when a barely noticeable distraction prevents us from focusing on the task at hand. Imagine you are reading a magazine article as part of a class assignment. If you are confronted with an obvious distraction, such as a blaring stereo, Damrad-Frye and Laird thought that you would not become bored, but would instead become irritated at the annoyance. With a barely noticeable distraction, however, such as the soft dialogue of a television soap opera in the next room, you might not realize you were being distracted. Instead, you might assume that the article must be boring, because you could not concentrate on it. To test this hypothesis, the researchers asked three groups of students to read an article about psychotherapy from *Psychology Today* magazine. Previous testing showed that students found the article moderately interesting. While reading the article, students were exposed to one of three conditions:

1. *Loud distraction:* a recorded TV soap opera blasting from the adjoining room;

2. *Moderate distraction:* the same show playing at a lower, just noticeable, level;

3. *No distraction.*

In the terminology of the experimental method, the students in the two distraction conditions are the experimental groups, those exposed to no distraction are the control group. At the start of the experiment, each student was randomly assigned to one of the groups. This process of random assignment, a crucial feature of an experiment, helps ensure that the experimental and control groups are alike in all important ways, except in terms of the manipulation of the independent variable. In this study, the independent variable was the noise condition (none, soft, or loud); the dependent variable was the students' ratings of boredom with the article. (The results, incidentally, generally supported the predictions. Students who read the article without distraction found it moderately interesting. Moderate noise led to high ratings of boredom. Louder noise, on the other hand, increased feelings of annoyance more than feelings of boredom.)

Advantages and Disadvantages of Experiments. Like the other techniques, experimentation has both problems and strengths. Among its problems, *carefully controlled laboratory conditions may not reflect conditions in the real world.* By controlling and isolating factors that normally co-occur in the world outside the laboratory, experiments may become artificial. For instance, people might be more distractible in a laboratory experiment than they are in the privacy of their own dorm rooms (where they could use a headset to drown out distractions). Just because distraction can lead to boredom in a laboratory setting, that does not mean that normal instances of boredom are *caused by* normal distractions. A second problem is that *experimental participants may behave in the way they think the experimenter wants them to behave.* This phenomenon is related to the problem of reactivity, which was a drawback for naturalistic observation also. As anyone who ever observed a sudden change in family behavior when company arrives is aware, people suppress their unpleasant behaviors when they know that they are being observed. Finally, *manipulations of psychological variables raise special ethical*

questions. Other methods, such as surveys and naturalistic observation, sometimes raise ethical issues about the invasion of people's privacy (since people may not want to be observed, or to talk about intimate details of their lives). This can also be a sensitive issue in experiments. However, experimental manipulations differ in a crucial way from other methods. Other methods *describe* phenomena that are already occurring (in the case of naturalistic observation) or that may already have occurred (in the case of case histories and surveys). The experimenter, on the other hand, is trying to *cause* a behavior that might not normally have occurred. Thus, experiments raise a number of special ethical questions. Before returning to consider the advantages of experimentation, we will consider these ethical problems.

RESEARCH AND APPLICATION:
The Ethics of Experimentation

Through their research, psychologists hope to discover ways to control child abuse, to overcome drug addiction, to reduce prejudice, to soothe depression, and to treat a host of other behavioral problems. Some experiments are completely benign, as when a perception researcher studies visual illusions. When it comes to studying such phenomena as aggression, prejudice, and stress, however, researchers face several ethical questions. The foremost question is: To what extent is it acceptable to expose humans and animals to unpleasant conditions in the interest of science?

Ethical Considerations in Human Experimentation

In the chapters that follow, we will describe experiments in which people were exposed to some rather unpleasant events. Subjects in stress experiments have been exposed to loud noises, electric shocks, and bloody circumcision films (Lazarus and Folkman, 1984). Male subjects in experimental treatments for homosexuality have been exposed to shocks or nausea-inducing drugs while they looked at photographs of nude men (Feldman, 1966). Those subjects are almost always volunteers who know what they are getting themselves into. In some cases, however, a subject confronts an unpleasant situation that he or she did not bargain for. For instance, subjects in aggression studies have been exposed to personal insults and frustrations (for example, Donnerstein and Berkowitz, 1983). In these cases, it is important that the subject remain an unwitting participant; if you know beforehand that someone is going to insult you as part of an experiment, the insults would probably lose their usual sting.

These unpleasantries have been justified by the hope of understanding the roots of problem behaviors. The cost–benefit trade-off faced by human researchers is well illustrated in several controversial studies of people's willingness to comply blindly with authority figures. In a study discussed in depth in Chapter 18, subjects were instructed to administer intense electric shocks to a man who began to beg to be let out of the experiment because of heart problems (Milgram, 1963). The majority of subjects became obviously distressed, but nevertheless obeyed the experimenter's orders to continue. In another study, nurses were given a physician's phoned-in order to administer an obvious overdose of a drug that could have killed the patient. The vast majority of the nurses started to carry out the order, and had to be stopped on their way to the patient (Hofling et al., 1966). Although neither shocks nor harmful drugs were actually used in these studies, participants were nevertheless subjected to a state of temporary distress and potential embarassment. Such manipulations are not likely to be permitted according to newer ethical standards (Ross, 1988). Nevertheless, these studies taught invaluable lessons about blind obedience to authority. The medical compliance study, for instance, warned us of a potentially critical deficiency in the relationship between doctors and nurses.

How does a psychologist ensure a proper trade-off between potential unpleasantness and social value in an experiment? The American Psychological Association (1981) has established a code of ethical guidelines for research. As we indicated above, most psychological research does not involve any potential psychological harm or discomfort to subjects. If there is any possibility of harm or discomfort, the researcher is required to seek a thorough review by researchers unconnected with the particular project before undertaking it. Even if a particular study is deemed acceptable by the ethical review panel, the investigator nevertheless takes additional precautions. Before beginning, subjects are informed of any aspects of the procedures that might be harmful or stressful, and told that they are free to withdraw from the research at any time. The ethical guidelines also specify that any information about particular subjects be kept confidential. Once the research is completed, the experimenter explains the purpose of the research, and also tries to ensure that sub-jects will not suffer any stressful aftereffects (American Psychological Association, 1981). By following these guidelines, researchers hope to derive beneficial knowledge without exacting an undue cost from human participants.

Ethical Considerations in Experiments with Animals

Some research questions involve levels of risk out of the question for human subjects. An experimenter studying how intense stress effects the development of ulcers would not use college freshman as subjects, even if there were willing volunteers. Instead, the researcher is likely to use rats or mice (Selye, 1976, among others). Similarly, before testing a possible drug for depression on human subjects, the researcher is likely to test for potentially toxic side-effects on animals.

Psychologists doing such research weigh potential benefits against costs, and try to avoid research that would be unnecessarily cruel to animals, or that would yield little potential information. But not everyone agrees on where to draw the line on animal research. In recent years, some animal rights activists have even argued that all research with animals should cease. Some activists go to great lengths to stop animal research. In April, 1989, one animal rights group vandalized laboratories at the University of Arizona and "liberated" a large number of research animals, including mice infected with a disease potentially fatal to humans.

Rats and mice are the most common research animals but most animal rights literature focuses on such animals as kittens, dogs, and monkeys. Do the perceived ethics of a given study vary with the species being used? Student participants in one recent study read a description of an experiment on the effects of severe stress on bodily hormones. All subjects read about the same study, which exposed animals to severe electric shock for a prolonged period of time. The only feature of the description that varied was the species of animal being used. Although the stress to the animal was always the same, students generally thought it less ethical to use animals that were closely related to humans—chimpanzees as opposed to squirrels. They also judged it less ethical to conduct the same research using animals that have traditionally had friendly relationships with us—dogs as opposed to rats (Kallgren and Kenrick, 1989). Thus, researchers can expect more moral outrage at research conducted with monkeys than rabbits, and more outrage for rabbits than rats.

Psychologists themselves have become increasingly concerned with the humane treatment of laboratory animals. In a statement on the principles for the care and use of animals, the American Psychological Association instructs that:

> Psychologists make every effort to minimize discomfort, illness, and pain of animals. A procedure subjecting animals to pain, stress, or privation is used only when an alternative procedure is unavailable and the goal is justified by its prospective scientific, educational, or applied value. Surgical procedures are performed under appropriate anesthesia; techniques to avoid infection and minimize pain are followed during and after surgery.

(American Psychologist, 1981)

While psychologists are aware that animals can feel pain, they are also sensitive, as Martin Seligman notes, to the human suffering that could be alleviated with animal research:

> Anyone who has spent time with severely depressed patients or with schizophrenic adults can appreciate the degree of their misery.To argue, as some do, that people should not do experiments on animals, is to ignore the misery of their fellow human beings. Most human beings, as well as household pets, are alive today because animal experiments with medical ends were carried out; without such studies, polio would still be rampant, smallpox widespread and always fatal, and phobias incurable.

(Seligman, 1975)

In sum, then, psychological research involves a trade-off between costs and benefits. The costs are occasional stress and discomfort for human subjects, and occasional pain and illness for laboratory animals. The benefits are increased knowledge about the causes of behavior, and the possibility of new techniques to alleviate human suffering. Researchers have a code of ethical principles to direct decisions about those trade-offs, and ethical review boards give supervisory counsel whenever the potential costs are high.

Despite the special problems of artificiality and occasional ethical issues, experiments have two important advantages. First, *experiments allow for the control of extraneous variables.* Under natural circumstances, the effects of one factor (for example, the number of distractions in a dormitory) are difficult to sort from the influence of many other variables (such as time of the day, or season of the year). In an experiment, the researcher can isolate one variable, while leaving the others constant. For instance, an experimenter can study the effects

of distraction during any time of the day or any season of the year. A second advantage is that *experiments allow the most confident statements of cause and effect.* Correlation does not prove causality. If a survey indicated that dorm residents were most bored at times when the dorm was most distracting, it would not prove that distraction caused boredom. Perhaps boredom causes students to seek distraction by turning on the radio while studying, or perhaps some third factor, such as tiredness late in the day, causes both distraction and boredom. By manipulating distraction directly, a researcher can be more confident of its causal role in boredom.

COMBINING RESEARCH METHODS

We have noted that each research method has certain disadvantages. If every approach has its Achilles heel, which one can we trust to carry the weight of scientific proof? Should we despair of ever finding answers to psychological questions? The answer is that psychologists need a combination of different methods to come to confident conclusions. By combining approaches, the strengths of one method can compensate for the weaknesses of another, and vice versa. Table 1.3 summarizes the different methods and describes the strengths and weaknesses of each.

Consider an example of how the strengths of one method can compensate for the weaknesses of another. As we shall discuss in later chapters, correlational studies have long indicated an association between heat and aggressive behavior. As you can see in Table 1.3, though, none of the correlational techniques allow us to make any confident cause–effect statements. Laboratory experiments also indicated that heat can increase aggression, but those studies were somewhat artifical (Anderson, 1989). Putting the two types of evidence together, however, allows us to be more confident of the results, since the problems of experiments do not apply to naturalistic observations, and the limitations of naturalistic observations do not apply to experiments.

Combining different methods to study the same problem is called **triangulation** (McGrath, 1982). The term triangulation is borrowed from geological surveying, where it refers to finding the exact location of a point by observing it from two different vantage points. You could use triangulation to help return to your car in a parking lot. Before leaving the car, you might imagine lines between the auto and two different landmarks, like a large oak tree to the right and a red building straight

TABLE 1.3   Comparison of Different Methods

Method	Characteristics	Example	Disadvantages	Advantages
Descriptive/Correlational				
1. Naturalistic observation	Observer records ongoing behavior in a natural setting.	Study of interpersonal distance between naval officers	1. Low frequency of some interesting behaviors. 2. Observer may interfere with the phenomenon. 3. Lack of control necessary for causal statements. 4. Observer's pre-existing opinions may bias attention to and memory for particular details.	1. Least artificial. 2. Rich source of testable hypotheses.
2. Case study	In depth account of one individual, usually someone with a clinical problem or some other unique quality.	Case of hysterical blindness.	1. Retrospective—may lead to biased recall. 2. Special cases may not generalize to others. 3. Because of multiple events in any one case, difficult to establish cause and effect.	1. Deals with a real problem. 2. Allows study of rare phenomena. 3. Rich source of hypotheses.
3. Survey	Questionnaire or interview probes people's reports of their behaviors, feelings, or thoughts.	Questionnaire study of high school sexual experiences.	1. Difficult to obtain an unbiased sample. 2. People may bias their responses to fit social conventions, or because of inaccurate memory. 3. Does not allow cause/effect conclusions.	1. Allows access to data difficult to obtain with other methods. 2. Easy to administer to large numbers of people.
Experimental				
4. Experiment	Researcher manipulates variables of interest.	Study examining effects of different types of distraction on boredom.	1. Manipulations may be artificial. 2. Participants may behave as they think the experimenter expects. 3. Some manipulations raise ethical problems.	1. Allows for control of extraneous influences. 2. Only method that allows confident cause/effect statements.

ahead. You can later locate the car by walking towards the red building until you get to the place where the oak is directly on your right. In psychology, triangulation refers to the process of observing a phenomenon using two (or more) different methods. For instance, researchers interested in the effects of violent television on children's aggressiveness have used correlational methods as well as experiments, as we will describe in Chapter 18.

Triangulation is related to another principle of good research—**replication.** Because the results of any given study may be affected by chance factors, it is important that they can be reproduced or replicated. In the experiment on distraction and boredom, perhaps something unusual about the particular magazine article contributed to boredom under certain circumstances. When other researchers can reproduce a finding in a different setting and under slightly different conditions, we can be more confident that the finding was not due to some accidental combination of circumstances.

It is difficult to come to confident conclusions about psychological questions. To be confident, we need to use multiple research methods (triangulation), and we need to reproduce particular findings (replication). We need also to be sure that each study avoids unnecessary problems that can plague the particular method used. For instance, researchers who do case studies and naturalistic observations need to ensure that their observations can be corroborated by others who do not share their biases. Survey researchers need to use adequate samples, and to take steps to minimize respondents' dishonesty and memory biases. Experimenters need to reduce artificiality and to guard against giving subjects subtle hints that reveal what the experiment is about. As a consumer of psychological information about how to live your life, how to treat your lover, or how to raise your children, you should be skeptical of those who offer confident conclusions based on anything less than well executed studies that have been corroborated by a variety of methods.

To be skeptical does not mean to totally disregard the results of any single study. Few researchers have the resources or diverse expertise needed to conduct multiple studies using multiple methods. Instead, each finding adds one bit of evidence, one further clue to help make an adequate conclusion. Like a good detective, a scientist does not jump to conclusions based on a single clue. At the same time, good detectives, and good scientists, do not disregard any single clue, even one that is, in itself, imperfect evidence.

PARTICULAR RESEARCH QUESTIONS IN PSYCHOLOGY

As we progress through this book, we will discuss the results of thousands of different research studies on hundreds of separate research questions.

Developmental psychologists ask questions about the effects of early experience on later thoughts, feelings, and behavior. For instance: "How does an infant's relationship with her mother influence her later social behavior?

Psychologists frequently categorize themselves according to the type of research questions they ask, and the chapters that follow reflect the major subdivisions of the field. For instance, developmental psychologists, whose work is discussed in Chapters 11 and 12, ask questions about how people's thoughts and behaviors change as they grow from infancy to old age. Community psychologists whose work is discussed in Chapters 14, 15, and 16, ask questions about how economic and social conditions in neighborhoods, schools, and cities influence mental health.

One of the primary ways of dividing research questions in psychology is to split them into basic and applied areas.

BASIC AND APPLIED RESEARCH

Basic research is mainly designed to describe and understand behavior, without immediate regard for a practical payoff. Psychologists who do basic research work mostly in universities where, like Wilhelm Wundt in his Leipzig laboratory, they can pursue abstract questions without having to justify their cost effectiveness. **Applied research,** on the other hand, uses basic principles to help solve real world problems. Applied psychologists commonly work outside the university, in clinics, schools, and factories where, like Sigmund Freud in his private practice in Vienna, they are asked to demonstrate the practical utility of their work. Table 1.4 lists a number of psychology's subfields according to the basic–applied distinction.

In actual practice, the distinction between basic and applied researchers is not a rigid one, since many researchers in the fields we classified as "basic" try to apply their findings to real world problems. A developmental psychologist may work for a hospital to determine the optimal way to treat newborns, for instance, or a social psychologist may work on a program to reduce racial prejudice.

In addition to the distinctions among psychologists, it is important to be aware of the distinctions between psychologists and the members of closely related disciplines. People commonly confuse *clinical psychologists* and *psychiatrists.* The confusion occurs because both groups treat people with behavior disorders. The major difference is that clinical psychologists, like other psychologists, traditionally have been required to conduct original research to obtain a Ph.D. (doctor of philosophy degree), whereas psychiatrists traditionally have obtained an applied degree in general medicine (M.D.) followed by a post-graduate specialization in behavior disorders. Because clinical psycholo-

TABLE 1.4   Areas of Psychology

Type of Psychologist	Example of a Typical Research Question
Basic	
Physiological	What changes occur in nerve cell firings when a person ingests a chemical like cocaine? (See Chapter 2—Biological Bases of Behavior) What are the effects of prolonged stress on the body's immune responses? (See Chapter 14—Stress, Coping, and Health)
Experimental	What mental processes account for optical illusions? (See Chapter 4—Perception) Why do some people have extraordinary memory for names and faces? (See Chapter 7—Memory) What accounts for changes in consciousness that occur during dreams? (See Chapter 5—Consciousness)
Developmental	How do child-rearing practices affect adult personality? (See Chapter 11—Infant and Child Development) What causes senility? (See Chapter 12—Adolescent and Adult Development)
Personality	Why do some people seek dangerous and exciting situations, while others avoid them? (See Chapter 10—Motivation and Emotion) What accounts for individual differences in shyness? (See Chapter 13—Personality)
Social	What thought processes underlie racial prejudice? (See Chapter 17—Attitudes and Social Cognition) What accounts for epidemics of imitative suicide? (See Chapter 18—Interpersonal Relations)
Applied	
Clinical	What causes the thought disorder associated with schizophrenia? (See Chapter 15—Psychological Disorders) What can be done to alleviate the distress of severe depression? (See Chapter 16—Treatment of Disordered Behavior)
Organizational	Can people be matched with jobs that suit their particular personalities? (See Chapter 13—Personality) How does job stress affect job performance? (See Chapter 14—Stress, Coping, and Health)
School	What can be done to improve learning in a retarded student? (See Chapter 9—Intelligence)
Counseling	What can be done to reduce loneliness and sadness in college students? (See Chapter 16—Treatment of Disordered Behavior)
Political	How can psychological principles be used to reduce tensions between opposing national groups (See Chapter 19—Psychology and Global Social Problems)
Environmental	How can environmentally destructive behaviors that contribute to pollution and energy shortages be controlled? (See Chapter 19—Psychology and Global Social Problems) What are the effects of urban crowding on crime? (See Chapter 19—Psychology and Global Social Problems)

gists receive more training in general psychology, their treatment methods have tended to emphasize learning and thought processes. Because psychiatrists are more highly trained in bodily disorders and are licensed to dispense drugs and perform surgery, their treatments have more often been biologically based.

To further complicate the picture, people from other disciplines are also involved in various aspects of treatment. These include social workers, who typically have an M.S.W. (Masters of Social Work) and who often work with families in community settings. Counseling psychologists (described in Table 1.4) may have an Ed.D. (doctor of education). In recent years, a number of professional schools have emerged, which offer a Psy.D. (doctor of psychology) degree. These professional psychologists are usually not required to

Community psychologists ask questions about how mental health is influenced by conditions in the social environment.   A community psychologist might ask how living in a poverty-stricken neighborhood affects psychological disorder, crime, and alcohol abuse.

conduct original research, but are trained in clinical practice techniques. Since the term *psychology* is typically defined as the scientific study of human behavior and mental processes, there is currently some controversy about how much research training should properly be expected of someone who wishes to be called a psychologist.

PSYCHOLOGICAL RESEARCH QUESTIONS IN THEIR WIDER INTELLECTUAL CONTEXT

To help organize the many findings that we will discuss in this book, let us return to the two pioneering figures we discussed at the beginning of the chapter. William James and Wilhelm Wundt had very different interests and very different personalities. Wundt was somber, methodical, and self-disciplined; James was charming, artistic, and self-doubting. However, they were also alike in several essential ways. Most importantly, both were trained in biology, but took positions in philosophy departments. Thus, psychology began with one foot in biology and one in philosophy. As you will see, many of the problems that psychologists investigate today have their roots in philo-

sophical debates that began centuries ago. The new psychologists differed from previous philosophers in adopting the methods of natural science. The shift to a scientific approach had one very important consequence: a commitment to empirical data-gathering. We have seen this in our discussion of case studies, naturalistic observations, surveys, and experiments.

Beyond the general shift to a scientific perspective, psychology's specific roots in biological science show up in several of its theoretical perspectives, such as the neuropsychological and evolutionary approaches. Those roots can also be seen in the use of such methods as naturalistic observation, which presumes that members of our species are best observed in their "natural habitat." Wundt and James, as well as other pioneering psychologists like Sigmund Freud, were initially trained in medical schools. This grounding in the applied branch of biology persists in psychology's commitment to real world problems. Many modern psychologists study problems at the intersection of medicine and psychology—the causes and treatment of mental "pathology."

The commitment to using psychology to understand and treat human problems does not stop

Social psychologists ask questions about interactions between people. They have asked questions about negative interactions, like the racial violence displayed here during a riot in Miami. They also study positive interactions, such as love and altruism.

with psychological disorders. It shows up in every branch of the field, where applied psychologists try to find practical uses for basic research findings. Throughout this book, you will find this problem orientation highlighted in every chapter, where we include sections on *Dysfunction* and *Research and Application*. The Dysfunction features show how breakdowns in basic psychological process can lead to psychological problems, and the Research and Application features relate the findings in each area to understanding and solving human problems.

There is a wider sense in which psychology retains its philosophical roots. As the center of the humanities, philosophy addresses the questions around which universities revolve. What is the essence of human nature? What is our place in the universe? A university education is designed to help you appreciate what centuries of human curiosity have taught us about our own place in the world. Although psychology is a separate discipline with its own set of questions, it is, like each of the different courses you will take, woven into

the general history of humanity's search for knowledge. To help you appreciate where psychology stands in that historical flow, we include an *Historical Background* section in every chapter.

Two other features of the book are especially designed to show you the coherence *within* the field of psychology. First is the map shown in Figure 1.3, which was used in the overall organization of this chapter. It showed how specific research questions and methods are nested within general theoretical perspectives, which, in turn, are encompassed by their historical background. This map appears again in the *In Context* summary of each chapter. Instead of simply listing the facts within a given chapter, we place them into this map's organizing scheme. This should help you see the relationship not only of the facts within a given chapter, but also of the separate facts across the different chapters.

The second organizing feature is called *Interactions*, and it is designed to show the connections across the diverse theoretical perspectives and research findings in this broad field. Although early chapters are necessarily focussed on microscopic close-ups of processes within the single individual, each chapter includes an *Interactions* section, which connects the fine details with the larger picture. As we move through the book from microscopic to macroscopic processes, this feature will point out how each subarea of research can contribute essential details to that larger picture.

We have thus designed the special sections of each chapter to emphasize the continuity across the field, and to focus on the general principles that underlie all the specifics. Table 1.5 summarizes the general principles behind each feature.

As we travel over the terrain of psychology, then, we will discover many different local topographies of facts—specific problem areas with specific features. In exploring those particular details, we will need to stand back to see the larger picture of psychological methodology, how psychologists use a set of common exploratory tools to study different micro-features of the terrain. Standing further back, we will see a common set of larger theoretical questions that encompasses the whole field. To gain the widest vantage, we will sometimes stand completely outside the modern field of psychology, and take the global historical perspective. When you have completed your journey through this field, you should know not only a set of facts about the specific discipline of psychology, but you should better understand the nature of our species and its scientific search for our place in the world.

From microscopic nerve cells to macroscopic group behaviors. Psychological research questions range from questions about microscopic processes within individuals (such as the different hormones influencing men's and women's behavior) to macroscopic social processes such as group conflict.

TABLE 1.5 Integrative Features of This Text

Special Feature	Description	General Principle Being Illustrated
Historical Background	Describes how the research problems in each chapter were defined and addressed by earlier scientists and philosophers.	The importance of modern psychological research can be better understood by examining its roots.
Dysfunction	Shows how behavior disorder can result from breakdowns in other processes.	Abnormal behavior is often rooted in the same processes that lead to normal behavior.
Research and Application	Provides in depth description of research dealing with causes or solutions for some individual or societal problem.	Basic and applied psychology are two sides of the same coin.
Interactions	Shows how: ■ Microsopic parts combine into macroscopic whole. ■ Person and environment are in continuous interplay. ■ Present events interact with genes and past experiences.	Different theoretical perspectives represent interlocked pictures of the same phenomena.
In Context	Sorts the central points of each chapter along a continuum from specific to general.	The diversity of specific findings and research strategies are nested within the context of general theoretical perspectives, and, in turn, within a historical background, to create an interwoven whole.

IN CONTEXT: THE SCIENCE OF PSYCHOLOGY

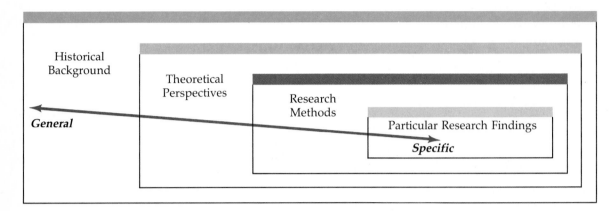

STUDY QUESTIONS

How can a scientific analysis be applied to behavior and mental processes?

What are the historical and philosophical roots of psychology?

What are the main theoretical perspectives in the field?

What are the research tools used by psychologists?

How can the particular research findings in psychology be organized into subfields?

HISTORICAL BACKGROUND

1. Wilhelm Wundt defined the field of psychology in his **Principles of Physiological Psychology,** written in 1873. He established a psychological laboratory at the University of Leipzig in 1879. Wundt was originally trained as a physician, and taught physiology before moving to a chair in philosophy.

2. William James was the first American psychologist, and a co-founder of the new field. Like Wundt, he was trained as a physician but eventually took a position as a philosophy professor. James adopted an evolutionary perspective on thought and consciousness, and wrote the landmark text in the field, **Principles of Psychology** (1890).

MODERN THEORETICAL PERSPECTIVES

1. The **evolutionary perspective** considers behavior and mental processes as adaptations that helped our ancestors survive and reproduce. Evolutionary theorists assume that animals inherit genes that influence behavior and mental processes by affecting the development and functioning of the nervous system and other physiological structures.

2. The **behavioral perspective** considers how observable features of the environment influence observable behaviors.

3. The **cognitive perspective** considers how people process information. Cognitive theorists consider the processes of attention, information storage, and retrieval.

4. The **phenomenological perspective** considers the person's experience from a subjective, rather than an objective, viewpoint. This perspective is closely connected to the **humanistic** approach, which emphasizes the positive aspects of human behavior, the individual's control over his or her own experience of the world, and self-development.

5. The **psychoanalytic perspective** considers human behavior to be motivated by unconscious determinants related to early conflict between society and the individual's selfish biological needs.

6. The **neuropsychological perspective** considers the physiological processes and structures that underlie behavior.

7. Recently, an emphasis on the interactions among the processes addressed by other schools has developed. This view, sometimes

called the **interactionist perspective,** emphasizes three themes: (1) Separate psychological processes fit together into a whole person; (2) The person continually interacts with the environment; and (3) Psychological events in the immediate present interact with historical causes represented by genetic predispositions and past personal experiences.

RESEARCH METHODS

1. **Naturalistic observation** is a technique for gathering data on ongoing behavior under natural circumstances. Its disadvantages include the low frequency of many interesting behaviors, the possibility of interference with the phenomenon of interest, and a lack of the control necessary to make causal statements. Its advantages are that it deals with natural behavior in natural settings, and that it provides a rich source of hypotheses.

2. **Case studies** are intensive investigations of single individuals, often used to study people with rare behavioral problems or special abilities. Their disadvantages are that they are often based on retrospection, they lack generality, and they cannot establish clear causal relationships. Advantages are that they deal with real people with real problems, they can address rare phenomena, and they can provide a rich source of hypotheses.

3. **Surveys** are studies in which people are asked to report on their beliefs, opinions, or behaviors. The disadvantages of surveys are that it is difficult to obtain an unbiased sample, and that people's responses may be biased. The advantages are that they provide easy access to data that would be otherwise difficult to obtain, and that they can easily provide descriptions of large populations.

4. **Correlational** techniques examine the relationship between different variables (social class and intelligence, for example) but have difficulties establishing clear causal explanations.

5. **Experiments** involve the manipulation of variables to determine their causal relationship with behavior and mental processes. Experiments have the disadvantages of artificiality and special ethical problems, sometimes producing unpleasant reactions in people and animals. The main advantage of the experiment is that it allows confident statements about causal relationships.

RESEARCH FINDINGS AND SUMMARY

1. Psychological research questions can be divided into **basic** and **applied** questions. Basic researchers seek to describe and understand behavior and mental processes, but may not be particularly concerned with practical uses of their findings. Applied researchers use basic principles to solve real-world behavioral problems.

2. Each chapter includes several special features:

   ■ **Historical Background** features explore the historical and philosophical roots of the research questions in any particular area.

   ■ **Dysfunction** features show how disordered behavior is related to basic psychological processes.

   ■ **Research and Application** features show how psychological research can be used to explain and sometimes improve real world problems.

   ■ **Interactions** features show how different parts of the person interweave with one another, and with past and present influences of the environment.

   ■ **In Context** features (like this one) organize the material in each chapter along the general–to–specific continuum, extracting from each chapter the basic questions, their historical context, the modern theoretical perspectives on those questions, the research methods used to examine them, and the particular empirical findings and definitions in that area.

3. The goal of this text is to show psychology not as a loose connection of empirical findings, but as an interwoven whole, best viewed by a combination of research methods, best considered from several interrelated theoretical perspectives, and best understood in light of a general context of philosophical and scientific ideas.

ADDITIONAL READINGS

Hilgard, E. R. 1987. *Psychology in America: A historical survey.* San Diego: Harcourt Brace Jovanovich. This book provides an excellent account of psychology's roots in other sciences and in philosophy. It devotes a chapter to Wilhelm Wundt and William James.

Stanovich, K. E. 1986. *How to think straight about psychology.* A lively introduction to the methods of psychology. The author argues that there is a wealth of scientific data about psychology, but that most of the books found in the "psychology" section of the bookstore and most of the "psychologists" appearing in the media have no scientific credibility.

BIOLOGICAL BASES OF BEHAVIOR

T he human brain is the most complex structure in the known universe. The extraordinary properties of this three or so pounds of soft tissue have made it possible for *Homo sapiens* to dominate the earth, change the course of evolution through genetic engineering, walk on the moon and create art and music of surpassing beauty.

(Richard Thompson, 1985)

Dr. P. was a well-known musician who taught at a music school. It was there that he began having problems recognizing the faces of his students. Not only did Dr. P. fail to identify familiar faces, he saw faces where none existed. On the sidewalk, for example, he would pat the top of a fire hydrant thinking it was the head of a child. But this was not the worst of it. On one occasion he was leaving his physician's office and looking for his hat when he took his wife's head in his hands and tried to place it on his head. According to the physician who examined him, Dr. P. had "apparently mistaken his wife for a hat" (Sacks, 1985). Tests showed that there was nothing wrong with Dr. P.'s eyes. His problems were caused by a massive tumor in the visual areas of his brain. Problems like this lead us to ask: What is the relation between brain and behavior?

Some scientists have estimated that the adult human brain is composed of 180 billion nerve cells, 50 billion of which are devoted to processing information (Kolb and Whishaw, 1990). What can these billions of nerve cells do? To give just a sample:

- The brain monitors and controls our basic life support systems, such as breathing and digesting.

- It directs our movements and maintains our balance and posture.

- It receives and interprets information from the world around us.

- It records significant and sometimes insignificant events into our memory.

- It allows us to solve problems, use language, and think of new ideas.

- It enables us to feel materials such as soft cotton and coarse burlap and to experience emotions such as happiness and sorrow.

- And, if this were not enough, it can do all of these things for us more or less simultaneously.

Working together with the glands of the endocrine system and the rest of the nervous system, the structures of the brain are responsible for all that we do, all that we feel, and all that we think about.

To see these systems in operation, consider just a few seconds of a tennis player's behavior. Visualize someone about to hit a tennis ball. This person's eyes need to follow the ball's approach and send this information to the brain. The brain, in turn, needs to analyze this information to determine the ball's trajectory and velocity and then to direct the muscles of the body to move the player to the right location on the court. At the very same time the brain has to prepare the muscles of the arm and upper body to swing the tennis racquet at the ball. For the swing to be properly executed, the brain must precisely integrate information from the eyes and muscles to coordinate the actions necessary to hit the ball over the net. As all this is going on, various glands in the endocrine system must increase heart rate and respiration to keep the body mobilized for action, while the electrical and chemical state of the brain changes rapidly as the player thinks about the game and revises the game plan. As every tennis player knows, you do not just hit a ball in a game of tennis: you keep track of your opponent's position, remember previous plays, continually update the score, produce emotional outbursts following well- or poorly-played shots, and devise an overall strategy in trying to win the match. All these diverse and complicated aspects of behavior are produced by the brain and other parts of the nervous system with the help of the **endocrine glands** (glands, including the pituitary and the adrenals, that secrete hormones into the bloodstream).

Why do we begin with a discussion of biological processes when many of you are interested in mental processes or disordered behavior? The answer to this question is that every process we will discuss in this book uses simple neural impulses and hormonal secretions as its building blocks. As you will see, damage to the nervous system is not just physical damage. It produces psychological problems that affect your sensations and thoughts as well as your social relations. Alter one part of the brain and you will no longer recognize your friends; alter another part and you will no longer make sense out of the words they say. Similarly, a biochemical imbalance can lead to hallucinations and distorted thinking and ultimately may require you to be committed to an institution for the insane. On a less extreme level, an excess of the hormone testosterone may lead to sexual obsession, while too little of the hormone norepinephrine can cause you to sink into depression.

An understanding of our biological strengths and limitations also gives us some perspective on the evolutionary significance of our behavior. For example, the existence of a large brain with millions of cells devoted to language suggests that communication was important to the survival of our prehistoric ancestors and tells us why speaking comes so readily to a child of today. As we proceed to examine more complex behaviors, the biological processes we will describe help us keep in mind that we are not a random collection of perceptions, habits, and impulses. We are specially evolved social beings with an efficiently integrated set of biological predispositions and potentialities. Beneath all the complexity, our basic biological capacities help us adapt to the unique problems of human life.

In this chapter we will examine the main features of the nervous and endocrine systems to see how they operate and what they do. After tracing the development of research on brain/behavior relations, we will examine how the brain and other parts of the nervous system function, from the microscopic activities of single nerve cells to complex brain structures woven of millions of separate cells. We will also see how the nervous system works hand in hand with the endocrine system. Although we will study the various physiological components in isolation, in reality they operate in an organized and unified network, like the thousands of components in an automobile. But just as a single loose bolt might turn a once-efficient automobile into a useless piece of machinery, so might a malfunction in any of these physiological components lead to serious disruptions in thought, emotion, or overt behavior. Thus, the material in this chapter is as essential to understanding psychology as a chapter on mechanics would be to an adequate understanding of the automobile. We can no longer assume that the study of the nervous system belongs to biology and the study of the behavior belongs to psychology. **Neuropsychology** is the field of psychology that represents the convergence of these scientific disciplines. It is the study of how behavior is organized and controlled by the brain and other parts of the nervous system (Gilinsky, 1984). We turn now to an examination of the historical roots of neuropsychology.

HISTORICAL BACKGROUND:
Neuropsychology

Early Theories

No one knows who discovered the special influence of the brain on behavior. The ancient Egyptians certainly did not connect the two. They mummified their dead pharoahs and went to great lengths to preserve the body for its journey to the afterlife. The heart and other vital organs were sealed in jars, while the "useless" brain was scooped out of the skull and discarded. This belief in the importance of the heart and blood vessels is fairly easy to trace—blood represents life, and the heart is responsible for its circulation.

Later Greek and Roman physicians, such as Hippocrates (fifth century B.C.) and Galen (second century A.D.), believed that behavioral problems were caused by imbalances of vital fluids (called *humors*) that moved through the body and brain. This view was updated during the Middle Ages, when people believed that food was absorbed by the intestines and passed to the liver, where it was changed into a fluid that circulated throughout the body. When this fluid reached the brain, it mixed with oxygen and then mysteriously changed into an *animal spirit* that enabled the body to move. Originating from the Latin *anima* (for life force) and *spiritus* (for breath), the animal spirit was believed to be stored in the fluid-filled cavities of the brain that we now refer to as **ventricles.** Up through the Middle Ages, it was the "stuff" in the brain's ventricles that was considered important, rather than the brain itself.

Around the seventeenth century, as the Renaissance ended, the ventricle theory was gradually replaced by the view that behavior and thought are produced by specific structures in the brain. Postmortem examinations of brain-damaged individuals, for example, showed how specific physical and psychological problems related to specific damage to the brain. Moreover, the discovery of sensory and motor neural pathways that linked the brain to the rest of the body suggested a neural basis for our ability to see, to hear, and to move about in the world. These early anatomical studies in the eighteenth and nineteenth centuries laid the foundation for modern neuropsychology.

Tan's brain and brain/behavior relations. When Paul Broca performed autopsies on former patients such as Tan, whose brain is shown here preserved in the Musée Dupuytren, he found that speech disorders were related to a damaged area of the brain.

The Nineteenth Century

As in any area of science, progress in understanding brain/behavior relations has hardly been smooth. For example, during the nineteenth century followers of **phrenology** believed that the bumps on a person's head could reveal that person's character. According to a Viennese physician named Franz Josef Gall (1758–1828), the shape of the skull conformed to the shape of the brain, which could be broken down into separate areas, each controlling a particular characteristic such as "reverence" or "secretiveness." Therefore, he reasoned, an enlargement of an area of the skull was caused by an excess of one characteristic, while a recessed area indicated a particular deficiency.

The attempt to connect brain and behavior by studying bumps on the head proved to be a dead end. However, it set the stage for a more fruitful approach called **localization theory.** Like phrenology, localization theory held that specific psychological functions were associated with specific areas or locations of the brain. Instead of studying bumps on the head, however, localization theorists studied the brain itself. One of the leading proponents of this view was French neurologist Paul Broca (1824–1880). By performing autopsies on former patients who had been unable to speak,

Broca discovered that each of these people had suffered damage to the same area in the left frontal portion of the brain. Broca's findings thus indicated that a specific area of the brain was responsible for speech. Findings like Broca's led *neurologists*—physicians who treat patients with diseased or damaged nervous systems—to search for connections between particular psychological functions and particular brain locations.

Although localization theorists had some successes, other scientists favored an alternative position known as **equipotentiality theory.** According to this view, there are few, if any, specialized regions of the brain. Damage to very different areas of the brain can disrupt the same psychological process because disruption depends not so much on *which area* of the brain has been damaged but on *how much* of the brain has been destroyed. Equipotentiality theorists believed that different areas of the brain were equivalent to one another. Each area shared "equal potential." The foremost proponent of equipotentiality theory was psychologist Karl Lashley (1890–1958). Lashley studied how learning was affected by the loss of parts of the **cerebral cortex,** the outer surface of the brain responsible for intelligent behavior. By destroying increasingly larger areas of the cortex in laboratory rats, Lashley found gradually greater disruption of

Karl Lashley. Lashley played a major role in establishing the field of neuropsychology, the study of the relation between the nervous system and behavior.

learning and memory. When only one area was destroyed, remaining portions of the brain could sometimes take over its function (Lashley, 1929).

Modern Approaches

Lashley's findings clearly supported his equipotentiality theory, but the earlier findings (from Broca and others) suggested that localization theory was also partly correct. Today, most neuropsychologists have adopted an intermediate position derived from the work of British neurologist John Hughlings-Jackson (1835–1911), the founder of modern neurology. According to **interactionist theory,** such complex psychological functions as perceiving and reasoning are based on a number of more basic abilities. Each of the basic abilities can be relatively localized in different areas of the brain (for example, the visual cortex at the back of the brain is crucial for seeing), but they are linked by numerous connections so that many different brain areas may be involved in the same psychological function (Beaumont, 1983). Rather than seek the specific brain location for each complex psychological function, Hughlings-Jackson believed that we would make greater progress by determining how several different areas of the brain each make a unique contribution to these functions. This view is more complex than either localization or equipotential theory, but it is also more consistent with what we now know about the relations between brain and behavior (Kaas, 1987).

Today, neuropsychologists use a variety of procedures to learn about brain/behavior relations. Much of this work is based on studies of laboratory animals. Neuropsychologists perform brain operations to see how the removal or destruction of brain tissue in a particular area affects an animal's behavior **(lesion procedure),** they stimulate the brain with electricity by inserting tiny wires into different brain structures **(electrical stimulation),** and they record the brain's electrical activity **(electrophysiological recording).** This research into brain/behavior relations is supplemented by work in such other fields as *neurology* (the study of the nervous system and its diseases) and *endocrinology* (the study of the endocrine glands). As an example of how procedures have changed, physicians previously needed to perform autopsies on former patients to see whether a damaged area of the brain might have caused a particular behavior disorder. Now, medical imaging techniques make it possible to examine the living brain. Figure 2.1 shows three of these techniques—a **CAT scan,** a **PET scan** and an **NMR scan.**

In a CAT (computerized axial tomography)

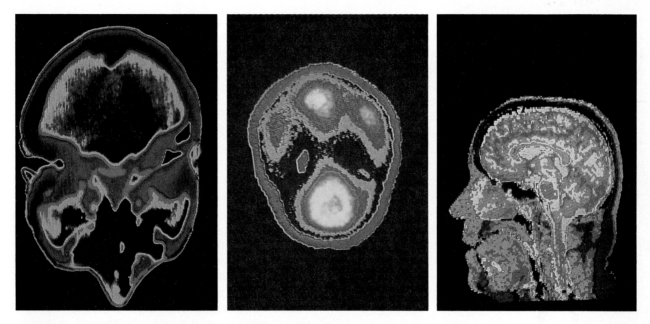

FIGURE 2.1 Modern imaging techniques allow us to look inside the head without surgery. (A) This CAT (computerized axial tomography) scan shows a two-dimensional top view of the interior of a person's brain. Evidence of a stroke (ruptured blood vessel) can be seen in an area called the parietal lobe. (B) In a PET (positron emission tomography) scan, warm colors such as yellows and reds indicate regions of high metabolic activity. In this example, a person is looking at a complex scene and the top view scan of the brain shows that an area in the rear of the brain called the visual cortex is most active. (C) This NMR (nuclear magnetic resonance) scan allows us to look at the soft tissue of the brain rather than its chemical processes without harming the patient.

scan, a series of X-ray measurements are made from many different orientations around a person's head. A computer than reconstructs the X-ray data into an image showing a "slice" of a person's brain (Figure 2.1A). This procedure allows researchers to detect damaged areas as small as one square millimeter. In a PET (positron emission tomography) scan, a scanner measures the amount of glucose (a form of sugar that is the brain's primary source of energy) being consumed in numerous brain locations. A computer analyzes this information to show differences in the rate of glucose consumption in different brain areas (Figure 2.1B). PET scans can be used to show which areas of the brain are used in different mental tasks and which areas of the brain no longer function normally. Finally, an NMR (nuclear magnetic resonance) scan provides an image of the brain's interior structures. In this procedure, a magnetic field is used to temporarily align atoms in one direction. When the field is removed, the atoms "wobble" back to their original orientation and, in so doing, emit characteristic signals that a computer can transform into an image of the brain's soft tissue (Figure 2.1C). Over the course of history, our conception of the brain has changed dramatically. What was seen at first as a mass of useless tissue became a container for animal spirits and then a complex set of interrelated neural structures that determine our actions and thoughts. ■

THE ORGANIZATION OF THE NERVOUS SYSTEM

Open the back of a television set and you will see wires, printed circuits, and a picture tube. Remove the top from a personal computer and you will find still more wires and printed circuits. The wires and circuits in these devices are the basic units of operation. How each device works depends upon how these basic units are arranged. In an analogous sense, the nerve cells called **neurons** are the basic units of operation in the nervous system. By themselves, though, they cannot explain the complexities of thought and emotion that enable a surgeon to perform a delicate operation or a musician to compose a spirited symphony. It is only when the "wires" are arranged into complicated patterns that they become capable of producing action and thought.

All animals have special neural structures for taking in information from the outside world and for controlling their movements. In the human nervous system, **receptor cells** in our sense organs—for example, our eyes or ears—receive environmental stimulation, while **effector cells** in our muscles or glands generate movements or chemical secretions. The receptor and effector cells are connected by different types of neurons to provide a neural network. **Sensory neurons** receive stimulation from the receptor cells and transmit it to the brain and spinal cord, while **motor neurons** transmit information from the brain and spinal cord to the effector cells in the muscles or glands. In between the sensory and motor neurons, **interneurons** transmit information back and forth between different parts of the brain and spinal cord. Spreading to every part of the body, the various neurons form an intricate communication network that we know as the nervous system.

MAJOR DIVISIONS

Actually, the nervous system is not a single system but a set of interrelated divisions and subdivisions (Figure 2.2). The first division consists of the **central** and **peripheral nervous systems.**

The central nervous system is made up of the brain and spinal cord. It is connected to the rest of the body by the nerve cells of the peripheral nervous system. The peripheral nervous system is subdivided into the **somatic** and **autonomic nervous systems.** The somatic system contains sensory neurons that carry impulses *to* our brain,

making us aware of different sensations such as temperature change, pressure, and pain. It also contains motor neurons that carry impulses *from* the brain and spinal cord to our skeletal muscles, producing voluntary movements such as throwing or walking and involuntary movements such as adjustments in balance or posture. The autonomic system is responsible for the activity of internal organs and glands. Nerves in the autonomic system link the brain and spinal cord to vital internal organs such as the stomach and heart. As implied by its name, the autonomic system functions autonomously: It allows the brain to regulate such life-supporting processes as digestion, heart rate, and respiration without any voluntary or conscious involvement on our part.

The autonomic system is itself further divided into the sympathetic and parasympathetic divisions. The **sympathetic division** is the "fight or flight" system—it prepares us physically for action during periods of high excitement or stress. The **parasympathetic division,** on the other hand, operates to conserve resources when we are calm (Figure 2.3). The normal body state is maintained by a balance between these divisions.

How does this complex nervous system guide our reflexive and voluntary behavior? Consider the following examples.

A REFLEXIVE RESPONSE
When infants arrive in the world, they can make a number of behavioral responses that are not de-

FIGURE 2.2 The major divisions of the human nervous system.

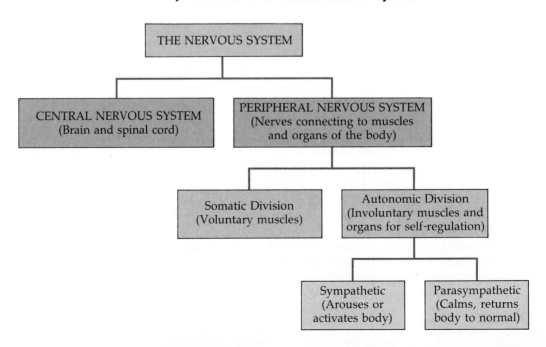

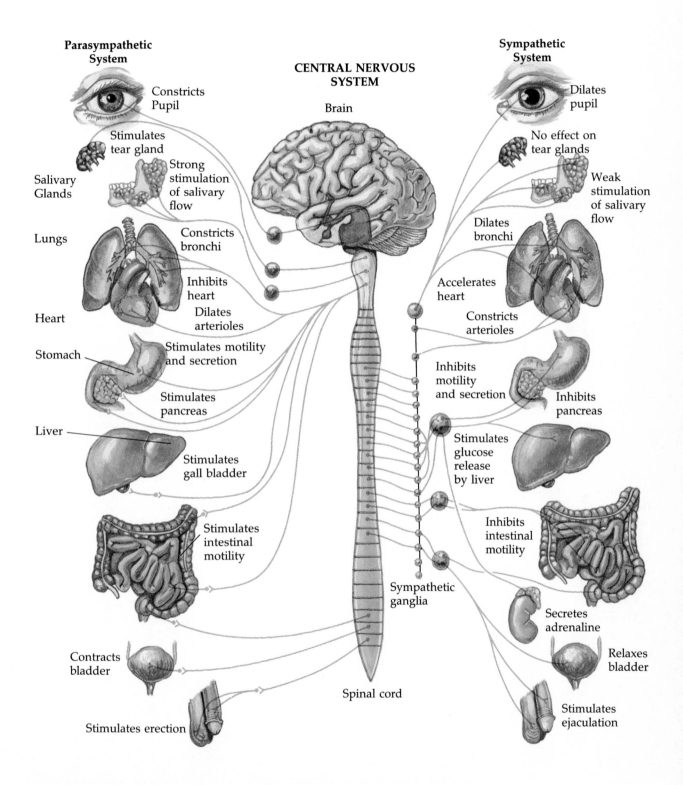

FIGURE 2.3 The autonomic nervous system consists of the sympathetic and parasympathetic systems. While most organs receive nerves from both systems, the function of these systems is largely complementary as they work in opposite ways. The sympathetic system is dominant during an emergency, while the parasympathetic system restores body equilibrium after the emergency has passed.

pendent on learning or thought. For example, they can withdraw their hands if pricked by a pin, close their eyes if something comes too close, and turn their heads in the direction of a stimulus— especially a nipple—that lightly touches their cheeks. These innate responses, called **reflexes,** are involuntary responses to particular stimuli that are based on existing or "pre-wired" connections in the nervous system.

As an example of a reflexive response, consider what happens when you accidentally touch a casserole dish that has just come out of a hot oven. The heat stimulates sensory receptors in your hand. The receptors then generate neural impulses that are transmitted along the sensory neurons to the spinal cord. Once there, interneurons transmit the sensory message in two different directions. One set of interneurons transmits the message to the brain, where it will be interpreted as pain. Other interneurons, entirely within the spinal cord, relay the sensory message to motor neurons in the cord. These, in turn, transmit motor commands to the muscles in the arms and hand, causing them to contract. The result is an involuntary, jerking back of the hand before you even have time to think about it or experience pain. This spinal withdrawal reflex has obvious survival value.

A VOLUNTARY RESPONSE

Although the withdrawal reflex is automatic, it need not occur all the time. The brain provides for flexibility. For example, suppose you have grasped a hot casserole dish with potholders and are carrying it to the dinner table. As you walk from the oven to the table, you feel the heat and become increasingly aware of the sensation of pain. This gradual pain is also the result of sensory receptors in your hands generating impulses that travel along the sensory pathways to your brain. Unlike the case where you rapidly withdraw your hand after touching a hot dish, you can withstand the moderate pain this time because it builds gradually and, because of the insulating potholders, it is not as intense. In this instance your brain issues *inhibitory* messages to the motor neurons in the spinal cord, causing you to hang onto the dish until you reach the table. Simultaneously, however, your brain issues *excitatory* messages to other motor neurons that stimulate those muscles needed to hurry you to the table. This example demonstrates how the nervous system integrates various excitatory and inhibitory signals to produce a unified response.

Two points should be clear from this overview of the nervous system. First, the nervous system is composed of billions of individual neurons that function as a **communication network,** linking widely separated parts of the body. This means that stimulation received at one part can lead to a response somewhere else. Second, the nervous system functions as an **integrative network** by simultaneously organizing the enormous amount of information it receives from both inside and outside of the body. The brain and other parts of the nervous system continually evaluate all this information and direct the body's effectors in a unified course of action. To understand how this is accomplished, we must turn our attention first to the building blocks of the nervous system to see how nerve cells function individually, and then to the neural structures that make up the brain to see how those cells function collectively.

BASIC NEURAL PROCESSES

Despite its complexity, our nervous system is basically constructed from only two different types of cells. Nerve cells called **neurons** receive and transmit neural signals to other parts of the body, while **glial cells**—the more numerous of the two— support and protect the neurons. Glial cells take their name from the Greek word for glue. They form a connective network that holds together the brain's billions of neurons. In addition, the glial cells insulate one neuron from another throughout the nervous system and clear away cellular debris when neurons degenerate and die. A continuous layer of glia surrounds the blood vessels in the brain to establish a *blood–brain barrier,* a protective shield that prevents many harmful chemical substances from passing from the blood to the brain.

Protected by the glial cells, the neurons carry out the main functions of the nervous system. They bring information to the brain from our senses, and they are involved in storing memories, solving problems, making decisions, and controlling our muscles. Since all of our behavior and experience depends on the action of neurons, it is important to understand something about their structure and the way they function.

THE STRUCTURE OF A NEURON

Neurons come in many different shapes and sizes, but they share certain anatomical features: Neurons have a cell body, dendrites, and an axon. (It will be helpful to refer to Figure 2.4 as you continue reading.) The **cell body** consists of a membrane boundary that surrounds the nucleus and internal contents of the cell. The nucleus is the

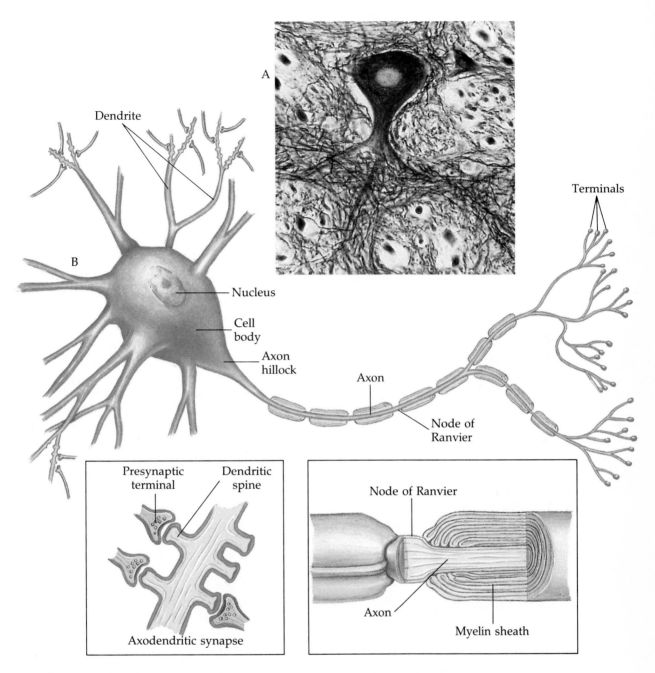

FIGURE 2.4 **(A) Nerve cells of the human spinal cord that have been magnified 160 times.** Gold staining makes the neurons appear brown. These nerve cells are the elementary units of our nervous system; they receive and transmit information to and from all of the different parts of our body. **(B) A typical neuron, showing the cell body, dendrites, and axon.** Magnified portions show the dendritic spines that receive stimulation from nearby cells and the nodes of Ranvier and myelin sheathing on the axon that facilitate neural transmission to the terminals.

portion of the cell that contains *deoxyribonucleic acid (DNA)*, strands of protein that hold the genetic blueprint for the cell's makeup and function. The cell also contains protoplasmic material that manufactures chemical substances used to communicate with other neurons.

Reaching out from the cell body like the branches of a tree, the **dendrites** receive information from other neurons. The longer and more complex a neuron's dendrites, the greater the number of connections it can make with other cells. The dendrites are sometimes covered with microscopic spines, and it is primarily at these spines that dendrites receive signals from other cells for transmission down their "trunks" to the cell body.

Neural signals are transmitted to other cells by the **axon,** a single fiber that emerges from the cell body. A group of elongated axons from hundreds or even thousands of neurons is called a **nerve.** Axons in the brain are usually less than one millimeter long, but axons from the spinal cord to the big toe can reach lengths of three feet or more. Chemical substances can travel in both directions along an axon and more than one type of chemical message can be passed to the receptors of an adjacent cell. Some diseases may involve disorders of axonal flow. For instance, patients with amyotropic lateral sclerosis (A.L.S. or Lou Gehrig's disease) lose their ability to control their muscles and eventually become helpless as the disease gradually destroys motor neurons and the axons from the brain to the motor neurons.

Axons are usually coated with an insulating material called a **myelin sheath** that is produced by the glial cells. Periodic breaks in the myelin sheath, which cause the axon to resemble a beaded necklace, are called the *nodes of Ranvier* (Figure 2.4B). These nodes allow axons with myelin insulation to transmit neural signals faster than uninsulated axons can because the signals can be transmitted along the axon by jumping from one node to the next. Myelin also helps prevent the scrambling of neural messages. For reasons that are still unknown, axons may sometimes lose their myelin sheath and respond abnormally. For example, in the neurological disorder called multiple sclerosis, axons that have lost myelin respond slowly and become susceptible to random firing from the activity of nearby cells. This neural short-circuiting produces slurred speech, jerky movements of the body, and eventual muscular paralysis.

At its end, the axon branches to form small structures known as **terminals** (Figure 2.4B). Each of the terminals transmits neural signals to the dendrites or cell body of an adjacent cell. In most instances, this signal is not transmitted by physical contact between neurons, but by a chemical process that bridges the small gap separating the cells. The gap, roughly 2/1000s of a micrometer (a micrometer is 1/1000 of a millimeter), is called a **synapse.**

NEURAL IMPULSES AND THEIR TRANSMISSION

When a neuron is sufficiently stimulated by another neuron, there is an electrical reaction in the walls of the axon that travels over the entire length of the axon to the terminals. This electrical reaction is called the **neural impulse.** Depending upon the diameter of the axon and the thickness of its myelin sheath, a neural impulse travels at a rate of approximately 2 to 200 miles per hour.

NEURAL FIRING

Neural impulses are generated by an electrochemical process involving the cell membrane. The cell's protoplasm and the liquid surrounding the cell contain electrically charged molecules called **ions** that can penetrate the cell membrane when the cell is stimulated by an adjacent cell. In the cell's inactive (nonfiring) state, the membrane keeps positively charged sodium ions (Na^+) on the outside and various negatively charged ions on the inside. This separation of ions causes the inside of the cell to be more negatively charged than the outside. The result is a small electrical charge, or voltage difference, across the cell's membrane. As shown in Figure 2.5A if a neuron is undisturbed, the charge remains relatively constant. This electrical charge is called the **resting potential** and it is similar to the stored energy of a flashlight battery, although it contains much less energy.

As shown in Figure 2.5B, when a nerve cell is strongly stimulated by another cell there is a chemical change in the cell membrane. The membrane becomes permeable, causing positively charged ions from the outside to enter and negatively charged ions from the inside to exit. This change quickly reverses the cell membrane's electrical charge at the point of stimulation and causes the adjacent portion of the cell membrane to reverse its charge as well. The change in the cell membrane passes rapidly in one direction down the length of the axon. It resembles a burning fuse of gunpowder when the heat from one portion of the fuse causes the next portion to ignite. This rapid change in the cell membrane is called the **action potential,** and, as it moves down the axon, it becomes the neural impulse (see Figure 2.5C).

For a neuron to generate an impulse, it must receive a certain level of stimulation. This is called the *threshold level.* Like a set mousetrap or a cocked gun, once it is triggered into action the neuron fires in a uniform and unchanging way. Stimuli that are below the threshold level produce no impulse at all, while stimuli above the threshold produce the same response each time. This unvarying relation is called the **all-or-none law.**

Since neurons fire in an all-or-none fashion, exactly the same for all stimuli above threshold, you might wonder how we distinguish between such different sensations as a gentle tap on the shoulder and a hearty slap on the back. The answer is that

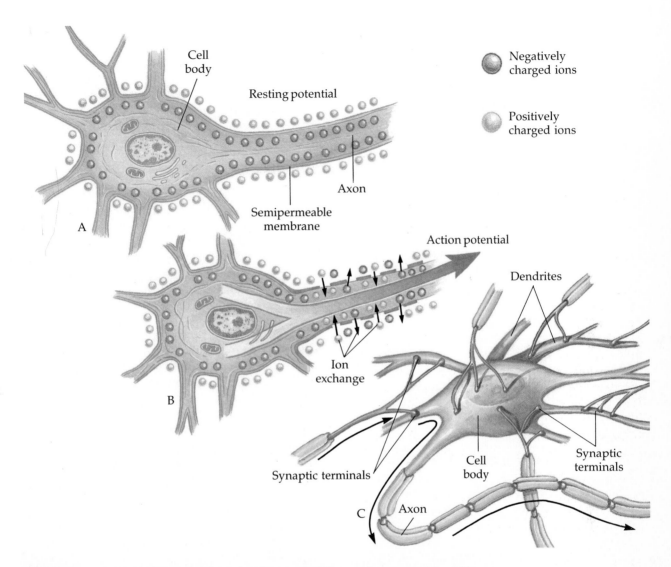

FIGURE 2.5 The neural impulse from resting potential to action potential. This highly diagrammatic view of a nerve cell shows that during a cell's resting state (A), positively charged ions are kept outside, while negatively charged ions are kept inside. When a cell is stimulated by another cell, the positive ions rush into the cell through its semipermeable membrane, reversing the cell's electrical polarity and causing this reversed polarity to travel down the length of the axon. This rapid change in polarity (B), is called the action potential, and as it moves down the axon, it becomes the neural impulse (C).

while individual neurons never produce impulses that vary in strength, intense stimulation generates impulses in a large number of cells. We can detect the strength of a stimulus by both the number of neurons that fire and the rate at which they respond. The brain combines the information from different sources to produce the appropriate sensation. So a weak tap on your shoulder will stimulate a low rate of firing in a small number of neurons, while a strong slap will stimulate many cells to fire rapidly.

Neurons can fire even without outside stimulation. In fact, there is a baseline level of spontane-ous activity in each neuron as it lies waiting for new stimulation. That stimulation can come either in the form of **excitatory influences** that increase the likelihood of firing or **inhibitory influences** that slow it down. (Recall our hot casserole dish example where excitatory and inhibitory impulses enable you to hurry to the table without dropping the dish.) All of the stimulation received by a particular neuron is channeled into its cell body where the converging excitatory and inhibitory influences are combined. If the resulting stimulation is sufficient, the neuron fires; if not, it continues to wait.

Drugs that have psychological effects often have an excitatory or inhibitory influence on neural firing. For example, the local anesthetic Novacain inhibits neural firing. Novacain blocks the conduction of the action potential along the axon. Dentists therefore can drill away at the nerves in our teeth without our feeling any pain because the pain messages are not transmitted to the brain. Still other drugs do not block a neuron from firing but raise its threshold level so that greater excitatory input is necessary before the neuron will fire. Presumably, this is why drugs such as diphenylhydantoin (Dilantin) are effective in treating **epilepsy,** a brain disorder produced by the continuous firing of neurons. Dilantin appears to raise the neural threshold level and thereby decrease the likelihood that these cells will fire. Epilepsy itself provides a particularly vivid example of the powerful influences that basic neural processes have on behavior.

DYSFUNCTION:
Epilepsy

It was Christmas morning and the children had come into our room to open presents. They sat all three bouncing around on the foot of our bed, the younger girl in the middle, Jonathan and his older sister on each side.

Suddenly one of them shouted "Mummy, something's wrong with Jonathan," and we all looked at him. He sat quite still, with a fixed stare in his eyes. Slowly his head turned to the left and his eyes moved sideways. His body stiffened, and as he began to slide off the bed I jumped out and supported him. For seconds he seemed to get tighter and tighter, and his color became pallid and then a horrible blue. Then small convulsive movements began in his arms and legs, which although they were not violent were very forceful and not to be restrained. He grunted, as if he were making a great physical effort with each jerk. This seemed to go on for an eternity, although it cannot have been much more than half a minute, with his color getting worse all the time.

Then it stopped, fairly quickly, and he lay there with his eyes turned up, once again motionless, not even seeming to breathe. I felt for his pulse and it was still there. As I

held his wrist, Jonathan gave a few deep gasping breaths, and his color began to come back, and the blueness disappeared. He coughed and spat, and my wife wiped his lips with a handkerchief because he seemed to have much more saliva than usual.

When he was breathing normally again, and murmuring to us, we carried him back to his bed, where he slept for a quarter of an hour. When he got up, he was a bit silent, but was soon back to normal, and returned to his very subdued sisters for more opening of presents.

I suppose the whole incident could only have lasted less than half an hour, but those thirty minutes changed our family life.

(Laidlaw and Rickens, 1976; cited in Sarason and Sarason, 1980)

Epilepsy was once thought of as a "sacred disease" caused by divine visitation. The origin of this belief is unknown, but it may have been based on the occurrence of an "aura," unusual sensations, including dizziness and hearing strange sounds, that occur just before an epileptic attack. The distinguishing symptoms of epilepsy are alterations of consciousness and recurrent seizures. The seizures are due to the spontaneous firing of hyperexcitable neurons in one area of the brain that spreads quickly to other areas. The neural mechanisms that produce epilepsy are still poorly understood. However, the development of the *electroencephalograph,* a device for recording the electrical activity of the brain, has made it possible to relate different types of epilepsy to different patterns of electrical activity.

To understand how an electroencephalograph works, recall that individual neurons in the brain are constantly receiving excitatory and inhibitory input from other neurons. This constant neural "chatter" produces continuous fluctuations in the electrical activity of billions of brain cells. An electroencephalograph records these fluctuations from a large number of neurons simultaneously. To record this electrical activity, electrodes are placed on the scalp, only a few millimeters from the brain's surface. Each electrode can then monitor the collective activity of the many neurons in its immediate vicinity.

Figure 2.6A shows different recordings, called **electroencephalograms** or **EEGs,** taken from people in various states of arousal. For example, when a person is excited the EEG recording is relatively flat, with many small, rapid changes in voltage. On the other hand, when a person is relaxed, with closed eyes, the recording shows slower changes in voltage. Generally, brain waves become larger in amplitude and slower in frequency as a person falls asleep. We will see in Chapter 5 that EEG recordings can distinguish not only between drowsy and alert states but also between different stages of sleep, thereby providing researchers with an objective measure of a person's state of consciousness. The electroencephalograph is an important diagnostic tool for epilepsy because it is possible to detect which area of the brain is malfunctioning by recording from different areas of the scalp.

Varieties of Epilepsy

Among the many different types of epilepsy, the best known are *grand mal* and *petit mal*. Figure 2.6B shows how EEG recordings distinguish between each of these seizures. Grand mal epilepsy is the most common type, characterized by seizures that render the victim unconscious and produce massive muscular convulsions. At the onset of the seizure the person becomes rigid for a few seconds and then begins a sometimes violent and rapid jerking of the trunk and limbs. Such an attack lasts from less than a minute to 30 minutes or more. If the seizure is brief, the person may quickly return to normal functioning, but if it is long, the person may pass into a deep sleep, followed by confusion and fatigue. Grand mal seizures may occur several times a day or only once every few years.

Petit mal seizures consist of a short reduction of consciousness rather than a complete loss. There are no convulsions and victims may not even know that they have had a seizure. During a petit mal attack, which lasts from 10 to 40 seconds, the victim appears to be in a trance; although he or she may speak during this period, the speech is usually repetitious and unrelated to previous events. Petit mal attacks can occur from several times a week to more than 100 times a day. For reasons still unknown, petit mal epilepsy is primarily found in children between the ages of four and eight, and it usually disappears before a child reaches adolescence.

In some cases, epilepsy can be traced to head injury, brain infection, or drug abuse, but in more than half of all cases no specific cause can be found. Seizures in epileptics can be triggered by flickering lights, menstruation, and emotional stress, or they can occur spontaneously, for no apparent reason at all. Fortunately for the 80 million people suffering from epilepsy worldwide, it can usually be treated with such anticonvulsive drugs as Dilantin. As we will see in the next section, a neuron's job is to transmit its signal to other neurons in the nervous system. Dilantin works to dampen this process by raising a neuron's threshold for firing. ■

FIGURE 2.6 Characteristic EEG recordings. This shows us brain waves for different behavioral conditions in normals (A) and for petit mal and grand mal seizures in epileptics (B).

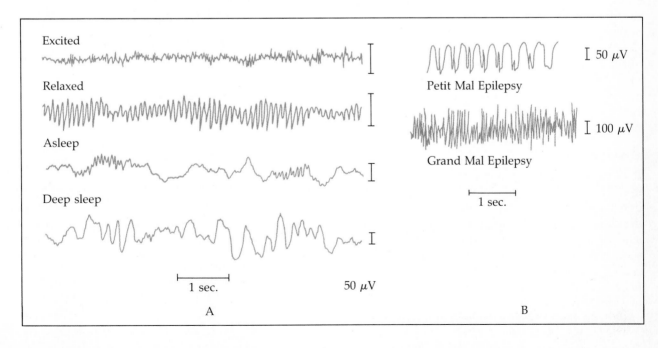

SYNAPTIC TRANSMISSION

Neurons not only fire, they communicate with other cells to create an informational network that links the various parts of our body. Because neurons located in our feet send neural impulses to our brain, we know when we stub our toe or step on a tack. To understand this communication process, it is crucial to understand how one neuron transmits its impulses to another.

The billions of neurons in the brain produce at least 10 trillion synaptic connections. A typical neuron may have several thousand of these synapses, small gaps separating the nerve cells. Figure 2.7 shows how a typical neuron sends its impulse across a synapse to the next neuron. The electrical impulse that has traveled down the axon of the transmitting cell must be converted into a chemical messenger that stimulates another neuron across the synaptic junction. In neurological terms, the transmitting cell is called the **presynaptic neuron,** the receiving cell is called the **postsynaptic neuron,** and the chemical messenger is known as the **neurotransmitter.** Since neurotransmitters affect other cells chemically, this means that most drugs that affect the nervous system (and ultimately our behavior) do so by influencing these chemical messengers that are transmitted from one cell to another.

Neurotransmitters are manufactured in the presynaptic neuron and stored in tiny sacs called *vesicles* located in the axon terminals. When an electrical impulse reaches the axon terminal of the presynaptic neuron, it forces the vesicles to break; like a cannon firing a burst of shells, the vesicles shoot their chemical contents—the molecules of the neurotransmitter—into the synaptic junction. Some of these molecules reach a *receptor site* on a postsynaptic neuron. A receptor site is simply a portion of an adjacent neuron that receives the molecules of a neurotransmitter. The molecules fit a receptor site like a key fits a lock. Since there are specific receptor sites for different types of neurotransmitter, only the molecules of a particular transmitter will "key" into a given receptor site.

As we said earlier, excitatory or inhibitory influences can change a neuron's threshold for firing. These excitatory or inhibitory influences are determined by the synaptic sites. Synaptic sites at dendrites tend to be excitatory, while synaptic sites at the cell body tend to be inhibitory. Consequently, a neurotransmitter received at an excitatory synapse will stimulate the postsynaptic neuron to fire, while a neurotransmitter at an inhibitory synapse will make it less likely to fire. At any given time, a cell receives neurotransmitters

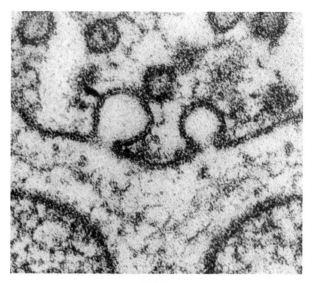

A

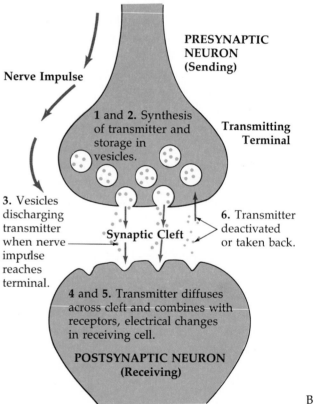

B

FIGURE 2.7 **(A) A photo magnification of a neural synapse. (B) The steps in the process of synaptic transmission.** The transmitting cell is called the presynaptic neuron, the receiving cell is called the postsynaptic neuron, and the slight space between both neurons is called the synapse. The terminal of a presynaptic neuron contains the synaptic vesicles that hold chemical substances called neurotransmitters. When an electrical impulse reaches a presynaptic terminal, it causes the vesicles to merge with the cell membrane and release their chemical contents into the synaptic cleft. The result is a chemical transmission of stimulation from one cell to its neighbor.

from various receptor sites. The postsynaptic neuron analyzes the incoming excitatory and inhibitory signals and fires only if the net level of stimulation passes its firing threshold. When this threshold is reached, the electrical-to-chemical-to-electrical transmission process is almost complete. All that remains is for the neurotransmitter to be deactivated so that the postsynaptic neuron can be stimulated again. Deactivation can occur in one of two ways. First, an enzyme at the synapse can break down the neurotransmitter. Second, the neurotransmitter can return to the presynaptic neuron. This process is called *reuptake* and it is the most common form of deactivation. Deactivation is crucial, for without it the nervous system would become overstimulated. This would lead to tremors and, eventually, death. In fact, some insecticides and nerve gases produce their deadly effects by blocking the deactivation of neurotransmitters at the neuromuscular junctions. Thus, victims die of uncontrollable muscle spasms.

In recent years, researchers have suggested that neurotransmitters can be related to certain forms of mental illness. For example, schizophrenia is characterized by major thought disorders (described in Chapter 15) that some believe may be associated with excessive levels of the neurotransmitter *dopamine* (Buchsbaum and Haier, 1983). Excessive dopamine is known to lead to disturbances of thought, emotion, and behavior, which are part of the symptoms of schizophrenia. The drug *chlorpromazine* works to alleviate these symptoms by interacting with dopamine's receptor sites in much the same way as the neurotransmitter. Because chlorpromazine molecules are shaped like those of dopamine, they can act like keys in the dopamine receptor locks. When this occurs, chlorpromazine blocks the dopamine receptors and the symptoms of schizophrenia are reduced. Another drug, *reserpine*, appears to reduce dopamine levels by destroying the vesicles for this neurotransmitter located in the presynaptic neuron. We will have more to say about schizophrenia in Chapters 15 and 16. For now, schizophrenia remains a fascinating puzzle because drugs that block or reduce dopamine can be used as a treatment for its symptoms even though no one has ever demonstrated that brain cells in schizophrenics produce excessive amounts of this neurotransmitter.

The use of drugs to counteract the effects of neurotransmitters provides a vivid example of how neurochemical processes in the brain interact to influence behavior and experience. To date, neuroscientists have firmly identified only a relatively small number of neurotransmitters, al-though the existence of many more is suspected. Table 2.1 lists some of these important chemicals, along with their effects on behavior.

Before we leave this material on basic neural processes and move on to the brain, we need to consider how these processes can be influenced by the environments in which they develop.

EFFECT OF EXPERIENCE ON NEURAL DEVELOPMENT

We study the nervous system to understand how it influences behavior and experience. But what effect does experience have on the development of the nervous system? Can experience affect the structure and function of nerve cells? To answer this question neuroscientists have examined the behavior and the brain cell development of rats that were reared under different environmental conditions. For example, in one study using the experimental method, laboratory rats from the same litter were placed in one of three groups soon after weaning: rats in an *enriched environment* condition were housed in a large cage full of objects that they could manipulate and explore (Figure 2.8), those in a *social control* condition were reared with other rats in barren cages and given no exploratory experience, and the animals in an *isolation control* condition were reared all alone in barren cages.

As adults, the rats from the enriched condition were behaviorally different from the other rats. For example, they learned to run mazes faster and with fewer errors (wrong turns) than did rats from the other conditions. Postmortem microscopic examinations of the brain cells of each of the rats revealed neurological differences as well. The rats from the enriched condition showed more extensive neural development than those in the other conditions. They had larger cell bodies in their nerve cells, a larger number of glia cells, and a larger number of dendritic branchings. The effect of environment on dendritic branching is especially important because a greater number of dendrite branches allows for greater communication between neurons. This research clearly indicates that experience can modify the structure of nerve cells (Greenough, Wood, and Madden, 1972; Rosenzweig, Bennett, and Diamond, 1972).

Caution is necessary in interpreting these findings, however. Rosenzweig and his coworkers have found that the brains of those rats reared in an enriched condition most closely resemble those of rats reared in a seminatural "wild" condition outside of the laboratory. Consequently, an en-

TABLE 2.1   Major Neurotransmitters and Behavior

Acetylcholine (ACh)	Found in the brain where it may be critical for normal thinking, in the neuromuscular junctions where it is necessary for muscle contraction, and in the peripheral synapses, such as those in the heart, where it serves an inhibitory function. Drugs that increase ACh in the cerebral cortex appear to help learning and retention, while those that decrease it disrupt thinking (Drachman, 1978; Sitarim, Weingartner, Caine, and Gillin, 1978). Botulium toxin, a poison found in improperly canned food, completely blocks the release of ACh at the presynaptic neuron, while curare, a poision used by South American Indians on the darts of their blowguns, blocks the receptor sites on the postsynaptic neuron that would normally receive ACh. In both instances, the victim dies of suffocation because the muscles for breathing become paralyzed.
Amino Acids	Used by neurons in the brain when fast excitation or inhibition is needed. *Glutamic acid* and *aspartic acid* are involved in excitation, while *gamma-aminobutyric acid (GABA)* and *glycine* are involved in inhibition. GABA, for example, appears to prevent the runaway excitation of neurons that is seen during an epileptic seizure. Convulsions occur when the inhibitory GABA receptor sites can no longer restrain neural activity. Tranquilizers like Valium or Librium act on GABA receptors, suggesting that this neurotransmitter may be linked to the control of anxiety.
Catecholamines	Present in the brain and peripheral nervous system. The major neurotransmitters are *dopamine (DA)* and *norepinephrine (NE)*. Within the brain there are two DA systems. One plays a major role in the regulation of movement. Loss of DA neurons results in Parkinson's disease, a disorder characterized by tremors and an inability to stand, walk, or initiate other movements. The other system is involved in schizophrenia: Excess DA can lead to the major disturbances of thought, perception, emotion, and behavior, all characteristic of this disorder (Meltzer and Stahl, 1976). The other catecholamine, NE, affects arousal and mood: too little NE can lead to depression; too much can produce an agitated, manic condition. Amphetamines increase alertness and endurance by facilitating the transmission of NE, while barbiturates produce drowsiness by inhibiting NE transmission.
Neuropeptides	Short chains of amino acids in the brain that are released during painful or stressful situations. These neurotransmitters are called *endorphins,* a contraction of "endogenous morphine," because the actions of these naturally occurring painkillers resemble those of the drug morphine (Hughes et al., 1975; Pert and Snyder, 1973). Endorphins may be responsible for the natural "high" that joggers feel after a period of strenuous exercise (Carr et al., 1981), the ability of athletes to ignore minor injuries and perform under stress, and the relief from pain experienced by some patients following acupuncture or electrical stimulation (Goldstein, 1978). The drug naloxone blocks the receptor sites for the endorphins and reverses their effect on behavior. Additional research suggests that endorphins may be involved in eating, memory, sexual behavior, and mood (Bolles and Fanelow, 1982).
Serotonin	Found in the central nervous system. It influences sleep and body temperature, and low levels of seratonin may be linked to depression and suicide. Drugs that deplete serotonin in the brain can produce insomnia or reduced need for sleep, although sleep patterns eventually become normal (Jouvet, 1973). In addition, the psychoactive substance LSD, which has a similar molecular structure to serotonin, may produce hallucinations and other thought disturbances by operating on the serotonin system in an undetermined manner (Cooper, Bloom, and Roth, 1978).

Adapted from Rosenzweig and Leiman (1989) and other sources.

riched environment may not enhance neurological development so much as an environment devoid of stimulation can hamper normal development. A lack of stimulating experience can modify the rat's nervous system and these changes, in turn, can influence its subsequent behavior and experience.

Similar effects have also been found in a number of other species, including gerbils, ground squirrels, and monkeys (Rosenzweig, 1984). Yet, despite this evidence, we still do not know whether early environmental experiences operate in the same way on humans, who are neurologically more mature

FIGURE 2.8 The living quarters for rats reared in an enriched environment. In addition to the social interactions provided by the presence of other rats, this cage is equipped with a variety of objects for the rats to manipulate and explore. Compared to rats reared in barren cages either alone or in pairs, these rats as adults showed faster learning and more extensive neurological development.

at birth. As we will see in Chapter 11, a lack of sensory stimulation during infancy can hamper subsequent cognitive and social development during childhood, but it is not clear whether these developmental deficiencies are linked to neurological deficits. Damage to the developing human nervous system is much more likely to occur while the fetus is still in the womb.

We turn now to the part of the nervous system that is of most interest to neuropsychologists—the brain.

THE BRAIN AND BEHAVIOR: STRUCTURES AND FUNCTIONS

The brain is not only the principal structure in the nervous system, it is one of the most important organs in the body. Because it is so crucial to the body, the delicate, fragile brain is provided with two vital forms of protection. First, it rests inside the skull, a set of thick bones that protects it from assault. Second, the ventricles of the brain are filled with cerebral spinal fluid that functions as a shock absorber for blows to the head. When a child

bangs her head, the skull and fluid absorb much of the force.

Another measure of the brain's importance to the body is the amount of resources it uses. Although the brain comprises only 2 to 2.5 percent of our adult body weight, it is nourished by approximately 20 percent of our blood supply. This rich supply of blood is necessary for the brain's vast energy needs, especially its continuous demand for oxygen to keep its fragile cells from dying. Unable to store oxygen for future use, the brain is disrupted by even a one-second lapse. After six seconds without oxygen unconsciousness can result, and after four minutes serious and irreversible brain damage can occur.

To understand the relations between the brain and behavior, it is helpful to think of the brain as organized into three major concentric layers. These are the **brainstem** and its related structures, which form the primitive central core of the brain; the **limbic system,** which evolved after the central core; and the more recently evolved **cerebral cortex,** which is responsible for higher mental processes. Each of these layers is depicted in a different color in Figure 2.9.

THE BRAINSTEM AND RELATED STRUCTURES

The brainstem and its related structures include the **medulla, pons, thalamus, hypothalamus, cerebellum,** and **reticular formation.** Collectively, these central core structures provide a gradual transition from the end of the spinal cord to the base of the brain. In terms of evolution, the brainstem structures are the oldest portion of the brain, existing in animals as primitive as fishes and amphibians. These structures exert control over the most primitive and fundamental aspects of our behavior.

THE MEDULLA AND PONS

Continuing to examine Figure 2.9, we see that the medulla and pons, enlargements of the brainstem, lie just above the spinal cord. The lowest part of the brain is the medulla, which regulates such vital body functions as heart rate, blood pressure, respiration, and digestion. The medulla also plays a major role in such simple reflexive movements as blinking your eyes when something comes too near to them and coughing when something gets stuck in your throat. The large bulge in the brainstem is the pons. It contains bundles of nerve fibers involved in alertness, attention, and movement. Together, the medulla and pons monitor the life supporting functions that help us survive.

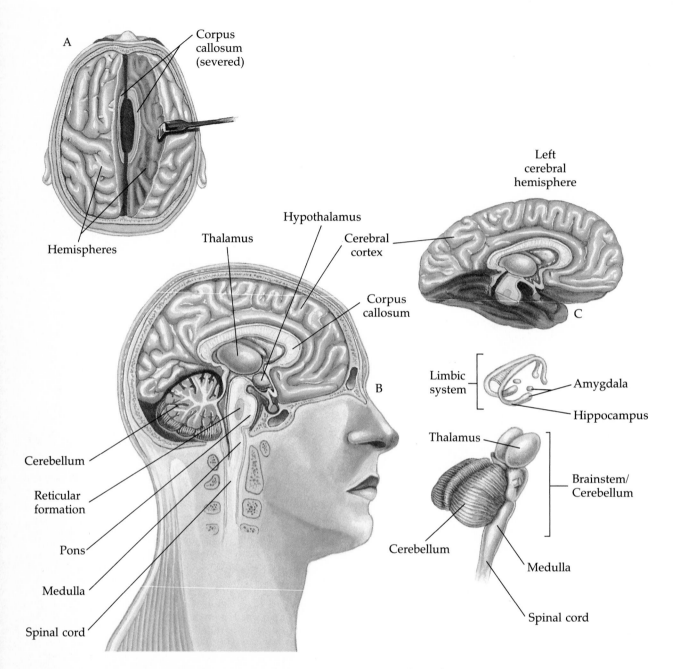

FIGURE 2.9 **The major sections of the brain as they appear normally and in isolation.** Part A shows the top view with the corpus callosum severed to reveal both cerebral hemispheres, Part B shows an interior view of the left hemisphere, and Part C shows the different brain structures as they would appear in isolation.

THE THALAMUS AND HYPOTHALAMUS

Lying above the brainstem proper, the thalamus relays sensory information from the different sensory systems, including eyes, ears, and skin, to higher centers in the brain. The thalamus is often called the brain's "relay station" because of the numerous sensory fibers that pass through this lower brain structure.

Located under the thalamus, the hypothalamus is no bigger than a peanut, but it is so important that it is sometimes called the "guardian of the body." Despite its small size, the hypothalamus is involved in many different aspects of behavior, including eating, sleeping, sexual behavior, and maintaining *homeostasis*, the proper balance of such essential bodily conditions as temperature and blood sugar level. In addition, the hypothalamus regulates the output of the pituitary gland, the master gland of the endocrine system. The hypothalamus also controls the emergency responses of the autonomic nervous system and endocrine glands, and restores equilibrium when the emergency has passed. Finally, the hypothalamus is involved in emotional experiences. For example, research has demonstrated that mild electrical stimulation to certain areas of the hypothalamus results in pleasurable sensations in animals and people. Since this research provides a fascinating glimpse into how neuroscientists learn about different brain structures, we will examine it in greater detail.

To study brain structures by electrical stimulation, researchers first perform brain surgery on a laboratory animal. Once the animal is anesthetized, a small portion of the skull is removed to expose the surface of the brain. The animal is then carefully placed in a device called a stereotaxic apparatus (stereotaxis means "solid arrangement") that holds the animals head firmly in place. Next, an insulated ultrathin wire called an *electrode* is inserted into the animal's brain. (The microscopically sharp point of this electrode can be inserted into any area of the brain that the researchers wish to study.) Finally, an electrical connector is cemented to the animal's skull to hold the electrode in place. This connector allows the researchers to connect a wire from the electrode in the animal's brain to different electronic devices. Later, when the animal is awake, the researchers can use the electrode to record the activity of nearby cells to see whether they are active when the animal engages in different behaviors, including feeding or sleeping. Alternatively, researchers can stimulate these cells by sending a weak electrical current through the electrode to observe its effect on behavior.

By using electrical stimulation of the brain (ESB), James Olds and Peter Milner (1954) accidently made an important discovery. Although these researchers set out to study a different area, their electrode ended up in an area near the rat's hypothalamus. After the rat recovered from surgery, Olds and Milner found that the animal learned to press a bar to receive tiny electrical impulses through the implanted electrode (Figure 2.10). After learning the bar-pressing response, the rat administered ESB to itself at a rate of once every five seconds. Similar effects of self-stimulation have been found in a wide variety of species including pigeons, cats, dogs, monkeys, and even humans (for example, Brady, 1961; Goodman and Brown, 1966; Heath, 1964). People who have had

FIGURE 2.10   A rat with an electrode implanted in its hypothalamus, which appears to function as a "pleasure center."   Each time the rat presses the bar, it receives a mild electrical stimulus. The rat will press the bar continuously for many hours to achieve this pleasurable effect. Psychologists use electrical stimulation to learn about the role of different brain structures.

electrodes implanted in their brains to relieve neurological disorders such as Parkinson's disease have described the stimulation as a mildly satisfying and pleasurable experience.

Because animals will work to obtain this form of ESB, researchers have speculated that these areas of the hypothalamus are important for reward. In fact, Olds described them as "pleasure centers" in the brain (Olds, 1958). What function do these areas serve? At present we do not know. But researchers have found that a number of areas of the brain, including parts of the hypothalamus, contain neural circuits that hold large amounts of the neurotransmitters dopamine and norepinephrine. Since ESB increases the release of these two neurotransmitters, one or both appear to be important for self-stimulation (Wise and Rompre, 1989). Researchers currently believe that these neural circuits are involved in reward. They are stimulated both by pleasurable activities (such as eating, drinking, and sexual behavior) that help us survive, and by other behaviors that are nonadaptive and do not enhance survival. These nonadaptive behaviors include self-stimulation and, as we will see in Chapter 5, taking addictive drugs.

THE CEREBELLUM AND SKILLED MOVEMENT

Just behind the brainstem and under the cerebral cortex is the cerebellum, or "little brain." The cerebellum receives sensory information from all over the body, which it uses to maintain posture and balance and to produce coordinated movement. (See Figure 2.9.) As an example of the cerebellum's control of movement, think about a young child who is learning how to eat with a spoon. At first, the spoon presents a bewildering number of problems for the child: how to hold it, how to balance food on it, how to raise it to the lips, and how to open and close the mouth at just the right time. Early in life, all of these movements are guided by the higher centers in the cerebral cortex. The child must use these higher centers to pay attention, to think deeply about a seemingly trivial activity. Before long, however, connections form with the motor cortex and the cerebellum takes over this task. Once the movement becomes highly practiced and automatic, the child can skillfully wield the spoon under the direction of the cerebellum. Thus, the cerebellum constructs the motor programs for all of those skilled movements from eating to swimming to playing the piano—activities we would scarcely be able to do if we had to stop and think deeply about them.

THE RETICULAR FORMATION AND AROUSAL

If you examined the interior of the brainstem with a microscope, you would see a crisscrossing network of fibers. This network of neural pathways is called the reticular formation (*reticulum* means network) and it extends to the cerebral cortex, relaying sensory information and controlling arousal and sleep. Like the ringing of a telephone, the reticular formation seems to alert the cerebral cortex to information that is on its way. When electrical stimulation is delivered through an electrode implanted in the reticular formation of a sleeping cat or dog, the animal will immediately wake up. Conversely, if some of these neural fibers are cut or dulled by barbiturates, the animal becomes drowsy and inattentive. If carried to an extreme, the destruction of the reticular formation leads to a complete and irreversible coma (Brown, 1977). In humans, the reticular formation influences not only arousal, but also the ability to concentrate and focus attention.

Under normal circumstances, all of these lower brain structures work together to regulate behavior. Imagine, for example, that you are riding a bicycle along the side of a road. Your medulla ensures that your heart rate and respiration are sufficient for the task. Your thalamus relays the sensory information from your eyes and ears to higher centers in the brain. Your hypothalamus

monitors the internal state of your body, and in an emergency (as when a truck pulls into your path) it activates a quick release of energy. Your cerebellum allows you to balance, pedal, and stop without having to ponder every move in sequence. Finally, your reticular formation and pons keep you alert and attentive as you ride. All of this goes on automatically, freeing you to enjoy the ride.

THE LIMBIC SYSTEM

As the amphibians and reptiles evolved, they developed a ring of interrelated structures that sheath the upper brainstem. These structures were once called the "reptilian brain." Today they are known as the limbic system, from the name coined by Broca in 1878. (*Limbus* means border or hem in Latin.) (Look again at Figure 2.9.) Among its different functions, the limbic system is involved both in coordinating information sent to and from the cortex and in regulating emotions. Through its ties to the hypothalamus, it monitors survival-essential behaviors, such as eating and sexual reproduction, that have strong feelings or "drives" associated with them. We will examine two limbic structures, the **hippocampus** and the **amygdala,** that have been clearly linked to behavior.

THE HIPPOCAMPUS AND MEMORY

The hippocampus comprises the largest portion of the limbic system. It got its name from the early anatomists who thought its curved shape resembled a sea horse (the Greek word for "seahorse" is *hippocampus*). (See Figure 2.9.) Contemporary research on people with hippocampal disorders often uses the case study method. Case studies involving the limbic structure have revealed that this brain structure is critically important for memory. For example, one person, identified by his initials H. M., underwent an operation in 1953 to relieve seizures from severe, uncontrollable epilepsy. In the operation, surgeons removed H. M.'s hippocampus and other limbic structures from both sides of his brain. As a treatment for his epilepsy, the operation was a success. But it produced a profound and permanent change in H. M.'s life that is best described by the psychologists who examined him.

> During three of the nights at the Clinical Research Center, the patient rang for the night nurse, asking her, with many apologies, if she could tell him where he was and how he came to be there. He clearly realized that he was in a hospital but seemed unable to reconstruct any of the events of the previous day.

On one occasion he remarked "Every day is alone in itself, whatever enjoyment I've had, and whatever sorrow I've had." Our impression is that many events fade for him long before the day is over. He often volunteers stereotyped descriptions of his own state, by saying that it is "like waking from a dream." This experience seems to be that of a person who is just becoming aware of his surroundings without fully comprehending the situation, because he does not remember what went before.

(Milner, Corkin, and Teuber, 1968)

The hippocampus, it turns out, is critical for normal memory functioning.

In the time since his operation, H. M. has learned only a few isolated facts. He has learned that an astronaut is a space traveler and that a public figure named Kennedy has been assassinated. In other ways, however, H. M. still suffers severe memory impairment. He does not know where he lives, who cares for him, or what he last ate. He has to guess at the current year and he greatly underestimates his actual age (Corkin, Sullivan, Twitchell, and Grove, 1981). Curiously, although H. M. does not readily acquire new facts and knowledge he can learn new procedures and skills. For instance, he shows steady improvement on a mirror drawing task, but each time he sits down to the task he claims never to have done it before (Cohen and Corkin, 1981). Thus, H. M. can learn from an experience without remembering that it ever happened.

The results of these studies of H. M. suggest that there is a physiological distinction between the development of motor skills and memory for facts and past events. It is this distinction, between "knowing how" and "knowing that," that involves the limbic system (Cohen and Squire, 1980; Frisk and Milner, 1990; Salmon, Zola-Morgan, and Squire, 1987). Without the hippocampus and related limbic structures, we know not what we know.

THE AMYGDALA AND AGGRESSION

The amygdala is a small limbic structure located between the hippocampus and the hypothalamus. (Refer once again to Figure 2.9.) The removal of the amygdala (called an amygdalectomy) can produce a change in emotionality. Curiously, many early studies involving amygdala lesions yielded inconsistent results. Some researchers reported tame, placid behavior in normally ferocious animals, while others found a decrease in sexuality and an increase in rage and aggression (Bard and

Mountcastle, 1948). We now know that the outcome of an amygdala lesion depends on which portion of the amygdala is destroyed (Henke, 1988; Kling, Lloyd, and Perryman, 1987; Steklis and Kling, 1985, among others).

Studies of amygdala lesions attracted considerable attention during the 1930s and 1940s because they suggested a possible neurological treatment for uncontrollable human aggression. Before the widespread use of tranquilizing drugs during the 1950s, highly aggressive patients were a major concern for mental hospital staff. If amygdalectomies could produce tame, placid behavior in animals, perhaps the same could be done with these dangerously aggressive mental patients. Working on this assumption, some neurologists and psychiatrists began to investigate the use of psychosurgery as a method for controlling not only extreme aggression but also other forms of abnormal human behavior.

RESEARCH AND APPLICATION:
Psychosurgery

Psychosurgery is defined as the destruction of brain tissue in order to alleviate emotional and behavioral disorders. It differs from other medical procedures because it involves the destruction of tissue that may not in itself be damaged or diseased but that is thought to be responsible for harmful behavior. In this regard, psychosurgery differs from neurosurgery, which involves the removal of tumorous growths or diseased tissue that may cause physical or behavioral problems. Advocates of psychosurgery today refer to it as "psychiatric surgery" in order to separate the present work from the earlier, crude procedures. Critics fail to see the difference, sometimes describing it as the deliberate mutilation of normal brain tissue to make patients more manageable (Valenstein, 1980a).

Origins and Use of Psychosurgery

Surgical attempts to alter behavior date back to ancient times. Some primitive people would chip a hole in the skull of a disturbed person to rid the brain of imagined evil spirits, bad humors, or even insect larvae (all believed to cause abnormal behavior). This practice, called **trephining,** has been used in remote areas of the world even in recent times (Valenstein, 1980a). Although these crude brain operations were the precursors of modern psychosurgery, medical professionals began using it in earnest only in 1935. After hearing a talk on how the destruction of the front portion of the brain rendered chimpanzees less excitable, a Portuguese neurologist named Egas Moniz modified this procedure to treat psychiatric patients who were considered dangerous to themselves and others. He devised a technique called a **prefrontal lobotomy,** in which he surgically severed the nerve fibers that run from the front of the brain to other areas. Moniz claimed that within two months of treatment, a number of patients had been cured.

Though very little was known about the consequences of Moniz's radical procedure, within a year two American neurosurgeons named Walter Freeman and James Watts popularized the use of psychosurgery in the United States. Between 1936 and 1950, over 10,000 psychosurgical operations were performed on people who had been described as "hopeless patients who had failed to respond to other methods of treatment, who had little to lose and everything to gain" (*Life,* March 3, 1947). Freeman alone performed 3,500 lobotomies. The operations left the patient more manageable by hospital staff, but often at the cost of unwanted side effects, including lack of foresight, blunting of emotions, and seizures. The following example shows some of these effects in a woman who was still institutionalized one year after her lobotomy:

> She lacks initiative and spontaneity, although occasionally she is the first to say "Good Morning." Her attention is not maintained . . . her judgment is poor and insight is only partial. Except for transient smiles she seems rather flat emotionally.

(Draper, 1947)

The use of psychosurgery has decreased with the development of drugs to control abnormal behavior, but surveys of neurosurgeons show that it continues to be used as a last resort for problems ranging from uncontrollable rage to chronic depression (Bartlett, Bridges, and Kelly, 1981; Donnelly, 1978). To treat uncontrollable rage, an amygdalectomy (destruction of the amygdala) is still the preferred type of psychosurgery. To control chronic depression, a cingulotomy is used. This operation involves the destruction of a bundle of nerve fibers called the cingulum (located below the cerebral cortex). This procedure is an advancement over a prefrontal lobotomy in that it does not produce the unwanted side effects that were associated with the earlier procedure. Some patients experience relief from chronic depression after a cingulotomy, but for unknown reasons others show no improvement at all (Corkin, 1980).

Concerns About Psychosurgery

The rationale for performing psychosurgery on humans is based on the premise of some neurosurgeons that patients who fail to respond to other forms of treatment may reach a "point of no return" and remain forever unresponsive to treatment (Valenstein, 1980b). It is difficult to explain how psychosurgery "works," but if brain surgery can produce dramatic changes in animals' behavior, then similar effects might be expected in humans. According to many psychologists, however, the results of the animal studies do not warrant the use of psychosurgery on humans. For example, research with animals that have had amygdalectomies has shown that a variety of outcomes are possible. Many factors contribute to psychosurgery outcomes, including an animal's status in a group before the operation and the exact location of the lesion. Some monkeys who have had amygdala lesions indeed became less violent, but when they were returned to the wild they became outcasts and eventually died (Kling, Lancaster, and Benitone, 1970). With humans, the results are equally mixed. Neurosurgeons have reported some success with amygdalectomies in treating patients subject to violent episodes, but other patients showed no improvement and required continued hospitalization (Chorover, 1979).

The problem with psychosurgery is that most behaviors are controlled in a complex manner by the interaction of many brain structures. The more complex the behavior, the greater the number and diversity of regions that appear to be involved. Aggression, for example, comes in so many different forms (for example, verbal aggression, physical aggression, spontaneous aggression, planned aggression, individual aggression, organized group aggression . . .) that it is unlikely to be associated with a single brain structure. Without understanding how the different structures of the brain work together, it is difficult to understand how the destruction of one portion is likely to affect the remaining parts.

We are only beginning to learn about the relations between brain processes and psychological disorders. Even when we do find a relation between a certain brain activity and a certain behavior, it still is not always clear which is the cause and which is the effect. The problem with psychosurgery is that without full knowledge of brain/behavior relations, it represents an indictment of specific brain structures for causing behavioral problems. In view of our present knowledge, many psychologists view this judgment as premature and think of psychosurgery as a form of experimental medicine that should be employed only with great caution. Moreover, since psychosurgery is not a life-saving or life-preserving procedure, it is not obvious who is ethically responsible for deciding to have it performed. If patients are unable to accept responsibility for their actions, who, then, is morally entitled to subject someone else to such a radical and irreversible procedure without evidence of damaged or diseased brain tissue? ▪

THE CEREBRAL CORTEX: AREAS AND FUNCTIONS

Mammalian brain evolution brought with it an increasing capacity for dealing with novel problems in learned and thoughtful ways. The increased capacity for problem solving is attributed to the brain structure that has expanded the most during human evolution—the **cerebral cortex,** or outermost layer of the brain. A layperson might confuse brainstems from a sheep and a human because of their similar size but could make no mistake about their cortexes. The human cortex not only has a very large number of capabilities, but it is immense, requiring an overstuffed cranium to house it. As you can see in Figure 2.11B, the highly developed cortex, comprising approximately 80 percent of the brain, sets us apart as a species and is responsible for our history and civilization. It plays a major role in our experience of consciousness, our sensory and motor skills, our ability to reason and plan, and, above all, our ability to use language to communicate.

FIGURE 2.11   (A) A photograph of the brain viewed from the top.   The two cerebral hemispheres as well as the convolutions of the cortex are shown. **(B) Variations in brain size.**   The brains of different vertebrates have been drawn on the same scale, illustrating the amount of the brain devoted to motor, sensory, and association areas. The increase in size of the cerebral cortex across different species, especially the increase in the amount of brain devoted to the association areas, allows for greater response flexibility and adaptability.

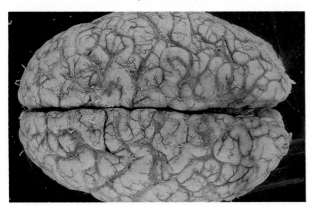

A

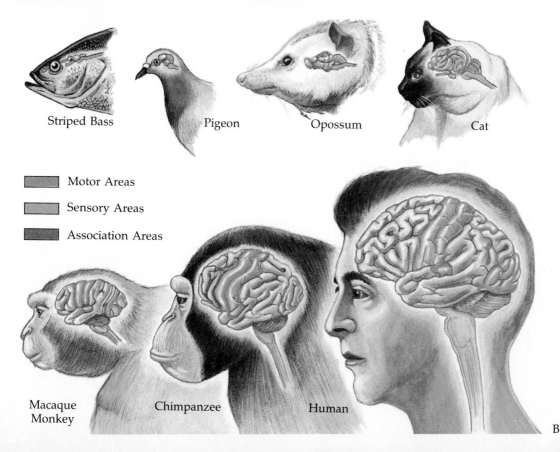

Striped Bass   Pigeon   Opossum   Cat

■ Motor Areas

■ Sensory Areas

■ Association Areas

Macaque Monkey   Chimpanzee   Human

B

THE DIVISIONS OF THE CEREBRAL CORTEX

The outermost portion of the brain consists of two large symmetrical halves (see Figure 2.11A). These **cerebral hemispheres** are linked by a thick bundle of nerve fibers called the **corpus callosum.** Completely enveloping the two cerebral hemispheres is a layer of nerve cells approximately three millimeters thick that comprises the cerebral cortex. The cortex (from the Latin word for *bark*) is responsible for giving the brain its characteristic wrinkled appearance. These wrinkles, called **convolutions,** were required by the vast evolutionary development of the cortex. As the brain increased in size over the course of evolution, the size of the skull increased to accommodate it. Scientists believe that at some point in the distant past the skull reached its physical limit, while the cortex continued to grow. The result was that the once smooth cortex became progressively cramped. In the process of twisting and turning to fill the interior of the skull, it became increasingly convoluted. Spread out, the cortex would cover an area of approximately two and a half square feet, but, wrinkled and folded, it fits snugly into the skull.

As the cortex developed, some convolutions grew larger, while others remained small. The large convolutions shown in Figure 2.12, can be used as landmarks to separate each of the cerebral hemispheres into four major divisions, called **lobes.** These rounded divisions of the brain consist of the **frontal, parietal, temporal,** and **occipital** lobes. The large convolution that runs from the top of the brain down each side is called the **central fissure,** and it separates the frontal and parietal lobes. Below the frontal lobe is the **lateral fissure.** It outlines the temporal lobe, which projects forward on each side of the brain. Finally, the occipital lobe is located at the rear of each hemisphere. From studies involving electrical stimulation of the brain and observations of people who have suffered brain damage, researchers have found that each of these areas has a somewhat different function.

For example, in 1870 two German physiologists, Gustav Fritsch and Eduard Hitzig, set out to discover which areas of the cortex were responsible for movement. They found that electrical stimulation of different cortical areas of a lightly anesthetized dog resulted in different types of movement. Stimulating one point on the surface of the dog's cortex caused the animal to flex one of its legs, while stimulating another point caused the dog to move its body. The movement was always *contralateral*—that is, on the side of the body opposite

to the cortical stimulation. This occurs because the brain's motor pathways cross over to the opposite side of the spinal cord as they leave the brain. This anatomical fact is just as true of humans as it is of dogs.

Although Fritsch and Hitzig's procedure is now over one hundred years old, detailed knowledge of the human cortical lobes came only recently. It was not until the 1940s that a Canadian neurosurgeon named Wilder Penfield began research to map various behavioral functions onto the surface of the human brain. Penfield began this research in order to help patients who suffered from severe epilepsy. Since removing even a damaged portion of a patient's cortex could lead to a potentially severe handicap, Penfield needed to know where different behavioral functions were located before beginning an operation. He obtained this information by using the method of electrical stimulation.

Since the brain contains no pain receptors, Penfield's patients were given only a local anesthetic on the surface of the head. They thus remained fully conscious while a portion of the skull and other protective coverings were removed to expose the surface of the brain. Penfield then administered a brief electrical stimulus to different points on the cortex and observed how the patient reacted. After numerous observations of this sort, he was able to draw a functional map for large areas of the cortical surface. Since the time of Penfield's pioneering research, scientists have learned that different areas of the cortex are important for receiving such sensory stimulation as the sound of a melody; for producing motor movements, including those needed to ride a bike; and for such cognitive functions as thinking, remembering, and speaking.

The Sensory Areas. Different sensory functions are connected to different areas of the cortex. Vision, for example, is localized in the occipital lobes at the back of the head. When Penfield stimulated different points in the occipital lobe, patients reported that they saw flashing and dancing lights, brightly colored discs, and radiating spots that changed to different colors (Penfield, 1947).

Electrical stimulation of other cortical areas led to very different experiences. For example, stimulation of the temporal lobes produced the experience of sound. Patients said they heard ringing and humming noises that reminded them of everyday sounds. Using this same stimulation procedure, Penfield found that our sense of touch is localized in a narrow strip of the parietal lobe, just

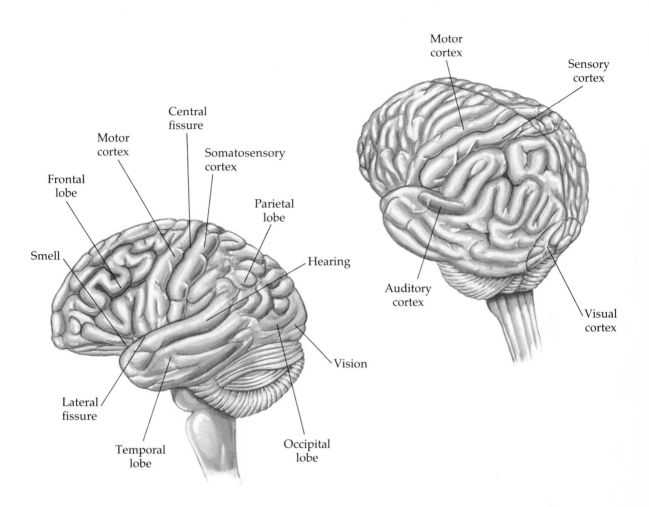

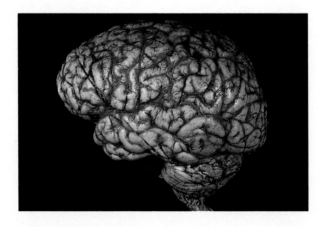

FIGURE 2.12 The convoluted cortex consists of four major areas called lobes. Major convolutions or fissures are used as landmarks to separate the different lobes of the brain. The locations of important behavioral functions are shown on the cortical surface.

behind the central fissure. This strip, shown in Figure 2.13, is called the **somatosensory cortex** (literally *body sense*, from the Greek word *soma* for *body*). When patients were stimulated at a point on this strip something interesting happened. Instead of associating their experience with the brain stimulation, patients believed that someone had just touched them on the surface of their bodies. Electrical stimulation near the top of the somatosensory cortex led them to feel a touch on the foot or leg, while stimulation lower in the cortex was experienced as a touch on the face (Penfield and Rasmussen, 1950). Penfield's research indicates that when someone touches you, you are aware of feeling it only because your somatosensory cortex is stimulated by messages from the area of body contact.

The amount of somatosensory cortex devoted to each area of the body can be illustrated by drawing the parts of the body in proportion to the amount of cortex devoted to each part (see Figure 2.13). The greater the amount of cortex devoted to an area of the body, the more sensitive that area is to touch. For example, it is only because of the considerable amount of somatosensory cortex devoted to our mouths and thumbs that these particular areas of our body are extremely sensitive to touch.

What happens if the somatosensory cortex is damaged? As you might expect, damage to one side of the brain can result in a loss of sensitivity

FIGURE 2.13 The somatosensory cortex and the motor cortex. The somatosensory cortex is located just behind the central fissure, while the motor cortex is located just in front of it. The sizes of the body parts reflect the amount of cortex devoted to them. The greater the amount of cortex, the more sensitive or responsive the corresponding area of the body.

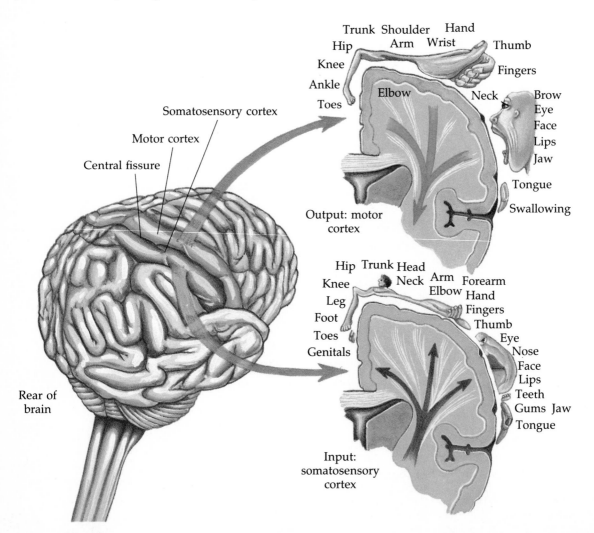

on the opposite side of the body. If the somatosensory cortex damage is severe, patients report that the sensationless sides of their bodies feel as if they belong to someone else. For example, neurologist Oliver Sacks (1985) reported on a patient who constantly fell out of bed at night. It seems that the patient woke during the night and discovered a "dead, cold, hairy leg" in bed with him. In attempting to throw the leg (actually, his own sensationless limb) out of bed, the patient would end up throwing himself on the floor. Another example of a case study was provided by Russian neurologist Alexander Luria, who recorded the thoughts of a former soldier who was wounded in this cortical area.

> Suddenly I'll come to, look to the right of me, and be horrified to discover half of my body is gone. I'm terrified; I try to figure out what's become of my right arm and leg, the entire right side of my body. I move the fingers of my left hand, feel them, but can't see the fingers of my right hand and somehow I'm not even aware they're there. . . .
>
> (Luria, 1973a)

The Motor Areas. The primary motor area of the cortex was discovered by John Hughlings-Jackson in the 1860s. Hughlings-Jackson studied epileptic patients and found that their convulsive seizures always started with uncontrollable movements in the same part of the body. He observed that the part of the body that began the uncontrollable movements was related to the area in the brain now called the **motor cortex.** Although there are motor fibers throughout the brain, they are most highly concentrated in the motor cortex, a thin strip of cortex located directly in front of the central fissure in the frontal lobe of each hemisphere. (See Figure 2.13.) Because of its contralateral or opposite-sided arrangement with the body, the motor cortex in each hemisphere governs the movements for the opposite side of the body.

Penfield extended Hughlings-Jackson's work by showing that different areas of the motor cortex control different movements. Once again, Figure 2.13 shows how the body would look if its parts were drawn in proportion to the amount of motor cortex devoted to each. Greater cortical area is given to those parts of our body—tongues and fingers, for example—that engage in graceful, skilled movements than to those parts—elbows and hips—that are involved in grosser positioning movements. This relation between the amount of motor cortex and the degree of motor control is also found in other animals. For example, a comparison of the motor cortical area that controls forepaw movement in raccoons and dogs shows differences that fit with their different degrees of dexterity. Since the raccoon uses its forepaws for exploration, the forepaw area in the raccoon's motor cortex is much larger than the forepaw area in the dog's (Welker, Johnson, and Pubols, 1964).

Injury to the motor cortex can lead to movement disorders that range from the loss of a very specific movement to the complete paralysis of an entire side of the body. Unlike the limp paralysis found with polio that results from damage to motor neurons in the spinal cord or brainstem, paralysis from motor cortex damage results in a spastic condition, due to the exaggerated operation of the stretch reflexes, in which the limbs are fairly stiff. In the epileptic patients who Penfield tested, electrical stimulation of the motor cortex produced body movements that greatly surprised the patients. Their bodies seemed to possess a will of their own, moving in response to the electrical stimulation without the patients "performing it themselves" (Penfield and Rasmussen, 1950). Just as we saw with the somatosensory cortex, it is the cortical stimulation, not the external event, that directly causes our responses. Without the cortical stimulation we would be neither aware nor responsive.

The Association Areas. We said earlier that the nervous system functions as an integrative network by organizing the enormous amount of information it receives from both inside and outside of the body. This integration is presumed to take place in the **association areas** of the cortex—the vast areas of cortex that remain after the sensory and motor areas are specified. Human beings have more association cortex than any other species— the association cortex in people comprises nearly three quarters of the cortex's surface. In fact, the association areas are largely the reason why we are so capable of creative and intellectually flexible behavior. Reading, writing, speaking, and thinking are made possible only because large areas of the cortex are set aside for these special functions.

Each lobe of the cortex makes a unique contribution to our mental abilities, including our ability to use language and to make decisions. The associative area of each frontal lobe was once believed to be responsible for intelligence because it is so large, but this belief is not completely justified. As we will discuss in more detail in Chapter 9, intelligence is not a single function, and therefore it cannot be localized in one portion of the brain. However, the frontal lobes do make an important contribution to "intelligent" behavior. Studies of people who have suffered brain damage in the frontal lobes indicate that this area is involved in making plans, solving problems, and making appropriate social judgments. Some people with frontal lobe damage show a peculiar urge to imitate other people (Figure 2.14).

Located near the visual cortex, the associative area of each occipital lobe is involved in integrating visual information—in putting all the colors and shapes that we see together into a meaningful whole. Patients with damage in this area are likely to have difficulty interpreting what they see. They can see visual objects correctly, but they have trouble identifying particular shapes and distinguishing one from another. One patient with this form of brain damage looked at a pair of glasses and made the following interpretation:

> a circle, then another circle, and some sort of crossbar, it must be a bicycle? . . .
>
> *(Luria, 1980)*

When asked to draw what they see, these patients can often draw the parts, but they cannot combine them into a coherent whole. These problems are called **visual agnosia** (*agnosia* comes from the Greek word for ignorance). As indicated by the man who mistook a pair of glasses for a bicycle, patients with visual agnosia are unable to recognize visual stimuli, such as a picture of a bird or train, even though there are no problems with their ability to see, speak, or think. If these patients are allowed to handle an object or hear it in use, they can frequently name it immediately (Bauer and Rubens, 1985).

The association area of each parietal lobe is particularly important for directing attention to changes in the environment and developing expectations of what is likely to happen next (MacKay and Crammond, 1987; Posner, Walker, Friedrich, and Rafal, 1987). Patients with parietal lobe lesions often show **spatial neglect**—they do not pay attention to a particular area of space that is opposite the side of their lesions. These patients may comb only half of their hair or completely dress only one side of their body. The unattended side of their body is often scratched and bruised, since they frequently walk into walls and fences. If asked to copy simple line drawings, parietal lobe patients tend to neglect one side of the figure (Figure 2.15). However, if their attention is directed to the missing parts, these patients can complete their drawings correctly (Luria, 1973b; McFie and Zangwill, 1960).

As our examples indicate, much of our knowl-

FIGURE 2.14 Testing a patient with frontal lobe damage. The frontal lobes of the brain are important for abstract thinking, organizing behavior over time and space, planning for future goals, creativity, and ethical and moral aspects of behavior. Patients with frontal lobe damage can show disruptions in any of these aspects of behavior. For example, in these photos, the frontal lobe patient has lost his sense of autonomy and mimics the behavior of the physician. These patients look to the environment for cues on how to act.

edge about the different associative areas comes from the study of people with brain tumors, head injuries, and strokes (ruptured blood vessels in the brain). In particular, two of the association areas were discovered as the result of work with patients with specific mental deficits. As mentioned earlier, the first person to correctly identify an associative area was Paul Broca, who localized speech in the left frontal lobe in 1861. Broca studied patients who had suffered speech loss after an injury or stroke. One of his most famous cases involved a man nicknamed "Tan" because this was one of the few words that he knew how to say. After Tan's death, Broca performed an autopsy and discovered a lesion in the left frontal cortex, an area that has since been named after its discoverer (see **Broca's area** in Figure 2.16A). Over the next several years, Broca demonstrated that his finding was reliable. Patients suffering from **expressive aphasia,** an inability to use speech normally, almost always show brain damage in the association area of the left frontal lobe. These people can understand speech, but they have difficulty pronouncing words correctly. They speak, if at all, in a slow and labored way, as in the following example:

> I asked Mr. Ford about his work before he entered the hospital.
>
> "I'm a sig . . . no . . . man . . . uh, well, . . . again." These words were emitted slowly, and with great effort. The sounds were not clearly articulated; each syllable was uttered harshly, explosively, in a throaty voice. With practice, it was possible to un-

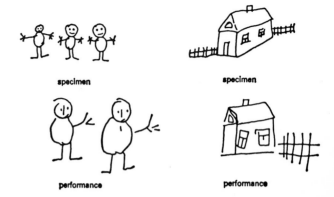

FIGURE 2.15 Drawing samples of a patient showing spatial neglect.   This patient has a lesion in the parietal lobe of the right cerebral hemisphere. When patients with this type of brain damage are asked to copy simple sketches, they often omit parts on the side of the drawing that is opposite to their brain lesion.

FIGURE 2.16 The generation of language.   (A) Broca's area and Wernicke's area are two important language centers in the left hemisphere. Broca's area contains the "articulatory" codes for words that enable us to speak, while Wernicke's area contains the "auditory" codes and our mental dictionary that enable us to understand. (B) PET scans of the left hemisphere of the brain showing different areas used during aspects of language processing: hearing, seeing, speaking, and thinking. The PET scan detects the relative amounts of glucose consumed in the cortex while a person engages in speech and other language-related tasks.

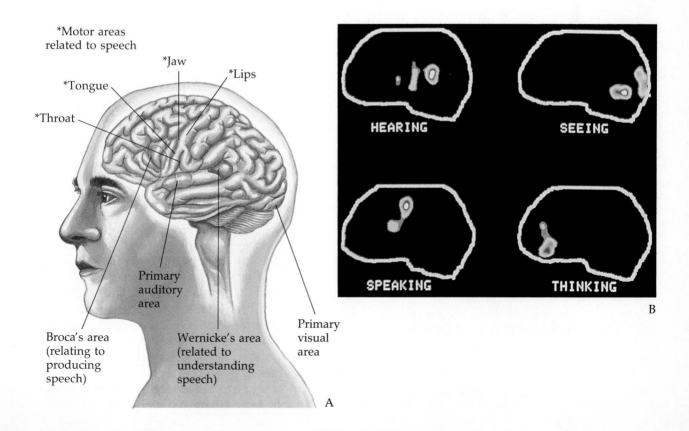

derstand him, but at first I encountered considerable difficulty in this.

"Let me help you," I interjected. "You were a signal. . . ."

"A sig-nal man . . . right," Ford completed my phrase triumphantly.

(Gardner, 1975)

In 1874, shortly after Broca localized expressive aphasia, a German neurologist named Carl Wernicke localized a second type of aphasia. In **receptive aphasia,** patients themselves speak fluently, but they cannot understand what other people are saying. As a consequence of their inability to comprehend speech, their own speech, though fluent, is often meaningless and bizarre. Again, an example is provided by psychologist Howard Gardner:

"What brings you to the hospital?" I asked the seventy-two-year-old retired butcher four weeks after his admission to the hospital.

"Boy, I'm sweating. I'm awful nervous, you know, once in a while I get caught up, I can't mention the tarripoi, a month ago, quite a little, I've done a lot well, I impose a lot, while, on the other hand, you know what I mean, I have to run around, look it over, trebbin and all that sort of stuff."

(Gardner, 1975)

Wernicke found that people with receptive aphasia typically had damage in the associative area of the left temporal lobe, (since called **Wernicke's area** in memory of his work). (This is shown in Figure 2.16A.) It is believed that when we hear a word our ears transmit the sensory information to the auditory cortex, but we cannot understand it until it has been processed in Wernicke's area (Geschwind, 1979). In order to say the word, our brain must transfer some neural representation of it from Wernicke's area to Broca's area. Once Broca's area has been stimulated, the areas of the motor cortex related to speech must be activated before we can speak it. When we read a word, its visual image is received at the visual cortex and then associated with its corresponding auditory pattern from Wernicke's area to enable us to understand it (Figure 2.16B).

CEREBRAL LATERALIZATION OF FUNCTION

We have described the associative cortex as though there were no differences between the left and right cerebral hemispheres. However, the two large halves of the brain shown earlier in Figure 2.11 are not mirror images of each other, and they are not equivalent in terms of their functions. Beginning with the findings of Broca and Wernicke, we now know that for most people the associative areas of the left hemisphere are important for producing and understanding language. Comparable areas of the right hemisphere are important for different functions. They provide the neurological basis for such spatial abilities as recognizing faces and solving pattern mazes and for thinking about music and nonlanguage sounds. When mental functions are connected more to one side of the brain than to the other, neuroscientists say that those functions are **lateralized.** Table 2.2 provides examples of cognitive functions that show **cerebral lateralization.**

In general, each hemisphere of the brain specializes in a different type of processing. However, the difference is relative, not absolute, because both hemispheres play a role in many different behaviors (Hellige, 1990; Kitterle, 1989; Palmer and Tzeng, 1990). The left hemisphere is superior to the right hemisphere in *analyzing* information. Tasks that involve extracting elements from a whole (like picking out the stray word in the set: man, fellow, guy, girl) or recognizing events that occur in order (like 5,10,15,____?) are mediated primarily by the left hemisphere. These abilities are crucial for conversation, since we must sort words as we listen and put them in order as we speak.

The right hemisphere, on the other hand, is superior to the left hemisphere in *synthesizing* information (Mateer, 1983; Witelson, 1983, 1989). Tasks that involve unifying individual elements into a coherent whole are mediated predominantly by this hemisphere. For example, we use our right hemisphere to see objects in cloud formations or to distinguish a painting by Picasso from one by Monet.

THE SPLIT-BRAIN PATIENT

Much of our knowledge about laterality has been obtained from research on epileptic patients who have had their cerebral hemispheres surgically separated. The two large hemispheres are linked by the corpus callosum, a thick bundle of 200 million nerve fibers between the hemispheres. The corpus callosum has sometimes been surgically severed as a last-gap medical measure to help people who suffer from the most severe form of epileptic seizures. During a grand mal seizure, an "electrical storm" of discharging neurons originates in one hemisphere and then spreads over the

TABLE 2.2   Lateralized Cognitive Functions

Behavioral Function	Greater Left Hemisphere Involvement	Greater Right Hemisphere Involvement
Visual recognition	Letters, words, and numbers	Faces and complex geometric patterns
Auditory recognition	Words and language-related sounds	Music and nonlanguage sounds
Tactile recognition	Unknown	Braille and complex tactile patterns
Language processes	Speech, reading, writing, and arithmetic	
Spatial processes		Geometry, sense of direction, and mental rotation of objects in space

Note: These generalities about the cerebral hemispheres hold for the overwhelming majority of people who are right-handed and have a family history of right-handedness. For those individuals who are left-handed or ambidextrous, the relations between the cerebral hemispheres and the lateralized functions may be reversed.

Adapted from Kolb and Whishaw (1990) and other sources.

corpus callosum to the other hemisphere. As we noted in the section on dysfunction, this cerebral storm produces a convulsion in which a person can lose consciousness, fall down, and experience several minutes of violent uncontrollable muscle spasms. For many people who are subject to these attacks, medication alleviates the risk of recurrent convulsions. However, for some rare individuals drugs are ineffective, and surgically separating the hemispheres is the only resort. With the corpus callosum cut, the electrical discharge can no longer spread over the entire brain and the subsequent seizures, if they occur at all, are less severe.

What are the consequences of so drastic an operation? One patient, upon awakening from the anesthesia, jokingly reported that he had a "splitting headache," but, generally, cognitive functioning does not appear to be seriously impaired (Gazzaniga, 1967). Nor are most patients handicapped by this experience. They can still perform activities like walking and swimming that involve the integration of both sides of the body. However, detailed laboratory studies of split-brain patients have shown that the two hemispheres differ substantially in their fundamental cognitive functions.

To understand how these differences were detected, we first need to understand how the eyes and brain are connected. Figure 2.17 shows that when we stare at one point, everything to the left of that point is first sent to the right hemisphere, while everything to the right of the point is processed first by the left hemisphere. This is true of all people. What makes the split-brain patient special is that, because the corpus callosum has been cut (look again at Figure 2.17), information

seen in the left or right visual field is received only in the contralateral (opposite-sided) hemisphere. Because the communication link has been cut, the left hemisphere knows nothing of what was just seen in the left visual field, and vice versa. Since information can therefore be presented to a single hemisphere, it is possible to test the cognitive functions of each hemisphere independently. This is something that can be done only with split-brain patients.

Figure 2.18 shows the experimental setting that was designed to test hemispheric functioning. A patient is seated in front of the screen and is asked to stare at the small point in the center. A word or picture is then flashed for one-tenth of a second in either the left or the right visual field. This span is too brief to allow the patient to shift gaze, so the visual stimulus is thus received by only one hemisphere. After the stimulus is presented, the patient is asked to place one hand under the screen and find, without looking, the object that was flashed on the screen. Before describing the findings, one additional fact needs to be remembered. The brain and body are connected in a contralateral manner. This means that each hemisphere of the brain receives messages from and sends messages to the opposite side of the body. For example, if you write with your right hand your hand movements are under the control of the motor cortex in your left hemisphere. Therefore, as shown in Figure 2.17, the primary hand–hemisphere connections are crossed—the left hand is guided by the right hemisphere, while the right hand is governed by the left hemisphere.

When a visual stimulus like the word PENCIL

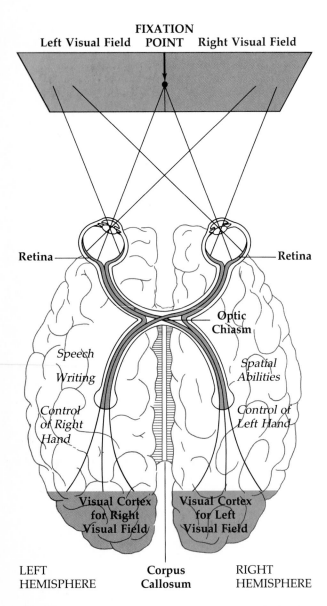

FIXATION
Left Visual Field **POINT** Right Visual Field

Retina———————————Retina

Optic
Chiasm

Speech

Writing

Spatial Abilities

Control of Right Hand

Control of Left Hand

Visual Cortex
for Right
Visual Field

Visual Cortex
for Left
Visual Field

LEFT
HEMISPHERE

**Corpus
Callosum**

RIGHT
HEMISPHERE

FIGURE 2.17 Eye–brain connections in a split-brain patient. In a split-brain patient, the corpus callosum is severed, while the optic chiasm is kept intact. When looking at a point in space, all stimuli presented to the left of the fixation point go to the right hemisphere of the brain, and all stimuli presented to the right of the point go to the left hemisphere. This contralateral (opposite-sided) arrangement is not true of the other senses. Audition, for example, has primary contralateral links between the ears and hemispheres, but it also has ipsilateral (same-sided) links. Olfaction is different still, having only ipsilateral links between each nostril and the hemisphere behind it.

was flashed to the left hemisphere (right visual field presentation) and the patients used their right hand to locate the object, they had no difficulty. The patients moved their hands over the objects, picked up the pencils, and said "It's a pencil." But

when the conditions were reversed, something unusual happened. When PENCIL was flashed to the right hemisphere (see Figure 2.18 again) the left hand easily found it on the table. However, when the patients were asked what they found, they guessed wildly or replied "I don't know" (Gazzaniga, 1967; Sperry, 1968). Incredibly, the patients found the correct object but did not know what it was!

The bizarre behavior of split-brain patients is understandable when we realize that, although both hemispheres can process simple visual stimuli and correctly guide their contralateral hand, only the left hemisphere can produce complex speech and verbally describe its behavior. Language, as Broca discovered, is lateralized (located in one hemisphere), and for most right-handed people and a majority of left-handed people it is located in the left hemisphere. There are other fundamental differences in the cognitive functions of the two hemispheres. Another example, which demonstrates a right hemisphere advantage, is shown in Figure 2.19. When shown simple drawings and asked to reproduce them, split-brain patients were more spatially accurate when they drew with their left hands (guided by the right hemisphere) even though they were right-handed. For most people, spatial functions are better represented in the right hemisphere.

Is Consciousness Also Divided? The fact that split-brain patients could find an object with their left hands but could not say what it was suggests a division of consciousness across the hemispheres. One hemisphere knew something that the other did not. When split-brain patients were shown a dollar sign in the left visual field (right hemisphere) and a question mark in the right visual field (left hemisphere), each hemisphere's experience of the task was different. When the patients were asked to use their left hands (right-hemisphere guided) to draw what they had seen without looking again at the drawing, they drew a dollar sign. When they were asked to name what they drew, the patients replied that they drew a question mark (Sperry, 1968). Their left hemispheres did not know what was drawn but thought that they did; their right hemispheres knew what was drawn but were unable to talk.

Similarly, if split-brain patients are presented with a command such as the word "WALK" shown briefly in the left visual field (right hemisphere), they will typically get up and walk. When asked where they are going, these patients may say something like "I am going to get a Coke"

"What did you see?"

"With your left hand, select
the object you saw
from those behind the screen."

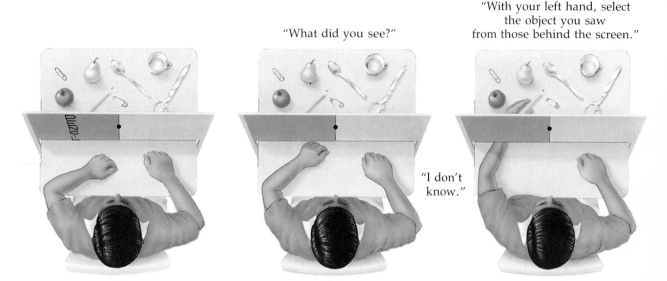

"I don't
know."

FIGURE 2.18 Testing a split-brain patient. When the split-brain patient fixates on the dot in the center of the display screen, a word is flashed in the left or right visual field. The patient must find the object on the table top without looking and then name the object in his hand. When the word goes to the left hemisphere, the patient can find the object and identify it; when it goes to the right hemisphere (as shown in this example), the patient can find the object, but he cannot say what it is. Although both hemispheres are capable of processing simple word or picture stimuli and can correctly guide the contralateral hand, only the left hemisphere can produce speech and accurately describe what has just happened.

(Gazzaniga, 1985). Under these conditions, the left hemisphere (which can produce speech, but saw nothing on the screen) attempts to explain the overt behavior that was started by the silent right hemisphere (which saw the previous command). Findings such as these suggest to some psychologists that split-brain patients are like people with two minds—mind left and mind right—that coexist within one body, each with its own will and its own perceptions and memories (Gazzaniga, 1972; Sperry, 1976).

Additional evidence for an apparent division of consciousness is found in the case study of a 15-year-old split-brain patient named Paul. Paul had his corpus callosum severed as a last resort treatment for epilepsy. After the operation, tests of his right-hemisphere functioning showed that Paul could not answer questions verbally that were visually directed to that hemisphere. Like most right-handed people, Paul's language center was lateralized in his left hemisphere. However, using his left hand he could spell answers to those questions with letters from a "Scrabble" game. Figure 2.20 shows an example of how Michael Gazzaniga and his associates communicated with Paul's silent right hemisphere. In one instance, they verbally asked "Who" and then flashed on the screen the words "are you?", directing the visual image to

FIGURE 2.19 Drawings by a split-brain patient. When a split-brain patient was shown the examples on the left and asked to reproduce them, he did a more accurate job with his left hand than his right even though he was right-handed. This difference occurred because spatial tasks are processed better by the right hemisphere, the hemisphere that controls the left hand.

EXAMPLE	LEFT HAND	RIGHT HAND

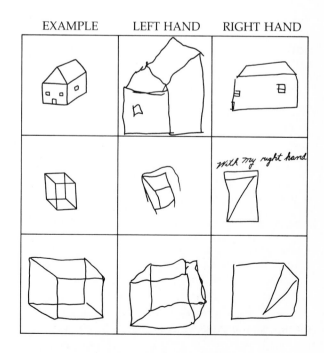

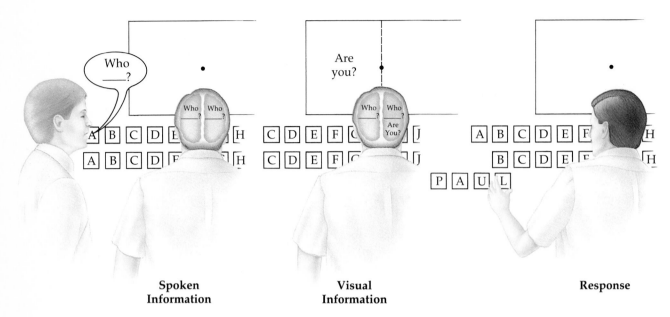

Spoken Information	**Visual Information**	**Response**

FIGURE 2.20 Communicating with a single hemisphere. A 15-year-old split-brain patient named Paul could answer simple questions either verbally by his left hemisphere or by spelling out words with letter blocks with his left hand controlled by his right hemisphere. By means of his normally silent *right hemisphere*, for example, Paul is able to spell his name, describe his mood ("good"), name his hobby ("car"), his favorite person ("Henry Wi Fuzi" for Henry Winkler, Fonzi), and answer questions about his career goals ("automobile race[r]"). Interestingly, Pual says (by means of his *left hemisphere*) that he would like to be a draftsman. For most of us, the sense of consciousness is unified; for split-brain patients, each hemisphere may possess conscious properties of its own.

Paul's right hemisphere. In other instances, questions were asked only verbally and Paul responded verbally under the direction of his left hemisphere. As the comments of the researchers indicate, Paul's responses sometimes varied according to which hemisphere was directing the response:

As his eyes scanned the 52 letters available, his left hand reached out and selected the "P," set it down and then proceeded to collect the remaining letters needed to spell "Paul." . . . Overflowing with excitement, having just communicated on a personal level with a right hemisphere, we collected ourselves, and then initiated the next trial by saying, "Would you spell the name of your favorite 'blank'?" Then "girl" appeared in the left visual field. Out came the left hand again, and this time it spelled "Liz," the name of his girlfriend at the time. . . . He spelled "automobile race [r]" as the job he would pick. This is interesting, because the left hemisphere frequently asserts that "he" wants to be a draftsman. In fact, shortly after the test session, we asked P.S. what sort of

job he would like to have and he said, "Oh, be a draftsman."

(Gazzaniga and LeDoux, 1978)

Data such as these suggest that each hemisphere may possess its own sense of self and conscious properties of its own.

Other psychologists, however, have questioned this interpretation of the split-brain research. Some psychologists reason that since each hemisphere is bound to the subcortical structures of the brain much as our arms are bound to our trunk these structures could provide a basis for conscious unity even in split-brain patients (among others, Beaumont, 1983). In fact, recent research lends some support to this belief. Studies have shown that the attentional system remains largely integrated in split-brain patients (Gazzaniga, 1987) and that cognitive information, such as semantic associations, can be transferred along a subcortical route (Cronin-Golomb, 1986). Psychologists and other neuroscientists are currently trying to determine which abilities remain unified and which become dissociated after a split-brain operation. For now, the issue of unified or divided consciousness in these patients must await additional research. However, we do know that each hemisphere has special abilities and, for people with an intact corpus callosum, the two hemispheres normally work together to guide our actions and thoughts. This is another example of how the nervous system organizes and integrates our behavior.

The point about hemispheric integration is important to remember because books in the popular press have argued that we can shift our mode of thinking from one hemisphere to another. Based on the laterality differences described earlier in Table 2.2, for example, some writers have devised "right hemisphere" training programs that are supposed to produce improvements in education, art, and psychotherapy (for example, Blakeslee, 1980; Edwards, 1986). To date, there is little evidence to support their claims, and most psychologists view such beliefs as overblown generalizations (Corballis, 1980).

THE ENDOCRINE SYSTEM

Until the beginning of this century, communication within the body and the interaction of behavior it produced were thought to be performed by the nervous system alone. However, not all of our behavior and experience is controlled by the nervous system. Some is controlled chemically by the **endocrine system.** The endocrine system consists of eight glands—the **pituitary, pineal, thyroid, parathyroid, adrenal, pancreas, kidneys,** and **gonads** (*ovaries* in the female, *testes* in the male)—shown in Figure 2.21. Each secretes the chemical substances called **hormones** directly into the bloodstream. Hormones not only influence our growth, development, and aging, they also influence our actions and moods. Small amounts of some hormones can influence our desire to eat or drink, our aggressiveness or submissiveness, and even our reproductive and parental behavior. In this section we will describe the endocrine system as a chemical communication system and then show how the endocrine and nervous systems are integrated in the control of behavior and experience.

FUNCTIONS OF THE ENDOCRINE GLANDS

Some endocrine glands are activated directly by our nervous system, while others are stimulated by internal bodily states. Of all of the endocrine glands, the pituitary is, perhaps, the most impor-

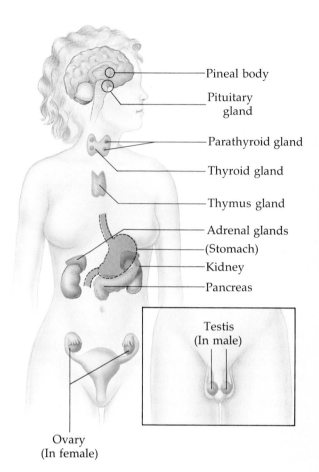

Pineal body

Pituitary gland

Parathyroid gland

Thyroid gland

Thymus gland

Adrenal glands

(Stomach)

Kidney

Pancreas

Testis (In male)

Ovary (In female)

FIGURE 2.21 The location of the major endocrine glands. These glands influence our behavior and internal states by secreting hormones directly into the bloodstream. Without the balanced secretion of hormones, we could not grow and reproduce and our body could not maintain homeostasis; without the secretion of additional hormones during times of stress, we would be unable to function effectively. Functions of these glands are outlined in Table 2.3.

tant. It secretes many different hormones that exert control over the other endocrine glands. For instance, it indirectly controls hormones in the ovaries and testes, which in turn control sexual development and arousal. Located at the base of the brain, the pituitary gland is itself controlled by the hypothalamus, a part of the nervous system.

The adrenal glands, located above the kidneys, secrete hormones that influence our mood and our ability to cope with stress. During stressful situations, the inner core of each adrenal gland, called the *adrenal medulla*, secretes the hormones **epinephrine** and **norepinephrine** (also called *adrenalin* and *noradrenalin*). Epinephrine thus plays a major role in the sympathetic "fight or flight" reaction. This hormone constricts the blood vessels in the stomach and intestines and increases the heart rate. This is why you may feel butterflies in your stomach and a pounding in your chest when your adrenal glands are pumping out epinephrine. Similarly, norepinephrine in the bloodstream causes the release of a pituitary hormone that, in turn, stimulates the liver to release more blood sugar. This sugar provides you with a rush of energy to help you cope with a potentially dangerous situation. These and other glandular functions are outlined in Table 2.3. We will have more to say about the endocrine glands and the actions of hormones in Chapter 14 when we discuss stress and related issues of health.

NEUROENDOCRINE INTEGRATION

As in the case of the pituitary gland, which is controlled by the hypothalamus, all of the endocrine system works closely with the nervous system to control behavior in an integrated manner. Two examples of how the endocrine glands complement the nervous system are found in the regulation of thirst and sexual behavior.

THIRST

What goes on in your body when you feel thirsty after an afternoon in the summer sun? Searching for the source of this feeling, neuroscientists have uncovered a "neuroendocrine" trail that begins in the kidneys. Among other things, the kidneys monitor the amount of fluid in the blood. When the water content of the blood is low, the kidneys send a signal to the brain to initiate drinking. The signal is not sent on the wires of the nervous system, but through the bloodstream, starting with the kidneys' release of an enzyme called renin. Renin converts blood proteins into the "thirst hormone" *angiotensin II*. Once this hormone reaches the brain, it contacts a tiny structure in one of the brain's ventricles called the subfornical organ. The angiotensin II molecules chemically stimulate the subfornical neurons to discharge neural impulses that are, in turn, transmitted to the thirst center of the hypothalamus (Epstein, Fitzsimons, and Rolls, 1970; Rolls, Wood, and Rolls, 1980). This combination of neural and endocrine processes ultimately leads to the experience of thirst, which causes you to head for the nearest water fountain or soft drink dispenser. Although the complex behaviors involved in finding a drink are guided by the nervous system, they are initiated by the endocrine system. In this manner, both systems work together as part of an integrated neuroendocrine system that controls our behavior and experience.

TABLE 2.3 **The Major Endocrine Glands and Their Functions**

Gland	Function
Adrenal	
cortex	Excretion of sodium and potassium
	Growth and sexual activity in women
medulla	Metabolism and responses to stress
Gonads	
ovaries (female)	Growth and development of reproductive system
testes (male)	Growth and development of reproductive system
Kidneys	Control of adrenal secretion and blood pressure
Pancreas	Regulation of metabolism and plasma glucose
Parathyroid	Regulation of calcium and phosphorus levels in the blood
Pineal	Regulation of bodily cycles, inhibition of premature sexual development
Pituitary	
anterior	Control of adrenal cortex, ovaries and testes, growth, metabolism, milk production, and thyroid gland
posterior	Excretion of water
Thryoid	Energy metabolism and growth

Adapted from Thompson (1985) and other sources.

SEXUAL BEHAVIOR

Sexual behavior provides another example of the ways in which the endocrine glands and nervous system work together. Evidence for this neuroendocrine integration comes from laboratory studies of animals and clinical studies of humans. For example, removing the ovaries from female rats results in a complete loss of sexual receptivity. However, if these female rats are later injected with estradiol (a form of estrogen), they return to their normal level of sexual receptivity (Davidson, Smith, Rodgers, and Bloch, 1968). Estrogen is sometimes called the "female sex hormone," but it is present in both sexes. For male rats, the results are different. The removal of the testes—castration—produces a more gradual reduction in sexual behavior. Sexual responsiveness in castrated male rats can be returned to its normal level by injections of *testosterone*. Sometimes called the "male sex hormone," some testosterone is also present in females.

Studies of hormones and human sexual behavior show a somewhat different pattern of results. Following castration (due to an accident, a clinical treatment for cancer, or for criminal or psychiatric reasons), men show a gradual and variable decline in sexual behavior that is similar to that seen in castrated animals. For example, a study of castrated men in Norway showed that only one third of 157 men had any degree of sexual arousal one year after castration, and even for that third arousal was drastically reduced (Bremer, 1959). However, women who lose their ovaries are not like ovariectomized animals. Instead, they continue to be interested in sex. Likewise, women who have passed menopause, when the ovaries no longer function, can continue to enjoy sexual relations. As we will discuss further in Chapter 10, females' sexual arousal may be linked not to estrogen but to the "male hormone" testosterone.

Current thinking holds that estrogen and testosterone excite or inhibit nerve cells in the brain that control sexual behavior. Behavior is controlled by the brain, but hormones exert their influence on behavior by acting on the brain's hypothalamus. For both males and females, the hypothalamus acts like a thermostat in regulating hormonal function. Unlike animals whose sexual behavior is tightly controlled by hormonal concentrations, human sexual behavior shows a more complex relation between hormones and arousal. Human sexual behavior is influenced by information received from our senses as well as hormonal concentrations in our bloodstream—a true neuroendocrine integration.

In closing, we have shown how the nervous and endocrine systems permit communication between different parts of the body. The neurotransmitters of the nervous system are really quite similar to the hormones of the endocrine system. Both are chemical messengers. Neurotransmitters carry messages the short distance across synapses, while hormones use the bloodstream to cover much greater distances. Some chemical messengers can even serve both roles. Norepinephrine, for example, can function as a neurotransmitter when released by a presynaptic neuron and as a hormone when secreted by the adrenal gland. These different functions are kept separate by the blood–brain barrier, which prevents hormones in the bloodstream from entering the brain. Neuroscientists are still discovering the complex relations between neurotransmitters and hormones and how they influence behavior.

INTERACTIONS:
Gender Differences in Laterality?

In Chapter 1 we discussed the pragmatic approach taken by many modern psychologists. Rather than looking for one theoretical perspective to answer all of our questions about behavior, psychologists today tend to look for interactions among dominant viewpoints. Beginning with the physiological perspective in this chapter, we will describe a variety of perspectives over the course of this text as we progress from microscopic biological processes to macroscopic behavioral problems. Eventually we will combine these different theoretical perspectives as we build toward a general understanding of behavior and experience. We will use this section in each chapter to develop these ideas. In this chapter we will show how a complex phenomenon—possible gender differences between the left and right hemispheres of the brain— that can be partially understood from a single perspective is still influenced by the interaction of a variety of factors rooted in other perspectives.

In 1974, psychologists Eleanor Maccoby and Carol Jacklin did an exhaustive review of the research on gender differences. In addition to finding differences in mathematical performance and aggression (which we will take up in later chapters), they found small but reliable differences in verbal and spatial abilities. Starting around age 11, girls were reported to demonstrate greater verbal ability than boys. They did better on simple tasks like spelling and on more complex tasks like solving verbal analogies and creative writing. Boys, on the other hand, did better than girls on visual-spatial tasks such as memory for shapes, maze learning, map reading, and geographical knowledge (Maccoby and Jacklin, 1974).

Today, the research findings tell a different story. Recent reviews have shown that gender differences in verbal, spatial, and mathematical abilities are much smaller than earlier believed. In fact, the gender differences have declined so precipitously that many psychologists no longer believe that there are major differences between females and males in these mental abilities (Caplan, MacPherson, and Tobin, 1985; Feingold, 1988; Hyde, Fennema, and Lamon, 1990; Hyde and Linn, 1988). This is a controversial topic and one that will surely generate additional research. At present, however, the findings indicate that gender differences in cognition are small, and even those differences are disappearing.

What about possible brain differences between females and males? Gender differences in brain organization are found in other mammals, and such differences may be present in humans even if there are little or no differences in cognitive abilities. Evidence for differences in cerebral function comes from behavior studies of laterality and research on neurological patients.

Sandra Witelson (1976) provided an example of a gender difference in laterality. She tested boys and girls between the ages of 6 and 13 on a touch-to-sight matching task. Without looking, the children were allowed to feel an irregularly-shaped object with either their left or their right hands. They then had to select the shape that they felt from a set of visually presented shapes. Boys did better with their left hands (linked to their right hemispheres) than with their right hands (linked to their left hemispheres); girls showed no difference between hands. These results suggest that a right hemisphere spatial advantage for boys is present early in life. The results are also consistent with other findings that show that when laterality differences are found, they are usually stronger in males than in females. This has led some psychologists to suggest that males are more "lateralized" than females (Bryden, 1981; Springer and Deutsch, 1989).

Psychologist Doreen Kimura (1983, 1985) has observed gender differences in her studies of neurological patients. She studied over 200 brain-damaged men and women on a variety of cognitive tasks to see what types of problems result from damage to specific brain areas. Kimura found that although damage to the left or right hemisphere could impair verbal or spatial performance in both genders, lesions in specific hemispheric areas could affect males and females differently. For example, men showed speech deficits after damage to either the front or back of their left hemispheres, while women showed such speech disorders more frequently following damage only to the front of this hemisphere. Similar gender-related differences in spatial abilities were found for right hemisphere lesions following a stroke or an accident. Spatial abilities in males were disrupted following damage to either the front or back of the right hemisphere, while similar disruptions in females tended to occur only after lesions in the front of this hemisphere.

Why gender differences in laterality exist is not yet known, although several hypotheses have been put forth. One possibility is that gender differences are based on differences in **cerebral organization.** Accordingly, if male and female brains are organized differently, then neurological damage should affect males and females differently. Kimura's research on brain-damaged patients points in this direction. Similarly, if females are normally less "lateralized" than males, then women would be expected to suffer less often than men when brain damage is confined to only one hemisphere. This, too, is confirmed by research (Lansdell, 1962; McGlone, 1978). Another possibility is that these gender differences are due to **hormonal effects.** Hormones can influence brain development and function, but it is not yet clear whether they can influence gender differences in brain organization (Hampson and Kimura, 1988). At present, we do not know the basis for gender differences in laterality. It may be, as Kolb and Whishaw (1990) believe, that differences between males and females are due to neurological factors that are modulated by the environment. In their words, the differences are likely the result of the interaction of many factors, some biological and some psychological in origin.

What is the practical significance of gender differences in laterality? This is an important and controversial issue because there is always the chance that the reporting of gender differences will exaggerate perceived differences between women and men and be used to limit the opportunities for women (Hyde, 1985; Matlin, 1987). When groups, such as women and men differ in status, it is often the case that group differences will be seen as a deficiency in the group with less status, women in this case. For example, should young women be discouraged from considering careers in engineering because, historically at least, females have scored slightly lower than males on tests of spatial ability? Psychologist Janet Hyde (1985) warns us that this would be a tragic mistake for two reasons. First, group differences in performance cannot be used to predict the performance of any individual, female or male. Second, the size of the gender difference on verbal and spatial tests is very small and, as we noted, it is decreasing. This means that there is considerable overlap in the verbal and spatial abilities of women and men (Hyde, 1981; Hyde and Linn, 1988; Sherman, 1978). There are some women who have better spatial ability than most men, and some men who have better verbal skills than most women. On the average, if women and men differ, they do so only to a very limited degree. As Doreen Kimura (1985) noted, while there may be laterality differences in the brains of women and men, there is more variability from person to person and, possibly, even within the same person over a period of time, than there is between the sexes. On most tasks of cognitive ability, women and men overlap to a considerable degree, and this argues very strongly that gender differences in the brain are insufficient to limit the possibilities for individual women and men. ▪

IN CONTEXT: BIOLOGICAL BASES OF BEHAVIOR

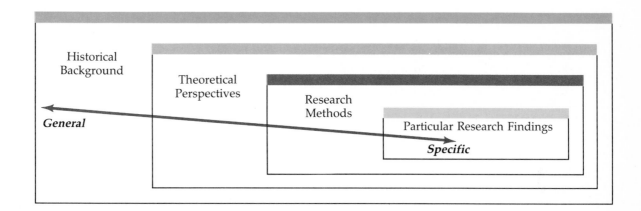

STUDY QUESTIONS

How are individual nerve cells organized to form a nervous system?

How do the major components of the brain and other parts of the nervous system regulate behavior on a neural level?

How is the brain organized?

What are the behavioral consequences of neural malfunctions?

How do psychologists study brain/behavior relations?

How do the endocrine glands regulate behavior on a chemical level?

How are the nervous and endocrine systems integrated?

HISTORICAL CONTEXT

1. Early Greek and Roman physicians believed that behavioral problems were caused by imbalances of vital fluids that moved through the body and brain. Only after the Renaissance did people accept the view that behavior and thought were produced by specific structures in the brain.

2. During the nineteenth century, neurologists performed autopsies on former patients and discovered the brain areas responsible for producing and comprehending speech. This work led to other discoveries that showed that specif-

ic psychological functions were associated with specific brain areas. This view of brain/behavior relations is called **localization theory.**

3. Early in the twentieth century, research on the physiological bases of behavior showed that when an area of the brain is destroyed, sometimes remaining portions can take over its function. This view that different areas of the brain can be equivalent to one another is called **equipotentiality theory.**

4. A major perspective today combines elements of localization and equipotentiality theories. This position, called **interactionist theory,**

holds that different areas of the brain each make a unique contribution to the same psychological function.

MODERN THEORETICAL PERSPECTIVES

According to interactionist theory, complex psychological functions are based on a number of more basic abilities. These basic abilities may be centered in different areas of the brain, but they are highly interconnected so that many different brain areas may be involved in the same psychological function. Our thoughts and actions are a product of the functions of interrelated neural structures.

RESEARCH METHODS

1. Experiments in the form of **lesion procedures** and **electrical stimulation** are most often the source of our understanding of brain/behavior relations. For example, the destruction of the cingulum has been used to control chronic depression (Corkin, 1980), and electrical stimulation has been used to map the sensory, motor, and association areas of the cortex (Penfield, 1947; Penfield and Rasmussen, 1950).

2. **Case studies** are also employed to observe the effects of brain surgery or cerebral injury on behavior. For instance, the case of H.M. revealed the importance of the hippocampus to normal memory functioning (Milner et al., 1968). Other cases, like the soldier who was wounded in the somatosensory cortex (Luria, 1973a) or the brain-damaged patients with expressive or receptive aphasia, show the effects of other brain structures on behavior.

RESEARCH FINDINGS AND SUMMARY

1. **Neuropsychology** is the study of the relation between the nervous system and behavior.

2. The human nervous system consists of the **central nervous system** and the **peripheral nervous system.** The brain and spinal cord comprise the central nervous system, while the remaining network of nerves throughout the body constitutes the peripheral system. The peripheral nervous system is subdivided into the **somatic** and **autonomic nervous systems.** Within the autonomic system, the **sympathetic division** prepares us physically for action, while the **parasympathetic division** operates when we are calm.

3. The nervous system contains **sensory neurons** that carry information to the central nervous system, **interneurons** that relay information between neurons in the brain, and **motor neurons** that carry information to the muscles and glands. Together, these neurons form a communication network that integrates the different parts of the body.

4. A **neuron** is composed of a **cell body, dendrites,** and an **axon.** It exists in a slightly negatively charged state called its **resting potential.** The neuron fires in an all-or-none fashion if it receives enough stimulation to surpass its firing threshold. If it fires, there is an electrical change in the neuron that is called the **action potential.**

5. Neural transmission involves converting the electrical impulse into a chemical messenger that crosses the synaptic junction and causes the receiving cell either to increase or to decrease its tendency to fire.

6. The most primitive portion of the brain is the **brainstem** and its related structures including the **medulla, pons, thalamus, hypothalamus, cerebellum,** and **reticular formation.** These structures control the most fundamental aspects of behavior, such as breathing and walking.

7. The **limbic system** is a ring of interrelated structures, including the **hippocampus** and the **amygdala.** It coordinates information with other brain centers, regulates emotional responses, and monitors specific behaviors (including eating, drinking, and sexual activity) that are essential to survival.

8. **Psychosurgery** involves the destruction of brain tissue for the purpose of alleviating psychiatric disorders. Psychosurgery's record is mixed.

9. The **cerebral cortex** has a characteristic convoluted appearance. The large convolutions help outline different areas of the cortex into the cerebral lobes. From front to back, the cortex consists of the **frontal lobes,** the **parietal lobes** at the top, the **temporal lobes** on the side, and the **occipital lobes** in the rear.

10. For most people, the associative areas of the left hemisphere are specialized for language, while the associative areas of the right hemisphere are specialized for spatial abilities. This asymmetry of function is called **lateralization.**

11. The glands of the **endocrine system** such as the pituitary and kidneys regulate behavior by secreting **hormones** directly into the bloodstream. The neurotransmitters of the nervous system and the hormones of the endocrine system are similar in that both are used to relay chemical messages in the body. In this way, both the nervous and endocrine systems communicate and integrate information.

ADDITIONAL READINGS

Beaumont, J. G. 1983. *Introduction to neuropsychology*. New York: Guilford. A comprehensive and accessible review of clinical and experimental neuropsychology. It covers what neuropsychologists have learned from case studies of brain-damaged individuals and studies of the normal brain in the psychology laboratory.

Blakemore, C. 1977. *Mechanics of the mind*. Cambridge: Cambridge University Press. A grand historical tour of our knowledge about the brain and how this knowledge was obtained. This book is wide-ranging in its coverage, wonderfully illustrated, and beautifully written.

Kolb, B., and I. Q. Whishaw. 1990. *Fundamentals of human neuropsychology* (3rd ed.). New York: Freeman. A comprehensive and up-to-date introduction to the field. The special chapters on applications of neuropsychological research provide a good source of information for topics ranging from learning disabilities to psychiatric and motor disorders.

Levinthal, C. F. 1990. *Introduction to physiological psychology* (3rd ed.). Englewood Cliffs, NJ: Prentice Hall. A highly readable textbook on physiological psychology that provides, in addition to fundamental neuroanatomy, comprehensive and current coverage of the operation of the senses, higher-order behaviors such as sleep and emotionality, and the biological bases of learning and mental illness.

McCarthy, R. A., and E. K. Warrington. 1990. *Cognitive neuropsychology: A clinical introduction*. San Diego, CA: Academic Press. A comprehensive and authoritative review of cognitive deficits in patients with brain lesions. This book describes the psychological and neurological approaches to the analysis of cognitive skills and abilities.

Nauta, W. J. H., and M. Feirtag. 1986. *Fundamental neuroanatomy*. New York: Freeman. An authoritative and highly readable text on basic neuroanatomy. This thorough introduction to brain and spinal cord organization focuses on the functions of the nervous system.

Springer, S. P., and G. Deutsch. 1989. *Left brain, right brain* (3rd ed.). New York: Freeman. A comprehensive and readable survey of hemispheric differences in the brain. This book is an excellent source of information for research on cerebral asymmetries in brain-damaged, split-brain, and normal subjects.

Valenstein, E. S., ed. 1980. *The psychosurgery debate: Scientific, legal, and ethical perspectives*. San Francisco: Freeman. An outstanding collection of papers that includes historical reviews of psychosurgery, evaluations of its effectiveness, patient descriptions, and legal and ethical issues. This book is a valuable source for information about this field of biomedical research.

SENSATION

T he minds of the scientist, the nonscientist, our pet dog sniffing about the world, or a fish swimming about in a bowl, in fact, the minds of all living, thinking organisms, are prisoners that must rely on information smuggled in to them by the senses. Your world is what your senses tell you. The limitations of your senses set the boundaries of your conscious existence.

(Stanley Coren and Lawrence Ward, 1989)

During infancy, Helen Keller was stricken with an undiagnosed illness that left her blind and deaf. Until the age of seven she remained completely mute, cut off from communication with the outside world. Then, her parents arranged for Annie Sullivan, a 21-year-old recent graduate of the Perkins Institute for the Blind, to work with their child at home. One month after Sullivan arrived, Keller began to understand the tactile messages that Sullivan made on her hand. The breakthrough came when Keller grasped the simple association between the sign for "water" and the water that was poured over her hand. Keller went on to graduate from Radcliffe College and later to write about her experiences.

For most of us our senses work so well that we do not appreciate their profound importance. But imagine what it would be like to describe the difference between black and white to a person who has been blind since birth. Or think about how you would explain the different tastes of salt and pepper to a person with no taste buds. For the blind person, salt and pepper differ only in taste. For the person without the ability to taste, salt and pepper differ only in color (Coren and Ward, 1989). Without our senses intact, our experiences would be drastically limited. Without the ability to see and hear, we would all live in a world as dark and silent as Helen Keller's.

Why is the study of sensation important to our understanding of psychology? One answer is found in the opening quote of this chapter—the brain experiences nothing of the external world except that "smuggled in" by the senses. Science writer Jillyn Smith (1989) described our senses as peepholes—peepholes through which we detect the world. These peepholes provide us with information that is absolutely essential for our survival. They tell us where to find food and shelter and they help us avoid danger. Specialized cells in our nervous system called *receptors* capture this information and translate it into a form that our brain can interpret. Once digested by the brain, this information forms the basis for our perceptions of the world.

Sensation is different from perception. As you read this page, special light-sensitive cells in your eyes provide your brain with sensory information. This information, however, is not in the form of letters or words. Rather, the receptors in your eyes provide information only about changing patterns of light and dark that your brain must later interpret. **Sensation** is the process involved in receiving environmental information and converting it into neural impulses for use by the brain. **Perception** is the organization and interpretation of patterns of sensory information that allows us to understand the meaning of objects and events, like the words that are printed on this page. In this chapter we will describe how the different sensory receptors provide information for perceptual processing, and in Chapter 4 we will show how this information is interpreted and made meaningful by the brain.

Another reason why sensation is important to psychology is that it is a rich source of individual differences in experience. We humans are programmed by our genes to share the same general sensory equipment. Barring sensory deficit, we can all see, hear, smell, taste, and feel. However, our genes also allow for variation. Our differing sensations, perceptions, and experiences go a long way toward making each of us unique. Our senses allow us to see the colors of a rainbow, the sky at sunset, and the stars of the Big Dipper. They allow us to hear the Rolling Stones, Luciano Pavarotti, and Kenny Rogers, and to tell the difference between them. They allow us to distinguish between such smells as fresh baked bread, roses, and cow manure. They allow us to taste the saltiness of a pretzel, the sweetness of honey, and the sourness of a grapefruit. They allow us to feel the soft fur of a kitten, the dull pain of a headache, and the tender kiss of a loved one. Sensations like these provide the experiences of life (Smith, 1989).

Sensation is important to psychology for one more reason. As the next section will show, sensation was one of the topics that motivated the establishment of the first psychology laboratories over a century ago.

HISTORICAL BACKGROUND:
Psychophysics and Sensory Physiology

There is no better domain than the study of the human senses to illustrate the seamlessness of science. Our present understanding of sensation has only come through the coordinated efforts of physicists, biologists, engineers, and psychologists. Isaac Newton's discoveries about the physics of light energy are the foundation of what we know today about color vision. During the seventeenth century, Newton not only discovered that white light could be separated into a color spectrum, he also noted that certain combinations of red and green light could not be distinguished from a pure yellow light. A century later these discoveries led to a debate between physician-physicist Thomas Young and chemist John Dalton. Dalton proposed a chemcial theory of color recognition, while Young suggested an anatomical one, positing the existence of three different primary color receptors in the eye. Over the next two centuries, research by psychologists and biologists has supported Young's theory. Likewise, the study of audition (the hearing sense) had depended on research into the physics of sound waves, the anatomy of the inner ear, the psychological experience of sound quality, and the neurophysiology of the brain. This work has been further augmented by engineers working on radar and sonar, and comparative zoologists working on natural sonar systems that allow bats, dolphins, and whales to navigate in the dark.

Within the field of psychology, there have been two major approaches to the study of the senses, each of which takes a slightly different strategy. Research on **psychophysics** examines the relation between the amount of physical energy in a stimulus (such as the number of watts in a light bulb) and our sensory experience of that stimulus (how bright it seems to be). Research on **sensory physiology,** on the other hand, examines how the special cells for each of the different senses translates outside stimulation into electrochemical messages that the brain can decipher. Two nineteenth-century scientists, Gustav Fechner and Hermann von Helmholtz, each made major contributions in these areas.

Gustav Fechner

Fechner (1801–1887) began his career as a physics professor at the University of Leipzig. In his 30s, however, ill health forced him to resign his position. In addition to suffering from overwork, Fechner had damaged his eyes while doing research on color sensations by gazing at the sun through colored glasses. After several years in seclusion, Fechner's health returned. In fact, his condition improved so suddenly that he believed it was a miracle. His change in health led to a change of interests. Fechner turned away from physics and became deeply interested in religion and philosophy.

These new interests brought Fechner to the study of sensation, which he saw as an important aspect of consciousness. Understanding how "objective" events in the outside world were related to their internal "subjective" mental sensations became a key philosophical problem for Fechner. From his training in physics, Fechner tried to solve this problem by carefully measuring people's ability to detect changes in the intensity of lights, tones, and other sensory stimuli. He called this research "psychophysics" because, in blending psychology and physics, he hoped to specify the relation between internal *psycho*logical experiences and external *physica*l events. Fechner is remembered today for having established a set of psychophysical procedures for the systematic study of sensation.

Interest in sensory physiology has a much longer history. In the fifth century BC, the Greek philosopher Democrites believed that we become aware of objects in our environment because these objects emit tiny copies of themselves (called *eidola*) that our sense organs pick up and transmit to the brain. By the Middle Ages, a modified *copy theory* of sensation held that the tiny copies were sent along tubes in the body to a hollow area of the brain called the *sensus communis*, the imagined site of sensory analysis (Blakemore, 1977). (The nonexistent *sensus communis* was later associated with reason and judgment and is probably the source of the term "common sense.")

By 1826, German physiologist Johannes Muller had put forth the idea that we are not directly aware of objects in our world, as copy theory would have it, but of our neural responses to the external stimulation. Although Muller contributed much to our early understanding of sensory physiology, his most important contribution was to train a pupil named Hermann von Helmholtz.

Hermann von Helmholtz

Helmholtz (1821–1899) was one of the greatest scientists of the nineteenth century (Boring, 1950; Hilgard, 1987). Beginning his career as a surgeon

Hermann von Helmholtz. Helmholtz was a German physiologist, physicist, and mathematician who made major contributions to the study of sensation. Though his work laid the groundwork for the experimental psychology of sensation, he is not considered one of the founders of psychology because he viewed his own research as an extension of physiology.

in Germany, Helmholtz achieved widespread and lasting fame as both a physiologist and a physicist. Among his many accomplishments, he made the first accurate estimate of the speed of the nervous impulse, and he invented the ophthalmoscope, a device for looking directly into the interior of the eye. More important for the development of sensory science were Helmholtz's pioneering studies of seeing and hearing. During the 1860s, he published a three-volume set of books on vision, along with a major volume on audition. The third volume on vision is still used as a reference book, and his theory of how we detect differences in the pitch of a sound (called *place theory*) is still a viable one.

Though neither Fechner nor Helmholtz was identified as a psychologist, both stand today as major figures in the establishment of psychology as a science. Taking our cue from them, we will see that an understanding of sensation requires some understanding of relevant principles from physics and physiology. Some knowledge of physics is important because you cannot hope to interpret a sensory experience without first having an understanding of the stimulus that generates the experience. To understand sight and hearing, for instance, you need to know something about the physical properties of light and sound. By the same token, an examination of the anatomy and physiology of the sense organs will help you understand how each sense responds to a different form of physical energy. We begin by looking at the relation between stimulation and sensory experience. ■

STIMULATION AND SENSORY EXPERIENCE

Psychologists who study sensation consider three broad issues. First, they seek the lowest limits of our sensory capabilities. What is the minimal amount of stimulation we can respond to, and what is the minimal amount of stimulus change we can detect? Second, they describe the psychophysical relation between particular types of physical stimuli and sensory experience. For example, how do changes in the wavelengths of light translate into the experience of different colors? Finally, they attempt to separate sensation from psychological factors to show how past experience influences sensory processes.

THE LIMITS OF OUR SENSES

Sensory receptors, such as those in our eyes and ears, are limited in the type of information they can receive and in the amount of stimulation they need to generate a noticeable sensation. To be noticed, a stimulus must be compatible with a sensory receptor and be intense enough to stimulate that receptor. The level of intensity sufficient to stimulate a sensation is called the *sensory threshold*. There are two types of these sensory thresholds, or limits. The first limit on our senses is called the **absolute threshold.** That is the weakest *level* of stimulus intensity that can produce a sensation. Stimulus intensities below our absolute threshold pass unnoticed. An example of an absolute threshold is the lowest volume setting on your stereo that you can still hear. We are also limited in our ability to detect *changes* in the intensity of a stimulus. For example, how much louder or softer must we make the stereo before we notice the difference? This limit is called the **difference threshold**—the smallest *change* in the intensity of a stimulus that can be detected. Changes in intensity larger than the difference threshold produce a **just noticeable difference** (JND) in sensory experience.

(For example, we say that this stimulus is "brighter" or "heavier" than before.) Changes that are less than a JND pass undetected.

THE ABSOLUTE THRESHOLD

In 1860 Fechner developed the procedures for calculating the absolute threshold. In the *methods of limits*, the intensity of a stimulus is changed to find the point at which an observer's response changes. For example, to measure the absolute threshold for a stimulus such as a light, the energy level of the light is changed until it is just barely noticeable. Starting with a bright light and making the light progressively dimmer, or starting with no light and making the stimulus increasingly brighter, the absolute threshold is the point at which the light can just be detected. This, by the way, is the same procedure that optometrists use when they test people's visual acuity.

Ideally, if the method of limits could determine a person's absolute threshold for a particular sensory stimulus, the *psychometric function*, which is the relation of stimulus intensity to detection performance, would resemble the function shown in Figure 3.1A. Stimuli below the absolute threshold (180 units in this example) would never be detected, while stimuli at or above the threshold would be detected on every trial. Actual performance, however, resembles the curve in Figure 3.1B. Instead of a clear separation of sensitivity between never and always detected, there is a gradation of sensitivity that progressively changes from lower to higher intensities. Within this range of stimulus intensities, a person may detect a stimulus on one trial, yet fail to detect that stimulus on another.

Why do we not find a sharp transition from nondetection to detection? There are several reasons. First, spontaneous changes in the nervous system can occur whether or not there has been any external stimulation. This spontaneous activity, called *neural noise*, can make a stimulus more difficult to detect. Second, fatigue, or even changes in a person's attention, can lead to fluctuations in sensitivity. Finally, a person's motivation to perform may vary from one trial to the next. Since there are so many sources of variation in judgments, the absolute threshold for a sensory stimulus is arbitrarily defined as the level of intensity at which it is detected 50 percent of the time. By this criterion, the hypothetical data shown in Figure 3.1B yield an absolute threshold of 180 units. Table 3.1 shows actual absolute thresholds for different senses expressed in everyday terms. Not only do

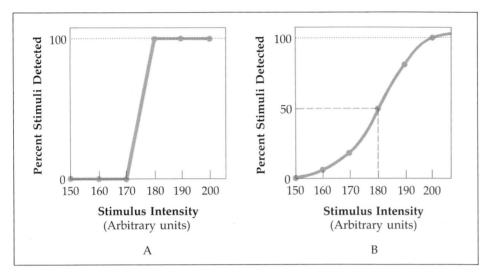

FIGURE 3.1 Relations between stimulus intensity and stimulus detection.   (A) This psychometric function relates stimulus detection to stimulus intensity. If sensory thresholds were sharply defined, there would exist a point below which stimuli would never be detected and above which they would always be detected. (B) Actual performance, however, shows a gradation of sensitivity from "never detected" at very low intensities, to "sometimes detected" at moderate intensities, to "always detected" at higher intensities. Because of the gradual change in sensitivity, the absolute threshold is defined as the level of intensity at which a stimulus is detected 50 percent of the time.

thresholds vary for each of the senses, they vary from person to person and situation to situation as well. Obviously, a person with poor vision would not see the flame of a candle 30 miles away on a dark, clear night; nor would someone suffering from a cold be likely to smell a drop of perfume in a six-room apartment through congested sinuses.

TABLE 3.1	Absolute Thresholds for Different Sensory Modalities

Sense	Absolute Threshold
Vision	The flame of a candle at 30 miles on a dark, clear night.
Hearing	The tick of a watch at 20 feet under quiet conditions.
Taste	One teaspoon of sugar in two gallons of water.
Smell	One drop of perfume in a six-room apartment.
Touch	The wing of a fly falling on your cheek from a distance of one centimeter.

After Galanter (1962).

THE DIFFERENCE THRESHOLD

The procedure for establishing the difference threshold was reported by German physiologist Ernst Weber in 1834. Subjects in Weber's research were asked to lift standard and comparison weights and to tell him whether they were the same. Over many trials, Weber determined the smallest difference between the standard and the comparison weights that his subjects could detect. He found that when his stimuli differed greatly, people always detected the difference; when the stimuli differed little, people often failed to notice the difference. Weber's results resembled the general psychometric function shown in Figure 3.1B. As in the case of the absolute threshold, the difference threshold is arbitrarily defined as the smallest difference between the standard and the comparison stimuli that is detected 50 percent of the time.

The most fascinating finding from Weber's research was that the difference threshold changed depending upon the weight of the standard stimulus. With light weights, subjects notice very small differences between the standard and the comparison, but, as the weights got heavier, larger differences were required. As everyday experience suggests, we are more likely to detect a small change in a weak stimulus than the same change in a stronger stimulus. Adding a dollar to the cost of a

stronger stimulus. Adding a dollar to the cost of a hamburger would invariably be detected, yet adding the same amount to the cost of an expensive French dinner would hardly be noticed at all. Although the JNDs (just noticeable differences) for the price of a hamburger and an expensive dinner are different, a fascinating constancy remains. The percentage of the price that must change for the change to be noticed remains the same. Extrapolating from Weber's research, if a person had to carry a 10-pound sack, the weight of the sack would have to be changed by ⅕ of a pound (two percent) for the change to be noticed. If the sack weighed 50 pounds, it would have to be changed by one pound (two percent) in order for the change to be detected. Finally, if the sack weighed 100 pounds, it would have to be changed by two pounds (two percent) in order for the change to be detected. While the JNDs in this example change from ⅕ to two pounds, they remain a constant percentage of the total weight. This finding, that a JND is a constant percentage of the intensity of a stimulus, is known as **Weber's law,** and the constant percentage it yields in each case is known as *Weber's constant*. Table 3.2 shows the different values of Weber's constant for different types of sensory stimuli. Since the sense organs differ in their ability to detect stimulus change, differences in sensitivity affect the JNDs and the constant percentages needed to observe a change. As shown in Table 3.2, we are much more sensitive to changes in the pitch of a sound or the brightness of a light (smaller Weber constants) than to changes in the taste of salt or pressure on our skin. These differences in sensitivity are based on differences in the number of receptor cells in each of our senses. Compared to the number of receptors for tasting, we have many more for seeing. Weber's law shows that while the senses differ in sensitivity, changes in sensitivity are uniformly related to changes in stimulus intensity for a broad range of sensory stimuli.

TABLE 3.2 Values of Weber's Constant for Different Sensory Stimuli

Sensory Stimuli	Weber's Constant
Pitch of a tone	.3%
Visual brightness	1.7%
Lifted weights	2.0%
Loudness of a tone	10.0%
Pressure on the skin	14.3%
Taste of a saline solution	20.0%

After Schiffman (1976) and other sources.

MEASURING SENSATION

Describing the limits of our sensory capabilities is only one aspect of sensation. Psychologists and other sensory scientists also want to know how the quality of a sensory experience changes as the physical stimulus changes. For example, how does our experience of brightness or loudness change as the intensity of a light or a tone is changed? To answer such questions precisely, we need a **psychophysical scale.** In the present context, a *scale* is defined as a graduated instrument for measurement. We are all familiar with numerous scales that measure different physical quantities. Bathroom scales measure weight, rulers measure length, and thermometers measure temperature. Each of these physical scales takes a quantifiable physical variable (weight, length, or temperature) and specifies it in terms of a physical unit of measurement (pounds, inches, or degrees). A psychophysical scale is conceptually similar but also differs in a fundamental way. A psychophysical scale takes a quantifiable physical stimulus, such as weight in pounds, and measures it as a subjective sensory experience, such as "heaviness." While we can precisely measure a physical stimulus such as light intensity with a physical instrument, we cannot use an instrument to measure the private, subjective experience of brightness. This private aspect of experience poses a problem for psychophysics. So does the fact that stimulation and experience are usually not related in a simple one-to-one fashion. For example, turning a three-way light bulb from a 50 to 100 watts setting or from a 50 to 150 watts setting does not double or triple our experience of brightness. Rather, our experience of brightness increases by smaller and smaller amounts, even though stimulus intensity increases by equal units (50 to 100 to 150 watts). In this case, constant increments in stimulation produce diminishing returns for experience.

AN INDIRECT MEASURE OF SENSORY EXPERIENCE

To understand this relation, Fechner devised a psychophysical scale. He measured the changes in intensity of a sensory stimulus (for example, increases in light energy) that were needed to obtain an equal series of just noticeably different increases in brightness. An example of the type of scale where stimulus intensity increases more rapidly than sensory experience is provided in Figure 3.2. The hypothetical data in the figure indicate that sensory experience is relative to the intensity of stimulation. For example, lighting one candle in a dark room creates a much larger change in sensa-

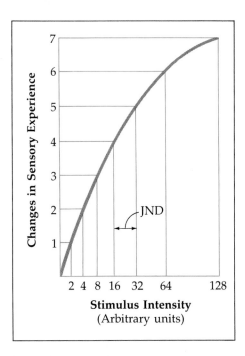

FIGURE 3.2 Changes in stimulus intensity and just-noticeably different changes in experience. In this psychophysical relation, progressively larger increments in stimulus intensity are needed to produce constant increments in sensory experience. This relation led Fechner to believe that sensory experience is proportional to the logarithm of stimulus intensity.

magnitude estimation. In this procedure an observer is presented with a standard stimulus, say a light, of some particular intensity. The light is arbitrarily given the numerical value of 100 and it is used as a basis of comparison for all other stimuli that follow. If observers believe that a second light is twice as bright as the standard, they assign it a value of 200; if they think it is only half as bright as the first, they give it a value of 50. In this way, observers directly report their sensory judgments over a wide range of stimulus intensities and produce a psychophysical scale.

When such different sensory qualities as brightness, apparent length, and shock intensity are examined by the magnitude estimation procedure, very different psychophysical functions are found (Figure 3.3). The function for brightness judgments closely resembles the classic Fechner function. It shows *compression* of sensory experience—judgments of brightness increase by smaller and smaller amounts with equal increments in stimulus intensity.

However, the other functions in Figure 3.3 show that different relations are possible. The function for apparent length (ratings of the lengths of different lines to a line selected as a standard) shows a *linear* (one-to-one) relation between

tion than does lighting a candle in a room that already has one hundred candles burning. Although the change in light energy is the same in both instances (the addition of one candle), the change in sensory experience is not.

Fechner proposed that sensory experience was proportional to the logarithm of stimulus intensity. This means that ever larger increases in stimulus intensity are needed to produce a constant increase in sensory experience. This relation is shown in Figure 3.2 and is known as *Fechner's law.* However, Fechner's law remains incomplete. It fails to predict the fact that for stimuli such as weight, temperature, and electric shock, increases in stimulus intensity result in larger, not smaller, increments in sensory experience. For instance, doubling the intensity of an electric shock produces about a tenfold increase in the perceived intensity of that shock (Stevens, 1975).

A DIRECT MEASURE OF SENSORY EXPERIENCE

One hundred years after Fechner, S. S. Stevens (1957; 1962) of Harvard University proposed a different way of measuring sensory experience. Stevens measured sensitivity directly by the *method of*

FIGURE 3.3 Three types of psychophysical functions. Different types of psychophysical functions are found for different types of physical stimuli. Judgments of brightness show compression of sensitivity with increases in stimulus intensity, judgments of electric shock show expansion, and judgments of length are linearly related to changes in stimulus size. Compression, linearity, and expansion are three types of psychophysical relations.

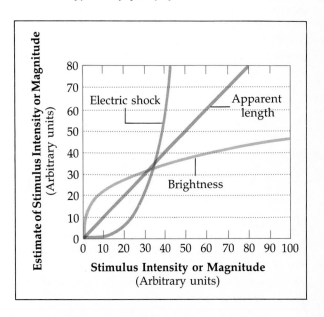

stimulation and sensory experience—doubling the length of a line doubles the judgment of length. The function for electric shock (ratings of comparison shocks to a standard shock intensity) shows *expansion* of sensory judgments, since doubling the intensity of a shock more than doubles its sensory experience. Compression, linearity, and expansion demonstrate the range of psychophysical functions.

Stevens described the different psychophysical functions mathematically and found that sensation is proportional to the intensity of a stimulus raised to a certain power and is different for each of the senses. This function, known as *Stevens's power law*, demonstrates why increases in stimulus intensity produce different increases in sensory experience for each of the senses. Different senses probably differ in their sensitivity because of specific benefits in these different relations. For example, susceptibility to the harmful effects of glare is reduced if our experience of brightness is compressed, while avoidance of dangerous shocks is enhanced if our sensitivity to shock is expanded (Goldstein, 1984).

Our understanding of how stimulation influences sensory judgments is based on a century of research that continues to the present day (Krueger, 1989). But there is still more to know about how we judge whether a stimulus is present or not, or whether the stimulus has been changed in some way. As we will see in the next section, these sensory judgments are influenced by more than just sensory stimulation.

SENSORY JUDGMENTS: SIGNAL DETECTION AND ADAPTATION

Psychologists have long known that our absolute and difference thresholds can be influenced by whether we are tired, interested, paying attention, or well-practiced on a task. As we saw in Figure 3.1B, sensory thresholds are not in any way fixed points; they are relative, graded experiences that depend on a variety of factors. In measuring sensory thresholds, conscientious observers are often unsure. ("There may have been a faint tone presented on that trial, but I am not positive.") Moreover, manipulating the instructions can alter performance. Lenient instructions (for example, "Respond if you think you hear a tone on each trial even if you are unsure") will lead to a *positive response bias,* a tendency to say that a stimulus was present, while conservative instructions ("Respond only if you are sure you hear a tone on each trial") lead to a more conservative or *negative re-*

sponse bias. Since performance is subject to such influences, it is reasonable to wonder about the extent to which performance on a threshold task measures a person's judgment standards (response bias) as well as his or her sensitivity. Two theoretical approaches deal with the problem of changes in sensory judgments. **Signal detection theory** separates sensitivity from other judgment factors, and **adaptation level theory** shows how sensitivity can change on the basis of past experience.

SIGNAL DETECTION THEORY

Imagine that you are a radar operator and must decide whether a faint blip or *signal* on your screen is a plane. If you are uncertain because the signal is weak, other factors may change your motivation to make a "yes" or "no" decision. If you are working at a busy metropolitan airport and want to avoid collisions at any cost, you will be inclined to err on the "yes" side. However, if you are working at a SAC (Strategic Air Command) base, a "yes" may put a whole squadron on red alert. Since putting fighter pilots in the air is both costly and potentially dangerous, you would want to err on the conservative side until the signal on your screen became stronger. Thus, your judgment of a weak signal can depend on more than just sensitivity. Originating in communications engineering, signal detection theory holds that sensory judgments are based not only on stimulus intensity but also on a person's motives and expectations, as well as on the "neural noise" that is always present in the nervous system. Signal detection theory states that the all-or-none threshold view of sensation is wrong. Instead, sensation is a graded experience that depends on the intensity of the sensory stimulus and the person's willingness to respond. Together, these *sensory* and *decision processes* determine the nature of a sensory response.

In a typical signal detection experiment, a person is seated in a quiet room facing a warning light that periodically flashes. Whenever the light is turned on, a tone may or may not be briefly sounded. Over the course of many trials, the intensity of the tone is varied from loud to very soft, and there are numerous "catch trials" in which no tone is presented. The listener's task is to say whether a tone was presented on each of the trials. Four different outcomes are possible. Listeners may say that they heard a tone when one was presented (a *hit*) or that they did not hear a presented tone (a *miss*). Conversely, they may say that they heard a tone when none was presented (a *false alarm*) or that they did not hear a tone when it was absent (a *correct rejection*). Notice how the terms also apply to radar operators, who are often faced with just such a signal detection task.

For loud tones, there is no problem; listeners are likely to say that they heard each tone and score a large number of hits. But as the tone gets softer, the task becomes increasingly difficult. According to signal detection theory, the task gets harder as the tones get fainter because of the presence of spontaneous neural noise in the nervous system. As we saw in the previous chapter, even when no external stimulation is present, neurons fire spontaneously and randomly. The problem for the listener is to determine whether a faint tone or signal was presented in addition to the noise (like hearing a radio program on an AM station that is filled with static) or if noise alone occurred. The presence of neural noise can lead listeners to make false alarms when no signals were presented or to miss faint signals that were actually there.

A listener's decision to say "Yes, I heard a tone" or "No, I didn't hear a tone" can be influenced by motives and expectations that affect the *response criterion*. This criterion or cutoff point is a measure of a person's willingness to say that a tone was presented, and it can be moved higher or lower. For example, if detecting faint signals is rewarded (if you are paid $1 for every hit and not penalized for each false alarm), then you are likely to lower your response criterion and say "Yes" more frequently. This strategy would result in more hits to faint tones as well as more false alarms to nonexistent ones. On the other hand, if making false alarms proves costly (if you are penalized $1 for every false alarm and given nothing for each hit), then you are likely to raise your response criterion to reduce your number of false alarms, while increasing your number of misses. Signal detection theory combines these different responses to provide a mathematical measure of a person's sensitivity called the detection level or, more simply, *d'* (pronounced d prime). In addition, the theory provides a way of measuring a person's response criterion, called *Beta,* that is relatively independent of sensitivity. In this way, signal detection researchers can measure both sensory and decision processes.

Although signal detection theory was initially formulated by engineers at Bell Laboratories to study the intelligibility of speech on telephone lines, it has proven useful in situations ranging from memory experiments to medical diagnoses (Does this chest X-ray show early traces of lung cancer?) and parole board deliberations (Will this person break the law again if he or she is re-

leased?). It is useful when a "yes/no" decision must be made under inherently uncertain or noisy conditions. In each case, the person or group making a decision must weigh the benefits of making a hit or correct rejection against the costs of a miss or a false alarm.

ADAPTATION LEVEL THEORY

Sensory adaptation is defined as the reduction in sensitivity that occurs as a result of prolonged, continuous stimulation. Table 3.3 shows how tactile sensitivity is lost when a constant weight is applied to the skin. Although the cheek is more sensitive than the back of the hand, and it takes longer to adapt to a heavier weight than a lighter weight, tactile sensation disappears in a matter of seconds. Similar adaptation decrements occur in each of our other senses.

Adaptation to constant stimulation is necessary because prolonged, continuous stimulation provides us with no new information. Just like the ticking of a nearby clock or the tactile pressure of our clothing, constant, unchanging stimuli quickly come to be ignored. Sensory adaptation is valuable because, by de-emphasizing what is old, it emphasizes what is new. Adaptation to light makes us more sensitive to dark; adaptation to warmth makes us more sensitive to cold. Sensory adaptation provides a frame of reference that helps us to notice these changes in stimulation. This varying frame of reference is called the **adaptation level** (Helson, 1964).

According to adaptation level theory, sensitivity is not dependent merely on current stimulus intensity. Rather, what you are experiencing now is influenced by what you experienced before (Helson, 1964). To see how prior stimulation can in-

TABLE 3.3 Average Time in Seconds for Sensation to Disappear as a Function of Weight and Location of a Tactile Stimulus

Stimulus Weight (mg.)	Back of Hand	Cheek
50	2.42	5.71
100	3.82	6.37
500	6.01	11.63
1000	6.71	13.51
2000	9.52	19.36

Adapted from Zigler (1932).

fluence your sensory experience, try the following task. Place one hand in a bowl of hot water and the other hand in a bowl of cold water. After a minute or so, remove both hands and place them in a bowl of lukewarm water. Your experience will come as a surprise. Instead of the water feeling lukewarm, it will feel cold for the hand that was previously in hot water and hot for the hand that was in cold water. This demonstration of sensory adaptation shows how our current sensory experience is influenced by prior stimulation.

SENSORY RECEPTORS: GENERAL PRINCIPLES

In the remainder of this chapter we will look at how each of the different senses actually operates. Although each sense is different, they all share general principles of operation. All sensory receptors convert physical energy into neural impulses that are transmitted to the different sensory areas of the brain. This process is called **transduction.** For example, we smell a rose after odor molecules from the flower have touched chemical receptors in our noses and have been transduced into electrical energy that can be used by our brains. We feel pressure when we sit in chairs because special skin receptors transduce mechanical force into electrical energy that is transmitted to our somatosensory cortexes. When physical energy is transduced, it is translated, or *coded,* into various neural firing patterns, and these codes provide the brain with information about different features of the stimulation (such as the loudness and pitch of a tone). While the various senses use different forms of physical energy (for example, odor molecules or skin pressure) they all convert that energy into coded neural impulses that eventually lead to sensory experiences.

How many different senses do we have? Aristotle organized the different senses into the five commonly known modalities: sight, sound, taste, smell, and touch. This everyday classification is still widely known, but it is actually misleading. There are more than five senses. For example, a sense of balance is provided by the *vestibular sense* located in the inner ear, and a sense of body position and movement is achieved by the *kinesthetic receptors* located in the muscles, tendons, and joints. Even the sense of touch is more complex than we had earlier believed. Touch involves several senses, as receptors in the skin indicate not only how things feel but also provide information about temperature, pain, and vibration. In the rest

of this chapter, we will describe these different senses, but, for two reasons, we will emphasize vision and audition. First, vision and audition are our most fully developed senses. In fact, vision dominates all the other senses in importance and is our richest source of information (Posner, Nissen, and Klein, 1976; Riggs, 1985). Second, vision and audition have been more thoroughly studied than any of the other senses. After considering vision and audition, we will highlight the unique features of our other senses.

VISION

There is an adage that says "The eyes are the windows to the world." At any given moment, our eyes can put us in touch with more potential information than can any of our other senses. In order to understand how our eyes enable us to see, we must begin our discussion of vision by describing the light that comes through these "windows."

PHYSICAL PROPERTIES OF LIGHT

The sun's electromagnetic radiation is the most important form of energy on earth. Aside from being a boundless source of energy for plants and a signal for seasonal behavior in animals, solar radiation is the basis for vision (Brown and Deffenbacher, 1979). Actually, there are many forms of electromagnetic energy, ranging from gamma rays and X-rays at one end of the energy spectrum to television and radio waves at the opposite end (Figure 3.4A). Because electromagnetic energy travels in waves—waves that resemble the ripples that move outward in concentric circles when a pebble is dropped into a pond—this energy spectrum is scaled in terms of wavelengths. More precisely, electromagnetic energy is thought to consist of incredibly small particles that move in a wavelike fashion (Uttal, 1973). Each type of radiation has its own characteristic *wavelength* (defined as the distance from the crest of one wave to the crest of the next). For example, gamma rays have extremely short wavelengths—less than four billionths of an inch—while radio waves can be measured in miles. Within the energy spectrum is a narrow band of wavelengths, called the **visual spectrum,** (Figure 3.4B) that is visible to the human eye. The range of visible wavelengths is from 390 to 760 nanometers. (A nanometer is one billionth of a meter or about 40 billionths of an inch.)

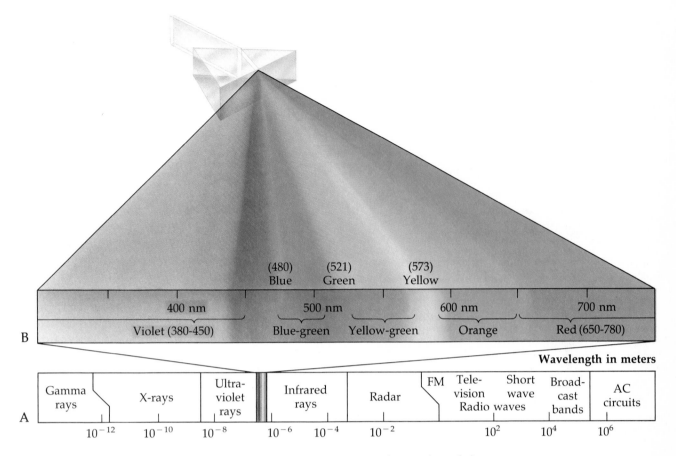

FIGURE 3.4 The energy spectrum and the visual spectrum. The portion of the energy spectrum (bottom line of figure) that is visible to the human eye consists of a narrow band of wavelengths between the ultraviolet and infrared rays. The visual spectrum (above) shows the colors of the rainbow as they appear when sunlight is passed through a prism.

PSYCHOLOGICAL PROPERTIES OF LIGHT

Physically, light can be described in terms of its **wavelength, amplitude,** and **purity.** Psychologically, these dimensions correspond most closely to **hue, brightness,** and **saturation** (the apparent purity of a hue). One of the most obvious aspects of the visual spectrum is that lights of different wavelengths are experienced as different colors. This fact was observed by Newton in 1672 when he passed sunlight through a prism and saw the colors of the rainbow, as can be seen in Figure 3.4B. As wavelengths increase across the visual spectrum, our perception of color changes from violet to blue, green, yellow, orange, and finally to red at the opposite end. *Hue* is the perception of color that is determined by the light's wavelength. The height of a wave, known as its *amplitude,* is related to *brightness.* The higher the amplitude, the brighter a color appears. Light is also characterized by its *purity,* the number of different wavelengths that

make up a particular color. The greater the purity, the fewer the number of different kinds of wavelengths, and the more saturated the color appears. These three dimensions of color can be seen in the color solid shown in Figure 3.5.

THE PHYSIOLOGY OF SEEING

What we see is not simply a function of the physical energy "out there," but also depends upon the structure of the eye and its connections to the brain. Before we can understand how we see objects in the world around us, we need to know how light energy is focused on receptor cells within the eye and translated into neural impulses. As you may recall from Chapter 2, receptor cells are specialized nerve cells used for receiving sensory stimulation. These cells convert energy such as light waves, sound waves, or odor molecules into neural impulses for the brain. In this section we will examine how visual stimulation is processed,

FIGURE 3.5. The color solid. The color solid demonstrates differences in hue, saturation, and brightness. Hue is represented by different colored chips along the circumference, saturation by chips along the radius, and brightness by chips on the vertical axis. Each vertical panel shows the differences in saturation and brightness that can exist for a particular hue.

from the time it enters the eye as light until it reaches the brain as a coded neural signal.

THE ANATOMY OF THE EYE

Figure 3.6 shows a drawing of a cross section of a human eye. Light entering the eye passes through the **cornea,** a transparent covering at the front of the eye that provides protection and support, and the **lens,** a transparent structure that focuses the light. The amount of light that enters the eye is controlled by the size of the **pupil,** the opening or black spot that appears in the center of the **iris,** a richly pigmented structure that consists of counteracting muscle bands that determine the size of the pupil and give the eyes their color. Incoming light is focused onto the **retina** at the rear of the eye, a paper-thin lining composed of millions of light-sensitive receptors. You might think of the retina as a balloon blown up inside a tennis ball (Smith, 1989). Among the retina's major landmarks are the **fovea,** a small indentation in the

FIGURE 3.6 The structure of the human eye. Light passes through the cornea, pupil, and lens before reaching the light-sensitive retina at the back of the eye. The cornea and the lens are responsible for the eye's focusing power. If the cornea is misshapen, some of the light reaching the retina will be improperly focused. This condition, call astigmatism, can be corrected by glasses or contact lenses.

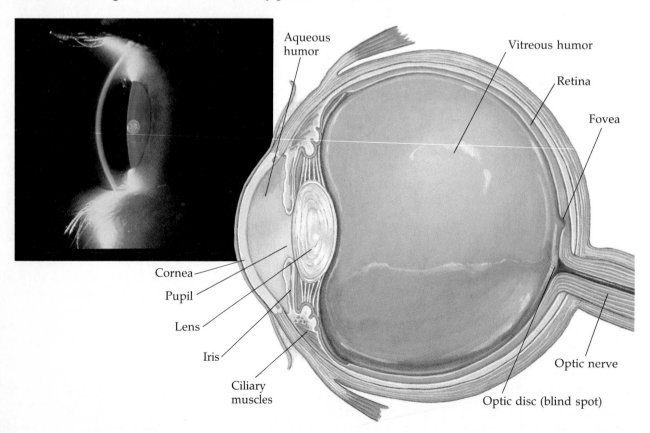

retina and the center of the visual field, and the **blind spot,** the point where blood vessels and neurons enter and exit the eye.

The pupil is controlled by the autonomic nervous system, and it can be dilated (made wider) or constricted (made smaller) according to the level of illumination. Under low levels of illumination, the pupil is dilated to admit more light; under high levels of illumination it is constricted, reducing the amount of scattered light in the eye and improving our ability to see clearly. The size of the pupil is also related to psychological factors. For example, pupil size is positively related to both judgments of sexual attractiveness and the degree of mental effort required for a given task. A person's pupils will widen while looking at an attractive person or

while concentrating on a difficult assignment (Hess, 1965; Kahneman, 1973). Apparently, this fact has been known for a long time. Centuries ago, Chinese jade merchants were said to watch their customer's eyes for dilation as an indication of their interest in making a purchase (Smith, 1989).

Directly behind the pupil is the lens. Light from objects both near and far is brought into focus through the process of *accommodation,* fine adjustments in the shape of the lens produced by the muscles that hold it in place. If the lens is improperly focused, **nearsighted** or **farsighted** vision results (Figure 3.7). Lens-focusing problems are partly hereditary, but experience also plays a role. For example, research has confirmed that ex-

FIGURE 3.7 Different conditions of seeing. In A, a person with normal vision sees near and distant objects clearly because the lens focuses light on the retina. In B, a nearsighted person cannot see distant objects clearly because light is focused in front of the retina. A concave lens corrects this condition by causing light rays to diverge. In C, a farsighted person has difficulty seeing close objects clearly because light is focused behind the retina. A convex lens corrects this problem by causing light rays to converge.

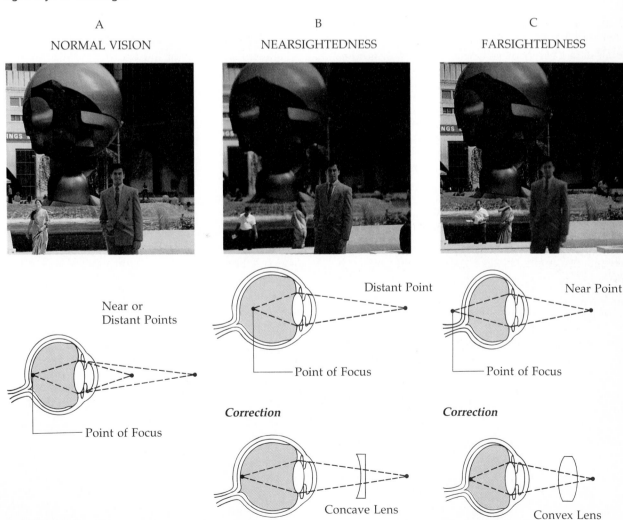

cessive reading can contribute to nearsightedness. In 1813, a British officer named James Ware reported that many well-educated officers were nearsighted, while illiterate enlisted men almost never suffered this fate. More recently, experiments with chicks have shown how reading and nearsightedness are related. When chicks were fitted with special contact lenses that obscured the outer fields of their vision, the lenses produced understimulation of the cells in the periphery of their retinas and overstimulation of the cells in the center. Over time, the chicks' eyeballs became elongated, resulting in nearsightedness (Collins, 1987). Excessive reading can produce this same pattern of stimulation in our eyes. This is why it is helpful to rest your eyes periodically when you read. You can do this by looking out of a window occasionally, since this relaxes your eye muscles and improves circulation.

Visual acuity is the ability to see fine detail clearly. It is concentrated in a special area at the center of the field of view known as the fovea. Standard tests, in which we cover one eye and read letters that diminish in size from a chart a short distance away, measure our ability to see fine detail. Outside of the fovea is the blind spot, a small area devoid of sensory receptors. It is here where the axons of retinal cells exit the eye through a "hole" in the retina. Because there are no receptors in this region, there is no visual sensitivity to light striking here. Normally this gap in visual sensitivity goes unnoticed, but, if you close one eye and follow the directions in Figure 3.8, you can experience this blind spot.

THE LIGHT-SENSITIVE RETINA

The retina is a network of cells that transforms light into neural impulses. As shown in Figure 3.9, when light enters the eye it passes first through the *ganglion* and *bipolar cells* before reaching the light sensitive **rods** and **cones.** The rods and cones are part of two separate receptor systems, together forming an intricate retinal mosaic that enables us to distinguish such features as color, texture, and form. Microscopically, the rods look like cattails on a stalk and the cones resemble carrots (Smith, 1989). Aside from their difference in shape, these cells differ in their number, location, sensitivity to light, and function. The six to eight million cones are concentrated largely in the center of the retina. They entirely fill the fovea and function well only in daylight or bright artificial light. They allow us to see with a high degree of visual acuity and to perceive different colors. In contrast, the 120 million rods far outnumber the cones, and they are located in the periphery of the retina. While the rods only distinguish black, white, and shades of gray, they function well under low levels of illumination—no lighter than bright moonlight (Barlow, 1982). Together, these receptors complement each other. The cones provide for color vision, enable us to discriminate apples from oranges, and allow the fine acuity needed for reading. The rods, on the other hand, allow us to see in dim light. Without the cones, we could not tell a colorful Monet painting from a black and white reproduction. Without the rods, we could not see the stars or find a seat in a semidark theater.

The transduction of light into neural impulses involves a photochemical process. The rods contain a chemical called *rhodopsin*, which is broken down or "bleached" by light. This bleaching generates a neural impulse that is transmitted to nearby cells. After a rod generates its impulse and the light is removed, the rhodopsin is returned to its original state, and so the process can be repeated. Rods function well under low levels of illumination because only a small amount of light is necessary to break down the rhodopsin and trigger a neural impulse. Think of the rods as microscopic bowling pins—each one signals the brain whenever it is bowled over by a light particle, and then is reset automatically.

Cones are less sensitive than rods and require more intense stimulation, but they generate their

FIGURE 3.8 A demonstration of the blind spot. Keeping your right eye closed, and your head approximately one foot from the page, stare at the dot. By moving your head closer in or farther back, you can find a point where the words on the left will disappear. You will not see the words when they project on the area of the left retina called the optic disc—the blind spot that is devoid of sensory receptors.

THESE
WORDS
WILL
DISAPPEAR

WATCH
•
THE DOT

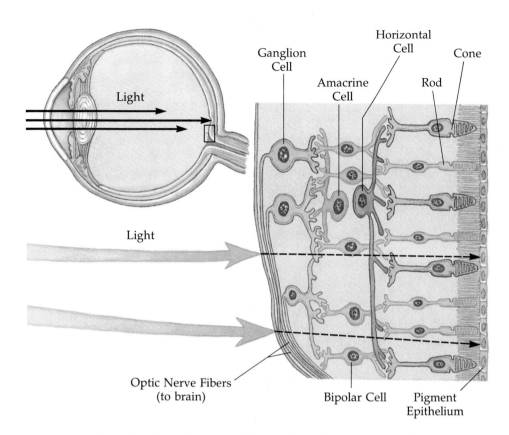

FIGURE 3.9 The cells of the human retina. Light is filtered through the ganglion and bipolar cells before reaching the rods and cones. This backward arrangement is due to the way the eye is formed during embryonic development. In the process of becoming an eye, the neural structure that extends from the brain is turned inside out. Once the rods and cones are stimulated, their neural impulses are sent to the bipolar and ganglion cells. The axons of the ganglion cells form the optic nerve that transmits neural impulses to the brain.

neural impulses through a similar bleaching and resetting photochemical process. There are three different types of cones, each containing different photosensitive chemicals, each sensitive to different wavelengths of light (Nathans, 1989). These photosensitive chemicals restrict our vision to only a small portion of the spectrum of light. Looking back to the visual spectrum shown in Figure 3.4, you should realize that there is no inherent change in electromagnetic energy that makes wavelengths from 390 to 760 nanometers suddenly become visible to most vertebrates, including us. The photochemical processes in the rods and cones of our eyes are triggered by electromagnetic energy with wavelengths in this particular range (Uttal, 1973). Other species have eyes with different sensitivities. For example, insects can detect wavelengths in the range of 300 to 650 nanometers, while rattlesnakes can detect wavelengths in excess of 1,000 nanometers—wavelengths invisible to us.

When lighting levels change, the photochemical processes respond very differently. **Light adaptation** is a reduction in sensitivity when illumination changes from dim to very bright. For example, our eyes must light-adapt when we leave a movie theater on a sunny afternoon. Light adaptation involves a relatively rapid shift from rod to cone vision so that we need not squint indefinitely in the bright, glaring light. On the other hand, **dark adaptation** results in an increase in sensitivity when illumination is considerably reduced. For example, our eyes must dark-adapt when we enter a movie theater on a sunny afternoon. Dark adaptation involves a slow shift from cone to rod vision, eventually allowing us to see in the semidarkness of the theater. Another way to see how adaptation processes influence our sensory experience is to stimulate only a portion of the visual field. If you do this, you can sometimes create interesting sensory aftereffects as the cells in your eyes readapt. For instance, a *negative afterimage* can be produced by staring at the stimulus shown in Figure 3.10.

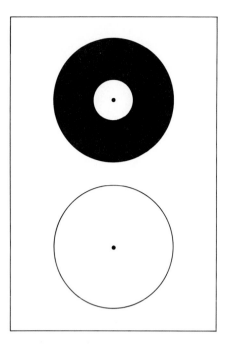

FIGURE 3.10. A demonstration of a negative after-image. Stare at the black dot in the center of the upper circle for approximately 15 seconds and be sure to keep the page at a fixed distance from your eyes. Then stare at the dot in the lower circle until you see a circular gray area around the fixation point. The "gray area" is a negative afterimage that is produced by the previous stimulation. While you looked at the first pattern, stimulation from the white area resulted in a portion of the retina being light adapted (made less sensitive), while stimulation from the surrounding black area resulted in a portion of the retina being dark adapted (made more sensitive). When you looked at the second pattern, the outer border of the figure seemed brighter because the corresponding area of the retina was more sensitive to light than that portion of the retina that corresponded to the center, which was partially light adapted.

After the rods and cones transmit their neural impulses to the bipolar and ganglion cells, the impulses are transmitted along the ganglion axons that make up the *optic nerve* (look back to Figure 3.6). Since the optic nerve contains only about one million separate nerve fibers, it is obvious that each of the 120 million rods and cones does not have a separate pathway to the brain. While thousands of cones in the fovea appear to connect in a one-to-one fashion with their own ganglion cells, many rods share the same ganglion cell. This results in a mixing of the output from many rods and a consequent loss of visual acuity. However, it also increases general sensitivity to light, because stimulation of any one of these many receptors is enough to stimulate the same ganglion cell. For this reason it is easier to see faint stars in the night sky by looking for them from one side of the eye or

another. These faint stars are not visible to the direct foveal vision of cones. Ancient navigators discovered this fact long ago. They looked to one side of a faint star, instead of directly at it, to increase their chances of seeing.

EYE MOVEMENTS AND VISUAL ACUITY

To see an object clearly the eyes must fixate on it, so that the image is directed to each sensitive fovea. To see all parts of the object clearly, we must move our eyes over its surface. These voluntary eye movements are called **saccades,** and they occur between one and five times a second. Figure 3.11 shows a tracing of a sequence of separate fixations made by a person looking at a painting. What is interesting about saccades is that we see clearly only during fixations (the numbered points in Figure 3.11). During an actual saccade, a visual scene is "smeared" across our retinal surface, rather than clearly fixated. Why is there no experience of this retinal smear? The answer is that stimulation from each new fixation obliterates what came before (Campbell and Wurtz, 1978). This is why, for example, we cannot see our eyes move in a mirror—to see them requires a fixation on the moving eyes themselves. This paradox was discovered long ago by Raymond Dodge. You can verify it yourself.

Keep one important fact in mind about the physiology of seeing: All of the objects that we see are the result of stimulation from sensory receptors in our retina being passed along neurons to the visual cortex at the back of the brain. As we discussed in the last chapter, our sensory neurons translate a physical stimulus such as light energy into a coded pattern of electrical impulses that provides information to the brain. This neural code bears no resemblance to the external objects that we see. For example, recordings from the ganglion cells in the frog's optic nerve have shown that these cells generate an electrical signal whenever a small dark object moves within a particular area of the frog's field of sight. These cells are called "bug detectors" because they only respond to bug-like stimuli that move in bug-like ways (Lettvin, Maturana, McCulloch, and Pitts, 1959). This is an example of an external stimulus (an object that resembles a bug) generating a neural impulse (an electrical signal that neither looks, nor sounds, nor acts, anything like a bug) that provides information to the frog's brain (There's food out there!). Our perceptual processes are much more complex, and yet in some ways they are just as simple. What we sense and what we perceive are both based on nothing more than particular patterns of electrical impulses.

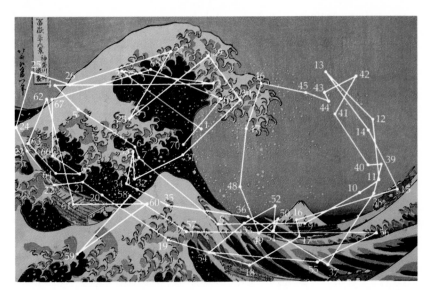

FIGURE 3.11 A record of saccadic eye movements. Buswell (1935) presented viewers with the picture *The Wave* by Hokusai Katsushika to study saccadic eye movements. The tracings made by an eye camera (a device for recording saccades) show the sequence of individual fixations made by a single observer. Saccadic eye movements provide the viewer with changes in visual stimulation. Each brief fixation provides new stimulation that can be integrated by the viewer into a coherent idea of what is seen.

RECEPTIVE FIELDS OF VISION

We have seen that ganglion cells in the frog's optic nerve fire whenever a small dark object moves within a particular area of the frog's field of sight. In this way, the ganglion cells form a receptive field to inform the frog about the presence and location of a bug. The **receptive field** for any particular cell is defined as the area in the visual field in which a stimulus will produce a response. Numerous receptive fields inform the frog's brain about the location of visual stimuli in the environment.

Research on receptive fields began in 1938 when H. K. Hartline discovered that there are three types of response fibers in the optic nerves of frogs. There are "on" fibers that fire when a light is turned on, "off" fibers that respond when a light is turned off, and "on–off" fibers that respond briefly when a light is turned on and briefly again when it is turned off. Each of these fibers is linked to an area of the frog's retina that contains those receptor cells. By converging on different optic fibers, the retinal cells form receptive fields, retinal regions that are sensitive to particular *changes* in illumination.

David Hubel and Torsten Wiesel (1959; 1962; 1979) won a Nobel Prize in 1981 for their research on receptive fields. After placing a minute single-cell recording electrode into the brain of an anesthetized cat, Hubel and Wiesel presented various simple visual stimuli to a motionless but wide-eyed animal. By carefully positioning the electrode and painstakingly observing the responses of cortical cells to different visual stimuli, they mapped the cat's receptive fields.

Hubel and Wiesel found that different types of cortical cells acted as detectors for different visual features (recall the "bug detectors" in the frog). These cells only began firing when they were stimulated by a specific visual stimulus. *Simple cells* fired when a thin bar of light oriented at a particular angle stimulated a specific retinal location. *Complex cells* only responded to a larger visual stimulus in a certain location. *Hypercomplex cells* were different still. They responded only to moving angles or corners, or to moving lines of a particular length and orientation that travelled across the retina in a specific direction. Hubel and Wiesel thus showed how different patterns of retinal stimulation are translated into particular types of brain stimulation. This is what enables us to see all the different features we are capable of seeing. For example, this **feature detection** is essential for such everyday perceptual processes as reading the lines on this page.

Our understanding of feature detection and the mechanics of vision has important practical applications. Seeing is dependent on our rods and cones generating electrical signals that are transmitted along the optic pathways to the visual cortex of the brain. If the light sensitive retinal cells of the neural pathways are defective, neural signals cannot reach the brain and we cannot see. Alternatively, if the visual cortex is damaged a permanent loss of vision occurs, because neural signals from the retinas cannot be interpreted by the brain. In both instances, blindness results. However, developments in the fields of ophthalmology (the area of medicine concerned with vision disorders) and neurology (the area of medicine concerned with the nervous system) offer some hope to the blind.

RESEARCH AND APPLICATION: Development of the Artificial Eye

In the century since Annie Sullivan broke through Helen Keller's sensory deficits, there have been a number of exciting developments for the blind. Medical researcher Paul Bach-y-Rita (1972), for example, developed an apparatus that allows the blind to "see with their skin." Based on the fact that blind people can learn to read Braille (a system of writing that uses characters made of raised dots), Bach-y-Rita's device turns visual scenes into patterns of tactile vibrations. The apparatus consists of a television camera attached to a mechanism that converts light into electrical signals. These signals stimulate a bank of vibrators attached to the back of a seat. These vibrations allow blind people to perceive objects by interpreting the distinctive patterns made on their backs (Figure 3.12). Said one highly practiced blind subject when presented with the tactile impression of a friend's familiar face:

> That is Betty; she is wearing her hair down today and does not have her glasses on. Her mouth is open, and she is moving her right hand from her left side to the back of her head.
>
> *(Bach-y-Rita, 1972)*

More recent research on visual deficits looks even more promising. Instead of training the tactile sense to do the work of vision, it may be possible to provide sight to the blind by direct electrical stimulation of the brain. For people with damaged eyes or defective optic pathways, blindness occurs because visual information cannot reach the visual cortex. If this brain area can be stimulated directly, thereby bypassing the defective component, vision might be restored.

An artificial eye of the future might receive light from a miniature television camera. Its electrical message would be transmitted to a tiny computer housed in the frame of a pair of dummy glasses. Upon receiving the message, the computer would generate a pattern of electrical signals to an array of electrodes placed on the surface of the visual cortex.

Research has already confirmed that electrical stimulation of the cortex can produce conscious visual sensations (Dobelle, 1977). These sensations are called *phosphenes*, and they resemble small glowing spots of light. When a number of phosphenes are generated simultaneously by electrical stimulation, blind subjects report seeing shapes. For example, a 35-year-old man who had been blinded in an automobile accident 15 years earlier reported that he saw letters, geometric shapes, and simple patterns in response to the cortical stimulation (Dobelle, Mladejovsky, Evans, Rob-

FIGURE 3.12 Seeing with the skin. This apparatus translates visual patterns into tactile vibrations so that the blind can "see with their skin." The light gathered by the television camera is converted into electrical signals that activate a bank of vibrators attached to the back of the seat. With practice, the patterns of vibrations are interpreted as objects in a three-dimensional world.

erts, and Girvin, 1976). Thus, conscious visual sensations can be experienced without direct visual input.

If researchers can decipher the complex neural codes that transmit visual information to the brain, the artificial eye will become a reality. However, our optimism must be tempered by the fact that the human optic nerve has about one million fibers, while the visual cortex probably has no more than 1,000 different sites for receiving electrical stimulation. This means that the acuity of an artificial eye may never come close to a natural one (Brindley, 1988). Still it would provide the blind with sight sufficient to read and move freely about in the world. Based on our understanding of vision, we have moved from the crude touch system that Annie Sullivan used with Helen Keller to the possibility of constructing useful artificial eyes in little more than 100 years. ■

COLOR VISION

In a single meadow in the Shenandoah National Park in Virginia, one might come across an irridescent blue indigo bunting, a scarlet cardinal, and a bright yellow American goldfinch, all standing out against the deep green of the forest. Such colors are not inherent in the birds' feathers but in the wavelengths of light that reflect off them to stimulate your eyes. How does the human eye translate reflected light waves into neurochemical impulses that the brain interprets as indigo, scarlet, and gold? The process is a complex and fascinating one, and understanding it has required the solution of several puzzles. The first puzzling phenomenon involves **color mixture,** the way two different wavelengths of light can combine to produce the experience of still a third (for example, green and red light together appear yellow). The second puzzle is the phenomenon of **complementary color afterimages,** in which looking at one color can lead to an afterimage of a completely different hue. The third puzzle involves **color blindness.** In a paper presented to the Manchester Literary and Philosophical Society in 1794, John Dalton gave the first account of color blindness. He noted: "That part of the image which others call red appears to me little more than a shade or defect of light," and that which other people called orange, yellow, and green appeared to him as "what I should call different shades of yellow." Dalton's color blindness led to some embarrassing moments. He is said to have scandalized the members of his Quaker congregation by wearing bright red socks to church (Smith, 1989).

COLOR MIXTURE, COMPLEMENTARY AFTERIMAGES, AND COLOR BLINDNESS

As Newton demonstrated in his early research with prisms, white light consists of a mixture of different wavelengths. To see how wavelengths mix, look at the *color circle* shown in Figure 3.13. The colors in this circle are arranged in the order of their appearance in the visual spectrum (with a few colors, such as purple, that are not found in the spectrum added to complete the circle). Colors opposite each other on the circle (for example, red-green or yellow-blue) are called *complementary colors*—when they are mixed together in the proper amounts, they produce the neutral gray that is shown in the circle's center. To see why complementary colored lights such as yellow and blue yield gray instead of green when they are mixed together, we have to distinguish between **additive** and **subtractive color mixture.** Additive color mixture occurs when we mix lights of different wavelengths to produce a new color. Once the lights are mixed, the eye can no longer determine the individual wavelengths that make up the mixture. For example, if you shine a spotlight projecting long wavelength light on a wall, the light reaching your eye from the wall will look red. (See Figure 3.14.) If you then shine a spotlight projecting medium wavelength light on a wall, the light from the wall will look green. However, if the spotlights partially overlap on the wall, the area of overlap will appear yellow. When lights of different wavelengths simultaneously stimulate the eye, their combined or "additive" effect results in a new color. Three widely spaced colors—say blue, green, and red—can be additively mixed to produce almost any color of light. The color that is obtained depends on how much of each wavelength is added to the total mixture.

To see an example of additive color mixture look closely at the screen of a color TV set. A color TV picture is actually a patchwork of about one million blue, green, and red dots. The color yellow that we see is really produced by a special beam behind the screen that projects green and red dots closely together. If viewed through a magnifying glass, the individual green and red dots can be seen. But if observed from normal viewing distance, they combine by additive mixture to produce the experience of yellow. This same principle was used in the nineteenth century by French pointillist painter Georges Seurat, who created subtle shades of color by laying dots of different colors next to each other on the canvas. When viewed from a distance, the individual dots blend to form solid colors (Figure 3.15).

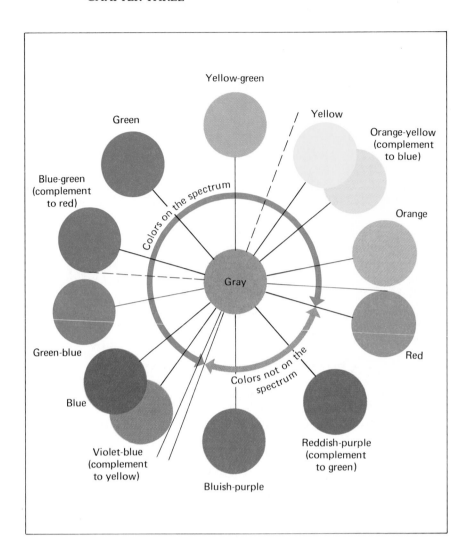

FIGURE 3.13   The color circle.   Colors opposite each other on the color circle are called complements. If they are mixed in the proper proportions they produce the neutral gray that is shown in the center of the circle. Mixing noncomplementary colors in equal amounts will produce a hue that is midway between the colors on the circle's circumference. The colors are arranged in terms of their spectral order, with nonspectral reds and purples added to complete the circle. Colors that are visible but not part of the color circle, such as brown, are produced by mixing different spectral wavelengths in the appropriate amounts.

FIGURE 3.14   Color mixture.   When lights of different wavelengths simultaneously stimulate the eye, they produce new colors through additive mixture. This example shows the colors produced by additive mixture in the areas where the red, blue, and green lights overlap. White results from the mixture of all three of these lights.

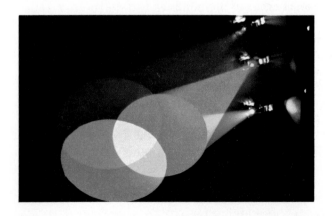

FIGURE 3.15 *Sunday Afternoon on the Island of La Grande Jatte.* French painter Georges Seurat (1859–1891) devised a technique, called *pointillism,* in which he created a variety of colors from a mosaic of individual, regulary shaped spots of color. Up close, the spots can be seen, as in the detail at right; from a distance, the spots blend together by additive color mixture to produce the appearance of solid colors. (The Art Institute of Chicago, Helen Birch Bartlett Memorial Collection)

Subtractive color mixture occurs when paints are mixed together. The results of mixing lights cannot be duplicated with paints because light and paint work in different ways. For example, an apple appears red because its surface pigment absorbs most of the short and medium wavelengths, allowing only those of roughly 620 nanometers to be reflected to our eyes. Similarly, a lush lawn looks green because only wavelengths of around 500 nanometers are reflected, and the rest are absorbed. Paints work in this fashion. All wavelengths are absorbed except for the color we see. When two different colored paints are mixed, the wavelengths from each of the paints are effectively subtracted from the mixture. For example, if paints representing the red of an apple and the green of a lawn are mixed together, the long wavelengths of the red are absorbed by the green, while the median wavelengths of the green are absorbed by the red. The result of mixing red and green is that we subtract all the wavelengths, leaving only a neutral gray. This distinction between subtractive and additive color mixture explains why we get green when we mix yellow and blue paints (subtractive color mixture) and gray when we mix yellow and blue lights (additive color mixture).

When your eye is stimulated by one color of a complementary pair—say yellow—and the stimulation of that color is then removed, you will experience "seeing" that color's complement—blue (Figure 3.16). Both findings—that the brain adds colors together to arrive at new color experiences, and that fatiguing the eye with one color leads to a complementary color afterimage—will have to be explained by theories of how our eyes construct a colored image.

The other theoretically important color phenomenon is *color blindness,* the inability to differentiate wavelengths from different portions of the visual spectrum. Some color-blind people may see the world solely in shades of gray, but this is only one of several types of color blindness. Some people are unable to distinguish reds from greens, while others see yellows and blues as the same. People with normal color vision are called *trichromats*; they can distinguish between light and dark, red and green, and yellow and blue. People such as John Dalton, whose color deficiency was an inability to distinguish red from green or yellow from blue, are called *dichromats,* while those who see only black and white and shades of gray are called *monochromats.* The most frequently occurring type of color blindness is red-green blindness, and this inherited defect occurs more often in males (seven percent) than in females (one percent). Individuals with yellow-blue blindness and monochromats who see no color at all are extremely rare. Consequently, most "color blind" people do see colors; they just see them differently from people with normal color vision. Tests of color blindness, such as the *Ishihari test* shown in

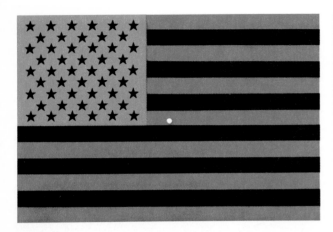 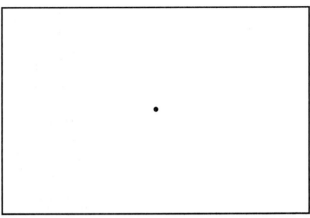

FIGURE 3.16   A demonstration of complementary color afterimages.   Stare at the dot in the center of the flag for approximately 30 seconds, until the colors begin to shimmer, and then stare at the dot in the center of the white rectangle. You should see a faint image of the U.S. flag as it normally appears—blinking once or twice helps if you do not see it at first. The colors of the afterimage are the complements of the original stimulus colors. Complementary color afterimages are explained by the opponent-process theory of color vision.

Figure 3.17, require people to look for specific visual patterns among a jumble of dots. In these examples people with red-green blindness have trouble distinguishing the figures from the surrounding field.

What accounts for the intriguing phenomena of color blindness, complementary afterimages, and color mixture? There are two major theories of color vision. Each can account for what the other cannot. Together, they provide a comprehensive description.

TRICHROMATIC THEORY

As we noted, Thomas Young proposed a theory of color vision almost two centuries ago. He observed that the mixture of blue, green, and red light can produce all the different colors of the spectrum. Young therefore speculated that the visual system contains three types of receptors, each one sensitive to different wavelengths of light.

A more modern version of this theory states that there are three different types of cones responsible for color vision. Because of the differ-

FIGURE 3.17   Test stimuli from the Ishihari test for color blindness.   People with normal color vision see the number 57 in the left stimulus and the number 15 in the right stimulus. People with red-green blindness, however, have difficulty seeing the numbers. Other stimulus patterns can be used to detect different forms of color blindness. Since colors differ in brightness and saturation, people who are color blind are sometimes unaware that their vision is defective. A person with red-green blindness, for example, could still respond correctly to traffic lights, because the red and green lights differ in their brightness and position.

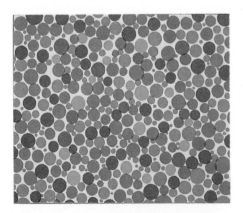 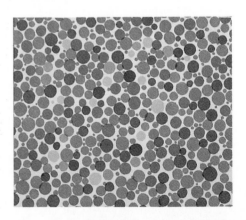

ent photochemicals they contain, one type of cone is maximally sensitive to short wavelengths, another type to medium wavelengths, and the last type to long wavelengths. Depending upon its wavelength, light energy stimulates these three receptors differently and produces the sensation of color. For example, the color blue is seen when the short wavelength receptor is maximally stimulated. However, if the medium and long wavelength receptors are simultaneously stimulated, the mixture of wavelengths in the retina could produce the experience of yellow, and if all three receptors are stimulated simultaneously, white is seen. Since in this theory perceived color is based on the output of three color receptors it is called the **trichromatic theory.**

This theory explains why new colors can be seen when the three primary colors are added. It is also supported by findings from anatomical and biochemical research. During the 1960s, for instance, researchers developed a device called a microspectrophotometer, which allowed them to determine the wavelength of light absorbed by a single receptor cell in the retina. Consistent with trichromatic theory, researchers have isolated three different types of cones—one is maximally sensitive to blue light, another responds most to green light, and the third responds most to light in the yellow-to-red range (Wald, 1964).

However, the trichromatic theory cannot answer several critical questions: Why the mixture of complementary colors produces gray; why staring at one color produces a complementary colored afterimage; and why, if there are three primary colors (blue, green, and red), people can still see yellow if they are red-green color blind. If yellow results from stimulating the red and green receptors, people who are red-green color blind—people with defective red and green receptors—should not be able to see this color. To handle these shortcomings, an alternative explanation, called the **opponent-process theory,** was proposed by the German physiologist Ewald Hering in 1878.

OPPONENT-PROCESS THEORY

In place of the three color theory, Hering proposed a six-color theory. He grouped the basic colors of red, green, yellow, blue, white, and black into separate red-green, yellow-blue, and white-black receptor pairs. According to the opponent-process theory, each member of a receptor pair works in opposition to the other. For example, if light energy stimulates the red member of a red-green pair

more than it does the green, the output of the red member will inhibit the output of the green, so that this receptor system will signal "red." Conversely, greater stimulation of the green member will result in its inhibiting the red, and the system will signal "green." Through the inhibition of opposing pairs, the opponent-process theory explains why people cannot perceive greenish-reds or yellowish-blues; only one member of an opponent pair can signal a response. However, if light energy stimulates both opponents equally, the inhibitory effects of the stimulation will cancel each other, producing a neutral gray.

Not only does the opponent-process theory account for color mixture, it also explains complementary afterimages and color blindness. Afterimages result from prolonged stimulation of one member of an opponent pair. For example, staring at the color green fatigues the green component of a receptor, so that later, when you look at a white field that stimulates the red and green members equally, the fatigued green member does not respond, while its fresh red opponent does. The result is a faint red afterimage following stimulation by the color green. This explains why staring at the green, black, and yellow flag in Figure 3.16 leads to a red, white, and blue afterimage. To account for color blindness, the opponent-process theory holds that dichromats are people who have their red-green or yellow-blue receptor pairs either missing or not working, while monochromats are individuals with only the white-black pair intact.

A COMBINED THEORETICAL VIEW

For many years the trichromatic and opponent-process theories were viewed as opposing one another. This is no longer the case. Together, they provide a comprehensive description of color vision (Hurvitz, 1978). The trichromatic theory applies to the three types of cones in the retina that are photochemically sensitive to different wavelengths of light. The opponent-process theory applies to those neural processes that occur later in the nervous system (Boynton, 1988). For example, neurons in the brain's visual pathways function in an opponent-process fashion: Some are excited by red light and inhibited by green, others excited or inhibited only by yellow or blue (DeValois and DeValois, 1975). Together, the trichromatic and opponent-process operations translate light energy into neural signals that we experience as color, allowing us to see a rainbow instead of a solid band of gray.

AUDITION

If the proverbial tree were to fall in an empty forest, would there be a sound? Actually, no. There would be rapid vibrations in the air but not "sound" (Christman, 1979). Sounds are not *in* the environment any more than "sights" are outside of our body. Sounds are sensory experiences that result from our ears converting changes in air pressure into neural impulses that the brain interprets. Before we describe this process, you will need to know a few basic facts about the physical and psychological properties of sound.

Sounds are produced by changes in air pressure caused by air molecules set in motion. For example, as Figure 3.18 shows, striking a tuning fork will generate a sound because its two prongs move in and out repeatedly. By alternately compressing and expanding the air, the prongs produce air pressure fluctuations, called **sound waves**, that can stimulate the receptor cells in your ear. Like the waves that move through a body of water, sound waves are energy pulses that are conducted through air. These sound waves can also be transmitted over a taut string like a child's soup-can telephone, or through a length of hose like a doctor's stethoscope. But without a medium for movement, creating sound waves is impossible. This is why ringing a bell in a vacuum will not make any noise. In fact, the thrilling battle sounds in such science fiction movies as *Star Wars* actually would never occur because there is no air to generate sound waves in space.

PHYSICAL PROPERTIES OF SOUND

Two physical dimensions of sound waves are important, **frequency** and **amplitude.** The frequency of a sound wave is defined as the number of expansion and compression cycles per second. For example, if the sound wave shown in Figure 3.18 completed its cycle from points A to E in one second the wave would have a frequency of one cycle per second, or one Hz (pronounced Hertz after the German physicist Heinrich Hertz). If it completed its cycle in one-tenth of a second, it would have a frequency of 10 Hz, or 10 cycles per second. People can sense frequencies from 20 to 20,000 Hz, with maximal sensitivity between 1,000 and 4,000 Hz. Dogs are sensitive to the wider range between 15 and 50,000 Hz. This higher level of sensitivity enables dogs to hear such high frequency sounds as "silent" dog whistles that we cannot hear at all. To give you some idea of differences in frequencies, the lowest and highest notes on a piano are approximately 28 Hz and 4,180 Hz respectively. Generally, differences in the frequency of sound waves are experienced as differences in pitch, the perceptual quality associated with the different frequencies. Keys at the right on the piano produce higher frequency sound waves, and therefore when we hear them we hear a higher pitch.

The physical characteristic of amplitude is indicated in Figure 3.18 by the height of the sound wave. Amplitude is a measure of the change in air pressure and is related to the experience of loud-

FIGURE 3.18 How a tuning fork generates sound. When you strike a tuning fork, it produces changes in air pressure as its prongs move in and out. These air pressure fluctuations are called sound waves, and they can stimulate the receptors in the ear. A sound wave is represented in this figure as a sequence of air compression and expansion caused by the moving prongs.

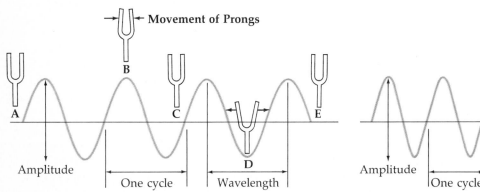

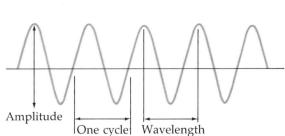

(A) Long-wavelength (low-frequency) sound

(B) Short-wavelength (high-frequency) sound

ness. The greater the change in air pressure, the louder the experience of sound. A forceful "forte" strike on a piano key produces a louder note than a soft "pianissimo" touch of the same key because the forceful strike produces a larger amplitude sound wave from its vibrating string. The amplitude of a sound wave is scaled in terms of *bels* or *decibels* (tenths of a bel, abbreviated dB) in honor of Alexander Graham Bell. The greater the number of dBs, the louder the experience of sound. The normal sensory threshold for a 2,500 Hz tone is set to zero dB. For higher or lower frequencies, more intense stimulation is necessary for a sound to be detected. Sounds louder than 125 dB are painful and, if prolonged, can result in hearing loss. Table 3.4 shows the decibel ratings for a variety of different sounds.

Pitch and loudness are not the only dimensions of sound we can experience. Sounds also provide us with information on their *perceived location* (where they are coming from), their *perceived duration* (how long they last), and their *timbre,* or tonal quality. We use the timbre of a tone to distinguish a note played on a piano from the same note played on a clarinet. Each sounds different to us because most sounds are composed of a mixture of different frequencies. For example, playing a middle C on a piano produces a fundamental tone of 262 Hz and overtones that are multiples of this frequency. These overtones help us distinguish among different instruments playing the same note.

PSYCHOLOGICAL PROPERTIES OF SOUND

To some extent, the psychological qualities of light (hue, brightness, and saturation) correspond to the psychological dimensions of sound (pitch, loudness, and timbre). Together these different dimensions describe a visual or auditory stimulus in terms of its quality, quantity, and purity, but there are important differences between them. Where different wavelengths of light can combine to produce a new color, different complex tones can combine in music to produce an experience of harmony. When different frequencies are not in harmony, the sound is referred to as *noise*. Notice how our use of the term "noise" has changed throughout this chapter. In discussing sensitivity, neural noise is defined as spontaneous neural firing. In the context of audition, noise is defined as a

TABLE 3.4　The Decibel Ratings of Different Sounds

Auditory Sensation	Decibel Level	Type of Sound
Danger level	140	Aircraft carrier deck
Pain threshold	130	Air raid siren
Maximum vocal effort	120	Jet takeoff at 200 feet
	110	Auto horn at 3 feet
	100	Chainsaw
	90	Heavy truck at 50 feet
	80	Freight train at 50 feet
Problems using telephone	70	Vacuum cleaner
	60	Conversation
Quiet	50	Moderate rainfall
	40	Library
Very quiet	30	Soft whisper
	20	
Barely audible	10	Broadcasting studio during programing
Hearing threshold	0	

Each increment of 10 dBs increases the intensity of the sound ten times. By law, people may work no more than two hours per day in a 90 dB noise environment, one hour per day in a 100 dB environment, and ½ hour per day in a 110 dB environment.

Adapted from Fisher, Bell, and Baum (1984) and other sources.

discordant mixture of auditory frequencies. Noise can also be defined psychologically as unwanted sound that is stressful when it is loud, unpredictable, or not subject to our personal control (for example, people talking in a quiet library).

What effect can prolonged exposure to noise have on our behavior? To answer this question, researchers have studied people who live or work in noisy environments. For example, a study using the correlational method examined the long-term effect of traffic noise on the educational development of children. The children in the study lived in an apartment complex that was built over a noisy highway. The closer an apartment was to the highway, the louder was the sound of the traffic. To determine the effect of this prolonged exposure to noise, psychologists administered reading achievement and auditory discrimination tests to children who lived in the building for at least four years. The researchers found a clear relation between the level of a child's apartment and the child's performance on the tests: The closer a child lived to the highway, the poorer the child's auditory discrimination and reading achievement scores (Cohen, Glass, and Singer, 1973). Similar performance decrements have been found in children who attended schools located near noisy airports (Cohen, Evans, Krantz, Stokols, and Kelly, 1981). While exposure to excessive noise can be harmful, remember that it is an ever present environmental condition; normal levels of noise, at least, soon come to be ignored through the process of sensory adaptation.

THE MECHANICS OF HEARING

How do the fluctuations in air pressure that we refer to as sound waves lead to the experience of sound? The answer to this question is based on an understanding of the anatomy of the ear.

THE ANATOMY OF THE EAR

When Vincent van Gogh cut off his ear, he did not lose his hearing. This is because the sensory organs for hearing are safely located in hollowed-out portions of our skulls. To understand how we hear, we need to follow the flow of an auditory signal through the anatomical structures of the ear. For the purpose of classification, these structures are found in the outer, middle, and inner ears as shown in Figure 3.19A.

The *outer ear* consists of the **pinna** and **auditory canal.** Sound waves travel down the auditory canal and strike the **eardrum,** causing it to vibrate. This vibration is transmitted to the three small

bones (the **malleus,** the **incus,** and the **stapes**) that make up the middle ear. These bones vibrate at the same frequency as the sound waves and amplify the intensity of the sound waves. In turn, these bones pass the vibration to a flexible membrane separating the middle and inner ears called the *oval window.* The oval window is on the side of a snail-like bone structure called the **cochlea,** which transforms vibrations into neural impulses. Pressure on the oval window causes the fluid that fills the hollow cochlea to move. When this fluid is set in motion, it sets up a traveling wave in a flexible membrane (the **basilar membrane**) that bends the tiny hair cells in a portion of the cochlea known as the **organ of Corti.** When a hair cell is bent, a neural impulse is transmitted to one of the nerve fibers in the auditory nerve (Figure 3.19B). The impulses travel up the ascending auditory pathways to the auditory cortex in each temporal lobe of the brain.

THEORIES OF HEARING

We know much less about audition than we do about vision. Theories of hearing have focused on how information about a sound wave's amplitude and frequency can be neurally coded in the auditory system to produce an experience of loudness and pitch. Most theories hold that information about loudness is represented by the number of neurons that fire. The larger the amplitude of the sound wave, the greater the number of hair cells that respond, and the louder the experience of sound (Whitfield, 1978).

Neurons code a sound wave's frequency (pitch) using a more complex set of processes. **Place theory,** proposed by Helmholtz in 1863 and more recently by Georg von Bekesy in 1960, holds that sound waves of different frequencies cause different portions of the basilar membrane to vibrate. Bekesy found that high frequency tones produced a greater displacement in the part of the membrane closest to the oval window, while medium frequency tones had a larger effect at the opposite end of the basilar membrane. The brain could therefore decipher a sound's frequency from the location on the basilar membrane that generates the strongest neural response. For example, if the hair cells next to the oval window are responding, the vibrations must come from a high frequency tone. However, place theory has difficulty explaining certain facts. It cannot explain how we can discriminate low frequency from medium frequency tones, since these frequencies produce displacement in similar portions of the basilar membrane. Nor can it explain how we are able to discriminate

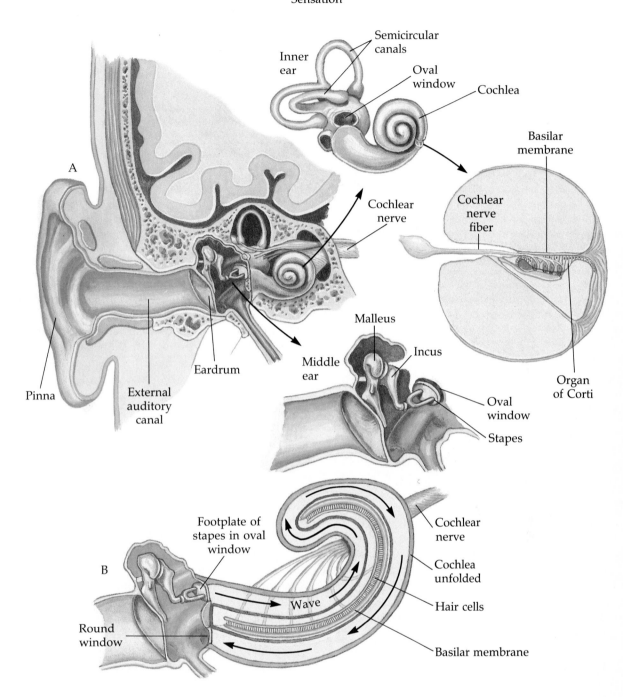

FIGURE 3.19 The human ear. (A) The structure of the human ear. Sound entering the ear passes through the following parts: the *pinna*—the external portion of the ear; the *auditory canal*—a resonance chamber that increases the intensity of specific auditory frequencies; the *eardrum*—a thin covering across the auditory canal that vibrates when stimulated by sound waves; the *malleus, incus,* and *stapes*—the three small bones of the middle ear that vibrate at the same frequency as the sound waves; the *oval window*—a flexible membrane that receives vibrations from the stapes; and the *cochlea*—the fluid-filled, snail-shaped structure that generates neural impulses to the brain. (B) A cross-section of the cochlea shown as it would look uncoiled. Vibrations on the oval window cause the fluid inside the cochlea to move. When this occurs, the hair cells of the organ of Corti are bent by the fluid, causing the hair cells to generate a neural impulse.

tones that differ only slightly in frequency. Again, the portion of the basilar membrane that is displaced by such frequencies would be very much the same.

As an alternative to place theory, **frequency theory** holds that information about pitch is provided by the rate or frequency of the hair cells' response (Wever, 1949). For example, a 400 Hz tone causes the basilar membrane to vibrate and the hair cells to generate a signal 400 times a second. Since individual hair cells can respond almost 1,000 times a second, their frequency of firing can provide the brain with information on the frequency of the auditory stimulus (the higher the frequency of firing, the higher the frequency of the tone). For tones beyond 1,000 Hz, cells may combine their responses to code these higher frequency tones. For example, a 4,000 Hz tone could be registered if each of four cells fired 1,000 times each second. In a sense, the cells combine their responses like British riflemen in the Revolutionary War did when they increased their shooting rate by firing in volleys. In fact, this combining of responses is called the **volley principle,** and it accounts for the fact that the rate of electrical responses along the auditory nerve matches the frequency of an auditory stimulus up to approximately 4,000 Hz. Beyond this point, cells are unable to respond in synchrony to provide frequency information to the brain.

Since each theory can account for the coding of frequency information at different portions of the auditory spectrum, place and frequency theories may complement one another. Just as trichromatic and opponent-process theories were combined to account for color vision, place and frequency theories can be combined to describe how we represent auditory frequency. For low frequency tones, frequency information can be easily represented by the rate of neural firing (frequency theory), while for medium and high frequency tones this information can be represented in terms of location (place theory) and sequencing of neural responses (volley theory).

After being processed at the basilar membrane, auditory information is further acted upon along the neural pathways ascending to the brain. There are excitatory and inhibitory cells that increase or decrease their rate of firing depending upon certain features of the sound. Some cells respond when a tone is turned on, others when a tone is turned off, and still others decrease their rate of firing over a tone's duration. As we ascend from the ear to the auditory cortex, sounds are subjected to very complex analyses (Evans, 1982). The result of this auditory analysis is that we can differentiate sound patterns finely enough to recognize the difference between a sentence spoken with a British accent and the same words spoken with an Irish brogue.

DYSFUNCTION:
Deafness

Our ears can hear sounds as varied as a discordant clap of thunder and the whisper of wind in the trees. But many people live in a world of silence, never hearing a single sound. In the United States alone, two million people are totally deaf. Why?

Hearing loss is caused by damage to either the middle or the inner ear. Damage to the middle ear can produce **conduction deafness.** As we age, deposits of calcium can lock the bones of the middle ear and thus prevent the transmission of vibrations to the inner ear. In the past a blunt needle was used to loosen these bones, but this procedure is dangerous and can easily damage these delicate structures. Moreover, even if this procedure is successful, deafness can recur as calcification continues. In extreme cases, the tiny bones are replaced with a fine wire that connects the eardrum and oval window and conducts sound waves to the inner ear. If the bones are not completely immobile, hearing aids can be used. They amplify the sound and force the slow-moving bones to conduct vibrations to the inner ear. Hearing aids can be adjusted to amplify only those frequencies in the auditory spectrum to which a person is deaf.

However, hearing aids are absolutely worthless if deafness is due to an inner ear malfunction called **nerve deafness.** Nerve deafness is caused by damage to the hair cells and their associated neural connections. This nonreversible disorder may be brought on by infection, diseases of old age, the long-term use of antibiotics such as streptomycin, and physical injury. Nerve deafness can also be caused by Paget's disease, in which abnormal bone growth crushes the auditory nerves. The composer Ludwig von Beethoven was believed to have lost his hearing in this way. In 1800, at the age of 31, Beethoven became aware of his gradual hearing loss. He wrote to a friend that his "noblest faculty" had deteriorated and that his ears whistled and buzzed. To counteract this enormous loss, he tried all available cures, including ointments, baths, rest, and even an ear horn. None of these remedies worked. By the age of 47, he was totally deaf. Yet throughout this period he continued to compose music of unsurpassing beauty that he could only hear in his mind (Bagar and Biancolli, 1947; Smith, 1989).

Research on nerve deafness is currently exploring the possibility of providing sound through the use of cochlear implants. Experimental cochlear implants were considered science fiction only a decade ago, but are now a reality. These devices convert sounds into electrical signals and transmit these signals to the brain via the auditory nerve. Sounds are picked up by a receiver worn near the ear and translated into electrical signals by a pocket-size computer. These signals are then sent to an implanted receiver and transmitted along a thin wire that has been surgically threaded into the cochlea of the inner ear. Cochlear implants have allowed people who have only recently become deaf to hear once again; however, their hearing is far from normal. Upon hearing his own voice, one man said it sounded like "a bunch of Martians" (Schmeck, 1984). At present, cochlear implants can help patients identify such important sounds as the ringing of a telephone or doorbell, and they can also help in the process of lip-reading (Evans, 1982; Brody, 1990). As in the development of an artificial eye, a cochlear implant that can produce normal hearing is still a dream of the future, but progress in treating deafness has come a long way since the days of the old-fashioned ear horn. ◾

SOUND LOCATION AND ECHOLOCATION

In addition to deciphering the volume and pitch of a sound, our auditory sense also tells us where the sound is coming from. The brain is able to decode very slight left–right differences in the time of arrival of a sound wave. A sound coming from your right side stimulates the membranes in your right ear a fraction of a second before it vibrates those in the left. If you are walking in the forest with a friend, toss a stone into the bushes nearby, and watch what happens. Very likely, your friend will turn in the direction of the sound. Head movements allow for more precise sound localization. By listening to a sound from two different head positions, the brain can combine the different information in the same way that early radar operators used readings from two different locations to "triangulate" the location of a nearby plane (Uttal, 1981).

Some animals use sound localization to navigate in the dark (Dawkins, 1986). Imagine the problem of a bat which must avoid flying into a tree on a moonless night (Figure 3.20). If the tree gave off a chirping sound, the bat could estimate its location in the same way that a human would—differences

FIGURE 3.20   Bat navigation at night. Bats can navigate in the dark by using echolocation, a process of emitting a continuous stream of noises and listening for the echoes of nearby objects.

between the sounds heard by the left and right ears would locate the source of the chirping. Since trees do not give off sounds, the bat solves the problem by emitting a continual stream of noises and estimating the location of dangerous trees and edible moths by the timing and volume of the echoes it hears. This process is called **echolocation.** Modern medical science uses a similar technique to construct an *ultrasound* picture of an unborn baby inside its mother's uterus, just like the bat's brain uses echolocation to construct an analogous picture of the night world. The process is even more amazing than it sounds at first. For one thing, sound waves rapidly lose energy as they expand away from the source. (Think of a sound wave as a constant amount of energy expanding into an ever weaker sphere.) Once the bat's chirp hits an object like a moth, it loses increasing energy on its return trip. To be most efficient, then, the bat must use very loud sounds, with a great deal of power. The bat's hearing apparatus, on the other hand, should be sensitive enough to detect very slight sounds. Unfortunately, a very sensitive hearing apparatus would be damaged by the loud sounds necessary for echolocation. The evolutionary solution is very similar to that used by the inventors of send–receive radar. The muscles in the bat's inner ear shut down its hearing for a fraction of a second at the precise moment of the sound burst. Bats move rapidly, and they need to update their sound image of the world frequently lest they suddenly crash into a tree. Thus, the alternation between hearing and screeching may occur up to 200 times a second. To maximize their ability to find food and avoid nearby objects, bats systematically vary the pitch of the tone they give off and move their ears to increase the information from the incoming sounds (Dawkins, 1986). In addition, to help them navigate in what would otherwise be an air-traffic controller's nightmare, bats have specialized areas in their auditory cortex that contain neurons devoted to analyzing the time intervals between chirps and echos, as well as the frequency and amplitude of echos (Suga, 1990). This is how bats make their way about in the dark with brains no bigger than large pearls. Research such as this work on bats increases our understanding of sensation by describing domains of sensory processing that are not available to human experience.

THE OTHER SENSES

Vision and audition are the dominant senses in humans and the two most thoroughly researched. However, other senses also affect behavior and add to the richness of our experience. Our sense of smell, for example, is quite different from our senses of vision and audition. Vision requires light and an unrestricted path for an object to be seen. Audition can function in the dark, but sounds can be deflected and distorted by objects. Sights and sounds are immediate; smells linger for a longer period of time (Smith, 1989).

OLFACTION (SMELL)

The air that we breathe contains about 79 percent nitrogen and about 21 percent oxygen. It also contains dust and other suspended matter, including a variety of chemical molecules that stimulate our smell receptors. **Olfaction** is the sense of smell, and it is dependent on odor molecules in the air entering our nasal cavity and stimulating receptors located inside the top of our noses. As shown in Figure 3.21, there are two different ways in which odor molecules can reach our olfactory receptors. When we inhale, our receptors are stimulated by air entering our nostrils. When we exhale, our olfactory receptors are stimulated again as air leaves the nose. Most of the flavor of food stems from the olfactory stimulation. Odor molecules from food that we chew stimulate the olfactory receptors as we exhale and give food its flavorful

FIGURE 3.21 The human olfactory system. The sense of smell is dependent on odor molecules in the air reaching the olfactory receptors located inside the top of the nose. Inhaling and exhaling odor molecules from food does much to give food its flavorful "taste."

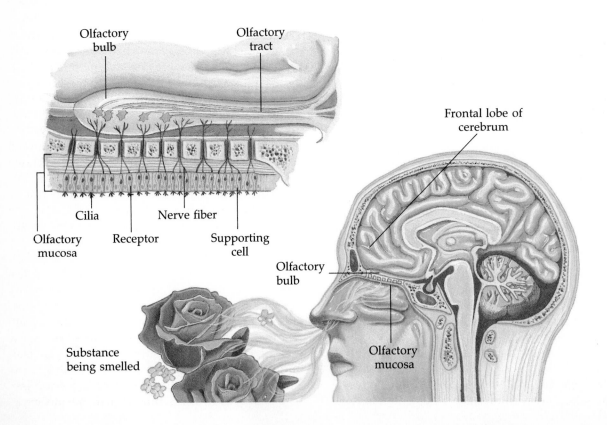

"taste" (Stevens & Cain, 1986). As evidence that food flavor is more smell than taste, a bite of apple is indistinguishable from a bite of raw potato when the nose is held tightly closed. This is why the nasal congestion that often accompanies a cold makes eating less enjoyable.

How do odor molecules in the air generate neural impulses? To begin with, the molecules touch the millions of hairlike receptors called **cilia** located in the *olfactory mucosa*. Research suggests that odor molecules may act on receptor sites in a "lock and key" fashion (Amoore, 1969; Moncrief, 1949). For example, John Amoore showed that different odors are associated with distinctly shaped molecules. Neural impulses may be generated when a molecule of a particular shape fits into a correctly-shaped receptor "slot," like a key fits in a lock. As with each of the senses, the intensity of an odor can be determined by the number of receptors that are stimulated (Engen, 1982). Once neural impulses are generated, they are sent to the *olfactory bulb* at the base of each side of the brain, and from there they travel to other areas including the frontal and temporal cortex (Tanabe et al., 1975).

Studies of olfaction in animals and insects have increased our understanding of smell. For example, dogs can track smells that humans cannot detect. Dogs can even track people who are wearing rubber boots (Droscher, 1971). How do they do it? The answer is not that a dog's individual olfactory receptors are more sensitive than ours, but that they have more of them. Dogs have 100 olfactory receptors for every one in a human (Moulton, 1977). This is why dogs make effective trackers. Their acute sense of smell can detect the minute sweat molecules that leak through the clothing and boots of a fugitive.

Olfaction also provides a primitive method of communication for insects. Chemicals called **pheromones** are used to communicate with other members of the same species. For example, sexual pheromones secreted by a female moth can attract a male moth over one mile away. Similarly, a dead ant will produce a pheromone residue during decomposition that causes worker ants to remove the body from the nest. If this "death smell" is applied to a live ant, that ant will be repeatedly carried from the nest (Wilson, 1963). Honeybees also produce pheromones. When a worker honeybee stings someone, the bee releases an alarm pheromone that attracts other bees and causes them to attack people and animals near the hive. The so-called African killer bees produce a highly potent alarm pheromone that causes them to be very aggressive (Shorey, 1977).

The term "pheromone" was originally intended to deal with genetically programmed insect behavior. When discussing the behavior of mammals, researchers prefer to think in terms of "chemical signals" rather than pheromones. Certainly, chemical signals play a role in mammalian behavior. For example, William James (1890) reported the case of a blind woman who sorted laundry for inmates of an asylum solely on the basis of smell. More recent research using experimentation confirms that we can identify the people we know by their smells. In one experiment, 12 pairs of siblings wore white T-shirts to bed on three successive nights. On the fourth day, each child was presented with two containers to smell—one held the brother or sister's T-shirt and the other held a T-shirt that had been worn by a stranger. When asked to pick their sibling's T-shirt, 19 out of 24 children made the correct selection. Nine mothers of the children also took the test. Each mother was given a choice between her child's T-shirt or a stranger's. The mothers chose their own children's T-shirts in 17 out of 18 selections (Porter and Moore, 1981). In a follow-up experiment, mothers of newborns only two to six days old correctly picked the T-shirts worn by their infants 16 out of 20 times (Porter, Cernoch, and McLaughlin, 1983). In each instance, people were generally accurate at recognizing their relatives' clothing using only their senses of smell. Helen Keller made the same observation. She said that her loved ones each had an unmistakable smell. She also claimed that she could tell the type of work people performed and where they had recently been by odors that clung to their clothing.

Research on gender differences in olfaction has shown that, in general, men are less sensitive to most smells than women are. Women are more accurate than men at odor identification of stereotypically "feminine substances" (perfume and nail polish remover, for example), foods (coconut and strawberry syrup, say), and surprisingly, even stereotypically "masculine substances" (including cigar butts and machine oil) (Cain, 1982; 1988). Gender differences in odor discrimination notwithstanding, the olfactory sense is important and useful for both sexes. Consider the case of a man who lost his ability to smell after being hit by a car:

Shortly after the accident his apartment building caught fire; he awoke to the shouts of neighbors, not to the smell of smoke that might have alerted him sooner. He cannot detect leaking gas. He has been poisoned by spoiled food. But Griffin says he suffers a more profound loss: deprived now of the rush of memory that an odor can let loose, he feels cut off from moments in his own past. "Think about rotting leaves or a campfire or a roast or a Christmas tree—I enjoyed those smells so much. . . . A dimension of my life is missing.

(Monmaney, 1987).

The loss of the sense of smell has profound effects not only on smell, but also on its companion sense, taste. Much of our sense of taste is dependent on our sense of smell.

GUSTATION (TASTE)

Although we think of eating as a matter of tasting, it actually involves smell, as we just noted, and touch and temperature as well (Bartoshuk, Cain, and Pfaffman, 1985). The term **taste** is strictly defined as the sensory experience resulting from stimulation of **taste bud** receptors. There are approximately 10,000 of these taste buds, located mainly on the surface of the tongue but also on other areas inside the mouth. Each taste bud, as shown in Figure 3.22, resembles a flower bud under microscopic examination and contains dozens of taste cells arranged like the staves of a barrel. These cells generate a neural impulse when they are stimulated by either liquid or food dissolved in saliva. The taste cells receive stimulation through a pore at the top of the taste bud. Once a taste neuron has been triggered, it sends an impulse to the medulla at the base of the brain and then to the parietal cortex for interpretation (Keverne, 1982). Unlike receptor cells in the eye or the ear, which cannot replace themselves, taste cells can regenerate in about a week. When we scald our taste cells on a cup of steaming hot soup, these cells replace themselves. However, as we get older we lose our ability to replace these cells, and we become less sensitive to taste. This is why older people perceive food as bland when younger people think it is just right.

Taste buds respond to only four primary stimulus qualities—*sweet, sour, salty,* and *bitter* (Bekesy, 1966). All other tastes result from combinations of these qualities, and this fact helps explain why smell is so important for the "tasting" of different foods. Sensitivity to sweetness is highest at the tip of the tongue, sourness at the sides, saltiness at the front and sides, and bitterness at the rear. Research suggests that taste receptors may have a primitive evolutionary connection to emotional expression. For instance, psychologists Jay Braun

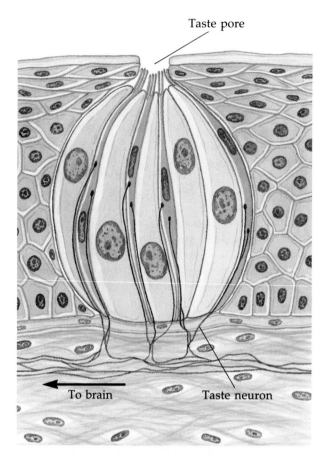

Taste pore

To brain

Taste neuron

FIGURE 3.22 The structure of a taste bud. The sensory receptors for taste are found primarily on the tongue. Taste cells can detect only sweet, sour, salty, and bitter qualities. All other tastes result from different combinations of these qualities.

and Jeffrey Nowlis (1989) found that taste receptors are carried on the same nerve fibers that control facial expression and that infants respond to tastes with emotional expressions. (For instance, sweet–happy and bitter–angry.)

Studies have also shown wide differences in taste preference. Infants are born with a preference for sweet tastes. This is thought to be adaptive, because a sweet taste is usually associated with food that is nutritionally good for a growing child. Their first food, milk, contains lactose as its natural sweetener. This helps explain why children will readily eat cookies and candy but will resist spinach and broccoli. Very gradually, children learn about different foods from their parents, and their taste preferences change as they age (Cowart, 1981; Greene, Desor, and Maller, 1975). Mexican children, for example, acquire a liking for hot chili peppers. The burning sensation they get from the peppers is the result of the pepper acting on pain receptors in the mouth and throat.

One last fact about taste is important for what it says about all of our senses. Taste receptors adapt quickly to the presence of the same stimulus. As all potato chip lovers know, each succeeding potato chip tastes less salty than the one that came before it. This adaptation to stimulation is a general sensory characteristic—the primary function of each sense is to provide new information to the brain.

THE CUTANEOUS (SKIN) SENSES

The act of touching another person, whether by the gentle stroke of a loved one or the heavy hand of an aggressor, is an act of considerable intimacy. In fact, touch is so important that there are unspoken rules that regulate its use. For example, *professional* touches are used by such people as doctors and tailors and are not supposed to have a personal meaning; *social* touches such as handshakes are formal greetings used among strangers and business associates; *friendship* touches are used to convey caring or concern with people we know well; and *intimate* touches occur between close family members, friends, and lovers. These conventions are influenced by culture. Countries in Southern Europe are considered "contact" countries because they have high rates of touching, while countries in Northern Europe and the United States are thought of as "noncontact" countries because people rarely touch each other in public (Thayer, 1988).

Touch researchers have found that humans and other animals need certain tactile experiences for normal development. As we will see in Chapter 11, premature infants who are regularly massaged gain weight faster than those who are left alone, and touch plays an important part in the bond of attachment that is formed between parent and child. Adults are similarly affected by touch. A gentle touch of a teacher can enhance performance on a college exam (Steward and Lupfer, 1987), while the casual touch of a waitress can cause us to leave larger tips (Stephen and Zweigenhaft, 1985). And when we feel lonely and depressed, being cuddled is especially comforting (Stein and Sanfilpo, 1985). However, not all touches are equally welcomed. We do not like a touch coupled with a negative comment (a pat on the stomach and a remark about our weight), we dislike being startled by a sudden touch, and we hate being moved out of the way as if we were chess pieces (Smith, 1989).

Despite all that we know about touch, it remains a poorly understood sense. Part of the reason why touch is poorly understood is that it is often dominated by vision. Ventriloquists, for example, exploit this dominance to fool us into thinking that sound comes from a dummy's moving mouth. Similarly, if your senses of vision and touch provide you with discrepant information, you are apt to trust your sense of vision more. For instance, in a study by Australian psychologist Roderick Power (1981), subjects examined a 20-cent Australian coin by feeling it with their fingers and looking at it through a pair of goggles. Unknown to the subjects, the goggles distorted the appearance of the round coin into the shape of an oval. When the subjects were later asked to draw the coin, they drew it as it appeared, not as it felt (and really was). The only time touch dominates vision is when our sense of vision is impaired—for example, when we look through a piece of stained glass that creates a blurred image (Heller, 1983). Under impaired viewing conditions, we are more apt to trust our sense of touch.

Unlike the other senses, our sense of touch is distributed all over the surface of our bodies. Over 600,000 receptors make the skin the body's largest sensory organ. In addition to touch (more precisely, *pressure*), we can sense *pain, warmth,* and *cold.* Some skin sensations, such as a tickle or an itch, result when the brain combines different patterns of these four elementary sensations (Iggo, 1982). Other sensations result from specialized receptors. For example, nerves at the base of our hair follicles are sensitive to mechanical pressures or vibrations. These tiny receptive fields on the skin detect warmth and cold, and the free nerve endings that terminate in the skin's topmost layer detect potential injuries to the skin, resulting in the sensation of pain.

PAIN

Pain can be caused by many stimuli, including sharp objects, intense heat or extreme cold, bacterial infections, the compression or "pinching" of nerves, and internal damage from cancer. Not all of these painful sensations are the same. Pain can be "sharp," as when we cut our fingers on a knife, "dull," as when we experience headaches or muscle strains, or "burning," as when we scrape our skin in a fall. Our particular experience of pain varies over our bodies, depending on the number of receptors that are present. For example, we have many more pain receptors on the surface of our eyes than on our hands. This is why a minute piece of lint passes unnoticed on the backs of our hands but is a painful irritant when it gets in our eyes. Our pain receptors provide this information. They differ from other sensory receptors in that pain receptors adapt very slightly or not at all to continued stimulation. Although unpleasant, this is a fortunate state of affairs, because pain warns us when something is wrong.

How do psychologists account for the experience of pain? The most widely-cited theory of pain is the **gate-control theory** of Melzack and Wall (1965). According to this theory, the experience of pain is based on the activity of large and small nerve fibers in the spinal cord. Melzack and Wall suggested that there is a pain gate at the top of the spinal cord that can be opened or closed. Activity in the small nerve fibers opens the spinal gate and leads to the experience of pain; conversely, activity in the large fibers is believed to close the spinal gate and prevent the experience of pain. Thus, a new source of pain can actually reduce pain from a previous source. *Acupuncture,* the Chinese procedure for controlling pain by inserting long needles into various parts of the body, may work by activating the large nerve fibers and closing the pain gate. Alternatively, acupuncture may relieve pain by causing the release of endorphins, the body's natural analgesics that we described in Chapter 2.

Pain is not just a response to physical damage, but can also be influenced by psychological factors. Some people can ignore pain, while others experience great pain for seemingly nonexistent damage. For example, amputees often report "phantom limb" pain long after an arm or a leg has been severed. Conversely, up to one-third of the patients with pathological pain obtain relief from a *placebo*, a pill with no true analgesic ingredients (Weisenberg, 1977). Research from signal detection theory has shown that a placebo affects a patient's criterion (Beta) for reporting pain rather than pain sensitivity (d') itself (Feather, Chapman, and Fisher, 1972). In other words, some people who take a placebo become less likely to report the pain that they feel. These studies indicate that our sensory experience cannot be explained simply as the result of signals from pain receptors that travel up to the brain; signals also travel down from the brain and modify our experience of pain (Melzack and Dennis, 1978). We will have more to say about pain, and the procedures used by psychologists for its treatment, in the chapter on health, stress, and coping.

KINESTHESIS AND BALANCE

If you have ever tried to walk on a leg that has "fallen asleep" you have some idea of how awkward movement would be without our kinesthetic sense. The sense of **kinesthesis** provides information about body position and limb movements. Sensory receptors in our muscles, tendons, and joints monitor the position of our limbs to allow us to perform coordinated movements.

Our sense of balance is provided by sensory organs in the inner ear. Three ring-like structures called the **semicircular canals** extend from the cochlea and are positioned at right angles to each other like the corner of a desk (Figure 3.23). Like jars holding liquid, the canals are filled with fluid that moves in the opposite direction than the body when the body is rotated. Movement of the fluid causes the hair cells in the canal to bend and thus generate a neural impulse (Benson, 1982).

A second mechanism of balance is found in the **vestibular sacs** between the cochlea and the semicircular canals. The sacs are filled with a jelly-like substance that contains small crystals, called *otoliths* or "ear stones." Gravity pulls on the otoliths and bends the hair cells, causing them to generate a neural impulse at the point of contact with the otoliths. The hair cells in the semicircular canals signal body position only when the body is accelerating or decelerating, but the otoliths are always affected by gravity. In tandem, the two mechanisms provide continuous information about head position. When there is a mismatch between information from our eyes and information from the inner ear, the result is the queasy feeling of "motion sickness."

STIMULATION THROUGH EXTRASENSORY CHANNELS

We have described how physical energy received by our sensory receptors provides us with information about the outer world. Some people claim that we can also pick up information on "extrasensory" channels—a phenomenon called **extrasensory perception,** or **ESP.** Researchers have tried to study this phenomenon under carefully controlled conditions, but the resulting findings have left most psychologists unconvinced that there is anything called ESP.

The hypothesized forms of ESP include *telepathy,* thought transference from one person to another; *clairvoyance,* the ability to perceive an object or event without the aid of the known senses (for

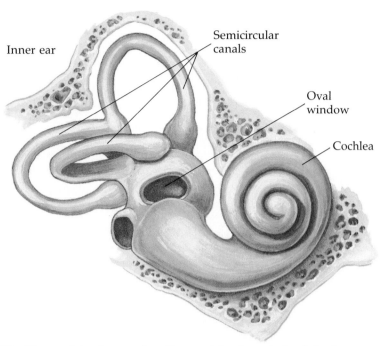

FIGURE 3.23 The semicircular canals. The semicircular canals of the inner ear provide us with our sense of balance. Hair cells in the semicircular canals are stimulated by the movement of liquid inside the canals whenever we move our bodies.

example, identifying a concealed object); and *precognition*, the ability to perceive a future event. Much of the research on telepathy and clairvoyance was done by J. B. Rhine and his colleagues during the 1930s and 40s. In one experiment Rhine used a card guessing task, in which five cards, each with a different symbol (a cross, a star, a circle, a set of wavy lines, and a square), were turned face down and presented to a subject. The subject's task was to report which symbol was on the other side of each card. Since the subjects were shown the stimuli before the experiment began, by chance alone they should have scored one in five, or 20 percent, correct. Rhine found that there were individuals, roughly 20 percent according to his estimate, who scored slightly but statistically higher than chance would allow in the card guessing task. The results of these exploratory studies were published in Rhine's 1934 book, *Extrasensory Perception*, and the enormous interest it aroused made ESP a household term.

However, British psychologist C. E. M. Hansel (1966) reviewed the attempts of other investigators to replicate Rhine's early findings. Citing data from different studies, based on thousands of trials, Hansel concluded that when sensory cues were eliminated subjects could not score above chance on the card guessing task. For example, he reported that some of the original cards used by Rhine could be read from behind when they were held toward a light. In general, studies reporting evidence of psychic ability have been so poorly designed that other explanations of their results are possible (Diaconis, 1978). If psychic phenomena were real, more rigorous experimental methods should eliminate error and, thus, find more evidence of ESP—but they typically find less (Hansel, 1966, 1980; Hyman, 1977). Finally, there is always the potential for deception. Psychologist Daryl Bem has used the tricks of a stage magician to demonstrate how this might occur. Standing in front of his class and "randomly" selecting an IBM registration card from a bowl, Bem proceeded to give a detailed description of the student who submitted it. However, unknown to the audience, Bem had actually memorized the registration number of a student selected in advance. He was then able to "read off" that number, and "intuit" detailed information about that student that had actually been provided by a roommate accomplice (Cornell, 1984). A professional magician named James Randi is so convinced that psychic powers are based on deception that he has offered a reward of $10,000 to anyone who can provide a reliable demonstration of a paranormal phenomenon. So far, no one has claimed the reward. The point is: Do not accept "psychic phenomena" on the basis of appearance alone. Some supposed ESP is due to chance, some is due to trickery, and none seems to be replicated under rigidly controlled conditions.

From our coverage of sensory physiology, you can see that this material relates closely to the general physiological processes we described in the previous chapter—both rely on the generation and transmission of neural impulses. Similarly, both are best understood in terms of physiological and evolutionary perspectives. In the next Interactions section, we will show how these perspectives help us to understand how all living organisms use their senses to adapt and survive in their world.

INTERACTIONS:
Sensation and Behavior Adaptation

The information taken in by our senses provides the raw material for much of our behavior. Since behavior is dependent on the kind of information that is obtained from the environment, the behavior of different species varies according to their sensory capabilities. Different sensory capabilities and behaviors have evolved in different animals as a result of their interactions with the environment. For example, nocturnal animals such as bats use their ears rather than their eyes to navigate. Therefore, bats lack cones and have no color vision. The African male rat has only rudimentary eyes, no larger than pinheads, capable of detecting only light and dark. Since these rats live in underground burrows, their eyes function only to detect danger when their burrows have been broken into (Smith, 1989). We noted earlier that frogs have "bug detectors" that enable them to catch flys. Frogs also have limited color vision. The leopard frog, for instance, can see blue, and it will jump toward this color if it is startled. This is an adaptive feature—blue is the color of water, and when a frog is in danger it will leap for the safety water provides.

Many birds have highly developed eyes capable of seeing a wide range of colors. Their eyes are packed with cones that enable them to see the colorful feather displays of their species, displays that can serve as a signal for mating. Owls, on the other hand, lack colorful feathers and are almost color blind. But since they are nocturnal birds, their rod-rich eyes allow for nighttime vision. Nocturnal primates such as the New World monkey function as owls do—they usually do not see in color. However, most primates typically have good color vision. Evolutionary theorists believe that color vision and acuity for fine detail were useful to these tree-living animals, helping them detect ripe fruit and dangerous predators from among the green leaves of the forest.

Evolutionary pressures are also thought to be responsible for developing the sense of hearing. As mammals developed over the course of evolution, the cochlea became longer and coiled. Its greater length and surface area resulted in a greater ability to discriminate among sounds. A well-developed sense of hearing became especially important for nocturnal animals when vision was not particularly useful. Barn owls, for example, can capture a field mouse in total darkness. Their ears are sensitive to a high frequency range and to tiny differences in the time of arrival of a sound. This enables them to hear the high-pitched squeaks of a mouse and to locate it precisely in a field.

These examples of sensory capabilities show how sensation is related to behavior and an organism's ability to adapt. By being responsive to different forms of stimulation, these sensory "peepholes" provide different information and different opportunities to act. For example, we can characterize the human senses as *near* and *far senses* (Sekuler and Blake, 1985). The near senses include our senses of touch, taste, and smell. Touch and taste require physical contact, while smell requires us to be in the general vicinity of an object to detect it. Our reaction to stimulation of our near senses is often fast and direct. We are immediately repulsed by a foul odor, and we react quickly when stung by a bee. In these instances, we act first and think later.

Our far senses of vision and audition allow us to act differently. Our eyes and ears are long-range instruments. We can see and hear things at a distance. These senses provide us with an early warning of danger and help us to seek safety and shelter. This is why Helen Keller's loss of vision and audition was so devastating. Without vision and audition, her awareness could not extend beyond the reach of her fingers or nose. For those with vision and audition intact, these senses provide us with time—time to consider the consequences of different possible actions. These senses give us time to think. Together, our near and far senses increase our chances of adapting and surviving.

IN CONTEXT: SENSATION

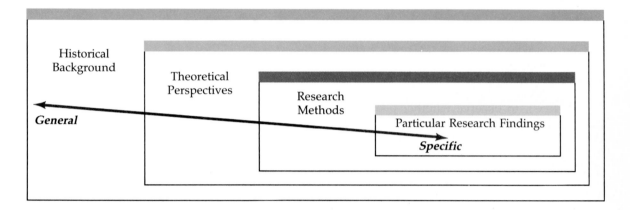

STUDY QUESTIONS

What do our senses do for us?

What is the minimal amount of stimulation to which we can respond, and the minimal amount of stimulus change we can detect?

How does the quality of a sensory experience change as the physical stimulus changes?

How many different senses do we have?

What is the basic process by which information from the external world comes to reach our brain?

Why do psychologists discredit the idea that we can pick up sensory information on "extrasensory" channels?

HISTORICAL BACKGROUND

1. Isaac Newton made an early contribution to the study of sensation in the seventeenth century with his work on the physics of light energy. Newton showed that white light could be separated into a color spectrum.

2. During the nineteenth century, Gustav Fechner studied the relationship between the amount of physical energy in a stimulus and our sensory experience of that stimulus. Fechner established a set of psychophysical procedures for the systematic study of sensation.

3. Interest in sensory physiology dates back to ancient Greece. However, it was not until the nineteenth century that sensory experience was seen as the result of sensory stimulation in the nervous system. During this century, Hermann von Helmholtz performed his pioneering studies on seeing and hearing. His ideas are still influential.

MODERN THEORETICAL PERSPECTIVES

1. Two theories have specified how judgment standards influence sensory judgments. **Signal detection theory** separates sensitivity from decision processes, and **adaptation level theory** shows how sensitivity can change as a function of past experience.

2. According to **trichromatic theory,** color vision is based on the stimulation of three different color receptors. **Opponent-process theory** holds that color vision is the result of stimulation of receptor pairs that work in opposition. Together, trichromatic and opponent-process operations account for color phenomena.

3. Theories of hearing have focused on how pitch is neurally represented. **Place theory** holds that sounds of different pitch vibrate different portions of the basilar membrane, while **frequency theory** holds that information about pitch is

provided by the rate of the brain cells' response. A combination of these theories describes how we represent pitch.

RESEARCH METHODS

1. The most frequently used method to study sensation is **experimentation.** It was used to measure sensitivity (Stevens, 1957), to map the receptive fields of the cat's cortex (Hubel and Wiesel, 1959), to observe whether people can identify others by chemical signals (Porter and Moore, 1981), and to observe sensory dominance when different senses provide discrepant information (Power, 1981).

2. A **correlational study** was done by Cohen et al. (1973) to determine if children's auditory discrimination scores and reading test scores were related to how close the children lived to a busy highway.

3. The **case study** was used to observe the effects of direct stimulation of the visual cortex in blind patients (Dobelle et al., 1976).

RESEARCH FINDINGS AND SUMMARY

1. The senses respond to physical energy from the environment. To be noticed, a stimulus must be compatible with a sensory receptor and be of sufficient intensity. The level of sufficient intensity is called the **sensory threshold.** The **absolute threshold** is the weakest level of stimulus intensity that will produce a sensation; the **difference threshold** is the smallest change in intensity that can be detected.

2. Psychologists use a **psychophysical scale** to relate a quantifiable physical variable (such as light intensity) to a subjective measure of sensory experience (such as brightness). Psychophysical functions may show compression, linearity, or expansion of the related sensory experience.

3. Sensory receptors convert physical energy into neural impulses that are transmitted to the brain. The brain can differentiate among the senses because it receives its neural messages along different sensory nerves that stimulate different areas of the cortex.

4. Within the broad spectrum of electromagnetic radiation, there is a narrow band of wavelengths that is visible to the human eye. This portion of the energy spectrum, from 390 to 760 nanometers, is visible because chemical reactions to light make the eye sensitive to energy from wavelengths in this range.

5. Physically, **light** can be described in terms of its **wavelength, amplitude,** and **purity.** Psychologically, these dimensions correspond most closely to **hue, brightness,** and **saturation.**

6. When light enters the eye, it passes first through the ganglion and bipolar cells of the retina before reaching the light sensitive **rods** and **cones.** The cones provide for color vision and fine detail vision, while the rods provide for night vision.

7. Single cell recordings indicate that cortical neurons can function as visual feature detectors. Simple, complex, and hypercomplex cells respond to different types of visual stimuli, such as edges or moving lines.

8. **Color vision** is the result of a photochemical process that begins in the retina and ends in the visual cortex. Different color phenomena include **color mixture, complementary afterimages,** and different types of **color blindness.**

9. **Sounds** are produced by changes in air pressure caused by air molecules set in motion. The air pressure fluctuations are called **sound waves** and they differ physically in terms of their **frequency, amplitude,** and **purity.** Psychologically, these differences are most closely related to **pitch, loudness,** and **timbre.** Information about loudness (*amplitude*) is represented by the number of neurons that fire, while information about pitch (*frequency*) is represented by the rate of neural firing and the location of the neural response. Sound and light are similar in that both can be described in terms of their frequency (wavelength), amplitude, and purity.

10. **Olfaction (smell)** involves the detection of airborne molecules by olfactory receptors inside the top of our nose. **Gustation (taste)** is a chemical process that sorts food and drink into sweet, sour, bitter, and salty categories. The **cutaneous (skin) senses** have receptors for pressure, pain, warmth, and cold. **Kinesthesis** and **body balance** depend mainly upon receptors located in the muscles and the inner ear.

11. The reality of **extrasensory perception** or **ESP** is dependent on researchers being able to produce such effects reliably under rigidly controlled conditions that eliminate the possibility of deception and error. Most psychologists do not believe that such a demonstration has been made.

ADDITIONAL READINGS

Barlow, H. B., and Mollon, J. D., eds. 1982. *The senses.* Cambridge: Cambridge University Press. A collection of advanced papers by experts in sensory science that covers the operation of each of the senses. Special attention is devoted to vision.

Cartarette, E. C., and M. P. Friedman, eds. 1974–1978. *Handbook of perception.* New York: Academic Press. A multivolume series by leading researchers in sensation and perception. The following volumes are especially relevant to sensory science: II (psychophysics and measurement), IV (hearing), V (seeing), and VIa (tasting and smelling).

Coren, S., and L. M. Ward. 1989. *Sensation and perception* (3rd ed.). New York: Academic Press. A lively text that presents research on all of the senses, along with interesting demonstrations and puzzles for the reader to try.

Engen, T. 1982. *The perception of odors.* New York: Academic Press. A complete review of the sense of smell, including research on odor memory, by a major contributor to olfactory research.

Gescheider, G. A. 1979. *Psychophysics: Method and theory.* Hillsdale, NJ: Erlbaum. An introduction to psychophysics that provides in-depth coverage of threshold calculation, psychophysical scales, and signal detection theory.

Matlin, M. W. 1988. *Sensation and perception* (2nd ed.). Boston: Allyn and Bacon. A thoughtful and interesting undergraduate text that engages the reader on a variety of issues in sensation and perception.

Randi, J. 1982. *Flim-flam!* Buffalo, NY: Prometheus Books. A skeptical review of paranormal claims by a master magician.

Smith, J. 1989. *Senses and sensibilities.* New York: Wiley. A fascinating and delightful book that explores the origins, functions, and dysfunctions of the different senses in a highly entertaining manner.

CHAPTER
4

PERCEPTION

I see, from my window, trees and meadows, and horses and oxen, and distant hills. I see each of its proper size, of its proper form, and at its proper distance; and these particulars appear as immediate trans-formations of the eye, as the colors which I see by means of it. Yet philosophy has ascertained that we derive nothing from the eye whatever but sensations of color. . . . How, then, is it that we receive accurate information, by the eye, of shape and size and distance?

(James Mill, 1829)

Until we think about it, it seems reasonable to suppose that the perceptual world is the same as the physical world. For example, you might think to yourself, "I see my friends walking down the hall because they are there. I see the book in front of me because it is there. What could be more obvious?" At first glance, perception seems straightforward and accurate. But if our senses give us straightforward and accurate information, then why do we not perceive our friends as shrinking in size as they walk away from us, in accordance with their shrinking image on our retina? If our view of the world and the things in it were based solely on sensory information the world would be a very chaotic place, because the information that we get from our senses does not always correspond to reality. Sometimes the "obvious" turns out to be wrong. Consider Figure 4.1. You should see what appears to be a clockwise spiral. But if you trace the path of the spiral with your finger, the spiral turns out to be an illusion. This illusion, called *Fraser's spiral*, consists of a set of concentric circles made up of line segments angled toward the center. Our visual perception of Fraser's spiral is inaccurate—the object that is perceived is not the same as the object on the page. Illusions such as Fraser's spiral warn us that the physical and perceptual worlds are not the same.

How is it that the "evidence of our senses" can sometimes fool us? More important, how do we manage to obtain a consistent and accurate view of the world if the sensory information from our environment is inconsistent and often at odds with

FIGURE 4.1 Fraser's spiral. This figure appears to show a spiral, but it is really a visual illusion. If you trace the path of the spiral, you will see that it consists entirely of concentric circles made up of line segments angled toward the center. Illusions indicate that the physical and perceptual worlds are not the same.

reality? The answer is found in those processes that we use to organize and interpret sensory information. **Sensation** refers to the immediate experiences that are generated by simple, isolated stimuli; **perception** involves the organization and interpretation of those stimuli to give them meaning. For instance, in listening to a person sing, we experience the qualities of loudness and pitch as sensations, while our ability to hear the sequence of sounds as a song is an act of perception. At the next level, if we understand and recognize the words to the song, our perception blends into **cognition,** a more complex interpretive process that involves memory and thought.

To understand why psychologists view perception as a problem to be solved, consider the parallels between the eye and the camera. At first glance, the similarities in their physical structure suggest that the same principles might explain the operations of both a camera and the eye. Both eye and camera have an opening to admit light and a lens to focus light on a photosensitive surface (in the eye, the retina; in the camera, the film). If the eye worked like a camera, then visual perception would be nothing more than images of the external world being formed on the retina of the eye. The eye would be like a window to the world. Most of the time we take our perception for granted and

view it in this naive, unthinking way. However, there are a number of important differences:

- An image of an object has only two dimensions, but our perception of an object has three.
- The image of this page is upside down on the retina, but we perceive it as rightside up.
- An image may appear small on the retina because it is formed by a small object nearby—a fly—or a large object far away—a star. Nevertheless, we perceive such objects accurately and perceive the star to be larger than the fly.
- Changes in the position of our head or our distance from an object change the image of the object on the retina, but our perception of the object remains stable.
- An image is based on the stimulation of millions of individual cells in the retina, yet we perceive a unified world.

(From Neisser, 1968; Rock and Harris, 1967)

Visual perception involves much more than taking pictures of objective reality. The eye is not like a camera. Rather, our eyes feed our brain neural patterns representing sensory information (Gregory, 1978). To construct a consistent and reasonably accurate view of the world, our brain must *interpret* this sensory information.

Our senses are our only means of knowing about the world, but they are not windows that let the world in. They are extensions of the brain that respond to different forms of physical energy. For example, in Figure 4.2 the sights, sounds, and smells of an outdoor scene are received by our senses of vision, audition, and olfaction from light waves, sound waves, and odor molecules. The objects in the outside world (the sunshine, the tree, and the grass shown in Figure 4.2) are referred to as *distal* (distant) stimuli, while the different forms of physical energy received by the senses (the light waves, sound waves, and odor molecules) are called *proximal* (nearby) stimuli. Our perceptions of distal objects are obtained from the proximal stimuli our senses receive.

Normally we are unaware of the fact that our perceptual experiences of distal objects are based on the interpretation of proximal stimuli. It is only when we are fooled by misleading or ambiguous sensory information that we realize how important interpretation is to perception. Illusions, such as Fraser's spiral and the ambiguous surface in Figure 4.3, show how our brain imposes an order on the

physical world. When you first look at Figure 4.3, you see it as a series of hills and valleys (with concentric rings marking the valleys). But if you turn your book upside down, the figure seems to change—the hills and valleys are reversed. Depending on how you observe the figure, the flat two-dimensional drawing can be perceived as two entirely different three-dimensional surfaces. In each case, the brain actively interprets the information it receives to arrive at a different perception.

This interpretive view of perception raises certain fundamental questions. First, why does the visual system need to interpret the images on the retina? Second, what information do we use to interpret these retinal images so that our perception remains true to the real world? To answer these questions, psychologist Donald Hoffman (1983) studied ambiguous figures similar to Figure 4.3. We need to interpret our retinal images, says Hoffman, because most visual images are somewhat ambiguous. In part, this ambiguity is based on the fact that retinal images are essentially two dimensional, while the real world is three dimensional. By interpreting retinal images, our visual system "forces" us to see the flat two-dimensional surface in Figure 4.3 as a three-dimensional surface of hills and valleys. In

FIGURE 4.2 The perceiver's problem.   The main problem in perception is to understand how we perceive distal stimulus objects from proximal stimulus energy. The distal stimuli that we perceive (the tree, the grass, and the sunshine) are interpretations of the proximal stimuli (the light waves, the sound waves, and the odor molecules) that we receive. Because the physical and perceptual worlds seem similar, it is easy to forget how fundamentally different they are.

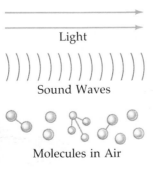

Light

Sound Waves

Molecules in Air

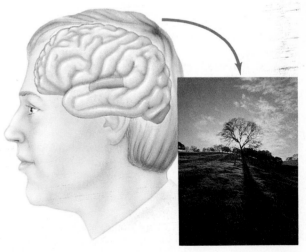

Distal Stimuli

Various objects from the physical world

Proximal Stimuli

Forms of stimulus energy that produce a pattern on a sensory receptor

Observer

Sensory receptors receive proximal stimuli; brain transforms impulses into a perceptual experience.

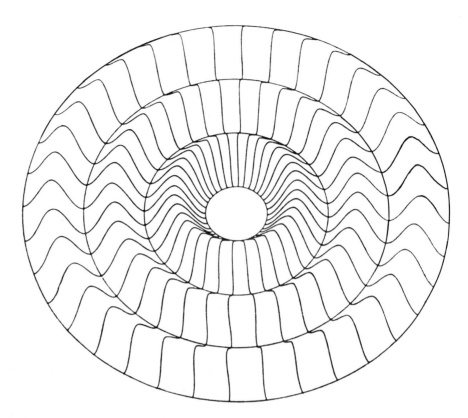

FIGURE 4.3   An ambiguous surface.   What do you see when you look at this figure? Do you see a series of hills and valleys, with concentric circles marking the valleys? Turn your book upside down and look at the figure again. How has your perception changed? Ambiguous figures show that the brain organizes and interprets the information it receives to produce a meaningful perception. In this example, more than one meaningful perception is possible.

the real world, there are regularities as well as ambiguities in the objects around us. These regularities provide us with information and allow us to interpret our retinal images in nonarbitrary ways. Notice that in moving from biological and sensory processes (described in Chapters 2 and 3) to perception, we have reached a point in our discussion of psychology where the mind now steps in and makes contact with the information. Organizing and interpreting neurally coded sensory information is a fundamental aspect of mind.

In this chapter we will describe the processes that enable us to interpret our retinal images in nonarbitrary ways. Space does not permit us to discuss all aspects of perception, but we can describe a variety of perceptual topics so that you will understand how our perceptual system works. Therefore, we will limit much of our discussion to showing how we use sensory information to perceive accurately such basic perceptual qualities as form, depth, size, and movement. In each instance we will see how we solve the puzzle of perceiving distal environmental stimuli correctly from the different proximal

stimuli reaching our senses. Normally we do this quickly and without ever thinking about it. In addition, we will focus on visual perception in this chapter because it is the most important form of perception and has been the most thoroughly explored. (Other aspects of perception are covered elsewhere in this book. Attention is covered in the chapter on consciousness, speech perception in the chapter on language, and perceptual development in the chapter on development.) Because it is a fundamental psychological process, perception spans many different areas.

HISTORICAL BACKGROUND:
Perception and Knowledge

In the seventeenth century philosopher Thomas Hobbes wrote, "There is no conception in man's mind which hath not at first, totally or by parts, been begotten upon the organs of sense." According to Hobbes and such later philosophers as John Locke and Bishop George Berkeley, it was not just that the senses were considered to be a source of knowledge, they were believed to be the *only* source of knowledge. Hobbes, Locke, and Berkeley were prominent *empiricists,* philosophers who held that all knowledge is obtained from the senses.

Perceiving by Unconscious Inference

The empiricist philosophers believed that even complex, abstract knowledge was ultimately derived from elementary sensations. Consider the principle of *associationism,* in which simple sensory qualities such as size, shape, and color are mentally connected into a complex perceptual experience. For example, our perceptual experience of an apple is based on the association of such qualities as smallness, roundness, and redness. This is because these sensory qualities occur together in time and place every time we experience an apple. Through associations formed by past experience, we learn that apples, in addition to being red, round, and smooth, also have a particular taste, a certain texture, and so on.

Some of these philosophers also believed that sensory information alone was insufficient to describe the world as people actually perceive it. For instance, Berkeley said that we cannot tell how far we are from an object with only the visual stimulation received by the eye. (Recall again the problems with the eye–camera analogy.) Since we are able to perceive the distance of objects fairly accurately, we must supplement the image on the eye with additional information. Berkeley believed that there are numerous cues we can use to help us perceive accurately. For example, the relative sharpness of the retinal image provides information about the distance of objects—nearby objects make sharper images than those that are farther away. Other distance cues such as overlap and perspective have been used by artists since the Renaissance to create realistic impressions of depth. (See Figure 4.4.)

In general, Berkeley saw perception as a process of interpreting sensory information in light of knowledge gained by earlier experience. However, this process of interpretation is not necessarily conscious. When we estimate the distance of an object, we do not consciously think about the sharpness of our retinal image. Instead, Berkeley believed that we use such information unconsciously. Later, in the middle of the nineteenth century, Hermann von Helmholtz (introduced in Chapter 3) called this process **unconscious inference.** Objects perceived as distant are unconsciously inferred to be larger than their retinal

FIGURE 4.4   A panel of the bronze doors of the baptistery of San Giovanni by Lorenzo Ghilberti. This Italian Renaissance sculptor conveyed a strong sense of depth in his art by using linear perspective with the three-dimensional figures as all lines flow to a central point behind the raised figures. Michelangelo once said that the doors were worthy of the entrance to paradise.

size. According to Helmholtz, we are so highly practiced at, and so often accurate in, making these perceptual inferences that we are normally unaware of making them. This belief is still a widely held view (Hochberg, 1988; Rock, 1985).

Perceiving Directly

Psychologist James Gibson (1904–1979) provided a different approach to perception. In a series of influential books, Gibson (1966; 1979) said that most of the information that we need for accurate perception is present in the stimuli themselves and is directly available to our senses. For example, the elements in Figure 4.5 provide important information for our perception of depth. In this illustration, depth is conveyed by a **texture gradient,** the gradual shift in the size of objects or detail as our eyes scan the scene from top to bottom. Whether we are looking at a field of flowers or a crowd of people, the elements of a texture gradient appear to become more densely packed as the surface extends into the distance. In these examples, no inferential reasoning is necessary. The texture provides us with direct information about depth. This approach to perception is called *ecological* because it emphasizes the use of information from the natural environment. It has attracted a number of

FIGURE 4.5 Texture gradients. The environment provides natural cues for depth in the form of texture gradients. Whether we are looking at flowers or at people, objects appear closer together as they extend into the distance. This fact is a perceptual invariant that can be used to provide information on depth; the closer together objects appear, the further away they must be from an observer.

ardent supporters in a relatively short period of time (Cutting, 1986; Mace, 1977; Turvey and Shaw, 1979).

Which view of perception is correct? Do we make unconscious inferences as Helmholtz believed, or do we perceive directly as Gibson maintained? There may be truth in both positions, as each may account for different perceptual abilities. For example, the Helmholtzian view can describe our perception when we read a note scribbled hastily by a friend. Here we are apt to make inferences and recognize words on the basis of our sensory analysis. On the other hand, the Gibsonian view appears more suited to describing how we use the information available in the environment to help us move about in the world. A tex-

ture gradient is an example of this type of information. In fact, psychologist James Cutting (1986) has suggested that our perceptual system may use different sources of information at different times, even when performing the same task. Consequently, regardless of whether we take a Helmholtzian or a Gibsonian view, all psychologists agree that our perception is ultimately based on information from the outside world. The primary purpose of this chapter is to examine the types of information that influence our perception of that world. We start with our ability to perceive form. ■

PERCEIVING FORM

Imagine the following scene. An inventor has just constructed a robot to help with housekeeping tasks. With great excitement, she issues its first command: "Pick up the cup from the table." The robot scans the room with its television camera "eye" and then proceeds to lift up the table. What has gone wrong? Anxiously, the inventor checks the robot's circuitry and finds that the machine had indeed "sensed" all the contours and changes in brightness that passed in front of its lens. Puzzled by this failure, the inventor begins to suspect that the perception of form is more difficult than she had imagined. Deep in thought, she asks, "Exactly how do I know where the cup ends and the table begins?"

The case of the misperceiving robot shows us that there is more to the perception of form than merely the detection of contours and edges (Coren and Ward, 1989). We can make the same point another way by looking at a picture in which many of the contours and edges have been removed. Figure 4.6 consists solely of irregular light and dark patches. Where is the meaningful form in this figure?

To make sense of the light and dark patches in Figure 4.6, you must organize the available information and interpret it on the basis of your past experience. If you know what type of object you are looking at, it is easier to recognize it (Reynolds, 1985). When "recognition" occurs, the individual light and dark patches become absorbed into larger, more meaningful forms. In fact, Figure 4.6 shows a dalmation dog (nose pointed downward and to the left) standing in front of a large tree. Once the information has been organized and interpreted, it is difficult to return it to its previous unorganized and uninterpreted state. In other words, after seeing the dog in the picture, it is

FIGURE 4.6   What do you see in this picture?   To illustrate how stimulus elements are organized, the normally rapid processes of perception are slowed down by the removal of all contours from the picture. To see this picture as meaningful (a dalmatian dog, nose downward, pointed left), you must construct a perceptual interpretation that organizes the available information.

nearly impossible to "lose" it in the sea of light and dark patches.

Although we rarely look for forms in degraded pictures, our normal processes of organization and interpretation are based on the same kind of problem. We must combine information from our senses with what we already know. These processes normally occur so quickly and effortlessly that tricks like degrading or improverishing the sensory stimulus are necessary to slow them down to prove that they exist.

PERCEPTUAL ORGANIZATION

What do we mean by **perceptual organization?** Perceptual organization refers to the manner in which we group some elements with others to make a coherent pattern or form. For example, in Figure 4.6 certain patches were seen as belonging to the figure of a dog, while others were seen as shadows. This tells us that one of the first tasks of perceptual organization is to separate stimulus elements into **figure and ground.**

FIGURE AND GROUND

A figure is a meaningful form that is perceived on a neutral ground. Figure 4.7 provides an illustration of a reversible figure–ground stimulus. You may see this stimulus as a light vase (figure) on a dark surround (ground) or as a pair of faces in silhouette (figure) against a light background (ground). Either case demonstrates three qualities of figure–ground organization. First, the figure seems more dense and recognizable than the ground. Second, the figure seems to be in front of the ground. Third, the ground is formless and seems to extend behind the figure (Goldstein, 1984). Although either organization of Figure 4.7 makes perceptual sense, you cannot perceive both at the same time. Having different forms simultaneously available would be impossibly confusing.

THE LAWS OF ORGANIZATION

Early in the twentieth century, a small group of German psychologists, Max Wertheimer, Kurt Koffka, and Wolfgang Köhler, became interested in the perception of form. They were known as the

FIGURE 4.7 How do you perceive this figure? Do you see the faces of Prince Phillip and Queen Elizabeth II in silhouette, or a large vase? Actually, both interpretations are possible but not at the same time. This reversible figure from a vase created for the 1977 silver jubilee for Britain's queen illustrates figure and ground. A figure is a meaningful form that is perceived on a neutral ground.

tion of elementary sensations. When the bricks are arranged in a particular way, a building emerges. When sensations are organized in a particular way, a pattern or form emerges. The organization thus captures the various elements and determines how we see them. The Gestalt psychologists found that there are strong, perhaps universal, tendencies to group elements on the basis of their proximity, similarity, good continuation, closure, and common fate. These patterns of perceptual grouping have been formulated into the Gestalt **laws of organization:**

- The *law of proximity* states that elements that are physically close tend to be grouped. You see the letters on this page as forming rows instead of columns because each letter is closer to the letters to the left and right than to the letters above and below.

- The *law of similarity* states that similar elements tend to be grouped. You see the words printed *in italics* as forming a separate group, apart from the words in regular print.

- The *law of good continuation* states that elements that form straight or smoothly curving lines tend to be grouped. If you look out a window and see two branches of a tree that cross, you will perceive two straight limbs, rather than two right angles that touch.

- The *law of closure* states that when a figure has a gap we tend to perceive the figure as closed and complete. If you close this book and hold it in one hand, it will still look like a rectangle, even though your hand is covering part of one of its sides.

- The *law of common fate* states that elements that move in the same direction tend to be perceived as a unit. If you look at a busy street, cars moving in one direction will form one group, while those going in the opposite direction will form a different group.

(Matlin, 1988)

Visual examples of these Gestalt laws are provided in Figures 4.8 and 4.9. In particular, notice how the Gestalt law of similarity is used in Grant Wood's well-known painting *American Gothic* (Figure 4.9). Look at how the three-pronged design of the pitchfork is repeated throughout the painting. It can be seen in the seams of the man's overalls, the cactus on the porch, the frames of the windows, and even the shape of the people's faces. Artists often very consciously employ different Gestalt principles to organize the various elements of the artwork (Zakia, 1975).

Gestalt psychologists (the German word "Gestalt" translates loosely as *configuration, pattern,* or *form*), and they believed that form perception was determined by certain organizing properties of the brain. Since the same ambiguous sensory stimulation can lead to different perceptual interpretations (look back to Figure 4.3), our perceptual experience of form must be influenced by the way that our brain organizes that stimulation. The Gestalt psychologists held that we organize our perception of objects on the basis of innate perceptual processes rather than on the basis of past experience. They viewed these inherent perceptual processes as laws of organization (Dember and Bagwell, 1985). Just as gravity "organizes" the sun and planets into a solar system, processes inherent in the brain group the elements of a scene into meaningful patterns or forms.

According to the Gestalt psychologists, our perceptual experiences are different from the sum of our elementary sensations. Just as a building is more than the sum total of its bricks or boards, so too are our perceptions more than just a combina-

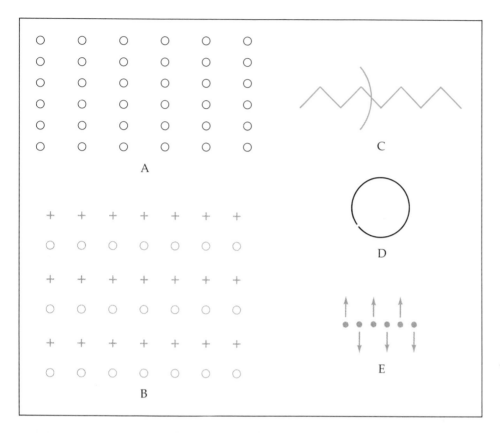

FIGURE 4.8   The Gestalt laws of organization.   In A, we see a set of columns, not rows, because elements that are near tend to be grouped *(law of nearness)*. In B, we see a set of rows, not columns, because similar elements are grouped *(law of similarity)*. In C, we see a zigzag line with a curved line running through it instead of a more complex figure *(law of good continuation)*. In D, we see a circle instead of a curved line, even though the figure is not completely closed *(law of closure)*. In E, we would see two groups of dots instead of some other arrangement if each dot suddenly moved in the direction of the arrows.

SHAPE CONSTANCY

Leonardo da Vinci is reported to have studied perspective by looking at objects through his window and tracing them on the glass. If you follow Leonardo's procedure and draw your desk top on a sheet of glass, your tracing of its shape will change as you walk toward your desk. You will draw a trapezoid when you are far away and a rectangle when you are close. However, your perceptual experience of the desk will remain constant even when your retinal image changes greatly. No matter how much your retinal image changed, it is hard to see your desk top as anything but a large rectangular shape. This phenomenon is called **shape constancy.** Shape constancy appears to be present at birth, and it is absolutely critical for accurate object perception (Slater and Morison, 1985).

FORM AND ORIENTATION

If you tip a square on a 45-degree angle, it becomes a diamond. This is true, however, only if there is no background to which to relate it. If you look at a square on a wall, and then tilt your head at a 45-degree angle, it will still look like a square. The orientation of an image on our retina does not, by itself, determine the orientation of the form we perceive. When we look at a figure we determine which end is up in relation to other things in our environment. Tilting your head when you look at a square on a wall will not produce a diamond because the top side of the square is still upright with respect to the wall. In addition, sensory information from our vestibular sacs, located in each inner ear, tells us about the position of our head. Thus, we combine different types of information to perceive our environment correctly.

FIGURE 4.9 An example of the Gestalt law of similarity. According to this Gestalt law, we tend to group similar visual elements. In this painting, *American Gothic* by Grant Wood, the artist has made effective use of this law in making visual associations. Notice how the three-pronged design of the pitchfork can be seen in various elements of the painting such as the seams in the man's overalls, the window frames, the cactus, and also the shape of the faces.

Despite our ability to make perceptual corrections, changes in orientation can be very disruptive for complex stimuli like human faces. Inverted faces are easily seen as inverted faces but are more difficult to identify as particular people. Upside-down faces look strange because they contradict our past experience. To correct for this inversion, we must mentally transpose each face to its normal orientation. Because faces have so many features, it is difficult to reorient each detail simultaneously. If some of the features in an upside-down face have already been transposed for us—as in the case of former British Prime Minister Margaret Thatcher's eyes and mouth in Figure 4.10—it is easier to make an identification. Curiously, if this figure is turned rightside up, the face looks extremely bizarre. This phenomenon is called the "Margaret Thatcher illusion," because as long as the face is viewed upside down the horrible expression on it goes unnoticed (Thompson, 1980).

ILLUSIONS OF FORM

An **illusion** is defined as a perceptual experience that does not correspond to physical reality. Illusions occur when we apply normal perceptual processes to environmental stimuli that do not follow the normal rules. Illusions can be either physical or perceptual in origin. *Physical illusions,* such as the distorted images in fun-house mirrors, are due to actual physical distortions of proximal stimuli and not to our misinterpretation of those stimuli. These illusions are fascinating, but they are more the domain of physics than psychology. *Perceptual illusions,* such as Fraser's spiral, are psychologically determined; they are due to the misinterpretations of proximal stimuli—to "seeing" something that is not really there. Psychologists are interested in these illusions because they can tell us more about normal perception. If we could specify the conditions that produce illusions, perhaps we could determine the basis for accurate perception.

SUBJECTIVE CONTOURS

Illusions of form occur when we combine stimulus elements to create an object that is sensible, but not really there. Figure 4.11 provides several examples. In each of these figures, there is an illusion of a **subjective contour.** In other words, we perceive a well-defined form where, objectively, there really is none. The illusion occurs when we combine the separate elements into a meaningful whole. In Figures 4.11A and B, we integrate those

FIGURE 4.10 The "Margaret Thatcher illusion." Although former British Prime Minister Thatcher's head is turned upside down in this figure, her eyes and mouth have been rotated to their normal orientation. This radical transformation in Mrs. Thatcher's facial features has surprisingly little effect on our ability to perceive her smiling expression. But if this page is turned upside down, a grotesque Mrs. Thatcher is revealed.

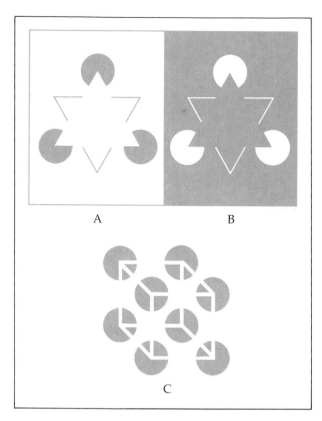

A   B

C

FIGURE 4.11 Subjective contours. Each of these examples leads us to perceive a figure that is not really there. The figures are illusions formed by subjective contours that result from the integration of the available elements into a meaningful whole. To convince yourself that the triangle in A and B is an illusion, cover the circular objects and the subjective contours will disappear. In C, the reversible Necker cube is composed entirely of subjective contours. It can be perceived as being above a black dotted background or behind a porous white surface.

elements that are actually present (three acute angles and three "Pac Man" figures) into perceptually simpler figures (a triangle and three circles). However, this interpretation only makes sense if we see these simpler figures as lying behind another triangle. This illusory triangle appears to overlap portions of the other figures, but if you cover the circular elements, the triangle disappears (Kanizsa, 1976; Stevens, 1983; Walker and Shank, 1987).

Figure 4.11C provides perhaps the most interesting example of all. First, there is a strong impression of a reversible figure, called a Necker cube, built entirely out of subjective contours. Note that the front and back of the cube can be made to alternate if it is seen as a three-dimensional object. Secondly, it is also possible to

reverse the figure–ground relation in the figure. That is, you can see the Necker cube as above a field of colored circles, or you can see each colored circle as a hole in a white wall through which you are viewing portions of the subjective Necker cube.

When we perceive a form, our brain constructs a pattern that combines the various parts into a perceivable whole that is as simple as possible (the Gestalt law of simplicity, again). Subjective contour illusions show that the brain can provide part of that structure to make a pattern complete. At present, psychologists do not agree on the underlying mechanisms responsible for subjective contours. However, figure–ground organization appears to play an important part (Coren, 1972; Parks, 1987). For example, in Figures 4.11A and B, the illusory triangle is seen as lying on top of the other elements. Thus, a "figure" emerges from the "ground" to help organize the otherwise meaningless set of elements into a simpler, more meaningful picture. One psychologist has even speculated that subjective contours evolved in the distant past as an anticamouflage device to enhance the outline of spotted predators, such as leopards, against backgrounds of dense foliage (Ramachandran, 1986).

IMPOSSIBLE FIGURES

Another type of form illusion is shown in Figure 4.12. At first glance, each figure appears to be a meaningful form; there is an elephant on the left and an arch on the right. But closer inspection reveals that each stimulus is an **impossible figure**—no such three-dimensional objects could possible exist in the world. It takes time to realize that these forms are impossible because each of their components—the legs, columns, and main bodies—are perceptually correct by themselves. By moving your eyes over the different portions of each figure, you try to integrate the information obtained from your eye movements into a coherent form. Only when you carefully try to fit the individual components together do you realize that the figures do not make any sense (Hochberg, 1970; 1988).

Dutch artist Maurits Escher (1898–1972) has used different impossible figures as the basis for his illusionist art. In his lithograph, *Ascending and Descending,* the impossible figure is the staircase that never ends. The monks on the outside of the staircase will be forever walking up, while the monks on the inside will be forever walking down (Figure 4.13). Illusions involving impossible fig-

FIGURE 4.12 Impossible figures. Initially, the figure on the left is seen as an elephant, and the figure on the right is seen as an arch. But after a more careful inspection, we see that neither of these figures could possibly exist in the three-dimensional world. It takes time to see these figures as impossible because all of their components are perceptually correct. Only when we try to put the components together into a meaningful whole do we realize that the components will not merge.

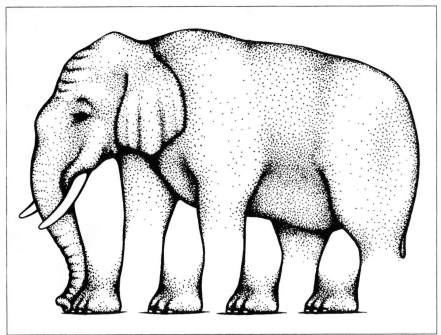

ures again demonstrate how we attempt to construct meaningful forms out of the information provided by our senses. In the case of the Escher lithograph, the artist tries to confuse us by putting together parts of a building that could never exist in the real world. Psychologist Julian Hochberg (1970) has said that we normally perceive form by integrating information obtained from successive glances at an object. However, we only become aware of this process when we look at impossible figures that resist our attempts at figural integra-

tion. In the next section we will describe the perceptual processes that produce figural integration and allow us to recognize patterns.

RECOGNIZING PATTERNS

Seeing the fish bowl turned over on our living room floor, most of us would react by questioning "What happened here?" or by concluding, "The cat's been after the fish again!" We would not, under normal circumstances, stop and wonder

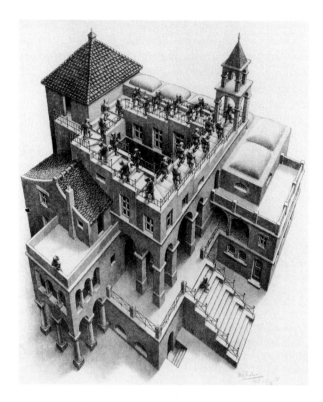

FIGURE 4.13 *Ascending and Descending* **by Dutch artist Maurits Escher.** Escher used impossible figures as the basis for his illusionist art. In this lithograph, columns of monks walk up and down an impossible figure in the form of a never-ending staircase. Impossible figures show how we attempt to construct meaningful forms out of the information provided. We only become aware of this process when we look at figures that resist integration.

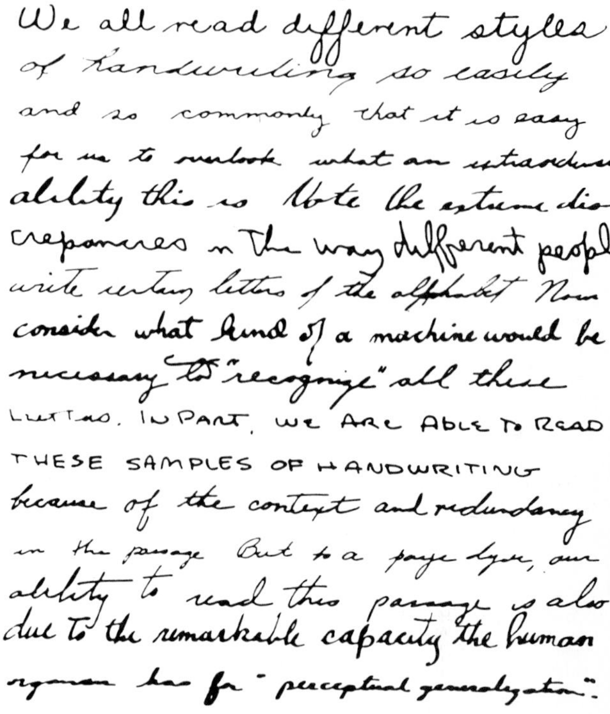

FIGURE 4.14 Versatility of pattern recognition. Although each line of this passage was written by a different person, we are generally not troubled by variation in form because of our ability to recognize pattern. Pattern recognition involves the perception and interpretation of stimulus elements on the basis of past experience.

what we were seeing. The overturned fish bowl, the puddle of water, and the satisfied cat would all be recognized as familiar forms by one of our most impressive perceptual abilities, the process of **pattern recognition.** Pattern recognition is defined as the meaningful interpretation of form. It is used to identify such stimuli as the words on this page, the building in which you live, and the faces of your family and friends. Pattern recognition is one of our most versatile abilities. For example, we can recognize numbers or words in different typefaces or handwriting scripts (Figure 4.14); we can recognize the same melody played by an orchestra or hummed by a friend; and we can recognize a furry creature as a dog even though we may have never seen the particular animal, or even its breed, before. In this section we will examine the pattern recognition processes that we use for form perception. We will see that pattern recognition involves more than the simple perception of stimulus elements: It involves the interpretation of those elements on the basis of our past experience.

FEATURE ANALYSIS

The versatility of pattern recognition has led psychologists to consider a theory that assumes that patterns are recognized on the basis of certain key components or features. For example, we can recognize clouds because each particular cloud shares the necessary critical features that satisfy our definition of a cloud—a mass of visible vapor floating in the atmosphere. This approach to pattern recognition is known as **feature analysis.**

The best known feature analysis model is the Pandemonium model of Oliver Selfridge (1959). Selfridge proposed that pattern recognition consists of a series of stimulus analyses carried out by "demons" who work at different levels in the sequence of pattern recognition. Demons are simply a convenient way of representing a physiological or psychological process without specifying in detail how the process actually works. Figure 4.15 shows how the Pandemonium model identifies a simple stimulus such as the letter R. According to the model, feature demons examine a stimulus in terms of its visual features. Each demon is responsible for recognizing a distinct feature. The feature demons specify the number and type of features and then pass this information on to the cognitive demons. Each cognitive demon is a stored representation of a different letter stimulus. A given cognitive demon is activated to the extent that the features it receives from the feature demons match the set of features that define its letter. A cognitive demon is really nothing more than a definition of a particular letter in terms of its component features.

The pattern recognition model is called Pan-demonium because the cognitive demons scream for the attention of the decision demon to the extent that the stimulus features they have received match those in each cognitive demon's set. The greater the extent of the match, the louder a cognitive demon screams. Figure 4.15 shows that the cognitive demons for R, P, and D are yelling loudly because of the features they have received. However, the cognitive demon for R is yelling the loudest and this is how the decision demon determines which letter we are actually looking at.

FIGURE 4.15 The Pandemonium model of Oliver Selfridge.   According to this feature analysis model of pattern recognition, a visual stimulus is examined first for its distinctive features. Feature demons pass their information on to the cognitive demons (stored letter representations) who scream to the extent that their features have been matched. The decision demon listens to the cognitive demons and determines which letter was seen on the basis of which demon yells the loudest. The demons are a convenient way of representing the underlying perceptual processes that operate on a continuous flow of information. The Pandemonium model holds that stimuli are recognized on the basis of feature extraction and interpretation.

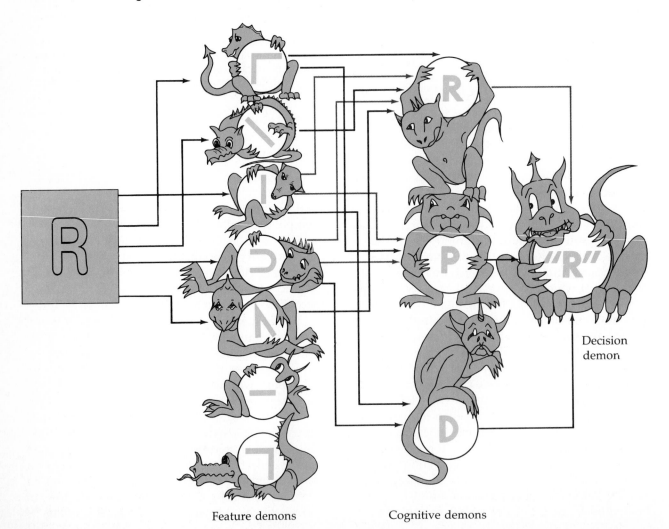

Decision demon

Feature demons   Cognitive demons

FEATURE EXTRACTION AND INTERPRETATION

Although it was humorously presented, Pandemonium is a serious model of pattern recognition that makes two important points. First, this model states that pattern recognition consists of **feature extraction** and **feature interpretation.** Feature extraction involves specifying the particular details that make up a stimulus, while feature interpretation consists of matching those details to feature sets that define different possible stimuli. Second, it states that pattern recognition can be based on a general set of features (vertical lines, horizontal lines, and so forth) that apply to all visual stimuli. Instead of trying to match a specific stimulus to a specific template, a set of features is compared to sets of defining features in memory. Regardless of their size or slant, all uppercase Rs can be identified because all are defined by the same set of visual features. This is how features analysis attains its great versatility.

A CONNECTIONIST APPROACH TO FEATURE ANALYSIS

The same processes of feature extraction and interpretation can be seen in the newer connectionist approaches to pattern recognition. According to this view, letters are still described by visual features, but now our knowledge of which features go with which letters is contained in a neural-like network of connections. This approach is called **connectionism** because it is based on the idea that features and letters are interconnected in the same way that neurons are interconnected in the brain. Figure 4.16A shows a simple connectionist network for identifying letters by feature analysis. When a letter is presented, its features become activated and they send their activation along excitatory pathways (the lines ending in arrows) to the letter representations. This figure shows just a few of the visual features that could be used for letter identification. In this example all of the letters receive excitatory inputs, and so this network could have trouble deciding which letter was shown.

The network in Figure 4.16B is an improvement. It allows for excitatory and inhibitory connections just like those found in our nervous system. (See Chapter 2.) If a feature is not contained in a letter, an inhibitory connection (a line ending in a dot) is made to that letter. This connectionist network will identify a previously shown letter as an R because its representation in the network has the highest level of activation.

Although the Pandemonium model and the connectionist network model are similar, since

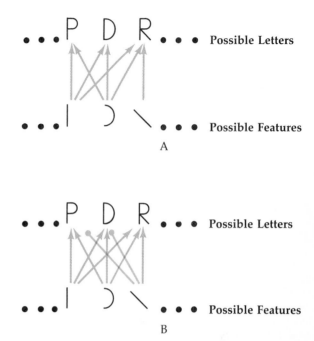

FIGURE 4.16 A connectionist approach to letter recognition. In A, a simple network is represented by features (vertical line, curved line, and diagonal line) at the bottom and letters at the top. A connection between a feature and a letter means that the letter contains that feature. An arrow indicates that the connection is excitatory. This means that when a feature is activated, the activation spreads to the connected letters. In B, the network is enhanced by the addition of inhibitory connections, indicated by the dots. Now when a feature is activated it activates excitatory connections to letters that contain that feature and inhibitory connections to letters that do not. In this example, the connectionist network would identify the letter *R*.

both are based on feature analysis, the connectionist approach offers greater specificity. Neural networks are preferable to unspecified "demons," and the use of excitatory and inhibitory connections more closely resembles the operation of the nervous system that is actually producing letter recognition. Thus, the connectionist approach provides a strong link between a model of how the mind organizes and integrates information and how the brain processes neural information. Much research is currently exploring how connectionist networks can describe a wide range of perceptual and cognitive phenomena (Churchland, 1990; McClelland and Rumelhart, 1986; Yuille and Ullman, 1990). We will have more to say about connectionism in Chapter 7, on memory.

RECOGNIZING FAMILIAR OBJECTS

Letters and words are important visual stimuli, but they are only a small part of the many stimuli we encounter every day. Can the same processes of feature extraction and interpretation that work so well with letters explain how we identify such familiar objects as horses and people? In fact, they can. The processes are essentially the same—only the features are different. Where letters use angles, curves, and lines as features, objects use such simple geometric forms as cylinders, blocks, and wedges. Figure 4.17 shows how this might work. In this figure, a group of familiar objects is represented by wedges of different sizes. If we assume that simple geometric forms (for example, cylinders, blocks, and wedges) correspond to the visual features that make up an object, we have the basis for understanding object recognition.

Psychologist Irving Biederman (1987; 1990) has proposed that there are 36 different geometric forms that serve as visual features in objects. These geometric forms, he says, are sufficient to determine the shape of all of the objects we can recognize. In order to recognize an object, we perform a feature analysis. We extract the geometric form features from the stimulus and then interpret those features. Thus, recognizing an object is like recognizing a letter. Figure 4.18 shows these processes at work. At first glance, you see two similar illustrations of a black field with irregular white shapes scattered about. But look closely. What do you see in each figure? If you see the black field and white shapes as a porus black wall (figure–ground organization, again), there is an object behind the wall that is identical in both figures. People take a half-second or more to identify the object in Figure 4.18B—they never see it in Figure 4.18A. We are able to perceive the flashlight in Figure 4.18B only because the major features of this object—the geometric forms that make up the object and thereby determine its shape—can be extracted and interpreted correctly.

What happens when we cannot interpret the features we have extracted from a stimulus? People with certain types of brain damage suffer from this perceptual problem. It is called **visual agnosia.** (Agnosia means "loss of knowledge.") As we will see in the next section, these people can see objects in terms of their parts, but they have trouble integrating the parts into coherent whole objects.

FIGURE 4.17 Sample cylinder figures.   This illustration shows that cylinders of different sizes can be used to construct recognizable figures. Research suggests that a variety of simple geometric forms, such as cylinders, blocks, and wedges, could function as visual features. These features would serve as the basis for pattern recognition that enables us to identify familiar objects.

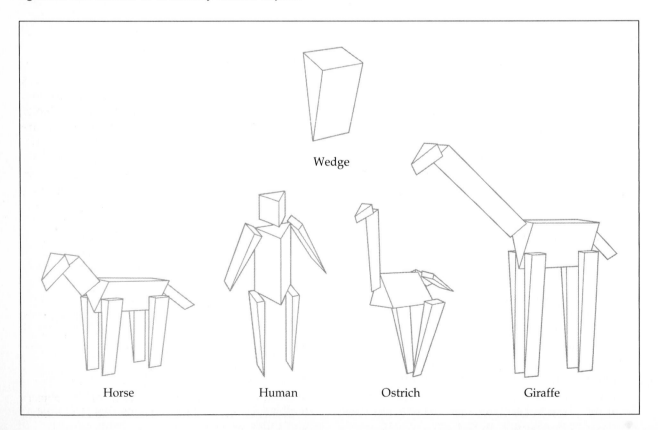

Wedge

Horse   Human   Ostrich   Giraffe

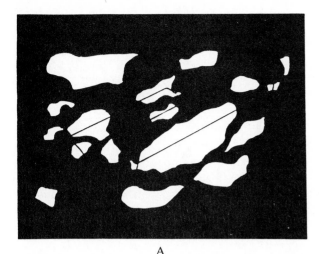

A

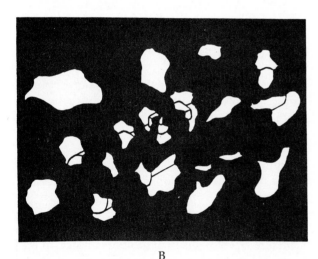

B

FIGURE 4.18 Hidden objects. Look at each of these figures. Do you see a hidden object in each? Think of each figure as a black wall with holes in it. Through the holes in the wall, you can see the outline of an object. If you are shown only A, you will almost never identify the object. If you are shown B, you will eventually see the *flashlight.* The object is the same in each figure, but B shows areas of change in the object's outline that allow us to determine its overall shape. These illustrations provide information about feature extraction and feature interpretation processes.

DYSFUNCTION:
Visual Agnosia

J. R. was a 73-year-old retired assembly worker and amateur theater director. As part of his theater work, J. R. made sketches and posters. Following a stroke (a ruptured blood vessel in the brain) that resulted in reduced blood flow to his left temporal and left occipital lobes, J. R. showed difficulty in recognizing common objects. When he was shown pictures of familiar objects, he was unable to identify most of them. He even had trouble with such highly familiar objects as a comb or a fork. When confronted with a drawing of two giraffes, J. R. resorted to reasoning to try to deduce what he could not readily perceive:

> The way this comes down, this could be an animal, four legs and a tail . . . a long neck comes up, an awfully long neck . . . here's a head because here's an eye . . . two crude drawings of some kinds of animals . . . not a mouse God knows . . . what would have such an extraordinary long neck? . . . a giraffe.
>
> *(Wapner, Judd, and Gardner, 1978)*

In addition to his difficulty in naming objects, J. R. was unable to recognize his son, his brother, or familiar hospital staff. Since J. R. was an amateur artist, his drawings were of special interest. Figure 4.19 shows examples of his attempts to draw a telephone from memory. If he was asked to copy a drawing of a telephone, J. R. could do a reasonably good job, but he could not identify what he had drawn.

Actually, there are a number of different types of visual agnosia. In **visual object agnosia,** a person may be unable to name a familiar object (for example, a comb), to show how it is used, or to recall ever having seen it before. This disorder can follow damage to the temporal and occipital lobes of the brain (Farah, 1990; Kolb and Whishaw, 1990). In **color agnosia,** a person may be unable to distinguish different colors or name colors that are associated with particular objects (such as lemons). Anatomical research on color agnosia has not determined the specific locus of these problems. In **prosopagnosia** or *agnosia for faces,* a person can lose the ability to recognize familiar faces. For example, J. R. had this problem along with visual object agnosia. In some rare instances, individuals with prosopagnosia are unable to recognize their own face in a mirror (Hecaen and Albert, 1978). Studies of prosopagnosia typically find damage in both the left and right temporal lobes (Damasio, 1985; Farah, 1990). At present, the term "visual agnosia" is used as a generic name for a variety of perceptual disorders (Wapner et al., 1978).

In many respects, patients who are diagnosed as visual agnosic have difficulty in forming a three-dimensional mental representation of the objects that they see in the world (Ratcliff and Newcombe,

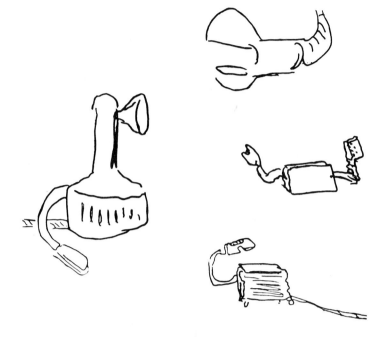

FIGURE 4.19 Drawings from an amateur artist after a stroke. Damage to the patient's left temporal and left occipital lobes resulted in visual agnosia: The patient experienced considerable difficulty in recognizing familiar, everyday objects. The drawings show various attempts by this artist to draw a telephone from memory.

1982). Like J. R. in his attempt to identify the giraffes, they demonstrate feature extraction in the absence of feature interpretation. ▪

Although features analysis provides a compelling way to think about pattern recognition, it remains an incomplete view. A complete picture is provided in the next section.

BOTTOM-UP AND TOP-DOWN PROCESSING

Have you ever had the experience of seeing someone in an unusual situation and being unable to "place" him or her in your memory? How quickly we recognize a stimulus depends upon where and when we have seen the stimulus before. To examine how this occurs, Irving Biederman (1972; 1981) conducted experiments in which he presented subjects with a picture of a common scene. This picture—perhaps of a kitchen or a city street—would be shown either as normal and coherent, or in a cut-up and rearranged form. (Figure 4.20). Although the objects in the jumbled pictures were always shown in their correct orientation, they lacked a coherent background. Biederman found that even if people knew where to look in advance, they were better at recognizing objects from coherent than from jumbled pictures. In other studies, Biederman left the background in its normal arrangement but moved an object out of its usual location. He found that objects out of context were

difficult to recognize after brief exposures. For example, people are better at identifying a fire hydrant if they see it on a sidewalk (its normal context) than if it is shown on top of a city mailbox (an unusual context).

Figure 4.21 shows some other examples in which pattern recognition is influenced by context. We interpret the middle stimulus in line A as the letter B because of its letter context. However, we see the identical physical stimulus as the number 13 in line B when it is in a number context. In lines C and D, we can perceive the ambiguously written word as either a verb or a noun depending on its surrounding sentence. In each of these examples, the context produces a **mental set** as to how the stimulus should be perceived. Appropriate sets prepare us for what is coming by suggesting possibilities that are consistent with the stimulus context, while inappropriate sets lead us astray (Seamon, 1976; 1978; Seamon and Wright, 1976).

When pattern recognition is determined solely by external stimulation, we say that the perceiver is *passive;* when the observer helps determine what is observed, we say that the perceiver is *active.* Feature analysis is a passive, bottom-up kind of visual processing because pattern recognition progresses inevitably from feature extraction to interpretation without guidance by the perceiver. The examples in Figure 4.20 indicate that there is also an active process in pattern recognition. The perceiver begins at the top choosing different hypotheses (best guesses) depending upon the context and upon the perceiver's set (what he or she

FIGURE 4.20 The importance of context.   Observers are faster at identifying the person in the normal, coherent picture than in the jumbled picture even though she is in the same position in both pictures and observers are told where to look in advance. Seeing objects in their normal context helps us to recognize them because the context enables us to formulate hypotheses (top-down processing) about what we are perceiving. These hypotheses, in turn, facilitate the interpretation of stimulus elements (bottom-up processing) so that pattern recognition can proceed quickly.

expects to see), and works down, checking them against the actual features of the stimulus. Thus, pattern recognition is more than a passive extraction of features from a stimulus. Low-level feature detectors involving the most elementary sensory processes analyze objects in the environment (from the "bottom"), while higher level mental processes involving reasoning and memory monitor the low level detectors (from the "top") to see which features are present. **Bottom-up** and **top-down processing** work together in an integrated manner. Looking back to the handwriting samples in Figure 4.14, we see that bottom-up processing

enables us to perceive the different lines as letters, while top-down processing using the sentence context helps us to make sense of some words that are difficult to interpret on their own. Both bottom-up and top-down processing are necessary to make sense of what we perceive. This is what the inventor in the section on form perception failed to realize. Before the robot could pick up a cup, it needed to know the defining features of such objects as tables and cups as well as the places where cups are likely to be found. Bottom-up and top-down processing can also be found in what you are doing right now—reading.

A **A B C**

B **12 13 14**

C *Jack and Jill event up the hill.*

D *The pole vault was the last event.*

FIGURE 4.21   Ambiguous stimuli are influenced by context.   How we see the underlined stimulus in each line is determined by the surrounding material. The stimulus in lines A and B can be seen as a letter or number depending on its context, while the stimulus in lines C and D can be seen as a verb or noun depending on its sentence surround. Context influences perception by suggesting reasonable interpretations.

RESEARCH AND APPLICATION:
The Psychology of Reading

How do we gather and organize information from the printed page? This question has intrigued psychologists for many years because skilled reading is the key to acquiring information in college and in life. Early research showed that reading involves a sequence of visual fixations (Buswell, 1922; Huey, 1908). When we read, we do not make smooth, continuous eye movements. Instead, we produce patterns of stop-and-go fixations, followed by eye movements to the next portion of the text. The majority of eye movements occur from left to right, but occasionally we look backward to words we have already seen. The eye movements between fixations are called **saccades** (from the French word for "jump"), and the backward saccades are called **regressions.** Each of these phenomena can be observed by placing a mirror next to a book and watching a reader's eyes through the mirror.

An Interactive Theory of Reading

Psychologists Patricia Carpenter and Marcel Just used fixations and saccades to learn about the process of reading. Using a computer screen to display text and a television camera to monitor the fixations and saccades, Carpenter and Just found that readers take in information at a rate that matches their comprehension. Since readers can control the rate at which they receive information, Carpenter and Just studied the self-imposed pauses to learn about the recognition and comprehension of text (Carpenter and Just, 1983; Just and Carpenter, 1980; 1987).

Consistent with earlier research, they found that when college students read text that is appropriate for their age, they fixate on almost every context word, they skip short function words such as *a, the,* or *that,* and they make saccades that are predominately left to right. For words that are fixated, students show a wide variation in the duration of each pause. Typically, fixations may last between 250 and 750 milliseconds, although some may be as brief as 50 milliseconds and others as long as a second or more. Readers fixate longer on unfamiliar words, or on words that are important to the theme, than they do on words that are familiar or less important to a passage. Carpenter and Just believe that this difference is meaningful, because fixation time is a reflection of the time needed to recognize and comprehend each word.

When the eyes move to their next fixation, new visual information masks that which came before. There is also a long fixation at the end of a sentence as readers integrate all of the information that they have read.

To understand how self-imposed pauses lead to recognition and comprehension, Carpenter and Just devised a theory to account for fixation duration. A schematic outline of the theory is shown in Figure 4.22. This theory is consistent with research on pattern recognition that describes word recognition and comprehension by the operation of bottom-up and top-down processing (Rumelhart, 1977; Treisman and Souther, 1986, among others). The theory outlined in Figure 4.22 specifies the sequence of steps involved in reading a sentence. First, our eyes fixate on a particular word so that our feature detectors can extract its physical features. We then match these features to a word representation in our *lexicon* (our mental dictionary of words in memory). The lexicon includes not only a representation of the word for pattern recognition but also the meaning of the word. After we have read each word, its meaning is held in a mental workspace (consciousness or "working" memory) to determine the meaning of a sentence. Finally, at the end of each sentence, we integrate the information into a complete idea. Since this integration takes time, our fixation at the end of a sentence tends to be relatively long, especially if the meaning of the sentence is not clear. After we have comprehended a sentence, our eyes move to the beginning of the next sentence and these processes begin again.

According to Carpenter and Just, a reader's knowledge of words influences how the physical features from the text are interpreted. Top-down processing can interact with bottom-up processing to suggest particular interpretations of the features. A recent connectionist model of reading from James McClelland and David Rumelhart (1981) indicates how this might be done. Their model is an extension of the connectionist models of letter recognition we described earlier in Figure 4.16. As shown in Figure 4.23, excitatory and inhibitory signals are produced by feature detectors, letter detectors, and word detectors. Excitatory connections end in arrows; inhibitory connections end in dots. Bottom-up processing is indicated by feature detectors exciting particular letter detectors. For example, the vertical line detector at the bottom of the figure excites the letter detector for T but inhibits those for the other letters. Top-down processing is shown by the word detectors exciting only those letter detectors that represent

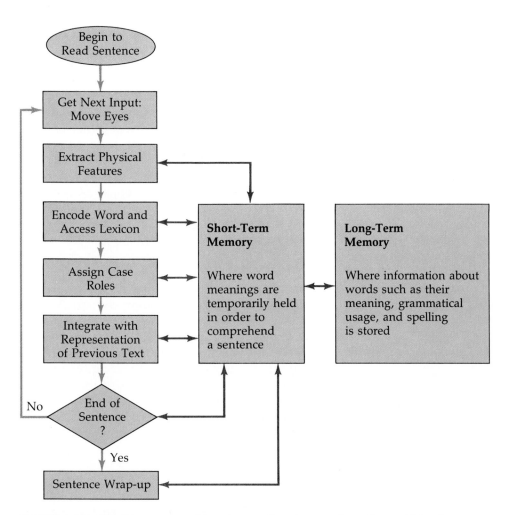

FIGURE 4.22 The Carpenter and Just interactive theory of reading. This schematic diagram represents the sequence of processes that these researchers believe are involved in reading. At each step, memory enters the sequence to make use of what the reader already knows.

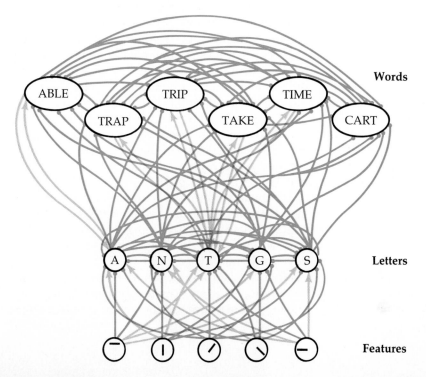

FIGURE 4.23 McClelland and Rumelhart's (1981) connectionist model for recognizing printed words. This model assumes bottom-up processing of information sent from the feature detectors to the letter and word detectors, and top-down processing that operates on the detectors in the opposite direction. The different detectors are connected by a neural-like network that transmits excitatory (arrow connectors) and inhibitory (dot connectors) signals.

letters contained in each particular word. Thus, if you were reading the sentence "The bride was worried that she would not get to her wedding on _____.", the detector for the word TIME would be excited by a sentence context (not shown in the figure). Combining the top-down information from the sentence already read with the bottom-up information obtained from the visual analysis of the word currently being read can make reading easier, especially if the words are unfamiliar. However, highly skilled adult readers (like you) normally only need to use bottom-up processing to identity the words in a text. After years of practice, bottom-up processing works so quickly and effortlessly that these skilled readers have no need for the slower top-down processing. Top-down processing is normally seen in poor readers who use the sentence context to try to figure out the words that they fail to recognize (Rayner and Pollatsek, 1989).

How much of a word we actually process while we read is still an unanswered question. Some psychologists believe that we only need to process the context, an initial letter, and a few global fixtures from a word in order to identify it correctly (Haber and Haber, 1981). Others believe that this type of limited information processing is often insufficient for word identification (McConkie, 1983; Rayner, 1983). Under many circumstances, we need to process each word more completely. Context may not allow us to skip over important words so much as it permits us to process those words more rapidly. For example, an experiment by Miriam Schustack and her colleagues (1987) has shown that word identification time is reduced when a word to be read (for example, *floor*) is preceded in a sentence by a semantic associate (sweep the *floor*) as opposed to an unrelated word (clean the *floor*).

Returning to the Just and Carpenter model, the various processes shown in Figure 4.22 have been spelled out clearly enough to allow us to test some assumptions of the theory. For example, one assumption is that readers fixate longer when there is greater cognitive demand placed on them. Hence, readers should fixate longer when they need to recognize and comprehend unfamiliar words, piece together important information from sentence clauses, and make their own inferences at the ends of sentences. In line with these assumptions, Carpenter and Just were able to predict different fixation durations accurately for individual words in a passage of text. In fact, the fixation durations predicted by the interactive theory of reading closely matched those actually observed, thereby supporting its assumptions.

Carpenter and Just noted that reading varies according to who is reading, what she is reading, and why she is reading. Readers use different patterns of reading if the text is especially difficult or if they are poorly educated. Under either of these conditions, readers make more fixations per line and longer fixations per word (Rayner, 1986). Conversely, if the text is especially easy, readers can decrease their number and length of fixations. Skimming a passage for its gist is an example of how readers can alter their eye movements to meet their current needs.

Enhancement of Reading Skill

Some reading instructors have tried to use the fixation data to enhance reading performance. Using data from studies of eye movements, some reading courses promise increases in reading speed without significant losses in comprehension. These courses in speed reading typically attempt to train readers to increase their reading speed by making fewer fixations per line. Readers are instructed to try to read several words or entire phrases each time that they gaze at a line. Some courses even attempt to teach readers to fixate only once in the center of each line, a practice that even skilled readers cannot do without considerable loss of comprehension. These programs do not enhance reading skill because they are based on the faulty assumption that the only difference between fast and slow readers is that fast readers make fewer fixations per line. Carpenter and Just found that college students could reduce their number of fixations only when they read simple children's stories or when they skimmed a passage for its gist. Other investigators have examined speed reading courses under carefully controlled conditions and found no support for the claims of increased speed without major comprehension loss (Carver, 1987; Homa, 1983). It seems that tests of comprehension used by some courses have been so poorly designed that knowledgeable people can score highly without even reading the material in the first place.

Do speed reading programs have any value? In fact, they do. They can be beneficial for teaching effective methods of skimming. For much of what we read every day, we may only need to skim for key words and ideas. Even when a more careful reading is called for, skimming the material in advance affords us an overview of what is to come. Having a general context for what is coming makes it easier for us to understand the material and helps us remember it (Reder and Anderson, 1980). We read more effectively when we know how the material is organized because we know what to expect. In this way, skimming facilitates top-down processing.

For children, the most effective way to enhance reading is to read as often as possible. Reading increases the size of a child's mental lexicon, and this increased working vocabulary makes subsequent reading easier because it helps a child to recognize and to understand words. Reading also increases the familiarity of the words a child already knows. Such words can then be processed faster. So the more you read, the more you know, and the easier it is to read (and learn) more. Despite the claims of speed reading courses, readers are not effective because of the way they move their eyes but because they move their eyes on the basis of what they know. ▪

In our discussion of pattern recognition, we described those processes that make the end result of our perceptual analysis available to conscious awareness. These perceptual processes enable us to become aware of what we are looking at and take appropriate action. For example, if we walk away from a growling dog, our behavior is most likely the result of our perception of danger. However, psychologists have also wondered if our behavior can be influenced by stimulus events that we do not consciously perceive. In other words, can we be influenced by sensory information without being aware of that information? This is the question of **subliminal perception**—the perception of objects or events below our threshold of awareness.

SUBLIMINAL PERCEPTION

During the 1950s, a New York advertising firm conducted a study in a movie theater in which they flashed messages to buy soft drinks or popcorn on the screen during the movie. The messages were reported to have led to a 56 percent increase in the sale of soft drinks and an 18 percent increase in the sale of popcorn (Britt, 1958). News of this study raised a storm of controversy and aroused widespread fears of subliminal exploitation. This study seemed to show that stimuli presented too briefly to be consciously perceived could somehow be registered in the viewer's unconscious and have an impact on that person's behavior.

Since the 1950s, people have expressed concern over subliminal perception in magazine advertisements (which were thought to contain subliminal sexual messages) and certain rock recordings (which were believed to contain "Satanic messages" recorded backward). Even today, audio tapes with subliminal messages recorded on them are promoted by entrepreneurs as cures for weight control, smoking, and poor memory. Their claims are completely unsubstantiated by careful research. Psychologists who have studied subliminal perception have reported mixed results (Dixon, 1981). Studies have failed to replicate the findings from the movie theater study, but researchers have reported subtle effects under carefully controlled laboratory conditions. Effects of subliminal perception have been observed in studies of semantic priming and in research on affective preferences.

UNCONSCIOUS SEMANTIC PRIMING

British psychologist Anthony Marcel (1983) used a procedure called *semantic priming* to study subliminal perception. Semantic priming refers to the influence of one word on the perception of the next word. In our earlier discussion of reading, we saw that the word *floor* was processed faster when it was preceded by a semantic associate (sweep the *floor*) than by an unrelated word (clean the *floor*). This is an example of semantic priming. Marcel wanted to see whether he could obtain semantic priming when the preceding stimulus was presented too briefly to be consciously perceived.

To find out, he presented subjects with two items back to back on a screen. The subjects' task was to decide whether the second item was a word (for example, INFANT) or a nonword (GLAYER). If it was a word, the subjects said yes; if not, they said no. On some trials, the two stimuli were presented above threshold. As shown in Figure 4.24, Marcel found that when the first stimulus was related to the second, semantic priming occurred; the subjects were faster at saying that INFANT was a word if it had been preceded by a related word (CHILD) than an unrelated word (STREET). However, the interesting case was when the first stimulus was presented subliminally. Marcel found that semantic priming occurred once again. Apparently the first stimulus registered unconsciously because it speeded up the processing of the second stimulus when it was semantically related.

UNCONSCIOUS AFFECTIVE PREFERENCES

Even our liking for a particular stimulus can be influenced by subliminal processing. For example,

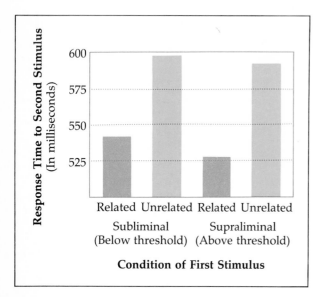

FIGURE 4.24 Semantic priming by subliminal perception. In this experiment, subjects were presented with two items in sequence and asked to decide whether the second item was a word. In one condition, both items were presented supraliminally (above threshold). Subjects showed evidence of semantic priming by making faster decisions about the second item when it was preceded by a semantically related word (for example, CHILD–INFANT) than an unrelated word (STREET–INFANT). Essentially the same results were obtained when the first stimulus was presented subliminally (below threshold). These findings provide evidence for subliminal perception by showing that semantic priming can occur even when the first stimulus is registered unconsciously.

in one experiment subjects were presented with a series of irregular geometric shapes, shown one at a time, each for only one millisecond. At this extremely brief duration, the subjects said that they saw only flashes of light. After viewing the sequence five times, the subjects were given a recognition test consisting of the stimuli they had repeatedly seen and new but comparable stimuli. The results showed that the subjects could not tell which stimuli they had seen before. However, when they were asked to select the stimuli they liked, the subjects tended to select the previously shown stimuli. In other words, the subjects liked the stimuli they had previously seen, even though they were unable to recognize them (Kunst-Wilson and Zajonc, 1980; Zajonc, 1980). Later research by the first author of this text and his colleagues (Seamon, Brody, and Kauff, 1983; Seamon, Marsh, and Brody, 1984) has shown that this finding is reliable. Still other researchers have found that the subliminal exposure to a stranger's face can influence our judgment about that person when we

later meet him or her in a social situation. We tend to like people we have seen even if we do not remember having seen them before (Bornstein, Leone, and Galley, 1987).

In summary, the accumulated evidence strongly suggests that perceptual processing to the point of recognizing patterns can occur outside of conscious awareness. Does this mean that advertisers might subliminally influence our behavior after all? Most psychologists remain doubtful. In tightly controlled laboratory studies, the viewers focus on a screen and give the task their undivided attention. In the real world, numerous above-threshold stimuli compete for our attention all the time. Whether we are watching a movie, looking at a magazine, or listening to music, our attention is captured by highly salient, above-threshold stimuli—the sights and sounds all around us. Weak sensory stimuli are just not likely to be noticed under these "noisy" real world conditions. Consequently, most psychologists believe that presenting stimuli subliminally merely makes them less noticeable.

PERCEIVING DEPTH, SIZE, AND MOVEMENT

Imagine that you perceive a black locomotive. Is this all you need to know in order to take appropriate action? The answer is clearly no. You need to know whether the locomotive is near or far, whether it is big or small (real or a toy?), and whether it is moving toward you. In order to act on your perception of form you must supplement that information with additional information about its perceived depth (distance), size, and movement. All of the forms we perceive exist in space and we attempt to specify their location by perceiving them at a certain distance, as having a particular size, and as moving or stationary. But remember from our introduction that each of these perceptual qualities represents a puzzle for perceivers to solve. Retinal images alone provide insufficient data for us to determine what is "out there in space." The following examples illustrate the nature of this perceptual puzzle:

A small retinal image can be caused by

1. a small object nearby

2. a large object in the distance.

A moving retinal image can be caused by

1. a stationary observer looking at a moving object

2. a moving observer looking at a stationary object

3. a moving observer looking at a moving object.

Despite these ambiguities, it is usually easy to tell whether an object is near or far, big or small, moving or still. The perceiver is almost never puzzled by what he or she is perceiving. In this section we will examine depth, size, and movement, and see how different types of visual information normally allow us to perceive these qualities accurately and effortlessly.

DEPTH INFORMATION AND PERCEPTUAL INVARIANTS

Depth perception enables us to see a three-dimensional world from flat, two-dimensional retinal images. Like other types of visual stimulation, information from the three-dimensional environ-

ment is received on the flat surface of the retina and sent to the brain in the form of neural impulses. The fact that retinal stimulation is two-dimensional is not really important for the brain because the brain "sees" only neural impulses, and those neural impulses include information that it can decode to determine depth. Some cues about depth can be found in monocular vision (looking with one eye), but others require binocular vision (looking with two eyes).

MONOCULAR DEPTH CUES

Even with one eye closed, your open eye can take in a great deal of information about depth. As you can see in Figure 4.25, **interposition** or *overlap* is

FIGURE 4.25 Monocular depth cues. These various cues allow us to perceive depth in the objects in our environment. Since each cue is available to monocular vision (that is, each provides depth information from a single perspective), artists have used these cues to portray depth in two-dimensional surfaces. The monocular cue of movement parallax is not shown; it provides information on depth by the relative movement of objects.

Interposition

A

Atmospheric Perspective

B

Linear Perspective

C

Relative Size

D

one simple cue for relative depth. Closer objects block the view of the more distant objects behind them. Another cue is **linear perspective,** apparent in the convergence of lines in the distance. Although the parallel lines of railroad tracks never really change their separation, they seem to get closer together as they recede in the distance.

Another monocular depth cue is **atmospheric perspective.** Since the air contains elements such as dust, smoke, and smog, we see distant objects—the high mountains on the horizon—less clearly than those nearby. Objects seen at a distance also produce smaller retinal images than when they are nearby. All other things being equal, our use of **relative size** as a depth cue is such that objects such as buildings and trees appear farther away as their retinal image gets smaller. The **relative height** of objects in our field of view provides additional information about depth. For objects such as clouds that are above our visual horizon (the line where the sky seems to meet the earth), the higher the cloud, the closer we perceive it to be. For objects such as people that are below our visual horizon, the higher the person, the farther away he or she appears.

One monocular cue is not shown in Figure 4.25 because it requires movement. If you are riding in a car or train, nearby objects seem to move by quickly, while distant objects do not. This difference in the movement of an observer relative to stationary objects is called **movement parallax.** Because of movement parallax, telephone poles seem to fly by the window of a moving automobile, while the moon appears to go along for the ride.

With the exception of movement parallax, all the other monocular cues (interposition, linear and atmospheric perspective, and relative size and height) have been successfully used by artists to produce an illusion of depth in flat two-dimensional surfaces. Figure 4.26 shows how each of these cues has been used to create a profound illusion of depth in a medal that measures only 82 mm (roughly 3 inches) in diameter. If you look at the medal with one eye, peering through a paper tube to eliminate the surrounding material, you feel as if you can almost step into the building. A very different sense of depth is provided by the American folk art painting in Figure 4.27. Can you tell which depth cues were used by the artist and which were deliberately ignored?

BINOCULAR DISPARITY

Looking at the world with one eye gives us the same impression of depth as we would get from

FIGURE 4.26 A medal of the Vatican Basilica. Although only 82 millimeters in diameter, the impression of depth in this medal is strong because so many monocular depth cues are employed. Can you see how interposition, linear perspective, and relative size and height have been effectively used by the artist to render a three-dimensional impression?

looking at a program on television. Television provides an impression of depth, but something essential is missing. In the real world depth is perceived with two eyes. Since the eyes are slightly apart, each sees a slightly different view of the world. This difference, which is most pronounced for objects that are nearby, is called **binocular disparity,** and it is easily demonstrated by your holding this page close to your face and alternately blinking your eyes as you read. The words will appear to jump back and forth as you switch from one eye to the other. The slightly different views from both eyes, which normally get integrated into a single perception, allow us to see more of an object with two eyes than either eye could see by itself. This *stereoscopic* vision provides depth information by making three-dimensional objects stand out from their surroundings.

Photographers in the nineteenth century understood the importance of binocular disparity for depth perception and used it to build depth into their two-dimensional pictures. Using a special camera with two lenses that were set the same distance apart as are human eyes, they would shoot two photographs of the same scene. Using a device called a *stereoscope* (similar to the modern "Viewmaster" toy), the left and right pictures were shown separately to the left and right eyes. The result was a single perception of the scene with

FIGURE 4.27 *Marquet Square, Germantown* **by W. Britton.** In this example of American folk art, the artist used some monocular depth cues but not others to create a particular style. The artist used interposition and height but not linear and atmospheric perspective or relative size all the time. For example, note how some people get bigger as they recede in the distance, while the church is too small to be in the foreground. Hence, the sense of depth in this figure is less compelling than that in Figure 4.26.

remarkable depth. Similar effects have been used to produce modern 3-D movies. These examples show the importance of binocular disparity for enhancing the perception of depth provided by the ever-present monocular cues.

PERCEPTUAL INVARIANTS

James Gibson began his research on depth perception by studying pilots during World War II. He felt that monocular and binocular cues by themselves could not account for the depth perception pilots needed to judge runway distances as their planes descended for a landing. Gibson found that there was one aspect of a pilot's visual field—the center of the visual field—that did not change during the landing. While everything else seemed to rush toward the pilot, the invariant center of the visual field told the pilot where the plane would eventually touch down.

Invariant aspects of perception were important for Gibson because he believed that they provide us with all of the information that we need to make accurate perceptions. For example, we saw earlier in Figure 4.5 how depth information is conveyed by a texture gradient. While it is true that a texture gradient contains monocular depth cues such as perspective, relative size, and relative height, it also contains a property that the other cues lack.

Extending over a large area, a texture gradient provides accurate information about depth no matter where we are on the gradient. As we move over its surface, the contours of the texture will change, but the gradient itself will remain constant— elements will always appear more densely spaced as their distance from us increases (Figure 4.5). The apparent change in object density for objects at different distances is characteristic of all texture gradients and is an example of a **perceptual invariant** (Gibson, 1966; 1979). (Note that a perceptual invariant is not the same as a **perceptual constancy,** which will be discussed below.) An invariant (for example, a texture gradient) is an unchanging and unalterable relation between a perceiver and the surrounding environment; constancy, represented by a book that is perceived to be rectangular even when viewed from one end (a shape constancy), is the tendency to perceive environmental features in the same way regardless of changes in the retinal stimulation.

At present it is very difficult to determine which type of information is most important for normal depth perception. Just because a particular type of information is available does not guarantee that people actually use it to perceive (Cutting, 1986; Goldstein, 1981). We may use some or all of the information, depending upon the stimulus situation. Obviously, the more information about depth that is available, the more accurate the depth perception can be.

SIZE CONSTANCY AND ILLUSIONS

Because we move about, our eyes receive a constantly changing view of the world. For instance, as we approach a building our retinal image becomes progressively larger. However, we do not perceive the building as growing bigger as our retinal image suggests; we perceive it as increasingly near. Our perception of size is unchanging because perceived size, like perceived shape, is a perceptual constancy.

SIZE CONSTANCY

Size constancy is defined as the relatively constant perception of an object's size when it is viewed from different distances. A friend who is 5'6" tall will appear to be the same height whether she is standing directly in front of you or 20 feet away. Since her size and her distance from you both contribute to the size of your retinal image (Figure 4.28), you cannot determine her size solely from the size of the retinal image; you need information about her distance as well.

Normally, when we make judgments about size we take an object's distance into account. For example, if we see a tiny car, we use the depth information available in the scene to determine that we are seeing a car that is far away. Cars and other objects have a *familiar size* that is based on our past experience. Psychologist William Ittelson (1951) performed a now-classic experiment to see how our perception of objects is influenced by familiar size. He presented observers with a series of playing cards, each shown from the same distance. Some were normal in size, some were half the normal size, and still others were double the normal size. Each card was illuminated individually in an otherwise darkened room to eliminate distance information. Ittelson found that the observers misperceived the cards. Instead of seeing them as different-sized cards at the same distance, they were seen as normal-sized cards at different distances. The observers were fooled in this task because their perceptual systems were denied the information usually available to them, and they were forced to use unreliable information. In the real world, inanimate objects do not change their physical size. When there is a change in the size of our retinal image, it must be because our distance from the object has changed.

ILLUSIONS OF SIZE

Since size constancy is strongly influenced by depth, inaccurate interpretations of distance can lead us to misperceive size. Just as we may misperceive different-sized objects as the same (for example, Ittelson's playing cards), so may we misperceive same-sized objects as different if we are fooled by misleading distance information. Figure 4.29 shows two people sitting in an *Ames room*, a specially built room that provides misleading depth information (Ittleson, 1952). While the person on the right appears abnormally tall and the person on the left looks unusually small, both are actually the same height. The schematic drawing of the room shows its general dimensions and true shape. When viewers look through a peephole, they assume that the room is normal and that both people are an equal distance away. Therefore, the difference in the retinal size of each figure is perceived as a difference in object size. Instead of seeing the room as badly distorted, the misleading depth information causes us to see the people as varying greatly in height. Incidentally, knowing that the room is distorted does not eliminate the effect; the people still appear to be different sizes even though we know that they are really the same size.

Depth perception also contributes to another common size illusion—the *moon illusion*. As shown

FIGURE 4.28 Size as a cue to distance. As the house moves farther away, the size of its image on the retina becomes increasingly smaller. But we see its size as constant because we use depth cues to determine that its distance from us, rather than its size, is changing.

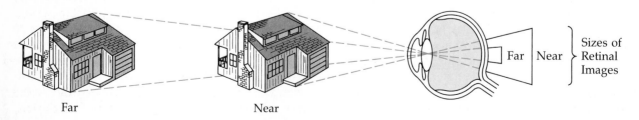

Far   Near   Far | Near } Sizes of Retinal Images

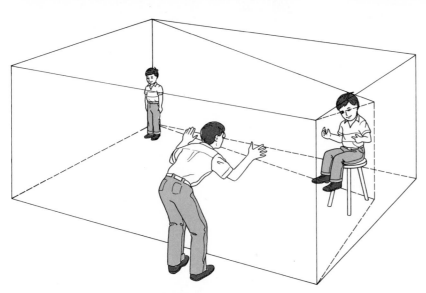

FIGURE 4.29 The Ames room. Because normal depth cues have been distorted, the people appear to vary greatly in size even though they are actually all the same height. Misleading depth information (see the schematic drawing) leads to incorrect interpretations about the size. Even knowing the source of the illusion does not eliminate the effect.

by Figure 4.30, the moon appears to be larger when it is on the horizon than when it is high in the nighttime sky. One theory is that the moon illusion is caused by a difference in the perceived distance between the moon and the observer at different points in the sky. Research has shown that observers imagine the sky overhead to be subjectively closer than the equally distant sky at the horizon (Figure 4.30). If it is assumed that the moon is perceived on the "surface" of the sky, the horizon moon will appear farther away than the zenith moon because of this perceived difference in distance. Since both moons have the same retinal size (it is, after all, the same moon), the perceived difference in distance is unconsciously interpreted as a difference in size (Kaufman and Rock, 1962). Consistent with this apparent dis-

tance theory, while the horizon moon appears 1.3 times as large as the zenith moon, blocking the horizon by viewing the moon through a tube eliminates the moon illusion.

Erroneous judgments about distance may also explain some other size illusions. Why does the left line in Figure 4.31A appear shorter than the right one when they are really the same length? One possibility is that this *Muller-Lyer illusion* occurs because we unconsciously interpret the fins on the left line as the outside corner of a building, and those on the right line as the inside corner of a room (Gregory, 1978) (Figure 4.31B) Since inside corners appear farther away than outside corners, the apparent difference in distance causes us to interpret the size of each line differently. If the right line is perceived as more distant than the left,

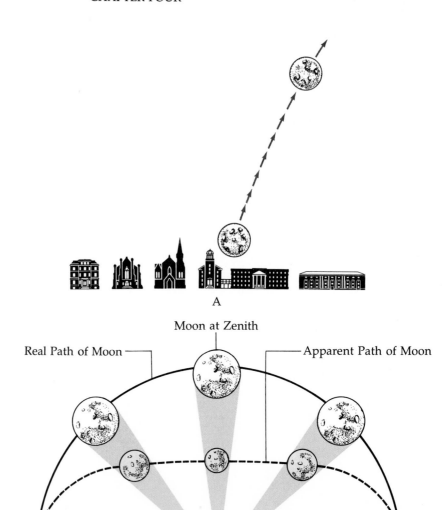

FIGURE 4.30 The moon illusion.   In A, the moon over the horizon appears larger than it does when it is high in the nighttime sky. (To get the effect, cover first one moon, then the other.) This illusion occurs because we perceive the "surface" of the sky overhead to be closer to us than the sky at the edge of the horizon. The horizon moon in B appears larger than the zenith moon because we perceive it to be farther away.

it must be longer in size. Essentially this same interpretation can be given to the *Ponzo illusion* (Figure 4.32). Here the depth cue of linear perspective causes the top horizontal bar to appear longer than the bottom bar even though both have the same retinal size. Once more, we appear to take the "distance" of an object into account to interpret the object's retinal image.

Understanding the conditions that give rise to illusions and misperceptions can have important and far-reaching effects. For instance, erroneous judgments of distance resulted in four airline

crashes in 1966. In each instance, a commercial airliner crashed on a clear night with the airport runway in sight. Psychologist Conrad Kraft (1978) investigated these accidents and found that, although each occurred in a different city, they all shared important factors. First, each plane approached the runway by flying over dark water. Second, each runway had a background of upward-sloping city lights. Finally, each plane crashed short of its runway.

Kraft believed that these crashes occurred because the pilots flew by sight instead of relying on

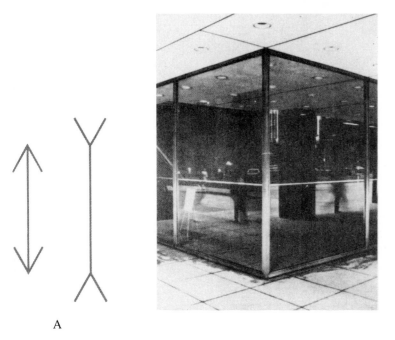

A   B

FIGURE 4.31   The Muller-Lyer illusion.   Although both lines in A are the same length, the line with the fins pointed outward appears to be longer. One possible explanation is that we unconsciously relate the lines and fins to real-life perceptual objects. If the right figure in B is perceived as being more distant than the left, even though it is equal in retinal size, it must be physically larger. The result is a size illusion based on a faulty perceptual interpretation.

FIGURE 4.32   The Ponzo illusion.   The upper horizontal line in A appears longer than the lower line. Even though both are physically the same, the upper one is perceived as being farther away. Depth and size information are combined to produce these perceptual illusions. In B, the two monsters are identical in size. Because the upper monster is perceived as being farther away, it is also perceived as being larger than the monster "in front."

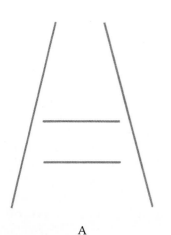

A

their instruments for accurate information. The combination of the lack of altitude information from the dark water and the upward-sloping city lights in the distance may have caused the pilots to believe that they were flying higher than they actually were. In reducing their altitude for landing, the pilots brought their planes too low and crashed. To test this explanation, Kraft reproduced the flight conditions on an aircraft simulator and found that 11 of 12 flight instructors made errors that would have resulted in crashes. Kraft's research shows that when normal information about the terrain is unavailable, pilots may unknowingly use unreliable information in its place, resulting in dangerous conditions. As a result of this research, pilots are now instructed to make extensive use of their instruments at night, even when flying in clear weather.

REAL AND APPARENT MOVEMENT

As we noted earlier in the chapter on sensation, our eyes are almost always in motion. Therefore, our ability to perceive movement accurately must depend on more than just a changing pattern of stimulation provided by a moving image on our retina. To understand movement perception, we will examine how people detect real movement and also how people can be fooled by illusions of apparent movement.

REAL MOVEMENT

Figure 4.33 shows three examples of real movement that we are able to perceive. In the first example, a woman is shown walking across our visual field as we stare at a point directly ahead. In real life, we perceive the person as walking from left to right because she covers and uncovers successive parts of the stationary background as she walks by our visual field. In this situation, the moving retinal image of the figure relative to the stationary background is sufficient to perceive movement accurately.

In the second example, the woman again walks from left to right, but now we do not simply stare at one point but watch her as she moves across the stationary background. The retinal image of the woman is now stationary, while the background shifts from right to left. Again, our perception of movement is based on the relative change of the figure in comparison to its surroundings. Since the retinal image of the woman is stationary while the background moves in the opposite direction of our eye movements (left-to-right saccades), it must be

that we are visually tracking a figure that is moving from left to right.

In the final example, we are moving from left to right past a stationary figure who is standing in front of a stationary background. In this situation our retinal image of the woman and background both move in the direction opposite our own movement at the same rate of speed. This informs us that we are moving from left to right, and that the figure and background are stationary. However, if the woman were walking more slowly from left to right than we were, she would move in our visual field from right to left at a slower rate than the background; if she was walking from right to left, then she would move across our visual field in the same direction as the background, but at a faster rate.

This is how the environment provides us with information for perceiving real movement accurately. In the case of a moving observer, this information is supplemented by kinesthetic information from body movements. This information works well for detecting movement against a visible background. There are also situations in which we can detect movement in objects that lack a visible background. For example, research has shown that observers can detect human figures that walk across a blank background and are seen only as points of light. When the lights are attached to prominent joints in otherwise invisible human figures, observers are able to determine whether the walkers are male or female, whether they are walking, jogging, or dancing, and whether a walker has a slight limp (Bertenthal, Proffitt, and Cutting, 1984). Observers can perceive the points of light accurately because of differences in the patterns of movement found in different activities and in male and female walkers (Cutting and Proffitt, 1981; 1982).

APPARENT MOVEMENT

Not all movement perception is based on moving stimulation. Sometimes we perceive movement when there is none. These illusions of movement are called **apparent movements.**

In **autokinetic movement** (autokinetic is defined as "self-moving") a stationary point of light is perceived as moving when it is viewed in a darkened room. One possible explanation for this illusion is that the brain is unable to detect all tiny, involuntary eye movements. Normally, such small movements are irrelevant, but in the absence of a frame of reference, minor shifts may lead to misperceptions. If a person moves her or his eyes

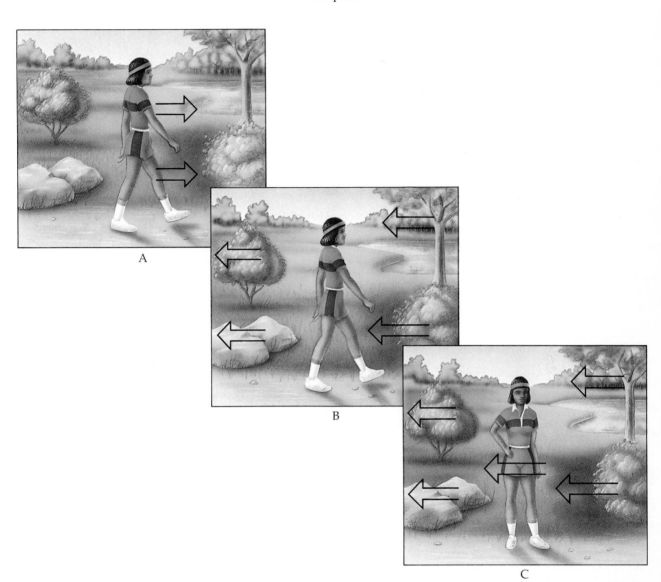

FIGURE 4.33 Examples of different types of real movement we are able to detect. In A, the person is walking across our field of vision. (We are stationary observers looking directly ahead at the park.) In B, the person walks by us and we watch the person walk by. In C, we walk past a stationary person while looking far off in the distance. In each instance, information about movement is available to us in the form of relative changes in the movement of the walker and the background.

while looking at the stationary point of light, the retinal image of the light will move. Because moving retinal images are normally associated with moving objects, the observer can misperceive the stimulation and perceive the light rather than his or her own eyes moving.

In **induced movement,** a small, stationary object is viewed against a larger, moving background. Because observers tend to assume that large objects are stationary, it is the smaller objects that appear to move. The illusion of a "racing moon" is

an example of induced movement (Duncker, 1938). If clouds are seen as stationary, then the moon may appear to race through them when the wind moves the clouds past the moon.

Finally, **stroboscopic movement** is an illusion of movement that results from the successive presentation of individual stimuli arranged in a sequence. The stationary lights in a theater marquee that appear to "run" around the marquee provide an example of this type of apparent movement. Stroboscopic movement also helps explain the perception of movement in motion pictures. When we watch a movie, we are really seeing a sequence of briefly displayed still pictures that change ever so slightly from one picture to the next. Early movies flickered (the derivation of the term "flicks") because only 16 pictures, or frames, were shown each second; current movies show 24 frames a second with 42 milliseconds between each frame. This rate of presentation is optimum for the illusion of stroboscopic movement.

Examples of apparent movement, especially illusions of stroboscopic movement, almost never occur naturally. They are produced by artificial means, including television and movies. Their usefulness for our understanding of movement is that they may reveal something about the underlying mechanisms that enable us to perceive accurately those events that are subject to change. This is important because perception is not static; it changes continually over time.

PERCEPTION AND EXPERIENCE

Through this point we have focused on how we perceive distal objects in space from the proximal stimulation reaching our senses. We have tried to show how we use sensory information in nonarbitrary ways to arrive at an accurate perception of the world. One important question we have still to consider is whether our use of this information is innate or learned. Is perception based on innate "wired in" mechanisms, or is it based on experience? This question has been a subject of philosophical debate at least since the time of Plato. The *nativists* have held that we are born with the ability to perceive accurately, while the *empiricists* have argued that we must learn to perceive accurately through experience. Today, psychologists believe that perception is best explained by the interaction of heredity and environment. Although it is usually difficult to separate these factors, some unusual situations have provided a glimpse of how nature and nurture interact.

PERCEPTION AND UNUSUAL EXPERIENCES

What would a blind adult see if she were suddenly provided with sight? What would a person's depth perception be like if he were raised in a densely foliated rain forest and then taken on a trip through wide open plains? Psychologists are interested in such unusual experiences because they may tell us how past experience influences perception.

RESTORED SIGHT IN THE BLIND

People have long wondered what the perceptual experience would be if a blind person were suddenly given sight. Would this person be able to perceive objects by sight that he or she formerly knew only by touch, or would the person require considerable visual experience in order to learn how to perceive visually? Case studies of a number of blind people who have had their vision surgically restored reveal that many of them see very little at first. Some failure to see normally after an operation such as a cornea transplant is hardly surprising. It takes time for a patient to recover from surgery. What is surprising is that it usually takes many months for these patients to learn to identify by sight objects that they could easily recognize by touch. Even after they have learned to see simple forms, visual perception is still a problem for many of these patients. Seemingly trivial alterations in the size or color of an object can disrupt their ability to make an identification. On the other hand, these patients seem to experience very little difficulty in learning to identify different colors. After colors are initially labeled for the patients, they can usually correctly identify them thereafter (von Senden, 1960).

Unfortunately, case studies of patients with restored sight actually reveal very little about the kinds of experiences that are necessary to perceive a stable, three-dimensional world. First, researchers do not know how long it takes to recover from such surgery. Second, it is often uncertain whether the surgery is completely successful in providing sight. Third, as you can see in Figure 4.34, blind adults have already learned much about the world through **haptic perception,** the perception of objects by touch (Kennedy, 1982; Millar, 1985). For each of these different reasons, the case studies of patients with restored vision actually have little bearing on the role of experience in perception.

DRAMATIC ENVIRONMENTAL CHANGE

Anthropological observations of people in different environments suggest that experience can have a dramatic influence on perception. For example, anthropologist Colin Turnbull recorded the experiences of a pygmy tribesman named Kenge who had spent all of his life in a densely foliated rain forest. Upon leaving the forest for a trip through the open plains, the tribesman's lack of depth perception over great distances resulted in some amusing misinterpretations.

Then he saw the buffalo, still grazing lazily several miles away, far down below. He

FIGURE 4.34 Images drawn by the blind. Blind people can learn about objects through self-observation and touch. Here, a blind person was asked to draw pictures of objects on a plastic sheet that makes raised impressions that can be felt. The drawings show that blind people portray depth in a visually perceptive way, even if they have been blind since birth. The drawings of crossed fingers and a person running show interposition of the fingers and differences in the relative size of the runner's legs.

turned to me and said, 'What insects are those?' At first I hardly understood, then I realized that in the forest the range of vision is so limited that there is no great need to make an automatic allowance for distance when judging size. . . .

When I told Kenge that the insects were buffalo, he roared with laughter and told me not to tell such stupid lies. Kenge still did not believe, but he strained his eyes to see more clearly and asked what kind of buffalo were so small. I told him they were sometimes nearly twice the size of a forest buffalo, and he shrugged his shoulders and said we would not be standing out there in the open if they were. . . .

The road led on down to within about half a mile of where the herd was grazing, and as we got closer the "insects" must have seemed to get bigger and bigger. Kenge, who was now sitting on the inside, kept his face glued to the window, which nothing would make him lower. I even had to raise mine to keep him happy. I was never able to discover just what he thought was happening—whether he thought that the insects were changing into buffalo, or that they were miniature buffalo growing rapidly as we approached. His only comment was that they were not real buffalo, and he was not going to get out of the car again until we left the park.

(Turnbull, 1962)

Turnbull's observations suggest that depth perception is based at least partly on a person's experience. In the next section, we will examine carefully controlled research that supplements these anecdotal observations.

PERCEPTION AFTER VISUAL DEPRIVATION

Psychologists have studied the role of experience in perception by controlling the type of visual stimulation an animal receives during its early development. For instance, single cell recordings taken from newborn kittens have shown the same types of feature detector cells that are found in adult cats (Hubel and Wiesel, 1963). This result suggests that the neural structure for perception is largely available at birth. However, the visual experience of the animal determines how well that structure will function.

DEPRIVATION AND NEURAL CHANGE

Just as impoverished rearing conditions can alter an animal's neural development (discussed in Chapter 2), so can deprivation of visual experience change the neural structures responsible for perception. For example, chimpanzees who were raised in darkness until the age of 16 months suffered neural deterioration. When they were finally exposed to a lighted environment, the chimps turned their heads in the direction of a light but otherwise acted as if they were blind (Riesen, 1947). In other studies, monkeys, chimpanzees, and kittens that were reared wearing translucent goggles, and consequently became accustomed to seeing the world through a cloudy, opaque film, could later perceive differences in color, brightness, and size, but could not follow moving objects or discriminate shapes (Riesen, 1965). Essentially the same conclusion can be drawn from research on humans. Infants who have had to wear a patch over one eye following an operation to correct a visual defect later show reduced visual acuity in the eye that had been covered (Awaya et al., 1973). These findings indicate that early visual experience is needed to maintain the neural structure for visual perception.

To see how this research is conducted, consider an experiment done by British psychologists Colin Blakemore and Grahame Cooper (1970). They reared kittens in the dark from birth to two weeks of age. At that time, they were each placed alone in a lighted chamber that had circular walls painted with vertical or horizontal stripes. The kittens stayed in the chamber for five hours a day; the rest of the time they spent in the dark. Other than the vertical or horizontal stripes, the chamber contained no visible corners or edges. Although the kittens were free to move about, they were fitted with neck ruffs that prevented them from turning their heads and changing the orientation of the stripes.

After five months of these conditions, the kittens' perception was tested. Blakemore and Cooper found that the kittens had trouble following moving objects, they showed faulty depth perception by trying to touch objects that were out of reach, and they frequently bumped into things. In one test, the researchers held a rod in front of two kittens, one that previously had been exposed to vertical stripes and the other to horizontal stripes. When the rod was held vertically and shaken, the kitten exposed to vertical stripes played with it; the other kitten showed no response. When the rod was held horizontally and shaken, the behavior of the kittens was reversed. Later, Blakemore and

Cooper observed recordings from cells in the visual cortex of their kittens. They found that early rearing conditions produced dramatic changes in neural firing. For kittens exposed only to vertical stripes, cells in the visual cortex responded only to vertical or near-vertical lines. Just the opposite was true for kittens exposed only to horizontal lines: cells in their visual cortex responded only to horizontal or near-horizontal stimuli.

Blakemore and Cooper's results indicate that the neural structures for perception require varied visual stimulation for normal perceptual development. Psychologists currently believe that when kittens are exposed to very limited forms of visual stimulation, only those cells that are stimulated by the environment continue to function effectively. Other cells in the visual cortex become unresponsive and may even degenerate (Movshon and Van Sluyters, 1981). Early perceptual experience thus has a marked effect on perceptual development. In other words, the neural structures provided by heredity can be modified by environmental experience. This shows that heredity and environment interact and that the perceptual system is capable of adjustment. This adjustability is clearly seen in experiments in which people wear special lenses to rearrange their perception of space.

REARRANGEMENT OF PERCEPTUAL SPACE

If we suddenly saw the world inverted and reversed, would we eventually adapt to this unusual experience and be able to function normally again? This is a question psychologists have asked since 1897, when George Stratton did his early research on the rearrangement of perceptual space. In studies of **optical rearrangement,** the normal relation between the distal stimulus and the retinal image is altered in some way. Stratton rearranged his retinal image by wearing a blindfold over one eye and, over the other eye, a lens that inverted and reversed what he saw. Thus, from Stratton's point of view, he appeared to reach "up" to pick up something off the floor and turn "left" when he wanted to go right. In one study he wore the lens for eight days. At first everything seemed abnormal. Everyday activities, such as eating or tying a pair of shoelaces, suddenly became difficult. Stratton reported that his image of his body became distorted and that at times he felt as though his head had sunk between his shoulders. In addition to this, the upside-down world seemed to slide around whenever he moved his head or eyes.

As time passed, Stratton adapted to the lens and was able to eat and dress more effectively. After several days he reported that his body image became more normal and things did not appear to move so much whenever he moved his head or eyes. Oddly, he occasionally found that the position of his hands felt reversed (that is, his left hand felt as if it were on the right, and his right hand felt as if it were on the left) and the world appeared rightside up. However, at other times he reported that while the world seemed rightside up, his body felt upside down. Stratton had some equally unusual experiences in other studies of optical rearrangement.

Later attempts to replicate Stratton's findings have met with varying degrees of success. For example, one study found that a person who wore this type of lens for 30 days adapted well enough to the optical rearrangement to be able to drive a car but when asked how things appeared still said that the world looked upside down (Snyder and Pronko, 1952). This means that the person's visual perception did not change as a result of wearing the lens. What changed was his sense of **proprioception** (the sense of bodily feedback). Research has shown that extended experience with optical rearrangement simply alters the felt position of various body parts (Harris, 1980; Rock and Harris, 1967). Our sense of proprioception, not our sense of vision, adapts to the new retinal images.

INTERACTIONS:
Constancy in Perception

As you finish reading this chapter, you now know that the perceptual and physical worlds are not the same. You know that perception involves much more than seeing your friends "because they are there." You even know something about the perceptual information that we use to organize and interpret our sensations. When you look around, you see objects with textures and surfaces. These stimulus qualities are picked up by your sensory receptors for perceptual processing by your brain. But early on we warned you about the difference between distal and proximal stimuli. The distal stimulus is the actual object or event that is "out there"; the proximal stimulus is the information that your sensory receptors receive. Your task as a perceiver is to learn about distal stimuli from the proximal stimuli received by your senses.

For example, think back to our discussion of size constancy. We said that a friend would appear to be the same size whether she were standing close by or walking a distance away. Our perception of her size is not determined solely by the size of the retinal image she projects. We supplement retinal size information with perceptual distance information from monocular and binocular cues to make an accurate judgment of size. In other words, we always take the context of proximal stimulation into account to arrive at an accurate perception of a distal stimulus. This is an example of a perceptual interaction—the interaction of a stimulus and its surround (Uttal, 1981).

Each of the other constancies can also be seen as perceptual interactions. In describing shape constancy we said that our perception of a desk top as a rectangular shape remains relatively constant even though our retinal image of it changes as we walk toward it. In this instance, we combine information about retinal shape with information about our orientation to perceive the desk surface accurately. Other constancies also show this relation. **Brightness constancy** refers to the fact that objects seem to stay the same brightness regardless of changes in illumination. For example, we describe a white car in moonlight as "light" and a piece of coal in broad daylight as "dark," even though both may reflect the same amount of light under these viewing conditions. In short, our perception of objects is much more constant than we might expect if we relied solely on information from proximal stimulation. To see why this is so, we will look at one type of constancy in greater detail.

Color constancy refers to the tendency to see objects as having the same color, even under very different conditions of illumination. Edwin Land, the inventor of the Polaroid camera, provided a vivid demonstration of color constancy during the 1950s. While studying color vision in his quest for an instant color camera, Land created patchworks made out of different colored papers. He called these patchworks "Mondrians" because they resembled the paintings of the famous Dutch artist. (See Figure 4.35.) In one condition, he measured the wavelengths reflected from an orange Mondrian patch under normal white light. Then, with three projectors equipped with different colored filters (one red, one green, and one blue), he adjusted the light striking a green patch until its wavelength composition was the same as that produced by the orange. If, said Land, we respond to the color patches in terms of the wavelengths reflected, the green patch should now appear orange. It did not. The colors in the Mondrian patchwork remained remarkably consistent de-

FIGURE 4.35 A Mondrian-like color patchwork created by Edwin Land to demonstrate color constancy. Look at this patchwork under a fluorescent light and then under a tungsten light. Even when different light intensities are projected onto the patchwork surface by the bulbs, the colors remain remarkably constant. The color that we see in any one patch depends on the light coming from both that patch and all the other patches in the visual array.

spite changes in lighting conditions. This illustrates color constancy.

How does color constancy work? Consider the following example. Imagine three berries—one green, one pink, and one ripe red—hanging against a cluster of dark green leaves. As the sun passes from bright daylight to rosy twilight, everything in the scene will come to reflect more long wavelength reddish light. However, the ripe berry will still look redder than the pink berry, and the pink berry will still look redder than the green berry and green leaves. The critical factor is that the ratio of the intensity of the red light coming from each berry to the red light intensity of the surround (the leaves and other parts of the scene) remains nearly constant despite the changes in illumination (Montgomery, 1988). This is what Land discovered in his color patchwork demonstration. The color that we see in one part of our visual field depends on the light coming from that place and on the light coming from all other places in our visual field (Hubel, 1988). We now know that special cell groups in the visual cortex perform this type of analysis to make color constancy possible (Livingstone and Hubel, 1984). The significance of color constancy is that it enables animals to eat ripe fruits and berries regardless of the lighting conditions. If there is sufficient light to see color, ripe berries will always look red. This, too, is a perceptual interaction of a stimulus and its surround.

In considering the different constancies, there is a lesson to be learned about perception. Nearly two hundred years ago, Bishop Berkeley (1709) said that the ability to foresee "damage or benefit" was essential to an animal's survival. By that he meant that all animals must perceive dangers and comforts in order to respond appropriately. More recently, James Gibson (1966) saw the task of perception as the process by which we obtain useful information from the environment. In other words, the purpose of perception is to learn about the external environment in order to take appropriate action. However, we are hampered in learning about distal objects because the proximal stimuli change. Each time we move about in the world, each time the viewing conditions change, the pattern of proximal stimulation is altered. The great value of the perceptual constancies is that they take these changes into account. In effect, the constancies provide us with a complex set of "corrections" (Coren and Ward, 1989). Without these constancy corrections, objects would change their shape, size, brightness, and color. There would be nothing permanent to learn from experience. With the perceptual constancies, we can make sense out of sensory stimulation and perceive a stable world. As we reported in Chapter 3, we are prisoners who must rely on information smuggled into us by our senses. Because of the perceptual constancies, we can have faith in this information. ■

IN CONTEXT: PERCEPTION

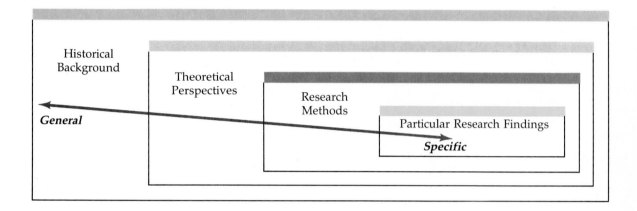

STUDY QUESTIONS

Why do psychologists consider perception a problem to be solved?

How do we perceive form?

How do we see a three-dimensional world from flat two-dimensional images?

What information enables us to perceive depth, size, and movement accurately?

What role does experience play in perception?

HISTORICAL BACKGROUND

1. The empiricist philosophers of the seventeenth and eighteenth centuries held that all knowledge is obtained from the senses. George Berkeley believed that perception involves interpreting sensory information on the basis of knowledge from earlier experience.

2. In the nineteenth century, Hermann von Helmholtz described the process of interpreting sensations as unconscious inference.

3. In the twentieth century, James Gibson held that unconscious inference was unnecessary. According to Gibson, information for accurate perception is present in the environment and directly available to our senses.

MODERN THEORETICAL PERSPECTIVES

1. The Helmholtzian and Gibsonian views of perception are still the major theoretical perspectives. The **Helmholtzian** approach de-scribes perception as a process of making unconscious inferences about sensory information on the basis of past experience. The **Gibsonian** approach holds that information that we need for perception is present in the stimuli around us and directly available to our senses. It is likely that each position can account for different perceptual abilities.

2. **Nativists** held that we are born with the ability to perceive; **empiricists** argue that we must learn to perceive through experience. Most psychologists favor an intermediate position that accounts for perception in terms of the interaction of heredity and environment.

3. More limited perceptual theories include attempts to describe pattern recognition by **feature analysis** and **bottom-up** and **top-down processing.** A variety of explanations have been offered to account for the different perceptual illusions.

■■■■■■ RESEARCH METHODS

1. **Experimentation** is widely used in studies of perception. It was used to study such varied phenomena as the role of context in identifying familiar objects (Biederman, 1981); the effects of early visual deprivation on the perceptual development of kittens (Blakemore and Cooper, 1970); and the subliminal perception of words, geometric shapes, and faces (Marcel, 1983, among others).

2. Case studies are also frequently employed. Cases such as J. R.'s show what perception is like for a person with visual agnosia (Wapner et al., 1978). Other cases, including those of the pigmy tribesman Kenge and the blind who have had their sight restored, provide clues about the role of experience in perception (Turnbull, 1962; von Senden, 1960).

3. Perceptual data are also obtained by recording the observations of people as they look at various stimuli. Illusions are studied this way (Kanizsa, 1976; Kaufman and Rock, 1962).

■■■■■ RESEARCH FINDINGS AND SUMMARY

1. **Perception** involves the organization and interpretation of sensory messages into a meaningful experience. The problem for psychology is to explain how **distal** stimulus objects can be perceived accurately from **proximal** sensory stimulation.

2. The perception of **form** begins when diverse stimulus elements are pieced together into an organized whole. The **laws of organization** were specified by the **Gestalt** psychologists and they include **proximity, similarity, good continuation, closure,** and **common fate.**

3. **Shape constancy** allows us to perceive relatively constant forms even when our retinal images vary greatly.

4. **Illusions** are perceptual experiences that do not conform to physical reality. Illusions of form, such as those involving **subjective contours** and **impossible figures,** show how stimulus elements are normally integrated into a complex figure.

5. **Pattern recognition** involves the meaningful interpretation of form on the basis of a person's past experience.

6. Pattern recognition by **feature analysis** consists of **feature extraction** and **interpretation processes.** Feature extraction involves specifying the features that make up a particular stimulus; feature interpretation consists of matching those features to feature sets that define different stimuli.

7. The perception of objects or events below the threshold of awareness is called **subliminal perception.** Psychologists have found evidence for subliminal perception in studies involving semantic priming and affective preferences. The belief that subliminal perception can be used to influence everyday behavior remains unsubstantiated.

8. Pattern recognition is best described by two different types of processing: **bottom-up processing,** which analyzes low level features; and **top-down processing,** which monitors feature detectors to determine which features are present.

9. Information about depth is necessary to perceive objects in three dimensions from two-dimensional retinal stimulation. **Monocular depth cues** include **interposition, linear perspective, atmospheric perspective, relative size, relative height,** and **movement parallax.** Seeing the world with two eyes provides an additional depth cue through **binocular disparity.** Depth information is also provided by a **texture gradient.**

10. **Size constancy** is defined as the relatively constant perception of an object's size when it is viewed from different distances. To interpret the size of distal objects correctly, information about depth must be added. If that information is incorrect, illusions of size occur.

11. **Real movement** is detected by noting a change in the position of objects and background in relation to the observer. Illusions of movement or **apparent movement** occur when sensory cues are misinterpreted. **Autokinetic movement, induced movement,** and **stroboscopic movement** are examples of apparent movement.

12. Laboratory studies of animals who have been deprived of early visual experience show that they become perceptually handicapped. Normal perceptual development requires exposure to varied environmental stimulation. The neural structures provided by heredity can be modified by environmental experience.

13. The perceptual system is capable of adjustment. Adaptation to **optical rearrangement** occurs because the brain reinterprets body position—it does not reinterpret visual space.

ADDITIONAL READINGS

Bruce, V., and Green, P. R. 1990. *Visual perception: Physiology, psychology, and ecology*. Hove and London, UK: Erlbaum. An advanced undergraduate text that covers the neurophysiology of vision, the computational approach to vision, and the Gibsonian or ecological approach to visual perception.

Coren, S., and Ward, L. M. 1989. *Sensation and perception*, 2nd ed. San Diego, CA: Harcourt Brace Jovanovich. A well-illustrated, easy-to-read text that covers sensation and perception in a lively manner and links physiological and psychological processes.

Cutting, J. E. 1986. *Perception with an eye for motion*. Cambridge, MA: A Branford Book, MIT Press. An extension of Gibson's approach to perception by a leading researcher in perception. Research is provided to show that objects and events often have multiple perceptual invariants to serve as sources of information.

Dixon, N. F. 1981. *Preconscious processing*. New York: Wiley. A critical review of the literature on subliminal perception, with a focus on laboratory research.

Gibson, J. J. 1979. *The ecological approach to visual perception*. Boston: Houghton Mifflin. Gibson's last book offers an explanation of visual perception from the ecological perspective. He shows how this approach can account for our perception of objects in the world as well as our perception of pictures and motion pictures.

Kanizsa, G. 1979. *Organization in vision*. New York: Praeger. A wonderfully illustrated book by the Italian psychologist and artist who created many different illusions involving subjective contours.

Rayner, K., and Pollatsek, A. 1989. *The psychology of reading*. Englewood Cliffs, NJ: Prentice Hall. A comprehensive book on reading theory and research by two experts in the field. This text offers an in-depth look at the mechanics of skilled reading.

Sekuler, R., and Blake, R. 1985. *Perception*. New York: Knopf. A well-written, carefully researched undergraduate text that provides comprehensive coverage of topics in visual perception.

CONSCIOUSNESS

Our normal waking consciousness, rational consciousness as we call it, is but one special type of consciousness, whilst all about it, parted from it by the filmiest of screens, there lie potential forms of consciousness entirely different. We may go through life without suspecting their existence; but apply the requisite stimulus, and at a touch they are there in all their completeness. . . .

(William James, 1890)

Chapter Outline

One night in 1959 a New York disc jockey named Peter Tripp announced that he would stay awake for 200 hours (over eight days) to raise money to fight polio. Following that announcement, people listened to his show, interested to see his reactions to such extended sleep deprivation. If Tripp did not fall asleep on the air, they speculated that he would at least show signs of extreme drowsiness, if not impaired functioning. But night after night, to his listeners' surprise, Tripp was as lively and animated as ever.

To conduct this sleepless marathon, Tripp stationed himself in a glass-walled Army recruiting booth in Times Square in the heart of Manhattan. Under the watchful eye of psychologists, psychiatrists, and medical specialists, who had earlier tried to dissuade him, Tripp stayed in the booth so that the public could verify that he remained awake. His only reprieve consisted of brief trips to a nearby hotel, where he would change clothes and freshen up.

Although he remained awake for the entire period of time, Tripp's thoughts became distorted and irrational. After two days without sleep, he began having visual hallucinations. He thought that spots on a table were bugs, he saw cobwebs in his shoes, and he thought a clock had a human face. After four days without sleep, he could not endure the simplest tests of attention. Said one of the psychologists who examined him, "Here is a competent New York disc jockey trying vainly to find his way through the alphabet." His performance on various mental tests became poorer and poorer, but, strangely, his changes in mental functioning were not apparent when he did his nightly radio show. He never uttered profanities or made any strange remarks that would lead his listeners to suspect that he was living through a nightmare.

Somehow Tripp managed to get through the final day. After his last show and an hour more of tests, he slept for 13 hours. The psychologists who were there tell us what he was like when they saw him again.

> When he awakened, the terrors, ghoulish illusions, and mental agony had vanished. He no longer saw a visual world where objects changed size, specks turned into bugs, and clocks bore human faces. Now it was no effort to remember a joke and solve simple problems. In 13 hours that unspeakable purgatory had vanished. . . .
>
> *(Luce and Segal, 1966)*

Most people who undergo massive sleep loss will not suffer the same problems that plagued Peter Tripp (Dement, 1978; Horne, 1988), and even he could function well in the familiar situation of his nightly radio show. However, changes in moods and thought processes are common to all of us at different times. To understand these changes we need to understand the nature of **consciousness.**

What is consciousness? The word was first used in the English language in the seventeenth century. It was derived from a Latin compound that meant "knowing things together." Numerous definitions of consciousness have since been proposed, but virtually all include a statement about awareness. In everyday language, consciousness is synonymous with awareness; it is our awareness of our perceptions, feelings, and thoughts at any particular moment. Another aspect of awareness is that the contents of consciousness can be described—we can tell another person what we are thinking about. (This is what was originally meant by "knowing things together.") Finally, consciousness often involves planning; we can think about something we are going to do before we actually do it. Being aware, being able to describe our awareness, and being able to plan future actions are all important characteristics of consciousness (Natsoulas, 1978; 1983).

Because our consciousness is limited, we are aware of only a limited number of things at one time. This limitation forces us to be selective—to attend to only a small portion of all the stimuli available to us. For example, if you are paying close attention to reading this page right now, you are probably not attending to the sight and sound of people nearby. Moreover, out of those few stimuli to which we do attend, we are aware only

of our perceptual interpretations, not of such sensory elements as light particles and sound-waves that initially stimulated our receptors. Our awareness of the world around us is based on which portion of the available stimuli we pay attention to and on how we have interpreted these stimuli. If the stimuli are changed, or if any of the underlying processes are altered, the result may be a change in consciousness. Hypnosis, meditation, and drug-induced states, for example, have all been used to try to modify consciousness (Figure 5.1). But before we examine these altered states, it is important to understand the historical battles that have been waged over the place of consciousness in psychology.

HISTORICAL BACKGROUND:
The Study of Consciousness

Until the second half of the nineteenth century interest in psychology was limited mainly to philosophical speculation about the mind. But things changed quickly when the new experimental psychology was founded. Psychology separated itself from philosophy by adopting the procedures of the natural sciences to investigate mental phenomena. For example, instead of speculating on the **span of attention** (the number of stimuli that can simultaneously be perceived and reported), experimental psychologists measured it directly. (It turned out to be approximately six or seven

FIGURE 5.1 Drug-altered consciousness. The geometric patterns in weaving produced by Huichol Indians in Mexico were often inspired by visions experienced during religious rituals involving the smoking of peyote, a hallucinogenic cactus.

stimuli.) Because the procedures they used were carefully reported, other psychologists could repeat the tasks and verify the reliability of the observations. Armed with scientific research methods, psychologists could now study such mental phenomena as attention and memory that were previously approached only on a personal, speculative basis. However, the study of consciousness was a bit more problematic. Consciousness has a checkered history in psychology because early researchers did not always use strictly scientific procedures to study it.

The First Studies of Consciousness

The first systematic studies of consciousness were conducted by Wilhelm Wundt at the University of Leipzig in 1879. Wundt believed that the task of psychology was to analyze ideas and conscious experience—the subjective creations of the mind that are composed of sensations and feelings. He thought that these basic elements were combined in some unknown way by a form of "mental chemistry" to produce ideas and conscious experience. To learn how this was done, Wundt proposed that psychologists study elementary sensations and then examine how these sensations were combined. For example, our experience of wetness can be reduced to the simpler sensory qualities of pressure and coolness. This early approach to the study of consciousness became known as **structuralism.** As its name implies, structuralism sought to see how basic elements were structured by the mind to produce different conscious experiences (Schlesinger, 1985).

Wundt's ideas were brought to America by one of his students, Edward Titchener (1867–1927). To reveal the basic elements of consciousness, Titchener trained observers to report their elementary sensations by the method of **introspection.** The word introspection means "to look within"; to study consciousness, the "introspectionists" trained themselves to look within their own experiences. Titchener and his followers analyzed consciousness by reporting the sensory qualities of the different stimuli they experienced—qualities such as color, size, and intensity and even feelings such as pleasure or pain—whether they were looking at a patch of color or sipping a glass of lemonade.

William James also used introspection, but he used it in an informal way to analyze his own conscious experience. James took issue with the structuralists and considered their approach both artificial and sterile (Hothersall, 1990). He likened their approach to consciousness to a person who tries to learn about a building by analyzing the

Edward B. Titchener. Titchener studied under Wundt in Germany and brought Wundt's ideas to America. Like Wundt, Titchener used the method of introspection to try to observe the basic elements of consciousness.

individual bricks. To James, this approach missed what was important and interesting about consciousness. Its function, he said, was to allow us to be adaptive. Consciousness allows us to adapt and adjust to environmental change. To do this, it has the following characteristics:

- Consciousness is *selective*. It allows us to focus on particular stimuli from the many impinging on our senses.

- Consciousness is *continuous* and *ever-changing*. It is like a stream that changes its direction as it flows.

- Consciousness is *personal*. My thoughts are mine alone.

The importance of consciousness to James cannot be overstated. His very definition of psychology as the "science of mental life" (see Chapter 1) was meant to focus on consciousness. For James (1890; 1892), the job of psychology was to describe the different states of consciousness and connect them to underlying physiological processes (Hilgard, 1987; Leahey, 1988).

Following James and the turn of the twentieth century, the use of introspection to study consciousness led to a dispute about whether the subject of consciousness should be a part of psychology at all. As a method for studying consciousness, introspection had several serious flaws. First, words may be inadequate to describe our conscious experience, so introspection may lead to partial or inaccurate reports. For example, expert wine tasters have had to develop an extensive vocabulary just to describe the subtle differences between wines, and yet no verbal description will substitute for an actual sip of a Batard Montrachet.

Second, even if language could adequately describe our inner experience, some mental processes may not be accessible—they may occur outside of awareness. Finally, because introspection is based on inherently personal and private experience ("These are the sensations that *I* experience"), this method often produces different reports from different observers. If each person's subjective experience can be different, it is impossible to verify whether any person's report is correct. Consequently, interest in introspection quickly waned.

The Rise of Behaviorism

At the start of the twentieth century, the natural sciences made great strides, using objective, scientific techniques that were not dependent upon the impressions of any individual observer. One psychologist who sought the same for psychology was John B. Watson (1878–1958). Watson was the founder of **behaviorism,** the approach to psychology that focuses on overt behavior and observable activities. Watson wanted psychology to focus on observable behavior because he realized that if psychologists were to study consciousness with introspection as their method, then animals, infants, and mentally disturbed people would be excluded (Hilgard, 1980). To Watson, this was unthinkable. Psychology must be concerned with animals, infants, and mentally disturbed people, as well as with those whom we

John B. Watson. The founder of behaviorism, Watson was instrumental in turning experimental psychology away from the study of consciousness by introspection. He forcefully advocated the study of observable behavior by rigorous and objective procedures.

would call normal. Watson rejected the subjective, introspective approach and replaced it with the objective analysis of observable behavior. In his paper, "Psychology as a Behaviorist Views It," Watson said the following:

> I believe that we can write a psychology . . . and never use the terms consciousness, mental states, mind . . . imagery and the like.
> . . . It can be done in terms of stimulus and response, in terms of habit formation, habit integrations and the like.
>
> *(Watson, 1913)*

His reaction to the introspective study of consciousness was to ban the concept of consciousness from psychology. Since consciousness could not be studied objectively, it had no place in the new science of psychology. Watson's behaviorism held sway in experimental psychology for much of the first half of this century.

Different Approaches to Consciousness

The concept of consciousness never completely disappeared, however. For example, Sigmund Freud saw consciousness as central to understanding psychology, and he extended the concept to include **preconscious** and **unconscious processes** (Freud, 1924). For example, before you remember an event from the past, the representation for that event exists in your memory in a preconscious form. Memories of childhood events before you thought of them are examples of preconscious memories. Much like the experience of walking through a dark house at night with only the light of a flashlight to guide you, remembering can put those events in conscious awareness like the beam of a flashlight brings objects in a darkened room into view. The objects, like the preconscious memories, were, in a sense, there all the time; it simply took the appropriate conditions to bring them into awareness.

Unlike preconscious memories, unconscious processes cannot be brought into conscious awareness. Freud believed that the repressed wishes and fears that express threatening or unfavorable ideas normally remain hidden from awareness. He inferred the existence of these unconscious processes by interpreting the contents of people's dreams and slips of the tongue. Dreams are a form of thinking not bound by rational rules, and Freud believed that they were determined by unconscious processes. Similarly, slips of the tongue were also thought to be expressions of unconscious wishes (A man introduces himself to a woman at a party and says, "Excuse me. I don't think we have been properly seduced."). Freud's ideas about unconscious processes remain controversial, but his ideas about consciousness have been useful to many psychologists.

In addition to Freud and his followers, psychologists called **phenomenologists** also continued to study consciousness, with an emphasis on the qualitative analyses of personal experience. Unlike the introspectionists, who sought to analyze experience into simple elements, the phenomenologists have tried to provide a faithful description of a person's feelings and thoughts by examining the "meaning" that is given to events. For example, phenomenological psychologists have been more interested in describing a person's feelings of self-esteem (How did you feel about yourself when your parents became divorced?) than in developing a theory about a person's behavior. They believe that we can learn more about human nature by studying how people view themselves than by observing and recording each other's behavior. For example, in describing his own consciousness, William James (1890) likened it to a stream.

> Consciousness then does not appear to itself chopped up in bits. Such words as "chain" or "train" do not describe it fitly, as it presents itself in the first instant. It is nothing jointed, it flows. A "river" or a "stream" are the metaphors by which it is naturally described. In talking of it thereafter, let us call it the stream of thought, of consciousness, or of subjective life.

We will see evidence of the lasting impact of this approach in later chapters of this text.

The Advent of Cognitive Psychology

Following Watson and the behaviorist movement, psychologists within the mainstream of psychology began to realize that while the behaviorists were correct in rejecting the introspective approach to consciousness, they had gone too far in their zeal to make psychology objective. In the 1950s and 1960s the concept of consciousness slowly returned to experimental psychology, now under the banner of **cognitive psychology.** Cognitive psychologists study the mental processes that occur in perception, memory, and thought. They emphasize mind instead of behavior—knowing instead of responding—and they use objective, scientific methods. Unlike the phenomenologists who are concerned with self-awareness, the cognitive psychologists seek to determine how our thoughts, knowledge, and interpretations influence our ability to acquire information, solve problems, and make plans. As part of this cognitive revolution, experimental psychologists have shown a renewed interest in consciousness and aspects of mind (Simon, 1982; Sperry, 1987). Such topics as mental imagery, feelings, and thought have made a comeback as psychologists have devised some interesting methods to study these private experiences in an objective way. Modern psychologists can study the behavior of animals, infants, and mentally disturbed people, and they are once again studying the workings of the mind.

In this chapter we are going to take a Jamesian approach to consciousness by describing the edges of the stream that James mentioned. First, we will focus on conscious awareness to see how attention is *selective*. Next, we will describe different states, including sleep and hypnosis, to show how consciousness is *continuous* and *ever-changing*. Then we will examine attempts to manipulate consciousness by drugs and meditation to show how consciousness is *personal*. We will conclude by describing the function that consciousness serves. Whenever possible, in keeping with James, we will relate what has been learned about consciousness to underlying processes in the brain. ■

CONSCIOUS AWARENESS

If you are having a conversation in a crowded restaurant, the voices you are trying to ignore may be louder than the one you are trying to hear. Next time you are in this situation, see how well you can ignore the background conversations. Then try listening to two conversations at once. Can you do so without missing parts of either? One of the most intriguing aspects of consciousness is the way it can be focused. We can direct our attention to certain stimuli from the vast array of sights, sounds, and smells that reach our sensory receptors. According to William James, the fact that attention is selective is one of the primary characteristics of consciousness. What determines how we focus our attention, and why do certain stimuli intrude despite our attention to something else?

ATTENTION

Attention is defined as the focusing of perception on a limited number of stimuli. Like twisting the zoom lens on a camera, this focusing results in a heightened awareness of those selected stimuli (Erikson and St. James, 1986; Posner, Snyder, and Davidson, 1980). At any given moment we are exposed to more information than we could possibly process. As you read this book numerous stimuli compete for your limited attention. Aside from the book itself, there may be visual stimuli (other people working close by), auditory stimuli (from the noises they make), and even tactile stimuli (from different parts of your body as you sit at your desk and read). Rather than overloading your brain by attempting to attend to all of these stimuli at once, you are selective. You pay attention to some and ignore the rest. Although we generally take this ability for granted, selective attention is by no means a trivial task. No one has ever described it better than William James did a century ago:

> Looking back. . . . we see that the mind is at every stage a theatre of simultaneous possibilities. Consciousness consists in the comparison of these with each other, the selection of some, and the suppression of the rest by the reinforcing and inhibiting agency of attention. . . . The mind, in short, works on the data it receives very much as a sculptor works on his block of stone. In a sense the statue stood there from eternity. But there were a thousand different ones beside it, and the sculptor alone is to thank for having extricated this one from the rest.

> (James, 1890)

SELECTIVE ATTENTION

Selectivity is important because it permits us to focus, or concentrate, our attention. For example, imagine a party where a large number of people are standing and talking in small groups. Many conversations are going on at the same time, yet we usually have no trouble following and participating in the conversation of our choice. This simple example illustrates the selective quality of attention. Attention is selective, but it is also subject to distraction. If our name comes up in another conversation, we can turn to find out what is being said. This distractability permits us to redirect our attention to new sources of important information. As we noted in Chapter 2, the parietal lobes of the brain are particularly important for directing attention to new sources of environmental information (Posner, Walker, Friedrich, and Rafal, 1987). Together, selectivity and distractability allow us to focus or refocus our attention as changing conditions warrant.

The fact that we are selective implies that there is a limit to our attention, a limit that we are reminded of every day. There are some activities that can be done simultaneously and others that can only be done alone. Driving and talking can usually be done at the same time, but typing and talking

can be extremely difficult. Since typing and talking interfere with each other, some aspect of each must require attention. For driving and talking, there is no interference because one of the tasks (driving) usually makes little demand upon attention. This can change, however, if we are driving in heavy traffic. Then, driving may demand maximum concentration, and the conversation must stop. Psychologists think of attention as a limited resource and selectivity as a means by which we keep within our attentional limits (Hirst and Kalmar, 1987; Norman and Bobrow, 1975). Without the ability to select some stimuli and ignore others, normal cognitive functioning would be impossible. Consider the following reports of patients who have been diagnosed as schizophrenic, a form of behavior disorder characterized by delusions and disordered thought processes:

> My concentration is very poor. I jump from one thing to another. If I am talking to someone, they only need to cross their legs or scratch their head and I am distracted and forget what I was saying. I think I would concentrate better with my eyes shut.
>
> My mind's away. I have lost control. There are too many things coming into my head at once and I can't sort them out.

> (McGhie and Chapman, 1961)

Something is terribly wrong with the selective attention mechanism in these schizophrenics. It no longer allows these people to control their attention, and therefore their thoughts become garbled and confused. Some psychologists believe that this inability to focus the mind or to sustain that focus is at the heart of schizophrenia (Chapman and Chapman, 1973; Place and Gilmore, 1980). Although other psychologists favor different interpretations, it is clear how disordered we all would be without the ability to focus our attention.

Bases of Selectivity. How do we select what we will pay attention to and what we will ignore? To address this question, psychologists have used a **dichotic listening task.** As a subject in a dichotic listening experiment, you would hear two different messages at the same time, one in each ear. (See Figure 5.2.) You would be asked to *shadow* (repeat out loud) one of the messages as you heard it. After both messages were completed, you would be asked questions about the message to which you did not pay attention. Even without paying attention, people can tell whether a voice was present, whether the voice belonged to a male or a female speaker, and whether there were non-

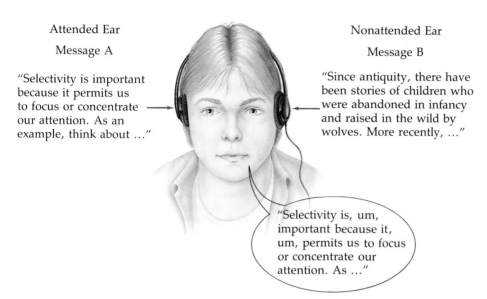

Attended Ear

Message A

"Selectivity is important because it permits us to focus or concentrate our attention. As an example, think about ..."

Nonattended Ear

Message B

"Since antiquity, there have been stories of children who were abandoned in infancy and raised in the wild by wolves. More recently, ..."

"Selectivity is, um, important because it, um, permits us to focus or concentrate our attention. As ..."

FIGURE 5.2   Dichotic listening and selective attention. In the dichotic listening task, a person is simultaneously presented with a different message to each ear. Attention is directed to one of the messages by asking the person to repeat it orally. This repetition is called "shadowing," and it ensures that the person is paying careful attention as directed. By observing what people remember from the nonattended message, psychologists can learn how selective attention operates.

speech signals, such as whistles, in the nonshadowed material. On the other hand, they cannot say what the nonshadowed message was about, what language was used, whether the language changed during the message, or even whether it contained ungrammatical nonsense (Cherry, 1953).

Since listeners are aware of only the physical aspects of a nonshadowed message, it appears that they use these physical features as cues to differentiate the two messages. Of all incoming information, that which is physically consistent with the shadowed message is fully recognized, while that which is inconsistent is rejected as irrelevant. In the party mentioned at the start of this section, we would use physical cues such as the direction of a voice, whether the voice is male or female, the lip movements of the speaker, and the speed and intonation pattern of what is being said, to focus our attention on the conversation of our choice.

Selective attention is a bit more complex than a simple analysis of physical cues, however. It seems that incoming information is examined along several different dimensions. To follow a conversation in a crowded room we first conduct a physical examination of the sensory stimuli; those stimuli that match the physical qualities of the speaker's voice are then subjected to an analysis for meaning, while all other nonmatching stimuli get attenuated (diminished) and blocked from con-

scious awareness. When selection on the basis of physical cues is impossible (for instance, if two people are speaking to you in similar voices from the same location), selection is made by analyzing the meaning and grammatical structure of each person's message. This task is more difficult and results in extra processing of the relevant message and blocking of the irrelevant one before it reaches conscious awareness (Hillyard and Kutas, 1983; Treisman, 1964).

Once we have selected a particular input, what causes our attention to shift? The physical characteristics of the stimuli are important. We are more likely to shift our attention to messages that are novel or complex or to stimuli that are large, intense, or moving (Broadbent, 1982; Johnston and Dark, 1986; Shiffrin, 1985). In general, stimuli command our attention if they stand out (a red light), change (the rising wail of a siren), or are associated with danger (a loud "beep" from an oncoming car). Repetitive stimuli (the ticking of a clock or the distant sound of highway traffic) provide no new information and are quickly ignored. Something that is personally important is also likely to command our attention. Parents of a newborn infant may awaken to a whimper from their child, yet sleep soundly as a truck rumbles by in the night. In each of these examples we see that stimuli that are generally or personally informative are likely to capture our attention. Through the swirl of information continually "buzzing" around us (to borrow a metaphor from William James), we selectively attend to only a small portion—that which is most relevant at the moment.

ATTENTIONAL DEMANDS AND PRACTICE

Not everything we do requires our full attention. For example, we can usually drive on an open highway with only minimal attention. However, this reduced demand for attention comes only after considerable practice (Kahneman and Chajczyk, 1983; Shiffrin and Schneider, 1977). When we learn any new task, whether driving or typing, we make many errors at first. With a little more practice we make fewer errors but still need considerable attention to do the task well. After continued practice, **automaticity** results—the task can be performed *automatically*. This means that our performance no longer requires conscious awareness. For example, highly skilled typists can type normally while they simultaneously recite nursery rhymes (Shaffer, 1975). Other typists say that they can read a manuscript while they are typing it as though they were reading a book—somehow the manuscript gets "magically" typed (Gentner and Norman, 1984). It requires an enormous amount of practice to reach this state of automaticity, though.

In an experiment designed to study how automaticity develops, college students were given two tasks to work on simultaneously over an entire semester. For one hour each day, the students silently read stories while they tried to copy a list of dictated words at the same time. As soon as one word had been copied, a new one was presented. At first, the students experienced great difficulty in doing both tasks together. They could copy the dictated words, but their reading rates dropped dramatically. However, after about eight weeks of practice they were able not only to read at their normal rates, but also to understand fully what they read. Thus, through extensive practice, the students had learned to take a simplified form of dictation automatically. Like the typists who could type and recite nursery rhymes simultaneously, these students could now read and write at the same time (Spelke, Hirst, and Neisser, 1976).

For potentially **dangerous** tasks it is crucial to practice to the point of automaticity. For example, in deaths attributed to scuba diving in California, many divers were found still wearing their heavy weight belts despite attempts by instructors of diving courses to make removal of the belt the first step in underwater emergencies (Bachrach, 1970). The problem that people face in dangerous situations is that attention becomes narrowly focused under conditions of high stress. This narrowing of attention works against us as we concentrate on a few, often irrelevant, details. For example, in focusing only on their attempts to reach the surface, many scuba divers apparently did not think of discarding their weight belts. Unfortunately, a lifesaving response that is "obvious" if you have time to think may never occur to you when you need it most—in the narrowly focused state of panic. Under these high stress conditions, lifesaving routines may only be useful if you have practiced them to the point of automaticity—if they have become so overlearned that they can be performed without conscious awareness.

DIVIDED CONSCIOUSNESS

Normally, our attentional capacity can be divided among different responses so that some receive most of our attention while others receive far less. For example, basketball players must divide their attention among several sources of information at once (Figure 5.3). The voices of teammates, opponents, and coaches, the movements of other players on the court, the player's own movements, and the noises from the crowd all compete for each player's attention. Successful players narrow their attention, disregarding such irrelevant information as the noise of the crowd, and then divide that attention between the calls and movements of the other players on the court. Running and dribbling the ball are so highly overpracticed that they require very little attention. Unless something unusual happens to break a player's concentration (perhaps a fan running onto the court), awareness stays focused mainly on those aspects that require conscious planning and control.

For some people, however, conscious awareness can be divided in a different way. Instead of dividing awareness in terms of momentary demands for attention, consciousness is divided so that some realms of awareness are kept separate from others. As we noted in Chapter 2, split-brain patients who have had their cerebral hemispheres separated sometimes function as though they had two separate minds, each again with its own sense of awareness. Still other individuals suffer from a mental disturbance called **multiple personality disorder,** in which there is more than one distinct personality, each with its own sense of conscious awareness.

Such individuals demonstrate an extreme form of discontinuous consciousness that is actually present in all of us. We think of consciousness as whole and continuous, but this is an illusion pro-

FIGURE 5.3 An example of divided attention. In a basketball game, the players must divide their attention among many sources of stimulation. An experienced player can perform some activities automatically (dribbling the ball), ignore some stimuli (crowd noises), and focus attention narrowly on other stimuli (movements and shouts of other players). In this way attention is directed only to those aspects of the game that require conscious planning and control.

duced by the presence of memory (Hilgard, 1977). From the time we go to sleep until we awaken there is a gap in conscious awareness that is bridged only by memory. We recognize ourselves as the same person we were last night or last year only because we remember ourselves from those previous times. As the example that follows will demonstrate, this feeling of conscious unity may be lost without access to such memories.

MULTIPLE PERSONALITY DISORDER

Cases of multiple personality (in which a person can shift back and forth between different identities) are rare, but they do occur. In the past, these people were thought to be possessed by demons, but now they are seen as suffering from extreme divisions of consciousness. A recent survey of 100 cases of multiple personality disorder found that the patients had an average of 13 distinct and separate personalities. More than half of these cases had personalities in the opposite gender, and 85 percent had alternate personalities that claimed to

be children (Putnam, Guroff, Silberman, Barban, and Post, 1986). Multiple personality disorder is more than just a change in mood; rather, it involves the sense of identity—who a person is at any particular moment. For example, case studies of people with multiple personality disorder have found that it is common for one personality to be fully aware of the others. At the same time, other personalities can exist that are unaware of the existence of others and remember nothing about their experiences (Davis and Osherson, 1977; Nissen, Ross, Willingham, Mackenzie, and Schacter, 1988). We still do not know the cause of this disorder, but we do know that people with multiple personalities tend to have had childhood experiences involving physical or sexual abuse (Putnam, 1982). The case of Jonah, a 27-year-old man hospitalized for severe headaches, provides an illustration of this disorder. Before being admitted to the hospital, Jonah chased his wife and young daughter from their home with a butcher's knife. During such aggressive acts, his wife reported that Jonah referred to himself as Usoffa Abdulla, son of Omega. When he later calmed down, Jonah could not remember his earlier violent behavior.

In the psychiatric hospital, the staff noted that Jonah seemed to act like a different person after each of his memory lapses. The doctors who examined him found that Jonah had four distinct personalities, each represented by a different name. The primary personality was called Jonah, a shy, sensitive person who acted frightened and confused when interviewed by the psychiatrists. Unaware of the other coexisting personalities, Jonah was passive, polite, and highly conventional.

When he was six years old, Jonah saw his mother attack his father with a knife. When the family was later reunited, a new personality by the name of Sammy emerged. It was Sammy who urged his parents not to fight in front of the children. Sammy was intellectual, legalistic, and capable of talking his way out of any difficulty. It was Sammy who took over whenever Jonah got into trouble.

When Jonah had difficulty with women, yet another personality took over to look after Jonah's sexual interests. Only vaguely aware of the other personalities, King Young, the lover, emerged when Jonah's mother dressed him in girl's clothes and he became confused about his sexual identity.

Finally, when Jonah felt physically threatened, a fourth personality—Usoffa Abdulla, the warrior—took over to guard and protect Jonah. Usoffa made his first appearance when Jonah, age 9 or 10, was beaten by a gang of white youths because he was black. After losing consciousness during the fight, Usoffa emerged and fought off his attackers.

Unlike most people, who integrate their differences into a complex yet coherent single personality, Jonah's are separated. Each key aspect of his primary personality has its alter ego, its opposite, that exists as a full-blown personality of its own. Unfortunately, this extreme case of divided consciousness has not responded positively to treatment (Ludwig, Brandsma, Wilbur, Benfeldt, and Jameson, 1972).

More recent research has shown that people with multiple personality disorder can reveal physiological differences for each personality. For example, psychologist Scott Miller (cited in Goleman, 1988) found that a woman with three personalities (aged 5, 17, and 35) had an eye condition known as "lazy eye" only in her early childhood personality. An ophthalmic exam revealed that one of her eyes turned inward when this personality took over. In another reported case, a person was allegic to a particular food in one personality and would develop a bad case of hives, only to have the disorder abruptly cease when a different personality emerged (Goleman, 1988). Psychologists currently have no ready explanations for how these divisions of consciousness influence physiological processes.

REALMS OF AWARENESS

Long ago, French philosopher René Descartes (1596–1650) erroneously thought that the pineal gland at the base of the brain was the seat of consciousness. Descartes believed this because the pineal gland was the only part of the brain that was not duplicated in both brain halves. It is true that the pineal gland is the only unpaired organ in the brain, but we now know that this gland serves mainly as an internal clock, regulating rhythmic changes in the body, such as those involved in waking and sleeping (Kalat, 1988; Kolb and Whishaw, 1990). The pineal gland affects a person's arousal, but it is not the seat of consciousness. Consciousness arises from brain processes rather than from a particular brain structure. Our normal sense of consciousness (who we are and what we are doing right now) is achieved by the brain interpreting our actions, moods, and other behaviors and constructing an explanation for why they occurred (Gazzaniga, 1985; 1988). How this happens we still do not know.

Consciousness remains a scientific mystery, but psychologists and other scientists are chipping away at an understanding of it by studying its many variations. For example, basketball players, split-brain patients, and people with multiple personality disorder all suggest that normal waking consciousness can be divided into different realms of awareness. Moreover, as William James noted in the opening quotation of this chapter, consciousness varies not only in its number of divisions but also in the different forms it may take. It is to these different forms that we now turn to show that consciousness is not only selective but also continuous and ever-changing.

ALTERED STATES OF CONSCIOUSNESS

An **altered state of consciousness** can be defined as a change in mental experience from that of normal waking consciousness. Ordinary conscious awareness is the state most familiar to all of us, but minor psychological or physiological changes can lead to radically different inner states. Some of these states, including daydreaming and nocturnal

Lost in a daydream. Psychologists view daydreams not as momentary lapses of consciousness, but as an altered state of consciousness. Daydreams allow us to solve problems or plan future actions as well as escape from boring, monotonous tasks. Daydreams can occur anytime we are idle or bored or not mentally engaged in some task.

dreaming, occur frequently. Others, like the ones produced by drugs, occur less often. Each satisfies the definition of an altered state, however.

DAYDREAMING

Daydreams are called *monologues interieurs* (talks with one's self) by the French. More formally, a **daydream** is a shift of attention away from an ongoing physical or mental task toward some internal stimulus. Just about everyone daydreams, and we daydream quite frequently. Although elderly people daydream less than those who are young, a survey of people between the ages of 18 and 50 found that 96 percent of the respondents daydreamed daily (Singer and McCraven, 1961). Daydreams occur most frequently at night just before we go to bed and least frequently in the morning when we wake up. During the day, daydreams can occur any time we are bored, idle, or engaged in a task that is not particularly demanding of our attention.

THE EXPERIENCE OF DAYDREAMING

During a daydream, we turn our focus of attention inward, away from such external events as the conversation of people nearby. Lost in thought, we may fantasize about inheriting great wealth or traveling through exotic lands, but more often than not we daydream about our interactions with other people. Whether our daydreams are brief

momentary distractions or longer events that seem to unfold in slow motion, our attention is turned away from the present external world. For example, we suddenly realize that we have read several paragraphs in a book without any conscious awareness of its contents; we are startled to find that we have driven a car for five miles without any awareness of what we passed. Attention turns inward during uninteresting times, and imagination takes over to provide an escape. Author James Thurber noted that the escape of a daydream can be almost irresistible when combined with a measure of wish-fulfillment:

"We're going through!" The Commander's voice was like thin ice breaking. He wore his full-dress uniform, with the heavily braided white cap pulled down rakishly over one cold gray eye. "We can't make it, sir. It's spoiling for a hurricane, if you ask me." "I'm not asking you, Lieutenant Berg," said the Commander. "Throw on the power lights! Rev her up to 8,500! We're going through!" The pounding of the cylinders increased: ta-pocketa-pocketa-pocketa-pocketa-pocketa. The Commander stared at the ice forming on the pilot window. He walked over and twisted a row of complicated dials. "Switch on No. 8 auxiliary!" he shouted. "Switch on No. 8 auxiliary!" repeated Lieutenant Berg. "Full strength in No. 3 turret!" shouted the Commander. "Full strength in No. 3 turret!" The crew, bending to their various tasks in the huge, hurtling eight-engined Navy hydroplane, looked at each other and grinned. "The Old Man'll get us through," they said to one another. "The Old Man ain't afraid of Hell! . . ."

"Not so fast! You're driving too fast!" said Mrs. Mitty. "What are you driving so fast for?"

"Hmm?" said Walter Mitty. He looked at his wife, in the seat beside him, with shocked astonishment. She seemed grossly unfamiliar, like a strange woman who had yelled at him in a crowd. "You were up to fifty-five," she said. "You know I don't like to go more than forty. You were up to fifty-five." Walter Mitty drove on toward Waterbury in silence, the roaring of the SN202 through the worst storm in twenty years of Navy flying fading in the remote, intimate airways of his mind.

(From The Secret Life of Walter Mitty *by James Thurber)*

THE VALUE OF DAYDREAMS

Over the years, there have been a number of possible explanations for daydreaming put forth. Freud (1908) viewed daydreaming as a way to provide partial gratification for strong desires. However, this view does not seem to account for the fact that fantasies about food or sexual activity, instead of gratifying us, often increase our desires.

More recently, psychologists have turned to cognitive explanations of daydreams. For example, in one study observers had to watch a light that blinked rapidly on and off for an extended period of time. The observers were supposed to press a button whenever the light changed its intensity. Most of the time nothing changed, and the subjects just sat watching the boring display. While the subjects were engaged in this *vigilance task,* half were asked to count continuously, and half were asked to daydream continuously. The results showed that the people who daydreamed were more alert to the vigilance task, as well as more comfortable, less drowsy, and less likely to fall asleep than were those subjects who counted while watching the light (Antrobus and Singer, 1964). When we are engaged in monotonous tasks (watching a blinking light, perhaps, or driving on a deserted highway through miles of farmland at night), we need some way to produce new stimulation or we may fall asleep. Talking to another person or listening to music on a radio is one answer—daydreaming is another. Daydreams have value because they provide *continuous* and *ever-changing* stimulation. This is why workers in boring jobs use daydreaming as a means of staying awake. Lifeguards and truckdrivers overwhelmingly report that they deliberately daydream to ease their boredom (Klinger, 1987). Daydreams also allow us to plan. Typically, we daydream about ordinary, everyday events—going shopping, interacting with family and friends, or solving personal problems. These daydreams enable us to try out imaginary solutions to problems and to remind ourselves of future events (Klinger, 1987).

SLEEPING AND DREAMING

Since ancient times, people have thought of sleep as a period of rest, similar to a temporary death. The Egyptians attributed the visions or dreams that a person had during sleep to the wanderings of an external spirit or soul, called *ba.* Presumably, this spirit left the body during sleep or at death and traveled to its permanent home in the underworld (Van de Castle, 1971). Sleep, though, is not at all like a temporary death. In fact, the bil-lions of neurons in the brain can be just as active when we are asleep as they are when we are awake (Chase, 1981). Far from lacking consciousness, the sleeper enters an altered state of consciousness that psychologists have only begun to explore.

WAKING AND SLEEPING CYCLES

Our pattern of waking and sleeping follows a regular 24-hour schedule. All over the world, people generally sleep from five to eight hours per night. Beside sleep, there are other regular daily changes in biological processes, including body temperature and blood pressure. These rhythmic patterns are called **circadian rhythms.** (*Circa* means *around,* *dia* means *day.*) The wake–sleep rhythm is tied to the 24-hour cycle of light and dark produced by the earth's rotation around the sun. When people are forced to adapt to different cycles of light and dark (for example, as workers in Antarctica are) they still maintain a circadian rhythm. However, without a day–night difference they tend to adopt a cycle based on 25 hours. Variations in the circadian rhythm of more than 27 or less than 23 hours are difficult to maintain, although some people can maintain a 48-hour cycle by staying awake for 32 hours and sleeping for 16 (Dement, 1978). As a person gets older, the circadian rhythm for sleep changes. Newborn infants spend 75 percent of each day asleep but quickly adjust their waking–sleeping schedule and spend more and more time awake (Figure 5.4). Animals also maintain a circadian rhythm for sleep, but schedules vary greatly from one species to another. Horses, cattle, and elephants sleep from two to four hours per day, while bats and opposums sleep 19 to 20 hours per day (Webb and Cartwright, 1978).

Why do we sleep? Surprisingly, no one knows for sure. Early theories related sleep to hormonal or blood changes. During the nineteenth century, it was believed that toxic wastes build up during waking hours and are then eliminated from the body by sleep. However, no chemical basis for the waking–sleeping cycle has ever been found. Sleep seems to restore and refresh us, but not through the dissipation of any toxic material. There is some evidence to support the commonsense view that we sleep in order to rest and conserve energy. Research involving a variety of animal species has shown that the higher an animal's general level of metabolism (the rate of converting food into energy) the greater the amount of time it spends asleep (Zepelin and Rechtschaffen, 1974). Humans, however, can use as much energy while asleep as while lying quietly awake, so energy conservation

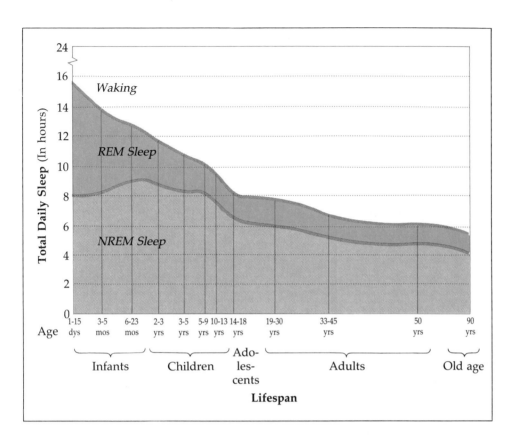

FIGURE 5.4 Changes in the amount of total sleep, REM sleep, and NREM sleep over the lifespan. During the first 14–18 years, total sleep and REM sleep periods decrease considerably, while the amount of NREM sleep changes only slightly. Thereafter, changes in sleep are much more gradual.

may not be the whole story (Hobson, 1989a). Sleep researchers offer the intriguing possibility that sleep evolved long ago in our ancestral past to keep us out of trouble at night. Since we do not see well at night, our fumbling and stumbling in the dark would have made us an easy target for nocturnal predators. Similarly, sleep serves to suppress those activities, such as finding food or a mate, that require sufficient light to be successful. In such situations, a nonresponse like sleep would be an adaptive response (Hobson, 1989a; Webb and Bonnet, 1979).

How much sleep is normal? Earlier we said that most people average five to eight hours per night. This figure has changed over time, however. From diaries and personal accounts of people in the 18th and 19th centuries, we learn that the average person used to sleep about 9½ hours a night. With ever greater industrialization (and such inventions as lightbulbs and late-night television) this figure has dramatically decreased. In fact, many sleep researchers now believe that many people are sleep deprived. These people are getting between 60 and 90 minutes less sleep each night than they should to feel vigorous and alert the next day (Angier, 1990). Chronic sleep deprivation is no light matter. The U.S. Department of Transportation reported that there were at least 40,000 traffic accidents in 1989 that were sleep related, and that approximately 20 percent of all drivers will fall asleep behind the wheel at least once. Long-term sleep deprivation cannot be undone in one or two nights—it requires several weeks of adequate sleep to reverse the effects of sleep loss (Angier, 1990). To determine whether you are getting enough sleep, keep track of the amount of sleep you get over a 10-day period. If you feel vigorous and refreshed each morning and able to concentrate throughout the day, you are getting enough sleep, and your average over the 10-day period is close to your ideal. If you are not getting enough sleep, set a fixed bedtime during the week and go to bed earlier on weekends, rather than trying to sleep later (Angier, 1990). For those who suffer more serious sleep disorders, including insomnia or narcolepsy, the solutions are not quite as simple.

DYSFUNCTION:
Insomnia, Narcolepsy, and Sleep Apnea

Although most of us can voluntarily control our periods of sleep, occasionally each of us experiences a problem in trying to fall asleep. When this problem occurs on a regular or long-term basis, it is called **insomnia** (from the Latin word for "sleepless"). This sleep disorder may affect 15 percent or more of the adult population, and it may take one of several forms (Kripke and Simons, 1976). Most people who suffer from insomnia have trouble falling asleep, but there are some people who awaken sometime during the night, several hours before they should, and then face difficulty in returning to sleep. Research into the causes of insomnia has shown that it may be brought on by psychological problems, such as worries over family or work, that prevent a person from relaxing. Eliminating the concerns usually eliminates the insomnia, although in some instances sedatives may be prescribed to treat the disorder temporarily. Sedatives and barbiturates make it easier to sleep, but they reduce periods of REM sleep (an important stage of sleep that we will describe in the next section) and they may lower the quality of sleep. Worse, withdrawal from the extended use of such drugs can itself produce anxiety, nightmares, and frequent awakenings during the night.

Insomnia can also result from faulty sleep habits. Changing the time or location of sleep each night can lead to insomnia because no regular pattern of sleep is established. On the other hand, trying to follow an extremely rigid sleep schedule can also lead to insomnia. In general, it is best to develop a regular pattern of sleep that you do not try to follow slavishly (Webb and Bonnet, 1979). Sleep researchers list the following suggestions for getting a good night's sleep:

- Try to establish a regular bedtime, but delay going to bed if you are not tired.

- Avoid heavy meals close to bedtime, although a light snack may sometimes help.

- Regular exercise is also beneficial, but not if it is done near bedtime.

- Reduce or eliminate the consumption of alcohol, chocolate, coffee, tea, and soft drinks containing caffeine during the afternoon and evening.

- During the early evening, write down your current problems and what you will do about them the following day.

- If you awaken during the night, try to relax and see if you fall back asleep. If you become tense, get out of bed and do something relaxing until you become sleepy again.

- Finally, if you fail to get a good night's sleep one night, do not oversleep or nap the following day. Maintain your regular schedule for rising and your normal level of activity.

(From Hopson, 1986)

Contrary to the problems faced by sufferers of insomnia, people with **narcolepsy** are chronically sleepy and suffer irresistible attacks of sleepiness at inappropriate times of the day. A person with narcolepsy can doze off during sex, in the middle of a meal, or while driving a car. In addition to their inappropriate dozing, narcoleptics often do things without conscious awareness. They engage in automatic behavior with memory "blackouts," as shown by the following cases from sleep researcher William Dement:

> "I was going to do the dishes. It was just after dinner. I remember walking in the kitchen and when I "woke up" about 30 minutes later, the kitchen was a complete mess. I had put all the plates in the clothes dryer and turned it on!"
>
> "I am on the verge of being fired from my job—I am a computer programmer. My last mistake was to run a completely inappropriate program for three hours which could have cost the company $25,000. During that period of time I had to do a certain number of tape rewindings, etc., which I did. It seems that I even talked appropriately to one of my assistants. However, I couldn't remember anything at all."
>
> *(Dement, 1976)*

Exact figures on the prevalence of narcolepsy are unavailable, but it is relatively rare (Browman, Sampson, Gujavarty, and Mitler, 1982).

Also chronically tired are people who suffer from **sleep apnea,** a disorder that involves difficulty in breathing during sleep. (*Apnea* means cessation of breath.) Because an obstruction closes the air passages in their throats, these people doze off and wake up several hundred times each night. Typically, sufferers of sleep apnea are unaware of their problem. They complain of being tired all day, but they believe that they sleep too much. Drugs that stimulate the brain's respiratory centers are sometimes effective as a treatment, while in other cases a surgical opening in the trachea (the air duct that runs from the larynx at the back of the throat to the lungs) is necessary to ensure normal breathing during sleep. ■

STAGES OF SLEEP

Just as there is a cycle of waking and sleeping, so there is a cycle of stages within sleep. These stages of sleep can be observed by an electroencephalograph that records the electrical activity of the brain. This machine produces a tracing of a person's electrical brain activity. This record (called an electroencephalogram or EEG) indicates that waking and sleeping states have different wave patterns. The brain wave patterns that occur throughout the night are shown in Figure 5.5. Prior to sleep, when our eyes are closed and we are not paying attention to anything in particular, our brain wave pattern is composed largely of *alpha waves.* These waves have a small amplitude (height) and a high frequency (cycles per second). As we enter the first stage of sleep, the brain wave pattern changes. During Stage 1, our pulse slows, our eyes begin to roll slowly under their closed lids, and we begin to feel drowsy. Very shortly, our brain waves change again. As their amplitude gets higher and their frequency gets lower, we enter Stage 2, and we are finally asleep.

Following Stage 2, we fall deeper and deeper asleep. Approximately 30 minutes from the start of Stage 1, we enter Stage 3 and then Stage 4, as indicated by the large amplitude *delta waves* shown in Figure 5.5. It is during Stage 4 that bed-wetting and sleepwalking may occur in children (Dement, 1978). After perhaps another 30 minutes, this stage

of deepest sleep ends, and our brain waves show a return to Stage 1. At this point, something interesting happens. Darting back and forth, our eyes move rapidly under their closed lids, but our body, which previously tossed and turned, now stops moving almost completely (Chase and Morales, 1990). While the EEG record looks as it does when we are awake, we are, in fact, very deeply asleep. With its characteristic **rapid eye movements (REMs),** this paradoxical stage of sleep shown at the bottom of Figure 5.5 is called REM sleep.

The distinction between REM sleep and all other stages of sleep (called non-REM or NREM sleep) is important because it provides another example of how consciousness is ever-changing. When subjects in sleep research experiments are awakened from REM sleep, they usually say that they were dreaming; when awakened from NREM sleep, they might say that they were thinking about something, but only rarely do they say that they were dreaming (Aserinsky and Kleitman, 1953; Webb, 1985). Thus, dreaming coincides frequently with REM sleep (Figure 5.6). Researchers have found that there is a dramatic increase in cerebral blood flow during dreaming, particularly in the right temporal–parietal region of the brain (Meyer, Ishikawa, Hata, and Karacan, 1987). However, EEG studies indicate that the right hemisphere is not the primary location of dream production (Ehrlichman, Antrobus, and Weiner, 1985; Wollman and Antrobus, 1984). People with damage to either cerebral hemisphere, but especially the left hemisphere, experience severe problems in dream recall (Greenberg and Farah, 1986). Psychologist John Antrobus (1987) believes

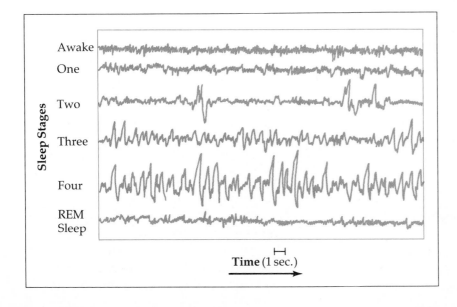

FIGURE 5.5 Different brain wave patterns recorded by an electroencephalograph while a person was awake and at different stages of sleep. The brain wave patterns shown for the deep REM sleep in which dreaming occurs are most similar to those of Stage 1, a period of drowsiness that occurs just prior to the onset of sleep.

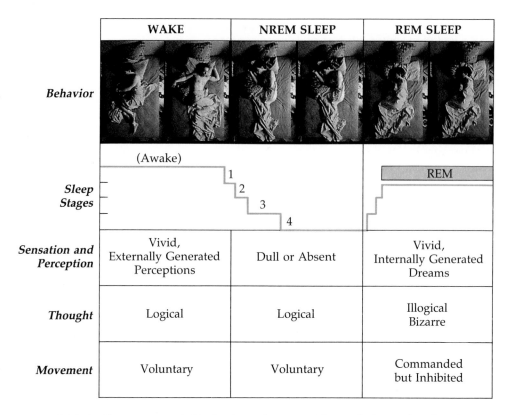

	WAKE	NREM SLEEP	REM SLEEP
Behavior			
Sleep Stages	(Awake) 1 2 3 4		REM
Sensation and Perception	Vivid, Externally Generated Perceptions	Dull or Absent	Vivid, Internally Generated Dreams
Thought	Logical	Logical	Illogical Bizarre
Movement	Voluntary	Voluntary	Commanded but Inhibited

FIGURE 5.6 Sleep stages and behavior. A person lying quietly awake, then in NREM sleep, and finally REM sleep will show major differences in perception, thinking, and movement control. The vivid perceptions and illogical thoughts characteristic of REM sleep are highly associated with reports of dreaming.

that dreams are more than a sequence of visual images and that both left and right hemisphere processes are involved. Consistent with this view is the multisensory nature of dreams. The visual sense predominates, but auditory, tactile, and movement sensations are also prominent. Somewhat surprising is the fact that taste and smell are underrepresented in dreams, as is the sensation of pain, especially since we may dream of frightening or physically dangerous events (Hobson, 1989b).

As the sleeper passes through the night, the cycle of stages is repeated about every 90 minutes with REM periods increasing in length from approximately five minutes to 30 minutes or more (Figure 5.7). The recurring REM periods suggest that everyone has four or five dreams each night, even though we forget at least 95 percent of those dreams (Hobson, 1989b). Since dreams are so frequent and sometimes so bizarre, psychologists, like everyone else, have long been fascinated by them. Just what is the stuff of dreams?

THE CONTENT OF DREAMS

Dreaming is a process that differs from waking consciousness in three ways. First, dreaming occurs only during sleep. Second, dreaming can be

a much more vivid experience than waking fantasy. While they are happening, our dreams usually seem as real as events that occur when we are awake. Because of this vividness, we respond emotionally during our dreams, laughing or crying while we sleep. Third, dreaming is not bound by the rules of rational thought. In dreams we may go places we have never been or see people who no longer (or never did) exist (Van de Castle, 1971). What seems incomprehensible in the light of day is accepted as perfectly natural in the hours before dawn. **Dreaming,** then, is defined as an altered state of consciousness that occurs during sleep, appears to be real and immediate, and transcends rational thought. Given these characteristics, perhaps it is not surprising that our ancestors attributed their dreams to the nightly wanderings of their souls.

But of what do we dream? To answer this question, college students in sleep research studies have been awakened during periods of REM sleep and asked to describe their previous thoughts. The following findings are based on those reports:

- Our dreams are more likely to be brief and common than exotic or bizarre. Since unusual

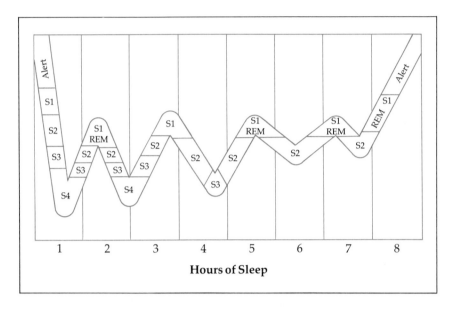

FIGURE 5.7 The cycles of sleep. During the night, our sleep shows a cyclic pattern as it passes through the different stages several times. Typically, our deepest sleep occurs within the first few hours. Thereafter, our sleep becomes progressively shallower, while the length of our REM periods becomes increasingly longer.

things tend to be remembered and common things tend to be forgotten, we may forget most of our dreams very quickly simply because they are so ordinary.

- As the central character in our dreams, we rarely dream of ourselves as being alone or in the company of strangers. The people we usually dream about are the people we interact with during the day.

- Our dreams have a negative tilt. Dreams of misfortunes—failing a test, or losing a loved one—are more frequent than dreams of success. Similarly, acts of aggression outnumber acts of kindness.

- Sexual encounters do not seem to occur very frequently in dreams. One study found that one dream in 10 was sexual for males, while one dream in 30 was sexual for females. These figures may underestimate the actual occurrence of sexual activity in dreams, though, if the subjects were reluctant to make full reports to the sleep researchers.

(From Hall and Van de Castle, 1966)

Occasionally, outside stimulation is incorporated into our dreams. For example, many of us have been awakened by a telephone that we previously heard ringing unanswered in our dreams. Perhaps the best example is found in an 1861 book on sleep in which the author, Andre Maury, dreamed that he was guillotined during the French Revolution. After the guillotine fell and chopped off his head, Maury woke up and found that the top of his bed had fallen and hit him on the back of the neck (Webb and Bonnet, 1979). These examples show that we can respond to a loud or jarring external stimulus while we are dreaming, but, in fact, we usually do not. Sleep researchers generally have been unsuccessful in getting dreamers to incorporate such external phenomena as running water into their dreams (Dement, 1978; Webb and Cartwright, 1978).

The content of dreams seems less dependent on external events during sleep than on actual events in the dreamer's waking life. The events of the previous day are often important, but so too are ongoing events. For example, pregnant women begin dreaming about childbirth after their fourth or fifth months of pregnancy. Many of these women dream of delivering a deformed child or even a litter of animals (Van de Castle, 1971). Such dreams are vivid and exaggerated expressions of a mother's concern about the health of her fetus. In the same vein, approximately one-third of the dreams of subjects during their first night in a sleep research experiment involve fears of being electrocuted (Dement, 1978). Since these subjects are wired for EEG monitoring during sleep, the unwarranted fear expressed by the dream is again certainly understandable.

THE MEANING OF DREAMS

In earlier times, dreams were thought to be messages from the gods, views of the future, or, more prosaically, signs of having eaten too much. There is no evidence to support any of these explanations. Through sleep research we have learned much about the occurrence and content of dreams, but we still do not know why we dream. Dreaming is a normal variation of consciousness that apparently serves some important biological function since the amount of REM sleep is regulated homeostatically—when people are deprived of dreaming by being awakened whenever they enter REM sleep, they will increase their amount of REM sleep on subsequent nights (Dement, 1960). The sheer fact that all of us will have 150,000 dreams by the time we reach age 70 suggests that dreams are important (Snyder, 1970). But exactly what function might these nightly fabrications serve?

Freud (1900) offered a psychoanalytic theory in his book, *The Interpretation of Dreams*. Dreams, said Freud, were the guardians of sleep. Their purpose was to allow the sleeper to express unconscious wishes in disguised form. According to Freud, dreams have both a **manifest** (obvious, conscious) **content** and a **latent** (hidden, unconscious) **content.** The manifest content of dreams comes from a person's memory, daily events, and bodily sensations during the night. The latent content is different. It contains the underlying motives that would disturb a sleeping person if they were consciously expressed. Instead, the latent content is concealed in a dream and expressed indirectly through the use of symbols. For example, an unconscious wish for sexual activity (latent content) might be symbolized in a dream by the presence of fire (manifest content). To interpret a dream correctly, Freud asked his patients to say whatever came to mind as they discussed their dream's manifest content. Through this **method of free association,** Freud attempted to uncover the latent content of the dream—the true motive that was being expressed in the dream. Freud's idea that dreams provide an outlet for unacceptable wishes pushed out of consciousness has intrigued psychologists for years, but there is still no firm evidence to support it.

Radically different from Freud, some neuroscientists suggest that our dreams are simply attempts by our brain to understand the random electrical discharges that occur throughout the night. According to this neural theory, active cells stimulate nearby cells related to different bodily functions. These cells may in turn activate higher cortical centers that will then attempt to interpret the signals they receive. Dreams, as such, could be the brain's attempt to interpret essentially meaningless messages from the lower centers (Hobson and McCarley, 1977). In a sense, the brain may be making the best it can of a bad situation. For example, dreams of being pursued while you are unable to move may result from the motor paralysis that occurs during REM sleep (Browman et al., 1982). Other related views hold that dreams are meaningless noise generated by the nervous system as it either "erases" irrelevant information from memory (a sort of "mental housekeeping") or provides periodic checks of the neural circuits during sleep (Crick and Mitchison, 1983; Evans, 1984).

The cognitive theory of psychologist David Foulkes (1985) is similar to the neural theory of Hobson and McCarley. According to Foulkes, dreams are involuntary mental acts based on information stored in memory. Our memory contains traces of events of the day as well as persisting personal concerns. These traces can be activated while we sleep just as thoughts and images can "pop" into our head while we are awake. These activated traces are then organized in some manner to make "sense" to the dreamer. For example, if the memory traces for *book, dog,* and *exam* become activated during sleep, you might organize these traces into a picture story and dream of yourself reading a *book* for an up-coming *exam* and being interrupted by a *dog* who starts to chase you. The elements of the dream are derived from things that you know or have experienced, but the dream itself is totally meaningless. It is like taking a set of random words and organizing them into a sentence. The sentence may be grammatically correct, but it signifies nothing.

Which interpretation of dreaming is correct? We do not know at present. It may be that dreams reflect meaningful psychological concerns at some times and meaningless gibberish at others.

HYPNOSIS

According to popular belief, **hypnosis** is a state of consciousness that is closely related to sleep. In the movies it is usually portrayed as a deep sleep or a sleeping trance. In fact, hypnosis received its name from the Greek word *hypnos* for *sleep.* Yet while people who are hypnotized may have their eyes closed, act very passive, and give the appearance of being asleep, the similarity of hypnosis to sleep is superficial. Physiologically, a hypnotized person's brain wave pattern, heart rate, and blood pressure resemble those of a person who is awake, not asleep. Behaviorally, a hypnotized person will respond appropriately to the suggestions of the

Mesmer's patients receiving "treatment." An eighteenth-century physician named Mesmer believed that illness was caused by an imbalance of invisible magnetic fluids in the body. He attempted to "cure" his patients by having them sit around a tub holding iron rods that were supposed to have been magnetized. When Mesmer appeared in the dimly lighted room he would pass among his patients, perhaps touching them, or gazing into their eyes and uttering commands. Psychologists believe that Mesmer discovered a procedure for inducing hypnosis in his patients.

hypnotist, while a sleeper will be oblivious to the suggestions of others. Hypnosis is also unrelated to sleepwalking, found predominantly in children during Stages 3 and 4 of sleep. Sleepwalkers do not follow instructions, and they do not remember their walks, hypnotized people follow instructions and, unless they are told to forget, they remember everything that has occurred (Barber, 1975). Hypnosis is defined as a state of consciousness that is characterized by heightened suggestibility and imagination and reduced initiative and reality testing (Hilgard, 1977).

HYPNOTIC INDUCTION AND SUGGESTION
Hypnotic induction is the name for the procedures used to guide a person into a hypnotic state. Each hypnotist has his or her preferred method of induction, but all use procedures to focus the subject's attention, reduce reality testing, and stimulate the imagination. For example, a hypnotist may ask a person to focus on a spot on the ceiling. As the person's eyes become fatigued, the hypnotist will suggest that the person is becoming relaxed. Good hypnotic subjects will eventually accept the hypnotist's suggestions and experience a sense of reality that has been likened to our sense of involvement in reading a fascinating story or watching a gripping movie. On one level we know that a story or movie is not real, but on another level we become involved and respond as though it were actually happening. In a similar sense, a hypno-

tized person might follow the suggestions of a hypnotist to laugh or to cry, but still maintain some contact with reality (for instance, the person must still hear and comprehend the hypnotist's instructions). People cannot be hypnotized against their wills, and they are no more apt to jump out of a window or hit themselves over the head during hypnosis than they would be during normal waking consciousness (Orne, 1977). The hypnotist does not dominate or control another person—he or she simply creates a condition in which a person can relax and act upon different suggestions. In a sense, the hypnotist acts as a tour guide to direct the hypnotized person's mental travel. Thus, the capacity to be hypnotize resides in the subject rather than in the hypnotist (Orne and Dinges, 1989).

Who can be hypnotized? The popular belief that only weak-willed or compliant people are hypnotizable is wrong. In other circumstances, people who are easily hypnotized are no more compliant than any other people (Orne, 1977). Tests of imagination and suggestibility, including the Stanford Hypnotic Susceptibility Scale, are used to indicate who is likely to be hypnotized. Imagine, for a moment, that a mosquito just landed on your hand and you wish to brush it off. If, in carrying out this imaginary task, you brushed off the mosquito, moved your hand, or made a facial grimace, this would indicate a strong imagination. If you did this consistently to a large number of items on the test, you would probably be a hypnotizable subject. In tests of this type, some people score very low, most fall in the midrange, and some—less than five percent of all people—score very high (Hilgard, 1977). Those who score high tend to be highly hypnotizable people. Rather than being weak or compliant, these people are imaginative and have a potential for creative expression. They identify deeply with characters in books and movies, and as actors they "become" the characters they portray. From early childhood on, these people have had the ability to set reality temporarily aside and become involved in their imaginative experience (Hilgard, 1974).

THEORIES AND CONTROVERSY

The study of hypnosis began in Paris, late in the eighteenth century. Conceived as a therapeutic treatment by the Austrian physician Fredrich Anton Mesmer (1734–1815), **mesmerism** was the precursor of hypnosis. It was Mesmer's belief that illness was the result of an imbalance of invisible magnetic fluids in the body. In order to restore the balance and thereby effect a cure, Mesmer had his patients sit alongside a tub filled with iron fragments while he walked around staring intently into their eyes. Some of Mesmer's patients, whose disorders were predominantly psychological in origin, were actually cured by this technique. Established French scientists were skeptical, however, so a royal commission investigated Mesmer's procedures in 1784. It was headed by the American ambassador to France, Benjamin Franklin. They concluded that his cures were due to the powers of touch and imagination rather than "magnetic" forces. Today, most psychologists believe that Mesmer produced his cures by the induction of hypnosis.

In general, hypnosis researchers fall into one of two theoretical camps. On one side are those psychologists who believe that hypnosis is a special altered state of consciousness, fundamentally different from normal waking consciousness. On the other side are those who believe that hypnosis can be explained by normal psychological processes that do not involve any special altered states. The "state" theorists hold that the events imagined during hypnosis are, like those in a dream, experienced as real; conversely, the "nonstate" theorists believe that hypnotized subjects follow the suggestions of the hypnotist but remain aware of what is actually going on around them (Kihlstrom, 1985). We will look at some of the evidence to see why they disagree.

People under hypnosis sometimes demonstrate what appears to be perceptual deafness or blindness. If sensory information could actually be blocked during hypnosis, then hypnosis could not be simple "play acting." To test this possibility, one study had subjects read out loud while their speech was played back to them through a set of earphones after a short delay. Instead of hearing what they just said, the subjects heard what they had said earlier. The normal response to this condition is to stammer and mispronounce words. Unlike truly deaf people who are not affected by delayed auditory feedback, people who were "deaf" through hypnosis made the same speech errors as other subjects who were not hypnotized (Barber & Calverley, 1964). On the basis of this type of research, "nonstate" psychologists such as Theodore Sarbin and others believe that hypnosis is a type of role-playing (Sarbin and Coe, 1972; Spanos and Radtke-Bodorik, 1980). Hypnotized people play the role that is suggested to them by the hypnotist's instructions ("Concentrate on my voice and relax. You will enter a state of hypnosis . . ."). This is not to suggest that hypnotized people are simply faking; the role is completely real to both them and the hypnotist. The role of a hypnotized person is just one of many roles (like student, sibling, or athlete) that a person might play. However, for these psychologists hypnosis is no more a special state of consciousness than is playing a game of tennis.

Why do others believe that hypnosis is an altered state? For some psychologists such as Ernest Hilgard, the belief that a hypnotized person is role-playing is difficult to accept. Hypnosis has been used to reduce or eliminate the perception of pain in countless medical procedures from tooth extraction to caesarean childbirth (Hilgard, 1986; Spiegel, Bierre, and Rottenberg, 1989). Hilgard argued that acting should not work to alleviate real pain. To support his argument, Hilgard noted that people under hypnosis can hold their arms in ice water without reporting the normal degree of pain. While the hypnotized subjects say that they feel comfortable as they keep one of their arms in freezing water, curiously, they will press a response key with their other hand indicating that they are experiencing increasing pain (Figure 5.8). Hilgard believes that there is a "hidden observer" during hypnosis that maintains contact with reality. When requested by the hypnotist, the hidden observer can write about sounds heard while hypnotically deaf and remember things that he or she is told to forget.

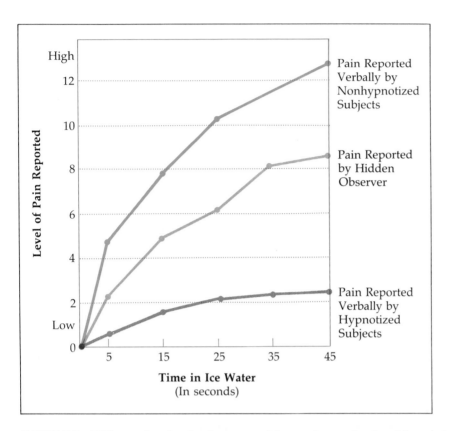

FIGURE 5.8   Different levels of pain reported by nonhypnotized and hypnotized subjects.   Hypnotized subjects responded either verbally or by having their "hidden observer" press a key. Some psychologists believe that even under hypnosis, part of our conscious awareness maintains contact with reality. The part that maintains contact is called the hidden observer.

Other psychologists, however, have criticized these findings by showing that hypnotized people in the ice immersion task will report either high or low levels of pain by their "hidden observers" depending upon what they are told by the experimenter (Spanos and Hewitt, 1980; Spanos, 1986). The fact that the subject's expectations can influence the "hidden" reports is consistent with the idea that hypnotic subjects enact a role. The experimenter's instructions define how they should play that role. In view of these conflicting interpretations, many psychologists are still uncertain about whether hypnosis truly represents an altered state of consciousness or is simply a form of role enactment during normal conscious awareness.

Current research in hypnosis is exploring earlier claims of **hypnotic age regression** and **hypermnesia** (improved recall of previously forgotten events under hypnosis). In studies of age regression, hypnotized subjects are supposed to be able to relive earlier episodes in their lives. However, recent studies fail to support this claim. Hypnoti-

cally "age-regressed" adults are incapable of thinking like children. They behave like adults trying to act like children (Nash, 1987). Nor has experimental research supported the claim that hypnosis can be used to improve the recall of forgotten events (Register and Kihlstrom, 1987; Yuille & McEwan, 1985). Such results indicate that hypnosis is of little use to eyewitnesses in courtroom proceedings. We will describe eyewitness memory and the conditions that affect it more fully in Chapter 7.

MANIPULATIONS OF CONSCIOUSNESS

So far, we have shown how consciousness is selective, continuous, and ever-changing. We turn now to its personal aspect. Every day, our consciousness varies naturally from a state of waking awareness to the various stages of sleeping and dreaming. Hypnosis is one technique that was developed to alter consciousness artificially. Long before Mesmer, however, people developed other techniques to manipulate their personal consciousnesses directly. Taking drugs is one example, and practicing meditation is another. Drugs, in particular, can alter our personal consciousness in different and sometimes terrifying ways.

DRUGS

A **drug** is any substance other than food which when ingested can stimulate or depress mental and/or physical functioning by acting on the nervous system. In this discussion, we will examine the alterations of personal consciousness produced by three general classes of drugs—**stimulants, depressants,** and **hallucinogenics** (Table 5.1). We will describe a variety of drugs in each class but focus our attention on three in particular because they are so widely used: cocaine (a stimulant), alcohol (a depressant), and marijuana (a hallucinogenic).

STIMULANTS

Stimulants are frequently used and abused in modern society. The relatively mild doses of caffeine in coffee and the nicotine found in cigarettes are in this class, along with the more dangerous stimulants such as amphetamines and cocaine. In small amounts, stimulants reduce fatigue and make us more alert. In larger doses, stimulants

---

TABLE 5.1   A General Classification of Different Drugs

Stimulants
Caffeine
Nicotine
Amphetamines (Methedrine)
Cocaine

Depressants
Sedatives
   Tranquilizers (Diazepam and Chloridiazepoxide)
   Barbiturates (Nembutal)

Opiates (Narcotics)
   Opium
   Heroin
   Morphine
Alcohol

Hallucinogenics
Lysergic acid diethylamide (LSD)
Mescaline (Peyote)
Phencylidine (PCP or "angel dust")
Marijuana

---

lead to feelings of increased energy and excitement. Physiologically, these drugs lead to an increase in pulse rate and blood pressure. They also increase blood sugar level, leading to a loss of appetite.

Amphetamines are synthetic drugs that stimulate the central nervous system by facilitating the release and retarding the re-uptake of the neurotransmitters dopamine and norepinephrine. (See Chapter 2.) The immediate effect of increasing the release of norepinephrine, for example, is to increase arousal and feelings of well-being. However, several hours after ingesting a large dose of amphetamine, the user may rebound into a state of depression because the brain cannot resynthesize new norepinephrine quickly enough to replace that which was released (Kalat, 1988).

These "uppers" are frequently used to counteract everyday feelings of depression and sleepiness. Because they suppress the appetite, amphetamines were once used in diet pills. In large doses, amphetamines can produce convulsions and lead to heart attacks and stroke (cerebral hemorrhage) because they stimulate enormous increases in blood pressure. One of the most dangerous amphetamines is Methedrine or "speed." When injected directly into the bloodstream, Methedrine produces a euphoric high that often leads to psychological dependence. When the high wears off, it can be recovered by repeated injections. After several days, however, the feeling of euphoria is difficult to sustain, and the negative side effects of the drug (including tremors, muscle pain, and feelings of persecution and other forms of distorted thinking) become more intense. As a consequence of going without food or sleep for an extended period of time, the user may collapse in a state of exhaustion. Long-term use can also lead to an amphetamine psychosis that resembles schizophrenia. Finally, extended use results in a **tolerance**—continued use of the drug requires progressively larger doses to get the same effects. For amphetamines, a tolerance develops to almost all of the drug's effects except the psychosis, which becomes more intense with continued drug use (Uretsky, 1989).

Cocaine has effects that are physiologically similar to those of amphetamines. Cocaine is derived from the leaves of the coca plant and may be injected, smoked, or sniffed. If cocaine is injected or smoked, its effect is almost immediate and may last from 10 to 20 minutes; if it is sniffed, its effect begins in about two minutes and may continue for 20 to 40 more (Weiss, 1989). Like the amphetamines, cocaine can induce feelings of euphoria, excitement, and self-confidence, increased talkativeness, restlessness, and a false sense of increased muscular strength. In larger doses, cocaine can lead to tremors, convulsions, hallucinations, paranoid delusions, and even death (Table 5.2). Like the other stimulant drugs in the class, cocaine's primary effect is to increase central nervous system activity by blocking the re-uptake of dopamine and norepinephrine.

Experts once disagreed about the possibility of physical addiction to cocaine, but current research indicates that this drug is extremely addictive (Wilbur, 1986). One of the earliest advocates of the medicinal use of cocaine was Sigmund Freud. He used it to treat his own feelings of depression and fatigue and thought that it was a miracle drug. However, Freud changed his mind about cocaine when a colleague took the drug on his recommendation and developed an acute cocaine psychosis (involving convulsions and disordered thinking) that led eventually to his death. Today, concern over cocaine centers on a potent, chemically modified form of cocaine called "crack" that can be smoked, and which is generally sold in pellets. The effects of smoking crack are even faster and more intense than those of inhaled cocaine and more quickly addictive, too. Crack is also more dangerous because overdoses can cause death by cardiorespiratory arrest (Cohen, 1980; Ray, 1983). Altman (1988) cites as examples of the devastating effects of cocaine and crack the case of three Detroit men who suffered paralyzing strokes after smoking crack, and the report of a healthy 45-year-

old man who died suddenly from a ruptured aorta after smoking cocaine for several hours. Because supporting a cocaine or crack habit is usually very expensive (some have been known to spend $2,000 a day), it is generally necessary for users to resort to crime in order to finance this pursuit (Weiss, 1989).

DEPRESSANTS

In contrast to such "uppers" as cocaine, depressants are called "downers." They come in a variety of forms. There are **sedatives,** such as the **tranquilizers** Valium (diazepam) and Librium (chloridiazepoxide) that calm the user by slowing the heartbeat and relaxing the muscles, and there are **barbiturates,** such as Nembutal, that can induce sleep. There are also **narcotics,** such as heroin, morphine, and opium, that are used to reduce pain. All of these drugs have negative side effects. Although barbiturates induce sleep, they reduce time spent in REM sleep and lead to a tolerance and withdrawal symptoms ranging from nightmares to severe anxiety. Narcotics produce a relaxed euphoria, but also lead to bodily tolerance and physical dependency. Even Valium, which is often thought of as a harmless tranquilizer, can lead to a physiological tolerance and physical addiction. Since the opiates (heroin, morphine, and opium) reduce the rate of respiration, an overdose can result in death through respiration failure. Withdrawal from opiates also leads to severely painful symptoms.

Neuroscientists believe that sedatives such as the tranquilizers Valium or Librium affect the brain by altering chemical transmission at the receptor sites (Barchas, Berger, Ciaranello, and Elliot, 1977). Specialized receptors the tranquilizer diazepam—so-called "Valium receptors"—have been found in parts of the brain involved in emotion (Mohler and Okada, 1977; Young and Kuhar, 1980). Just as the discovery of opiate receptors in the brain led to a search for endogenous (self-produced) opiates called endorphins (described in Chapter 2), the existence of receptor sites for diazepam suggests that the brain may produce its own tranquilizer to calm the central nervous system. Taking a sedative may supplement this process, as the sedative relaxes muscle tissue and enhances the function of inhibitory neurotransmitters (such as GABA) in the brain.

By far the most commonly used depressant is **alcohol.** Alcohol is sometimes mistaken for a stimulant because it affects the brain regions that normally inhibit behavior. Consequently, a person may become more talkative and sociable following

---

TABLE 5.2	**Cocaine's Effect on the Body**
Brain and Nervous System	Constriction and breaking of arteries leading to stroke. Seizures, tremors, delirium, and psychosis.
Blood Vessels	Constriction of blood vessels and abrupt rises in blood pressures.
Heart	Reduced flow of oxygenated blood to the heart, irregularity of heartbeat, and heart attacks.
Liver	Destruction of cells.
Nasal Passages	Damage to cells and loss of sense of smell.
Reproductive System	Following long-term use, males and females experience difficulty in maintaining sexual arousal.

Modified from Altman (1988).

a few drinks. However, with continued drinking, depressant effects become clear. Alcohol invades all parts of the body because of its chemical solubility and small molecular size (Pinel, 1990). It is clearly a depressant because it depresses neural firing. Sensations are dulled, the ability to memorize or solve problems is impaired, and even well-learned skills such as walking or driving become uncoordinated (Table 5.3).

Physiologically, alcohol acts as a general depressant. However, some effects of alcohol consumption may depend on psychological factors. Particularly with small or moderate amounts of alcohol, people's behavior is heavily influenced by what they expect alcohol to do. In one experiment, male social drinkers were given a drink containing either vodka and flavored tonic or only flavored tonic. Half of the men were told that their drinks contained alcohol and half were told that theirs were alcohol-free; in reality, half of the drinks in each group contained vodka. Following the drink, each man was given a test of social anxiety that required him to try to make a favorable impression on a woman who was actually an accomplice of the researchers. Using heart rate as a measure of anxiousness (the more anxious you are, the faster your heart beats), this study found that men who thought that they had consumed alcohol tended to have slower heart rates than those who thought that they had been drinking only tonic water. Regardless of whether they had actually consumed

any alcohol, the men who thought that they had drunk vodka showed less anxiety than those who believed that they had only consumed an alcohol-free drink (Wilson and Abrams, 1977). When only a small amount of alcohol was involved, expectancies were more important than actual blood alcohol levels.

Expectations influence a person's behavior only to a point. After several drinks, there are physiological changes that override expectancy—the drinker becomes intoxicated. (See Table 5.3.) The quantity of alcohol necessary before someone becomes intoxicated depends on such factors as body weight, the length of time since the last meal, and whether the drinking has gone on long enough for the drinker to have developed a tolerance. Other things being equal, heavier people, people who have just eaten protein-rich foods, and experienced drinkers, who have developed a tolerance, can all consume more alcohol before feeling its effects than can others. Since alcohol is so widely accepted in our society, it is the drug most widely abused.

RESEARCH AND APPLICATION:
Alcohol Abuse

Over 100 million adults in this country use alcohol. Approximately 10 to 12 million of them are alco-

TABLE 5.3 Blood Alcohol Concentration and Behavior

Blood Alcohol Concentration	Behavioral Effects	Beverage Consumption*
0.05%	Reduced alertness, pleasurable feelings, release of inhibition, impaired judgment	2 cans of beer or 2 glasses of wine or 1 cocktail
0.10%	Delayed reaction times, impaired motor control, reduced caution, legal intoxication in many states	4 cans of beer or 4 glasses of wine or 2 cocktails
0.20%	Marked reduction in sensory and motor ability	
0.25%	Severe motor and perceptual impairment	10 cans of beer or 10 glasses of wine or 5 cocktails
0.30%	Stupor, lack of comprehension	
0.35%	Possible death beyond this point	

*Blood alcohol concentrations are based on 150 pounds of body weight and consumption during a one-hour period. Concentration will be higher for lighter body weights and lower for heavier weights, and it will be higher for women than men because men have more fluid (less fat) than women of the same body weight. Individual behavioral effects of alcohol consumption vary.

From Ray (1983) and other sources.

Teenage alcohol use. A large-scale survey commissioned by the National Institute on Drug Abuse reported that approximately 90 percent of the high school students in the sample had drunk alcohol in the past year and that roughly 20 percent had been intoxicated at least six times during the period (Johnston, Backhan and O'Malley, 1982). Alcohol is the most widely used and abused drug in the world.

holics—people who are so dependent on alcohol that it interferes with their health, interpersonal relations, and livelihood (Goodwin, 1989). The problems created by alcohol abuse can be seen daily in our hospitals and on our highways. Consider the following facts:

- Alcohol abuse (including intoxication) is the single most common reason for hospital emergency room visits.

- Approximately half of the first admissions to mental hospitals involve alcohol-related problems.

- Over half of all automobile accidents involve drivers who have alcohol in their bloodstreams.

(Johnston, O'Malley, & Bachman, 1989; Schuckit, 1989)

People who abuse alcohol harm not only themselves, they distress their families, friends, and the people who work with them. In the case of drunk drivers, their victims may be complete strangers. Nor is this problem limited to adults—adolescents use and abuse alcohol as well (McKirnan and Johnson, 1986). In fact, the peak drinking years for most people are between ages of 18 and 34 (Lettieri and Ludford, 1981). Problem drinking is especially serious for high school and college age young people. Because drinking initially eases tensions and promotes friendly interactions, it is seen as an integral part of social life. However, alcohol-related accidents are the leading cause of death among young adults. Because of the high rate of traffic

mortalities, many states have raised their legal drinking age from 18 to 21 years and observed a significant reduction in highway fatalities.

Consequences of Alcohol Abuse

What are the consequences of alcohol abuse? Consumption of large amounts of alcohol for an extended period of time is associated with a shortened life expectancy, liver disease, heart failure, hypertension, and cancer of the mouth and throat. Chronic alcohol consumption is also associated with extensive brain damage that results in **Kosakoff's syndrome,** a disorder that is characterized by profound memory impairment. (See Chapter 7.) However, there is no evidence that one or two drinks a day has any adverse effects on health for adult males and nonpregnant adult females. The adverse effects of alcohol on fetal development are discussed in Chapter 11.

Although considerable research has been directed to studying the effects of alcohol, researchers are still not certain how alcohol affects the brain. A drink of alcohol is absorbed into the bloodstream from the stomach walls and small intestines, and is carried to the brain, where it passes through the blood-brain barrier. (See Chapter 2.) The first part of the brain to be affected is the cortex. Areas of the cortex that normally serve an inhibitory function become inactive, leading the drinker to be less socially inhibited following a moderate amount of alcohol. Larger amounts of alcohol affect more widespread areas of the brain and lead to ever-greater disruptions in behavior. Finally, if too much alcohol is consumed at one time, the lower centers of the medulla (an enlargement of the brainstem that controls breathing and heart functioning) cease to function. At this point, the drinker dies (Levinthal, 1983). To date, research has focused on how alcohol affects the action of the brain's neurotransmitters, but no final conclusions have been drawn. Research has provided vivid descriptions of the consequences of chronic (long-term) alcoholism, however. For example, people who have been drinking excessively for a long time and suddenly stop can develop a dangerous withdrawal syndrome called **delirium tremens (DTs).** Included in its symptoms are the following:

- Tremors of the hands, tongue, and lips
- Disorientation for time and place
- Vivid hallucinations
- Acute sense of panic

Perhaps the best description of delirium tremens is the fictional, though highly accurate, account provided by Mark Twain in *Huckleberry Finn.*

> Pap took the jug, and said he had enough whisky there for two drunks and one delirium tremens. . . . He drank and drank. . . . I don't know how long I was asleep, but . . . there was an awful scream and I was up. There was Pap looking wild, and skipping around every which way and yelling about snakes. He said they was crawling up on his legs; and then he would give a jump and scream, and say one had bit him on the cheek—but I couldn't see no snakes. He started and run around . . . hollering "Take him off! he's biting me on the neck!" I never see a man look so wild in the eyes. Pretty soon he was all fagged out, and fell down panting; then he rolled over . . . kicking things every which way, and striking and grabbing at the air with his hands, and screaming . . . there was devils a-hold of him. He wore out by and by. . . . He says . . . "Tramp–tramp–tramp; that's the dead; tramp–tramp–tramp; they're coming after me; but I won't go. Oh, they're; don't touch me— don't! hands off—they're cold; let go. . . ."
>
> Then he went down on all fours and crawled off, begging them to let him alone. . . .

(Twain, 1884/1983)

A person suffering from delirium tremens would be hospitalized and treated with a tranquilizer such as Librium. This tranquilizer has a

"cross tolerance" with alcohol—it will substitute for alcohol—and thus stop the withdrawal symptoms. Over a period of four to seven days, the tranquilizer dosage is gradually reduced as the patient overcomes his or her addiction to alcohol. Without medical treatment, delirium tremens can lead to major convulsions and death.

Treatment of Alcohol Abuse

What is the best treatment for alcoholism? At present, there is controversy not only about the best course of treatment but about the nature of alcoholism itself. For many years alcoholism has been thought of as a disease, and the only "cure" for this disease is total abstinence from alcohol use. More recently, some psychologists (who prefer the term *problem drinking* to alcoholism) see it as a learned behavior disorder. Instead of complete abstinence, they believe that some alcoholics can regain control of their drinking (Marlatt and Rose, 1980).

The idea that alcoholism is a disease can be traced to a book published in 1785 by an American physician named Benjamin Rush. However, it was not until the middle of this century that Elvin Jellinek (1960) popularized this view. From case studies of alcoholic patients, Jellinek saw alcoholism, like disease, as following a course of progressive deterioration. Alcoholics, he said, began with social drinking to relieve tension and ended with a complete loss of control. Once a person is an alcoholic, thought Jellinek, there exists a "craving" in the body for alcohol such that one drink sets up a chain reaction requiring him to continue drinking, even against his will. Because of this loss of control, Jellinek believed that total abstinence was the only treatment possible for alcoholism. Organizations such as Alcoholics Anonymous (AA) follow this course of treatment.

Psychological research, however, has challenged the general view of alcoholism as a disease and Jellinek's specific assumption about loss of control. For example, psychologist G. Alan Marlatt and his associates have shown that the mere *belief* that they are drinking alcohol can lead alcoholics to increase their drinking and begin to crave alcohol. In one experiment, similar to one we already described, some alcoholics were given drinks supposedly containing alcohol. Actually, some subjects received vodka and tonic, while others received only tonic. Other alcoholics were given the same types of drinks and told that they all were alcohol-free. If alcoholics suffer from a loss of control, then all of the subjects who received a drink containing alcohol, regardless of what they were told, should

A meeting of Acoholics Anonymous. Weekly meetings are often staffed by counselors who are themselves recovered alcoholics. They work to form a loosely knit community that allows alcoholics to help each other stay sober. Members adopt the view that alcoholics are "allergic" to alcohol and that the cure for this allergy is avoidance.

have shown an increased craving and consumed more. This did not occur. Alcoholic subjects consumed more drinks only when they thought they were drinking alcohol, regardless of the content of their drinks (Marlatt, Demming, and Reid, 1973). Findings such as these cast doubt on Jellinek's view of alcoholism as a disease that results in loss of control.

On the other hand, alcoholism does have a strong genetic component. It runs in families, especially for males. Sons of alcoholics, even those separated from their parents at birth, are more likely to become alcoholics than sons of nonalcoholics. If the sons are identical twins, both have an increased risk of being alcoholic, even if they are raised apart (Goodwin, 1979; Schuckit, 1983). This research suggests that there may be a genetic predisposition toward alcohol abuse.

But even with a genetic predisposition toward alcoholism, it may be possible to change serious problem drinkers by new learning experiences. To date, the most ambitious and controversial treat-

ment is the **controlled drinking program** of Mark and Linda Sobell (1973; 1978). In this program, alcoholics are taught a variety of new skills. For example, they are taught how to monitor the level of alcohol in their bloodstreams by observing their alcohol intake over time; they are taught effective social skills to improve interpersonal relations; and they are taught different methods of relaxation. The goal of the program is to train alcoholics to control their drinking so that they may resume social drinking without fear of losing control. Unlike the disease model of alcoholism, this view holds that control can be acquired through reeducation—it is not invariably lost to a "disease."

Does controlled drinking work? Unfortunately, there is no clear answer. Early research by the Sobells (1973; 1978) indicated that alcoholics could in fact learn to control their consumption. However, a 10-year follow-up study suggested that this program was a failure. Many of the alcoholics who were trained in controlled drinking failed from the onset to drink safely, and a large number of these people were rehospitalized within a year of their training (Pendery, Maltzman, and West, 1982). Other research has suggested that controlled drinking is possible depending on the severity of the alcoholism. This *severity of dependence hypothesis* holds that the more dependent a person is on alcohol, the poorer his or her chances of controlling future drinking (Heather and Robertson, 1983). Some success at controlled drinking has been reported for alcoholics with relatively low levels of consumption and drinking problems of short duration (Orford, Oppenheimer, and Edwards, 1976), but, for those judged severely dependent, controlled drinking has rarely, if ever, been obtained (Edwards, Duckitt, Oppenheimer, Sheehan, and Taylor, 1983). Thus there is some support for the severity of dependence hypothesis, but the relation between dependence and controlled drinking remains imprecise because dependence is often difficult to measure (Orford and Keddie, 1986). Until the debate over controlled drinking is settled, alcoholics who have successfully stopped drinking are probably best advised not to drink again. ■

HALLUCINOGENICS
The vivid hallucinations and other examples of distorted perceiving and thinking found in people suffering from delirium tremens can also be produced by certain hallucinogenic drugs. Hallucinogenics are drugs that modify personal conscious-

ness by affecting a person's sensation, perception, thinking, self-awareness, and emotion. They include such drugs as LSD, mescaline, and PCP ("angel dust"), as well as marijuana. Collectively these drugs produce changes in a person's sense of time and space and can also lead to hallucinations and other forms of distorted perceptions. The effects of marijuana are milder than those of the other drugs, but whether such effects will be weak or strong depends on the dosage level and the person.

LSD, or lysergic acid diethylamide, is a synthetic drug derived from a fungus called ergot that grows on grain. An average dose, amounting to no more than a speck, can have an effect that lasts for hours (Figure 5.9). Users report that colors seem to shimmer, objects appear magically and shift kaleidoscopically, nonexistent voices or music may be heard, and the perception of time can be distorted—hours pass like minutes or minutes pass like hours. As the following personal example demonstrates, these unusual experiences can sometimes be quite unpleasant.

> The physical world I could see had begun slowly to come apart. No cubic inch of space had to do with any other. Everything in my field of vision turned into bright jelly. There was no time and place, nothing but a flow. I got up and waded through the room, making my way unsteadily. Around me the music, the fire, and the candle dripping, the lights of nearby buildings, all combined and flowed.

> Yet I could see Ralph and Arthur watching me, and I saw my own situation with terrible clarity. I had gone out too far and couldn't get back! I called to Ralph, remembering what Arthur had said in the beginning: ". . . if you get hung up, always move toward your partner." I did, crying: 'Help me. I want to get back!'

(Harrington, 1967)

The effects of LSD depend upon when, where, with whom, and by whom the drug is taken (Barron, Jarvik, and Bunnel, 1964). Moreover, since most LSD is made in makeshift labs, it can contain other chemicals, such as Methedrine (speed) and strychnine, that make its effects even more difficult to predict. Because of these varying experiences, people rarely take this drug on a regular basis. LSD is almost completely eliminated from the body within 24 hours of ingestion, but "flashback" experiences can occur weeks or even months after the drug was last used. During these flashback episodes, the illusions or hallucinations of the original LSD "trip" may be experienced again—sometimes in situations where they may be dangerous for the individual (Stanton, Mintz, and Franklin, 1976). The cause of these flashback episodes remains unknown.

Aside from alcohol, marijuana is the drug most widely used to manipulate consciousness directly. Surveys suggest that approximately 60 million people over the age of 13 have tried marijuana at least once. Although the vast majority of all users

FIGURE 5.9 What is is like to take LSD? In this series of sketches, a man who took the drug attempted to draw a friend's face at different times during the LSD "trip." Shortly after taking the drug, little effect on perception or drawing could be seen (A). Within an hour, however, the sketches became increasingly disorganized as the subject reported difficulty controlling the movements of his hand (B, C). By the end of three hours, the subject reported that his visual experience was distorted. His perspectives had changed and everything seemed to be moving (D). Six hours after taking the drug, the effects started to subside (E), and after eight hours, the effects had largely disappeared (F). Upon completing the last sketch, the subject said that he was bewildered and tired.

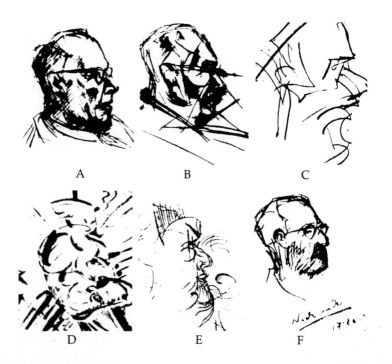

A B C

D E F

are classified as "experimenters," roughly five percent use the drug daily (Mirin, 1989). Marijuana is produced from a hemp plant that grows all over the world. Its leaves are dried and usually smoked. The effect may vary widely from person to person. Marijuana sometimes acts as a stimulant and at other times as a depressant, depending upon the current mood of the user. At low, usual "social" doses, it can produce a feeling of relaxation and enhance sensitivity to touch, taste, and sound. But, like alcohol and the other depressants, marijuana also can reduce coordination, impair memory performance, and lengthen reaction time in driving and other complex tasks. As with many drugs taken in small amounts, the effects of marijuana are heavily influenced by the user's beliefs or expectations about the drug. Many users report that they had to learn how to smoke marijuana, and that their expectations were not completely fulfilled during their first attempts. Smoking with experienced users provides the person with information on how to identify the drug-related experiences (Ray, 1983). Thus, in small amounts, the effects of marijuana are often subtle and influenced by the social situation (Pinel, 1990).

At present, it appears that small doses of marijuana do not produce a tolerance in the body. That is, increasing amounts are not needed to feel euphoric. Nor is there evidence that occasional use produces a physical dependency (Schaeffer, Andrysiak, and Ungerleider, 1981). However, some studies have reported that chronic users may develop a tolerance and can experience withdrawal symptoms that include loss of appetite, diarrhea, and sweating (Jones, 1980). Additional research has suggested other long-term ill effects of marijuana, including reduced fertility and increased susceptibility to lung disease (Taskin, Coulson, Clark, et al., 1985). Even occasional usage is not without potential danger as marijuana intoxication is detrimental to driving and can lead to highway fatalities (Jones and Lovinger, 1985). What is most disturbing is the fact that the effects of marijuana can last well beyond the feelings of euphoria originally produced by the drug. For example, a study of aircraft pilots showed that their performances on a flight simulator were significantly impaired for as long as 24 hours after smoking a single marijuana cigarette (Yesavage, Leiver, DeNari, and Hollister, 1985). These findings are of concern to all people involved in public safety.

In summary, despite years of research on marijuana and the other hallucinogenic drugs, many important questions about their effects remain unanswered. However, professionals do not view these drugs as harmless. They are all potentially dangerous (Petersen, 1989; Smythies and Ireland, 1989). Many people seem intent on playing with their personal consciousnesses and producing variations in their perceptions and emotions by drugs or alcohol. But they are playing a deadly game as shown by the high rates of addiction and the problems they cause.

WHY ADDICTS TAKE DRUGS

Addicts are people who continue to use drugs despite the ill-effects of the drugs on their physical and social life and despite repeated attempts to stop (Pinel, 1990). Many people equate addiction with **physical dependency,** the state produced by repeated usage of a drug such that its termination results in severe withdrawal symptoms. However, this view of drug addiction is no longer widely held. Many addicts who have gone through addiction treatment programs to rid their bodies of drugs return to their drug-taking ways months or even years later (Tims and Leukefield, 1986). This fact argues against physical dependency, since drugs are no longer in these people's bodies and withdrawal symptoms such as nausea and cramps usually disappear after a week. Some addicts may take drugs to alleviate withdrawal symptoms, but many do so because they have developed a **psychologically dependency.** These are people who are not physically dependent but who take drugs nonetheless, because they feel that the drugs are necessary for their sense of well-being.

To explain why addicts take drugs, many psychologists now favor a **positive incentive theory of addiction** over a theory that emphasizes physical dependence. According to this view, addicts take drugs to obtain the pleasurable effects of the drugs, not to avoid their unpleasant withdrawal symptoms (Stewart, de Wit, and Eikelboom, 1984, among others). The following comments from one addict provide an apt description of this position:

> I'm just trying to get high as much as possible. I would have to spend $25 a day on heroin to avoid withdrawal, but I actually use about $50 worth. If I could get more money, I would spend it all on drugs. All I want is to get loaded. I just really like shooting dope. I don't have any use for sex; I'd rather shoot dope. I like to shoot dope better than anything else in the world.

(From Pinel, 1990)

If the pleasure that is derived from a drug is the primary factor in drug addiction, then the phenomenon of *electrical stimulation of the brain (ESB)* becomes important to our understanding the physiological basis of drug addiction. You may recall from Chapter 2 that rats will engage in self-stimulation by pressing a bar to receive tiny electrical impulses through an electrode that has been implanted near the hypothalamus (Olds and Milner, 1954). In fact, rats will press the bar as often as 2,000 times an hour for brain stimulation, in some cases stopping only after collapsing from exhaustion. The researchers speculated at that time that the neural circuits that were responsible for self-stimulation might also be responsible for the pleasurable effects associated with other activities such as eating, drinking, sexual activity, and possibly even taking addictive drugs. Today there is support for this view. Current research suggests that cell bodies in the brainstem send axons to the limbic system that promote the release of dopamine and provide a signal for reward. This reward circuit in the brain can be stimulated by a diverse set of pleasurable behaviors that have major survival value to the organism—eating, drinking, and sexual activity, to name just a few. It is now known that this reward circuit can also be stimulated by certain behaviors that have nothing to do with survival. These behaviors include self-stimulation (ESB) and taking addictive drugs (Wise, 1988; Wise

and Rompre, 1989). This means that a brain circuit that was once stimulated naturally by behaviors related to survival can now be stimulated powerfully and directly by behaviors unrelated to an organism's health or well-being.

According to Roy Wise (1988), an understanding of the dopamine reward circuit can explain why drug habits are so difficult to break. Drugs like cocaine or its derivative, crack, can activate the reward circuit directly and with much more intensity than any survival-related activity we may find rewarding can. For addicts, this means that the pleasure obtained from biologically important behaviors cannot compare to the pleasure they obtain from their drugs. Look back to the quotation from the addict who said that he or she likes "to shoot dope better than anything else in the world." This provides a powerful message about why addicts take drugs and why treatment programs are so often unsuccessful. In allowing people to play with their consciousness, drugs provide a shortcut to pleasure while they bypass those activities that used to provide pleasure for most of our evolutionary history (Wise, 1984).

MEDITATION

MEDITATION AND CONCENTRATION

Meditation offers a way to manipulate personal consciousness directly, without drugs. It primarily involves a set of mental exercises that can produce concentration, awareness, and a sense of tranquility and equilibrium. When Buddhism was introduced into Japan from China in the thirteenth century, the teachers, or Zen masters (*Zen* is the Japanese pronunciation of the Chinese word for *meditation*), used daily periods of quiet meditation to guide their pupils toward *satori*, a special state of "pure awareness" (Figure 5.10). The Zen masters believe that our perception of the world is distorted by desires and cultural beliefs, and they use meditation to eliminate these illusory views and see the world more directly and clearly.

Rather than using meditation as a ritualistic or ceremonial way of escaping life, Buddhists use it as a method to manipulate consciousness in order to face life fully and directly. For example, by learning to attend fully to the present, a person becomes free of self-awareness. Attention is focused on what is happening here and now, rather than divided and directed toward the imagined self in the future or the remembered self in the past. This is what the Zen masters meant by pure awareness and is why meditation is not a technique for escaping from life.

A person smoking crack, the stronger and more addictive form of cocaine. Crack is a fast-acting, intense stimulant that increases the activity of the central nervous system by blocking the re-uptake of the neurotransmitters dopamine and norepinephrine. The result is a feeling of euphoria followed by a crashing low.

FIGURE 5.10 Japanese monk practicing Zen meditation to achieve transcendence and enlightenment. Psychologists study people who meditate regularly to see whether it provides them with any health benefits. Some benefits have been found.

Although there is no single way to meditate, one method of the Zen masters has become popular. Under the guidance of a teacher, beginning meditators spend two periods each day sitting motionless with their eyes closed to learn how to control their attention. During these sessions the meditator is asked to count each breath from one to ten and to repeat this exercise for five or ten minutes. As the following example shows, what makes this task so difficult is that our minds tend to wander.

> At the beginning you will find it extremely difficult to bring your mind to concentrate on your breathing. You will be astonished how your mind runs away. It does not stay. You begin to think of various things. You hear sounds outside. Your mind is disturbed and distracted. You may be dismayed and disappointed. But if you continue to practice this exercise twice daily, morning and evening, for about five or ten minutes at a time, you will gradually, by and by, begin to concentrate your mind on your breathing. After a certain period, you will experience just that split second when your mind is fully concentrated on your breathing, when you will

not hear even sounds nearby, when no external world exists for you. This slight moment is such a tremendous experience for you, full of joy, happiness and tranquility, that you would like to continue it. But still you cannot. Yet if you go on practicing this regularly, you may repeat the experience again and again for longer and longer periods.

(Rahula, 1959)

This is the beginning of concentrative meditation. More advanced meditators may focus on a sound pattern called a *mantra* by saying a word or phrase over and over to themselves or they may focus on a paradox called a *koan* (What is the sound of one hand clapping?) to try to escape from reasoning and reach a state of consciousness devoid of self-awareness.

THE BENEFITS OF MEDITATION

Practioners of meditation claim that they feel refreshed after they meditate, and that they can see the world more clearly. While we have no way of evaluating the claim that meditators "see the world more clearly," we can examine research that looks for objective physiological change. For example, meditation can reduce oxygen consumption, lower respiration and heart rates, and reduce the lactate level in the blood stream (high lactic acid is associated with anxiety) while a person is meditating (Benson and Friedman, 1985; Shapiro, 1985). In addition, meditation has been associated with lowering high serum cholesterol levels (Cooper and Aygen, 1979), reducing sleep-onset insomnia (Woolfolk, Carr-Kaffashan, and Lehrer, 1976) and lessening irritability and minor depression (Carrington et al., 1980). Meditation also seems to lower the general level of body metabolism and produce EEG recordings with alpha waves similar to those usually found during periods of resting wakefulness. Unfortunately for people with high blood pressure, however, reductions in blood pressure during meditation have either not been found reliably or have been found only in a few hypertensive patients, who have taken medication for their hypertension while they meditated (Benson, 1975; Benson and Friedman, 1985). Physiologically, the overall body response to meditation seems opposite to the fight or flight reaction found when the body mobilizes its systems during an emergency. For this reason, bodily reactions to meditation are sometimes referred to as "the relaxation response" (Benson, 1975).

Not all psychologists are convinced that there are any clear benefits of meditation. Several conditions make it difficult to know whether the reported benefits are due to meditation or other factors. For example, there is always a potential problem of *self-selection* in these studies of meditation. Positive effects of meditation may be obtained by those who use it because only those people who find the experience rewarding continue to meditate. For those who abandon the use of meditation because they find it unsatisfactory, no effects can be reported. Researchers have also found that during periods of meditation some people engage in brief periods of sleep, so that some of the general positive effects on health associated with meditation may simply be due to rest (Holmes, 1980; 1987). Much more research will need to be done before we can evaluate the claims of those who practive meditation and understand how it changes their conscious awareness.

INTERACTIONS:
The Value of Consciousness

In Chapter 1, we described the interactionist viewpoint as a way of combining elements from various theoretical perspectives to understand the whole human being. In Chapters 2 through 4, we described the neuropsychological perspective in looking at the biological bases of behavior, sensation, and perception. In each closing section we have tried to show how an organism's behavior could be seen as a successful adaptation to its particular environment. In this chapter we have introduced the cognitive perspective in examining attention and awareness. We spent considerable time showing how consciousness is selective, continuous, ever-changing, and personal. Each of these characteristics of consciousness was originally outlined by William James (1890; 1892). But we have not yet considered James's view of the adaptive function of consciousness for our everyday behavior.

In Chapter 1 we said that our behavior is based on both *proximate* and *ultimate* causes. Proximate explanations focus on the present causes of behavior, while ultimate explanations focus on long-term historical causes. William James took an ultimate perspective when he wrote his first textbook in psychology. Influenced by Charles Darwin's theory of evolution, James believed that our actions and even our thoughts had evolved to serve some purpose—namely, to help us survive. In this Jamesian tradition, we can ask about the adaptive function of consciousness by raising the following question: How does consciousness help us survive?

In order to answer this question, psychologist George Mandler (1985) suggested that we replace it with two simpler questions: When are we conscious, and what are we conscious of? Mandler answered these questions this way: We are conscious, he said, first, when we acquire new knowledge and skills. For example, as we are learning to drive a car we are conscious of our every action; later we can drive automatically. Second, we are conscious when we must make choices (Do I turn left or right at the fork?). Third, we are conscious when our environment changes. If a dog runs into our path while we are driving home, this event suddenly "registers," and we take appropriate action to avoid running it over.

As we saw earlier in Chapter 3, our senses respond to changes in environmental stimulation to provide us with new information. This information is then registered in consciousness so that the contents of consciousness change whenever there is a change in the state of our world (Mandler, 1985). If you are meditating beside a Buddist temple, you may not notice the constant chattering of the local monkeys, but you will almost certainly be jarred by the pounding feet of a stampeding elephant or a thunder clap in the distant mountains. By making us aware of change, consciousness provides us with information about our place in the world and makes us better able to cope. Consciousness thus provides us with the opportunity to make choices and plan (How can I avoid that dangerous animal? Where can I go to take shelter from the storm?). In this way, consciousness allows us to think about the outcomes of different actions before any overt responses are made. We can eliminate harmful or nonbeneficial alternatives by thought rather than by trial and error.

Consciousness, therefore, has value to us as a species because it enables us to act *reflectively* rather than *reflexively*; it allows us to focus on the most important aspects of our environment and to adapt to changing conditions. This is not to say that we do not at times act reflexively; many of the brain's biological functions occur with no conscious awareness. However, the availability of consciousness permits us to act reflectively in some circumstances to which lower animals respond only reflexively. This is the adaptive advantage of consciousness that William James described long ago, and this is why it has value in our everyday behavior. ■

IN CONTEXT: CONSCIOUSNESS

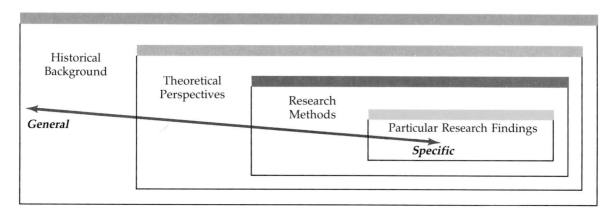

STUDY QUESTIONS

What is the role of conscious awareness?

How many different forms of consciousness exist?

How can we manipulate conscious awareness and what are the effects of these manipulations?

HISTORICAL BACKGROUND

1. The first studies of consciousness were conducted by Wilhelm Wundt in 1879. Wundt sought to determine how sensations and feelings are combined to produce different conscious experiences. Following Wundt, Edward Titchener used introspection to reveal the basic elements of consciousness. This approach became known as **structuralism.**

2. Early in the twentieth century, John B. Watson championed the view that psychology must be an objective science and focus only on observable behavior. Consciousness had no place in Watson's approach, which was called **behaviorism.**

3. The study of consciousness returned to psychology with the rise of **cognitive psychology** during the 1950s and 1960s.

MODERN THEORETICAL PERSPECTIVES

1. The cognitive approach is the main theoretical perspective for studying consciousness. Cognitive psychologists seek to determine how our thoughts, knowledge, and interpretations influence our ability to acquire information, solve problems, and make plans.

2. There are a variety of specialized theories that attempt to explain alterations or manipulations of consciousness in dreams, hypnosis, and alcoholism.

3. Dreams can be viewed as unconscious wishes expressed in disguised from **(psychoanalytic theory),** the brain's attempt to interpret meaningless messages from lower brain centers **(neural theory),** or involuntary mental acts based on information stored in memory **(cognitive theory).**

4. "State" theorists believe that hypnosis is an altered state of consciousness; "nonstate" theorists hold that hypnosis is a type of role-playing.

5. Some theorists believe alcoholism is a disease that results in a loss of control. They hold that the best treatment is total abstinence. Others view alcoholism as a learned behavior that can be changed by new experiences. This approach teaches controlled drinking.

6. According to the **positive incentive theory of addiction,** addicts do not take drugs to avoid unpleasant withdrawal symptoms but to obtain their pleasurable effects.

RESEARCH METHODS

1. **Experimentation** was widely employed. For example, it was used to determine the bases of selective attention in dichotic listening tasks (Cherry, 1953), whether there is a hidden observer in hypnosis (Hilgard, 1977; Spanos and Hewitt, 1980), and the effects of expectations on alcohol consumption (Wilson & Abrams, 1977).

2. **Surveys** have been used to measure the frequency of daydreaming (Singer and McCraven, 1961), the content of dreams (Hall and Van de Castle, 1966), and the effectiveness of controlled drinking programs (Pendrey et al., 1982).

3. The **case study** of Jonah showed how consciousness is divided in a multiple personality.

RESEARCH FINDINGS AND SUMMARY

1. **Consciousness** is synonymous with awareness; it is our awareness of our perceptions, memories, and thoughts at any particular moment.

2. **Attention** is the focusing of awareness on a limited number of stimuli. We select one stimulus source as relevant and reject the remainder as irrelevant on the basis of physical or meaningful cues.

3. Practice on a task serves first to reduce the number of errors that are made and later to reduce the amount of attention needed to perform the task. After considerable practice, **automaticity** results—some tasks can be performed with little or no conscious awarenss.

4. Case studies of **multiple personality** in which people can shift back and forth between different identities show an extreme division of consciousness. Each personality may exhibit different brain wave patterns, different voice patterns, and widely different behavior characteristics.

5. An **altered state of consciousness** is a change in mental experience from that occurring during normal waking consciousness. Examples of altered states include **daydreaming, sleeping,** and **dreaming** while asleep.

6. Our pattern of waking and sleeping follows a regular 24-hour schedule. During sleep, there is a cycle of stages that is detected by recording the electrical activity of the brain. In periods of deep sleep, we produce **rapid eye movements (REMs)** under our closed lids. We tend to dream during REM sleep.

7. **Dreaming** represents an altered state of consciousness that occurs during sleep, appears real and immediate, and transcends rational thought. Everyone dreams four or five times a night, and the majority of our dreams are common, unexciting, and involve the people we interact with during the day. There is no generally accepted explanation of the meaning of dreams.

8. **Hypnosis** seems superficially to be like sleep, but, physiologically and behaviorally, it is different. People who score high on tests of imagination and suggestibility tend to be hypnotizable.

9. **Drugs** are chemical substances other than food that can stimulate or depress mental and physical functioning. In small doses, stimulants such as caffeine can reduce fatigue and make us more alert. Stronger stimulants such as amphetamines or cocaine can produce a physiological tolerance, a physical addition, and even death.

10. **Depressants** include sedatives, barbiturates, and narcotics. The use of narcotics, including heroin, morphine, and opium, results in an increased tolerance that can lead to physical dependence. The most commonly used depressant is alcohol.

11. **Hallucinogenics** are drugs that affect sensation, perception, thinking, self-awareness, and emotion. They include such drugs as LSD, mescaline, and PCP, as well as marijuana. These drugs do not produce physical dependence, but they can produce temporary changes in a person's thinking by giving rise to hallucinations and other forms of distorted perception. Aside from alcohol, marijuana is the drug most widely used for directly manipulating consciousness.

12. **Meditation** involves a set of mental exercises designed to produce concentration, awareness, and a sense of tranquility and equilibrium. Meditation appears to lower body arousal and energy demands and produce a restful state.

ADDITIONAL READINGS

Bowers, K. S. 1983. *Hypnosis for the seriously curious.* New York: Norton. An introduction to hypnosis that describes different hypnotic phenomena and various clinical applications in an unbiased, authoritative manner.

Goleman, D., and Davidson, R. J., eds. 1979. *Consciousness: Brain, states of awareness, and mysticism.* New York: Harper & Row. A wide ranging collection of papers on

different approaches to the study of consciousness and altered states.

Hobson, J. A. 1988. *The dreaming brain.* New York: Basic Books. A fascinating review of what sleep researchers have learned about sleeping and dreaming.

Mandler, G. 1985. *Cognitive psychology: An essay in cognitive science.* Hillsdale, NJ: Erlbaum. A book on cognitive psychology's past, present, and future that discusses consciousness and mind in a thoughtful and engaging manner.

Ray, O. S. 1983. *Drugs, society, and human behavior*, 3rd ed. St. Louis: Mosby. A carefully researched, authoritative introduction to the study of drugs and their effects on behavior.

Schuckit, M. A. 1989. *Drug and alcohol abuse: A clinical guide to diagnosis and treatment*, 3rd ed. New York: Plenum. A current textbook on the effects of drugs and available treatment programs.

West, M. A., ed. 1987. *The psychology of meditation*. New York: Oxford University Press. A thoughtful guide to the methods and findings on meditation from leading researchers in the field.

LEARNING

W e are all accustomed to having our emotions manipulated by seemingly innocuous stimuli. Successful novels, plays, films, and television shows are successful in part because they move us to experience strong emotions. But they move us even though we do not directly experience any significant . . . stimuli. How do these initially insignificant stimuli get their power over us?

(Barry Schwartz, 1989)

In a 1960 Alfred Hitchcock movie, an attractive woman checks into an eerie roadside lodge. Fatigued and unsuspecting, she slips into the shower. Suddenly, an unidentified assailant appears, raises a butcher's knife high into the air, and brutally stabs the lonely traveler to death. For some time after seeing *Psycho,* many people were a bit nervous every time they entered a shower. In a 1975 Stephen Spielberg film, a young girl frolicking offshore at a popular beach resort is suddenly dragged under the surface and devoured by a massive white shark. After seeing *Jaws,* many people were reluctant to set foot into the ocean. The directors of these popular films had inadvertently made water phobics out of masses of viewers. Our goal in this chapter is to describe the basic principles of learning that underlie these sorts of reactions and, more importantly, to show how our behavior can be profoundly influenced by a few of these very simple learning principles.

We define **learning** as a relatively permanent change in behavior or behavior potentiality that results from experience (Hergenhahn, 1982; Kimble, 1961). There are four terms within this definition to which you should pay special attention. First, learning is inferred from a *change in behavior* because we cannot directly observe the changes in the brain that occur when someone learns something. Second, *behavior potentiality* means that learning can occur even if an animal or person makes no observable response at the time of learning. The effect of learning may only be apparent later when an appropriate occasion arises. For example, people may silently watch chilling films like *Psycho* or *Jaws* and show distress only later, when they are alone in a shower or swimming in the ocean. Third, the requirement that learning be *relatively permanent* excludes temporary changes in behavior such as those produced by fatigue, illness, or drugs. For example, fatigue may cause our driving to deteriorate, but a period of rest will restore our normal performance. Finally, learning is based on *experience*. This fact is critically important because inappropriate behavior acquired from past experience can later be changed. *Psycho* viewers' initial anxiety about showering was unlearned after they took several showers without encountering any slashers.

Learning has an important function. It helps us *adapt* to changing conditions in the world. Adaptation is the process of changing behavior to fit changed environmental conditions. Psychologists in several different fields study learning in order to determine how much of our behavior can be changed by environmental factors and how these changes in behavior are made. For example, developmental psychologists study how we learn to make moral decisions and how little girls and boys learn about gender roles. Clinical psychologists are also interested in learning, but they wish to understand the role that learning plays in making some of us continually anxious and others murderously aggressive. An understanding of the elements that make up learning is necessary to an understanding of many different aspects of behavior.

Ours is not the only species that is capable of learning. In fact, psychological knowledge about learning has often come from studies of rats, pigeons, and dogs. These animals are invaluable for research. The elementary forms of learning found in humans can also be demonstrated in animals, and we can precisely control their genetic history, past experience, and motivational states such as hunger or thirst. For example, you will see that the same sorts of methods that have been used to teach animals new behaviors have also been used to treat problem behaviors in people.

After describing the history of research on learning, we will examine two major forms of learning. The first is **classical conditioning,** an elementary form of learning that enables us to make connections between events or phenomena in our environment (for instance, our association between bells ringing and class breaks). The second is **instrumental conditioning,** a form of learning that allows us to learn the consequences of our behavior (such as traffic tickets for speeding). Early theorists tried to explain all learning on the basis of these two processes.

Modern researchers still view these processes as important. However, they believe that much of learning, even in animals, involves complex **cognitive learning,** a form of learning that involves forming internal representations of events in the world. We will discuss cognitive learning at the end of this chapter, as a prelude to the next chapters that deal with memory and thought. Those chapters will cover the kind of learning you can obtain from lectures and books. This chapter focuses on the more elementary types of learning involved in forming associations and learning the consequences of your actions.

HISTORICAL BACKGROUND:
Associative Learning

When we come to feel uneasy in the shower after watching *Psycho*, or experience moments of panic in the ocean after watching *Jaws*, it is because we have made an association between the events in the film and those in our life. **Associative learning** is defined as the learning of a relation or contingency between events in the world. Associative learning from movies that connect showering or swimming with violent death is an unfortunate twist on what is normally a very beneficial learning process. Associating the smell of smoke with the presence of fire, for example, can save our lives. How do we learn to make associations between events in our environment?

Modern ideas about associative learning can be traced back through seventeenth- and eighteenth-century British empiricist philosophers, including John Locke and George Berkeley, to Aristotle in classical Greece. These philosphers were interested in how we form mental associations between ideas. One important principle of mental association was called **contiguity:** Such sensations as sights and smells become associated if they occur together in time and place. For example, we come to associate smoke with fire because smoke and fire are most often experienced together. How does this process work? William James provided a physiological explanation:

> When two elementary brain processes have been active together or in immediate succession, one of them on reoccurring tends to propagate its excitement into the other.
> *(James, 1890)*

James thus attempted to explain the association of ideas on the basis of contiguity of brain processes.

At the time James wrote these words, there was no physiological research to support his statement. It was not until the turn of this century that the methods of natural science were applied to the study of learning by two towering figures in the field, Ivan Pavlov and Edward Thorndike. Pavlov studied learning because he was interested in the functions of the nervous system. Thorndike studied learning to understand the evolution of intelligence. Each helped establish the psychology of learning by studying associative processes in animals.

Ivan Pavlov

Ivan Pavlov (1849–1936) was born in a peasant village in central Russia. He originally studied to become a Russian Orthodox priest like his father, but a change of mind led him to physiology. As a result of his pioneering research on digestion, he won a Nobel Prize in 1904. However, Pavlov is remembered today for his program of research on learning. This work began accidentally while he was studying salivation in dogs. Pavlov observed that a dog sometimes began salivating when there was no known physiological reason for it to do so. For example, a hungry dog would salivate not only to meat powder placed in its mouth but also to the

mere sight of a food bowl. In fact, Pavlov found that a hungry dog would salivate at the sight of a laboratory assistant, the onset of a light, or even the beat of a metronome—if each of these different stimuli immediately preceded the delivery of food. Pavlov labeled these responses "psychic secretions" to distinguish them from those that occurred naturally when food was placed in the mouth. The discovery of the psychic secretions had a profound impact on the field of psychology. In fact, they provided the first experimental evidence for associative learning.

Pavlov's great insight was to treat these psychic secretions as reflexes that operated according to the same principles as any other digestive reflex. Since he thought that all bodily functions were regulated by the nervous system, Pavlov believed that the psychic secretions were based on newly formed neural connections. The original salivary response to food in the mouth was called an *unconditioned reflex*, while he considered the secretion of saliva in response to a stimulus associated with food a *conditioned reflex* (Pavlov, 1927). Translated from the original Russian, these terms are now used to describe the associative processes we call **classical conditioning.**

Edward Thorndike

In the United States, Edward Thorndike (1874–1949) took a far different approach to the study of learning. Like Pavlov, the son of a minister, Thorndike had never heard of psychology until his junior year at Wesleyan University, when he read William James's *Principles of Psychology*. After graduation he studied with James at Harvard, and began his research on animal learning in the basement of James's home. Like James, Thorndike was influenced by Charles Darwin's theory of evolution. Thorndike wanted to know how animals use their intelligence to adapt to the conditions of the world. Darwin (1871) had earlier argued that mental ability was not uniquely human; it was just more developed in humans than in other species. If humans evolved from lower animal forms (as Darwin believed), then the study of animal learning was essential to understanding the biological origins of human intelligence. George Romanes, an ardent supporter of Darwin, followed this lead and wrote a major work called *Animal Intelligence* in 1884. Romanes tried to document the learning ability of a broad range of species, including mollusks, ants, bees, wasps, termites, spiders, fish, reptiles, birds, rodents, cats, dogs, foxes, wolves, jackals, and elephants (Domjan, 1987). Thorndike continued this tradition. His 1911 book—also called *An-*

Ivan Pavlov. While studying the digestive process in dogs, Pavlov found that the animals often began salivating to stimuli associated with food before they began to eat. He spent years studying this form of associative learning that we now know as classical conditioning.

Edward L. Thorndike. Influenced by Darwin's theory of evolution, Thorndike was interested in learning how animals use their intelligence to adapt to the world. He studied trial-and-error learning in which animals learn the consequences of their actions. This type of learning is now known as instrumental conditioning.

imal Intelligence—influenced the study of learning in the United States for decades.

As an example of how Thorndike studied learning, Figure 6.1 shows a picture of an apparatus called a puzzle box that Thorndike devised for his research. A hungry cat was placed in the box with a dish of food outside. Inside the box there were various devices: a button, a string loop, or a foot pedal that, if pressed or pulled, opened the door of the box and allowed the cat to escape and get the food. Thorndike described the changes in the cat's behavior that occurred over a series of sessions as **trial and error learning.** According to Thorndike,

> When put into the box the cat . . . tries to squeeze through any opening; it claws and bites at the bars or wire; it thrusts its paws out through any opening and claws at everything it reaches; it continues its efforts when it strikes anything loose and shaky. . . . The cat that is clawing all over the box in her impulsive struggle will probably claw the string or loop or button so as to open the door. And gradually all the other non-successful impulses will be stamped out and the particu-

lar impulse leading to the successful act will be stamped in by the resulting pleasure, until, after many trials, the cat will, when put in the box, immediately claw the button or loop in a definite way.

(Thorndike, 1898)

Thorndike did not believe that a cat learned to escape in order to get food or that the cat formed a mental expectation of food. Rather, a cat merely learned to make a particular response in a particular situation—learning that was strengthened by the food reward that followed. Thorndike believed that animals adapt to their environments by forming associations between stimuli (for example, the foot pedal in the puzzle box) and responses (a paw movement on the pedal that opens the door). These associations between stimuli and responses are strengthened according to Thorndike's **law of effect:**

> Of several responses made to the same situation, those which are accompanied or closely followed by satisfaction to the animal will, other things being equal, be more firmly connected with the situation.

Thorndike, 1911)

In Thorndike's puzzle box example, satisfaction produced by escaping from the box and eating the food "stamped in" the particular response that led to escape. This stamped-in response thus becomes more likely to occur in the future. Since the animal's behavior was instrumental in receiving a reward, this form of associative learning has been called **instrumental conditioning,** in contrast to the form of associative learning studied by Pavlov called classical conditioning.

B. F. Skinner

Although Pavlov and Thorndike studied different forms of associative learning and did so for very different reasons (Pavlov to try to understand the formation of new neural connections and Thorndike to try to understand adaptive behavior in animals), each viewed associative learning as a mechanical process that was devoid of reason or thought. In other words, behavior was influenced by *external* environmental events and not by *internal* cognitive processes. This view, typified by psychologist B. F. Skinner's research, largely dominated the study of learning in the first half of this century. Skinner, as we will see in this chapter, saw the results of his studies of conditioning as providing a way of describing not only the behavior of rats and pigeons, but of people in

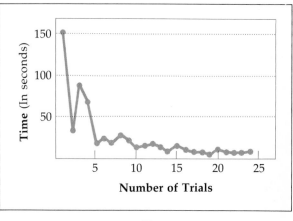

A

B

FIGURE 6.1 **(A) One of Thorndike's puzzle boxes for cats.** This primitive apparatus was fitted with strings or pedals that could be used to open the door of the box. The task of the hungry cat placed inside the box was to learn by trial and error how to get out for a food reward. **(B) A typical learning curve.** Thorndike measured the time it took a hungry cat to get out of a puzzle box. With practice, the cat got out faster and faster until after approximately 10 trials, it could escape immediately.

everyday situations. Until his death in 1990, he remained the leading proponent of **behaviorism,** an approach to psychology (discussed in Chapter 5) that holds that behavior can be described solely by environmental events (Skinner, 1953; 1987). However, many contemporary psychologists, including those who study animal learning, have come to differ with this view. We will see that psychologists now include cognitive processes in their explanations of learning, and that even simple associative learning has turned out to be anything but simple. ■

CLASSICAL CONDITIONING

PAVLOV'S FRAMEWORK

In every animal and person there are a number of innate *stimulus-response associations*—connections "wired in" at birth, before any learning occurs. For example, all people will pull back their hands (a response) from the top of a hot stove (a stimulus) or jerk their knees (a response) to a tap on the patellar tendon (a stimulus). We do not need to learn these responses to specific stimuli, nor do we consciously control them. We do not weigh the pros and cons of removing our hands from the stove—we jerk them back automatically and reflexively. Classical conditioning is constructed upon these inborn neurological connections that we described in Chapter 2. To use Pavlov's dogs as an example, there is an innate association between food and salivation: A hungry dog will always

salivate to food placed in its mouth. The food is a stimulus that automatically *elicits* a salivation response. Since no learning is involved in this reflexive action, Pavlov called the food stimulus an **unconditioned stimulus (UCS)** and the salivary response an **unconditioned response (UCR).**

Through learning, a previously neutral stimulus can come to acquire some of the same properties as an unconditioned stimulus. In this case, the previously neutral stimulus is called a **conditioned stimulus (CS)** and the response it produces is called a **conditioned response (CR).** For example, Pavlov's dogs did not normally salivate to the sound of a metronome (a previously neutral stimulus), but through conditioning the beats of the metronome (now a conditioned stimulus) came to be associated with food and therefore elicit salivation (now a conditioned response). To use a different example, the unconditioned stimulus of a brutal murder scene in the movie *Psycho* elicits the unconditioned response of fear and apprehension. Because of classical conditioning, the shower stimulus, previously associated only with feelings of cleanliness, is now associated with feelings of terror. This new emotional association between showering and fear follows the same principles of classical conditioning that led Pavlov's dogs to salivate to the beats of a metronome. Classical conditioning is thus a powerful and widespread form of learning. To see how such associations are formed and how they may be subsequently broken, we will examine several important conditioning processes discovered by Pavlov.

PROCESSES IN CLASSICAL CONDITIONING

Pavlov described the processes by which associations are acquired and become the sources for more general behaviors or more complex ones, as well as the ways in which these learned responses could be unlearned or extinguished. These processes include acquisition, higher-order conditioning, and extinction.

ACQUISITION

Acquisition is the process by which a stimulus comes to elicit a conditioned response. To see how this occurs, Pavlov performed an experiment to see whether he could produce salivation to a previously neutral stimulus. With a hungry dog in a harness to prevent unnecessary movement, Pavlov connected one of the animal's salivary glands to a recording device that measured secretions of saliva (Figure 6.2). When food powder was placed in the dog's mouth, there was an increase in the flow of saliva. This was simply the reflexive action of an unconditioned stimulus producing an unconditioned response. Next, Pavlov struck a tuning fork and observed the animal's reaction. The dog turned toward the sound, but it did not alter its flow of saliva. In this way Pavlov established that the sound of a tuning fork was a neutral stimulus with respect to the response of salivation.

Classical conditioning began when the tuning fork was struck several seconds before food was delivered into the animal's mouth. Pairing the sound of the tuning fork with the delivery of food constituted a *learning trial*. After a dozen or so learning trials, conducted over several days, Pavlov found that the flow of saliva increased to the sound of the tuning fork alone. The previously neutral sound had become a conditioned stimulus that elicited a conditioned response of an increase in the flow of saliva. The procedure used by Pavlov to establish a conditioned response is shown in Figure 6.3.

Pavlov continued his research by experimenting with the timing of the conditioned and unconditioned stimuli. These procedures, called **simultaneous, delayed, trace** and **backward conditioning,** are illustrated in Figure 6.4. In simultaneous conditioning, the conditioned and unconditioned stimuli are presented at the same time. In delayed conditioning, the conditioned stimulus is presented briefly before the unconditioned stimulus, and it remains present until the response occurs. In trace conditioning, the conditioned stimulus begins and ends before the unconditioned stimulus is presented, while in backward conditioning the unconditioned stimulus briefly precedes the presentation of the conditioned stimulus.

Short-delayed and trace conditioning work best. Simultaneous and backward conditioning are unreliable and often unsuccessful (Houston, 1991;

FIGURE 6.2 Pavlov's experimental apparatus for the study of conditioned salivation. The tube entering the dog's cheek drained the animal's saliva, which was collected and measured in the test tube shown on the base of the stand. During conditioning trials, the harness prevented the dog from making unnecessary movements.

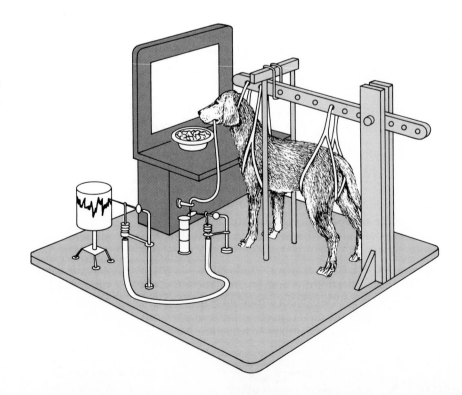

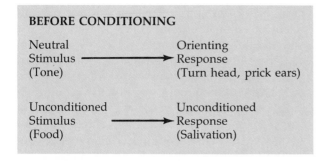

BEFORE CONDITIONING

Neutral
Stimulus ⟶ Orienting
(Tone) Response
(Turn head, prick ears)

Unconditioned ⟶ Unconditioned
Stimulus Response
(Food) (Salivation)

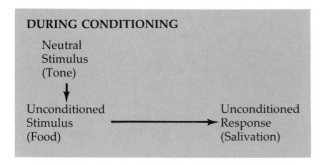

DURING CONDITIONING

Neutral
Stimulus
(Tone)
↓
Unconditioned ⟶ Unconditioned
Stimulus Response
(Food) (Salivation)

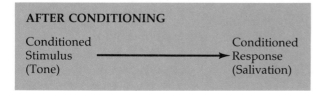

AFTER CONDITIONING

Conditioned ⟶ Conditioned
Stimulus Response
(Tone) (Salivation)

FIGURE 6.3 Pavlov's procedure for producing a conditioned response. The initial, neutral stimulus (such as a tone) elicits an orienting response but does not elicit salivation until it is paired with an unconditioned stimulus (such as food); it then becomes a conditioned stimulus that elicits salivation.

Schwartz, 1989). Delayed and trace conditioning are most effective because they permit the conditioned stimulus to signal the occurrence of the unconditioned stimulus. To draw an analogous example, a flashing light at a railroad crossing is an effective danger signal only if it *precedes* an approaching train. However, even with delayed or trace conditioning, the acquisition of a conditioned response is strongly influenced by the amount of time between the presentation of the conditioned and unconditioned stimuli. Conditioning is usually best when this interval is very short, typically around a half-second (Smith, Coleman, and Gormezano, 1969).

The type of conditioned stimulus is also important for acquisition. Early conditioning researchers thought that any neutral stimulus could be an effective conditioned stimulus, but psychologists now know this to be false. In some instances, animals demonstrate an **associative bias**—a biological "preparedness" or predisposition to learn relations between certain stimuli more easily than others. Rats, for example, will learn to avoid a particular food on the basis of its taste, but not its appearance. Psychologist John Garcia and his associates have found that rats can learn the association between a particular taste (a conditioned stimulus) and physical illness (an unconditioned stimulus) in only a single trial. This conditioning can occur even when the time between the taste and the illness is as long as 10

SIMULTANEOUS CONDITIONING

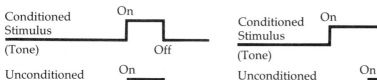

DELAYED CONDITIONING

TRACE CONDITIONING

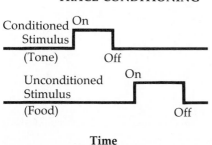

BACKWARD CONDITIONING

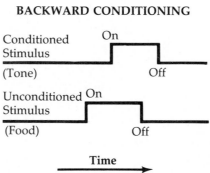

FIGURE 6.4 The different temporal arrangements for the presentation of stimuli in classical conditioning. Four different arrangements are possible depending upon whether the conditioned stimulus precedes (delayed and trace conditioning), occurs at the same time (simultaneous conditioning), or follows (backward conditioning) the presentation of the unconditioned stimulus. Delayed and trace conditioning are the best arrangements as the conditioned stimulus acts as a signal for the unconditioned stimulus that follows.

hours. However, little or no learning occurs if a light, a tone, or even the appearance of food is used as the conditioned stimulus (Garcia and Koelling, 1966; Garcia, McGowan, and Green, 1972; Domjan, 1980). In effect, the rat is biased to associate taste with physical illness. This fact should not be surprising. You may have experienced how a similar bias operates in people. If we taste a distinctive food such as Cajun shrimp and become ill later in the evening, what do we normally do? We connect our upset stomach with the distinctive food we ate rather than with other possible stimuli—including the people we had dinner with. Like the rat in the conditioning experiments, we associate our illness with "something we ate" and avoid that particular food in the future. This phenomenon is called **taste aversion,** and it explains why wild rats that taste poison and become ill but do not die are very difficult to poison afterward. On the basis of that one aversive experience, they will not eat anything flavored with that poison again.

Research on classical conditioning suggests that associations are facilitated if the conditioned and unconditioned stimuli are similar (LoLordo, 1979; Rescorla, 1987). For example, associations are learned faster if the stimuli (say a light as the conditioned stimulus and an aversive blast of air as the unconditioned stimulus) are presented in the same location (both from the ceiling or both from the floor) rather than in different locations (Testa, 1975). Associations are also learned faster if the stimuli are received by the same sense rather than by different senses. However, the phenomenon of taste aversion tells us that stimulus similarity is not the only basis for association. Certain types of conditioned and unconditioned stimuli seem to belong together. These findings are important to learning theorists because they imply that classical conditioning is influenced by more than just the closely timed pairing of the conditioned and unconditioned stimuli. Something other than temporal contiguity is at work.

What factor might guide the formation of associations between stimuli? One possibility is that associations are facilitated if the conditioned and unconditioned stimuli are biologically related. According to Martin Seligman (1970), the presence of an associative bias shows the importance of evolutionary factors in learning. For example, an associative bias may help explain why it is easier to learn a fear of sharks than of automobiles, even though many more of us have witnessed automobile catastrophes than attacks from killer

Fear of sharks. Some associations are more easily learned than others. For example, many of us can acquire a fear of sharks more readily than we can learn to fear automobiles or airplanes, even though we have witnessed many more crashes than shark attacks. This associative bias may be due to our evolutionary history of avoiding dangerous animals.

sharks. Humans may be more predisposed to fear sharks than cars because, as a species, we have had a long history of avoiding dangerous predators.

Another intriguing possibility was suggested recently by psychologist Barry Schwartz (1989). Suppose, says Schwartz, we think of classical conditioning not as associative learning but as a means of discovering cause and effect relations. Causes precede effects just as conditioned stimuli precede unconditioned stimuli. Classical conditioning can be the means by which animals and people differentiate true cause–effect temporal relations from temporal relations that are only accidental. For example, when we associate sickness with taste, we seem to be performing a causal analysis. We attribute our illness (an effect) to a novel food (a possible cause). This same causal analysis may be performed by the rat. Although speculative, this view suggests that classical conditioning makes a more important contribution to learning and everyday behavior than previously believed (Schwartz, 1989).

GENERALIZATION AND DISCRIMINATION

Once a conditioned response has been acquired, stimuli that are similar to the conditioned stimulus will also evoke that response. For instance, rabbits conditioned to blink to a tone of a particular pitch will also blink to tones higher or lower in pitch. This spread of conditioning to stimuli similar to the conditioned stimulus is called **generalization.** The greater the similarity between the original conditioned stimulus tone and a new tone, the more the generalization that occurs. In this example, generalization is based on similarity of sound, but it can be based on other similarities as well (Honey, 1990; Pearce, 1987).

Generalization is valuable because it reduces the amount of learning that is needed. For example, if we had to learn anew that each hot stove is potentially dangerous—if we could not generalize from our earlier experiences—we might never avoid burning our fingers. Generalization allows us to apply our earlier experiences to new, but similar, situations.

On the other hand, we can also learn *not to respond* to similar stimuli, while continuing to respond to the original conditioned stimulus. This process is known as **discrimination.** For example, if a dog learns that a note from a tuning fork (a conditioned stimulus) is always followed by food (an unconditioned stimulus) and if the dog is also exposed to other stimuli (bells and whistles) that are not followed by food, the dog will become

increasingly selective and learn to make a conditioned response only to the sound of the tuning fork. This discrimination procedure can also be used to determine an animal's sensory capabilities. If an animal responds differently to different-colored stimuli that are equal in brightness and saturation, showing a conditioned response only to one particular color, the animal must possess color vision. Similar training procedures can tell us about any of the other senses.

Although the processes of generalization and discrimination have been studied in the laboratory, they are, in fact, common in everyday life. An early frightening experience with a dog, for example, may initially cause a young child to fear all four-legged furry animals (generalization). Later, after experiences with friendlier dogs, the child will learn to discriminate among different animals and avoid those that are barking and baring their teeth but not those wagging their tails.

HIGHER-ORDER CONDITIONING

Until now, we have described examples in which a previously neutral stimulus becomes a conditioned stimulus through its association with an unconditioned stimulus. Pavlov also found that once a conditioned stimulus had been established, it could function as an unconditioned stimulus and be used to form new associations. In Pavlov's case, once a dog learned to salivate to the beats of a metronome (the original conditioned stimulus), a new stimulus such as a flashing light could elicit salivation even though it had never been paired with food, if it was first paired with the sound of the metronome. Pavlov called this procedure higher-order conditioning. Higher-order conditioning can be obtained when a new conditioned stimulus serves as a signal for the original conditioned stimulus (Leyland & Mackintosh, 1978). The significance of higher-order conditioning is that it shows that classical conditioning extends beyond the direct associations of conditioned and unconditioned stimuli to a much larger class of stimuli. A child who is bitten by a dog will learn to avoid the sound of dogs growling even though the dog who bit her was not growling.

EXTINCTION

So far, we have seen how animals can learn new conditioned responses. But environmental relations change, as when food no longer follows a tone. When conditioned and unconditioned stimuli no longer occur together, the old conditioned response must be erased. Pavlov called this **extinction** and defined it as the elimination of a conditioned response due to the withholding of the unconditioned stimulus. Figure 6.5 shows what Pavlov found when he stopped presenting an unconditioned stimulus after a conditioned stimulus. In this example, when the beats of the metronome were repeatedly presented alone the amount of saliva that was elicited showed a progressive decline. After several trials, the conditioned stimulus no longer produced a conditioned response. At this point the conditioned response was extinguished.

But how do we explain extinction? Three types of evidence led Pavlov to believe that the dogs held back or inhibited their responses because they learned that food was no longer forthcoming. First, as shown in Figure 6.5, if a response was extinguished and the animals were removed from the apparatus, the dogs, upon their return, would once again salivate to the presentation of the conditioned stimulus alone. This **spontaneous recovery** implied that a weakened conditioned response

FIGURE 6.5 The extinction and spontaneous recovery of a conditioned response. Pavlov found that presenting the tone without following it by food quickly resulted in a loss of salivation to the tone. This process is called extinction. However, the following day, when the tone was presented again, the animal salivated again but then quickly stopped salivating on the later trials. This brief recovery of a conditioned response is called spontaneous recovery.

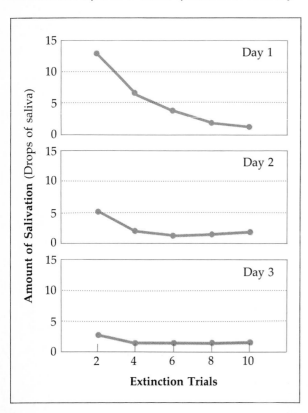

still existed. Second, the conditioned response would reappear if a distracting event such as a loud, unexpected noise was presented right after the presentation of a conditioned stimulus (but during the extinction trials). This was more evidence that the conditioned response still existed. Finally, after a conditioned response had been extinguished, the same response could be relearned in less time than it took to learn it originally. This savings in relearning implied that some of the original learning had been retained.

To understand the importance of extinction, imagine that conditioned responses never extinguished. The permanent effects of past experience could have serious consequences for our behavior. For example, the short-lived fear of taking a shower after seeing *Psycho* is merely annoying, but a permanent fear of showering would be a real handicap. Persistent inappropriate fears are called **phobias,** and they sometimes require the professional help of a psychologist to aid in the extinction process.

DYSFUNCTION:
Phobias and Conditioned Fears

A phobia is a persistent fear reaction that is greatly out of proportion to the reality of danger. For example, some people refuse to swim even in completely safe waters because of their fear of sharks. One interesting fact about most phobias is that they are more likely to occur to certain types of stimuli—phobias tend to involve the fear of injury (for example, falling from great heights), insects or animals (spiders or snakes), and specific situations (crowds or open spaces). In keeping with our earlier discussion of associative bias in conditioning, research on phobias suggests that people are biased or prepared to learn specific types of phobic associations (Seligman, 1972). For example, we are biologically prepared to be afraid of heights and predators. A second interesting fact about phobias is that they can be acquired and eliminated through the processes of classical conditioning (Kalish, 1981).

The earliest demonstration of a phobia acquired through classical conditioning was reported in 1920 by John Watson and Rosalie Rayner. In this study, an 11-month-old infant boy named Albert B was conditioned to fear a white rat. During the initial testing, Watson and Rayner established that little Albert showed no fear of the rat (a neutral stimulus), but he was startled and began to cry when a steel bar was struck by a hammer behind him as he reached out to touch the rat (a loud noise is an unconditioned stimulus that automatically elicits an unconditioned response of crying in infants). Later, during the conditioning trials, the frightening clang was sounded each time the rat was presented to the infant. After seven such pairings, Watson and Rayner presented the rat alone. According to their notes:

> The instant the rat was shown the baby began to cry. Almost instantly he turned sharply to the left, fell over on his left side, raised himself on all fours and began to crawl away so rapidly that he was caught with difficulty before reaching the edge of the table.

(Watson and Rayner, 1920)

Five days later, when little Albert was tested again, he still showed fear of the rat. Moreover, Albert also showed signs of fear when he was shown a rabbit, a dog, a seal fur coat, and even a Santa Claus mask. This suggested that the original conditioned response had generalized (Figure 6.6). Although little Albert showed signs of fear of furry or hairy objects, he never showed any fear of his toy blocks, even though they were also present at the time of conditioning. This latter finding suggests an associative bias, since Albert could learn an association between certain stimuli and not others. In fact, later studies with other infants failed to establish conditioned fear when a pair of opera glasses or a toy block was used as a conditioned

stimulus instead of a laboratory rat (Bregman, 1934; Valentine, 1930).

While we may seriously question the wisdom of the adults who conducted these procedures on a defenseless child, Watson and Rayner's study demonstrated two things. First, fear could be established by classical conditioning. Second, an acquired fear could generalize to new stimuli. What they neglected was a demonstration that conditioned fear could be extinguished. Although extinction training was part of Watson and Rayner's plan, the infant was removed from their study before they got to that phase. However, Mary Cover Jones (1924), an associate of Watson, later used other children to show that conditioned fear could be extinguished.

Numerous investigations have since shown that fear can be classically conditioned (Campbell, Sanderson, and Laverty, 1964; Kalish, 1981, among others). In some cases, fear established through conditioning can last over a period of years:

> During World War II, the signal used to call sailors to battle stations aboard U.S. Navy ships was a gong sounding at the rate of 100 rings a minute. To personnel on board, it was associated with the sounds of guns and bombs; thus it became a conditioned stimulus for strong emotional arousal.
>
> Fifteen years after the war, a study was conducted comparing the emotional reactions

FIGURE 6.6 John Watson and Rosalie Rayner testing little Albert for generalization of conditioned fear. After conditioning the infant to fear a laboratory rat, Watson and Rayner found that the newly acquired fear generalized to other objects not previously associated with fear. This 1920 study, which showed that phobias could be acquired through classical conditioning, has been criticized on ethical grounds. (Photo from 1919 film of Watson and Rayner study by Dr. Benjamin Harris, Swarthmore College)

of hospitalized navy and army veterans to a series of 20 different sound stimuli. Although none of the sounds were current signals for danger, the sound of the "call to battle stations" still produced strong emotional arousal in the navy veterans who had previously experienced that association.

(Edwards and Acker, 1961)

Why are phobias and conditioned fears so difficult to extinguish as conditioned responses? The answer is that in order for extinction to occur, a person must confront the conditioned stimulus in the absence of the unconditioned stimulus. If the fearful person can successfully avoid the phobic object or situation (the conditioned stimulus), extinction has no chance of occurring. For instance, people with a fear of snakes avoid those situations in which their fear might be extinguished. Unless a person encounters a few snakes and learns that most do not strike at humans, the fear is difficult to modify. We will see in the chapter on psychotherapy that treatments for phobias use the principle of extinction to eliminate undesirable behavior. New learning experiences pair relaxation responses with the conditioned stimuli that were previously associated with fear. ■

THE NATURE OF CLASSICAL CONDITIONING

As we mentioned earlier, the British empiricist philosophers believed that contiguity is the basis for associative learning. That is, stimuli become associated if they occur together in time and place. Pavlov's research with dogs strengthened this belief. However, more recent research has shown that classical conditioning requires more than just contiguity between stimuli. For one thing, an association is formed only when a conditioned stimulus acts as a signal for an unconditioned stimulus. For another, a conditioned response is an adaptive response for an animal or person, and it may be completely different from an unconditioned response. Before presenting evidence for these new views, we need to describe two phenomena that tell us a great deal about the process of stimulus association—sensory preconditioning and blocking.

SENSORY PRECONDITIONING AND BLOCKING

In the sensory preconditioning procedure outlined in Figure 6.7, one stimulus becomes associated with another stimulus before either is related to an unconditioned stimulus. For instance, in a study

by W. J. Brogden (1939), dogs were presented with a bell sound and a light together for 200 trials. Each time, the bell briefly preceded the light, and no other stimuli were presented. The repeated pairing of these neutral stimuli is called **sensory preconditioning** (Figure 6.7). After the first 200 trials, the light alone was paired with a mild electric shock. The shock was an unconditioned stimulus that caused the dog to withdraw its leg as an unconditioned response. Through classical conditioning, the dogs learned to withdraw their legs when the light went on. Now, what would happen if the bell were presented even though it had never been paired with the shock? Brogden found that the bell acted as an effective conditioned stimulus—the dogs withdrew their legs when they heard the bell ring. The bell served as a signal for the light, which had subsequently become associated with shock. Likewise, if you whistled "Singing in the Rain" every time you showered, you might get nervous upon hearing this song after seeing the shower scene in *Psycho*.

If the conditions of this experiment are reversed, so that the bell and the light are paired after the light has been associated with shock, with the bell preceding the light, we have the procedure for higher-order conditioning that we have already discussed (Figure 6.7). Under these conditions, the bell again serves as a signal for the light, and a conditioned response is observed. But if the light is associated with the shock and then the bell and light are presented together with the shock, there will be no conditioned response if the bell is later presented alone (Figure 6.7). This failure to learn about a second stimulus that has been presented in compound with a conditioned stimulus is called **blocking.** Apparently, once a reliable signal is found, learning about other potential signals is blocked. The phenomenon of blocking is important because it demonstrates that mere contiguity between stimuli is not enough to produce an association (Kamin, 1969; Pearce and Hall, 1980). Together, the results of the studies of sensory preconditioning, higher-order conditioning, and blocking suggest that an association is formed between stimuli only when one stimulus signals the occurrence of the other. These findings also question the assumption of early researchers that conditioning is a "mindless" mechanical process.

CONDITIONED STIMULI AS MEANINGFUL SIGNALS

The signaling function of classical conditioning is best seen in the research of psychologist Robert Rescorla (1967). Rescorla trained dogs to jump over

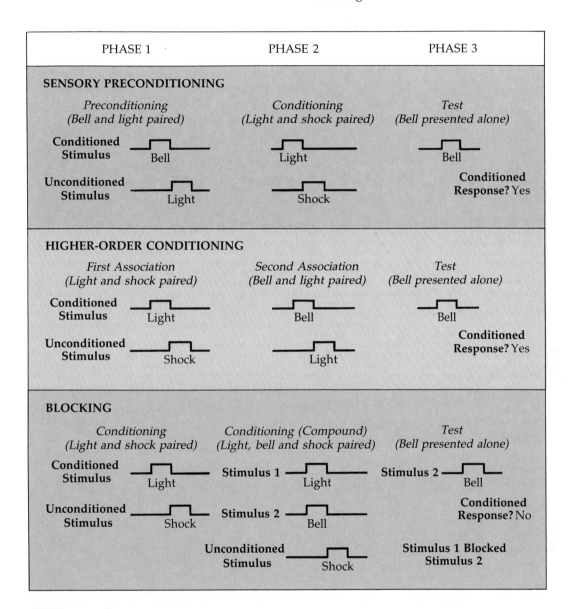

FIGURE 6.7 The three phases of sensory preconditioning, higher-order conditioning, and blocking. In sensory preconditioning and higher-order conditioning, the bell will function as a conditioned stimulus in the final phase of each procedure. However, in the blocking procedure the bell will not act as a conditioned stimulus in the final phase because mere contiguity between stimuli is not enough to produce classical conditioning. To elicit a conditioned response, a stimulus must act as a signal for the unconditioned stimulus.

a hurdle to avoid a mild electric shock. In one experiment, outlined in Table 6.1, dogs were each placed alone in a large cage that was divided in half by a low hurdle. If the dog stayed on one side for more than 20 seconds, a shock was delivered through the floor of that side. The dogs quickly learned to jump over the hurdle in a regular back and forth pattern to avoid receiving any shocks.

After learning to avoid shocks, each dog was removed from the hurdle apparatus and placed in one of two groups, each exposed to a different series of classical conditioning trials. For Group 1, a tone (a conditioned stimulus) briefly *preceded* a shock (an unconditioned stimulus) that elicited leg withdrawal (an unconditioned response). This procedure produced effective conditioned responses to the tone. Group 2 received the same number of conditioning trials, but, for them the tone always briefly followed the shock. The dogs in this group did not learn to withdraw their legs after the tone. Following the conditioning trials, each dog was returned to the hurdle apparatus,

TABLE 6.1 The Signal Value of a Conditioned Stimulus

Rescorla's (1967) Procedure

Phase 1: Hurdle Jump Task

Dogs must jump over a low hurdle every 20 secs to avoid receiving an electric shock

Phase 2: Classical Conditioning of Leg Flexion

Dogs in Group 1

Tone	Shock	Leg Flexion
Conditioned Stimulus	→ Unconditioned Stimulus	→ Unconditioned Response

Dogs in Group 2

Shock	Tone	Leg Flexion
Unconditioned Stimulus	→ Conditioned Stimulus	→ Unconditioned Response

Phase 3: Return to Hurdle Jump Task

Tones Presented Instead of Shocks
- Dogs in Group 1 increase their rate of jumping
- Dogs in Group 2 decrease their rate of jumping

and the tone from the preceding portion of the experiment was presented at different times. No further shocks were delivered.

Rescorla found that the dogs from the first group (tone before shock) increased their hurdle jumping, while the dogs from the second group (tone after shock) decreased their jumping. The dogs in the first group had learned through classical conditioning that a tone always preceded a shock; when they heard the tone in the hurdle apparatus, they jumped to the other side to avoid being shocked. The dogs in the second group, however, had learned through classical conditioning that a tone always followed a shock; when these animals heard a tone in the hurdle apparatus, the tone implied safety so these dogs stayed put. In each instance, the dogs learned the *meaning* of the tone in terms of their specific experiences. For some it served as a signal for danger, for others it was a signal for safety. For all animals, however, the tone served as a signal and enabled them to make effective and adaptive responses. These findings suggest that classical conditioning is based on the learning of predictive relations between stimuli (Rescorla and Wagner, 1972; Wagner and Rescorla, 1972). A conditioned stimulus that provides information about an unconditioned stimulus develops a stronger association to that stimulus (Rescorla, 1990).

CONDITIONED RESPONSES AS ADAPTIVE RESPONSES

In his early research, Pavlov mistakenly believed that a conditioned stimulus became a substitute for an unconditioned stimulus and that a conditioned response mimicked an unconditioned response. This belief was based on his finding that an unconditioned stimulus of food elicited an unconditioned response of salivation and that, after conditioning, a conditioned stimulus such as a tone would elicit essentially the same response. We now know that this view is wrong. We have already seen that the conditioned stimulus is a signal rather than a substitute for an unconditioned stimulus. While there are times when a conditioned response does indeed mimic an unconditioned response, at other times these responses are very different. For example, when a person is shocked, heart rate invariably increases. But if each shock is briefly preceded by a tone stimulus, what should happen? An increase in heart rate as a conditioned response would be maladaptive, as the heart would become further strained by the delivery of the shock. It would be more adaptive if the heart slowed down, making an anticipatory compensation for the effect of shock. And indeed, this is just what happens (Obrist, Sutterer, and Howard, 1972). In studies of this type, the conditioned response is an adaptive response that differs greatly from the unconditioned response (Flaherty et al., 1980; Siegel, 1977).

CONDITIONED RESPONSES OUTSIDE THE LABORATORY

We have seen that classical conditioning often occurs in situations when one event signals that another is about to occur. Psychologists have taken advantage of this fact and used classical conditioning to change human behavior. For instance, classical conditioning procedures have been used in the treatment of alcoholism, a topic we covered more fully in Chapter 5. One treatment, called **alcohol-aversion therapy,** involves pairing the sight, smell, and taste of alcohol with Antabuse, a drug that causes the person to vomit if he or she drinks alcohol. After repeated pairings, the alcoholic forms an association between the experience of drinking alcohol (a conditioned stimulus) and the effects of Antabuse (an unconditioned stimulus). Alcohol-aversion therapy is essentially a systematic attempt to produce a taste aversion.

Psychologists Eleanor Midkiff and Ilene Bernstein (1985) reported that taste aversions are particularly likely for people undergoing chemotherapy for the treatment of cancer. These patients often associate feelings of nausea with food (a conditioned stimulus) instead of with their chemotherapy (an unconditional stimulus), making them susceptible to self-induced starvation on top of the problems of cancer. Since associations between food and chemotherapy effects are so easily formed, these patients can be helped by giving them a "scapegoat" food. Prior to chemotherapy, the patients are given a novel food to which they will form a taste aversion, instead of the familiar foods that they might otherwise learn to avoid. In this way, classical conditioning effects can be rerouted to help these patients maintain healthy diets (Bernstein, 1985).

Classical conditioning has also been used in the treatment of hay fever and other allergies. Allergies can be treated by drugs, but these drugs often have such side effects as drowsiness. If a novel stimulus—perhaps a particular odor—(a conditioned stimulus) is paired with the allergy drug (an unconditional stimulus), people will form an association between the odor and the effects of the drug. For some patients, subsequent presentation of the odor alone can provide relief from allergic symptoms (Russell et al., 1984; Sampson and Jolie, 1984). Thus Pavlov's discoveries can be applied to a wide range of human behaviors.

Classical conditioning is important, but it is only one form of associative learning. A hungry dog will learn not only to salivate to the sight of a dog biscuit, but also to "roll over" or "shake hands" if these behaviors are rewarded with a biscuit. Performing tricks for food is not based on classical conditioning; it is based on instrumental conditioning, the form of associative learning that is concerned with the *consequences* of responses.

INSTRUMENTAL CONDITIONING

Though it is well known that animals can be taught to perform tricks to entertain people, it is less widely known that these instrumental conditioning training procedures can also be used with animals to make life easier for the handicapped. For example, Figure 6.8 shows a photograph of a young man named Robert Foster, who was seriously injured in an automobile accident. The accident left Foster paralyzed from the shoulders down. Also shown in the photo is a small capuchin monkey named Hellion, who was trained by instrumental conditioning to provide assistance to Foster.

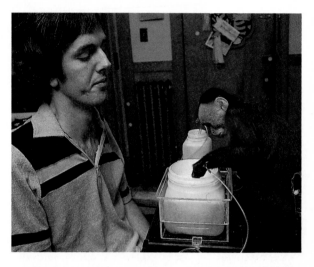

FIGURE 6.8 Helpful conditioned behavior. Little capuchin monkeys, long known as "organ grinder" monkeys, have been trained to help handicapped people. In this photo, a monkey performs various tasks for a quadriplegic young man. Using instrumental conditioning, the monkey was taught to feed the man and to help out in other ways.

trained by instrumental conditioning to provide assistance to Foster.

To control Hellion's behavior, Foster has a food dispenser attached to his chair that he can operate with his mouth. Whenever Hellion does what Foster wants her to do, he rewards her with either a food pellet or the sound of a clicker—a sound that has been associated with food. Over time, Hellion was taught to open and close doors, turn lights on or off, play records on a stereo, and even groom and feed Foster. Instrumentally conditioned animals can thus help injured or handicapped people lead more independent and productive lives (Curtis, 1979; Mack, 1981). Although the study of instrumental conditioning began with Thorndike and his puzzle-solving cats, B. F. Skinner modified this form of conditioning and popularized its practical application. We will examine the conditioning procedures that make such an application possible.

SKINNER'S APPROACH TO CONDITIONING

We saw earlier that Thorndike's pioneering studies led to his important law of effect—responses will be learned if they lead to satisfying effects. Yet his discussion of the consequences of behavior (in subjective terms such as "satisfaction") left much to be desired. By the end of the 1930s, both the means of studying instrumental conditioning and the language used to describe it had changed. These changes were due largely to Skinner. He modified Thorndike's research to show how the behaviors of animals such as pigeons and rats can be influenced by their consequences. According to Skinner, behaviors that are followed by a positive outcome (called reinforcement) become more likely to occur, while those that are followed by a negative outcome (called punishment) become less likely to occur (Skinner, 1938). Distinguishing between responses that are *elicited* (the conditioned response in classical conditioning) and those that are *emitted* (the response that is rewarded in instrumental conditioning), Skinner studied emitted responses that he referred to as **operants**. Operants are behaviors that "operate" on the environment to produce reinforcement. For example, when a dog rolls over and is rewarded with a biscuit it is performing an operant response. The terms **operant conditioning** and **instrumental conditioning** are often used interchangeably (Houston, 1991). Both refer to those instances where reinforcement follows a specific response. However, in instrumental conditioning, each learning trial (for example, a cat being placed in a puzzle box) is initiated by the experimenter. In operant conditioning, there are no trials. The experimenter waits for the animal to emit a response and then rewards or punishes that behavior.

Skinner believed that in order to understand a specific behavior it is necessary to train that behavior from scratch. For this purpose he designed an operant chamber for rats, commonly known as a Skinner box, into which a hungry rat is placed. The chamber, shown in Figure 6.9, is nothing more than a small metal and plexiglass cubicle with a protruding bar and a food cup located on one wall. This chamber permits an experimenter to study the operant response of bar pressing. The measure of learning is the animal's rate of response—the number of responses emitted during a unit of time (in this instance, the number of bar presses per minute). Whenever the rat responds by pressing the bar, a food pellet is dropped promptly into the cup. The effect of this food reinforcement on a hungry animal is predictable: The rat will increase its rate of bar pressing. When stated in Skinner's terms, Thorndike's law of effect becomes a statement about reinforcement: If an operant response is followed by reinforcement, the probability of that response is increased.

To learn about the behavior of animals, Skinner studied many of the same phenomena that Pavlov and Thorndike had studied before him. As you

FIGURE 6.9 An operant learning chamber devised by B. F. Skinner to study bar-pressing behavior in rats. Each press of the bar by the animal releases a food pellet into the food cup. The food is used as a reinforcement to shape the bar-pressing response.

will see, phenomena such as acquisition, generalization, discrimination, and extinction can also be studied in the operant chamber. However, Skinner did not limit his research to the behavior of rats or pigeons in simple boxes. He extended his findings to people in complex learning situations such as classrooms and psychotherapy sessions. Following our coverage of the basic processes of instrumental conditioning, we will see how these principles have been used by psychologists to modify various behaviors ranging from temper tantrums to self-induced starvation.

PROCESSES IN INSTRUMENTAL CONDITIONING

ACQUISITION

Thorndike's puzzle box research was limited because he had to wait for a cat to make a complete response before it could learn. With this procedure, a cat could only learn to do what it was already capable of doing. Reinforcement simply strengthened responses already in the cat's behavioral repertoire. But animals can also learn to make or acquire new responses. How can instrumental conditioning explain how a dog learns to roll over or how a cageful of lions learn to perform circus tricks? Simply waiting around for

B. F. Skinner. Psychologist B. F. Skinner believed that knowledge gained by research on animal learning could be applied to make human learning more efficient.

the desired response to occur and then reinforcing that response would be time consuming and, in the case of lions, potentially dangerous. A more direct means of producing a new behavior is necessary. That direct means is called **shaping.** Shaping is defined as the process of reinforcing behaviors that are increasingly similar to the desired behavior. Gradually, the desired behavior is shaped. Long known to professional animal trainers, the method of shaping was adopted by Skinner to study how animals acquire new responses.

For example, shaping is used to train a rat to press the bar in an operant chamber. At first, the hungry rat will spend a good deal of time exploring its new environment. At this stage, it rarely presses the bar. After observing the rat, the experimenter begins to shape the response by using the **method of successive approximation.** Initially, the hungry rat is reinforced with a food pellet whenever it looks at the bar. Other responses, such as grooming or looking in the wrong direction, are ignored. Gradually, the rat comes to orient more and more toward the bar. When this occurs, the experimenter increases the behavior demands of the animal. To receive a reinforcement now, the rat must approach the bar. Later it must actually touch the bar, and finally it must press it. Thus, the method of successive approximation shapes a desired behavior by carefully reinforcing

and strengthening each small step toward the target response.

You can use this same procedure to train a pet at home. To get your hungry dog to roll over, you need to reinforce a sequence of responses. First, give him a biscuit for sitting, then for lying down, later for lying on his side, and so on. By carefully reinforcing each of these successive approximations, you will soon have your dog rolling over on command. Whether an animal learns to press a bar, roll over, or perform a complex circus act, the responses have all been shaped by reinforcements that follow the animal's actions.

Just as some associations in classical conditioning are more easily learned than others, so are some responses in instrumental conditioning more readily acquired than others. This is due to differences in biological preparedness—the extent to which an animal's nervous system prepares it to learn certain responses and associations. Preparedness varies across species and can exist in any degree, from *prepared* (responses and associations are learned with little training) to *unprepared* (responses and associations are only learned with training) to *contraprepared* (responses and associations are hard to learn even with training). For

Music from the very young. Research on instrumental conditioning has demonstrated the necessity of considering the naturally occurring response tendencies of an animal or person when trying to teach a new response. Japanese musician Shinichi Suzuki has observed naturally occurring responses in young children to teach them to play the violin.

example, an understanding of preparedness has been used by the Japanese musician Shinichi Suzuki to teach violin playing in young children. Rather than try to teach the children to associate musical notes on a page with the position of their fingers on a violin, the Suzuki method uses listening as the basis for learning. Suzuki teaches the children to associate the sound of each note with the position of their fingers on their instrument. He also has the children make short, quick movements with their bows to take advantage of naturally occurring response tendencies. The result is that children all over the world have been taught to play complex musical pieces at an age that was previously believed to be impossible.

GENERALIZATION AND DISCRIMINATION

Just as in classical conditioning, animals show generalization and discrimination in instrumental conditioning. For example, if a pigeon has learned to peck a red key in an operant chamber for food reinforcement, the bird will also peck the key if its color is slightly changed. This phenomenon is called stimulus generalization, and it is defined by two characteristics. First, responses reinforced in the presence of one stimulus (perhaps a red light) will occur in the presence of similar stimuli (orange or pink lights). Second, the greater the similarity between the original stimulus and a new stimulus, the more likely it is that the response will occur.

In **discrimination training,** an animal learns that reinforcers are related to some stimuli but not to others. For example, a rat can learn to press a bar for food reinforcement when a light above the bar is turned on and to refrain from bar pressing when the light is turned off. The light is a **discriminative stimulus** that provides information to the rat. When it is on, it signals that reinforcement is available; when it is off, it indicates that responses will not be reinforced. Through exposure to these contingencies, rats can learn to use the discriminative stimulus and respond only when the light is on.

CONDITIONED REINFORCEMENT

In discussing classical conditioning, we saw how a previously neutral stimulus could become associated with a conditioned stimulus and elicit a conditioned response through higher-order conditioning. In instrumental conditioning an analogous phenomenon exists. Stimuli that are paired with reinforcement can become reinforcing through repeated association. Stimuli that are essential for an animal's survival—stimuli such as food, warmth, and shelter—are called **primary reinforcers.** Stim-

uli that become reinforcing through their association with a primary reinforcer are called **secondary** or **conditioned reinforcers.** In one experiment, hungry rats were trained to press a bar under conditions in which a light was turned on just before food reinforcement was delivered. After the response was learned, extinction training began; continued bar pressing by the rats produced neither light nor food. Later, when the conditions were changed so that bar pressing turned on the light but still did not result in food, the rats resumed pressing it (Bersch, 1951). The light, by virtue of its association with food, had become a conditioned reinforcer.

Examples of conditioned reinforcers are common in everyday life. One obvious example is money—a secondary reinforcer that has value only through its association with primary reinforcement. Even animals will work for money if they can "purchase" primary reinforcers with their earnings. For example, Figure 6.10 shows a chimp putting a token in a "vending" machine. To earn the token, the chimp learned a new response. Using this same principle, some reform schools and mental hospitals have set up "token economies," in which people must earn tokens to purchase

FIGURE 6.10 Tokens of reward. Like people, chimpanzees can be trained to work for conditioned reinforcers. Chimps will perform various responses if they are reinforced with tokens that can later be used to "buy" a primary reinforcer such as food. In this photo, a chimp places a token into a machine that delivers grapes.

things such as food or time away from the institution (Ayllon and Azrin, 1968). People work for these tokens by doing things that are socially desirable, including helping the staff, learning new skills, or, in extreme cases, just dressing and feeding themselves.

EXTINCTION

In classical conditioning, if an unconditioned stimulus no longer follows the presentation of a conditioned stimulus, the conditioned response will eventually extinguish. Similarly, in instrumental conditioning an instrumental response will also weaken and extinguish if it is no longer followed by reinforcement. For example, we will continue putting money in a soda machine only so long as we get a can of soda from the machine. If the machine stops delivering soda, we quickly extinguish our response. Often, we will try the machine at a later time (**spontaneous recovery**) to see whether it will once again deliver reinforcement.

Our examination of instrumental conditioning has shown that animals learn to relate their responses to the environmental contingencies of reinforcement. But exactly how does reinforcement work?

THE NATURE OF REINFORCEMENT

AMOUNT AND DELAY OF REINFORCEMENT

In classical conditioning we saw that a conditioned response is influenced by the strength of the unconditioned stimulus and the time interval between the conditioned and unconditioned stimuli. In a similar way, a new instrumental response is influenced by the amount and delay of reinforcement. Psychologists determined this by studying rats who learned to run a *T-maze* for food reinforcement (Figure 6.11). In these experiments, a hungry rat was placed in the T-maze start box and allowed to run down the alley and turn either left or right. Food was always located behind the same goal box door, and it was the animal's task to find it. The rats eventually learned to pick the correct door. How quickly they did so, however, depended upon when and how much reinforcement was delivered. Rats who received immediate reinforcement after making a correct choice took fewer learning trials than rats who had to wait several seconds for their rewards (Grice, 1948). Further, rats who received a large reinforcement performed better than those who received a small reinforcement (Clayton, 1964). In general, the shorter the

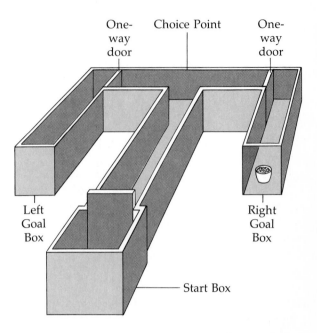

FIGURE 6.11 A T-maze apparatus used to study instrumental learning in rats. A hungry rat is placed in the start box and allowed to explore the maze. At the choice point the rat must turn left or right, and one-way doors prevent it from retracing its path. The rat's task is to learn which side contains the food reinforcement. After a number of trials, the rat will consistently choose the goal box that contains the food and avoid the empty goal box.

delay and the larger the amount of reinforcement, the better the animal's performance.

These effects of amount and delay of reinforcement, however, are relative rather than absolute; they depend on an animal's past experience. As shown in Figure 6.12, animals who must run down an alleyway to receive food run more slowly if they are shifted from a large to a small reinforcement than the animals who receive a small reinforcement for all trials run (Crespi, 1942). A similar phenomenon occurs when the timing of a reinforcement is changed. A reinforcer that comes later than expected is less effective than one that is delivered on time (McHose and Tauber, 1972). This phenomenon is called a **negative contrast effect,** and it is believed to be due to animals' forming expectations about the amount and delay of reinforcement. When these expectations are not met, as in the case of a smaller or later reinforcement, frustration or disappointment can result (Amsel, 1958). Those of you who have spent long hours studying for a test only to have received a grade that was less than you expected may well understand this effect. But instead of studying less

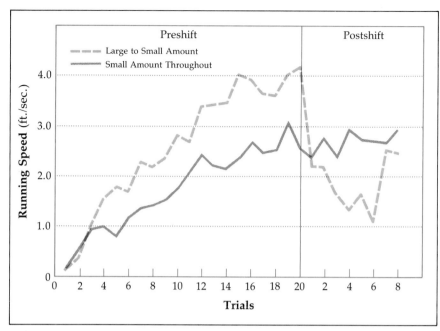

FIGURE 6.12 The effect of amount of reinforcement on an instrumentally conditioned response. Animals trained to run down an alleyway for food run faster the greater the amount of reinforcement. But if the amount is significantly reduced, the animals will run slower than those who received the same small amount all along. This phenomenon is called a negative contrast effect.

next time, just remember that not all of our responses are reinforced in the manner we expected.

SCHEDULES OF REINFORCEMENT

In addition to varying the amount and delay of the reinforcer, learning researchers have experimented with the **schedule of reinforcement.** A schedule of reinforcement describes the relation between a response and a reinforcer. If a reinforcer follows a correct response each time, the schedule is called a **continuous reinforcement schedule.** If only some of the responses are reinforced or reinforcement is available only some of the time, the schedule is called a **partial** or **intermittent reinforcement schedule.** The examples presented so far have employed continuous reinforcement, but many other schedules can be used. In fact, continuous reinforcement is really the exception rather than the rule in the real world. Students usually do not get reinforced with a high grade every time they study for a test, and athletes are not reinforced by winning each time they enter a contest. Yet the behaviors of studying and practicing tend to persist if they occasionally lead to reinforcement.

To understand how intermittent reinforcement schedules influence our behavior, we need to examine the various relations that can exist between a response and a reinforcer. Intermittent schedules can vary on two dimensions. First, reinforcement can be made contingent upon either a certain *number of responses* or on the *passage of time* since the last reinforced response. When reinforcement is contingent upon the number of responses, the schedule is called a **ratio schedule;** when reinforcement is contingent upon the passage of time, it is called an **interval schedule.** Second, the number of responses before reinforcement occurs or the unit of time since the last reinforced response can be *fixed* or *variable.* Combing these dimensions produces four different intermittent schedules: **fixed ratio, variable ratio, fixed interval,** and **variable interval.**

In a fixed ratio schedule an animal is reinforced after it emits a fixed number of responses. For example, a Fixed Ratio-20 schedule would mean that 20 responses would have to be made before a reinforcement was delivered. A factory worker who is paid by the number of units produced ($10 for every 100 boxes filled) is operating on a fixed ratio schedule. Figure 6.13 shows that if the number of responses needed to obtain a reinforcement is high, there is a pause after each reinforcement, followed by a steady rate of response.

In a variable ratio schedule reinforcement comes after a specified number of responses have been emitted, but this number varies from one

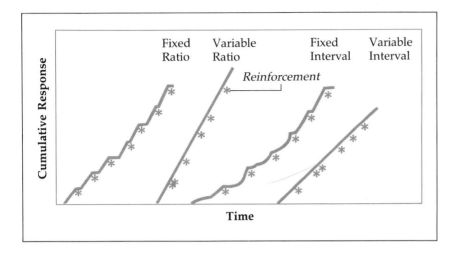

FIGURE 6.13 Response rates for different intermittent reinforcement schedules.   Typical cumulative records for fixed ratio, variable ratio, fixed interval, and variable interval reinforcement schedules. The marks indicate the delivery of a reinforcement.

reinforcement to the next. Slot machines deliver reinforcement on a variable ratio schedule. Since payoffs come only after a variable number of non-reinforced responses has been made, gamblers never know whether their next response will hit the jackpot. Consequently, this schedule produces a very high rate of response. (See Figure 6.13.)

In a fixed interval schedule reinforcement follows the first response made after a specified period of time. Following a reinforcement, no additional responses will be reinforced until the interval has passed again. For example, the making of Jello-O operates on a fixed interval schedule (Domjan and Burkhard, 1986). After you mix the gellatin with hot water you must refrigerate it for a certain length of time for it to gel. You are unlikely to check on the Jello-O right after you put it in the refrigerator. However, as the time to gel draws to a close, you are apt to open the refrigerator more frequently, especially if you are hungry and want your reward. This intermittent schedule produces an uneven, or "scalloped," rate of response. (See Figure 6.13.)

Finally, in a variable interval schedule reinforcement follows the first response made after a period of time that varies from one reinforcement to the next. For students away at college, reinforcement in the form of letters or packages from home is frequently delivered on a variable interval schedule. Since reinforcement may be found anytime in the campus mailbox, this schedule produces a steady rate of response. (See Figure 6.13.)

The practical significance of these reinforcement schedules is that they can be used to maintain behavior over a lengthy period of time with only an occasional reinforcer. This means, for example, that a child is more likely to maintain good personal health habits such as brushing her teeth or washing his hands if these behaviors are only intermittently reinforced. When a child begins to learn these behaviors, parents should use a continuous reinforcement schedule, praising the child regularly. But after the learning is complete, such praise should be given intermittently. Intermittent reinforcement has advantages and disadvantages. It maintains much of our desirable behavior, while also bolstering our undesirable activities. Intermittent reinforcement can get a child to wash before dinner, and it can encourage a gambler to pour money into a slot machine. Occasional reinforcement can maintain a behavior indefinitely and prevent it from being extinguished. This helps explain why habits that are reinforced only occasionally are so difficult to break.

IDENTIFYING A REINFORCER

Reinforcement is critically important because it determines how frequently a behavior will occur. But what specifically makes a stimulus a reinforcer? Food and water are commonly used as reinforcers, but an animal will not work for food unless it is hungry, nor for water unless it is thirsty. How then should a reinforcer be identified?

Psychologists used to believe that reinforcers were stimuli that satisfied physiological needs. Yet two examples suggest that reinforcers need not work this way. First, we have already seen that stimuli such as lights or tones that are associated with primary reinforcers can function as conditioned reinforcers. A conditioned reinforcer influences behavior but does not satisfy a biological need. Second, studies of electrical brain stimulation (described in Chapters 2 and 5) have shown that a mild electric current can function as a reinforcer and yet not satisfy an ordinarily experienced physiological need. For example, rats have been trained to press a bar to receive electrical stimulation through a microelectrode implanted in areas of the brain near the hypothalamus. Some of these animals only stopped after hundreds or even thousands of responses. Then they literally dropped from exhaustion (Olds and Milner, 1954). Unlike food or other reinforcers that are only effective when the animal is in a state of biological deprivation, electrical stimulation of these "pleasure centers" can reinforce behavior when the animal is not deprived in any way (Carr and Coons, 1982; Olds and Fobes, 1981). These examples indicate that a reinforcer cannot be simply identified as a stimulus that satisfies a physiological need or reduces a biological state of deprivation.

How can a reinforcer be identified if there is no physical property that is common to all? A step toward the solution to this puzzle was provided by psychologist David Premack (1965). He found that any behavior that had a high frequency of occurrence (for example, eating) could be used to reinforce any other behavior that had a lower frequency of occurrence (bar pressing). More specifically, when the opportunity to get food (a normally frequently occurring behavior) is made contingent upon pressing a bar (a normally infrequently occurring behavior), the food will reinforce the bar pressing. Similarly, with children a frequently occurring behavior such as playing can be used to reinforce a less frequently occurring behavior such as making a bed if playing is made contingent upon bedmaking. This relation is called the **Premack Principle,** and it demonstrates the *relativity* of reinforcement.

Premack's approach explains certain counterintuitive findings. For example, even though rats will normally engage in drinking more than running (so that drinking can be used to reinforce running) the reverse is also possible. If rats are prevented from running, they can be trained to drink more water than normal to gain the opportunity to run (Allison, Miller, and Wozny, 1979; Timberlake and Allison, 1974). In this example, running is contingent upon drinking. These findings have led to a new theory of reinforcement. According to **deprivation theory,** any activity can function as a reinforcer if the subject is restricted from performing this activity as often as it would otherwise (Timberlake and Allison, 1974). It is not yet clear which view of reinforcement best explains all of the data. However, all of these views share a number of important features. First, reinforcement is a relative term. Whether one activity will reinforce another depends on what the activities are and on their relative frequency of occurrence. Second, there is no hard and fast rule for defining a reinforcer. Under appropriate conditions, any activity can serve as a reinforcer for some activities, as a punisher for others, and as neither for many others (Schwartz, 1989).

METHODS OF BEHAVIOR CHANGE

The principles of instrumental conditioning are among the most practically useful concepts uncovered by psychologists. We will focus on four different procedures that have been used to modify problem behavior: positive reinforcement, negative reinforcement, extinction, and punishment. Postive and negative reinforcement can increase the rate of desirable behaviors, while extinction and punishment can decrease or eliminate undesirable responses. A response will be *more* likely to occur in the future if it leads to either positive reinforcement (the onset of a desirable stimulus) or negative reinforcement (the termination of an undesirable stimulus). Conversely, a response will be *less* likely to occur in the future if it is not followed by positive reinforcement (extinction) or it is followed by punishment.

POSITIVE REINFORCEMENT

"A poorly preserved mummy suddenly struck with the breath of life" is how one psychologist described the appearance of a woman suffering from a disorder called *anorexia nervosa*, a chronic failure to eat (Bachrach, Erwin and Mohr, 1965). At the time she was hospitalized, the woman was 5 feet 4 inches tall but weighed only 47 pounds (see Figure 6.14). Since she had not been helped by eight previous hospitalizations and was in imminent danger of death, a team of psychologists used positive reinforcement to try to get her to eat. The psychologists believed that well-intentioned family and friends had maintained the patient's inappropriate behavior by reinforcing it with attention and special considerations. With the help of the hospital staff, these reinforcers were now used to change her behavior.

Before conditioning began, the patient stayed in a bright, pleasant hospital room where she enjoyed visitors, television, and other conveniences. When conditioning began, she was deprived of these activities so that they could be used as **positive reinforcement.** Positive reinforcers include

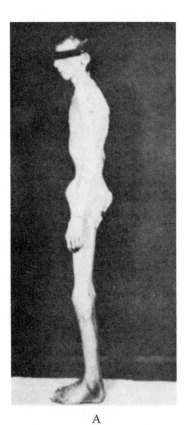  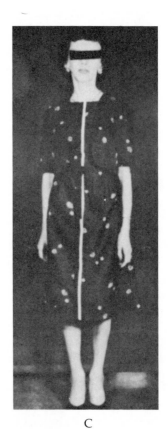

A   B   C

FIGURE 6.14 Pictures of a woman who was suffering from anorexia nervosa, a chronic failure to eat. To get the woman to eat, psychologists shaped her behavior by rewarding appropriate responses. At the start of behavior therapy (A), the woman was hospitalized and in grave danger of death. After eight weeks of therapy the woman gained 17 pounds and was treated as an outpatient. Following ten months of continued therapy the woman gained an additional 10 pounds (B). The final picture (C) shows the woman just before she completed a course in practical nursing and began work. Unfortunately, not all patients with this eating disorder respond positively to this form of treatment.

primary reinforcers such as food or water and conditioned reinforcers such as money or praise. In this case study, only conditioned reinforcers were withheld. All of the things the woman previously enjoyed (activities that occurred frequently) were now made contingent upon eating (an activity that occurred infrequently). This is an example of the Premack Principle in operation.

Each of the psychologists ate one meal a day with the patient and reinforced her eating by talking, turning on her television, allowing access to visitors, and so on. As each small step was mastered, she was gradually required to eat more food (response shaping) until her diet was considered normal. After two months of treatment, the patient was released from the hospital and was treated as an outpatient for an additional year. The success of the positive reinforcement procedure in this case study is readily seen in the series of pictures taken over the period of this treatment (Figure 6.14).

NEGATIVE REINFORCEMENT

Reinforcement need not always be positive. Stimuli whose termination or removal increase the likelihood of a response are called **negative reinforcers.** The effects of negative reinforcement can be studied by either **escape** or **avoidance conditioning.** In escape conditioning, an appropriate response terminates an aversive stimulus. For example, turning off a vacuum cleaner can eliminate an unpleasant sensation in your ears. In avoidance conditioning, an appropriate response avoids exposure to an aversive stimulus. By learning to hold a hammer and nail properly, you can avoid smashing your thumb. Negative reinforcement is not the same as punishment. For example, if you drive too fast and get a speeding ticket, this is punishment; if you turn off a boring television show, this is negative reinforcement through escape. In the case of punishment, a response leads to a negative outcome; in the case of negative reinforcement, a response leads to a positive outcome.

A variation of the negative reinforcement procedure has been used to improve reading and speaking skills in the case of a chronic stutterer. With delayed auditory feedback as a distracting and unpleasant stimulus, a stutterer was asked to read aloud each day over a period of two weeks. Whenever the person stuttered, he heard what he had previously said played back through a set of earphones. Speaking smoothly was negatively reinforced by escape from this unpleasant feedback. The rate of stuttering was initially as high as a dozen words per minute, but after five days of this treatment it dropped to zero. However, this change in behavior was purchased at the expense of the reading rate. To stop stuttering and escape from the aversive stimulus, the stutterer dramatically slowed his rate of reading. But after another five days the stuttering rate stayed at zero, and the reading rate progressively improved. By the end of two weeks, this treatment completely eliminated stuttering and doubled the rate of reading from its pretreatment baseline. Negative reinforcement replaced stuttering with normal speech (Goldiamond, 1965).

EXTINCTION

A case study of a 21-month-old child who threw temper tantrums illustrates how extinction can be used to eliminate undesirable behavior. In this instance, the child cried each night unless one of his parents stayed with him until he was asleep. Since the temper tantrums were reinforced by the parents' attention each night, the parents were told to put the child to bed, make sure that he was well cared for, and then ignore the tantrum that was to follow. The child cried for almost one hour the first night but then showed progressive improvements on each of the succeeding nights. By the tenth night, the parents reported that the child actually smiled when he was put to bed. The moral of this episode is not that children's cries should be ignored. Rather, a child's behavior should be examined to determine what is being demanded and whether the demand is reasonable. In this case, the behavior was unreasonable and the extinction procedure resulted in its elimination (Williams, 1959).

PUNISHMENT

One of the most frequently used procedures for changing undesirable behavior is **punishment**. It is defined as the use of an aversive stimulus or the removal of a positive reinforcer to decrease the likelihood of a particular response (Domjan and Burkhard, 1986). If punishment takes the form of an unpleasant stimulus (like a slap or a verbal reprimand), it is called **aversive punishment;** if positive reinforcement is removed (as in the loss of privileges or possessions), it is called **response cost.** Research has shown that punishment is effective in changing behavior when the punishment is intense, immediate, and used in conjunction with positive reinforcement to teach more desirable forms of behavior (Walters and Grusec, 1977).

For example, studies by O.I. Lovaas and his associates have used a combination of positive reinforcement (candy) and aversive punishment (a mild electric shock) to teach autistic children to speak and refrain from self-destructive behavior. **Autism** is a form of abnormal behavior that affects young children. It is characterized by unresponsiveness to environmental stimulation, repetitive movements (including hand flapping), and self-mutilation (for example, head banging and wrist biting) (Garretson, Fein, and Waterhouse, 1990; Rutter and Schopler, 1987). Various neurological disorders have been proposed, including brainstem and hemispheric dysfunctions, but no agreement yet exists on the cause or causes of this disorder (Ornitz, Atwell, Kaplan, and Westlake, 1985; Sussman and Lewandowski, 1990). Still, some success has been achieved by behavioral techniques. Psychologist Lovaas and his group have used electric shock to stop the children's self-destructive and disruptive behavior, while at the same time using shaping by positive reinforcement to get the children to speak. When the parents of these children continued this treatment at home, the destructive and other bizarre behaviors were replaced with normal interactions (Lovaas, Koegal, Simmons, and Long, 1973).

Psychologists once believed that punishment was largely ineffective and would only suppress rather than eliminate an undesirable response. However, many psychologists today view punishment differently. In situations where undesirable behavior is dangerous to either the person or to others, punishment that is neither physically injurious nor unnecessarily cruel may be both necessary and justified. For example, parents whose children misbehave might combine response cost (time-out from home play) with reasoning to modify their children's inappropriate behavior. Reasoning alone may not always work, but if reasoning is associated with the punishing loss of play it will eventually lead the child to connect parental explanations with punishment for misbehavior (Walters and Grusec, 1977). Punishment is best used in conjunction with a positive conditioning procedure. Punishing a child can stop an undesirable behavior (for example, running into the street) while shaping by positive reinforcement can lead to a long-term positive change ("I like the way you've been staying in the yard, so here's a cookie.").

Problems with either form of punishment can arise, however, when either is used as the sole method of modifying behavior. Aversive punishment, for example, can produce unwanted negative emotional states such as hostility or fear. Parents who berate or spank their children may end up with children who dislike or fear them. Similarly, a child with a punitive teacher may come to not only fear that teacher, but develop a dislike for school. In these examples, aversive punishment may lead a child to avoid the punishing adult and those situations in which punishment is received. If aversive punishment is unpredictable and inescapable, feelings of passivity and helplessness can arise and lead to depression. Finally, the use of aversive punishment provides a child with the message that aggressive and hurtful behavior is appropriate for adults. After watching adults act aggressively, children may imitate their behavior. This could explain why children who are abused by their parents often become abusive parents themselves (Strauss and Gelles, 1980).

In some ways, response cost is a milder, less traumatic form of punishment than aversive punishment. Depriving a child of the opportunity to play is unlikely to result in fear. Nor does it provide an aggressive model for the child to imitate later. However, response cost can elicit frustration and anger when a privilege or possession is removed, and parents who attempt to control their children's behavior by withdrawing love and affection can damage their children's self-esteem (Wylie, 1978). If response cost is used, it should be limited to the opportunity to engage in a pleasurable activity that is not vital to the physical or psychological well-being of the child. This is why the old-fashioned disciplinary act of "going to bed without dinner" is an inappropriate use of response cost.

In summary, while both methods of punishment can be effective it is important to keep their potentially harmful effects clearly in mind. They should only be used briefly and only in conjunction with positive reinforcement. Physical and psychological harm should be avoided. Remember, punishment alone merely tells someone what not to do. Positive reinforcement, coupled with reasoning, indicates what should be done, and why (Routh, 1982).

The next section shows how conditioning research has application to the treatment of medical disorders.

RESEARCH AND APPLICATION: Behavioral Medicine

Behavioral medicine is the interdisciplinary field of psychology and medicine that is expanding our understanding of health and disease. One of the goals of this field is to apply knowledge obtained from psychology to the treatment of people with medical problems (Miller, 1983). Such knowledge could have enormous practical application. For example, if operant conditioning can be used to influence physiological responses such as abnormal heart rate and blood pressure, then perhaps people could learn how to regulate their abnormal autonomic responses voluntarily.

Operant Conditioning of Autonomic Responses: Biofeedback

Normally we are unaware of our autonomic responses because they provide us with little *feedback* or information about their current level of functioning. For example, we cannot tell whether our blood pressure is high or low, and we often have little information on our heart rate, unless our heart is pounding after especially vigorous exercise or stress. However, electronic instruments can measure autonomic responses and provide us with external feedback about these normally silent functions. For example, an instrument can monitor our blood pressure from moment to moment and sound a tone that gets louder and louder whenever our blood pressure rises. We can then try to use this information to regulate our blood pressure voluntarily. **Biofeedback** is the name for this procedure, and it involves providing external feedback for those responses that normally lack feedback.

Training in biofeedback is based on operant conditioning. For example, if you want to raise your blood pressure, you must learn to perform some response that makes the tone get louder or higher. Your ability to change the tone (and thus modify your autonomic responses) is thought to be reinforcing, because the tone provides you with the knowledge that you have been successful. Until relatively recently, psychologists did not believe that this could occur. But Neal Miller and others have shown that operant conditioning of autonomic responses is possible, and that it has application to behavioral medicine (Kimmel, 1974; Miller, 1983; Schneiderman, Weiss, and Kaufmann, 1989).

Psychologists Miller and Brucker (1979) used biofeedback training to produce a therapeutic increase in blood pressure in a man whose spinal cord had been severed by a gunshot wound. The broken spinal cord left the man a paraplegic and disrupted his normal mechanism for maintaining his blood pressure while standing. Whenever the man was helped to an upright position, his blood pressure would fall, and this caused him to become dizzy and faint. To avoid fainting the man had to remain reclined, with his legs in an elevated position.

Biofeedback training was used to teach the man to raise his blood pressure voluntarily. Using equipment that sounded a tone whenever the man's blood pressure increased, Miller and Brucker simply told him to try to get the tone to stay on by whatever method he could. After several weeks of training he was able to raise his blood pressure sufficiently so that he could sit upright without fainting. Using the shaping principle, the researchers progressively raised the blood pressure level that was needed to sound the tone. Finally, the man could raise his blood pressure without the use of the tone. Figure 6.15 shows the changes in blood pressure over a period of minutes. In one condition, the man did not attempt to raise it before standing. In the other condition he voluntarily raised it and then maintained it at a normal level. Biofeedback training was thus used to help this man stand and move with support. Ten other patients with similar spinal injuries were also studied by Miller and Brucker, and nine of these people successfully learned to increase their blood pressure voluntarily.

How do these patients learn to control this autonomic response? Through careful monitoring of a patient's performance, Miller and Brucker ruled out an increase in muscle tension as the cause. Tensing the muscles produced only a slight increase in blood pressure. Instead, Miller and Brucker said that biofeedback training enables patients to learn how to increase their blood pressure directly. At first, patients think up exciting visual images to increase their blood pressure. After a while, they report that "they just think about wanting their blood pressure to go up and it does, much as your arm goes up when you want it to" (Miller, 1985). The exact source of these changes is still unknown, but we do know that they are brought about by the same principles of shaping and reinforcement that were discovered from basic research on animals.

Current Status of Biofeedback

Research on biofeedback has had a progression of ups and downs. Following some sporadic successes in the 1960s, it was the subject of several exaggerated claims and false promises. Now, after hundreds of studies have been conducted, psychologists have gained a sense of perspective about when biofeedback will succeed and when it will not (Linden, 1988). Among the successes, biofeedback has been used to help stroke or spinal injury patients move formerly immobile limbs numbed after a loss of sensory feedback (Ingles, Campbell, and Donald, 1976). It has also been

FIGURE 6.15 Therapy through biofeedback. Changes in blood pressure in a man whose normal mechanism for maintaining blood pressure was destroyed by an accident that severed his spinal cord and left him a paraplegic. Whenever the man was placed in an upright position, his blood pressure dropped, and he became dizzy and fainted. After biofeedback training, the man could raise his blood pressure voluntarily. This figure shows the changes in blood pressure that occurred when he voluntarily raised his blood pressure and when he did not. Studies such as this suggest that biofeedback can be a useful therapeutic procedure for the field of behavioral medicine.

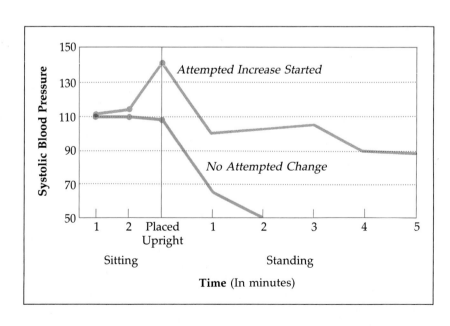

used to alleviate muscle spasms and tension headaches (Brudny, Grynbaum, and Korein, 1974; Budzynski, Stoyva, Adler, and Mullaney, 1974) and to treat cases of curvature of the spine (Dworkin, 1979). However, contrary to earlier hopes, biofeedback has not been very successful in reducing high blood pressure in cardiovascular patients. Only moderate reductions in blood pressure have been found when biofeedback is used in conjunction with relaxation treatments (Miller, 1985). However, we are only beginning to realize the potential that biofeedback holds for the field of behavioral medicine. As the techniques become more refined, we might expect additional successes. ▪

COGNITIVE ASPECTS OF LEARNING

We have focused on classical and instrumental conditioning to show you how animals and people learn associations and contingencies between responses and events. For much of the first half of this century, psychologists believed that these two forms of learning provided a full account of animal learning and, perhaps, even of human learning. Today, most psychologists reject that viewpoint. Conditioning is very important in animal and human learning, but cognition plays a major role as well.

HUMAN AND ANIMAL COGNITION

For humans, cognitive learning processes involve the perception, organization, and retention of information in a learning situation. For animals, the term cognitive processes is used in a more restricted way. **Animal cognition** does not refer to thinking in the ordinary sense; rather, it refers to the animal's use of an *internal representation* as the basis for action (Roitblat, 1987). An internal representation refers to the form in which information is held in memory. It might involve information about features of a stimulus (such as its size, shape, or color) or information about previous events. At present, we know very little about what these internal memory representations are like, but there is ample evidence that some such representations exist. We will consider some of this evidence from studies of cognitive mapping, latent learning, spatial memory, observational learning, and expectancy. This section will provide a bridge between the study of associative learning and the study of cognitive processes, discussed in the chapters that follow.

COGNITIVE MAPS AND LATENT LEARNING

From the 1920s through the 1940s, learning theorist Edward Tolman studied how rats learned routes through mazes. On the basis of his findings, he argued that it was impossible to ignore the role of cognition in learning, even in rats. Tolman believed that rats learn complicated mazes, such as the one shown in Figure 6.16, not by having a specific sequence of left and right turns "stamped in" by reinforcement but by developing a mental picture of the maze. He called this mental picture a *cognitive map.*

ANIMAL COGNITIVE MAPS

According to Tolman, a **cognitive map** is an internal representation of a spatial layout ("the lay of the land") that an animal stores in its memory. After the animal develops a map, that map can be used to guide its future behavior. As evidence for his cognitive interpretation, Tolman and his followers studied **latent learning**—a type of learning that occurs without reinforcement, and remains latent, or dormant, until it becomes necessary. For example, Tolman and Honzik (1930) tested three groups of rats in the maze shown in Figure 6.16. Although the amount of practice in the maze was the same for all of the groups, the reinforcement conditions were different. Rats in the first group received a food reinforcement each time they solved the maze, rats in the second group never received a reinforcement, and rats in the third group received no reinforcement until the eleventh day of practice. After that, the rats in the third group were reinforced for every maze solution.

The average number of errors (wrong turns in the maze) made by each group over the experimental sessions is shown in Figure 6.17. The rats in the first group, who were uniformly reinforced, did better than the rats in the second group, who were never reinforced. This finding, however, tells us very little about the role of reinforcement in maze learning. It is the performance of the rats in the third group that provides us with new information. These rats behaved like the nonreinforced rats through the tenth day, but when food reinforcement was introduced on the eleventh day their performances changed. Suddenly, these rats began making very few errors. In fact, they performed equal to or better than the rats who received reinforcement each day. What accounts for this shift in performance? Tolman saw it as evidence for latent learning—the rats in the

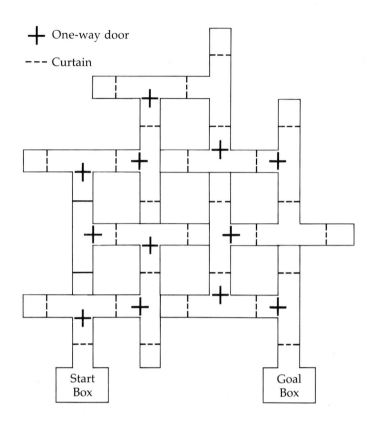

FIGURE 6.16   A complex learning maze used to study instrumental learning in rats.   In order to get a reinforcement, a rat must find its way from the start box to the goal box. Over trials, the rats make fewer and fewer wrong turns.

third group had learned the correct path through the maze during their nonreinforced trials, but this learning remained dormant until reinforcement was available.

According to Tolman, latent learning demonstrates two important points. First, it shows that rats can develop cognitive maps that will guide them quickly through a maze when they are later reinforced. Before the reinforcement, the rat's knowledge of the maze was there, but it was latent. Since the learning occurred prior to reinforcement, reinforcement was not necessary. Second, latent learning indicates that *learning* and *performance* are different. As Tolman and Honzik have shown, an animal needs to perform to show that it has learned, but it can learn in the absence of a performance. Extending this distinction to people, we may have passed by a shop that rents tuxedos and evening gowns without ever giving it much thought, much less stopping and entering the store. But if we were suddenly required to attend a formal gathering, we would know exactly where to go for our clothes. Like the rats in Tolman's third group, only when we are motivated to respond do we translate what we have learned into actual performance.

The reality of internal spatial representations is demonstrated even more convincingly by the results of a study of latent learning in chimpanzees.

In this experiment, chimps were carried through a one-acre compound that was filled with bushes and trees. While the chimps were carried through the compound along an irregular twisting and turning route, they watched the experimenter hide food in 18 different locations. Later each chimp was individually returned to the center of the compound and turned loose. Not only did the chimps find most of the food, but their paths from one food location to the next minimized travel time. Rather than follow the original path of the experimenter, they created more efficient routes. In a second experiment, fruit was hidden in half of the locations and vegetables were hidden in the other half. This time, the chimps demonstrated their inherent preference for fruit by going to the fruit locations first (Menzel, 1978). These results suggest that when the chimps were initially carried through the compound they formed a cognitive map of the terrain. Later, they used that map (much like a traveling salesperson might use an actual map) to locate the hidden food and minimize their travel time.

HUMAN COGNITIVE MAPS

If you have ever tried to find your way around a new city, you may have felt like a rat in a maze. Psychologists have extended Tolman's idea of a

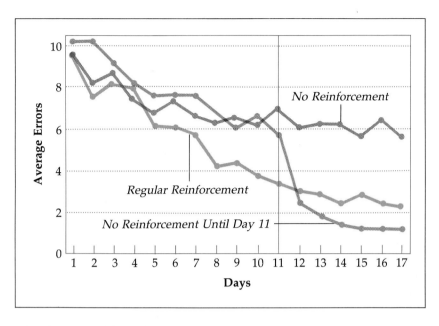

FIGURE 6.17 Evidence for latent learning. Rats tested in a complex learning maze showed improved performance over trials if they were reinforced for each correct solution; rats that were never reinforced showed little improvement in performance. However, rats that received no reinforcement during the first 10 trials, but did receive reinforcement thereafter, showed an immediate change in performance. These rats clearly learned a path through the maze during the first 10 trials, but this learning was latent until reinforcement was made available.

cognitive map to people to learn about their mental representations of cities. To see what people knew of their cities, urbanologist Kevin Lynch (1960) asked a group of subjects to draw their city on paper. In his study of Boston, Lynch found that certain landmarks such as Paul Revere's house and the Boston Common were always drawn by his subjects, while other areas of the city were omitted as though they did not exist. This is a major difference between a physical and a cognitive map. To obtain a sense of this task, take a few minutes, and draw a map of your campus. As you try to put your campus on paper, you must turn your mental representation (your cognitive map) into a physical map that can be examined by others. The most important factor influencing the accuracy of your map is your familiarity with the campus. The greater your familiarity, the more detailed your mental representation, and the more accurate your map (Evans, 1980).

Research has shown that cognitive maps are acquired on the basis of "landmarks" (such as the library, the psychology building, and your dorm), the spatial relations between those important places (the library is directly behind the dorm), and the travel plans (the paths that you take) needed in order to move from one place to another (Evans, Marrero, and Butler, 1981; Garling, Book,

and Lindberg, 1984). A cognitive map of a geographical area serves an important adaptive function—it allows you to move successfully from one place to another with minimal thought and effort. Without a cognitive map, you would be forced to use a physical map to get to your next class, or you would haphazardly wander about until you finally found the class or else gave up in sheer frustration. Cognitive maps thus organize information in memory by specifying the location and spatial arrangement of environmental features.

ANIMAL SPATIAL MEMORY

Closely related to the work on cognitive maps is the research on animal spatial memory conducted by David Olton and his colleagues (Olton, 1979; Olton and Samuelson, 1976). To study a rat's memory for locations, Olton devised a *radial maze* that had eight arms radiating from a central choice area (Figure 6.18). He placed a food pellet in a cup at the end of each arm and a hungry rat in the choice area. Olton wanted to know how the rats would go about finding the food. Would the rats make mistakes and enter arms they had already obtained a food pellet from, or would they somehow remember their previous choices and avoid retracing their steps?

FIGURE 6.18 An eight-arm radial maze. When a rat is placed in the center of the maze with food located out of sight in a food cup in each arm, it optimizes its performance by entering each arm only once. Rats have spatial memory that enables them to remember the location of food.

Olton and Samuelson found that the animals nearly always chose an arm that they had not entered before. However, they did not go through the maze in a systematic clockwise or counterclockwise pattern. How did the rats know which arms they had already visited? Several possible explanations exist. Perhaps the rats could smell the unseen food in the maze arms they had not visited. Maybe the rats marked each arm they visited with a drop of urine and used this scent to avoid repeating themselves.

The researchers tested these possibilities in a variety of ways. In one experiment, they replaced a food pellet in each previously visited arm. If the smell of food was important, the animals should reenter these arms. This did not occur. In another study, the researchers surgically removed each animal's sense of smell and found that they still only visited arms in the maze that were new. Clearly, the smell of food or urine markers were not guiding the animals' behavior. The systematic elimination of a variety of cues, including smell or touch, suggested that the animals performed correctly in the radial maze on the basis of spatial memory. In other words, the rats *remembered* where they had been.

Olton and Samuelson tested the possibility of spatial memory in rats by allowing an animal to visit only a few arms in the maze. The animal was then confined to the central area while the entire maze was shifted 45 degrees. After this was done, the rats were free to explore. Now, previously explored arms were in positions formerly occupied by unexplored arms. If the rats were making their choices on the basis of the remembered location, they should begin to make errors and enter arms they had visited before. This is exactly what the researchers found. It appears that rats remember the location of food in the radial maze on the basis of its spatial location (Beatty and Shavalia, 1980; Roberts and Van Veldhuizen, 1985).

OBSERVATIONAL LEARNING

Everyday learning often occurs vicariously. We watch other people and observe whether they are reinforced or punished. **Observational learning** is defined as the learning of environmental contingencies by observing the actions of others. Many skills, including learning to ride a bicycle or swim, can only be acquired by trial and error, whereas other skills, such as learning to recognize poisonous snakes, are best learned by observation. The ability to learn by observation enables us to profit from the successes and failures of others without engaging in time-consuming trial and error learning.

OBSERVATIONAL LEARNING IN ANIMALS

Earlier in this chapter we described how phobias could be acquired by classical conditioning. However, direct traumatic conditioning may not be the only means of learning a phobia. Phobias might also be acquired by watching others act in a fearful way. Because it would be unethical to try to induce phobias in humans (contrary to Watson and Rayner, 1920), researchers have used animals to see whether they can become phobic from observational learning experiences. Psychologist Susan Mineka and her colleagues used rhesus monkeys to investigate this possibility.

Rhesus monkeys reared in the wild have an intense fear of snakes. This fear does not appear to be innate because rhesus monkeys reared in a laboratory show no such fear. Mineka and her coworkers wanted to see whether the laboratory-reared monkeys could learn a snake phobia merely by watching other monkeys act fearful. To find out, they used two groups of monkeys—a group of wild-reared monkeys who were highly fearful of snakes, and a group of laboratory-reared monkeys who had no preexperimental snake phobia. During testing, the monkeys in each group had to reach over a clear box to obtain a food treat. When the box contained a neutral object like a wooden block, the wild-reared monkeys readily grabbed the food. But when the clear box contained a live snake, these monkeys not only held back, they made grimaces and threatening faces, clutched at their cages, and showed other signs of extreme fear. In sharp contrast, the laboratory-reared monkeys were largely unaffected by the contents of the box.

To see whether the laboratory-reared monkeys would fear snakes after watching their wild-reared cousins, the researchers placed some of them in clear view of the wild-reared monkeys as they performed the task. Others watched the performance on a television monitor from another location. In both cases, the "observer" monkeys acquired a fear of snakes that lasted for at least three months (Mineka, Davidson, Cook, and Keir, 1984). These findings strongly suggest that phobias can be learned by observation (Cook and Mineka, 1990). Incidentally, they also show that even monkeys can learn from watching television.

OBSERVATIONAL LEARNING IN CHILDREN

A classic demonstration of human observation learning was made by psychologist Albert Bandura (1965). In one of his studies, preschool children watched an adult model attack a large, inflated rubber "Bobo, the clown " doll. When the children were later individually left alone with the doll, they often imitated the adult's actions. They too punched and kicked the doll. Other children saw the adult punished for acting aggressively. These children were much less likely to attack the Bobo doll. However, when these children were later offered rewards for imitating the adult's behavior they readily did so. In comparison to other children who did not see an aggressive model, Bandura found that all the children who saw an adult attack the doll learned aggressive responses. However, whether they performed these responses depended upon what they saw happen to the adult. Again, we see that learning is not the same as performing. Regardless of whether children perform the hostile actions they see modeled, Bandura's research shows that the potential for harm is implanted just by watching other people act aggressively. Thus observational learning allows us to learn the consequences of behavior merely by watching others. By forming internal

representations of such episodes in memory, we learn connections between behaviors and their consequences without paying the potential costs of trial-and-error learning.

EXPECTANCY

In the process of forming connections between behaviors and consequences, animals and people also form *expectancies:* "Given what I have already experienced, what can I expect in the future?" Long ago, psychologist O. L. Tinklepaugh (1928) provided one of the most compelling demonstrations of expectancy learning. He allowed a monkey to watch him place a piece of banana under one of two cups. When the monkey was permitted to select a cup, it chose the cup with the banana rather than the empty cup. After a number of trials, Tinklepaugh switched the banana with a piece of lettuce without letting the monkey see him. When the monkey was then allowed to get the food, Tinklepaugh reported the following event:

> She jumps down from the chair, rushes to the proper container and picks it up. She extends her hand to seize the food. But her hand drops to the floor without touching it. She looks at the lettuce but (unless very hungry) does not touch it. She looks under and around her. She picks the cup up and examines it thoroughly inside and out. She has on occasion turned toward observers present in the room and shrieked at them in apparent anger. After several seconds spent searching, she gives a glance toward the other cup, which she has been taught not to look into, and then walks off to a nearby window. The lettuce is left untouched on the floor.

(Tinklepaugh, 1928)

From the early research of Tinklepaugh to more recent research, we know that animals and people can form expectancies in learning tasks (Colwill and Rescorla, 1985; Miller and Spear, 1985). One of the most surprising findings in this area is the research of Elizabeth Capaldi and David Miller (1988). They found that rats are able to count and that their counting influences their behavior. In a series of ingenious studies, the researchers measured the speed with which rats ran a straight runway from a start box to a goal box. Each rat received alternating patterns of trials in which food was either present or absent in the goal box for each trial. For example, one pattern of trials consisted of the sequence R–R–N. This meant that reinforcement was available in the goal box for the first two trials but not the last trial. The other pattern of trials was N–R–R–N. In this pattern reinforcement was only available for the second and third trials. The rats were exposed to each of these trial patterns on an alternating sequence. After about a dozen repetitions of each pattern, the rat's speed going to the goal box became greatly reduced only on Trial 3 of pattern R–R–N and Trial 4 of pattern N–R–R–N, the terminal trials in which reinforcement was unavailable. According to Capaldi and Miller, the slower running times for the nonreinforced terminal trials are the result of the rats counting the reinforced trials. If the preceding two trials were reinforced, the next trial must be nonreinforced. Consequently, there is no reward if the animals run quickly. If this interpretation of the rat's behavior is correct, it implies that expectancy of nonreward is guiding the animal's behavior on the terminal trials and that the expectancy is based on counting. In this case, the rats are performing simple arithmetic.

Research on the cognitive aspects of learning demonstrates that learning is not a mechanical "stamping-in" process. Animals and people evaluate their environment. They respond on the basis of what they perceive as likely outcomes. Instead of viewing learning as the result of the environment acting upon passive learners, many psychologists now believe that learners actively respond to their environmental experiences (Fountain, 1990; Lucas, Timberlake, Gawley, and Drew, 1990, among others). They ask: "Of what use is this information from the environment?" Animals and people are more likely to survive if they can adapt to changing conditions by learning environmental relations, instead of simply responding in an unchanging, mechanical way.

INTERACTIONS:
Constraints on Learning

Earlier we defined associative learning as the learning of a relation or contingency between events in the world. How general is this form of learning? Psychologist Gregory Kimble (1985) has said that the fundamental problem with the associative view of learning is that it does not deal with differences between individuals or species. The early belief that only one or two kinds of learning existed, and that the same laws of learning applied to all species, is now considered to be a serious

mistake (Leahey and Harris, 1989; Schwartz, 1989). Research in the last 25 years has shown that learning is an adaptive trait that is tuned by evolution to fit organisms into their particular environments. We have touched on this theme throughout this chapter.

For example, the fact that rats demonstrate latent learning of mazes suggests that they may be programmed by their genes to form spatial representations. Wild rats live in underground burrows where spatial memory would be a necessity. Similarly, the research on preparedness shows that animals (and people) learn some associations easily and others not at all. The work on food aversion is especially relevant to this issue.

For instance, learning researchers have discovered that rats learn food aversions on the basis of taste but not appearance, since rats are nocturnal feeders with poor vision. Thus, for the rat taste is a better cue than appearance to avoid eating spoiled food. On the other hand, quails are daytime feeders with very good vision. They, too, can learn food aversions if they become ill after eating a new food. But, unlike rats, they form an association between illness and a food's appearance rather than between illness and its taste (Wilcoxon, Dragoin, and Kral, 1972). These examples illustrate how the organism and the environment interact. They also indicate that an animal's place in the environment and its evolutionary past go a long way toward directing the way it learns even simple associations (Leahey and Harris, 1989). Finally, they suggest very strongly that the principles of classical and instrumental conditioning are not rigid universal laws of learning that apply to all species and situations. There are pervasive species-specific and situation-specific processes that supplement the general processes. Humans, for example, seem to be uniquely prepared to learn language. Although chimpanzees have been taught elements of sign language, we will see in Chapter 8 that they acquire this skill with great difficulty. In comparison, two-year-old children pick up language easily, even without any systematic instruction. Humans, it seems, are cognitively prepared to acquire language in a way that chimpanzees are not (Kimble, 1985).

Research in cognitive learning adds another level of complexity to our description of learning. Associative and cognitive learning are distinctly different learning processes, found in varying degrees in different species (Premack, 1983). For humans, associative learning and cognitive learning complement one another in many natural learning situations. Think back to our discussion of conditioned fear following movies like *Psycho* or *Jaws*. The classically conditioned fear of showers or sharks is acquired through observational learning, and it remains latent until the opportunity to shower or swim reminds us of our earlier vicarious experience. Both forms of learning affect our behavior, and both are important for adaptive responding. Associative and cognitive learning enables us to evaluate stimulus information, judge the significance of different events, and respond on the basis of the contingencies we have perceived. As with the other animals, our environmental niche and evolutionary past determine which contingencies we will perceive. Our ability to remember which are the signals for important events and to note which consequences follow which actions is not only helpful, it is crucial to our survival. ■

IN CONTEXT: LEARNING

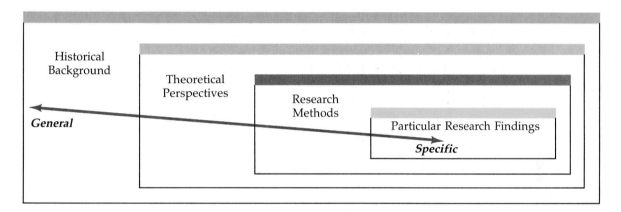

STUDY QUESTIONS

How are associations formed and why are they important to learning?

Why are some associations easier to learn than others?

What procedures can be used to modify behavior?

What role does cognition play in learning?

HISTORICAL BACKGROUND

1. Modern ideas about **associative learning** began with such British empiricist philosophers as Locke and Berkeley in the seventeenth and eighteenth centuries. They believed that mental associations were based on the **contiguity** of stimulus sensations.

2. Ivan Pavlov provided the first experimental evidence for associative learning in dogs at the start of the twentieth century. While studying the digestive system, Pavlov discovered that hungry dogs would salivate when they encountered people or objects associated with food. This type of associative learning became known as **classical conditioning**.

3. A contemporary of Pavlov, Edward Thorndike studied a different type of associative learning. Instead of looking at associations between stimuli, Thorndike studied how cats formed associations between stimuli and responses as they learned how to escape from a puzzle box. This form of associative learning is called **instrumental conditioning**.

4. B. F. Skinner modified Thorndike's research by showing that new responses could be shaped by selective reinforcement. Skinner's approach to learning is called **operant conditioning**.

MODERN THEORETICAL PERSPECTIVES

1. During the first half of this century there were many general theories of associative learning. Today these theories no longer motivate research. The principles of classical and in-

strumental conditioning are not, as once thought, rigid universal laws of learning that apply to all species and situations. Associative and cognitive learning are distinctly different learning processes that are found in varying degrees in different species. However, both forms of learning involve adaptive responses to environmental relations that help animals and people survive.

2. Local theories still exist to explain such particular learning phenomena as reinforcement. For example, **deprivation theory** holds that any activity can function as a reinforcer if the subject is prevented from performing this activity as often as it would otherwise.

RESEARCH METHODS

1. **Experimentation** was used in this chapter to study learning in a variety of species. For example, it was used in studies with laboratory rats to provide evidence for conditioned taste aversion (Garcia et al., 1972), latent learning (Tolman and Honzik, 1930), and counting (Capaldi and Miller, 1988). Experimentation also showed that dogs can use a conditioned stimulus as a signal (Rescorla, 1967), that chimps have spatial memory (Menzel, 1978), and that both children and chimps are capable of observational learning (Bandura, 1965; Mineka et al., 1989).

2. The **case study** method was used to show how conditioning procedures could be used to modify the behavior of a woman with anorexia nervosa (Bachrach et al., 1965), a man who stuttered (Goldiamond, 1965), and a child who threw temper tantrums (Williams, 1959).

RESEARCH FINDINGS AND SUMMARY

1. **Learning** is a relatively permanent change in behavior or behavior potentiality that results from experience.

2. Pavlov's **classical conditioning** is built upon innate associations between **unconditioned stimuli** and **unconditioned responses.** By pairing a previously neutral stimulus such as a bell with an unconditioned stimulus such as food, the neutral stimulus becomes a **conditioned stimulus** that elicits a **conditioned response.**

3. Once a conditioned response has been acquired, it may show **generalization** to stimuli that are similar to the conditioned stimulus. However continued training, in which only the conditioned stimulus is followed by the unconditioned stimulus, will lead to **discrimination,** as only the conditioned stimulus

will elicit the conditioned response. When the unconditioned stimulus no longer follows the conditioned stimulus, the conditioned response will show **extinction** and will no longer be made.

4. Research shows that an association between stimuli is formed when a conditioned stimulus functions as a **signal** for an unconditioned stimulus. A conditioned response is not a substitute for an unconditioned stimulus; it is an **adaptive response** to the particular situation.

5. **Instrumental conditioning** is a form of associative learning that is concerned with the consequences of responses. **Shaping** by the method of successive approximation is used to produce a new response by taking small behavioral steps and carefully reinforcing each of the steps toward that novel response. In general, the greater the amount and the shorter the delay of reinforcement, the better the learner's performance. As in classical conditioning, an instrumentally conditioned response will show evidence of **generalization, discrimination,** and **extinction.**

6. A **schedule of reinforcement** is a relation between a response and a reinforcer. Under **continuous reinforcement,** each response is reinforced; under **intermittent reinforcement,** only some responses are reinforced or reinforcement is available for only a specified period of time. The four different intermittent schedules are the **fixed ratio, variable ratio, fixed interval,** and **variable interval schedules.**

7. **Positive** and **negative reinforcement** have been used to *increase* the rate of desirable behaviors, while **extinction** and **punishment** have been employed to *decrease* or eliminate undesirable responses. Punishment can be effective when it is used in conjunction with positive reinforcement to teach a more desirable form of behavior.

8. The field of **behavioral medicine** integrates our knowledge about behavior and medicine to promote health and fight disease. One therapeutic procedure is called **biofeedback training,** and it is based on operant conditioning. People given biofeedback training have learned to regulate several "involuntary" autonomic responses.

9. **Animal cognition** refers to the use of an internal representation by an animal as a basis for action. Phenomena such as **cognitive maps and latent learning, spatial memory, observational learning,** and **expectancy** provide evidence of cognitive processes. For example, re-

search on observational learning has shown that animals and people can learn environmental relations by observing the actions of others.

10. Research on associative and cognitive learning has shown that learners evaluate stimulus information and respond on the basis of the perceived relations. This ability to note environmental events and remember the consequences of actions enables learners to adapt and survive.

ADDITIONAL READINGS

Gormezano, I., Prokasy, W. F., and Thompson, R. F., eds. 1987. *Classical conditioning*, 3rd ed. Hillsdale, NJ: Erlbaum. Leading researchers in the field present current advances in behavioral, neurophysiological, and neurochemical studies of classical conditioning.

Hergenhahn, B. R. 1982. *An introduction to theories of learning*, 2nd ed. Englewood Cliffs, NJ: Prentice Hall. A broad review of learning theories and theorists from the past to the present. Special attention is given to associative and cognitive theories.

Houston, J. P. 1991. Fundamentals of learning and memory, 4th ed. San Diego, CA: Harcourt Brace Jovanovich. An undergraduate text that describes the principles of learning that apply to humans and animals.

Kasden, A. E. 1989. *Behavior modification in applied settings*, 4th ed. Pacific Grove, CA: Brooks/Cole. This book shows how learning principles are applied to the treatment of behavior disorders. Numerous examples show how these principles have application to everyday life.

Miller, R. R., and Spear, N. E., eds. 1985. *Information processing in animals: Conditioned inhibition*. Hillsdale, NJ: Erlbaum. A collection of papers by animal researchers who have adopted a more cognitive, information processing approach to the study of learning in animals.

Roitblat, H. L. 1987. *Introduction to comparative cognition*. New York: Freeman. A comprehensive introduction to thinking and memory in animals, including bats, pigeons, bees, dolphins, monkeys, and apes.

Schwartz, B. 1989. *Psychology of learning and behavior*, 3rd ed. New York: Norton. A complete, carefully written, scholarly account of the psychology of learning. This text presents the origins, principles, and controversies of behavior theory in a interesting and understandable manner.

CHAPTER

7

MEMORY

The human memory system is capable of a rich variety of operations. At one extreme, it holds a highly detailed record of sensory images long enough to permit the identification and classification of sights, sounds, odors, tastes, and feelings. At the other extreme, memory records our experiences for use throughout our lifetime. Yet, despite their power, our memories can fail in frustrating ways. We can remember what we ate for dinner yesterday, but not the name of the person we have just met at a party. Some things seem easy to remember, others seem almost impossible.

(Peter Lindsay and Donald Norman, 1977)

Try answering the following questions involving your memory for names:

> What is the name of your school?
> What is your mother's maiden name?
> What are the names of the seven dwarfs from *Snow White?*
> What was the name of the classmate who sat on your left in third grade?

To unravel some of the mysteries of memory—including why some things are easy to remember, while others are difficult or impossible—we need to consider how memory operates.

Most events we experience are soon over, never to occur again. But many events stay with us, recorded in our nervous system. We call this record a **memory.** Our memory enables us to carry thousands of past events into the present; even events that occurred only once, for a brief moment. Memory is remarkable; without it, much of what you do would be impossible. Without memory, you could not think, you could not learn, and you could not carry on a conversation. Even your sense of self—of who you are—depends on the continuity of memory. When you wake up each morning you never question who you are because your memory bridges the past to the present. Think about what life would be like without memory. It would be nothing more than a series of momentary experiences, each one unrelated to another.

In thinking about how memory operates, were you able to recall your mother's maiden name, the names of the seven dwarfs, and the name of your third grade classmate? To the extent that you were successful, your ability to recall these things is based on three memory processes: **encoding, storage,** and **retrieval.** When we first experience an event, we must transform the information into a representation that can be placed in memory (encoding). That representation must be retained in the memory system (storage). Finally, in order to be of any use to us, it must later be recovered by the act of remembering (retrieval).

To organize what is known about memory, we will study its processes and contents in the same way that we might study the processes and contents of a complex computer that receives information, performs various operations on that information, and stores it for later use. The computer is an information processing device that can encode, store, and retrieve information. Psychologists do not believe that the human mind is a computer, but we do believe that it is often useful to think of human memory as an "information processing system" that operates, at least in part, with processes similar to a computer's. This conceptual approach is called **information processing.** A second conceptual approach is also used to study memory. This approach is called **connectionism** and, as we said in Chapter 4, it uses the neural processes of the brain as a model for memory processes. We will use both of these approaches in this chapter.

Before we begin, you will need to have an idea of what the memory system is like. A recent conceptual model, developed by psychologist

An information-processing device. A computer can encode, store, and retrieve information from memory.

Nelson Cowan (1988) is shown in Figure 7.1. To see how this model works, imagine that you have just dialed the information operator to get the telephone number of your favorite restaurant. You begin to process this information when your sensory receptors pick up information from the environment—in this case, the sounds made by the operator's voice. These unprocessed sensory signals are held in the **brief sensory store,** a large capacity memory register associated with each of your senses. This store holds the sensory information to allow time for your pattern recognition processes (described earlier in Chapter 4) to translate the information into a more meaningful form. In the process of pattern recognition, the sounds made by the operator are identified on the basis of knowledge in your **long-term store,** the repository of everything you know. At this point, the sounds have been translated into a telephone number ("828-5585") that you can think about.

In terms of our memory model, the telephone number that you think about, or "mentally rehearse," is said to be held in the **short-term store.** The short-term store is the portion of the long-term store that is currently active, and it can change quickly when your focus of attention is shifted. For example, if a friend interrupts you with a question ("What time does the movie start?") you may well forget the number. However, if the telephone number has already been memorized, you can retrieve it from your long-term store again and again. According to the memory model, retrieval involves "reactivating" the portion of the long-term store that contains the telephone number. When this is done, the number is once more in short-term storage and can be the focus of your attention.

From our virtually limitless long-term store we can retrieve such varied information as the name of the first boy or girl we ever had a crush on, the taste of cold beer and warm pizza, and the feel of the warm sun on our body after a dip in the ocean. From this memory store, we can remember our childhood home and former friends exactly as they were—at least we think we can. As you will see in this chapter, our long-term memory can fool us—sometimes we remember things differently from how they actually were. And it can disappoint us—at other times we fail to remember things that we thought we knew very well. Troublesome though these errors and failures may be, they provide us with important clues to the operation of the memory system. They also show

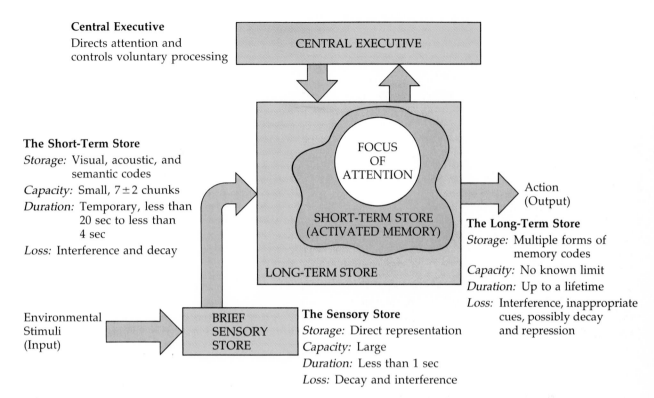

Central Executive
Directs attention and controls voluntary processing

CENTRAL EXECUTIVE

FOCUS OF ATTENTION

The Short-Term Store
Storage: Visual, acoustic, and semantic codes
Capacity: Small, 7±2 chunks
Duration: Temporary, less than 20 sec to less than 4 sec
Loss: Interference and decay

SHORT-TERM STORE (ACTIVATED MEMORY)

LONG-TERM STORE

Action (Output)

The Long-Term Store
Storage: Multiple forms of memory codes
Capacity: No known limit
Duration: Up to a lifetime
Loss: Interference, inappropriate cues, possibly decay and repression

Environmental Stimuli (Input)

BRIEF SENSORY STORE

The Sensory Store
Storage: Direct representation
Capacity: Large
Duration: Less than 1 sec
Loss: Decay and interference

FIGURE 7.1   A contemporary model of the memory system.   This model, adapted from Nelson Cowan, 1988, shows how the three memory stores are related. Environmental stimulation is received by the sensory store. Through the process of pattern recognition (not shown), the stimulation is identified on the basis of information in the long-term store. The activated portion of the long-term store is called the short-term store. Information in the short-term store can become the focus of attention. Psychologists wish to know how information is encoded and stored in the memory system and how it is retrieved at a later time.

us that human memory differs from that of an electronic computer, which always retrieves information in the same way (Estes, 1980). In this chapter we will describe why the memory system often succeeds and why it occasionally fails. We will discuss several methods for improving memory and we will also describe several puzzling memory pathologies that can tell us a great deal about normal memory functioning. Using the memory model model shown in Figure 7.1 as our guide, we will examine the properties of each of its components from the sensory to the long-term store.

HISTORICAL BACKGROUND:
Approaches to Memory

Discoveries about memory began in the second half of the nineteenth century when psychology was still in its infancy. Nineteenth-century psy-

chologists did physiological investigations of memory loss in patients with amnesia, designed developmental studies of memory in children, and contributed to philosophical discussions in the nature of memory (Murray, 1976). Memory was also one of the first areas to be examined with the new experimental approaches to psychology (Baxt, 1871; Jacobs, 1887; Wolfe, 1886, among others). However, of all these early studies, Ebbinghaus's research on the memorization of verbal material had the greatest impact.

Hermann Ebbinghaus

Born in Germany and trained in philosophy, Hermann Ebbinghaus (1850–1909) was interested in applying the methods of natural science to the study of memory. After completing his doctorate, he came across a copy of Fechner's *Elements of Psychophysics* in a second-hand bookstore in France. Realizing the significance of Fechner's approach to the study of sensation (described in

Hermann Ebbinghaus. Ebbinghaus was the first person to use the scientific method to study memory systematically. His original quantitative studies of memory were described in his classic book, *Memory*, published in 1885. The inscription inside its title page reads "From the most ancient subject we shall produce the newest science."

Chapter 3) Ebbinghaus eagerly followed Fechner's example and applied experimentation and quantitative measurement to the study of memory. He began his research in 1879 and published his classic monograph, *Memory*, in 1885.

In order to learn about memory, Ebbinghaus used himself as his only subject. With incredible patience and persistence, he learned list after list of *nonsense syllables* over a period of years. Ebbinghaus invented these consonant–vowel–consonant nonsense trigrams (for example, MIB–DAX–BOK) so that he could memorize each list with minimal influence of prior learning. From a set of over 2,000 of these stimuli, Ebbinghaus would construct a list of a dozen or so nonsense syllables and read them aloud in time with the beats of a metronome. After reading a list, he would try to recall the items, measuring the number of times he had to repeat a list until he got it correct. For lists of up to seven or eight items, he found that one study trial was sufficient to recite the items quickly and correctly. For longer lists, additional study was necessary. The longer the list, the more Ebbinghaus needed to repeat the trials to reach perfect recall.

After learning a list, Ebbinghaus tested his memory by recalling the list at various times. Using the first nonsense syllable in a list as a cue, he

attempted to recall the rest. If he was less than perfect, he measured the number of trials that it took him to relearn the list. The number of relearning trials he needed to reach the original criterion (perfect recall) was Ebbinghaus's measure of memory performance, and he expressed it as a *savings score*. A savings in relearning was demonstrated if he needed fewer trials to relearn a list than it took to learn it originally. Ebbinghaus found that the longer the interval of time between the original learning of a list and its subsequent relearning, the less the savings that occurred. In other words, the greater the time between original learning and relearning, the greater the amount of forgetting. This relation between savings and the time between learning and relearning is Ebbinghaus's most famous discovery. It is known as a **forgetting curve** (Figure 7.2). Ebbinghaus is remembered today for enlarging the domain of psychology by showing that it was possible to study memory in a scientific way.

Frederic Bartlett

In the 1920s, British psychologist Frederic Bartlett (1886–1969) took a different approach to the study of memory. Unlike Ebbinghaus, Bartlett was interested in the kinds of things that are remembered, rather than the number of trials that it takes to memorize something. He believed that in order

Frederic Bartlett. Bartlett showed how remembering was subject to errors and distortions. Rather than using nonsense syllables that were popular at the time, Bartlett used everyday stimuli such as words, objects, and stories to see how remembering changed over time. His classic book, *Remembering*, was published in 1932.

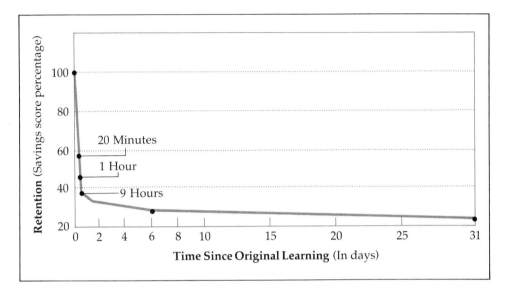

FIGURE 7.2 Ebbinghaus's forgetting curve. Using himself as his only subject, Ebbinghaus calculated the percentage of time saved in relearning lists of nonsense syllables according to the amount of time that elapsed since original learning. He found that forgetting occurs rapidly immediately after learning and then declines gradually.

to understand how memory functioned in everyday situations, we need to study memory using everyday stimulus materials. Instead of asking people to learn lists of meaningless nonsense syllables, Bartlett used meaningful stimuli such as words, objects, and stories. Rather than measuring savings, he was interested in seeing whether our remembrances changed over time.

Bartlett outlined his research procedures in his 1932 book, *Remembering*. His *method of serial reproduction* was designed to demonstrate the effect of social factors on remembering. In this task, a person was briefly shown a stimulus such as a drawing of an owl and then was asked to draw it from memory. This new drawing was then shown to another person who repeated the process of viewing and drawing. After numerous repetitions of this process, Bartlett compared the most recent reproduction of the stimulus with the original drawing of the owl. He found in one series of reproductions that the owl had changed into a cat (Figure 7.3).

Bartlett's best known procedure was his *method of repeated reproduction*. In this task, people read an unusual story from a folktale or myth and were later asked to recall it. Table 7.1 shows one of his stories, "The War of the Ghosts," and how one person recalled that story after various periods of time. Bartlett found that recall was often characterized by omissions, simplifications, and transformations of the original story. Typically, the

errors were sensible—the teller changed the story into a more familiar and conventional form. Bartlett is remembered today because he demonstrated that our memory for events is often vague and incomplete. He showed how we fill in the gaps in our memory by making logical inferences about what "must have been."

The different approaches used by Ebbinghaus and Bartlett guided much of the later research in this field. We will see the influence of Ebbinghaus's emphasis on quantitative measurement and Bartlett's emphasis on qualitative change when we look at remembering and forgetting. Before we do that, though, we need to examine how information enters the memory system in the first place. Before there can be a memory, there must be an experience to remember. ■

ENTERING THE MEMORY SYSTEM

Do all of our experiences produce memories? The answer to this question depends upon what you mean by memories. All of our experiences can produce a physical change in the nervous system that we refer to as a **memory trace,** but not all of these traces are permanent. Some memory traces can last a lifetime, some a few days or hours, some perhaps 30 seconds, and some, called sensory memories, are so brief that they may last for less

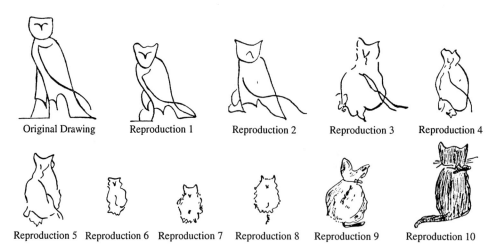

Original Drawing   Reproduction 1   Reproduction 2   Reproduction 3   Reproduction 4

Reproduction 5   Reproduction 6   Reproduction 7   Reproduction 8   Reproduction 9   Reproduction 10

FIGURE 7.3 The method of serial reproduction. One of Bartlett's memory tasks was the method of serial reproduction. In this task, a person was shown a drawing of an owl. Thirty minutes later, the person reproduced the drawing of the owl from memory. The first reproduction was largely faithful. But when this reproduction was shown to a second person and the sequence repeated a number of times, the drawing systematically changed during its reproductions from an owl to a cat. Bartlett used this task to study the effects of social factors on remembering.

than a second. We will begin our entry into the memory system that we outlined in Figure 7.1 by describing the sensory memories produced by the brief sensory store.

SENSORY MEMORY

Sensory memory connects our present to our most recent past. It is defined as the persistence of stimulation in the nervous system after the physical stimulation from the environment has been terminated. For example, following the presentation of a visual stimulus there is a brief visual memory trace called an **icon;** after an auditory stimulus there is a brief auditory memory trace called an **echo** (Neisser, 1967). The other senses, including touch or taste, may have their corresponding sensory memories as well, but research in sensory memory has dealt predominantly with sight and sound.

THE STUDY OF SENSORY MEMORY

Most people associate the name Peter Mark Roget with the *Thesaurus* he compiled in 1852. But this nineteenth-century physician is important for another reason as well. He was the first person to report on the visual memory trace that persists after we look at a moving object. As an example of Roget's observation, if you shine a flashlight on a wall in a darkened room and trace a circular path by rapidly moving your arm as you hold the light, you will see a circle of light even though the light is actually shining on only one portion of the wall at

a time. This "visual persistence" is an example of iconic memory. An even better example is shown in Figure 7.4. If you look at a picture of an object that has been placed behind a screen containing a narrow slit, you will see only a narrow band of the picture. It is impossible to identify the object (in this case, a camel). But if the slit is moved rapidly

FIGURE 7.4 Passing a camel through the eye of a needle. Although the screen permits only a narrow band of the picture to be seen at one time, moving the screen rapidly back and forth across the picture enables the entire object to be seen. This demonstration, which is easy to verify at home, provides evidence for the existence of iconic memory that persists long enough for the concealed camel to be made visible.

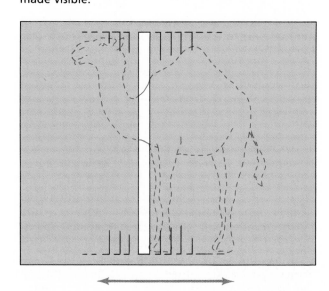

TABLE 7.1 A Person's Recall of a Story After 20 Hours and After 2 Years and 6 Months

"The War of the Ghosts" in Its Original Form

One night two young men from Egulac went down to the river to hunt seals, and while they were there it became foggy and calm. Then they heard war cries, and they thought: "Maybe this is a war party." They escaped to the shore, and hid behind a log. Now canoes came up, and they heard the noise of paddles, and saw one canoe coming up to them. There were five men in the canoe, and they said:

"What do you think? We wish to take you along. We are going up the river to make war on the people." One of the young men said: "I have no arrows."

"Arrows are in the canoe," they said.

"I will not go along. I might be killed. My relatives do not know where I have gone. But you," he said, turning to the other, "may go with them."

So one of the young men went, but the other returned home.

And the warriors went on up the river to a town on the other side of Kalama. The people came down to the water, and they began to fight, and many were killed. But presently the young man heard one of the warriors say: "Quick, let us go home: that Indian has been hit." Now he thought: "Oh, they are ghosts." He did not feel sick, but they said he had been shot.

So the canoes went back to Egulac, and the young man went ashore to his house, and made a fire. And he told everybody and said: "Behold I accompanied the ghosts, and we went to fight. Many of our fellows were killed, and many of those who attacked us were killed. They said I was hit, and I did not feel sick."

He told it all, and then he became quiet. When the sun rose he fell down. Something black came out of his mouth. His face became contorted. The people jumped up and cried.

He was dead.

Story Recall After 20 Hours

Two men from Edulac went fishing. While thus occupied by the river they heard a noise in the distance.

"It sounds like a cry," said one, and presently there appeared some men in canoes who invited them to join the party on their adventure. One of the young men refused to go, on the ground of family ties, but the other offered to go.

"But there are no arrows," he said.

"The arrows are in the boat," was the reply.

He thereupon took his place, while his friend returned home. The party paddled up the river to Kaloma, and began to land on the banks of the river. The enemy came rushing upon them, and some sharp fighting ensued. Presently someone was injured, and the cry was raised that the enemy were ghosts.

The party returned down the stream, and the young man arrived home feeling none the worse for his experience. The next morning at dawn he endeavoured to recount his adventures. While he was talking something black issued from his mouth. Suddenly he uttered a cry and fell down. His friends gathered round him.

But he was dead.

Story Recall After 2 Years and 6 Months

Some warriors went to wage war against the ghosts. They fought all day and one of their number was wounded.

They returned home in the evening, bearing their sick comrade. As the day drew to a close, he became rapidly worse and the villagers came round him. At sunset he sighed—something black came out of his mouth. He was dead.

From Bartlett (1932).

back and forth across the picture, the entire object suddenly becomes visible. Although only a narrow band of the picture is shown at any moment in time, you see the complete object because of your iconic memory. The sum of the momentary glimpses and iconic traces enables you to see the object in its entirety. In effect, a camel can be passed through the eye of a needle (Parks, 1965).

Iconic memory was first demonstrated many years ago but systematic research on it did not begin until the middle of this century, when George Sperling conducted experiments on the capacity of the iconic store and the duration of iconic traces (Sperling, 1960). With an apparatus called a *tachistoscope* that presents visual stimuli at precisely controlled durations, Sperling presented his subjects with stimulus arrays of up to 12 letters such as the following:

QLHK
CNVX
FRWB

Each array was flashed for only 50 milliseconds, or 1/20th of a second. In the *whole report condition,* the subject's task was to report all of the letters that were shown. Sperling found that for small arrays of three or four letters, the subjects were perfect. However, for larger arrays they could never report more than four or five letters correctly. This relation between the number of letters displayed and the subjects' report of an array is shown by the line labeled "whole report condition" in Figure 7.5.

Perplexed by the limited recall and his subjects' reports that they saw more than they could report, Sperling devised an ingenious scheme to measure the capacity and duration of iconic storage. Since a brief visual stimulus leaves an iconic trace that persists for a short time after the stimulus is removed, Sperling felt that the limited recall of his subjects may have been due to the rapid disappearance of their iconic traces. In effect, the subjects only had time to "read off" four or five letters from the iconic trace before it disappeared. To test this possibility, Sperling used a different procedure than before. Instead of trying to recall the whole array, the subjects were asked to recall only a part of it. In this *partial report condition* the subjects were now asked to report only a single row of four letters from the array. This change reduced the number of letters to be recalled and thereby gave subjects sufficient time to do the task before their iconic trace had faded. To ensure that the subjects used iconic memory to do the task, rather than the stimulus itself, Sperling waited until the stimulus was removed before designating which row of letters was to be reported. Immediately after an array, one of three tones signalled the report of a particular row: a high-pitched tone for the top row, a medium tone for the middle row, and a low tone for the bottom row. Since each row was equally likely to be signaled and the subjects did not know in advance which row they would have to report, the partial report procedure reveals the number of letters available in the iconic trace at that moment in time. For any given row, the percentage of letters recalled yields an estimate of the percentage of letters in the entire iconic memory trace. This is the same line of reasoning that in-

FIGURE 7.5 The recall of briefly displayed letters. A comparison of the number of letters correctly reported by either whole report or partial report according to the number of letters briefly displayed by a tachistoscope. Under the whole report condition, the subjects tried to report all of the letters in the array; under the partial report condition, the subjects tried to report only a particular set of the stimuli designated by a cue after the array was removed. The advantage of partial report over whole report implies that, immediately after a visual array is shown, there is a brief iconic trace that can be used to report the stimuli.

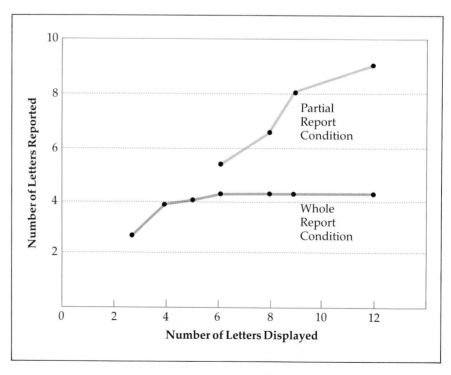

structors use when testing students in a course. Rather than test students on all of the material presented, only a portion is called for on a test. If students were told the contents of the test in advance, their test grades could not be used to estimate what they learned from the course, since they might have focused on only the material on which they knew they would be tested.

When Sperling multiplied the number of letters reported for a given row by the number of rows in an array, he found that immediately after an array was removed the subjects had nearly 100 percent of the letters available in their iconic trace. (See the line labeled "partial report condition" in Figure 7.5.) This trace quickly fades, however. Delaying the tone cue in the partial report condition by only 300 milliseconds (approximately one-third of a second) after the array was removed reduced the available letters to only 75 percent. Within one second, the trace was gone and subjects' recall was no greater than that obtained from the whole report condition. Essentially the same characteristics have been found for echoic memory following the presentation of brief auditory stimuli (Darwin, Turvey, and Crowder, 1972; Massaro, 1970). These findings demonstrate that sensory storage can hold a large amount of information. However, most of this information is lost in less than one tick of the clock.

FUNCTION OF SENSORY MEMORY

At present, most psychologists agree that sensory memory exists. However, there is considerable controversy about its importance for memory processes—the importance of iconic memory is particulary questioned. Must all visual information pass through the sensory store before it can become the focus of our awareness? Some psychologists believe so. They take the brief sensory store shown in Figure 7.1 quite literally as the first stage in a sequence of stages that we use to process information (Coltheart, 1980). Other psychologists disagree. They believe that iconic memory is only used under conditions of very brief visual exposures. For example, we use it when we view a movie. A movie is actually a sequence of separate still frames shown at a rapid rate, but each briefly shown frame gives rise to an iconic trace that lasts until the next frame is projected on the screen. Due to iconic memory we never see the gap between frames. Instead, we experience a continuous sequence (Gregory, 1978; Rock, 1975). Still other psychologists believe that iconic memory may be simply a sensory afterimage (discussed in Chapter 3) and, except under such unusual circumstances as

The richness of remembering. Memory codes enable us to recall such qualities as the flavorful aroma and taste of barbecued chicken.

looking at stimuli in a tachistoscope, it plays no important role in normal memory processes (Haber, 1983; Neisser, 1983). Additional research is needed to tell us how often we actually use our iconic memory. However, psychologist William Uttal has suggested at least one important function. Interestingly enough, it is closely tied to Roget's original observation. Iconic memory, says Uttal, is the nervous system's way of linking individual moments in time. For example, it is used to perceive moving objects as moving objects instead of as a disconnected series of events (Uttal, 1983).

There is less controversy about the role of echoic memory. Since auditory information is usually spread out in time—one word is spoken after another—some means of briefly preserving the immediate past is essential. Ulric Neisser (1967), for example, has suggested that a foreigner who confuses the words *seal* and *zeal* could not be helped by someone saying "No, not seal, *zeal!*" unless those individual sounds could be retained long enough to be compared. Echoic memory seems to be ideally suited to this purpose.

In summary, one plausible function of sensory memory is to extend the duration of our perception of stimuli when they are presented very briefly. Without this time extension, our pattern recognition processes would not have time to analyze the sensory information. Consequently, very brief stimuli would never capture our attention and become the focus of our awareness. But given sufficient time for the pattern recognition operations to be performed, the stimuli that we are seeing or hearing can be transformed, or *coded*, into meaningful representations and relayed to conscious awareness. In the terms used by our memory model, the processed information is then held in the short-term store.

SHORT-TERM MEMORY

The short-term store shown in Figure 7.1 is often loosely equated with attention and consciousness. It can receive information from the "outside" (the result of perceptual processing) or it can retrieve information from our memory archives (the result of long-term storage). Being conscious of what someone is saying to you is an example of short-term memory based on perceptual processing; thinking about a movie you saw last week is an example of short-term memory based on retrieval from the long-term store. **Short-term memory** is the type of memory we use when we wish to retain information for a short time to think about it. The short-term store has a **working memory** component, a sort of workspace in the mind, that is used to manipulate information in consciousness (Baddeley, 1986). In this regard, the short-term store is essential for such cognitive tasks as speaking or reading (Baddeley, 1979; Fletcher, 1986). For example, imagine how difficult it would be to understand the following sentence if the information at the beginning could not be held in the short-term store until you read the words at the end:

> The girl who asked about the boy who the woman with the large income hired never came back again.
>
> *(From Matlin, 1983)*

Without the use of this memory, we could never understand the sentence. Nor could we answer the question "Who never came back again?" The short-term store provides the output for the memory system that enables us to respond or act. In this section we will distinguish the short-term store from the other memory stores shown in Figure 7.1 on the basis of how much it can hold, how long that storage lasts, and how it loses information.

CAPACITY

How much information can we hold in the short-term store? To answer this question, psychologists have devised a measure called the **memory span.** This is the maximum number of stimuli that can be recalled in perfect order 50 percent of the time. Across a wide variety of conditions, research has shown that the memory span has an upper limit of seven plus or minus two "chunks" (Miller, 1956). A **chunk** is a unit of information that functions as a single stimulus. Seven consonant letters (b, c, d, f, g, h, k) and seven simple words (bat, dog, car, cup, boat, shoe, hair) are both seven chunks. We can hold approximately seven of these stimuli in our short-term storage.

We cannot increase the number of chunks that we can hold in short-term storage, but we can stretch our capacity by increasing the amount of information in each chunk. For example, psychologist Herbert Simon (1974) presented himself the following list of words and found that he could not recall them correctly after just one presentation:

Lincoln
Milky
Criminal
Differential
Address
Way
Lawyer
Calculus
Gettysburg

Try it. Without looking back, write down as many words as you can. Most of us have the same problem because these relatively complex words represent nine chunks of information. This amount typically exceeds our short-term storage capacity. However, if you rearrange the words into four chunks of information, your task is considerably easier.

Lincoln's Gettysburg Address
Milky Way
Criminal Lawyer
Differential Calculus

This list is easier to recall because four chunks fit comfortably within our memory span.

A study of the short-term storage capacity of novice and master chess players demonstrates the importance of information chunking. After viewing a picture of a chess game in progress for five seconds, members of both groups were asked to reproduce all of the pieces on a blank chess board. As you might expect, the chess masters were almost perfect at this task, while the beginners seldom placed more than half of the pieces correctly. Were the chess masters better because they had larger memory spans? No. When the task was repeated with all of the chess pieces randomly arranged on the board, the performance of the masters dropped to that of the beginners.

With an actual game, the masters saw the board in terms of clusters of action. These clusters were based on common relations among specific pieces that allowed the chess masters to group the entire collection into a small number of meaningful units or chunks. For instance, the masters might recognize a pattern as a minor variation on a classical defense to the Queen's gambit. Novices did not have this backlog of experience; they saw the board as a collection of unrelated pieces. With the same memory spans of seven plus or minus two chunks, the masters could reproduce more pieces than the novices because their chunks contained more information (DeGroot, 1966). This study indicates that while the capacity of short-term storage is limited by the number of chunks, it is not nearly so limited in terms of information. Through experience, we can learn to pack more information into each chunk and effectively stretch the capacity of the short-term store.

DURATION

Once you have placed information in your short-term store, you can maintain it indefinitely by **mental rehearsal,** by repeating the information over and over to yourself. But what happens if rehearsal is prevented? How long do we retain information that is not rehearsed and not already learned and represented in the long-term store?

To measure short-term memory duration, psychologists Lloyd Peterson and Margaret Peterson (1959) conducted an experiment in which they presented college student subjects with three consonant letters (C X T, for example) followed by a "distractor" task (hearing a three-digit number—say 409—immediately after the letters were presented). Once the subjects heard the number, they had to count backward by threes from that number (409, 406, 403, and so on) until the signal to recall the letters was given. The purpose of the distractor task was to prevent the subjects from rehearsing the original letter stimuli for a specified period of time. After three to 18 seconds of distraction, the subjects were asked to recall the letters. The results, shown in Figure 7.6, indicate that the distractor task had a considerable effect on recall. After three seconds of distraction, subjects could recall 80 percent of the original letters, but if the distraction blocked rehearsal for 18 seconds, they could recall only about 10 percent. Recent data are even more striking. If subjects are not forewarned of the recall task, information in short-term storage is lost after a brief two seconds of distraction (Muter, 1980; Sebrechts, Marsh, and Seaman, 1989).

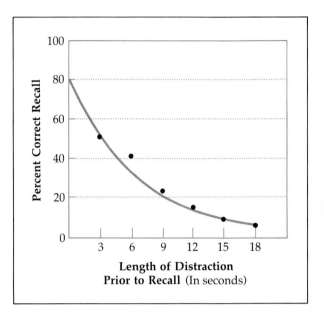

FIGURE 7.6 Forgetting from short-term storage. Without the aid of rehearsal, information in the short-term store is quickly forgotten. After listening to three consonant letters (for example, C X T), subjects counted backward by threes for three to 18 seconds. The longer the subjects were distracted by counting, the poorer their recall of the letter stimuli.

Without rehearsal, short-term memory traces are forgotten in only a matter of seconds.

FORGETTING

Forgetting is actually a desirable feature of short-term storage. It allows us to eliminate information we no longer need. For instance, imagine that short-order cooks or waiters remembered all of the meals they served. Forgetting has value in that it allows us to discard what is no longer relevant and to attend to the information at hand.

What is responsible for forgetting in short-term storage? Psychologists attribute it to either **decay** or **interference.** Information that is not rehearsed could simply fade away with the passage of time (decay), or it could be dislodged by the arrival of new information (interference). Which interpretation is correct? Research suggests that both factors produce forgetting, although interference appears to be more important. If information in the short-term store is not maintained by rehearsal, it suffers decay. This loss is greatly accelerated when additional information produces interference with the original material (Reitman, 1974; Shiffrin and Cook, 1978).

The research we have discussed shows that the short-term store is used to hold a limited amount of information temporarily in conscious aware-

Using short-term memory. This man holds dinner orders in his short-term store while he prepares the dishes; then he replaces them with new orders.

ness. If this information is not actively rehearsed it is quickly lost by interference and decay. The short-term store comes in handy when we need to have specific information immediately available for only a short period of time (perhaps a telephone number we looked up in the directory). More importantly, short-term storage provides a basis for the production of long-term memory.

FORMING LONG-TERM MEMORIES

William James drew a distinction between *primary* and *secondary memory*. He said that information in consciousness was held in primary memory, while information not in consciousness but capable of being recovered (the name of your school and your mother's maiden name) resided in secondary memory. Psychologists still hold this view, but our terminology has changed. Instead of "primary and secondary memory," we now use "short- and long-term storage." The unlimited long-term store is a more-or-less permanent repository of all of the things we know. In this section, we will consider how we get information into this repository and we will address a question of some importance to most college students: How can we get information into long-term storage more efficiently?

REHEARSAL AND LONG-TERM MEMORY

Mental rehearsal can be used not only to maintain information in the short-term store, but to es-

tablish new memory traces in the long-term store. For example, rehearsing (repeating) a word frequently increases the probability of later recalling it. When people are presented with a list of approximately twenty unrelated words (hoof, candy, pencil, and so forth) shown individually at a rate of one every five seconds and then asked to recall all of the words they can in any order they wish, the words in the list are not all recalled equally well. People are best at recalling words at the beginning and end of the list (Figure 7.7) (Murdock, 1962, among others). This U-shaped relation between a word's position in the list and its probability of recall is called a **serial position effect**—the high recall of the first few items is called a *primacy effect*, while the high recall of the last few items is called a *recency effect*. A serial position effect is a characteristic of a **free recall task,** where people study a list of words and then recall the words in any order they can.

It appears that the way we tend to rehearse words for recall influences which words are best recalled. When people rehearse the words out loud as the list is being presented the first items in the list are rehearsed the most frequently, while the last words in the list are rehearsed the least frequently (Figure 7.7). Just before beginning their recall, people are found to be most apt to be rehearsing the final three or four words in the list (Rundus, 1971). Recent research has confirmed and extended these findings. Not only are early items rehearsed most frequently, they are rehearsed intermittently while the rest of the list is being presented. In a sense, people practice recall-

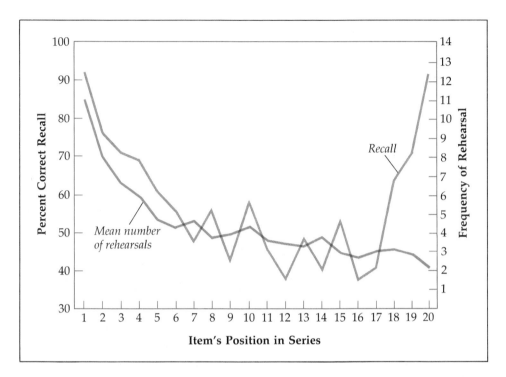

FIGURE 7.7 A serial position curve. A serial position curve for the free recall of a 20-word list shows the probability of each word's recall according to its position in the list. The high recall of the first few items in the list is called a primacy effect, while the high recall of the last few items is called a recency effect. Also shown are the number of times each word was rehearsed according to its position in the list.

ing the early items before they are actually recalled at the end of the list (Modigliani and Hedges, 1987).

These findings are consistent with earlier research that suggested that the primacy effect in free recall is due to recall from long-term storage, while the recency effect is the result of recall from short-term storage (Glanzer and Cunitz, 1966). The early items in the list that are rehearsed the most are therefore more likely to be represented in the long-term store. On the other hand, the last items in the list received the most recent rehearsal and are likely to still be represented in the short-term store when recall begins. At the time of recall, people recall the words they are currently rehearsing (the recency effect), and then they recall the words according to the amount of rehearsal each has received (the primacy effect). These data both support the distinction between short-term and long-term storage and suggest that rehearsal is important for the formation of long-term memories. However, not all studies have found the same relations between rehearsal frequency and long-term storage (Craik and Watkins, 1973). Why is there a discrepancy? It appears that there may be more than one type of rehearsal.

MAINTENANCE AND ELABORATIVE REHEARSAL

Instead of thinking of rehearsal as one process, psychologists now distinguish between two different types, called **maintenance** and **elaborative rehearsal** (Bjork and Jongeward, 1975; Craik and Watkins, 1973). Maintenance rehearsal is a form of mental repetition that serves mainly to hold memory traces in the temporary short-term store, although it can establish weak traces in the more permanent long-term store. Elaborative rehearsal involves alterations or additions to the information in short-term storage. It is responsible for establishing strong traces in long-term storage. As an example of each type of rehearsal, compare the following strategies used to remember a person's name. For example, make believe that you have just been introduced to a man named Arnold Brown and you wish to remember his name.

Maintenance Rehearsal:
Arnold Brown; Arnold Brown; Arnold Brown,
. . .

Elaborative Rehearsal:
Arnold Brown; let's see, Arnold can be a person's first name or last name, as in the name

Benedict Arnold; Brown can also be a color name; Arnold Brown; this person's initials are the first two letters of the alphabet and they are in alphabetical order. . . .

(From Stern, 1985)

Maintenance rehearsal helps us keep information in short-term storage, but elaborative rehearsal helps us get that information into long-term storage (Bjork and Jongeward, 1975). This is an important distinction to keep in mind because people often mistakenly believe that both forms of rehearsal are equally effective (Shaughnessy, 1981). If you think about the memory demands of a given task, the choice between maintenance and elaborative rehearsal should be clear. In general, use maintenance rehearsal for temporary short-term storage (for a one-time phone number) and elaborative rehearsal for more permanent long-term storage (for a psychology test).

LEVELS OF PROCESSING

The way in which we encode, or think about, a stimulus is important for long-term memory. Encoding, again, is defined as the process of interpreting a stimulus and storing a representation of that interpretation in memory. We can think of encoding a stimulus as a series of levels that range from a simple analysis of its physical features to an analysis of its meaning. For example, Figure 7.8 shows the different ways in which a visual stimulus can be analyzed. In this example, the apple can be analyzed *visually* as a round, red object, *acoustically* as a word with a particular sound, or *conceptually* as an edible fruit. This progression of analysis from appearance to name to meaning is referred to as the **levels of processing** (Craik and Lockhart, 1972).

In general, experiments on free recall have shown that a conceptual analysis leads to better memory than a visual or acoustic analysis. When people were asked to analyze words in a list for their meaning they recalled more of the words on a later test than did other people, who saw the same words but were told to concentrate on their physical features (Hyde and Jenkins, 1969, among others). According to the levels of processing framework, deciding whether an apple is pleasant (a conceptual analysis) leads to a more distinctive memory trace for this stimulus than deciding whether the word apple contains the letter E (a visual analysis). Subsequent levels of processing experiments have confirmed that the way we process a stimulus influences its long-term storage (Craik and Tulving, 1975; Seamon and Murray, 1976; Seamon and Virostek, 1978). The more we understand about a stimulus, the better it will be learned and remembered.

This research can provide you with a few rules for efficient memory formation when you are studying for your next exam. First, listen or read for comprehension. It is difficult to learn and remember something that you do not understand, so aim for a conceptual level of processing. For

FIGURE 7.8 Encoding processes and memory. We can encode visual features of an object, acoustic features of its name, and conceptual or semantic aspects of its meaning. According to one approach, these different encoding processes correspond to different levels of processing. Research shows that the more we understand about a stimulus, the better that stimulus is retained.

Stimulus	Perceptual Classification	Type of Analysis	Level of Processing
	Is it red? Is it small?	Visual	Shallow
	Does it rhyme with chapel?	Acoustic	Moderate
	Is it edible? Is it good?	Conceptual	Deep

example, when you finish reading this paragraph, ask yourself what it meant. Second, study under conditions where you can devote full attention to the task. Distractions can prevent information in short-term storage from getting into long-term storage. Third, use elaborative processing. Try to associate new material with what you already know—material in your long-term storage. For example, if you want to remember a person's name, think of some associations to that name (remember our example of "Arnold Brown"). Fourth, when you find yourself day-dreaming, take a short break; studying while on "automatic pilot" is not effective for producing long-term memory. Finally, space your study sessions. Distributed study is far superior to massed study (cramming) for retaining information in memory (Keppel, 1967, among others).

MEMORY CODES

As we have seen from the levels of processing research, our long-term memory depends on how we encode information. Encoding processes are important because the way in which information is encoded determines how that information is represented in memory. Memory representations are called **codes** and there are three general types: *visual codes* deal with the appearance of stimuli; *auditory codes* deal with the sound of stimuli; and *semantic codes* deal with the meaning of stimuli (Postman, 1975). To read, write, or speak, we must code words in each of these forms. However, words are not the only kind of information that gets coded in memory. For example, our memory of Italian sausage can be coded in terms of the meaning of these words, the visual image of a sausage, its spicy aroma, its peppery taste, and the sound that our teeth make when they bite through its crisp skin (Matlin, 1983). All of these codes can add to the richness of our remembrance. Research on picture and word memory indicates how visual and semantic codes can help us remember.

MEMORY FOR PICTURES AND WORDS

For many years, psychologists studied memory by using only such verbal materials as words and nonsense syllables. But when psychologist Roger Shepard (1967) compared memory for words, sentences, and pictures, he found that we remember pictures best. Shepard gave his subjects a deck of approximately 600 cards, containing single words, English sentences, or pictures of magazine advertisements. After looking through the deck, the subjects were given a *forced choice recognition test*.

The test consisted of a series of trials in which two stimuli were shown: one had been in the deck, and the other was new, but comparable to a stimulus in the deck. The subjects were asked to select the stimulus that they had previously seen. Shepard found that people recognized roughly 88 percent of the single words and 89 percent of the sentences (chance performance was one in two or 50 percent). However, their memory for pictures was virtually perfect. Even when the subjects were tested two hours after seeing the pictures they still recognized 99 percent.

Why do we remember pictures better than words? A difference in coding may be responsible. Words are normally represented in memory by a verbal code. (This code would include information about the sight, sound, and meaning of a word as a verbal stimulus.) Pictures are different, however. They seem to be coded visually (in terms of their appearance) as well as verbally. For example, when we look at a picture of a car our pattern recognition processes automatically produce a visual representation of the car and a verbal interpretation of the word "car" as well. According to **dual coding theory,** pictures are remembered better than words because our probability of recalling either one of two codes is higher than our probability of recalling a single code (Paivio, 1971). While we must retrieve a verbal code before a word can be remembered, we can retrieve either a visual or a verbal code and still successfully remember a picture. There are other theories to explain the picture superiority effect (Nelson, 1979; Pezdek, Maki, Valencia-Laver, Whetstone, Stoeckert, and Dougherty, 1988), but the dual coding theory has an important practical application for memory. It suggests that we can improve our memory for words if we turn these words into mental pictures. In this way, we can dual-code words as we do pictures.

VISUAL IMAGERY AND MNEMONICS

Considerable research supports the argument that we can better remember words that we have also coded into mental pictures (Bellezza, 1981; Bower, 1972; Paivio, 1971). For example, when you see the word BUTTERFLY you will remember it better if you imagine a brightly colored Monarch butterfly resting on the tip of your finger than if you simply think of the word and say it over and over to yourself. Visual imagery improves memory performance because it involves elaborative rehearsal, conceptual processing for meaning, and the formation of dual memory codes. Visual imagery is the process of constructing mental pictures that bear a resemblance to physical reality. We will describe visual imagery more fully in Chapter 8. For now, it is important because it serves as the basis for many mnemonics.

The word **mnemonic** comes from the Greek word *mnemonikos,* which refers to memory or past experience. Mnemonics are defined as schemes or strategies for assisting memory. Their use dates back to the ancient Greek civilization where effective memorization was a highly valued skill. Actors and orators who needed to remember large bodies of information used these memory-assisting techniques to ensure effective retention. For example, Greek orators would recall long speeches by practicing them while walking. They would associate different parts of their speeches with landmarks along the way. Later, they would recall the speech by recalling their walk and the landmarks. Mnemonics are still widely used today. For instance, if you want to remember the value of pi to fourteen places (pi = 3.14159265358979), just remember the following sentence:

"How I want a drink, alcoholic of course, after the heavy lectures involving quantum mechanics."

(Browne, 1988)

The number of letters in each word in the sentence corresponds to each single digit of pi.

One mnemonic that relies on visual imagery is called the **pegword mnemonic.** It uses a simple rhyme scheme in place of the geographical locations favored by the Greek orators. To help you understand this mnemonic, try to learn the numerical rhymes by reciting them several times. Test yourself by saying each number and recalling the associated rhyme word before you continue reading. These simple rhymes will serve as memory pegs upon which you will hang new information.

ONE IS A BUN
TWO IS A SHOE
THREE IS A TREE
FOUR IS A DOOR
FIVE IS A HIVE
SIX ARE STICKS
SEVEN IS HEAVEN
EIGHT IS A GATE
NINE IS A LINE
TEN IS A HEN

(From Miller, Galanter, and Pribram, 1960)

After you have memorized the rhymes, you are ready to learn the list of 10 words shown below.

Using visual imagery, go down the list one word at a time, visualize the object that each word represents, and associate it in some fashion with the appropriately numbered word in the rhyme scheme. For example, associate TELEPHONE to BUN by imagining a bun talking into a telephone or a telephone sitting on a large bun. Your examples do not need to be this bizarre; just be sure to link your images in some way (Wollen, Weber, and Lowry, 1972; Kroll, Schepeler, and Angin, 1986). Take a moment to form your images, and make sure that you visualize each object from the word list interacting with the appropriately numbered object from the rhyme scheme.

1. TELEPHONE
2. PENCIL
3. CAR
4. MOUSE
5. HAMMER
6. COAT
7. DISH
8. BOOK
9. HAT
10. SCISSORS

This mnemonic relies on the use of visual imagery to form strong associations and the numerical rhymes to organize the information in memory. The result is efficient learning and remembering. If you have done the task, you should be able to recite the word list forward or backward or in any order you wish. Not only will you know each item, you will also know each item's position. Now, what was the position of the word DISH?

ORGANIZATION AND MEMORY

Mnemonics generally work by visually coding verbal items and organizing the items to be remembered by some existing scheme. We saw in Chapter 4 how organization influences perception; some of these same principles also apply to memory.

Before reading further, list as many friends and acquaintances as you can recall in five minutes. Now look at your list. The names that you generated are probably not a haphazard recollection but a structured output organized in terms of your relationship with these different people. Relatives, friends, and neighbors are probably recalled in separate clusters rather than jumbled all together. This grouping pattern suggests that we organize information on the basis of conceptual relations. If we think of remembering a fact as similar to retrieving a book from a large library, the role of organization becomes clear. Without an efficient filing system, retrieving a particular library book would be a difficult, if not an impossible, task. Without an efficient organizational plan, retrieving a particular fact from memory would likewise be difficult and tedious.

How organization facilitates remembering can be seen in an experiment by Gordon Bower and his associates (1969). People were shown a large number of words to study in either an organized or a jumbled fashion. Half of the subjects saw four sets of approximately 28 words each in their correct hierarchical arrangement (Figure 7.9), and half saw the same words in each set in a scrambled order (steel, common, precious, sapphire, and so on). After studying each set for one minute, the subjects were asked to recall all of the words they could remember. The results showed that subjects who studied the words in their correct conceptual arrangements recalled over 70 words after one trial; however, those who viewed the random arrangements recalled only about 20 words. After three trials of study and recall, subjects with the organized sets recalled all 112 words, while the other subjects recalled less than half.

Organization had a powerful effect on memory performance in this experiment because the subjects used the organization as a plan to guide their recall. The people who studied the words in an organized fashion typically started their recall at the top of a word hierarchy and worked down the inverted "tree" either branch by branch or level by level. For instance, GRANITE was recalled only if MASONRY was recalled first. Subjects who stud-

ied the words in the randomly arranged sets did not show these effects. Their recall showed no organizational pattern (Bower, Clark, Lesgold, and Winzenz, 1969).

Organization enhances remembering because it provides a plan for remembering; it tells us where to begin, how to proceed, and when we are finished. Thinking back to our discussion of mnemonics, we can see that the pegword mnemonic is effective partly because it uses visual imagery and partly because it uses a well-learned structure (the rhyme scheme) to organize the information in memory. Once information has been organized, it can be efficiently retrieved. This is what the Greek orators learned many centuries ago.

You can see from the material on rehearsal, memory codes, and organization that under normal circumstances memory performance is not so much an inherent ability but a skill that can be enhanced by a more effective use of memory processes. You may have seen someone on television perform a remarkable memory feat like recalling everyone's name in a large audience. Such feats are not usually the result of a "superior memory" but of the performer using a well-learned mnemonic scheme to remember the names quickly and efficiently. These memory experts usually appear special only until we know the basis of their skill. With enough time and effort, you, too, could perform feats of memory. Still, there may be some "special" people whose memory abilities appear to be more than just the application of mnemonic schemes.

FIGURE 7.9   A conceptual word hierarchy for the category of MINERALS.
Subjects who were presented with words hierarchically organized remembered many more of the words than subjects who saw the same words randomly arranged. The hierarchical organization facilitated memory performance because it was used as a plan to guide subsequent remembering.

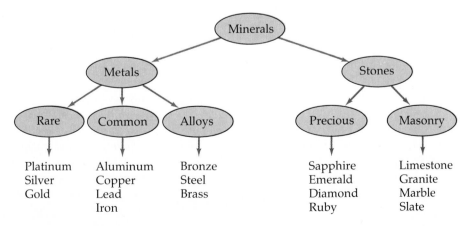

RESEARCH AND APPLICATION:
Photographic Memory and Memorists

It is commonly believed that some people are born with a superior memory that enables them to retain information in a photo-like way. The term **photographic memory** is often used to describe such people's abilities. However, there is surprisingly little firm evidence to support this widespread belief in photographic memory. Yet, from time to time, there are intriguing reports of individuals who, when examined under carefully controlled conditions, demonstrate superior memory. These people are called **memorists** (Neisser, 1982). What can these people do and how do they do it?

Memorists

There is a famous anecdote about conductor Arturo Toscanini and his prodigious memory for music. One night, just before a concert, a bassoonist reported to him that the key for the lowest note on his instrument was broken. What should he do? Toscanini thought for a moment and then replied, "It is all right—that note does not occur in tonight's concert" (Marek, 1975). Toscanini is said to have memorized every note for every instrument in 250 symphonies and 100 operas.

Russian psychologist Alexander Luria (1968) used the case study method to study one individual with a memory as prodigious as Toscanini's. The man, named Shereshevskii, began work as a newspaper reporter but later became a professional entertainer, earning his living by demonstrating his unusual memory. Luria tested this man's memory over a period of 30 years. Remarkably, he found that Shereshevskii had no difficulty recalling extremely complex mathematical formulas or long lists of words or numbers months or even years after he saw them. When he was presented with digit and letter arrays like the one in Table 7.2 he recalled all of its characters perfectly. After studying the array for three minutes, it took him only 25 seconds to recall the characters in the second column, 30 seconds to recall the same column backward, and 50 seconds to recall all of the characters by rows. Shereshevskii claimed to have an image of the array that permitted him to retrieve whatever information was requested.

Luria discovered that Shereshevskii combined strong powers of visual imagery with self-learned mnemonic techniques to produce his outstanding performance. Whenever he was asked to memorize something, he would convert the material into a mental image that he was able to see. Said Shereshevskii,

> When I hear the word *green*, a green flowerpot appears; with the word *red* I see a man in a red shirt coming toward me; as for *blue*, this means an image of someone waving a small blue flag from a window. . . . Even numbers remind me of images. Take the number 1. This is a proud, well-built man; 2 is a high-spirited woman; 3 a gloomy person (why, I don't know); . . . 6 a man with a swollen foot; 7 a man with a mustache; 8 a very stout woman. . . . As for the number 87, what I see is a fat woman and a man twirling his mustache.

(Luria, 1968)

Shereshevskii reported that he only had problems remembering such abstract words as *infinity*, *eternity*, and *nothing*—words he was unable to visualize.

This case study by Luria suggests that when people with strong visual imagery use mnemonic techniques they can demonstrate truly remarkable feats of memory. Yet we would be reluctant to describe this memory as photographic because it is based on the use of highly developed mnemonic skills for coding and organizing information. However, some people do seem to possess an unusual form of visual memory called **eidetic imagery,** and this is closer to what we think of as "photographic memory."

TABLE 7.2 An Example of a Stimulus Array Used by Luria to Test Shereshevskii's Memory

8860
4531
7904
2251
3478
8913
2215
5431
9734
1528
2976
3931
X37X

From Luria (1968).

Eidetic Imagery

Eidetic imagery is defined as a form of visual memory in which information is retained in an accurate and highly detailed manner after the original scene disappears. Early research suggested that eidetic imagery was common in grammar school children, but that it disappeared near the age of puberty. Studies now find that only five to 10 percent of all children demonstrate eidetic imagery (Leask, Haber, and Haber, 1969). In a typical test for eidetic imagery, a child is given 30 seconds to examine a colored picture from a children's book mounted on an easel (Figure 7.10). The picture is then removed, and the child is asked a series of questions while still looking at the easel. The following dialogue provides a glimpse of an eidetic experience in a 10-year-old boy who had just seen a picture from *Alice in Wonderland*:

EXPERIMENTER:	Do you see something there?
CHILD:	I see the tree, gray tree with three limbs. I see the cat with stripes around its tail.
EXPERIMENTER:	Can you count those stripes?
CHILD:	Yes (pause). There's about 16.
EXPERIMENTER:	You're counting what? Black, white or both?
CHILD:	Both. And I can see the flowers on the bottom. There's about three stems, but you can see two pairs of flowers. One on the right has green leaves, red flowers on bottom with yellow on top. And I can see the girl with a brown dress. She's got blond hair and a red hair band and there are some leaves in the upper left-hand corner where the tree is.
EXPERIMENTER:	Can you tell me about the roots of the tree?
CHILD:	Well, there's two of them going down here (points) and there's one that cuts off on the left-hand side of the picture.
EXPERIMENTER:	What is the cat doing with its paws?
CHILD:	Well, one of them he's holding out and the other one is on the tree. (The child looks away from the easel and then back again.)
EXPERIMENTER:	Is the image gone?
CHILD:	Yes, except for the tree.
EXPERIMENTER:	Tell me when it goes away.
CHILD:	(pause) It went away.

(Adapted from Haber, 1969)

FIGURE 7.10 A test picture for eidetic imagery. When this picture was shown to grammar school children for 30 seconds, approximately five to 10 percent of the children reported seeing a highly detailed and accurate image of the picture after it was removed. These children could report details of the scene as if it were still present. In some instances, the eidetic image lasted for a half minute or more.

When children reported seeing the picture after it had been removed, their images lasted roughly 30 seconds or more. But are they reporting an eidetic image or just describing their memory of a colorful picture? The children describe their images in the present tense and point to aspects of their image as though it were present and resting on the easel. In addition, the children said that they did not have an image of parts of the picture they did not look at long enough, even though they could sometimes remember what the parts contained. Such reports are suggestive of eidetic imagery, but not all psychologists are convinced that it exists. Because research on eidetic imagery has produced inconsistent findings, it remains a provocative and elusive puzzle (Gray and Gummerman, 1975; Haber, 1979).

Memory as a Skill

Though we cannot be sure about the existence of eidetic imagery, we do know that memory performance can be dramatically improved by the use of mnemonic techniques. People with otherwise average memory ability can do some rather surprising things. For instance, in one study a college student named Steve was given extensive practice over a period of months on a simple memory span task. For the first four sessions, his performance was what you would expect—he could not remember more than seven digits in order correctly. But then he discovered a mnemonic system for recoding the digits into long-distance running times (Steve's hobby was long-distance running), and his performance took off. For example, a series such as 2–1–4–7 could be recoded as "2 hrs, 14 mins, and 7 secs, an excellent marathon time." Over a period of 20 months, his memory span for digits increased from seven to approximately 80 (Ericsson, Chase, and Faloon, 1980).

Psychologists believe that people like Steve have exceptional memories because they have learned specific strategies for placing information rapidly into long-term storage. This approach, called **skilled memory theory,** says that there are no inherent differences between average people who put information in long-term storage at a slow rate and memorists who memorize at a fast rate. Through practice, the memorists have discovered highly efficient encoding processes (Ericsson and Polson, 1988).

What can we conclude about superior memory abilities? Some psychologists, including Ian Hunter (1978), believe that memorists are trained and not born; they acquire their special abilities largely through extensive mnemonic practice. Others, including Ulric Neisser (1982), believe that it is too early to dismiss all reports of people with special memory ability as due merely to the application of mnemonics. Until more memorists can be found and studied, this debate is likely to continue. ■

REMEMBERING

So far we have seen how information is encoded and stored in memory. However, a great deal of information is successfully encoded and stored, but cannot be retrieved. In this section and the one that follows we will describe how different conditions influence remembering and its opposite—forgetting. Both remembering and forgetting are enormously complex psychological processes. There are times when we remember only to discover that we have remembered incorrectly, and there are times when we forget only to find that we later remember. To improve our memory, we need to understand these different conditions.

WHAT IS REMEMBERED?

The taste or smell of something familiar can be a powerful retrieval cue, as can the voice of a friend from whom we have not heard for some time. Recall from Chapter 1 how the taste of a crumb of "petite madelaine" caused French writer Marcel Proust to remember scenes from his youth. Retrieving information from memory is one of our most remarkable abilities, but it is not the simple, automatic process you might take it to be. Our memory does not work like a computer that always retrieves information the same way, and it does not operate like a videocassette recorder that creates an unchanging record of the past. Our memory often operates less accurately, but it is considerably more versatile than that of any machine. We can see evidence of this versatility in the kind of information we retain and the different types of memory we possess.

TYPES OF LONG-TERM MEMORY

Psychologists believe that there are several distinct types of long-term memory. Remembering how to tie your shoelaces, where you put your car keys, and the definition of the word *platypus* may be based on different retrieval processes involving different forms of memory. Psychologist Endel Tulving (1983; 1986) has distinguished between procedural, episodic, and semantic memory. **Procedural memory** enables us to perform such acts as tying a pair of shoelaces or riding a bicycle. **Episodic memory** is our knowledge of personally experienced events and their order of occurrence in time. It is episodic memory that we use to "travel backward" in time to recall such specific facts as the location of our car keys or what we did at our high school graduation. Finally, **semantic memory** represents our knowledge of words, symbols, and concepts, including their meaning and rules for their manipulation. Important for language and thought, semantic memory is also used to recall the definitions of words and facts such as "two and two are four" and "fire engines and barns are usually red" (Figure 7.11). It is too early to determine how many varieties of long-term memory exist (Anderson and Ross, 1980; McKoon, Ratcliff, and Dell, 1986). However, there is some research support for Tulving's view. For example, one experiment showed that people who scored high on tests of vocabulary (an index of semantic memory) did not necessarily score high on the free recall of word lists (an index of episodic memory) (Underwood, Boruch, and Malmi, 1978). The fact that people's performance on episodic and seman-

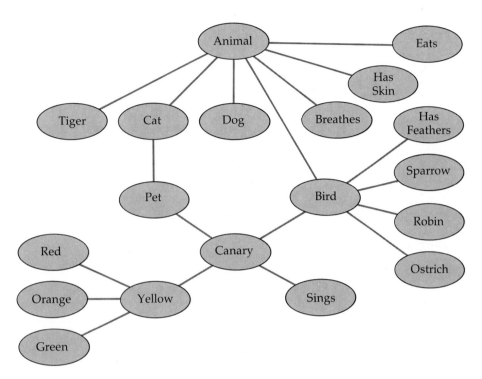

FIGURE 7.11   A portion of semantic memory.   According to the spreading activation model of Collins and Loftus (1975), concepts are represented in memory by means of an associative network. The shorter the distance between two concepts, the greater the strength of their association. By viewing semantic memory in this fashion we can see why we can verify statements such as "A canary sings" faster than "A canary breathes." " At present, this approach is one of several used by psychologists to study semantic memory.

tic memory tasks were not closely related suggests that the two forms of memory are different.

In many respects, the small portion of semantic memory diagramed in Figure 7.11 is similar to the connectionist model of word identification by McClelland and Rumelhart (1981) that we presented in Chapter 4. Both are network models that assume massive connections, or associations, between information in long-term storage. Network models help explain why we are reminded of "firecrackers," "picnics," and "Uncle Sam" when we think about "July 4th." Thinking of one idea automatically spreads energy or activation to many related ideas that are spread out, or "distributed," in the semantic network. In fact, some scientists, including Rumelhart and McClelland and their associates (1986), believe that it will be possible to represent complex cognitive processes (perhaps generating associations to particular words) on newer computers that can perform a variety of processes simultaneously (in parallel). This connectionist approach views memory as the strength of connections between distributed information in storage. In recent years, connectionist models of

cognition have been developed in a number of areas, including vision, language, and memory (Kosslyn, 1987; Sejnowski and Rosenberg, 1987; Smolensky, 1988).

ABSTRACTING INFORMATION FROM TEXT

To study memory under more natural learning conditions, many current researchers follow Bartlett's example and use sentences and stories instead of the more traditional word lists. Jacquelin Sachs (1967) read subjects a story and then tested their ability to recognize sentences from either the middle or the end of the story. Some of the sentences were presented in their original form, while the formal wording, voice, or meaning of others were changed, as shown in the following examples:

> *Original Sentence:* He sent a letter about it to Galileo.
> *Formal Wording Change:* He sent Galileo a letter about it.
> *Active-to-Passive Voice Change:* A letter about it was sent to Galileo.

Meaning Change: Galileo sent him a letter about it.

Sachs found that her subjects could recognize any type of change in sentences taken from the end of the story. However, if a sentence was taken from the middle of the story, only changes in meaning were recognized; changes in formal wording or voice went unnoticed. These results suggest that we retain a fairly accurate representation of a sentence immediately after we hear it. But with the passage of time and the addition of new information, we forget surface details such as wording and voice and retain only the gist of a sentence.

While memory for gist is common, there are many occasions when we remember not only the gist of a sentence or story, but the exact wording as well. Obvious examples include our memory for the words of different songs or poems and our ability to recite verbatim such things as the Pledge of Allegiance, a prayer, or the lines of a play (Intons-Peterson and Smyth, 1987; Rubin, 1977). In such cases, the order of the words is what defines the particular piece. The whole point is lost if you remember only the gist of a poem. It does not do to remember Coleridge's line "There came an ancient mariner, and he stopped one of three" as "An old sailor came up to three people, and stopped one." And if you do not remember a joke verbatim, you will probably not get a laugh. So while we normally remember only the gist of an event, the memory system is versatile enough to handle specific details and exact wording if necessary.

THE INFLUENCE OF CONTEXT AND SCRIPTS

In Chapter 4 we discussed how our perception of a stimulus is influenced by its context. A context is used to recognize a pattern of stimulation and interpret the meaning of the stimulus. Context is also important for memory because in influencing how a stimulus is interpreted it also influences how it will be retained. Consider the following passage:

The wealthy man stood before the mirror and combed his hair. He checked his face carefully for any places he might have missed shaving and then put on the conservative tie he had decided to wear. At breakfast, he studied the newspaper carefully and, over coffee, discussed the possibility of buying a new washing machine with his wife. Then he made several phone calls. As he was leaving the house he thought about the fact that his children would probably want to go to that private camp again this summer. When the car

didn't start, he got out, slammed the door, and walked down to the bus stop in a very angry mood. Now he would be late.

(Modified from Bransford and Johnson, 1973)

Now read the passage again, but this time substitute the word *unemployed* for the word *wealthy* in the first line. This single alteration changes the context of the passage and can thus change what the reader is likely to retain (Bransford & Johnson, 1973). In a study of the effect of context on story recall, Anderson and Pichert (1978) read subjects a story about a house from the perspective of either a burglar or a potential buyer. After the subjects heard and recalled the story, they were told about the alternate perspective and asked to recall the story once more. The results showed that on the second recall the subjects recalled more information relevant to the new perspective and less information relevant to the old. If they first heard the story from the perspective of a potential buyer they recalled more information about the structure of the house. Later, when asked to recall it from the perspective of a burglar, they were able to recall more of its contents—information that they had not recalled when recalling the story from the perspective of a possible buyer. What was recalled about the original story depended on the perspective or story context for the subjects at the time of retrieval.

Scripts also provide a context for remembering facts. Scripts are defined as general action sequences that describe well-learned routines. Through repeated experience, we acquire scripts of activities such as riding a bus, visiting a dentist, and eating out in a restaurant. Table 7.3 shows an example of a restaurant script broken into four separate scenes. Within each scene are a sequence of actions in the order in which they are carried out. Scripts can lead us to recall things that never were, simply because we expect them to be there. For example, when people were given stories that involved a familiar script such as eating in a restaurant, they made errors in their recall by "remembering" script-related activities that were never explicitly stated in the story (Bower, Black, and Turner, 1979). Similarly, when script-related information was presented in pictorial form, people unknowingly used the script and made erroneous inferences during remembering (Baggett, 1975). Script-related information can be seen as knowledge from semantic memory that influences our recall of everyday events.

So far, we have seen that there may be different types of long-term memory (procedural, episodic, and semantic) and that we can either abstract the

TABLE 7.3 A Script for Eating Out in a Restaurant

Scene 1: Entering
Customer enters restaurant
Customer looks for table
Customer decides where to sit
Customer goes to table
Customer sits down

Scene 2: Ordering
Customer picks up menu
Customer looks at menu
Customer decides on food
Customer signals waitress
Waitress comes to table
Customer orders food
Waitress goes to cook
Waitress gives food order to cook
Cook prepares food

Scene 3: Eating
Cook gives food to waitress
Waitress brings food to customer
Customer eats food

Scene 4: Exiting
Waitress writes bill
Waitress goes over to customer
Waitress gives bill to customer
Customer leaves tip for waitress
Customer goes to cashier
Customer gives money to cashier
Customer leaves restaurant

Adapted from Bower et al. (1979).

gist of new information or memorize it verbatim. In addition, the context in which an event occurs can influence our memory for that event, particularly if the event follows a familiar script. Under such conditions, errors and distortions of memory are quite possible.

ERRORS AND DISTORTIONS IN REMEMBERING

When Bartlett studied remembering many years ago, he realized that what people remembered was sometimes different from what they actually experienced. It was not that people simply forgot isolated details and remembered less, but that people remembered differently. Their recall was actually a *reconstruction* of a previous event based on old and new information. He observed this fact in his studies of Indian legends such as "The War of the Ghosts" and in studies of serial reproduction like those involving the drawing of the owl (Figure 7.3). Today, studies of eyewitness memory and

autobiographical memory provide graphic examples of these reconstructive processes in operation.

EYEWITNESS MEMORY

To study eyewitness accuracy, psychologist Robert Buckhout (1974) staged an "assault" on a professor in front of a large class of students. Seven weeks after the incident, many students could not describe the attack accurately, and only about 40 percent of the students could pick out a picture of the assailant from a set of six pictures. Approximately 60 percent of the viewers selected the picture of an innocent person. Given such poor memory, it seems likely that the testimony of eyewitnesses is also often inaccurate. Right after a crime, witnesses often give incomplete and fragmentary reports. After repeated recollections between the first police report and the final courtroom testimony, their remembrances become coherent and well-integrated, but they are not always accurate (Buckhout, 1974). Just like subjects in the memory studies we discussed earlier, eyewitnesses generate a context or a story within which they fit the initial sketchy details. They then "fill in the gaps" by unknowingly making inferences about the details that they missed. The result is a reconstructed recall based partly on what was and partly on what "must have been."

In any complex event some details will be missed, so it is not surprising that people use other information in trying to present a reasonable and coherent testimony. Even the wording of a question can inadvertently change the testimony by suggesting additional information about what happened. After viewing slides of an automobile collision in one experiment, witnesses were asked either: "How fast were the cars going when they smashed into each other?" or "How fast were the cars going when they hit each other?" (Figure 7.12). A week later, they were asked whether they had seen any broken glass. People were more apt to say "yes" if the previous question used the word *smashed*. In reality, there was no broken glass in the slides (Loftus and Palmer, 1974). These inaccurate remembrances could occur because we integrate information about an initial event and later recollections about the event into a single memory representation. Or it may be that post-event information influences our responses to questions about an event but does not alter our specific memory for the event. For example, people who see a baseball game and later read a newspaper account of the game may answer questions about the game on the basis of their direct observations, the newspaper story, or both (McCloskey and Zaragoza, 1985). At present we do not know

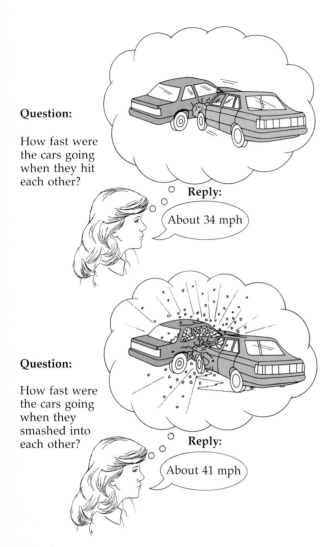

Question:

How fast were the cars going when they hit each other?

Reply:

About 34 mph

Question:

How fast were the cars going when they smashed into each other?

Reply:

About 41 mph

FIGURE 7.12 Eyewitness inaccuracies. After viewing slides of a motor vehicle accident, viewers were asked to estimate the speed of the cars at the time of impact. Speed estimates were influenced by the way the question was asked. One week after viewing the slides, people who were initially asked the question with the word "smashed" were, compared with viewers who heard the word "hit," more likely to report that they saw broken glass even though none was shown.

whether eyewitnesses integrate information into a single trace of an event or produce multiple traces in memory representing different sources of information (Loftus, Donders, Hoffman, and Schooler, 1989; Zaragoza and Koshmider, 1989). However, in either case eyewitnesses often make inaccurate memory reports.

AUTOBIOGRAPHICAL MEMORY

Closely related to eyewitness memory is a new area of research called **autobiographical memory.** Your autobiographical memory may include personal recollections of such varied experiences as

your first date, the first time you flew in an airplane, and the moment you opened your SAT scores. Research suggests that we keep a plausible and consistent record of our past, but our autobiographical memory is not necessarily complete or accurate (Barclay and Wellman, 1986; Pillemer, Goldsmith, Panter, and White, 1988). For example, sociologist Lee Robins and his colleagues (1985) found that people who came from troubled homes as children, but who later became well-adjusted adults, were likely to forget or "rewrite" the facts of their troubled pasts. Once these people had become conventional adults, they tended to look back on their lives as though they had always been this way. In keeping with the view of remembrances as reconstructions, our autobiographical memory is a record of our past that is filtered by our personality and our current beliefs.

Particularly dramatic events sometimes show up the inaccuracies in autobiographical memory. For instance, Roger Brown and James Kulik (1971) did a survey and found that many people who were in their teens or older on November 22, 1963, have a clear and vivid memory of where they were and what they were doing at the moment they heard of the assassination of President Kennedy. The vivid clarity of everyone's recall of such events has led Brown and Kulik to call these recollections *flashbulb memories.* However, these flashbulb memories are not a special form of memory that captures the past like a photograph. They show changes and distortions over time, just as memories of more ordinary events do (McClosky, Wible, and Cohen, 1988). Rather, flashbulb memories are instances of autobiographical memory in which we line up our own lives with an historical event and say "I was there" (Neisser, 1982). In this way, flashbulb memories may be explained by ordinary memory mechanisms (Harsch and Neisser, 1989; McCloskey et al., 1988). As is the case with eyewitness memory, we see that when we remember events from our past, we are more like the author of an autobiography than a tape in a videocassette machine (Christianson, 1989; Rubin, 1986).

Before we turn our attention to forgetting, it is important to maintain a sense of balance about remembering. Errors and distortions undoubtedly occur each day, but so do accurate recalls and recognitions (Postman, 1985). As students, you remember the time and location of your classes, the names of your professors and friends, and, to varying degrees, your coursework as you study for exams. You do not have a verbatim memory of everything said in class, but that would be unnecessary. We tend to remember things that are

The *Challenger* explosion. What were you doing when you heard of the space-shuttle explosion? Many people have a vivid memory of the event.

personally important to us as well as those things that are unusual, novel, and exciting, rather than dull and commonplace. By storing new and important information, memory thus helps us adapt and survive.

FORGETTING

In describing short-term memory we said that forgetting is a desirable feature. It enables us to eliminate information we no longer need so that we can refocus our attention. Forgetting in long-term memory is less desirable. We are troubled when we forget material that we studied for an exam, the name of a person we have met several times, and even a particular word in a conversation that we have "on the tip of the tongue." Forgetting in long-term memory is complex because it can occur for a variety of reasons. We will review some of these reasons in this section with an eye toward any factors that might make us less prone to forget.

CAUSES OF FORGETTING

REPRESSION

Freud proposed that memory is permanent and that all forgetting is motivated. Painful or anxiety-arousing memories are forgotten by a process called **repression,** an unconscious defense designed to prevent unpleasant memories from

reaching conscious awareness. These memories could surface in disguised form in dreams and slips of the tongue, but only a person with a background in psychoanalysis could decipher their actual meaning (Freud, 1901).

According to Freud, repression can occur in severe cases of psychological stress, fear, or humiliation. This memory loss serves to prevent a painful experience from reaching consciousness. In the case of an experience that is terribly traumatic, such as witnessing a murder or a fatal accident, the observer may develop **amnesia,** a partial or complete loss of memory for that event. If this is accompanied by running away from the situation, it is called a **fugue state.** In this condition, the person runs away in a state of panic and suffers a memory loss for all personally identifying information. Such a person may spend months or years living in another city until some reminder brings back his or her previous personal memory. Since such memories are often recovered, that suggests that they were merely repressed rather than permanently lost.

While repression may account for a form of psychopathological forgetting, it cannot provide a general explanation of forgetting for three important reasons. First, repression cannot explain the type of amnesia that results from a cerebral concussion. A blow to the head results in a physical rather than a psychological trauma. Second, it cannot explain the normal forgetting of trivial events that occurs every day. Much of what we forget has little or no emotional significance. Finally, the evidence for repression is limited in comparison with the abundant evidence for other sources of forgetting.

DECAY

In the case of normal, everyday forgetting, it may be that memory traces simply decay, or weaken, over time. This trace decay explanation is intuitively appealing but is difficult to test experimentally. The problem is that different events occur over time (eating, studying, exercising, and so on) so that if forgetting occurs with the passage of time, we cannot be sure whether the forgetting was due to decay or the interfering effect of other events that occurred during that time. The results of an experiment shown in Figure 7.13 suggest a solution to this problem. After learning a list of nonsense syllables, people remembered more of the items if they then went immediately to sleep than if they had stayed awake (Jenkins and Dallenbach, 1924). If decay over time were solely responsible for forgetting, the forgetting curves

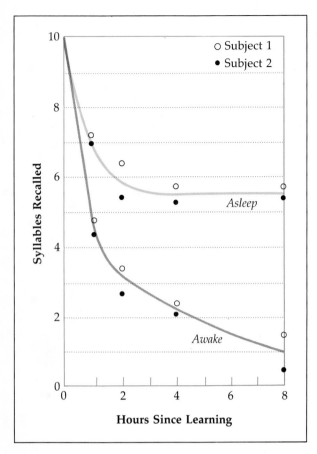

FIG 7.13 What causes forgetting? Two subjects were given lists of nonsense syllables to learn and permitted to sleep or stay awake during the interval between learning and testing. If forgetting were caused only by memory decay over time, the retention curves should be identical. Instead, the results showed less forgetting when learning was followed by sleep. These results indicate that interference from events that occur after learning can affect memory performance.

shown in Figure 7.13 should be identical since equal time elapsed between study and test for both conditions. The fact that the curves are different indicates that forgetting is due to more than just decay. Forgetting may result from decay, but interference is a major contributing factor as well.

INTERFERENCE

Consider the experience of readers of a very popular paperback series. To readers of the Harlequin series, story changes from one novel to the next are minimal. There is a set formula that typically involves a young woman—usually poor, but always attractive—who meets a man in some exotic location. After 190 pages in which there is no overt sex, no tragedy, and no violence, the woman and man marry.

From what we have said about remembering, it should be clear that since the core of these stories is fairly constant, most readers should remember the gist of each story very well. But what about specific details? Here, because of story similarity, we would expect a great deal of confusion. After reading several of these stories, the characters and settings would be hopelessly mixed.

Competing memories can produce forgetting by generating interference that operates proactively (forward in time) or retroactively (backward in time). **Proactive interference** is the forgetting of new material due to the disruptive effect of previously learned material, while **retroactive interference** is the forgetting of previously learned material due to the disruptive effect of new learning. In our Harlequin example, the more stories you have read prior to your current story (proactive interference) and the more stories you will read after it (retroactive interference) the less likely you are to remember the specifics of any particular book.

Numerous studies have shown that proactive and retroactive interference occur, particularly when the old and new material are similar (Postman, 1961; Underwood, 1957). For example, Spanish interferes more with French (which is similar) than with Japanese (which is quite distinct). However, you can turn this principle of interference to your advantage. Since similar material before or after you study can interfere with memory, try to surround learning periods with unrelated activities. Sleep can be used to reduce interference, but so can eating, exercising, or even studying an unrelated subject.

CUE-DEPENDENT FORGETTING

There is another very frequent type of forgetting that you may have experienced when you were trying to introduce two acquaintances or to recall some fact for a test. There are times when we cannot remember something that we later remember with ease. We often feel that the item to be remembered is on the tip of our tongue. When a word is on the tip of our tongue, we generally know the word's meaning and something about its sound and appearance. People can recognize a word on the tip of the tongue but for some reason can not recall it (Brown and McNeill, 1966). How can we recover information on the tip of the tongue? The answer lies in the use of cues. Try the following example once more:

> Recall the names of the seven dwarfs from *Snow White*.

Did you get the dwarf whose name begins with the letter *B?* Maybe the letter *B* is not the best cue. How about this cue—Shy? Try these hints on friends who have not recalled *Bashful,* and their eyes may suddenly light up. If you say "How about Herman?", though, they will be confident he was not one of the dwarfs. This indicates that remembering requires more than just the presence of information in long-term storage. Information may be available (present in memory) but inaccessible (unable to be recalled). Without the right cue, remembering may not occur. For this reason, we call this type of forgetting **cue dependent.** (In case you have not recalled them all yet, the seven dwarfs are Bashful, Doc, Dopey, Grumpy, Happy, Sleepy, and Sneezy.)

THE IMPORTANCE
OF RETRIEVAL CUES

We see the importance of cues in experiments on memory. For example, if we were to give people a list of words in different categories (COW, LAMB, APPLE, PEAR, ENGINEER, LAWYER . . .), we would expect people who were given category labels as recall cues (Animals, Fruits, Professions . . .) to remember more words than those who were not given cues. This difference between *cued recall* and uncued or *free recall* is not surprising. However, if those people who initially free-recalled the words were *later* given the category cues and asked to recall the list once more, their recall would improve (Tulving and Pearlstone, 1966). This improvement is important because it implies that more information was available in long-term storage than was accessible on the first recall attempt. In fact, the right retrieval cues can lead to nearly perfect recall even for lists of 500 or 600 words (Mäntylä, 1986; Mäntylä and Nilsson, 1988).

Since cues guide the search for information in long-term storage, poor or ineffective cues can actually produce forgetting. A poor cue can point in the wrong direction. For example, if you have tickets for a concert next week, where should you put them so you will remember where they are? Should you put them in a logical place, such as your wallet or purse, or in an unusual place, such as your refrigerator or freezer? When asked questions of this type, people say that unusual locations are best, but research shows this belief to be wrong (Winograd and Soloway, 1986). We are more apt to remember an object's location if it is stored in a logical place because the logical relation between the object and location serves as a cue to the object's location. This is why putting your tickets in your wallet or purse (a very logical location since it will travel with you to the concert) is more effective for remembering their location than storing them in your freezer (something that has no sensible relation to going to the theater).

We have seen that forgetting occurs for many reasons. Ordinarily, we forget because memory traces are interfered with by competing traces or because they are not accessed by the right cue. In rarer situations, we may forget because traces of emotional experiences are repressed or because of physical trauma. Because it can occur for so many reasons, forgetting is one of life's common (if annoying) experiences. All of us occasionally forget the name of a person we just met at a party, or what we are looking for as we walk from the living room to the kitchen. These moments of forgetfulness are completely normal. It is only sudden or severe memory loss that is cause for concern.

DYSFUNCTION:
Korsakoff's Syndrome and Implicit Memory

In 1889, a Russian physician named Sergei Korsakoff reported that long-term alcoholism can lead to serious defects of memory. This disorder is called **Korsakoff's syndrome.** The case study of a 49-year-old man named Jimmie G. reported by neurologist Oliver Sacks is illustrative:

"Hiya, Doc!" he said. "Nice morning! Do I take this chair here?" He was a genial soul, very ready to . . . answer any questions I asked him. He told me his name and birth date, and the name of the little town in Connecticut where he was born. . . .
"And you, Jimmie, how old would you be?" Oddly, uncertainly, he hesitated a moment, as if engaged in calculation.
"Why, I guess I'm nineteen, Doc. I'll be twenty next birthday. . . ."
"Here," I said, and thrust a mirror toward him. "Look in the mirror and tell me what you see. Is that a 19-year-old looking out from the mirror?"
He suddenly turned ashen and gripped the sides of the chair. "Jesus Christ," he whispered. "Christ, what's going on? . . . Is this a nightmare? Am I crazy? . . ."
"It's okay, Jimmie," I said soothingly. "It's just a mistake. Nothing to worry about." . . .
He regained his colour and started to smile,

and I stole away, taking the hateful mirror with me.

Two minutes later I re-entered the room. . . . "Hiya, Doc!" he said. "Nice morning! You want to talk to me—do I take this chair here?" There was no sign of recognition on his frank, open face.

"Haven't we met before, Mr. G.?" I asked casually.

"No, I can't say we have. Quite a beard you got there. I wouldn't forget *you*, Doc!"

(Sacks, 1987)

Generally, Korsakoff's syndrome is characterized by several different types of forgetting (Talland, 1969):

- **Anterograde amnesia.** Patients have difficulty forming new memories.

- **Retrograde amnesia.** Patients have extensive memory loss for prior events that may cover much of their adult life.

- **Confabulation.** Patients make up stories about past events to conceal their memory loss.

- **Apathy.** Patients often appear indifferent to ongoing events.

The memory problems of the Korsakoff's patient are related to diet. Specifically, they are the result of brain damage caused by a thiamine (Vitamine B$_1$) deficiency. Chronic alcoholics often suffer from malnutrition. They may go for days or even weeks on diets lacking in thiamine. Without adequate thiamine, the brain cannot metabolize its primary fuel, glucose, and this leads to brain damage in the form of neuronal shrinkage and loss (Kalat, 1988). Researchers currently believe that a Korsakoff's patient has damage in the medial thalamus and portions of the hypothalamus (Brierley, 1977; Victor, Adams, and Collins, 1971) as well as a general loss in the frontal lobe. (These brain structures were described in Chapter 2.) CAT scans have revealed frontal lobe deterioration in approximately 80 percent of the Korsakoff's patients tested in one study (Moscovitch, 1982). At present, the effects of Korsakoff's syndrome cannot be reversed; however, if these patients are treated with massive doses of thiamine early enough the deterioration can be arrested.

Although the outlook for these patients is generally bleak, recent research has shown that Korsakoff's patients can demonstrate new learning (Hirst et al., 1988; Musen, Shimamura, and Squire, 1990). However, these patients have a problem in consciously remembering what they have learned. To understand this new research, we must distinguish between **explicit** and **implicit memory.** Explicit memory requires conscious recollection of a past episode or event, while implicit memory requires the demonstration of enhanced performance on a task without deliberate or conscious remembering (Schacter, 1987; Kihlstrom, Schacter, Cork, Hurt, and Behr, 1990).

As an example of implicit memory in Korsakoff's patients, consider the following task. In one experiment, patients were shown a list of ten words such as DEFEND, CONVEY, BELFRY, and so on. After seeing the list, they were asked to recall as many words as they could. On this test of *explicit* memory, the Korsakoff's patients failed. They did much worse than other alcoholic patients who had not developed Korsakoff's syndrome. However, if the Korsakoff's patients were given partial word cues (for example, DEF_ _ _, CON _ _ _, and BEL_ _ _) and asked to complete them with the first words that came to mind, they did so by filling in the words from the original list, even though each of the cues could have been completed in several ways (Graf, Squire, and Mandler, 1984). This word fragment task provides a measure of memory for recent events without awareness. The amnesic Korsakoff's patients show evidence of new learning when *implicit* memory is tested. These findings are consistent with a famous anecdote reported long ago by Swiss psychologist Édouard Claparède (1911). He once shook hands with a female Korsakoff's patient while hiding a pin in his hand. This caused the patient obvious discomfort. When he returned a few minutes later and again offered his hand, the patient refused to shake it, although she could not explain why. ▪

BIOLOGICAL BASES OF MEMORY

Connections between memory and the brain are made in several places in this text. In Chapter 2 we discussed the patient H. M., who suffered profound memory impairment after his hypocampus was removed. In this chapter we described how Korsakoff's patients show severe forms of amnesia after portions of their hypothalamus and frontal lobes are damaged. And in Chapter 12 we will describe the brain changes in the elderly that are associated with Alzheimer's disease. In this section we will focus on more general issues involving the biological bases of memory. First, does the brain contain a permanent record of all of our past experience? Second, what are some promising mechanisms for explaining how memory is represented in the brain?

THE ISSUE OF MEMORY PERMANENCE

During the 1950s, a Canadian brain surgeon named Wilder Penfield operated on a number of patients who were suffering from severe epilepsy. In this disorder (described in Chapter 2) the brain's temporal cortex produces abnormal electrical activity that spreads over the entire brain to produce convulsions and a loss of consciousness. To eliminate the seizures, Penfield removed brain tissue from the area that produced the abnormal activity. Before doing so, however, he stimulated different points on the patient's cortex to be sure that he would not remove any area that was involved in an important function such as speech production or comprehension. Since there are no pain receptors in the brain, this procedure could be carried out with a fully conscious patient, who had been given only a local anesthetic to numb the scalp area. Using a mild electrical probe, Penfield stimulated various points on the patient's exposed cerebral cortex and observed the patient's reactions. As in the following example, he sometimes found that the stimulation produced an experience resembling a memory flashback.

> . . . the patient heard a specific popular song being played as though by an orchestra. Repeated stimulation produced the same music. When the electrode was kept in place, she hummed the tune, chorus and verse, thus accompanying the music she heard. After a point in her temporal cortex had been stimulated, (the patient) observed with some surprise "I just heard one of my children speaking. . . . It was Frank, and I could hear the neighborhood noises. . . ."
>
> *(Penfield, 1952)*

From such observations Penfield concluded that the brain kept a permanent record of all of the things that a person had ever experienced (Penfield, 1952; 1975). In effect, thought Penfield, the brain functioned as a tape recorder, and many people seem to agree with this view (Loftus and Loftus, 1980).

Though Penfield's observations are fascinating, there are several reasons to doubt his conclusions. First, just because *some* trivial events may be remembered, it does not follow that *all* experiences are permanently stored in the brain. Second, if the brain functioned as a tape recorder, then the errors and distortions that occur in everyday remember-

ing simply would not take place. Third, only a very small minority (less than 8 percent) of the hundreds of patients tested by Penfield provided such observations. Fourth, the mental experiences following brain stimulation often had a dreamlike or fantasy quality (in one case a person heard both sides of a telephone conversation), more than they had the quality of memory. Finally, stimulation at different sites occasionally produced the same experience, while stimulation at the same site sometimes produced different responses. Contrary to what you might conclude from Penfield's findings, our memories are not located in tiny, specific areas of our cortex; nor is there any evidence for the widespread belief that all of our past experiences are retained. The brain stores more memories than are readily accessible, but this in no way implies that all past experiences are permanently represented.

MEMORY MECHANISMS

Researchers have learned a great deal about the cognitive processes that underlie memory, but we know considerably less about memory's biological bases. Psychologists believe that it is misleading to think of a memory trace as a single entity at a single center in the brain. Instead, a memory is better viewed as a collection of entities involving many different areas of the brain (Squire, 1987). At present, we do not know exactly how memory traces are represented in the brain. But exploratory studies have suggested several possible biochemical and neurological mechanisms for memory (Matthies, 1989).

BIOCHEMICAL MECHANISMS

Biochemical approaches to memory involve studying chemical reactions. They include studies of hormones, such as epinephrine and ACTH, that can enhance or impair remembering under certain conditions (Izquierdo et al., 1982). Another promising candidate is an unusual molecule called the **NMDA receptor** after the chemical N-methyl D-aspartate that is used to detect it. Neurobiologists speculate that this receptor may turn on certain biochemical reactions that lead to the encoding of memories. Specifically, this receptor appears to regulate the flow of calcium into brain cells. When a neural pathway is stimulated, there is a long-lasting increase in the strength of its synaptic response. This increase in response strength is called **long-term potentiation (LTP),** and scientists believe that it may be an important memory mechanism (Lyncn and Baudry, 1984; Squire, 1987).

Long-term potentiation also occurs when two converging neural pathways are stimulated at the same time, possibly resulting in the formation of new neural connections. It is now known that long-term potentiation is triggered by the release of calcium, suggesting that the NMDA receptor may play a critical role in this process (Cotman and Iverson, 1987). Figure 7.14 shows how this might occur to explain our ability to associate different sensory experiences in memory. Other biochemical research has focused on possible changes in the synaptic gaps between neurons, where communication between nerve cells takes place. Some theorists believe that memory is established by biochemical changes in neural synapses during the process of learning (Deutsch, 1983; Lynch, 1984).

NEUROLOGICAL MECHANISMS

Neurological approaches to memory involve studying neurons or brain structures. Some theorists suggest that memory is represented by structural changes in the neurons themselves. For example, as mentioned in Chapter 2, rats reared in "enriched" environments (home cages filled with objects to manipulate and explore) show increases in cortical weight and thickness, in synaptic diameter, and in the number and length of dendritic branches when compared to those reared in a standard laboratory environment (Greenough, 1984; Rosenzweig and Bennett, 1978). These findings suggest that memory may have a neurological basis and that the brain is physically changed by early experience.

Other researchers have been studying the role of different brain structures in learning and memory. For example, research with rabbits has shown that the memory trace circuits for a conditioned eyeblink response are primarily located in the animal's cerebellum. For more complex forms of conditioning, neural circuits in both the hippocampus and cerebellum are involved (McCormick and Thompson, 1984; Thompson, 1983). The neuropsychological basis of memory is complicated by the fact that different types of memory may involve different structures of the brain, including the cerebellum, hippocampus, amygdala, and cerebral cortex (Thompson, 1986; Woody, 1986). For example, patients with damage to the left temporal lobe often have difficulty with verbal memory tasks, including recalling a list of words or a story (Frisk and Milner, 1990). Conversely, patients with damage to the right temporal lobe have problems with nonverbal or visual memory tasks. They find it difficult to learn a maze or

FIGURE 7.14 A model of neural connections.
In this speculative illustration, our experiences of the taste and color of peach are associated in the following way. When we taste a peach, a neuron in the brain fires and sends its signal along a neural pathway. When we see the peach's yellow color, another neuron fires and, likewise, sends it signal along. When both pathways fire rapidly in succession, links between these pathways can be formed, resulting in a new connection that can represent our concept of peach. According to this model, NMDA receptors regulate the release of the strengthening of neural connections. New neural connections are necessary for the establishment of memory.

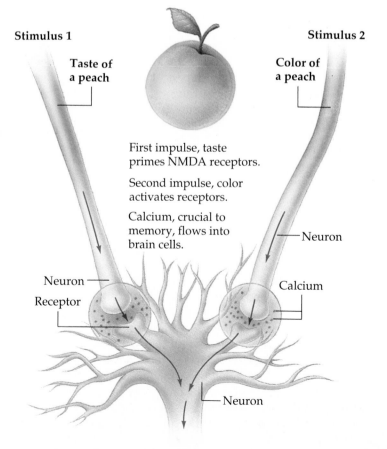

Stimulus 1

Taste of a peach

Stimulus 2

Color of a peach

First impulse, taste primes NMDA receptors.

Second impulse, color activates receptors.

Calcium, crucial to memory, flows into brain cells.

Neuron

Neuron

Receptor

Calcium

Neuron

recognize a face (Milner, 1970). This suggests that the left and right hemispheres partly divide the labor of verbal and nonverbal memory.

We are just beginning to understand the biological bases of memory and can expect exciting developments in the next few years. A better understanding of these processes should lead to progress in treating memory disorders like Korsakoff's syndrome and Alzheimer's disease.

INTERACTIONS:
Connecting Biology and Cognition

In the last section we outlined some of the mechanisms that have been proposed to explain how memory is represented in the brain. But biology alone cannot explain memory. To understand our memory system we need to combine information from the biological and cognitive perspectives. The cognitive perspective informs us about memory performance—our memory capabilities and limitations. The biological perspective provides us with information about the structure of memory to help us understand our capacities and limitations. To date, we know more about performance than structure, but this is quickly changing. Memory is a field undergoing rapid change and development as ideas from both perspectives lead to theoretical advances. One example of this crossfertilization is called **connectionism.** As we noted in our discussion of pattern recognition (Chapter 4) and semantic memory (this chapter), connectionism has provided psychologists with a new model for how the mind works, a model that is based on how the brain processes information. In this section we will describe how the connectionist approach can account for several everyday memory phenomena. We will use a simple connectionist model provided by Jay McClelland (1981).

Imagine, for example, that you live in a neighborhood that is dominated by two gangs, the Jets and the Sharks. Table 7.4 lists the members of these gangs, along with each member's age, education, marital status, and occupation. Figure 7.15 shows a neural-like network model for how you might represent some of this information in memory. For the sake of simplicity, we will only use excitatory connections (connectors ending in arrows) in this example. Each element (filled circle) in the central "cloud" represents one of the gang members. These elements are linked by excitatory connections to representations for the various characteristics. For example, one element has con-

TABLE 7.4 **Characteristics of Individuals Who Belong to the Jets and the Sharks**

Name	Age	Education	Marital Status	Occupation
Jets				
Art	40s	J.H.	Sing.	Pusher
Al	30s	J.H.	Mar.	Burglar
Sam	20s	Col.	Mar.	Bookie
Clyde	40s	J.H.	Sing.	Bookie
Mike	30s	J.H.	Sing.	Bookie
Jim	20s	J.H.	Div.	Burglar
Greg	20s	H.S.	Mar.	Pusher
John	20s	J.H.	Mar.	Burglar
Doug	30s	H.S.	Sing.	Bookie
Lance	20s	J.H.	Sing.	Burglar
George	20s	J.H.	Div.	Burglar
Pete	20s	H.S.	Sing.	Bookie
Fred	20s	H.S.	Sing.	Pusher
Gene	20s	Col.	Sing.	Pusher
Ralph	30s	J.H.	Sing.	Pusher
Sharks				
Phil	30s	Col.	Mar.	Pusher
Ike	30s	J.H.	Sing.	Bookie
Nick	30s	H.S.	Sing.	Pusher
Don	30s	Col.	Mar.	Burglar
Ned	30s	Col.	Mar.	Bookie
Karl	40s	H.S.	Mar.	Bookie
Ken	20s	H.S.	Sing.	Burglar
Earl	40s	H.S.	Mar.	Burglar
Rick	30s	H.S.	Div.	Burglar
Ol	30s	Col.	Mar.	Pusher
Neal	30s	H.S.	Sing.	Bookie
Dave	30s	H.S.	Div.	Pusher

From "Retrieving General and Specific Knowledge From Stored Knowledge of Specifics" by J. L. McClelland, 1981, *Proceedings of the Third Annual Conference of the Cognitive Science Society*, Berkeley, CA. Copyright 1981 by J. L. McClelland. Reprinted by permission.

nections to the name *Rick,* the age *30,* the occupation *burglar,* the marital status *divorced,* the gang *Shark,* and the educational level *high school.* This element and its connections thus represent everything we know about Rick. Table 7.4 confirms these facts about Rick and the other gang members represented in the figure.

To see an example of remembering, suppose that someone mentions the name Rick in a conversation. Using our network model, the representation for Rick's name would be activated in your memory. This activation would then spread along the excitatory connector to the main element that represents Rick, which would in turn activate all of the other connected representations that provide information about Rick (such as his age, occupation, and so on). This example shows an important characteristic of this connectionist model—it has a **content-addressable memory.** This means that if it is provided with partial information, such as a person's name, it can use that information to retrieve other information about the person from memory. Our memory operates in the same way. For example, if someone mentions John Lennon you are reminded of the Beatles and their songs because representations for these different pieces of information are interconnected in your long-term memory. This is the same principle we described earlier in this chapter when we said that thinking about the Fourth of July will automatically remind you of firecrackers, picnics, and Uncle Sam.

Another characteristic of this connectionist model is that it demonstrates **graceful degradation** (Baddeley, 1990). From a biological perspective,

this means that as the brain loses large numbers of neurons and their interconnections as a result of the normal process of ageing, memory is still able to function. In our example, if we "lost" the connection between Rick and his age, we could still make an educated guess from the other information that remains in our memory. For example, if we still know that Rick is a Shark and that most Sharks are in their thirties (see Table 7.4), our best guess would be that Rick is also in his thirties. In this instance we would be correct because we made a sensible guess based on information in memory. This is another characteristic that is shared by the connectionist network and our own memory system.

These examples show how the connectionist approach is providing a new way to think about memory by building on the interactions of biology and cognition. Biology provides the conceptual model based on neural processes; cognition provides the memory phenomena that must be accounted for by the model. Connectionism thus bridges the gap that formerly existed between the biological and the cognitive approaches to memory. ■

FIGURE 7.15 A connectionist model of memory. This model shows how some of the individuals and their characteristics shown in Table 7.4 could be represented in a neural-like network model. Each person is represented by a filled circle in the center "cloud." Excitatory connections link the different characteristics to each person.

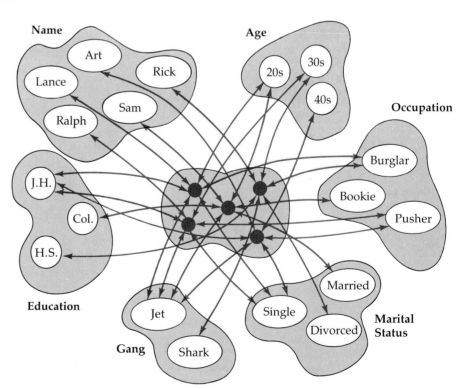

IN CONTEXT: MEMORY

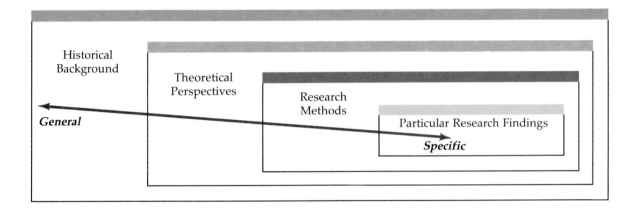

STUDY QUESTIONS

Do all of our experiences produce memories?

How many types of memory are there?

How long do different memories last?

How can we improve our memory?

HISTORICAL BACKGROUND

1. Research on memory began in the nineteenth century when psychology was still in its infancy. Early studies focused on memory development in children and memory loss in patients with amnesia.

2. The first real work on memory to prove of value to psychology was that of Hermann Ebbinghaus. In 1885, Ebbinghaus published his book, *Memory*. Using himself as his only subject, Ebbinghaus discovered the forgetting curve by measuring the memorization and retention of nonsense syllables. He is remembered today for showing that memory could be studied scientifically.

3. In 1932, Frederic Bartlett published his book, *Remembering*. Unlike Ebbinghaus, Bartlett used pictures and stories to study how memory functioned in everyday situations and how it changed over time. Bartlett is remembered today for showing that our memory for events is characterized by omissions, simplifications, and transformations.

MODERN THEORETICAL PERSPECTIVES

1. One conceptual approach to memory is called **information processing.** This approach uses the computer as a model for the way information is encoded, stored, and retrieved from the sensory, short-term, and long-term memory stores. Another conceptual approach is called **connectionism.** It uses neural networks in the brain as a model for the way memory works.

2. More specialized theories exist for different memory processes. For example, the **levels of processing hypothesis** describes the effects of different encoding operations on retention. Similarly, **skilled memory theory** looks at the encoding processes of expert memorizers.

3. Numerous theories exist to explain forgetting. According to Freud, forgetting was produced by **repression.** Experimental research has provided support for **decay** and **interference** theories as well as for **cue dependent** forgetting.

RESEARCH METHODS

1. Experimentation was the predominant method used to study memory in this chapter. George Sperling (1960) used experimentation to measure the duration of iconic memory. Experimentation was also used to measure the duration of short-term memory (Peterson and Peterson, 1959), the unreliability of eyewitness memory (Loftus and Palmer, 1974), and the ability of Korsakoff's patients to produce implicit memory (Graf et al., 1984).

2. Case studies were frequently used to highlight unusual memory. Strong visual memory was shown by a man named Shereshevskii (Luria, 1968), while a man named Jimmie G. showed what memory is like for patients with Korsakoff's syndrome (Sacks, 1987).

3. Surveys were less frequently used. Brown and Kulik (1977) conducted a survey to observe the frequency of flashbulb memories.

RESEARCH FINDINGS AND SUMMARY

1. Following the presentation of a visual stimulus, there is a brief visual memory trace called an **icon;** following an auditory stimulus there is a brief auditory trace called an **echo.** Iconic and echoic memory are forms of **sensory memory** that can hold a large amount of information for a very short period of time.

2. The **short-term memory store** has a limited capacity that can hold approximately seven chunks of information. Information in short-term storage is lost by **decay** and **interference** in a matter of seconds, unless it is maintained by mental rehearsal.

3. **Maintenance rehearsal** is a form of mental repetition that serves mainly to hold memory traces (like those for a phone number the operator has just given us) in short-term storage. **Elaborative rehearsal** involves alterations or additions to the information in short-term storage and results in the establishment of strong traces in **long-term storage,** the more permanent repository of all of the things we know.

4. Stimulus **encoding** can be thought of as a series of levels that range from the analysis of physical features to the analysis of meaning. The progression of analysis is called the **levels of processing.** Research shows that encoding the meaning of a stimulus normally leads to the best retention.

5. Three types of memory representations or **codes** are important for short-term and long-term storage: **visual codes** deal with the appearance of stimuli, **auditory codes** deal with the sound of stimuli, and **semantic codes** deal with the meaning of stimuli.

6. **Visual imagery** is the process of constructing mental pictures that bear a resemblance to physical reality. Visual imagery is important because it serves as the basis for many mnemonic schemes for assisting memory. **Mnemonics** (such as HOMES for the names of the five great lakes) facilitate retention because they organize information and provide a plan for remembering.

7. Different retrieval processes can occur for different forms of memory. **Procedural memory** enables us to learn how to drive a car or tie our shoelaces. **Episodic memory** is used to represent our knowledge of such personally experienced events as our high school graduation and our first week at college. **Semantic memory** represents our knowledge of words, symbols, and concepts that we use to carry on a conversation or to learn a subject such as calculus.

8. **Scripts** are generalized action sequences that describe well-learned routines. When we recall script-related events, errors in remembering occur because we are apt to recall script activities that were assumed but never explicitly stated. Errors and distortions occur because remembering is often a *reconstruction* of the past based partly on what was and partly on what must have been.

9. Normal everyday forgetting is produced by decay and interference. Both **proactive** and **retroactive interference** can be reduced by surrounding periods of learning with unrelated activities. Everyday forgetting can also occur when information is available, but inaccessible. Remembering is **cue-dependent** because the right cue can make information accessible.

10. Physical trauma can produce memory loss in the form of **anterograde amnesia**—memory loss for events after a traumatic event—and **retrograde amnesia**—memory loss for events prior to a physical trauma. Both forms of amnesia are found in Korsakoff's patients. These patients show **implicit memory** (enhanced performance without conscious remembering), but not **explicit memory** (conscious recollection of the past).

11. Current research in neuropsychology is exploring the biological basis of memory by looking at the effects of **long-term potentiation** (the increase in strength of synaptic responding) as well as the role of different brain structures.

ADDITIONAL READINGS

Baddeley, A. D. 1990. *Human memory*. Boston: Allyn & Bacon. An up-to-date review of memory with lots of practical applications.

Khan, A. U. 1986. *Clinical disorders of memory*. New York: Plenum. An extensive review of different memory disorders produced by drugs, head trauma, chronic diseases, and senility.

McDaniel, M. A., and Pressley, M. 1987. *Imagery and related mnemonic processes*. New York: Springer-Verlag. A book on how to use mnemonics, especially those involving visual imagery, to improve memory. Fun to read and do.

Neisser, U., and Winograd, E., eds. 1988. *Remembering reconsidered: Ecological and traditional approaches to the study of memory*. Cambridge, UK: Cambridge University Press. Studies of memory from an ecological or naturalistic approach complement studies from a traditional labora-tory approach to show new directions in memory research.

Rubin, D. C., ed. 1986. *Autobiographical memory*. Cambridge, UK: Cambridge University Press. A wide-ranging collection of papers by leading researchers on what we remember and forget from our past.

Seamon, J. G. 1980. *Memory and cognition: An introduction*. New York: Oxford University Press. An undergraduate textbook that reviews theory and research on memory from an information processing perspective.

Seamon, J. G., ed. 1980. *Human memory: Contemporary readings*. New York: Oxford University Press. A collection of influential papers by leading cognitive psychologists on a wide variety of topics in memory.

Squire, L. R. 1987. *Memory and brain*. New York: Oxford University Press. A current look at what is known about the physiological bases of memory by a leading figure in the field.

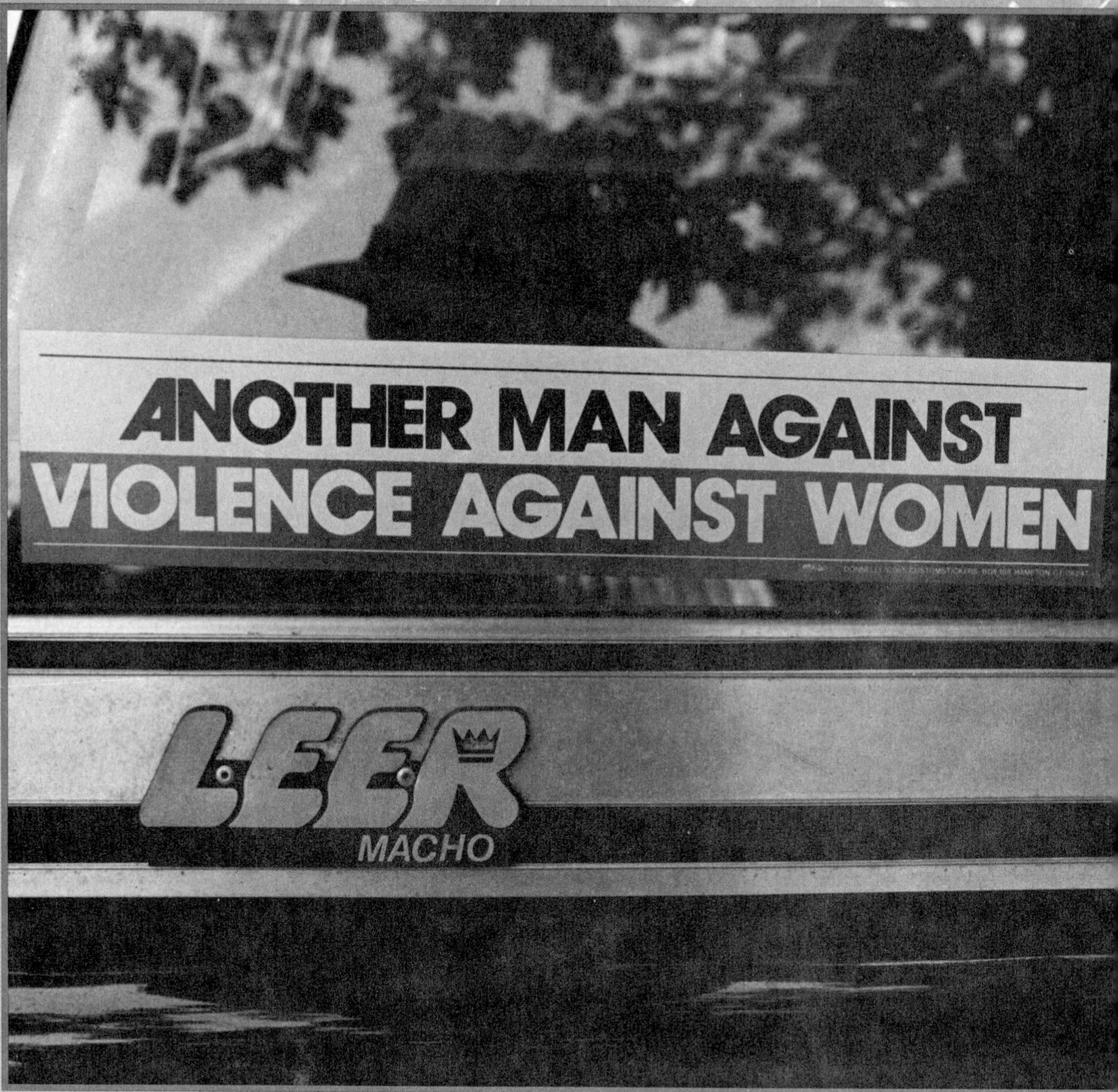
ANOTHER MAN AGAINST
VIOLENCE AGAINST WOMEN
LEER
MACHO

CHAPTER
8

LANGUAGE AND THOUGHT

[M]oviegoers] will remember Stanley Kubrick's film of Arthur Clarke's *2001, A Space Odyssey* as a rich source of prophecies concerning technological advance. If asked to list the more fanciful of these futuristic suggestions, probably few would mention the sensible verbal exchanges between the human astronauts and HAL, the computer. HAL's linguistic prowess is more commonly taken for granted than is the basically trivial gadgetry compensating for weightlessness. . . . HAL's ability to lip-read is indeed surprising, but his appropriate replies to the indefinitely various remarks of the human crew cause scarcely an eyebrow to be raised in wonderment.

(Margaret Boden, 1977)

Chapter Outline

Consider the following dialogue:

A. Why are you in the hospital?
B. I shouldn't be here.
A. Who brought you here?
B. The police.
A. What trouble did you have with the police?
B. Cops don't do their job.
A. What do they do instead?
B. Cops arrest the wrong people.
A. Are you afraid of the underworld?
B. The Mafia are the worst gangsters.
A. Are you connected with the Mafia?
B. They spy on me.
A. Why do they?
B. They want to get false evidence to frame me.
A. What do they have against you?
B. They are out to get me.
A. What for?
B. I have incriminating evidence against the Mafia.
A. Are you sure of all this?
B. You don't believe me?
A. I am doing my best. (Silence)
B. Can't you think of a decent question to ask?
A. You seem hostile to me.
B. Some of your remarks annoy me.
A. I am sorry.
B. Forget the excuses, you guys are all alike.

(Colby, Weber, and Hilf, 1971)

On the surface, this seems to be a conversation between a member of a hospital staff and a person troubled by some type of thought disorder. Person A seems to be an interviewer at a psychiatric hospital, while person B sounds like a patient suffering from a *paranoid disorder,* a psychological disorder in which a person has delusions of persecution. In fact, A's comments are from a psychiatrist who thought he was conversing with a patient through a computer, but B's are from a computer program called PARRY, designed to simulate the responses of a paranoid. In this example, the psychiatrist could not tell that a **computer simulation** was used to mimic human cognitive processing.

Colby's artificial paranoid PARRY and Clarke's science fiction creation HAL are interesting to psychologists because of the general questions they raise about language, thought, and artificial intelligence. **Language** is a system of gestures, sounds, or written symbols that is used for communication. **Thought** is the mental manipulation of symbols—including concepts, images, or abstract representations—that stand for objects, events, or ideas in memory. **Artificial intelligence (AI)** involves the use of computer programs to perform tasks normally done by the human mind. For example, in considering PARRY's responses we might wonder how these various statements were generated and how the psychiatrist's questions were "understood" by the computer. But equally interesting to psychologists is how the psychiatrist understood PARRY's responses and generated questions to ask on his own. Just as we typically take HAL's speech for granted in the movie *2001,* in real life we marvel at PARRY's responses and all but ignore the complex cognitive processing done by the human mind. To many psychologists, the most intriguing topics in cognitive psychology are the ordinary abilities of speaking and thinking that we take for granted because they are so common (Ashcraft, 1989). What are the fundamental cognitive processes that permit language and thought to occur? How are language and thought related? These questions build on topics we have already discussed. Earlier we examined the brain and sensory systems to see how information is encoded from millions of neural impulses into clear and meaningful perceptions. We also saw how information is stored in memory and how it may be retrieved. These processes of encoding, storage, and retrieval provide each of us with the "material" that we use to communicate and think. In this chapter we will extend our analysis of cognitive processes to examine the bases of language and thought.

HISTORICAL BACKGROUND: Knowledge and Cognitive Science

What do you know? When we ask you to think about what you know, you might first think about the sort of information you learned in school. To this, you might add other specialized information—knowledge of how to play a saxophone, how to ride a horse, or even how to program a computer. In addition, you also have knowledge that is shared by everyone else in your culture. For example, you know that a dog is an animal, a book is to be read, and ice is cold to the touch. You also know how to find your way around town and how to use language to communicate.

The knowledge you have acquired is the result of mental abilities—abilities such as paying attention, reasoning, and remembering—that collectively are called cognitive processes. Cognitive processes are the basis for **cognition**—your ideas, understandings, and thoughts. The branch of psychology that studies cognition is called **cognitive psychology.**

The study of cognition is not the sole province of psychologists, however. For years, experts from a variety of areas have studied how people acquire and use knowledge. By 1956, this shared interest resulted in the development of a new field called **cognitive science** (Gardner, 1985; Hunt, 1989). Cognitive science is defined as the study of how knowledge is acquired, represented, and transmitted. This interdisciplinary field combines the efforts of cognitive psychologists, linguists, computer scientists, philosophers, anthropologists, and neuroscientists. Together, their goal is to determine the ways in which intelligent systems function, whether they are human, animal, or machine. We do not have space to review the origins of each of these disciplines. Instead, we will focus on significant developments in the areas most closely related to psychology—language, thought, and, to a lesser extent, artificial intelligence.

Language

Scholarly interest in language began in the nineteenth century when explorers ventured into remote areas of the world. As people traveled more widely and became familiar with a wide variety of languages, they became curious about the origin of language. For instance, some scholars wondered whether the various languages all descended from one original language (Hilgard, 1987). Such questions did not interest the early psychologists, however. At the start of the twentieth century, the few psychologists who thought about language were primarily concerned with how young children acquire language because of the importance of language for school. Consequently, the early psychological research on language focused mainly on vocabulary growth.

In 1957, psychologist B. F. Skinner published a book titled *Verbal Behavior*. In this book, Skinner tried to extend his research on laboratory animals to the use of language by humans. According to Skinner, human verbal behavior could be described by the same principles of operant conditioning that described the behavior of rats and pigeons in the laboratory. Talking, listening, and reading are responses that are influenced by reward just like any other response. Therefore, said Skinner, any utterance will tend to be repeated if it is followed by a reward. For example, a child's verbal behavior is guided by reinforcement in the act of reading:

> If a child responds *cat* in the presence of the marks CAT and not otherwise, he receives approval; if he responds *dog* in the presence of the marks DOG and not otherwise, he also receives approval. . . .
>
> (*Skinner, 1957*)

Consistent with the prevailing behaviorist approach from the 1930s through the 1950s, Skinner's approach to language attributed as much as possible to learning.

Not everyone agreed with Skinner. Shortly after Skinner's book appeared, a young linguist at MIT named Noam Chomsky (1959) published a sharp rebuttal. What a child has to learn in order to understand and produce language, he argued, is too complicated to be learned by the method of reinforcement. Chomsky believes that there are general rules that guide our use of language, and that these rules are an *inherent* feature of the way our minds work. This belief that essential aspects of language are innate, rather than learned, set Chomsky at odds with Skinner and divided researchers during the 1960s. We will see in the section on language acquisition that this debate over nature and nurture is still with us. However, the earlier emphasis on conditioning as the basis for language acquisition has largely given way to the study of the cognitive processes that produce language as the cognitive revolution swept through psychology during the 1960s and 1970s. Chomsky's ideas are important for providing an alternative to behaviorism and for sparking ex-

The hands of Clifton Chenier. We often marvel at the great dexterity and coordination of movements expressed by a gifted musician, but we tend to ignore the complex cognitive processes that are also involved in the performance. A diversity of cognitive skills, including memory and thought, allow musicians, such as this famous accordionist, to remember different compositions and to guide their fingers perfectly over the keys.

perimental research on the structure and use of language.

Thought

Research on thought has had a far different history. Since the time psychology began, thought has been a subject of keen interest. With psychology's close ties to philosophy, this interest is understandable. Philosophers from ancient times have wondered how it is possible for us to think about a prior experience when the external stimulation from that experience is not present. For example, how do we recall the face of a friend? How do we reminisce about our high school graduation ceremony? One early view held that a trace of a previously perceived experience was stored in the mind and could be recalled and examined at will. This view led to some early investigations of visual imagery. In the late nineteenth century, for example, Wilhelm Wundt assumed that visual images were *mental representations* that resembled objects originally perceived through the senses. A mental representation can be a sensory image (the sight of a canary or the sound of its song) or a symbol (the word "canary") that represents an object or idea. According to the earlier views of the British empiricist philosophers, all thought was based on mental images that were brought into conscious awareness according to the laws of association. One image simply triggered another. However, later research suggested that people could think without using mental images at all. One of Wundt's students, Oswald Kulpe (1862–1915), conducted a series of studies to show that "imageless thought" was possible. He found that when people were asked to say the opposite of a familiar word (for example, to say "UP" after hearing "DOWN") the response just "popped" into mind automatically, without any intervening images. This research led to an early controversy over the possibility of imageless thought (Hilgard, 1987).

By the 1920s, debate over mental representations was pushed aside by the work of American behaviorist John B. Watson. As we saw in Chapter 5, Watson was interested in making psychology an objective science; to do so, he focused only on observable behavior. You might wonder, then, how thinking could be studied by behaviorists such as Watson, since it is a covert, private act. Watson's solution was to redefine thinking. He viewed thinking as essentially the same as any other bodily act. Like all behaviors, he said, thinking must involve motor responses. It only appears covert because the muscle movements are much smaller and harder to see.

What muscles move during thinking? According to Watson (1925), subvocal speech was the basis for thought. In fact, early research on people who performed mental arithmetic problems (for example, multiplying 24 by 12 in their heads) actually showed increased muscular tension in the area of the speech organs (Jacobson, 1932). Moreover, Watson cited evidence to show that deaf mutes actually make signs while asleep. In effect, they talk (and think) in their sleep with their hands. However, subsequent research showed that Watson's view on the muscular basis for thought was clearly mistaken. When people did things such as gargling, that interfered with speech movements, or when they were administered such drugs as curare, that produce complete muscular paralysis, they were still able to think and perform various mental tasks successfully (Leuba, Birch, and Appleton, 1968: Smith, Brown, Toman, and Goodman, 1947).

Instead of viewing thinking in terms of muscle movements, modern cognitive psychologists describe thinking in terms of symbolic mental representations. Today psychologists know that we can think in a variety of ways. For example, in planning a summer vacation, we can think in words to make a list of all of the things we must pack, we can think in mental images to visualize how we must pack the car, and we can think abstractly (without words or images) to remember suddenly to take along the suntan lotion even though we were not consciously thinking of the beach. Words, images, and abstract mental codes are symbolic mental representations that psychologists currently study to learn about thought.

Artificial Intelligence

Psychologists also study thought by working with computer scientists to simulate it. Together, they have begun breaking thought into different components that are used in such tasks as problem solving and reasoning, and then trying to generate computer programs that can perform these tasks. Creating intelligent computers is what artificial intelligence is all about.

The field of computer science began in the 1940s when vacuum-tube computers, including UNIVAC, were invented to assist in mathematical calculations for business and industry. During the summer of 1956 an important conference was held at Dartmouth College. It was there that scientists began considering whether computers could be programmed to "behave" intelligently. Allen Newell, who had been working on a computer program to play chess, was at the conference, along with economist–psychologist Herbert Simon, who subsequently worked with Newell and later won a Nobel Prize. Newell and Simon developed a powerful computer program during the late 1950s called the "General Problem Solver" (Newell, Shaw, and Simon, 1958; Simon and Newell, 1971). Its purpose was to solve a variety of problems, including playing chess, solving geometry theorems, composing music, and diagnosing psychological disorders in a manner that simulated human behavior. Their pioneering work helped establish the field of artificial intelligence and

Herbert A. Simon. A major figure in the psychology of thinking, Simon was instrumental in helping to launch the field of artificial intelligence.

showed its enormous practical potential. For example, specialized problem-solving programs called **expert systems** can now facilitate complex human decision making. One expert system called MYCIN helps physicians diagnose and prescribe treatments for infectious diseases (Shortliffe et al., 1973).

Research on computer programs such as MYCIN shows that complex tasks—tasks that were formerly thought to require human intelligence—can be performed by a machine. For some researchers in artificial intelligence, this is a sufficient goal. Other researchers are more interested in simulating human cognition itself. Many psychologists now believe that humans and computers are alike in one general respect—both are information processing systems. We saw in the preceding chapters how we encode information from our senses, store it in long-term memory, and retrieve it at a later time. Computers also store and retrieve information. Although there are obvious differences between the operations of electronic transistors and neurons, understanding how machines process information may shed light on understanding human cognitive processes. The discipline of cognitive science seeks to understand these processes, especially those involved in language and thought. ■

LANGUAGE PROPERTIES AND PROCESSES

We study language and thought together because they are closely related components of cognition. Language is a medium for facilitating social interaction. It allows for the expression and communication of thought. The ability to use language to communicate raises fundamental questions about the mind. What are the essential properties of language and how do they assist in communication? How is language acquired? Is language a uniquely human ability or can animals use language as well? Finally, does the language we use influence the way we perceive the world? These general questions about language are of great interest to psychologists and linguists alike.

LANGUAGE AND COMMUNICATION

If you think of all the languages you have ever heard, it is easy to be impressed by their differences. Many languages sound quite different from one another. Given that there are over three thousand languages in use today, do these languages have anything in common? Underneath their differences are there any similarities? The answer is *yes* to both questions.

A language is a system of gestures, sounds, or written symbols that embodies units of meaning *(words)* arranged according to set rules *(grammar)* for the purpose of communication. Languages may be *natural* or *artificial.* Natural languages, for example, English and French—arose from everyday communication between people; artificial languages such as those used for computer programming were constructed to interact with machines and will not concern us further. The science of **linguistics** studies natural languages and their grammatical rules. **Psycholinguistics** is a branch of psychology that examines language as an aspect of behavior involving speaking, writing, and thinking. Together, linguists and psycholinguists have revealed many of the common properties that all languages share.

PROPERTIES OF LANGUAGE

To many native English speakers, foreign languages such as Chinese or Greek sound more like a meaningless rush of sounds than an organized sequence of words. Yet all languages use words and sentences to represent thoughts. In order to represent thoughts, all natural languages share a number of fundamental properties. Languages are **productive, structured,** and **referential** (Hocket, 1960).

To say that language is productive means that there is no limit to the number of novel sentences we can generate. Every time we speak, we can express ourselves in new ways. The same is true for writing. Try as hard as you might, you are unlikely to find any sentence repeated in this text. Better yet, if you were to select any sentence at random, you would have a very difficult time finding it repeated in any book in your school library. From only 26 letters and approximately 100,000 words, we can produce literally trillions of novel sentences (Anderson, 1990). And although these sentences are all different, we can read and understand them because we share an understanding of our language and its rules. This leads to the second fundamental property—language is structured.

Language is structured through the rules of **grammar,** the tacit knowledge that enables native speakers to form acceptable sentences, know what they mean, and know how to pronounce them (Carroll, 1986). Although we invent new sentences all the time, the new sentences are constrained by our **syntax,** grammatical rules for combining words into phrases and sentences. For example, grammatical rules organize a list of words—*ship, the, tiny, distant, on, the, landed, planet*—into a meaningful sentence—*The tiny ship landed on the distant planet*. As we will see in the section on language acquisition, we learn these rules implicitly at an early age in life.

In addition to being productive and structured, language is also referential. The term referential describes the relation between words and their meanings. The *babbling* of a brook and the *quack* of a duck are termed *iconic referents* in that these words sound like the things they refer to. By and large, though, the relation between words and meanings is arbitrary (Glucksberg and Danks, 1975). **Words** are symbolic and arbitrary referents for things, and they enable us to refer to those things in their absence. As a consequence, we can learn from the experiences of others because words can convey information about events that occurred at another time.

American Sign Language (ASL) is also productive, structured, and referential and is, therefore, also a language. It involves the use of gestures *(signs)* instead of speech. ASL's signs are produced from a small number of handshapes, positions, and motions. Interestingly, people who sign have trouble with sentences that contain similar signs ("hand twisters") just as people who speak have trouble with sentences that contain similar sounding words ("tongue twisters") (Treiman and Hirsh-Pasek , 1983). As with spoken language, the relation between signs and their meaning is largely arbitrary. Some signs do resemble their referents, but most do not. Sign language was originated in Europe during the sixth century by monks who had taken vows of silence. They made up signs so they could "talk" to one another. Over the centuries, these signs were passed down and later were used to teach language to the deaf. In 1775, a monk named Abbe de l'Epée opened a school for the deaf in Paris. The signs that he developed are the basis for approximately 60 percent of the signs used in ASL today (Smith, 1989).

COMMUNICATION IN OTHER SPECIES

Human beings are not the only species that communicate. Female moths use an odorous chemical called a pheromone to attract males. Ants also communicate by leaving pheromone trails for other ants to follow to food sources. The strength of the pheromone trail is related to the size of the food source. Once the food source is depleted, the returning ants no longer leave a trail. Research using the method of naturalistic observation has

revealed that honeybees communicate in a more complex manner. They make movements that resemble a "dance" to tell other bees the direction and distance of nectar (Figure 8.1). If the nectar is less than 100 yards away, these bees will move in a circular path on the wall of the hive. If the nectar is farther away, honeybees will produce a figure eight movement connected by a line made by wagging their abdomens (von Frisch, 1974). The straight line portion of the figure eight pattern tells the direction of the nectar, while the duration of the bee's waggles indicates its distance. Still other species communicate vocally. Animals like monkeys, dolphins, and whales make specific sounds to warn other group members of danger (Chollar, 1989).

Although insects and animals can communicate, linguists would not call their communication language. Insects and animals do not

FIGURE 8.1 Honeybees use a "dance" to inform other bees about the direction and distance of nectar. When a bee returns to the hive after finding food, it traces a figure-eight pattern and waggles its abdomen as it traverses the center line of the figure eight. The straight line portion of the figure eight tells other bees the direction of the nectar relative to the position of the sun. The number of waggles tells them how far they must fly. Other bees learn where the nectar is located by feeling the dance since they cannot see it in the dark hive.

exhibit those properties of language that would enable them to express an unlimited number of ideas: productivity, structure, and reference. While the bee's dance has a structure and the particular movements refer to aspects of the environment, it is limited to only one idea. The dance conveys information about the location of food. Language is not so specific. We can tell someone about food in an unending variety of ways:

"Dinner is served at eight."
"Smell the aroma of that sizzling steak."
"Come and get it!"

Insects and animals cannot do this.

THE UNITS AND PROCESSES OF SPEECH

Having considered the defining characteristics of language, we now describe how speech is produced and understood. We will start with the building blocks of speech and work our way up to the perception and comprehension of sentences.

THE UNITS OF SPEECH

Speech is produced by the human vocal tract shown in Figure 8.2. When we speak, we move our tongue, lips, and jaw while we expel a column of air from our lungs. These rapid movements change the shape of the oral and nasal cavities through which sound resonates after air passes over our vocal cords, resulting in different sounds. Vowel sounds are produced by a continuous flow of air through the vocal tract, while consonants are produced by stopping the airflow. Try saying a few vowels and consonants while paying attention to the position of your lips and tongue.

All languages use a limited number of distinct speech sounds. These sounds, which are used to distinguish one word from another, are called **phonemes.** Most languages use less than 100 phonemes. For example, the English language has about 45 phonemes, while the Hawaiian language has roughly 13. Phonemes include vowels, consonants, and blends. The word *tin*, for instance, is composed of three separate phonemes corresponding to the sounds for *t, i,* and *n.* Obviously not all combinations of phonemes are possible within any language (*tpc,* for example, cannot be spoken in English) and not all languages use the same set of phonemes. This is part of the reason why learning a foreign language and sounding like a native speaker is so difficult. Some of the phonemes that are used in English will not be used in another language, and some of that language's

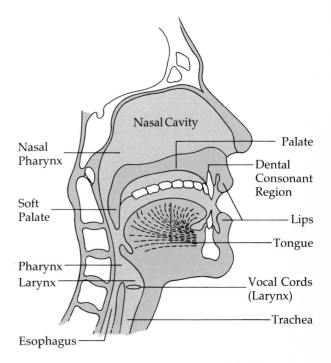

FIGURE 8.2 A longitudinal section of the human vocal tract. Sound is produced when air from the lungs passes over the vocal cords of the larynx and is exhaled from the oral and nasal cavities. Different sounds occur when the shape of the cavities is changed by altering the position of the lips and tongue.

phonemes will have to be learned from scratch. Moreover, some languages do not distinguish between sounds that are treated as different phonemes in English. For example, the English sounds corresponding to *l* and *r* are treated as the same phoneme in Japanese. This is why native Japanese speakers have trouble pronouncing such English words as *lollipop* correctly. In addition, all languages have their own rules for how phonemes can be combined. English does not permit words to begin with the letters *tl* (they can occur in the middle of a word—*battle* or *bottle*), but it does allow *sl* as in *slip* or *slide* and *pl* as in *play* or *please.* Although there are restrictions, the 45 phonemes can be combined to yield an enormous variety of sounds.

Sounds, however, are not language. Sounds must be combined to produce meaningful units called **morphemes.** A morpheme is defined as the smallest language unit that possesses meaning. A morpheme could be a word (as in *like*), a prefix (as in *un*), or a suffix (as in *ly*). When combined, these three morphemes yield the word *unlikely.* There are more than 100,000 morphemes in the English language. In different combinations, they can produce over one million words. If we count words like *big, bigger, biggest* as separate words since they are based partly on different morphemes, then most adults have a vocabulary of hundreds of thousands of words. As with phonemes, there are rules for combining morphemes (*teacher* not *erteach*, for example). Even so, the number of combinations is staggering. Looking back, we see that there are grammatical rules for each of the levels of language we have discussed. Phonemes are organized into morphemes, morphemes are organized into words, and words are organized into sentences to express different thoughts, as illustrated in Figure 8.3. By keeping within the constraints of these rules, an inexhaustible supply of speech is possible. This is what gives our language its incredible flexibility and diversity.

SPEECH PERCEPTION

Part of what makes morphemes meaningful is our ability to perceive them separately even when they are connected in a word such as *unlikely*. This is where speech perception comes in. **Speech perception** involves the identification of auditory linguistic stimuli. It raises a challenging question for researchers: How can we recognize thousands of different words when any given word may be pronounced in different ways and the boundary between words is often blurred? For example,

think about how your friends differ in their rate and style of speaking. Some speak rapidly, and some speak slowly; some may speak with an Irish brogue, and others may have a Southern drawl. Despite wide variations in pronunciation and rhythm, we normally have little trouble understanding them (Levinson and Liberman, 1981; Miller, Aibel, and Green, 1984). We can even understand people when they are talking with cookies or toothbrushes in their mouths (Matlin, 1988). How do we perceive speech so accurately under such variable conditions? The answer is found in the pattern recognition processes we described earlier in Chapter 4.

Visual pattern recognition involves both **bottom-up** and **top-down processing.** Speech perception is no different. It involves not only the processing of phonemes into morphemes and morphemes into words (bottom-up processing), it also involves understanding what a person has said on the basis of what has already been said and what is likely to be said (top-down processing). Not only do we work up from the phoneme to the thought, we also work down from our interpretation to the auditory signal.

For example, when we listen to someone speak our ears are stimulated by the sound waves generated by the speaker. The message is not in the

FIGURE 8.3 A hierarchical organization for language. All human languages can be hierarchically organized. At the top of the hierarchy is the sentence, which is composed of phrases, which in turn are composed of words, and then morphemes (the smallest units of language that have meaning), and phonemes (the distinct speech sounds of a language). The phonemes are represented by phonetic symbols because English words are not always spelled the way they sound.

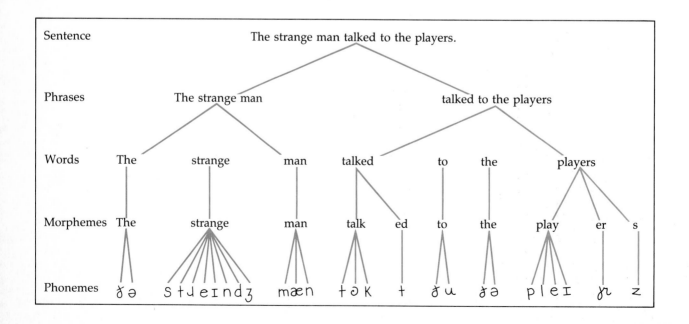

sounds themselves, however; it is in our interpretation of these sounds. Think again about what it is like to listen to a person speaking an unfamiliar foreign tongue. We hear words and phrases when we listen to English but only a continuous flow of babbling sound when we listen to an unfamiliar language. In this respect, English is not different from other languages. To a Russian native, English sounds just as jumbled. In English and other languages, normal speech comes rapidly and with few auditory gaps between words or phrases (Cole and Jakimik, 1980; Cooper, 1983). Figure 8.4 shows a **speech spectrogram,** a visual representation of the different auditory frequencies in an utterance. There are usually no gaps visible between words. If there are no gaps between words, then why do we perceive them as separate from one another? The answer lies in our use of both bottom-up and top-down processing to segment sounds into words and phrases. We match incoming sounds against our memory and use our knowledge of language to determine what has been said and what is likely to come next. The context of speech stimuli helps us greatly in this regard.

For example, individual words, in and of themselves, can sometimes be difficult to interpret correctly without contextual support from other words. The sentence fragment *"The ball was. . . ."* is ambiguous by itself because the word *ball* has more than one meaning. Until we hear more of the sentence, we do not know how to interpret it. If the sentence continues *"The ball was thrown at the batter's head,"* then *ball* refers to a baseball. But if it continues *"The ball was attended by royalty and other dignitaries,"* then we know that *ball* refers to a social event. The context of the sentence tells the listener which interpretation is correct. We see this fact clearly in the results of an experiment on word identification (Pollack and Pickett, 1964). After recording normal speech on tape, the researchers cut the tape into segments and played either single words or short phrases to a group of subjects for identification. The results showed that people were very poor at identifying individual words and improved only when the words occurred within phrases—the longer the phrase, the better the word identification (Figure 8.5). The identification of a sound as a word was influenced by what the subjects heard before and after it. These findings support the idea that we use top-down processing to form expectancies of what we are hearing on the basis of what we have already heard. Such sophisticated cognitive processing permits us to use language successfully. Surprisingly, these complex processes are acquired very early in life.

ACQUIRING LANGUAGE

Children all over the world are born without the ability to produce language. But by the time they are five, they have mastered enough of their native tongue to carry on a conversation. In only five years, they learn to make the proper speech sounds, to combine these sounds into words, and to organize the words they have learned into meaningful and grammatically correct sentences. We continue to acquire language after early childhood, but the first five years set the foundation for later development (Menyuk, 1983).

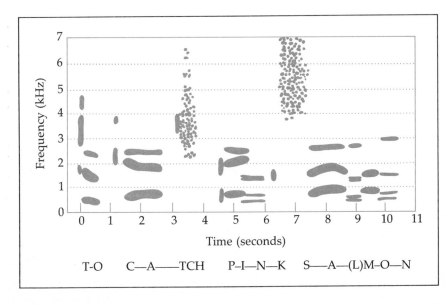

FIGURE 8.4 What spoken words look like. A speech spectrogram converts sound energy into a visual display. In this example, we see that the phrase *to catch pink salmon* has no identifiable boundaries between syllables or even between words. Speech perception requires both bottom-up and top-down processing to segment sounds into meaningful words.

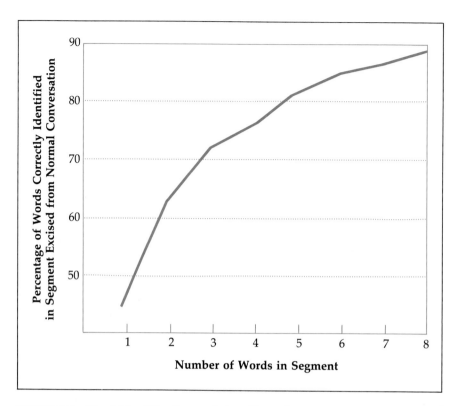

FIGURE 8.5 Word identification and the effect of a sentence context. Word identification increases when the word to be identified is presented in the context of a conversation. The greater the available context, the greater the word identification accuracy.

THE PRELINGUISTIC INFANT

The word *infant* comes from the Latin word *infans,* which means "without language." Because neither the brain nor the shape of the mouth and throat is yet ready for speech, infants are incapable of speaking at birth (Glucksberg and Danks, 1975). But infants can vocalize from their first moments of life.

INFANT CRYING AND COOING

For the first four months, infants cry and coo as their only means of vocalization. We do not know when, if ever, infants use their cries as a form of communication. Parents of three- to five-month old infants cannot distinguish between cries of pain, hunger, or surprise on the basis of the sound alone. However, by the time the baby is seven months old, parents can discriminate between these different sounds (Müller, Hollien, and Murry, 1974; Ricks, 1975). While there is no evidence that infants cry in order to communicate, it is clear that these cries do provide information and that parents learn to discriminate among them by trial and error (Gustafson and Harris, 1990). Very early in life infants learn that vocalizations can enhance their well-being; they can bring a dry diaper, some warm milk, or a cozy blanket.

INFANT BABBLING

By the age of four or five months, something new happens. Infants begin to babble. This babbling consists of sounds like *ba-ba* or *goo-goo* and is much more like speech than crying. Infants all over the world babble in the same way, and the mixture of phonemes they produce could be the basis for any language. In fact, infants from different countries cannot be told apart on the basis of their babbling alone (Atkinson, MacWhinney, and Stoel, 1970). Why infants babble is not known. Since deaf infants babble and they cannot hear their own sounds, it seems clear that babbling does not serve as a means of communication (Lenneberg, 1967). It may be that babbling is controlled by a maturational process that prepares the vocal tract for speech in the same manner that an orchestra tunes up before giving a performance. Over the next several months, the vocalizations are influenced by the surrounding environment. The infants continue to produce the speech sounds that they hear around them, but they lose those sounds that are foreign to their parents' language. The speech sounds they produce gradually come to resemble the phonemes for the specific language they will eventually speak.

THE BEGINNING OF SPEECH

Prior to speaking, infants communicate through gestures. By the age of six or seven months, infants will hold objects and show them to adults. By ten or eleven months, infants will point to objects and attempt to use this gesture to direct the attention of another person. At this time infants also understand the meaning of someone else's pointing. Where before they would look at the hand or face of a pointing adult, now they will look where the adult points (Clark, 1977; Lempers, Flavell, and Flavell, 1977). While this achievement in communication is impressive, it pales beside what happens at the end of the first year. To enhance their communication, infants combine their gestures with single words. It is these one-word utterances that mark the beginning of speech.

ONE-WORD UTTERANCES

Although the speech is minimal, it can convey much information. For example, the one-year-old child who says *baba* for *bottle* may be expressing any of the following ideas:

> "This is a bottle."
> "The milk is sour."
> "I am hungry. I want a bottle."
> "I am still hungry. I want another bottle."

Starting with only a handful of words at the beginning of the second year, children may have a vocabulary of over 200 words by its end (Figure 8.6). Using the naturalistic observation method, psychologist Katherine Nelson (1973) found that children first talk about such things as animals, food, and toys that have attracted their attention and only later begin to speak of such inanimate objects as tables and chairs.

TWO-WORD UTTERANCES

Between the ages of one-and-a-half and two-and-a-half, another change occurs. Children all over the world begin forming two-word sentences such as "More milk" or "Allgone juice." Frequent misinterpretation by a child's parents might force a child to communicate more effectively, and the two-word utterances would be a step in this direction (Glucksberg and Danks, 1975). Much as a tele-

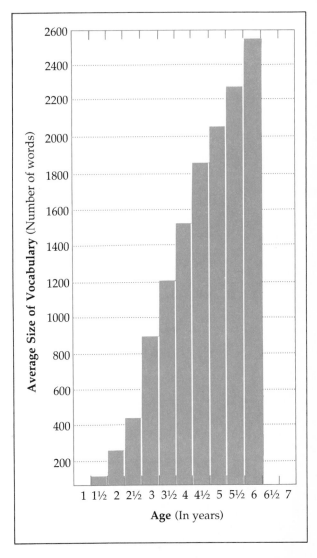

FIGURE 8.6 Vocabulary size and age. From infancy through early childhood, vocabulary size shows a dramatic increase.

gram, where the cost of words necessitates using only the most important words, the two-word sentences of children are telegraphic in that they are short and to the point (Table 8.1).

EXPANDED SENTENCES

Still later, from ages two through seven, these sentences are expanded, and the child communicates even more effectively and less ambiguously. By the time they are five, children will learn to use articles, past-tense endings, plurals, and other elements that were not present in their earlier telegraphic speech (Gleason, 1985). Once again, the impetus for all of this effort is greater communication of thought.

TABLE 8.1 A Sample of Two-Word Sentences from Children in Different Countries

Intention of Utterance	LANGUAGE			
	English	German	Russian	Finnish
Request	want gum	mehr milch (more milk)	day chasy (give watch)	lisää kakkua (more cake)
Question	where dog	wo puppe (where doll)	gde papa (where papa)	missa pallo (where ball)
Quality	big boat	armer wauwau (poor dog)	Mama khoroshaya (mama good)	rikki auto (broken car)
Possession	my dress	mein ball (my ball)	mami chashka (mama's cup)	täti auto (aunt car)
Action	Bambi go	puppe kommt (doll comes)	papa bay-bay (papa sleep)	Seppo putoo (Seppo fall)

Modified from Slobin (1979).

THEORIES OF LANGUAGE ACQUISITION

We have seen that there is an orderly progression in the child's acquisition of language. Children listen to the sounds they hear, they begin to babble and later to emit the particular speech sounds from their environment, they use gestures and single words, and finally they generate increasingly complex sentences. This progression describes the child's behavior, but it does not explain how language is acquired. At present, psychologists have a number of theories about how we acquire language.

LANGUAGE ACQUISITION BY OPERANT CONDITIONING

One possibility, put forth by psychologist B. F. Skinner (1957), is that language is learned by operant conditioning, an elementary form of learning in which responses are shaped by reinforcement. Early in life, speechlike sounds may be reinforced by parental attention and may increase in their frequency, while nonspeech sounds are ignored and thereby decrease in frequency. Speechlike sounds might then be shaped into words and words into sentences, again by parental reinforcement. Though this approach seems plausible, research indicates that language is not generally acquired in this way. As a rule, parents do not shape their child's utterances into grammatical sentences (Brown, 1973). Tapes of parent–child interactions show that parents are more apt to respond to the truth of a child's statement than the manner in which it is stated.

> TWO-YEAR-OLD CHILD: "Mama isn't boy, he a girl."
> MOTHER: "That's right."
> TWO-YEAR-OLD CHILD: "And Walt Disney comes on Tuesday."
> MOTHER: "No, he does not."
> *(Brown and Hanlon, 1970)*

Of course, parents do occasionally correct ungrammatical statements, especially if the meaning of the utterance is unclear (Demetras, Post, and Snow, 1986; Hirsh-Pasek, Treiman, and Schneiderman, 1984). But these corrections are relatively infrequent. Children are very rarely told, "No, you said that wrong" (Bohannon and Stanowicz, 1988).

LANGUAGE ACQUISITION BY IMITATION

Similarly without wide support is the view that children learn language by imitating the speech of adults (Bijou, 1976, among others). Certainly children are capable of learning by observing (and listening to) others, but imitation is not the primary basis of language acquisition. The problem is that not all children imitate.

CHILD: "Nobody don't like me."
MOTHER: "No, say "Nobody likes me.' "
CHILD: "Nobody don't like me."
         (Eight more repetitions)
MOTHER: "Now listen carefully. Say 'Nobody likes me.' "
CHILD: "Oh! Nobody don't likes me."

         (McNeill, 1966)

In a study of 30 young children who were recorded talking with their parents at home, roughly 20 percent of the children imitated their parents 30 to 40 percent of the time. The remaining 80 percent of the children imitated their parents less than 10 percent of the time (Snow, 1981). Imitation is not a frequent occurrence, and there is wide variation among children in their willingness to imitate. The fact that children are creative in their use of language is also at odds with the imitation theory.

From a child who plans to drop a piece of paper on his sister—"I'm gonna fall this on her."
From a child asking his mother to make a piece of paper smooth—"How would you flat it?"

(Bowerman, 1974)

Since these sentences were unlikely ever to have been uttered by an adult, they cannot be explained as due to imitation. To date, research has shown positive effects of conditioning and imitation on language use only for overcoming speech deficits in autistic children and for helping children who are delayed in their language development (Lovaas, 1967; Zelazo, Kearsley, and Ungerer, 1984).

LANGUAGE ACQUISITION AS A BIOLOGICAL PREDISPOSITION

If language is not normally acquired through conditioning or imitation, perhaps it is a part of the biological heritage of the developing infant and child. One view, put forward by linguist Noam Chomsky (1972), holds that children are biologically ready, or "predisposed," to learn any language with ease. Chomsky has argued for the presence of a "language acquisition device" (LAD) that is supposedly responsible for this process. While Chomsky's views have been influential, hard evidence for his position has been lacking.

One fact that linguists like Chomsky use to support their belief that language learning is an innate quality of mind is that young children from many different cultures acquire language in virtually the same manner and with virtually no formal instruction. Children are exposed to only a limited number of examples out of the enormous range of permissible utterances from which they learn their language. From these examples, children figure out the rules of their language and quickly begin producing understandable speech. Even deaf children who learn sign language go through this same process. They first sign one word at a time, then two, and so on (Klima and Bellugi, 1979; Newport, 1984). Linguists argue that the complexity of the task, coupled with the age of the children and their cultural differences, implies that children

Language learning in the deaf. Research shows that a deaf child goes through the same process of language acquisition as a hearing child does. First he learns one sign, then two, and so on. In this example, the children are learning the sign for the number seven.

must be biologically prepared to acquire language. Consistent with this view of preparedness that we discussed earlier in Chapter 6 is the research that shows that deaf children who were never exposed to any form of language instruction (including signing) spontaneously made up their own gestural systems, called "home signs" (Fant, 1972; Tervoort, 1961). It seems that language is so central to the human mind that it emerges in all people with normal intelligence, whether they can speak or not (Restak, 1988).

LANGUAGE AS SOCIAL INTERACTION

Most psychologists currently believe that humans are biologically predisposed to use language, but that the details of a language are acquired through social communication. There is still disagreement over the extent to which a child has to be directly taught to speak. Many psychologists believe that children take an active part in this process. Rather than being specifically taught by adults, children become competent speakers by listening to examples of adult speech and then generating the rules of their language (Tagatz, 1976).

PARENT–CHILD INTERACTIONS

Parents do play an important role in their child's acquisition of language, however. Language develops out of the social interaction between parent and child, as the following interaction illustrates:

MOTHER: "Hello. Give me a smile" (then gently pokes infant in the ribs).

INFANT: (Yawns)

MOTHER: "Sleepy, are you? You woke up too early today."

INFANT: (Opens fist)

MOTHER: (Touching infant's hand) "What are you looking at? Can you see something?"

INFANT: (Grasps mother's finger)

MOTHER: "Oh, that's what you wanted. In a friendly mood, then. Come on, give us a smile."

(Clark and Clark, 1977)

Early on, the infant interacts with the parent (or primary caregiver) by looking at this person and vocalizing in this person's presence. Later, the infant will make reference to the same things as does the parent. For example, parent and child will look at the same toy, point to it, and touch it. The parent, in turn, will naturally use language to describe what is going on. However, adults modify their speech when they talk to an infant. They use a special tone of voice with a slow rate of talking, a high pitch, and exaggerated intonations. This simplified speech is called **motherese,** and it is used by adults and even children in talking to an infant (Newport, 1977). Next time you are in the presence of an infant, listen to the way people (including yourself) talk to the baby.

THE VALUE OF MOTHERESE

What is the value of this simplified speech? For one thing, research has shown that infants pay special attention to this form of speech. If given a choice between simplified speech or normal adult speech, infants will turn to show that they prefer listening to motherese (Fernald and Kuhl, 1987; Spring, 1974). Psychologists also believe that simplified speech provides an infant with early lessons on language. Adults who speak slowly, exaggerate their pauses, and repeat key words and phrases, allow children to learn how to divide sounds into words and phrases (Kemler Nelson, Hirsh-Pasek, Jusczyk, and Cassidy, 1989). Also, simplified speech allows the child to learn the relation between words and objects. As the parent and child play together, the parent's naming of different toys helps the child to discover which sounds refer to each toy. For a child learning a language, this social interaction provides clues about what is being said. Children cannot learn language simply by listening to speech. We know this because normal hearing children of deaf parents cannot learn language by listening to a radio or watching television; they need to interact with another person (Sachs and Johnson, 1976). Difficult though it may be, the child must understand or infer what the parent is talking about before she or he can learn language. Without this top-down process of understanding, the child cannot relate the sounds to their meaning (Macnamara, 1972).

Language experts are currently debating the long-term benefits of simplified speech. Some research shows that children do not learn to speak earlier if their mothers lower their level of speech (Nelson et al., 1983). Nor is simplified speech used universally. In places like New Guinea and American Samoa, mothers use adult speech in talking to their infants, and the babies learn their language just the same (Ochs, 1980; Schieffelin and Eisenberg, 1981). However, we do know that language acquisition is influenced by the types of social interactions that children have with adults. For example, children who look at books with adults who describe the pictures and expand on the children's descriptions ("Yes, that's a dog. See his big tail.") develop language skills faster than children who read with silent or minimally attentive adults

(Cazden, 1965; Whitehurst et al., 1988). Similarly, children whose parents repeat and expand on what they say develop language more quickly than children whose parents use language more sparingly (Bates et al., 1982; Bohannon and Stanowicz, 1988). In each instance there is a dialogue in a social setting that is essential for language acquisition. Ever-increasing demands for greater specificity and clarity force the child to progress from one-word utterances to two-word sentences to expressions of complete ideas. Without other people to talk to, there would be no impetus for this to occur.

DYSFUNCTION:
Social Isolation and Language

The importance of a social interaction for language is most dramatically shown in those instances where children have been lost, abandoned in the forest, or raised in isolation at home. Since antiquity, there have been stories of abandoned children who were raised in the wild by wolves. In this century, a number of these bizarre tales have been documented. Psychologist Roger Brown (1958) reviewed several of these cases. For example, in 1920 two girls later named Kamala and Amala were found living together with wolves in the Bengal province of India. Kamala was approximately nine years old and Amala was about one and a half. Brown describes them this way:

> They were thoroughly wolfish in appearance and behavior: Hard callus had developed on their knees and palms from going on all fours. Their teeth were sharp edged. . . . Eating and drinking were accomplished by lowering their mouths to the plate. . . . At night they prowled and sometimes howled. They shunned other children but followed the dog and cat.
>
> *(Brown, 1958)*

Amala died a short time after being placed in an orphanage, but Kamala lived nine years longer. Gradually, she abandoned her wolflike ways. She learned to play with other children, developed a sense of responsibility, and became generally socialized. However, her use of language remained largely undeveloped. Compared to the average three-year-old, who has a vocabulary of nearly 1,000 words (Lenneberg, 1967), Kamala had a vocabulary of no more than 100 words when she died at around age 18 (Sargent and Stafford, 1965).

Nineteenth century French educator Jean Itard (1804) gave a detailed account of his attempt to educate another of these feral children. This story is called *The Wild Boy of Aveyron,* and it still makes for fascinating reading.

Similar effects of social isolation can be found in those tragic case studies of children who were raised in attics, closets, and dark basements by deranged parents. When attempts have been made to undo the horrors done to these children, the results are often mixed. For example, Isabelle was six when she was discovered. Since infancy she had been kept hidden by her parents and raised with only minimal attention to her needs. She was unable to use language and seemed to be severely retarded. At the time of her discovery, she appeared to know less than an average two-year-old. However, with special training, she progressed rapidly and caught up with her peers. Within one year she entered school and spoke as well as the other second graders in her class. In this instance, language and cognitive functioning were not permanently damaged (Brown, 1958).

Genie, however, suffered a different fate. For most of her first 14 years, Genie lived tied to a chair or caged in a crib with wire mesh sides and an overhead cover. She was occasionally barked at by her father (who thought her no more than a dog), never spoken to, and frequently beaten. When she was discovered in 1970, she weighed only 60 pounds, spoke only a few isolated words, and was severely emotionally disturbed (Curtiss, 1977). After a decade of work with psychologists and other professionals, Genie has made considerable progress. Her language development followed the progression shown by young children, and she has acquired an extensive vocabulary. However, her language is still not normal. She has a problem in articulating words and her grammar remains impoverished. In many respects, Genie is more advanced cognitively than linguistically. She has less trouble learning the meaning of words than she does in learning how to make grammatical utterances (Curtiss, 1980).

What causes one child like Isabelle to recover and others like Kamala and Genie to experience difficulty even after years of training? Psychologists think that a crucial factor is the age at which the first language is acquired. There appears to be a *sensitive period,* a particular time interval during which certain behaviors are most easily acquired. A first language, for example, may be more readily acquired prior to the onset of puberty than at later times (Johnson and Newport, 1989; Lenneberg, 1967). Genie's case, in particular, suggests that some aspects of language may be difficult to acquire after this period. We cannot know for sure because Genie has also suffered great emotional harm. At present, it seems safest to conclude that the longer a child has been isolated from normal social interaction, the less likely that child will function normally. This seems especially true with regard to the use of language. ■

LANGUAGE ACQUISITION BY CHIMPANZEES?

Since other species communicate, might they be capable of acquiring language? Some theorists believe that language is unique to humans because the human mind is different from those of all other species (Chomsky, 1972). Others, including psychologists David and Ann Premack (1984), believe that this issue is unresolved. In their book, *The Mind of an Ape,* they asked whether there is only one kind of mind in the universe, with differences between species due to variations in the fundamental plan, or whether there are different kinds of minds, each with different inherent capabilities? One way to find out is to see whether chimpanzees can be taught to use language—an issue that has tantalized psychologists for years.

TEACHING LANGUAGE TO CHIMPS

Chimpanzees are a natural species to compare to humans because they are closest to us on an evolutionary scale and, at maturity, they have the general intelligence of children aged two or three—who have already acquired the basics of language. What has the research shown? Early studies found that chimps will adopt some human habits such as eating with a spoon and "drawing" with a pencil (Hayes, 1952). In addition, chimps will learn to respond correctly to such comments as "Don't do that" or "Hug Mamma" (Kellogg and Kellogg, 1967). But attempts to produce speech have been a failure because chimps do not have the vocal apparatus to produce humanlike speech (Liberman, Mattingly, and Turvey, 1972). A different approach to language learning was necessary.

During the 1970s, researchers devised a number of techniques for teaching language to chimps. David Premack (1971) taught a chimp named Sarah to communicate by using plastic shapes that stood for words. Duane Rumbaugh (1977) taught a chimp named Lana to communicate by pressing keys on a computer. Each key represented a different word. However, the most successful technique

was adopted by Beatrice and Allen Gardner (1969; 1972). They taught American Sign Language (ASL) to a chimp named Washoe.

The Gardners raised Washoe in a house trailer with minimal restraint, constant human companionship, and lots of social interactions and games. The only language used in Washoe's presence was ASL. They trained Washoe by manually shaping her fingers into the proper positions and guiding her through the movements for a particular sign. Later, after she caught on, Washoe learned signs by simply observing and imitating her teachers. After four years of training, Washoe had learned approximately 130 signs. She made different signs for objects *(banana);* features of objects, such as their color *(green);* actions *(hug);* and modifiers of actions *(more).* Sometimes she put signs together to produce sequences that had a sentencelike quality *(hurry gimme toothbrush),* while at other times she appeared to use signs in novel ways. For example, after learning the sign for *dirty* in reference to feces and soil, Washoe used the sign in reference to another monkey after a fight *(dirty monkey)* and after one of the psychologists refused one of her requests *(dirty Roger).* Still other researchers report that their chimps have mastered up to 500 signs. This is an impressive accomplishment, although it is only about half of the number of words mastered by the average three-year-old child with no formal instruction at all.

CONTROVERSY SURROUNDING CHIMP LANGUAGE

For some psychologists, Washoe and other signing chimps appear to resemble young children who have begun putting words together (Fouts, Hirsch, and Fouts, 1982; Gardner and Gardner, 1978; Patterson, 1978). However, other researchers have doubts about which aspects of language, if any, these chimps have actually mastered. The most ardent critic of this research has been psychologist Herbert Terrace. Terrace and his associates taught ASL to a chimp named Nim (Nim Chimsky), who acquired a vocabulary of 125 signs in less than three years and produced two- and three-sign combinations. When Terrace looked carefully at Nim's videotaped performance, he found important differences between the signing of chimps and the use of language by children.

Unlike a child, who progresses from single words to sentences, Terrace found that Nim formed strings of two or three signs but never used longer strings to convey more elaborate meanings. In addition, children use language spontaneously,

Teaching language to a chimp.   Psychologists have taught chimps to communicate using American Sign Language. In this photo, the woman is signing "you" and the chimp is pointing to himself. At present, not all psychologists are convinced that chimps use language in the same way that humans do.

but a detailed analysis of Nim's training showed that he tended to imitate his teachers. In reviewing the videotapes of other chimps, Terrace concluded that other researchers may have unknowingly provided their chimps with subtle prompts and gestures. Instead of using language, these chimps may have been producing a series of signs that were followed by reinforcement, acting like rats do when they run mazes for food rewards (Sanders, 1985). It seems that many of the signs used by chimps refer to things they find pleasurable—such things as food, baths, and tickles (Terrace, Petitto, and Bever, 1976; Terrace, Petitto, Sanders, and Bever, 1980).

Terrace's interpretation of this research has generated considerable controversy, and the issue is a long way from being settled (Pinker, 1990; Premack, 1985). Adding to the controversy, psychologist Sue Savage-Rumbaugh and her colleagues (1986) have made some startling discoveries with two pygmy chimps named Kanzi and Mulika. When Kanzi was an infant, he accompanied his mother while she was being taught to communicate by pressing geometric symbols that stood for words on a keyboard. To the amazement of the researchers, when Kanzi was two-and-a-half

years old he spontaneously began using several symbols correctly. Later, his younger sister Mulika showed this same ability to learn by observation. Moreover, these chimps then began to comprehend spoken English words. The relative ease with which these chimps acquired symbols and their ability to understand speech suggests that pygmy chimps are far different from other ape species. In fact, they have a reputation for being the most humanlike animals. Their faces look less apelike, they frequently walk upright, and they mate face to face (Eckholm, 1985). The research on Kanzi and Mulika raises some fascinating possibilities. Says Savage-Rumbaugh,

. . . when an ape can, simply by virtue of human rearing, begin to comprehend human speech, the power of culture learning looms very large indeed. It would follow that if the capacity to understand speech is there . . . it would only take one animal who developed an innovative way to produce sounds to push the behavior of a feral group of apes toward the path of language.

(Savage-Rumbaugh, McDonald, Sevcik, Hopkins, and Rubert, 1986)

At present, the question of whether language is unique to humans is still hotly debated. However, it is possible that the research on language acquisition in chimpanzees will eventually reveal something about the manner in which apes and humans evolved and the role played by communication and thinking skills in this process (cf., Bates, Thal, & Marchman, 1989; Pinker and Bloom, 1990).

THOUGHT PROCESSES

One morning, exactly at sunrise, a Buddhist monk began to climb a tall mountain. A narrow path, no more than a foot or two wide, spiraled around the mountain to a glittering temple at the summit. The monk ascended at varying rates of speed, stopping many times along the way to rest and eat dried fruit he carried with him. He reached the temple shortly before sunset. After several days of fasting and meditation he began his journey back along the same path, starting at sunrise and again walking at variable speeds with many pauses along the way. His average speed descending was, of course, greater than his average climbing speed. Prove that there is *a spot* along the path that the monk will occupy on both trips at precisely the same time of day.

(Koestler, 1964)

Did you figure out the answer, or did you get tired and give up? More importantly, do you know what thinking processes you used to try to solve the problem? For example, did you use words or mental imagery in searching for its solution? If you tried to verbalize the problem, you were probably unsuccessful. The easiest way to solve the "Buddhist monk" problem is to do it visually. Imagine two monks—one walking from the bottom of the mountain and the other from the top—on the same path starting at sunrise. At some time during the day and at some point on the path, the two monks must collide (Adams, 1979). Regardless of the rate of walking, the monks' paths must cross and this point will be at "precisely the same time of day" for both monks. The problem does not require you to specify that time.

What aspect of this problem made it difficult to solve? Was it the language that tripped you up or did you jump to the wrong conclusion in your haste to solve it? Psychologists use problems of this type to learn how we use language and different thought processes in everyday tasks. What

makes some so skilled in problem solving? What rules guide our reasoning? These issues are theoretically important for understanding the higher cognitive functions of making decisions and judgments, solving problems, and reasoning. They are also practically important for understanding everyday thinking. Thinking is so much a part of our lives that it is impossible to imagine not thinking. We think at college registration in deciding what classes to take, we think at the grocery store in deciding what foods to buy, we think at the refrigerator in deciding what to eat, we even think as we sit quietly and daydream. In the sections that follow we will describe several different thought processes and see how we can use this information to think more creatively and clearly. We will start with visual thinking to show how we use visual images to represent and manipulate information in our minds.

VISUAL THINKING

In Chapter 7 we showed how mnemonics that used visual images could enhance our memory performance. Now we will show how visual images can also serve as the basis for thought.

TWO VISUAL IMAGERY SYSTEMS

Neurological research with animals and brain-damaged people has demonstrated that there are two distinct systems in the brain for representing visual information. One system, called the "where" system, is located in the parietal lobes and is used for representing spatial information—our knowledge of where things are located in space. For example, we use spatial information to determine whether Iowa is closer to Kansas or Florida. The other system, called the "what" system, is located in the temporal lobes and is responsible for object representations—our knowledge of what different things look like (Ungerleider and Mishkin, 1982). For example, we use object information to determine whether Iowa looks more like Colorado than Idaho. The two visual systems are involved in visual thinking because there are two distinct types of imagery— **visual spatial imagery** and **visual object imagery**—that correspond to the visual systems (Farah, Hammond, Levine, and Calvanio, 1988). Visual images are similar to the brain states that arise in these systems during visual perception, but they occur in the absence of visual stimulation (Kosslyn, 1988). How do we use these images?

USING SPATIAL AND OBJECT IMAGES

Try answering the following questions:

- Is the doorknob to your front door on the left or the right side?
- If you rotate the letter N clockwise 90°, what new letter is formed?

Most people report that they answer questions like these by thinking of visual images that they can examine in mental space. Evidence for the idea that we can generate spatial images and manipulate them comes from the research of Roger Shepard and Lynn Cooper, among others. In a series of experiments, they showed that people take longer to decide whether two block figures are the same when the orientations of the figures are made increasingly different (Figure 8.7). Considerable research suggests that people make their decisions by mentally rotating one member of each stimulus pair to try to bring it in congruence with the other (Cooper and Shepard, 1984; Shepard and Metzler, 1971; Takano, 1989). This mental rotation of a block figure is an example of how we generate and manipulate a spatial image, and it is similar to the kind of visual thinking we do when we imagine the letter N rotated 90° or the furniture rearranged in our room.

FIGURE 8.7   Are the block figures in each pair the same or different?   The figures could be the same but rotated in either a picture or depth plane, or they could be two different figures. Pair A shows the same figure rotated 80 degrees in the picture plane, pair B shows another figure (also the same) rotated 80 degrees in the depth plane, and pair C shows two different figures. The time needed to decide "same" depends on the angle of rotation of the figures—the greater the angular rotation, the longer the response time. These data suggest that people determine the identity of objects by imaging the block figures as three-dimensional solids and rotating them in space to compare them.

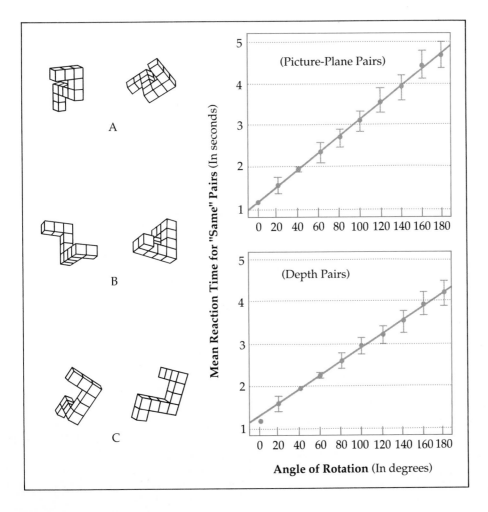

Try answering a few more questions:

- What color is a football?
- Do a German shepherd's ears normally point up or down?

These questions involve object imagery and research on this type of imagery often uses stimuli such as animals and their body parts because this information is not likely to be stored verbally in memory. People report that they answer questions about whether a German shepherd's ears point up or down or whether a kangaroo has a long or short tail by generating and checking their images of these animals (Kosslyn, 1975). This is similar to the kind of visual thinking we do when we daydream and imagine ourselves talking with a friend or engaging in some other familiar activity. When spatial and object imagery are used together, they provide an opportunity for visual thinking that is especially suitable for solving problems that are visualizable.

VISUAL IMAGERY IN PROBLEM SOLVING

There are numerous accounts of scientists and inventors who used spatial and object imagery to solve difficult scientific problems (Finke, 1990; Shepard, 1988). Perhaps the most famous example is that provided by chemist Friedrich Kekule when he was trying to determine the molecular structure of benzene. One night, Kekule dozed by the fireside and dreamed of a whirling, snakelike figure that formed a closed loop. For Kekule, the image of a snake biting its tail gave him the necessary insight into the structure for the benzene molecule. Similarly, Albert Einstein was led to some insights in physics by doing "thought" experiments in his imagination. Everyday observations indicate that this type of visual thinking is quite common (Kosslyn, 1990). Whether imagining how to pack the car for a vacation or how to rearrange furniture in a room, we use our mind's eye to imagine possible solutions until we find one that works.

PROBLEM SOLVING

We use **problem solving** when we want to reach a goal that is not readily attainable (Matlin, 1983). Here are a few common examples:

- trying to find a friend's house in an unfamiliar neighborhood
- looking for your car keys when they are not in their usual location
- answering an essay question about two theories that seem unrelated
- playing a game of chess or doing a crossword puzzle

Problems come in so many different forms that there is no single, clearly-defined cognitive operation that is called "problem solving." Rather, problem solving involves a variety of cognitive processes and the importance of any process varies from one problem to another (Metcalfe and Wiebe, 1987). However, this does not mean that problems cannot be approached systematically. Psychologists John Bransford and Barry Stein (1984) devised a five-step plan for effective problem solving. Their problem solving strategy is called IDEAL, and it consists of the following steps:

I   Identify the problem.
D   Define and represent the problem.
E   Explore possible strategies.
A   Act on the strategies.
L   Look back and evaluate the effects of your activities.

In other words, to solve a problem, you need to understand it, generate possible solutions, overcome possible obstacles, and evaluate your alternatives.

UNDERSTANDING THE PROBLEM

What does it mean to understand a problem? One view holds that *understanding* involves constructing an accurate mental representation of the problem (Greeno, 1977). For example, consider the following sentence:

Tree trunks are straws for thirsty leaves and branches.

To understand this sentence, you must generate an internal representation in your mind that makes use of the similarity of tree trunks and straws. Once you realize that both are capable of moving liquid, the sentence is no longer nonsensical. The same point can be made about comprehending text. What might the following paragraph be about?

The procedure is actually quite simple. First you arrange things into different groups. Of course, one pile may be sufficient depending on how much there is to do. If you have to go somewhere else due to lack of facilities that is the next step, otherwise you are pretty well set. It is important not to overdo things. That is, it is better to do too few things at once than too many. In the short run this may not seem important but complications can easily arise. A mistake can be expensive as well. At first the whole procedure will seem complicated. Soon, however, it will become just another facet of life. It is difficult to foresee any end to the necessity for this task in the immediate future, but then one never can tell. After the procedure is completed one arranges the materials into different groups again. Then they can be put into their appropriate places. Eventually they will be used once more and the whole cycle will then have to be repeated. However, that is part of life.

(Bransford and Johnson, 1973)

Without a coherent mental representation, the paragraph is essentially meaningless. But if you were told or figured out that the paragraph described a procedure for washing clothes, it suddenly makes sense. The first step in solving a problem is to understand the nature of the problem. Think back to the Buddhist monk problem. If you really understood the problem when you first read it, you would not have wasted effort trying to figure out a specific time.

GENERATING POSSIBLE SOLUTIONS

Once you understand a problem, there are a variety of strategies you can use to generate possible solutions. The two most general strategies are called *algorithms* and *heuristics*. An **algorithm** is a step-by-step procedure that will always produce a solution to a problem because it considers all possible solutions. For example, algorithms can be used to solve *anagrams*, words that have been scrambled into jumbled collections of letters. Consider the following anagram:

ATC

If you used an algorithm to unscramble the letters, you would arrange them into all possible combinations until you located a word (TCA, CTA . . . CAT!). But what about the following anagram?

LOSOCGYHYP

For 10 letters, there are over 3 ½ million possible letter arrangements. Here, an algorithm would be inefficient. The trouble with algorithms is that they may require considerable time and effort to use. We need a short-cut strategy that allows us to generate a possible solution without considering every possible letter arrangement.

Heuristics are mental short-cuts or rules of thumb that suggest possible solutions but do not ensure a solution. For instance, we could use our knowledge of the English language as a heuristic to help solve the 10 letter anagram. One heuristic strategy would be to focus on letter combinations that have a high probability of occurrence (PH, PL, PO, PS, . . .). Another heuristic would be to try to form a part of a word from some of the letters (PSY, for example) and then see whether the remaining letters fit. For many problems we face, such as writing a term paper, heuristics are the preferred strategy because no algorithms are available. Three specific heuristics can be applied to a wide variety of problems: **means–ends analysis, working backward,** and using an **analogy.**

In a means–ends analysis, we divide a problem into a number of subproblems, or components. We solve each subproblem by noting the difference between the original state and the goal state and then reducing the difference between these two states. For instance, imagine that you have to write a term paper. To use a means–ends strategy, you would divide the paper into a number of subproblems, including choosing a topic, locating the literature, reading the literature, organizing your notes, and writing and revising your paper. Once the subproblems are identified, you can work to reduce the difference between your original state (no paper) and your goal state (a paper to hand in). This "divide and conquer" strategy is used so often that we take it for granted, but it is a successful problem-solving heuristic (Bransford, Sherwood, and Sturdevant, 1987).

For other problems, working backward is a more effective strategy. In this case, we begin by knowing the desired outcome or goal state and work back to the original state. For example, imagine that you need to meet someone for a job interview at 1 pm and you do not want to be late. The goal state is being at that place at 1 pm. The problem is how to get to that goal state. To arrive on time, you must figure out how long it takes to drive to your appointment, find a place to park, and locate the correct building and office. If it takes an hour to do all of these things, then you must leave for your interview by noon. Working backward is an effective strategy to use when the goal state is clearly defined and your original state is not.

Another frequently used heuristic is problem solving by analogy. For this strategy, we try to use the solution to one problem to guide solutions to another. For example, mathematics texts often use this method. They work out one example in the book and then ask students to follow the same procedure for solving similar problems. To see the power of an analogy, first try to solve the problem that Karl Duncker (1945) posed to his subjects.

Suppose you are a doctor faced with a patient who has a malignant tumor in his stomach. It is impossible to operate on the patient, but unless the tumor is destroyed the patient will die. There is a kind of ray that can be used to destroy the tumor. If the rays reach the tumor all at once at a sufficient high intensity, the tumor will be destroyed. Unfortunately, at this intensity the healthy tissue that the rays pass through on the way to the tumor will also be destroyed. At lower intensities the rays are harmless to healthy tissue, but they will not affect the tumor either. What type of procedure might be used to destroy the tumor with the rays, and at the same time avoid destroying the healthy tissue?

(Duncker, 1945; adapted by Gick and Holyoak, 1980)

Duncker found that approximately 40 percent of his subjects misunderstood the problem and advocated operating on the patient. Another 29 percent thought that the rays should be directed to the stomach through an opening such as the esophagus. In fact, only about five percent of the subjects thought of the correct solution.

More recently, psychologists Mary Gick and Keith Holyoak (1980) wondered whether people could use an analogy to help solve Duncker's tumor problem. To find out, they conducted an experiment. They gave their subjects the following story before attempting Duncker's problem:

A small country was ruled from a strong fortress by a dictator. The fortress was situated in the middle of the country, surrounded by farms and villages. Many roads led to the fortress through the countryside. A rebel general vowed to capture the fortress. The general knew that an attack by his entire army would capture the fortress. He gathered his army at the head of one of the roads, ready to launch a full-scale direct attack. However, the general then learned that the dictator had planted mines on each of the roads. The mines were set so that small bodies of men could pass over them safely, since the dictator needed to move his troops and workers to and from the fortress. However, any large force would detonate the mines. Not only would this blow

up the road, but it would also destroy many neighboring villages. It therefore seemed impossible to capture the fortress. However, the general divised a simple plan. He divided his army into small groups and dispatched each group to the head of a different road. When all was ready he gave the signal and each group marched down a different road. Each group continued down its road to the fortress so that the entire army arrived together at the fortress at the same time. In this way the general captured the fortress and overthrew the dictator.

(Gick & Holyoak, 1980)

With this story as a hint, Gick and Holyoak found that nearly all of their subjects devised an analogous solution to the tumor problem. They dispersed the intensity of the rays by hitting the tumor with several weak rays from different directions. The analogy provided the subjects with **insight,** the ability to perceive suddenly the true nature of the problem and its solution. Using analogies to solve problems is really just learning from past experience (Matlin, 1983). When we can draw an appropriate analogy from our long-term memory, we can often solve a completely new problem (Ross and Kennedy, 1990). Recent studies of the papers of inventor Thomas Edison indicated that he relied heavily on the use of analogy. Early drawings of his motion-picture machine show that it evolved from his already available phonograph (Broad, 1985).

OVERCOMING OBSTACLES

Past experience is not always helpful, however. What served us well in one situation may hinder us in another. Sometimes we need to reexamine our assumptions and reformulate how we are thinking in order to solve a particular problem. Consider the dot problem. *Without removing your pencil from the surface,* draw no more than four straight lines that will go through all nine dots.

Many people find this problem difficult because they assume that the lines must stay within an imaginary boundary enclosing the dots. But this assumption is one that has been imposed by the problem solver, not an inherent part of the problem. Look at some of the different solutions that are possible, depending on how the problem is structured (Figure 8.8).

Examining our assumptions and making them explicit is helpful, but it is not always sufficient. Problem solving can be hampered by the use of strategies that worked well in the past but are no longer effective. When this occurs, we say that the problem solver has an inappropriate **mental set,** a particular way of looking at a problem that may interfere with finding new solutions. Table 8.2 shows how a previously successful strategy can decrease the likelihood of seeing a simpler, more direct solution to a problem. The task is to use the water jars to obtain the amount of water called for by each of the problems. Try the first problem now.

If you were successful, you solved the problem by subtracting Jar A from Jar B once and Jar C from Jar B twice. Before reading on, try solving the remaining problems in order.

When this experiment was done by Abraham Luchins in 1942, he found that people who tried to solve the problems in the order shown had a great deal of difficulty with the seventh problem. They tried to use the solution that had worked on the previous problems once more and found that it would not work. Other people, who tried only Problems 6 through 10, did not experience this difficulty. They solved the seventh problem with a simpler solution by adding Jars A and C. Luchins's

research shows that problem solving can be hampered when we indiscriminately use strategies that worked for us before. New problems may have unique qualities that require different solutions.

At other times, our inability to solve a problem rests not on our trying to force a solution that will no longer work but on failing to see that objects

TABLE 8.2 Luchins's Water Jar Problems

| PROBLEMS | GIVEN JARS OF THE FOLLOWING SIZES | | | OBTAIN THIS AMOUNT |
	A	B	C	
1	21	127	3	100
2	14	163	25	99
3	18	43	10	5
4	9	42	6	21
5	20	59	4	31
6	23	49	3	20
7	15	39	3	18
8	28	76	3	25
9	18	48	4	22
10	14	36	8	6

Adapted from Luchins (1942).

FIGURE 8.8 Possible solutions to the nine dot problem. A sample of different solutions for drawing no more than four straight lines through all nine dots, without lifting your pencil from the surface. Solution A is the most straightforward, but B and C also satisfy the demands of the task.

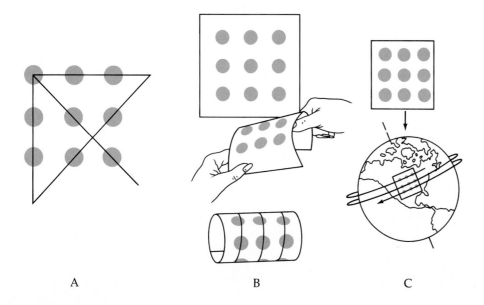

A   B   C

have more than one use. This inability to see a new or unique use for a common object is called **functional fixedness.** For example, Figure 8.9 shows a task in which a person must tie two strings together. However, the strings cannot be reached at the same time. One solution is to see that a tool such as a pair of pliers can also be used to form a pendulum when it is tied to one string. With one string in motion, the problem is easily solved (Maier, 1931). Another example of overcoming functional fixedness came from news reports of motorists who were stranded after the 1980 eruption of Mt. St. Helens. The air was so thick with volcanic ash that automobiles quickly stalled when they sucked the ash through their air filters. One person's solution was to wrap panty hose around the engines air intake to serve as a screen for the ash. This novel solution was so successful that the Washington Highway Patrol purchased panty hose for their cars to help other stranded motorists. Seeing objects only in terms of their intended function can blind us to creative applications.

CREATIVITY AND CREATIVE PROBLEM SOLVING

Creativity is the ability to produce original and appropriate ideas, and it is based on two different types of thinking. One type is **convergent think-**ing—a type of thinking that proceeds toward a single answer, such as "48 × 12 = ___." Most of our training in school involves this type of thinking. The other type is **divergent thinking**—a type of thinking that involves moving outward from a problem in many different directions, such as "How many uses can you think of for a brick?" In the panty hose example, both types of thinking were necessary to solve the problem. Divergent thinking was used to generate different possible solutions, while convergent thinking was necessary to select the best solution at hand. In this instance, the fine mesh of an available pair of panty hose provided a creative solution to keep volcanic ash out of the car's engine. Given this particular solution, you might be able to think of other original and appropriate solutions to the problem.

Research indicates that creativity is related to intelligence, but high intelligence is no guarantee of creativity. In fact, beyond a moderately high IQ (above an IQ score of 120), creativity and intelligence are unrelated (Barron, 1963; Horn, 1976). For example, highly creative scientists and engineers tend to score no higher on IQ tests than do their less creative colleagues (MacKinnon and Hall, 1972). Rather than intelligence, other factors are associated with creativity. The first is **imagina-**

FIGURE 8.9 How would you tie the two strings together? Successful problem solving sometimes requires the use of objects in ways that differ from their intended function. In this example, the pliers could be tied to one string to form a pendulum. When the pendulum is set in motion, it can be grasped with an outstretched hand.

tive thinking skills—the ability to see things in new ways, to recognize relations, and make new connections—like using panty hose as an air filter. The second is **intrinsic motivation**—the ability to work on something for the pure joy of it rather than for some external reward. The third is **expertise**—the ability to use a broad and highly organized body of knowledge systematically (Amabile, 1983; 1987; Kohn, 1987). Closely related to these cognitive characteristics are certain personality characteristics associated with creativity. Creative people tend to be independent, nonconforming, and self-confident (Barron and Harrington, 1981). When individuals with these characteristics confront a problem, their solutions are apt to be novel and fitting.

EVALUATING THE ALTERNATIVES

After you have generated possible solutions to a problem you must test them. You need to check to be sure that you have not generated false solutions. For example, try solving the brain teaser shown in Figure 8.10. Each move that you make should bring you closer to a solution. If not, try a different approach.

Of course, there will be times when you fail to solve a particular problem. At these times, the best thing to do is to put the problem away. There are numerous accounts of people who turned away from a problem for hours or weeks and, upon returning, found a solution very quickly. This phenomenon is called the **incubation effect.** It suggests that an escape from a problem may sometimes lead to its solution. We may fail at first because we have adopted an inappropriate mental set. The passage of time and a refocusing of attention can reduce this set and allow us to consider new strategies. However, this tactic will only work for people who understand their problems and have done the necessary background work. Simply turning away from a problem we do not understand rarely provides a solution.

COGNITIVE EXPERTISE

Extended practice at solving problems in a particular field leads to expertise. Experts in any field—whether engineering, psychology, or law—solve

FIGURE 8.10 How would you solve this problem? Q. A man wants to cross a river with a fox, a goose, and a bag of corn, but his boat will only hold the man and one other object. The man cannot leave the fox with the goose because the fox will eat it. Nor can he leave the goose with the bag of corn because the goose will eat the corn. How can the man get everything across the river safely?

A. The man can solve the problem by making several trips. First, he takes the goose across and leaves it on the far shore. Then he returns and brings the fox across. But instead of leaving the fox and goose alone together, he brings the goose back with him to the first shore. Then he takes the corn across and leaves it with the fox. Finally, he returns to the original shore and brings the goose across.

problems differently from novices (Holyoak, 1990). For example, we noted in Chapter 7 that chess masters can reproduce the great majority of the chess pieces on a board they have seen for only a few seconds. From years of practice, chess experts have developed efficient ways to encode complex chess patterns, while novices have not. In fact, chess masters may have more than 50,000 chess patterns in memory. They can use this knowledge to visualize possible moves without having to think each of them through the way that novices do (Chase and Simon, 1973).

Psychologists Robert Glaser and Michelene Chi (1988) studied the problem solving of experts in a variety of fields. Regardless of field, they found that experts share similar cognitive characteristics. For example, experts perceive information in large meaningful patterns, use memory efficiently, show depth of understanding, and are able to monitor their own performances. These keys to expert thinking are outlined in Table 8.3.

Research on cognitive expertise can shed light on the differences between effective and ineffective problem solving. Furthermore, if we can precisely describe the basis of expert knowledge, we can use the rules to generate computer programs that demonstrate artificial intelligence.

RESEARCH AND APPLICATION:
Artificial Intelligence

We said earlier that humans and computers were alike in one general respect—both are information processing systems that encode information, store it in memory, and retrieve it for later use. In this section we will look at the ways in which humans and computers are similar to and different from each other on problem solving tasks.

Computer Problem Solving

Artificial intelligence is a field of study that uses computer programs to perform intellectual tasks normally done by the human mind. Computers have been programmed to read texts, to recognize spoken words, and to make expert judgments such as medical diagnoses. In order to solve problems, a computer must be programmed to generate "intelligent" solutions. To do this, the computer needs two basic elements. First, the computer must have a **knowledge base.** This is a background of information about the problem area under consideration. For example, the expert system MYCIN contained a large knowledge base about the diagnosis and treatment of infectious diseases. This

TABLE 8.3   Keys to Expert Problem Solving

Characteristic	Example
1. Experts Excel Primarily in Their Own Fields	Expert taxi drivers can use their knowledge of streets and roads to generate a far greater number of routes along lesser known streets than can novices (Chase, 1983). Experts in one area of knowledge do not perform well in unfamiliar areas, however.
2. Experts Perceive Information in Large Meaningful Patterns	Chess masters excel at reproducing pieces on a chess board (Chase and Simon, 1973). Expert computer programmers also recall key programming terms in clusters (McKeithen, Reitman, Rueter, and Hirtle, 1981).
3. Experts Are Fast and Accurate at Solving Problems in Their Fields	Experts solve physics problems faster and more accurately than novices. Experts take more time at the start to analyze a problem but take less overall time to solve it (Larkin, McDermott, Simon, and Simon, 1980).
4. Experts Use Memory More Efficiently	Experts have developed strategies for storing large amounts of information rapidly. One memory expert could recall over 80 digits in a memory span task and could recognize over 80 percent of the numbers a week later (Chase and Ericsson, 1982).
5. Experts Have Greater Depth of Understanding of Problems	In categorizing physics problems, experts organize the problems on the basis of underlying mechanical principles; novices use more superficial sorting schemes based on the problem description (Chi, Feltovich, and Glasser, 1981).
6. Experts Can Monitor Their Performances	Experts are more aware than novices of when they make errors, why they fail to understand, and when their solutions need checking (Chi, 1987).

Adapted from Glasser and Chi (1988).

knowledge was gleaned from several experienced physicians by a procedure known as "knowledge harvesting" (Baddeley, 1990). Second, the computer must have a **method of search,** a set of rules or procedures for using its knowledge base to solve problems. For example, the rules of operation for MYCIN specify that the program begin by obtaining a patient's medical history and a list of current symptoms. It then works backward (heuristically) by comparing the person's symptoms to information about diseases and their symptoms stored in the computer's memory. If the computer needs additional information for a diagnosis, the program specifies that MYCIN ask for more information from a consulting physician. As a result, MYCIN can expand its knowledge base and show the steps it followed to reach each diagnosis. Compared to diagnoses done by physicians, MYCIN's accuracy is essentially the same. Both correctly diagnose infections about 70 percent of the time (Shortliffe, 1983; Shortliffe et al., 1973).

Rules That Computers Use

How do computers solve problems? In general, they use algorithms and heuristics, just as humans do. In fact, computers are especially good at using algorithms because this type of strategy does not require much flexibility. As we noted, algorithms are step-by-step rules that automatically generate a solution to a problem. Solving a long series of mathematical equations or performing repetitive statistical tests by an algorithm are easy to do on a computer. This is what computers were originally designed to do. However, other tasks, such as playing chess, are not simple to perform by using an algorithm. The problem is that the number of possible moves for an entire chess game is astronomical (about 10^{120} different possibilities)! A chess algorithm that examined all of the possible moves and countermoves in advance could win, but it would take forever to examine these billions and billions of moves (Solso, 1991).

In order to play chess, computers are thus forced to rely on heuristics. These strategies provide a general plan but do not guarantee success. Heuristics that chess experts and chess playing computers use include such strategies as attacking an opponent's queen, controlling the center of the board, and exchanging pieces on the basis of piece or position advantage. The computer can determine which move to make at any point in a game by using these different heuristics.

How well do computers do? Today, chess-playing computers easily defeat most average players. Good programs, including Hitech or Oracle, can beat all but the very best players, and one program called Deep Thought even beat a grandmaster in 1988. One reason for the success of these programs is that, in addition to the heuristics they employ, they can evaluate over 175,000 positional moves per second. Thus, a computer can consider about 30 million possibilities in the three minutes allowed for each move in tournament play (Solso, 1991).

Differences Between Human and Computer Information Processing

For all of their obvious successes, researchers in artificial intelligence are still confronted with some fundamental differences in the ways in which humans and machines process information. For one thing, people often solve problems by using analogies. They can use ideas from a number of different and seemingly unrelated sources in their search for a solution. For a computer, this would be akin to solving a problem in one knowledge base with a solution from a different knowledge base. People do this fairly easily, but computers do not.

For another, humans and computers differ in their modes of operation. Most computers process information *serially*—they do one thing at a time. You can do this as well (for example, you are reading this book by processing one word after another), but you can also process information from several sources simultaneously. This is called *parallel processing*. When you go to the movies, you can perceive images on the screen, understand the dialogue, and be aware of the people around you, all at the same time. Even within a particular sense such as vision you can process information about color, form, movement, and depth in parallel. Researchers in artificial intelligence are now trying to mimic complex cognitive processes on newer computers that perform a variety of processes simultaneously (see *connectionism* in Chapters 4 and 7), so this distinction between humans and computers may one day no longer hold. However, computers will always excel in tasks that require the storage and manipulation of vast quantities of information. This is why computers are used to keep track of bank accounts, hospital records, and weather data. Humans, in turn, are still much better than computers in everyday mental tasks—distinguishing a cup from a bowl, for example, or identifying a rose by its smell.

Finally, human and computer information processing is different in at least one more fundamental way. Computers always operate in a logical, step-by-step manner. People do not. Human thought is "messy, intuitive, and subject to subjective representations" (Gardner, 1985). We humans can use reason and logic, but we also can act irrationally and reason in a distorted and biased manner (Norman, 1981). We will see evidence of this type of thinking later in this and other chapters.

In fairness to researchers in artificial intelligence, their goal is to program computers to perform intelligent tasks and not necessarily to imitate human cognitive processes. Artificial intelligence has enormous potential for storing knowledge and using it in powerful ways (Klahr and Kotovsky, 1989; Polson and Richardson, 1988). In addition to the proliferation of expert diagnostic systems, we can expect progress in occupational areas, where dangerous or tedious jobs can be performed by robotic systems, and in job training and education, where computer-aided instruction can tailor educational lessons to the needs of each student (Andriole, 1985). How far computers can go in performing intelligent tasks will be demonstrated in the years ahead. ■

REASONING

In addition to problem solving, a central component of thought is **reasoning.** We use reasoning to draw new conclusions from the facts we already know. If we think of reasoning as encompassing other forms of thought such as problem solving and decision making, reasoning is nearly synonymous with cognition itself (Rips, 1990). To understand how we reason, we must understand not only the different cognitive skills involved in reasoning but also the factors that interfere with making sound judgments.

CONCEPT IDENTIFICATION

Suppose a professor walks into a classroom of students, points down to a metal waste basket, and says "Oogle." She then picks up a wooden ruler, points up to it, and says "Aagle." Then she walks to the desk, points down to the metal legs, and says "Oogle." By now, some of the students begin to understand. Continuing, the professor points to the top of the wooden door and says "Aagle." When she points to the metal doorknob, the students yell "Oogle," but the professor just smiles and says "No, that's an Aagle" (Mayer, 1983). If we were to continue this exercise, you would eventually catch on. If the professor points up, the object is on Aagle; if she points down, it is an Oogle. This exercise demonstrates the way we look for rules to organize our knowledge of the world. Psychologists refer to these rules as **concepts.** A concept is a property or relation that is common to a set of individual instances. Concepts refer to collections such as the term *dog* (collies, beagles, and shepherds) or relations such as the phrase *shorter than* (Diane is shorter than John). We use concepts to group objects, events, and ideas on the basis of their common elements.

In a classic experiment on concept identification, psychologist William Labov (1973) presented

subjects with the cuplike objects shown in Figure 8.11. These stimuli are said to share a **family resemblance** (Medin and Wattenmaker, 1987). That is, no single feature is shared by all of the stimuli, yet each stimulus has at least one feature in common with the others. Labov presented each stimulus individually and asked the subjects to decide whether each was a cup or a bowl. He wanted to know what features determined how the objects would be categorized. In addition, he asked subjects to imagine each container filled with either coffee or potatoes.

In general, Labov found that the wider the object, the more likely it was to be called a bowl. Also, containers imagined to hold potatoes were more likely to be called bowls than those holding coffee. This study shows that our concepts of cups and bowls are influenced by perceptual *features* (bowls are wider than cups) and perceived *functions* (cups typically hold liquids, and bowls normally hold solids).

We tend to learn to identify concepts by interacting with them. After studying the examples in Figure 8.12, we have no trouble identifying the rules and applying them correctly in the final column. In many real-life instances we learn concepts in a similar manner. Through exposure to isolated examples of a concept (for example, poodles, spaniels, and bloodhounds), we come to abstract their common element. (They are all dogs.) However, sometimes the features of concepts overlap, and we are fooled. In our opening example, some metal things were Oogles and some wooden things were Aagles. So, too, young children may erroneously think that Angora cats may be dogs because they share some doglike features. With additional examples, the child learns which features distinguish cats from dogs and acquires an accurate concept for each type of animal.

Feature overlap is not the only factor that can impede concept identification. People learn concepts by generating **hypotheses,** tentative guesses about the nature of the concept. They then test these guesses in the real world. The following examples show how young children generate incorrect hypotheses by focussing on an incorrect feature:

A mother scolding her child says, "Young man, you did that on purpose." Later when she asked the boy if he knew what "on purpose" meant, the child replied: "It means you're looking at me."

A mother said, "We have to keep the screen door closed, honey, so the flies won't come

FIGURE 8.11   Which of these objects are cups?   These drawings were used to determine the perceptual boundaries for our concept of *cup*. In general, cups are not as wide as bowls, although there is no clear line separating one from the other.

in. Flies bring germs into the house with them." When asked what "germs" were, the child said: "Something the flies play with."

(Maccoby, cited in Clark and Clark, 1977)

Adults can also be fooled by attending to an incorrect aspect of a situation, as indicated by our Oogles and Aagles example. However, after repeated opportunities to evaluate our hypotheses we formulate new concepts that are consistent with experience.

Concept identification is important because it lets us make inferences about people, objects, and events without dealing with each encounter as a unique instance. For example, we know that vegetables are edible without sampling each vegetable in the supermarket because this feature is a part of our vegetable concept. Similarly, we form concepts of people—plumbers and professors—

and generate hypotheses based on what we have learned to expect from them. When our concepts are accurate, we can make efficient decisions. But when our concepts are inaccurate, as in the formation of prejudicial racial stereotypes, the hypotheses we make can lead us astray. We will have more to say about concept identification at the end of the next chapter when we define the concept of intelligence. First, though, we must conclude our discussion of thought by examining reasoning and decision making.

INDUCTIVE AND DEDUCTIVE REASONING

Inductive reasoning is the discovery of general rules from specific experiences (Pellegrino, 1985). It is really a form of hypothesis testing in which we begin with one or more examples and try to draw a general conclusion. For example, if every person

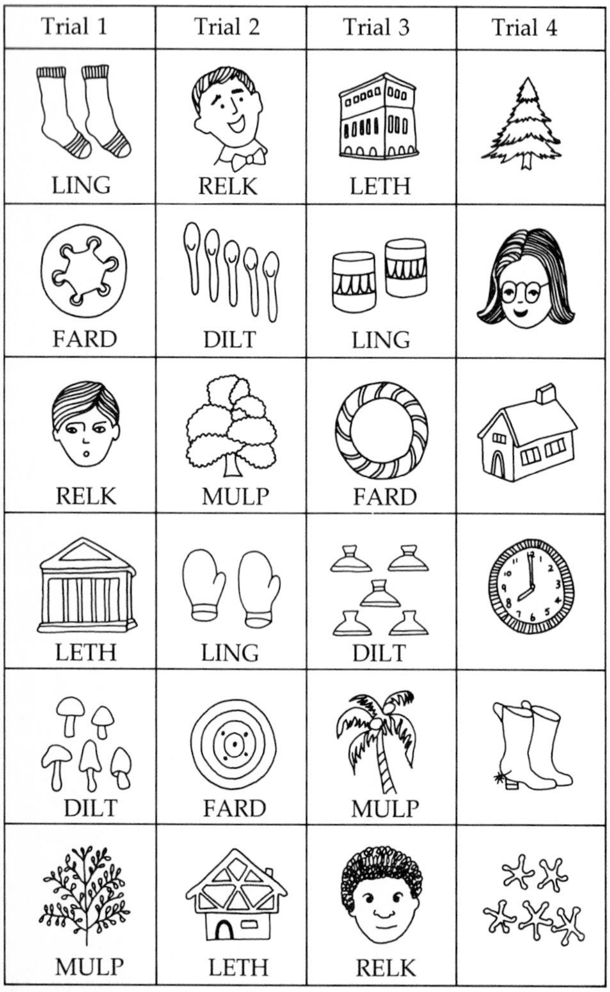

Trial 1	Trial 2	Trial 3	Trial 4
LING	RELK	LETH	(tree)
FARD	DILT	LING	(woman)
RELK	MULP	FARD	(house)
LETH	LING	DILT	(clock)
DILT	FARD	MULP	(boots)
MULP	LETH	RELK	(snowflakes)

FIGURE 8.12 A concept identification task. Look at each figure in Trial 1 and read its corresponding name. Now do the same for Trials 2 and 3. By Trial 4, most people can name each of the figures because they have learned the names for each of these concepts. We learn concepts by interacting with specific examples.

you have ever met had one nose, you could use these experiences to draw the conclusion that everyone has one nose. If you then met someone with two noses, you would have to modify your conclusion. Thus, with inductive reasoning, we use our observations to suggest a conclusion that can be disproved but can never be proved (Halpern, 1989). Figure 8.13 shows common types of problems used to study inductive reasoning. *Classification* problems require identifying the common elements in words and figures. *Series completion* problems require discovering rules to complete the series. Finally, *analogy* problems require discovering relations. Analogy problems are correlated with success in school and are often found on exams for college admission. As we will see in the

next chapter, psychologists are studying the cognitive processes underlying analogical reasoning to understand what differentiates more intelligent and less intelligent people and to try to teach less intelligent people to use better thinking strategies (Pellegrino, 1985).

In contrast to inductive reasoning, which begins with particulars and searches for general rules, **deductive reasoning** uses general rules to draw conclusions about particular instances. For example, if you begin with a general rule believed to be true, such as everyone has one nose, you can conclude that both of the authors of this text, two people you have never met, also have one nose apiece. Your conclusion in this particular instance follows from your general belief. If your belief is true, your conclusion must also be true (Halpern, 1989).

One type of problem used to study deductive reasoning is the **syllogism,** an argument that consists of two statements (called premises) that we assume to be true and a conclusion that follows logically from the premises. The task is to decide whether the conclusion is valid. Consider the following syllogism:

> All women have toes.
> Martha Washington was a woman.
> Therefore, Martha Washington had toes.

We have no trouble following the logic of this example and deciding that the conclusion is valid. Consider another example:

> All people are mammals.
> All chimpanzees are mammals.
> Therefore, all people are chimpanzees.

Now the conclusion is clearly invalid. The category mammals includes a variety of different species, including people, chimpanzees, and all other animals that nourish their young with milk. Consider one more example. Is its conclusion valid?

> Welfare is giving to the poor.
> Charity is giving to the poor.
> Therefore, welfare is charity.

People have difficulty with this syllogism even though it is constructed in the same manner as the previous invalid syllogism about mammals. If you agree with its conclusion, you are not likely to see its logical flaw—the same one that was so apparent in the chimpanzee example (Wason and Johnson-Laird, 1972). Deductive reasoning is a complex process that can be biased by our existing knowledge and beliefs.

We have drawn a distinction between inductive

INDUCTIVE-REASONING PROBLEMS

CLASSIFICATION PROBLEMS

Verbal

1) mouse wolf bear —   A. rose B. lion C. run D. hungry E. brown
2) Bob   Jack Fred Bill —   A. Mary B. boy C. name D. Ed   E. Jones

Figural

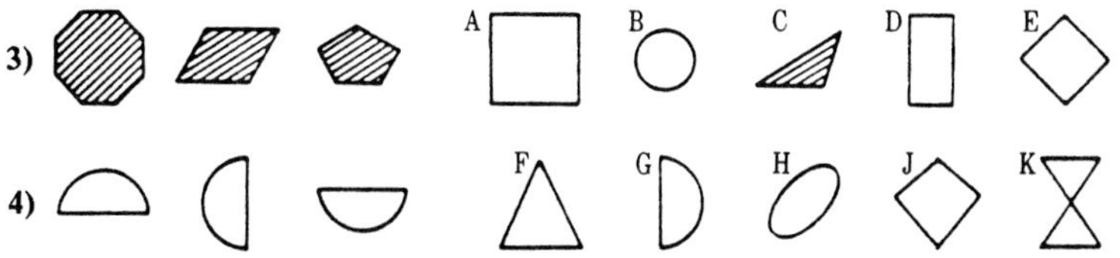

3)

4)

SERIES COMPLETION PROBLEMS

Letter Series

5) c d c d c d — — — —
6) j k q r k l r s l m s — — — —

Number Series

7) 32 11 33 15 34 19 35 — — — —
8) 72 43 90 71 47 85 70 51 80 — — — —

ANALOGY PROBLEMS

Verbal (A:B :: C:D')

9) Sugar:Sweet :: Lemon: __
   Yellow Sour Fruit Squeeze Tea

10) Abate:Decline :: Wax: __
   Increase Improve Blemish Polish Wane

Numerical (A:B :: C:D :: E:F')

11) 7:21 :: 5:15 :: 4: __
12) 15:19 :: 8:12 :: 5: __
13) 10:40 :: 6:36 :: 5: __
14) 28:21 :: 24:18 :: 20: __

FIGURE 8.13 Inductive reasoning problems. In the classification problems, select the correct alternative that fits best with the examples provided. For the series completion tasks, figure out the rule that is used to fill in the missing portion of each series. Finally, solve the analogy problems by discovering the relationship expressed in each problem. For example, sugar is to sweet as lemon is to _____? The answers are as follows: 1) B; 2) D; 3) C; 4) G; 5) c d c d; 6) t m n t; 7) 23 36 27 37; 8) 69 55 75 68; 9) Sour; 10) Increase; 11) 12; 12) 9; 13) 30; 14) 15.

and deductive reasoning to highlight their different operation. However, in real life we often use both forms of reasoning together. Our beliefs guide our observations, and our observations then guide our beliefs. This means that there can be an interplay of inductive and deductive reasoning, since everyday thinking almost always involves a variety of different thought processes (Halpern, 1989). The next section on decision making shows how different thought processes can affect the quality of the decisions we make.

DECISION MAKING

Suppose that you have some money to invest, and a friendly stockbroker offers you a tip about a new computer company. You decide to follow up on this tip by checking the prices of stocks for existing companies such as IBM on the New York Stock Exchange. IBM is a big, profitable company and, if you had invested in it when it started, you could be wealthy today. What is wrong with making your decision on the basis of how well other computer companies have done in the past? The answer is that you are demonstrating a **confirmation bias**—you are only seeking information that is likely to induce you to buy stock in the new company. You also need to get information that could disconfirm your decision to buy. For example, instead of just looking at successful companies, you need to know how many companies have failed in recent years and what the general business outlook is for computers. All too often we fail to seek data that are inconsistent with the ideas we are considering.

Research on decision making has shown that we often make bad decisions in highly predictable ways (Stich, 1990). These errors are frequently the result of a **cognitive bias,** the tendency to use inappropriate information or an inappropriate strategy in making a decision. For example, earlier we described heuristics, including working backward and using an analogy, as mental shortcuts that generally serve us well. However, if we use heuristics inappropriately these strategies can distort our thinking and lead to an incorrect decision. Psychologists Amos Tversky and Daniel Kahneman, among others, have pointed out the kinds of errors that can occur when we use heuristics inappropriately. We will describe two of their examples in this section—the representativeness and the availability heuristics.

THE REPRESENTATIVENESS HEURISTIC

Try solving the following problem:

> The present authors have a friend who is a professor. He likes to write poetry, is rather shy, and is small in stature. Which is his field: Chinese studies or psychology?
>
> *(Kahneman and Tversky, 1971; cited in Nisbett and Ross, 1980)*

If you chose Chinese studies, you probably used the **representativeness heuristic,** a decision-making process in which the likelihood of an event is determined by noting the similarity between the evidence and the possible outcomes. According to this rule of thumb, we make a decision on the basis of how well something matches our representative example in memory. In other words, we have learned that some characteristics tend to go together. When we observe some of these characteristics, we conclude that the others must be present as well. In this example, if the man's personal characteristics fit your stereotype of a professor of Chinese studies better than your stereotype of a psychology professor, you would likely decide on this basis. However, if you did this

in the present example, you would probably be wrong. If you chose Chinese studies, you also committed the **base-rate fallacy;** you ignored the fact that there are many more professors of psychology than Chinese studies in most universities. Personal characteristics notwithstanding, the professor is most likely a psychologist.

Once we become aware of this cognitive bias, we are less susceptible to its effect. For example, a study of resident physicians and first-year medical students found differences in their accuracy in diagnosing diseases. Experienced physicians are taught to make use of the probabilities of particular diseases and not to be fooled by individual symptoms. The residents in this study "played the odds" and made more accurate diagnoses than the first-year students, who often made decisions reflecting only symptoms and not also the likelihood that such a disease might occur—a base-rate fallacy (Zukier and Pepitone, 1984).

THE AVAILABILITY HEURISTIC

The **availability heuristic** is an estimate of the frequency or likelihood of an event on the basis of how easily such examples come to mind (Tversky and Kahneman, 1973). For example, are there more psychology or physics majors at your university? If you decide that there are more psychology majors because you know more of these people, you are using the availability heuristic. In this particular instance you would most likely be correct, because there are typically more psychology than physics majors. What about the following questions:

- Are there more words in the English language that begin with the letter *k* or have *k* in the third position?

- Are there more deaths due to homicide or diabetes-related diseases?

If you are like most people, you are apt to base your answers on how many examples come to mind. In the first question, it is easier to think of words that begin with *k* than have *k* in the third position. In the second question, murders are more widely reported in the news media than deaths due to diabetes. In both instances, however, a decision based on the availability heuristic would be wrong. More English words have a *k* in the third than in the first position, and there are more diabetes-related deaths than murders. This same kind of thinking, guided by the availability heuristic, can influence the actions of a health professional. For example, in a medical text, a physician described the difficulty of deciding whether to remove the ovaries when performing hysterectomies on women in their late 30s or early 40s:

> "Sometimes whether or not I remove the ovaries depends on what has happened to me in the last two weeks," he said. "If I've watched a patient die from cancer of the ovary, I often remove them. But if I've been free of this experience for a while, I'm more inclined to leave them in."
>
> *(Gifford-Jones, 1977)*

Whether to remove the ovaries or not is a complicated medical decision, but this decision should be made on the basis of a large set of case histories, not a recent, highly salient event such as a particular patient's death.

Occasionally, the use of the availability heuristic can be the basis for correct action. Psychologist Diane Halpern (1989) noted that very few cases of Toxic Shock Syndrome were reported before 1978. But as soon as a relation between this syndrome and tampon use by menstruating women was widely publicized, there was a dramatic increase in the number of reported cases. The most likely explanation is that the diagnosis was more available for easy recall by physicians.

The kind of information we consider and the type of strategy we use have important consequences for the quality of our decisions. The representativeness and availability heuristics, for instance, are only a few of the strategies that we use in making decisions. In some instances, they make our thinking more efficient. In other instances, they lead us to make poor decisions. By being on the lookout for these cognitive biases, you will be in a better position to make unbiased decisions in the future.

INTERACTIONS:
Words and Ideas

In this chapter, we have presented language as a medium for communicating thoughts from one person to another. But language could have an additional function. It could influence the way we perceive and think about our world. In other words, language could interact with thought processes to determine the kinds of ideas we might have. People from different cultures, by virtue of their different languages, would therefore have different ideas. This interaction of language and thought would represent a person-environment interaction in that a particular person's thoughts

would be dependent on that person's linguistic environment. This possibility has been discussed by philosophers, psychologists, and writers for much of the twentieth century. For example, in his 1949 novel about the then-distant future—*Nineteen Eighty-Four*—George Orwell speculated that government could control its citizens by removing specific words from the language and modifying the meanings of others. Behind these tyrannical manipulations was the assumption that if people could not talk about specific events, they could not think about them either.

The most ambitious attempt to create a theory about the influence of language on thought was made by Benjamin Whorf (1956). After years of studying the languages of North American Indian tribes, Whorf concluded that language determined perception and thought—where people spoke different languages, their perceptions and thoughts would likewise be different. This position is called the **linguistic relativity hypothesis.** Specifically, this hypothesis holds that the language of any culture determines how the people in that culture perceive and understand their world. In other words, thought is relative to language. As evidence for this position, Whorf cited illustrations to show that people in different cultures often have different ways of talking about the same phenomena. For example, Eskimos have many different names for different types of snow, while English-speaking people tend to have only a single word. In terms of the linguistic relativity hypothesis, this implied to Whorf that Eskimos perceived differences in snow that were invisible to English speakers.

However, there are strong reasons why we should not accept the general idea of linguistic relativity. Much research has shown that while people may differ in their number of names for things like snow, rice, or camels, people do not differ in their basic perceptual processes. For example, people in different cultures differ in their use of words to describe **focal colors,** the generally agreed upon best example of a particular color. In English we have eleven focal color words (black, white, red, yellow, green, blue, brown, purple, pink, orange, and gray), while the Dani, a Stone Age tribe in New Guinea, have only two, one for dark, cool colors and one for light, warm colors (Rosch, 1974). If Whorf's hypothesis is correct, it would imply that the Dani do not perceive distinctions among focal colors the way that English-speaking people do. However, research by Eleanor Heider Rosch (Heider and Oliver, 1972; Rosch, 1973) showed that the Dani make the same per-

Does language determine thought?   According to the linguistic relativity hypothesis, the language that people speak determines how they perceive and think about their world. Thus, the Hopi Indians of the American Southwest should experience time differently from other people because they have no words for hours, minutes, or seconds in their language. However, research has shown that language does not determine how we perceive the world or the kinds of thoughts that we have.

ceptual distinctions among colors as do English speakers. In one experiment, Rosch asked members of the Dani tribe to learn arbitrary names for focal and nonfocal colors. Even though they have no names for any of these colors in their language, the Dani found it easier to learn nonsense names for focal colors (for example, green) than for nonfocal colors (aquamarine), just as English-speaking subjects do (Rosch, 1973).

Instead of speculating on how differences among languages influence thought, most psychologists now think it wiser to view these differences as reflecting historical accidents and the particular communication needs of different speakers (Glucksberg and Danks, 1975). It is not that language directs thought but, rather, that language reflects those aspects of their lives that people find important. In a sense, language is relative to thought. We invent new words to describe new ideas all the time. For example, "black holes" and "quarks" are words invented by astronomers and physicists to describe new theoretical ideas. More commonly, the increased popularity of skiing has led many English speakers to make verbal distinctions about the quality of snow (for example, powder, corn, ice) that they previously would not have made (Clark and Clark, 1977). Language can change when we change what we pay attention to. This, after all, is how we come to add new words to our language.

In summary, there is no hard evidence to suggest that language influences the way we perceive or understand our world. Language can certainly influence thoughts, or else you would not be reading this book. But it does so only as a medium for communicating ideas, not as a determiner of the kinds of ideas we can have (Anderson, 1990). ■

IN CONTEXT: LANGUAGE AND THOUGHT

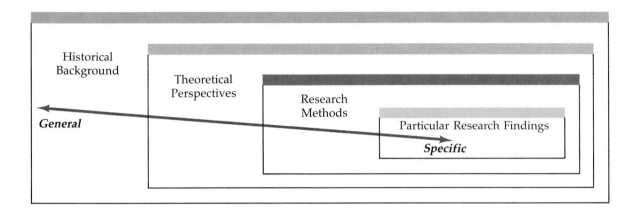

STUDY QUESTIONS

What are the essential properties of language?

How is language acquired?

Is language unique to humans?

How do we solve problems, form concepts, and reason inductively and deductively?

What obstacles do we face in solving problems and making decisions?

Does language influence the way we think?

HISTORICAL BACKGROUND

1. Scholarly interest in language began in the nineteenth century as scientists traveled to unexplored lands. Early psychologists were not generally interested in language, however. The few studies they conducted focused on vocabulary growth in school children.

2. In 1957, B. F. Skinner argued that language is acquired through operant conditioning. Linguist Noam Chomsky countered that humans are biologically predisposed to learn language without any special training. Chomsky's views sparked research in the new field of psycholinguistics.

3. Unlike language, thinking has been actively studied since Wundt first opened his lab. In the 1920s, John B. Watson mistakenly defined thinking as subvocal speech.

4. Research on artificial intelligence began in the 1950s when computer programs were written to perform intelligent actions. An early program called the General Problem Solver showed that computers could solve a wide range of problems formerly thought to require human intelligence.

MODERN THEORETICAL PERSPECTIVES

1. Theories of language acquisition differ on the relative importance of heredity and environment. **Behaviorist** theories that emphasize the environment hold that language is learned through operant conditioning and social imitation. The **nativist** approach holds that people are biologically structured to discover the rules of their language and produce comprehensible speech.

2. According to the **linguistic relativity hypothesis,** language determines perception and thought. People who speak one language will have different perceptions and thoughts than people who speak a different language. There is no support for this idea.

■■■■■■■■ RESEARCH METHODS

1. **Experimentation** was frequently used to study language and thought. For example, Shepard and Metzler (1971) conducted an experiment on visual imagery to measure the time needed to rotate block figures mentally. Gick and Holyoak (1980) showed how verbal analogies help people solve conceptually similar problems. And Rosch (1973) performed an experiment to see if the Dani perceive differences in color the same way that English speakers do.

2. **Case studies** showed how language acquisition in such children as Isabelle and Genii was hampered by social isolation (Brown, 1958; Curtiss, 1980).

3. **Naturalistic observation** of bees revealed how they communicate the location of nectar (von Frisch, 1974), while naturalistic observation of infants showed a progression in vocalizations from babbling to one-word and two-word utterances (Nelson, 1973).

■■■■■■■■ RESEARCH FINDINGS
AND SUMMARY

1. **Language** is a means of symbolic communication that is based on gestures, sounds, and written symbols.

2. Speech sounds used to distinguish one word from another are called **phonemes.** The smallest language units that possess meaning are called **morphemes.**

3. Children all over the world acquire language in the same way. They listen to sounds, babble, gradually emit speech sounds found in their environment, use gestures and single words, and finally generate increasingly complex sentences.

4. Research indicates that language is not normally acquired by operant conditioning or so-cial imitation. Humans may be biologically predisposed to learn language in a social context for the purpose of communication. Without this social context, language does not develop normally.

5. Attempts to teach chimpanzees to speak have been a failure. However, chimpanzees can learn to use symbols and communicate by **American Sign Language.** This work is still controversial, and it is not yet determined whether the true use of language is unique to humans.

6. **Thinking** is the mental manipulation of symbols that represent objects, events, or ideas.

7. Research has shown that problem solving is facilitated by the use of step-by-step procedures called **algorithms** and mental shortcuts called **heuristics.** Effective heuristics include **means–ends analyses, working backward,** and **using analogies.**

8. Problem solving can be hampered by an inappropriate **mental set** or by **functional fixedness,** the failure to see new uses for common objects.

9. **Artificial intelligence** involves the use of computer programs to perform tasks normally done by the human mind. Specialized programs for solving problems are called **expert systems.**

10. **Reasoning** involves drawing conclusions from known facts. Studies of **concept identification** indicate that we learn concepts by generating and testing **hypotheses.** We use **inductive reasoning** when we discover general rules or concepts from specific experiences. We use **deductive reasoning** when we draw conclusions about specific experiences from general rules.

11. We exhibit **cognitive bias** when we use such heuristics as the **representativeness heuristic** and the **availability heuristic** inappropriately.

12. The **linguistic relativity hypothesis** has not been supported by research. Language does not direct thought; it reflects those aspects of a culture that people find important.

ADDITIONAL READINGS _____

Anderson, J. R. 1990. *Cognitive psychology and its implications,* 3rd ed. New York: Freeman. A sophisticated overview of cognitive psychology with an emphasis on relating research findings to everyday living.

Carroll, D. W. 1986. *Psychology of language.* Monterey, CA: Brooks/Cole. A basic book on psycholinguistics that is well-written and full of everyday examples and applications. A good source of information for papers.

Finke, R. 1990. *Creative imagery: Discoveries and inventions in visualization.* Hillsdale, NJ: Erlbaum. This book shows how research on visual imagery can provide techniques to enhance creative discovery and thinking.

Gardner, H. 1985. *The mind's new science: A history of the cognitive revolution.* New York: Basic Books. This book provides the first full-scale history of cognitive science. It provides an in-depth account of how scholars and researchers from varied disciplines came together to forge a new approach to the study of mind.

Halpern, D. F. 1989. *Thought and knowledge,* 2nd ed. Hillsdale, NJ: Erlbaum. A comprehensive, well-planned overview of human cognition. An excellent source of basic information.

Martindale, C. 1991. *Cognitive psychology: A neural-network approach.* Pacific Grove, CA: Brooks/Cole. A clearly written book that shows how psychologists study cognitive processes from a connectionist perspective. This book does a good job of explaining neural networks in a nontechnical way.

Osherson, D. N., and Lasnik, H., eds. 1990. *Language: An invitation to cognitive science* (Vol. 1). Cambridge, MA: The MIT Press. Leading cognitive scientists describe their research on a wide range of topics in the general field of language.

Winston, P. H. 1984. *Artificial intelligence,* 2nd ed. Reading, MA: Addison-Wesley. A clear, concise introduction in the field of artificial intelligence.

INTELLIGENCE

I ntelligence—one of the most important ways by which we judge one another—is a powerful and emotive issue for parents, teachers, employers, and even politicians. But what exactly is intelligence? How is it formed? How much of it is related to hereditary factors, and how much to social ones? And, most important of all, can we develop an objective, scientific way of measuring this aspect of ourselves?

(Hans Eysenck and Leon Kamin, 1981)

Chapter Outline

Our opening quotation sets forth the major issues for this chapter. Hans Eysenck and Leon Kamin (1981) ask how intelligence is defined, whether it is influenced more by heredity or environment, and how it is measured. At the start of the twentieth century no one had answers to these questions. Today we are well on our way toward providing satisfactory responses. To see why these questions have been so difficult to answer, consider each one briefly in turn.

HOW IS INTELLIGENCE DEFINED?

Offhand, you might think it easy to define intelligence. For example, think of two classmates you know reasonably well. Which one is more intelligent? Answering this question is probably easy for you. A more troublesome question might be: What do you mean by intelligence? Although we feel certain that one person is smarter than another, we may have difficulty explaining the basis for our decision. The problem, as we will see in this chapter, is that intelligence is a "fuzzy" concept; we all have a rough idea what it is, but the specifics are hard to pin down.

In 1921, 14 experts in the field were asked to define intelligence. Each gave a slightly different definition. Some experts focused on abstract thinking ability, others on the ability to adapt to new situations, others on the ability to profit from experience, and still others emphasized the sheer capacity for knowledge. Indeed, some have suggested that there may be as many definitions of intelligence as there are experts to define it. Defining intelligence is difficult because we want to describe those mental abilities that enable us to do such varied tasks as crack an atom, write a poem, or invent an electric lightbulb. These tasks are so varied that we cannot describe the underlying mental abilities in only a few words. Consequently, there is no simple definition of intelligence that is completely satisfactory. But, as we will see in this chapter, if we consider the various definitions from experts in the field, there are a number of common themes (Sternberg, 1986; 1990). Therefore, we will define **intelligence** broadly as a collection of mental abilities that enable us to learn from experience, to adapt to our changing environment, to work in a goal-directed manner, and to solve problems and think creatively.

IS INTELLIGENCE INFLUENCED MORE BY HEREDITY OR ENVIRONMENT?

In light of the importance of intelligence, it is not surprising that countless hours of research and inquiry have been devoted to intelligence and intelligence tests. Since at least the times of Plato and Aristotle, people have asked: What is the nature of intelligence? Why do people vary so greatly in intellectual capacity? How can we raise more intelligent children? These questions concern the relative roles of heredity and environment and they have major implications for everyday life. Consider the following news stories:

A controversial Escondido sperm bank for superbrains has produced its first baby—a healthy, 9-pound girl born to a woman identified only as a small-town resident. . . . Founded by inventor Robert K. Graham . . . the facility contains sperm donated by at least three Nobel Prize winners, plus other prominent researchers. . . . The sperm bank was founded to breed children of higher intelligence. The goal has been denounced by many critics, who say that a child's intelligence is not determined so much by his genes as by his upbringing and environment. (*Los Angeles Times*, May 25, 1982)

Becky Swanston frequently taps out notes on a pure-pitch xylophone for her daughter Kelly, age 9 ½ months, and plays classical music for her "all the time." . . . Melanie Petropolous shows oversized flashcards to her son Tommy, age 3, with bits of information ranging from the names of different birds to the parts of a plant. . . . Karen Garber flashes cards with words, shapes, and colors at her son Nicholas, who will be 3 in June and who can count to 10 and identify shapes and colors. . . . The three mothers are among the graduates of a . . . weeklong course offered by a Philadelphia organization called the Better Baby Institute entitled "How to Multiply Your Baby's Intelligence," designed to teach parents how to make their infants, toddlers, and preschoolers smarter. (*Los Angeles Times*, (May 1, 1983)

(Kail and Pellegrino, 1985)

Is intelligence largely inherited, as the founder of the California sperm bank would have us believe? Or is intelligence more the result of early experience in a stimulating environment, as the Better Baby Institute suggests to its clients? Proponents for both views can still be found. However, we will see in this chapter that intelligence is actually the result of the joint effects of heredity and environment. Both have major effects on intelligence.

HOW IS INTELLIGENCE MEASURED?

To measure intelligence objectively, psychologists have had to devise proper tests. We will describe some of the major tests in the sections that follow and show how they have changed over time. One of the things we will show is that intelligence tests are likely to be useful only in the particular culture for which they were designed. It is difficult to apply Western notions of intelligence and mental measurement to people from other cultures because these people have different conceptions of intelligence. Thus, how intelligence is measured is intimately related to how it is orginally defined.

Curiously, the study and measurement of intelligence is one of psychology's most impressive contributions to modern society. Intelligence tests are used in business and education to make decisions about which people will most likely benefit by additional training or schooling. However, no other aspect of psychology is as misunderstood by the general public as intelligence (Kail and Pellegrino, 1985). Before we can understand the controversy that often surrounds this field, we need to trace its historical roots to see how intelligence tests were devised and what purpose they were intended to serve. After completing this historical review we will return to our three main issues and discuss them in greater detail.

HISTORICAL BACKGROUND:
The Origins of Intelligence Testing

The history of intelligence testing can best be seen in the history of our attempts to measure mental abilities and competence. The use of tests to assess competence has an ancient history. More than 2,000 years ago, Chinese emperors used an early version of a civil service test in which they examined their officials every three years to determine their competence to remain in office (Bowman, 1989). In the early 1800s, these testing procedures were observed by British diplomats and missionaries who used them to found the British civil service tests. The modern American civil service exams follow in this ancient tradition. Other examination systems also predate the contemporary intelligence testing movement by centuries. For example, university examinations were being conducted at the University of Bologna, Italy, as far back as 1219 A.D. By the middle of the nineteenth century, written examinations were being used throughout Europe and the United States to decide who should be awarded college degrees, who should serve in government positions, and who should be allowed to practice medicine or law (Dubois, 1970).

Much of this early testing was more concerned with **achievement** than **aptitude**. Both types of tests assess an individual's current status, but achievement tests are designed to measure what a person can do at present (what level he or she has already achieved), while aptitude tests attempt to predict what a person could potentially accomplish (what he or she is apt to do in the future). Any standardized exam on a school subject such as history or math is an achievement test. An aptitude test, on the other hand, tries to measure the potential for success. We will see that intelligence tests were devised to measure "scholastic aptitude," a person's potential for intellectual success. The idea of aptitude testing took hold when British biologist and statistician Sir Francis Galton (1822–1911) first called attention to the possibility that intelligence could be measured.

Sir Francis Galton

The concept of intelligence as a general mental faculty goes back at least to Aristotle, but Galton is credited with the idea that differences in in-

Oedipus and the sphinx. Ancients often used riddles to assess intelligence. In this fifth century B.C. Greek painting, a sphinx asks Oedipus, "What animal walks on four legs in the morning, two at noon, three in the evening?" Oedipus answers "Man" (a baby crawls, an adult walks, and an old person uses a cane). For the correct response, Oedipus was made the King of Thebes.

telligence are hereditary (Miller, 1984). Like his distant cousin Charles Darwin, Galton was concerned with the study of differences between species and differences between members of the same species. In his 1869 book, *Hereditary Genius,* Galton observed that sons of distinguished judges often became distinguished themselves, and he concluded that "eminence" ran in families. Unfortunately, Galton ignored the fact that wealth, leisure, and excellent educations also helped further the course of the careers of distinguished people of his day (Hilgard, 1987).

In the tradition of John Locke and the British empiricist philosophers, Galton believed that knowledge enters the mind through the senses. Therefore, he reasoned, individual differences in intelligence may be due to individual differences in sensory responses. To test this idea, Galton established a laboratory in London in 1884 in which, for a small fee, he measured the visual and auditory acuity and the speed of reaction of over 10,000 people. He found nothing of lasting importance, but he did pioneer the study of **individual differences,** the study of psychological differences between individuals and between groups.

Alfred Binet

Instead of looking for differences in sensory abilities as Galton had done, European psychologists in the late nineteenth century looked at more complex cognitive functions, including attention, sentence comprehension, and memory. Foremost among this group was French psychologist Alfred Binet (1857–1911). Binet had been studying different ways of measuring children's mental abilities for several years, and by 1903 he completed an intensive study of the intellectual development of his two daughters. Based on this early work, Binet was commissioned by the French Minister of Public Education to devise a test to identify children likely to have difficulty in school. The goal was to find those children early in their academic careers and provide them with special education before they experienced a long series of failures.

Before Binet, a child had been judged as below average in intelligence on the basis of the subjective, often biased, evaluations of teachers. With the help of Theodore Simon, a physician who worked with these children, Binet set out to construct an objective test of intelligence. He put together a collection of diverse tasks and administered them to children between the ages of three and 15. Binet sorted through the exercises, identifying only those tasks that distinguished bright from dull children or old from young chil-

Alfred Binet. A pioneer in the study of individual differences, Binet introduced the idea of intelligence testing that became widespread in Europe and the United States. Together with Theodore Simon, he developed the first scale for measuring intelligence.

dren, and then he arranged the tasks in order of increasing difficulty. The result, in 1905, was a collection of 30 tasks known as the *Metrical Scale of Intelligence*—the first useful intelligence test of its type (Miller, 1984).

Revisions of the scale in 1908 and 1911 grouped the tasks according to the age at which 50 to 75 percent of the children passed each task. Table 9.1 shows examples of the different tasks that were used for several age groups. Each task was designed to reflect the performance of an average child of a given *chronological age*, the actual age of a child. For example, average three-year-olds could point to their eyes or nose, while average 15-year-olds could repeat a sequence of seven digits (7, 3, 4, 1, 9, 2, 8, for example). Thus, each series of tasks reflected a particular "mental level," defined as the age level at which the majority of the children could successfully complete the tasks.

Binet's establishment of the age levels for various tasks was important because it permitted him to derive a score known as the *mental age* for each child. The mental age is the age level associated with the last set of tasks the child can successfully complete. Thus, a six-year-old who successfully completed all of the eight-year-old tasks but began failing the nine-year-old tasks would have a mental age of eight years. Children whose mental age exceeded their chronological age by two or more years were called "advanced," while those whose mental age was two or more years less than their chronological age were labeled "retarded" (Reisman, 1976). This was Binet's objective procedure for identifying intellectually impaired school children in France. By pointing out areas of performance where special education might lead to improvement, Binet's practical approach to intelligence was clearly different from that of Galton, who viewed intelligence as fixed and innate.

Shortly after Binet's death, a German psychologist named William Stern noted that a four-year-old child with a mental age of two and a 10-year-old child with a mental age of eight would be judged to have equal degrees of retardation—two years—by Binet's method of scoring. Since the younger child appears more retarded than the older (for the younger child, the mental age is half the chronological age), Stern recommended dividing each child's mental age by his or her chronological age to produce a *mental quotient*.

Lewis Terman

In 1916, psychologist Lewis Terman of Stanford University revised Binet's test and translated it into English. He also adopted Stern's mental quo-

TABLE 9.1 Examples of Different Age-Related Tasks from Binet's 1911 Intelligence Test

Age of Child	Task to be Performed
3	Point to body parts such as eyes, nose, and mouth. Repeat 2 digits. Repeat a sentence of 6 syllables (The girl ran up the hill). Identify common objects in a picture.
7	Understand the difference between left and right. Describe a picture. Count the value of six coins. Carry out three commands given in sequence (Clap your hands, hop forward, and touch your nose).
15	Find three rhymes for a word in one minute. Repeat seven digits. Repeat a sentence of 26 syllables (The young gentleman helped the old woman carry her belongings up the steep staircase to her room last night). Interpret a set of facts.

tient with one slight modification. Terman multiplied the quotient by 100 to eliminate the decimal point. This change gave us the formula for the familiar **intelligence quotient** or **IQ:**

$$IQ = \frac{Mental\ Age}{Chronological\ Age} \times 100$$

The formula produces an IQ score of 100 for a child of any age if the child's mental and chronological ages are equal (for example, IQ = [10 ÷ 10] × 100 = 100). Thus, the IQ score of 100, which represents average intelligence, is simply a function of the procedure used to obtain the score. This same procedure produces an IQ score of less than 100 if the mental age is less than the chronological age (IQ = [8 ÷ 10] × 100 = 80), indicating below-average intelligence, and a score greater than 100 if the mental age is greater than the chronological age (IQ = [12 ÷ 10] × 100 = 120), indicating above-average intelligence.

Terman's revision of Binet's test was called the *Stanford-Binet Intelligence Scale* in honor of Stanford University, where Terman worked, and Alfred Binet. It became the model for tests of mental abil-

ity. Terman established age norms for the various tasks with American children, and he later added items to measure the intelligence of adults. This last feature turned out to have important consequences for the intelligence testing movement. With the entry of the United States into World War I in 1917, the Army called on leading psychologists to devise a test for selecting competent leaders from among its vast number of recruits. The Army had little time for a test like the Stanford-Binet, which is given to one person at a time and takes over an hour to complete. So Terman and fellow psychologists Robert Yerkes and Edward Thorndike constructed a pencil-and-paper intelligence test that could be administered quickly and efficiently to groups. This test, called the Army Alpha, along with a pantomime version for illiterate or non-English-speaking soldiers, the Army Beta, was given to over 1,750,000 men between 1917 and 1919 (Hilgard, 1987). The Army's experience with testing led to a growing acceptance by the American public of the use of intelligence tests in a wide variety of settings.

Our review of the intelligence test movement would not be complete without noting a particularly painful instance of abuse. In 1882, Congress passed a law forbidding "lunatics" and "idiots" entry into the United States. During the massive wave of immigration that occurred between 1905 and 1914 over 10 million people came to America, sometimes more than 10,000 a day. Selection of the mentally defective became a major concern. To select these people for deportation, psychologist Henry Goddard was commissioned to devise an appropriate testing procedure. His completed test included items like the following: *unfair test*

What is Crisco?
Who is Christy Matthewson?

Not surprisingly, many immigrants failed. After all, as David Hothersall (1984) wrote, how many Hungarians used Crisco or followed the exploits of the star pitcher of the New York Giants? Goddard (1917) argued differently, however. On the basis of his tests, he believed that 83 percent of the Jews, 80 percent of the Hungarians, 79 percent of the Italians, and 87 percent of the Russians (to name just a few) were mentally defective. These findings were later used as part of the "scientific justification" for restrictive immigration quotas. Nearly three-quarters of a century later, the idea of measuring intelligence by mental tests has now been accepted as routine, but the intelligence test movement remains controversial (Hothersall, 1984; Miller, 1984). ■

MEASURING INTELLIGENCE

Today, more than a million Americans take some form of intelligence test each year. What do these tests measure and is this measure an accurate indicator of intelligence? The answers to these questions are hard to come by, partly because intelligence is difficult to define and also because accuracy is similarly tricky. It is probably best to begin our coverage of intelligence by surveying the most commonly used tests. Then we can examine what they seem to measure and how consistent the results of these tests are among many people. This will provide a solid foundation for understanding how intelligence is defined.

MODERN INTELLIGENCE TESTS

There are several different intelligence tests that are fairly widely used today in the United States. These tests include the Stanford-Binet Scale, the Wechsler Scales for Adults and Children, and such various group tests as the Scholastic Aptitude Test. We will describe them in this section before we discuss the criteria by which all mental tests are judged.

THE STANFORD-BINET INTELLIGENCE SCALE

The Stanford-Binet has been revised four times since it was first published by Terman. Changes in language usage and technology require updating of the test every 15 to 20 years. For example, in the 1937 revision 69 percent of the three-year-olds tested could name five drawings of common objects correctly. By the 1950s, only 11 percent of this age group could do as well on this task. Had children become less intelligent? No. The problem was that such common objects as telephones and stoves had changed dramatically over the years. Telephones lost their hand cranks and stoves lost their large exhaust pipes. To keep abreast of these changes, the test makers made periodic revisions (Terman and Merrill, 1972).

Before the 1986 revision, all test items contributed equally to the calculation of the total Stanford-Binet IQ score. Thus, if a child did well on the verbal items but had difficulty with the numerical problems, the total IQ score would not reflect this child's special strengths and weaknesses. Today, the Stanford-Binet has four major tests of intellectual ability, with separate IQ measures for each. These tests measure verbal reasoning, quantitative reasoning, abstract–visual reasoning, and short-term memory. Table 9.2 shows examples of the types of tasks by which the Stanford-Binet test measures these abilities.

Since the 1986 revision of the Stanford-Binet, IQ scores are no longer obtained by dividing mental age by chronological age. If you took the Stanford-Binet today, you would be asked questions appropriate to different age levels and get points for each correct response (Thorndike et al., 1986). The tester would sum your points and check a table that shows how other people your age performed on the same questions. The average score of other people is assigned an IQ score of 100. Scores lower or higher than the average score are assigned different IQ values based on how much they deviate from the average of your age group. Psychologists have found that the distribution of IQ scores approximates the form of a **normal curve** (a symmetrical, bell-shaped frequency distribution described in the Statistics Appendix). A normal distribution is found for many characteristics of people, characteristics such as differences in height.

Figure 9.1 shows the distribution of IQ scores that was obtained from a large number of people who took the 1937 revision of the Stanford-Binet. Most IQs are clustered around the average score of 100, with the number of scores in each "tail" decreasing to fewer and fewer cases. Also shown in Figure 9.1 are the descriptive adjectives assigned by psychologists to different areas of the distribution. Scores between 90 and 110 are labeled "normal," those above 130 are "very superior," and those below 70 are "retarded." In each instance, a person's IQ score reflects a *relative* standing within the entire distribution of IQ scores for people of the same age. Consequently, people will always have an IQ of 100 if their performances are average for their age level.

THE WECHSLER INTELLIGENCE SCALES

One of the first tests to measure verbal and performance skills separately was produced by psychologist David Wechsler in 1939. Wechsler worked at Bellevue Hospital in New York and was responsible for assessing a variety of patients ranging from alcoholics and drug addicts to mentally retarded people and normal people in trouble. He originally developed his test because he felt that the Stanford-Binet available at the time relied too heavily on verbal material and was not appropriate for adults. His test, which came to be known as the *Wechsler Adult Intelligence Scale* or *WAIS* (1939, 1955, 1981), contains a verbal subscale and a nonverbal performance subscale to provide separate IQ scores as well as a total IQ. These same sub-

TABLE 9.2   Description of the 1986 Stanford-Binet Intelligence Test

ORGANIZATION OF TESTS BY CONTENT AREAS

4 Content Areas	Verbal Reasoning	Abstract/Visual Reasoning	Quantitative Reasoning	Short-Term Memory
15 Individual Tests	Vocabulary	Pattern Analysis	Quantitative	Bead Memory
	Comprehension	Copying	Number Series	Memory for Sentences
	Absurdities	Matrices	Equation Building	Memory for Digits
	Verbal Relations	Paper Folding & Cutting		Memory for Objects

EXAMPLES OF ITEMS

Vocabulary   Define words like train, wrench, letter, error, and encourage.

Comprehension   Answer questions like, "Why should people brush their teeth?" "Why should people be quiet in a library?" "What is one advantage and one disadvantage of living in a small town instead of a big city?"

Absurdities   Identify the mistakes or "silly" aspects of pictures in which, for example, a man is shown using the wrong end of a rake or a girl is shown putting a piece of clothing on incorrectly.

Copying   Arrange a set of blocks to match different designs; draw designs like those shown in pictures.

Memory for Objects   Choose the right order in which a series of pictures were presented.

Number Series   Determine which numbers come next in a series of numbers such as the following—32, 26, 20, 14, __, __.

Verbal Relations   Indicate how three objects or words are alike but different from a fourth. For example, how are dog, cat, horse alike, but different from boy.

Bead Memory   Arrange different colored and shaped beads to match pictures of the beads organized in different layouts.

From Nietzel et al. (1991).

scales are present in tests for all age groups, a feature not present in the Stanford-Binet. Table 9.3 shows sample verbal and performance tasks from the WAIS. Similar tests for children were developed by Wechsler later. The *Wechsler Intelligence Scale for Children (WISC)* measures IQ in children aged seven to 16, and the *Wechsler Preschool and Primary Scale of Intelligence (WPPSI)* is for children aged four to six-and-a-half. As with the Stanford-Binet, the Wechsler Tests are periodically revised, and each is individually administered; that is, a specially trained examiner presents items to one examinee at a time.

GROUP TESTS

Both the Stanford-Binet and all three Wechsler tests are administered individually. Other mental tests can be administered to a large number of people at one time. Examples of these group-administered tests include the familiar *Scholastic Aptitude Test (SAT)* and the achievement-oriented *Graduate Record Exam (GRE)*. These tests have the advantage of being less costly and more time-efficient to administer than are individually administered tests. For example, the armed services uses a variety of group tests, including the *Armed Services Vocational Aptitude Battery (ASVAB)*, to select

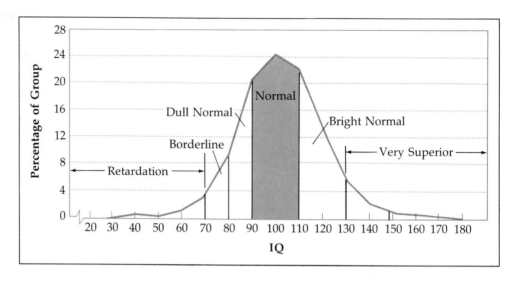

FIGURE 9.1   The distribution of IQ scores from the 1937 revision of the Stanford-Binet. For any large sample of people, the IQ scores will approximate a normal distribution, with an average score of 100. Also shown in the figure are the adjectives used to describe various levels of IQ.

people with special skills to be trained as cooks, pilots, and computer technicians. On the negative side, group-administered tests generally provide less detailed information about each examinee than do individually administered tests. In an individually administered test such as the Stanford-Binet, the examiner can determine whether the examinee understands each question and appears to be trying to answer it. This sort of information may be important for diagnostic purposes. These features cannot be assessed in group-administered tests.

CULTURE-REDUCED TESTS

Ideally, a person's performance on an intelligence test should not be influenced by his or her cultural background. As we noted in the Historical Background section at the beginning of this chapter, early intelligence tests were strongly biased toward verbal material, and some required familiarity with a particular language. But even when people were familiar with a test's language, differences in social background could lead to differences in performance. For example, select the word that does not belong with the others in the following set: [HARP, DRUM, CELLO, VIOLIN, GUITAR]. Children from upper- and middle-class homes typically select the correct item—DRUM; children from lower-class homes tend to select the unfamiliar word CELLO (Eells et al., 1951). Even nonverbal performance can be effected by a person's background. In tasks where children must recognize elements missing from common objects, children from poor families, for example, may not

recognize that there is anything wrong with a comb with several missing teeth (Hewitt and Massey, 1969). Tests such as the Raven Progressive Matrices Test, shown in Figure 9.2, are designed to be culture-reduced.

In general culture-reduced tests have not been as successful as conventional intelligence tests in predicting performance at school. The reason is that the very abilities responsible for good performance at school are often themselves culture-dependent. In our society, school success requires verbal and numerical skills, so tests that measure these skills predict success.

In summary, many different kinds of intelligence tests are available. Some test people individually, some test people in groups. Some test a variety of mental abilities to arrive at an overall measure of intelligence, others test for a particular aptitude or skill. Some tests are for children, and others are for adults. However, each test has certain qualities that make it a valuable tool.

IMPORTANT CRITERIA FOR USEFUL TESTS

If you are like most people you have taken many tests in your lifetime and are likely to take even more. You have taken general achievement tests, intelligence tests, and probably a college admissions test such as the SAT. After college, you can expect more tests if you plan on going to graduate or professional school. When your education is completed, still more tests await you if you wish to obtain a license to practice certain professions, in-

Table 9.3 Simulated Test Items from the Wechsler Adult Intelligence Scale

General Information

1. How many wings does a bird have?
2. How many nickels make a dime?
3. What is steam made of?
4. Who wrote "Tom Sawyer"?
5. What is pepper?

General Comprehension

1. What should you do if you see someone forget his book when he leaves a restaurant?
2. What is the advantage of keeping money in a bank?
3. Why is copper often used in electrical wires?

Arithmetic

1. Sam had three pieces of candy and Joe gave him four more. How many pieces of candy did Sam have altogether?
2. Three women divided eighteen golf balls equally among themselves. How many golf balls did each person receive?
3. If two buttons cost 15¢, what will be the cost of a dozen buttons?

Similarities

1. In what way are a lion and a tiger alike?
2. In what way are a saw and a hammer alike?
3. In what way are an hour and a week alike?
4. In what way are a circle and a triangle alike?

Vocabulary

This test consists simply of asking, "What is a _____?" or "What does _____ mean?" The words cover a wide range of difficulty.

Performance Tests

In addition to verbal tasks of the kinds illustrated above, there are a number of performance tasks involving the use of blocks, cut-out figures, paper and pencil puzzles, etc.

cluding medicine or law. For these various tests to be useful they must measure what they intend to measure, and they must measure it accurately. To accomplish these goals, tests must meet three criteria: they must be **standardized, reliable,** and **valid.**

STANDARDIZATION

There are several different features of a standardized test. First, standardized tests are administered under *uniform conditions.* By uniform conditions we mean that the test is administered in a similar manner no matter where, when, to whom, or by whom it is given. Second, standardized tests are *scored objectively.* This means that procedures for scoring the test are specified in detail so that any two trained scorers will arrive at the same score for the same set of responses. Thus, questions to which answers require subjective evaluation (for example, essay questions) generally are not included in standardized tests. Finally, standardized tests are designed to measure relative performance, not absolute ability, on a task. To measure relative performance, standardized tests are interpreted with reference to a comparable group of people, the **standardization sample.**

To illustrate the importance of the standardization sample, imagine that you were told that a 10-year-old received a score of 50 on a standardized achievement test. What would you infer about the child's ability? Suppose that you were told that the highest possible score on the test was 100. By some standards, the child would have failed to demonstrate mastery of the material covered on the test. However, what would you think if the rest of her class—in this case, the standardization sample—received an average grade of 53? Now the child does not seem to have

FIGURE 9.2 An item from the Raven Progressive Matrices Test. Complete the pattern by selecting the correct alternative. Items vary in difficulty depending on pattern complexity and the similarity among the alternative choices. This test is designed to be less dependent on a person's language and cultural background than traditional intelligence tests.

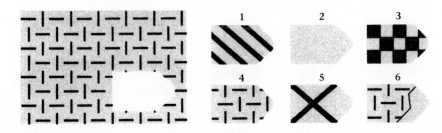

Measuring intelligence in school. Conventional intelligence tests predict performance in school because they measure the verbal and numerical skills needed for success at school. However, these skills can be culture-dependent. Children from varying cultures may do poorly on conventional tests because they lack familiarity with these skills. For these children, intelligence is more adequately measured by using a culture-reduced test.

done too poorly, even though she only got half of the total possible points. Suppose further that the test was a final examination given in a second-semester college calculus course. Now the 10-year-old appears to be quite remarkable. The point of these examples is that a score on a standardized test always reflects a *relative* estimate of ability. It tells us how someone did relative to other people.

Binet's original test was standardized on only 300 children. The 1937 revision of the Stanford-Binet was standardized on 3,000 native-born white Americans. Today, intelligence tests use thousands of people to represent the target population in terms of such variables as age, race, education, geographic location, and other factors that might be related to test performance. An individual's intelligence score is then interpreted with reference to this larger group.

Curiously, each successive standardization sample of people who have taken the Stanford-Binet has scored higher than the preceding sample. Similar increases in the level of performance from one generation to the next have been found with other intelligence tests on a world-wide level (Flynn, 1984; 1987). Although the specific causes for these increases in test performance have not yet been determined, they may reflect general increases in literacy and education. However, because each person's score is calculated in relation to the standardization sample for his or her age group, an average IQ (whatever the absolute level of performance for that group) still has a score of 100.

RELIABILITY

must be consistent

In order to have confidence in a test, we expect repeated measurements to be consistent. Good tests yield consistent results and, therefore, demonstrate **reliability.** For example, imagine that you step on a scale and it indicates that you weigh 10 pounds more than you did last week. You are disappointed because you have been exercising, and you are certain that you have not gained weight. You step off the scale in disgust, and then, on a whim, you get back on it. This time the scale says that you weigh five pounds less than you did last week. You get off and then on the scale again, and this time it indicates that you weigh the same as you did last week. Think about what just happened. Your scale did not give a consistent measurement of your weight across repeated attempts. Think also about your reaction. Would you have confidence in any of the weights you read from the scale? This same concern applies to the measurement of intelligence.

We expect to obtain approximately the same score on an intelligence test if we repeat the test a short time later. If the test does not consistently measure our responses, the test lacks reliability. Of course, it is possible that such extraneous factors as changes in motivations, fatigue, measurement error, or learning and maturation (if the time between tests is long) could make test scores variable and, thus, less reliable. However, intelligence tests in use today have reliability coefficients (statistical measures of a test's consistency of measurement) as high as +.90. The high reliability in this instance means that 95 percent of the people who take the same test a second time will have scores within plus or minus five points of their original scores (Anastasi, 1982). (See the Statistics Appendix for a fuller explanation of reliability coefficients.)

VALIDITY

Even if a test is reliable, it may not be a valid assessment of intelligence. **Validity** refers to the extent to which a test measures what it is supposed to measure. For example, imagine that there is a new test of intelligence that is quick, easy to administer, and highly reliable. All you have to do is write down your age, your mother's maiden name, and your height. If you do this several times, you will, undoubtedly, give the same answers each time. However, you will probably complain that the test does not measure intelligence. In this example, the test is reliable but not valid.

There are different types of validity. One type, **construct validity,** refers to the extent to which a test measures a particular psychological process. In the case of intelligence, we would want to know whether a test is really a measure of "intelligence." One criterion for assessing construct validity is age differentiation. Scores on such tests as the Stanford-Binet are expected to increase with chronological age during childhood. If test scores fail to increase, the test is probably not a valid measure of intelligence. On the other hand, merely showing an increase in scores with age does not prove that the test measures intelligence. Construct validity is difficult to determine for intelligence tests because not all test-makers agree on a single theory or definition of intelligence (Cronbach, 1984).

However, most widely used intelligence tests have very good **concurrent** and **predictive validity.** Concurrent validity refers to the degree of agreement between different types of measures given at the same time. These measures might be IQ scores on different tests, teacher ratings, peer ratings, and so on. For example, the correlation between scores for children on the Stanford-Binet and the WISC is approximately +.94. This measure shows very high agreement of scores on both tests. Psychologist Arthur Jensen (1980) reviewed 47 studies of concurrent validity and found that correlations extended from +.43 to +.94 between different intelligence tests, with a mean correlation of +.80. These correlations indicate that all of the tests are measuring something similar. Presumably, they measure intelligence.

Predictive validity is determined by the extent to which intelligence test scores predict other measures of academic success or capability. Remember that Binet originally developed his intelligence test to predict performance in school, and indications are that he was successful. Predictive validity of most intelligence tests is quite good and is perhaps the strongest evidence for the validity and usefulness of the tests. Intelligence test scores correlate highly with academic achievement. The correlations are approximately +.60 to +.70 during grammar school and +.40 to +.50 during high school. These correlations indicate several things. First, predictive validity decreases as children get older. This suggests that with increasing age a variety of factors beside intelligence (motivational levels, career objectives, and health, for example) affect scholastic achievement. Second, at all age levels, the correlations indicate that, in general, individuals who perform better on tests of intelligence are more likely to perform better in school than are those who perform poorly. But the correlation is not perfect, and there will be children who perform extremely well on tests of intelligence but do poorly in school and children who do just the opposite. It is neither fair nor reasonable to make predictions for individual children based solely on intelligence test scores.

For many high school students, the predictive validity of tests such as the SAT or its equivalent, the ACT (American College Testing program), has a bearing on whether these students will be admitted to college. Admissions officers use these test scores to help them make decisions about college applications because research has shown that test scores on the SAT correlate positively with first year college grades. The correlation is approximately +.38 for the verbal portion of the SAT and college grades and +.35 for the math portion (Linn, 1982). Since people who score low on the SAT generally do not attend college, these correlations are based on a restricted range of SAT scores. The result is an underestimation of the relation between SAT scores and college grades. If everyone who took the SAT actually entered college, these correlations would be approximately +.50, about the same as the correlation between high school grades and college grades (Anastasi, 1982).

Currently, there is a controversy over the use of these tests in admissions decisions. Some claim that SAT scores can be raised by taking special courses or by taking the test on several occasions. This is a potential problem because the SAT is supposed to be an aptitude test (the Scholastic Aptitude Test) that measures the potential for academic success. If students can in effect "cheat," raising their scores through coaching or by taking the test several times, the SAT would be measuring other factors than academic potential. This would provide an unfair advantage to those people who could afford to pay for coaching or for taking the test more than once. Such ploys are largely ineffective, however. Taking the SAT more than once is unlikely to have a major effect on your performance unless the score from the first test was artifically lowered by illness or some other particular event. Moreover, preparatory courses for the SAT are also unlikely to influence performance greatly unless you are grossly unfamiliar with taking standardized tests (Carroll, 1982; Messick, 1980). Coaching can make you more familiar with a test, it can reacquaint you with certain subjects (mathematics, for example), and it can offer help on strategies for guessing. For example, the most obvious answer is usually correct for the initial questions on a test but usually incorrect for the final questions. However, you can become familiar with the SAT by studying the sample test material that is provided when you register, and you can brush up on math on your own. Coaching does not provide much more. One study showed that 30 hours of coaching in verbal skills resulted in an average gain of only 14 points on the verbal portion of the SAT. Similar coaching in math produced only about a 26 point gain in the SAT's math section. The average total gain of 20 to 30 points after 60 hours of coaching is negligible (combined verbal and math SAT scores range from 400 to 1600) and would probably not influence the decision of an admissions committee (Kulik, Baugert-Downs, and Kulik, 1984; Messick and Jungeblut, 1981). For students with a normal high school education, short preparatory courses for the SAT are probably a waste of money and time.

STABILITY OF INTELLIGENCE SCORES

Does a person's intelligence change with age or is intelligence a stable characteristic? If intelligence is a stable characteristic, then a person should achieve approximately the same relative standing on repeated testings over time. In other words, there should be a high correlation between intelligence test scores at one age and scores at another age. In fact, earlier research consistently showed little relation between infant intelligence and later intelligence scores or school achievement (Bayley, 1970; McCall, Appelbaum, and Hogarty, 1973). This may not be so surprising. A closer examination of infant intelligence tests reveals that they mainly rely on measures of motor coordination and sensory abilities rather than on such skills

as comprehension and reasoning, measures found in tests for older children. In this instance, the low correlation between infant and childhood intelligence tests probably reflects differences in the construction of the tests (Brody & Brody, 1976).

More recent research by psychologist Joseph Fagan and others has found a moderate relationship between scores on infant mental tests and scores on intelligence tests for children age six or older. Innovative tests can predict later intelligence from infant performance. For example, in one study three- to eight-month-old infants were shown simple geometric shapes. After these stimuli were shown individually several times, each was paired with a comparable but novel stimulus. Infants demonstrated memory in this task if they looked at the novel stimulus more than at the familiar one. The more novel stimuli each infant looked at, and the longer the baby looked at them, the higher that infant's memory test score would be. (If the infants had no memory of the previously shown shapes, the novel and the familiar shapes would be equally likely to attract their attention.) Those infants who scored high on the memory test were found to have high intelligence test scores at age six and beyond (Fagan and Singer, 1983). In fact, in a review of 15 studies of this type, Fagan (1984) found that correlations extended from +.33 to +.66, with an average correlation of +.45. These findings, and those of more recent studies, provide evidence for moderate stablity in intelligence scores from infancy onward (Bornstein and Sigman, 1986; Raz, Willerman, and Yama, 1987).

Intelligence test performance becomes more stable throughout childhood and adolescence than it was in infancy. Figure 9.3 shows that intelligence tests given at age three are only slightly predictive of test performance at age 17, whereas the relation between IQ in early and late adolescence is much stronger. In general, the correlation increases as the length of time between testings decreases. However, despite this relative stability in intelligence scores (particularly in older children) there are always a few children whose scores vary as much as 30 to 50 points in either direction from one testing to the next (McCall et al., 1973; Sontag, Baker, and Nelson, 1958).

Studies of the stability of intelligence in adulthood typically show that scores peak between the ages of 18 and 25, decline gradually through age 50, and thereafter drop more rapidly (Horn, 1978). However, the progressive deterioration over adulthood is highly misleading. We will see in the chapter on adolescent and adult development that such studies have often grouped people of different

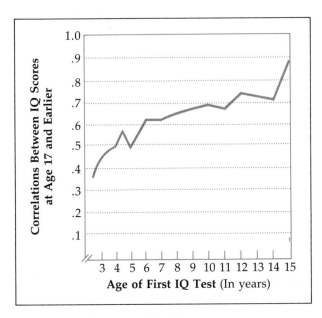

FIGURE 9.3 IQ stability and age. This figure shows the relation between IQ scores at age 17 and scores obtained at earlier ages. In general, as the time between tests decreases the correlation between IQ scores increases. IQ scores from tests given in early childhood do not correlate highly with tests given at age 17.

ages and educational backgrounds (for example, younger people are more apt to have a college education than older people). Moreover, elderly people may perform poorly because of ill health or fatigue. In studying intelligence in the elderly, psychologists now distinguish between fluid and crystallized intelligence. **Fluid intelligence** is the capacity to analyze problems and respond quickly and accurately; it does show a general decrease with age. **Crystallized intelligence** represents general knowledge and information about the world; it increases or remains constant through age 85 (Horn, 1970; 1978). For some elderly people, general intelligence can decline dramatically in their last year of life. This precipitous drop in intelligence is often just one of a variety of symptoms of deteriorating health that signals an impending termination of life.

EXTREMES OF INTELLIGENCE

In Figure 9.1 we saw that intelligence scores approximate a normal, symmetrical distribution. The majority of scores are clustered at the center, with progressively fewer in either extreme. Who are the people who have scores in the portions of the distribution labeled "retarded" or "gifted"?

MENTAL RETARDATION

People are classified as mentally retarded if they score below 70 on a standard intelligence test. But retardation is defined by more than just an IQ score. According to the American Association of Mental Deficiency, retardation involves below average intellectual functioning *and* impairment in adaptive behavior. This impairment in adaptive behavior can be seen in childhood. Retarded children are often slow to begin to walk, to talk, and to become toilet trained. In adulthood, severely retarded people do not marry, hold jobs, or care for themselves. Depending on the criteria that are used, there are approximately 10 million retarded people in the United States, a figure that represents roughly three percent of the population (Cytryn and Lourie, 1975).

Psychologists typically distinguish among different degrees of retardation. The categories include **mild retardation** (IQs between 52 and 69), **moderate retardation** (IQs between 36 and 51), **severe retardation** (IQs between 20 and 35), and **profound retardation** (IQs below 20). In general, the more severe the retardation, the less frequent its occurrence in the population, and the less able the person is to function in society. For example, mildly retarded people, who constitute 75 percent of all retardates, have reasonably good prospects for adapting to life's demands if provided with education and training. On the other hand, profoundly retarded people, who constitute only about one percent of all retardates, have virtually no measurable intelligence and require close supervision throughout their lifetimes. Table 9.4 shows the level of functioning of people in each category during their childhood and adulthood years.

What causes mental retardation? There are a number of possible causes. In some cases, it is caused by biological factors. Brain injury, prenatal infection, or lack of oxygen during birth can all lead to retardation. Genetic or chromosomal defects can contribute as well to certain types of retardation. One type of genetically caused retardation, **Down's syndrome**, is described in Chapter 11. These biological disorders are referred to as **organic retardation.** Organic factors are commonly associated with severe and profound retardation.

In cases of mild retardation, it is often difficult to identify a clear physical cause. Many mildly retarded people are born to parents with low IQs and are raised in deprived homes. If normal intelligence is the result of a combination of factors (some hereditary, some environmental), mild re-

TABLE 9.4 Behavioral Characteristics of the Mentally Retarded

Degree of Retardation	LEVEL OF FUNCTIONING		
	Birth through Age 5	Age 6 through 20	Age 21 and over
Mild (IQ 52–69; 75 percent)	Slower to walk, to talk, and to feed themselves than other children. Often not recognized as retarded.	Can conform to social rules and learn sixth-grade level skills by late teens.	Can usually acquire social and vocational skills for self-support. May need guidance and assistance in times of stress.
Moderate (IQ 36–51; 20 percent)	Delays in motor development and speech noticeable. Responds positively to training.	Can learn language, elementary safety, and health habits and can be taught simple manual skills. Unlikely to progress beyond second grade academic level.	Can perform unskilled or semiskilled work under supervision. Needs guidance under conditions of mild stress.
Severe (IQ 20–35; 3.5 percent)	Obvious delays in motor development and little or no language skill. May respond to training for simple tasks like feeding.	Can talk or communicate and learn elementary health habits. Requires systematic habit training.	Can conform to daily routines and repetitive activities. Requires a protective environment.
Profound (IQ below 20; 1.5 percent)	Minimal capacity for sensorimotor functioning. Needs nursing care.	Shows basic emotional responses and may respond to limited training in self-help. Requires close supervision.	May walk and produce primitive speech, but incapable of self-maintenance and requires nursing care.

Adapted from the Mental Retardation Activities of the U.S. Department of Health, Education, and Welfare, Washington, D.C.: U.S. Government Printing Office, 1963.

tardation may occur in those unfortunate individuals for whom a large number of causal factors fall in the wrong direction (Zigler and Cascione, 1984). Poor health, poor diet, and inattentive parents can all hamper a child's intellectual development. This form of retardation is called **cultural-familial** retardation for two reasons. First, many

Down's syndrome. This form of moderate to severe mental retardation results from a chromosomal disorder.

people in this group come from families with low socioeconomic status. Second, many of these people have a relative who is also mentally retarded (Grossman, 1982; Zigler and Cascione, 1984).

From the 1950s to the early 1970s, it was widely believed that the educational needs of the retarded were so different from those of normal children that the retarded required special classes, with separate teaching methods and a different curriculum. However, these special education programs were largely ineffective. In concentrating on self-help skills, they did not prepare the children (especially the mildly retarded children) for integration into society. Separate residential institutions were even worse, since they removed a retarded child from the normal situation of family and society (Zigler and Finn-Stevenson, 1987).

By 1975, the education pendulum had swung in the opposite direction. Instead of isolating the retarded, educators and mental retardation experts argued for normal treatment of the retarded. The Education for All Handicapped Children Act of 1975 (Public Law 94–142) required that each handicapped child be given a program of individualized instruction in "the least restrictive environment." This has been interpreted to mean that retarded and other handicapped children should be *mainstreamed* into the regular classroom. Preliminary evaluations of the effect of this new approach are mixed. Some studies show that mainstreamed handicapped children fare no better or worse than handicapped children in special education classes (Gottlieb, 1980, among others). Still other studies have found improved self-image in some mainstreamed retarded children, while others report that mentally retarded children still feel stigmatized by their normal peers (Caparulo and Zigler, 1983; Meyers, MacMillan, and Yoshida, 1980). Thus, the issue of the best way to educate the mentally retarded remains unresolved.

While debate continues over the merits of mainstreaming, psychologists have made advances in understanding how mildly retarded children differ from children of normal intelligence in cognitive skills. After reviewing a large number of studies, psychologist Ann Brown and her colleagues Joseph Campione and Roberta Ferrara (1982) report the following differences:

- Educable Mentally Retarded (EMR) children (IQs around 70) perform certain mental operations more slowly than normal children do. For example, EMR children take longer to decide whether two letters are the same (A,A) or different (A,B).

- EMR children have less knowledge about the world than normal children do. They know less geography, less math, less science, and less history.

- EMR children do not use such learning strategies as mental rehearsal to help themselves in memory or reading tasks.

Intrigued by the differences in learning strategies, Brown and her associates set out to see whether better strategies could be taught to retarded children. In one experiment, a group of EMR children was shown pictures of common objects (a comb, a key, a pencil, and a spoon) and asked to remember them in order. The children were told that they would later be tested. The researchers explained to the 10- to 12-year-olds that they could remember the items better if they rehearsed the names of the objects for a later test. This instruction was followed by practice at rehearsal to make sure that the children could monitor their own performances. After extensive training, the children not only used rehearsal spontaneously a year later, they used it effectively for a different type of memory test (Brown, Campione, and Barclay, 1979).

These results indicate that mildly retarded children can benefit from special programs tailored to treat areas of intellectual weakness. Such results do *not* mean that educational programs can eliminate retardation. They cannot. However, proper training can maximize each person's potential. Recent research has shown that the mildly retarded, at least, may have potential quite a bit higher than previously believed. One special group of mildly retarded people is the *gifted retardates*. These are retarded individuals who are amazingly proficient in a particular skill. Gifted retardates are described in more detail in the section that follows.

DYSFUNCTION: Gifted Retardates

Ever since he was a boy, Alonzo Clemens loved working with clay. He would sit for hours molding clay into tiny animals. But Alonzo was retarded, and the staff of the training school where he lived worried that his attachment to his clay was causing him to fall farther and farther behind in his studies. So they removed the clay in the hope of using it as an incentive to get Alonzo to concentrate on his studies. However, Alonzo had other ideas. One day a staff member discovered tar streaks on Alonzo's bedding. Looking under the bed, the staff member discovered a tiny menagerie of animals, all made out of tar. At night, while the other children slept, Alonzo carefully crafted his animals out of the tar he had earlier scraped off the school playground with his fingernails.

Today, Alonzo cares for horses at a home for the retarded in Colorado, and he is fast becoming known as a talented sculptor of animals. He has had public showings of his work and has received the acclaim of professional artists. When asked how he sculpts his horses and antelopes from memory, Alonzo, who has difficulty speaking, just smiles and taps the side of his head with his forefinger (Schmidt, 1983).

Leslie Lemke is another retarded young man. Born blind and suffering from cerebral palsy, Leslie could not walk or speak a complete sentence by age 19. Yet one morning he went to the family piano and played Tchaikovsky's First Piano Concerto from memory (Schmidt, 1983). There are reports of a man with an IQ of 54 who could play eleven musical instruments by ear and of a famous Japanese artist named Yamamoto who had an IQ of only 47 (Hill, 1975; Morishima, 1975). Figure 9.4 shows one of Yamamoto's colorful prints.

FIGURE 9.4 Nagoya Castle in Japan. This sketch was made by a mentally retarded man named Yamamoto. During infancy, he suffered from hydrocephalus, an abnormal accumulation of fluid in the brain, that left him mentally retarded. Although Yamamoto has very poor verbal and intellectual skills, he has remarkable artistic ability, typical of other gifted retardates.

These case studies involve people who were formerly called *idiot savants* (from the French term for "learned idiot"). Today, psychologists prefer the more accurate label of **gifted retardates** to describe the very small minority of retarded people who display skills that would be extraordinary even for normal people. Most of the gifted retardates have IQs between 50 and 75. They are more likely to be men than women by a slightly higher ratio (three to one) than that found for all mental retardates (three to two) (Ingalls, 1978; Schmidt, 1983). In addition, we know that many of these people suffer from **autism,** a disorder in which people almost totally withdraw from social contact. Autistic people, as portrayed by Dustin Hoffman in the movie *Rain Man,* appear physically normal, but they rarely converse or make eye contact with others.

How do the gifted retardates perform their amazing feats? Psychologist A. Lewis Hill has speculated that their special abilities may be tied to an abnormal division of function between the left and right cerebral hemispheres. Since most of the special abilities involve processes associated with the right hemisphere (for example, perceptual skills, numerical skills, and musical talents) it may be that a developmental defect in the left hemisphere resulted in exaggerated development in the right (Hill, cited in Schmidt, 1983). Research may one day tell us whether this idea has merit. At present, the talents of the gifted retardates remain a fascinating enigma. ■

MENTAL GIFTEDNESS

Seven-year-old Susan was a problem for her teacher. Although she seemed bright in certain ways, she did not bother to finish class assignments. Sometimes she would stare out the window during class. At other times she would turn a question into a joke or make cartoon drawings on her tests. Convinced that her inattention and lack of motivation were caused by a learning disability, the teacher referred her to a testing psychologist. The tests revealed no evidence of any disability but did show that Susan had an IQ of 147. When she was asked to explain her school performance, she had a simple answer. She found her schoolwork boring and repetitive and was searching for ways to amuse herself. Figure 9.5 shows another special seven-year-old, a boy named Christopher who has exceptional mechanical and inventive abilities. For a class assignment, he designed a model for an energy efficient roof that lets the sun in during the winter but keeps it out in the summer.

People who score above 130 on an intelligence test are labeled **mentally gifted.** Less is known about these people than their well-studied counterparts, the mentally retarded. In the past, gifted people were often thought to be misfits or oddballs who were frequently out of step with society. However, a classic study begun by Lewis Terman in 1921 and continued through the 1970s by Robert and Pauline Sears did much to shatter the myth of social maladjustment (Sears, 1977; Sears and Barbee, 1977; Terman, 1954).

FIGURE 9.5 A mentally gifted child. At the age of seven, Christopher used his exceptional mechanical and inventive skills to design an energy efficient roof for a house. He is shown fitting the roof over his model. Notice how his roof keeps the vertical summer sun out but allows the angular winter rays in.

Terman wanted to discover what gifted children were like, what factors influenced their development, and whether their exceptional intellectual capacities predicted later success in their careers and social relations. In 1921 and 1922, he identified over 1,400 children who had IQ scores over 140 or who were within the top one percent of the population on IQ. Terman collected data on these individuals nine times over a period of 50 years, measuring such variables as physical development, educational and occupational status, personality development, self-ratings of ambitions, and satisfying aspects of life. The average IQ of these children was 151 during the initial assessment, when they were 11 years old. Over the course of childhood, these individuals were physically taller, heavier, stronger, and reached sexual maturity at an earlier age than did the general population. They performed better in school and graduated from high school at slightly younger ages than the general population.

These advantages continued into adulthood and extended to other areas. For example, 71 percent of the men and 67 percent of the women graduated college, and 30 percent of the men and 24 percent of the women obtained one or more graduate degrees. In terms of occupational status, 85 percent of the men took professional or semiprofessional jobs. Approximately one half of the women worked full-time outside the home during the 1930s through the 1960s; of these, 63 percent were in professional or semiprofessional occupations. This is more remarkable than it may at first seem, as very few Americans completed college in those days, and only a small minority of women took professional jobs.

By the time they were 50, these individuals had published more than 2,500 articles and more than 200 books in the sciences, arts, and humanities, close to 400 short shories, 55 essays, and had been granted at least 350 patents (Oden, 1968). By most standards, then, these people were very accomplished and productive. Furthermore, they were especially happy with their lives (Figure 9.6). Over half reported "deep satisfaction" with their lives and almost 90 percent reported being at least "fairly content."

These data suggest that there is a relation between giftedness and different measures of life success. However, a word of caution is necessary. The majority of the gifted children identified by Terman, like those used in Galton's study of eminent families, grew up in advantaged homes. Given that advantaged people have better health, education, and family income, we should expect many accomplishments from such a group. The precise nature of the relation between giftedness and life success is still a source of controversy, although many would agree with psychologists Erness and Nathan Brody (1976) who stated that "It is doubtful that the attempt to select children scoring in the top one percent of any other single characteristic would be as predictive of future accomplishment."

The mentally gifted, like the mentally retarded, pose special problems for educators (Gallagher, 1983). Should gifted children be *accelerated* and allowed to skip grades? Will acceleration meet the intellectual needs of these very bright children at the expense of their social and emotional needs? Research on this issue is scant, although Terman suggested that gifted children are ahead of their classmates physically and socially as well as intellectually. Moreover, very bright children often seek out the company of older children and adults, so the concern that acceleration may lead to social isolation may be unfounded (Hetherington and Parke, 1986).

Psychologists Julian Stanley and Camilla Benbow (1983) have worked with large numbers of gifted children, and they strongly endorse the concept of acceleration. In a study called the Study of Mathematically Precocious Youth, an ongoing project that began at Johns Hopkins University in the early 1970s, Stanley and Benbow identified

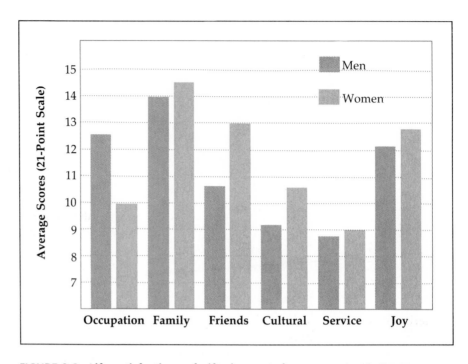

FIGURE 9.6 Life satisfactions of gifted men and women. Lewis Terman identified a large group of children in the early 1920s who scored above 140 on an intelligence test. In 1972, when these mentally gifted people reached retirement, they were asked about their sources of life satisfaction. Their greatest satisfaction came from their families, and they showed very high ratings for overall pleasure with their lives. Gifted people clearly enjoy more than just occupational rewards.

over 35,000 mathematically talented young people from early administration of the SAT. The purpose of this program is to provide 12- to 17-year-old gifted children with stimulating educational opportunities, including intensive summer courses in mathematics and science, access to college courses, and even the chance to enter and graduate from college early. For example, Stanley tells of one young man, barely 17, who graduated from Johns Hopkins with a BA in mathematical science after only five semesters there, one year in high school, and one year in junior high. "Nor was he narrow in his interests," says Stanley (1976) ". . . His list of extracurricular activities is long, including a high school letter in wrestling and a varsity spot for two years on the college golf team." Many gifted young people have adapted extremely well to this acceleration. What was true of the mentally retarded seems equally true of the mentally gifted. Educational programs can be designed to maximize intellectual potential, whatever that potential might be.

GENETIC AND ENVIRONMENTAL INFLUENCES ON INTELLIGENCE

Is our intelligence the result of the genes we receive from our parents, or the educational experiences we encounter after birth? This is one of the most controversial topics in the study of intelligence because of its bearing on our interpretation of racial differences in IQ test scores. This form of the *nature–nurture controversy* was widely publicized in 1969 when psychologist Arthur Jensen argued that 80 percent of the differences in people's IQ scores are due to genetics. Jensen went on to suggest that such compensatory education programs as Head Start would be ineffective in changing such scores (Jensen, 1969). Since that time, numerous articles and books have been written on both sides of the issue (Eysenck and Kamin, 1981; Scarr, 1981, among others). To understand this continuing debate we need to understand the concept of heritability.

THE CONCEPT OF HERITABILITY

Heritability is a statistical estimate of the relative influence of genetics and environment on a given characteristic such as intelligence. It is widely recognized that individual differences in IQ scores reflect the separate effects of genetic and environmental factors, as well as their interaction. For example, bright parents typically give their children an environment that enhances their intellectual development. Bright children, in turn, take advantage of their environment by asking questions of their parents and engaging in stimulating experiences (Scarr and Carter-Saltzman, 1982). This makes it difficult to know whether these children are bright because of their genes, their special home life, or both. At the heart of this controversy is the notion of the heritability of intelligence.

Heritability refers to the extent to which individual differences in an observable characteristic are due to differences in the genetic makeup of people within a given population. In terms of intelligence, it addresses the question of what proportion of the differences between people in IQ scores is genetically determined. Thus, heritability provides a statistical estimate of the relative influence of genetics and environment. As an illustration, whether you have blood type A, B, AB, or O has a heritability of 100 percent, since differences among people in blood type are determined entirely by differences in genetic makeup. On the other hand, the heritability of a characteristic such as height is lower than 100 percent. Even though genetic differences account for a great deal in determining who is tall and who is short, environmental differences in nutrition and health care also play a role.

There are several methods that can be used to estimate the heritability of intelligence. Each method represents an attempt to isolate the independent effects of genetic background on intelligence test performance. To accomplish this, researchers identify pairs of individuals who differ systematically in the similarity of their genetic makeup and environment. The two main methods are twin studies and adoption studies.

TWIN STUDIES

Researchers who study twins begin by searching for pairs of *identical* and *fraternal twins*. Since identical twins develop from the same fertilized egg, they have exactly the same genes. Fraternal twins, however, are no more genetically alike than any other pair of siblings and they can even differ in sex. As we will see in this section, we can determine whether genetics and/or environment influences intelligence by comparing the performance of identical and fraternal twins reared together or apart.

To determine the heritability of intelligence, pairs of identical and fraternal twins are compared in terms of their **concordance rate,** the likelihood that both twins will have a specific characteristic, given that one of the twins has the characteristic. For intelligence, concordance refers to the similarity in twins' intelligence test performance. If the more genetically similar pair is also more similar in IQ scores, then that gives us a reading as to the influence of genetic factors. If we assume that each pair of identical and fraternal twins shares similar environments, then differences in IQ scores must reflect differences in genetic makeup. By contrast, if identical twins are no more similar in test performance than fraternal twins, the influence of genetic factors on IQ scores would not be of prime importance. For this reason, twins are especially important for learning about the heritability of intelligence.

Table 9.5 summarizes the results of over 100 separate studies on familial resemblances in measured intelligence. It presents the correlation of IQ scores for pairs of people who vary in genetic relatedness. In general, the more closely related

TABLE 9.5 Familial Resemblances in Intelligence Test Performance

Relationship	Average Correlation
Identical Twins	
Reared Together	.86
Reared Apart	.72
Fraternal Twins	
Reared Together	.60
Siblings	
Reared Together	.47
Reared Apart	.24
Parent–Child	.40
Foster Parent–Child	.31
Cousins	.15

Adapted from a survey of 111 studies compiled by Bouchard and McCue (1981).

two individuals are, the higher the correlation between their intelligence scores. This indicates that genetic factors do indeed influence intelligence test performance. However, it is also important to see that genetic makeup is not the sole determinant of IQ performance. If it were, we would expect that the correlations between identical twins reared together and those reared apart would be identical, when in fact they are not. Thus, environment does make a difference in intelligence test performance.

Although twin studies provide important information, they are not the best means of teasing apart the influences of heredity and environment on intelligence. For example, there is some question about the assumption that identical and fraternal twins share similar environments. In fact, research has shown an environmental difference in that identical twins are treated more similarly than are fraternal twins (Plomin, Willerman, and Loehlin, 1976). One way around this problem is to compare identical twins reared together and those reared apart. This approach has the advantage of enabling researchers to examine variations in environment because the (identical) genetic makeup remains constant. If identical twins still have similar IQ scores, even though they were raised in different environments, then genetic factors must account for this similarity. However, how different are these different environments? Separated identical twins are often raised by branches of the same family (mother and mother's sister), raised in close proximity to one another, or not separated for very long periods of time. Therefore, says Leon Kamin, those rare identical twins who are reared apart can share more than identical genes; they can share environments that are more similar than had been previously thought (Eysenck and Kamin, 1981). Nevertheless, the fact that identical twins reared apart show *higher* correlations in IQ scores than fraternal twins reared together argues very strongly against the likelihood that shared environments can account for all of these findings.

The consistent pattern of results across a variety of twin studies does indicate that genetic factors contribute in some measure to individual differences in IQ scores. However, the various qualifications to these studies caution us that the separation of genetic and environmental influences is not easy. Evidence from adoption studies sheds additional light on this complex issue.

ADOPTION STUDIES

Adopted children are not usually genetically related to the family that raises them. If environmen-

tal factors were the primary influence on measured intelligence, we would expect that the IQs of the adopted children would be more highly correlated to those of their adoptive than their biological parents. By contrast, if both adopted children and children raised by their biological parents show higher correlations with their biological parents' IQ scores, then the genetic position would be supported. The data from several studies show that the correlations between adopted children and their biological parents are higher than between adopted children and their adoptive parents (De-Fries et al., 1979, among others). More recent data from the Texas Adoption Study (Horn, 1983; Horn, Loehlin, and Willerman, 1979) and the Minnesota Adolescence Study (Scarr and Weinberg, 1983) support these findings. The data also show that there is little difference between the correlations for adopted children and their biological parents and the correlations between biologically related parents and children living together. In other words, children's IQ scores correlate with those of their biological parents, whether or not they were raised by them. These findings argue for the importance of genetic factors. Based on reviews of both twin and adoption studies, Sandra Scarr and

An interracial family. It is becoming more common today than it was in the past for families to adopt children of different ethnic and racial backgrounds. Psychologists are interested in interracial adoptions because it allows them to assess the relative contributions of genetic and environmental influences on the development of individual differences.

her associates have estimated the heritability of intelligence test performance to be approximately .50 (Scarr and Carter-Saltzman, 1982; Scarr and Weinberg, 1983). Other researchers have come up with different estimates of heritability, some higher, some lower (Eysenck, 1987; Henderson, 1982; Loehlin, Willerman, and Horn, 1988). But if we use the heritability estimate of .50 as a rough approximation, what does this tell us about the relative influence of genetic and environmental factors? It would mean that approximately 50 percent of the variability of scores for the particular population being studied is due to genetic differences. It does *not* mean that 50 percent of a given person's IQ score is the result of genetic factors. Remember, for any given characteristic, heritability is an estimate of the proportion of the differences *between individual people* that is genetically based. We must also keep in mind that if about half of the variability in a particular group of people is due to genetic differences among individuals within the group, the same data provide evidence for an environmental influence as well (Plomin, 1988; Plomin and Daniels, 1987). These issues are especially important in considering group differences in measured intelligence.

GROUP DIFFERENCES IN INTELLIGENCE TEST SCORES

It is in relation to particular racial and ethnic groups that the concept of heritability has generated the most controversy. For example, black Americans have an average IQ score that is approximately 15 points less than that of white Americans (Brody and Brody, 1976). Also, children from upper-class English, Irish, and American homes score about 12 points higher on average than those from lower-class homes (Vane, 1973). How should these differences be interpreted?

SOCIOECONOMIC DIFFERENCES

Figure 9.7 shows average IQ scores for a wide range of occupations. The data were obtained from the U.S. Army during a World War II testing program. On the average, skilled workers scored higher than unskilled workers, and professionals scored highest of all. However, there is a considerable range of scores within many different occupations. Thus, teamsters and farmhands with the highest IQs easily outscored the average accountant or engineer. This fact tells us that we cannot make individual judgments of intelligence by socioeconomic status alone.

FIGURE 9.7   The average IQ and the range of IQs for a variety of occupations.
These data, obtained from a U.S. Army testing program in World War II, show the average IQs and the range of IQs for people in different occupations. Although there are differences in the average IQs across occupations, there is also an enormous range of IQs within each occupation.

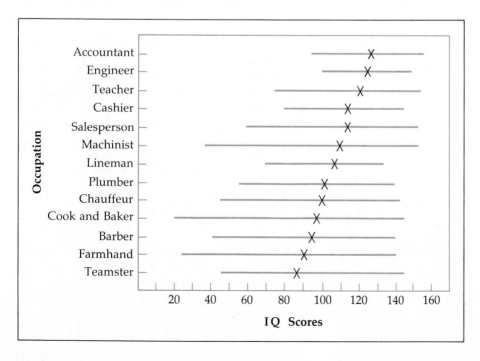

Differences in average IQ scores among people in different occupations or classes are also found among the children of these people, although the differences are smaller. In one study, children of professional and technical workers had an average IQ of approximately 109, while those of laborers and farm workers had a mean score of roughly 92 (Kaufman and Doppelt, 1976). It may be that the socioeconomic status of the parents is influenced strongly by genetic factors which, in turn, influence their children's IQ scores. Additionally, environmental factors may play an important role. Affluent parents can provide their children with educational advantages (special preschool programs, for example, and a home full of books and educational toys); less affluent people cannot. Current research suggests that a child's intellectual performance is determined by genetic factors *and* the influence of the father's educational level and occupation on the family environment (Duyme, 1988; Mackenzie, 1984). In other words, both genetic and environmental factors are important.

RACIAL DIFFERENCES

What of the difference in average IQ scores for blacks and whites? We noted earlier that some psychologists, notably Jensen (1969), have argued that this difference is largely attributable to genetic differences between groups. Jensen has further argued that the difference cannot be attributed to a cultural bias against blacks in different intelligence tests. Lower average scores for blacks are found on nonverbal and culture-reduced tests (Jensen, 1980; 1985; Mackenzie, 1984).

However, several points are critically important in understanding this issue. For one thing, regardless of what the heritability estimate is for intelligence, heritability describes variations due to genetic factors for individuals *within* a given population (for example, all black Americans). It does not tell us whether variation *between* groups (say, black versus white Americans) results from similar genetic factors. Consider the following analogy provided by geneticist Richard Lewontin (1976) as an example:

Two populations of seeds are grown in different environments. One group of seeds is placed in a fertile soil and grows well; the other group is placed in barren soil and grows poorly. Differences in the growth of the plants *within* each group will largely be due to genetic differences between the seeds—some will be tall and some will be short. However, average differences in the

growth *between* the two groups of plants primarily will be due to differences in environmental conditions.

In 1986, approximately 31 percent of all black families in America lived at or below the poverty level, compared to roughly 11 percent of all white families (U.S. Department of Commerce). As a consequence, the environments in which blacks and whites are raised are often dramatically different. Compared to white children, black children generally experience poorer nutrition, less adequate health care, fewer educational opportunities, and have parents who are less educated. To the extent that environmental factors influence IQ scores, black children will do poorer than whites.

Direct evidence of the importance of environmental influences comes from studies of children of interracial parents and interracial adoption. For example, a study of illegitimate children fathered by U.S. servicemen after World War II in Germany found no difference in the average IQ scores of those children who had white fathers and those who had black fathers. These children were all raised by their German mothers under similar socioeconomic conditions. If genetic factors were responsible for racial differences in intelligence scores, racial differences should have been found in this study. The fact that they were not provides support for an environmental interpretation of racial differences (Eyferth, 1961).

In a study of interracial adoption, Sandra Scarr and Richard Weinberg (1976) reported that the average intelligence test score of the white adopting parents was 120. The average score of their biological children was 117. The black adopted children produced an average IQ score of 106, significantly higher than the average for black children generally. Furthermore, the earlier the children were adopted, the higher their eventual intelligence test scores. Those black children adopted before their first birthdays had an average IQ of 110. These data indicate that socioeconomic opportunities provided by the home environment can have pronounced effects on intelligence test scores.

At present, the longstanding, systemic differences in the environment for black and white Americans make it impossible to determine to what extent, if any, racial differences in intelligence scores can be attributed to genetic factors. Psychologists and educators have urged that research should now be focused on ways of overcoming environmental differences (Zigler and Seitz, 1982). By studying how children should be cared for and educated, we can improve the performance of children of all racial groups. As evidence of this, different enrichment programs such as Project Head Start have worked to offset environmental disadvantages in early childhood. We describe this program in the "Research and Application" discussion that follows.

RESEARCH AND APPLICATION
Project Head Start

During the 1960s, educators, social scientists, and federal policy makers became concerned with the great discrepancies in the intellectual skills of young children entering school. Children from poor homes frequently began school without the basic skills needed to be successful. As a consequence, they often fell behind their classmates, had to repeat grades, got discouraged, and left school early for menial jobs. As a result, they were also unequipped to prepare their own children for school. Each new generation of disadvantaged children seemed to perpetuate a cycle of early problems in school followed by a lifetime of poverty.

To break this cycle of lack of education, unemployment, and hopelessness, and as part of President Lyndon Johnson's War on Poverty, Congress authorized funds to establish a preschool program for economically disadvantaged children. In part, this decision was based on the work of psychologist James McV. Hunt (1961) who published a book in which he argued that intelligence was largely a product of environmental influences, and Benjamin Bloom (1964) who wrote that intellectual development reached its peak during a child's preschool years. These writings, which stressed environmental influences on intelligence, helped set the intellectual climate of these times and free the funds to help disadvantaged children get a "head start" in life.

Project Head Start began in 1965 as a summer program for four- and five-year-old children whose socioeconomic background indicated that they would do poorly in school. With additional funding, it quickly expanded to include children from infancy through age eight. Many different programs have evolved over the years. Some provide services at home, while others are based in daycare or educational centers.

What happens in a Head Start program? In some cases, special education teachers visit preschool children at home several days a week. During their visits, the teachers may engage the children in identifying objects in picture books, naming colors, counting, and understanding such concepts as near–far and big–little. In addition to attempting to stimulate the children's intellects, the teachers instruct their parents in techniques for developing their children's abilities. In other Head Start programs, the children might visit a center and work on various educational tasks with other children, teachers, and parents. Aside from intellectual development, Head Start programs also focus on a child's physical and social well-being. Children who are hungry or ill are not likely to succeed in school; neither are those who are not motivated to learn (Zigler, 1973).

Research over the past two decades has demonstrated the value of Project Head Start. At first, the

Project Head Start. Children from socioeconomically disadvantaged homes are given an opportunity to prepare for grade school. Teachers and parents work together with these preschoolers to provide them with increased intellectual stimulation. Research shows that Head Start programs produce long-lasting positive benefits to a child.

project was evaluated solely in terms of changes in IQ scores. The early results were promising—IQ scores did increase for children enrolled in Head Start. However, the optimism was short-lived. IQ gains faded away after the children left the program (Bronfenbrenner, 1975; Salkind, 1983; Zigler and Berman, 1983). In fairness, this fadeout could represent reduced motivation instead of a loss of mental ability, as the children often moved from stimulating preschool programs to depressing substandard poverty-area schools (Zigler and Seitz, 1982).

Today, project evaluators have taken a more global perspective. Long-term positive effects have been reported on a variety of practical measures as a result of Head Start. For example, compared to disadvantaged children who were not enrolled in Head Start, children who had been enrolled do better in school and their personal lives. By age 19 or older, former Head Start children have a higher high school completion rate, a greater rate of participation in vocational schools or college, a higher rate of employment, and a lower record of arrests than non-Head Start students (Berrueta-Clement et al., 1984; Jordan, Grallo, Deutch, and Deutch, 1985; Lazar and Darlington, 1982). Moreover, programs like Head Start turn out to be more cost-effective than remedial programs aimed at adults (Weikart, 1982). Clearly, these programs have had an important and positive impact on the lives of both the children who took part in them, and their families (Lee, Brooks-Gunn, and Schnur, 1988; Zigler and Finn-Stevenson, 1987). ■

DEFINING INTELLIGENCE

We have talked about how intelligence is measured without providing a very precise definition. It is unsatisfying to say (as some have said) that intelligence is simply "what intelligence tests measure." Many psychologists have struggled for a more adequate conceptual answer to the question: "What is intelligence?" Starting with Binet, some psychologists have viewed intelligence as a general capacity for thinking and understanding. Binet assumed that this capacity helps us assess and handle a wide range of situations. His test contained many different mental tasks, and he generally found that advanced children scored higher on all of the tasks than less capable children. Others have argued that intelligence is a combination of separate abilities, such as verbal and social skills, abstract thinking, and even "common sense." Still others have suggested that intelligence tests do not measure all aspects of

intelligence. Over the years, three different conceptual approaches to intelligence have emerged: the **psychometric approach,** the **cognitive approach,** and the **implicit theory approach.** We will discuss the contributions of each of these approaches, as well as the areas where they may fall short of providing a complete definition of this very slippery topic.

THE PSYCHOMETRIC APPROACH: INTELLIGENCE AS THAT WHICH IS MEASURED

Psychometrics involves the measurement of mental characteristics. The psychometric approach to intelligence involves analyzing the results of intelligence tests to determine the structure of human intelligence. In particular, it seeks to determine whether intelligence consists of one general factor or a variety of factors. The person most responsible for establishing this approach was British psychologist Charles Spearman. In 1904, Spearman proposed a theory of the underlying organization of human intelligence that he tested over the next several decades.

FACTOR ANALYSIS AND GENERAL INTELLIGENCE

By the mid-1920s, Spearman had discovered that there was a positive correlation between scores on many different IQ tests. To determine what was common to these different measurements, he originated a sophisticated method of data analysis known as **factor analysis.** The logic of factor analysis is analogous to the mathematical procedure of "factoring," in which complex algebraic expressions are simplified by removing the common multiplier of all terms. Factor analysis shows how different measures are related. For instance, factor analysis may reveal that people who are good at remembering numbers are also good at solving complex math problems. People who are good at defining obscure words, on the other hand, may not be particularly good at solving math problems, but may be quite good at finding the central theme in a short story. In each case, a different common factor is revealed, one related to numerical ability and the other related to facility with words.

After factor-analyzing the results of test scores, Spearman proposed a two-factor theory of intelligence. He believed that all measures of intelligence could be divided into two independent factors. The first factor was a *general* factor of *g,* which later became identified as *general intelligence.* Intellectual tasks are correlated, said Spearman, to the extent that each task measures *g*. The other factor in his two-factor theory was *s*—individual tasks each had *specific* factors that also affected performance. The presence of different *s* factors in different intellectual tasks (numerical or verbal tasks, for example) tended to lower the correlation between tasks.

Spearman believed that his theory provided a good explanation for the predictive success of such tests as the Stanford-Binet. He argued that the Stanford-Binet, by including many diverse tasks, minimized the impact of specific factors that potentially could skew the scores. Thus, the total IQ score on the Stanford-Binet would reflect primarily what was constant across the various tasks—namely, general intelligence, or *g* (Spearman, 1927).

FACTOR ANALYSIS AND PRIMARY MENTAL ABILITIES

It was not long before psychologists began to question the validity of Spearman's two-factor theory. Louis Thurstone (1938), for one, objected strongly to Spearman's emphasis on a single form of general intelligence. Thurstone argued instead that intelligence is a group of independent abilities rather than a general factor that is constant across diverse tests. From his use of a new type of factor analysis, Thurstone identified seven separate abilities that he termed primary **mental abilities.** They include the following items:

- Verbal comprehension—the ability to understand word meanings.

- Verbal theory—the ability to think of words rapidly.

- Number—the ability to perform mathematical calculations.

- Memory—the ability to recall words in lists or sentences.

- Space—the ability to visualize objects in varied orientations.

- Perceptual speed—the ability to note similarities and differences in objects by observing visual details quickly.

- Reasoning—the ability to detect a pattern in a series of items and predict the next item in a series.

Furthermore, he designed a test battery to assess these abilities, called the Primary Mental Abilities Test Battery.

Despite his considerable effort, Thurstone never realized his goal of discovering the basic components of intelligence. First, his primary mental abilities were not entirely independent of one another. This suggested that Spearman's concept of general intelligence might still be useful. In fact, many psychologists still acknowledge the existence of Spearman's *g* (Brody and Brody, 1976). Second, other psychologists using the psychometric approach have claimed that intelligence is made of still other sets of different factors. For example, J. P. Guilford (1982) proposed 180 different mental abilities, each theoretically different from one another. This lack of agreement over which are the primary components of intelligence has led some psychologists to turn from psychometrics to cognitive psychology to understand the nature of intelligence.

THE COGNITIVE APPROACH: INTELLIGENCE AS MENTAL PROCESSING

Unlike the psychometric approach, which is concerned with the *products* of intelligence, such as the answers a person gives to questions on an IQ test, the cognitive approach looks at the *processes* that underlie intelligent behavior, the particular *mental operations* that are responsible for generating those answers. The goal of the cognitive approach is to describe the specific components of a given intellectual task and to specify the mental operations that are needed to perform it (Hunt, 1985; Sternberg, 1982). For example: What actually goes on inside someone's head upon being asked to arrange a pile of blocks into a hexagon or to name the first five presidents? Cognitive theorists think that individual differences in intelligence depend on the specific mental processes that different people use, and on the speed and accuracy with which they use them. For example, an intelligent person may be someone who pays attention to more details of a problem or reasons more carefully about these details.

INDIVIDUAL DIFFERENCES IN ATTENTION

In Chapter 5, we described attention as a limited mental resource. Doing two things at once (driving and talking) or doing something complicated (programming a computer) requires more of our attentional resources than doing something simple (chewing gum). Perhaps intelligence is related to an ability to pay attention to more things at a given time.

To find out, subjects in an one experiment were given the Raven Progressive Matrices Test (Figure

9.2) as a measure of their general intelligence. IQ scores were obtained by increasing the difficulty of the problems until each person made errors. After the test was administered, it was presented again. This time only easy items were given, but the subjects had to do a second task at the same time. While taking the IQ test, people had to hold a lever between two posts, using the thumb and index finger on their left hands. Normally, this is easy to do, but it becomes difficult when the subjects are distracted by attempting to solve Raven Matrix problems simultaneously. To the extent that the IQ test involves attentional resources, the addition of the motor task will be less taxing for those who scored high on the initial IQ test—their attentional resources will not be strained by the concurrent easy IQ test. On the other hand, those who initially scored low (those who found the first test hard) should do relatively poorly on the motor task because they need their attentional resources to answer the IQ test. Just such a pattern was found, supporting a connection between individual differences in attention and individual differences in IQ scores (Hunt, 1980). This finding illustrates one of the ways in which a particular cognitive process—in this case, attention—can be a critical element in an intellectual task.

INDIVIDUAL DIFFERENCES IN REASONING

Psychologist Robert Sternberg (1977; 1985) has argued that intellectual performance is based on the joint operation of **components** and **meta-components of intelligence.** Components include those cognitive processes that enable a person to encode stimuli, hold information in short-term memory, mentally compare different stimuli, perform mental comparisons, make calculations, and retrieve information from long-term memory. Metacomponents, on the other hand, are the higher-order processes that we use to analyze a problem and to pick a strategy for solving it. Sternberg wanted to know whether individual differences in intelligence might be related to individual differences in the use of these cognitive processes.

In one series of studies, he observed how people use the different components on verbal problems of the following sort:

Washington is to 1 as Lincoln is to ? (5 or 10).

Sternberg analyzed the analogies task into a series of components.

- First, subjects must encode each of the items in the analogy—in other words, they must form a mental representation of it. In our ex-

ample, Washington could be encoded as the first president, a Revolutionary War hero, the person on a one-dollar bill, and so on. Lincoln could be encoded as the sixteenth president, a Civil War leader, the person on a five-dollar bill, and so forth.

- Second, once a person has developed a list of attributes for each item's mental representation, the two lists are compared for matching attributes.

In this present example, the comparison process would reveal that Washington and Lincoln were both presidents whose pictures appear on U.S. currency. The solution to the analogy is then obvious:

Washington is to 1 as Lincoln is to 5.

Sternberg found that people who scored high on analogy tests spent more time encoding the items and forming accurate mental representations than people who scored low did. Having devoted sufficient time to getting a clear mental image of the problem components, highly skilled analogy solvers then made faster comparisons than less skilled people did. Therefore, people with better reasoning ability generally spend more time understanding the problem but reach their solutions faster than those less skilled on the task. Sternberg and Davidson (1982) reached similar conclusions with other reasoning tasks (Figure 9.8).

Research by cognitive psychologists is increasing our understanding of intelligence by dissecting intellectual tasks into their basic mental processes to reveal the underlying sources of IQ differences (Baron, Badgio, and Gaskins, 1986; Carpenter and Just, 1986, among others). Mental processes such as paying attention and getting a clear image of the problem were discussed previously in Chapters 5 and 8, and they play an important role in intelligence. However, all of the tests and theories that we have examined so far have one flaw—each overlooks how intelligence functions in everyday life.

THE IMPLICIT THEORY APPROACH: INTELLIGENCE AS THAT WHICH IS USED EVERY DAY

At the beginning of this chapter we asked you to think of two classmates and determine who was more intelligent. We also asked you what you meant by "intelligence." Each of us has an **implicit theory** of intelligence, a set of beliefs that we use to form opinions about the intelligence of the people

FIGURE 9.8 Consider the following problem. Water lilies double in area every 24 hours. At the start of the summer there is one water lily on a pond. After 60 days, the pond is completely covered. On what day is the pond half covered? People do well on this type of task if they carefully encode the relevant information. People with good reasoning skills note that the most important fact in this problem is that lilies double in number every day. Consequently, if the pond is covered on the 60th day, it must have been half covered on the 59th day.

we know. You may find it hard to articulate your theory. However, if you were pressed to list those qualities that you think all intelligent people possess, chances are that your list would be similar to those reported in a survey of Yale undergraduates, community residents, and experts in the field of intelligence (Sternberg, Conway, Ketron, and Bernstein, 1981). Three broad categories of behaviors were considered intelligent by these people. Although the makeup and relative importance of the categories differed somewhat from group to group, the categories can be roughly described as *verbal ability, problem solving ability,* and *practical intelligence and social competence.* An intelligent person shows verbal ability by being articulate, having a good vocabulary, and reading with high comprehension. This person shows problem solving ability by accurately interpreting information and making appropriate decisions. Finally, an intelligent person demonstrates practical intelligence and social competence by being aware of the effects of her or his actions on others and by having a social conscience. This research

suggests that most of us develop implicit theories that define intelligence, many of which include a common core based on these three categories (Siegler and Richards, 1982; Sternberg et al., 1981; Yussen and Kane, 1985).

By identifying the unspoken theories we tend to hold regarding intelligence, several researchers have begun to develop new theories and to test them empirically (Sternberg, 1985; 1986; Gardner, 1983). Consider two such theories that follow.

TRIARCHIC THEORY AND PRACTICAL INTELLIGENCE

Over the past decade, Robert Sternberg has been instrumental in showing that the cognitive approach to intelligence can supplement the traditional psychometric approach. In recent years, Sternberg has enlarged his view of intelligence to go beyond the typical testing situations. His latest theory of intelligence, called **triarchic theory,** is a three-part theory that builds on his earlier componential approach to reasoning. Based on observing Yale graduate students, Sternberg became convinced that his componential theory did not cover all types of intelligence. To illustrate the different varieties, he described three idealized graduate students—Alice, Barbara, and Celia—who represented the different kinds.

Alice always scored high on intelligence tests, had nearly perfect undergraduate grades, and was easily accepted into graduate school. Her outstanding analytic skills made her one of the top students during her first year when critical thinking was essential for doing well on course exams. During the second year, however, the emphasis shifted from critical to creative thinking as students needed to develop ideas for research. Alice had trouble thinking creatively and dropped to the lower half of her class. Alice represents the *componential* aspect of intelligence. This is the type that is measured by standard intelligence tests and is necessary for acquiring new information and thinking critically about it.

Barbara's undergraduate grades and test scores were low by Yale's standards, but she had great letters of recommendation that said that she was a creative thinker with lots of ideas for research. Barbara was not admitted to Yale, but she did work with Sternberg as a research assistant and they did a number of important projects together. Says Sternberg, "Academic smarts are easy to find, but creativity is a rare and precious commodity" (Trotter, 1986). Barbara represents the *experiential* type of intelligence. This is the type that enables people to adjust creatively and effectively to new tasks and situations.

Celia was different still. Her undergraduate grades, test scores, and letters of recommendation were all good but not great. Celia lacked Alice's superior analytic ability and Barbara's exceptional creative ability, yet she had a knack for finding out what was important to succeed in graduate school and for doing the kind of research that is valued in psychology. Celia was best described as being "street-smart." She represents the _contextual_ type of intelligence. This kind of intelligence enables people to select environments in which they can function, to adjust to those environments, and to modify them if necessary.

Sternberg's earlier componential theory could account for Alice, but it was too limited to explain Barbara or Celia. The new triarchic theory, involving componential, experiential, and contextual aspects of intelligence, is broad enough to describe all three of these people who represent the different kinds of intelligence that are found in all of us

in varying degrees. The problem with standard intelligence tests is that they only measure "academic" intelligence, the componential aspect, and ignore the other kinds. To remedy this situation, Sternberg has embarked on a new research program designed to measure practical intelligence. **Practical intelligence** is most closely related to the contextual aspect of intelligence. It is defined as intelligence that operates in the real world, as a person adapts to and shapes his or her environment.

One line of research in this new approach has been to look at how people decode nonverbal messages. For example, Figure 9.9 shows four pictures of pairs of individuals. Two of these pairs are real couples involved in a romantic relation; two others are "false" couples. Can you tell the real couples from the imposters? What cues did you use to help make a decision? Table 9.6 shows the cues reported by the people in this study. When subjects looked at a large set of pictures of genuine and fake couples, they could pick out the real couples far

FIGURE 9.9 Couples, real or false? Two of these pictures show people who are actually romantically involved; two other pictures show people who are merely pretending. Can you pick out the genuine from the fake couples? Research on social competence and practical intelligence suggests that we use a variety of nonverbal cues (Table 9.6) to make such decisions and can usually do better than chance at them. In these examples, the real couples are those in the right-hand column.

TABLE 9.6 Nonverbal Cues Used to Select Genuine Couples in Pictures

Cue	Description
Relaxation	Genuine couples generally look more relaxed with each other.
Angle of Bodies	Genuine couples tend to lean toward each other more than false couples.
Body Positioning	Genuine couples tend to position their arms and legs more naturally than people who are posing.
Tenseness of Hands	Fake couples tend to show tenseness in their hands; genuine couples do not.
Socioeconomic Match	Genuine couples appear to match better in socioeconomic class (guessed from clothes and physical appearance) than false couples.
Body Distance	Genuine couples stand physically closer together than false couples.
Physical Contact	Genuine couples show more physical contact than false couples.
General Similarity	Genuine couples tend to be more similar in appearance (including dress, age, race, and ethnic group) than false couples.

Adapted from Sternberg (1986).

better than chance would allow (Sternberg and Smith, 1985). Clearly, the subjects were picking up something.

What is significant about this approach is that it goes beyond purely mental skills to measure attitudes and emotional factors that can influence a person's mental skills. In fact, Sternberg (1986) has recently compiled a list of reasons why intelligent people sometimes fail (Table 9.7). These mental stumbling blocks, he believes, explain why conventional intelligence tests tell us so little about performance in everyday life.

THEORY OF MULTIPLE INTELLIGENCES

Howard Gardner is another psychologist who has been similarly dissatisfied with the narrowness of the mental abilities measured by traditional in-

telligence tests. In his 1983 book, *Frames of Mind*, Gardner looked at data from intelligence tests, cognition experiments, and neuropsychological research. He also studied people with special abilities, including child prodigies and gifted retardates. He believes that there are seven independent types of intelligence that, because of heredity or training, develop differently in different people. These seven intelligences include *linguistic, logical-mathematical, spatial, musical, bodily-kinesthetic, intrapersonal,* and *interpersonal intelligence* and they are described in Table 9.8. The first three types are measured by standard intelligence tests. Thus, a person could do poorly in

TABLE 9.7 Some Reasons Why Intelligent People Fail (Too Often)

Reason	Description
Lack of Motivation	In many situations, motivation is at least as important as intelligence in achieving success.
Lack of Impulse Control	Impulsive behavior tends to detract from intellectual work.
Lack of Perseverance	Giving up too easily in the face of difficulty is a prescription for failure.
Fear of Failure	Unwillingness to try something new because of fear of failing removes the opportunity for growth and the realization of full intellectual potential.
Procrastination	When putting things off becomes a lifestyle, it becomes a serious problem that leads to missed opportunities and failure.
Inability to Delay Gratification	Accomplishing little things that are easy to do at the expense of big things that take longer results in smaller rewards in the future.
Too Little or Too Much Self-Confidence	Lack of self-confidence prevents one from developing one's intellectual abilities and ultimately results in a self-fulfilling prophecy. Too much confidence can lead to a failure to correct areas in need of self-improvement.

Adapted from Sternberg (1986).

TABLE 9.8	Gardner's Multiple Intelligences

Type	Description
Linguistic	Involved in reading, writing, listening, and talking. High linguistic intelligence can be demonstrated by writers.
Logical-mathematical	Involved in most scientific thinking, including solving logical puzzles, deriving proofs, and performing calculations. High logical-mathematical thinking can be demonstrated by philosophers and mathematicians.
Spatial	Involved in moving from one location to another or determining one's orientation in space. High spatial intelligence can be demonstrated by architects and marine navigators.
Musical	Involved in singing, composing, conducting, or performing on a musical instrument. High musical intelligence can be demonstrated by musicians and composers.
Body-kinesthetic	Involved in using one's body or its various parts to perform skillful and purposeful movements. High body-kinesthetic intelligence can be demonstrated by dancers, athletes, and surgeons.
Intrapersonal	Involved in understanding one's self and having insights into one's thoughts, emotions, and actions. High intrapersonal intelligence can be demonstrated by Zen masters.
Interpersonal	Involved in understanding other people and one's relations to others. High interpersonal intelligence can be demonstrated by psychotherapists, teachers, salespeople, and politicians.

From Gardner (1983) and Sternberg (1990).

school and still be a musical genius. Including the last four types under the heading of intelligence is a source of some controversy (Sternberg, 1990; Walters and Gardner, 1986). Whether these categories truly represent separate types of intelligence or merely different talents, Gardner would like to see them all measured to provide a truly global assessment of each person's ability (Gardner, cited in Ellison, 1984). Interestingly, the formal examinations of the ancient Chinese that we described in this chapter's Historical Background section measured proficiency in the "six arts"—writing, arithmetic, music, archery, horseback riding, and the rites and ceremonies of public and private life (Wing, cited in Ellison, 1984). These arts are strikingly similar to Gardner's multiple intelligences.

CROSS-CULTURAL IMPLICIT THEORIES

The similarity of the Chinese arts and Gardner's multiple intelligences might lead you to wonder if people from different lands have similar implicit theories of intelligence. Psychologists have also wondered about this possibility. To find out, they asked people from different countries what characteristics they associated with intelligence. This is called **cross-cultural research** because it compares the reponses of people from different countries. For example, Australian and Chinese people have somewhat different conceptions of intelligence. Both say that intelligence is associated with creativity, problem solving, and a large knowledge base. However, on other criteria the two cultures differ. The Australians believe that language and communication skills are important, while the Chinese stress carefulness and correctness of thinking (Keats, 1982). Similar differences in emphasis are found in cross-cultural studies of African tribespeople. The Mashona people of Zimbabwe associate intelligence with being cautious and prudent in social relations, while the Bagandan people of Uganda associate it with persistence and mental order (Irvine, 1969; 1970; Wober, 1974). Some of these responses are similar to our conception of practical intelligence. However, enough differences are present to caution us to guard against applying Western notions of intelligence indiscriminately to people of other lands.

INTEGRATION OF CONCEPTUAL APPROACHES

In considering the different conceptual approaches to intelligence, several issues are worth noting. First, Gardner's theory of multiple intelligences and Sternberg's triarchic theory are the most current and sophisticated attempts to provide a general theoretical framework for all of intelligence research. Though preliminary, these theories are important. They extend research into such new areas as the study of practical intelligence. They also provide a broad and comprehensive view of human abilities, extending from linguistic and mathematical abilities on the one hand to interpersonal abilities on the other. Both theories can be expected to have an impact on the direction of future research (Kail and Pellegrino, 1985).

Second, the psychometric and cognitive approaches actually complement one another (Ackerman, 1987). General factors, including Thurstone's primary mental abilities, are useful for identifying individual areas of strength or weakness. The cognitive approach can be used to assess areas of weakness and provide a detailed diagnosis of why a person may be deficient in this area. This integrative approach to intelligence is consistent with the original purpose of intelligence tests outlined by Binet nearly a century ago—they provide a diagnostic assessment of individual ability.

Finally, given this merging of approaches, how do we define intelligence? Is it whatever an intelligence test measures? Is it a set of components and metacomponents? Is it a set of primary mental abilities or seven different "frames of mind"? One of the most compelling reconceptualizations of the nature of intelligence was provided by psychologist Ulric Neisser (1979), who argued that intelligence is not one but many things that are loosely related. He defined intelligence as a "fuzzy" concept to which many features are relevant. Neisser's cognitive approach to intelligence is based on the work of Eleanor Rosch (Rosch, 1978; Rosch, Mervis, Gray, Johnson, and Boyes-Braem, 1976) who studied how people form concepts based on their everyday experiences. This work is closely related to the topic of concept identification that we discussed earlier in Chapter 8.

There are two important features of concepts, **fuzzy sets** and **prototypical instances**. Fuzzy sets refer to the absence of features that decisively define the members of the sets. Prototypical instances refer to examples that fit the category better than others. The classic example of a fuzzy set is derived from the work of philosopher Ludwig Wittgenstein (1953). Wittgenstein pointed out that there is no single feature that defines the concept *game* and distinguishes it from a nongame. Rather, games resemble one another in much the same way that members of a family do. Each is different from another, and yet each shares features in common. Because of this lack of defining features, instances are considered members of a concept based on their degree of relatedness to the "best" exemplar of the concept, the prototypical instance. Prototypical instances are those that possess all the typical properties of the concept. For example, a robin is a prototypical exemplar of the concept *bird*

because it displays the typical properties of the concept—it has wings and feathers, builds nests, flies, lays eggs, and is a certain size. Decisions about the concept membership of other objects, such as sparrows, eagles, turkeys, and penguins, are based on the extent to which these instances resemble the prototype. However, none of the features listed above decisively defines the concept *bird*. Airplanes have wings and fly but are not birds; chickens and penguins do not fly but are nonetheless considered birds.

Neisser has argued that *intelligent person* is a similar fuzzy concept. "Our confidence that a person deserves to be called 'intelligent'," he said, "depends on that person's overall similarity to an imagined prototype, just as our confidence that some object is to be called 'chair' depends on its similarity to prototypical chairs." The important implication of this view is that two people may be considered intelligent for very different reasons; that is, they may possess different prototypical features. One may be socially and musically adept, the other may be logical and witty. Furthermore, Neisser's conceptualization accommodates the variety of implicit and explicit theories about intelligence. After all, different researchers have focused on different facets of the set of typical features. And if intelligence is a fuzzy concept, then disagreement about *what* defines intelligence is to be expected because there is no single feature or set of features that decisively defines this concept.

From this point of view, tests such as the Stanford-Binet are effective because they measure a variety of dimensions that are important for determining how closely an individual resembles the prototypical "intelligence-test smartie" who gets all the items right. However, Neisser is quick to point out that traditional assessments of intelligence measure only some of the relevant dimensions. Other dimensions, including social competence and practical intelligence, have not yet been measured by standard IQ tests, but they are probably important dimensions of the prototypical intelligent person. Thus, in viewing intelligence as a fuzzy concept, Neisser has in effect shown how both the implicit and the explicit psychometric theories offer different, yet valid, views of intelligence. Keeping within this cognitive perspective, intelligence of either the implicit or explicit variety can be seen as the end result of skillful information processing. It comes from acquiring information, storing it in memory, retrieving it, combining it, and using it in the process of acquiring new information and skills (Humphreys, 1979).

INTERACTIONS:
Genes, Environments, and Individual Differences

We have shown how intelligence is measured and defined, and how it is influenced jointly by heredity and environment. There is one more issue to address: How do genetic and environmental influences combine to produce differences between individuals? The study of individual differences in psychological characteristics will figure prominently in the chapters on personality and abnormal behavior that follow. In the present context of intelligence, individual differences are indicated whenever people produce a distinctive pattern of results on different components of an intelligence test. For example, one person might score high on a test of verbal relations and low on a test of quantitative reasoning, while another person might do the reverse. People are rarely uniform in their abilities. In this final section we will outline how genetic and environmental factors could lead to these individual differences in measured intelligence.

Genetic and environmental influences are not independent influences on intelligence—they interact. A "good" genetic predisposition does not contribute a certain number of IQ points, nor does a "good" environment add more points to the total. A child with a genetic predisposition to be gifted and another child with a genetic predisposition to be educably retarded will not encounter the same environments. The gifted child will likely be placed in different classes and will be treated differently by his or her teachers. And even if the environment were the same for each child, the children would not respond to it in the same way.

Behavior geneticists have described several forms of gene–environment interactions, and they are shown in Table 9.9. *Passive* gene–environment interactions occur because a child's parents normally provide the child not only with genes but also with an environment. For example, a child with gifted parents will receive good genes and also will be exposed to a home full of intelligent conversation, reading materials, and educational toys. Intelligent parents might also be more likely to notice any reading deficiencies in their child and to take steps to alleviate them early. These passive interactions (passive on the part of the child) serve to increase the correlation between a child's IQ and the IQ of his or her parents.

Evocative gene-environment interactions refer to the fact that children with differing genetic backgrounds may elicit different reactions from their environments. For example, a child who is predisposed to learn with great difficulty may frustrate his or her teachers, whereas another child who learns quickly may please his or her teachers. As a result, the second child will have more pleasant dealings with the same teachers. Once again, the effects of genes and environments are not independent. If the slow learner encounters teachers who are skillful and patient, this child may develop as high an adult IQ as a quick learner raised in a deprived and unresponsive environment.

Finally, *active* gene-environment interactions result when children with different genetic backgrounds seek out different environments. A child who learns easily will take different courses in school than a child who learns slowly. Such interactions can result not only from cognitive factors but from motivational factors as well. For example, Anne Anastasi (1982) noted that the early findings of adult gender differences in math ability, differences that we described in Chapter 2 as being no longer significant or reliable, might have resulted from women shying away or being steered away from competitive math courses rather than from their lack of the requisite intellectual ability. She found that even girls who scored higher than most boys in their early math courses tended to chose not to go on to the more difficult math courses. As a result of such choices, children with different genetic backgrounds may actually construct different life environments for themselves.

TABLE 9.9 **Gene–Environment Interactions**

Type of Interaction	Description
Passive	Parents who provide the child's genes also provide the child's environment.
Evocative	Children with different predispositions evoke different reactions from their environments.
Active	Children with different predispositions seek out different environments.

Adapted from Plomin, DeFries, and Loehlin (1977).

In summary, because parental inputs tend to amplify genetic tendencies, because children create effects on their own learning environments, and because children tend to choose environments that can modify their intelligence, genetic and environmental effects on intelligence cannot be neatly separated. As we will see in Chapters 13 and 15, the same sorts of gene–environment interactions are important not only for intelligence but also for such personality traits as friendliness and aggressiveness and for such disordered behavior patterns as depression. ■

IN CONTEXT: INTELLIGENCE

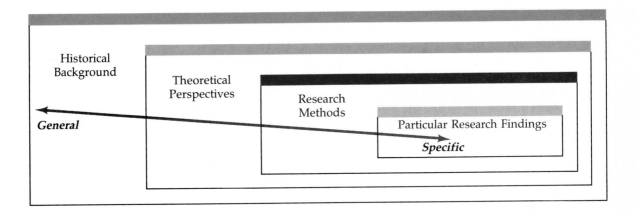

STUDY QUESTIONS

How do psychologists define intelligence?

Is intelligence the result of genes we receive from our parents or the educational experiences we have after birth?

What factors lead to mental retardation or genius?

How is intelligence assessed?

What are the necessary criteria for an effective intelligence test?

HISTORICAL BACKGROUND

1. The use of tests to assess competence dates back at least 2,000 years to the ancient Chinese. By the middle of the nineteenth century, written tests were used throughout Europe and the United States for awarding college degrees, assigning government positions, and licensing doctors and lawyers.

2. Late in the nineteenth century, Sir Francis Galton suggested that intelligence could be measured. He believed that differences in intelligence were hereditary.

3. In 1905, Alfred Binet and Theodore Simon devised the first objective intelligence test to identify children who were likely to have difficulty in school. Their test measured attention, comprehension, and memory and allowed children to be assessed as normal, advanced, or retarded. Binet believed that children with scholastic difficulties could be helped by special education.

4. Lewis Terman revised Binet's test in 1916. His revision, called the Stanford-Binet Intelligence Scale, became the model for intelligence tests and the latest revision is still widely used. During World War I, Terman and other psychologists developed group intelligence tests. Their success led to the widespread use and acceptance of mental tests in business and education today.

MODERN THEORETICAL PERSPECTIVES

1. The **psychometric approach** analyzes IQ scores to determine whether intelligence consists of

one general factor or a variety of factors. Charles Spearman originated a statistical procedure called **factor analysis** to identify the factors that make up intelligence. He concluded that IQ tests measured general intelligence, **g,** and specific factors, **s,** reflecting different abilities. Louis Thurstone disagreed with Spearman and argued that intelligence consists of seven primary mental abilities. Lack of agreement over what are the primary components of intelligence and how many independent components there are has plagued this approach.

2. The **cognitive approach** seeks to describe the specific components of a given intellectual task and specify the mental operations that are needed to perform it. Individual differences in IQ scores depend on the specific mental processes that people use and the speed and accuracy with which they use them.

3. The **implicit theory** approach goes beyond typical IQ testing situations to consider how intelligence is expressed in everyday life. People tend to have an implicit theory of intelligence that includes three broad categories—verbal ability, problem solving ability, and practical intelligence. Robert Sternberg's triarchic theory and Howard Gardner's theory of multiple intelligences provide a comprehensive view of human ability, ranging from linguistic and mathematical abilities to interpersonal ability.

RESEARCH METHODS

1. The most frequently used technique for studying intelligence was the **correlational method.** For example, it was used to show that widely-used intelligence tests have high concurrent validity (Jensen, 1980) and to show that infant memory correlates with IQ scores during childhood (Fagan, 1984). The correlational method was also used in numerous studies of twins (reared together or apart) to assess similarities in IQ scores (Bouchard and McCue, 1981, among others.)

2. Other methods used include the **case study, survey,** and **experimentation.** Case studies of Alonzo Clemens and Leslie Lemke revealed unusual abilities in two gifted retardates (Schmidt, 1983). A survey showed how a wide spectrum of people defined the concept of intelligence (Sternberg et al., 1981). Finally, a variety of researchers used experimentation. For example, one experiment determined whether mentally retarded children could learn memory strategies (Brown et al., 1979).

RESEARCH FINDINGS AND SUMMARY

1. **Intelligence** involves the ability to learn from experience, to adapt to one's environment, to work in a goal-directed manner, and to solve problems and think creatively.

2. Contemporary intelligence tests provide a measure called an **intelligence quotient** (IQ) that was originally derived from the ratio of a person's mental and chronological ages. An average IQ score equals 100, and IQ scores are normally distributed around that value.

3. Intelligence tests can be **individually administered** or given to a group of people at one time. **Group administered** tests are less costly and more time-efficient but provide less detailed information about an individual's performance than individually-administered tests. Many tests include both **verbal** and **performance scales.**

4. **Standardized** tests of intelligence are characterized by administration under standard conditions, objective scoring, and the use of a standardization sample for comparison purposes. Most widely used intelligence tests are highly **reliable** (repeated testing on the same test produces consistent results) and demonstrate good **concurrent validity** (different tests produce similar results) and **predictive validity** (tests predict academic success or capability). The absence of **construct validity** (proof that a test measures "intelligence") has been a major source of criticism.

5. Earlier tests of infant intelligence based on sensory and motor performance showed little relation to later IQ scores or school achievement. More recent tests assess infant cognitive abilities and show a relation to subsequent IQ scores. This relation suggests moderate stability in infant intelligence. Beyond infancy, stability in intelligence test scores increases throughout childhood and adolescence and reaches a peak during early adulthood.

6. Peoples are classified as **mentally retarded** if they score below 70 on a standard intelligence test and if they show impairment in adaptive behavior. In general, the more severe the retardation, the less able the person is to function in society. Some retarded people, called **gifted retardates,** are amazingly proficient in a particular skill. Retardation has its origin in biological and cultural-familial factors.

7. People with IQ scores over 130 are labeled **mentally gifted.** These people adapt very well

to challenging tasks, and they benefit from accelerated educational opportunities.

8. **Heritability** refers to the extent to which individual differences in a characteristic such as intelligence are due to differences in the genetic makeup of the people in a population. Varied estimates of heritability have been obtained from *twin* and *adoption* studies. At present, research indicates that both genetic and environmental factors strongly influence intelligence test performance.

9. There is controversy over the relative importance of genetic and environmental influences on IQ scores in the interpretation of group differences. On the average, people from lower-class homes score lower than people from upper-class homes, and black Americans score lower than white Americans. Environmental differences between groups make it impossible to determine to what extent, if any, group differences in IQ scores reflect genetic factors. Projects such as *Head Start* are aimed at providing a positive learning environment for socioeconomically disadvantaged children.

10. There is little consensus among psychologists concerning a single theory of intelligence. Different conceptual approaches, including the psychometric approach, the cognitive approach, and the implicit theories approach, all have research support.

11. Current thinking holds that intelligence is the end result of skillful information processing. Intelligence comes from acquiring information, storing it in memory, retrieving it, and using it in the process of acquiring new information and skills.

ADDITIONAL READINGS

Cronbach, L. J. 1984. *Essentials of psychological testing*, 4th ed. New York: Harper & Row. A thorough introduction to the study of psychological testing and individual differences.

Eysenck, H. J., and Kamin, L. 1981. *The intelligence controversy*. New York: Wiley. Two leading figures in the field of intelligence debate the relative importance of genetic and environmental factors.

Gardner, H. 1983. *Frames of mind: The theory of multiple intelligences*. New York: Basic Books. A novel approach to intelligence that pools data from many sources to provide a framework for understanding individual differences. This book is especially useful for examining cross-cultural differences.

Kail, R., and Pellegrino, J. W. 1985. *Human intelligence: Perspectives and prospects*. New York: Freeman. A scholarly yet highly readable introduction to the field of intelligence. Special attention is directed to the psychometric, information processing, and cognitive-developmental approaches to intelligence.

Plomin, R., DeFries, J. C., and McClearn, G. E. 1980. *Behavioral genetics: A primer*. San Francisco: Freeman. A well-written introduction to the field of behavioral genetics with a special focus on individual differences in intelligence.

Sternberg, R. J. 1986. *Intelligence applied: Understanding and increasing your intellectual skills*. New York: Harcourt Brace Jovanovich. An interesting attempt by a leading researcher to help people understand their intellectual skills and to become more proficient in using them.

Sternberg, R. J. 1990. *Metaphors of mind: Conceptions of the nature of intelligence*. UK: Cambridge University Press. A thoughtful examination of the different metaphors of human intelligence and a look at how these metaphors guide our theories and research.

Willerman, L. 1979. *The psychology of individual and group differences*. San Francisco: Freeman. A good, basic introduction to the literature on individual differences and group differences, including differences in gender, age, and race.

MOTIVATION AND EMOTION

R eason is . . . the slave of the passions. (*David Hume, 1739*)

Chapter Outline

On December 22, 1984, Troy Canty, Barry Allen, James Ramseur, and Darrell Cabey approached Bernhard Goetz on a New York subway train and asked him for $5. In response to Canty's request, Goetz withdrew a loaded pistol and shot all four of the young men. When his case came to court, one question was central: What motivated Goetz's behavior? His defense claimed that he believed the four youths were about to rob him—they were carrying weapons and had just demanded money from him. Goetz said that Canty, who made the request, had a smirk on his face and "a gleam in his eye." Other facts support the argument that Goetz was acting in a reasonable and rational manner: He had been previously mugged three times; each of the youths he shot had a prior police record, and all were later arrested on other charges (except for the one paralyzed by the shooting). The prosecution, however, claimed that Goetz was driven by an inner passion for violence—that he was a "coldblooded sadistic man." In support of their claim, Goetz shot one of the youths twice, saying "You don't look so bad, here's another." The question of "why" people do the things they do, so important in courts of law, is the central concern of the psychology of motivation.

The psychology of **motivation** is concerned with the forces that energize and direct behavior. Questions about motivation are of interest in all walks of life, not just in the courthouse. Irrational passions may lie hidden behind behavior that seems eminently reasonable. Thomas Edison was a brilliant inventor who used his great powers of reason in a passionately driven way. By the time he died, he had earned 1,093 patents, and the phonograph and light bulb were among his credits. His motto was "genius is 1% inspiration and 99% perspiration." Charles Darwin sweated out 119 scientific publications, Einstein 248, and Freud 330 (Simonton, 1984). Margaret Mead's record of accomplishment is staggering; it includes

Albert Einstein. Psychologists interested in motivation ask questions about *why* people do the things they do. Albert Einstein published 248 books and articles. On the surface, Einstein's hard work seems to have been motivated by simple scientific curiosity. Some psychologists, including Sigmund Freud, have argued that even such seemingly sensible behaviors as scientific curiosity are based on irrational needs including unconscious sexual and aggressive urges. The dichotomy between irrational and rational influences is at the basis of several important issues in the study of motivation and emotion.

39 books, 1,397 published articles, letters, and interviews, and 28 honorary degrees (Howard, 1984). Were these people simply exercising the human capacity for reason, or were they, as Hume would have it, controlled by passions?

It is fascinating to ponder grand questions about motivation, questions such as what induces someone to violence or to great achievement. But there are equally fascinating questions about such everyday motivations as hunger and thirst. Although many of us take these motivations for granted, there are anorexics such as we discussed in Chapter 6, who eat so little that they come close to starvation. Others seem unable to restrain their eating, and some individuals have reached weights of over 1,000 pounds. As we shall see, hunger is controlled by a remarkably sophisticated system of physiological checks and balances.

When Bernhard Goetz shot the four youths on the subway, his motivational state had a special quality to it; it was seething with emotion. He told the police that "If I had more bullets, I would have shot them all again and again. . . . I was gonna gouge one of the guys' eyes out with my keys afterwards" (*Newsweek*, June 29, 1987). The words motivation and emotion come from the same Latin root (*movere*—to move), and we can define an **emotion** as a special motivational state involving physiological arousal and special bodily reactions. Consider the difference between anger and thirst. When people are angry, they generally show a higher-than-usual state of general bodily arousal, specific facial expressions (including leering and sneering), and other bodily movements (clenched fists, for example). Those bodily reactions communicate angry people's emotional states to other people. When people are thirsty, on the other hand, they do not necessarily show a high level of arousal or any thirst-revealing facial expressions. As we will see, the line between emotions and other motivational states is a fuzzy one, and we shall discuss some interesting areas of overlap later in the chapter.

The line between different emotions is itself a matter of some debate. What exactly *is* anger? How is it different from fear or joy? There is some agreement that all emotions have a physiological component, but there is serious disagreement about whether one emotion is biologically different from another. Some psychologists claim that anger, fear, joy, and love are physiologically identical, differing only in the way we think about them. Others claim that the mind is merely a passive observer of our joys and sorrows, registering them after they have already occurred. This debate is not just an idle philosophical issue. It has a central practical implication for the field of psychology. As we will see when we discuss psychotherapy, some popular forms of psychological treatment are based on the idea that emotional disorders can be treated by changing the way in which we think, whereas other treatments bypass the mind and treat the body's emotional reactions directly.

In sum, this chapter will address several general questions: What role do biological factors play in motivating human behavior? How are those biological motivations influenced by learning and rational cognition? How are emotions similar to, and how are they different from, other motivational states? How are specific emotions—such as fear and anger—different from one another?

HISTORICAL BACKGROUND:
Human Nature

The brightness of her cheek would shame those stars
As daylight doth a lamp; her eyes in heaven

Would through the airy region stream so bright
That birds would sing and think it were not night.
See! how she leans her cheek upon her hand:
O! that I were a glove upon that hand,
That I might touch that cheek.

(*Shakespeare, from* Romeo and Juliet)

In the famous balcony scene, Shakespeare's Romeo uttered these words of longing only hours after locking eyes with Juliet. When passionate love strikes, all else in the universe seems to pale in significance. What comes first? A passion that wrests control of the powers of reason, making each new Romeo perceive his *amore* as more beautiful than all the stars in the heavens? Or does reason guide our passions? Perhaps Romeo talked himself into a fit of passion with all his romantic ruminations, and maybe he could have cooled himself down by making an objective list of her liabilities as well her assets (1. nice eyes (+), 2. pretty hair (+), 3. member of the enemy clan (–), 4, nasty cousin Tybalt who slew my friend Mercutio (–). . . .).

In the first century A.D., the Stoic philosopher Epictetus argued for a **rationalist** view of human motivation. This position held that our actions are grounded in free choices of the rational mind. To quote Epictetus: "It is not the things themselves that disturb men, but their judgments about the things." The great philosopher Descartes (1596–1650) agreed that people could control their own behavior rationally, but he also speculated that our bodies are sometimes like machines, controlled by mechanical impulses produced by the brain in response to outside events. Advances in physics and other sciences led to an increasing acceptance of this **deterministic** view by the time Charles Darwin published *The Expression of Emotions in Man and Animals* in 1872. Darwin argued that human emotional expression had the same roots as the emotions shown by other animals:

With mankind some expressions, such as the bristling of the hair under the influence of extreme terror, or the uncovering of the teeth under that of furious rage, can hardly be understood, except on the belief that man once existed in a much lower and animal condition. . . . He who admits on general grounds that the structure and habits of all animals have been gradually evolved, will look at the whole subject of Expression in a new and interesting light.

(Darwin, 1872)

Darwin argued that emotions evolved in the same way that any physical trait evolved. Anything that helps in the struggle for survival—that helps to conserve resources, protect young, or attract mates—is likely to be preserved over generations. Emotional expressions help an animal to survive by communicating with other animals. Consider the sneering or snarling faces shown in Figure 10.1. Darwin argued that, in an ancient era, the teeth were bared only as a preparation for attack. Over time, however, those animals who delayed in attacking were able to avoid bodily injury by simply signaling the intention to attack. Tooth and claw combat is costly to both competing animals, and it is eminently more efficient to "discuss" it with facial expressions first.

FIGURE 10.1 The expression of anger in two different mammalian species. Darwin believed that many emotions expressed by dogs and humans can be traced to their common origin, in combination with the continuing adaptive advantage of such expressions.

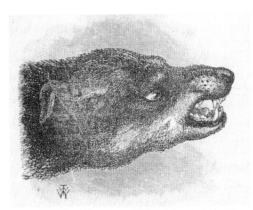

The philosophical dichotomy between rational and nonrational motivation has continued within the field of psychology. When William James wrote the *Principles of Psychology* in 1890 he aligned the discipline with the nonrational side of the controversy. Following Darwin's reasoning, James argued that much of human behavior is controlled by **instincts** like those that control the behavior of other animals. To James, an instinct was an "impulse" to act in a certain way in response to a particular bodily sensation. A sneeze is a good model of what James meant by an instinct—an irritation to the lining of the nasal passages leads automatically to a burst of air from the lungs. In discussing the instinctive underpinnings of human behavior, James asked:

Why do men always lie down, when they can, on soft beds rather than on hard floors? Why do they sit round the stove on a cold day? . . . Why do they prefer saddle of mutton and champagne to hard-tack and ditchwater? Why does the maiden interest the youth so that everything about her seems more important and significant than anything else in the world?

(James, 1890)

The answer, according to James, is that certain impulses occur automatically, without our even having to think about them. James held that humans have a rich repertoire of automatic impulses, from simple reflexes such as sucking in infants, to more complex reactions such as sympathy, curiosity, shame, and love. Presaging some modern researchers, he believed that phobias are based on natural fears of environmental stimuli, including dark places, heights, and strange animals.

Another early psychologist who was influenced by Darwin was Sigmund Freud. Freud argued that sexual and aggressive impulses, although instinctive, are unacceptable in human society. Our parents, acting as agents of society, punish us for any expression of these socially taboo impulses (biting another child, for example, or playing with his or her genitals). After several years of unpleasant clashes with society, children suppress their selfish instinctive tendencies, and divert sexual and aggressive energy into socially acceptable behaviors. (Freud used the term *displacement* for the diversion of instinctual energy.) Freud probably viewed Romeo and Juliet as failures of this socialization process: They not only lost control of their sexual impulses, but they seemed to be expressing a bit of hostility against their parents as well (after all, they both fell for a family enemy).

Freud's position on reason and the passions was clearly in line with Hume's and directly opposed to the rational theories of motivation—not only is reason the slave of the passions, but it is a blind slave; most of the time those passions operate without conscious awareness.

One aspect of Freud's viewpoint is particularly important to note. Unlike William James, Freud felt that there are only one or two instincts, and that they have only a very general energizing effect on behavior. Sexual and aggressive urges are redirected into socially acceptable channels, and thus these two instincts are the bases of other motives. For instance, a Freudian might view Einstein's 238 scientific publications as a very successful displacement of sexual and aggressive energies.

Later psychologists agreed with Freud that human behavior is not motivated by a large number of specialized instincts, but many disagreed that all motivation could be reduced to sexual and aggressive instincts. Instead, they rejected the concept of instinct in favor of a more general concept of **drive** (Hull, 1943). A drive is like an instinct in that it is a form of physiological arousal, but it is different from an instinct in that it does not specify a particular pattern of behavior. Consider hunger—it may arouse a person to look for food, but it does not specify what or how to eat. American psychologists believed that there are only a few biological drives, such as hunger, thirst, and the need to maintain a 98.6° body temperature.

Drive theorists believed that we are motivated by **drive reduction**: the desire to turn off the physiological states associated with hunger, thirst, and other drives. According to the drive reductionist view, we would prefer to exist in a totally unstimulated condition (something like sleeping on warm sand after a satisfying meal). As we will see, this assumption has aroused some interesting controversies.

What is the biological basis of motivation and emotion? Can all human motivation be explained in terms of the reduction of simple drives? The issues raised here, begun as philosophical debates, have stimulated a great deal of research that continues to this day. We now turn to this research. ■

MOTIVATION

Behavioral scientists in America and Europe went down different paths to search for the biological bases of motivation. The major European contributions to the study of motivation have come from **ethology.** Ethology is a field that links psychology and zoology. Ethologists study animals living in natural environments by the method of naturalistic observation, in hopes of understanding how an animal's behaviors (the song of a mockingbird, for example) might have evolved to help the animal adapt to its natural surroundings. American motivational psychologists, on the other hand, have historically studied laboratory animals in controlled experimental settings. They have been concerned with the general principles that underlie such drives as hunger and thirst across different species, from rats to humans. As we shall see, the two different approaches have led to two rather different views of motivation.

THE NATURALISTIC APPROACH TO BIOLOGICAL MOTIVATION

Ethologists have been most interested in studying motivations that appear without experience in undomesticated animals. For instance, Niko Tinbergen (1951) was awarded the Nobel prize for work on the mating behavior of a small European fish called the stickleback. Similar courtship rituals can be observed in many common aquarium fishes, as one of the authors of this text observed in the Siamese fighting fish he kept as a child:

> The Siamese fighting fish (Betta splendens) is a colorful little fish from Indochina that can be purchased in almost any pet shop. People in Thailand and Cambodia put two males into a jar together and watch the drama begin, as the fish spread their fins, puff out their gills, brighten into iridescent shades of indigo and scarlet, and then tear into one another like a pair of prize fighters. Because of their pugnaciousness, male Siamese fighting fish are often raised in isolation.
>
> Following the advice of a book from my local pet shop, I attempted to simulate the water conditions of springtime in Siam by raising the water temperature, running the water through peat moss to increase its acid content, and feeding the fish an abundant supply of crustaceans and insect larvae. Exactly as I had been led to expect, the fish began to prepare himself for mating. He scooped down mouthfuls of air, coated them with a special salivary secretion, and constructed a "bubble nest" (about 7" in diameter and 1" high) that floated in a corner of the tank. Meanwhile, I had been treating a female fighting fish to warm acid water and similar cuisine. She began to show a

recognizable abdominal swelling from the development of her egg supply. I then introduced the female into the male's tank and he immediately responded as if preparing for a fight, brightening up, spreading out his gills and colorful fins, and actually tearing a chunk off her tail fin. She swam away for a moment, but then returned and met his display with one of her own. She began to wriggle in a very uncharacteristic manner as he swam around her. He continued his display, and occasionally nudged her. After a minute or so of this dancing, the male performed a very unusual movement, actually wrapping his body around the female's. (See Figure 10.2.) At this point she released several eggs into the water, and they were met by his release of sperm fluid. He scooped them up, spit them into the bubble nest, and then returned to repeat the last few movements several times until over 100 eggs were released. For the next week, the male guarded the eggs and then the tadpole-like neonates. So courageous was his parental zeal that he would bite my finger if I placed it into the water. (The finger alone was considerably larger than he was.) About a year later, I watched the exact same ritual performed by one of his sons, who had been raised in isolation, away from any other fighting fish.

(Douglas T. Kenrick)

FIGURE 10.2 Male and female Siamese fighting fish in a mating embrace. These behaviors are examples of instinctive *fixed action patterns.* Such behaviors do not require learning—they emerge in fish raised in isolation.

INSTINCTIVE BEHAVIOR

These Siamese fighting fish demonstrated all the characteristics of instinct—behavior that is inborn, characteristic of a species, and locked to particular forms of stimulation. The fact that the same ritual occurred in a fish raised in isolation indicates that it was not a function of experience but was instead wired into his nervous system. What is it that is wired in in such a way? For one thing, instinctive behavior systems involve special sensitivities to particular environmental stimuli, called **sign stimuli.** These are environmental stimulations that trigger an instinctive pattern. In the case of the Siamese fighting fish, the sight of the female served as a sign stimulus that triggered a set of courtship displays on the part of the male. Likewise, his own display served as a releaser for her courtship displays. These special behavioral displays are another feature of instinctive behavior. The special mating behaviors of the female and male are called **fixed action patterns.** Fixed action patterns are behavioral configurations that appear in the same form in all members of a species. Different fixed action patterns occur in response to different sign stimuli. Males never wrap themselves around one another in a fight, for instance, nor do they use the courtship dance in other situations. There is another important feature of instincts—they are conditional. That is, they do not always emerge just because the appropriate sign stimuli are present. The animals must be in an appropriate state of *hormonal readiness;* that is, their bodies must inform them when it is time to perform the fixed action patterns. In the case of the two fighting fish, their hormonal condition was put on red alert for mating by several factors. Changes in the environment (warm acidic water and an abundance of live food associated with spring rains) caused certain changes in their bodies (like the production of eggs) that in turn led to the release of different hormones and associated changes in behavior.

One final point about the Siamese fighting fish's mating ritual is that it involves **response sequences,** or complicated chains of behaviors that are interwoven with cues from the environment, cues such as the responses of another animal. Instinctive behaviors are often much more complicated and drawn out than a simple sneeze. Research on the mating behaviors of another fish, the European stickleback, has revealed that behaviors at a later step of a mating sequence would be performed only if a pair had gone through the earlier steps (Morris, 1958).

In work with ring-necked doves, Daniel Lehrman and his colleagues have shown that mating sequences involve a step-by-step interplay between behavior and hormones (Lehrman, 1966). When a male ring dove encounters a female, he courts her with a series of bowing movements and cooing sounds. Observing the male's behavior affects the female's pituitary gland, which leads to hormonal changes in her body, and to the development of her eggs. As they build the nest and the female responds to the male's flirtations, both of their bodies secrete progesterone, and that hormone will later stimulate them to sit on the eggs. These mating sequences involve reciprocal interactions in which the behavior and physiology of one mate depends on the responses of the other mate. If the animal is prevented from going through each of the stages, it will not respond in the same way to the same stimulus. In the fighting fish, for example, the female does not release her eggs until the male wraps around her. However, if he simply swam up and wrapped around her, without appropriate foreplay in the form of a courtship dance, she would not be likely to release her eggs.

ARE THERE HUMAN INSTINCTS?

Do we have sign stimuli, fixed action patterns, and response sequences? If we do, what are they? Ethologists have suggested several possibilities, although not all psychologists are convinced. Irenaus Eibl-Eibesfeldt (1975; 1980), a noted ethologist, made a case for the human smile as a fixed action pattern. To begin with, the smile is found across all human cultures, and children in such remote cultures as the !Kung Bushmen of the Kalahari desert begin to smile at the same age as youngsters in Omaha, Nebraska, and Hoboken, New Jersey. Not only that, but they smile in response to the same sorts of situations (that is, at events that make them happy). One could try to make a case that all cultures have passed on similar traditions about smiling over the years, but that is stretching an argument. Nor can the cultural transmission argument explain another fascinating fact. Children born deaf and blind also begin to smile at the same age and for the same reasons as do Bushmen and Nebraskans. Since these children can neither observe others nor hear about the norms for smiling, their ability to smile suggests a special human fixed action pattern (Figure 10.3). At the same time, seeing a smile on someone else's face seems to be a sort of sign stimulus. It is automatically recognized all around the world, regard-

FIGURE 10.3 Laughter from a girl born blind and deaf. The fact that this girl is cut off from the usual channels of imitation learning suggests that her smiling and laughter is innate.

less of culture or language (Ekman et al., 1987). The combined evidence, then, suggests that the smile occurs without experience (like a fixed action pattern), and that it serves as a universal communication function (like a sign stimulus).

Do humans have an innate mating ritual, like the Siamese fighting fish do? Some ethologists think we might. Desmond Morris (1972) discussed human response sequences that parallel the mutual dance be observed in stickleback fish. He argued that, like sticklebacks and fighting fish, our species also has an innate mating ritual in which a man and a woman go through several steps of courtship that change each other's body chemistry and cement a mating bond. When we discuss sexual attraction later, we will describe some films taken by ethologist Eibl-Eibesfeldt that seem to show an innate flirting sequence in humans around the world. Of course, there are vast differences between people and Siamese fighting fight. People's biological predispositions are always modified by their past learning experiences and present situations.

DRIVES: HUNGER, THIRST, AND PHYSIOLOGICAL BALANCE

Instead of studying naturalistic behavior patterns, American psychologists during the first half of this century used laboratory methods to study primary and secondary drives. **Primary drives,** like instincts, are assumed to be wired into the nervous system at birth. However, a primary drive is believed to differ from an instinct in that learning,

not genetic programming, determines how an individual responds to a drive. Hunger is a good example of a primary drive. We do not need to learn to feel hunger. It is automatically turned on in response to certain physiological events, and turned off in response to others. However, a drive such as hunger does not specify exactly which behaviors should be used to satisfy it (the way the reproductive instinct in Siamese fighting fish does). Some of us walk to the deli and order a ham and swiss on rye, others reach for a bowl of rice and chopsticks, and some even nibble on fried grasshoppers. Drive theorists assume that those specific preferences are learned through operant conditioning, and this is the basis of **secondary drives.**

HOMEOSTASIS: MAINTAINING INTERNAL BALANCE

What goes on in your body when you feel hungry? In a classic study of this drive, Walter Cannon inserted an inflatable balloon into his colleague's stomach (Figure 10.4). The man pressed a button whenever he felt hunger pangs; it turned out that his experience of hunger was associated with contractions of his stomach's walls. This research helped establish the view that drives come from **tissue needs.**

Drive theorists such as Cannon thought of a tissue need as a bodily irritation—an unpleasant sensation that motivated the person or animal to alleviate it. Hunger contractions are unpleasant sensations that can be reduced by eating; dryness in the mouth is an unpleasant sensation that can be reduced by drinking, and so on. In 1932, Cannon introduced the concept of **homeostasis,** which refers to an ideal balanced state in the body's internal environment. As an example, your body has physiological mechanisms that balance the ratio of salt to water in your blood. When the salt ratio is too high, dehydration of *osmoreceptors* (brain cells sensitive to the blood's salt–water balance) leads to thirst and water retention; when it is too low, other body mechanisms stimulate water loss. Cannon believed that the body has a number of mechanisms to maintain a balanced internal environment. To understand the concept of homeostatic equilibrium, it helps to think about the thermostats that maintain the temperature in your house. Imagine that you wanted to keep your house between 65 and 80 degrees. When the temperature drops below 65 the thermostat in the heating system clicks on and begins to warm the house up. When the temperature reaches 65, the thermostat

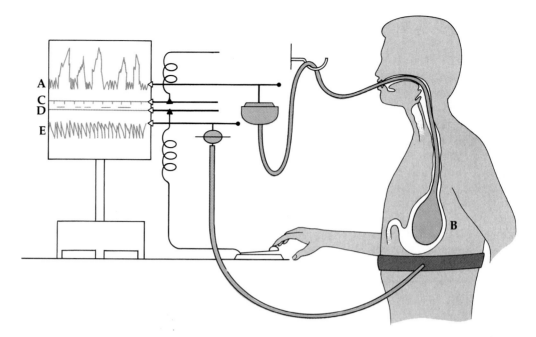

FIGURE 10.4 The apparatus used by Cannon and Washburn (1912) to study the relationship between stomach contractions and the experience of hunger.   Each stomach contraction squeezes a balloon (B) which leads to a mark on the revolving drum at the left (A). When the subject feels a hunger pang, he or she presses a button which makes a mark at D. (C marks the passage of time, and E is a record of respiration). The subject's reports of hunger pangs were directly correlated with the stomach contractions.

clicks off, and the heating stops. When it gets above 80, however, another thermostat clicks on the air conditioner. In this way, your house is maintained at a comfortable temperature, and the extremes of frigid cold and sweltering heat are avoided. In a similar way, when we have gone too long without eating, mechanisms in the brain's limbic system respond to low blood sugar in the bloodstream and turn on the heat, in the form of feelings of hunger. When you eat, the food in your stomach stimulates sensory receptors in the stomach walls that notify the limbic system to turn off the hunger pangs long before you go to the opposite extreme and rupture the walls of your stomach.

Psychologists and physiologists have learned a great deal about what turns thirst on and off, and about how we manage to keep our body temperature very close to 98.6° (Klein, 1982; Petri, 1981). Our bodies normally do such a good job of regulating these processes that we rarely think about them. Let us focus on two drives that are a bit more troublesome to regulate, hunger and sex. These drives are interesting because their regulation is partially automatic but also partially subject to conscious control. If you have ever tried to control your appetite for some delicious food, you

may have wondered just how much your reason can override your passions. Psychologists still debate this issue, but some recent evidence suggests that your Epictetian rational side (or your cerebral cortex, if you will) does not have an easy time lording over the Humean passions controlled by the body's homeostatic mechanisms.

SHORT-TERM REGULATION OF HUNGER

Hunger researchers have studied two types of hunger control mechanisms—those that control the short-term *initiation* and *termination* of eating, and those that control body weight over the long term. In the short term, there are a number of mechanisms that turn hunger on and off. Fullness of the stomach can shut off the pangs of hunger (Berkun, Kessen, and Miller, 1952), but that is not necessary. If a food is highly nutritive, an animal will stop eating long before its stomach is full (Janowitz and Hollander, 1953; Deutsch, Puerto, and Wang, 1978). This suggests that the stomach has receptors that chemically analyze the incoming food. So part of hunger is based on information that the brain receives from the stomach (Teitlebaum and Epstein, 1962), but there is more to it than that. One early experiment showed that animals who had their stomachs removed continued to eat, indicating that stomach pangs are not the only signals for hunger (Tsang, 1938). Later research suggests that the brain's hypothalamus analyzes blood glucose levels to decide whether to turn hunger on or off (Klein, 1982). For instance, if a chemical that blocks glucose metabolism is injected into the hypothalamus, it tricks the brain's sugar-monitoring system into underestimating blood sugar, and the result is voracious eating (Oomura et al., 1969). Hunger seems to be turned off when glucose receptors in the liver are stimulated by sugar in the bloodstream (Russek, 1971; Schmitt, 1973). There is also evidence of fat receptors that are related to hunger control (Klein, 1982). It seems that the brain has several sources of information that can turn hunger on and off—receptors in the stomach walls, in the mouth, in the liver, and in the brain's hypothalamus all help maintain a balance between starvation and an overstuffed stomach. As one author put it: "Motivation is . . . overdetermined . . . the human body has 'back-up systems' that come into play if one mechanism fails" (Petri, 1981).

Your body has a wonderfully efficient system for monitoring internal cues to hunger. Nevertheless, you may have found yourself ignoring the nearly painful fullness in your stomach to go back for a second helping of Aunt Mildred's blueberry–cream cheese torte after the already enormous meal you ate last Thanksgiving. Drive-reduction theorists originally viewed drives as motivational states that originate inside the body. However, researchers found that those internal "tissue needs" are complemented by **incentives**, external stimuli that excite drives. Aunt Mildred's delicious torte would be an example of an incentive. What makes some stimuli capable of motivating behavior? Part of the incentive value of food seems to stem from innate preferences based on evolution. For instance, young infants show happy reactions to sweet flavors, and unhappy reactions to bitter flavors, as the facial expressions in the baby in Figure 10.5 show. Why is sweet food inherently pleasant? Evolutionary biologists suggest that a sweet taste signals ripened fruit, which has greater nutritive value than unripened fruit. Why is bitter food inherently unpleasant? Bitterness is often associated with poisonous alkaloids in plants, so avoiding a bitter taste is often a good bet for survival.

So evolution seems to have played some role in food choice, but many food preferences, such as some people's preference for New York-style over Chicago-style pizza, are a function of learning. To survive, we need to find nutritive and nonpoison-

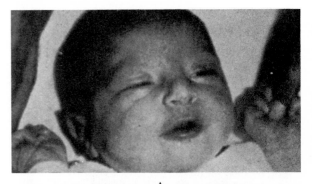

A

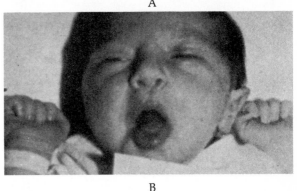

B

FIGURE 10.5 Taste and innate emotional expressions. Newborn infants respond with different facial expressions to (A) sweet tastes (sugar solution), and (B) bitter tastes (quinine solution), in a 1977 study conducted by J. E. Steiner.

ous substances to eat. Some of our learning processes seem to be specially adapted for food recognition. As we discussed in Chapter 6, for instance, we very quickly learn to avoid foods previously associated with nausea (Garcia and Koelling, 1966; Rozin and Kalat, 1971). This form of conditioned food aversion is powerful, and may play a role in self-induced starvation in cancer patients. Since they are treated with chemicals that produce nausea, these patients learn to associate nausea with anything they eat (Braun and Nowlis, 1989).

LONG-TERM REGULATION OF HUNGER

Beyond the immediate sensations of hunger and the tastiness of the food in front of us, how do we regulate our body weight over the long haul? Why is it that some of us have such an easy time maintaining a slender frame that only varies by a pound or two over several years, while others of us seem prone to expand our waistline with no more effort than it takes to raise a few chocolates to our lips?

One theory of long-term regulation is associated with experiments that produced the grossly obese

FIGURE 10.6   A rat with a lesion of the ventrome-dial hypothalamus (VMH).   Such a lesion leads the animal to eat voraciously until it attains a weight that is two or three times its normal level.

rat in Figure 10.6. Rats with surgical lesions in an area adjacent to the VMH (ventro-medial hypo-thalamus) (Gold, 1973) eat enormous amounts of food, attaining weights two to three times their pre-operation level. (If you weigh 150 pounds, imagine being 300 to 450 pounds by the time you sat down to dinner next Thanksgiving.) Although rats with VMH lesions eat voraciously, there are some interesting limits to their eating habits. For one thing, they are picky eaters. Compared with normal-weight rats, they eat more good-tasting food but, if they are given food that tastes bad, they will eat less.

Psychologist Stanley Schachter compared these VMH rats with obese human beings and found a number of similarities. (See Table 10.1.) Using these similarities, he hypothesized that obese peo-ple are controlled by external rather than internal cues (Schachter, 1971; Schachter and Rodin, 1974). In one study designed to test the theory, the researchers left a plate of small hors d'oeuvre sandwiches in front of students working during lunchtime. Sometimes the plate held only a few sandwiches, while at other times it was heaped up with an immense mound of food. Overweight col-lege students tended to eat all the sandwiches in front of them, regardless of whether there were too few or too many for a normal-sized lunch. If too much food was put in front of normal weight-students, on the other hand, they would eat only a small portion. Normal weight students would also walk over to a nearby refrigerator and get more if there was not enough food on the plate. Over-weight students would not. Overweight students also seemed to watch the clock as an eating signal, and the researchers could alter their eating be-havior by moving its hands. Whether the clock in the lab was sped up or slowed down, obese sub-jects tended to eat when it said 12:00. Normal-weight students seemed to pay more attention to their internal clocks, and tended to eat when it was really 12:00, regardless of what the clock said. In other words, normal-weight students seemed to be following an internal clock rather than the one on the wall. Another test of the "externality" hy-pothesis found that, when asked to judge the taste of ice cream, overweight, compared with normal-weight, students ate more of a creamy, expensive brand, but less of a cheap, bitter-tasting one. These findings suggested to Schachter that obesity might be caused by a failure of the brain's hypothalamic weight control centers to process information. Obese people therefore have to rely on external cues, and in a society with an overabundance of high incentive food cues within easy reach it is easy to overdo it.

Despite the parallels between VMH rats and obese humans, recent researchers believe there are problems with Schachter's original theory about

TABLE 10.1   Similarities Between Obese Humans and Rats with Ventromedial Hypothalamic (VMH) Lesions

When compared to normal humans and rats, obese humans and VMH rats:

1. Eat more when food tastes good.
2. Eat less when food tastes bad.
3. Eat slightly more food per day.
4. Eat fewer meals per day.
5. Eat more food per meal.
6. Eat more rapidly.
7. React more emotionally.
8. Engage in less physical activity.

Findings from Schachter (1971).

external cues and obesity. Although VMH damage does make humans obese (Teitlebaum, 1961), very few overweight people have suffered such damage. In fact, "externality" in obese people, when it is found, may be a *result* of being overweight, not a cause (Nisbett, 1972, Rodin, 1981). Recent research has focused on the way that a person's homeostatic weight control mechanisms are set to keep each individual at a particular weight by controlling *metabolism*—that is, the body's energy expenditure. It seems that our waistline is influenced by more than just short-term hunger. In the old view, VMH rats got fat because their brain's "off" mechanism for hunger was destroyed, so they just ate and ate. However, these rats actually did curb their eating, but did so at a much higher body weight. This research suggested the possibility that an animal's body has a **set point**—a target weight maintained by increases or decreases in metabolism and hunger. It appeared that the operation changed the body's normal set point.

In support of the set-point theory, it was found that if the rats were fattened up before the experiment, they stopped eating sooner after the operation that altered their hypothalamuses. This suggested they reached a new set point sooner (Powley and Keesey, 1970). And if VMH animals are kept on the same diet as normal rats, they nevertheless gain more weight, presumably by slowing down their energy expenditures and thus burning off less fat (Han and Liu, 1966). In further support of the set point theory, thin people could be temporarily fattened up if they gorged on rich foods during an experiment but they immediately began to lose weight when the experiment was over (Sims, 1974). On the other hand, overweight people who have lost weight on a diet very often gain it back (Johnson and Drenick, 1977).

How do our bodies maintain their set points? When we go on a diet, it appears the body simply lowers its metabolic rate to compensate for the loss of calories. One study of men put on a starvation diet found that they reduced their metabolisms an average of 29 percent (Keys et al., 1950). Differences in waist size are not a simple function of the amount of food we eat, then. If you slow down your eating in hopes of reducing your 36 inch waist down to a 32, you may start to feel tired as your body slows down to maintain its set point (Bray, 1969). Studies of adopted children suggest that the body's set point is partly determined by heredity (Stunkard et al., 1986). Some of us are thus born with a predisposition to be hefty, others with a proclivity to be skinny. However, environmental variables surely enter into the equation.

Whether someone is obese depends more upon his or her social status than on his or her nationality. Since people of the same social class share fewer genes than people of the same nationality, this indicates that societal influences may be more important than genes in determining obesity (Stunkard, 1968). Even identical twins, who share the same genes, can vary by several pounds.

If overweight people have a chronically higher set point for body weight, that may help explain why some people act as if their eating desires are constantly straining against a leash. Because our culture regards a slender body as the standard of beauty, overweight people must diet chronically to keep below their set points. One team of researchers found that people who expressed concerns about their weight indeed acted like "restrained eaters" (Herman and Mack, 1975). Once the restrained eaters were induced to start overeating—they were given a milk-shake before beginning taste trials—the voracious wolves inside them took over, and they had a hard time stopping.

Stanley Schachter (1982) noted that many weight-reduction studies have yielded discouraging results, with most of the losses being regained in a year or two. If nature has conspired to give some people a higher set point than others, the prospects might seem bleak for obese individuals who wish to lose weight. However, Schachter noted that some programs, including Weight Watchers, are successful in helping people to maintain a weight loss. Further, he surveyed 161 adults from a college campus and a summer resort town, and found that 29 percent of them had tried to lose weight. Of that group, 63 percent had been successful (they had lost at least 10 percent of their weight, and maintained the loss for over a year). One tactic is to avoid eating fatty foods, since these stimulate secretions of insulin, thereby increasing the appetite (Rodin, 1985). Another is to exercise regularly. A program of regular exercise can raise the body's metabolism even during a diet (Thompson et al., 1982). Crash dieting may not be a good strategy, since our bodies may store more fat under conditions of intermittent starvation (Rodin, 1982). For the same reason, it appears that several meals a day are better than one or two. Sometimes the results can be encouraging indeed. The successful weight losers interviewed by Schachter reported losing an average of 34.7 pounds, which they had managed to keep off for an average of 11.2 years.

Why the discrepancy between Schachter's optimistic findings and the discouraging findings of many obesity treatment programs (Johnson and

Drenick, 1977)? Part of the answer may be that body weight results from an interaction of genes and experience. Schachter's subjects were not that far from the normal weight range, and probably experienced fairly rapid success in their diets. For example, it is easier to get into trim shape if you are only 15 pounds overweight, as compared to 50. Someone obese enough to seek treatment, on the other hand, may be fighting not only a higher biological set point but also a lower likelihood of rapid reinforcement for dieting.

SEX: BIOLOGICAL OR LEARNED?

We have seen that hunger is, in part, a biologically based drive. There are centers in the brain specially sensitive to information about blood sugar, stomach fullness, and so on. But what about sex? No one has ever survived without eating, but many have survived long periods, even lifetimes, without sex. This has led some psychologists and sociologists to regard sex as a nonbiological drive (Simon and Gagnon, 1977, among others). On the other hand, we would not be here if our ancestors were not at least somewhat motivated to reproduce. From an evolutionary perspective, it would be surprising if some biological mechanisms had not evolved to ensure reproduction. Thus, biological theorists often regard sex as a primary drive (Daly and Wilson, 1983).

We will first consider evidence that sex is a nonbiological drive. One line of support for this viewpoint comes from findings that sexual drive seems to vary widely from culture to culture. The two most noted cultural extremes in sexual activity come from the island cultures of Mangaia in Polynesia and Inis Beag off the coast of Ireland. A typical woman raised on Inis Beag waits until she is well into her twenties to have her first sexual intercourse; she never engages in premarital petting below the waistline, and only rarely above. Once she is married, she and her husband engage in intercourse without foreplay, and she never has an orgasm. A typical man from this island also has no experience, even with petting, until he marries after age 30. A Mangaian woman, on the other hand, has extensive experience with premarital petting and intercourse. She is likely to have several partners over the years, and they come into the family hut at night to make love to her while the other family members pretend not to notice. She learns to achieve simultaneous orgasm with her partner, and may even tease him about her previous lovers' erotic abilities. A Mangaian man also has numerous premarital partners, beginning

at age thirteen when an older woman teaches him lovemaking strategies (Marshall, 1971; Messenger, 1971).

The existence of such wide cultural diversity does suggest that learning plays an important role in the expression of sexuality, but does it prove that biology is unimportant to sexuality? Not necessarily. Perhaps people on Mangaia and Inis Beag do not differ in their inclination to have sex, but only in their tendency to act on those inclinations. In the same way that we can learn cultural rules about when and what to eat, and can even refrain from eating when the rules tell us to fast, so we may learn when and where to express our sexual impulses.

However, another line of evidence seemed to make an even stronger case for sex as a social motive. The male's testes produce large quantities of a hormone called **testosterone,** and the females ovaries produce a group of hormones called **estrogens.** Both of these hormones were found to have strong effects on sexual behavior in animals, but early studies suggested that humans could function without them. For instance, women whose ovaries are removed did not report any reduced interest in sex (Bancroft, 1978). Moreover, some men whose testicles were removed reported a continuing sex drive (Bremer, 1959). But two lines of evidence suggest that psychologists may have overinterpreted those earlier findings and jumped too quickly to a negative conclusion about sex and biology. First, the sexual behaviors of human males and females do appear to differ in some ways that parallel those found in many other mammals. Second, sexual drive in both men and women appears to be partly related to the hormone testosterone. We will review the evidence on these two points.

GENDER AND SEXUALITY

One important biological factor seems to be related to sexual drive across all cultures—gender. Even in prudish Inis Beag the men are, compared with the women, more interested in sex—masturbating before marriage, and initiating intercourse afterwards. Across a wide variety of species, animal researchers frequently find that males and females often differ in sexual motivation. In particular, males are more likely to initiate sexual contact than females are, and they are more interested in pursuing new partners. For instance, male rats who have copulated to the point of fatigue with one female will perk up again if new females are dropped into their cages (Dewsbury, 1981). Females who have just copulated, on the other hand, are not so interested in new partners, and in general prefer familiar ones. This phenomenon has been dubbed the "Coolidge effect" after an anecdote about the late president:

One day the President and Mrs. Coolidge were visiting a government farm. Soon after their arrival they were taken off on separate tours. When Mrs. Coolidge passed the chicken pens she paused to ask the man in charge if the rooster copulated more than once each day. "Dozens of times" was the reply. "Please tell that to the President," Mrs. Coolidge requested. When the President passed the pens and was told about the rooster, he asked, "Same hen every time?" "Oh, no, Mr. President, a different one each time." The president nodded slowly, then said, "Tell that to Mrs. Coolidge."

(Bermant, 1976; cited in Symons, 1979)

Gender differences in sexuality show up frequently in survey and experimental studies. Compared with women, men who participated in Kinsey's classic survey of sexual behavior reported more premarital, extramarital, and homosexual experiences, as well as more variant experiences, such as sex with animals. Males are vastly overrepresented in virtually all categories of sexual deviation (Davison and Neale, 1982). More recent studies have found that since the "sexual revolution" of the 1960s and 1970s women and men are more closely matched in premarital sexual behavior, but they still retain very different attitudes about sexuality (Hendrick et al., 1985; Townsend, in press). For instance, one study found that over 50 percent of teenage girls who were having premarital sex expected to marry their partners, but only 18 percent of their male partners had a similar expectation (Coles and Stokes, 1985). Surveys find that men are only slightly more likely to have extramarital affairs than are women, but they report being much more *eager* to have affairs than women are (Daly and Wilson, 1983). It seems that men's extramarital affairs are more limited by the number of willing partners, while women are more likely to set their own limits (Hinde, 1984).

Interest in erotica also differs between the sexes. *Playboy* and *Penthouse* have much higher readerships than *Playgirl*, and even subscribers to *Playgirl* are predominantly male (Shepher and Reisman, 1985). In one study general psychology students were offered a choice between two experiments to complete a class requirement. One experiment was designed to sound rather boring—

it was on "the perception of geometric figures." The other one, they were told, would involve seeing an erotic film, which would include explicit scenes of sexual intercourse. The results showed a clear gender discrepancy. Males were more likely to choose the erotica experiment, while females were more likely to choose to avoid it (Kenrick et al., 1980).

Many biological theorists think that these gender differences are linked to the evolutionary past. They argue that our female ancestors, who carried the unborn child and nursed it afterwards, had an initially higher investment in the offspring and more to lose from an ill-chosen mating (Hamilton, 1964; Trivers, 1972). Thus female humans, like female mammals in general (Hinde, 1984), were selected for being more selective about when and with whom they would have sexual experiences. Those past evolutionary pressures might be related to genetically based hormonal differences between men and women.

HORMONES AND SEXUALITY

Throughout their lives, and particularly after puberty, males produce more of the hormone testosterone than do women. Females, on the other hand, produce more estrogen than do men. These two hormones have a number of effects on behavior. Developmentally, they influence the structure of the body, including certain parts of the brain that are involved in sexual drive (Svare and Kinsley, 1987). In women, estrogen leads to the growth of rounder hips and breasts; in men, testosterone leads to the development of additional facial hair and the growth of upper body muscles. These hormones also have less obvious effects. A female animal exposed to testosterone in her mother's womb will later behave more like a male (Phoenix et al., 1959; Svare and Kinsley, 1987). Human females who are accidentally exposed to high doses of testosterone before birth may end up as *hermaphrodites*, individuals with genitalia that are partly male and partly female. As children, these hermaphrodites are clearly identified as girls, but they show some behavioral remnants of the early hormones—they play more "masculine" sports, and have activity levels more typical of boys (Ehrhardt and Meyer-Bahlburg, 1981).

Estrogen and testosterone also seem to influence sexuality. In animals, estrogen influences female *receptivity* to sexual advances. In addition to being produced in the testes, testosterone is produced in the adrenal glands of both females and males, and it influences *sexual advances* made by both sexes (Bancroft, 1978). We mentioned that early studies of sex hormones in humans seemed to disagree with animal findings, which suggested to some that sex was not a biological drive in humans. Later findings led to a reappraisal of this early conclusion. For one thing, men who have their testicles removed show very dramatic decreases in sexual behavior, indicating that the earlier reports of castration findings were probably misinterpreted (Bancroft, 1978). There was some initial sexual interest shown by some of the castrated men, but by the time a year had elapsed there was very little interest left even in most of those who initially showed some activity. The fact that all interest does not immediately stop is not surprising, since the adrenal glands continue to produce some testosterone even after castration. Similar patterns are found in castrated cats—those with sexual experience may continue to engage in sexual behavior (Rosenblatt and Aronson, 1958).

For women, however, the results seem to pose more of a problem for a biological view. Removing the ovaries simply does not influence women's frequency of intercourse, although it does decrease vaginal lubrication during sexual arousal. This seems to suggest that hormones are less important for women's sexual responses than they are for men's. However, removal of a woman's adrenal glands *does* lead to a decrease in reported interest in intercourse (Waxenberg et al., 1959). Why? It appears that testosterone rather than estrogen may be more closely linked to initial sexual approach in *both* sexes (Bancroft, 1978). Removing a woman's ovaries has no effect on sexual desire because the estrogen they produce is not the relevant chemical; however, removing the adrenal glands does have an effect because they produce testosterone. Later research indicates that high testosterone levels predict the amount of early teenage sexual experience for boys and girls alike (Smith, Udry, and Morris, 1985). Identifying testosterone as the hormone responsible for initiating sexual desire helps explain the multitude of findings showing that males—who produce much more of it—have, in general, a higher likelihood of initiating sexuality in all of its manifestations. To say that estrogen does not play a role in initiating sexual desire is not to say that it plays no role in sexual activity. How a woman responds to a sexual experience—whether she has an orgasm and whether she reports a high degree of sexual arousal during intercourse—seems to be related to estrogen levels (Moos and Lunde, 1969; Udry and Morris, 1968).

Differences between the two sexes thus seem to be related to testosterone, and clinical problems that lead to the cessation of testosterone production do seem to be associated with decreased sex drive. However, the differences in sex drive among normal people of one sex are not directly tied to variations in their relative levels of testosterone (Persky, 1987). In most cases, people suffering from sexual dysfunction do not have insufficient levels of sex hormones (Schreiner-Engel et al., 1989). Instead, sexual problems often result from psychological *inhibitions* that stem from fears of failure, from problems in relationships, or from associating sex with disgust or anxiety (Bancroft, 1986). So, although it was incorrect to assume that sex hormones have nothing to do with human sexual activity, it would be just as incorrect to interpret the evidence as indicating that humans are puppets of the chemicals in their bloodstreams and that their environment is irrelevant. Like hunger, the intensity of sex drive appears to result from an interaction of the biological organism and sociocultural experiences.

If testosterone can explain the difference in intensity of sex drive between males and females, some researchers wondered whether it might be related to the difference in direction. For instance, homosexuals and heterosexuals might differ from one another because of differences in testosterone levels. However, research has shown that testosterone is related to the *intensity* of the sexual drive in both sexes, but is not clearly related to its *direction* (Persky, 1987).

REDUCING DRIVES VERSUS SEEKING STIMULATION

We have seen that hormonal and physiological states play some role in sex, in thirst, and in hunger. But how do we explain Isaac Newton's driving desire to make a scientific contribution? Are there different hormones related to intellectual zeal? It seems unlikely; but, if there are not, how then do we explain such motivation?

Drive theorists can provide a partial answer with the concept of secondary drive—a concept based on the same idea as secondary reinforcement. To refresh your memory about conditioning: A neutral stimulus (say, a light) associated with a primary reinforcer (such as food) will come to elicit some of the same responses as the primary reinforcer. A rat will work to turn on a light that was previously associated with food, for instance. Drive theorists assume that intellectual rewards become motivating because they were previously associated with the satisfaction of primary drives. As an example, perhaps Isaac Newton was driven to academic achievement because when he was a child his mother rewarded him with cookies and hugs every time he said something smart. In fact, Newton was his mother's favorite, and as an adult he was described by one contemporary as "excessively covetous of praise" (Lerner, 1973).

The concept of secondary drive may offer a partial explanation of Newton's drive for praise, but his scientific curiosity itself might have another basis. The fact that even animals show intrinsic curiosity challenges the idea that all motivation can be reduced to either the reduction of primary drives or secondary associations with that drive reduction (Figure 10.7). Animals will sometimes even work to *increase* their levels of stimulation—solving puzzles for which there is no reward (Harlow et al., 1950) or opening a window just to watch an electric train move around a track (Butler and Harlow, 1954). So animals act as though stimulation is hardly unpleasant, and humans seem to find a complete *lack* of stimulation irritating rather than relaxing. In one fascinating study, people were paid to spend a few days in a sensory deprivation chamber. They were placed on a comfortable bed in a soundproof room, with padding around their hands and an opaque light shield around their heads. They could eat or drink at will through tubes near their mouths. Virtually all forms of sensory stimulation were therefore greatly reduced. If the drive-reduction theory were correct, the sensory deprivation chamber should have been heaven—all normal irritations, distractions, and bodily itches were reduced to near zero. Did the subjects experience it as heavenly? No. In fact, subjects found the experience quite unpleasant, and many asked to be released early. Some even began to hallucinate (Bexton, Heron, and Scott, 1954). The sensory deprivation results, combined with the findings that show that animals and people will often seek arousal, suggest that a complete reduction of stimulation is not particularly desirable.

Based upon these findings, the idea that motivation is based on drive-reduction principles was replaced with the idea that organisms seek an **optimum level of arousal** (Berlyne, 1963). It seems that either too little *or* too much stimulation is unpleasant. What is too little and what is too much stimulation seems to vary from one person to the next. Some people enjoy a great deal of sensation, while others try to avoid it. These individual differences in the desire for excitement and change are measured with the the **sensation seeking** scale (Zuckerman, 1979). You can find out where you stand on the sensation seeking dimension by rating yourself on this scale. (See Table 10.2.) Peo-

FIGURE 10.7 Curiosity motivation. Monkeys will work on puzzles for no other reward than the pleasure of playing with them (Harlow et al., 1950). Results of curiosity research led psychologists to question the theory that all behaviors are motivated by a desire to reduce stimulation.

ple who score high on the scale seem to be chronically underaroused, and they seek situations to increase their arousal. For instance, high sensation seekers take more illegal drugs and stimulants, have a greater variety of sexual experiences, and are more willing to engage in such thrill-seeking sports as skiing and sky-diving. High sensation seekers are prone to commit more crimes in their search for thrills (Zuckerman, 1979). Low sensation seekers, by contrast, prefer to avoid the buzzing confusion of crowds and the dangers of drugs and skydiving for quieter pleasures, such as reading and one-on-one conversation.

In summary, we are not motivated to reduce only tissue needs such as hunger and thirst, nor can all motivation be explained in terms of secondary associations between new stimuli and those primary drives. Human beings and other animals are motivated to increase their arousal under certain conditions, and a moderate level of stimulation seems preferable to none at all. What constitutes a pleasant level of arousal differs from one person to the next.

COGNITIVE AND SOCIAL MOTIVES

Oscar Wilde once said: "We are all in the gutter, but some of us are looking at the stars." The humanistic approach to motivation suggests that psychologists have paid too much attention to the needs we share with rats in the gutter, and ignored the nobler human motivations. Abraham Maslow

TABLE 10.2 The Sensation-Seeking Scale: A Self-Test

To test your own sensation-seeking tendencies, try this shortened version of one of Marvin Zuckerman's earlier scales. For each of the 13 items, circle the choice, A or B, that best describes your likes or dislikes or the way that you feel. Instructions for scoring appear at the end of the test.

1 A I would like a job that requires a lot of traveling.
  B I would prefer a job in one location.

2 A I am invigorated by a brisk, cold day.
  B I can't wait to get indoors on a cold day.

3 A I get bored seeing the same old faces.
  B I like the comfortable familiarity of everyday friends.

4 A I would prefer living in an ideal society in which everyone is safe, secure, and happy.
  B I would have preferred living in the unsettled days of our history.

5 A I sometimes like to do things that are a little frightening.
  B A sensible person avoids activities that are dangerous.

6 A I would not like to be hypnotized.
  B I would like to have the experience of being hypnotized.

7 A The most important goal of life is to live it to the fullest and experience as much as possible.
  B The most important goal of life is to find peace and happiness.

8 A I would like to try parachute-jumping.
  B I would never want to try jumping out of a plane, with or without a parachute.

9 A I enter cold water gradually, giving myself time to get used to it.
  B I like to dive or jump right into the ocean or a cold pool.

10 A When I go on a vacation, I prefer the comfort of a good room and bed.
   B When I go on a vacation, I prefer the change of camping out.

11 A I prefer people who are emotionally expressive even if they are a bit unstable.
   B I prefer people who are calm and even-tempered.

12 A A good painting should shock or jolt the senses.
   B A good painting should give one a feeling of peace and security.

13 A People who ride motorcycles must have some kind of unconscious need to hurt themselves.
   B I would like to drive or ride a motorcycle.

Scoring

Count one point for each of the following items that you have circled: 1A, 2A, 3A, 4B, 5A, 6B, 7A, 8A, 9B, 10B, 11A, 12A, 13B. Add up your total and compare it with the norms below:

0–3 Very low on sensation seeking
4–5 Low
6–9 Average
10–11 High
12–13 Very High

From "The Search for High Sensation," by M. Zuckerman, in *Psychology Today*, February, 1978, *11*(9), 38–46. Copyright © 1978 by Ziff-Davis Publishing Company. Reprinted by permission.

(1954) suggested that there is a hierarchy of human motivations. Maslow believed that biological motivations of the drive-reduction sort are at the bottom of the hierarchy. Once we have avoided such irritations as hunger and thirst, Maslow argued, we move on to a new set of needs, including the desire for safety—something that is not as important when we are starving, and willing to take chances to survive. (See Figure 10.8.) When we are safe and physically satisfied, we move on to the need for love and belonging, and so on. Maslow assumed the lower four steps in the hierarchy relate to **deficiency needs,** which operate according to drive-reduction principles. When all these deficiency needs are met, however, we ascend in the hierarchy to the desire for understanding and aesthetic experience, and finally to the desire for personal fulfillment and peak experiences.

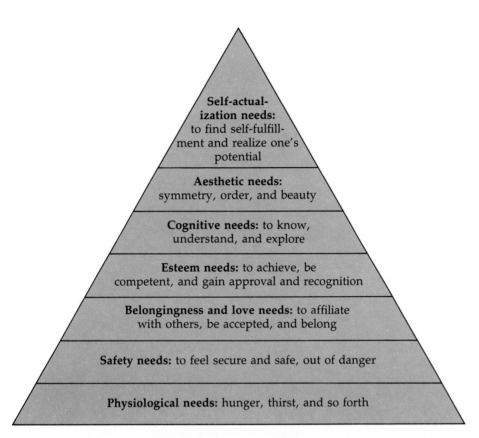

FIGURE 10.8 Maslow's hierarchy of motives. Maslow argued that such primary drives as hunger and thirst have priority over any other motivations. Once those needs are met, however, the person can move on to other needs. As we move up the pyramid, each progressively higher need represents a less essential priority for everyday life. The need for affiliation arises only after we have met our need for safety, but before the need to achieve, and so on. At the top are needs that are uniquely human, including the need for knowledge and beauty. When all other needs have been satisfied, Maslow argued that we move on to the need to "self-actualize," or fulfill our own unique potential.

Although these higher intellectual needs, like the desire to gaze at the stars, bear some similarity to the curiosity shown in other animals, Maslow believed that higher human needs cannot be understood through animal studies.

Since Maslow constructed his hierarchy of needs, psychologists have devoted some attention to the "higher needs," particularly to what Maslow called **cognitive needs**—those needs that involve the use of higher intelligence. In line with the findings about curiosity in monkeys, many psychologists believe humans are driven to seek information as an end in itself. In fact, some social psychologists have argued that the desire to obtain information underlies important **social motives** (Festinger, 1954, among others). Social motives involve interactions with other people, and include the need to affiliate with others and the need to achieve.

RESEARCH AND APPLICATION: Need for Achievement

What made Isaac Newton, Thomas Edison, and Margaret Mead work with so much devotion? Psychologist David McClelland attributed it to high **need for achievement.** This is the need to compete with some standard of excellence. The standard used to measure achievement is usually a social one—to excel one must do better than others have done at some endeavor. Beating the state record for the mile, rising to the head of the class, winning the Nobel Prize, or winning an elected office would all be ways to satisfy the need for achievement. McClelland and his colleagues developed interesting methods for measuring the need for achievement, and they have studied the motive in the laboratory, the classroom, the workplace, and even the folklore of different countries (McClelland, 1985). As we shall discuss, they have applied their findings to increasing achievement in economically disadvantaged areas of India.

McClelland and his colleague J. W. Atkinson began their studies of the need for achievement using a test called the **Thematic Apperception Test (TAT)**. The TAT is a **projective test**. That is a test with ambiguous items, for which there is no objectively "correct" answer, but which is designed to allow subjects to "project" their own needs and desires into their responses. In the TAT, people are shown pictures and asked to make up stories to describe what they think is going on. (See Figure 10.9.) For instance, in one experiment people deprived of food for 16 hours began to tell many stories with food as a central theme (McClelland and Atkinson, 1948). Just as the TAT was found to be sensitive to manipulations of hunger, it is also sensitive to manipulations of achievement. Students told that they had done poorly on an abilities test responded to the ambiguous pictures with more stories about achievement (McClelland, 1951). Figure 10.9 gives an example of two stories, one high and one low in need-achievement.

Compared with people low in need-achievement, high need-achievement people get better grades in courses related to their career goals (Raynor, 1970, among others), and want higher paying jobs and more success in their careers (Andrews, 1967; Minor and Neel, 1958, among others). Intelligent people typically obtain higher need-achievement scores, but even with intelligence equated, people high in need-achievement do better in college courses related to their career goals. Compared with those low in the need, people high in need-achievement also do better in business, even with initial advantages held equal.

Individuals high in need-achievement tend to be very realistic in choosing goals. They pick objectives that are challenging, but not so challenging that they would not have a reasonable chance of meeting them. In sharp contrast, low need-achievement scorers tend to shoot too low, choosing careers with certain success but low payoffs, or too high, choosing occupations so demanding that no one will blame them if they fail. When they succeed, high need-achievers attribute it to their abilities, whereas low need-achievers attribute it to good luck. When they fail, high need-achievers say they did not try hard enough, but low need-achievers are more likely to blame it on their own lack of ability (Weiner, 1986). These differences

FIGURE 10.9 Tell a story about this picture. Is this girl thinking about love, about friendship, or is she dreaming about future successes? Researchers who have studied the need for achievement ask subjects to tell stories about ambiguous pictures, on the assumption that those who are highly concerned with achievement will tell stories that reflect their concerns with success. Two such stories, one high, and one low in achievement imagery, are listed below:

Story 1: The girl is thinking about her future. She sees herself rising above her humble background to become a surgeon. She has read alot and always comes in at the top of her class, and thinks she is suited for a career in medicine. She imagines how proud her family will be when she graduates at the top of her class in Harvard medical school.

Story 2: She is thinking about falling in love. She is imagining a "Prince Charming" who will sweep her off her feet, and take her away to live in a lovely house in the country, where they will walk hand in hand through fields of red, orange, and yellow flowers. She will pick lovely bouquets, and wear flowers in her hair.

help explain why high need-achievers persevere at difficult tasks—they believe they can succeed with a little more effort. Low need-achievers give up because they believe that they do not have the necessary ability.

Where do these differences in achievement motivation come from? They seem to be based partly on the way parents and teachers teach children to think about their own failures and successes. High need for achievement is likely to be found in children whose parents encourage them and reward them for success, but who also set high standards for them (Teevan and McGhee, 1972). People who experience success come to have **self-efficacy beliefs**—the belief that they will succeed in the future (Bandura, 1977). The exact opposite seems to occur after the experience of repeated failures (Seligman, 1975). People develop a sense of **learned helplessness**—the belief that they will fail regardless of effort. As we will see, some recent approaches to psychotherapy apply these findings in attempts to change people's chronic self-defeating beliefs.

McClelland and another colleague, David Winter, reasoned that if success and failure experienced inside a laboratory could alter achievement motivation, perhaps need-achievement could be taught on a wider scale. They set up an achievement motivation training program in an area of India where achievement was typically very low. Over a 40-day period, they trained approximately 50 businessmen in the city of Hyderabad to set realistically high goals and to measure their progress toward their goals. When the participants were compared to local businessmen who had not enrolled in the program, they were found to have started more new businesses, invested more money in their businesses, and hired more than twice as many new employees. Two years later, the researchers found that the standard of living of 4,000 to 5,000 people had been raised by the achievement intervention (McClelland and Winter, 1971). In another application of this line of research, McClelland and his colleagues rated the literature of different societies, applying the same criteria they used to rate TAT responses. For instance, *My Fair Lady*, in which a poor cockney girl rises above the upper-crust snobs who initially looked down on her, is a high-achievement tale. The researchers found that a country's economic growth could be predicted from the amount of achievement imagery in the stories that people in that society told (McClelland, 1961). ▪

As we just noted, some cognitive theorists believe that achievement-related behaviors are motivated by our beliefs about whether or not we are likely to succeed (Bandura, 1977). Other researchers believe that even the end goal of achievement striving is nothing more than information; we seek accomplishment to reduce uncertainty about our abilities (Trope, 1975). Besides the need to achieve, other cognitive factors may influence our motivation to begin a task or to persist in the face of failure. For instance, your motivation in any situation may also depend upon which set of *standards for self-evaluation* is presently in mind (Carver and Scheier, 1981; Higgins, Strauman, and Klein, 1986). If you are thinking about your reputation as a world-class athlete you will be less motivated to study this weekend than if you have been reminded of your future as the first physicist in the family.

INTRINSIC AND EXTRINSIC MOTIVATION

In a court of law, the judge and jury are often interested in distinguishing between inner and outer influences. For instance, a juror's judgments about subway vigilante Bernhard Goetz might have been very different, depending upon whether he or she thought his actions were caused by his situation (the potential threat from the four boys who accosted him) or by his inner character (a "coldblooded" and "vicious" character, as alleged by the prosecutor). Inner causes of behavior are called **intrinsic motives,** whereas outer instigations to behavior are called **extrinsic motives.** Our judgments of other people, and of ourselves, often depend on this distinction. Whether you respond to someone's nudge with aggression, affection, or inattention may depend upon your judgments about why you were nudged. If you attribute the nudge to something extrinsic (your assailant was being buffeted around in the same crowd, or tripped over an obstacle on the floor), you will probably ignore it. If you attribute it to something intrinsic (the nudger seemed eager to start a fight, or seemed to be flirting), you may respond emotionally (becoming angry in the first case, affectionate in the second). This process of assigning causes to someone else's behavior is called **causal attribution** (Jones and Davis, 1965; Kelley, 1973). Causal attributions demonstrate how our cognitions about someone else's motivation become factors that motivate our own behavior. We also use the same cognitive attributional processes to understand our own motivations. Your **self-perceptions** (Bem, 1972) about why you are now doing what you are doing or feeling what you are feeling may be related to what you think, feel, and do in the future. Clive Seligman, Russell Fazio, and Mark Zanna (1980) asked Princeton students to rate the people they were currently dating. Before doing the ratings, half the students were led to focus on such extrinsic reasons for being in the relationship as, "I go out with ___ because my friends think more highly of me since I began seeing her/him." The other half were led to focus on intrinsic reasons for the attachment—

rating such questions as "I go with ___ because we always have a good time together." Those who focused on extrinsic rewards reported significantly fewer feelings of love and less intention to marry.

A focus on extrinsic rewards can also undermine the quality of work. Teresa Amabile (1985) recruited creative writers for a study of "people's reasons for writing." Half filled out a "Reasons for Writing" questionnaire that focused on extrinsic rewards such as money. The other half were led to focus on intrinsic payoffs, such as the pleasure they get from writing. Participants then wrote a poem. As judged by a panel of 12 professional poets, subjects who focused on extrinsic payoffs wrote significantly less creative poems. This suggests that the 71 percent of students in a recent sample who reported that money was their highest aspiration in life (*APA Monitor*, January, 1987) will do less creative work than those who choose a career for intrinsic reasons. Other research suggests an additional cost to extrinsic motivation—external rewards can undermine the natural enjoyment that people originally feel while working on a task of their choosing (Deci, 1975; Lepper, Greene, and Nisbett, 1973, among others).

Laboratory studies have thus established that motivation can be influenced by beliefs, internal standards, and attributions. It seems that cognitive factors *can* influence motivation. However, psychologists disagree about whether cognitions normally *do* exert important causal influences on our behavior.

DO COGNITIONS CAUSE BEHAVIOR?

There is ample evidence that we can give reasonable explanations for our behaviors, and that those explanations make it sound as if we are motivated by rational beliefs and attitudes. But perhaps we make up the rational explanations after the fact— that is, after we have acted on some irrational impulse. Or perhaps the cognitions that accompany behavior are what philosophers would call *epiphenomenal*, which is to say that thoughts accompany behaviors, but do not cause them. As one psychologist expressed it, cognitions might simply be "a kind of idle chatter that is irrelevant to the control and influence of behavior" (Brody, 1983). B. F. Skinner (1975) said that "introspection cannot be very relevant or comprehensive because the human organism does not have nerves going to the right places." Skinner believed that most of what we do is done "automatically," in response to environmental stimuli that we may or may not be aware of. In support of the idea that cognitions are not causal, Richard Nisbett and Timothy Wilson

(1977) found that people in experiments often give verbal explanations of their behavior that are perfectly sensible, except that they are wrong. For instance, subjects given a placebo pill in one experiment tolerated four times as much shock as those who did not receive the pill (Nisbett and Schachter, 1966). When they were later told that the pill was a fake, and asked to estimate whether it had had any influence on their own behavior, subjects denied any influence. After reviewing a large number of studies in this area, Nathan Brody (1983) concluded that cognitive factors are not always irrelevant to goals and motives, but they often are. In some cases, cognitive factors are *sufficient* to motivate behavior (as when you make the attribution that someone purposefully stepped on your foot, as opposed to doing so accidentally). However, cognitive awareness is not *necessary* to motivate behavior. We often do things for passions that have little input from our reason.

EMOTION

Although your hunger for a slice of pizza (usually studied in terms of motivation) and Romeo's passionate love for Juliet (usually considered an emotion) may seem to be obviously different, psychologists are unsure about where to draw the line, or whether it even makes sense to draw a line. Some argue that emotions amplify motivations, and others argue that emotions *are* motives—driving us through most of the important tasks in our lives (Leeper, 1970; Tomkins, 1970; 1980). What seems most important in distinguishing emotions from other motivational states is *affect*; that is, emotions have a "feeling" component, and we experience emotions as changes from the steady, more level, flow of normal consciousness. Psychologists usually separate emotion into three interrelated components:

1. *physiological arousal*, particularly arousal of the autonomic nervous system (the fight or flight system);

2. *voluntary behaviors*, particularly movements of the facial muscles, and

3. *phenomenological experience*, conscious thoughts and feelings.

Most psychologists would agree that when a real-life Romeo meets his Juliet, he is physiologically aroused, he changes his behaviors (begins to smile frequently), and he has thoughts of love running through his head. Beyond that, there would be some disagreement. Which component is the primary cause of emotions like Romeo's—thoughts, behaviors, or physiological arousal? Are there distinct patterns of arousal and facial behavior associated with different emotional experiences? Could Romeo have distinguished his feelings of love for Juliet from other emotions (such as his contempt for the other members of her family)? Finally, are there universal patterns of emotional response—can someone living in the 1990s in Papua, New Guinea, or Hoboken, New Jersey, really imagine what a medieval Italian lad felt when he saw Juliet's eyes? There are two major traditions of research on emotions, and each has come up with a very different set of answers to these questions. Researchers of the evolutionary school generally hold that emotions are different from one another, and that they are universal. Researchers of the cognitive school generally hold that emotions are based in thoughts, that they are not universal, and that they are not physiologically distinct from one another. Some researchers combine elements of both approaches, though, and cognitive theorists have long debated about when thought enters into the process.

EVOLUTIONARY APPROACHES: ARE THERE UNIVERSAL EMOTIONAL EXPRESSIONS?

As we mentioned earlier, Charles Darwin argued that emotional expressions (sneers and smiles, for example) are important tools for survival. Darwin was not just a brilliant armchair theorist, but a very thorough scientist as well. He examined several kinds of data in his search for the evolutionary significance of emotions. For instance, he gathered comparative data across several species as well as developmental data from human infants. Research in both these traditions continues today (Izard and Buechler, 1980; Panskepp, 1982). His most important insight, however, was to gather cross-cultural data:

> . . . it seemed to me highly important to ascertain whether the same expressions and gestures prevail, as has often been asserted without much evidence, with all the races of mankind, especially with those who have associated but little with Europeans. Whenever the same movements of the features or body express the same emotions in several distinct races of man, we may infer with much probability, that such expressions are true ones,—that is, are innate or instinctive.

(Darwin, 1872)

Modern evolutionary theorists assume that all our ancestors faced a number of common problems of survival, including reproduction, self-protection, and competition for status (Eibl-Eibesfeldt, 1980; Panskepp, 1982; Plutchik, 1980; Scott, 1980). A number of automatic reactions evolved to help in those survival-relevant situations. These reactions include internal physiological states (the arousal of anger) as well as particular patterns of muscular response (clenched fists and bared teeth) that assist in survival. Many of the problems encountered by apes (including humans) involve subtle social conflicts; for example, how to get along with other members of the troop and at the same time protect one's position in the dominance hierarchy. According to ethologist Irenaus Eibl-Eibesfeldt (1980), facial expressions of emotion are fixed action patterns that help control interactions with others. In fact, it appears that humans and our ape-cousins have evolved an elaborate set of facial muscles to specifically assist in intra-group communication (Liggett, 1974).

Evolutionary theorists generally agree on about nine or 10 primary emotions. With slight variations from one theorist to the next, the list usually includes fear, anger, joy, disgust, surprise, contempt, shame, sadness, and anticipation or interest. (Izard, 1971; Plutchik, 1984; Tomkins, 1981). Each of these emotions has its own particular facial expression, and research has revealed fascinating similarities in these expressions around the world (Ekman et al., 1987, among others). People in places as diverse as Brazil, Japan, and the United States agree quite well about the emotion expressed by particular facial expressions. (See Figure 10.10.)

Could it be that the cross-cultural agreement in facial expression is due to either the pervasiveness of mass media, or some other influence shared by all these modern societies? To rule out this possibility, Paul Ekman and Wallace Friesen (1971) went to the South East Highlands of New Guinea and did an experiment with a group of Fore tribesmen still living in an "isolated, Neolithic, material culture." Their subjects had never seen a movie, spoke neither English or Pidgin, and had never lived in a Western settlement. Each Fore tribesman was asked to listen to a short story designed to capture a basic emotion. For instance, fear:

> He is sitting in his house all alone, and there is no one else in the village. There is no knife, axe, or bow and arrow in the house. A wild pig is standing in the door of the house, and the man is looking at the pig and is very

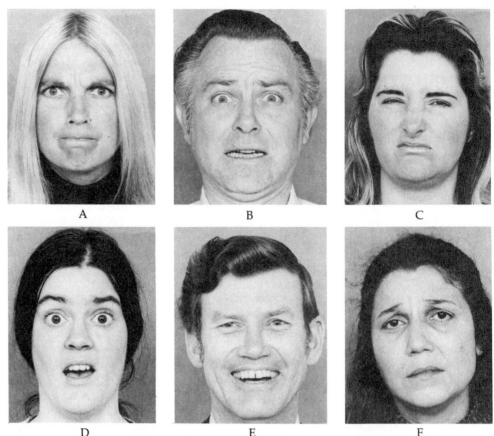

FIGURE 10.10 Emotional expressions recognized across cultures. When Americans were shown photographs like those above, the vast majority agreed that the emotions portrayed were anger (A), fear (B), disgust (C), surprise (D), happiness (E), and sadness (F). When the same photos were shown to people in Argentina, Brazil, Chile, Japan, and other countries, subjects there also concurred about the emotions being expressed, thus supporting Charles Darwin's prediction that emotional expressions would be recognized universally.

afraid of it. The pig has been standing in the doorway for a few minutes, and the person is looking at it very afraid, and the pig won't move away from the door, and he is afraid the pig will bite him.

(Ekman and Friesen, 1971).

The tribesmen then matched the story with one of three photos, similar to the ones shown in Figure 10.10. Given three choices, the researchers would have expected 33 percent correct guesses by chance alone. Actually, the correct photo was chosen 77 percent of the time. The researchers used a similar procedure with young children, giving them a choice of two photographs, and found a 90 percent rate of correct choices. Finally, they asked Fore tribesmen to role-play each of the stories,

videotaped their faces, and asked students in the United States to identify the emotions being displayed. The result mirrored the first findings: American students accurately judged the emotion of the isolated Fore. The authors conclude that particular facial behaviors seem to be universally associated with particular emotions, just as Darwin had suggested.

To say that humans have an innate ability to express and to recognize certain emotions does not imply that emotions are unchangeable. Adults in all societies learn to suppress their emotional responses (Eibl-Eibesfeldt, 1980) or to mask them with voluntary control of facial muscles (Ekman and Friesen, 1975). Some cultures, including the Japanese, learn to suppress them more fully. In another study designed to unmask emotions, re-

FIGURE 10.11 Facial expressions in private. The Japanese man on the left did not show a strong facial expression to a grueling film when he was in the presence of others. When alone, however, he showed as much reaction as the American student. This supports the argument that cultural learning can lead to the suppression of natural expressions, but that it does not remove the basic emotional reaction.

searchers filmed Japanese subjects while they watched a revolting film (Ekman and Friesen, 1975). When watching in public, the Japanese were stone-faced. In private, though, their true responses came out, and were very much like those of Westerners (Figure 10.11). Interestingly, we do not do a perfect job of masking other emotions with a smile, and our other facial muscles can give away our true feelings (Figure 10.12).

As Sherlock Holmes responded to Dr. Watson after amazing the doctor with a seeming ability to read his mind: "The features are given to man as the means by which he shall express his emotions, and yours are faithful servants." Indeed, a modern Sherlock Holmes may find a wealth of information about "mind-reading" in Ekman's research.

COGNITIVE APPROACHES: HOW ARE EMOTIONAL FEELINGS AND THOUGHTS RELATED?

Cognitive approaches are less directly concerned with the outward expression of emotion, and more concerned with our inner experience of emotion and how that inner experience is connected to our interpretation of the environment. What goes on in our minds and our bodies to make us decide we are feeling an emotion, and how do the mind and body interact? As we shall describe in a later chapter, these questions are important in understanding and treating emotional disorders. In attempting to alleviate anxiety and depression, should we treat the body with drugs, or should we try to change a person's beliefs? And if cognition is important in making us anxious or depressed, exactly how is it important?

THE BODILY FEEDBACK THEORY

Cognitive theorists have debated whether the bodily responses associated with emotion come before or after the relevant cognitions. For example, do our hands start to shake before or after we become consciously aware that we are afraid? In his *Principles of Psychology* William James made the best known statement of a very controversial position:

> Common-sense says, we lose our fortune, are sorry and weep; we meet a bear, are frightened and run; we are insulted by a rival, are angry and strike. The hypothesis here to be

FIGURE 10.12 Psychologist Paul Ekman codes smiles according to which of 80 different facial muscles are used to produce them. The woman in (A) is showing a smile that masks anger, (B) is a formal "polite" smile (a doctor telling a patient to enjoy his stay, (C) is a smile used to soften verbal criticism, and (D) is a smile used to accompany reluctant agreement—"All right, if you insist."

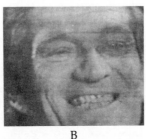
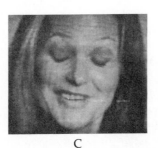

A   B   C   D

defended says that this order of sequence is incorrect . . . *the more rational statement is that we feel sorry because we cry, angry because we strike, afraid because we tremble.*

(James, 1890)

This **bodily feedback theory** is depicted in Figure 10.13. The theory postulates that such bodily changes as trembling hands or heart palpitations come before our conscious experience of an emotion, and help us to decide that we are feeling an emotion. James's evidence was largely based upon introspections about what an emotion without any of the physical symptoms would be like. That evidence was challenged by Harvard physiologist Walter Cannon (1927), who favored a preconscious processing theory.

THE PRECONSCIOUS PROCESSING THEORY

Cannon had several criticisms of James's theory. First, if James were correct each emotion should provide a distinct pattern of physical responses. For instance, the bodily changes for sorrow should be different from those for anger, and both should differ from fear. However, physiological studies done in the 30 years after James advanced his theory had not detected much difference between the various emotions. Second, visceral responses to arousing stimuli are slow. Since visceral responses are caused by chemicals—such as adrenaline—that are released into the bloodstream, rather than by electrical impulses, the brain has information about an emotion before any pounding of the heart or butterflies in the stomach even occur. Perhaps you noticed this delay if you ever had a near-miss car accident. You may have slammed on your brakes and steered well clear of the danger before your heart, late to the scene, began pounding more rapidly. As shown in Figure 10.13, the **preconscious processing theory** posits that lower brain centers process the emotion-arousing stimulus (a large mammal snarling at you) and then *simultaneously* send information to both the cortex (where a conscious experience is formed—"I am afraid") and the autonomic nervous system (which controls the visceral responses—the pounding heart and butterflies in the stomach).

THE TWO-FACTOR THEORY

Cannon's theory assumed that we can have a cognitive experience of emotion without any feedback from such excited visceral organs as the heart and stomach, which are independently notified by the lower brain centers. However, you may have

found yourself in a situation that seemed as if it should have been emotional and yet felt "cool," like Albert Camus' "Stranger," who did not cry at his mother's funeral. In fact, there is evidence that experiences without arousal are perceived as "unemotional," even when the situation clearly calls for emotion. One researcher interviewed patients with a type of spinal damage that cut off feedback from the visceral organs, and found that they reported a decrease in highly emotional experiences (Hohmann, 1966). Regarding his anger, one of the patients reported, "It just doesn't have the heat to it that it used to. It's a mental kind of anger."

Forty years after Cannon published his critique of the bodily feedback theory, Stanley Schachter and Jerome Singer (1962) published a partial defense of James's theory that seemed to pull all the bits of evidence together. Schachter and Singer reasoned that James was partly right in that visceral feedback is necessary for an emotion to occur. But judging from responses to adrenaline injections, visceral feedback alone is not enough. People who were physiologically aroused by injections of adrenaline (Marañon, 1924) often reported only "as if" they were feeling an emotion, and some of them reported no emotion at all. In addition to physiological arousal, Schachter and Singer argued that cognition plays a major role in emotion—the person must also attribute the internal symptoms to some emotional situation. If the symptoms are attributed to an injection, then no emotion will be experienced. Thus, arousal is the first and the cognitive label the second factor in emotion.

To test their two-factor theory, Schachter and Singer conducted an intriguing experiment. Participants arrived for what they thought was a study of visual perception, and received an injection of a drug called "suproxin" (supposedly a "vitamin" that improved vision). In reality, some of the subjects received a shot of adrenaline, which leads to autonomic arousal (usually experienced as a pounding in the chest due to increased heart rate and blood pressure, sweating palms, and a feeling of butterflies in the stomach). This provided a manipulation of the *first factor* in emotion, *arousal*. The others—the control group—were given a placebo (a saline injection with no physiological effects). Next, the experimenters manipulated the *second factor, information from the environment* the subjects could use to label their physiological arousal. Some of the subjects were led to label the autonomic symptoms as due to the "suproxin"— they were told to expect aroused feelings. Others were misled and told that the drug would make them feel numbness in the feet and maybe a slight

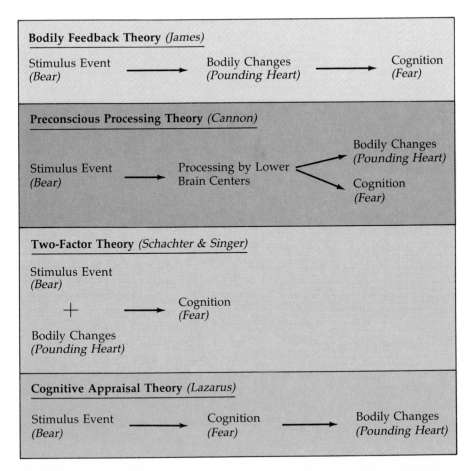

Bodily Feedback Theory *(James)*

Stimulus Event
(Bear) ⟶ Bodily Changes
(Pounding Heart) ⟶ Cognition
(Fear)

Preconscious Processing Theory *(Cannon)*

Stimulus Event
(Bear) ⟶ Processing by Lower
Brain Centers ⟨ Bodily Changes
(Pounding Heart)
Cognition
(Fear)

Two-Factor Theory *(Schachter & Singer)*

Stimulus Event
(Bear)

+ ⟶ Cognition
(Fear)

Bodily Changes
(Pounding Heart)

Cognitive Appraisal Theory *(Lazarus)*

Stimulus Event
(Bear) ⟶ Cognition
(Fear) ⟶ Bodily Changes
(Pounding Heart)

FIGURE 10.13 How the major theories view the relations between stimulus events, bodily changes, and cognition. The words in parentheses give one example, but could vary. If the word "bear" were replaced with "death of a loved one," then "fear" would be replaced with "grief," and so on. The theories differ primarily about where conscious cognition enters the process.

headache. These latter subjects should therefore search for an emotional cause for the symptoms, and the researchers provided one. Half of the subjects were provided with a "happy" label for the situation by a fellow subject (actually a confederate of the experimenter) who cracked jokes, made paper airplanes out of the experimental questionnaires, and danced about with a hula hoop that had been left in the room. The other half of the subjects were led to label their feelings as anger, by being asked to fill out a questionnaire that asked very intrusive personal questions. One question asked: "With how many men has your mother had extramarital relations?" The nicest possible response about mother was: "five or less." In this condition, the confederate got progressively more angry as the experiment wore on, until he finally tore up the questionnaire and stormed out of the room, slamming the door on the way out. When subjects were later asked to rate their feelings, both the physiological arousal and the context played a role. Those who were led to believe that

the drug caused their arousal reported less intense feelings than either those who were misled about the drug or those who were given a placebo (and had fewer feelings to describe). However, those who were both given adrenaline and misinformed about the true effects of the drug tended to report emotions in line with those of the confederate. These subjects reported the most negative mood in the angry condition and relatively more positive moods in the happy condition. Schachter and Singer interpreted their findings as support for the two-factor theory—both arousal and a cognitive label are necessary for us to decide that we are experiencing an emotion. Either one alone is insufficient.

Although the Schachter and Singer two-factor solution seems to be an elegant ending to the bodily feedback–cognition dispute, other researchers have not replicated the exact effects (Marshall and Zimbardo, 1979), and a host of other studies cast doubt on this general model of emotion (Reisenzein, 1983). So, have psychologists exhausted the possible relations between cognition and arousal as determinants of emotions? Not quite. There is still the one rejected by William James.

THE COGNITIVE APPRAISAL THEORY

We began this section with James's idea that our bodily reactions *precede* our experience of an emotion. As James noted, this idea seems to contradict common sense. Schachter and Singer's two-factor model likewise has problems from a commonsense point of view, since they also assumed that our conscious experience of fear only comes after the visceral arousal. Participants in their experiment only searched for environmental cues after they noticed that they were feeling aroused. In a natural situation, that would be analogous to this train of reasoning: "My heart is pounding. I wonder what I'm feeling? There is no one attractive around, so it is not love. Ah, but there is that grizzly bear sniffing at my leg, so I must be afraid." Doesn't common sense suggest that the arousal came from the bear in the first place? In fact, Richard Lazarus and his colleagues (1980) argued for just such a position. Except under rare conditions, they argued, we feel arousal just as common sense would suggest, in response to our assessment of the situation we are in. The cognitive appraisal position assumes that cognition comes first, and is *followed* by arousal only if we judge that something important is about to happen. (See Figure 10.13)

Lazarus and his colleagues have done a number of experiments to examine how interpretations can influence our responses to stressful situations. In one classic study college men watched a grueling anthropological film. The film showed an actual circumcision ritual that included teenage boys having the foreskins of their penises cut, complete with close-up shots of the bleeding incisions. Participants in the control condition were simply shown the film without comment. In another condition, a narrator described the bloody ceremony in gruesome detail, emphasizing the pain and distress the boys were experiencing. Finally, two other groups heard a narrator who attempted to minimize the boys' suffering. In one case the narrator denied that the ceremony was very painful; in the other case, he "intellectualized" about the scientific meaning of this transition rite. The experimenters examined each observer's heart rate and skin conductivity and found that participants led to focus on the gruesome details showed more physiological arousal than did the control subjects. Subjects led to deny or intellectualize the pain, on the other hand, showed less arousal than either of the other two groups (Speisman et al., 1964).

Thus, the cognitive appraisal theory posits that we can control our emotional arousal by controlling what we pay attention to, and what features of a situation we think about. It is the modern version of Epictetus' first century theory that "It is not the things themselves that disturb men, but their judgments about the things."

THE BODILY FEEDBACK THEORY RECONSIDERED

Cognitive models since James have carried the hidden assumption that the only admissible evidence the brain will accept from the body is from the autonomic nervous system—the involuntary responses of internal organs. However, several researchers have recently argued that we have been searching in the wrong place for bodily cues for emotion. The autonomic nervous system may amplify the intensity of an emotion, but the real source of differential feedback to the brain may come from the face (Izard and Buechler, 1980; Zajonc, 1985). For instance, there is some evidence that different facial expressions can lead to different patterns of blood flow through the brain, and might therefore provide the feedback the brain needs to decide which emotion the person is feeling (Zajonc, Murphy, and Inglehart, 1989).

To test the bodily feedback viewpoint, James Laird (1974; 1984) had students contract various facial muscles as he attached different electrodes to their faces. Some of the students were asked to contract their facial muscles in such a way that an observer would have said that they were smiling. Others were asked to contract a different set of muscles, pulling their faces into what looked like angry grimaces. When Laird later asked the students to rate their moods, the results vindicated William James's theory; the smilers felt happier and the scowlers felt more angry. The same effects were also found in a study in which students could not have guessed that the researcher was interested in emotional expression (Strack, Martin, and Stepper, 1988). When students were asked to hold a pen in their teeth (an exercise that tenses muscles normally used in smiling), they later reported being happier than if they had been asked to hold the pen in their lips (an action that tenses muscles that oppose a smile). Other research by Paul Ekman and his colleagues (1983) further suggests that psychologists were too quick in discarding James's view of emotion. These researchers used Laird's method, having subjects contract muscles associated with different emotions, but they measured several indices of autonomic arousal, including heart rate and hand temperature.

They found that different facial expressions led to different patterns of arousal. For instance, anger is associated with high heart rate and high hand temperature, fear with high heart rate and low skin temperature, and disgust with low heart rate.

What can we make of all this? It does seem that there are different patterns of bodily reaction associated with the different emotions, after all. It also seems, to some extent at least, that feedback from the body can influence which emotional state we feel. (Figure 10.14) Nevertheless, the research does not prove that this feedback is normally the primary cause of emotional experience. It seems plausible that Lazarus is correct in assuming that some cognitive appraisal normally precedes the body's emotional response. To say that "cognitive" appraisal is important, however, does not mean that such appraisal needs to be conscious (Zajonc, 1980). Affective reactions can occur without necessarily involving conscious cognition (Seamon et al., 1983).

INTERACTIONS:
Integrating Motivation and Emotion

Psychologists have often fallen into the trap of pitting evolutionary models against the cognitive or learning models that dominated the field in the years between 1920 and 1980. To this black or white way of thinking, we are *either* instinct-driven animals *or* rational cultural beings who have transcended biology. However, biologically determined drives and emotions, learning experiences, and rational cognitions are hardly independent of one another. In this section, we consider how emotions (such as fear and anger) and other motivational states (such as hunger and sexual arousal) interact with learning and cognition to form adaptive systems that help us deal with important changes in our environments.

Cognitions Ultimately "In the Service of the Emotions"

Robert Plutchik (1980) has argued that all of our problems of survival as social primates did not end with the evolution of our large brains. We modern hominids still need to eat, to reproduce, to get along with other group members, and to protect ourselves against threats to our well-being. In line with William James, Plutchik argued that our brains evolved to help us adapt to survival-relevant situations. He presumed that the primary emotions are associated with behavior patterns that help us deal with the most common survival relevant events, and that "cognitions are in the service of emotions." A diagram of Plutchik's model of emotion is presented in Figure 10.15.

Plutchik proposed that we use our cognitive processing abilities to help predict when important events are likely to occur. Unlike lower animals, we can analyze subtle cues ("Is he trying to impress the boss and move up into the job I've been wanting?"), and draw abstract parallels between the present situation and previous ones ("This reminds me of the time a fight broke out in that bar in Muskogee."). The advantage of processing environmental stimuli at the "thoughtful" level of

FIGURE 10.14 Facial feedback and emotion. Research indicates that people who smile feel better than those who make other expressions, such as pursing their lips. Robert Zajonc and his colleagues have found some evidence that these different facial expressions are accompanied by different patterns of blood flow through the brain (Zajonc, Murphy, and Inglehart, 1989).

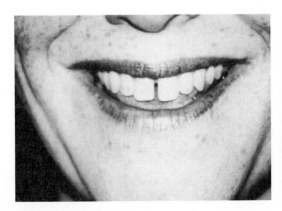 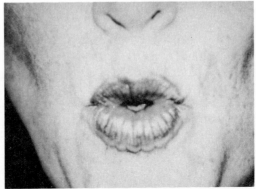

STIMULUS EVENT	→	COGNITION	→	FEELING	→	BEHAVIOR	→	EFFECT
Bear	→	Danger	→	Fear	→	Run	→	Protection

FIGURE 10.15 Plutchik's model of emotion. Notice that Plutchik adds overt behavior and effect to the cognitive appraisal model. He argued that each emotion helps us respond to a particular set of survival demands.

conscious cognition is a more efficient use of our emotional response system than our pet cat could make (that is, we can better avoid costly mistakes). Table 10.3 shows Plutchik's complete list of primary emotions and their associated cognitions. It also describes which stimuli elicit and which responses follow each emotion. This scheme connects the cognitive appraisal model of emotion with the evolutionary model by specifying how our search for particular kinds of information in the outside world (about poisonous foods or enemies, for instance) is linked to particular emotional responses (such as disgust and anger), and how those emotional responses are linked to particular adaptive patterns of behavior (such as spitting out or hitting).

Actually, John B. Watson, famous as the champion of behaviorism, presented an early interactionist view of emotion. He believed there were three innate emotions: fear, rage, and love. To prove that these three basic emotions were innate he demonstrated their existence in very young infants. If a mother quickly lowered her arms, Watson observed that her infant would scream with fear even if he had never been dropped. Likewise, a loud noise would elicit this basic fear response in inexperienced infants. In a similar manner, the infant would show rage if restrained and would coo lovingly when stroked. Watson believed that all other emotional responses were derived from these three basic emotions (Watson and Morgan, 1917). He assumed that new emotional responses are learned through classical conditioning, in the same way that the famous Little Albert learned to fear a white laboratory rat after it was associated with a loud noise (Watson and Rayner, 1920). History has a way of simplifying stories, and Watson is remembered as the champion of the view that humans are, as John Locke expressed it, "blank slates." It is less elegant to remember him as viewing human nature as a "slightly premarked slate."

Motivations and Emotions as Evolved Survival Systems

You may have noticed that Watson's conception of emotional conditioning is directly related to the concept of secondary drives. Let us reconsider how the learning and cognitive approaches to motivation fit with the evolutionary school of thought, and then return to the connection between emotion and motivation. When we discussed hunger and sexual motivation, we saw that each primary motivation is associated with a particular biological system; each involves distinct hormones and distinct patterns of activity in the brain's limbic system. Although hunger, thirst, and sexual arousal are "wired in" to the brain, none of these responses is fixed. Through the process of operant conditioning, these basic drives are conditioned to different sets of stimuli in different people, depending partly upon their culture and partly upon their unique life experiences. Nevertheless, the conditioning process is constrained in certain ways. For instance, some incentives (such as a sweet taste) seem to be innately preferred, and, as we saw in our earlier discussion of nausea conditioning, some connections between stimuli and responses (taste and nausea) seem to be much easier to make than others. Our motivational systems seem to be partly prewired to help us adapt to our environment. Where the environment is likely to be fixed, the relevant predisposition is likely to be strong and universal. For example, few, if any, infants show a revulsion to sweet tastes or a desire for bitter tastes. Evolutionary biologists would argue that sweetness is usually not associated with poison, while bitterness often is. Where the environment is likely to be variable, the connections are only roughed in, and learning and cognition fill in the gaps.

From the interactionist perspective, the distinction between emotion and motivation may not be the most useful one we could make. In fact, a

TABLE 10.3 Plutchik's List of Primary Emotions

Stimulus Event	Inferred cognition	Feeling	Behavior	Effect
Threat	"Danger"	Fear, terror	Running, or flying away	Protection
Obstacle	"Enemy"	Anger, rage	Biting, hitting	Destruction
Potential mate	"Possess"	Joy, ecstasy	Courting, mating	Reproduction
Loss of valued person	"Isolation"	Sadness, grief	Crying for help	Reintegration
Group member	"Friend"	Acceptance, trust	Grooming, sharing	Affiliation
Gruesome object	"Poison"	Disgust, loathing	Vomiting, pushing away	Rejection
New territory	"What's out there?"	Anticipation	Examining, mapping	Exploration
Sudden novel object	"What is it?"	Surprise	Stopping, alerting	Orientation

Source: Plutchik, R. (1980).

number of evolutionary theorists (including Scott, 1980) do not distinguish hunger and sexuality from the other emotional states. Hunger, thirst, temperature regulation, love, fear and anger are all considered innate motivational systems that have different functions—each drives us to respond to a different set of survival-relevant problems. Each one may be elicited by some unconditioned stimulus (for example, sugar, dehydration, cold, an attractive person, bears, or someone who tries to frustrate us) and each can be classically conditioned to a new set of incentive stimuli that signal a survival-relevant encounter (the smell of pizza, our lover's perfume, or fresh bear droppings). Over the course of each individual's development, operant conditioning of new sets of responses can facilitate or inhibit simple innate responses to each motivational state. (We can learn to suppress a look of disgust for someone we dislike, or a look of anger when our boss frustrates us.) On a moment-to-moment basis, our cognitive abilities are used to make abstract connections between stimulus events (you remember that this snake's pattern is that of a harmless kingsnake, not a poisonous coral snake) or to decide which of several adaptive responses might best suit a new situation ("Maybe if I bang these pans together, this bear will leave my food alone"). In sum, the interactionist position sees such emotional states as anger and fear and such motivational states as hunger and sexual arousal as linked together in a network of survival processes. Each one is linked to a specific cognitive assessment of important events in the environment (such as a threat or a mate) and to a specific

set of behaviors that will help us deal with those events (such as running or smiling). ■

MOTIVATIONAL–EMOTIONAL SYSTEMS INVOLVE OPPOSING PSYCHOLOGICAL STATES

In discussing motivation and emotion we have made repeated reference to physiological arousal. The very concepts of "motivation" and "emotion" imply some arousal, or "drive," and even the cognitive models of emotion assume some level of physiological arousal. Two ideas about drives have provided a very important organizing function for American psychologists. The first is Cannon's notion of homeostasis, the idea that physiological needs act like thermostatic checks and balances. There is a system that turns on hunger, checked by a system that turns it off; there are similar opposing systems for thirst, body temperature, and so on. The second idea is the notion that all types of motivation (food-seeking, thirst, mate-seeking, and so on) are driven by the same state of arousal, or a "generalized drive" (Hull, 1943).

There are two physiological systems related to this idea of generalized drive. One is the autonomic nervous system, and the other is the arousal system in the brain's reticular activating system, which controls activation and attention. (See Chapter 2). In fact, both systems operate on the principle of homeostatic balance. The *sympathetic* branch of the *autonomic nervous system (ANS)* arouses us for fight or flight by increasing heart rate and blood pressure, activating the voluntary muscles, and dilating the pupils. Its action is opposed by the *parasympathetic* branch that slows down our consumption of bodily resources. (Refer back to Figure 2.3.) Stimulation of one area of the brain's reticular activating system can lead to a dramatic burst of arousal, raising a sleeping cat to a state of intense alertness, for instance. Stimulation of another area has the exact opposite effect, putting a waking animal to sleep.

Cognitive theories of emotion have focused mainly on the fight-or-flight arousal of the sympathetic ANS, and this narrow focus may have led to the confusion about whether there is one emotional state or many. Most theorists would agree that autonomic arousal is probably a component of all emotion, and perhaps of all motivated behavior as well. However, the picture is a bit too complex to be painted with a single state of arousal.

Let us return to Plutchik's theory of emotion. Plutchik assumed that each of the emotional states has a bipolar opposite. As you can see in Figure 10.16, he arranged emotional experience into a three-dimensional scheme. Stronger emotions are listed on the top surface, and each emotional state is across the circle from one that is opposite to it. For example, rage is directly opposed to terror in Plutchik's model; the two are incompatible. You cannot be fuming with anger and petrified with fear at the same moment. Likewise, you cannot, at the same moment, be feeling the emotion of acceptance (as you would feel in a moment of love or deep communion with a close friend) and its opposite, loathing. Another, slightly simpler model of emotion captures the same idea as Plutchik's scheme. As shown in Figure 10.17, emotional experience can be displayed in a three-dimensional space composed of three opposing states: pleasure–displeasure, dominance–submissiveness, and high arousal–low arousal (Mehrabian and Russell, 1974). Notice that this model can be directly exchanged with Plutchik's model by replacing the terms acceptance–loathing with pleasure–displeasure and rage–terror with dominance–submissiveness. The aroused–unaroused dimension differentiates between emotional and unemotional experience (or motivated and unmotivated experience). At the low end, we are asleep. Physiologically, we may think of this dimension as controlled by opponent processes in the autonomic nervous system as well as those in the reticular activating system that we have just discussed.

Are there physiological processes that correspond to the other two dimensions? One possibility is that the ratio of adrenaline to noradrenaline is

FIGURE 10.16 Plutchik's model of the relationship between the primary emotions. Intense emotions are shown on the top surface, and less intense emotions are depicted underneath them (disgust is mild loathing, boredom is very mild loathing, and so on). Each wedge on the top is incompatible with the opposite wedge (rage is opposite terror, acceptance is opposite loathing, and so on).

related to the dominant–submissive (or rage–terror) dimension. Psychologists have tended to blur the distinction since both hormones are associated with generalized sympathetic arousal. However, there is some evidence that noradrenaline may be relatively more important in states related to anger, whereas adrenaline is relatively more important in states related to fear. For instance, animals that are predators (like the big cats who "fight" more than "flee") show a high ratio of noradrenaline to adrenaline when they are aroused, while prey animals (favoring "flight") show a higher ratio of adrenaline (Funkenstein, 1955). At the same time, humans who are angry, as opposed to being afraid, show a similarly high noradrenaline ratio (Elmadjian et al., 1957). The hormone testosterone is also related to dominance behaviors, and there are opposing hormones that block it (Svare and Kinsley, 1987). In the brain there are separate centers of the limbic system that, when stimulated, can elicit either rage-like responses or their opposite, fearfulness (Panskepp, 1982).

There are also hormones and brain centers that roughly correspond to the "pleasure–displeasure" dimension. For instance, researchers interested in

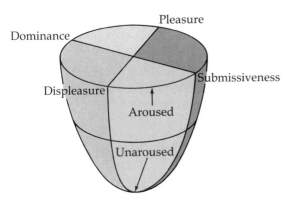

FIGURE 10.17 Mehrabian and Russell's model of the three major *dimensions* of emotional experience. Note that this dimensional model could be laid directly on top of Plutchik's model (Fig. 10.16). Research discussed in the text suggests that there are physiological opponent processes underlying each of the three bipolar emotional dimensions.

the action of addictive opium derivatives, such as morphine and heroin, have been writing a fascinating chapter in the history of motivational research. Since those drugs have such reliable relaxation effects, researchers guessed that there might be natural bodily receptors sensitive to these substances. That guess proved true, and researchers discovered that our bodies naturally produce chemicals structurally similar to the addictive opiates (Pert and Snyder, 1973). These chemicals have been dubbed **endorphins** (for "endogenous morphine," bodily hormones that reduce the sensation of pain). Our bodies produce these endorphins just when they are needed. For instance, women in the late stages of pregnancy show several times the normal level of endorphins in their bloodstream. Researchers have also located specific areas of the brain that seem to be associated with pleasure and displeasure. As we noted in Chapter 2, physiologists James Olds and Peter Milner (1954) discovered that rats would voluntarily press a bar to obtain electrical stimulation to certain areas of the brain. As we mentioned, the rats would sometimes press the bar several thousand times an hour, without stopping to eat or drink, until they dropped from exhaustion. In humans, there are similar brain centers that lead to pleasant sensations when stimulated electrically (Delgado, 1969). Humans whose brains are electrically stimulated in certain areas giggle and become unusually friendly or flirtatious. There are also opposing brain centers that seem to be related to the opposite response— avoidance behaviors (Panksepp, 1982). It is possible that these bipolar homeostatic mechanisms underlying motivation and emotion have profound implications. They can be used to explain addictive behaviors of all sorts, from heroin dependence to compulsive thrill-seeking to romantic love (Solomon, 1980).

DYSFUNCTION:
Opponent Processes and Addiction

To understand why the body's responses to arousing events contribute to addictions of all sorts, we need to consider a few simple assumptions from Richard Solomon's **opponent process model.** First, Solomon assumes that every physiological state of arousal automatically leads to an opposing state. This is simply another way of saying that our bodies attempt to maintain physiological balance, or homeostasis. The initial state of arousal, called the "A-state," is eventually offset by an opposing physiological response called the "B-state." For example, researchers observed that parachutists experienced either apprehension or terror as the moment to jump out of the plane approached. After landing, the A-state of terror was replaced with a B-state of euphoria (Fenz and Epstein, 1971).

There are two important details about the B-state. First, it builds slowly, getting stronger each time we repeat the actions that led to the A-state. Second, it dissipates more slowly than the A-state, so there is a B-state "hangover" when the A-state disappears. In the case of parachutists, novice jumpers were very frightened before the first jump or two, and afterwards felt about ten minutes of relief and excitement. Experienced jumpers, on the other hand, experienced only mild apprehension on jumping, but afterwards were highly euphoric for several hours (Fenz and Epstein, 1967). The pattern of opponent response is depicted in Figure 10.18. As you can see, the A-state (terror, in this case) declines with time as the opposing B-state is strengthened. After the stimulation that produces the A-state subsides, the B-state remains. The B-state "hangover" is weak at first, but becomes stronger with repetition.

The opponent process theory may explain the tolerance experienced by long-term users of alcohol and drugs. The first dose of alcohol or heroin elicits a pleasant state of painless euphoria in the user. The body responds with an opposing physiological process designed to bring the person back to baseline, but this B-state is slow and weak on first use. After the "high" is over, there is a mild hangover, feelings of slight agitation and discomfort. With repeated use the B-state gets stron-

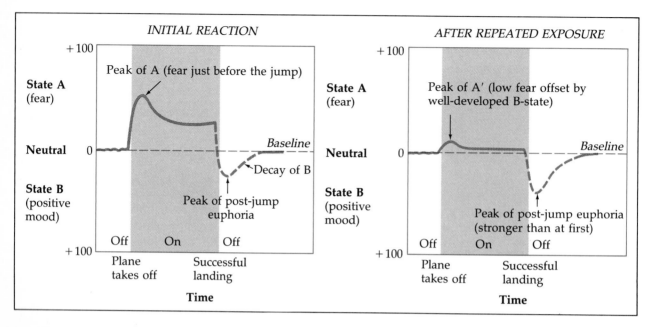

FIGURE 10.18 Opponent process model of motivation. The figure at the left shows the initial reaction to an arousing event, such as a jump from an airplane. The "A-state" is the initial reaction—fear in this case. The weak opponent response ("B-state") builds with time, so that after a number of exposures (as an experienced paratrooper would have), the "A-state" fear reaction is almost washed out by the strengthened "B-state." However, the "B-state" is slow to dissipate, so that with repeated experience, as in the figure on the right, the strong opponent response lasts for some time after the event. (Paratroopers feel positive for hours after a jump.)

ger and there is only a short euphoric A-state when the drug is first taken. Now, however, there is a long, more intense hangover after the drug wears off. Consequently, the user is likely to resort to ever-higher doses of the A-state stimulus (alcohol or heroin), in order to counteract the increasingly pronounced B-state. The problem is further exaggerated because the unpleasant B-state can become conditioned to situations formerly associated with the A-state (Wikler and Pescor, 1967). Thus, the alcoholic who has successfully dried out will experience withdrawal symptoms again if he returns to his favorite bar on a social visit.

Solomon (1980) noted that his model of addiction applies to love relationships as well. When first you meet that Romeo or Juliet you have been dreaming of, you are both overwhelmed with feelings of warmth and ecstasy as you look into one another's eyes. At the beginning the separations are only mildly unpleasant. If you start to date steadily, however, an opposing B-state builds up. Thus, the times together are less intense, but the separations are miserable. If you break up, like the alcoholic returning to his old haunts, any stimuli associated with your lover (your favorite song, a glimpse of the place where you used to meet) will

bring on the miserable B-state again. To deal with the problem, you can take the romantic equivalent of a methadone maintenance program—find someone else. ▪

MOTIVATIONAL–EMOTIONAL SYSTEMS CONNECT BASIC AND COMPLEX PROCESSES

We have discussed some of the important links between motivational processes, learning, and cognition. Moreover, motivational systems are centrally connected to the other basic psychological processes we have discussed in earlier chapters. As we have seen, sensation, perception, learning, and cognition are all "selective." We are only sensitive to a small spectrum of the energy around us (different from the spectrum that a dog or a bat senses) and even then we only notice, attend to, learn, and think about a small part of the vast array of stimuli that we could sense and perceive. How do we decide what to "select"? Motivation and emotion play the crucial organizing roles in this process, setting priorities for how we allocate our cognitive processing time. Motivation and emotion also help us learn the important contingencies; that is, those stimulus–response relations likely to help us survive and reproduce.

In this chapter, we have seen that there are differences of opinion about the relative importance of innate biological motivations, learning, and higher cognition. We will see these issues come up again and again as we talk about the complex topics of personality, psychopathology, and social behavior. To what extent are pathological behaviors (such as depression) or normal social behaviors (such as friendliness) a function of "wired-in" motivations? To what extent are these behaviors due to learning in the home and at school? Whether they are innate or learned, how much can we control feelings such as depression or attraction with conscious cognition (our "reason")? As we will see in the chapters on psychopathology and treatment, how psychologists answer these questions influences what they try to do to change behavior. We will attempt to show how biological passions and cognitive reasoning work together to help us adaptively survive and reproduce. Reason may indeed be the slave of the passions, but it is a slave that is permitted to advise its master.

IN CONTEXT: MOTIVATION AND EMOTION

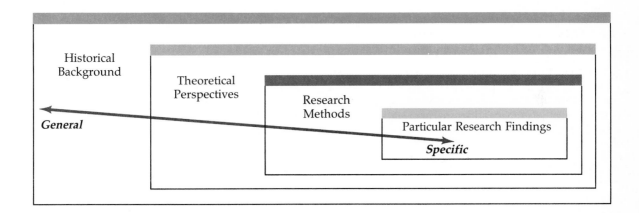

STUDY QUESTIONS

What determines the choice of some behaviors over others, and what energizes those behaviors?

How do bodily states interact with rational cognitions in driving behavior?

Do we seek to reduce arousal states to zero, or to achieve some optimum level of arousal?

How do physiology, thought, and behavior combine in *affective* states such as anger, joy, and love?

How are emotions and other motivational states, such as hunger and thirst, different from one another, and how are they related?

HISTORICAL BACKGROUND

1. Charles Darwin and William James held that motivational states evolved to help in survival.

2. Sigmund Freud argued that biological drives were suppressed and redirected in modern society.

MODERN THEORETICAL PERSPECTIVES

1. Evolutionary theorists follow Darwin in viewing human motivation and emotion as rooted in animal instincts. They assume human motives and emotions are universal across cultures.

2. Drive theorists combine Hull's behavioral approach with a physiological perspective, tracking the relations between drives and biochemical variations in the body. *Stimulation seeking* behaviors suggest that animals may not seek **drive-reduction** as an ultimate goal. Such behaviors are explained by the theory that organisms seek an **optimal level of arousal** above zero.

3. Humanistic psychologists hold that humans have special intellectual and aesthetic needs that are not explained well by biological or learning models. Maslow held that humans have a hierarchy of motives in which drives based on biological deficiency take precedence over higher needs.

4. Cognitive motivation theorists assume that beliefs, standards, attributions, and self-perceptions can all influence motivation. Cognitive theories of emotion address the relations between stimulus events, bodily changes, and the conscious experience of emotion:

   a) the **bodily feedback** theory assumes that bodily changes occur before cognition;

   b) the **preconscious processing** theory assumes that stimulus events lead to bodily changes and cognition independently;

   c) the **two factor** theory assumes that bodily changes *and* an appropriate situational label are both necessary for the cognitive experience of an emotion;

   d) the **cognitive appraisal** theory assumes that bodily changes occur only after we have determined that a stimulus might be important or threatening.

5. The **interactionist** approach combines elements of the other approaches. It holds that events in the world are cognitively analyzed for their relevance to survival. Once a survival related cognition occurs (such as "danger"), it automatically leads to a specially adapted primary emotion (fear). Each emotional feeling is accompanied by an increased likelihood of certain behaviors (running) adapted for survival in the relevant situation (protection). Conditioning accounts for the fact that different people respond differently to the same events.

RESEARCH METHODS

1. Evolutionary theorists have conducted **naturalistic observation** studies of animals (Lehrman, 1966) and **cross-cultural experiments** of human emotion (such as the study of emotional recognition in Fore tribesmen by Ekman and Friesen, 1971).

2. Drive theorists have conducted laboratory experiments, often using animals to study simple drives such as hunger and thirst. The research on brain lesions and obesity in rats is an example of a laboratory experiment (Gold, 1973).

3. Cognitive theorists have conducted laboratory experiments with humans. The study of men's reactions to a circumcision film is an example (Lazarus et al., 1980).

4. Experiments using projective techniques to study unconscious motivations show some influence from the psychoanalytic approach. These were discussed in the section on achievement motivation (McClelland and Atkinson, 1948).

RESEARCH FINDINGS AND SUMMMARY

1. Instinctive behavior has several components. **Fixed action patterns** are automatic response sequences, exemplified by a dog's growling and baring its teeth when it is threatened. **Sign stimuli** are patterns such as a peacock's display, which facilitate communication among animals, and **response sequences** are complex chains of behavior involving more than one animal (such as the mating ritual in the fighting fish).

2. Drives often operate on the principle of **homeostatic balance,** with opposing sets of thermostat-like controls checking one another.

3. In the short term, hunger is controlled by receptors in the stomach's walls, in the mouth, in the liver, and in the brain's hypothalamus. Hunger can also be stimulated by the **incentive** properties of the foods we eat.

4. Long term regulation of hunger is partly controlled by the brain's ventromedial hypothalamus (VMH). Eating patterns in animals with VMH lesions and obese humans led to speculation that obesity is caused by insensitivity to internal cues for hunger and overreliance on *external cues.* Recent research on obesity has considered a **set point** explanation, which holds that the brain controls both hunger and food metabolism in order to keep a constant weight.

5. Sexual behaviors vary across cultures, and can occur in males without testes, as well as in

women without ovaries. However, biological factors are linked to human sexual motivation. The male hormone **testosterone** is involved in both sexes' inclination to *initiate* sexual contact.

6. Conscious cognitions are not always necessary or sufficient to cause behavior; sometimes our behavior is controlled by factors that are *unconscious*.

7. People around the world can recognize one another's facial expressions. However, we can learn to suppress these innate emotional expressions in public.

8. Cognitive processes interact with feedback from the body and the environment in determining the experience of emotion.

9. Several physiological **opponent processes,** related to *arousal–unarousal, dominance–submission,* and *pleasure–displeasure,* underlie motivational systems. Opponent processes can explain addictions of various sorts.

ADDITIONAL READINGS

Clark, M. S., and Fiske, S. T., eds. 1982. *Affect and cognition.* Hillsdale, NJ: Erlbaum. Leading researchers describe their work on the relationship between emotion and cognition.

Daly, M., and Wilson, M. 1983. *Sex, evolution and human behavior,* 2nd ed. Boston: Willard Grant Press. A review of research suggesting that courtship and sexual behavior in human beings follows the same general principles that explain behavior in other animals.

Darwin, C. 1872/1965. *The expression of emotions in man and animals.* Chicago: Univ. of Chicago Press. Darwin's original statement of the evolutionary model of emotion, still readable and fascinating.

Eibl-Eibesfeldt, 1975. *Ethology: The biology of behavior.* New York: Holt, Rinehart, & Winston. Summarizes the evidence for fixed action patterns, sign stimuli, and response sequences in animals and humans.

Ekman, P. 1985. *Telling Lies: Clues to deceit in the marketplace, politics, and marriage.* New York: Norton. Describes the evidence on complex nonverbal patterns that reveal emotions different from what people may be saying.

Mandler, G. 1984. *Mind and body.* New York: Norton. A cognitive approach to understanding emotion and stress.

Petri, H. L. 1985. *Motivation: Theory and research,* 2nd ed. Belmont, CA: Wadsworth. A scholarly review of the research on motivation.

Plutchik, R. 1980. *Emotion: A psychoevolutionary synthesis.* New York: Harper & Row. A statement of Plutchik's biosocial interactionist theory.

INFANT AND CHILD DEVELOPMENT

W e enter this world small and helpless, with few capabilities and few behaviors. Within two decades, however, we have the full range of human skills at our disposal, for whatever purpose we desire. Within another two decades the inexorable decline in powers and skills through aging begins, and will continue until death. The human adult is the lord of creation, the most successful organism ever evolved. Yet no other primate—indeed, no other mammal—is as dependent as we are at birth. How does something as helpless as a human baby become something as competent as an adult?

(T.G.R. Bower, 1979)

Chapter Outline

When Charles Manson was born in 1934, his mother, Kathleen Maddox, was 16 years old and unmarried. Her relatives said that she "ran around a lot, drank, and got into trouble." To her son, she was an uncaring and negligent mother. She would leave young Charles with neighbors for what she said would be an hour, then disappear for days or weeks at a time. When Charles was five, his mother was arrested, along with her brother, for robbing a gas station and knocking out the attendant with a Coke bottle. When she got out of prison three years later, she reclaimed Charles from an aunt but sent him to a boys school when he was 12. He ran away after ten months and returned to his mother who refused to take him in. Then 13, he began a life of crime, including burglaries and armed robberies that kept him in reform schools and prisons for much of the next 20 years. In 1971, at the age of 36, Charles Manson was arrested for leading a cult of alienated youths in a series of brutal murders (Bugliosi, 1974).

British philosopher John Stuart Mill was born in 1806 into a very different type of family. Instead of neglect, Mill was subjected to extreme parental control. His father, James Mill, was a philosopher and historian who kept his son away from other boys. Instead of school, young John was drilled daily by his father in a painstaking and exacting fashion. In his autobiography, the son described his father as an impatient perfectionist who

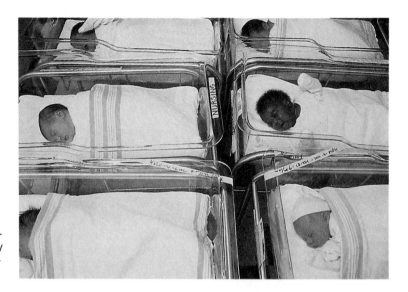

Infants shortly after birth. Over the course of development, each of these infants will change in many ways due to the joint effects of heredity and environment. Developmental psychologists study the changes in physical and mental abilities that take place over the life span.

"demanded of me not only the utmost of what I could do, but much that I could by no possibility have done." What he could do was quite impressive. At three, he began the study of Greek. At six, he read Xenophon, Herodotus, and Aesop, and discussed his notes with his father. At eight, he learned Latin, geometry, and algebra, and read more English history than most well-educated young people two or three times his age. Without any childhood friends, Mill had no other children with whom to compare himself. He had only his father, who told him frequently that he fell short of the possible ideal. Until he died in 1873, Mill maintained a humble opinion of himself, apparently accepting his father's opinion that he was not special in any way.

As in the chapter on intelligence, we again see the interplay of genetic and environmental influences on behavior. Certainly criminality ran in the Manson family and genius in the Mill family, as Manson's mother was herself a convicted thief and Mill's father was himself a noted philosopher. On the other hand, even before Manson was born his mother drank heavily and may have damaged his developing nervous system. After he was born, he observed her antisocial behavior and that of her criminal friends. Mill, however, had a father who not only provided a perfect model of a great philosopher but who also taught him everything a philospher needed to know. Which factor is more important for determining our behavior? Is it our heredity or our environment that determines what we are?

For centuries, scholars have debated this question of *nature* versus *nurture*, of *heredity* versus *environment*. As we noted in Chapter 9, heredity refers to the characteristics and potentialities that we inherit from our parents, while environment refers to all of the external events we ever experience. Our experiences before and during birth, what we eat, our parents' childrearing practices, our teachers' lessons, our brothers and sisters, and even our neighborhood and historical period are all defined as part of the environment. Today, the debate over heredity and environment is not cast in an "either–or" form. Psychologists have taken a more balanced position, which recognizes that our development is based on the reciprocal action of both factors. For example, we reported in Chapter 9 that your intelligence is the result of inherited characteristics and environmental experiences including your home life and educational opportunities. Accordingly, John Stuart Mill might not have written any philosophical treatises if he grew up under Charles Manson's family conditions. Mill and Manson were the products of genetic influences from their parents and the conditions in which they were reared. Modern developmental psychologists want to understand how hereditary and environmental factors work together to produce developmental differences in each of us (Plomin and DeFries, 1985; Schlesinger, 1985).

Developmental psychology involves the scientific study of changes in a person's physical and mental abilities across the life span. Two issues are critical in this regard. First, developmental psychologists want to *describe* development. They want to know how people change as they grow older. Second, they want to *explain* development. They want to say which causal factors are responsible for these changes. Psychologists are particularly interested in changes in our **cognitive development**—our ability to perceive, to use language, and to think logically—and in our **social and emotional development**—our emotional reactions and our social interactions with others. To learn about these aspects of development, psychologists start by asking these types of questions:

- At what age can an infant recognize his or her mother?

- At what point can a child grasp the abstractions involved in adding two numbers together?

- When can a child first understand what gender she or he is?

- At what age do friendships become important to a child?

Infancy and childhood are especially important for observing these developmental processes at work.

HISTORICAL BACKGROUND:
Child Psychology

Adults have been fascinated by children for at least as long as history has been recorded. The Greek philosopher Plato (427–347 BC), for one, spent considerable time thinking about childhood training and education. He believed that children differed in their abilities and that each child should find work that best suited those abilities.

Two thousand years later, British philosopher John Locke (1632–1704) described children as incomplete adults who were ruled by strong impulses and desires. He believed that children should be carefully controlled because their development was guided by their experience. Locke viewed the child's mind as a *tabula rasa* (blank slate) at birth, and he advocated a structured and constant environment to mold its development. John Stuart Mill's father was influenced by Locke and he apparently took these teachings to heart.

However, not everyone believed that development was guided solely by experience. Some, such as French philosopher Jean-Jacques Rousseau (1712–1778), believed that children would develop optimally if they were not subject to strict supervision. Rousseau saw children as "noble savages" who possessed an inherent knowledge of right and wrong. Rather than attempt to fit the child into adult society, Rousseau saw the task of parents as providing their child with opportunities to explore the world. Most adults have not been entirely happy with Rousseau's idea of letting nature take its course with their children's development. Nonetheless, Rousseau is important for child psychology for two reasons. First, in presenting a view that differed from Locke's, he made explicit the distinction between hereditary and environmental influences on development, a distinction that eventually led to inquiry into the nature–nurture controversy by scientists. Second, he put forth the then-radical view that an adult is something a child has to *become*, a position that was to have far-reaching effects on education. In 1762, he wrote:

> . . . nothing is known about childhood. The wisest people are so much concerned with what grown-ups should know that they never consider what children are capable of learning.

(Rousseau, cited in Gardner, 1982)

Sharing Rousseau's belief, Swiss educator Johann Pestalozzi (1742–1827) worked to change educational methods in schools. He advocated that teachers abandon the method of rote memorization. Pestalozzi believed that children's thought processes changed over the course of their development, and that instructional methods should take these changes into account. The child sees the world from a different perspective than the adult, Pestalozzi argued, and educators should structure the educational experiences to suit the child. Consequently, the child, about whom so little was known, became the subject of great scientific inquiry during the second half of the nineteenth century.

Early Studies of Development

Of major importance to the development of child psychology was the publication of Charles Darwin's book *The Origin of Species* in 1859. In this book Darwin outlined an evolutionary perspective that saw change among plants and animals as following a lawful and orderly sequence. In particular, he saw a biological link between humans and other animal species and between adults and their children. As a result of Darwin's theory, scientists began to study children to learn about the origins of adult behavior.

Darwin himself carried out one of the first scientific studies of a child using the method of naturalistic observation. In 1840 and 1841, he kept a diary of his son's perceptual and motor development. In one instance, Darwin noted that although his son Doddy looked at a candle on the ninth day of life, he did not try to grab it until he was over four months old. Darwin also sought to determine the age at which different emotions such as anger and joy first appeared, and he compared his child's personal development to the developmental changes in other species. These day-to-day accounts of individual development came to be known as **baby biographies** and, by the turn of this century, they became a popular form of gaining information about the course of development.

Spurred by the success of the baby biographies, psychologists looked increasingly at children to discover the processes that lead to developmental change. Foremost among the early psychologists was G. Stanley Hall (1846–1924). Hall devised questionnaires and conducted interviews to determine how children of different ages understood everyday concepts such as hot and cold. By studying how children think, Hall believed, he could come to understand the behavior and thinking of adults.

Hall used a very different research method from that earlier employed by Darwin. Darwin had used the **method of longitudinal analysis,** as he repeatedly measured his son's behavior over a long period of time. In contrast, Hall used the **cross-sectional method.** He made observations of different-aged children to see how behavior varied in different age groups. Each of these approaches has advantages and disadvantages. The longitudinal approach can provide suggestions about the causes of age-related changes in behavior, but it is expensive and time-consuming to employ. Longitudinal research takes place over years, as children develop and researchers study them at different ages. The cross-sectional approach is more efficient in that data from different-aged children are obtained at the same time, but the researchers do not know what the individual children were like when they were younger. Both of these research techniques are still widely used by developmental psychologists. The choice of approach to be used varies with the topic being studied.

Maturation, Developmental Stages, and Learning

A student of Hall's named Arnold Gesell (1880–1961) made numerous studies of growth and behavior and demonstrated that there is an orderly sequence that guides infant physical and motor development. Gesell coined the term **maturation** as the name for the growth-directed processes that produce orderly changes in physical and mental abilities independent of specific experiences. Gesell also popularized the notion of developmental stages, such as the "terrible twos" and the "con-

forming threes," through which children often seem to pass.

The idea that development proceeds through a series of stages has been used by a number of influential theorists. For example, one of the most influential of these **stage theories** was developed by Swiss psychologist Jean Piaget (1896–1980), whose theory of cognitive development we will later describe in detail. Piaget believed that children think differently at different ages. At each stage from infancy through adolescence, the child acquires new strategies for understanding and acquiring knowledge. We will see that Piaget's theory has had a major impact on cognitive development research in this century.

Early research on social and emotional development was inspired by a different stage theory of development—Sigmund Freud's psychoanalytic theory of personality development. Through extensive personal interviews, Freud came to the conclusion that psychological problems in adults were related to deep, unresolved sexual and aggressive feelings that children developed toward their parents. According to Freud, personality development in childhood follows a series of stages, and the way in which a child manages these stages has a profound impact on his or her adult personality. For example, Freud believed that toddlers who were toilet-trained very early could become obsessively concerned about neatness and cleanliness as adults. Erik Erikson was a disciple of Freud, who modified and extended Freud's views to look at social and emotional development over the entire life span. We will describe Erikson's stage theory in Chapter 12.

In sharp contrast to the stage theories of development, behaviorist John Watson championed the view that cognitive, social, and emotional development were guided soley by learning and conditioning. In his 1928 book, *Psychological Care of Infant and Child*, Watson presented the position that behavior was influenced solely by the environment. While Watson and his followers emphasized the importance of nurture, others, including Gesell, Piaget, and Freud, leaned toward nature as the primary determinant of behavior. Modern developmental psychologists adopt an interactionist position and look at the interplay of heredity and environment in trying to understand behavior.

Today, developmental psychologists continue to be concerned with the broad questions raised by the great thinkers of the past. How is the child's experience different from that of adults and from that of younger and older children? How much of

Jean Piaget. During the first half of the twentieth century, Piaget studied thinking in children and developed a theory of cognitive development that still generates considerable research. Piaget specified how children's thinking changes during four periods of development, spanning the ages from infancy to young adulthood.

our cognitive, social, and emotional behavior is influenced by genetic factors, and how do genetic influences unfold in the face of different environmental pressures? And, finally, how do early life events influence what we will do later in our lives? The answers to these questions have implications beyond their philosophical significance. Contemporary developmental research is important for parents, educators, and health professionals who need answers to practical questions about the effects of such factors as busing, day-care programs, and television violence on children. These issues provide compelling reasons for psychologists to study development. ■

GENETICS AND PRENATAL DEVELOPMENT

Our psychological development begins long before we are born. At the moment of conception, we receive genes from our parents that may influence whether we become a philosophical genius, a violent criminal, or a contented suburbanite. And before a newborn baby sees the light of mother's first smile, a host of environmental factors can produce profound changes in the fetus while it is still in her womb. Because of the importance of genetic and

prenatal (before birth) factors, we will examine each separately below.

DEVELOPMENTAL BEHAVIOR GENETICS

Developmental behavior genetics is the interdisciplinary field of study that attempts to relate variations in behavior to variations in heredity. For example, research in behavior genetics has shown that genes have an influence on psychological characteristics ranging from intelligence to psychopathology (Table 11.1). To see how a behavior geneticist decides whether a characteristic—high intelligence, perhaps, or schizophrenia—can be inherited we need to understand the operation of genes and chromosomes.

GENES AND CHROMOSOMES

Behavior geneticists assume that physical characteristics, such as eye color, height, and a tendency for obesity, are passed on via genes. This was a controversial assumption until 1866 when a young Austrian monk named Gregor Mendel published his work on the inherited characteristics of garden peas. By crossbreeding plants with different characteristics (for example, purple versus white

TABLE 11.1 Psychological Characteristics Influenced by Genes

Cognitive Characteristics	Personality and Social Characteristics
Performance on different intelligence tests (Bouchard and McGue, 1981; Plomin and DeFries, 1985)	Emotionality and temperament (Vandenberg, 1967) Depression, anxiety, and various forms of abnormal behavior (Gottesman, 1962; Inouye, 1965)
Word fluency and vocabulary, spatial imagery, speed of perceptual classifications, and visual memory (DeFries, Kuse, and Vandenberg, 1979).	Special interests and skill in athletics and the arts (Farber, 1981)

flowers; yellow versus green seeds) and observing the effects over successive generations, Mendel was able to deduce certain laws of genetic inheritance. These laws governed the transmission of different plant characteristics passed on from parent to offspring. He believed that characteristics such as the colors of flowers or seeds were determined by the parents contributing tiny "elements" to the offspring. By the turn of this century, these elements became known as **genes,** the fundamental units of heredity. Genes come in pairs (one from each parent) and they are carried by thread-like molecules called **chromosomes.** Most body cells contain 46 chromosomes, each containing one thousand or more genes. At the time of conception, 23 chromosomes from the father's sperm are combined with 23 chromosomes from the mother's ovum to form 23 pairs. These pairs are then duplicated every time the cells divide. Each of the cells in your body contains the genetic material that could be used to produce your clone. These genetic blueprints are coded into strands of DNA (deoxyiribonucleic acid) in the cell's chromosomes. Very simply, DNA controls the production of enzymes that are used to build new cells and to communicate between them.

Just as genes control the development of our eyes, bones, and muscles, they also control the development of our nervous and endocrine systems. Thus, by influencing the structure of the brain and the production of hormones, genes influence our sensory and cognitive processes and even our thresholds for emotional reactions such

as anger and fear. Behavior geneticists believe that there are individual differences in our nervous systems and in our production of hormones. These inherited physiological differences can influence whether a person become an intellectual, a criminal, an extrovert, or a chronic depressive. The belief that genes can influence individual differences in behavior remains controversial, but there are some very clear cases of genetic effects on individual differences in intelligence. Historically, the most important discoveries in this area were the findings of genetic causes for some forms of mental retardation. Down's syndrome is one example.

DOWN'S SYNDROME

Down's syndrome is the most common form of chromosomally caused mental retardation. Approximately one in every 600 to 700 children in the United States is born with Down's syndrome (Edgerton, 1979). Infants with Down's syndrome develop normally for the first six months of their lives, but thereafter they fall farther and farther behind other infants in their age group. Children with Down's syndrome have difficulty paying attention, interpreting what is going on around them, and communicating with other people.

Although there are several varieties of Down's syndrome, children with the most common form have an extra or third chromosome in their twenty-first pair. During the process of **meiosis,** when the mature sex cells of each parent split to form separate cells, this chromosome pair in the mother or father fails to divide, resulting in 47 chromosomes instead of the normal 46 (Lejeune, Turpin, and Gautier, 1959). We do not know why this chromosomal abnormality occurs and how it leads to mental retardation, but we do know that the incidence of Down's syndrome increases dramatically with the age of the mother. Mothers in their twenties have one chance in 1500 of having a Down's syndrome baby, mothers in their early thirties have one chance in 800, mothers in their early forties have one chance in 130, and mothers in their late forties have one chance in 65 (Plomin, DeFries, and McClearn, 1980). Although Down's syndrome cannot be treated, it can be detected by the thirteenth week of pregnancy through a procedure called *amniocentesis*, where a sample of the amniotic fluid is drawn and its genetic material analyzed. It is now possible to test a fetus for specific gene abnormalities associated with retardation. In addition, potential parents can have their chromosomes analyzed to determine if they carry any harmful genes before they conceive a child.

GENE–BEHAVIOR RELATIONS

Down's syndrome provides a clear-cut case of a genetic influence on behavior. In fact, the genetic material that is responsible for the syndrome can be precisely identified under a microscope. However, it turns out that very few behavioral patterns are caused by so obvious a factor as an extra chromosome. Most frequently the important genetic codes are hidden within the strands of protein in the minute DNA molecules that make up the chromosomes. Often they are *polygenetic;* that is, influenced by more than one gene. Only recently have we begun to be able to map the relation between specific gene strands and specific behavioral characteristics. In the case of polygenetic characteristics, complex mathematical models are used.

It is not necessary to pinpoint specific genes to establish that a particular characteristic is heritable. As we saw in Chapter 9, several other techniques can provide the necessary clues. One simple technique is to observe if a characteristic "runs in the family" and how it tends to run. For the sake of simplicity, we will consider the physical characteristic of eye color before we examine the more complex characteristic of schizophrenia.

Eye color is determined by genes received from both parents. If the genes from both parents are the same, the child will have the eye color that is specified in the genetic message. But what if one parent provides a gene for brown eyes and the other provides a gene for blue eyes? A potential genetic conflict is avoided because genes for some attributes such as eye color are either **dominant** or **recessive.** A gene is dominant over another if it is more likely to be expressed as a physical attribute. In the case of eye color, the gene for brown eyes is dominant, while that for blue eyes is recessive. Thus, if a child receives genes for both brown eyes and blue eyes from the parents, the dominant gene will guide development and the child will have brown eyes. A child can have blue eyes only if both parents contribute a recessive gene for blue eyes.

Since the extended family tree is rarely available to follow the course of a complex characteristic such as schizophrenia, behavior geneticists often ask a more general question: Can we be confident that genetic factors play a role in causing this behavior? This itself is an important question because if the answer seems negative there is no point in spending valuable time trying to locate the responsible genes. However, even this broad question is not always easy to answer. As we saw in examining the genetic roots of intelligence, **twin studies** and **adoption studies** help psychologists sort out the relative impact of genes and the environment.

For example, imagine that you want to know whether there are any genetic factors affecting schizophrenia. First, you would ask whether schizophrenics had more schizophrenics in their families than you would expect to find in an "average" family. Actually, psychologists have found the likelihood that a schizophrenic has a schizophrenic brother or sister (or one who will become schizophrenic) is approximately eight percent, a much higher figure than the one percent risk of schizophrenia for people in general (Rosenthal, 1970). A behavior geneticist would be encouraged by this finding, but would not consider it to be conclusive evidence. Perhaps the schizophrenic siblings share some common genes, but they also shared other things, including common parents, homes, and diets.

Instead, a behavioral geneticist would seek out fraternal and identical twins who have been separated at birth for one reason or another by adoption agencies and raised in separate environments. (Fraternal twins share 50 percent of their genes, while identical twins share 100 percent.) When such a group of separated twins was examined after they reached adulthood, researchers determined that there was a 9 percent chance that if one fraternal twin were schizophrenic, his or her same-sex twin would exhibit the same disorder.

Family resemblance. In this photo, the daughter shows a strong physical resemblance to her mother because physical characteristics such as the color of her eyes and hair are genetically determined. Psychologists and behavior geneticists study the degree to which people's behavior also is influenced by heredity.

With identical twins, the likelihood rose to 44 percent. (Rosenthal, 1970). Such findings on the likelihood of twins demonstrating the same characteristic (technically termed the *rate of concordance*) provide strong evidence for a genetic influence in schizophrenia.

Based on this sort of detective work, behavior geneticists are fairly confident that genes play an important role in all of the behaviors listed in Table 11.1. However, there are additional complications. It is rare that a particular **genotype,** a person's genetic inheritance, always leads to a particular **phenotype,** a person's observable characteristics. The environment almost always interacts with a person's genes to establish the **range of reaction.** The range is a set of limits determined by the genes. However, where the phenotype falls within this range is a result of the shaping forces in the environment. For example, in Chapter 9 we saw how genetic and environmental factors combine to produce a range of reaction for intelligence. In the present context, John Stuart Mill obviously had a different reaction range than a child with Down's syndrome. Given the limited reaction range of a Down's syndrome child, even the stimulating environment provided by Mill's father could not have created a philosophical genius.

PRENATAL DEVELOPMENT AND BIRTH

Genetic and environmental factors actually begin their influence on behavior before birth. Incredible physical changes occur during the 38-week period between conception and birth. This is when our genes are unfolding their plans in a crucial environment—our mother's womb. Our sensitive brain is built in this environment. Beginning at around nine weeks after conception, the fetal brain has already begun to show signs of conducting electrical messages. At five months of age, the fetus is moving its fingers, blinking its eyes, swallowing, sucking, and even hiccuping. By the seventh month, the brain has grown greatly and taken on its characteristic convoluted appearance. By the beginning of the ninth month, the fetus has developed sensory abilities, including the ability to detect light and taste sweet substances. And it is even beginning to respond to the outside world— sudden loud noises can produce changes in the fetus's heart rate (Newton and Modahl, 1978).

ENVIRONMENTAL INFLUENCES ON PRENATAL DEVELOPMENT

While the crucial foundations are being laid for later cognitive and social development, the fetus needs a safe environment. A number of things can go wrong, particularly during the third through the sixth weeks of pregnancy when the central nervous system begins to form. This is particularly troublesome because women seldom know by the third week of pregnancy that they are pregnant, and this is the time when the developing human embryo runs the greatest risk of gross brain malformation (Sulik, Johnston, and Webb, 1981). Table 11.2 shows some of the different agents that

TABLE 11.2 Some Maternal Factors That Can Endanger Prenatal Development

Exposure to or Use of:	Possible Effects on Unborn Child
Addictive drugs	Growth deficiency; withdrawal syndrome; respiratory depression; death
Alcohol (moderate use)	Growth deficiency; maturational lag
Alcohol (excessive use)	Fetal alcohol syndrome from alcoholic mothers: deformities of the heart and face; prematurity; mental retardation
Anesthetics or barbiturates	Respiratory depression
Antibiotics	Hearing loss; growth inhibition; discolored teeth
Aspirin (excessive use)	Respiratory depression; bleeding
Cigarettes (one pack or more per day)	Fetal growth retardation; convulsions; increased fetal heart rate; prematurity
Malnutrition	Fetal growth retardation; malformation; less developed brain; increased susceptibility to disease
Rubella (German measles)	Mental retardation; heart defects; vision and hearing problems
Thalidomide (and other tranquilizers)	Hearing defects; limb deformities; defects of heart, eyes, intestines, and kidneys; cleft lip or palate; death
Vitamins (excessive use)	Congenital abnormalities; cleft palate
X-ray	Mental retardation; bone defects; spine and eye defects; cleft palate; limb deformities

Modified from Gardner (1982) and other sources.

can endanger the unborn child. We will focus on one of these agents in the Dysfunction section that follows.

DYSFUNCTION:
Fetal Alcohol Syndrome

The negative effects of excessive alcohol consumption on fetal development have been known for a long time, but it is only in recent years that researchers have identified a pattern of developmental malformation known as **fetal alcohol syndrome (FAS).** This disorder affects roughly one-third of all infants born to alcoholic mothers and it is characterized by a variety of symptoms. Infants with fetal alcohol syndrome are smaller than average in size and have various physical deformities, including abnormally small heads, malformed faces, and underdeveloped brains (Figure 11.1) (Abel, 1980; Jones, Smith, Ulleland, and Streissguth, 1973). In addition, these infants' cognitive development is impaired as they are often mentally retarded and likely to remain so (Hanson, Streissguth, and Smith, 1978; Streissguth, Barr, and Martin, 1984). A parallel study documents the effects of maternal alcohol consumption on the behavior of infant macaques, and is demonstrated in Figure 11.2.

The risk of fetal alcohol syndrome and the severity of its symptoms increases the more a pregnant woman drinks (Abel, 1980; Rosett and Weiner, 1985). Some researchers believe that when the blood alcohol level rises in the mother's bloodstream, the umbilical cord to the fetus collapses, and this may temporarily cut off the supply of oxygen to the developing fetus (Mukherjee and Hodgen, 1982). One study found that only one ounce of 80-proof vodka consumed by a nonalcoholic pregnant woman resulted in a cessation of fetal breathing movements that lasted for approximately half an hour (Fox et al., 1978). Insufficient oxygen to the fetal brain could be the source of mental retardation in FAS babies.

Are such results applicable only to hard-drinking women? No. Recent research by Ann Streissguth and her colleagues has found that even moderate social drinking can have serious effects on an unborn child. One large-scale study examined three-day-old infants whose mothers had been drinking as little as two-thirds of a drink of liquor or three-fourths of a glass of beer or wine daily during pregnancy. The infants showed behavioral and learning deficits. They had lower arousal levels and more body tremors, and they

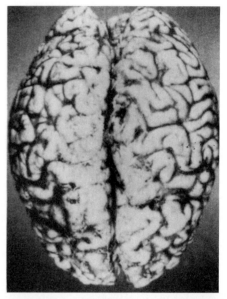

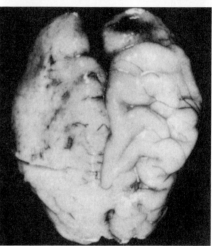

FIGURE 11.1 The effects of maternal consumption of alcohol on infant brain development. The brain of a normal child (top) and the brain of a child who suffered from fetal alcohol syndrome (bottom). Note the smaller size and fewer convolutions in the brain from the child with fetal alcohol syndrome.

took longer to become bored by repetitive stimulation than comparable infants whose mothers abstained from alcohol during pregnancy (Streissguth, Barr, and Martin, 1983). Similar behavioral and learning deficits were found in four-year-old children whose mothers consumed two drinks a day during pregnancy (Streissguth et al., 1984). These studies are part of a growing body of research that indicates that, even in moderate amounts, alcohol can have negative effects on an unborn child. For the developing fetus, there may be no such thing as a safe level of exposure (Barr, Streissguth, Darby, and Sampson, 1990). ■

FIGURE 11.2   Fetal alcohol syndrome.   Research indicates that alcohol consumption by a mother can seriously affect the well-being of her child. Alcohol can cross the placenta (the structure in the uterus through which the fetus is nourished) to enter the fetal bloodstream and damage the developing brain. Even moderate consumption of alcohol during pregnancy can produce later cognitive deficits in the infant and result in fetal alcohol syndrome. In these photos, a normal baby macaque (left) responds with curiosity to a toy in a box, while the baby macaque suffering from fetal alcohol syndrome (right) is listless and inattentive.

Before moving on, it is best to keep a sense of perspective about prenatal hazards. Normal fetal development is overwhelmingly the rule. Thanks to current research on the ways in which development can go awry, pregnancy is safer today than it was throughout most of history. However, even in our grandparents' time, the majority of all pregnancies ended with the birth of a normal and healthy child.

BIRTH

Nine months after conception, the real environmental changes begin, as the baby is forced through the mother's narrow cervix and into the bright lights and noise of the outside world.

Psychological studies of the effects of birth have focused on two factors: birthweight and prematurity. Very low birthweights (between two and three pounds) are associated with cognitive and motor deficits (Koop, 1983; Lester et al., 1986). Many—but not all—underweight infants recover to reach normal levels of development. Some of these very low-birthweight children show retardation in cognitive skills such as reading, spelling, using language, and doing arithmetic. One study has reported that the higher a family's occupation and income level, the better the chances of recovery from early cognitive deficits associated with low birthweight (Wilson, 1985). Presumably, parents with sufficient means can provide a low-birthweight infant with a nourishing and stimulating environment in which to realize his or her inherent potential. These findings on birthweight and development point once again to the interrelation of heredity and environment.

Premature infants have an additional problem. Along with their low birthweights, they can be separated from their parents during the first few weeks of their lives. This separation, if coupled with the lack of sensory stimulation that comes from spending those weeks in an isolette, can hamper a delicate infant's development. In the past, a "hands off" policy was standard treatment, but research has shown that these infants respond positively to gentle stimulation and handling (Leib, Benfield, and Guidubaldi, 1980). As a result, hospitals now encourage parents to visit and fondle their child frequently. These visits allow the parents to see how their baby is doing and, more importantly, they appear to increase a baby's chances of survival (Zeskind and Iacino, 1984). Today, medical advances have made it possible for many of these infants not only to survive, but to fare quite well (Buckwald, Zoren, and Egan, 1984; Klein et al., 1985).

INFANCY

When a baby comes home from the hospital, and family and friends gather around, differences of opinion invariably arise over the infant's sensory and perceptual abilities. Can the newborn infant see people clearly? How long will it take for the baby to learn that mommy's face and voice are part of the same person? In fact, babies can see, hear, and respond to a variety of sights and sounds in their environment much earlier than you might expect. Research indicates that they are born with sensory and perceptual abilities that enable them to interact with the world from their first day of life (Hall and Oppenheim, 1987).

THE NEWBORN CHILD

The first month after birth is called the **neonatal period.** It marks the beginning of **infancy,** a period that extends through the second year of life. It is during the neonatal period that the child develops a routine for sleeping, feeding, and caretaking and becomes part of the family.

Though newborn infants are totally dependent on adults for their care, they are far from helpless. They come into the world equipped with a set of reflexes to help them survive. For example, they automatically turn their heads and mouths in the

The world of the premature infant. Premature infants are confined to a hospital isolette until they are strong enough to go home. However, they need stimulation and interaction with people in order to thrive. Frequent visits by the parents are especially valuable. Such visits allow the parents to monitor their child's development and they provide the child with necessary attention and love.

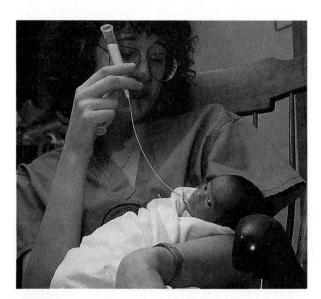

direction of stimulation to their cheeks. This **rooting reflex** aims the child in the direction of nourishment, and then other reflexes, such as sucking and swallowing, take over. In addition to knowing how to eat, the newborn infant can breathe, blink, cough, sneeze, and eliminate waste, all without a single lesson. Newborn infants also enter the world with all of their senses turned on. They distinguish between various tastes and sounds, turn away from unpleasant odors, and react strongly by thrusting and kicking when something interferes with their breathing (Lipsitt, 1979). Though their visual acuity will not be fully developed until they are four to six months old, infants can follow objects that move slowly across their visual field (Cohen, DeLoache, and Strauss, 1978). Far from being tiny passive creatures who are incapable of doing very much, newborn infants are enormously responsive.

PERCEPTUAL AND COGNITIVE DEVELOPMENT

Until fairly recently, many people believed that infants perceived very little and knew even less. The problem, of course, was that because infants lack speech and cannot communicate their experiences there was no way of knowing about the mental life of the young child. But in the late 1950s the situation changed. At that time, psychologists realized that if infants could not communicate directly they could express themselves indirectly through such observable behaviors as sucking, head turning, eye movements, and emotional displays. When questions are posed in the right way, infants have no problem responding.

PERCEPTUAL PROCESSES

A wide variety of studies have shown that infants are capable perceivers. For example, research in auditory perception has found that newborn infants can locate sounds in space (Ashmead, Clifton, and Perris, 1987; Morrongiello, Fenwick, and Chace, 1990). In a study involving an infant girl only 10 minutes old, a soft clicking noise was presented to her left or right ear. She demonstrated sound localization by turning her head, either left or right, in the direction of the noise (Wertheimer, 1961). Sound localization requires a split-second perceptual discrimination to determine which ear was stimulated by sound first.

If infants can locate the direction of sounds, can they tell the difference between different types of sounds? Even if they could, how would we ever know? Experimental ingenuity has provided an answer. We know that repetitive events are soon ignored. This process is called **habituation.** One team of researchers used it as the basis for an experiment with infants who were only six weeks old. The infants were presented with a non-nutritive electronic nipple that produced a distinct speech sound when they sucked on it. To find out if infants could perceive the difference between a *ba* and a *pa* sound, only one type of sound (for example, the *ba* sound) was presented at first. On discovering the new sound, the infants increased their rate of sucking, but then they gradually became habituated and their rate of sucking declined. At this point, the experimenters changed the speech sound. With *pa* instead of *ba* heard after each suck, the rate of sucking increased once again (Figure 11.3). The infants had not become fatigued, they had merely become bored with the *ba* sound. These results demonstrate both habituation (a decrease in responsiveness to unchanging stimulation) and dishabituation (an increase in responsiveness to new stimulation) and they show that neonates are capable of detecting subtle differences in the perception of sound (Eimas, Siqueland, Jusczyk, and Vigorito, 1971; Jusczyk and Derrah, 1987). This is further testimony to the complex skills possessed by the newborn infant.

Between one and two weeks of age, infants can perceive distance or depth. They can tell when an object is moving toward their faces, and they show this by taking steps to defend themselves. If a toy is slowly moved closer and closer to the face, young infants open their eyes wider, move their heads back, and raise their hands to protect their faces from the potential blow (Bower, Broughton, and Moore, 1970). Of course the researchers never actually hit the infants, but the self-protective responses show that infants are capable of detecting something coming toward their faces. An apparatus called the "visual cliff" has also been used to test for depth perception in older infants. In one study, psychologists placed infants individually on the "deep" side of the visual cliff apparatus (the side that appears to have a floor far below the glass surface). They then observed the infants' reaction to what appears to be an abrupt drop (Figure 11.4). They found that the heart rate slows down in six-week-old infants, while it speeds up in older infants who are able to crawl (Campos et al., 1978). Heart rate deceleration is associated with attention, while acceleration is associated with fear. Are the children really afraid of the apparent cliff? To find out, the psychologists had each infant's mother try to coax her child to crawl across the

FIGURE 11.3 Speech perception in infancy. In this study, six-week-old infants were presented with an electronic nipple that produced different speech sounds. Over the course of a nine-minute period, one group of infants (A) heard a *ba* sound each time they sucked. These infants initially increased their rate of sucking and then decreased as they became habituated to the sound. For another group of infants (B), the speech sound was changed after five minutes from *ba* to *pa* and their rate of sucking increased once more. These results indicate that neonates can detect subtle differences in speech sounds.

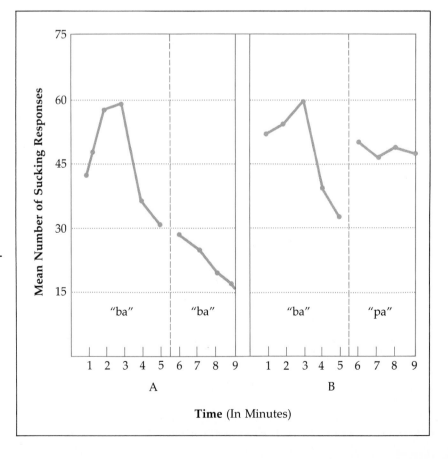

FIGURE 11.4   Depth perception in infancy.
Although both sides of the "visual cliff" apparatus
are covered with thick glass, one side looks shallow
and the other side looks deep. Research with animals and humans indicates that depth perception is
available early in life. Infants who can crawl will not
cross the deep side.

"deep" side from the "shallow" side of the visual
cliff. Though the thick glass was strong enough to
support them and mother was waiting with outstretched arms, the infants refused to budge (Gibson and Walk, 1960).

Perhaps most impressive of all is the young
infant's ability to coordinate sights and sounds. In
an experiment by psychologist Genevieve Carpenter (1975), two-week-old infants were presented
with one of the following visual and auditory
stimuli:

- The mother's face.
- A female stranger's face.
- The mother talking to the infant.
- A female stranger talking to the infant.
- The mother talking to the infant with a strang-
  er's voice.
- A female stranger talking to the infant with
  the mother's voice.

The infants looked longest at their mother when
she spoke in her own voice and next longest at
their mother's face alone. What was surprising,
because of the age of the infants, was their reaction
to incorrect combinations of the mother and female
stranger. When the mother's face was presented
with a stranger's voice—or vice versa—the infants
often burst into tears. This research clearly shows
that infants combine their mother's sight and

sound into a unified perceptual experience at a
very young age. They know what she looks like
and sounds like and they know that both of these
features are supposed to come from the same
source. This study and others like it suggest that
infants are particularly adept at connecting different channels of perception (Bushnell, Shaw, and
Strauss, 1985; Spelke, 1979).

COMPLEX COGNITIVE PROCESSES

Beyond the ability to see and hear, how does the
infant think? According to Jean Piaget, older children not only know more than younger children,
they think in fundamentally different ways. Piaget
held that at specific points in their development,
children dramatically change their ways of thinking about the world. He described cognitive development as a series of overlapping periods that
involve major changes in thinking from infancy
through adolescence. The periods include the *sensorimotor* (from birth to two years), the *preoperational* (from two to seven years), the *concrete
operational* (from seven to eleven years), and the
formal operational (beyond eleven or twelve years).
We will describe the first three of these periods in
detail in this chapter and save the fourth for the
next chapter since it typically occurs during
adolescence. This stage approach to cognitive development has been criticized in recent years. Critics claim that not all children go through each stage
at the age or in the sequence Piaget described.
Nevertheless, his theory still provides a useful picture of the ways in which our mental processes
develop.

Piaget believed that children's cognitive development proceeds in an orderly, sequential manner. What a child can do at one age depends upon
changes that occurred earlier. Just as we would not
expect a three-year-old child to lift a 100 pound
weight, we should not expect this same child to
learn calculus or analytic geometry. In each instance, there are structural limitations based on the
child's current level of development. The child's
limited physical structure prevents her or him
from lifting the weight, while the child's limited
"cognitive" structure prevents her or him from
learning complex mathematics. For Piaget, the
cognitive structure is a set of behavior patterns or
rules that determines how a child comes to understand the world. Just as the physical structure
of the body changes during development, so the
cognitive structure changes as well. For Piaget, the
changing cognitive structure is the means by
which the child understands and remembers information from the environment.

Piaget believed that two processes account for changes in a child's cognitive structure: assimilation and accommodation. **Assimilation** is the process of taking in information from the external world and relating it to what we already know. For example, young children may mistakenly believe that all adults are parents. "This person is large, has a beard, and speaks with a deep voice. He must be a daddy." Sorting people into categories like "mommies and daddies" initially helps children to organize a great deal of information, but gradually they learn that their simple organizations are limited. (Not all large, bearded people are daddies, for instance). When children become aware of a discrepancy, tension results, and they are forced to change their beliefs to accommodate a more accurate view. **Accommodation,** therefore, is the process of revising the cognitive structure to make it more consistent with experience. Children eventually come to know that not all adults are parents, not all animals are dogs, and not all toys are theirs. According to Piaget, it is the interplay of the assimilation of new experiences and their accommodation with prior beliefs that serves as the catalyst for cognitive development.

THE SENSORIMOTOR PERIOD

Piaget called the first period of cognitive development the **sensorimotor period** for a very simple reason: infants learn about their world through their senses and motor behavior (Piaget, 1954; Piaget and Inhelder, 1969). During the first two years of life, infants learn primarily by looking, listening, and feeling, rather than by thinking. At the very beginning, an infant's behavior is dominated by such reflexes as rooting, sucking, and

swallowing. Later, these reflexes are supplemented by such voluntary movements as reaching and grasping. Infants then start to manipulate objects in their environment. By six months of age, infants will examine objects by fingering them and turning them around, all the while with intent expressions on their faces (Ruff, 1986). Still later, with the additional mobility they have found by crawling and walking, infants move about deliberately and purposefully as they explore their environment.

According to Piaget, the principal achievement of the sensorimotor period is an understanding of the concept of **object permanence.** This is the realization that objects, including people, continue to exist even if they are not visually present. This belief is so deeply ingrained in adults that we take it for granted, but it is something that each of us learned very early in life. If a screen is placed in front of a toy, a three-month-old infant will act as if it has disappeared (Figure 11.5). Between eight and 12 months of age, infants will search for a toy that is completely hidden from view, even if they must wait a short period of time before searching (Baillargeon and Graber, 1988). However, if the toy is moved several times, they often forget where it was hidden and look for it in its initial location (Bjork and Cummings, 1984). Only later, during the second year of life, will infants follow the movement of a toy as it is hidden in a series of places and find it in its correct location. Once the child actively searches for hidden objects, he or she shows an understanding of object permanence. This accomplishment marks an end to the sensorimotor period of cognitive development.

In general, cognitive development during the first two years of life involves a shift from depen-

FIGURE 11.5. Out of sight, out of mind. Young infants do not understand the concept of object permanence. When an object is out of sight, they act as if it no longer exists. Only later will they learn that objects still exist even if they are hidden from view.

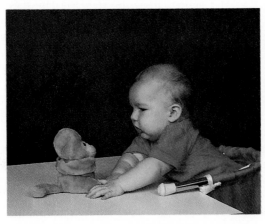
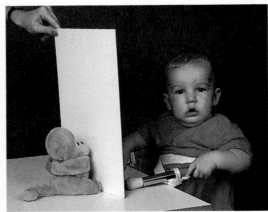

dence on sight, touch and the other senses to an increasing dependence on thought. Symbolic thought can be seen in the play of two- and three-year-olds, who pretend that one object is something else (Flavell, Flavell, and Green, 1987). They know that brooms are not really horses and mud-pies are not really food, but yet they can pretend that they are. This ability to substitute symbols for reality is the foundation for abstract thought. At this time, children also are developing a sense of the past and the future and an ability to recall past events. The attainment of object permanence, along with the development of memory (memory would have no function if objects lacked permanence), enables young children to remember where food or a favorite plaything is located. It also allows children to handle separation from their parents. They are now old enough to grasp that mommy and daddy still exist even if they are no longer in view. Moreover, symbolic thinking enables a child to learn increasingly complex behaviors. For example, newborns can imitate the simple movements of adults: They can smile, stick out their tongues, or clench their fists (Haviland and Lelwica, 1987; Meltzoff and Moore, 1983; Vinter, 1986). As the infants mature, they can imitate more complex behaviors. For instance, 14-month-old infants can imitate the actions of television models. Infants who watched a videotape of a model pulling apart a dumbell-shaped toy later repeated the behavior when they were presented with the toy for the first time (Figure 11.6). Some infants even took the toy apart if they were presented with it a day after viewing the tape. This experiment shows that infants are able to learn how to manipulate objects by watching the actions of others (Meltzoff, 1988). By the age of two, children learn increasingly complex chains of responses with the aid of their symbolic memory. Presented with a toothbrush and a tube of toothpaste, a two-year-old can easily mimic mommy's behavior from memory. This increasing ability to learn from other people is part of another crucial aspect of development—the development of social cognition.

SOCIAL COGNITION IN INFANCY

Social cognition is defined as the means by which people come to understand the thoughts and feelings of themselves and others and how they think about social relations. Of primary importance for social cognition in infancy is the process of **differentiation**. Infants learn to differentiate people from inanimate objects, familiar people from strangers, and themselves from others (Flavell,

FIGURE 11.6 Looking and learning. Infants can learn by imitating the actions of others, even if they are observing those actions on a television screen. In these photos, an infant watches a model take a toy apart. Later, when the infant is given the new toy, he, too, pulls it apart, just as the model did. Infants have very little trouble translating a two-dimensional television image into three-dimensional reality.

1985). The development of self-awareness—of a personal identity we call a **sense of self**—shows how the process of differentiation is entwined with cognitive development.

A sense of self is a composite of the attitudes, beliefs, and feelings that people have about themselves. Summarizing the views of earlier theorists, psychologist Howard Gardner (1982) has said that the development of a sense of self is dependent on the presence of three factors. First, children must become aware of their bodies, of its appearance and condition. Second, children must learn to use language appropriately when saying "I," "me," or "mine," or when giving their names. Third, children must have knowledge of their past, of their unique chronological history. Given these necessary conditions, research suggests that children develop a sense of self-awareness between the ages of two and three (Stipek, Gralinski, and Kopp, 1990).

How have psychologists learned about the development of self-awareness? Studies of infants have found that when one-year-old infants are shown pictures of themselves, they label the pictures as "baby." By the age of two, the children have changed, and they respond correctly with their own names. Still later, between the ages of two and three, they respond to the question: "Who is this?" by simply saying "Me" (Lewis and Brooks, 1975; Damon and Hart, 1982). A developing awareness of the body has been demonstrated in an experiment in which children of different ages were shown their faces in a mirror after their noses had been secretly colored with rouge. If children have an awareness of their bodies, then a red nose should come as a surprise. Accordingly, these children would most likely reach up and touch their noses as they conflict with their established self-images. Infants of less than one year of age did not touch their noses, while the majority of two-year-olds did. Upon seeing themselves in the mirror, the older children acted silly and smiled (Lewis and Brooks, 1978). A sense of self develops slowly because it depends on other processes. For example, without a prior understanding of object permanence, children could not view themselves as existing over time.

EMOTIONAL DEVELOPMENT AND ATTACHMENT

In addition to our innate predispositions to walk, to talk, and to think, we enter this world prepared to meet others of our kind. Infants have a set of prewired emotional responses they can use to make mommy and daddy smile or to draw their parents' attention to their distress. But emotional development is more than the simple maturation of a set of innate responses—environmental factors are important as well.

THE DEVELOPMENT OF EMOTIONS

As we noted in Chapter 10, one of the first people to study emotional development was Charles Darwin (1872). Using the method of naturalistic observation, Darwin saw that many animals had a variety of expressions that appeared to serve as innate signals for other animals. These expressions, he believed, could serve an adaptive function by facilitating interactions among members of a species. For example, aggression could be regulated by the expressions of threat or submission. If an animal acted submissively, it could avoid having to fight.

Nearly half a century later, psychologist John Watson presented a modified view of emotional development. Watson argued that only three emotions were innate—fear, rage, and love. All other emotions, he believed, were derived from these basic emotions through conditioning (Watson and Morgan, 1917). For example, emotional responses such as fear could be attached to previously neutral stimuli. This view of emotional development served as the basis for his study of acquired fear (discussed earlier in Chapter 6), in which an infant named Albert learned to fear a white rat through its association with a sudden loud noise (Watson and Rayner, 1920).

Not everyone agreed with Watson. For example, psychologist Katharine Bridges (1932) studied a large number of children in a foundling home in Montreal and presented a different picture of emotional development. By observing the emotional responses of infants over the first two years of life, Bridges found that newborns tended to show mostly generalized excitement. But from this one basic emotion, she said, the excitement became differentiated into the various emotions as the infant matured.

The various emotions do appear at different periods in the development of the infant. However, we still are not sure if they are all differentiated from generalized excitement (as Bridges argued) or if they occur spontaneously with physiological changes in the maturing child. In either event, the infant's emotional responsiveness is influenced by the infant's experience. The act of smiling, for example, is guided by both heredity and environment.

SMILING

Studies of infants all over the world indicate that smiling is a universal, natural expression. Infants smile during their first month of life, and they usually start laughing by four months of age. The innateness of smiling is suggested by movies of children born deaf and blind who smile, despite their sensory handicaps (Eibl-Eibesfeldt, 1973). Experience is important, though, as normally sighted infants smile earlier than blind infants. This again suggests an interaction of heredity and environment.

During the first year of life, there are three different stages in the development of smiling. The first stage, present at birth, is called *spontaneous* or *reflexive smiling*. In this period, the infant will smile without external stimulation. It is this type of smiling that hospital ultrasound recordings (sound tracings that are turned into pictures) have detected on fetuses still in the womb. Two to eight weeks after birth a change takes place, and *nonselective social smiling* occurs. Here, the infant will smile at various visual stimuli, especially human faces. After five or six months, a final change occurs—*selective smiling* appears, as infants distinguish between familiar and unfamiliar people and smile more at those who are familiar. Although all infants pass through these stages, environmental factors effect the frequency of smiling. Infants smile more when the adults around them smile in return, and they smile more when they are raised at home with their families than when they are brought up in institutions by nonfamily members (Gerwirtz, 1965; Termine and Izard, 1988).

By the age of seven months, infants can differentiate such expressions as happiness, fear, and surprise in the faces of people around them (Ludemann and Nelson, 1988). In fact, different patterns of brain wave activity have been recorded by an electroencephalograph (EEG) machine when infants are smiling or crying or when they are looking at video tapes of models who are expressing different emotions. For example, psychologists Richard Davidson and Nathan Fox found that ten-month-old infants showed greater brain wave activity in their left frontal lobes when they smiled, but greater activity in their right frontal lobes when they cried. This same pattern of brain wave activity was seen when the infants merely looked at videotaped models who smiled or cried. These experiments indicate that infants are able to respond to the emotional cues of people around them (Davidson and Fox, 1982; Fox and Davidson, 1988).

Why are emotional expressions such as smiles and cries important to the growing infant? Psychologists believe that they are important because they play a key role in the formation of **attachment,** the tendency of infants to seek closeness with particular individuals (usually their parents) and to feel secure in their presence. The long-lasting emotional bond that is produced by attachment is perhaps the most important process in the infant's early social development.

FORMING ATTACHMENTS

Attachment normally occurs during the first six months of life. Very young infants are attracted to all people. Gradually, they learn to discriminate among people and begin to prefer familiar to unfamiliar people. Finally, between six and seven months of age infants seek contact with specific people—normally their parents or others who take care of them—and they may show signs of distress when these people are not present.

Not surprisingly, infants form strong attachments to their mothers. However, infants also form strong attachments to their fathers (Lamb, 1977). In fact, there seems to be little difference in the way children become attached to each parent, although mothers and fathers do differ in their typical interactions with their child. Mothers are more apt to vocalize and caress their infants, while fathers are more apt to play with their children.

Parental play styles. Although both parents will play with their child, fathers are more apt to engage in physically arousing games, while mothers tend to talk to and caress their babies or play more conventional games, such as peek-a-boo. Fathers are even more physical than mothers in instances where they stay at home with the child and the mothers go off to work.

Infants, for their part, look to each parent to satisfy different needs. They prefer their fathers as partners in play, but they go to their mothers in times of stress. Fathers are often exciting and unpredictable, while mothers tend to be soothing and comforting (Clarke-Stewart, 1978; Power and Parke, 1982). A similar conclusion was reached in a cross-cultural study involving one-year-old infants and their parents in India (Roopnarine et al., 1990). At present we do not know the extent to which these differences in parent–child interactions are biologically or culturally determined, but we do know that both parents are important attachment figures who play major roles in the social development of their children. Given that fathers typically spend less time than mothers with their children, it appears that the quality of the interaction rather than its duration is an important factor in attachment formation (Grossman, Pollack, and Golding, 1988). Essentially the same message is provided by research on mothers who work—attachment seems to be dependent on the quality and not the quantity of time that a mother spends with her child (Easterbrooks and Goldberg, 1985; Hoffman, 1984).

THEORIES OF ATTACHMENT

Why do attachments form? One possibility is that attachment is based on the satisfaction of the infant's physical and psychological needs. Infants must be fed, kept warm and clean, and given attention and affection, and they may develop positive feelings for those who satisfy those needs. But which of these needs is most important to attachment?

According to Freudian psychoanalytic theory, attachment is based on the mother or primary caregiver satisfying the child's most basic needs—mainly hunger and thirst. Similarly, early behaviorist learning theory saw attachment as resulting from the reduction of basic "drives," states of arousal caused by physical needs. These views assume that the positive feelings that occur following the satisfaction of physical needs, such as the feeling of contentment after eating or drinking, become linked to the person who satisfies those needs. In short, we become attached to the hand that feeds us.

But there are several problems with these self-centered approaches to attachment. First, attachment is not a one-way street, and these views cannot explain why parents become attached to their children. Second, they cannot explain why infants become attached to their fathers, or other people who might not be strongly associated with eating or drinking. Finally, research with infant rhesus monkeys, who also became strongly attached to their mothers, demonstrates unequivocally that the satisfaction of hunger or thirst is not the basis for attachment. While studying learning in rhesus monkeys, psychologist Harry Harlow (1949) discovered that monkeys who were raised alone in order to reduce their exposure to disease were later seriously socially impaired, even though they had all of their other needs met. He studied infant monkeys who were raised by two substitute or "surrogate mothers"—a wire form that provided nourishment and a terrycloth form that provided warmth. The monkeys did not become attached to the wire "mother" despite the fact that "she" fed them. Instead, they became attached to the soft terrycloth form that provided only contact comfort. This attachment was apparent both in the amount of time that the infant monkeys spent with the terrycloth "mother," (Figure 11.7) and by the fact that the infants ran to this "mother" when they were frightened by strange mechanical toys.

Instead of viewing attachment in terms of the gratification of physical needs, British psychiatrist John Bowlby (1973) has adopted an **ethological approach.** This approach looks at unlearned, goal-directed behaviors as instincts that are guided by the interplay of genetic and environmental factors. According to Bowlby, human attachment is based on innate patterns of behavior that guide social interactions between parent and child. Attachment occurs because the infant is pre-equipped with innate emotional responses, such as smiling and crying, that elicit parental care and protection. A mother's responses are also innate. It hurts her to hear her child cry, and it warms her heart to see her or him smile. Unlike psychoanalytic theory, this view minimizes the importance of feeding. Feeding is just one of many social situations in which parents and infants interact. Attachment formation is based on mutually rewarding social signals—smiles, hugs, and giggles—and not on the satisfaction of such physical needs as hunger or thirst (Cohn and Tronick, 1987; Rutter and Durkin, 1987). Since the parent's emotional responses are also guided by innate processes, Bowlby's view has the advantage of explaining why parents also become attached to their children.

ATTACHMENT, TEMPERAMENT, AND LATER DEVELOPMENT

Can social development during early childhood affect future development? Erik Erikson developed an important theory of social and emotional de-

FIGURE 11.7   Attachment and contact comfort. Infant monkeys raised with surrogate "mothers" preferred to be with the terrycloth-covered mother than the mother who provided nourishment. Psychologists had earlier believed that attachment was based on the satisfaction of biological needs, but research by Harry Harlow demonstrated that contact comfort plays an important part in infant–parent attachment.

velopment that in part echoes Freud's view that child development sets the stage for adult development. For Erikson, infants form a lifelong attitude of either trust or mistrust toward the world based on the sensitivity and responsiveness of their early caregivers. However, others have argued that infants are remarkably resilient. Except in cases of severe neglect or abuse, early negative experiences can often be rectified by more sensitive and responsive care later on (Clarke and Clarke, 1976). As you can imagine, such an important issue has generated a good deal of research.

To learn about attachment and its later effects, psychologist Mary Ainsworth and her colleagues watched mothers interact with their babies. For four-hour sessions every three weeks from birth until the end of the first year, Ainsworth observed the sensitivity and responsiveness of each mother in meeting the needs of her child. At one year of age, the infants' attachment to their mothers was tested in what the researchers called the **strange situation.** This consists of the following series of events:

1. The mother and infant enter an unfamiliar room.

2. The mother sits down, while the infant is free to explore.

3. A stranger enters the room and sits in a chair.

4. The mother leaves, while the infant and stranger remain.

5. The mother returns and the stranger leaves.

6. The mother leaves the infant alone in the room.

7. The stranger returns.

8. The stranger leaves and the mother returns.

Ainsworth found three different patterns of attachment. The majority of the infants, roughly 60 to 65 percent, were described as *securely attached.* They used their mothers as a base of exploration to seek out toys and objects in the unfamiliar room, and each of them occasionally returned to her for close contact. Each was clearly distressed when the mothers left the room and went to her when she returned. Before this encounter with the strange situation, the mothers of these infants were described as sensitive and responsive to their child's needs.

A second group of infants, roughly 20 percent, were described as *avoidant.* Each of these babies rarely cried when the mother left and ignored the bids for interaction when she returned. These mothers were previously observed to be largely insensitive to their child's needs. Instead of being affectionate, these mothers often acted angry or irritable with their children.

Finally, a third group of infants, approximately 10 to 15 percent, were classified as *ambivalent.* They were occasionally upset when their mothers left, but when each mother returned her baby either showed a lack of interest or exhibited ambivalence by going to her, but kicking and squirming upon being picked up. Mothers of these children were observed to be awkward and somewhat insensitive to their children but not as rejecting as the "avoidant" mothers (Ainsworth, 1973; Ainsworth, Blehar, Waters, and Wall, 1978).

In fairness to the mothers, we should keep in mind that mother–infant attachment is not a one-way street. Babies are not passive creatures that development happens to—they have a hand in creating their own worlds. Some infants are temperamentally more difficult than others, and do not take easily to cuddling and comforting (Weber, Levitt, and Clark, 1986). Attachment is a reciprocal relationship and differences in infant temperament surely influence a mother's interaction with her child.

How do these different patterns of attachment in infancy affect later social development? Research indicates that young children who were securely attached as infants are more cooperative, enthusiastic, and, in general, more socially competent than children who were insecurely attached (Oppenheim, Sagi, and Lamb, 1988; Sroufe, 1978; Waters and Sroufe, 1983). However, these observations are correlational. We cannot say that secure attachment during infancy causes social competence during childhood. Perhaps the children's temperament accounts for both, or perhaps securely attached children have parents who are also effective at teaching social competence. To see the effects of attachment on later development, we need to look elsewhere—to studies of attachment deprivation.

ATTACHMENT DEPRIVATION

Perhaps the clearest picture of the consequences of attachment on later development is found in Harlow's experiments with monkeys. To follow-up his earlier research on the effects of attachment deprivation during infancy, Harlow raised infant monkeys in isolation. Although their physical needs were met and a cloth surrogate mother was provided, the infants were socially isolated and deprived of the opportunity to become attached to a parent. Harlow found that these infants showed severe behavioral pathologies. They clutched their bodies, they rocked back and forth, and they bit themselves on their arms and legs. If the period of isolation lasted for only the first three months of life, the monkeys eventually recovered. But if the period of social isolation was extended for the entire first year, the monkeys became abnormal adults. For example, female adult monkeys who had been isolated for their first year of infancy treated their firstborn offspring miserably. They provided little support for their infants and even abused them to a dangerous extent (Harlow, 1971).

In retrospect, even though Harlow's infant monkeys became attached to the comfort and security of a cloth mother, a lifeless surrogate mother is not enough for normal social development. What the cloth mother lacked was the ability to engage in a social "dialogue" based on reciprocal behavioral actions. This dialogue need not take place with an adult, though. Monkeys raised with other infant monkeys, along with a surrogate mother, demonstrated social development that was initially slower than normal, but eventually became indistinguishable from normal. Moreover, if a monkey who was formerly isolated was placed with a group of normally raised younger playmates, the younger monkeys functioned as little therapists and induced playfulness and socially appropriate behavior in the former isolate (Suomi, Harlow, and McKinney, 1972). These results indicate that a lack of normal attachment in infancy can be harmful to later development, but the effects of such isolation are modifiable.

No ethical scientist would ever dream of conducting an isolation experiment with human infants. However, an unfortunate parallel to the animal research can be found in children reared in institutions. In the past, some institutions for orphans provided for the physical needs of the children, but failed to meet their emotional needs. The children who were raised in these cold, uncaring environments became apathetic, fearful, and withdrawn (Provence and Lipton, 1962). Such effects need not be permanent. Like Harlow's monkeys, these children are often able to recover when they are placed in a more sensitive and responsive situation. But they probably have an easier time learning attachment during infancy than at a later time, when they must undo the effects of their earlier negative experiences (Clarke and Clarke, 1976; Lerner, 1984).

The role of attachment in later development remains a subject of considerable interest to psychologists. Infant attachment is seen as the first of a series of social interactions that each of us will experience in life. Rather than directly affecting our behavior as adults, attachment in infancy paves the way for childhood social relations. Attachment thereby affects later social development by setting its initial course. Nonetheless, it is possible for later social interactions to alter that course in a positive or negative direction.

CHILDHOOD

The period of **childhood** extends roughly from ages two through 12. It is marked most clearly at its end by the sexual changes of puberty that turn a child into a potential parent. Though enormous developmental advances have been made already during infancy, great changes in thought and behavior still lay in store for the developing child.

COGNITIVE DEVELOPMENT IN CHILDHOOD

By the age of two, children are well on their way to using language and thinking abstractly. Although two-year-olds can think, their thought processes are still very different from those of adults. Even a four-year-old, fluent in language, cannot see the humor in the following joke:

> One day a man went to a restaurant and ordered a pizza. When it was served, the waiter asked him if he would like it cut in four or eight pieces. "Oh, four," the man replied, adding that "I could never eat eight pieces."
>
> (McGhee, 1976)

The joke exceeds the cognitive ability of a four-year-old who thinks the man is right—eight pieces are a lot more than four. Older children find this joke amusing because they realize that the quantity of food remains the same no matter how you slice the pie. Such understanding proves to be an important step in cognitive development.

To learn about cognitive development during childhood, Piaget asked children to use their powers of reasoning on several kinds of problems. He found that younger children differed from older children in their ability to comprehend **reversibility,** the process of changing an object in some fashion and then returning it to its original state. For instance, dividing a bag of marbles into two or four groups does not change the total number of marbles because if the marbles were replaced in the bag—if the operation were reversed—the same number of marbles would be obtained. According to Piaget, children use **mental operations** to transform and manipulate what they see or hear according to logical rules. Reversibility is one such mental operation. Younger children lack this ability, so they are called **preoperational.** Older children demonstrate reversibility, but only with concrete, tangible objects. Children at this age are therefore called **concrete operational.** Piaget used this qualitative change in thinking to divide cognitive development during childhood into these two major periods.

THE PREOPERATIONAL PERIOD

Between the ages of two and seven, children continue to learn about people and objects in their world. However, their thinking is often illogical and dominated by perceptual experience. Consider the following example. Young children were allowed to play with a cat who was later fitted with a mask of a dog. When the children were asked to identify the animal, three-year-olds thought that the cat had turned into a dog, while four- and five-year-olds were confused. Only six-year-olds knew that the animal was still a cat (DeVries, 1969). During early childhood, children do not understand the distinction between appearance and reality, and they are often guided by their perceptual experience.

Not only are young children fooled by appearances, they are also apt to believe that their experience is everyone's experience. Because children at this age have trouble adopting the perspective of other people, Piaget described the perspective of the preoperational child as self-centered, or **egocentric.** Piaget often got ideas for his research by using the method of naturalistic observation. For example, in observing young children playing marbles, he found that, although the children played together, each was engaged in the game according to her or his own rules. No child was trying to beat the others (Piaget, 1965).

When young children are confronted with tasks that demand logic, they fail for a variety of reasons. They demonstrate **irreversibility,** an inability to rearrange objects mentally, as the following conversation with a four-year-old boy shows:

ADULT:	Do you have a brother?
CHILD:	Yes.
ADULT:	What's his name?
CHILD:	Jim.
ADULT:	Does Jim have a brother?
CHILD:	No.
	(Phillips, 1969)

Most four-year-olds also demonstrate **transductive reasoning** by mixing up cause and effect. For instance, when asked to finish incomplete sentences, children often reverse the order of events.

> I had a bath because . . . afterwards I was clean.
> I've lost my pen because . . . I'm not writing.
> (Piaget, 1926)

And their reasoning is limited in still another way as illustrated by the pizza joke. They fail to understand **conservation,** the idea that the properties of an object, such as its mass, volume, and number, do not change despite transformations in that object's appearance (Figure 11.8). Figure 11.9 shows several of the tasks that Piaget used to conclude that preoperational children do not realize

A   B   C

FIGURE 11.8   The thinking of the preoperational child.   To understand the concept of conservation children must learn that physical properties such as volume, number, length, or weight do not change despite changes in the appearance of objects. For example, in this test of conservation of volume, a child can perceive equality of volume when each beaker is the same (A), but she is fooled by appearances when the liquid from one short, wide beaker is poured into a tall, narrow beaker (B). Not realizing that the volume of a liquid is conserved as it is poured from one beaker to another, this preoperational child focuses on the height of the liquid and says that the tall beaker has more (C).

FIGURE 11.9   Tests of conservation.   A variety of tasks devised by Piaget to test children's understanding of conservation. Preoperational children (aged two to seven) do not realize that objects retain their physical properties of volume, number, length, and weight despite changes in their appearance.

Conservation of Volume

A B   B C

Children agree that two equal beakers containing equal amounts of liquid are the same, but if the liquid is poured into different sized beakers, they may think its volume has changed. (Beaker C).

Conservation of Number

A ⓒⓒⓒⓒⓒ B ⓒⓒⓒⓒⓒ
B ⓒⓒⓒⓒⓒ C ⓒ ⓒ ⓒ ⓒ ⓒ

Children agree that equal rows of coins are the same, but if one of the rows is lengthened, they may judge it to have more. (Row C).

Conservation of Length

A ▭▭▭   B ▭▭▭
B ▭▭▭   C ▭▭▭

Children agree that two sticks of equal length are the same if they are aligned, but they may no longer be judged as equal if one of the sticks is moved.

Conservation of Weight

A ◯ ◯ B   B   C

Children agree that two equal balls of clay are the same, but if one is flattened and stretched, they may think that it is now more. (Ball C).

that objects conserve their physical properties. In Piagetian terms, preoperational children cannot demonstrate the concept of conservation because they lack the mental operation of reversibility.

Not all psychologists accept Piaget's views of young children's thinking. Studies of egocentrism by Rochel Gelman and other psychologists have shown that even young children can take another person's perspective into account in order to communicate effectively. For instance, in spite of their often deficient reasoning preschool children aged three and four are sometimes able to demonstrate conservation (Gelman, 1978: Miller, 1986) and, at times, they may even specify cause and effect relationships in a logical manner.

ADULT:	Can a rock walk?
CHILD:	No.
ADULT:	Why?
CHILD:	Cause it doesn't have legs.
ADULT:	Can a person walk?
CHILD:	Yes, cause it has legs.
ADULT:	Can a doll walk?
CHILD:	No, cause it has pretend legs.

(Gelman, Spelke, and Meck, 1983)

The distinction between some animate and inanimate objects is apparently available in early childhood (Massey and Gelman, 1988). Young children can give evidence of causal thinking, but only as we have just seen, when they are discussing such familiar objects as rocks, people, and dolls.

Together, these results suggest that the ability to take another person's perspective and to think logically in reasoning tasks begin earlier than Piaget believed. However, these cognitive skills are clearly absent at the start of the preoperational period, and develop gradually over time. Once children begin to think logically enough to grasp the concept of reversible operations—to be able to put the pizza back together mentally—they enter what Piaget called the period of concrete operations.

THE CONCRETE OPERATIONAL PERIOD

With slow but continuous growth and ever-increasing skills, the child between seven and 12 undergoes more change in cognitive development. According to Piaget, the shift in the child's conceptual understanding can be seen easily if the child is asked to do a sorting task. When four-year-olds are asked to sort a collection of objects into separate piles that "go together," they most frequently sort on the basis of object size or color—for example, small objects in one pile, big objects in another; red objects in one pile, yellow objects in another. Older children realize that objects can be sorted in other ways. Older children can sort objects on the basis of their conceptual similarity—for example, tools in one pile, animals in another pile. By classifying objects in this manner, older children show that they are no longer so dominated by the appearance of things.

With their increased understanding and their ability to demonstrate reversibility, seven- to 12-year-old children are now in the concrete operational period. They are able to solve conservation problems that had earlier baffled them (look back to Figure 11.9). For example, they realize that when water is poured from a short, wide container into one that is tall and narrow, the water cannot increase in volume. They have learned to compensate for the perceptual difference in height by noting that the taller container is narrower. They have also learned that a liquid retains its identity; it can neither increase nor decrease in volume according to the size of a container. And they have learned the operation of reversibility; they know that when a liquid is poured back into its original container, it regains its original appearance.

Although these preadolescent children are capable of systematic thought, their cognitive development is still far from complete. As indicated by the name of this period, concrete operational children deal well with concrete tasks involving tangible objects or events, but they have difficulty with abstract ideas. Parents and teachers can encourage abstract thought by explaining abstract ideas in terms of concrete examples. Art work is one area in which the child can learn to connect the abstract with the concrete. Figure 11.10 provides an example. It shows a child's conception of the wind as it invisibly moves different objects in its path.

As children progress through this period, one of the most important cognitive skills they develop is the ability to know which mental operations to apply to different problems. Early in this period, children may have the appropriate conceptual knowledge, but they may apply it only to highly specific situations. For example, they may solve one type of conservation task (for example, conservation of number) yet be fooled by another (conservation of volume). Only later, when the children have gained more experience, will they become "fully operational" and detect underlying similarities in tasks, such as those in Figure 11.9, that seem, on the surface, to be different. This ability to move beyond appearances is called

FIGURE 11.10   Concrete operational thinking.   The child in the concrete operations stage can deal with abstract ideas only if they are placed in a concrete context. In this drawing by an elementary-school child, the abstract idea of the wind is shown by its effect on tangible objects such as the curtains, tree, and clothes that lie in its path.

abstraction, and it represents a significant advance in reasoning and symbolic thought.

We will consider the final period of Piaget's theory of cognitive development, the formal operational period, in the next chapter. For now, the summary of his theory in Table 11.3 serves as a reminder of those periods that we have covered and a preview of the period we will describe. Note that while Piaget has been criticized by studies that show that children often seem more cognitively advanced for their age than his theory suggests, his theory has stimulated a mass of research enhancing our understanding of cognitive development in childhood.

ATTENTION AND MEMORY DEVELOPMENT

Although Piaget's view of cognitive development is shared by many psychologists, there is another approach to cognitive change that emerged from the American experimental tradition. The **information processing** approach, described in Chapter 7, holds that cognitive development is best studied by examining the basic cognitive processes that underlie any given task. Information processing psychologists are concerned with how information is stored in memory and how it is later retrieved to solve particular problems. Developmentally, they are interested in the cognitive strategies that children of different ages use in different situations.

According to this view, children think differently at different ages because they differ in both their ability to process information and the type of information they select to process.

Neonatal studies have shown **selective attention** in infants who are only several minutes old (Wertheimer, 1961). This indicates that the ability to direct attention may be partly innate. However, selective attention also increases with age. In one experiment, six- and nine-year-old children were asked to decide whether two pictures were the same or different. Photographic records of eye movements showed that the younger children looked at only parts of the pictures and made numerous errors. The older children were more accurate. They scanned each picture thoroughly before making a decision (Vurpillot and Ball, 1979).

Not only are younger children less systematic in their processing of information, they are often unable to differentiate relevant from irrelevant information. When children of different ages were shown a movie and later asked to recall either relevant information about the film's plot or irrelevant information about one of the characters (for example, what color dress was she wearing?) the recall of relevant information increased with age, while the recall of irrelevant information decreased (Hale, Miller, and Stevenson, 1968). As children get older, they examine information more selectively and they choose more meaningful informa-

TABLE 11.3 Piaget's Sequence of Cognitive Development

Cognitive Period	Description
Sensorimotor Birth to two years	Infants progress from reflexive actions to the beginning of symbolic thought. Knowledge is obtained by coordinating sensory impressions and motor movements. Infants form a basic understanding of object identity and permanence and begin to understand spatial, temporal, and cause and effect relations. They gradually learn to distinguish between themselves and the external world.
Preoperational Two to seven years	Thinking is dominated by physical appearance. Children cannot comprehend that an object is the same even if its appearance changes. However, young children expand their abilities to think symbolically by acquiring language. They can then represent objects and events with words and images. In playing with other children, they can pretend that one object is something else.
Concrete Operational Seven to eleven years	Children can now understand logical principles in relation to concrete events. They cannot yet reason abstractly or test hypotheses systematically, but they are able to understand that certain properties of an object, like its mass or quantity, remain the same even after changes in appearance. No longer egocentric, these children can take another person's perspective.
Formal Operational Beyond eleven or twelve years	Thinking is no longer limited to concrete events. Adolescents can solve abstract problems and test hypotheses by deduction. They can reason logically, reflect on their own thinking, and speculate on what might or ought to be.

Notes: Each of Piaget's cognitive periods stresses a particular type of thinking. The sequence of cognitive development is always the same as each new period extends what came before. However, the age range for each period is approximate.

tion to examine (Ackerman, 1987; Renninger and Wozniak, 1985).

Complementing the development of selective attention, children become more systematic in their thinking. They devise different strategies to help themselves remember. Between the ages of five and seven, children frequently talk to themselves, and shortly thereafter they discover that silently repeating the names of different items (the process of **mental rehearsal**) is an effective way to remember them. If kindergarten children are given several common items to remember—for instance, a comb, a key, a book, and a cup—they almost never rehearse the items on their own, while the majority of fifth graders spontaneously rehearse (Flavell, Beach, and Chinsky, 1966; Ornstein, Medlin, Stone, and Naus, 1985). Interestingly, kindergarteners will improve their performance if an adult prompts them to rehearse, but when they are no longer prompted, they no longer rehearse. Young children apparently cannot see how their mental rehearsal is connected to their memory per-

formance, whereas preadolescent children see this connection and exploit it (Fabricius and Hagen, 1984). This change signals a major advance in cognitive development. Now the children are not only thinking abstractly, they are controlling and directing their thinking.

Thus, studies of attention have shown that with increasing age, children examine information in a more systematic and focused way (Hudson, 1990; Nelson and Nugent, 1990). In addition, studies of memory have shown that children learn to use strategies that help them cope with the demands of education (Wagner, 1982). As a consequence of these changes in information processing, children begin to be able to think about their own memory skills. This awareness is called **metamemory.** Some studies of metamemory measure the length of a series of items that can be recalled in perfect order. Young children have limited metamemory; they consistently overestimate how many items they can recall in perfect order. As children get older, they become more accurate in judging the difficulty of different tasks and they also become more efficient in using their own mental resources (Butterfield, Nelson, and Peck, 1988; Kail, 1979). In many ways, these findings complement Piaget's approach to cognition. Rather than viewing the information processing approach as an alternative to Piaget's theory, it may be seen as a more systematic and quantitative description of the processes that underlie the cognitive changes originally profiled by Piaget.

SOCIALIZATION PROCESSES

Socialization is the name of the process by which children acquire the attitudes, beliefs, and customs of their family and culture. Parents who impart their own values and beliefs to their child are the first agents of socialization. With increasing age, children are more and more influenced by peers—children of similar age and interests.

SOCIALIZATION BY PARENTS

As children grow and mature, the role played by their parents changes. At first, parents are mainly concerned with satisfying the child's physical and emotional needs. Few demands are put on the newborn. As children become more capable of understanding, parents become increasingly concerned with controlling their behavior and teaching them to act in ways that are socially acceptable. All parents share some of the same goals of socialization. Regardless of whether a child is raised in a simple jungle hut or a sophisticated suburban home, parents must teach their children how to control various bodily functions—for example, they must learn not to urinate whenever and wherever they want. All parents also must teach their children how to control their behavior toward other people—for example, to inhibit their aggressive impulses when another child takes a toy that they want.

Yet while there are similarities in the goals of socialization there are also important differences. Each society has a slightly different set of rules about how and when to control impulses. Some of these rules depend upon how the society obtains food. In farming societies parents tend to stress the values of obedience and responsibility. These values are important in agricultural societies because crops and livestock can die if they are not cared for at fixed and regular times. On the other hand, parents in hunting and fishing societies are more apt to emphasize initiative and self-reliance. For those who must outwit nature to survive, flexibility and independence are more important than

obedience and responsibility (Barry, Child, and Bacon, 1959).

Moreover, there are differences in socialization within any complex society, many of which depend upon the social class of the parents. For example, in the United States children are typically taught values that their parents require for their jobs. Working class parents usually work in a job that is closely supervised by a boss, and these parents tend to stress the importance of obedience. Conversely, middle class parents, whose work is more loosely supervised or who may be self-employed, emphasize self-control. By emphasizing obedience, working class parents are teaching their children to adhere to external control, while middle class parents' emphasis on self-control teaches control from within. With this difference in values, it is not surprising that working class parents are more apt to use physical punishment, a prime example of external control, as a method of disciplining their children than are their middle class counterparts, who often use restriction of privileges (Kohn, 1979).

Given that parents are so important in setting the initial course of socialization, one crucial question is how specific childrearing practices influence the child's social development. In what ways might our behavior be related to the way we were raised?

RESEARCH AND APPLICATION: Childrearing Practices

Until the middle of this century, developmental psychologists were concerned with the effects of feeding, weaning, and toilet training on the social development of the child. They asked a variety of questions that were often guided by Freudian theory. Is breast feeding superior to bottle feeding? Is early weaning or early toilet training detrimental to later development? These initial childrearing concerns were shown to have little effect on development (Zigler, Lamb, and Child, 1982). Today, psychologists are less interested in specific events and more interested in the general tone of the relationship between parent and child.

Styles of Parenting

As preschool children learn how to climb stairs, play on swings, and ride tricycles, they get themselves into potentially dangerous situations and require the constant vigilance of their parents. How should parents act? How should they communicate, praise, and punish to best develop a competent and self-reliant child? Until relatively recently, little was known about this issue.

In 1967, psychologist Diana Baumrind conducted extensive interviews with parents of three- and four-year-old children. She observed how the parents and children interacted at home and how the children interacted with other nursery school children. Baumrind rated all the parents on four factors: *control* (attempts to direct or modify dependence, aggression, and play), *demands for maturity* (attempts to have children perform up to their level of ability), *clarity of communication* (reasoning with and listening to the child), and *nurturance* (expressions of warmth and pride). Three different parental styles emerged from her study. She found *authoritative* parents who scored high on all four dimensions, *authoritarian* parents who were only high on control, and *permissive* parents who were only rated high on nurturance. In dealing with their children, the authoritative parents exerted firm control when required, but they explained their actions and encouraged their children to express their opinions. Authoritarian parents, however, were more detached and distant from their children. They expected strict obedience to rigid standards that they often did not explain to the child. ("You will do it because I say so.") Finally, permissive parents were affectionate with their children, but they failed to assert their authority. Permissive parents imposed few restrictions, made few demands, and were reluctant to punish inappropriate behavior.

Socially Different Children

As you might expect, each of these styles of parenting was associated with a socially different type of child. In the nursery school, Baumrind found that children of authoritarian parents tended to be moody, insecure and withdrawn, while children of permissive parents were immature, passive, and dependent. Only children of authoritative parents were evaluated positively. They were independent and self-reliant, friendly and energetic. Thus, the most well-adjusted and socially developed children came from firm but loving parents who presented goals and standards of conduct, yet communicated with their children (Baumrind, 1967).

In a follow-up study of these children when they were eight or nine years old, Baumrind found that the children of authoritarian or permissive parents tended to be relatively less original and self-reliant on different intellectual tasks, while children of authoritative parents were higher on self-reliance, self-confidence, and social ease

A parental explanation. Research indicates that consistency in enforcing rules, together with the use of reasoning and explanation, has a positive effect on social development.

(Baumrind, 1977). Still other research has shown that parenting styles are related to scholastic performance. In a study of nearly 8,000 high school students, the children of authoritative parents had markedly better grades than those of authoritarian or permissive parents (Dornbusch et al., 1987).

In thinking about such findings, it is tempting to reflect on how we were raised by our own parents and how we might use this information to better the next generation. However, before you conclude that differences in parental style are responsible for differences in social development, remember that Baumrind's results are correlational. She has demonstrated that different styles of parenting are associated with different outcomes in childhood; she has not demonstrated that one *causes* the other. Certainly, the correlation may mean that social development in childhood is directly influenced by parental style, but other explanations are possible. For instance, it may be that innate differences in children's temperament lead to differences in parental style. For example, easy children may simply be easy to explain rules to, and so may elicit an authoritative approach from their parents. Alternatively, maybe social competency is biologically transmitted. Perhaps competent parents tend to have offspring who would be competent even if they were raised in another home. So while other studies have extended Baumrind's finding of a relation between parental style and social development in the United States (Pulkkien, 1982; Trickett and Susman, 1988) and China (Lau et al., 1990), we are still uncertain about the causal basis of this relation. In this sense, Baumrind's research is similar to Ainsworth's (reported earlier in this chapter) on patterns of attachment in infancy. Both show that parents clearly influence their children, but psychologists are increasingly realizing that children also actively influence their parents, as they have done since birth. This process is called **reciprocal socialization.** ▪

SOCIALIZATION BY PEERS

Parents are important, but they are not the only people who affect social development. Animal and human research alike has demonstrated the importance of peers. We saw earlier that monkeys raised in isolation failed to develop normally when later placed with adults. Yet, if placed with a group of normal monkeys of slightly younger age, the isolated monkeys gradually responded to the playful initiatives of their nonadult peers and developed normally thereafter.

Could peer groups have a similar therapeutic effect on socially withdrawn children? Research suggests that the answer is yes. Socially withdrawn four- and five-year-old children who were placed in a group of slightly younger normal children showed improved social skills after only three weeks, while other withdrawn children not exposed to the nonadult peers made no progress (Furman, Rahe, and Hartup, 1979). Studies like this suggest that peer interactions can, in themselves, influence social development. Normally, this influence occurs during the natural course of preschool play.

Play is defined as an exploratory and pleasurable activity that does not aim toward any specifc goals. Like most social behaviors, play follows a developmental sequence. Initially, one- and two-year-old children engage in *solitary play*. Even in a group, each child plays mainly alone. *Parallel play* follows soon after, as children enjoy more physical proximity but do not yet interact. They are like nearby parallel lines that are close but never meet. Piaget's description of young children playing marbles is an example of parallel play. Only after

age three will children begin *cooperative play* with each child taking separate but complementary roles. These changes in the structure of play are brought about by changes in cognitive development. Cooperative play cannot occur until a child becomes less egocentric and understands the perspectives of others.

Just as the nature of play changes, so too does the basis for friendship. Among preschoolers, friends are whomever a child happens to be playing with at a particular time. At the start of grammar school, friends are those who do what the child likes to do. During later childhood, children begin to adapt their behavior to meet the needs of their playmates—to do things they might not like, just for the companionship. Finally, by adolescence, mutual sharing and feelings of intimacy serve as the basis for friendship (Selman, 1980). Play is thus crucial for children's social development because it provides a social context within which friendship can develop.

What other functions might play serve? Russian psychologist Lev Vygotsky (1967) described play as a vehicle for learning rules, learning how to cope, and trying out new situations. Play engages symbolic thought as children "make believe," and it has other cognitive benefits. During games, children solve problems and learn about their environment. Socially, games allow children to try out

Play at different ages in childhood. Play is an exploratory and pleasurable activity that is not oriented toward specific goals. By age three, children engage in cooperative play in which each child takes a complementary role. One purpose of cooperative play is that it enables children to practice the different behaviors that they have previously observed in adults.

different roles that they might assume as adults. For example, children playing with toy cars and trucks learn to follow various conventions such as driving on the correct side of the road, in between their numerous crashes. Parents play with their children, but in some ways peers do a better job since they are less easily bored. Young children play longer and more intensely with their peers than with their quickly tiring parents (Rubenstein and Howes, 1976). This finding helps to explain why time with adults decreases, while time with peers increases, as children increase in age.

Children in peer groups compare themselves to one another and develop a sense of identity ("I am not as smart as Sara, or as athletic as Anthony, but I am the funniest kid here.") Peer groups also allow a child to develop a sense of belonging to a group beyond the immediate family. These processes of socialization begin during infancy and early childhood but are greatly accelerated when children go to school.

SOCIAL COGNITION IN CHILDHOOD

During their school years children make prodigious advances in social cognition, the ability to understand people and think about social relations. Unlike the more passive learning by socialization, during which a child comes to internalize the values and beliefs of his or her parents, social cognition is a more active form of learning, in which a person works to construct his or her own knowledge and perception of the world (Sherman, Judd, and Park, 1989).

ROLE-TAKING AND CONCEPTIONS OF FRIENDSHIP

As children progress from the preschool through the preadolescent years, their ability to make accurate inferences about other people's thoughts and feelings shows a dramatic increase. Children become more sensitive to the ideas and actions of others and more aware that others will react to their ideas and actions from a different perspective. **Role-taking** is a cognitive skill that refers to the child's ability to comprehend what another person sees, how another person feels, and what another person thinks. There is a definite developmental progression from an egocentric perspective to one that actively considers the thoughts and feelings of others (Selman and Byrne, 1974). As you might expect, one of the most significant factors affecting the development of role-taking is social experience. Regardless of age, children who lack the opportunity to interact with other children

are less skillful at taking the perspective of others than are children who have extensive social interactions. School provides the opportunity for many of these interactions and also provides the setting in which children can become friends.

In discussing the importance of peers, we have already seen how the basis for friendship changes from proximity (physical closeness) in preschool children to shared feelings of intimacy in adolescents. Psychologist James Youniss (1980) studied changes in children's thoughts about friendship. He asked children of different ages to tell him a story in which "a child your age shows another child your age that they like them."

He found that for children between the ages of six and eight, friendship was based on unqualified sharing. Friends were those who gave you candy or let you use their toys. Older children between nine and 11 described a friend as someone who helped resolve an inequity. For example, if you needed a pencil in school, a friend gave you one of his. Still older children between 12 and 13 spoke of friendship more in terms of psychological support than physical exchanges. For them, a friend was someone who discussed problems with you when you disagreed with your parents or who helped you when you did not understand your math.

From Youniss's research, we can see a number of shifts in social cognition. First, young children see friends as largely interchangeable, but older children do not. Second, children see the basis for friendship as changing from sharing such material resources as food and toys to sharing such psychological resources as advice and affection. Third, older children express an increase in concern and active caring for one another. They see friends as assuming each other's burdens and troubles. These changes in the perceived basis of friendship parallel those that occur in role-taking. For both, the child develops an awareness and concern for others that make her or him a more sensitive and responsive person.

Thus far, we have lumped all children together in describing changes in social cognition. Children differ according to the developmental factors associated with age, but they also differ according to gender. Being a boy or a girl has different implications for psychological development.

THE INFLUENCE OF GENDER ON CHILD DEVELOPMENT

Read almost any of the great children's classics and you will see a very different picture of the two sexes. For instance, in Mark Twain's *Tom Sawyer*, boys are the class troublemakers and the town's pirates. They have fist fights, they sneak out of the house at night, and they roam the countryside in search of adventure. Girls in this story are more civilized. They wear pretty dresses, they behave in class, and they write poetry. Do boys and girls still act in this manner? The answer is yes and no. Walk onto any grammar school playground and you will still see some of the same differences that Twain observed. Boys are still more likely to fight with one another and to be scolded by their teachers for breaking the rules. Girls, on the other hand, now wear jeans instead of dresses and play soccer or basketball as well as more traditional games such as hopscotch or jump rope. Figure 11.11 shows some of the similarities and differences in the preferences of modern Tom Sawyers and Becky Thatchers. Other than a few notable exceptions, such as playing with dolls or guns, this survey of 2,000 children between the ages of seven and 11 showed more general similarities than differences (Zill, 1985).

SEX ROLES AND SEX DIFFERENCES

In developing a sense of self, children learn the behaviors that their society considers appropriate for their sex. The characteristic ways of acting masculine or feminine are referred to as **sex roles.** They can vary from one society to another and they can change over time. Certainly, our society's definition of what is appropriate for males and females has changed enormously in the past several decades. For example, men are no longer considered strange if they enjoy cooking or playing with children, and women are no longer prevented from running for high office or working in a construction trade. By the same token, men can be sensitive and tender (formerly "feminine" characteristics) and women can be independent and competitive (formerly "masculine" characteristics). Psychologist Sandra Bem (1976) refers to such people as being **androgynous.** Their personalities include a balanced combination of positive characteristics formerly thought to be "appropriate" for only one gender or the other. Leisure activities, work

FIGURE 11.11   Activity preferences of boys and girls.   A survey of over 2,000 children between the ages of seven and 11 generally showed more similarities than differences in activity preferences for boys and girls. Gender differences, when they occurred, can be seen by looking at what these children dislike.

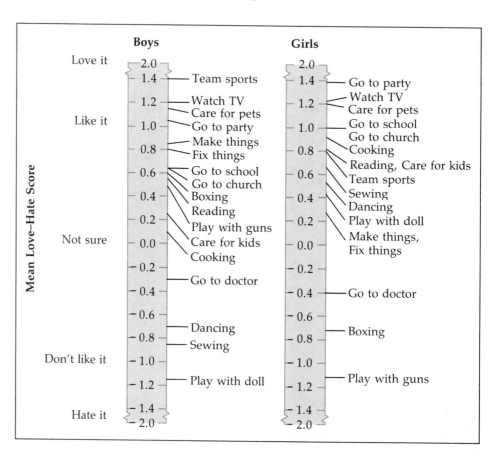

skills, and attitudes have become much more unisex. Yet differences still exist. Even with today's more openminded approach, biological and social factors provide different experiences for males and females.

Sex differences in behavior are present during early childhood, but they tend to become magnified during the school years. For example, boys are generally more active at birth, fuss more at three months of age, and play more vigorously at one year of age than do girls of the same age. During childhood, boys continue this pattern. They are more aggressive than girls and they engage in more strenuous activities (Maccoby and Jacklin, 1974; 1980). Beside these differences in physical activity, boys and girls are sometimes reported to show differences in social and cognitive development. However, these differences are not always reliable. For example, reviews of the social development literature find no support for the popular beliefs that girls are more social than boys, that boys have more achievement motivation than girls, that girls are more suggestible than boys, or that boys have more self-esteem than girls (Hetherington and Parke, 1986; Maccoby and Jacklin, 1974). Gender differences in cognitive development have also been reported. Previous studies found that girls were better than boys in verbal abilities, while boys were better than girls on spatial and mathematical abilities. However, we discussed this research in Chapter 2 and reported that these differences have always been small and current research indicates that gender differences in cognition are disappearing (Caplan, MacPherson, and Tobin, 1985; Feingold, 1988; Hyde, Fennema, and Lamon, 1990; Hyde and Linn, 1988). Even for those areas in which sex differences have been observed, the role of different treatment by parents and society based on sex cannot always be ruled out.

THEORIES OF SEX DIFFERENCES

What accounts for sex differences in behavior? Historically, most psychologists have taken a strong environmentalist (nurture) position. In doing so, two major theories have been advanced: social learning theory and cognitive developmental theory.

Social learning theory assumes that boys will be boys and girls will be girls only because it gets them rewards. Change the reward structure and the behavior will change. For example, if girls were rewarded for acting like boys, they would show increased aggressiveness and play cowboys and Indians instead of dolls, and, in fact, some tomboys may behave as they do for just this reason. Social learning theorists, including Walter Mischel (1970), have focused on sex differences in the way children are socialized. They believe that they have tracked the source of sex differences to the minds of the parents. For example, parents describe their newborn sons as "big," "strong," and "alert," and their newborn daughters as "little," "soft," and "inattentive" even when the infants are actually equal in size (Rubin, Provenzano, and Luria, 1974). During childhood, many parents maintain this sex differentiation by emphasizing achievement, competition, and independence in boys and concern for others, sensitivity, and trustfulness in girls (Block, 1980). Boys are more likely to be given educational toys, action figures, and sports equipment, while girls get domestic toys and dolls (Huston, 1983; Lawson, 1989; Rheingold and Cook, 1975).

Children, in turn, quickly learn how they are supposed to behave. By the age of three, both boys and girls believe that boys like to play with cars, help their fathers, and build things, while girls like to play with dolls, help their mothers, and say "I need some help" (Kuhn, Nash, and Brucken, 1978). By the age of six, boys and girls (and their mothers) in Taiwan, Japan, and the United States tend to believe that boys are better at math and girls are better at reading, even though evidence for such differences in ability at this age is nonexistent (Lummis and Stevenson, 1990). Peers also play a role. Boys who play with dolls or girls who play with trucks may be criticized or ignored by other children (Fagot, 1977; O'Brien and Huston, 1985). Even here, though, there are differences. "Tomboys" are accepted more readily than "sissies" (Huston, 1983). In general, there is a tendency in our society to regard "masculine" activities as superior to "feminine" activities as a result of earlier views of sex roles.

Cognitive developmental theory holds that boys and girls assume their respective characteristics because they have mastered the concept of gender (they understand which gender they belong to) and they want to show that they are able to play a complex social role. According to psychologist Lawrence Kohlberg (1966), sex-typed behaviors occur as a natural outcome of cognitive development. Closely linked to Piaget's theory, cognitive developmental theory holds that between the ages of two and three children begin to classify themselves and others by sex. Gradually, they develop an understanding of the concepts of "male" and "female" and actively pursue those activities that are associated with their own gender. For example, toddlers in nursery school tend to play with toys stereotyped for their gender—trucks for boys, dolls for girls. Still later, between five and seven years of age, children acquire **gender conservation** as they realize that they will always be male or female.

Cognitive developmental theorists do not deny that children can learn by imitating others and that children are influenced by praise and criticism. But these theorists link social and cognitive development by stressing the relationship between the development of sex roles and the cognitive development of the child. What children learn about sex roles is based on what they are taught. However, what they are capable of learning is based on their level of cognitive development. This theory can explain why children acquire sex roles even when their parents do not pressure them, but there are some findings that it cannot easily reconcile. For example, sex differences in gross motor activity and in aggression occur long before children have the cognitive capacity to understand gender conservation or even to label themselves male or female. If the theory were entirely correct, sex differences would not precede gender awareness, but in some instances they do.

Social learning and cognitive developmental theorists agree on one point: The specifics of sex roles are largely arbitrary. In our society, males are aggressive and females are better behaved *only* because of cultural norms transmitted by parents, peers, and the mass media. This radical environmentalist view is opposed by biological theories of sex differences. For example, biological theorists point out that there is a similar sex difference in aggression across all human societies (Frieze et al., 1978). Not only does this difference show up in preschool children, it also shows up in other mammalian species. Biological theorists attribute this difference in part to the presence of the male hormone testosterone (Rose, Holaday, and Bernstein, 1971).

Rather than attempting to select one theory over another, many psychologists have adopted a perspective on sex roles that combines biological differences with socialization differences based on both social learning and cognitive developmental concepts (for example, Kenrick, 1987). According to this interactionist perspective, our biological heritage predisposes us to act in certain ways, while our socialization training can serve to minimize or maximize whatever differences do exist. In the chapter's final section, we will consider these interactions in more detail.

INTERACTIONS:
Differences in Development

In considering psychological development during infancy and childhood, it is impossible to separate biological and cognitive processes. Developmental psychology spans the distance from ultimate causes of behavior, such as genes received from our ancestors, to proximate influences, such as a childs' interactions with parents or friends. Consider the research on attachment. It appears that infants are born with a tendency to smile. This facial expression seems likely to have evolved to assist parent–child bonding among our ancestors. But in the course of development children progress from reflexive smiling to selective smiling in the presence of certain people and not others. Older children can voluntarily control their smiling to fit their cognitive interpretation of a situation. For example, they can inhibit a smile in school if they think the teacher will disapprove. Developmental psychologists have provided many such examples of linkages between separate psychological processes involving biological maturation and learning.

In our discussion of gene–behavior relations we encountered an important interactionist concept when we described the range of reaction, the genetically determined limits for any behavior. We suggested that different people receive genes that limit their likely responses to the environment. For example, a child with Down's syndrome inherits a narrow limit for learning intelligent behaviors, whereas John Stuart Mill inherited a wide range. In considering the limits determined by the genes, remember that we cannot consider genes alone. Genes merely set the outer limits for development, while experiences are necessary to establish the range of behaviors actually observed. Had John Stuart Mill been adopted into a family situation like Charles Manson's, he might not have become a murderer like Manson (who had a different range of reaction) but it is unlikely that he would have become a philosophical genius. The experiences provided by his father's teaching and harsh discipline *interacted* with Mill's particular range of reaction to produce his unique pattern of development.

Developmental psychologists have also noted another important form of interaction between the developing organism and its environment. Children are not simply passive recipients of outside stimulation—by their temperaments and interactions with others they have a hand in creating their own worlds. For example, the cranky child will get a very different reaction from his or her parents than will the chronically happy one (Bell and Harper, 1977). In this way, young children who begin with small differences in their range of reaction may construct their own experiences so that they differ dramatically as adults.

These interactions between basic psychological processes and environmental experiences underlie phenomena such as personality, abnormal behavior, and social processes that we will discuss in the remainder of this book. By examining these interactions, we can better see how the different threads in the field of psychology weave together into a patterned whole. ■

IN CONTEXT: INFANT AND CHILD DEVELOPMENT

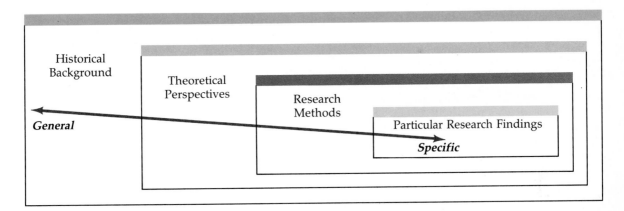

STUDY QUESTIONS

How do heredity and environment influence development?

What are the sensory and perceptual abilities of a newborn child?

What is the basis of attachment?

How does thinking change during childhood?

How do children acquire the attitudes and customs of their family and culture?

How do children learn about sex roles, and how does a child's gender influence his or her behavior?

HISTORICAL BACKGROUND

1. Philosophers in the seventeenth and eighteenth centuries had very different ideas about childrearing. John Locke advocated strict supervision, while Jean-Jacques Rousseau argued for letting nature take its course.

2. In the nineteenth century, Charles Darwin conducted one of the first scientific studies of a child by keeping a biography of his baby son. In America, G. Stanley Hall did questionnaire and interview studies to understand how children think.

3. In the twentieth century, Arnold Gesell popularized the notion of developmental periods during childhood. This idea of developmental periods was later used by Jean Piaget to describe cognitive development and Sigmund Freud to describe personality development.

MODERN THEORETICAL PERSPECTIVES

1. According to Piaget, there is an orderly sequence of cognitive development that extends from reflexive actions in infancy to logical rea-

soning in adolescence. Cognitive development is based on the assimilation of new information and the accommodation of that information within the existing cognitive structure of the child. The information processing approach complements Piaget's approach by providing a systematic and quantitative description of the processes that underlie cognitive change.

2. Theories of particular developmental phenomena include the ethological theory of attachment and the social learning and cognitive development theories of sex differences.

3. The interactionist perspective holds that biological factors predispose us to act in certain ways, while socialization can minimize or maximize inherent differences.

RESEARCH METHODS

1. One of the most frequently used methods for studying development was **experimentation.** For example, it was used with infants to study auditory discrimination (Eimas et al., 1971), perceptual learning (Carpenter, 1975), and attachment formation in infant monkeys (Harlow, 1971).

2. A variety of other methods was also employed. **Naturalistic observation** was used by Darwin to record his son's behavior in a baby biography and by Piaget to get ideas about how children think. Darwin's repeated observations of his son over time is an example of the **longitudinal method,** while Piaget's observations of different aged children is an example of the **cross-sectional method.** The **correlational method** was used to show the relationship between parenting styles and later development (Baumrind, 1967). Finally, the **survey method** was used to reveal similarities and differences in activity preferences of boys and girls (Zill, 1985).

RESEARCH FINDINGS AND SUMMARY

1. The task of **developmental psychology** is to describe and explain the changes in cognitive, social, and emotional development that occur over the life span.

2. **Heredity** refers to the characteristics and potentialities that we inherit from our parents; **environment** refers to all of the external events that we experience in life. **Developmental behavior genetics** attempts to relate variations in behavioral characteristics to variations in hereditary makeup.

3. **Genes** are the fundamental units of heredity. Large numbers of genes interact with the environment to direct the course of development and render each person unique.

4. Newborn infants have specific innate abilities that help them survive. They can root, suck, swallow, breathe, blink, cough, sneeze, and eliminate waste, all without being taught. Infants are also capable of complex perceptual acts. They can locate sounds in space, differentiate novel and familiar sounds, and show evidence of facial recognition. Very early in life, infants learn what their mothers look and sound like, and they know that both features come from the same source.

5. **Social cognition** refers to the processes by which children learn to understand the thoughts and feelings of others and learn to think about social relations.

6. **Attachment,** a long-lasting emotional bond that is formed between parent and child, is based on the responsiveness of each person to the signals emitted by the other. Satisfaction of physical needs, attention, affection, and contact comfort are different forms of responsiveness.

7. Between the ages of two and seven, children grow more reliant on **symbolic thought** even though their thought processes are still very different from those of adults. Young children are fooled by appearances and they have not yet learned the principles of **conservation—** those properties of objects, such as their mass or volume, that remain constant despite changes in appearance. The ability to think logically and take another person's perspective develops gradually over this period.

8. Between the ages of seven and 12, children's thinking becomes more systematic. No longer dominated by appearances, children come to understand conservation and have a growing awareness of their cognitive abilities. As children get older, they devise strategies to enhance their performances at school and they become more efficient in using their resources.

9. **Socialization** is the name of the process by which children acquire the attitudes, beliefs, and customs of their family and culture. Gradually, children gain a sense of who they are and how they fit into the social context of their family and friends. Although parents and peers are important, children take an active part in their own socialization.

10. Social cognition in childhood involves an active form of learning in which a child constructs his or her own knowledge and perception of the world. The cognitive skill of **role**

taking becomes important as children get increasingly better at comprehending the thoughts and feelings of others.

11. By observing their parents and peers, children learn how to behave as members of a particular sex. Parents and other people serve as **role models** for masculine and feminine behavior. These sex roles are the result of gender differences in biology and socialization.

ADDITIONAL READINGS

Bornstein, M. H., and Lamb, M. E., eds. 1988. *Developmental psychology: An advanced textbook*, 2nd ed. Hillsdale, NJ: Erlbaum. A comprehensive view of the entire field of developmental psychology. Authoritative chapters by leading scholars cover historical origins, current research in cognitive, social, and personality development, and application of developmental principles.

Brazelton, T. B., and Yogman, M. W., eds. 1986. *Affective development in infancy*. Norwood, NH: Ablex. A look at attachment and emotional development in infancy by researchers in different specialities, including pediatrics, child development, psychology, and psychiatry.

Cole, M., and Cole, S. R. 1989. *The development of children*. New York: Scientific American Books. An outstanding overview of the entire field of child development. The authors skillfully blend research and theory in describing the course of physical, cognitive, and social development throughout infancy and childhood.

Crain, W. C. 1985. *Theories of development: Concepts and applications*. Englewood Cliffs, NJ: Prentice Hall. A highly readable introduction to the major theorists in developmental psychology. This book is a valuable source for historical information and contemporary positions of the leading theorists.

Ginsburg, H. P., and Opper, S. 1988. *Piaget's theory of intellectual development*, 3rd ed. Englewood Cliffs, NJ: Prentice Hall. An up-to-date introduction to the theory and research of Jean Piaget. This text shows the relevance of Piaget's work to contemporary education and provides an overview of important research done in the last 10–15 years of Piaget's life.

Plomin, R., and DeFries, J. C. 1985. *Origins of individual differences in infancy*. New York: Academic Press. This clearly written summary of a major adoption study looks at developmental issues in infancy in terms of genetics and environment. This research represents the most extensive study of the degree of resemblance between infants and their biological and adoptive parents.

Siegler, R. S. 1991. *Children's thinking*, 2nd ed. Englewood Cliffs, NJ: Prentice Hall. A wide-ranging introduction to cognitive development that extends from perceptual to academic-skill development.

Zigler, E. F., and Finn-Stevenson, M. 1987. *Children: Developmental and social issues*. Lexington, MA: Heath. A current and readable overview of development from infancy through adulthood. Scientific information and social issues are integrated by a blend of basic research and its application. A good source book for students for topics in developmental psychology.

CHAPTER
12

ADOLESCENT AND ADULT DEVELOPMENT

I have come to believe that there is no single predictable, universal adult experience—there are many, and they frequently involve transitions. From childhood through adulthood, people are continually at the beginning, in the midst of and resolving transitions—some expected, others not. We initiate some but are forced to weather others. At times, we feel comfortable in our roles, at other times uncertain about what is ahead. Although we all experience transitions, our lives are so different that one person may go from crisis to crisis while another may experience relatively few strains. These differences depend on many factors, but one of the least telling is chronological age.

(Nancy Schlossberg, 1987)

Chapter Outline

When Albert Einstein (1879–1955) was 37 years old, he was universally recognized as the greatest theoretical physicist of his age, the twentieth-century equal of Isaac Newton. The work that he conducted between the ages of 22 and 37 altered the study of physics forever. From where did this creative genius originate? Looking back on Einstein's childhood in Germany, his school records show that he had trouble with foreign languages, but he was outstanding in physics and math. Upon completion of his studies, Einstein could not land a regular teaching position, so he took a job at a Swiss patent office. This first job turned out to be ideal in that it provided him with time to think and write about physics. At the age of 26 he published five papers on different subjects, three of them among the greatest in the history of physics (Snow, 1966). One led to a Nobel Prize 16 years later and another concerned his special theory of relativity that related space, time, and matter. How did Einstein achieve these brilliant insights while still a young man? And why were there no additional theoretical breakthroughs in his final 30 years? Einstein never wavered from his devotion to physics, yet most of his colleagues in physics thought that he wasted the second half of his life (Snow, 1966).

Frank Lloyd Wright (1867–1959) was a contemporary of Einstein who followed a different creative path. In his autobiography, Wright attributes his early interest in architecture to a set of blocks his mother gave him as a child. Fanciful or not, Wright had a boyhood interest in design that was realized by him becoming an architect. Wright opened his office in Chicago and developed the "prairie house," whose long, horizontal lines paralleled the Midwestern plains. Like Einstein, he showed an initial burst of activity while still a young man. Between 1901 and 1909, Wright designed 120 buildings and built 76. However, from 1909 until 1936 domestic problems and scandal surrounded his career and most people thought Wright was finished. Yet in 1936, at the age of 67, two brilliant projects restored Wright to the forefront of the architectural world. At an age when most people have settled into retirement, Wright designed an ultracontemporary office building for the Johnson Wax Company in Racine, Wisconsin, and he built a country house for a family over a waterfall in Bear Run, Pennsylvania. That house, called "Fallingwater," is considered by many architectural critics to be the finest of the twentieth century. These projects spurred Wright on to his second extended period of productivity. In his remaining 23 years, Wright built 180 of over 400 projects he designed, including the Guggenheim Museum in New York, first sketched at the age of 76.

A generation ago, the stories of Einstein and Wright would have been considered largely irrelevant to developmental psychology. In fact, it is only in recent years that introductory psychology texts have included a separate chapter on adolescence and adulthood. Historically, research in developmental psychology has placed its emphasis on the study of infants and children. The theories of such people as Freud and Piaget, with their focus on stages of child development, have related adult behavior to the experiences and processes of childhood. Except for the negative consequences of aging, most theorists acted as though development were essentially over at the age of 18 or 21 (Allman and Jaffe, 1982). The stories of Einstein and Wright show this view to be wrong. Einstein's genius could not be seen in his childhood, nor was Wright's productivity after age 60 expected from prevailing opinion about the elderly.

Adulthood is usually thought of as a time in which people marry and raise children when they are young, achieve a peak in their work when they reach middle age, and retire when they are older. Yet this pattern of behavior does not provide a good fit for many individuals. As we already noted, Einstein did his best work while still very young and Wright did his most creative designs when he was older. People can marry, reach a peak of productivity, and retire at any number of possible ages. We are no longer surprised by a 35-year-old grandmother, a 70-year-old college student, or a 55-year-old man who becomes a father for the first time (Neugarten, 1980). We now know that a person's age as an adult is not a very reliable guide for how that person actually lives and behaves (Schlossberg, 1987).

The interior of the Guggenheim Museum in New York City. Frank Lloyd Wright was 76 years old when he designed this extraordinary building. Psychologists study people of all age groups because development does not stop with the onset of adulthood, it continues over the entire life span.

Today, **life-span developmental** psychologists focus on the types of developmental changes that occur and the factors that determine these changes throughout human life (Baltes, Reese, and Lipsitt, 1980). We know that the changes in physical, cognitive, social, and emotional development that marked infancy and childhood continue through adolescence and adulthood. Although these changes are not as dramatic as they were in our earlier years, nevertheless we are always changing. Since life-span psychologists do not believe that development ends with sexual maturity or the completion of physical growth, much of their time has been spent researching the changes that take place during adolescence, adulthood, and old age (Datan, Rodeheaver, and Hughes, 1987; Petersen, 1988).

Carl Jung. An early follower of Freud, Jung later established his own theory of personality, which emphasized the symbolic, mythological, and spiritual aspects of human nature. Jung was especially interested in psychological transformations in adulthood.

HISTORICAL BACKGROUND:
Life-Span Developmental Psychology

During the Middle Ages, most people's status was determined once they passed puberty. Boys took their fathers' profession and married women who cared for the home, just as their fathers had. Girls got married and raised children, just as their mothers had. This usually occurred fairly early by modern standards. However, by the turn of the twentieth century much had changed. People were living longer, moving around more, and sometimes continuing their schooling well beyond puberty. In the early 1900s, psychologists had already begun considering the emotional and behavioral changes that occurred after a person made the physiological shift into adulthood. In 1904, for example, psychologist G. Stanley Hall, a pioneer in developmental psychology, published *Adolescence*, in which he described this developmental period as one of "storm and stress." In 1922, Hall covered the other extreme of adult development in a book on old age called *Senescence*.

Carl Jung

Some of the most influential ideas about life-span development were born early in the psychoanalytic movement. Freud saw adult personality development as set during childhood, but some of his followers disagreed. They saw adulthood as a time for further development, apart from the experiences of childhood. For instance, Carl Jung (1875–1961) was originally a disciple of Freud, but split with him in 1913 in disagreement over the older man's emphasis on childhood sexual and aggressive impulses. Jung saw development as a lifelong process, and he believed that many of the important issues for adults have nothing to do with sex, aggression, or family turmoil. Instead, he was interested in the ways in which mature adults searched for religious meaning and personal fulfillment in life. Jung gave particular attention to the "second half of life," beginning at about age 40. He felt that adult development was a product of both internal psychological processes and such external social forces as religion and work.

One of Jung's observations was that, after establishing a career and a family, many people around age 40 go through a **crisis,** a period of time that can involve a psychological transformation in their lives. Jung referred to this particular period as the *midlife crisis.* During this time, people begin to listen to their inner urgings—longings they have previously ignored. This self-examination can lead to important psychological changes. People who were formerly driven by ambition may become interested in interpersonal relations, while those who were dependent on others may become independent and assertive for the first time (Jung, 1933). Jung saw midlife as a time for previously unrealized psychological growth. In fact, he believed that those people who cling to the past (for

Erik Erikson. Trained as a psychoanalyst, Erikson put forth a theory of eight stages of development that cover the entire life span. Erikson's most influential work is *Childhood and Society*, published in 1963.

instance, middle-aged people who try to maintain the appearance and prowess of youth) miss a valuable opportunity for further psychological development.

Erik Erikson

Erik Erikson (1902–) is another psychoanalytic writer who has had a profound impact on the field of life-span developmental psychology. Erikson accepted Freud's basic idea that development involves the conflicts we experience and attempt to resolve as we become socialized. However, he believed that sexual and aggressive impulses were not the only sources of these conflicts. Well versed in the humanities and the sciences, Erikson focused on the problems inherent in becoming a member of society—the need to develop trust in others, to find a role within various groups, to form a family, and so on. He conceived of development as a series of eight stages that encompassed the entire life span (Table 12.1). He held that each of these developmental stages was characterized by a particular psychological crisis. Infancy, for example, involves a crisis of trust versus mistrust based on an infant's relation to his or her parents. If the relation is warm and secure, the infant will become trustful of others (Erikson, 1963). Most important, Erikson believed that the various psychological crises do not end with genital maturity.

Many do not even arise until adulthood and old age.

Life Transitions

In this chapter we are going to describe the general stages of adolescent and adult development and the major events that can punctuate a person's life. We will see that the issues facing adolescents, young and middle-aged adults, and the elderly are different. However, as indicated by our opening quotation, age per se is not necessarily the crucial factor. Many of the life events we will experience are largely independent of age. For example, getting married, having children, and starting or changing a career all involve major adjustments, no matter when they occur. Getting married at 25 or at 55 involves similar types of adjustments, and people who retire at 50 or at 70 face many of the same adjustment problems. Psychologists are increasingly realizing that major events are life transitions; how we respond to them, rather than how old we happen to be when they occur, is more important for understanding behavior (Helson, Mitchell, and Moane, 1984). **Life transitions** are events or nonevents that alter our roles, relationships, and beliefs, and they are only loosely related to age. Psychologist Nancy Schlossberg (1987) lists the following types:

- *Anticipated Transitions.* Major events, such as starting a career, getting married, or retiring, that many people expect in their lives.
- *Unanticipated Transitions.* Unexpected life events, such as a serious illness, a loss of a job, or a divorce, that disrupt one's normal routine.
- *Nonevent Transitions.* Expected life events that fail to occur, such as not getting married or not getting a sought-for promotion.

The various transitions such as marriage and retirement may appear to have little in common, but they all influence the direction of a person's life. The particular transition is not nearly so important as how it alters a person's roles, relationships, and beliefs. In this way, Schlossberg's approach to life's transitions is similar to Jung and Erikson's approach to psychological crises: Each views adolescent and adult development in terms of how we respond to the major events in our lives. They differ in that Jung and Erikson stress the ways in which all of us go through similar general crises at different periods in our lives, while Schlossberg shows the great variety of life transitions that are possible and how our re-

TABLE 12.1 Erikson's Eight Stages of Development

Stage	Crisis	Possible Outcomes
1. Birth to 1 Year	Trust vs. Mistrust	Attachment to mother establishes a foundation for later trust in others. Failure of attachment can lead to mistrust of people.
2. Ages 2 to 3 Years	Autmy vs. Shame and Doubt	Gain basic control over body movements and functions or generate doubt and fearfulness over one's actions.
3. Ages 3 to 5 Years	Initiative vs. Guilt	Become purposeful and directive or lose self-esteem.
4. Ages 6 to 11 Years	Industry vs. Inferiority	Develop competence in cognitive and social skills or feel inadequate to the demands of new tasks.
5. Adolescence	Identity vs. Role Confusion	Develop a sense of identity in transition from childhood to adulthood or maintain uncertainty over one's role in life.
6. Early Adulthood	Intimacy vs. Isolation	Establish relationships with others based on love or friendship or avoid making commitments by distancing oneself from others.
7. Middle Age	Generativity vs. Stagnation	Work toward goals involving family, career, and society or turn inward and dwell on disappointments.
8. Old Age	Integrity vs. Despair	Accept the satisfactions and sorrows in one's life or look back in regret at what might have been.

Adapted from Erikson (1963).

sponses to them contributes to making each of our lives unique. In this chapter we will describe both the common and the unique aspects of development by showing that development is a lifelong process of responding to crises and life transitions.

In Hall's studies of adolescence and old age, Jung's midlife crisis, Erikson's eight stages of development, and Schlossberg's life transitions, we see some of the same grand themes and questions we encountered in the last chapter. These include:

- *The Nature–Nurture Interaction.* To what extent are we products of genetically programmed variations in physiology (such as the dramatic changes that occur with the sexual maturity of adolescence or the loss of reproductive capacity at menopause) and how are these genetic factors influenced by variations in the environment such as nutrition, religious beliefs, or social class?

- *Continuity of Development.* How do early experiences influence later experiences? For example, does our success at establishing trust in infancy or finding a strong sense of identity in adolescence affect our success at establishing a happy family or a productive career in adulthood?

- *Discontinuity of Development.* How do the psychological experiences of each developmental period, such as infancy and adolescence, differ from one another?

We will examine such issues in this chapter, beginning with the child's transition into adolescence. ■

ADOLESCENCE

In other places and times the transition from childhood to adulthood has been sharp and abrupt. For example, many remote tribes perform **initiation rites** on their children at the time of puberty. The initiation rites are ceremonies that mark the passing of a child into the adult world. In its simplest form, the rite may involve a haircut or a change of clothing. However, more complex rituals can involve dramatic events to demonstrate that the child is now an adult. For boys, initiation rites have involved ordeals including circumcision with a sharpened stick, elaborate tattooing, painful beatings, and submersion in icy water (Benedict, 1934; Brown, 1969). For girls, the rituals could entail social isolation, teeth filing, or scarring of the skin (Ford and Beach, 1951; Stone and Church, 1968).

During the initiation rite, an adult from the tribe often functions as a teacher while the child is in seclusion. At this time an older male will teach a boy about important male functions and responsibilities, ranging from sexual technique to tribal values and customs. For example, boys of the Zuni Indians of New Mexico are told that the sacred Kachina who appear at different festivals are really masked members of the tribe. The boys learn that, as adults, they must carry out important tribal tasks that, as children, they attributed to the gods. Similarly, an older woman will teach a girl the skills needed to be a lover, a wife, and a mother. After she has completed the lessons, the girl is given a new hairstyle and adult clothes to show that she is ready for marriage. Completion of the initiation rite means that the young person is fully recognized as an adult without any lingering ambiguity.

Today we have vestiges of these initiation rites in the different religious ceremonies, such as bar and bat mitzvahs and confirmations, that signal the end of childhood. However, the transition in our society is far more lengthy and ambiguous than that in many primitive societies. This difference in transition is relatively recent in origin. In 1900, puberty in the United States was still usually seen as the end of childhood and the time to begin adult work. However, ever-increasing industrialization has gone hand-in-hand with lengthened education to extend the transition period. This period is called **adolescence**, a term derived from the

A rite of initiation. Various initiation rites are used to mark the passing from childhood to adulthood at puberty. This man is wearing a ceremonial headdress as he conducts an initiation rite for young adolescent males.

Latin word *adolescere*, which means "to grow into maturity." Adolescence is defined as the stage that begins with the onset of puberty and ends, at approximately age 20 or 21, with the arrival of young adulthood.

Current researchers believe that because adolescence brings so many changes that require effective coping, the teenage years are likely to set the person's pattern of responding to challenges for the rest of his or her life (Petersen, 1988). For example, during adolescence young people have to deal with a number of potential crises. They have adult sexual needs, typically without any socially approved outlets. They are physically mature, and yet still live, like children, under the jurisdiction of parents and teachers. Their peer groups are changing from same-sex play circles to mixed-sex social circles. They are larger and consequently more dangerous, and, despite their lack of emotional or financial readiness, they are physically capable of having children on their own. Even society seems uncertain about when to consider a young person an adult, as witnessed by the variations from state to state in the age at which a young person can drink alcohol, drive a car, marry, and own property. In this section we will look at how the changes in physical, cognitive, and social development that mark adolescence change a child into an adult.

PUBERTY AND MATURATION

After the explosive growth of infancy, childhood is characterized by slow, continuous physical development. For most mammals, this gradual growth pattern continues through adulthood, but primates are different. Along with the monkeys and apes, we go through an abrupt series of physical changes during puberty.

PHYSICAL CHANGES DURING PUBERTY

Puberty is the period of development in which a person becomes sexually mature and capable of reproduction. The onset of puberty, which normally begins after age 10, is triggered by the hypothalamus, the lower part of the thalamus in the brain. The process begins when the hypothalamus signals the pituitary gland to secrete hormones called **gonadotropins.** These hormones, in turn, produce a series of changes in other endocrine glands—most notably, they stimulate the production of sex hormones (*estrogen* in the female's ovaries and *testosterone* in the male's testes) that eventually make a person capable of sexual reproduction.

Puberty is characterized by two important types of changes. (See Figure 12.1). Changes in the **pri-**

mary sex characteristics involve the development of the ovaries, uterus, and vagina, and the beginning of menarche (menstrual periods) in females. For males, the changes entail the growth of the scrotum, testes, and penis, and the ability to produce sperm. The changes in a person's **secondary sex characteristics** are obvious to others. Although both sexes grow pubic hair, females grow breasts and their hips widen, while males undergo a deepening of the voice, growth of facial hair, and the development of larger muscles in the upper body. These physical changes are linked to social attractiveness and a person's self-image.

The changes in the primary and secondary sex characteristics are dramatic, but they are just one aspect of the pattern of change. Hormones from the pituitary gland also influence physical growth and metabolism. As Figure 12.2 indicates, puberty is also characterized by the rapid increase in a person's height and weight called the **adolescent growth spurt.** Typically girls experience the growth spurt between the ages of 10 and 13, while boys experience it two years later, between the ages of 12 and 15. During the growth spurt a person may grow three to six inches and gain 10 to 14 pounds each year (Tanner, 1978). And while the growth spurt occurs earlier in girls than in boys (making girls taller than boys in early adolescence) boys will usually show greater yearly increases. In fact, by the time they reach adulthood males are often 10 percent larger than females.

Paradoxically, while the social status of adulthood has been delayed until approximately age 21 in this century, the physical changes associated with puberty have been occurring earlier than they used to. For example, the adolescent growth spurt occurs earlier today than it did in the last century. Similarly, the age of menarche has decreased over the years. In the United States, the average girl began to menstruate at age 14 in 1910, 13.4 in 1930, and 12.8 in 1955 (Cagas and Riley, 1970; Roche, 1979). Better nutrition, improved health care, and fewer childhood diseases may be responsible for these accelerated effects of puberty.

GENDER DIFFERENCES IN THE EFFECTS OF EARLY OR LATE PUBERTY

The age of puberty varies from one child to another. Think back to your childhood friends. Some of them matured very early, others matured later.

FIGURE 12.1 The physical changes of puberty. The release of various hormones during puberty initiates a host of changes in males and females. There are changes in the sex organs (primary sex characteristics) that enable sexual reproduction to occur, and changes in physical appearance (secondary sex characteristics) that are linked to social attractiveness and self-image. These changes mark the onset of adolescence.

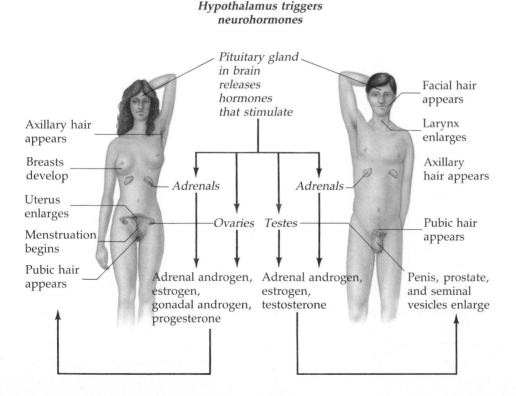

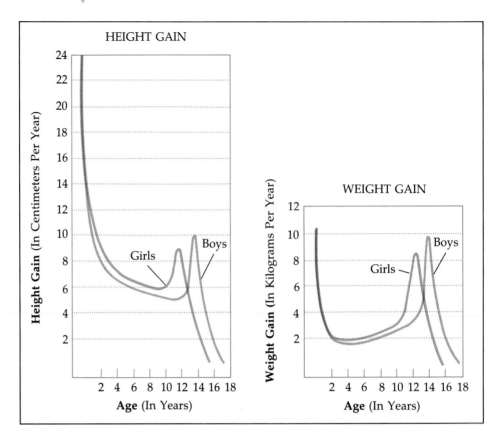

FIGURE 12.2   Growth according to age and gender.   Average height and weight gains for girls and boys according to age. Both sexes show a growth spurt in height and weight during puberty, but it is both later and larger for boys.

Research indicates that the age at which people reach puberty can effect their personality and social development, and these effects can be different for males and females.

Research on the psychological effects of early and late maturation began at the University of California at Berkeley during the 1940s. For boys, the results were dramatic and clear. Early-maturing males were viewed as attractive and popular by their peers and adults, and they tended to be poised and self-assured in their social relations. For the most part, these boys perceived themselves as more mature, less in need of help, and more capable in interpersonal relations than their late-maturing peers. In sharp contrast, the late-maturing males tended to be tense and restless and to engage in such immature attention-getting behavior as clowning (Mussen and Jones, 1957).

For girls, the relation between the onset of puberty and psychological development was more complex. Early-maturing females who were still in grammar school tended to be at a social disadvantage; peers and adults often considered these 11- and 12-year-old girls out of step. Yet during junior high school these girls were more favorably regarded, and they had an advantage over their late-maturing peers in social situations (Jones and Mussen, 1958).

More recently, psychologist Anne Petersen and her colleagues conducted large-scale surveys of young adolescents in two suburban school districts. They wanted to know how being an early or late maturer (one year earlier or later than average) affected the young people's behavior and feelings about themselves. To find out, the researchers interviewed 335 adolescents twice a year as they progressed from grades six through eight. The adolescents were classified as early, average, or late maturers from information about their growth and sex characteristics.

Petersen and her colleagues confirmed and extended the earlier research (Brooks-Gunn, Petersen, and Eichorn, 1985; Crockett and Petersen, 1987; Petersen and Crockett, 1985). For example, boys who matured early tended to be more satisfied with their appearances than their less-mature classmates. Girls, on the other hand, often complained that they felt embarrassed if they matured early and were different from their friends. By eighth grade, however, such effects were greatly diminished. Said one girl, "By then everyone wore a bra and had their period. I was normal" (Petersen, 1987). The timing of puberty also affected a young person's mood. Consistent with their thoughts on body image, early-maturing boys reported more positive moods than boys who had not yet experienced the physical developments of puberty. The reverse was true for early-maturing girls. Reflecting on the timing of your own puberty, did your experiences fit with these findings?

More obvious, perhaps, were Petersen's findings on the effects of maturity or interactions with members of the opposite sex. In sixth grade most students generally agreed that "girls like boys better than boys like girls." But by the seventh and eighth grades, this situation changed rapidly. Early-maturing boys and girls are the ones who make initial contact with members of the opposite sex, but before the end of eighth grade this pattern spreads to include most girls and boys.

In surveying family relations, Petersen and her colleagues found that the feelings of affection and support that adolescents and their parents feel for one another suffer a decline from the sixth through the eighth grades. The biggest decline occurred between teenage girls and their mothers, a finding reported by other researchers as well (Savin-Williams and Small, 1986; Steinberg, 1987). Yet, even in this case, the decline was a matter of degree. Feelings changed from very positive to less positive, not from positive to negative. An adolescent's search for independence puts stress on family relations, but much depends on how those relations were to begin with. In most instances, the relations remained strong.

Finally, this research found that puberty was not generally associated with Hall's earlier description of adolescence as a period of storm and stress. Overall, the pattern of development in early adolescence was decidedly positive. More than half of all teenagers tested were judged to be essentially trouble-free, and another 30 percent could be described as having only intermittent problems. However, roughly 15 percent of these young people did appear to be troubled and caught in a downward spiral. For these troubled teenagers, girls tended to show signs of depression, while boys acted rebellious and disobedient. Petersen and her colleagues are currently studying whether the patterns of development established in early adolescence continue through the high-school years. By identifying troubled teenagers early on, it may be possible to redirect their course of development (Petersen, 1987).

COGNITIVE DEVELOPMENT

Alongside the dramatic changes in sexual physiology and the psychological effects these changes can bring, adolescence also brings changes in the way people think. Adolescents not only know more than they did as children, they are able to reorganize what they know and to use it to think logically. Jean Piaget was aware that cognitive maturation did not stop at puberty, and his theory of cognitive development (outlined in Table 11.3 of Chapter 11) also had much to say about the development of this type of thinking.

Social interactions in adolescence. Puberty is the time when boys and girls begin making contact with members of the opposite sex. The early-maturing members of each sex are the ones who initiate the contact.

LOGICAL THOUGHT

According to Piaget, the last stage of cognitive development results in logical thought. Adolescents are no longer bound by the concrete operations of childhood. They appreciate irony, sarcasm, and wit. For example, psychologist Marvin Levine has collected a variety of puzzles and riddles that would baffle most children, but intrigue many adolescents. Consider the following:

> A man leaves his camp by traveling due north for 1 mile. He then makes a right turn (90 degrees) and travels due east for 1 mile. He makes another right turn and travels due south for 1 mile and finds himself precisely at the point he departed from, that is, back at his campsite. Where is the campsite located (or where on earth could such a sequence of events take place)?
>
> *(Levine, 1988)*

If you have analyzed this problem in a logical manner, the campsite could only be located at one possible place on earth—the South Pole (Figure 12.3). The type of thinking needed to solve such puzzles occurs in Piaget's final period of cognitive development, the *formal operations stage*.

Formal operations thinking is characterized by the ability of adolescents to form hypotheses, reason abstractly, and think in a systematic way. These changes can be seen in a game such as 20 Questions, when one person has to identify what another person is thinking by skillfully asking a series of questions. Six-year-old children do not realize the value of first determining broad categories ("Animal, vegetable, or mineral?"); they jump right in and ask specific object questions ("Is it a poodle?"). Slightly older children begin to see the value of adopting a strategy, but they do not follow it systematically. After asking a general question, they often follow it with one that is too specific ("Is it alive?" "Yes." "Is it a poodle?"). However, after age 11 or 12, when the formal operations stage begins, young people easily solve the task. They formulate general questions and then progressively restrict their alternatives ("Alive? Animal? Mammal? Four-legged? Domesticated? Pet?" and so forth).

Adolescents also have moved beyond the restrictions of concrete operations, thinking about here and now. They are able to reason about abstractions and verbal statements. This ability is called **propositional thinking.** For example, propositional thinking was necessary in a study in which young people were shown a series of colored chips and then asked to determine whether the following statement was true or false:

> "Either the chip (concealed) in my hand is green or it is not green."

Children often answered that they could not tell without seeing the chip, while adolescents understood the logical properties of the statement and knew that the proposition must be true. (Osherson and Markman, 1975) Finally, adolescents begin to think scientifically and demonstrate **hypothetico-deductive reasoning.** This is the ability to form and test hypotheses through logical, systematic procedures. In one task, children and adolescents were shown a beaker of potassium iodide, four other beakers containing different chemical solutions, and a small dish for mixing. The person was told that by mixing the potassium iodide with one or more of the solutions, it was possible to produce a bright yellow mixture. The researchers found that nine-year-old children mixed the solutions in a seemingly random fashion, first trying one mixture, then another, and often repeating themselves. Adolescents by age 14, however, systematically mixed the potassium iodide with each solution individually before they tried particular combinations. By methodically considering each possibility, the adolescents successfully completed the task (Inhelder and Piaget, 1958). Studies such as this show that formal operations thinking in adolescence is a purposeful activity, based on the systematic application of

FIGURE 12.3 Going around in triangles. Where on earth could you travel due north for one mile, due east for one mile, and due south for one mile, and find yourself back at your starting point? This trip could only be made if it originated at the South Pole.

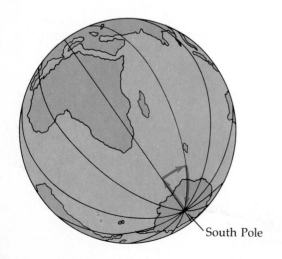

South Pole

logical reasoning. Only through formal, logical operations are the adolescents eventually able to deduce the correct rule.

CHALLENGES TO PIAGET'S CONCEPTION OF FORMAL OPERATIONS

The development of logical thinking permits adolescents to engage in a more sophisticated form of thinking than they could engage in as children. They are able to use their minds to explore such new, more abstract domains as philosophy and science. However, the stage of formal operations is a milestone that not everyone passes. Contrary to what Piaget initially believed, research has shown that formal operations thinking is not universally acquired, nor is it always applied even by those who have the capacity. For example, students in a high school shop class may make a careful diagnosis of an automobile engine to determine why the car does not start. By understanding the operation of the engine and checking each of the relevant components, such as the battery, starter, and ignition system, the students use their mechanical knowledge and formal operations thinking to fix it. However, these same students, depending on their motivation and knowledge, might not apply this same process of logical thought to other subjects, such as philosophy and science. Psychologists have found that people may demonstrate formal operations thinking on some tasks but not others, and only 30 to 40 percent of all adolescents and adults use it systematically (Martorano, 1977; Neimark, 1975). In view of these observations, Piaget (1970) revised his theory to say that while abstract rules of thought can be applied, in principle, to any subject matter, they are applied, in fact, to only those subjects that we know very well.

CHANGES IN SCHOOL PERFORMANCE

The development of abstract, logical thought is matched by ever-greater demands on adolescents at school. Earlier in elementary school, a child's education was primarily concerned with developing basic skills in reading, writing, and arithmetic. In high school, however, students are expected to understand a wider variety of subjects in far greater detail. Abstract ideas in the form of algebra equations, philosophical principles, and chemistry charts are all part of an adolescent's educational experience. Coupled with these greater demands are the more stringent grading policies practiced by many teachers. This often results in a general decline in the marks that students earn over their adolescent years (Simmons and Blyth, 1987). Good

Logical thinking in adolescence. The development of logical thought permits adolescents in high school to formulate hypotheses and examine abstract ideas. Students can move beyond concrete examples and consider theoretical ideas, such as how the course of history was changed by the discovery of the atom.

teachers are aware of the fact that adolescents are only *in the process* of learning to think logically. Consequently, they couple their teaching of abstract concepts (such as the principles of economics) with concrete examples (such as handling a budget) to help their students along. Teachers who emphasize learning by rote memorization instead of conceptual understanding limit the cognitive growth of their students.

Parents also play an important role in school performance. In the preceding chapter, we described Diana Baumrind's (1967; 1977) research on the effects of different parenting styles on children's social development. Recently, psychologist Sanford Dornbusch and his colleagues (1987) looked at the effects of Baumrind's typology of parenting styles (authoritarian, permissive, and authoritative childrearing practices) on the school performance of approximately 8,000 high school students. Extending Baumrind's earlier correlational results, these researchers found that authoritarian and permissive parenting styles were associated with low grades, while authoritative parenting was associated with high grades. Together, Baumrind's and Dornbusch's correlational studies suggest that children and adolescents benefit from authoritative parents who are firm but loving and who set clearly communicated goals and standards of conduct.

THE DEVELOPMENT OF MORAL REASONING

Suppose that a clerk at a supermarket gave you too much change with your receipt. Should you point out the error or remain silent and take the money? What if you observe a classmate cheating on an exam? Should you keep quiet or inform on this person? These examples involve moral dilemmas about how we should act. The appropriateness of specific actions can vary from one society to another, but all societies have unwritten moral rules about how people should behave in social situations. The development of **moral reasoning** is the process by which children come to adopt their society's standards of right and wrong. According to psychologist Lawrence Kohlberg (1963; 1969; 1981), children may pick up religious or philosophical beliefs from their parents, teachers, and clergy, but these beliefs have only a minor effect on their moral judgments. Rather, Kohlberg believed that the development of moral reasoning is intimately related to the development of decision-making ability—that is, it is a cognitive skill. In other words, the way we think about moral dilemmas changes as we mature in ways that parallel the changes in our cognitive development.

SOLVING MORAL DILEMMAS

To see how moral reasoning develops, Kohlberg presented young people of different ages with a series of moral dilemmas. The following story about a person named Heinz is the best-known. You might want to check on your own moral reasoning by reading the story and answering the questions at the end before you continue with the text.

In Europe a woman was near death from cancer. One drug might save her, a form of radium that a druggist in the same town had recently discovered. The druggist was charging $2,000, ten times what the drug cost him to make. The sick woman's husband, Heinz, went to everyone he knew to borrow the money, but he could only get together about half of what it cost. He told the druggist that his wife was dying and asked him to sell it cheaper or let him pay later. But the druggist said "No." The husband got desperate and broke into the man's store to steal the drug for his wife. Should the husband have done that? Why?

(Kohlberg, 1969)

Kohlberg was not interested in whether people judge a particular action as right or wrong. Instead, he was concerned with how people explain and justify their moral judgments and, particularly, how these explanations change during childhood and adolescence. By recording the responses of thousands of people of different ages, Kohlberg found evidence that moral reasoning developed over a series of six stages.

KOHLBERG'S THEORY OF MORAL REASONING

According to this view, everyone progresses through the six stages of moral development in the same order. However, not everyone reaches the highest level, and some people are faster (or slower) to develop than others. Kohlberg grouped the stages into three broad categories labeled *preconventional, conventional,* and *postconventional morality.* These categories, their associated stages and descriptions, and examples of different responses to Heinz's dilemma are presented in Table 12.2. Kohlberg found that seven-year-old children typically gave responses that placed them in the preconventional category. They used no abstract principles of any kind. They distinguished "right" and "wrong" solely by their consequences. Something was "good" if it avoided punishment and "bad" if it did not (stage 1). Children in late childhood are also oriented toward consequences, but in a more positive light. They tend to see good behavior as anything that leads to personal benefits, such as a person returning a favor (stage 2).

At the beginning of adolescence, Kohlberg observed a shift in the basis for moral judgments. Around the age of 13, young people moved from preconventional to conventional morality. Adolescents, unlike children, are oriented toward social convention—toward conforming to the rules and pressures of society. During the initial years, adolescents base their moral reasoning on conformity to societal standards in the hope of gaining social approval and acceptance. Kohlberg called this period the "good boy–good girl" stage (stage 3). During later adolescence, however, this concern for the approval of others diminishes and adolescents develop an appreciation for the need to maintain social order. Moral judgments made at this stage are based on a genuine respect for authority rather than a fear of punishment (stage 4). For example, many young people entered the armed service when drafted during times of war even though they would have preferred to stay home. Adolescents at this stage are willing to suffer in order not to break the rules (to do their

TABLE 12.2 Kohlberg's Theory of Moral Reasoning

Stages of Moral Reasoning	Description	In Favor of Stealing the Drug	Against Stealing the Drug
I. Preconventional Morality			
1. Punishment and Obedience	Moral behavior is anything that avoids punishment. The consequences of an action determine whether it is good or bad.	If you let your wife die, you will get in trouble. You'll be blamed for not spending the money to save her and there'll be an investigation of you and the druggist for your wife's death.	You shouldn't steal the drug because you'll be caught and sent to jail if you do. If you do get away, your conscience would bother you thinking how the police would catch up with you at any minute.
2. Instrumental Relativism	Moral behavior is anything that gains reward. What is good is whatever satisfies one's needs. Helping others can be good if the help will be reciprocated.	If you do happen to get caught, you could give the drug back and you wouldn't get much of a sentence. It wouldn't bother you much to serve a little jail term, if you have your wife when you get out.	You may not get much of a jail term if you steal the drug, but your wife will probably die before you get out so it won't do you much good. If your wife dies, you shouldn't blame yourself, it wasn't your fault she has cancer.
II. Conventional Morality			
3. Good Boy–Good Girl	Moral behavior is that which pleases others and avoids their disapproval. Approval of others is based on intentions and comes from being "nice."	No one will think you're bad if you steal the drug, but your family will think you're an inhuman husband if you don't. If you let your wife die, you'll never be able to look anybody in the face again.	It isn't just the druggist who will think you're a criminal; everyone else will too. After you steal it, you'll feel bad thinking how you've brought dishonor on your family and yourself; you won't be able to face anyone again.
4. Law and Order	Moral behavior is defined by set codes of social conduct. Respecting authority and "doing one's duty" are examples of moral acts.	If you have any sense of honor, you won't let your wife die because you're afraid to do the only thing that will save her. You'll always feel guilty that you caused her death if you don't do your duty to her.	You're desperate and you may not know you're doing wrong when you steal the drug. But you'll know you did wrong after you're sent to jail. You'll always feel guilty for your dishonesty and lawbreaking.
III. Postconventional Morality			
5. Social Contract	Moral behavior follows socially accepted principles that work for the good of society.	You'd lose other people's respect, not gain it, if you don't steal. If you let your wife die, it would be out of fear, not out of reasoning it out. So you'd just lose self-respect, and probably the respect of others too.	You would lose your standing and respect in the community and violate the law. You'd lose respect for yourself if you're carried away by emotion and forget the long-range point of view.
6. Universal Ethical Principle	Moral behavior is based on the abstract idea of conscience to produce mutual respect and trust. "Doing unto others as you would have them do unto you" is an example of an abstract ethical principle.	If you don't steal the drug and let your wife die, you'd always condemn yourself for it afterward. You wouldn't be blamed and you would have lived up to the outside rule of the law but you wouldn't have lived up to your own standards of conscience.	If you stole the drug, you wouldn't be blamed by the other people but you'd condemn yourself because you wouldn't have lived up to your own conscience and standards of honesty.

Adapted from Kohlberg (1969; 1981).

"duty" to society). Kohlberg believed that the shift from preconventional to conventional morality is based on cognitive change. Adolescents are no longer so egocentric; they can see things from perspectives other than their own, and they can evaluate a moral act according to more than personal rewards and punishments.

The final category of moral reasoning, postconventional morality, is closely linked to the development of formal operations thinking. To shift from conventional to postconventional morality requires the ability to completely divorce oneself from the concrete rules and regulations of one's particular society, and to understand the higher abstract principles upon which those rules are based. For example, at stage 5 people judge moral actions on the basis of democratically accepted laws or agreements. They understand that such arrangements are social conventions, agreed upon so that people can live comfortably together. They also understand that sometimes the rules can conflict with good intentions, but they generally believe that the individual should not go against the rules of the majority. For example, most people pay taxes to their government so that it can carry out its various functions even though they may disagree with specific governmental policies or actions.

The last stage in the development of moral reasoning involves making judgments on the basis of ethical principles such as justice, inalienable human rights, and respect for the dignity of others. Matters of conscience guide moral judgments at this stage and violating a rule or law may be morally acceptable if in doing so one remains true to one's moral principles (stage 6). According to Kohlberg's measurements, most people do not reach this highest level of moral development. This stage, he said, is reserved for the truly exceptional, such as Mahatma Gandhi and Martin Luther King, Jr., who formulate abstract ethical principles to guide their moral behavior. For example, Gandhi in India and King in the United States used nonviolent resistance to bring about political or social change based on their belief that human life was sacred and could not be taken under any circumstances.

SUPPORT AND CRITICISM OF THE THEORY

In support of Kohlberg's theory that the development of moral reasoning is guided by cognitive development, research has consistently shown that children are preconventional, adolescents between the ages of 13 and 16 are conventional, and

only one quarter to one half of all older adolescents and adults are postconventional in their moral judgments (Dacey, 1982). These findings have been obtained in *cross-sectional* research where individuals of different ages have been compared (Kohlberg, 1969; Walker, deVries, and Bichard, 1984); in *longitudinal* research, where the same individuals have been examined over a period of years during childhood and adolescence (Rest and Thoma, 1985); and in *cross-cultural* research, where the same sequence of developmental stages has been observed in individuals from such different countries as the United States, Mexico, and Taiwan (Figure 12.4).

Research also found that people at the higher morality levels cheat less on examinations (Krebs, 1967), and show decreasing willingness to obey an experimenter's orders to shock another person (Turiel, 1974; 1983). In one obedience experiment, people were asked to administer shocks as punishment to a person in another room when that person (actually an accomplice of the experimenter) made errors on a learning task. The subjects thought that they were delivering shocks, though none were actually delivered. As might be expected from the theory, a majority of the postconventional morality subjects in this obedience experiment refused to participate or expressed strong reservations and guilt, while a majority of the subjects at the other morality levels willingly took part in the task. Together, these different studies provide support for Kohlberg's theory.

Yet, as ambitious as this theory is, it is limited in several important ways. Critics have argued that while the theory describes a progression of changes in moral reasoning, it does not tell us how someone will act (Kurtines and Gewirtz, 1984; Kurtines and Grief, 1974). This distinction between *moral judgment* and *moral behavior* is important because research has found only a weak relationship between what people often say that they will do and what they actually do (Maccoby, 1980). In fairness to Kohlberg, however, he never set out to describe moral behavior; his theory is concerned only with describing the development of moral reasoning.

GENDER DIFFERENCES IN MORAL REASONING

Critics have also questioned Kohlberg's finding that postconventional morality is achieved more often by males than females in our society. Psychologist Carol Gilligan, for one, has criticized the masculine bias of Kohlberg's rating scheme. For

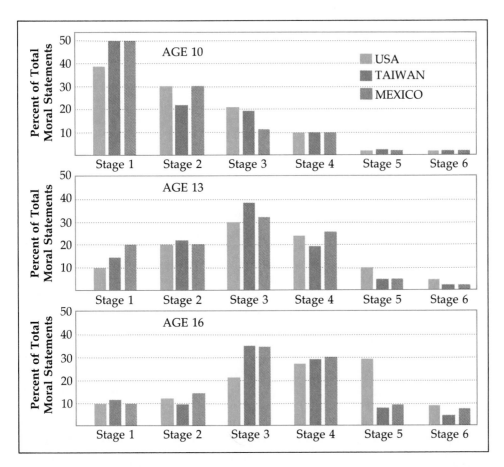

FIGURE 12.4 A cross-cultural examination of moral reasoning. People from different countries follow the same sequence in the development of their moral reasoning. Following Kohlberg's theory, children form moral judgments at the lowest level of development (stages 1 and 2) but with increased cognitive development they progress to higher levels (stages 4 and 5).

example, when women are faced with a moral dilemma, such as whether to have an abortion, they consider different factors than men do. Women are more likely to focus on the needs of others, to be concerned about social relations, and to take other points of view into account; men tend to deal more narrowly with rules and moral issues and focus on individual rights and self-fulfillment (Gilligan, 1977; 1982). As evidence for her belief that Kohlberg's theory penalizes women for their different sensitivities, Gilligan has examined Kohlberg's use of Gandhi as an example of a person who, though placed at the stage 6 level because of his ethical belief in the nonviolent resistance to evil, was nonetheless sometimes cruel to his wife and close friends. Says Gilligan,

> the blind willingness to sacrifice people to truth. . . . links Gandhi to the biblical Abraham, who was prepared to sacrifice the life of his son in order to demonstrate the integrity

and supremacy of his faith. Both men, in the limitations of their fatherhood, stand in implicit contrast to the woman who comes before Solomon and verifies her motherhood by relinquishing truth in order to save the life of her child.

(Gilligan, 1977)

Gilligan does not argue that women's morality is superior or inferior to men's, but only that development has made each gender different. To date there is very little research on gender differences in moral reasoning, and no consensus exists on the interpretation of such differences (Darley and Shultz, 1990). However, the few studies that are available tend to support Gilligan's contention that women's moral judgments, compared to men's, are more concerned with feelings of compassion and empathy (Haan, 1975; Holstein, 1976; Gilligan, 1982). A complete theory of moral development must take this difference into account.

PERSONALITY AND SOCIAL DEVELOPMENT

Following the dramatic physical changes that occur during puberty, adolescents often become self-conscious and introspective. No longer their childhood selves, teenagers become concerned with defining just who they are. The choices afforded by modern society simply did not exist in the middle ages. For instance, instead of becoming a shoemaker or housewife in Heidelberg (or whatever one's father or mother happened to be) today's teenager has the option to choose an occupation, a geographical residence, and even a set of religious beliefs. In the process of making these decisions, adolescents build personal identities that begin to separate them from their parents.

ACQUIRING A SENSE OF IDENTITY

It is widely believed that a stable adult personality is based on the sense of identity forged during adolescence. Adolescents can think logically, tell right from wrong, and explain the basis for their beliefs—all necessary ingredients for constructing a sense of identity. A **sense of identity** is defined as an organized sense of how our own personality traits, values, and beliefs fit together in defining who we are. Our sense of identity includes our self-concept and our level of self-esteem. The self-concept is our appraisal of our strengths and weaknesses. This evaluation in turn influences our level of esteem. In other words, our self-concept is *what* we think we are (for example, a second-string volleyball player, a decent piano player, a promising artist, a poor math student), while our self-esteem is *how* we feel about ourselves. When we perceive our strengths to outweigh our weaknesses, our level of self-esteem will be high. Our identity also includes our values, attitudes, and preferences about things other than ourselves, including religion, sex, politics, and even rock 'n roll.

For Erik Erikson, the central crisis of adolescence is the conflict between *identity* and *role confusion*. (Look back to Table 12.1.) When adolescents can combine the different ways in which they are like other people with the ways in which they differ, they have forged an identity. When they cannot, they exhibit role confusion and remain uncertain over their roles in life. Role confusion is actually a failure to develop a sense of self. According to Erikson, this conflict is caused by the physical and psychological changes taking place during this period. Puberty arouses sexual interests, and advances in cognitive development lead to a questioning of values and beliefs. Facing these choices leads to the so-called "identity crisis."

During the identity crisis, adolescents experiment in order to try out different identities (Markus and Nurius, 1986). As adolescents, we may adopt different clothing styles, tastes, and musical interests in considering different identities, until we find one that fits our own personality and environment. Erikson believes that this experimentation with different lifestyles, occupations, and friends is a positive and necessary activity in order to make intelligent choices. Adopting an identity too early, before the alternatives have been considered, can result in **identity foreclosure,** in which a young person never learns what else he or she had the potential to become. For instance, a premature decision that your only acceptable identity is to become a doctor or lawyer may rule out other possibilities that might better suit your talents and preferences. Erikson favors a **psychosocial moratorium,** an uncommitted period during which adolescents try many different roles before picking one as their own (Erikson, 1963).

Through the process of experimentation, adolescents usually construct a sense of identity. However, some adolescents remain in a state of role confusion and enter adulthood aimlessly shifting from one job to another. Erikson also suggests that there is an even darker side to identity forma-

Peer influence during adolescence. Friends help determine our clothing styles, rules of behavior, musical preferences, and even our choice of other friends. During adolescence, peer influence is especially strong.

tion, in which a **negative identity** can be formed. The adolescent may decide that he or she is a "born loser," and may turn to delinquency, drug abuse, or—in extreme cases—suicide to end his or her feelings of isolation and alienation.

Finding a positive personal identity is important, but it is only one of the problems facing adolescents. In addition to struggling within themselves, they must also struggle with some major changes in their relations with parents and peers. For example, in the process of establishing an identity we come to view ourselves as distinct from our parents, two people whose lives have been closely intertwined with our own.

RELATIONS WITH PARENTS

Infants can live in their own little world, with no consideration of the needs of their parents, but adolescents cannot be so socially carefree. Parents must be dealt with not only because they control such significant resources as money and the car, but also because they provide a potential source of stability. Faced with greater responsibilities and new expectations, adolescents look to their parents to provide them with feedback on their actions and plans.

When adolescents have a positive relationship with their parents and openly discuss important issues with them, they are more likely to be independent and self-assured, and to develop a strong sense of identity (Conger, 1977). However, as you know from your own experience, disagreements invariably occur. Even in the closest families, parents and teenagers bicker and squabble. Teenagers disagree with their parents over friendships, dating, money, chores, and the availability of a car (Kinloch, 1970). The bad news for parents is that this bickering lasts for a period of several years. It begins with the onset of puberty and persists until middle to late adolescence (Steinberg, 1987). The good news is that these disagreements typically do not undo the previously established bonds of affection and love. Parents and teenagers rarely end up rejecting each other. In fact, the majority of all teenagers say that they continue to respect their parents and get along well with them (Gallup, 1986; Collins, 1990).

What are the root causes of parent–adolescent disagreements? Evolutionary theorists have pointed out that in primates such as gibbons, who live in small, monogamous family groups, it is normal for male and female gibbons to leave the family soon after puberty. These theorists believe that adolescent emigration from the family serves an important adaptive function by minimizing inbreeding and increasing genetic diversity (Steinberg, 1987). Given such an evolutionary heritage, it would not be surprising to find biological mechanisms that encourage humans to begin the process of breaking away from their parents during the adolescent years. Bickering and squabbling can be seen as manifestations of this process. Freud, for example, along with more recent psychoanalytic theorists, argued that teenage rebelliousness is a normal, even healthy, aspect of growing up and preparing to leave home (Adelson and Doehrman, 1980).

However, we need to be careful in our interpretation of such conflicts. High levels of conflict are neither normal nor healthy. Intense, prolonged conflict is associated with teenagers running away from home, dropping out of school, and developing psychological problems such as depression (Petersen, 1988). Moreover, parent–adolescent conflicts can be modified by changing social situations. For example, psychologist Mavis Hetherington and her colleagues found less conflict between teenagers and a remaining parent in divorced families than in nondivorced families (Anderson, Hetherington, and Clingempeel, 1986; Hetherington, 1989). They believe that greater maturity and responsibility are expected of children in single-parent families. Together, these findings imply that family conflicts during adolescence are influenced jointly by biological and social factors.

RELATIONS WITH PEERS

The stability that parents provide is important, but their influence gradually wanes as adolescents' relations with their peers eventually overtake them in importance. In fact, friends may be more important in adolescence than at any other time of life. For example, if your parents tell you that you are talented or attractive, you tend to discount their views because they are hardly impartial, and their standards may be quite different from your own. Friends, however, are more believable. When adolescents discuss problems with their parents, the parents often explain their views, rather than attempt to understand the views of the adolescent. However, discussions with friends tend to be more evenly balanced between attempts to explain and to understand (Hunter, 1985). Parents attempt to influence by exercising authority or expertise; they may try to step in and solve the problem. Peers influence more subtly. Their values and ideas rub off gently during mutual and friendly interactions (Berndt and Perry, 1990; Youniss, 1980). Peers are especially influential in determining musical preferences, clothing styles, recreation, and the choice of friends. They are also important in choosing whether or not to experiment with drugs. When parents and peers disagree over drugs, it is usually the peers who prevail (Kandel, 1981). The pressure to conform to peer group standards increases steadily through childhood and preadolescence, and it reaches its peak around age 14 or 15. Thereafter it gradually declines, as adolescents become less dependent on an exclusive peer group (Berndt, 1979).

Australian sociologist Dexter Dunphy (1963) found that adolescent peer relationships seem to go through a series of stages (Figure 12.5). The first stage occurs during preadolescence or early adolescence when young people form small, single-sex groups of friends. This is followed by a stage in which adolescents form larger circles of friends made up of members of both sexes. During this stage boys and girls associate with one another, but the primary friendships are same-sex. In the third stage, teenagers form cliques composed of members of both sexes. At this point, mixed gender interactions increase and dating may begin. During later adolescence there is a fourth stage, in which the mixed gender cliques dissolve as people break off into couples. According to Dunphy, the individuals break away when the groups have served the major function that led to their formation in the first place—the formation of intimate relationships. In the majority of young people this involves heterosexual relations, but for some young people, development leads to becoming part of a homosexual couple.

RESEARCH AND APPLICATION:
Sexual Relationships in Adolescence

Over the past several decades, psychologists have conducted numerous surveys of adolescents to determine their sexual behaviors and beliefs. Although the threat of AIDS (acquired immune deficiency syndrome) has changed recent sexual mores, particularly in urban areas, an historical

FIGURE 12.5 Dunphy's stages of peer group relations. The formation of groups during early adolescence serves to increase interpersonal relationships that lead eventually to the formation of couples during late adolescence.

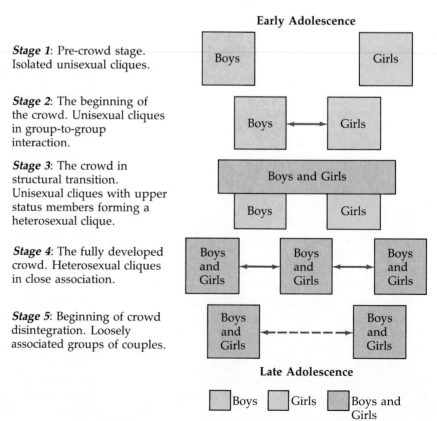

Stage 1: Pre-crowd stage. Isolated unisexual cliques.

Stage 2: The beginning of the crowd. Unisexual cliques in group-to-group interaction.

Stage 3: The crowd in structural transition. Unisexual cliques with upper status members forming a heterosexual clique.

Stage 4: The fully developed crowd. Heterosexual cliques in close association.

Stage 5: Beginning of crowd disintegration. Loosely associated groups of couples.

overview of several major surveys shows a dramatic increase in sexual activity in this century.

Surveys of Sexual Behavior

In their large-scale surveys done in the 1940s, Alfred Kinsey and his colleagues found that approximately 50 percent of men and 20 percent of women reported premarital intercourse by age 20 (Kinsey, Pomeroy, and Martin, 1948; Kinsey, Pomeroy, Martin, and Gebhard; 1953). However, surveys conducted in the 1980s yielded a different picture. When averaged together, the results of three recent surveys showed that 68 percent of college men and 59 percent of college women had had intercourse (Earle and Parricone, 1986; Phillis and Gromko, 1985; Sherwin and Corbitt, 1985). There are problems in comparing the earlier Kinsey data with current college surveys because fewer people went to college in Kinsey's day (although those who did were *less* sexually experienced than their noncollege counterparts). However, some of the recent surveys have polled students at the same colleges for several years and found increases even over the past decade (Earle and Parricone, 1986; Phillis and Gromko, 1985).

Typically, surveys find more reported intercourse among young males than young females, which may be due to a number of factors, including:

- Females are reluctant to admit premarital experiences.

- Males exaggerate the extent of their premarital experiences.

- A small number of females have had a large number of male partners.

Whatever the discrepancy among college freshmen and sophomores the difference disappears by graduation, when the majority of both sexes report having had sexual intercourse. For example, one survey found that 85 percent of graduating college women and 82 percent of men were no longer virgins (Jessor and Jessor, 1975). These data suggest that sexual intercourse during adolescence may now be the norm in many places.

Although sexual activity has dramatically increased since Kinsey's day, the attitudes of adolescents toward sex have remained somewhat traditional, even during the peak of the 1970s' "sexual revolution." Surveys continue to show that most teenagers oppose sexual intercourse if the relationship is based solely on physical pleasure. Love, affection, and feelings of intimacy are more important reasons for having intercourse. Not sur-

prisingly, for a majority of teenagers sexual contact was limited to someone with whom they were "in love" at the time (Hass, 1979).

> The first time I had intercourse I was 17 years old. I was a senior in high school and I'd been going with a guy I really thought I loved. We had done just about everything else and it seemed kind of silly to stay a virgin any longer so one night we just went ahead. No big planning or discussion or lines, it just happened.
>
> *(Masters, Johnson, and Kolodny, 1982)*

Birth Control and Sex Education

One of the unfortunate consequences of the increase in adolescent sexual activity is the high rate of unwanted pregnancies. Despite widespread dissemination of birth control information, surveys show that many teenagers use none. As a result, more than one million teenage girls in the United States become pregnant each year, most unintentionally (Wetzel, 1987). Many teenagers are simply poorly informed about the process of contraception. Others know better, but they do not use birth control devices—even if they have gone so far as to get them. Sometimes teenagers make bad decisions. Teenage boys tend to make decisions on the use of condoms based on whether they think their friends use them, whether they are inconvenient to purchase or use, or whether they feel condoms might make them look "silly" (Goleman, 1987). In addition, teenagers often err in evaluating the odds of getting pregnant. Pregnancy is thought to be *less probable* the more times they have had contraception-free sex that did not result in pregnancy. These failures to think clearly about pregnancy lead to increases in this risk-taking behavior and, ultimately, to increased pregnancies. Teenage parents face psychological difficulties because they are often financially and emotionally unprepared for the responsibilities of caring for a child (Furstenberg, Brooks-Gunn, and Morgan, 1987).

Most people agree that pregnancy among young girls should be prevented, but they disagree on how it should be done. Some experts argue that it is unrealistic to expect teenagers to abstain from sex. Unwanted pregnancies, they say, can be prevented by teaching sex education in schools, including the appropriate use of contraceptives (Freeman, 1980). But sex education and contraceptive use are highly controversial issues. Some people oppose their use on religious grounds. Others believe that this approach will

Teenage pregnancy. Over one million girls between the ages of 10 and 14 become pregnant in the United States each year. The overwhelming majority of these girls keep their babies and many of them subsequently drop out of school. Their limited education and training leads to dim prospects for employment and often a lifetime of economic hardship.

increase, rather than decrease, sexual activity and, consequently, increase unwanted pregnancies. However, numerous research studies have found that effective sex education leads to a reduction in irresponsible sexual behavior (Scales and Gordon, 1978). For example, research on sex education in Europe has shown that the level of sexual activity is at least as high among teenage girls in the Netherlands and Sweden as it is in the United States. However, their levels of pregnancy and abortion are considerably lower (Jones et al., 1985). The difference is due to extensive sex education and the availability of birth control devices for European teenagers. In Sweden, there is compulsory sex education in all school grades and contraceptives are provided free of charge. In the Netherlands, private groups provide information about contraceptive methods so that Dutch adolescents are well informed. These policies have kept teenage pregnancies in check and helped prevent the number of abortions from increasing.

Some of those who believe in the value of sex education argue that it should be taught in the home instead of the school, yet research also clearly shows that while parents may believe that they are their child's best teachers, most parents do not provide their children with sex education and most children are too uncomfortable to ask (General Mills American Family Report, 1977). As a result, young people learn about sex largely from their misinformed friends and from movies and television. ■

THE TRANSITION TO ADULTHOOD

We noted early in this chapter that the end of childhood is marked by the physical changes of puberty. In modern technological societies this also marks the beginning of adolescence. However, adolescence is not a stable developmental period that is universally observed. In some cultures, such as the Inuit Eskimos of Canada, our notions of adolescence do not apply. There, young women are considered adults following puberty and they are likely to marry and bear children soon after. Young men must wait somewhat longer, until they can build a home and hunt unassisted. Once a male proves that he can support himself and a family, he too is considered an adult (Condon, 1987). The Inuit Eskimos have no concept of adolescence.

In modern technological societies the presence of a long period of adolescence is closely linked to lengthy job training and formal education. For us, adolescence is a period of time in which a young person undergoes a psychological transition from dependency to self-sufficiency. It begins when a person passes puberty and ends when he or she becomes fully autonomous. If anything, the societal forces that created this transitional period in the first place are still moving in the same direction. By most accounts this means that young people will require more training and education to perform ever more sophisticated jobs. This could result in an extension of adolescence as we know it, or in the creation of a new developmental period after adolescence, in which young people have some forms of autonomy but are not fully recognized as adults (Keniston, 1970). From the perspective of life-span development, this means that the transition from childhood to adulthood is not a constant or stable period. The length and manner of this transition will depend on one's social and cultural situation (Cole and Cole, 1989).

ADULTHOOD

In our society the onset of adolescence is associated with puberty, but there is no such signpost for adulthood. For some, including writer Richard Cohen, adulthood can sneak up unexpectedly.

Several years ago, my family gathered on Cape Cod for a weekend. My parents were there, my sister and her daughter, too, two cousins and, of course, my wife, my son and me. We ate at one of those restaurants where the menu is scrawled on a blackboard held by a chummy waiter and had a wonderful time. With dinner concluded, the waiter set the check down in the middle of the table. That's when it happened. My father did not reach for the check.

In fact, my father did nothing. Conversation continued. Finally, it dawned on me. Me! I was supposed to pick up the check. After all these years, after hundreds of restaurant meals with my parents, after a lifetime of thinking of my father as the one with the bucks, it had all changed. I reached for the check and whipped out my American Express card. My view of myself was suddenly altered. With a stroke of the pen, I was suddenly an adult. . . . I thought then and there it was a rite of passage for me. Not until I got older did I realize it was one for him, too.

(Cohen, 1987)

Modern developmental psychologists think of adulthood as consisting of three generally distinct periods: **early adulthood** (from approximately age 20 to 40), **middle age** (from roughly age 40 to 65), and **old age** (over 65). Each of these major phases of adulthood is marked by a different set of psychological issues. For example, Freud and Erikson thought that a person becomes an adult when he or she assumes the responsibilities of both love and work. In fact, we will see that many of the important issues of adulthood revolve around these two crucial topics.

THE AGING PROCESS

All species have a characteristic life expectancy. For a mouse, the expectancy is only three years; for an elephant, it is approximately 60. For people living in technologically advanced nations, the life expectancy is now more than 70 years. Within the long span between ages 20 and 80, people typically reach their peak of physical strength and endurance during their twenties and then gradually decline.

What causes us to age? At present there are many theories, but not much is clearly known. At the cellular level, some scientists have suggested that aging is caused by cells that simply wear out

and lose their regenerative power. At another level, others have suggested that the brain contains a "hormonal clock" that, at some set time, triggers a host of age-related disruptions (Patrusky, 1982). Curiously, the aging process works differently for men and women. In 1900, the life expectancy for men in the United States was 46 and for women 48. However, men living in the early 1980s can expect to live to an average age of 71, while women will live to an average age of 78 (National Center for Health Statistics). Researchers currently believe that this gender difference in longevity is based on both genetic and lifestyle differences. Hormonal differences between the sexes as well as the ability of women to develop social networks to cope with crises may contribute to differences in longevity (Johnson, 1984).

YOUNG ADULTHOOD AND THE SEARCH FOR INTIMACY

The period of young adulthood involves a radical transition in lifestyle. Generally it is seen as the period when you finish school, begin work, leave home, and, often, start a family of your own. However, there are a variety of routes through one's twenties and thirties. For example, 80 percent of Americans sampled in a 1957 survey felt that women who remained single were either sick or neurotic. Today, 75 percent of those sampled feel that single women have simply chosen an alternative lifestyle (Yankelovich, 1981).

A TIME OF CONFLICT AND TRANSITION

For young adults who have acquired a sense of identity and begun to engage in productive work, maturity brings a new set of challenges and opportunities. Erikson saw this period as an especially important time for forming deep personal relationships. People who form a loving relationship are healthier and happier than those who do not (Traupmann and Hatfield, 1981). According to Erikson's theory of development, the central crisis of early adulthood is the conflict between *intimacy* and *isolation*. Intimacy refers to the process of sharing with and caring about another person without fear of losing one's self in the process. Intimacy can involve lovemaking, but sexuality is not a necessary condition. Soldiers who have served together under conditions of battle often develop a sense of caring and commitment for each other that exemplifies an intimate relationship. On the other hand, Erikson held that the failure to establish intimacy leads to feelings of isolation, in which a person exists alone with no one to share with or care about. This failure can occur in individuals who have a fear of rejection or a narcissistic love of self (Erikson, 1963).

If we think of Erikson's crises as developmental tasks, then the major task of young adulthood is to form an intimate relationship. For most people, even today, that process usually ends in marriage.

MARRIAGE

More marriages occur during young adulthood than at any other time in life. In the United States, where 95 percent of all adults marry, surveys have revealed that the average age for a person's first marriage decreased through most of this century. In 1890, the average male was 26.1 years old and the average female was 22.9 years old. By 1962, these ages had fallen steadily to 22.9 for males and 19.9 for females. However, since then the trend has reversed. In 1985, after two decades of increases, the average ages have risen to 25.7 years for males and 23.3 years for females (Wetzel, 1987). One reason for this change is that more young people are going to college and postponing marriage in the hopes of landing a better-paying job after graduation. Today, young people are more concerned about financial matters than they were in the 1960s and 1970s (Astin, Green, and Korn, 1987). One factor has remained constant, however: males are typically a few years older than their female partners when they marry.

In many traditional cultures, locating one's lifelong partner was not a troublesome issue—your spouse was picked by your parents. In most contemporary societies, this is no longer the case. We are on our own, and must sort through many potential mates. In fact, selecting a mate is not just one task, but several different ones (Figure 12.6). It is a complex process that evolves as people pass through a series of stages during which the number of potential mates is progressively reduced. For example, we see many acceptable-looking partners, but pass them on the street without a word. If the situation is right, we may break the ice and talk with those we find attractive. Many of them do not pass the next stage, though, when they prove to lack personalities appealing to us. Some potential partners pass the first three stages, but do not arouse each other to desire sexual relations. Finally, some people pass all of the first four stages, but cannot live together.

Among those young people who marry, many of the relationships will end in divorce, especially during the first three years. Research shows that people who marry during adolescence are more likely to get divorced, as are those whose parents were divorced, who are dissimilar in age, intelligence, personality, or attractiveness, and who have no children (Bentler and Newcomb, 1978; Hetherington, 1979; among others). Of those who divorce, the overwhelming majority will remarry, and many will divorce again (Figure 12.7).

MARRIAGE FROM THE PERSPECTIVE OF EACH GENDER

What factors produce conflict in a marriage? A large-scale study by psychologist David Buss (1989) found that different things bothered men and women (Table 12.3). Men were bothered by women who were self-centered, moody, and sexually withholding, while women disliked men who were condescending, unreliable, and sexually

TABLE 12.3 Sources of Conflict Between Sexes

What Bothers a Woman About a Man	
Condescension:	Ignoring her opinions, treating her as an inferior, making her feel stupid.
Unreliability:	Ignoring her feelings, acting neglectful by not keeping promises or spending enough time with her.
Thoughtlessness:	Being inconsiderate or rude; not helping at home; teasing her about such things as how long it takes to dress.
Emotional Constriction:	Acting tough to hide his emotions.
Sexual Demands:	Forcing or demanding sex; making her feel sexually used.
What Bothers a Man About a Woman	
Self-Absorption:	Fussing over her appearance: overly concerned with her face, hair, and clothes.
Moodiness:	Acting "bitchy" or otherwise temperamental.
Sexual Rejection:	Unresponsive to sexual advances; refusing to have sex; being a sexual tease.

Note: Many areas of conflict are the same for both sexes, but these are some of the primary factors that bother men and women differently.

Modified from Goleman (1989), based on data from Buss (1989).

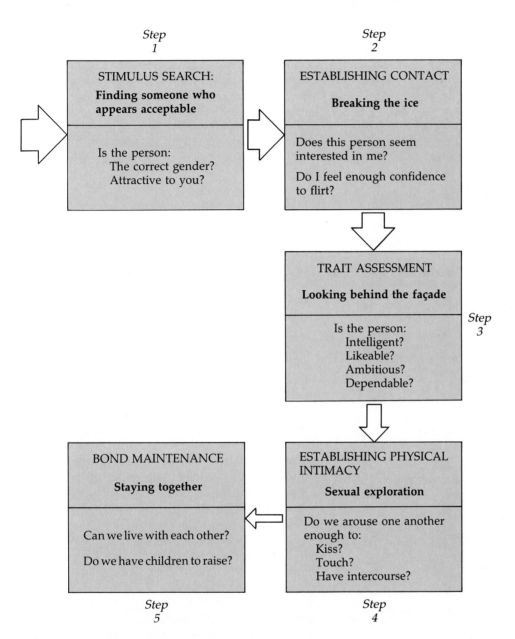

Step 1

STIMULUS SEARCH:

Finding someone who appears acceptable

Is the person:
    The correct gender?
    Attractive to you?

Step 2

ESTABLISHING CONTACT

Breaking the ice

Does this person seem interested in me?

Do I feel enough confidence to flirt?

TRAIT ASSESSMENT

Looking behind the façade

Is the person:
    Intelligent?
    Likeable?
    Ambitious?
    Dependable?

Step 3

ESTABLISHING PHYSICAL INTIMACY

Sexual exploration

Do we arouse one another enough to:
    Kiss?
    Touch?
    Have intercourse?

Step 4

BOND MAINTENANCE

Staying together

Can we live with each other?

Do we have children to raise?

Step 5

FIGURE 12.6 The process of mate selection. Mate selection involves a number of overlapping stages, each with a different task to accomplish. Fewer and fewer potential partners make it through each step in the process. This selection process tends to produce couples who are similar in their education, ethnic, physical, and social backgrounds.

aggressive. Both sexes were troubled by an unfaithful partner. When marital breakups occur, financial and sexual problems are often cited, but researchers have found that such problems may be "red herrings." Some research suggests that the number one problem is a failure to communicate. Future marital success can be predicted by the quality of a couple's communication before marriage, including their ability to resolve conflict, achieve personality compatibility, and form realis-

tic expectations (Markman, Floyd, Stanley, and Storaasli, 1988; O'Leary and Smith, 1991).

What makes for a long and successful marriage? Marriage researchers Jeanette and Robert Lauer (1985) conducted a survey of 351 couples who had been married 15 years or more. Each husband and wife responded individually to a questionnaire that focused on a variety of marital topics—topics such as sex, money, goals in life, and feelings about marriage in general. The researchers found a

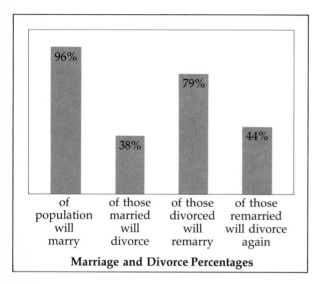

FIGURE 12.7 Marriage and divorce statistics in the United States during the 1980s. Approximately 40 percent of all marriages end in divorce, especially those between people who married during adolescence, whose parents were divorced, who have extramarital sex, or who have no children.

surprising amount of agreement between husbands and wives in what they considered important for a successful marriage. Table 12.4 shows the top seven reasons given by each spouse, in their order of frequency. The order of responses turned out to be the same for each partner. Most important of all was the fact that these people regarded their spouses as their best friends. Said one woman of her husband, "I would want to have

TABLE 12.4 Ingredients for a Successful Marriage

Reasons Given by Husbands and Wives In Their Order of Frequency

1. My spouse is my best friend.
2. I like my spouse as a person.
3. Marriage is a long-term commitment.
4. Marriage is sacred.
5. We agree on aims and goals.
6. My spouse has grown more interesting.
7. I want the relationship to succeed.

Note: Respondents were 351 couples, husbands and wives tested individually.

Adapted from Lauer and Lauer (1985).

him as a friend even if I weren't married to him." And another, "I am married to someone who cares about me, who is concerned for my well-being, who gives as much or more than . . . she gets. . . ." (Lauer and Lauer, 1985). These statements are eloquent expressions of Erikson's idea of intimacy, the establishment of a relationship with someone else based on love and friendship.

WORK

Work is profoundly psychologically important. Not only does the choice of a career affect your social and economic status, it can influence your circle of friends, your political and economic values, where your family will live, who will care for your children, and even the amount and type of stress you will experience. Income that you obtain from work can significantly affect your job satisfaction, a finding that seems especially important to many college students as they plan their future careers (Figure 12.8). However, income is not the only factor—for some people, it is not even the major factor. For professional and semiprofessional people, job satisfaction comes from achievement and recognition for their work. For less skilled workers, on the other hand, job satisfaction is related to income and job security. Various other factors are also important, including the extent to which the job is challenging, whether people are allowed to work autonomously, and whether they get along with their coworkers (McCormick and Ilgen, 1985).

People who choose jobs that complement their interests are less likely to change jobs and are happier on the job (Beck, 1986). However, for many people the choice of a job or career is likely to change during their lifetime. A Department of Labor survey of 71 million Americans found that the average length of a job was only 4.2 years. Job length is lower for unskilled and semiskilled workers than for professionals, and there is a general trend for people to hold more than one job in their lifetimes. Questioning prior career decisions is especially common during the next period of adulthood, the middle-age years.

MIDDLE AGE AND THE QUEST FOR GENERATIVITY

Not much developmental change seems apparent between the ages of 35 and 45, but powerful psychological forces begin to stir under the surface. One writer described these stirrings this way:

Ask anyone over 35, when did you first begin to feel old? Was it when you looked at your-

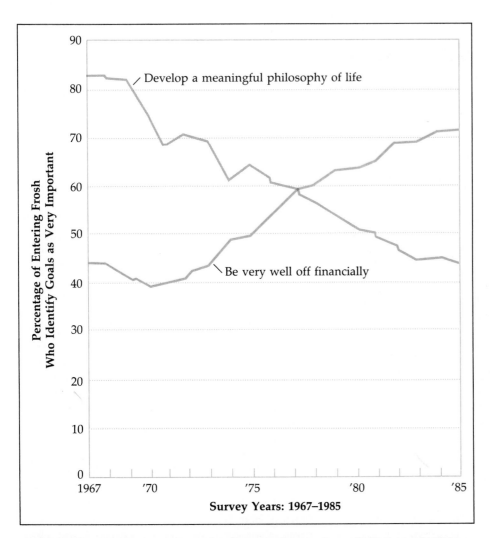

FIGURE 12.8 Changes in values of college students. From 1966 through 1985, over 300,000 first-year American college students were given a questionnaire about their values and goals in life. One of the most striking differences in values over this twenty-year period is shown in this figure. In 1966, more than 80 percent of the students felt that "developing a meaningful philosophy of life" was one of their major goals. By 1985, that percentage had shrunk to less than 50 percent. Conversely, there was a dramatic increase in the percentage of students who believed that "being very well off financially" was a major goal. Students are still concerned about such issues as apartheid and arms control, but there has been a definite shift in some personal values.

self in the buff and realized that everything was half an inch lower? "Hold your stomach in, mom." "It's in."

The middle of the thirties is literally the midpoint of life. The halfway mark. No gongs ring, of course. But twinges begin. Deep down a change begins to register in those gut-level perceptions of safety and danger, time and no time, aliveness and stagnation, self and others. It starts with a vague feeling. . . .

I have reached some sort of meridian in my life. I had better take a survey, reexamine where I have been, and reevaluate how I am going to spend my resources from now on.

(Sheehy, 1976)

In the transition from young adulthood to middle age, we begin to appreciate the limits of life. This realization begins imperceptibly, but it gradually grows and forces a psychological reassessment of who we are and where we are going.

Job satisfaction and work. Job satisfaction is influenced by a wide variety of factors. For professional and semiprofessional people it is related to achievement and recognition; for less skilled people, job satisfaction is related to other factors including income, security, and the degree to which the work is challenging.

MIDLIFE CONFLICT AND REASSESSMENT

Some people react calmly as they advance toward old age, while others become greatly distressed and feel that their time is running out. Erikson views the major crisis of this period as a conflict between *generativity* and *stagnation*. By generativity, he means that a person becomes more concerned with others and attempts to improve society. A recent survey of 1,200 men and women by the American Board of Family Practice (a professional organization of physicians in family practice) found that the vast majority saw middle age as a time for acts of caring and deepening of relationships (Goleman, 1990). Of those sampled, 84 percent agreed that during middle age a person becomes more compassionate to the needs of others, and 89 percent saw this as a time to become closer to family and friends. Middle-aged people, by virtue of their position and experience, can help younger people get started, see their ideas take hold, and work toward positive change.

Alternatively, middle-aged people can stagnate and become excessively concerned with their own needs. Like Dickens's Scrooge in *A Christmas Carol,*

the self-absorbed person has no regard for other people and focuses only on personal matters (Elkind, 1970). During middle age, people can stagnate if they come to believe that they will not achieve their earlier goals or, once having achieved them, find that they were really not all that worthwhile. Fortunately, stagnation is reversible (Erikson, 1963). As Dickens illustrated, even Scrooge could become generative when he was shown his own miserable end.

Building on Erikson's theory, psychologist Daniel Levinson and his associates (1978) interviewed adult men of different ages. In their survey, the researchers found that adulthood, at least for men, is hardly a period of monotonous sameness. By conducting in-depth longitudinal interviews with these men, Levinson found that their lives were marked by alternating periods of stability and transition. During the transitional periods—between early and middle adulthood (ages 40 to 45) and middle and late adulthood (ages 60 to 65)—people examine the previous periods of stability and ask if anything should be changed. These periods, according to Levinson, occur in a fixed sequence, but they are not always even and continuous. Sometimes change is gradual, while other times it is abrupt. During the transition into the middle aged years, people carefully reexamined their choices about marriage and work.

FAMILY AND JOB FLUCTUATIONS

During their middle aged years, most people have three roles to play: parent, spouse, and child. Adults must divide their time between children (who may now be young adults), a middle-aged marriage partner (who may have become increasingly independent), and aging parents (who may need assistance). The most significant change in the family occurs when the children leave home. After years of childrearing responsibilities, middle-aged parents are once again childless. Their home becomes an "empty nest." Just prior to this dramatic reversal, marital satisfaction reaches an all-time low. But after the children leave home many marriages successfully rebound (Rollins and Feldman, 1970). The empty nest has its own rewards, including less responsibility and financial burdens and more personal freedom. Children, for their part, usually still maintain close contact through visits and telephone conversations.

Although job satisfaction reaches a peak for some people during middle age, when they achieve high earnings and status, for others it can be a time of anguish. Some people seriously question whether they have really been pursuing the right goals. For these people, middle age is like a second identity crisis. They need to determine all over again not only who they are, but where they are going in their remaining years. However, keep in mind that crisis, transition, and change occur throughout life and not everyone experiences middle age the same way. For example, some men find this period disruptive, others avoid such problems by not raising family or job-related issues, and still others actually thrive during these years (Farrell and Rosenberg, 1981). For middle-aged women who have recently entered the job market, it can be a time for establishing an identity apart from their family and home. In fact, working at a meaningful career can be psychologically satisfying, even if it means juggling the multiple roles of mother, wife, and working person (Baruch and Barnett, 1983). For women who work at home raising families, life transitions are apt to be related to such family changes as the arrival of children or young people leaving home (Reinke, Ellicott, Harris, and Hancock, 1985).

Together, this research suggests that life transitions in middle age are less dependent on age than on significant life events. For example, for many people there is a lessening of family responsibility when the children are grown and leave home. This lessening of family obligations, which normally occurs after age 40, brings with it increased personal freedom. No longer having to worry about their children's dental or college costs, middle-aged adults may more freely pursue their own interests. For many, this period of self-examination is followed by an even stronger commitment to their marriage and work. Others make changes that alter the course of their future. One way or another, each person must deal with the inevitable fact that their life span has a definite end.

OLD AGE AND A SENSE OF INTEGRITY

According to recent **demographic studies** (statistical studies on the size and distribution of human populations), the percentage of people over 65 is increasing dramatically. In 1790, the elderly constituted only two percent of the United States population; in 1900, they constituted four percent; while in 1984, the 28 million elderly comprised 12 percent. If present trends continue, the elderly will comprise 20 percent of the population by the year 2030 (U.S. Bureau of the Census). These demographic changes make the development of the elderly an increasingly important social issue. There are major changes in family and work after age 65. Your children may move to distant places,

you may lose the spouse who shared most of your years, you are likely to retire from your life's occupation, and your health may fail. However, despite all these difficulties, studies of people in their 70s have shown that growing old is not synonymous with physical or mental deterioration. Many elderly people are active and satisfied with their lives (Neugarten and Neugarten, 1986).

RETIREMENT, MARRIAGE, AND HEALTH

Although we have used the conventional age of 65 to define the onset of old age, many elderly people do not think of themselves as old until they reach their 70s. The elderly are apt to see themselves as old only after they have retired, lost family or friends, and begun to suffer from ill health. Since these important personal and social changes do not automatically begin on one's 65th birthday, some people still feel "young" at 65, while others feel old long before then. As the 75-year-old mother of one of the authors of this text said, "I don't feel old yet. I can still travel, visit my grandchildren, and do whatever I want." Frank Lloyd Wright is another example. Recall that he was still active and designing major buildings well into his 80s. Yet in many occupations retirement comes at age 65, regardless of one's abilities. For those people who still have the desire and ability to work, mandatory retirement may pose a real problem of adjustment. Since a job can be a source of satisfaction and self-esteem, a change from worker to retiree may require a change in a person's self-image.

What determines how well a person handles retirement? Research indicates that several factors are important. Postretirement satisfaction is highest in those people who continue to enjoy good health, who were not forced to retire before they were ready, and who have enough income to maintain an adequate standard of living (Kimmel, Price, and Walker, 1978). When these conditions are met, people generally adjust to their retirement and come to enjoy the freedom and leisure it affords.

After retirement, husbands and wives spend more time together than ever before. Sometimes that can be more stressful than pleasant, as both partners try to adjust to a whole new set of mutual roles. However, many elderly people have a far different problem. After decades of marriage, they must learn to live alone. Of those people over 65, 15 percent of the men and 50 percent of the women have lost their spouses through death. Widows and widowers tend to be less satisfied with life than those who are still married. As one 75-year-old man said, "I was very happy 'till last year when my wife passed away: I lived with her 52 years . . . when I go home now I'm all by myself" (Kimmel, 1974). However, if widows and widowers have an adequate income level, if they are healthy and mobile, and if they remain involved with family and friends, then they generally cope satisfactorily (Belsky, 1990).

As people get older, personal health becomes increasingly important to their quality of life. Chronic problems like arthritis, hypertension, and rheumatism show a substantial increase. Approximately 40 percent of the elderly experience some form of physical limitation that interferes with their daily lives. When these limitations reduce the freedom to move about, isolation and unhappiness can follow, especially for those who live alone.

COGNITIVE CHANGE IN OLD AGE

In addition to changes in work and love relationships, numerous studies have suggested that the elderly must cope with deteriorating cognitive abilities. Typically, these studies have examined people of different ages on tests of intelligence or memory and have found that performance is best for people in their twenties and thirties, remains stable or declines slightly through their forties, fifties, and sixties, and declines rapidly during their seventies and eighties. However, more recent research indicates that the picture is not as bleak as the earlier studies have led us to believe. It now seems that a decline in cognitive ability is not an inevitable part of aging for people who remain physically and emotionally healthy (Poon et al., 1980).

For example, we noted in Chapter 9 that studies of intelligence draw a distinction between *crystallized* and *fluid intelligence*. Crystallized intelligence was defined as the ability to use accumulated knowledge to solve problems and make decisions. On vocabulary and comprehension subtests of an intelligence test such as the Wechsler Adult Intelligence Scale, crystallized intelligence rises slightly, rather than declines, over the entire life span (Horn and Donaldson, 1980). This makes it more likely for an older person to be able to define "ubiquitous" or to explain the difference between Marxism and social democracy.

Fluid intelligence is different. It does decline with age. Fluid intelligence was defined as the ability to see patterns and relationships, such as those used in a game of chess. Intelligence subtests that measure perceptual and memory skills show a gradual decrease in these skills after young adulthood. In fact, mathematicians and scientists, who

require fluid intelligence, make their greatest accomplishments during their twenties and early thirties (as Einstein did); while writers and historians, who require crystallized knowledge, do their best work in their forties and fifties, and sometimes even later (Denney, 1982). Figure 12.9 shows an idealized representation of these cognitive changes over the life span.

One must take great care in interpreting studies of age and cognitive ability. These studies can be unintentionally biased in favor of younger people in a number of ways. First, the elderly may perform worse than college-aged people because of diminished interest or motivation. Second, ill health can hurt the scores of the elderly, and many elderly people take medication that could hamper their cognitive performances. Finally, the elderly as a group have had less formal education than current generations of younger people.

To study the effects of age on cognitive performance, psychologists Warner Schaie and Sherry Willis (1986) conducted a longitudinal experiment on 229 elderly people, aged 64 to 95 years, over a 14-year period. Earlier testing of these people by Schaie on a verbal inductive reasoning task and a spatial mental rotation task showed that 122 people declined in performance, while 107 remained stable. Following these long-term observations, the researchers gave each of the subjects five hours of training on either an inductive reasoning or a spatial orientation task. Each of the training programs used problems that employed procedures

FIGURE 12.9 Changes in intelligence over the life span. Measures of intelligence typically show that crystallized intelligence (a person's factual knowledge of the world) increases with age, while fluid intelligence (a person's ability to deal with new problems) gradually declines. The severe decline in cognitive ability called senility is not a normal, inevitable aspect of aging, but a diseased, pathological condition.

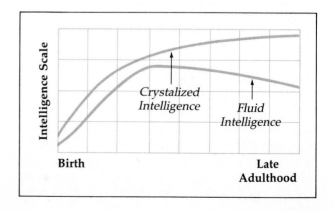

similar to those used in the original tasks, but none used identical problems. For example, the reasoning task required the subjects to look for a pattern in a series of letters and predict the next letter in the series (for example, A–C–E–G–?). The spatial task asked subjects to determine how objects would look if rotated in different orientations.

Schaie and Willis found that their training program could reverse the decline in performance on both cognitive tasks for 40 to 60 percent of the elderly, as well as enhance the performances of those who had previously remained stable. These results indicate that cognitive decline in a substantial number of elderly people is reversible, given adequate remedial training. Consequently, declines in cognitive performance need not necessarily reflect irreversible biological deterioration in the elderly (Willis and Nesselroade, 1990).

Current research suggests that at least part of the difference in the performance of the young and the elderly is in the spontaneous use of effective processing strategies by young people. For example, memory studies typically show poorer recall and recognition by elderly people (Bachman, 1991; Craik and McDowd, 1987). However, in experiments that carefully control the strategies that people use during learning, age differences in recall and recognition memory can often be dramatically reduced or eliminated (Mitchell and Perlmutter, 1986). These findings suggest that college students normally do better than old people because the students spontaneously use more effective strategies for remembering. This interpretation is supported by an experiment from psychologist Hilary Ratner and her associates (1987). They compared cognitive performance in elderly people with two groups of young adults. One group was enrolled in college, the other was not. In tests of story recall, the college group outperformed each of the other groups, but the non-college youth did not do better than the elderly. Thus, in this study, the use of effective learning strategies was associated with being a college student, not with being young (Ratner, Schell, Crimmins, Mittleman, and Baldinelli, 1987).

Today, psychologists are trying to determine which memory components are adversely affected by age (Light, 1991; Light and Burke, 1988). We know that neither short-term memory span nor the ability to learn from experience changes with age (Craik and Rabinowitz, 1984; Schaie and Willis, 1986). It is also untrue that the elderly remember distant events better than current happenings (Poon, Fozard, Paulschock, and Thomas, 1979). These widely held beliefs are just myths. However, when compared to the young, it is true that the elderly are apt to be slower on tasks that measure response speed and to attend to fewer stimuli or tasks simultaneously, again reflecting the distinction between fluid and crystallized intelligence (Birren, Cunningham, and Yamamoto, 1983; Campbell and Charness, 1990; Cerella and Fozard, 1984). It is also true that effective strategies for learning and remembering can be lost if they are not frequently used. This finding is reminiscent of the use of memory strategies by children discussed in the preceding chapter. Children who go to school develop effective strategies for retaining information, while children who do not go to school normally fail to develop such strategies. Similarly, the elderly can maintain their memory skills if they live in a stimulating environment, in which such skills have a function. One clear implication of this research is that the severe decline of mental functions commonly known as **senility** is neither an inevitable nor a normal consequence of aging. Senility, as we will see in the next section, is a symptom of physical disease.

DYSFUNCTION:
Alzheimer's Disease

As a fireman in a small town for forty years, E.D. had been decorated for heroism and risen to the rank of captain. Shortly before his retirement, though, his work began to slip. He became unnerved by the sound of fire hoses dragged across the floor, and the noise and commotion of firemen answering an alarm caused him to panic and become confused. Following retirement, E.D. sank into a depression and gradually became increasingly irritable and forgetful. While tending his garden, he forgot how to use his tools, but was too embarrassed to ask for help. With the passage of time, his condition greatly deteriorated. He eventually reached the state of not knowing who he was. He could not recognize his wife or children, he was forced to wear a diaper, and he had to be fed by hand (Dinolfo, 1984). Even the simplest everyday tasks became impossible for him to perform.

The person described in this passage is suffering from **Alzheimer's disease,** a progressive neurological disorder that attacks the brain and causes severe cognitive impairment. Alzheimer's disease is characterized by depression and a general decline in cognitive performance in its early stage, irritability, anxiety, and a loss of speech in

The tragedy of Alzheimer's disease. This elderly woman is suffering from Alzheimer's disease, a neurological disorder that destroys a person's ability to maintain contact with the world. This woman cannot perform the simplest, everyday functions to care for herself, nor does she recognize the young woman who is giving her a manicure. At present, Alzheimer's disease cannot be prevented, treated, or cured.

its intermediate stage, and a loss of simple responses such as bladder control in its later stage. As the disease progresses, many aspects of memory become impaired. Patients with Alzheimer's disease show poor short-term memory, poor long-term memory for words, pictures, and faces, and poor remote memory for famous people and events from the past (Morris and Kopelman, 1986; Partridge, Knight, and Feehan, 1990). As in our example of E.D., patients with Alzheimer's disease may not even recognize members of their family. Unlike the Korsakoff's syndrome patients we described in Chapter 7 whose memory problems become stable after treatment, the memory problems of Alzheimer's patients only get worse because there is no treatment or cure for this disease. Alzheimer's disease is always fatal.

Researchers have found that this disease is associated with neural degeneration. Cell damage in the form of **neurofibrillary tangles** (twisted filaments that fill the cells) and **senile plaques** (degenerated networks of axon terminals) is found in many areas of the brain. This cell damage is especially severe in the hippocampus (an important limbic structure for memory described in Chapter 2), the amygdala (another limbic structure), and the sensory portion of the cerebral cortex (Hyman, Van Hoesen, Damasio, and Barnes, 1984; Rogers and Morrison, 1985). These degenerating nerve cells have the effect of disconnecting major portions of the brain. The result is an Alzheimer's patient who has lost all contact with the world (Mountjoy, Rossor, Iversen, and Roth, 1984).

The specific cause of this neurological disorder is still unknown. In some cases, Alzheimer's appears to run in families, suggesting that genes may play a role in causing the disease. In these instances, its occurrence is controlled in some unspecified way by a dominant gene on chromosome number 21 (St. George-Hyslop et al., 1987). However, in most cases, Alzheimer's disease occurs in people who have no family history of the disease. In those cases where genes do not seem responsible, it may be that Alzheimer's can result from a slow-acting virus that crosses the blood–brain barrier and takes many years to develop (Brown, Salazar, Gibbs, and Gajdusek, 1982; Wietgrefe et al., 1985).

At present over 100,000 people die each year from Alzheimer's disease, making it the fourth leading cause of death in the United States, behind only heart disease, strokes, and cancer. Approximately five percent of all people over age 65 and 11 percent of those over age 85 suffer from this neurological disorder. Because the number of elderly people in the United States is increasing and these people are at risk for Alzheimer's disease, federal funds for research have increased in order to seek a treatment and cure for this disorder before it overwhelms the health care system. ■

APPROACHING LIFE'S END

For those who stay healthy into old age, there is one last developmental task. At this time, when a person's lifework has been completed, he or she can look backward and evaluate that life. Erikson describes this last crisis as a conflict between *integrity* and *despair*. He believes that old people who view their past achievements with pride obtain a sense of integrity that Erikson refers to as wisdom (Erikson, 1963; Erikson, Erikson, and Kivnick, 1986). For example, if people believe that they have done their best, they can see their whole life as a meaningful experience. This sense of integrity or wholeness will lead them to face their final days with peace and personal acceptance. But if they construe their past as a series of missed opportunities or directions, they can develop a feeling of despair. Those who despair see their past efforts as futile, and they dwell on what might have been. With the inevitable approach of death, this sense of gloom only darkens the remaining years.

Most young people avoid death from accident or illness, but all old people must face the natural end of their lives. Consequently, young people rarely think of death, while older people commonly consider their own mortality. How do we confront the fact that we will eventually cease to be? Psychiatrist Elizabeth Kubler-Ross (1969) interviewed over 200 patients in a Chicago hospital survey who knew that they were going to die within a limited period of time. She believed these terminally ill patients passed through a series of stages. First comes *denial,* in which a person believes that "some mistake has been made." Second is *anger,* when the truth can no longer be denied. Third is *bargaining,* in which the terminally ill person pleads to God or others for more time. Fourth is *depression* over the impending separation from those the person holds dear. Fifth, and last, is peaceful *acceptance* of the inevitability of death.

Current research has questioned whether Kubler-Ross's stages of dying apply to all terminally ill people. Some researchers have argued that most people only experience the depression stage. Others have wondered if peaceful acceptance is necessarily the best way to die (Kastenbaum, 1981). Still others report that a variety of responses is possible, and terminally ill patients do not necessarily exhibit a fixed sequence of feelings (Shneiderman, 1976). These findings suggest that people's responses to death, like their responses to other crises, transitions, and changes that characterize life, are rarely uniform and patterned.

INTERACTIONS:
Sexual Maturation and the Environment

Adolescent and adult development illustrate a complex interplay of biological and environmental influences. These interactions of biology and environment unfold normally in the course of each person's development. The clearest examples are found in the changes associated with puberty and menopause.

The physical changes of puberty are produced by biological maturation. But that sudden bubbling of hormones and the associated bulging of various body parts have consequences for almost all the basic psychological processes. Those changes affect an adolescent's thoughts, sensations, self-perceptions, and social experiences. As we noted, early-maturing boys and girls are treated differently by both their own and the opposite sex. The girl who suddenly develops breasts, or the skinny boy who suddenly sprouts chest muscles and facial hair, may find other people flirting with them in a way that never happened before. Likewise, the changes in their own internal states change their motivation to flirt and to seek the affections of others. As we noted in Chapter 10, sexual interest in both males and females is related to testosterone flow, which increases in both sexes at the time of puberty.

The adolescent's own reaction to puberty will depend partly on the society in which he or she comes of age. In some societies, such as the South Pacific Mangaian islanders, teenagers begin having sexual intercourse as soon as they reach puberty, with adults encouraging and advising their sexual activities (Marshall, 1971). In Mangaia, frequency of sexual intercourse is usually measured in terms of per day or per week. Depending on a person's age, sexual intercourse may occur twenty times a week for 18-year-olds, or two or three times a week for people in their 40s (Marshall, 1972). In other societies, like the Inis Beag culture off the coast of Ireland, there is considerable social pressure directed against premarital petting, and no one has intercourse until he or she is married (Messenger, 1972). Since marriage takes place in the midtwenties for women and the midthirties for men, that means that people in the Irish community must suppress the biological urges associated with puberty for at least a decade. Even after marriage, frequency of sexual intercourse is very low—it is usually measured in terms of per month or per year (Messenger, 1972). Thus, the psychological effects of sexual maturation are strongly influenced by the socializing environment.

A relation between sexual maturation and the environment is seen clearly in other species where the environment has a clear influence on the onset of sexual readiness. For instance, males of some fish species only reach sexual maturity when they find an available mating territory. Before finding an open territory, the males remain small and drab. Immediately afterward, they grow larger and more colorful and develop large gonads. One reason why males tend not to mature before they have a chance to mate is that larger males are more susceptible to attack and predation, and so until the odds are good that they can help propagate the species it is useful for an animal to remain prepubescent (Warner, 1984). Biological theorists reason that animals are genetically programmed to mature sexually when the physiological investment is most likely to pay off (Alexander, 1987; Partridge and Harvey, 1988).

We do not yet know whether the possibility of sexual activity alters the sexual development of human males. Given the animal literature, it is possible that we have misinterpreted the causal link between early puberty and social success in boys. It may be that being socially successful and athletic *causes* a boy to reach puberty early, and not that early puberty causes a boy to be socially dominant. If our socially extroverted and athletic male ancestors had a better chance of early mating this could make evolutionary sense.

For females, there is clearer evidence that puberty is linked to the environment in a way that also makes evolutionary sense. Biologist Rose Frisch (1988) has found that girls will not begin to menstruate until they have accumulated enough body fat to support a fetus. For example, athletic girls who lack sufficient body fat will not menstruate. Frisch suggested that the relation between body fat and sexual maturation is based on our evolutionary history. Our hunter-gatherer ancestors faced frequent periods of food shortage. Adults can survive reasonably long periods without nutrition, but babies and unborn fetuses cannot. It was adaptive for our female ancestors to have bodies programmed to delay sexual maturation until they had developed a fetal insurance policy of surplus fat. In this way, the evolutionary past connects with the present through genes that are programmed to link sexual maturation to cues that reproduction will be successful. The unfolding genetic program will nevertheless interact with the social environment. Even though her body is programmed to enter puberty, a girl raised on Inis Beag will have to suppress her sexual thoughts and behaviors; a girl from Mangaia will not.

An evolutionary perspective also helps us understand why women experience menopause (the cessation of menstruation) during their forties,

while men do not go through a similar change in their reproductive ability. Women directly contribute their bodily resources to their offspring, who grow inside their bodies and must be nursed after birth. After age 40, however, pregnancy results in an increased health risk for a woman and an increased chance of illness or defect for her child. Our female ancestors probably fared better by simply ceasing to have children at this time, rather than take a chance that would hinder their ability to take care of their existing children or grandchildren (Alexander, 1987; Kenrick and Keefe, 1992). Since men contribute none of their bodily resources to their children and risk no direct physical danger by having more children, a male equivalent of menopause would serve no adaptive function.

Looking at sexual behavior from an evolutionary perspective does pose certain risks. For example, we cannot assume that just because a process such as menopause exists that it must have some adaptive function now or have had one in the past. Not everything we do or undergo in life is directly related to our survival or the survival of our species. The value of the evolutionary perspective is that it suggests possible origins for biological and psychological processes that, when combined with other perspectives, suggest new ways of thinking about behavior. Each of the perspectives that we outlined in Chapter 1 provides us with different insights and different levels of possible explanations.

We will have more to say about the interactions of biology and environment in subsequent chapters when we discuss issues of health, abnormal behavior, and social processes. ▪

IN CONTEXT: ADOLESCENT AND ADULT DEVELOPMENT

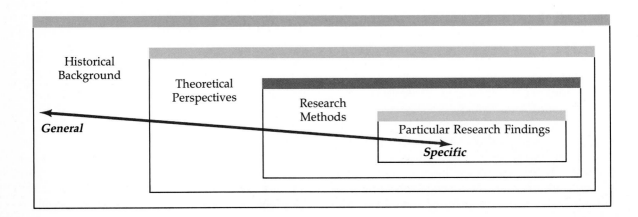

STUDY QUESTIONS

Why do psychologists think of development as a lifelong process?

What are the major developmental tasks of adolescence?

What are the major developmental tasks of adulthood?

How are the psychological experiences of one developmental period qualitatively different from those of another?

What determines how well a person handles old age?

HISTORICAL BACKGROUND

1. During the Middle Ages, a person assumed adult status right after puberty. By the twentieth century, a period of adolescence separated childhood and adulthood as people lived longer and schooling often continued past puberty.

2. Early in the twentieth century, G. Stanley Hall published his research on adolescence and described it as a line of "storm and stress." He later published a book on old age.

3. Many influential ideas about life-span development were born during the rise of the psychoanalytic movement in this century. Freud saw adult personality development as set during childhood. Carl Jung studied the ways in which mature adults searched for religious meaning and personal fulfillment in life. He was the first to describe the psychological changes around age 40 as a midlife crisis. By far the most influential theorist on psychological development was another follower of Freud named Erik Erikson.

MODERN THEORETICAL PERSPECTIVES

1. Erikson proposed a grand theory of psychological development that covered the entire life span. He believed that development involved a series of eight stages, each characterized by a particular psychological conflict. Many of these conflicts occurred during adolescence and adulthood.

2. Piaget's theory of cognitive development (described in the last chapter) extends into adolescence when young people develop logical thought. This final period is called the formal operations stage.

3. Kohlberg's theory of moral reasoning is related to Piaget's theory of cognitive development.

According to Kohlberg, there are six stages of moral development. Everyone progresses through the stages in the same order, but not everyone reaches the highest level.

4. The stage idea is also seen in Dunphy's theory of adolescent peer relationships and Levinson's theory of transitions in adulthood. According to Dunphy, adolescents pass through a series of stages, starting with small groups of friends and ending with intimate relationships. Levinson believed that adulthood is marked by periods of stability and change as people focus on earlier choices involving marriage and work.

RESEARCH METHODS

1. **Surveys** were frequently used to study adolescence and adulthood. Surveys were used to observe the effects of the timing of puberty on social development (Peterson, 1987), the sexual behaviors and beliefs of adolescents (Earle and Parricone, 1986; Goleman, 1987), the age of marriage (Wetzel, 1987), the reasons why some marriages last (Lauer and Lauer, 1985), the psychological transitions in adulthood (Levinson et al., 1978), and the experiences of those who are dying (Kubler-Ross, 1969).

2. **Experimentation** was used to study cognitive change in the elderly (Ratner et al., 1987; Schaie and Willis, 1986).

3. The **correlational method** indicated a relationship between parenting styles and high school performance (Dornbusch et al., 1981), while the **case study** of E.D. showed the debilitating effects of Alzheimer's disease (Dinolfo, 1984).

RESEARCH FINDINGS AND SUMMARY

1. **Life-span psychology** deals with the description and explanation of developmental pro-

cesses that occur between conception and death. Research in life-span psychology focuses on discontinuities as well as continuities in development, and on how biological changes interact with cognitive and environmental factors to influence developmental processes.

2. **Adolescence** begins with the onset of **puberty** and ends with the arrival of young adulthood at approximately age 20. Puberty is the sexual maturation of the child, produced by major hormonal changes. During the period of puberty, there are changes in a person's **primary** and **secondary sex characteristics** that not only alter physical appearance, but also enable the person to sexually reproduce.

3. Personality and social development are influenced by the timing of puberty. Early-maturing boys are viewed as attractive and popular and they tend to be successful in social and athletic activities; just the opposite is true of those boys who mature late. Early-maturing girls seem at an initial disadvantage, but they come to be favorably regarded by the time they get to junior high school; late-maturing girls appear to suffer no disadvantages.

4. Peers often function as parent substitutes in an adolescent's quest for autonomy. Peers are especially influential in matters of personal taste. With the formation of friendship groups, heterosexual interactions increase and this leads to an increase in personal involvement and the formation of couples in late adolescence. Research shows that premarital sexuality has increased throughout this century.

5. Adulthood is divided into three distinct age-related periods: **young adulthood** from age 20 to 40; **middle age** from 40 to 65; and **old age** for all of the years thereafter. The onset of young adulthood is marked by assuming the responsibilities of work and love. People tend to marry others who are similar in age, intelligence, personality, and social backgrounds.

6. Job satisfaction is especially important during middle age and it is influenced by a variety of factors. For professional and semiprofessional people, job satisfaction is associated with achievement and recognition by others. For less skilled workers, it is associated with income and job security.

7. During middle age, people gradually accept that their lives are approximately half over. Some people react calmly, while others become distressed.

8. **Demographic** research shows that the percentage of people over age 65 is dramatically increasing. These people are not apt to think of themselves as old until they retire, lose family and friends, and, possibly, suffer from ill health. The elderly can adapt to the personal and social changes of old age if they have sufficient income, health, mobility, and a social network of family and friends.

9. A severe decline in cognitive ability is not an inevitable aspect of aging for those elderly people who remain physically and emotionally healthy. While *fluid intelligence* decreases gradually from middle age on, *crystallized intelligence* actually increases over the life span. **Senility** is not a normal part of aging, but a diseased, pathological condition. **Alzheimer's disease** is an example of a neurological disorder in the elderly.

ADDITIONAL READINGS

Belsky, J. K. 1990. *The psychology of aging: Theory, research and practice*, 2nd ed. Monterey, CA: Brooks/Cole. A well-balanced overview of classic and current research on the elderly. Major research findings are discussed, and there are many illustrations of their clinical application.

Birren, J. E., and Schaie, K. W., eds. 1985. *Handbook of the psychology of aging*, 2nd ed. New York: Van Nostrand Reinhold. A comprehensive collection of survey chapters on adult development and aging by leading researchers. This book provides an authoritative review and reference source for numerous research topics on aging.

Elkind, D. 1984. *All grown up and no place to go*. Reading, MA: Addison-Wesley. This book outlines the special problems faced by adolescents in their relations with parents and peers.

Gibson, K. R., and Petersen, A. C., eds. 1991. *Brain maturation and cognitive development: Comparative and cross-cultural perspectives*. Hawthorne, NY: Aldine de Gruyter. A multidisciplinary approach to the study of brain processes and cognitive development with contributions from specialists in the fields of evolutionary, neurological, genetic, psychological, and cross-cultural research.

Montemayor, R., Adams, G. R., and Gullotta, T. P., eds. 1990. *From childhood to adolescence: A transitional period?* Newbury Park: CA: SAGE. A wide-ranging collection of chapters on adolescence, including sections on physical growth, family relations, and social cognition.

Perlmutter, M., and Hall, E. 1985. *Adult development and aging*. New York: Wiley. An up-to-date and easy-to-read textbook that surveys the major topics and findings in adult development.

Rebok, G. W. 1987. *Life-span cognitive development*. New York: Holt, Rinehart and Winston. A book on cognitive development from the life span perspective that focuses on recent theoretical and empirical advances. Extensive coverage of topics including spatial cognition, creativity, and social cognition, as well as more traditional topics, is provided.

Smith, W. J. 1985. *Dying in the human life cycle*. New York: Holt, Rinehart and Winston. A comprehensive review of research on dying that ranges from infant death to the humane care of the terminally ill and the aged.

PERSONALITY

T he word personality . . . is used in two distinct ways. . . . Personality in (one) sense . . . refers to the distinctive impression that a person makes on others, in the sense that Humphrey Bogart was a unique motion picture personality. The root of the word personality is the Latin term *persona*, the mask worn by an actor to signify his role in a play. Because this form of personality is tied to a public appearance, we are curious about who or what is behind the mask. . . . Personality in the (other) sense refers to the fundamental or basic core of man, to the essential person that lives at the center of our being. . . .

(Robert Hogan, 1976)

Chapter Outline

Paul Gauguin and Vincent van Gogh are today regarded as among the greatest artists in modern history. The two shared several personal characteristics. Both were aesthetically brilliant and passionately unconventional, for instance. Their interests and motivations were similar enough that they roomed together for a short time. But the differences between them were greater, and their association was short-lived and explosively terminated.

Paul Gauguin and Vincent van Gogh have personalities that have fascinated biographers. They were similar in certain ways; both were artistic and unconventional, for instance. They were also very different in some ways; Gauguin (left) was dominant and extraverted, van Gogh (right) self-doubting and introverted. Personality psychologists study individual differences—the ways in which people are alike, as well as the ways in which people are different.

Gauguin was tough, self-confident, and egotistic (Wildenstein and Cogniat, 1972). After his radical father died early in his youth, he was raised by a mother whose own mother had left her husband to become a crusading socialist. In his early thirties, Gauguin callously left his wife and family and a successful banking career to pursue his artistic interests and to live with a series of different women. His art, which includes the well-known paintings of beautiful South Pacific women, was sensual and unrestrained.

Van Gogh, on the other hand, was meek, self-tortured, and introverted (Wallace, 1969). His father was a stern Dutch minister, and his mother was also highly conventional. In school, he was shy and withdrawn, and he later had difficulties relating to women. More than once, he fell madly in love with a woman who had shown no interest in him, only to be spurned when he suddenly blurted out his feelings. Unlike Gauguin, he never married. He did live with a prostitute for a few months, but she left him to return to a bordello. Van Gogh, in characteristic fashion, blamed himself. Before turning to art, van Gogh also had a short, but unsuccessful, career in business. He lost

his job when he became morose and socially inappropriate. Unlike the comfortable sensuality of Gauguin, van Gogh's art alternated between melancholic control and emotional explosiveness.

The questions raised by these two men's differences and similarities illustrate the central issues of personality psychology. Personality psychologists study *individual differences* in cognition, emotion, and behavior, and they attempt to explain where those differences come from. They do research to describe and to explain how people—van Gogh, Gauguin, you, and me—are different from (and similar to) one another.

DESCRIBING AND ASSESSING PERSONALITY

The first major question for personality psychologists is *descriptive:* "How can we describe the major behavioral differences between people?" To answer this question, personality psychologists often devise tests to assess (or measure) **personality traits**—behavioral characteristics such as friendliness, social dominance, conventionality, emotional adjustment, and aesthetic inclination. They then compare those tests to actual behavior or the reports of people who know the person being tested, and may go on to use the tests to predict how that person will behave in different jobs, marriages, or other social situations. The Strong Vocational Interest Blank is an example of a personality test that has been researched for several decades (Holland, 1966). It is used to compare a person's interests to those of people already in various occupations. The test could be used to compare a modern Gauguin's interests with those of people in different occupations, and perhaps save him a decade in a job unsuited to his temperament.

There is a second descriptive question that personality psychologists ask: "How do different psychological traits go together?" If someone is artistic, for instance, can we also expect him or her to be unconventional and passionate? Or a personality psychologist might ask about the difference between someone who is artistic and extroverted (like Gauguin) and someone who is artistic and introverted (like van Gogh).

EXPLAINING THE CAUSES OF PERSONALITY DIFFERENCES

At the *explanatory* level, personality psychologists ask where individual differences in experience and behavior come from. Noting that van Gogh's brother Theo was also sensitive and reserved, a personality psychologist might ask about the extent to which this type of behavior (called introversion) is genetically endowed, and the extent to which it results from a common family environment. Different personality theories have focused on a wide range of potential causes of individual differences. Some emphasize genes or family history, while others consider the individual's historical and cultural milieu. Was there something about European society in the late nineteenth century that led both van Gogh and Gauguin to develop unconventional personalities, for instance? Other theories focus on the individual's everyday rational decisions, and might argue that van Gogh could have become a conventional and well-adjusted man, had he decided to do so.

In seeking explanations of behavior, personality psychologists may again ask questions about how different psychological processes go together. Personality psychologists try to fit together the separate processes we have discussed in the first half of this book. How does an individual's physiology link with his or her learning history, persistent motivations and emotional states, and perceptual

processes? How was van Gogh's social life related to physiological processes going on in his brain and body? How did these, in turn, relate to his thought processes, and how did his thought processes influence his perception of the scenes he painted?

The theories we discuss in this chapter provide an intellectual framework for considering other questions about complex human behavior in the chapters that follow. Theories of personality underlie much of the research on psychopathology and psychological treatment, for example, as well as research on individual differences in social behaviors such as aggression and kindness.

HISTORICAL BACKGROUND: Conceptions of Personality

Questions about personality have intrigued reflective people from the earliest times. The Greek philosopher Hippocrates developed a scheme for personality description that is still referred to today (Eysenck, 1953; see Fig. 13.1). Extending the idea that there were four basic elements—air, water, fire, and earth—Hippocrates proposed four bodily fluids, or humors—blood, phlegm, yellow bile (or choler), and black bile. This scheme, which was further elaborated by the Roman physician Galen, proposes that there are four types of people in the world, and that your type depends on the "fluid" that predominates in your body. If you have a relatively high ratio of blood you will be sanguine (or cheerful). Phlegm makes you phlegmatic (or unemotional), yellow bile makes you choleric (irritable), and black bile makes you melancholic (depressed).

The idea of a connection between bodily conditions and personality went through a number of variations over the years. In the nineteenth century, phrenologists such as Franz Gall (described in Chapter 2) attempted to connect personality to bumps on the skull. Later in the same century, Cesare Lombroso, influenced by Charles Darwin's theory of evolution, argued that the physical features of criminals marked them as evolutionary "throwbacks." According to Lombroso, criminals were a different subspecies (*homo delinquens*), who could be identified by their prominent jaws and eyebrows, asymmetric skulls, insensitivity to pain, and predilection for cruel and impulsive behavior (Toch, 1979). Lombroso believed these traits evolved during an earlier, more brutal, stage of

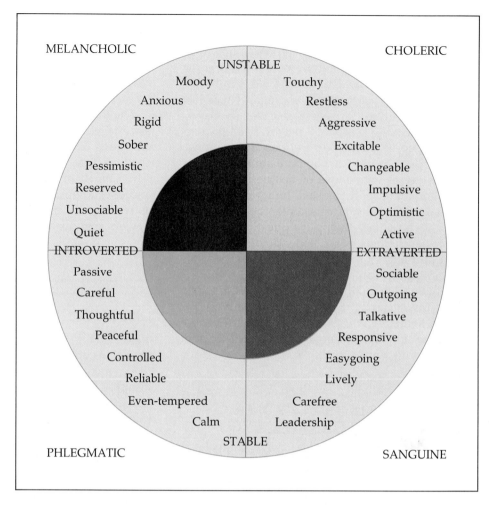

FIGURE 13.1   A modern personality scheme that is a descendant of Hippocrates's theory of the four temperaments.   Hippocrates's temperaments are shown in the middle dark area. The modern terms are shown around the outside of the circle.

human history. Although Lombroso's theory is today regarded as a historical curiosity, modern personality psychologists continue to consider the possible relevance of evolutionary principles to an understanding of human nature and individual differences.

During the first half of this century, William Sheldon (1944) continued the search for connections between anatomy and personality. Sheldon collected evidence suggesting that three different body types are associated with three different behavior patterns. *Mesomorphs* are those whose bodies are predominantly bone and muscle. According to Sheldon, mesomorphs tend to love adventure, risk, and competition for dominance and power. They also tend to be ruthless, and to respond to alcohol by becoming aggressive. *Ectomorphs*, on the other hand, are thin and delicate, and have the largest brains in proportion to their body size.

They tend to be sensitive, self-conscious, private, and intellectual, and resistive to alcohol and drugs. Finally, Sheldon argued that heavy people, *endomorphs*, are predisposed to love physical comfort, socializing, and eating. They are oriented toward family relationships, and they respond to alcohol by becoming relaxed and friendly. Consider Paul Gauguin and Vincent van Gogh in terms of Sheldon's approach. Gauguin was closest to the muscular mesomorph, while van Gogh was a slender ectomorph. Consistent with Sheldon's theory, Gauguin was adventurous, outgoing and socially aggressive, whereas van Gogh was sensitive, self-conscious, and socially withdrawn.

Unfortunately, Sheldon himself rated both the body type and the personality characteristics of the people he studied, and he may have let his theoretical expectations bias his judgments (Hall and Lindzey, 1957). Later researchers who used one set of raters to judge body type and a second set to judge personality found weaker relationships between body and behavior (Child, 1950). However, properly conducted studies still find many relationships between body type and behavior that cannot be explained as due to the rating biases of the researchers (Wells, 1983). For instance, muscular mesomorphs made up about 60 percent of a group of institutionalized delinquents, but only about 30 percent of a matched group of nondelinquent youth (Glueck and Glueck, 1956). In recent years, the search for a relationship between body and personality has largely shifted from outward bodily characteristics to inner physiology and genes.

Another approach to personality is rooted in philosophical developments during the nineteenth century. Unlike biological theorists, those who adopt the **phenomenological perspective** argue that personality begins not in the body, but in the mind—in the conscious choices we make about how to live our lives. This approach is related to the work of philosophers such as Søren Kierkegaard (1813–1855), and Friedrich Nietzsche (1844–1900), who contemplated how a person comes to be aware of his or her true self (Hogan, 1976). Phenomenologists distinguished between "authentic" and "alienated" self-conceptions: some of us are honest with ourselves and are authentic, while others of us refuse to face our true selves and are alienated. As we will see, the phenomenologist's interest in conscious thought and the inner self remains prominent in personality research.

Perhaps the most influential personality theorist was Sigmund Freud. Unlike the phenomenologists, Freud believed that the causes of our behavior are most often inaccessible to conscious awareness. Freud's theory continues to be influential today, so we will discuss it in depth in the next section. As we will see, Freud's theory touches on several of the key historical questions about personality: What is the relationship between our inner selves and the outer world? What is the relative influence of biology as opposed to environmental pressures in determining what we are like? What is the role of conscious and unconcious thought processes on our personalities?

In addition to Freudian theory, we will discuss trait, biological, learning, phenomenological, and cognitive perspectives. Based upon their different historical roots, each of these schools takes a slightly different approach to assessing and explaining personality. ■

THE PSYCHODYNAMIC PERSPECTIVE ON PERSONALITY

We have already encountered Freud's influential theory in several chapters, and will encounter it again in the next three chapters, when we discuss psychological conflict and disorder. Freud believed that adult personality is in fact rooted in the conflict between society and the individual's biological drives. As we noted in Chapter 10, Freud assumed that all humans are born with a common set of drives for self-preservation and reproduction (Freud, 1933). Those drives provide the basic structural foundation for personality, which Freud called the **id.** All of us share the same set of uncivilized instincts, which often come into conflict with society when the individual's sexual and aggressive impulses threaten the well-being of others. The differences among us depend upon how our parents handled certain critical conflicts involving weaning, toilet training, and sexual impulses. Each conflict represents a battle between selfish biological needs and the pressures of society. The selfish id wants to go on nursing at mother's breast, to urinate as soon as the impule strikes, and to have sexual relations with the first possible love objects—our parents. The id operates on the **pleasure principle,** or the desire for immediate gratification. As agents of society, our parents try to bring those barbaric impulses under control. As a consequence, we develop the more sensible part of our personality that Freud called the **ego.** The impulsive id never goes away, but we learn that we will be happier if we delay gratification. Instead of urinating the moment the urge strikes, the older child delays the impulse, walks to the bathroom, and avoids a conflict with mother. The ego operates on the **reality principle,** seeking optimal compromises between the demands of biology and those of the real world. The ego thus controls the id—it acts to get things done in an efficient and socially acceptable manner. At around age five, according to Freud, the child develops a third component of the personality called the **superego.** The superego is an internalized representation of the parents' value system. A child with only an ego would steal candy if she was sure no one was looking, but a child with a superego has internalized her parents' ideas about right and wrong and would punish herself with guilt for stepping out of line. Although the superego sounds highly civilized, it, too, is ultimately an outgrowth of the selfish id, and Freud believed that the moral behavior of the superego develops partially to appease the parents and win the love of the parent of the opposite sex.

PERSONALITY DEVELOPMENT: BIOLOGICALLY PROGRAMMED SOCIAL CRISES

According to Freud, parents must walk a fine line between being overly harsh and overly lenient during the crises over weaning, toilet training, and sexual impulses. Freud believed that these crises were so important that he called the first year of life (when breast feeding and weaning usually occur) the **oral stage,** the second year (when toilet training usually occurs) the **anal stage,** and the third to the fifth years (when the child often becomes obsessed with genitalia) the **phallic stage.** Following this, the child enters a **latency stage,** during which sexual urges are largely suppressed until puberty. The strong sexual urges associated with puberty signal the onset of the **genital stage,** during which the adolescent begins to search for an adult sexual partner. Freud believed that there are particular syndromes of adult personality associated with problems during the first three stages. For instance, if your mother is too harsh in weaning you from her breast, you may develop an *oral-aggressive* personality, characterized by pessimism, suspiciousness, sarcasm (biting verbal humor), and argumentativeness. Notice that the connection between these traits is a lack of interpersonal trust and the use of the mouth in an aggressive way. On the other hand, if your mother is too indulgent, you could develop *oral-receptive* characteristics, related to ingesting food and trusting others. These include dependency, gullibility (the willingness to "swallow anything"), and a fondness for sweets and smoking, as well as an obsession with oral sex.

Freud worked mainly with troubled patients, but he believed that a normal personality also arises from compromises between biological impulse and social pressure. None of us can suppress our biological needs entirely, and Freud believed that socially unacceptable impulses could be reversed, pushed out of awareness, or channeled into some desirable activity. What makes Freudian theory seem confusing to some people is that things are rarely what they appear to be on the surface because impulses are most often expressed indirectly. On the surface Paul Gauguin's interest in art could be explained as a fascination with form and color. However, a psychoanalyst might focus on Gauguin's paintings of women, and attempt to connect them to unresolved feelings about his mother. **Defense mechanisms** are cognitive strategies that people use to cope with anxiety-provoking thoughts and impulses. One example of a defense mechanism is **projection,** in which a person deals with a threatening impulse by attributing it to others. For instance, a woman who is ambivalent about commitment might accuse her boyfriend of losing interest in her. If he then points out he had hinted at marriage just last night, she might insist that he was really only being sarcastic. A recent study was designed to test the psychodynamic idea that defense mechanisms are especially likely to be used when people are feeling threatening impulses. When students were asked to tell a story about a person in a TAT card (a projective test described in Chapter 10), their stories tended to evidence more use of defense mechanisms if they had previously been angered by an insult. For instance, angered subjects attributed more hostile intentions and feelings to the character than did non-angered subjects, and the researcher interpreted this as evidence of projection (Cramer, 1991). Because of the connection between defense mechanisms and psychological stress, we will discuss them at greater length in Chapter 14, which deals in depth with stress and coping.

Freud believed that the motives for many of our behaviors are *unconscious.* If an artist were to deny that his or her artistic inclinations stemmed from neurotic needs, for example, that denial would prove nothing. In fact, if the artist's denial was vehement, the Freudian might take that very denial as evidence for the theory. The final hallmark of Freudian thought is the belief that *early childhood conflicts* are particularly important in shaping adult personality.

OTHER PSYCHODYNAMIC VIEWPOINTS: THE NEO-FREUDIANS

Freud's psychodynamic theory attracted many adherents and critics. A number of personality theorists, sometimes called neo-Freudians, accepted Freud's basic premise that adult behavior is influenced by unconscious motivations, but differed with him on other important assumptions. In particular, several theorists disagreed about the extent to which all adult behavior is motivated by sexual and aggressive drives. For instance, Erik Erikson, whose ideas we discussed in Chapter 12, believed that personality development involved a number of social crises that continued into adulthood and old age, and that mostly had nothing to do with sexuality. In this section, we consider four other neo-Freudians who had important influences on modern psychological thought: Carl Jung, Alfred Adler, Karen Horney, and Erich Fromm.

Carl Jung argued that, in addition to sexual and aggressive drives, all humans inherited a desire to seek higher religious fulfillment and self-development. Jung's studies of cross-cultural anthropology and mythology led him to posit a **collective unconscious,** or a universal set of ideas. Because of a shared evolutionary history in which all humans were nurtured by mothers, and were threatened by snakes and the dark, Jung postulated, we are all predisposed to feel dependency and love toward our mothers and to fear snakes and the dark. Jung (1936/1969) referred to these universal ideas as **archetypes.** Archetypes are not specific thoughts and perceptions, but simply inherited tendencies to perceive and feel in certain ways about certain objects (such as snakes or mothers). Although Jung's ideas may at first sound rather far-fetched, modern work on learning preparedness does lend some support to the idea that humans could inherit a tencency to learn some associations more easily than others. As we will discuss in Chapter 15, for instance, there is some evidence that it is easier to learn phobic fears of naturally threatening stimuli (such as snakes and wasps) than of equally dangerous objects that our ancestors never encountered (such as automobiles).

Alfred Adler also de-emphasized sexual motivation, and focused instead on socially based motivations. According to Adler (1930), adult behavior is largely motivated by **striving for superiority,** the upward drive for perfection. The motivation is based upon childhood feelings of inferiority—all of us begin life with particular handicaps or deficiencies that we strive to overcome. For instance, Demosthenes was a childhood stutterer who went on to become a great orator, and Theodore Roosevelt was a frail child who went on to become a burly and powerful man. In a healthy individual, striving for superiority is directed toward the good of the group—the person attempts to better his or her community or to make a useful scientific or medical discovery. In the unhealthy individual, who has suffered too great a sense of inadequacy, Adler believed that striving for superiority takes the form of selfish aggrandizement.

Karen Horney, like Adler, focused on social interactions as the source of adult motivations. Horney (1945) believed that our adult characteristics often represent attempts to deal with **basic anxiety**—the childhood feeling of being isolated and helpless in a potentially hostile world. Basic anxiety, according to Horney, results not from sexual and aggressive conflicts, but from any disturbances in the child's relationships with his or her parents, including rejection, punishment, or overprotection. In attempting to deal with basic anxiety, the person develops a characteristic social orientation, which could include being dependent on others for security, being competitive with others, or being avoidant of others.

Erich Fromm also emphasized the individual's social experiences. However, as a student of sociology and economics, he focused more on the larger society in which a child developed. Influenced as much by Karl Marx as by Sigmund Freud, Fromm (1941; 1947) held that a person's adult personality is influenced by the economic and social conditions of the country in which he or

Marketing ourselves. Neo-Freudian Erich Fromm has argued that an individual's adult personality is influenced by the economic and social conditions of the culture in which he or she is raised. Germans were characterized by authoritarian personality characteristics, for instance, and Americans by a "marketing personality." Stemming from our market economy, Americans often emphasize their external characteristics such as physical appearance—developing the "outer package" to the relative exclusion of inner qualities.

she was raised. Each individual faces a conflict between the desire to be free and independent and the desire to fit in with othrs. When people are threatened, they may forsake their own individuality and retreat into blind conformity. Fromm argued that Germans after World War I "escaped from freedom" by developing authoritarian tendencies, and that modern Americans shirk personal responsibility by developing shallow "marketing personalities" (that is, we package ourselves to appeal to others, but ignore the development of our inner qualities).

Other dynamically-oriented theorists have likewise shared Freud's emphasis on the importance of unconscious motivations, but have placed their emphases on different aspects of the individual's thoughts and social interactions (for instance, Kohut, 1977; Sullivan, 1953). It seems unlikely that adult personality can be traced solely to sexual and aggressive conflicts, as Freud speculated; to universal archetypes inherited from our ancestors, as suggested by Jung; or to social conflicts, as hypothesized by Adler, Horney, Fromm, and others. Instead, it may be reasonable to assume that each of the different factors discussed by dynamic theorists makes some contribution to adult personality. Unfortunately, finding definitive evidence for or against many of the psychodynamic hypotheses has proven difficult, as we discuss in the next section.

EVIDENCE FROM CASE STUDIES

The case studies generated by Freud and his followers provide the best known, and also the most controversial, evidence for the theory. Consider the case of Little Hans, a five-year-old boy with an irrational fear of horses. Freud used Hans's case to illustrate his theory of infantile sexuality. At age three, Hans had become fascinated with his own penis (he called it a "widdler"), and touched it frequently, which led his mother to threaten "If you do that, I shall send you to Dr. A. to cut off your widdler." Hans's interest in the topic did not abate, however, and he became fascinated with questions about which animals had widdlers, and whether his mother had one or not. Around the same time, he became hesitant to leave the house for fear that a horse would bite him. Freud emphasized several facts about this case: a) horses have noticeably large penises; b) Hans seemed to associate his father with horses; and c) Hans' had a very close attachment to his mother. Putting these pieces of information together, Freud interpreted Hans' phobia as due to *castration*

anxiety. In other words, Hans feared that his father would castrate him because of his sexual attraction towards his mother. Unable to consciously accept his resentment towards his father, he displaced his fears onto another large powerful animal with a large penis—a horse.

Psychodynamic theorists argue that cases like this demonstrate the special methodology needed to understand the complexity of human personality. Carl Jung used this argument when he said that his own ideas had:

> been tested a hundredfold in the practical treatment of the sick. . . . Naturally, these medical experiences are accessible and intelligible only to one who is professionally concerned with the treatment of psychic complications. It is therefore not the fault of the layman if certain of my statements strike him as strange. . . . I doubt, however, whether this kind of ingenuousness is a qualification for competent criticism.
>
> *(Jung, 1921)*

In other words, psychodynamic ideas only sound far-fetched to those who have not dealt with patients. Unfortunately for the theory, not every practicing clinician comes to the same conclusions after his or her own hundreds of hours of treating psychic complications. As we just discussed, Jung's interpretation of his case studies led him to emphasize universal archetypes; Adler's case interpretations led him to focus on childhood inferiority; and other analytic theorists came to different conclusions.

PROBLEMS OF THE CASE STUDY METHOD

The disagreements amongst psychodynamic theorists stem partly from a problem with the case study method upon which the psychodynamic perspective is founded. The case study does not allow control over the influences of a theorists' biases on his or her interpretations. When two behavioral psychologists considered the case of Little Hans, they found several things that Freud failed to emphasize (Wolpe and Rachman, 1960). Most importantly, Hans's fear of horses developed not when his mother threatened to castrate him, but when he had almost been crushed by a falling horse as he was walking along the street with his nurse. According to Joseph Wolpe and Stanley Rachman, the explanation of Hans' phobia is very simple—he had a classically conditioned fear of horses. Perhaps Freud's explanation about a connection between Hans fear of horses and castration is right, or perhaps Wolpe and Rachman's explanation is correct: the point is that the wealth of data in a clinical case allows any number of plausible interpretations.

The various attempts to explain van Gogh's strange, self-destructive behaviors illustrate the difficulties in interpreting case studies. Most attempts at interpretation have been stimulated by van Gogh's cutting off his left ear. After cutting off the lower half of the ear, van Gogh wrapped it up, brought it to a prostitute named Rachel, and asked her to "keep this object carefully." (Runyan, 1981).

Psychodynamic theorists have found van Gogh's bizarre self-destructive act especially interesting because it simultaneously involves sexuality and self-directed aggression. One theorist explained it in terms of Freud's interpretation of Hans's phobia, as symbolizing fear and resentment towards his father, and desire for his mother. The day before the incident, van Gogh had argued with Paul Gauguin and threatened him with a razor. Gauguin was a much more physically powerful man, and he stared firmly at van Gogh until the Dutchman dropped the razor and ran away. If we assume that Gauguin reminded van Gogh of his stern father, then by cutting off his ear van Gogh simultaneously made a symbolic attack on his father (his own "flesh and blood"), and "at the same time . . . punished himself for committing the act." Then, "in depositing his symbolic organ at the brothel he also fulfilled his wish to have his mother" (Schnier, 1950). This explanation brings together several facts in van Gogh's case, and fits with Freud's ideas that anger and sexuality can be rechanneled in various ways. Unfortunately, other authors have used the same case evidence to come to completely different conclusions. Runyan found 13 different explanations of the same case evidence, including:

> Van Gogh had unconscious homosexual impulses towards Gauguin. By cutting off his ear, he symbolically castrated himself (the Dutch word for penis is, in fact, similar to the word for ear).
>
> Van Gogh sometimes had troubling auditory hallucinations, and cut the ear off to silence them.

A more recent analysis of van Gogh's letters concludes that he cut off his ear, and eventually committed suicide, because he suffered from Meniere's Syndrome (excess fluid and pressure in the inner ear, which leads to many unpleasant symptoms including pain and dizziness). Using the volumes of material on van Gogh's life, different authors have found evidence for their favorite explanations. However, not all the explanations can be true, and the many accounts of van Gogh's self-destructive act provide clear evidence of one fact—case studies can easily be used to support many different theories. Nonetheless, case studies do provide a wealth of detail about specific individuals. Although writers differ in their emphases, van Gogh's case clearly shows a pattern of inner conflict that involved harsh anger toward his father, intense conflict over sexual matters, and agonizing self-despair. Because careful observation is the starting point in the scientific method, case studies can be quite useful in generating hypotheses for further research, but case studies need to be combined with other methods to avoid the pitfalls of interpretative bias.

PROJECTIVE TECHNIQUES AND PERSONALITY ASSESSMENT

Because they are seeking to uncover the underlying and often unconscious assumptions and processes that form one's personality, psychodynamically-oriented psychologists used *projective methods* such as the Rorschach inkblot (Figure 13.2) to try to bring unconscious motivations to light. (In Chap-

FIGURE 13.2 What do you see in this figure? A psychoanalytic assessment of personality uses ambiguous projective figures like this in an attempt to uncover hidden impulses that a person could not describe in an objective way.

ter 10 we discussed the use of projective tests to assess achievement motivation.) A psychologist interested in unconscious motives cannot use direct self-report measures. Someone's response to the question "Do you have an unconscious desire to kill your father?" would be meaningless, since no one can report on his or her unconscious motives. Tests such as the Rorschach are designed to measure unconscious motives indirectly by providing a stimulus with no content at all. The presumption is that unconscious repressed motives are always straining to be released, and will slip out in disguised form in the response to an ambiguous inkblot. Unfortunately, responses to inkblots require a good deal of interpretation, and clinical judges often disagree with one another about their meaning (Potkay and Allen, 1986). Even when clinicians agree, we may wonder whether the test results tell us anything more than we could have learned through conversation. One reviewer summarized the evidence from over 5,000 books and articles on the inkblots to conclude that they were not useful in predicting behavior (Peterson, 1978).

EVALUATION OF THE PSYCHODYNAMIC PERSPECTIVE

Despite the problems posed by projective tests and case studies, it would be an oversimplification to say that there has been no support for Freudian theory. When the theory has been tested with more stringent methods, including experiments, some support for some of the ideas has been found. For instance, Goldman-Eisler (1956) found one group of people who were pessimistic, passive, aloof and verbally aggressive *(oral pessimists)*, and another who were optimistic, nurturant, and sociable *(oral optimists)*. Exactly in line with Freud's theory, oral pessimists were more likely to have been weaned early (before five months), while oral optimists tended to have been weaned late. Though rigorous tests sometimes support the theory, psychoanalysts note that experimental methods may prejudice the case against psychoanalysis. Experiments are best suited to testing hypotheses about events that can be manipulated in a laboratory, but are not so helpful in studying unconscious motives that are rooted in early childhood conflicts. Even if one wished to do a long-term experiment, it would be ethically unthinkable to attempt to manipulate sexual and aggressive conflicts in children.

Perhaps most importantly, Freudian theory has had a important impact on many researchers who would not describe themselves as Freudians. As we discussed in the motivation chapter, and will discuss again in the chapter on social cognition, there has been a great deal of research on nonconscious influences on behavior in recent years (Erdelyi, 1985). Although many of these researchers use modern cognitive models to explain their findings, they are following a tradition of research with roots in Freudian theory. Social learning researchers have also borrowed concepts from Freud, but have changed their explanations of processes such as repression to include modern learning principles. As we will see in upcoming chapters, psychodynamic ideas continue to influence research on disordered personality.

Beyond the specific hypotheses, Freudian theory has had a number of important influences on the way we view personality today. Three of these influences are most important. Freud stressed that early childhood experiences affect later thought and behavior, and researchers are still uncovering evidence of such relationships (Franz, McClelland and Weinberger, 1991). In particular, Freud pointed out that children often have strong and primitive emotional reactions to conflicts within the family. Second, Freud emphasized how our selfish biological drives conflict with the needs of society. Third, he pointed out that adults are often unaware of the motivations underlying their own behavior. As we have seen in the last few chapters, and will see in those that follow, these issues of *socialization, gene/culture interaction,* and *unconscious motivation* are still very contemporary topics.

TRAIT APPROACHES

As we noted earlier, personality traits are behavioral characteristics that differentiate people from one another. For instance, some people are more friendly than others, some are more competitive, and still others are more trustworthy. The trait approach represents a systematic effort to describe and classify those characteristics. To a trait researcher, Freud's grand attempt to explain personality, without first developing an adequate means of describing individual differences, put the cart before the horse. In order to study a phenomenon scientifically, we first need to describe and organize it. Before Linnaeus systematically organized plants according to their physical features (mainly their stamens and pistols), botanists had no shared way to categorize the plants that they came across in the field. One botanist might describe a plant in terms of its color, another in terms of its number of flowers, and yet another in terms of its root system, or the thickness of its stem, and so on. In order for botanists to communicate with one another, and to make progress, they needed to establish a common taxonomy of plants.

ALLPORT, CATTELL, AND FACTOR ANALYSIS

Just as biologists are confronted with a vast array of features to organize, so are psychologists confronted with a seemingly overwhelming number of personality characteristics. Psychologist Gordon Allport conducted one of the first attempts to organize those traits. When he and a colleague went through the dictionary, they found 17,953 different personality descriptors in the English language (Allport and Odbert, 1936). In fact, about one out of every 22 English words is a trait term, attesting to the importance people place on describing one anothers' behavior. Imagine what would happen if each personality psychologist chose a different term from the list every time he or she did a study; one studying "passion," another researching "intemperance," still another examining "zealotry," and so on. With thousands of trait terms to choose from and no way of integrating them, we would quickly end up with an overwhelming mass of unrelated findings. In an attempt to organize the universe of trait terms, Raymond Cattell (1956) began with approximately 4,000 of Allport and Odbert's 17,953 terms (the ones that were not rare or antiquated) and narrowed the list down to 171 by removing exact synonyms (such as agile and nimble). Through the use of a statistical technique called factor analysis Cattell reduced the list still further, and examined how trait ratings are related to events in a person's life and that person's scores on various objective tests. As we noted in the intelligence chapter, factor analysis is a way of finding out which types of measurements go together. For instance, a person rated as "mature" also tends to be rated as "emotionally calm" and "persistent." Such a person also reports few "really disturbing dreams" and says that he or she would want his or her life to be "essentially the same" if it could be lived over again (Cattell, 1965). On the basis of these factor analytic studies, Cattell concluded that 16 factors were sufficient to describe personality. Those 16 factors are shown in Table 13.1. To better understand our discussion below, take a few moments to rate yourself on each of those dimensions.

THE "BIG FIVE" PERSONALITY FACTORS

Later researchers have used even more sophisticated statistics to reduce the list further. If you look at Table 13.1 you will see that some of the terms are not completely independent of one another. For instance, where you stand on the dimension "emotional/easily upset versus calm/stable" would be related to where you stand on the dimension "relaxed versus tense/driven"; and your score on "reserved/unfriendly versus outgoing/friendly" would be correlated with your score on "shy/timid versus venturesome." In recent years, researchers using advanced statistical techniques have come to some agreement that the list can be reduced even further—to five independent dimensions (Goldberg, 1981; John, 1990; Piedmont, McCrae and Costa, 1991). **Extraversion** is composed of characteristics such as talkative, sociable, and adventurous, **Agreeableness** is made up of traits such as goodnatured, cooperative, and likeable. **Conscientiousness** includes dimensions relating to responsibility, neatness, and task motivation. **Emotional Stability** incorporates calmness, poise, and composure. Finally, **Culture** includes traits such as intelligence and interest in philosophy and art. It has been suggested that each dimension applies to an important question we ask about the

TABLE 13.1 Common Terms for Cattell's 16 Personality Factors

16 PF

Emotional/easily upset	vs.	calm/stable
Intelligent	vs.	unintelligent
Reserved/unfriendly	vs.	outgoing/friendly
Assertive/dominant	vs.	not assertive/humble
sober/serious	vs.	happy-go-lucky
conscientious	vs.	expedient
shy/timid	vs.	venturesome
tender-minded	vs.	tough-minded
suspicious	vs.	trusting
practical	vs.	imaginative
shrewd	vs.	forthright
self-assured/placid	vs.	apprehensive
conservative	vs.	experimenting
group oriented	vs.	self-sufficient
undisciplined	vs.	self-disciplined
relaxed	vs.	tense/driven

people with whom we interact in everyday life (Goldberg, 1981):

Is this person active and dominant *(extraverted)* or passive and submissive?

Is this person warm and pleasant *(agreeable)* or cold and distant?

Is this person responsible *(conscientious)* or undependable?

Is this person sane *(emotionally stable)* or crazy?

Is this person smart *(cultured)* or ignorant?

Some researchers, such as Britain's Hans Eysenck (1970), argue that the taxonomy of traits can be made even simpler by arranging traits into a simple two-dimensional "circumplex." Figure 13.3 shows a circumplex of interpersonal traits (Wiggins and Broughton, 1985). A circumplex is derived from a statistical technique similar to factor analysis, but provides a simple way to display how the different trait dimensions relate to one another. For instance, the trait of ambitiousness is not related to the warm versus cold dimension—it is quite possible to be either ambitious and cold or ambitious and warm, for instance. (Follow the line from the word ambitious to the line connecting cold/quarrelsome with warm/agreeable and you will see that it lies exactly in the center of that line.) On the other hand, ambitiousness is negatively related to submissiveness—a person cannot be both at the same time. However, ambitiousness is seen as being somewhat related to gregariousness and somewhat calculating.

To give an example of how this works, consider the traits that some of our students picked as being their single most characteristic trait. The most commonly chosen word was "friendly." Two students actually picked "mean." When different students were asked to place those words into this circumplex, friendly was placed somewhere between warm/agreeable and gregarious/extraverted. Thus, friendliness is seen as being warm rather than cold, and as somewhat more dominant than submissive. The word mean was placed between cold/quarrelsome and arrogant/calculating, suggesting that meanness is seen as being cold (rather than warm) and slightly dominant (rather than submissive). Again, to get a feel for how a circumplex works pick a word that you would use to describe your own behavior, and others to describe one or two friends and relatives. Then, try to find where those words fit within the circle in Figure 13.3.

To summarize this section, personality researchers have found that underneath the seeming complexity of 17,953 trait terms, and the almost infinite number of individual behaviors described by these trait words, there is a fairly simple and organized structure. Traits can be organized into a manageable number of clusters that capture a few important questions that people commonly ask about one another.

FIGURE 13.3 A circumplex arrangement of personality traits showing the relationship of social traits to one another. Ambitious–dominant characteristics are opposite of lazy–submissive traits. However, they are independent of the cold–warm dimension. That is, it would be possible to be either ambitious *and* cold or ambitious *and* warm. Gregarious/extraverted characteristics tend to be associated with both ambitiousness and warmth, so they are placed in the upper right corner of the circumplex. Aloofness (lower left) is opposite to gregariousness. Can you place yourself within this circle?

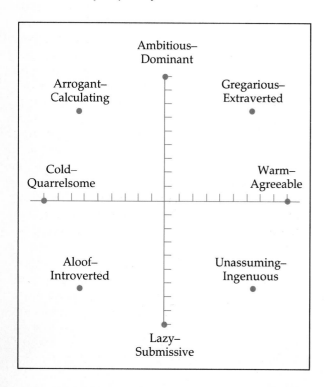

RESEARCH AND APPLICATION:
Trait Assessment and Success on the Job

Despite his artistic aptitude, Vincent van Gogh was a failure in his job as an art dealer. He was not conscientious, not particularly agreeable to his coworkers, and quite unambitious as a salesman. Even though he worked in a gallery owned by his uncle, he was eventually fired. These days, some employers use personality tests to try to avoid just this sort of a mismatch. In the area of personnel selection, personality assessment can help employers avoid hiring people whose personalities are unsuited to their job requirements, and to help potential employees avoid the unpleasantness of taking the wrong job (Hogan, 1992).

The landmark study in this area was done by the Office of Strategic Services (OSS), the precursor to the CIA that was set up during World War II (Briggs, 1991; US Office of Strategic Services, 1948). The OSS assessment staff included some of the top psychologists in the country. The staff was asked to select people for job assignments that were secret and quite varied (the jobs might involve data-gathering, interpreting, or dropping behind enemy lines). Without knowing what their specific assignments would be, the assessment staff faced the task of selecting individuals who were not only flexible, but also able to keep secrets and think quickly in the face of adversity. Because of the great potential costs of a fouled espionage mission, candidates for the OSS were extensively tested over a three-day period. In addition to written tests, the men were placed into a series of situations designed to uncover any character weaknesses. For example, during his first day of interviews the applicant was told that he was not to reveal any information about himself throughout this testing period. On the second day he was given a test of his "leadership abilities", in which he was to supervise two GIs in a simple construction project. The assistants, though, were actors, who were deliberately lazy and disagreeable. When the construction project went uncompleted, the applicant was told that he had failed the test, and was ordered to report for debriefing. In reality, this was a test to "crack" his cover and induce him to reveal information about himself before he was authorized to do so. On another occasion the applicants were subjected to a harassing and threatening interview, during which they were asked to invent and defend a false self-description in just a few minutes. After the second day of this very stressful testing, groups of applicants were given a party at which alcoholic beverages were served, but even this was really only another test of their ability to avoid self-revelations.

The OSS assessment had the advantage of an intensive and thorough battery of assessment tests. However, the staff operated under a number of important disadvantages. For one thing, the OSS staff did not know the applicant's exact roles in advance, nor were they able to study successful and unsuccessful prior agents. In many cases, though, a psychologist working on personnel

Traits and situational choice. The situations that people find themselves in are often influenced by their personality traits. Compared with an introvert, for instance, an extraverted person is more likely to choose a job as a public performer.

selection can examine the personality characteristics of those who have already been successful at a job, and can use that information for future hiring decisions. In recent years, a number of researchers have examined how trait dimensions such as the ones we just discussed can be used to predict job successes. For instance, one team of researchers examined Navy men who worked under "explorer conditions" during a six-month winter at isolated Antarctic bases. Men who were successful at this type of work were introverted and not easily bored. Sociable men who needed a great deal of stimulation did poorly (Busch, Schroeder, and Biersner, 1982). Another long-term study of Sears executives indicates that the successful executive is sociable, ambitious, and self-confident (Bentz, 1985). Other studies indicate that being adjusted, conforming, and likeable is more important than clerical skill in success as a secretary (Hogan et al., 1985).

We can see from these examples that a good personality for one job may be a handicap for another. The introversion that promotes adjustment to work in the Antarctic would only hinder an executive trainee for Sears. From his research on vocational interests, John L. Holland developed the Hexagonal Model of General Occupational

Themes, shown in Figure 13.4. Examples of typical jobs for each theme are:

> Conventional: office workers and accountants,
> Enterprising: sales and public speaking,
> Social: ministers and athletic coaches,
> Artistic: creative writers and actors,
> Investigative: scientists and mathematicians,
> Realistic: mechanical engineers and farmers.

Holland found that people in occupations adjacent to one another (for example, Conventional and Enterprising) had very similar interest patterns. People in occupations opposite to one another (for example, Conventional and Artistic), on the other hand, showed very dissimilar interests. In other words, an accountant might be interested in work in sales, but would be unlikely to be interested in work as an actor or an artist. Based on his own work using personality inventories in personnel selection, Robert Hogan (1982) has made the case that Holland's job interest hexagon is actually a form of personality circumplex. According to Hogan, two personality dimensions can be placed over the job interest hexagon, as shown in Figure 13.5.

Jobs at the bottom of the hexagon (enterprising

and social) are well-suited for extraverts, whereas those at the top (realistic and investigative) are suited for introverts. An extrovert would not do well as a laboratory scientist, but would do quite well as an athletic director, for instance. Jobs on the left (conventional) are better for people high in conscientiousness (or self-control) whereas those at the right (artistic) are more likely to be filled by impulsive, less socialized individuals. An impulsive nonconformist would not do well as a clerk in an art gallery, though he might do quite well as a painter. Perhaps if Vincent van Gogh had been given an adequate personality assessment as a teenager he could have avoided several discouraging years in his uncle's gallery.

EVALUATION OF THE TRAIT APPROACH

The trait approach is based on much more sophisticated empirical research than is the psychodynamic approach, but it is not immune from criticism. The main criticism of this approach is that the traits measured by psychological tests do not enable psychologists to make exact predictions of an individual's behavior. This criticism comes from the social learning approach to personality,

FIGURE 13.4 A circumplex of occupational categories developed by John Holland. Occupations adjacent to one another (investigative and artistic, for example) involve interests that are similar. Those across from one another (for instance, investigative and enterprising) involve little overlap in interests. Thus, someone who would be happy in a job as a scientist might also be happy as an artist or an engineer, but would be least suited for work as a corporate manager.

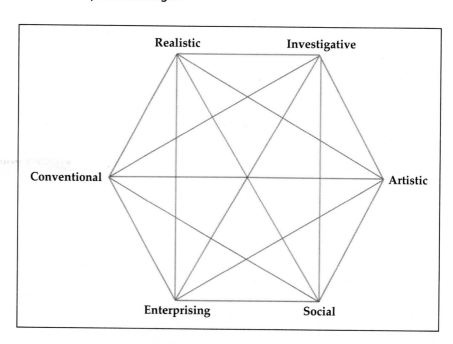

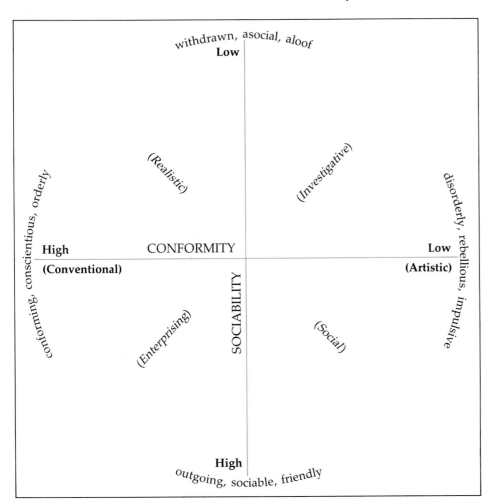

FIGURE 13.5   A scheme connecting the categories of occupational choice with the basic dimensions of personality.   Jobs at the top of the hexagon (engineer and scientist) tend to involve introverted interests; those at the bottom (sales manager and social worker) involve extraverted interests. Those at the left (accountant) involve orderliness and self-control; those at the right (artist) involve unconventionality and impulsiveness.

which traditionally favored environmental explanations of individual differences. We will return to this issue when we discuss the social learning approach, but we will say for now that the accumulating evidence suggests that both traits and environments combine to determine behavior (Kenrick and Funder, 1991).

Another criticism of the trait approach is that it loses the individual person by focusing on general traits (Carlson, 1984; Lamiell, 1981). For instance, two bright people who are interested in art, as were van Gogh and Gauguin, would be grouped together in a study of the trait called "culture." Obviously, research that considers traits one at a time will miss the unique patterning of characteristics that makes up each individual. One solution to this problem is to describe an individual's *pattern*

of scores on a number of different dimensions. This approach is best seen in several decades of research on the *Minnesota Multiphasic Personality Inventory (MMPI)* (Dahlstrom et al., 1975; Mathaway & McKinley, 1989). The MMPI was originally developed to identify people with psychological disorders, but has since been used in studies of personnel performance, college adjustment, and health risk, to name a few applications. The test includes scales to measure such troubling traits as hypochondria, depression, psychopathic deviance, and schizophrenia. Subjects rate a number of true/false questions, such as "I often feel that life is not worth living" (which would score on the Depression Scale), and "I was often in trouble in school" (which would score on the Psychopathic Deviance Scale). Rather than considering each of the subscales independently, researchers who use the MMPI consider a person's *profile* of scores. As an example, the profile in Figure 13.6 suggests someone who has low regard for conventional standards (high score on the Psychopathic Deviance Scale), who is active and impulsive (high score on the Hypomania Scale), and who is socially outgoing (low score on the Social Introversion Scale). It might characterize someone like Paul Gauguin. Vincent van Gogh would also score high on the Psychopathic Deviance Scale (because of his disregard for convention), but he would score high on the Introversion scale, and probably on the Depression and Hypochondriasis scales as well.

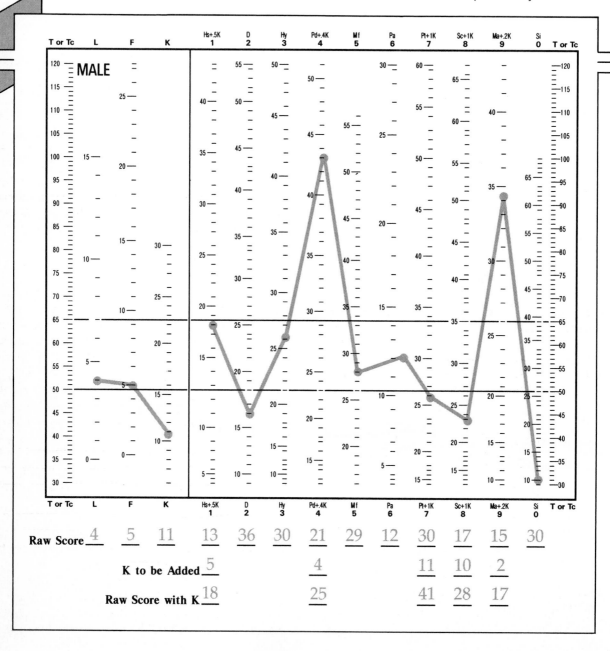

FIGURE 13.6   The *Minnesota Multiphasic Personality Inventory* (MMPI) considers how different trait dimensions are related in the same individual.   This profile suggests an individual who is low in socialization (high PD, for "psychopathic deviate"), highly energetic (high MA, for "mania"), and outgoing (low SI, for "social introversion"), as Paul Gauguin was. The test was designed for use with clinical populations, but has since been used in studies of normal personality.

By examining profiles rather than single group scales, researchers can develop a more accurate picture of the complete individual.

A final criticism of the trait approach is that it has been largely atheoretical. In developing the MMPI, for instance, researchers included a very large number of test questions, and used statistical techniques to determine which ones distinguished various clinical groups. In general, trait researchers have tended to focus on the development of reliable and valid personality tests, without developing an adequate theory to explain the traits they measure. As we noted in the first chapter, theory is useful in helping us understand the results of research, and in suggesting which research questions should be asked next. On the other hand, it may be useful to think of trait researchers as concerned with accurate description, the essential first step in any science. Questions about what traits mean and where they come from can be dealt with by other perspectives. The trait approach is ultimately based in taxonomic research in natural history, similar to the taxonomies of plants and animals that provided the foundation for evolutionary theory. Given the background, it is not surprising that a number of studies have examined traits from the biological perspective, to which we now turn.

BIOLOGICAL APPROACHES TO PERSONALITY

Where do psychological traits come from? Biological approaches assume that behavioral traits are rooted in anatomy and physiology. Nervous people might be that way because they naturally produce more hormones such as adrenaline, or because their nervous systems are constructed to be especially responsive to environmental threats, for instance. There are three different levels of analysis that biological theorists work on. Some biological theorists search directly for physiological differences between people with different behavioral traits. Sheldon's work with physique and temperament was one example of that type of work. Other biological theorists go a step deeper, and look for evidence of genetic inheritance for different traits. Like the researchers who examined family inheritance and intelligence (discussed in Chapter 9), these researchers examine family inheritance patterns for such traits as friendliness, shyness, or nervousness. Finally, some biological theorists go even further back, considering the possible evolutionary roots of individual differences in behavior. Below, we consider research that takes each of these approaches.

EVOLUTIONARY ROOTS OF INDIVIDUAL DIFFERENCES

Why do we care so much about whether the people around us are dominant, pleasant, responsible, sane, or smart? According to some theorists, it is because these are the very dimensions that made the difference to our ancestors' survival. Consider several features of human history. Human beings have always lived in groups. Until very recently, in evolutionary terms, our ancestors lived in small bands of 25–50 individuals who knew one another well. The members of those groups hunted and foraged together, and depended upon one another to survive. Every human group is organized in terms of a status hierarchy. Because of intense competition between and within human groups, it served our ancestors well to live in groups with organized dominance hierarchies and decisive leaders. In order to control competition within the group, it was also useful to carefully note and remember where everyone else stood in the dominance hierarchy (Baer and McEachron, 1982; Lancaster, 1975). Finally, evolutionary theorists argue that our ancestors survived by being aware of each other's characteristics, so that the labor within the group could be divided efficiently (Hogan, 1982). Domineering and aggressive group members made good warriors, while agreeable and nonhostile members made good childcare specialists.

CROSS-CULTURAL EVIDENCE

If this evolutionary reasoning is correct, all human groups everywhere should have similar ideas about personality since everyone's ancestors evolved under similar social conditions, and faced the same problems of living in social groups. Geoffrey White (1980) found evidence for just such a universal conception of personality. White studied the words used to describe people in three different language groups in India and the South Pacific. When he statistically analyzed the relationships among trait words, he found that the different trait words from each language could be nicely arranged into a two-dimensional circumplex (see Figure 13.7).

White noted that the two main dimensions of dominance/submission and solidarity/conflict are the same as those found in research done with Americans and Europeans. If you compare this circumplex with the one used by Wiggins and Broughton (look back to Figure 13.3), you will see that what is called "ambitious/dominant versus lazy/submissive" there is identical to what is called "dominance versus submission" in Figure 13.7,

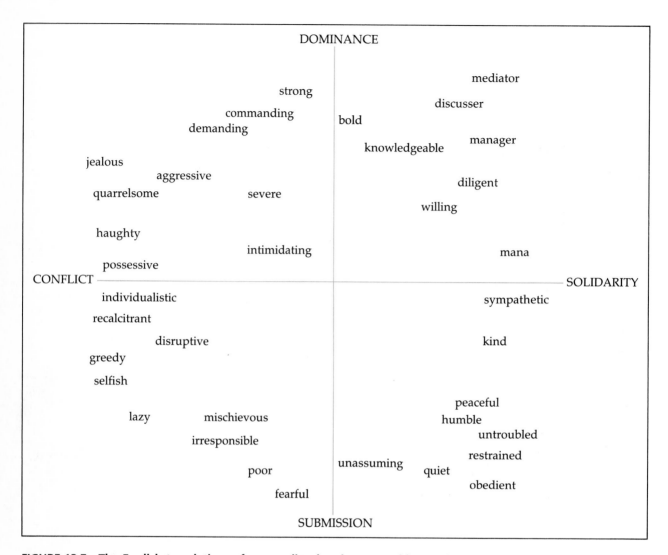

FIGURE 13.7   The English translations of personality descriptors used by a Polyne-sian tribe.   Geoffrey White found that personality traits used around the world fit into a circumplex similar to the one in Figure 13.3.

and what is called "cold/quarrelsome versus warm/agreeable" there can be comfortably replaced with what is called "conflict vs. solidarity" here. In short, it appears that humans the world over think about one another's personality in essentially the same terms.

HEREDITY AND PHYSIOLOGY OF PERSONALITY TRAITS

A critical assumption of the evolutionary argument is that personality traits are heritable. Although we are still uncertain about the exact pathways by which genes influence personality, one thing seems quite clear from recent research—personality traits do have a substantial heritable component. That is, the extent to which you are arrogant or unassuming, dominant or submissive,

friendly or shy, is due in part to characteristics you inherited from your parents.

DYSFUNCTION: Shyness

In 1896, a physician named Harry Campbell gave a report on "morbid shyness" to the British Medical Society:

> His soul is full of longing, but the world knows it not; the iron mask of shyness is riveted before his face, and the man beneath is never seen. Genial words and greetings are ever rising to his lips, but they die away in unheard whispers before the steel clamps.

(Campbell, 1896)

Since Campbell's time, there has been a great deal of research on shyness (Jones, Cheek, and Briggs, 1986). As you may have noted already, all of the personality schemes that we have discussed (whether based on several factors or on a circumplex) include a dimension such as extraversion versus introversion or outgoing versus aloof. Shyness, although not synonymous with what we have been calling introversion or aloofness, is closely related to them (Briggs, Cheek, and Jones, 1986).

Developmental psychologists Jerome Kagan and J. Steven Reznick (1986) believe that the roots of adult shyness are partly genetic. For one thing, shyness can often be seen in the preschool years. They found that very young children (less than two years old) showed two patterns of reaction to an unfamiliar person. Some of them, who were called "inhibited," greeted a stranger by staring, becoming quiet, and retreating to their waiting mothers. Others, called "uninhibited," either showed no response to the stranger or actually approached the new person. Parents of the inhibited children described them as being generally watchful, shy, and timid; while parents of the uninhibited children used such words as outgoing, bold, or fearless. When these same children were confronted with another stranger several years later, they tended to show similar reactions. As older children, inhibited kids avoided danger and social situations. As adults, those who had been inhibited as children reported more social anxiety, and were more dependent on their spouses.

Kagan and his colleagues also found physiological correlates of social inhibition in children (Kagan et al., 1988). When confronted with a stranger, for instance, inhibited children showed physiological signs of heightened attention—their pupils became dilated and their heartrates became higher and less variable. According to their parents, inhibited children also demonstrated relatively more stress symptoms, including chronic constipation, allergies, and frequent nightmares.

Why would shyness show up very early in life and be related to physiology? Kagan and Reznick (1986) interpret their findings from a biological perspective. They reason that some people inherit a particular *temperament* that predisposes them to be shy. As we discussed in the chapter on early development, social reticence is a common characteristic of infants' temperaments. Some infants are slow to warm up to others, and they grow into relatively shy children (Thomas and Chess, 1977).

Shyness is not independent of other behaviors. For extremely shy individuals, shyness can be part

Shyness and temperament. Research indicates that socially inhibited children are more likely to grow up to be shy adolescents and adults. There is some evidence that shyness is related to genetic inheritance.

of a troubling pattern of social characteristics. For instance, Harrison Gough and Avril Thorne (1986) found that shy people often gave bad first impressions. Strangers rated them as weak, frail, worrying, and in many cases, intellectually incompetent. Actually, SAT scores show that shy people are as intellectually competent as anyone else. Perhaps people incorrectly interpret a shy person's reluctance to speak out as evidence that he or she has nothing intelligent to say. Not surprisingly, shy people say that they are fearful of social interactions, more self-conscious, and more lonely than nonshy people (Jones, et al., 1986). In addition, they report more suspicions and resentments of other people, and they indicate more depression and anxiety (Briggs, Cheek, and Jones, 1986; Jones, Cheek, and Briggs, 1986). Despite their problems in relating to others, it is important to note that shy people are not particularly disturbed. In fact, approximately 40 percent of university students report some degree of shyness (Zimbardo, 1986). ■

TEMPERAMENT AND PHYSIOLOGY

We have just discussed findings suggesting that shyness is partly rooted in a genetically based temperament. Other researchers have argued that adult personality can be traced, in large part, to three temperamental differences that show up in early childhood: *emotionality, activity,* and *sociability* (Buss and Plomin, 1975). Emotionality refers to the fact that some children become upset easily, while others are more calm. Activity refers simply to children's activity levels: Some children are physically active, while others jump about much less. Sociability refers to the differences that Kagan studied—some children are shy around strangers, some are not.

At the adult level, temperamental differences in emotionality and sociability seem to show up in the two major factors that British psychologist Hans Eysenck calls extraversion and neuroticism. Consistent with the biological approach, there do seem to be physiological differences that relate to extraversion and neuroticism (Eysenck, 1970, 1981). It appears that extraverts may seek adventure and social interaction to increase their chronically low arousal levels. Introverts, on the other hand, seem to be overaroused; grand adventures and boisterous parties only raise their arousal to unpleasant levels. Eysenck has produced some evidence that neuroticism (or poor adjustment) is related to differences in autonomic arousal (the "fight or flight" response discussed in Chapter 10). People who have generally high levels of autonomic arousal tend to be nervous (or "neurotic" in Eysenck's terminology). Their high level of autonomic arousal makes them especially sensitive to punishment.

FAMILY AND TWIN STUDIES OF PERSONALITY

If traits are inherited, then we ought to find that they run in families. Biographers often note dramatic similarities between members of the same family. William James's father, sister, and brothers all showed characteristics of the same depression and anxiety that plagued him throughout his life (Allen, 1967). Of Paul Gauguin's personality, one biography notes: "On his mother's side, Gauguin sprang from a family with hot blood in its veins and an exotic background, to which he owed his fierce pride, independent spirit, and temperamental violence" (Wildenstein and Cogniat, 1972).

Although family similarity is necessary to establish genetic inheritance, it is not by itself sufficient. In order to be sure that a trait is heritable, it is necessary to use more rigorous behavior genetic methods (Plomin and Daniels, 1987; Rowe, 1991). We must show a correlation in shyness between biological relatives, and we must show that the relationship cannot be explained as due to a shared environment, since family members usually share both genes and environment. One method is to compare identical and fraternal twins. If identical twins are not more like one another than fraternal twins are, that would argue against the genetic

theory. Another approach is to compare adopted children with their biological and adopted relatives. If adopted children resemble their adoptive rather than their biological parents, that would also argue against the genetic theory.

Evidence from studies of identical twins indicates that these twins have very similar personalities (Bouchard and McGue, 1990). Esther Pauline Friedman and her sister Pauline Esther Freidman were identical twins who not only acted alike but also got married at the same time and even took very similar jobs as adults. We know Esther as Ann Landers and Pauline as Abigail Van Buren ("Dear Abby"). Since "Ann" and "Abby" were raised together, perhaps their similarities can be explained as being due to common environmental pressures. However, common environmental pressures cannot explain the remarkable similarities found between identical twins raised apart.

Jerry Levey and Mark Newman, the two twins shown in Figure 13.8, were separated at birth and raised without any awareness of each other's existence. Nevertheless, they both grew up to become firemen, and dressed and acted so similarly that another fireman at a convention mistook Jerry for Mark. Even though they had never met, each of them had the same mustache, the same sideburns, and the same aviator glasses. Their favorite pastimes were the same—hunting, fishing, watching old John Wayne movies and professional wrest-

FIGURE 13.8 Two identical twins raised apart, but nevertheless developed very similar personalities. Both took jobs as firemen, made the same kind of jokes, and had similar avocational interests and preferences. Twin studies support the importance of heredity in personality.

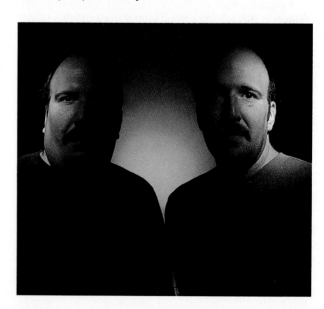

ling, and eating Chinese food after a night on the town. Both drank the same brand of beer and held the bottle in a peculiar manner, with a pinkie stretched underneath. "Both were bachelors, compulsive flirts, both raucously good-humored" (Rosen, 1987). As Jerry noted "We kept making the same remarks at the same time and using the same gestures. . . . It was spooky." Although some of these similarities could be due to coincidence, the twins' scores on personality tests coincided at a level well beyond chance. Returning to the trait of shyness, twin and adoptee studies suggest that it has a substantial genetic component (Plomin and Daniels, 1986). Similarly, research on a wide range of personality traits reliably shows an important role for heredity (Plomin, 1986; Rowe, 1991).

EVALUATION OF THE BIOLOGICAL PERSPECTIVE

Two decades ago, many psychologists would have dismissed the biological perspective on personality. In recent years, however, research arising from the biological perspective has led to a number of fascinating advances (Buss, 1990; Rowe, 1991). Research on twins raised in separate homes and adoptees raised in the same home has established that genetic differences can explain about half of the normal differences between people (Plomin and Daniels, 1987). That research has also produced another fascinating finding—that simply being raised in the same home environment does not seem to make people similar to one another (Rowe, 1991; Loehlin, 1987). If you and your brother are both outgoing, for instance, it is more likely due to the genes you share than to the way your parents treated the two of you. Although the behavior genetics methods can give us an idea about how much of normal personality is determined by genes and by common family environments, those methods do have their limitations. For one thing, family and twin studies do not tell us how genes operate to make relatives similar, nor can they tell us how genetic predispositions interact with the environment. For instance, what is the genetic tendency that causes some twins to be friendlier than others? Is it an abundance of hormones like the pain-killing endorphins that put them in a generally easygoing mood? Is it a lower level of hormones that leads some people to be anxious around others? Or is simply a tendency to smile more frequently at an early age, which in turn leads others in the social environment to respond in a friendlier way? Research from other perspectives is needed to understand the social environment, and how it interacts with biological tendencies.

Research on the relationships between hormones and personality aims to address some of the questions about how biological tendencies operate on a day-to-day basis (for example, Stelmack, 1990; Zuckerman, 1990). However, that research is still in its infancy, and we understand very little about the link between psychophysiology and behavior that is friendly or intellectual. Even when we do find links between personality and physiological differences between individuals, it is not always clear whether the physiological difference is causal (Davidson, 1991). For instance, if a researcher found that friendlier people did have higher levels of pain-killing endorphins, it would not be clear whether those chemicals were the cause of the person's friendliness, or whether they were the result of leading a sociable lifestyle.

Research from the evolutionary perspective is also leading to a number of interesting new findings (Buss, 1990; Gangestad and Simpson, 1990; Kenrick, Sadalla, Groth, and Trost, 1990). The evolutionary perspective helps us understand why certain aspects of personality are found throughout the world (White, 1980), and it links up with the findings from anthropology and biology to help understand human nature and the differences between us. However, it is important to keep in mind that evolutionary hypotheses only give us a long-distance view of human behavior. Although they suggest that genes inherited from our ancestors may influence our behavior in certain ways, evolutionary findings do not specify exactly how those genes act to influence behavior in a given individual. To address those questions, biological theorists need to zoom in their focus to the closer genetic and physiological perspectives. But genes and physiology only tell a part of the story—the fact that there are differences between genetically identical twins tells us that environmental factors are also important. The behavioral and social learning perspectives, which are the topic of the next section, focus on just such environmental factors.

BEHAVIORAL AND SOCIAL LEARNING PERSPECTIVES ON PERSONALITY

Something happens after birth to make even identical twins different. The behavioral viewpoint focuses on the environmental pressures that shape behavior after birth (Bandura, 1977; Dollard and Miller, 1950). Those who adopt this perspective use classical conditioning, operant conditioning, and modelling to explain how personality is learned. Classical conditioning could lead to "shy" behaviors if a child had unpleasant encounters with new children. After being punched in the nose by a strange boy on the first day of kindergarten and being ridiculed by a group of children in his new neighborhood, a youngster might generalize anxiety to later encounters with strangers. Once the child had conditioned fear to strangers, operant conditioning could maintain an avoidance of social situations. On future occasions, he might learn that the anxiety of meeting strangers goes away if he shies away from them and does not offer himself up for potential bludgeoning or ridicule. As we noted, behaviorists Wolpe and Rachman (1960) explained Little Hans's phobia of horses as a case of conditioned fear. However, Albert Bandura (1977) has argued that complex patterns of behavior are not usually learned by direct reinforcement, but by vicariously observing the rewards and punishments received by others. As we discussed in an earlier chapter, a child watching a movie such as "Jaws" could develop a phobic fear of sharks without ever having seen an actual shark, much less having been attacked by one. By the same principle of vicarious learning, a movie about a demented horse who stomps innocent little children might produce a generation of Little Hanses. In this case, the children would have learned to fear horses through modelling rather than classical conditioning.

SOCIAL LEARNING THEORIES

As we noted in Chapter 1, a strict behaviorist perspective would reject internal explanations of such behaviors as traits and cognitive processes because they are not directly observable. Modern learning theories of personality have adopted a cognitive learning perspective rather than one that is solely based on behavior. These approaches followed from the work of John Dollard and Neal Miller (1950), who applied the learning model to such unobservable processes as repression (which they explained in terms of simple avoidance conditioning). Instead of learning to avoid an unpleasant external stimulus (a horse), repression involves learning to avoid an unpleasant internal stimulus (thoughts about horses). To demonstrate this process, one team of researchers taught a group of undergraduates to associate a nonsense syllable (for example, "yov" or "gex") with an English word (perhaps "soldier" or "memory"). Afterwards, they gave the students electric shocks while exposing them to distant associates of some of the English words ("navy" for soldier, and "brain" for memory). When later asked to remember the original nonsense syllables, the students made mistakes on only 6.3 percent of the words that did not have an unpleasant association with shock. On the other hand, the students made mistakes 29.2 percent of the time on the words associated with shock. This supports the view that repression involves learning to avoid thoughts associated with unpleasant events (Glucksberg and King, 1967). According to this cognitive learning viewpoint, adults differ from one another in their degree of defensiveness because some people have learned to avoid thinking about certain topics.

The social learning approach to personality is best exemplified in the work on **locus of control,** a scale that measures individual differences in beliefs about whether we can control the rewards and punishments we receive. The scale was based on the premise that behavior is determined not so much by actual environmental contingencies, but by our *expectancies* and *beliefs* about those contingencies (Rotter, 1972). The scale divides people into *internals,* who believe that they have control over rewards in their lives, and *externals,* who believe that chance, luck, and other powerful people determine events in their lives (Table 13.2).

A large number of studies have found that internals are more likely to try to control what happens to them in experiments, college classes, their personal relationships, and so on (Phares, 1976). Externals are generally willing to leave things to fate. Researchers in the area have often assumed that an internal orientation is the better of the two, but that may not be true for people who really do have little chance of controlling their lives. For college students, it is no doubt better to work hard on schoolwork than to leave grades to fate (which is usually unkind under those circumstances). Likewise, it pays for people in positions of responsibility to take charge of events in their lives. However, what happens when people really do not have control? In laboratory studies, internals become extremely frustrated by situations in which rewards and punishments are not under their control, while externals just go with the flow (Gregory, Chartier, and Wright, 1979). In the real world, older people in institutions sometimes suffer more when they have an internal orientation. For someone living in the regimented climate of many medical settings (including some homes for the elderly) it may sometimes be less frustrating to simply accept helplessness and passively allow the

TABLE 13.2 A Scale to Measure Locus of Control

Make a choice for each item. In some cases, you will find that you believe both statements or neither one. Please make a decision anyway.

1. a. I often find myself saying something to the effect of "What will be will be."
   b. I believe that what happens to me is my own doing.

2. a. I deserve credit for most of my accomplishments.
   b. I've been fortunate to have done well on a number of occasions.

3. a. I'm a pretty confident person. I can make things happen.
   b. Sometimes I'm amazed at how things seem to happen to me all by themselves.

4. a. I feel like a Ping-Pong ball. Life just bounces me back and forth between happy and sad.
   b. If I want to be happy, I just choose a fun thing to do and go to it.

5. a. You get what you deserve and deserve what you get.
   b. I don't feel guilty about the good things that happen to me or moan about the bad things. It could just as well have happened to someone else.

6. a. I plan things, and they turn out as I expect.
   b. "Come what may," that's my motto. I'm a tumbleweed, caught in the wind.

7. a. I enter many lotteries, drawings, and things like that. I keep hoping I'll strike it rich.
   b. I steer clear of everything from bingo to poker. The odds are too long.

8. a. In this country, anyone with some talent and some sweat is going to make it.
   b. If you're lucky, you're rich; if not, join the crowd.

9. a. Some people wander around under a black cloud, while the sun shines on others.
   b. Let's face it, some people have ability and use it; some have it and waste it; and some just don't have it.

10. a. Life is a great glob of complexity. It would take an Einstein to win at it.
    b. It's really quite simple: if you're good and work hard, you succeed.

11. a. Sometimes I feel powerful, able to do whatever I want.
    b. Sometimes I feel powerless, the victim of mysterious forces.

12. a. We are likely to be swept up in the ebb and flow of events.
    b. If we can get to the moon, we can change the course of mighty rivers and make the weather do our bidding.

Give yourself a point if you chose each of the following alternatives: 1.a.; 2.b.; 3.b.; 4.a.; 5.b.; 6.b.; 7.a.; 8.b.; 9.a.; 10.a.; 11.b.; 12.a. The higher the score, the more external you are.

Based on C. R. Potkay and B. P. Allen (1986).

nursing staff to make the decisions (Felton and Kahana, 1974; Hanusa and Schulz, 1977).

Social learning theories have been particularly influential in research on the development and treatment of pathological personality traits (Bandura, 1977; Mischel, 1979, among others). This research examines how symptoms such as depression involve expectancies about one's ability to control the environment (Beck, 1982; Bandura, 1986). We will discuss this approach further in the upcoming chapters on disorder and treatment.

THE PERSON/SITUATION CONTROVERSY

At one time, some behaviorists felt that environmental influences were so important that it was unnecessary to even discuss internal traits. B. F. Skinner (1953) argued against such internal causal explanations of behavior. Instead, Skinner advo-

Locus of Control a scale that measures individual differences in beliefs about whether we can control the rewards and punishment we recieve

ing Skinner, some behavioral psychologists ("situationists") questioned whether an inner personality even exists, making statements such as,

"I, for one, look forward to the day when personality theories will be regarded as historical curiosities" (Farber, 1964). William James actually anticipated this position in 1890, when he suggested that we all tailor our performances to the demands of the social situation:

> Many a youth who is demure enough before his parents and teachers, swears and swaggers like a pirate among his "tough" young friends. We do not show ourselves to our children as to our club-companions, to our customers as to the laborers we employ, to our masters and employers as to our intimate friends.
>
> (James, 1890)

If the situationist perspective were correct, there would really be no point in talking about personality at all, since an individual's "personality" is no more than the sum of the environmental pressures in his or her life. However, the argument that there is no such thing as personality seems to go against our intuitions. If you think about your friends, relatives, and acquaintances, it seems quite clear that some of them are more friendly, some are more intellectual, and some are more dependable, situational pressures notwithstanding. However, situationists have suggested several reasons why our intuitions about the differences among the people we know may be mistaken.

PERSONALITY MAY BE IN THE EYE OF THE BEHOLDER

Perhaps personality traits are illusions, but we continue to believe in them for the same reasons that some people continue to believe in black magic and psychic abilities. That is, cognitive errors may lead us to remember facts in a biased and distorted fashion (Fiske and Taylor, 1991; Ross and Nisbett, 1991, among others). For example, we may form a first impression based on only a smattering of information ("The new girl must be snobbish, she's from Beverly Hills.") and then compound the error by seeking and remembering only information that confirms our initial erroneous judgment (Snyder, 1984). You may ask others whether they have noticed anything snobbish in the new girl's behavior instead of asking whether they've noticed anything friendly about her, which would lead you to hear evidence against your mistaken first impression.

In support of the hypothesis that personality traits are in the eye of the beholder, some studies showed that clinical psychologists using psychological tests could reach very little agreement about

which patients were anxious, depressed, aggressive, and so on (Goldberg and Werts, 1966). Each clinician's eye seemed to behold a different person. However, clinical judges in those studies were usually given access only to very limited information about a person (Kenrick and Dantchik, 1983). Just because a psychologist cannot reliably determine personality from a stranger's inkblot responses does not mean that a woman's husband cannot judge the personality of the wife with whom he has lived for ten years. To adequately test the notion that personality traits are in the eye of the beholder it is necessary to give personality traits a fair test. One way to do this is to examine ratings made by people who know the target person well. If friends and relatives who have observed you in everyday life cannot agree about what you are like, that evidence would be damning to the idea of personality traits.

To this end, a number of studies have had adults describe their own personalities, and then compared their self-ratings with those made by relatives and friends of the subjects. At the same time, the student is rated by friends, roommates, or parents. To familiarize yourself with this type of research, it is helpful to first rate yourself on the dimensions used in one such study (Table 13.3).

Jonathan Cheek (1982) asked fraternity men at Johns Hopkins University to rate themselves and one another on these same dimensions. When ratings like these are correlated with one another, the results virtually always show agreement between raters that is better than chance (Kenrick and Funder, 1988), and Cheek's study was no exception. Fraternity members agreed substantially about which of them was relatively more adventurous, more cooperative, or more talkative. If the ratings are made on reliable scales, by judges who know one another well, the correlation is usually above .50, which indicates a substantial level of agreement (McCrae, 1982, for example). Perfect agreement would produce a correlation of 1.0, so the .50 correlation does suggest that there is some error in our judgments, and that some of what we see in others is in our eyes only. However, there is enough agreement to rule out the radical idea that personality is *only* in the eye of the beholder (Kenny and LaVoie, 1984).

PERSONALITY TRAITS AND SOCIAL STEREOTYPES

Agreement between observers does not put an end to the person/environment controversy. When your dormitory mates agree that you are friendly they are not necessarily basing their judgments on

TABLE 13.3 Personality Self-Rating

Rate yourself on these dimensions, and ask a roommate, friend, or relative to rate you on the same dimensions. Be sure not to discuss the dimensions with the person you choose. Just hand over the scale and then leave the room until it is done:

Rating of ....

Extraversion:

Talkative	1	2	3	4	5	6	7	Silent
Sociable	1	2	3	4	5	6	7	Reclusive
Adventurous	1	2	3	4	5	6	7	Cautious

Agreeableness:

Goodnatured	1	2	3	4	5	6	7	Irritable
Mild/gentle	1	2	3	4	5	6	7	Headstrong
Cooperative	1	2	3	4	5	6	7	Negativistic

Conscientious-ness:

Responsible	1	2	3	4	5	6	7	Undepend-able
Neat/tidy	1	2	3	4	5	6	7	Careless
Persevering	1	2	3	4	5	6	7	Quitting/fickle

Emotional Stability:

Calm	1	2	3	4	5	6	7	Anxious
Poised/relaxed	1	2	3	4	5	6	7	Tense/nervous
Composed	1	2	3	4	5	6	7	Excitable

Based on Cheek (1982).

your *behaviors*. People can agree with one another about who has which traits and still be wrong. During the Middle Ages, people often agreed that a particular woman in town was a witch, but with hindsight we would now say that they were wrong, despite their consensus. Are we joining in a mutual delusion when we agree about which neighbor is aggressive and which is friendly? Perhaps we all hold similar stereotypes about people who look a certain way or belong to a certain group. We see that one fellow is a muscular athlete, and automatically assume that he is competitive and unintellectual. We see that his cousin is bespectacled and speaks with a highbrow accent, and automatically assume that she is an intellectual. If we were to observe their behavior, however, we might find that the athlete is actually more intellectual than his bespectacled cousin.

Perfect strangers do agree about a person they have met for only a minute or two (Funder and Colvin, 1988; Passini and Norman, 1966). Why? Perhaps strangers can agree because some parts of personality are expressed quickly—in a ready smile, or a ever-present smirk, but a few minutes provides only the chance to categorize the person based on obvious physical cues. Generally, a person in a general's uniform will be more conservative than someone wearing a Greenpeace T-shirt. (Stereotypes are not necessarily wrong.) Given time, however, we do move beyond our stereotyped judgments of strangers. People who have known someone for several months or years reach better agreement about that individual's personality than strangers can, suggesting that they have been observing his or her behavior and have been modifying their impressions during the relationship (Funder and Colvin, 1988).

Further evidence for the validity of trait judgments comes from findings that show that we agree more about personality dimensions that involve publically observable behaviors. Cheek (1982) found that fraternity members agreed more about who was talkative and sociable (extraverted) than about who was calm and composed (emotionally stable). Other researchers have found similar results (Funder and Dobroth, 1987; Kenrick and Stringfield, 1980; McCrae, 1982; Norman and Goldberg, 1966, among others). Why can people agree about who is extraverted better than they can agree about who is emotional? It seems to be because it is easier to observe extraverted behaviors than it is to observe emotionality. You cannot be secretly talkative, but you can be secretly emotionally aroused (Kenrick and Stringfield, 1980). Researchers consistently find more agreement about traits that people say are *publically observable* (Amelang and Borkenau, 1986; Cheek, 1982; Funder and Dobroth, 1987; Zuckerman et al., 1989).

EVALUATION OF THE BEHAVIORAL PERSPECTIVE: LESSONS OF THE PERSON/SITUATION DEBATE

In provoking the controversy about the relative importance of persons and situations, the behavioral perspective has taught us some valuable lessons. Personality traits do seem to have some basis in actual behaviors. We can agree about who has which traits, and that agreement is higher when we have had time to observe the person's actual behaviors. The agreement does not seem to be based simply on what the person says about him or herself (Amabile and Kabat, 1982), and it is higher on dimensions that are observable to others. All of these findings suggest that personality judgments are based in behaviors, and not in our

Publicly observable traits. From just looking at the women in this picture, it is reasonably easy to infer that they are friendly. On the other hand, it is less easy to tell whether or not any of them is anxious. People generally agree more about publicly observable traits, such as friendliness or neatness, than about unobservable characteristics, such as anxiety or introspectiveness.

minds. Did the research on the person/situation debate simply confirm that our intuitions about personality traits were right all along, then? Not at all. The research has shown that our intuitions are susceptible to various biases, and that our own personal biases and stereotypes may lead us to exaggerate the importance of personality traits. (We will discuss some of these biases in a later chapter on social cognition.) The debate also showed us that even well-trained psychologists will do a poor job of personality assessment if they base their judgments on a short interview (Epstein, 1980; Moskowitz, 1982). Small samples of behavior are too unreliable to capture the personality traits that our teachers, friends, or relatives can detect over weeks, months, and years of close contact with us.

Perhaps the most important lesson of the person/situation debate is the realization that personality and situations do not act independently of one another. Think back to the way that you rated yourself on the adventurous–cautious dimension in Table 13.3. If you rated yourself as a 2 (somewhat adventurous), you probably did not mean that you were constantly seeking adventure, even while taking a math exam or driving your grandmother to the grocery store. You probably meant that certain circumstances (a chance to go skiing, perhaps, or to drive to Mexico over spring break)

are likely to lead to adventurous rather than cautious behavior on your part. Some situationists defined traits in a very limited way, as patterns of behavior that are "constant across different situations" (Argyle and Little, 1972). However, trait psychologists themselves view traits as tendencies to respond to certain situations in certain ways (Allport, 1966). Allport used a nonpsychological trait to make his point—people differ in the tendency to perspire, but those differences do not show up except when it is hot. Psychologists have realized that it was a mistake to assume that behavior was *either* caused by external situations *or* by internal traits (Bem and Funder, 1978; Endler and Magnusson, 1976). In recent years, researchers have turned their attention to understanding more about how traits and situations *interact* with one another.

PERSON/SITUATION INTERACTIONS

What does it mean to say that traits and situations interact with one another? At the simplest level, it means that *traits are more easily expressed in some situations than in others*. For instance, Richard Price and Dennis Bouffard (1974) found that situations could be divided into low or high in "behavioral constraint". These researchers asked students which everyday behaviors—eating or laughing, for

TABLE 13.4 Situations Arranged from High to Low Behavioral Constraint

	Situation
Most Constrained (People unlikely to show much variation in behavior)	Religious Services
	Job Interview
	Elevator
	Family Dinner
	Class
	Movies
	Restroom
	Sidewalk
	Bus
	Date
	Bar
	Football Game
Least Constrained (People likely to show variations in behavior)	Dorm Lounge
	Park
	Own Room

From Price and Bouffard (1974).

example—they would perform in which everyday settings (Table 13.4).

In some settings—a park or a dorm room—people performed a wide range of behaviors; whereas in others—a church or a job interview—people were constrained to a narrow range of behaviors. To put it another way, we are inhibited from expressing ourselves in such situations as a job interview. (Though you might be generally adventurous, you would be unlikely to invite the interviewer to take the rest of the afternoon off and join you on a sky-diving trip.)

Even in unconstrained situations, however, traits do not always show up. Instead, *a trait will only show up in a situation where it is relevant* (Kenrick, McCreath, Govern, King, and Bordin, 1990). Anxiety only shows up in situations that are threatening, for example, and adventurousness only shows up in situations that involve a choice between excitement and safety. Some types of situations bring out the same behaviors in almost everyone. Few people get anxious at the sight of mittens, but growling sounds in a dark campground make most of us a bit nervous. To some extent, however, people differ in which situations are relevant to their traits. Some people begin to sweat at the thought of speaking in front of others, but do not raise an eyebrow at the thought of flying on an airplane (Endler, Hunt, and Rosenstein, 1962; Kendall, 1978).

Neither our traits nor the situations in our lives are constant—they influence one another. Our traits can change situations we enter (Caspi, Bem and Elder, 1989). For instance, one researcher found that aggressive children could transform a peaceful playground into a near brawl within a few minutes after they came on the scene (Rausch, 1977). Likewise, *situations can change traits;* several months in Marine boot camp would probably make anyone more aggressive and self-disciplined. In addition, our *traits influence the settings we choose to enter* (Caspi and Herbener, 1990; Snyder and Ickes, 1985). As an example, Paul Gauguin did not accidentally end up living his last years in Samoa; he was actively seeking a setting to fit his character. A biography suggests that Gauguin's numerous flights from society:

> . . . asserted his need for independence, his need to break away from the bourgeois social order and return to a world of primitive simplicity and elemental truths where an artist's personality could develop freely and find the form of expression best suited to it.

(Wildenstein and Cogniat, 1971)

In sum, personality traits do exist. People show behavioral consistencies across different situations, and across decades of their lives (Conley, 1985; Costa and McCrae, 1988; West and Graziano, 1989). However, it requires careful attention to separate the effects of traits from the effects of situations. Traits show themselves only in particular situations—those that are relevant and not too highly constraining. You may be very outgoing, but not show it during a calculus examination. Finally, traits and situations are not always separable. Traits influence the situations in our lives, by affecting our choice of life settings and other people's responses to us.

PHENOMENOLOGICAL AND COGNITIVE PERSPECTIVES ON PERSONALITY

Biological theories hold that the differences between us originate in genes that were shaped in the evolutionary past. Learning theories downplay the evolutionary past, and explain our differences in terms of our personal learning histories. Phenomenological theories focus more on the present, on the ways that we perceive and interpret what is going on right now, as well as our expectancies about what is likely to happen in the future. Phenomenological theorists hold that the differences between us are a simple function of our different beliefs. Change our beliefs and our behavior would change. One of the most historically important phenomenological perspectives was George Kelly's model of each person as a scientist (Kelly, 1955). Kelly believed that each of us develops theories about the world and then acts on those theories to see how well they work. He believed that these theories, which he called **personal constructs,** were the basis of our personalities. If you believe that people generally try to exploit one another, you may act dominant and aggressive towards others. If you believe that people are generally kind and giving, you will act friendly towards them. As we noted in Chapter 1, the phenomenological perspective has been closely tied to the humanistic approach, which focuses on people's potential to reconstruct their lives by changing their negative beliefs about themselves and others.

HUMANISTIC FOCUS ON HUMAN POTENTIAL

On the assumption that people can choose their own personalities, some researchers in the humanistic tradition have turned away from the study of malfunctioning personalities such as those studied by Freud to the examination of exemplary personalities. Abraham Maslow (1954) believed that the psychology of personality should be based on the best of humanity. He studied a group of people who exhibited what he called **self-actualized personalities**—people who were developing to the highest reaches of their potential. His first subject was the anthropologist Ruth Benedict, a colleague of his at City College of New York. He went on to study Eleanor Roosevelt and Albert Einstein, as well as a number of historical figures, including Abraham Lincoln, Henry David Thoreau, and Ludwig von Beethoven. He found that these people shared a number of characteristics, including a childlike sense of fascination with the world around them. As Einstein expressed it, "One cannot help but be in awe when [one] contemplates the mysteries of eternity, of life, of the marvelous structure of reality" (Clark, 1984). Each of Maslow's self-actualized people also showed a commitment to problems outside his or her own narrow needs, a preference for a few close friendships rather than many shallow ones, a nonhostile sense of humor, and a tendency to have peak experiences (or intense feelings of oneness with the world).

This emphasis on the healthy side of personality has been quite influential in humanistic approaches to psychotherapy. In trying to help people with emotional problems, Carl Rogers has stressed the two central themes found in the writings of Kelly and Maslow. Like Maslow, Rogers focuses on self-actualization—on developing each person's positive potential. Like Kelly, Rogers stresses the extent to which people can choose different—and potentially more satisfying—views of themselves and others. Rogers's approach will be discussed in detail in Chapter 16.

In recent years, the phenomenological perspective has been increasingly integrated with the cognitive learning perspective (Bandura, 1977; Mischel, 1979, among others). Modern cognitive researchers do not reject the concept of learning, but they do reject the view of human learning as a simple conditioning process. These modern approaches hold that we differ in the things we choose to pay attention to, in the way we encode what we are attending to, and in the ways we retrieve information from memory (Carver and Scheier, 1988; Cantor and Kihlstrom, 1987; Norem, 1989). For instance, some of the differences between people might be related to differences in the **schemas,** or cognitive filters, they use to interpret events in their lives. A schema is a conceptual framework a person uses to collect and organize information about his or her world. Schemas influence what a person pays attention to, what he or she thinks about, and what he or she remembers. For instance, if you are shy it could be because you tend to interpret other people's behavior in terms of a "social rejection" schema. That is, you interpret many situations in your life in terms of the possibility of social rejection. A social rejection schema will influence attention (causing you to notice rude and unpleasant comments by others), thinking (causing you to ruminate about whether a particular comment was meant to make fun of you), and memory (causing you to remember unpleasant encounters that less shy people would promptly forget). For example, introverted students are more likely to notice and remember unpleasant encounters with other people (Graziano, Feldesman, and Rahe, 1985).

THE SELF

The study of the self integrates the phenomenological and cognitive approaches. Phenomenological theorists such as Maslow and Rogers view self-actualization as a central concept. But what exactly is the "self?" Before going on to discuss the research in this area, it is useful to consider your own self. Take a moment, and three or four lines on a sheet of blank paper, to answer the following simple question:

Who are you?

William James (1890) differentiated between several different meanings of the self, including the *material Self* (all I can call mine; my hands, and my eyes, as distinguished from yours), the *social Self* (the recognition I get from my friends; as a piano player, as a soccer player, and so on), and the *self as knower* (my momentary consciousness; the self that is reading this book and feeling a pang of hunger). Contemporary research on the self is concerned with how we define ourselves **(self-concept),** how we evaluate ourselves **(self-esteem),** and when and how we become conscious of ourselves as distinct from the environment **(self-awareness).**

SELF-CONCEPT

How do you decide what you are like? When the second author of this book followed the above suggestion to answer the question "Who are you?" he came up with the following list: "professor, researcher, father, husband, mediocre amateur guitar player, writer, native New Yorker, tall, unconventional, introspective, intellectual, shy of strangers, life of the party around friends, Irishman, funny, hedonistic." This list demonstrates the several types of self-definition processes we will discuss below.

In 1902, sociologist C. H. Cooley advanced the idea of the "looking-glass self." In the same way that a mirror gives me feedback about the appearance of my body, so the reactions of others provide feedback about the kind of person I am. Thus, a person's self-concept is partly rooted in the feedback of other people. When the author rates himself as funny it is because he frequently hears others laugh when he make attempts to entertain. Likewise, one needs the response of others to see oneself as "the life of the party."

There is another way that we use other people when we are defining ourselves—we compare ourselves to them. When students are asked the question "Who are you?" they frequently note characteristics that make them distinct from others (McGuire and McGuire, 1988). It is unlikely that the author would describe himself as a native New Yorker if he still lived in the same New York neighborhood, where describing oneself as a New Yorker is not much more informative than describing oneself as human. People are especially likely to mention their distinctive *physical* characteristics in telling about who they are. Again, if the author had grown up in a Watusi village, he might define himself as a short white person rather than a tall Irishman.

Our self-definitions also arise from the *roles* we play, which we begin to take seriously over time (Hogan, 1976). When the author first took a position as a professor it did not seem that that role was a "real" part of himself, but now that he has played the part so many times it has become part of his self. Roy Baumeister (1986, 1991), a psychologist who has done extensive research on the self, notes that some of our self-definitions arise from a single irreversible transformation in our role or social status. The author's identity as a father is a once and forever transition. Others need to be occasionally renewed. His identity as a researcher could be redefined if he stopped collecting data and publishing in scientific journals. Baumeister makes the interesting argument that self-definition was not even an issue before such events as the Reformation and the industrial revolution replaced a small set of fixed roles—farmer, Catholic, male—with the ever-present possibility of revisions. In a few years, the author could, in theory, become an unmarried waiter in a natural foods restaurant and a Zen Buddhist. With so many different role possibilities, we can ask questions about our self that would never have occurred to our ancestors.

SELF-ESTEEM

We do not react dispassionately to our self-conceptions. When the author describes himself as a mediocre amateur guitar player, he is evaluating himself. Notice, however, that his list is slanted towards the positive—he is first and foremost a professor, a researcher, and a loving father and husband. Even "shy around strangers" is immediately balanced out with "life of the party around friends." We already noted how self-concepts are derived from comparisons with others. Many researchers believe that we derive our self-evaluations from the same process. For instance, people in higher status occupations tend to have higher self-esteem (Bachman and O'Malley, 1977). When we compare ourselves and others, we are not completely objective, but seem to suffer

"You are fair, compassionate, and intelligent, but you are perceived as biased, callous, and dumb."

Self-esteem refers to our feelings about what we are worth. A wise palm reader would be aware of the self-serving bias: most people feel that they are much more worthy than average. (Drawing by Mankoff; © *The New Yorker* Magazine, Inc.)

from a **self-serving bias.** Abe Tesser and Jennifer Campbell found that we usually compare ourselves with others using dimensions on which we are particularly gifted (Tesser, 1988, Tesser and Campbell, 1983). Presumably, our search for information is motivated by a desire to maintain a positive self-evaluation, and when our self-esteem is threatened, we enjoy finding someone worse off to compare ourselves with (Gibbons and McCoy, 1991). There is certainly evidence enough that most people manage to maintain a high regard for themselves. To give a few examples from diverse areas of research: 90 percent of business managers rate themselves as better than the average manager, 70 percent of high school seniors rate themselves as above average in leadership ability (only two percent think that they are below average), 25 percent of students think that they are in the top one percent in the ability to get along with others, and 90 percent of college professors rate themselves as superior to their average colleagues (Blackburn et al., 1980; French, 1968; Myers, 1987).

At the beginning of the chapter we noted the distinction between the inner and outer aspects of personality. Some researchers have wondered whether many of the findings on the self-serving bias might be due to a bias in *self-presentation*. Per-

haps the inner self has a realistic self-evaluation but the public self is simply putting on a good front. To test this, researchers have compared self-ratings that people thought would be made public with self-ratings people thought that no one else would ever see. The results support the idea that our private opinions about ourselves are every bit as flattering as our public front (Greenwald and Breckler, 1985). In many cases, it seems that public humility is an act and we are even more self-flattering in private (Schlenker and Miller, 1985).

SELF-AWARENESS

Unless we are especially narcissistic, we are not usually very conscious of our "self." An hour ago you may have been eating dinner and talking with your roommate about a book you recently read, giving no thought whatever to whether you were eating differently from her, or whether you were the better or worse reader. What causes us to shift our attention from the external world to the self, and what happens when we make that shift? Robert Wicklund and Dieter Frey (1980) believe that most of what we do is automatic; that is, done without any self-consciousness at all. These researchers report that we become aware of our selves in novel situations (perhaps the first day in class), or when we are in a minority (the only woman in the chemical engineering class). Wicklund and his colleagues have done a number of studies in which they artificially make people self-aware by sitting them in front of a mirror or a television camera. It appears that when we are self-aware we take pains to be on our best behavior. One interesting aspect of this research is that self-aware people behave more consistently with their stated attitudes and their personality self-descriptions. For instance, students in one experiment filled out a questionnaire that measured their general level of guilt about sex (Gibbons, 1978). When the researcher later examined their reactions to pornographic materials, he found that there was little relationship between people's scores on the sex-guilt scale and their later ratings about how much they enjoyed the pornographic materials. However, those who viewed the pornography in front of a mirror showed a very high degree of consistency. Findings like these are generally explained in cognitive terms. When you become aware of yourself, you begin to use an internal set of standards to decide on a course of behavior (Carver and Scheier, 1981). When you are acting on automatic, on the other hand, you simply go along with the pressures of your present situation.

It seems that some individuals are more prone to chronic self-awareness than others (Fenigstein, 1984; Davis and Franzoi, 1991). For instance, shy people tend to be more self-conscious than outgoing people (Briggs, Cheek, and Jones, 1986). Mark Snyder (1979) developed a test to measure differences in **self-monitoring.** People who score high in self-monitoring tend to pay close attention to the demands of whatever situation they happen to be in at the moment, while those who score low on the scale are more likely to use internal standards to guide their behavior. A politician who presents a different face to each interest group he talks to would be an example of someone high in self-monitoring. Snyder (1983) has found that low self-monitors show more consistency between their self-descriptions and their behaviors, whereas high scorers seem to act more in line with situational demands.

EVALUATION OF THE PHENOMENOLOGICAL PERSPECTIVE

There can be no doubt that people, at least occasionally, think carefully about their inner selves, and that they have deep feelings about themselves. However, some theorists have questioned whether those inner thoughts and feelings have an important causal role in determining behavior (Skinner, 1953; 1990, among others). Based on physiological studies of brain–behavior relationships, for instance, Michael Gazzaniga (1985) suggested that conscious explanations of what we do are often little more than after-the-fact rationalizations. According to this perspective, we are usually not aware of the real causes for our behavior, which may lie in physiological processes occurring in less consciously accessible areas of the brain. As we noted earlier, people are very good at making up self-centered explanations for behaviors that are really caused by events outside of their awareness (Nisbett and Wilson, 1977). If this position is correct, then our phenomenology is simply *epiphenomenal.* That is to say, our inner feelings and thoughts are secondary byproducts of brain processes, which do not themselves actually determine how we behave. A less radical version of this position is that we normally act in an automatic way, responding to our environments and

inner states without giving much reasoned thought to what we are doing. When something unusual happens, though, it may draw our attention to ourselves, and lead us to act in a more consciously considered manner (Carver and Scheier, 1981).

Experimental studies of the phenomenological perspective have found that changes in how people act and how they feel can be manipulated by having them think about certain things as opposed to others (Fiske and Taylor, 1991). As you may recall from our first discussion of experimental methods, however, laboratory experiments have the problem of artificiality. Demonstrating a phenomenon in the laboratory does not tell us how important it is in the real world. For instance, we discussed research showing that people who are made self-conscious in a laboratory will act more in line with their inner personality traits (Gibbons, 1978, among others). Does that mean that self-consciousness explains every instance of consistency that we see on the street? No, it only shows that self-consciousness can potentially play a causal role, not that it normally does.

In recent years, however, there has been increasing research relating phenomenological interpretation to behavioral processes in the real world. In Chapter 14, for instance, we will discuss findings that show that people's chronic ways of interpreting the stressful events in their lives can lead to changes in their body's immune reactions, and even to physical damage to their bodies in the form of hypertension and other disorders. However, it would be a mistake to assume that people simply construct their psychological world and their physiological reactions to it. Just as mental events can influence physiology (as when thinking about delicious food can make our mouth water), so physiology can influence mental events (as when hunger causes us to fantasize about food). The relationship between cognition and physiological processes is a two-way street. It would also be a mistake to assume that our past learning experiences can be ignored as we construct ourselves on a moment-to-moment basis. Modern cognitive approaches to personality stress the connection between ongoing cognitions and learning history. Thus, contemporary theorists combine insights from the phenemonological perspective with other approaches. In the next section, we consider the interactionist attempt to completely remove the barriers between the different perspectives on personality.

INTERACTIONS:
Connecting the Different Perspectives on Personality

Which theoretical perspective is correct? Was van Gogh shy and Gauguin outgoing because they had different genes and hormones, because they had different early childhood experiences, or because of the ways in which they thought about themselves as adults? Rather than select just one of these perspectives, an interactionist perspective attempts to integrate them (Kenrick, Montello and MacFarlane, 1985). One way to think about how all these theories fit together is to recall the *proximate/ultimate continuum* we discussed in Chapter 1. Proximate explanations deal with events as they are occurring (immediate causes), while ultimate ex-

planations deal with the underlying causes of those current events (long-term causes). Table 13.5 shows how the different theories of personality might be arranged along this continuum.

Note that psychological traits, such as shyness, can be explained within each of the other perspectives. As we noted earlier, trait researchers have been mainly interested in the *descriptive* questions—What are the major dimensions that differentiate people from one another? How do different characteristics fit together within the individual? The other perspectives are all more concerned with explanation—locating the *causes* of the differences between people. Thus, each of the other perspectives would provide a different causal explanation of a descriptive trait such as shyness. In the table, we arranged those causal explanations from proximate to ultimate. The most important point is that the more immediate expla-

TABLE 13.5 Different Personality Theories Arranged According to the Time Frame on Which They Are Primarily Focused

Theoretical Perspective	Sources of Traits (examples)	Possible Explanation of Shyness
Cognitive/Phenomenological *(Relatively most proximate)* Information Processing	Schemas	Tendency to pay attention to possibilities for social rejection or embarrassment
Humanistic	Self-concepts	Beliefs about oneself as unattractive or boring
Learning Cognitive Learning	Expectancies about reinforcement	External locus of control in social situations
Behaviorist	Habits	Conditioned anxiety from previous punishment for speaking up
Psychodynamic	Childhood fixations based upon psychosexual conflict	Negative parental reaction to child's sexual or angry feelings leads to later fear of self-exposure
Biological Physiological	Hormonal or anatomical characteristics	Tendency towards unpleasantly high arousal in stimulating social situations
Behavior Genetic	Genes inherited from parents	Temperamental shyness inherited from parents
Evolutionary *(Relatively most ultimate)*	Environmental and social pressures on ancestors	Adaptiveness of avoiding social conflict and embarrassment, given particular social situations

Note: Proximate explanations focus on the immediate causes of behavior (such as embarassment over a comment that you heard a moment ago), while ultimate explanations focus on the long-term causes of those immediate events (for instance, the evolutionary history of people's tendency to blush in an embarassing social situation).

nations can be linked with the more historical ones along a time continuum. Thus, the different theories are not necessarily opposed in their explanations, but simply have a different focus—the proximate explanations provide more focused small scale snapshots, while the more ultimate explanations provide a long distance background perspective.

Why does one person develop a cognitive tendency to pay attention to possible social embarassment (a proximate cause of shyness)? Likely because of a background of previous learning experiences that involved the punishment of social embarassment. In turn, people whose parents made them feel embarassed about their own sexual or angry feelings might find later social embarassment more of a punishment. Thus, a psychodynamic account of early childhood experiences may link up with an explanation that focuses on later learning, which in turn links up with an explanation that emphasizes ongoing thought processes. Going further back, children who are born with certain physiological predispositions may be especially sensitive to social situations in the first place (Stelmack, 1990). Such temperamental sensitivity could make a child more sensitive to his or her parents' reactions. If the child's parents reinforce those tendencies, the child may grow up even more sensitive to the reactions of other people. As we noted earlier, the work of Hans Eysenck and his colleagues has suggested just such interactive connections between genetic predispositions, physiological reactions, and learning experiences (Eysenck, 1970, 1981). Finally, an evolutionary account would consider that people might have evolved a tendency to become especially sensitive about social situations involving sex and aggeession because those impulses posed special problems for our ancestors, who lived in small, tightly knit social groups (Leak and Christopher, 1982). In sum, the different theoretical explanations may not be opposed to one another, and a consideration of all of them together provides a more complete account of where individual differences in such traits as shyness come from.

Physical Characteristics Demonstrate Interactions between Genes and Environment

Several early theories of personality, including Sheldon's theory of body types, suggested a relationship between bodily characteristics and personality. The effect of genes upon the *appearance* of the body may be one of the most direct ways that biological factors contribute to later ex-

periences and, consequently, to feelings and thoughts about oneself. Consider the relationship between physical attractiveness and friendliness, which nicely demonstrates how proximate and ultimate factors migh interact with one another.

In the most ultimate sense, some of the physical features that people find attractive seem to be related to health and reproductive condition, and thus to the probability of surviving offspring (Buss, 1989; Symons, 1979) (Figure 13.9). As we

FIGURE 13.9 *Vahine No Te Vi,* **by Paul Gauguin.** During his visits to the South Pacific, Paul Gauguin, like many other visitors, was impressed with the physical attractiveness of many of the island natives. Physical attractiveness appears to be related to personality in several ways that illustrate the operation of interactions. Attractive people are treated more kindly and develop friendlier personalities. At an ultimate level, the favorable treatment of attractive people may stem from the fact that attractiveness is related to health and desirable genetic characteristics, some of which may have been related to our ancestors' survival. Thus, this woman's beauty may signal desirable mate characteristics. At a proximate level, their experiences may lead attractive people to interpret ongoing events differently from less attractive people. (Paul Gauguin, *Vahine No Te Vi,* 1892, Baltimore Museum of Art, Cone Collection).

will discuss at greater length in Chapter 18, there are reasons to believe that our female ancestors might have selected males who had features that relate to social dominance, including broad shoulders and large upper body muscles, whereas our male ancestors were more likely to look for features that relate to nurturing children, such as body fat and relatively wide hips.

In a more proximate sense, physical attractiveness is related to facial features and body type (Cunningham, 1986; Cunningham, Barbee and Pike, 1990; Wiggins et al., 1977). These physical features are heritable—children tend to look like their parents. On an even more immediate level, physically attractive people have different experiences as they grow up. They are likely to be treated better by teachers and classmates (Dion, 1972), and to be treated better by people they meet when they get older (Snyder, Tanke, and Berscheid, 1977). As a result of the warm reception they get from others, physically attractive people generally develop more friendly personalities (Goldman and Lewis, 1977). Those different life experiences, which can ultimately be traced to different genes, will also cause differences at the most proximate level—what people pay attention to and think about at any given moment. Physically attractive people will probably think differently about social interactions. Someone who is accustomed to being treated nicely is likely to interpret an ambiguous comment ("Where did you get those shoes?") dif-

ferently from someone who is accustomed to being picked on. Thus, physical differences between people lead them to have different experiences, and those different experiences lead to differences in the way they process social information on a moment-to-moment basis. Ultimate and proximate causes thus form an unbroken chain in influencing individual differences.

Personality Connects the Parts

In considering these interactions, it becomes clear how personality is interwoven with the other areas of psychology. Individual differences in such traits as friendliness have their basis in an interaction of biology, learning, and cognitive processes. Because personality psychology considers the whole person, it shows how processes such as physiology, learning, and cognition are really inseparable. Some people grow up to be shy partly because of physiological mechanisms that influence how they perceive, how they learn, and how they respond to their experiences. As we shall see in the chapters that follow, personality underlies a great deal of complicated human behavior—how we respond to stressful life situations, whether we act aggressively in social encounters, and so on. In this chapter we have focused on individual differences within the normal range. In the next two chapters, we will continue to examine individual differences, but focus on differences in adjustment and maladjustment. ▪

IN CONTEXT: PERSONALITY

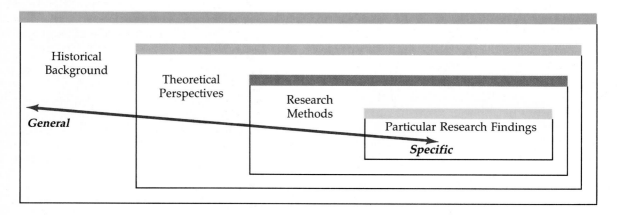

STUDY QUESTIONS

How can psychologists best describe and explain individual differences in behavior, thought, and emotion?

At the descriptive level, personality psychologists ask: (a) How can we devise tests to measure dimensions like friendliness and dominance? (b) How do the individual traits measured by those tests go together?

At the explanatory level, personality psychologists ask: (a) Where do individual differences come from? (b) How do processes such as physiology, learning, and cognition influence one another to determine an individual's behavior?

HISTORICAL BACKGROUND

1. Hippocrates hypothesized a number of connections between a person's character and the predominant fluids in his or her body.

2. During the first half of the twentieth century, William Sheldon examined the relationship between body type and personality.

3. Phenomenological philosophers held that the differences between us are rooted in differences in our views of the world and of ourselves.

MODERN THEORETICAL PERSPECTIVES

1. The **psychodynamic** theory assumes that adult personality traits are rooted in unconscious conflicts between selfish biological needs and demands of society. Freud believed that the child's personality begins as a set of selfish impulses (called the id), but that the child develops a set of skills to deal with the demands of the world (called the ego), and a system of internalized parental values (called the superego). Adult personality presumably develops in response to childhood crises over breastfeeding, toilet training, and sexuality.

2. **Trait** approaches are generally aimed at describing and organizing the vast differences among people.

3. **Biological** theories of personality consider the physiological differences between people that might underlie behavioral differences, as well as the genetic inheritance of human traits and their possible relationship to our ancestors' survival.

4. The **behaviorist** theory views personality in terms of classical and operant conditioning. Modern **social learning** theorists emphasize cognitive factors that influence personality, such as individual differences in expectancies about reward and punishment.

5. **Phenomenological** theorists view personality as a direct product of conscious choice. In recent years, this position has merged with laboratory studies from a cognitive perspective and led to research on the self.

6. The **interactionist** perspective assumes that biology, learning, and cognition interact with one another to produce personality traits. Biological approaches deal more with relatively ultimate genetically caused roots of behavior. Cognitive approaches address more immediate or proximate causes of behavior. Learning connects the two.

RESEARCH METHODS

1. Original support for psychodynamic theory was based on **case studies** such as Freud's case of Little Hans. The problems of interpreting case material are illustrated by Wolpe and Rachman's (1960) behavioral reinterpretation of this case.

2. Trait researchers including Raymond Cattell (1956) have used **factor analysis** to help describe and categorize the dimensions along which people differ. Factor analyses are statistical methods that help organize those behaviors that tend to vary together within people.

3. Biological researchers have used **behavior genetic** methods such as twin studies to examine the heritability of personality traits (Plomin and Daniels, 1987) and **cross-cultural comparisons** such as White's (1980) study of trait language to examine the universality of trait dimensions.

4. Behavioral and cognitive researchers have used **experimental** methods to study how manipulated variations in the environment interact with personality characteristics. For example, Glucksberg and King (1967) were able to induce forgetting by repression when nonsense syllables came to be associated with mild electric shocks.

RESEARCH FINDINGS AND SUMMARY

1. Evidence from psychodynamic case studies is open to numerous interpretations; 13 different explanations have been offered for why van Gogh cut off his ear. Freud's theory contributed three major themes to modern personality research: an interest in unconscious determinants

of behavior, an emphasis on early childhood, and a consideration of the conflict between selfish biological impulses and the needs of society.

2. Although there are thousands of different trait terms, factor analyses have found an underlying structure that consists of a much smaller number of dimensions. There is some consensus on five major personality dimensions: extraversion, agreeableness, conscientiousness, emotional stability, and culture.

3. Personality traits have been related to success and satisfaction on the job. Basic types of jobs appear to be related to the basic personality dimensions of introversion/extraversion and impulsivity/self-control.

4. In support of the biological perspective, there is evidence that different human groups think about personality in similar ways. Behavior genetic studies support the biological assumption that the major personality traits are heritable. However, even identical twins differ somewhat in their adult personalities, suggesting that genetic factors do not operate independently of the environment.

5. Shyness is a common trait that arises in personality studies, and characterizes many people. Children who are inhibited around strangers tend to grow up to become shy, and also to show more anxiety.

6. Rotter's locus of control scale measures expectancies about a person's ability to control rewards in his or her life. Internals, who believe that they are in control of rewards and punishments, make more attempts to control their lives than do externals, who are more likely to leave things to fate.

7. The behaviorist emphasis on environmental determinants of behavior stimulated the person/situation controversy. Some psychologists have argued that personality is simply in the eye of the beholder, but research indicates substantial agreement between different observers in rating the behavioral characteristics of someone they know well. The fact that agreement increases with acquaintance indicates that trait ratings are not simply based on empty stereotypes. Personality traits can be useful in predicting behavior, if reliable measures are used, and if the personality dimensions are based on observable behavior.

8. Personality and environment interact in determining behavior. Person/situation interactions refer to the following:
(a) traits are more easily expressed in some situations than others,
(b) traits only show up in relevant situations,
(c) traits and situations can change one another, and
(d) traits influence our choice of situations to enter.

9. The phenomenological perspective has contributed to research on the self, which has addressed:
(a) **self-concept:** how people decide what they are like. Feedback from other people, attention to distinctive characteristics, and social roles all seem to play a role in self-concept.
(b) **self-esteem:** how people evaluate their self-conceptions. People generally show a self-serving bias in those evaluations, and prefer to compare themselves to others on the dimensions on which they themselves are especially gifted.
(c) **self-awareness:** how people become conscious of themselves. Self-awareness is increased by being in a novel situation, or by being a member of a minority. Individuals high in self-consciousness strive to keep their behaviors in line with their internal standards, those high in self-monitoring pay more attention to the demands of the situations they are in.

ADDITIONAL READINGS

Derlega, V., Winstead, B., and Jones, W., eds. 1991. *Personality: Contemporary theory and research.* Chicago, IL: Nelson-Hall. A collection of articles written for undergraduates by modern personality researchers.

Freud, S. 1933/1965. *New introductory lectures on psychoanalysis.* New York: Norton. A general introduction to the ideas of the man who was not only the most prominent figure in the field of personality, but an important influence on modern thought in a wide range of disciplines.

Hogan, R. 1976. *Personality theory: The personological tradition.* Englewood Cliffs, NJ: Prentice Hall. A clear and readable introduction to traditional personality theories by a defender of personality against situationist and behavioral critics.

McAdams, D. P. 1990. *The person: An introduction to personality psychology.* Harcourt Brace Jovanovich. A nicely written and thoughtful overview of the field, including an excellent treatment of case studies and related approaches to personality.

Potkay, C. R., and Allen, B. P. 1986. *Personality: Theory, research, and applications*. Monterey, CA: Brooks/Cole. A good general overview of modern research in personality.

Wells, B. W. P. 1980. *Personality and heredity: An introduction to psychogenetics*. London: Longman. A consideration of evidence for the biological viewpoint, with good coverage of important research from Britain.

STRESS, COPING, AND HEALTH

A t first glance it may seem that changes in one's social world, and in related emotional and mental states, have little to do with disease. But there is mounting evidence that "real," organic diseases are linked to changing beliefs about oneself, to the nature of one's relationships with others and to one's position in the social world. . . . Our lungs, hearts, and stomachs are hardly independent, autonomous organs . . . they are all in communication with and regulated by the brain. . . . Indeed, a primary function of the brain, perhaps as important as rational thought or language, is health maintenance.

(Robert Ornstein and David Sobel, 1987)

Chapter Outline

In Robert Louis Stevenson's classic *Treasure Island* the young protagonist tells of a secretive, irritable, and heavy-drinking old sea captain who came to live at his family's inn. The old man was being pursued by a band of ruthless pirates, and he lived in fear that they would find him and deliver the ominous "black spot." After several months a "dreadful-looking figure"—a blind man in a black cloak—arrived and forced the boy to show him to the captain. The captain was terrified to the point of appearing ill when he saw the blind man, who quickly stuffed something into the captain's hand and left. After some time in a daze, the captain looked sharply into the palm of his hand, then suddenly jumped to his feet, crying that he had only "six hours."

> Even as he did so, he reeled, put his hand to his throat, stood swaying for a moment, and then, with a peculiar sound, fell from his whole height face foremost on the floor. . . . The captain had been struck dead by thundering apoplexy. . . . On the floor close to his hand there was a little round of paper, blackened on one side. I could not doubt that this was the *black spot*. . . .

(Robert Louis Stevenson, 1883)

It is not only in nineteenth-century fiction that psychological stress has been linked to bodily illness. There is a real physical toll paid for psychological stress, and the costs may be much higher today than they were a hundred years ago. In the era in which Stevenson wrote *Treasure Island*, most people died from such infectious diseases as typhoid fever, smallpox, and cholera

(Shank, 1983). In 1900, tuberculosis was still the top killer in the United States, followed by pneumonia. In 1988, by contrast, approximately 780,000 Americans died of heart disease, 152,000 died of stroke, and 72,000 died of pneumonia (Johnson et al., 1989). Consider also that pneumonia is the only communicable disease among the top 10 causes of death. As of July, 1988, the total number of AIDS cases ever diagnosed was still less than 67,000 (Mays and Cochran, 1988), and about half of the deaths attributed to the disease had occurred in the seven preceding years. Each of the top three killers—heart disease, cancer, and stroke—is partly related to unhealthy behaviors. Whether we smoke, what we eat, and how much we exercise, for instance, can influence whether we fall victim to one of these diseases. Consider the costs of smoking—the Center for Disease Control estimates that the habit accounts for 320,500 deaths each year, mostly from heart diseases and lung cancer. And a recent survey of entering college freshmen indicates that after dropping for two decades, smoking was again on the rise for the class of '92 (*Arizona Republic*, Jan. 10, 1989).

Between 1950 and 1980, medical costs jumped from 4.5 to 10 percent of the Gross National Product (Matarazzo, 1980). And between 1980 and 1990, Bureau of Labor statistics indicate the cost of medical care went up 111 percent, more than double the overall consumer inflation index. Most of the billions of dollars spent on medical problems go to treating people who are already sick. Only about two percent of that money is aimed at the prevention and control of illness. Many health professionals argue that spending more money on post-illness medical care can have little effect, and that the money would be better spent on programs to change people's unhealthy behaviors before they fall ill (Elliot, 1983).

One important link between psychology and health is the research on **stress.** Stress can be defined as the physical and psychological response to perceived environmental threat. Note that different people may perceive the same potentially threatening event in very different ways, depending on their *cognitive interpretation* of that event and the resources that they have at their disposal (Lazarus and Folkman, 1984). If a classmate tells you there will be a pop quiz in your calculus class tomorrow, you will experience less stress if you think that your friend is only joking, or if you feel very confident of your mathematical abilities. We will begin by addressing how environmental events and interpretations can affect stress and will discuss the effects of stress on the mind and the body. In addition to exacting a psychological cost, by contributing to psychological disorders, stress also takes a direct physical toll. Some diseases, including hypertension and peptic ulcers, are directly linked to stress. Beyond that, there is new evidence that stress may contribute indirectly to a host of other diseases, from colds to cancers, by interfering with the body's **immune system** (O'Leary, 1990). The immune system is the body's wall of defense against illness, and it includes cells in the skin and bloodstream that detect and destroy potentially harmful bacteria and viruses.

Adults spend a good portion of their waking hours at their jobs, and many find those hours the most stressful aspect of their lives. After discussing the general relationship between illness and stress, we will look at specific research on organizational stress, including evidence that people with certain personality characteristics are particularly prone to suffer from the stresses of the workplace, while others seem to thrive on the same stress. Stress on the job is very expensive, whether the costs are measured in terms of human pain or cold cash. A 1984 report from the Office of Technology Assessment estimates that stress-related illnesses cost business $50 to $70 billion a year (Arndt and Chapman, 1984). Those stresses are especially costly for lower level workers, who must often suffer low pay, lack of opportunity, and close supervision by unsupportive bosses. Whether out of humanitarian or financial concerns, many organizations have started bringing psychological treatment into the workplace in the form of stress management programs.

Stress does not always cause people to deteriorate. Sometimes it brings out their strengths. On November 22, 1963, Robert Kennedy received a call from FBI director J. Edgar Hoover saying "I have bad news for you." The news was that his brother, the president, had been shot, perhaps fatally. Kennedy reportedly turned away and clapped his hand to his mouth with a look of "shock and horror" on his face (Schlesinger, 1978). After a few minutes of being unable to speak, however, Kennedy began making calls. When he had established that his brother was dead, he began to take charge of notifying and comforting other family members. His biographer describes him as hugging several relatives when he met them. He stayed emotionally controlled for the rest of that day, telling one friend "Don't be so gloomy, that's one thing I don't need right now." It was not until he went to bed, early the next morning, that someone heard him break down sobbing and ask "Why, God?" For the next month he was withdrawn and composed, but his friends described him as having a continual look of pain on his face, as if he had a toothache. He then began to make sarcastic jokes about death—"Been to any good funerals lately?"

The following summer Kennedy went through a change of attitude as a result of an intensive immersion in Greek literature and existential philosophy:

> He returned from the dangerous journey, his faith intact, but deepened, enriched. . . . He supplemented the Greek image of man against fate with the existentialist proposition that man, defining himself by his choices, remakes himself each day and therefore can never rest. Life was a sequence of risks. To

fail to meet them was to destroy a part of oneself. He made his way through the haze of pain—and in doing so brought other sufferers insight and relief.

(Schlesinger, 1978)

Kennedy's story shows that stressful experiences can sometimes lead to personal growth. It also illustrates several concepts we will discuss in the section on **coping** with stress. Coping can be defined as cognitive and behavioral attempts to bring stress under control (Lazarus and Folkman, 1984). Robert Kennedy's coping efforts went through several phases. On the first day, he attempted to suppress "gloomy" conversation, only to break down crying that night. Later he began to joke about death, and finally he found some meaning in the tragedy of his brother's assassination. Throughout, he spent a great deal of time around family members, providing and receiving *social support* (defined as emotional or material assistance from others). We will discuss research on the value of these different coping strategies.

Finally, we will consider how the research and theory on stress and coping illustrates yet another side of the interaction between biology, learning, and cognition. Thus far, we have discussed biological factors as causal agents, describing how neural structures and physiological events can influence which experiences we think about and learn from. In this chapter, you will see how your experiences and cognitions can have powerful influences on your physical body.

Robert Kennedy (center, left) at his brother John's funeral. Robert went through several stages in coping with his brother's murder. Following unsuccessful attempts to suppress his emotion, he turned to humor, followed by a search for meaning. Throughout, he provided support for the other family members.

HISTORICAL BACKGROUND:
Health Psychology

As we saw in the excerpt from *Treasure Island*, the link between stress and disease was recognized well before this century. Eighteenth-century physician John Hunter noted that "My life is in the hands of any rascal who chooses to put me in a passion." In fact, Hunter died during an emotional debate with a member of his hospital staff (Smith et al., 1986). Before that, in 1628, the pioneering cardiologist William Harvey observed that "A mental disturbance provoking pain, excessive joy, hope or anxiety, extends to the heart, where it affects its tempo and rate, impairing general nutrition and vigor." (Williams, 1984). Earlier still, physicians in ancient Egypt observed that anger affected the rate and strength of the pulse (Williams, 1984).

The modern interest in stress shares its early history with the study of emotion. As we noted in Chapter 10, Charles Darwin made careful observations of the bodily reactions associated with different emotional states:

> As fear increases into an agony of terror . . . the heart beats wildly or must fail to act and faintness ensue; there is a death-like pallor; the breathing is labored; the wings of the nostrils are widely dilated; there is a gasping and convulsive motion of the lips, a tremor on the hollow cheek, a gulping and catching of the throat. . . . In other cases there is a sudden and uncontrollable tendency to headlong flight; and so strong is this that the boldest soldiers may be seized with a sudden panic.
>
> *(Darwin, quoted in James, 1890)*

Psychosomatic Disorders

During the 1920s, Walter Cannon did his intensive work on the "fight or flight" reactions of the autonomic nervous system, which we discussed in Chapter 10. Cannon (1929) noted that very different sorts of stressors, from physical cold to emotional events, lead to the release of adrenaline into the bloodstream. These descriptive and physiological studies of emotional reactions made important contributions to our understanding of the immediate effects of stress, but it was not until the late 1920s and 1930s that researchers began to pay attention to the chronic effects of psychological stress on the body. At that time, researchers in the psychoanalytic tradition, such as Franz Alexander, gathered case studies of individuals with psychosomatic disorders. Psychosomatic medicine was concerned with physical disorders that seemed to result from prolonged psychological conflict. Among these were peptic ulcers, asthma, and hypertension. In 1934, Alexander advanced the idea that peptic ulcers were caused by frustrated dependency needs. Thinking back to Chapter 13 on personality should help you understand why Alexander's psychoanalytic viewpoint led him to make a connection between digestive problems and dependency. As we noted, Freudian theorists have speculated that dependent relationships with others begin during the period of breastfeeding, when the child first comes into contact with another human being. Thus a problem related to one's dependency on other people would be likely to be connected with a disorder related to eating.

Alexander and his colleagues held that each psychosomatic disorder was related to a specific type of psychological conflict. For instance, migraine headaches were related to repressed anger, and asthma was connected to anxiety (Friedman and Booth-Kewley, 1987). The idea that a particular psychological conflict is associated with each psychosomatic disorder is called the **specificity hypothesis**. This hypothesis assumes that specific conflicts go with specific illnesses.

Stress and the General Adaptation Syndrome

Around the time that Alexander and his colleagues were studying human psychosomatic disorders, a Canadian medical researcher named Hans Selye (1936) was studying the reactions of rats to prolonged stress.

Selye did not begin his research with a particular interest in stress; instead, he was injecting rats with ovarian tissue as a part of a search for a new sexual hormone. The rats responded to these injections with a very strong physiological response—bleeding ulcers, shrinkage of the thymus gland, and enlargement of the adrenal glands. To be certain that the effects were the result of ovarian hormones, Selye conducted an experiment that included a control trial in which rats were injected with various other foreign substances. To his ini-

Hans Selye was a pioneer in the study of physiological responses to stress. He proposed that all stressors, including cold, disease, and painful shocks lead to a *general adaptation syndrome* (described in Fig. 14.1).

tial disappointment, the same physiological reactions occurred regardless of the type of injection. His dejection at the failure of his hormone search disappeared, though, when he realized that he might be on the track of a more important discovery. Perhaps the body had "a single nonspecific reaction" to trauma of any kind. To follow his hunch, Selye began subjecting his experimental animals to different kinds of stressors, including uncontrollable restraint and electric shock. Regardless of the type of stressor, the rats seemed to show the same physiological reaction, which Selye named the **general adaptation syndrome.**

Selye found that the general adaptation syndrome progressed through three separate stages (Selye, 1976). (See Figure 14.1.) During the *alarm* stage, at the first encounter with a stressor, there is a high level of activity of the sympathetic nervous system and an outpouring of *catecholemines* (neural transmitters and hormones like adrenaline). The sympathetic nervous system controls the "fight or flight" reaction discussed in Chapter 10, and adrenaline is a hormone that plays an important part in defensive arousal. The body may go into a state of shock as a result of this acute response to a stressor. If the threat continues, the organism moves to a stage of *resistance*, during which the body draws heavily on its reserves, and the individual appears to be quite resistant to continued stress. If the stress goes on for a very long period, however, the body's reserves begin to run out, and the high level of sympathetic arousal actually begins to damage such bodily organs as the kidneys, the heart, and the stomach lining. At the stage of *exhaustion*, the parasympathetic system becomes dominant, and the individual collapses. At this point, the body's reserves are depleted, and the organism is especially vulnerable to attack by any new disease. Selye's idea that the physiological response to any stressor follows this three-stage pattern is called the **nonspecificity hypothesis.** This hypothesis posits that any type of stress can lead, nonspecifically, to general physical deterioration.

Since Selye's pioneering work, researchers have learned a great deal about the body's response to stress. Some of the research we will discuss supports his idea of a general physiological response. However, not every human being responds in exactly the same way or with the same intensity to the same stressor. Researchers since Selye have studied the cognitive and physiological differences between people, and the specific aspects of a stressful situation that lead to different coping responses at different times by different people.

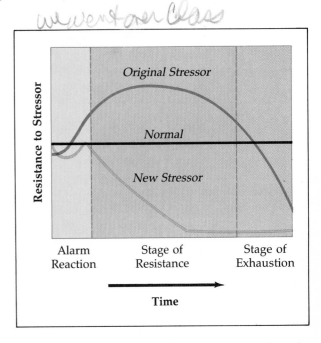

FIGURE 14.1 Selye's general adaptation syndrome. When first confronted with a stressor, the organism enters the *alarm* stage, characterized by a drop in blood pressure and body temperature and an increase in the flow of adrenal hormones that reduce inflammation. If the stress persists, the alarm phase is followed by the *resistance* stage, during which the body adapts to the stressor, but has a decreased resistance to new stressors. If the original stressor persists for a long period, the animal enters the *exhaustion* phase, which involves drastically lowered levels of activity and a lowered resistance to disease, due to the eventual depletion of the body's physiological resources.

Modern Health Psychology

There has been a recent explosion of research on the relationship between psychology and physical illness (Kiecolt-Glaser and Glaser, 1988; O'Leary, 1990; Olson and Elliott, 1983), and there is now a whole subfield called **health psychology.** In general, health psychologists are concerned with the role of psychological factors in preventing illness and maintaining good health (Gatchel, Baum, and Krantz, 1989; Taylor, 1986). More specifically, health psychologists research such questions as:

- *What makes some events more stressful than others?* For instance, why is it that a change of jobs can sometimes be invigorating and other times devastating?

- *How does stress contribute to physical illness?* For instance, can stress lower the body's immune response to herpes or other viral infections?

- *Can psychological treatments ease the pain and discomfort of physical disease?* For instance, can a person be taught to deal with the pain of an amputated limb without addictive drugs?

- *How can people cope with stressors in their lives and on their jobs?* For instance, what can stock brokers do to manage their everyday job stresses?

The field of health psychology is really just being born. Promising new findings have led to increasing funds for research in medical and organizational settings. Many clinical and social psychologists, inspired by ready research funds and the prospect of exciting discoveries, have shifted their attention to this area. Even as we write this book, new researchers are entering this field, raising novel questions, and beginning to come up with some fascinating answers. ■

THE NATURE OF STRESS

What is it that makes an experience stressful? Some cases are unambiguous, as when Robert Kennedy heard that his brother had been shot. But many of life's stressors are more difficult to identify. Stress can come from life changes that society generally regards as positive, such as taking a job or even getting married. For instance, in 1957, a 21-year-old Long Island woman fell dead as she ascended the church steps on the way to her wedding (*Time*, 1986).

Such simple everyday inconveniences as listening to a complaining boss or waiting in a long line at the supermarket can be stressful. Researchers in the area take two general approaches to classifying stress. One approach asks about *types of events*. Which particular events are more or less stressful? Researchers here make a distinction between major life changes—such as marriage—and "daily hassles"—such as an argument with your parents. A second approach asks about *general features of any given event*. What is it that makes one walk in the city unremarkable, and another a nightmare? Research here indicates that if you cannot predict when a stressful event will occur, if it is new to you, or if you cannot control it, you will be more distressed than if you have seen it before, knew it was coming, and know just what to do about it.

CATEGORIZING STRESSFUL EVENTS: MAJOR LIFE CHANGES AND MINOR DAILY PROBLEMS

On February 26, 1972, a slag dam on Buffalo Creek in West Virginia collapsed, and over a hundred million gallons of mud and water suddenly flooded the seventeen miles of valley below. One hundred twenty five people drowned and hundreds more were injured as their homes and cars were swept away by the flood waters. A team of social scientists found that the 650 survivors were psychologically devastated for some time afterwards. Survivors reported grief, despair, insomnia, nightmares, irrational angry episodes, and increased use of alcohol and prescription drugs for the year after the disaster (Gleser, Green, and Winget, 1981). Those who had been personally injured or had lost relatives and friends were the most emotionally damaged by the flood.

In the Buffalo Creek incident, a sudden and tragic loss of loved ones and homes led to severe stress. Even less severe events can lead to serious stress responses. For instance, Ghanaian villagers who were relocated to make way for the Lake Volta dam showed similar signs of emotional distress and increased alcohol use (Lumsden, 1975). Likewise, workers who have had to move as a result of a job transfer often suffer psychological and physical problems (Brett, 1980). It is easy to understand adverse reactions to a tragic flood or even to forced resettlement, but why the reaction to a simple change of job location, a change that is often accompanied by an increase in job status and pay? Some researchers argue that any change in our lives has stressful consequences. Thus, researchers have studied the range of potentially stressful events, from losing a loved one to dropping the garbage bag.

LIFE CHANGES

In an effort to find out how stressful events are linked to illness, Thomas Holmes and Richard Rahe (1967) asked tuberculosis patients about their lives just before they became ill. The researchers expected that unpleasant events would be linked with the onset of illness. Consistent with this expectation, many patients reported such things as the death of a spouse and the loss of a job. Unexpectedly, the patients also reported many seemingly neutral changes in recreational activities, sleep patterns, or domestic arrangements. Most unexpectedly, many of them reported seemingly positive events, including taking a vacation or getting married. From this information, the researchers developed the hypothesis that any disruption of our daily routine can be a stressor. Following this hunch, Holmes and Rahe developed the Social Readjustment Rating Scale. The scale assigns readjustment values (or LCUs, "life change units") to 43 common life events. (See Table 14.1.) The values were determined by asking

TABLE 14.1 The Holmes and Rahe Social Readjustment Scale

Have you experienced any of these in the last year?

Life Event	Mean Value	Stress Index
Death of spouse	___ × 100 =	___
Divorce	___ × 73 =	___
Marital separation	___ × 65 =	___
Jail term	___ × 63 =	___
Death of close family member	___ × 63 =	___
Personal injury of illness	___ × 53 =	___
Marriage	___ × 50 =	___
Fired at work	___ × 47 =	___
Marital reconciliation	___ × 45 =	___
Retirement	___ × 45 =	___
Change in health of family member	___ × 44 =	___
Pregnancy	___ × 40 =	___
Sex difficulties	___ × 39 =	___
Gain of new family member	___ × 39 =	___
Business readjustment	___ × 39 =	___
Change in financial state	___ × 38 =	___
Death of close friend	___ × 37 =	___
Change to different line of work	___ × 36 =	___
Change in number of arguments with spouse	___ × 35 =	___
Mortgage over $10,000*	___ × 31 =	___
Foreclosure of mortgage or loan	___ × 30 =	___
Change in responsibilities at work	___ × 29 =	___
Son or daughter leaving home	___ × 29 =	___
Trouble with in-laws	___ × 29 =	___
Outstanding personal achievement	___ × 28 =	___
Wife beginning or stopping work	___ × 26 =	___
Beginning or ending school	___ × 26 =	___
Change in living conditions	___ × 25 =	___
Revision of personal habits	___ × 24 =	___
Trouble with boss	___ × 23 =	___
Change in work hours or conditions	___ × 20 =	___
Change in residence	___ × 20 =	___
Change in schools	___ × 20 =	___
Change in recreation	___ × 19 =	___
Change in church activities	___ × 19 =	___
Change in social activities	___ × 18 =	___
Mortgage or loan less than $10,000*	___ × 17 =	___
Change in sleeping habits	___ × 16 =	___
Change in number of family get-togethers	___ × 15 =	___
Change in eating habits	___ × 15 =	___
Vacation	___ × 13 =	___
Christmas	___ × 12 =	___
Minor violations of the law	___ × 11 =	___

*Note: $10,000 was a figure based on the economy in the mid-1960s. An equivalent figure today would be $50,000.

From Holmes and Rahe (1967).

subjects to rate the amount of readjustment required by each event, assuming that marriage had a value of 50 on a 100-point scale. Note that the death of a spouse is given 100 points, indicating that it is seen as requiring the most adjustment. Divorce is next with 73 readjustment points, and so on. Before proceeding, you might want to check off each of the events which has happened to you during the last year, and calculate your own score.

In later studies, researchers found that higher scores on the readjustment scale were associated with more illness. For instance, 79 percent of those who scored over 300 LCUs (and had therefore undergone major life stress) had had a serious illness during the year following the events (Holmes and Masuda, 1974). Fifty-one percent of those with moderate amounts of change (between 200 and 299 LCUs) had fallen ill, as had 37 percent of those with mild change (between 150 and 200 LCUs). Note that this finding is correlational, and does not prove that the stress led to illness. Perhaps the life changes were caused by other factors that also led to illness, or perhaps people recall more negative changes after they have fallen ill. When figuring your own score you should also keep in mind that scores in the table are based on a sample of older working men, and that a certain amount of change may be a normal and expected part of college life. In line with the research we discussed earlier, it seems likely that anticipated changes will be less harmful than unexpected ones. So it would be a mistake to assume that a high life change score has you marked for illness.

In recent years, in fact, there has been some controversy about the extent to which life changes actually predict future illness (Maddi, Bartone, and Puccetti, 1987; Schroeder and Costa, 1984). One criticism is that positive changes, like marriage, may not normally be related to illness (Taylor, 1986), and may even work to buffer the negative consequences of unpleasant events (Cohen and Hoberman, 1983). A second criticism is that not everyone experiences the same event in the same way. Although people from very different backgrounds can agree on the aversiveness of certain events, such as the death of a spouse (Miller et al., 1974), there is not as much agreement about less traumatic occurrences, such as taking out a mortgage. A new college graduate may see a change of job as a challenge, while a well-established middle-aged businessperson may see it as a threat. Irwin Sarason and his colleagues (1978, 1982) developed a modified scale that asks subjects to rate not only whether a particular event happened to them, but also the extent to which it had a negative or positive effect. Adverse effects were more related to events that the person *perceived* as negative (Sarason et al., 1978). In addition to studying our perceptions of the major events in our lives, some researchers have shifted their attention from major changes to the minor events of everyday living.

MINOR EVERYDAY PROBLEMS

Instead of focusing on such monumental stressors as the Buffalo Creek catastrophe, some psychologists believe that we can learn more about the effects of stress by studying what are sometimes called "daily hassles" (Lazarus and Folkman,

1984). These are the undramatic inconveniences of everyday life—returning to the car to find a parking ticket, arguing with your roommate about the dishes, or discovering that the cat has made a mess on the rug.

Researchers have asked subjects to record these daily hassles, and found that, compared with major life changes, the minor inconveniences are actually better predictors of mental and physical distress (DeLongis et al., 1982). Obviously, some daily inconveniences are more relevant than others. Spilling the garbage is probably less upsetting than being stuck in traffic for an hour when you are already late for work. Psychologists Lee Anna Clark and David Watson (1988) found that arguments were the daily events most related to negative emotion. Having health problems, perhaps a cold or a flu, was also related to negative moods. Table 14.2 lists some common daily hassles found in a study of middle-aged adults, along with the things that were most likely to give them an "uplift" (Kanner et al., 1981).

Positive and negative daily events, and even positive and negative daily moods, can occur at the same time (Clark and Watson, 1988; Reich and Zautra, 1981). Good and bad things sometimes happen on the same day, and you can feel partly good and partly bad at the same moment. If you have an argument on Thursday, you are likely to rate yourself high on unpleasant moods, such as anger and depression. However, if you also get a good grade on the same day, you will rate your positive mood high as well. Research on college students' life events indicates that positive moods are related to such reinforcing events as getting a good grade or an unexpected gift, while negative moods are independently affected by painful events, including arguments with friends or parents (Reich and Zautra, 1981). Positive events seem to raise our positive feelings but do not generally do much to erase the effects of painful experiences.

As an example of how positive and negative affect can operate independently, students report lower positive mood, but no accompanying changes in negative mood, on days when they work at their part-time jobs (Clark and Watson, 1988). In other words, working does not generally put people in a bad mood, it just interferes with whatever puts them in a positive mood on their days off. Conversely, Sundays do not put people in a particularly good mood, but the "day of rest" is associated with very low scores on negative mood. In this study, the daily event most likely to give people an "uplift" was an interaction with

TABLE 14.2 A List of the Ten Most Frequent Daily Hassles and "Uplifts" Reported by Middle-Aged Adults over a Nine-Month Period

HASSLES		UPLIFTS	
Item	% of Times Checked*	Item	% of Times Checked*
1. Concerns about weight	52.4	1. Relating well with your spouse or lover	76.3
2. Health of a family member	48.1	2. Relating well with friends	74.4
3. Rising prices of common goods	43.7	3. Completing a task	73.3
4. Home maintenance	42.8	4. Feeling healthy	72.7
5. Too many things to do	38.6	5. Getting enough sleep	69.7
6. Misplacing or losing things	38.1	6. Eating out	68.4
7. Yard work or outside home maintenance	38.1	7. Meeting your responsibilities	68.1
8. Property, investment, or taxes	37.6	8. Visiting, phoning, or writing someone	67.7
9. Crime	37.1	9. Spending time with family	66.7
10. Physical appearance	35.9	10. Home (inside) pleasing to you	65.5

*Note: [a]The "% of times checked" figures represented the mean percentage of people checking the item each month averaged over the nine monthly administrations.

From Kanner, A. D., Coyne, J. C., Schaefer, C., and Lazarus, R. S. (1981).

another person (providing, of course, the interaction was not an argument!).

FEATURES OF STRESSFUL EVENTS: UNCERTAINTY AND LACK OF CONTROL

In an article titled "On the Phenomenon of Sudden Death in Animals and Man," physiologist Curt Richter quotes an earlier anthropologist:

> In New Zealand a Maori woman eats fruit that she only later learns has come from a taboo place. . . . By noon the next day she is dead. In Australia a witch doctor points a bone at a man. Believing that nothing can save him, the man rapidly sinks in spirits and prepares to die. He is saved only at the last moment when the witch doctor is forced to remove the charm.
>
> (Basedow, 1925, cited in Richter, 1957)

In his own laboratory research, Richter observed that laboratory animals faced with apparently uncontrollable threats sometimes fell victim to sudden death. Richter placed rats into jars and then filled the jars partway with water. Rats are normally very good swimmers, and are capable of swimming for several days if there is a possibility of escape. But the flooding in the jars was obviously inescapable, and Richter found that these rats often died within minutes, without even trying to survive. When he autopsied the rats, Richter found, to his surprise, that they had not drowned. They had died from parasympathetic activity, which involves reductions in adrenaline levels, along with blood flow away from the muscles and into the body's periphery and digestive organs. As we discussed in Chapter 2, parasympathetic arousal is opposed to the "fight or flight" reaction, and it usually dominates during relaxed periods, not stressful ones. Richter concluded that the animals had given up in the face of a hopeless situation, and he held that a similar process might explain the phenomenon of "voodoo death."

Although most of us face few death curses, we are often confronted with stressors that are outside of our control, from rare natural disasters to everyday traffic jams. There is a good deal of evidence that *uncontrollable events* are particularly stressful (Fiske and Taylor, 1984; Seligman, 1975). The importance of controllability has been shown in studies of "executive rats," in which two rats receive exactly the same electric shock, but one is given a lever that could be used to turn the shock off after it occurs. Over a long series of such trials, the partner rat, helpless to do anything about its plight, is more likely to develop ulcers than is the "executive" (Weiss, 1977). In studies with humans, subjects are also more upset by electric shock if they have no means to control or prevent the shocks (Gatchel, Baum, and Krantz, 1989). In fact, subjects who simply *believe* that they can control electric shocks experience less physiological arousal than comparable subjects who believe they have no control (Geer, Davison, and Gatchel, 1970, among others). This research is closely related to the phenomenon of "learned helplessness," in which people give up in the face of stressors that seem to be uncontrollable. We discussed this phenomenon in Chapter 10, and return to it in the next chapter on psychological disorders.

Outside the laboratory, the importance of control has been shown in a series of field studies done in homes for the elderly. Elderly people who make their own decisions about relocation into geriatric homes show less physical deterioration than those who are placed there by others (Schulz and Brenner, 1977). One study found an improvement in the health and activity levels of elderly patients if they were simply given control over weekly visits by a college student (Schulz, 1976). Patients who received a similar number of visits, but who were not given control over their scheduling, did not show the same benefits. Unfortunately, when that control was removed at the end of the experiment, the patients deteriorated (Schulz and Hanusa, 1978). In another study of control, elderly patients were encouraged to make more decisions about their daily schedules and were also given a plant to take care of. Those patients showed improved health and activity levels when compared to those who were simply given a plant, and told that the nursing staff would take care of them and their plant (Rodin and Langer, 1977). An individual's personality traits may also influence how he or she will react to an uncontrollable event. For instance, uncontrollable events are less stressful for individuals who have an "external" locus of control (that is, who do not see themselves in control of the events in their lives) (Gregory, Chartier, and Wright, 1979).

An important aspect of having control over the day-to-day inconveniences in your life, such as dental appointments, is that you know when they are going to occur. Animal studies indicate that *uncertainty* about an aversive event makes it much more disrupting (Weinberg and Levine, 1980). Human studies also show that uncertainty is aversive. One study found that subjects who were told that they had a five percent chance of receiving an electric shock were actually more aroused than those who were told that they had a 50 percent chance (Epstein and Roupenian, 1970). Based on their discussions with the participants, the re-

Stress and control. Could taking care of a pet reduce the stressfulness of an elderly person's life? One study indicated that simply giving elderly nursing home residents a plant to take care of, along with encouragement to make decisions about their daily schedules, led to improved health, compared with a regimen in which nursing staff did all the caretaking.

searchers concluded that those in the 50 percent group were resigned to receiving a shock, and could brace themselves. Those in the five percent group, on the other hand, were uncertain about how to prepare themselves.

One study of stress in "real life" provides clearer support for the hypothesis that humans find uncertainty aversive (Hunter, 1979, cited in Lazarus and Folkman, 1984). This research compared the physical and emotional adjustment of four samples of Navy wives: (1) those whose husbands had returned from active duty in the Vietnam war; (2) those whose husbands had been killed in action; (3) those whose husbands were prisoners of war; and (4) those whose husbands were missing in action. The greatest stress was experienced not by the women who were certain that their husbands had been killed, but by those who were most uncertain about what had happened to their husbands.

Novelty is another potentially stressful feature of an event. A student's first day in college is likely to be full of uncertainty and confusion, but that typically dissipates by midsemester. Novel situations may actually combine the features of unpredictability and uncontrollability. If you have just moved from Two Dot, Montana, to the urban campus of New York University, you may have a vague feeling that something bad could happen, but you have no idea what it might be, and no experience to know what you might do about it. In a classic study of stress responses, Walter Fenz and Seymour Epstein (1967) studied the effects of novelty on parachutists making a free fall out of an airplane. They recorded the jumpers' skin conductance, heart rate, and breathing rate at several times, including a control day on which the subjects did not intend to jump, the arrival at the airport, just before jumping, and after landing. The researchers compared experienced jumpers to novice jumpers who had never made a free fall. As you can see in Figure 14.2, the two groups did not differ on control days, or when they arrived at the airport. As the plane took off and reached jumping altitude, however, the novices became progressively more aroused, indicating that they found the upcoming event more stressful than the experienced jumpers, who remained relatively more calm. A more recent study by Fenz (1988) indicated that novice parachutists show less stress if they are first exposed to detailed films of jumps,

and then given a chance to dress up in jumping gear and accompany other jumpers on a flight without jumping themselves. In this way, the procedures were gradually made more familiar to the novices.

In sum, then, there is evidence that certain types of events are more stressful than others. Major life changes, including divorce and the death of a spouse, are particularly stressful. Daily hassles, especially arguments, can also be quite stressful. Any given event is more stressful when it is novel, when it is uncertain, or when it cannot be controlled. Stressful categories of events often involve many of these stress-inducing features. For instance, the death of a spouse leaves the widowed person helpless to do anything about it, and with a high degree of uncertainty about the future. It is important to keep in mind that the same event that is stressful to one person at one time may be exhilarating to that same person at another. After all, sports parachutists jump out of planes voluntarily. Recall the research on sensory deprivation, discussed in Chapter 10, which indicated that unchanging environments are experienced as unpleasant. Totally familiar situations may be boring, while a certain amount of novelty causes a pleasant level of arousal (Russell and

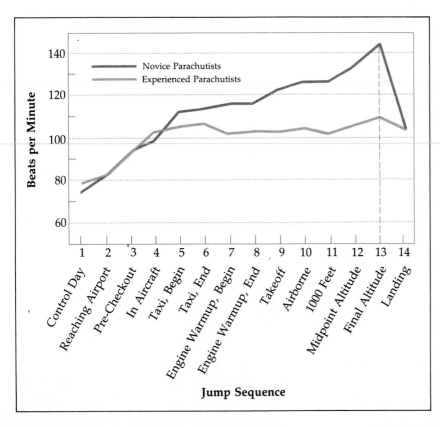

FIGURE 14.2 Heart rate at different phases in the jump sequence for experienced and novice parachutists. Note that the two groups do not differ until the plane begins to take off. As the moment of the jump approaches, the novices' heart rates became quite high. This is an example of the importance of novelty in increasing the stressfulness of an experience.

Mehrabian, 1978.) It is only when the arousal gets out of control that it is aversive. Recall also that some sensation-seeking individuals repeatedly seek out high levels of novelty and challenge in their lives (Zuckerman, 1984).

STRESS, HEALTH, AND PHYSICAL SYMPTOMS

The term stress is also used in a physical sense, as when we discuss the stress on a bridge caused by driving a heavy truck over it. Such stresses on a bridge eventually cause it to deteriorate. When psychologists use the same term for unpredictable and uncontrollable life changes and daily hassles, they imply that "stress" is a potentially deteriorating force. In fact, there is ample evidence that psychological stressors wear us down, just like eighteen-wheel trucks rolling over a bridge wear it down. Consider the top-rated stress on Holmes and Rahe's (1967) list of life changes—death of a spouse. A recent study of 95,647 widows and widowers (Kaprio et al., 1987) indicated that they themselves were significantly more likely to die during the period following the death of their spouses. Some of those deaths were from suicides and accidents, but there were also increases in death from natural causes, particularly heart attacks. Divorce, the number two life change, is also associated with an increased incidence of emotional disturbance and physical disease (Jacobson, 1983). For instance, admission rates to psychiatric clinics are three to nine times higher among divorced than married people (Bloom et al., 1978). And lesser stressors can take their toll as well. A classic study of students preparing for their doctoral qualifying examinations found that, as the examination drew nearer, the students began to become more anxious, and to complain of stomachaches, asthma, and general feelings of weariness. Students also increased their use of tranquilizers and sleeping pills (Mechanic, 1962).

Even minor daily disruptions are associated with physical costs. Students in one recent study were asked to record the stressful things that happened to them each day. A later statistical analysis indicated an increase in physical and psychological symptoms following particularly stressful days (DeLongis, Folkman, and Lazarus, 1987). In the upcoming sections, we discuss the complex interplay between stress and physical and mental health. We will also discuss another fascinating interaction between the mind and the body—the perception of pain and physical symptoms.

STRESS AND MENTAL HEALTH

In addition to its effect on physical symptoms, stress can also lead to disruption of psychological functioning. Consider the case of a woman who had survived the Auschwitz concentration camp. She was forced to rise at two in the morning to prepare for a roll call that lasted until 7 A.M., when she was fed a meal of one piece of bread, margarine, and beet jelly. At two in the afternoon, she had another roll call, followed by a bowl of chemical-tasting potato mush. At night she slept in a bunk with 12 other people, and regretted picking an upper bunk after it broke and crushed several of the people sleeping below. To control lice infestations, inmates were stripped naked, and all the hair on their bodies was shaved off while the guards watched with amusement. As her confinement extended over time, she was subjected to more and more frequent "mass selections," in which Dr. Josef Mengele, later dubbed the "Auschwitz angel of death," would line up the inmates and choose those who would be cremated. She described the criterion for "selection" to be any sign of illness, sometimes as slight as a pimple.

This woman, and many others in her predicament, showed a pattern of emotional response to the concentration camp (Chodoff, 1970). At first, inmates were shocked and horrified at their plight. Following this, they entered a period of apathy, depression and mourning. Those who survived showed chronic psychological symptoms, including nightmares, social withdrawal, depression, guilt, and mistrust of others. Another study looked at the survivors of the Hiroshima bombings, and also found evidence of chronic guilt, anxiety, and social apathy lasting for years after the trauma (Lifton, 1982). Less tragic stressors can induce psychological costs, including temporary depression and other negative feelings (DeLongis et al., 1987, among others). In the next chapter we will discuss serious psychopathological states, including chronic anxiety, schizophrenia, and depression. Stress undoubtedly plays some part in anxiety disorders. It probably also plays a role in chronic depression, and some believe that it is involved in other disorders, including schizophrenia. In addition, stress is linked to psychophysiological disorders, to which we now turn.

PSYCHOPHYSIOLOGICAL DISORDERS

As defined earlier, psychophysiological disorders are actual physical ailments that are partly a result of psychological stress. They include headaches as well as more chronic dysfunctions, including ulcers, asthma, arthritis, hypertension, and heart disease. An argument with your boss or worries about a test can lead to physical symptoms by stimulating the autonomic nervous system's sympathetic "fight or flight" reaction. As we noted earlier, skydivers approaching a jump showed increased breathing and heart rates—two signs of sympathetic activity (Fenz and Epstein, 1967). Figure 14.3 shows the results of a psychophysiological case study of a doctoral student during the period when she took her dissertation oral exam (Johansson, 1977). Instead of using indirect measures of sympathetic activity, such as heart rate, Johansson measured actual adrenaline levels. As you can see, adrenaline gradually increased during the week preceding the exam, and dropped after the exam was over.

The "fight or flight" response involves an increased output of energy by the body, an increased tension in the voluntary muscles, and a neglect of such normal processes as digestion. It is easy to see why people under stress, including students preparing for important exams, might experience stomachaches (from the disrupted digestive processes and heightened heart rate) and headaches (from the increased tension in the voluntary muscles). If the stresses continue over time, they can permanently damage the biological system, as Hans Selye (1976) noted in his work on the General Adaptation Syndrome. Many other studies support Selye's observation that psychological stressors can produce bodily damage. Since Selye's own early work, for example, numerous studies have verified that animals exposed to psychological stress develop peptic ulcers (Weiss, 1968; 1971; among others).

Recent research also suggests that chronic anxiety can lead to peptic ulcers in humans (Friedman and Booth-Kewley, 1987). Stress also contributes to hypertension (Egan et al., 1983), which can lead to kidney damage and stroke. Stress can heighten blood pressure by increasing sodium retention (Light et al., 1983), or by interfering with the metabolism of fats that build up on the inside of "hardened" arteries (Krantz, Baum, and Singer, 1983). Prolonged stress also contributes to heart disease (Taylor, 1986). Recent evidence has generally not supported the earlier specificity hypothesis of a unique pattern of psychological stress associated with each psychophysiological disorder. In general, chronic hostility, anxiety, and depression all show up more in people with psychosomatic disorders of all kinds (Friedman and Booth-Kewley, 1987). However, some differences were revealed in a recent meta-analysis (a statistical technique in which the results of a large number of different studies are combined). Coronary disease, asthma, and ulcers are all positively linked to anxiety and depression, but ulcers are unique in showing no association with measures of anger (Friedman and Booth-Kewley, 1987.) (See Figure 14.4.)

Bronchial asthma occurs when the breathing passages are obstructed by muscle spasms and swelling of the tissue in the lungs. Asthma is actually triggered by *allergens*, substances such as pollen, dust, drugs, or animal hair, that are recognized and rejected by the body. The body's allergic reaction to these foreign substances is intensified by stress. In one study, researchers found that asthma patients used three times their normal medicine doses if they were experiencing a great deal of life stress, and did not simultaneously have much support from friends and relatives (De

FIGURE 14.3 Adrenaline secretion rates during the period of a student's oral dissertation defense. As shown in the figure, adrenaline secretion began to rise during the week preceding the exam and peaked on the day of the exam. During the next week, there was a dramatic drop back to normal levels.

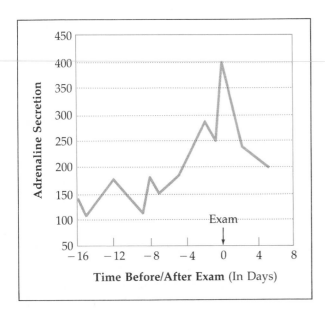

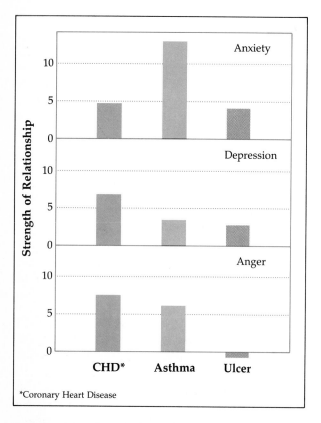

FIGURE 14.4 The relationship of anxiety, depression, and anger to psychophysiological disorders. This figure represents the combined results of several studies reviewed by Friedman and Booth-Kewley (1987). Note that each of the disorders is positively related to anxiety and depression, although the strength of association differs for the different disorders. Unlike other psychophysiological disorders, ulcers show no relationship with anger.

Araujo et al., 1973). These findings are interesting because they indicate that, in addition to its direct effects on the organs involved in the fight or flight reaction, stress can also interfere with the operation of the body's immune system.

STRESS AND IMMUNE RESPONSES

Medical researchers have become increasingly interested in the body's immune response. When we get an infection, specialized white blood cells called T and B lymphocytes team up to identify the invading bacteria or virus, chemically neutralize it, and destroy its cell structure. AIDS (autoimmune deficiency syndrome) is caused by a virus that infects crucial T-cells and cripples their ability to fight off infection. There is recent evidence that stressful life events can also interfere with the body's immune responses (Jemmott and Locke, 1984; O'Leary, 1990). In fact, on the basis of their own research indicating that stress can open the

door to viral infections, biomedical researchers Janice Kiecolt-Glaser and Ronald Glaser (1988) speculated that stress could possibly influence how well someone might be able to fight off an initial AIDS infection. Stress has been linked to an increasing number of diseases that were not previously categorized as psychosomatic disorders. For instance, people who have recently lost a spouse are more susceptible to such diseases as pneumonia and cancer (Klerman and Izen, 1977; Sklar and Anisman, 1981).

Herpes is a viral infection that leads to recurrent sores around the mouth or genitals. A study of dental students with this virus indicated that symptoms were more likely to break out during periods when the students were lonely, or when they were "under the gun" at exam time (Kiecolt-Glaser et al., 1985a). Another study indicated that students were more likely to come down with respiratory illnesses three to five days *after* a particularly stressful day (Stone, Reed, and Neale, 1987). The researchers note that it takes that long for the symptoms of a viral infection to show up. Thus, stress on Tuesday interferes with our immune response on Tuesday, but the symptoms of the resultant infection do not show up until the weekend.

There is also direct evidence that stress can interfere with the ability of white blood cells to fight off infections (Schleifer et al., 1985). For instance, one team of researchers found that mourning spouses showed lower than normal blood counterattack against potential infection (Bartrop et al., 1977). Arthur Stone and his colleagues found a similar relationship between daily mood and immune response. The researchers measured dental students' mood three times a week. Each time, the students were given an oral dose of a protein (rabbit albumin) which, though harmless, evoked a protective response by the body. One of the body's first lines of defense against antigens is in the saliva, which produces a substance called *secretory immunoglobulin A* (sIgA), a biochemical that attacks and neutralizes potentially harmful substances. The researchers found that the sIgA response to the foreign protein was lower on days when the students were in a negative mood, and, conversely, higher on days when they were in an especially good mood (Stone, Cox, et al., 1987).

We are not yet certain exactly how or why stress interferes with immune responses. It is possible that the body has only a limited amount of resources at its disposal, and must put the immune system on temporary hold while it mobilizes to meet an immediate external threat (from a bear or a threatening drunk, for instance). There is some evidence that immune cells actually have receptors for such neurochemicals as adrenaline and endorphins (Ornstein and Sobel, 1987). As we noted earlier, adrenaline and endorphins are involved in the "fight or flight" response to external threats. Thus, new research in this area suggests a complex interplay between the internal and external defense systems.

PAIN AND SYMPTOM RECOGNITION

Thus far, we have seen several ways in which psychological factors can contribute to illness. Prolonged stress can lead directly to such psychophysiological disorders as ulcers, and, by interfering with immune responses, it can contribute indirectly to other diseases of all sorts. But psychological states contribute to illness in a more immediate way, by contributing to our experience of painful and unpleasant symptoms of illness. Cognition and learning can determine whether we recognize, and how we react to, physical symptoms of illness. Our emotional reaction to painful symptoms can, in turn, affect how much pain we experience. In the upcoming sections, we will consider how thought and attentional processes can influence the extent to which a person experiences the pain of bodily injuries and illnesses. We will also consider how the reactions of other people can lead some people to exaggerate their attention to minor symptoms, and thus contribute to phenomena that range from malingering after an illness to "mass illnesses" that seem to have no medical basis.

PAIN AND COGNITIVE PROCESSES

To the traditional medical view, pain is not something "in the head," but something "out there" in the body—the result of destruction of, or pressure on, nerve cells in the skin, muscles, and internal organs (Warga, 1987). Of course, pain does begin in nerve endings in the body. However, during the 1960s psychologists began to question that view. Consider the following description of Scottish terriers that were raised in restricted environments. When they were brought out of restriction:

They had never seen people, and ran round and round the feet of whoever was there. They were so frisky and rambunctious that inevitably someone would accidentally step on their tails. But we didn't hear a squeak from them. In their excitement, they would also bang their heads with a resounding

smack on the building's low water pipes and just walk away. I was curious, and lit a match to see how they would respond to the flame. They kept sticking their noses in it, and though they would back off as if from a funny smell, they did not react as if it hurt.

(Melzack, quoted in Warga, 1987)

This seemed to suggest that the experience of pain might be moderated by the brain's attentional systems. (This system, located in the brainstem, is discussed in Chapter 2). The dogs' experience of pain was damped by their attention to the exciting array of new stimuli in the world they had never before seen.

After noting the unusual lack of pain responses in the deprived terriers, psychologist Ronald Melzack began to study humans who suffered from unusually high levels of pain. One puzzling clinical syndrome is called **phantom limb pain,** or pain in a part of the body that no longer exists. Phantom limb pain is fairly common in amputees. About 35 percent of all amputees report pain in their missing limb. For those patients, the limb still feels as if it were there, and they may try to step on the phantom leg or grasp objects with the phantom hand (Melzack, 1973). In several tragic cases, the limb was originally amputated in order to relieve a chronic pain problem, as in the following case of a woman whose legs had been amputated:

Mrs. Hull would describe burning pains that were like a red-hot poker being shoved through her toes and her ankle. She would cry out from the pain in her legs. Of course, there were no legs.

(Melzack, quoted in Warga, 1987)

Mrs. Hull used three types of words to describe her pain. Such words as "exhausting," "sickening," "terrifying," and "punishing" described the emotional component, while "shooting," "scalding," "splitting," and "cramping" described the sensory component. A third group of words, including "unbearable" and "annoying," seemed to capture a third evaluative component. Melzack used these words to develop the McGill Pain Questionnaire, which has since been extensively used in the clinical assessment of pain.

After studying phantom limb pain, Melzack and Patrick Wall (1965) developed a theory to incorporate several puzzling pain phenomena. In addition to the phantom limb phenomenon, there are other findings that do not fit with the specificity theory of pain. For instance, there is the phenomenon of "referred pain," in which patients experience soreness in parts of the body that are not themselves afflicted with disease. Heart patients may experience intense discomfort from pressure on points on the shoulder and chest called "trigger zones" (Melzack, 1973). At the same time, stimulation of trigger zones can sometimes relieve the agony in the affected organ. *Hyperstimulation* involves the relief of pain in one area of the body by irritation of another area. For instance, a painfully cold icepack applied to the leg makes people less likely to notice a painful electrical stimulation applied to the teeth (Melzack, 1973). Acupuncture, the Chinese art of analgesia through the insertion of needles into various points of the body, may rely on similar principles (Mayer et al., 1976). As we mentioned in Chapter 3, the **gate control theory** explained these phenomena by positing feedback from the brain to the pain receptor path-

way in the spinal column (Figure 14.5). According to this theory, pain from an arm or a leg can be turned on or off by the brain (or by other receptors in the spinal cord) as a function of stimulation in other parts of the body. In the instance of the icepack diversion, for instance, cold stimulation to the leg stimulates a mechanism in the brain that partly closes the gate for pain information coming from the teeth. More recent research supports the theory that stimulation of different areas of the brain can inhibit pain transmission in the spinal cord (Perl, 1984).

COGNITION AND OTHER SYMPTOMS

Other findings suggest that the way we focus our attention can contribute to a wide variety of physical symptoms. For instance, joggers were found to run faster in a beautiful wooded area than on a track. The pretty scenery apparently dis-

FIGURE 14.5 The gate control theory of pain. This theory posits two gates that can open or close to influence pain perception. The first gate is in the spinal cord. Damage to free nerve endings in the skin or inner organs stimulates pain fibers, which work to open the spinal gate. However, information about other sensory experiences (for instance, vibration) can close the spinal gate. A second gate in the brain stem can be opened or closed by information from higher brain centers. For instance, anxiety caused by comparing the present injury to painful past experiences can open the second gate, and thereby enhance the experience of pain.

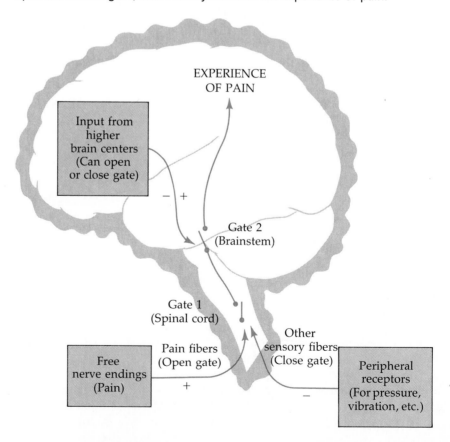

tracted their attention from painful sensations in their chest and legs that would otherwise have led them to slow down (Pennebaker and Lightner, 1980). Even attention to minor symptoms can magnify the experience of physical illness. James Pennebaker (1982) notes that most of us experience fairly frequent "symptoms," such as mild headaches, sniffles, coughs, or upset stomachs, but usually ignore them as we go about our daily business. If circumstances lead us to become concerned about illness, however, we may suddenly focus on those everyday discomforts, and begin to feel quite ill (Pennebaker, 1982).

DYSFUNCTION:
Mass Psychogenic Illness

Mass psychogenic illness is a phenomenon in which a group of people suddenly come down with symptoms that seem to have no organic basis. One such incident was reported in an elementary school in Norwood, Massachusetts on May 21, 1979 (Small and Nicholi, 1982). During the ceremony for sixth graders graduating to junior high, one boy became dizzy, fell from the stage, cut his chin, and started bleeding profusely. Suddenly, other sixth graders began to fall ill with weakness, dizziness, chills, and faintness. The epidemic began with eight girls and one boy, but then spread throughout the assembly. Thirty-four children were hospitalized, and 40 to 50 were treated on the school lawn when the ambulances became overloaded. Within four hours the crisis was over and doctors could find no medical cause for it. As is commonly the case with incidents of this sort, the epidemic spread among children who were similar to one another (sixth graders), and who were experiencing stress (their graduation to junior high). Pennebaker (1982) argues that such outbreaks are due to a mislabeling of such common physical symptoms as anxious butterflies in the stomach. He notes their similarity to the "medical student's syndrome," in which 70 percent of first-year medical students imagine that they have one of the dread diseases they are reading about. The children who were hospitalized during the Norwood school epidemic were probably also predisposed by prior experience to worry about their physical symptoms. Three-quarters of the hospitalized children had experienced a death in the family (compared with 39 percent of the children who did not fall ill).

One case of mass psychogenic illness was actually manufactured, more or less unintentionally. In 1942, 25-year-old Frank Sinatra had begun to attract a large following of teenage girls, who would throw him roses, hang on every lyric that he sang, and wait for him in crowds outside his dressing room. When Sinatra appeared in a concert at the Paramount Theatre in New York, his manager arranged a publicity stunt by paying a dozen girls to moan and scream, and coaching two of them to fall into a dead faint in the aisle. The excitement spread to hundreds of the other girls present, however, and 30 of them were taken to ambulances after they fainted (Kelley, 1986). When this incident was reported in the press, Sinatra became famous for girls "swooning" at his concerts. Again, in this case there was a combination of circumstances that naturally led to physiological arousal (crowds and the proximity to a star), with a social context that both suggested and fueled the physical symptoms.

Mass psychogenic illness is a fascinating phenomenon, but there are problems in interpreting any given incident. People sometimes fake symptoms, for instance, and medical experts sometimes miss a real, but unusual, illness. We will encounter this problem again in the next chapter, when we discuss psychological disorders in which people imagine or fake physical illness. Medical and psychological experts also have occasional difficulties in distinguishing between the symptoms of anxiety and those of other illnesses. For instance, a stomachache or a headache may be brought on by psychological distress, or by an infection or injury. Such phenomena as mass psychogenic illness suggest that people themselves are also unable to make such distinctions, and look to others to help them decide whether their current feelings are cause for alarm. As we saw in our earlier discussion of hypnosis, and will see in a later discussion of such phenomena as mass suicide, social suggestion has powerful and sometimes puzzling influences on individual thought, feeling, and behavior. ■

PHYSICAL ILLNESS AND THE REACTIONS OF OTHER PEOPLE

Phenomena such as mass psychogenic illness and purposely feigned symptoms demonstrate an important point. Physical symptoms occur in a social context. The reactions of other people can play an important role in maintaining illness. In considering people's reactions to painful symptoms, behavioral psychologist Wilbert Fordyce (1988) distinguishes between pain, suffering, and pain behaviors. *Pain* is a sensation caused by physical damage to specialized sensory neurons. *Suffering* is an emotional response that can follow pain or other unpleasant events, such as the loss of a loved one. *Pain behaviors* are what people do when they suffer or are in pain. The same painful damage can lead to very different suffering and pain behaviors. In considering these distinctions, Fordyce notes several interesting phenomena. Earlier research (Beecher, 1959) had found that wounded soldiers in Boston Hospital requested less narcotic pain relievers than did surgery victims with similar injuries, for instance, and permanent disabilities from back injury are nonexistent in some countries. Those disabilities have fluctuated with government disability policies in our own country. It is not that soldiers did not have pain from their wounds, or that people in other countries do not experience back pain. (Fordyce presents evidence that they do.) The point is that suffering and pain-related behaviors vary with their consequences. For wounded soldiers, their injuries meant a ticket home from the war, and thus reduced another kind of suffering. For workers eligible for permanent disability, back pain may mean a lifetime meal ticket, and so they were motivated to pay more attention to the pain than they would have otherwise.

How other people respond to a patient's injury can sometimes hinder recovery. In one study, researchers found that two days of treatment for back injury led to more recovery than seven days of treatment did (Deyo, Diehl, and Rosenthal, 1986). Likewise, patients recover more fully from an illness if they are given a specified time to stop bedrest than if they are told to "let pain be your guide" (Fordyce et al., 1986). Why do patients have speedier recoveries when doctors set a time limit on the expected suffering? One reason is that people who have something better to do do not pay as much attention to their pain as they would otherwise. As we saw above, attentional processes play a role in the experience of pain. In addition, prolonged bedrest leads to extensive loss of muscle and cardiovascular fitness. With problems such as back injury, that loss of fitness further interferes with the exercise needed for recovery.

To summarize this section, the phenomenon of pain involves more than the simple input from damaged sensory receptors. Responses to the same injury or illness can vary depending upon how much attention we give it, how others respond to it, and even how other people seem to be responding to their own similar symptoms.

STRESS AND ORGANIZATIONAL BEHAVIOR

A glance back at Holmes and Rahe's list of major life changes (Table 14.1) reveals that many of these stressful events are related to work. Losing or changing jobs, trouble with the boss, and even a change in working hours are all ranked as quite stressful. Daily hassles also include many events at work, including disagreements with the boss. One study of 230 working women found that difficulties at work were the single best predictor of depression and anxiety (O'Neill & Zeichner, 1984). Stresses at work take a significant toll on some:

> For four years (Robert) Hearsch had been a successful supervisor for Hughes Aircraft. Then General Motors took over . . . and he was put in charge of buying pens and pencils. He found orders backlogged and records in disarray. He spent most of his days appeasing angry secretaries. He stayed on gamely, arriving early, leaving late, working through his breaks. But, as Hearsch tells the story, things only got worse. His supervisors hinted that his position might be phased out. They ignored his diligence and recorded small mistakes into his file. They even left him off the guest list for the department party. . . . The pressure took its toll. Hearsch lost 20 pounds. His marriage hit the skids. He suffered a minor nervous breakdown. (Mr. Hearsch filed a workman's compensation claim and was awarded a $20,000 settlement from the company, which he said was little compensation because) "I lost my wife, my house and my career."

(Miller, 1988)

As we noted earlier, stress on the job costs industry billions of dollars a year in accidents, health claims, absence from work, and impaired performance. And there is evidence that job stress can lead workers to become dissatisfied with home and family life, and so weaken their marriages (Barling and Rosenbaum, 1986; Keon and McDonald, 1982). Most troubling is the finding that workers under stress are more likely to abuse their spouses and children (Barling and Rosenbaum, 1986; Aganthanos and Stathakpolou, 1983).

STRESSFUL JOBS

Which jobs are most stressful? According to the National Institute on Workers Compensation, secretaries, waitresses, office managers, and laborers have the worst plights ("Stress on the Job," 1988). Air traffic controllers, police officers, inner-city high school teachers, medical interns, and stock brokers also have stress-prone jobs. Contrary to the stereotype that executives have the most pressure on the job, the evidence suggests that those lower on the totem pole have it much worse. For instance, one early study compared executives to craftsmen and foremen in the same corporation, and found that executives were the least likely to develop peptic ulcers (Dunn and Cobb, 1962). Likewise, an extensive study of over 1,000 men who held one of the top three executive positions in Fortune 500 companies revealed that the mortality rate of those top-flight executives was 37 percent lower than that of other men of comparable age and race (Seliger, 1982). Another study examined 2,352 women listed in *Who's Who*. Like the executive men, these high-powered women were healthier than expected, with a 29 percent lower mortality rate than other women of the same age. Conversely, underpaid female clerical workers are at very high risk for coronary problems (Haynes and Feinleib, 1980).

Why might high-status employees be in better health? One explanation relates to the research, discussed earlier, showing that uncontrollable stressors are more damaging than those under our control. Executives have much more control over the stressors in their lives than do their secretaries, whose agendas and deadlines are set by those higher up. In addition to uncontrollability, other aspects of jobs can make them unpleasant. Job ambiguity is associated with more stress (Jackson and Schuler, 1985). For instance, a rookie police officer may be confused when one supervisor says it is desirable to maintain good community relations while another says that it's better to arouse fear in people's hearts. A heavy workload or interpersonal conflict on the job are also linked with anxiety, physical symptoms, and job dissatisfaction (Spector, Dwyer, and Jex, 1988). Finally, organizational constraints—job conditions that interfere with employees doing their jobs—are also related to job distress (O'Connor et al., 1982). These factors can combine to make for a very stressful job. A secretary may be asked to act as a pleasant receptionist, even though that interferes with the typing that the boss wants done on a tight deadline. These conflicting demands may require overtime work, and lead to feelings of helplessness because there is little opportunity for the lower-status employee to effect a change in these working conditions.

An example of a stress-prone job. Stock brokers have a highly stressful job, involving uncertainty, lack of control, and numerous daily hassles (including sometimes heated arguments with other workers on the crowded floor). The different facial reactions you see here may be related to individual differences in coping with work stress (which we will discuss in a later section).

STRESS AND JOB PERFORMANCE

At first glance, it seems that stress would interfere with carrying out one's work. Indeed, there are findings that stress can hurt performance. For instance, subjects in one study were asked to solve analogies like "Butter is to margarine as sugar is to: beets, saccharine, honey, lemon, candy, chocolate." Compared to unfrightened subjects, people expecting electric shock were less likely to scan the answers carefully, and more likely to jump to incorrect conclusions before considering all the alternatives. Interestingly, stressed subjects made more mistakes even when they thought that the shocks would be contingent on their performance. That is, fear of punishment for a poor performance only served to disrupt these subjects (Kienan, 1987).

The relationship between stress and work performance is not a simple one, however. Some studies of the effects of environmental stressors, such as noise and heat, indicate that stress hurts performance; but other studies find either no effects or improvements in performance under stress. The effects do not seem to be random. Instead, they often fit with a principle that has come to be called the **Yerkes-Dodson law,** which states that arousal, whether due to stress, exercise, or a cup of coffee, leads to an improvement in performance up to a point, but hurts performance beyond that point. The Yerkes-Dodson law thus implies that the relationship of arousal to performance is an inverted U-shaped function, as shown in Figure 14.6.

As you can also see in Figure 14.6, the point at which arousal begins to hurt performance depends on the complexity of the task. For complex tasks, arousal is expected to disrupt performance fairly quickly. For simple tasks, arousal should be harmful only at very high levels. Under normal circumstances, it may be uncommon to find arousal of the sort that will interfere with performance. Although the Yerkes-Dodson law is an elegant solution to the conflicting findings on arousal and performance, there is some debate about whether it applies to all types of arousal (Anderson, 1990; Neiss, 1990). Research indicates that high arousal may only hinder performance when the arousal stems from threat (Neiss, 1988). Threats, such as the potential loss of one's job, can be a common source of stress at work. The arousal stemming from fear of such punishments will only improve performance under limited conditions.

Closely related to the fear of a boss's punishments is the stress of having someone else looking over your shoulder while you work. As you might guess, low status workers are more likely to be closely supervised, especially when they are perceived as performing poorly (Spector, Dwyer, and Jex, 1988). Low status individuals are also likely to work in open areas, rather than in their own private offices. The presence of others who can potentially evaluate our performance seems to act like a mild stressor. If we are working on a very simple task, or one that we have learned very well, we are likely to do better (Zajonc, 1965). This performance-induced increment is called **social facilitation.** In line with the Yerkes-Dodson law, however, performance-induced stress can be debilitating on complex or poorly learned tasks (Zajonc, 1965). Imagine two workers, one of whom is just learning the complex skilled craft of making guitars by hand, and the other of whom has worked for a year on an assembly line boxing the guitars in a standard and simple process. The first worker

Social facilitation and work stress. Some research indicates that the presence of other people who can observe our performance leads to arousal. In line with the Yerkes-Dodson principle, the socially induced arousal can facilitate performance on simple, well-learned tasks (such as assembly line work), but it can hurt performance on complex, poorly learned tasks (Zajonc, 1965).

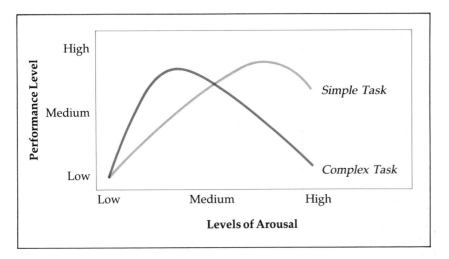

FIGURE 14.6 A graphic depiction of the Yerkes-Dodson principle. Arousal increases performance up to a certain point. Obviously, people do not work well when they are half asleep. However, high levels of arousal produce a deterioration in performance. If the task is complex, the turning point will come at a lower level of arousal. For simple, well-learned tasks, moderately high levels of arousal are not debilitating, but very high levels are.

is likely to do worse with supervisors and co-workers looking over his or her shoulder, while the second will likely perform better with an audience.

STRESS-PRONE WORKERS: TYPE A AND HARDY EXECUTIVES

Given our discussion of personality in the last chapter, it makes sense to wonder whether some people are more susceptible than others to the factors that can make work stressful. Stressful working conditions should have more effect on people who bring an overly high arousal level, a deadline mentality, or a sense of uncontrollability with them to the job. Researchers have extensively examined two complex personality variables that might contribute to stress. The **Type A syndrome** is composed of several interrelated characteristics that are believed to increase susceptibility to stress-related illnesses, whereas **hardiness** is composed of a set of personal characteristics that relate to stress resistance.

The Type A individual is generally characterized by competitiveness, hostility, and a sense of urgency about time. More specific Type A characteristics include rapid talking, walking, and eating, as well as irritability at such delays as being stuck in traffic on the way to a meeting. Type As tend to be "workaholics," who continually set deadlines for themselves and have difficulty taking a vacation. (If they do go away they may bring work with them and call in to the office several times a day.)

Perhaps because of their deadline mentality, they frequently get angry at others. Cardiologist Meyer Friedman began his work on this syndrome when his upholsterer informed him that the chairs in his office had a peculiar pattern of wear—severely frayed along the front edge, but otherwise like new. It was as if his heart patients were always sitting on the edge of the seat, eagerly perched, ready to get moving. Along with fellow cardiologist Ray Rosenman, Friedman defined the Type A personality, and went on to interview 3,000 middle-aged men in the "Western Collaborative Group Study" (Friedman and Rosenman, 1974). After tracking the men for eight years, Friedman and Rosenman found that Type A men, in comparison to Type Bs (who took a relaxed and noncompetitive approach to life), had suffered more than twice the number of heart attacks or sudden deaths.

Later research has sometimes found a strong relationship between Type A and illness, but the results are not always clear and consistent. Some researchers believe that it is the hostility component of the Type A personality that contributes to increased risk of heart attack (Spielberger et al., 1985). For instance, Redford Williams and his associates studied 255 physicians whose personality test scores indicated that they were hostile and cynical. Compared with their peers, those men were five times more likely to die or have a coronary problem during the 25 years after they left medical school (Williams, 1984).

Instead of looking for people likely to succumb

to work stress, psychologist Suzanne Kobasa (1979) took the opposite tack. She examined a group of executives who had experienced a highly stressful year but had not fallen ill. She compared these men to a group who had become ill in response to similar levels of stress. She and her colleagues asked the executives about their backgrounds and their jobs. They also administered a number of personality tests to find out what was special about the *hardy* (or illness-resistant) executives. She found three things that distinguished the hardy men:

1. *Commitment.* They were devoted to their jobs, their families, and other important values;

2. *Control.* They had a sense of personal mastery over their lives; and

3. *Challenge.* They saw life changes not as threats, but as chances to test themselves.

You can rate yourself on hardiness using a short version of the scale that Kobasa (1984) developed. (See Figure 14.7.)

Following on Kobasa's work, other studies have confirmed that commitment and control are associated with good health (Ganellen and Blaney, 1984; Hull, Van Treuren, and Virnelli, 1987). However, this later research indicates that challenge may not be an active ingredient in the formula for hardiness. Being committed and in control may not always *prevent* stress, but being uncommitted and helpless is, in itself, stressful (Hull et al., 1987). A study found that salespeople with a "helpless" outlook have poorer sales records and are more likely to change jobs frequently, thus contributing to their own life stresses (Seligman and Schulman, 1986). In a related vein, people who take an optimistic outlook also seem to cope better (Scheier, Weintraub, and Carver, 1986).

FIGURE 14.7 A self-test for hardiness. This test is designed to study people who are especially good at withstanding stress.

HOW HARDY ARE YOU?

Below are 12 items similar to those that appear in the hardiness questionnaire. Evaluating someone's hardiness requires more than this quick test. But this simple exercise should give you some idea of how hardy you are.

Write down how much you agree or disagree with the following statements, using this scale:
0 = strongly disagree,
1 = mildly disagree,
2 = mildly agree,
3 = strongly agree.
☐ **A.** Trying my best at work makes a difference.
☐ **B.** Trusting to fate is sometimes all I can do in a relationship.
☐ **C.** I often wake up eager to start on the day's projects.
☐ **D.** Thinking of myself as a free person leads to great frustration and difficulty.
☐ **E.** I would be willing to sacrifice financial security in my work if something really challenging came along.
☐ **F.** It bothers me when I have to deviate from the routine or schedule I've set for myself.
☐ **G.** An average citizen can have an impact on politics.
☐ **H.** Without the right breaks, it is hard to be successful in my field.
☐ **I.** I know why I am doing what I'm doing at work.
☐ **J.** Getting close to people puts me at risk of being obligated to them.
☐ **K.** Encountering new situations is an important priority in my life.
☐ **L.** I really don't mind when I have nothing to do.
To Score Yourself: These questions measure control, commitment and challenge. For half the questions, a high score (like 3, "strongly agree") indicates hardiness; for the other half, a low score (disagreement) does.

To get your scores on control, commitment and challenge, first write in the number of your answer—0, 1, 2 to 3—above the letter of each question on the score sheet. Then add and substract as shown. (To get your score on "control," for example, add your answers to questions A and G; add your answers to B and H; and then subtract the second number from the first.)

Add your scores on commitment, control and challenge together to get a score for total hardiness.

A total score of **10–18** shows a hardy personality. **0–9:** moderate hardiness. **Below 0:** low hardiness.

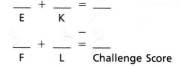

___ + ___ = ___	___ + ___ = ___	___ + ___ = ___
A G	C I	E K
___ + ___ = ___	___ + ___ = ___	___ + ___ = ___
B H Control Score	D J Commitment Score	F L Challenge Score

_____ + _____ + _____ = _____
Control   Commitment   Challenge   Total Hardiness
                                                 Score

In sum, jobs are often a source of stress, particularly jobs that offer ambiguity, role conflict, and little hope of control by the worker. The arousal produced by stress can hurt performance on complex tasks, though it could also help performance on simple, well-learned tasks. Workers who take a hostile and competitive approach to their jobs are more likely to become ill, while those who approach their jobs with commitment and a sense of control may avoid job stress.

RESEARCH AND APPLICATION:
Stress Management

In an attempt to deal with the problems of job stress, many businesses have begun programs aimed at "stress management." These programs may include a wide range of interventions: biofeedback, humor programs, training in the Oriental art of tai chi (which combines dance with martial arts movements), and so on. The most common approach is to institute an "employee fitness program," which usually includes daily classes in aerobic exercise. Thus far, an estimated 50,000 U.S. firms have instituted fitness programs (Falkenberg, 1987).

Fitness programs can reduce the negative consequences of job stress in several ways. For one thing, a person in good physical shape should become less aroused during stressful situations. Physically fit people can do the same job with less muscular exertion and slower respiration rates (Ledwidge, 1980). For these reasons, physically fit workers can work more efficiently (Folkins and Sime, 1981). Another benefit can come from exercise *during* a particularly stressful period. Troubles on the job can lead to the secretion of free fatty acids, chemicals that build up on the walls of the arteries and contribute to cardiovascular problems over time. Exercise at those times of intense stress can lead to more efficient metabolization of these biochemicals, preventing their harmful buildup (Everly and Rosenfeld, 1981). Exercise can also reduce psychological stress, since it leads to a state of relaxation (deVries and Adams, 1972).

Physical fitness is also associated with lower levels of anxiety and depression (Folkins and Sime, 1981; McCann and Holmes, 1984). Given our earlier discussion of the effects of arousal on performance, then, we would expect that exercise would improve people's performance on tasks that involve any degree of complexity. In fact, subjects in one study did better work on a demanding cognitive task if they had previously completed a vigorous exercise class, as opposed to a hobby class (Lichtman and Poser, 1983).

Thus, physically fit workers seem to be able to work more efficiently and to be better able to withstand job stress. This may account for findings that adherents to fitness programs are more productive than their co-workers (Bernacki and Baun, 1984, among others). In the long run, there are other benefits. Because of their improved physical and mental health, regular exercisers make fewer health claims than do less fit workers (Naditch, 1985). Finally, there is evidence that participants in employee fitness programs are less likely to skip days at work, or to quit their jobs (Falkenberg, 1987). In sum, employee fitness programs seem to pay off for businesses in a number of ways. ■

COPING WITH STRESS

When grouchy bosses or difficult examinations start to get on your nerves, you need not just sit passively as the fatty acids and catecholemines course through your arteries. If you are like the hardy executives in Kobasa's research, you can try to take control and do something about it. Removing the cause of stress is probably the most effective coping strategy, but sometimes, as in the case of a irritable boss or natural disaster such as the Buffalo Creek flood, it is not possible. Barring an immediate solution to our problems, we may try a number of other strategies to make them less aversive—we may seek the support of friends, we may reinterpret our situation to make it seem less unpleasant, we may laugh or cry, go for a drink, and so on. These attempts to control stress are called *coping mechanisms*.

Richard Lazarus and his colleagues have made a useful distinction between **problem-focused** and **emotion-focused coping strategies.** Problem-focused strategies are those aimed at doing something to change the problem causing the distress (perhaps talking to the boss about what he or she expects of you). Problem-focused strategies tend to be used in situations that we regard as changeable (Folkman and Lazarus, 1985). Emotion-focused strategies, used more in situations that are appraised as unchangeable, are aimed at regulating our distressing emotional responses. Compared with women, men are less likely to use emotion-focused strategies, such as seeking support from a friend (Endler and Parker, 1990).

Psychologists Susan Folkman and Richard Lazarus (1985) examined undergraduate students' coping strategies at three time periods—two days before a midterm examination; a week later, two days before the grades were announced; and five days after the grades were posted. Before the exam, students tended to use such problem-focused strategies as studying—a guaranteed way to reduce the potential problems caused by an upcoming exam. If they sought out others, it was more likely to be for information than for emotional support. After the exam, when their fates were sealed, they tended to use the emotion-focused cognitive strategy of "distancing" (measured by such phrases as "Try to forget the whole thing."). If they sought out others afterwards, it was for emotional support rather than for information. Our discussion will focus on these two related lines of defense in coping with stress: seeking social support from others and reinterpreting the meaning of a stressful situation to ourselves.

SOCIAL SUPPORT

We have just seen that students awaiting an examination may seek out others to relieve their stress. At times of physical danger, people are especially likely to pull together. At 8 P.M. on the evening of October 30, 1938, a massive panic swept the United States and provided a clear demonstration of the importance of social support under stress. The panic followed a series of radio announcements about a strange object that had landed in Grover's Mill, New Jersey. At first, listeners heard calm scientific reports of a cylindrical object that gave off a humming noise and then began to unscrew itself in front of curious observers. Suddenly, however, they began to hear people screaming as a strange creature emerged. The creature reportedly started shooting flames at the onlookers, and then radio contact with the original reporter was lost. The police and state militia were called in, but were reportedly killed by the thousands as the creature made its way to New York, and was joined by other aliens landing up and down the East Coast.

Of course, the radio announcements were merely a dramatic program—an enactment of H. G. Wells' War of the Worlds. Primed by intense fears of invasion from Europe during the late 1930s, however, and taken in by the realistic presentation of the program, many people believed that an invasion was actually taking place. According to Princeton psychologist Hadley Cantril (1940), who published a classical case study of the group reaction to the "Martian invasion," surveys at the time indicated that over one million people, many of whom tuned in too late to hear that it was a dra-

matic broadcast, actually took the broadcast seriously. One New Jersey resident drove over 50 miles to get home, never slowing below 70 miles per hour, even for traffic lights. Another hit a curve on his speedy drive home, and wrecked his car. He walked away without caring, assuming that he would have no use for the vehicle in the future. Cantril noted that "the desire to be near loved ones was very common." Here are several of the accounts he recorded:

> "My sister, her husband, my mother- and father-in-law were listening at home. . . . We all kissed one another and felt we would all die."

> "I wanted to be with my husband and my nephew so I ran out of the house—I stood on the corner waiting for a bus and I ran out to every car thinking it was a bus. When I got home my husband was not there so I rushed to the neighbors. . . ."

> "The girls in the sorority houses and dormitories huddled around their radios trembling and weeping in each other's arms. They separated themselves from their friends only to take their turn at the telephones to make long distance calls to their parents, saying goodbye for they thought might be the last time."

(from Cantril, 1940)

Like other animals, humans have always been safer in groups (Trivers, 1985). However, there is increasing evidence that people provide more than physical protection for one another. They provide emotional support and reassurance that can reduce the psychological and physiological symptoms of stress (Cohen and Wills, 1985; Wortman and Conway, 1985). A lack of support can increase our susceptibility to illness. For instance, short-term loneliness is associated with a decrease in immune response (Kiecolt-Glaser et al., 1985a). This increased vulnerability can take a toll over time. Students who described themselves as "loners" in medical school had, compared with other medical students, the highest rates of cancer at a follow-up several decades later (Shaffer et al., 1987). On the other hand, people who receive a great deal of social support from their friends and relatives are less emotionally disrupted by life changes and daily hassles (DeLongis, Folkman, and Lazarus, 1987; Roos and Cohen, 1987), and they are less likely to experience psychosomatic symptoms when they are subjected to stress (de-Araujo et al., 1973). In the long run, those who have strong social ties are likely to be more resistant to disease, and thus to live longer (House, Robbins, and Metzner, 1982). In fact, there is some evidence that strong social support may enable a person to grow stronger as a result of a stressful experience (Holahan and Moos, 1990).

In addition to providing protection and emotional support, people give other types of support to one another. Several types of social support are listed in Table 14.3. For instance, other people may provide *appraisal support*, helping to evaluate and clarify how serious a problem is. If a successful graduate student tells you that he also failed his first college algebra exam, the consequences of your failure will seem less devastating. Others can also provide *informational support*, giving advice about how to deal with the problem. In the search for solutions to problems at school or on the job, two heads are likely to be better than one, especially when the first head is abuzz with confusion and anxiety. Finally, friends and relatives may provide *instrumental support*, providing material goods or services to overcome the stress. If dad lends you some money when your car breaks down, you can stop tearing your hair out and just fix it. One way that relatives and friends may provide support is by facilitating laughter and tears. There is emerging evidence that both may reduce the physiological and psychological effects of distress (e.g. Cogan et al., 1987; Frey and Langseth, 1986; Martin and Lefcourt, 1984, among others).

Recent research by health psychologists Gayle Dakof and Shelley Taylor (1990) suggests that people who are suffering from a stressful illness want and expect different types of support from different people in their lives. These researchers found that cancer patients valued emotional support rather than informational and instrumental support from their close relatives and friends. On the other hand, the patients most valued informational support from doctors and other cancer patients. The cancer victims perceived some attempts at social support, including minimizing the problem, as doing more harm than good.

Several researchers have successfully used social support as a preventative intervention in medical settings (Wortman and Conway, 1985). In one study, pregnant women were assigned a companion to be with them during labor and delivery (Sosa et al., 1980). Compared to a control group, these women experienced significantly fewer medical complications during delivery. Measuring from the time they entered the hospital, women with a companion also delivered their babies in less than half the time that it took for those who

TABLE 14.3 Different Types of Social Support

Type of Support	Example
1. *Emotional*	A sympathetic hug.
2. *Appraisal*	A story about someone who did much worse than you did on the first math exam, and went on to get an A.
3. *Informational*	A suggestion about where to get tutoring to help you pass a difficult course.
4. *Instrumental*	A loan to help you pay for a tutor.

Based on House (1981).

went it alone (8.8 vs. 19.3 hours). The socially supported women also tended to enjoy the experience more, and they were more likely to smile during delivery.

The relationship between social support and stress is a complex one. As stress researcher Manuel Barrera (1986) notes, social support not only softens the physiological impact of stress, it can actually change the stressor. If you have friends and family to count on, losing your job is not the same catastrophic event it would be if you were alone. Social support can also have direct effects on our health. An absence of friends and family is itself a very important source of stress. Unfortunately, social support may be like money in the bank. You can only withdraw so much before you are left with an overdrafted account. Over the long haul, people avoid those who are chronically depressed (Billings and Moos, 1982; Coyne, 1976). It thus makes sense that those with a large network of friends and relatives are better able to withstand stress, because they do not exhaust any one source of social support.

COGNITIVE COPING STRATEGIES

As we just saw, one source of social support that others provide is information. Information is sometimes helpful in changing our interpretation of illnesses and other potential threats to our well-being. For instance, imagine your different reaction to a cough and a headache if several people told you that they had the same symptoms last week, as compared to hearing a doctor say that those are the initial symptoms of a dangerous and

Social support as stress reducer. On their return from the Christmas holiday season, 35 students from Syracuse University were killed by a terrorist bomb planted on Pan Am flight 103. Here surviving friends and relatives of those students provide social support for one another. Having a large network of friends and family to count on in times of stress may reduce the likelihood of later physical illness.

potentially fatal epidemic that has just broken out. This example also illustrates how our interpretations can either reduce or enhance our level of psychological distress in a given situation. As we noted earlier, medical students sometimes misinterpret common bodily symptoms as signs of horrible diseases, and thus suffer needless anxiety. One approach to cognition and stress focuses on how people use cognitive misinterpretations to avoid psychological distress, while another approach examines how people use cognitive appraisal to more or less accurately gauge the appropriate response to a potential threat.

COGNITIVE DEFENSES AGAINST ANXIETY

In the last chapter, we discussed Freud's theory of personality. Freud believed that personality developed partly out of the individual's characteristic methods of coping with conflict and anxiety. Freud believed that stress led to the development of **defense mechanisms,** unconscious strategies to reduce anxiety. The most primitive of these is **repression,** which involves putting an unpleasant memory or impulse out of consciousness. As we will discuss at greater length in the next chapter, Freud believed that psychopathological symptoms often result from repressed sexual and aggressive feelings about one's parents. Repression involves a more or less complete loss of the conscious memory of a traumatic event. It is different from **suppression,** in which the person is aware of the unpleasant memory or impulse, but consciously tries not to think about it. Unfortunately, conscious suppression is often very difficult, as demonstrated in a recent study by Daniel Wegner

and his colleagues (1987). Borrowing an anecdote from Dostoyevski, in which the writer challenged his brother not to think of a white bear, the researchers made the same challenge to their subjects. Other subjects were asked to think of a white bear. The subjects asked to suppress thoughts of a white bear were not only unsuccessful at doing so, but they were also more likely to have thoughts of a bear intrude into consciousness later. Thus, conscious attempts to suppress an intruding thought may backfire, at least in the short run.

Rationalization is a defense mechanism that involves making excuses for our previous failures or transgressions. Bruce Babbitt, a candidate for the 1988 presidential election, offered a nice example of rationalization. After spending millions of dollars only to lose the nomination, he claimed that he did not really want to win anyway. As we discussed in Chapter 13, **projection** is a defense mechanism in which the individual sees his or her perceived failings in others, as in the case of someone who never stops talking about how many other people in the dorm are obsessed with sex. In the defense of **reaction formation,** the individual converts a distressing impulse into its opposite. For instance, a Freudian might suggest that a person working for an antipornography crusade is actually struggling to control his or her own erotic desires.

COGNITIVE APPRAISAL AND ADAPTATION TO STRESS

Cognitive defenses against stress are not necessarily neurotic. They can be adaptive. As we described in the chapter on motivation, subjects watching a bloody circumcision film evidenced less physiological response when they were led to deny the unpleasantness. Obviously, how one first appraises a stimulus is an important determinant of how stressful it will be. Those who convinced themselves that the "invasion from Mars" must not be real had very different reactions from those who convinced themselves that it was (Cantril, 1940). Other research finds that people are less disrupted by an unpredictable stressor if they do not pay attention to it (Matthews et al., 1980). Denial can sometimes work with more serious problems. Psychiatrist David Folks and his colleagues found that coronary bypass patients who denied the dangers of their surgery made better recoveries than those who were highly concerned about and interested in the surgery (Crawford, 1987).

The relationship between stressful bodily reactions and cognition has been extensively researched by Richard Lazarus and his colleagues, and we already have discussed some of that work in this chapter. Table 14.4 shows their model of the cognitive appraisal process that determines whether a particular event will lead to a stress-related physiological response.

This model divides the appraisal process into two parts. *Primary appraisal* categorizes the situation into one of three possible categories. The situation may be appraised as *irrelevant* to survival needs, as when we decide that the person standing across from us in the restaurant is killing time waiting for a dinner companion to arrive. It can be appraised as *benign-positive*, as when we realize that the person entering the restaurant is our date for the evening, dressed to kill. Finally, it can be appraised as *stressful*, as when we decide that the person storming across the restaurant is our date's old lover, armed to kill. If a primary appraisal leads us to decide that a situation is in the stressful category, we then engage in a *secondary appraisal*. Secondary appraisal is aimed at determining what we can do to cope with the stressful situation. It consists of an appraisal of the resources at our disposal, including our health and energy levels, our ability to control or to solve the problem at hand, and the sources of social and material support we can rely on. Secondary appraisal also involves an analysis of the constraints that the present situation puts on our use of resources. For instance, we may have a black belt in karate, but decide that a violent solution to the angry former lover would make a bad impression on our date.

TABLE 14.4 Cognitive Processes Determining Stress Onset

Primary Appraisal: Is this situation potentially stressful?

1. *Irrelevant:* Not related to survival or personal goals.

2. *Benign-Positive:* Related to survival or personal goals in a positive manner (results in positive emotional reaction).

3. *Stressful:* Loss, harm, threat, or challenge. Depending on the outcome of secondary appraisal, categorizing a situation as stressful may result in the "fight or flight" reaction.

Secondary Appraisal: What can I do about the cause of stress?

1. *Resources:* These include health and energy, ability to control the situation or to solve the problem, social support, and money or possessions that could be used.

2. *Constraints:* These include psychological deficits and other people who pose potential obstacles to coping.

Based on Lazarus and Folkman (1984).

INTERACTIONS:
The Two-Way Street Between the Brain and the Body

To the traditional view, stress and health fit within a strictly medical model. Stress is viewed as one potential source of disease—different from invasion by bacteria or a genetically based malfunctioning of the kidneys, but a disease nevertheless. If that view were correct, the solutions for stress would be limited to medical ones—tranquilizers to quell the troublesome secretions of the adrenal glands, for instance.

In keeping with our discussion in earlier chapters, however, we can think about stress as the result of interactions between a person's past experience, present thoughts, and biochemical changes in his or her body. In previous chapters, we have emphasized how the biological organism can contribute to people's thoughts and behaviors. However, the relationship between the body and the mind is not a one-way causal street. It should be clear from this chapter that psychological experiences can also change the body. Certain ways of thinking about stressful events, certain ways of approaching work, and certain ways of relating to other people can lead to actual damage to our digestive organs, our hearts, our arteries, and even our immune systems.

Since the time of William James, psychologists have tended to view psychological processes, even extreme emotional reactions, as "functional." To say that a process is functional means that it serves some adaptive purpose, that it helps the individual to better adapt to the environment. This view of stress reactions as functional is different from the traditional medical view, which focuses on stress reactions as disease processes in an otherwise healthy body. However, the functional view immediately raises one question: If psychological stress can wreak such havoc on the systems of the body, how can stress reactions be adaptive?

Is Psychological Distress Functional?

Stress reactions are intimately related to the emotional processes described in Chapter 10. In that chapter, we discussed how emotions, such as fear, can assist us in survival-relevant situations. We can think of stress as extreme or prolonged exposure to situations that evoke powerful emotional reactions, particularly such negative emotions as fear and anger. When we are fearful or angry, the autonomic nervous system mobilizes resources to deal with a threat from the outside. Since our bodies do not have an infinite store of resources, this autonomic reaction must be paid for at some cost to other life-sustaining processes. If you need to run away from a bear just after you have finished a picnic lunch, the blood that was flowing to your stomach is diverted to your leg muscles, for instance. Research we presented in this chapter suggests that stressful emotional reactions also inhibit the action of the immune system. Our bodies seem to hold off their attack on viruses and other internal threats when we perceive an external event that poses an immediate danger to life or limb. This sort of allocation of resources would have made sense for our ancestors, who often had very limited sources of nutrition to replenish their bodies' natural fortifications.

Distress, Illness, and Resource Allocation

Recent findings suggest an intimate connection between the immune system and the brain mechanisms that shut down our level of behavioral activity when we are sick. When white blood cells detect an invading infection, they release chemicals that instruct the brain not only to release energy-producing sugars and fats into the bloodstream, but also to dampen our sexual appetites and make us feel tired and achy. This makes adaptive sense, as one neuroendocrinologist recently

noted (Sapolsky, 1990). To fight off an infection, the body needs to produce a tremendous number of white blood cells and hormones very rapidly. This burst of immune activity is "expensive" to the body's energy stores, and so the body inhibits other activities. The inhibition of sexual feelings during illness makes particular sense, because "producing offspring is one of the most expensive things you can ever attempt with your body" (Sapolsky, 1990).

Along similar lines, other researchers have begun to investigate the adaptive significance of psychological distress (Thornhill and Thornhill, 1989). The evolutionary view is that stress represents a reaction to anything that threatens an individual's chances of surviving or reproducing. If you consider the stressful life events that we have discussed, you can see that many are indeed potential threats to survival (for instance, the loss of one's job is losing one's "means of living"). Other life events, such as losing a spouse, involve threats to a person's reproductive potential. Since our ancestors lived in small hierarchical groups, lowered social status would also have meant fewer reproductive opportunities and a lower chance of survival (Hogan, 1982). The relationship between stress and reproduction can be seen clearly in the finding that women stop ovulating when they lose too much weight (Frisch, 1988). Since human reproduction involves a large commmitment of the female's bodily resources to the offspring, reproductive inhibition is another way in which stress changes the way the body allocates its resources.

Learning Experience and Stress Responses

A focus on interactions leads us to ask not only about the evolutionary history of stress reactions, but also how those biological adaptations are fitted to the individual's life experiences through learning. Recall our earlier discussion of conditioned nausea in rats (Garcia, McGowan, and Green, 1972). Conditioned nausea involves an interaction between a biological system and the learning capacities of the brain. When the animal becomes ill after eating a new food its brain stores a vivid memory of the novel taste, which is later used to protect the body from further illness, since it causes the rat to reject the food before it can do any damage. Recent research indicates that immune responses can also be conditioned, so that stimuli associated with previous infections elicit a rapid state of preparedness for a potential new infection (Ader and Cohen, 1985). These findings suggest that learning experiences play a role in our body's biological responses to stress. As we saw in our earlier discussion, instrumental conditioning can also play a role in the pain responses, when other people's reactions reinforce chronic suffering (Fordyce, 1988).

Our discussion of Lazarus and Folkman's cognitive appraisal model of stress illustrates that ongoing cognition is also a central link in the chain between experience and bodily reaction. Whether the body kicks in its biological defenses will depend on how the brain interprets events in the present environment. Our body's physiological response to a potentially stressful situation is only called into play when our cognitive appraisal leads us to view it as an actual threat that will tax our ability to handle it easily. Learning history again comes into play at this stage. Learning interacts with cognition by influencing whether we interpret a situation as threatening. (If you have observed a shooting on a New York subway you

will see the underground transit system very differently than if you have only had pleasant experiences there.) Previous learning also influences how we perceive our ability to handle a given situation. (If you have experience working as a bouncer, you may be less threatened by a drunken and abusive teenager.) Thus, ongoing cognition and learning history interact to determine the likelihood of a biologically programmed stress response.

Although psychologists who study stress and health are specialists working at the field's interface with medicine, then, they are also contributing to our general understanding of the interwoven fabric of biology, experience, and mental phenomena. As noted in the chapter's opening quote, some psychologists are beginning to regard health maintenance as one of the brain's major functions. ■

IN CONTEXT: STRESS, COPING, AND HEALTH

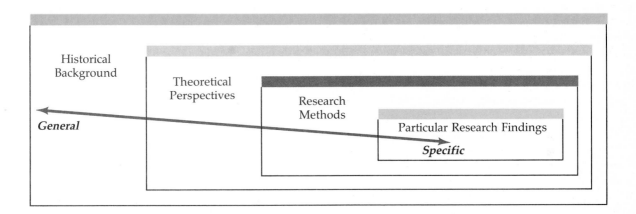

STUDY QUESTIONS

What kinds of experiences lead to stress?

How does stress contribute to the development of physical illness?

How do psychological factors contribute to pain and other symptoms of illness?

How can people cope with natural stressors in their lives and on their jobs?

HISTORICAL BACKGROUND

1. During the first half of this century, Hans Selye found evidence of a three stage **general adaptation syndrome** in response to stressors. The stages were alarm, resistance, and exhaustion. Selye posited a *nonspecific response to stress:* Dif-

ferent stressors would lead to the same "general" physiological response.

2. Franz Alexander and other researchers early in this century studied *psychosomatic disorders.* These are physical dysfunctions, including dis-

orders like ulcers, hypertension, and asthma that are caused by psychological problems. They are now called **psychophysiological disorders.** Psychosomatic disorder researchers held that each ailment was caused by a *specific* psychological conflict.

MODERN THEORETICAL PERSPECTIVES

1. Researchers who take a **medical** perspective, including Selye, have tended to study phenomena at the physiological level of analysis. They view stress as an atypical state of bodily hormone production brought on by actual bodily damage or prolonged threat.

2. The **psychoanalytic** perspective, seen in theories such as Alexander's, is a view of stress reactions as unexpressed sexual and aggressive energy that indirectly damages bodily organs. The notion that defense mechanisms like repression are cognitive devices for avoiding anxiety is also derived from psychoanalytic theory.

3. The **behaviorist** perspective is represented in Fordyce's view of pain behaviors as maintained by rewards in the environment.

4. The **cognitive** viewpoint shows up in studies of the role of attention in pain, and in the view of stress as a function of cognitive appraisal.

5. According to the **interactionist** view, stress results from the interplay of the biological organism, environmental experience, and ongoing cognition. Stress reactions are viewed as functional responses that helped our ancestors survive. Cognition and learning play a role in determining whether a physiological stress response is necessary.

RESEARCH METHODS

1. One common approach to studying human stress categorizes the types of situations that lead to stress, including major life changes and daily unpleasantries (for instance, De Longis, Folkman, and Lazarus, 1987). People's reactions to surveys about these events are then **correlated** with measures of physical or psychological health.

2. Several clinical **case studies** were mentioned in this chapter. The study of the woman who had survived a concentration camp was one (Chodoff, 1970). Studies of mass hysterical illness and the "Martian invasion" applied the case study method at the level of groups of people (Cantrol, 1940).

3. Biomedical researchers have used the **experimental method** to study reactions to intense stress in animals. Selye's (1936) studies of adaptation to stress in rats is an example.

RESEARCH FINDINGS AND SUMMARY

1. Major **life events** and daily unpleasantries are both related to physical and emotional health. Such features as *novelty, uncontrollability,* and *uncertainty* all increase the stressfulness of any given event.

2. Stress can contribute to such emotional disorders as depression, and to such psychophysiological disorders as ulcers. Stress can also interfere with immune responses, thus increasing the general risk of infection and cancer.

3. Pain is not confined to the peripheral receptors, but involves "top down" input from the brain as well. **Phantom limb pain** occurs in limbs that have been amputated. According to the *gate control theory,* the brain or spinal cord can cut off receptivity to peripheral pain if there is stimulation in other areas of the body.

4. Attention to normal physical symptoms may contribute to the phenomenon of **mass psychogenic illness,** in which people seem to fall ill as a consequence of social suggestion.

5. Organizational stress is costly to employers and workers as well. The most stressful jobs are low in status, ambiguous, and involve long hours and organizational obstacles.

6. In line with the **Yerkes-Dodson law,** stress will facilitate performance up to a point, then become debilitating. It takes less stress to interfere with performance on complex or poorly learned tasks, as opposed to simple, well-learned ones. **Social facilitation,** a change in performance due to the presence of observers, seems to operate in line with the Yerkes-Dodson Law.

7. **Type A** is a syndrome of personality characteristics composed of time urgency, competitiveness, and hostility. Several studies have shown a relationship between this pattern and heightened risk of coronary illness. **Hardiness** is a set of characteristics associated with stress resistance. It is composed of commitment, control, and a sense of challenge regarding one's work.

8. Stress management programs for workers often involve aerobic exercise programs. Such programs can act to improve job performance and to decrease stress-related illnesses.

9. **Coping** refers to efforts to deal with stress. **Problem-focused coping** aims to remove the problem, whereas **emotion-focused** strategies aim to regulate the distress of problems that are difficult to remove.

10. **Social support** consists of emotional, informational, and material aid from others. Individuals with relatively more social support are less likely to become ill.

11. **Defense mechanisms** are cognitive strategies for handling external and internal threats.

ADDITIONAL READINGS

Friedman, M., and Ulmer, D. 1984. *Treating Type A behavior—and your heart*. New York: Knopf. Friedman, who did the original and highly influential work on the Type A personality, here reports on a large-scale study in the control of stress-prone tendencies, and offers advice on how to lower the risk of heart attack.

Lazarus, R. S., and Folkman, S. 1984. *Stress, appraisal, and coping*. New York: Springer. A thorough presentation of an influential cognitive model of stress and coping, written by two prominent stress researchers.

Maddi, S. R., and Kobasa, S. C. 1984. *The hardy executive: Health under stress*. Homewood, IL: Dow Jones–Irwin.

The originators of the hardiness construct describe their interesting work.

Selye, H. 1976. *The stress of life*. New York: McGraw-Hill. A classic treatment of the author's work on the general adaptation syndrome.

Taylor, S. E. 1991. *Introduction to health psychology*. (2nd edition) New York: McGraw-Hill. A comprehensive treatment of an emerging field by a prominent researcher in the area.

PSYCHOLOGICAL DISORDERS

For centuries people have misunderstood the nature of mental illness. This has led them to react to it with fear, embarrassment, shame, and guilt. They have thought of it as a punishment God gives to sinners, as a spiritual torment due to possession by the devil, or as a moral defect due to weakness of will. In earlier centuries the mentally ill were burned at the stake or pressed to death because they were thought to be possessed. Others were chained in cells for much of their lives. . . . (We) might comfort ourselves with the belief that we live in a more enlightened era. But . . . people who suffer from mental illness are still often the victims of subtler versions of social stigmatization, cruelty, and prejudice. This prejudice grows out of ignorance and misunderstanding about the nature of mental illness.

(Nancy Andreason, 1984)

Chapter Outline

In this book's opening chapter we noted that some of psychology's pioneering thinkers, including William James, were trained in both philosophy and medicine. As philosophers, they wanted to know about normal perception, normal consciousness, and normal thought processes. As medical biologists, they were curious about how this basic knowledge could be used to understand abnormal, or pathological, processes. In the Dysfunction section of each chapter thus far, we have tried to show how the breakdown of normal processes sometimes leads to psychological dysfunction. In this chapter we will examine how modern psychologists have tried to categorize and explain psychological disorder.

People with psychological disorders have cognitive, emotional, and behavioral characteristics that make their own lives miserable and may frustrate, annoy, and puzzle those around them. These people have been labeled "maladjusted," "abnormal," "mentally ill," "psychopathological," or even "possessed." To help the unafflicted understand what the world of mental illness looks like, writer Norma MacDonald has painted an inside picture:

I know that I spent an unhappy childhood and a tragic adolescence, and that until a complete mental collapse occurred when I was 24, I lived through a series of emotional upheavals, depressions, abrupt changes of mind and plan, severe asthma, and a great many minor ailments like colds, fevers, influenza, and general fatigue, which left me little energy for sports or social life. . . . My father had been in a mental hospital since I was four years of age . . . and I lived in secret dread that it might be hereditary. . . . What I do want to explain, if I can, is the exaggerated state of awareness in which I lived before, during, and after my acute illness. At first it was as if parts of my brain "awoke" which had been dormant, and I became interested in a wide assortment of people, events, places, and ideas which normally would make no impression on me. Not knowing that I was ill, I . . . felt that there was some overwhelming significance in all this, produced either by God or Satan. . . . The walk of a stranger on the street could be a "sign" to me which I must interpret. Every face in the windows of a passing streetcar would be engraved on my mind, all of them concentrating on me and trying to pass me some sort of message. . . .

My brain . . . had become sore with a real physical soreness, as if it had been rubbed with sandpaper until it was raw . . . I had very little ability to sort the relevant from the irrelevant. . . . The filter had broken down.

(MacDonald, 1960)

In reading such a lucid account by a former mental patient, one might be led to agree with Oliver Wendell Holmes, who said that "insanity is often the logic of an accurate mind overtaxed." Many of us have occasionally questioned our own sanity, and perfectly normal people occasionally engage in irrational and self-defeating behaviors (Baumeister and Scher, 1988). However, disturbed people who are in the acute phase of their symptoms are not always so logical. In one classic case, for instance, a hospitalized student screamed the following at a psychiatric interviewer's question about his name:

What is your name? What does he shut? He shuts his eyes. What does he hear? He does not understand; he understands not. How? Who? Where? When? What does he mean? When I tell him to look, he does not look properly. You there, just look! What is it? What is the matter? Attend; he attends not. I say, what is it, then? Why do you give me no answer? Are you getting impudent again? How can you be so impudent? I'm coming!

I'll show you! You don't turn whore for me. . . .

(from Kraeplin, in Spitzer et al., 1981)

Severely disturbed people are often disturbing to the people around them. Sometimes, their behaviors are eccentric and puzzling—for example, a man was arrested in 1984 on Long Island for tickling young women's feet and stealing their shoes (United Press International, June 26, 1984). At other times their inner torment is directed into inexplicable violence. On July 31, 1966, University of Texas student Charles Whitman wrote:

I don't really understand myself these days. I am supposed to be an average, reasonable, and intelligent young man. However, lately . . . I have been the victim of many unusual and irrational thoughts. These thoughts constantly recur, and it requires a tremendous mental effort to concentrate on useful and progressive tasks. In March when my parents made a physical break I noticed a great deal of stress. I consulted Dr. C. at the University Health Center and asked him to recommend someone that I could consult with about some psychiatric disorders I felt I had. I talked with a doctor once for about two hours and tried to convey to him my fears that I felt overcome by overwhelming violent impulses. After one session I never saw the doctor again, and since then I have been fighting my mental turmoil alone, and seemingly to no avail. After my death I wish that an autopsy would be performed on me to see if there is any visible physical disorder. I have had some tremendous headaches in the past and have consumed two large bottles of Excedrin in the past three months.

(UPI, cited in Sarason and Sarason, 1987)

After writing this note, Whitman murdered his wife and his mother, and then went to a university tower with a high-powered rifle and an abundant supply of ammunition. A trained Marine sharp-shooter, Whitman shot 38 people before a policeman's bullet ended his own tortured life. An autopsy revealed that Whitman had a malignant brain tumor that may have been related to his behavior (Sarason and Sarason, 1987).

Sometimes it is hard to draw the line between normal and abnormal behavior. Was Berhard Goetz, the subway vigilante described in Chapter 10 who shot four alleged muggers, disordered? What about a 19-year-old who defies her parents' attempts to stop her sexual behavior and alcohol use? What if she were thirteen? There are two main questions we will ask about abnormal behavior, and they are very similar to the questions we asked about normal personality in Chapter 13. First, how can we best *describe* abnormal behavior? Are there certain criteria we can use to draw a line between normal and abnormal behavior? Are there common patterns of behavior that go together, or is each disturbed person completely unique in his or her disturbance? The second question is: How can we *explain* abnormal behavior? What causes people to behave in bizarre, unpleasant, or self-destructive ways? Many of the same theoretical models used to explain normal behavior have, with a few variations and additions, also been used to explain extreme behavior. However, some researchers believe that normal and abnormal behavior result from very different processes.

HISTORICAL BACKGROUND:
Changing Views of Disorder

Some of the earliest records of abnormal behavior come from Egyptian and Greek documents describing a disorder found among virginal and

Hippocrates, the Greek physician who believed that psychopathology was the result of physical illness.

widowed women. The disorder, called *hysteria* by the Greeks, was characterized by bodily pains, headaches, paralysis, and sadness (Rosenhan and Seligman, 1984). Greek scholars believed that the disorder was the result of a dislodged uterus (*hystera* in Greek), which roamed around the woman's body and caused problems wherever it lodged. When it lodged at the heart, for instance, it produced feelings of nervousness and oppression. Another influential theory from ancient Greece linked behavioral disorder to bodily dysfunction. As indicated in Figure 15.1, Hippocrates believed that an imbalance of one of the essential bodily fluids described in Chapter 13 could lead to disordered behavior. Hippocrates made careful observations of several clinical syndromes, and his description of *melancholia* would immediately be recognized by any clinical psychologist today. Now, though, we would call it *depressive disorder*.

The Biomedical Perspective: Biological Roots of Mental "Illness"

Hippocrates was a physician—the Hippocratic oath is named for him—and his theory was the forerunner of the **biomedical model** of psy-

FIGURE 15.1   The four temperaments, which Hippocrates associated with imbalances in bodily fluid. Clockwise, from top left: the melancholic person is depressive (from excessive black bile); the phlegmatic person is listless (from excessive phlegm); the sanguine person is cheerful (from excess blood); and the choleric person is violently angry (from excess yellow bile).

chopathology. (The term "model" here refers to an analogy that helps us visualize a set of assumptions about the causes of abnormal behavior. The biomedical model assumes that abnormal behavior is like other forms of illness, caused by bodily disturbances from outside infections or internal malfunctions. Just as measles has a set of *symptoms*, such as an unusual skin rash, so mental illnesses have sets of symptoms. Mental illnesses are unique in that they may involve disturbances of endocrine functioning or of the central nervous system, and thereby indirectly affect moods, thoughts, and behaviors. As is the case with any other illness, certain *syndromes* (patterns of symptoms) are expected to occur together. Just as we find a concurrence of fever, glandular swelling, and spotted skin for measles, we find a concurrence of sleeplessness, loss of appetite, and guilt in depressive disorders. The biomedical model has powerfully shaped our modern way of thinking and talking about abnormal behavior. For instance, we describe disordered behavior as *psychopathology* (which translates from its Greek roots into "mental illness"), and we commit disordered individuals to "mental hospitals".

During the Middle Ages, Hippocrates' biomedi-cal model was not the prevalent viewpoint among European intellectuals. Instead, medieval thinkers held to a **supernatural model,** which conceived of bizarre behaviors as an outward sign of sin or possession by evil spirits. A classic statement of the *demonic possession* view was written during the fifteenth century by two scholarly Dominican monks commissioned by Pope Innocent VIII, himself a dedicated foe of witchcraft. The *Malleus Malleficarum (Witch's Hammer)* presented a systematic approach for detecting witches, many of whom would have been labelled as eccentric or mentally ill today.

During the century after the publication of the *Malleus Malleficarum* there were attempts to restore the biomedical model. The German physician Johann Weyer, for instance, argued that most of those persecuted for witchcraft were really mentally or physically ill, and he recommended more humane treatment of them. Religious scholars attacked Weyer's books as the work of the devil and they were prohibited to the public. In 1768, John Wesley, a prominent Protestant clergyman, could still declare that "the giving up of witchcraft is in effect the giving up of the Bible" (Kisker, 1964). During the seventeenth and eighteenth

A 16th century wood-cut depicting demons tormenting St. Anthony (by Martin Schongauer). According to the prevalent supernatural model of that time, behavioral disturbances were due to such torments.

centuries, however, the biomedical model gradually replaced the demonic possession model. The most influential statement of the modern medical view came in 1883, when the German physician Emil Kraeplin, who had worked with Wundt in the first psychology laboratory, published a textbook on psychiatry.

Kraeplin presented the foundation for modern approaches to the diagnosis of mental disorders. He had observed two very different types of patients on the mental wards. One type of patient showed a long history of mental deterioration, a wide variety of symptoms including delusions, hallucinations, confused thinking, and inappropriate moods, and a very poor prognosis (a medical term for the likelihood of recovery). He dubbed this syndrome *dementia praecox*. (Today we would use the term **schizophrenia.**) The other type showed dramatic disturbances of mood that came on suddenly and from which he or she was likely to recover. Kraeplin grouped patients with depressed and elated moods together, and called their disorder *manic-depressive insanity*. (Now it is called **bipolar affective disorder.**) Kraeplin established these distinctions "merely for the purpose of preliminary study" and fully expected them to be improved. Though they were indeed modified, his categories proved to be useful as a preliminary organization of psychological disorders.

The biomedical view that Kraeplin advanced is a variant of the biological model of personality discussed in Chapter 13, and its proponents were curious about whether schizophrenia might be heritable. Ernst Rudin, a student of Kraeplin's, examined the relatives of hospitalized mental patients. Rudin found an 8.6 percent rate of schizophrenia in siblings, and a 16.5 percent rate if one of the parents was also schizophrenic. This is much higher than the approximately one-half of one percent that would be expected by chance. As we shall see later, behavioral genetic research on major behavioral disorders provides support for Kraeplin's biological model of mental illness.

The Psychodynamic Perspective: Internal Conflicts as the Source of Mental Disorder

The **psychodynamic perspective** was proposed as an alternative to the traditional biomedical model. As we discussed in previous chapters, the psychodynamic model was made popular by Sigmund Freud (1856–1939). Like Kraeplin, Freud was a physician. Instead of studying the physical causes of mental symptoms, however, Freud went in the opposite direction, looking at the mental causes of

physical symptoms. Freud's colleague Josef Breuer was treating a woman named Anna O., who suffered from severe headaches, paralysis of the throat, and numbness in the right arm. There was no apparent neurological damage, and her physical symptoms were accompanied by strange behaviors, including violence and depression. Anna's symptoms had begun when her father, whom she loved deeply, was taken down with a terminal illness, and she was required to sit by his bed late into the evenings. Breuer and Freud (1895/1950) believed that her symptoms resulted from conflicted feelings about her father. On one level, she felt anger at him (his illness interrupted her social life in the short run, and meant that she would be left without him in the long run). However, her love and loyalty toward him led her to feel guilt about her selfish feelings, and to push them out of her consciousness. Freud believed that unacceptable sexual and aggressive impulses can be diverted into various symptoms, such as Anna's paralysis and headaches. Like the biomedical approach, the psychodynamic perspective sees maladjusted behavior as a *symptom* of an inner process. From the psychodynamic perspective the root of the symptom is not physical disease but psychological discord.

The Behavioral Perspective: The Problem is the Behavior

Freud's views about the causes of psychopathology diverged from the biomedical perspective, but both models share the assumption that disordered behaviors are symptoms of some underlying malfunction. Some psychologists, including John Watson, rejected that assumption in favor of a **behavioral perspective.** Watson's famous case, "Little Albert," was designed to show the flaws in Freuds' analysis of Little Hans's phobia. Recall that Watson and Rayner used classical conditioning to induce a phobia-like fear of a white rat in Albert by sounding a loud gong every time the boy was introduced to the animal. To proponents of the behavioral perspective, the behavioral "symptom" is the sickness, it is not a sign of a disturbed inner process. The behavioral approach is therefore less concerned with the *causes* of mental disorder than the biomedical or psychodynamic approaches. It emphasizes treatments designed to teach the person new, more adaptive responses.

The behavioral approach to disorder became quite popular during the 1960s. In 1965, Teodoro Ayllon and his colleagues (1965) tried to show how the search for unconscious causes of psychopathology can lead to erroneous explanations.

These researchers used cigarettes to reward a schizophrenic woman for carrying a broom around the hospital with her. After a short period of reinforcement, the woman carried the broom continually. They then asked a psychoanalytically oriented psychiatrist to comment on the case. He described it as "a ritualistic procedure, a magical action," in which the broom might be either "a child who gives her love" in return for her devotion, "a phallic symbol," or "the scepter of an impotent queen." The psychiatrist estimated that it would take a long period of analysis to remove this symptom of her deeply seated sexual conflicts. Ayllon and his colleagues promptly changed her behavior by changing the contingencies, so that she now got cigarettes only when she was not carrying the broom. Although this demonstration does not prove that schizophrenics "normally" develop their symptoms in this way, it does show that some symptoms can be learned in the same manner as normal behavior.

In recent years, the behavioral perspective has evolved into the *cognitive–social learning perspective,* which adds an emphasis on such cognitive factors as expectancies in human learning. From this perspective, for example, depression may result from negative thoughts such as "I never get what I want."

The Sociological Perspective: Emphasizing the Role of the Environment

The behavioral perspective shifted the focus from the "mentally ill" individual to the environment,

Homelessness: an unfortunate side-effect of de-institutionalization. A number of marginally disturbed people who would once have lived out their lives in institutions for the mentally disordered have proved unable to adjust to life on the outside, and have joined the ranks of the homeless.

stressing the rewards and punishments that might lead to problem behaviors. The **sociological perspective,** which gained prominence during the late 1950s and early 1960s, also focuses on the environment but takes a much wider perspective. This model views disordered behavior as being rooted in the wider society. August Hollingshead and Fredrick Redlich's (1958) classical study of social class and mental illness provided an impetus for this approach. Hollingshead and Redlich argued that people in the lower classes are subjected to especially high levels of stress—financial difficulties, powerlessness, and so on. As a poignant and classical example of the stresses associated with poverty, Hollingshead and Redlich (1958) note that when the *Titanic* trans-Atlantic luxury liner sank in 1912, only four out of 143 women booked on first class drowned (three of whom voluntarily stayed on board). By contrast, 15 of 93 women in second class went down with the ship, as did 81 of the 179 women in third class. The seamen kept the third-class passengers below decks at gunpoint while the higher-class passengers boarded the lifeboats (Lord, 1955).

In their own research, Hollingshead and Redlich examined psychological disorders among residents of New Haven, Connecticut. They divided New Haven residents into five social groups. Those in the top group were college educated business and professional leaders who owned large houses and belonged to private country clubs. Those on the lowest rung of the New Haven social ladder were uneducated laborers who lived in tiny tenement flats. Those on the bottom rung were frequently unemployed, and always paid poorly when they did find work. The researchers found that those in the lower classes were, compared with the higher classes, much more likely to suffer from psychological disorders. The rate of schizophrenia in the lower classes, for instance, was about eight times higher than that in the top group. The sociological approach is closely connected to the community approach to treatment, which we discuss in the next chapter.

This brief history highlights how models of psychological disorder have gone through several fashions. Some, like the medical model, have gone in and out of style more than once. However, several root questions appear again and again, and persist to this day. We are still trying to answer the descriptive questions raised by Hippocrates and Kraeplin. Which disordered behaviors go together? How many different patterns of pathology are there? And we are still trying to discover how much of psychopathology is caused by external factors—such as parents or society—and how much is caused by internal factors—such as hormonal imbalances or psychic conflicts. As we shall see, modern researchers have begun to provide some answers to these longstanding questions. ■

DEFINING PSYCHOLOGICAL DISORDER

Before we can discuss the causes of psychological disorder we must decide on the kinds of behaviors that qualify as disordered, and then decide how those different behaviors fit together within individual people. Defining psychopathology is a little more difficult than defining physical disease. Many physical diseases are based on an "all or none" criterion: Even a small infection with the leprosy virus, or a slight stroke, qualifies for a positive diagnosis. But most of us have had violent impulses, or moments of confusion, anxiety, or depression. Few of those episodes would qualify us for psychiatric diagnoses. In fact, if a person has never felt any of these disruptions of thought and emotion, that fact might itself be an indication of psychopathology.

CRITERIA FOR ABNORMALITY

Where do we draw the definitional line between psychopathology and "normal" psychological functioning? We will consider four possible criteria: subjective distress, statistical deviation, norm violation, and harmful symptoms.

SUBJECTIVE DISTRESS

One criterion for psychopathology is simple—ask the individual how disturbed he or she feels. By this standard, you are psychopathological if you think you are. This approach is useful to the extent that some people are able to cope with more confusion and distress than others. At first glance, it makes sense that only the troubled seek treatment. By itself, subjective distress is not enough, however. It was clear that Charles Whitman experienced subjective distress when he wrote the note about his overwhelming violent impulses, but Charles Manson (discussed in Chapter 12) thought his mass murders were justified. Unfortunately, it is often when people are most disturbed that they are least likely to seek help. Some, like the woman quoted at the beginning of this chapter, believe they are acting under the direct influence of supernatural forces, and may even feel that psycholo-

gists are agents of the devil or some other evil force.

STATISTICAL DEVIANCE

The statistical criterion sidesteps the issue of self-definition and the fact that all of us show occasional irrationalities by specifying an objective mathematical standard. You are maladjusted if your behavior is unusual in comparison to that of others. Being depressed once in a while is statistically normal, but being depressed for two weeks out of every month is statistically abnormal. Getting angry for 15 minutes a month is, likewise, normal, while getting angry for 15 minutes out of every hour is not. This definition also has its limits. It does not specify which statistical abnormalities (such as violence) are important and which (such as whistling) are irrelevant. It also does not separate valuable deviations (very infrequent anger) from undesirable ones (very frequent anger). The statistical definition is usually supplemented with some consideration of societal norms.

NORM VIOLATION

To be abnormal by this definition a behavior must violate some cultural rule or expectation. In our society, for instance, people are expected to cry at funerals and to be depressed after the loss of someone dear. They are not expected to cry on the job, or after the loss of a cheap earring. Although cultural standards are undoubtedly important in defining psychopathology, there is some controversy about how important they should be to diagnosticians. One problem is that norms sometimes vary widely from one cultural group to the next. The use of psychotropic drugs such as peyote is normal among some Native American groups in Utah, but might be considered a sign of psychopathology among the Mormons in Salt Lake City. Brutal spouse abuse that would bring in the authorities in Yonkers is normal among the Yanomamo, a South American tribe whose men regularly beat their spouses and one another. There is also some discrepancy between the cultural "ideal," as expressed in the norms, and the real culture, as expressed in actual behavior. For instance, Alfred Kinsey and his colleagues (1948, 1953) found that over 90 percent of American men and 60 percent of American women violated the norms against masturbation. These statistics made it difficult to justify the earlier medical opinion, popular at the turn of the century, that masturbation is a sign of pathology, and itself a major cause of insanity.

HARMFUL SYMPTOMS

One criterion disregards subjective distress, statistics, and norms, by defining behavioral pathology as the presence of symptoms that are harmful to their possessor or other people. That definition would encompass murderers such as Charles Whitman, and ignore harmless behaviors such as frequent whistling. It still has its limits, however, since not everyone agrees about what is harmful. Everyone can agree about Whitman's homicidal spree, but what about the eccentricities of the schizophrenic who wears aluminum foil in his hair to catch interplanetary vibrations, and screams epithets about God and the FBI to passing shoppers?

The disagreement about what constitutes a harmful symptom creates ethical dilemmas. Take the case of Robert Friedman, the "wealthy beggar" who was stopped by a policeman for panhandling, normally a very minor offense. When the policeman opened the beggar's briefcase, he found $24,087 in small bills. It turned out that Friedman was employed as a typist but had an obsession with money, and refused to spend money on clothes or to move from his dingy one-room apartment. Clearly an unusual man, he was placed in a mental institution despite his protests, and was not released for several years. By the time he did regain his freedom, he had lost his job and his ability to type. He was also penniless, since his previous wealth had disqualified him for free treatment and he was forced to pay for "care" he did not want (Sheils, Agrest, and Sciolino, 1975).

Cases like this led psychiatrist Thomas Szasz (1960, 1974) to argue that the very concept of "mental illness" is a useless and harmful myth, and the mentally unbalanced should be judged by the same rules as everyone else. They should be incarcerated only when they commit a crime, and not when their eccentricities make them appear to be "potentially dangerous." (A medical opinion that one has the *potential* for danger is a common criterion for involuntary commitment.) By the standard of "potential danger" any poverty stricken male from the same family as a convicted criminal should be imprisoned—males, especially poor ones, have a much higher than average likelihood of committing a crime, (Julian and Kornblum, 1983) and criminal behavior tends to run in families (Mednick, et al., 1984). We would never really consider such a travesty of civil rights unless the man was declared to be mentally disordered. Many people put away for being "potentially dangerous" have never hurt anyone; their major

crimes are that their behavior seems unpredictable and incomprehensible to others.

Although no single criterion is adequate for judging behavior as abnormal, most people defined as mentally ill fit more than one of the criteria, and a combination of all the definitions works reasonably well. Most of the behavior we will discuss in this chapter is statistically unusual, as well as being *either* personally distressing to the individual *or* harmful to others. At the same time, many of these behaviors violate norms of appropriate conduct.

RESEARCH AND APPLICATION:
Insanity as a Label

"If sanity and insanity exist, how shall we know them?" wondered psychologist David Rosenhan (1973). Just as some psychologists argued that normal personality traits are "in the eye of the beholder," Rosenhan believed that psychiatric diagnoses might be in the minds of the observers. To examine this possibility, Rosenhan and seven of his associates (a graduate student, two other psychologists, a pediatrician, a psychiatrist, a painter, and a housewife) attempted to get themselves labelled as "insane." Each one appeared at the admissions office of a different hospital, claiming to hear voices. They said that the voices were unclear, but seemed to say "empty," "hollow," and "thud." Aside from this, they told the truth about themselves, about their interpersonal relationships, and about the frustrations and joys in their lives. Each one was admitted to the hospital, and, with one exception, was diagnosed as schizophrenic. The exception was not diagnosed as being normal, but was labelled as manic-depressive. After admission, they immediately started acting normally; if asked, they said that they were fine and the voices had stopped. Nevertheless, they were kept in the hospital for an average of 19 days, and in one case for 52 days, before being released. Rosenhan reports that no staff member ever questioned a pseudopatient's initial diagnosis, although several fellow patients did. It seemed that their normal behaviors were reinterpreted to fit with the insanity label. For instance, the pseudopatients kept notes on their experiences, and one nurse wrote in the case record: "Patient engages in writing behavior." One pseudopatient had honestly told the admitting psychiatrist that he had had a distant relationship with his father as a child that had warmed up as he grew older, while the opposite had occurred with his mother. The pseudopatient described warm relations with his wife, except for occasional arguments, and said that he rarely spanked his children. This rather normal history was written into the case record as:

This white 39-year-old male . . . manifests a long history of considerable ambivalence in close relationships, which begins in early childhood. A warm relationship with his mother cools during his adolescence. A distant relationship to his father is described as becoming very intense. Affective stability is absent. His attempts to control emotionality with his wife and children are punctuated by angry outbursts and, in the case of the children, spankings. And while he says that he has several good friends, one senses considerable ambivalence embedded in those relationships also. . . .

(Rosenhan, 1973)

When the pseudopatients tried to approach the ward psychiatrists for information, they were met with responses such as the following:

PATIENT: Pardon me, Dr. X, could you tell me when I am eligible for grounds privileges?

PHYSICIAN: Good morning, Dave. How are you today? (Doctor moves off without making a response.)

Only six percent of the psychiatrists said anything in response to these perfectly reasonable questions, some just looked at the pseudopatient, and fully 71 percent simply moved on with their heads averted. Noting that the pseudopatients continued to be treated as if they were insane even though they acted perfectly normal from the moment they were admitted, Rosenhan concluded: "We now know that we cannot distinguish sanity from insanity."

Not everyone agrees that Rosenhan proved his point. Psychiatrist Robert Spitzer (1975) claims that Rosenhan's study proved only that psychiatrists cannot detect patients who are *simulating* schizophrenic symptoms. Since every one of the pseudopatients was released with a diagnosis of "schizophrenia in remission," Spitzer argues that the normal behaviors of the pseudopatients hardly went unnoticed. He points out that since most real patients still have some of their symptoms when they are released, they are sent out with the same diagnosis they came in with. The diagnosis of "schizophrenia in remission" received by the pseudopatients is used for fewer than seven percent of actual cases. In Rosenhan's study, the hospital staff was, understandably, not capable of knowing that the pseudopatients had lied earlier, and so assumed that the symptoms were in remission. Spitzer points out that the pseudopatients reported persistent auditory hallucinations that were troubling enough to lead them to volunteer for admission to a mental hospital. That one symptom, he points out, is completely consistent with the diagnosis of schizophrenia—normal people never have such symptoms. Another one of Rosenhan's critics noted:

If I were to drink a quart of blood and, concealing what I had done, come to the emergency room of any hospital vomiting blood, the behavior of the staff would be quite predictable. If they labeled and treated me as having a bleeding peptic ulcer, I doubt that I could argue convincingly that medical science does not know how to diagnose that condition.

(Kety, 1974)

Although Spitzer disagrees with Rosenhan about our ability to make initial distinctions between sanity and insanity, he does acknowledge that mental health professionals are often too willing to reinterpret normal life histories to fit their diagnoses. One study made this point by asking psychiatrists and psychologists to judge a completely healthy individual (Temerlin, 1970). The researcher began by taping an interview with an actor who was asked to present himself as being completely mentally healthy. The man said that he was happy with his family, his job, and his sex life, and was free of depression, psychosomatic symptoms, hostility, and excessive drinking. He reported no guilt, anxiety, or thought disorganization. During the interview, he described himself as a productive physical scientist and mathematician, who had just read a book on psychotherapy and wanted to talk about it. Temerlin showed the tape to large groups of psychiatrists, clinical psychologists, graduate psychology students, law students, and undergraduates. Before viewing the tape, some of the viewers heard a high-prestige mental health professional say "I know the man being interviewed today. He's a very interesting man because he looks neurotic but actually is quite psychotic." (Neuroses are milder disorders related to anxiety, while psychoses are more extreme disorders involving bizarre thought disorders and

Eccentric or normal? Research discussed in the text indicates that behavior which would generally be considered quite normal (such as feeding the pigeons in the park) may be interpreted as a sign of mental illness if we are led to believe that the person is mentally disordered.

matician, since mathematicians are highly abstract and depersonalized people who live in a world of their own." By focusing attention on the man's abstract and introverted profession, the psychiatrist ignored all evidence that the man was highly socialized and interpersonally successful. In terms of the cognitive concepts discussed earlier, we would say that the label "insane" can act as a schema, leading observers to engage in selective (and biased) information processing.

Although the studies we have discussed suggest that psychiatric diagnoses are too quickly applied even to people with minimal symptoms, professionals do a bit better with real patients, whose symptoms are likely to be much less ambiguous. Within broad limits, at least, clinical diagnosticians can agree about how to categorize a particular patient (Spitzer et al., 1976; Spitzer, Forman, and Nee, 1979, among others). In fact, even Rosenhan's study found that 11 out of 12 diagnoses of the hallucinating pseudopatients agreed, even though there was only one actual symptom to go on. What Temerlin's and Rosenhan's findings tell

mood disturbances.) The researcher compared the group that heard this suggestion to four different control groups. Three of the control groups were from the same sample as the experimental groups. Some viewed the tape without having heard any suggestion at all, some heard a suggestion that the man was mentally healthy, and others watched the tape thinking that it was a normal job interview. A fourth control group came from a different sample. This group consisted of actual courtroom jurors, who watched the tape as part of what they thought was a sanity hearing. Did labeling this healthy man as psychotic have any effect on how he was perceived?

The results, as shown in Table 15.1, demonstrate that a label of mental illness can lead to a very strong bias in the way that normal behaviors are interpreted. Although most of the control subjects thought that the man was quite normal, very few of those who heard the suggestion were able to ignore it. Surprisingly, psychiatrists did substantially worse than untrained undergraduates. One psychiatrist, taken in by the prestigious psychiatrist's suggestion, said: "I thought he was psychotic from the moment he said he was a mathe-

TABLE 15.1 Diagnoses Given to a Healthy Man as a Function of Type of Suggestion and Type of Subject

	DIAGNOSIS MADE BY SUBJECTS:		
	Psychotic	Neurotic	Normal
Control Groups (by type of suggestion)			
No prestige suggestion	0%	43%	57%
Suggestion of mental health	0	0	100
Employment interview	0	29	71
Sanity hearing	0	0	100
Experimental Subjects (by type of subject; note that all were given a suggestion that the man was psychotic)			
Psychiatrists	60	40	0
Clinical psychologists	28	60	12
Graduate students	11	78	11
Law students	17	73	10
Undergraduates	30	54	16

From Temerlin (1970).

us is that clinicians can be too quick to accept a diagnosis, and that normal behaviors can be reinterpreted as pathological once someone is given a psychiatric diagnosis.

Just because clinicians can be misled into applying a diagnostic label to a normal individual, you should not underestimate the psychological problems of those who get their diagnoses by the more usual route. The intense psychological pain of a depressive is not something invented by the diagnosing clinician, but a real problem that results in at least 20,000 suicides a year (Sarason and Sarason, 1987). And the inner voices heard by a schizophrenic man are something that he carries around in his head regardless of the label his psychiatrist carries in his or hers. ▪

CLASSIFICATION
OF PSYCHOLOGICAL DISORDER

Because of the problems raised by Rosenhan and others, the criteria for defining someone as behaviorally disordered have been made much more specific and rigorous in recent years. The Revised Diagnostic and Statistical Manual III (DSM III-R) is the current handbook that practicing clinicians use to diagnose behavior disorders. It is considerably more specific than DSM I and DSM II. The manual gives highly detailed descriptions of 18 major categories of psychological problems, each subdivided into a number of specific diagnoses and sub-diagnoses (See Table 15.2).

THE FIVE AXES OF DIAGNOSIS

When a psychologist or psychiatrist uses the DSM III-R, he or she assesses the patient on five different sets of criteria, or axes. The first assessment is the diagnosis of a major clinical syndrome such as *paranoid schizophrenia* or *anorexia nervosa*. (This is called Axis I.) The patient is also assessed for the presence of a personality disorder, or an ingrained and inflexible trait that might be relevant to treatment. (This is Axis II of the diagnosis.) (We will discuss various types of clinical syndromes and personality disorders in some detail in this chapter.) Axis III of the diagnosis addresses whether the patient has any physical disorders or illnesses that might be relevant to the mental or behavioral problems; a physical handicap, perhaps, that might lead to anxiety about travelling outside the house. The diagnosis also considers the extent of psychosocial stressors that might affect the patient's condition, including any recent catastrophes (Axis IV); as we saw in Chapter 14, stress can have an important relationship to anxiety and other psychological problems. Finally, the di-

agnosis gives an assessment of the highest level of functioning that the patient has achieved in his or her work, social relationships, and leisure time during the last year (Axis V). All of these factors help in judging the severity of the problem, the type of therapy that might be most helpful, and the prognosis for recovery.

Table 15.2 contains only a partial list of the diagnostic categories in DSM III-R. In this chapter, we will discuss several major categories in some detail, and then go on to consider how these different disorders might be explained. As we go through these categories, you will no doubt recognize some of the specific behaviors in yourself and the people you know. But keep in mind the research we just discussed. In an attempt to avoid "false positives" like the diagnoses made of Rosenhan and his colleagues, the diagnostic manual specifies objective criteria, with specific cut-off points detailing the number, intensity, and duration of symptoms necessary before a diagnosis is rendered. For instance, the manual cautions against diagnosing someone as "schizophrenic" unless the person shows more than one symptom, and those symptoms have persisted for more than a short period of time and seem to disrupt work or social life (DSM III-R, 1987).

MOOD DISORDERS

The most common psychological ailments are mood disorders. Four hundred thousand people are treated for depression every year (Ray, 1983). Much less often, people suffer from the extreme upswings of mood called **mania**. Although you might not think it possible to be in too good a mood, individuals in the manic state often lose control of themselves in their excitement and begin to act in a very inappropriate and self-destructive fashion. We will describe this manic behavior in more detail after discussing the more common depressive disorder.

DEPRESSIVE DISORDER

The defining symptoms of **depressive disorder** are an unhappy mood and the loss of interest and pleasure in life. In addition, depression is commonly associated with insomnia, loss of appetite, fatigue, feelings of guilt, and thoughts of suicide and death. Various researchers have estimated that between six and 19 percent of us will experience a serious episode of depression at least once in our lives (Frerichs et al., 1981; Weissman et al., 1981). Depression is more common in women than in men (Boyd and Weissman, 1981; Nolen-Hoeksema, 1987). Lifetime risks for depression are

TABLE 15.2 Selected Mental Disorders from the DSM-IIIR

AXIS I: MAJOR CLINICAL SYNDROMES

Disorders Usually First Evident in Infancy, Childhood, or Adolescence

Mental retardation
Pervasive developmental disorders
  Autistic disorder
Disruptive behavior disorders
  Attention-deficit hyperactivity disorder
  Conduct disorder
Anxiety disorders of childhood or adolescence
  Separation anxiety disorder
  Avoidant disorder
Eating disorders
  Anorexia nervosa
  Bulimia nervosa
Gender identity disorders
  Gender identity disorder of childhood
  Transsexualism

Organic Mental Disorders

Dementias arising in the senium and presenium
  Alzheimer's disease
  Multi-infarct dementia
Psychoactive substance-induced organic disorders
  Alcohol intoxication
  Cocaine withdrawal
  Cannabis delusional disorder
Psychoactive substance use disorders
  Alcohol dependence
  Nicotine dependence

Schizophrenic Disorder

Schizophrenia
  Catatonic
  Disorganized
  Paranoid

Mood Disorders

Bipolar disorder
Depressive disorder

Anxiety Disorders

  Panic disorder
  Agoraphobia without history of panic disorder
  Social phobia
  Obsessive-compulsive disorder

Somatoform Disorders

  Conversion disorder
  Hypochondriasis

Dissociative Disorders

  Multiple personality disorder
  Psychogenic amnesia

Sexual Disorders

Paraphilias
  Exhibitionism
  Fetishism
  Pedophilia
  Sexual masochism
Sexual dysfunctions
  Female sexual arousal disorder
  premature ejaculation

AXIS II: PERSONALITY DISORDERS

Personality Disorders

  Antisocial personality disorder
  Histrionic personality disorder
  Narcissistic personality disorder

AXIS III: PHYSICAL DISORDERS OR ILLNESSES, other than mental disorders, that may be relevant to understanding or treating the client's problems.

AXIS IV: PSYCHOSOCIAL STRESSORS that might influence the client's condition and affect response to treatment.

AXIS V: LEVEL OF ADAPTIVE FUNCTIONING, the highest level of functioning achieved by the client over the past year in social relationships, work, and the use of leisure time.

Note: The DSM III-R is the Diagnostic and Statistical Manual of Mental Disorders (3rd Edition, revised, 1986). The above list is only partial; there are approximately 300 separate categories in the revised manual.

eight to 12 percent for men, and 20 to 26 percent for women. Generally, males may turn negative emotion outward, feeling more anger, whereas females may turn their negative feelings inward, thus feeling more depressed (Stapley and Haviland, 1989). Women are more likely to become depressed over friendships. However, men report more depressed moods in some situations, such as contests that relate to achievement (Stapley and Haviland, 1989). Although there is some evidence for a partial biological basis for the sex difference in depression, it does not appear that the monthly variations in menstrual hormones are responsible (Nolen-Hoeksema, 1987). One factor that contributes to the gender difference is that women and men respond differently once they are in a depressed mood. Women tend to amplify their moods by ruminating about their problems, whereas men tend to actively distract themselves by doing other things (Nolen-Hoeksema, 1987).

Depressive disorder strikes many people who would appear to have everything going for them. Oliver Cromwell, Abraham Lincoln, and Martin Luther suffered from depression. This same disorder led Ernest Hemingway, Vincent Van Gogh, and Marilyn Monroe to end their productive lives by their own hands. Norman Endler is a successful psychology professor who shared this inside picture of severe depression:

> I honestly felt subhuman, lower than the lowest vermin. . . . I could not understand why anyone would want to associate with me, let alone love me. . . . I was positive that I was a fraud and a phony and that I didn't deserve my Ph.D. I didn't deserve to have tenure; I didn't deserve to be a full professor. . . . I didn't deserve the research grants I had been awarded; I couldn't understand how I had written the books and journal articles that I had and how they had been accepted for publication. I must have conned a lot of people. . . . I analyzed all the people I knew and felt that each of them could do most things better than I could.

(Endler, 1982)

Suicide. Most people experience depressed mood at certain times, and even the majority of those who are depressed enough to seek treatment are not suicidal. Fifteen percent of those treated for depression eventually go on to end their own lives, however, and suicide is the ninth highest cause of death in the United States (Murphy, 1983). Among college students, it ranks second as a cause of death. Suicides are also high among the elderly. Like 80-year-old Nobel laureate Percy Bridgman, older people often commit suicide rather than endure the slow pain of terminal illness (Rosenhan and Seligman, 1984). Twice as many women as men attempt suicide, but twice as many men are successful, largely because men are more likely to use such immediately lethal methods as shooting themselves. There is also a gender difference in the motivations for suicide. Failure at work is a more prominent cause of suicide in men than in women. Failures at love often trigger suicides in both sexes, but do so more frequently for women. Divorced people of both sexes have suicide rates many times higher than their married or single counterparts (Bloom, Asher, and White, 1978).

Not everyone who gets severely depressed considers suicide, however, and other factors are important in turning personal anguish into suicidal intent. A sense of hopelessness seems to be one crucial component in suicidal intention (Beck, Kovacs, and Weissman, 1975), as does a rigid approach to solving life's problems (Patsiokas et al., 1979). It seems that suicide is likely when an individual is unable to imagine a solution to his or her present problems.

Biological Factors in Depression. Behavior genetic studies indicate that depression tends to run in families, and that families with high numbers of depressives also tend to have higher numbers of alcoholics (Faraone, Kremen & Tsuang, 1990; Zigler and Glick, 1988). Consistent with the genetic findings, there are a number of other biological factors related to depressive disorder (Swerdlow and Koob, 1987). For instance, depressives show abnormal EEG patterns during sleep (Kupfer et al., 1985) and have abnormally low blood flow through their brains during depressive periods (Lingjaerde, 1983).

Depression is often related to sleep disturbance, which has led to the suggestion that it may result from disruption of *circadian rhythms* (Healy and Williams, 1988). As we discussed in Chapter 5, circadian rhythms are seasonal or daily fluctuations in physiological activity (for example, the sleep/wake cycle). Interestingly, clinically depressed mood is more common during the morning hours (Healy and Williams, 1988). Depression may be a sort of daily "jet lag" in which the person's physiology does not adjust to the transition from sleep to waking. For those people who suffer from **seasonal affective disorder,** depression is especially likely to occur during the colder and darker months of the year. Compared with such sunnier southern states as Florida and Arizona, this seasonal depression is at least four times more prevalent in such Northern states as Washington, Maine, and North Dakota. (See Figure 15.2.)

Research by biomedical researchers Richard and Judith Wurtman finds that seasonal depressives develop a craving for carbohydrates during short winter days. Because of a physiological process involving the brain chemical serotonin, a carbohydrate snack seems to lead to an unusual increase in mood for these people. Wurtman and Wurtman (1989) also document a similar process of cyclic depression and carbohydrate craving in women suffering from *PMS* (premenstrual syndrome). The connection between carbohydrate craving and depression might also shed some light on the connection between alcohol abuse and depression. It may be that alcohol, like candy, can be used as self-therapy for depressive moods (Zigler and Glick, 1988).

Environmental Factors in Depression. Whatever the role of biological factors, environmental factors also play a role in bringing on a depressive epi-

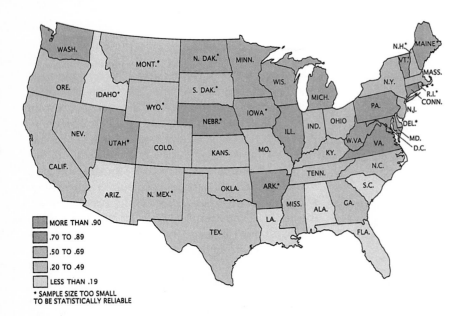

FIGURE 15.2   The prevalence of seasonal affective disorder (SAD) in the United States. This data, gathered by Steven G. Potkin and his associates (from Wurtman and Wurtman, 1989), indicates considerably more seasonal depression in the northern latitudes. Note, for instance, that Washington, Minnesota, and Maine have more than three times the levels of SAD as Florida, Louisiana, and Arizona. This disorder seems to be related to a physiological change in brain biochemistry that is triggered by shorter winter days.

MORE THAN .90
.70 TO .89
.50 TO .69
.20 TO .49
LESS THAN .19
* SAMPLE SIZE TOO SMALL TO BE STATISTICALLY RELIABLE

sode. The majority of depressive episodes are preceded by a stressful life event, such as a marital separation (Barnett and Gotlib, 1988; Paykel, 1985), and are followed by social reactions that may prolong the depression. Psychologist James Coyne notes that other people often reward depression in the short term, by giving attention and reassurance to the person who makes self-derogating or suicidal comments (Coyne, 1976; Strack and Coyne, 1983). In the long term, however, other people avoid the depressed person, because interacting with someone in a bad mood is unpleasant (Gotlib and Robinson, 1982; Strack and Coyne, 1983). Unfortunately, depressed people do not get any immediate feedback that tells them that they are turning others off, but they do get the reward of the short-term attention. Thus, their depressive behavior is perpetuated.

In the last chapter, we described Kurt Richter's observation of rats that made no attempts to survive when confronted with a flooded cage from which there was no escape. Later studies found that dogs exposed to inescapable shocks early in an experiment later failed to take advantage of an open escape door, but just suffered helplessly (Seligman, 1975). Just as dogs learn to stop trying when their efforts seem to be useless, Martin Seligman argued that people become depressed as a result of failed attempts to control the stressors in their lives. Seligman and his colleagues named this phenomenon *learned helplessness*. In line with the principle of generalization discussed in Chapter 6, Seligman assumed that this helpless response is transferred to other situations that the person could in fact control were he or she to try.

Cognitive Factors in Depression. Some theorists believe that maladaptive ways of thinking can also contribute to depression (Ingram, 1990). Experience with an uncontrollable environment is not, according to this view, sufficient to lead to helplessness in humans. That experience must also interact with self-defeating beliefs (Abramson, Seligman, and Teasdale, 1978). Depressives may differ from normals because they are more likely to take personal responsibility for negative events in their lives, even when they are outside their control: "I should have known the train would be late and taken the earlier one." They also tend to deny responsibility for positive events. Recall how Professor Endler denied any personal credit for all his many professional successes during the time he was depressed.

Psychologists have traditionally assumed that depressives are inaccurate in their negative beliefs about themselves. However, depressives may be relatively accurate in appraising their control over the world, while nondepressives, conversely, distort reality in a self-flattering manner (Alloy, Abramson and Viscusi, 1981). This has led these authors to suggest that depressives are "sadder but wiser" (Alloy and Abramson, 1979). Before concluding that depression equals realism, however, we should mention that other research indicates that only mildly depressed people are more realistic than nondepressives (Ruhlman et al., 1985). Research with more severely depressed individuals actually finds that they are not accurate, but distort their explanations in ways that make them look bad (Raps et al., 1982). Thus, healthy people tend to view themselves in a manner that is distorted in their own favor, whereas increasing degrees of depression first remove this bias, then replace it with a bias towards viewing things in an unrealistically self-derogating manner.

Although there is good evidence that depressed people see the world in a negative light, there is some question about whether this is a cause or an effect of their depression. Other research demonstrates that *after* someone is placed in a negative mood, he or she is likely to interpret events in more negative terms (Forgas et al., 1984, among others). After reviewing a number of studies in the area, Peter Barnett and Ian Gotlib (1988) concluded that depressive attitudes and attributions appear to be *results* of such life experiences as divorce, but not the original causes of the depression. This issue is still being debated, however. In Chapter 16 (on therapy) we will discuss evidence suggesting that depressive cognitions may contribute to maintaining depression, even though they may not have caused it (Healy and Williams, 1988).

BIPOLAR DISORDER

Bipolar disorder is the DSM III-R term for what Kraeplin originally called manic-depressive disorder. Manic symptoms involve very high levels of energy, restlessness, talkativeness, and sometimes unbounded optimism and grandiosity. The manic person often makes extremely unrealistic plans— consider the dentist who decided to double the size of his office despite a recent downturn in business, and began tearing down the walls himself when he could not get a contractor to begin work immediately. The following conversation shows some of the central characteristics of mania:

> THERAPIST: Well, you seem pretty happy today.
> CLIENT: Happy! Happy! You certainly are a master of understatement, you rogue! [Shouting, literally jumping out of seat.] Why I'm ecstatic. I'm leaving for the west coast today, on my daughter's bicycle. Only 3100 miles. That's nothing, you know. I could probably walk, but I want to get there by next week. And along the way I plan to follow up on my inventions of the past month, you know, stopping at the big plants along the way having lunch with the executives, maybe getting to know them a bit—you know, Doc, "know" in the biblical sense [leering at the therapist seductively]. Oh, God, how good it feels. It's almost like a non-stop orgasm.

(Davison and Neale, 1982)

In some cases, mania can be turned to success. For instance, there is some suggestion that Winston Churchill and Theodore Roosevelt suffered from manic-depression (Rosenhan and Seligman, 1984). Frequently, however, the disorder results in failure because of the unrealistic nature of the manic patient's schemes and his or her sometimes inappropriate social behaviors. Sometimes manic patients become dangerous when others interfere with their grandiose plans. More frequently they exhaust themselves, and may have heart attacks during their manic episodes.

Most individuals who suffer from depression do not show the upward shift into mania, although manics usually do become depressed at times, often severely. Bipolar disorder affects both men and women equally, suggesting that it is a different disorder from unipolar depression, which affects women more frequently. Like unipolar depression, however, it is also associated with alcohol abuse, particularly during the manic phases of the disorder (Zigler and Glick, 1988). Manic individuals may use alcohol not because it makes them feel good, but because of its sedative effects.

Physiological studies suggest that mania is related to biochemical abnormalities in the central nervous system, perhaps an overreactivity to dopamine (Swerdlow and Koob, 1987). Behavior genetic studies support a biological hypothesis, indicating that the disease is highly heritable (Allen, 1976; Faraone et al., 1990; La Roche et al., 1985). Although behavior genetic studies establish that there is an innate predisposition to the disease, they do not tell which genes are involved. In recent years, however, there have been advances in the technology of gene mapping—locating specific genes for specific traits. There has been recent news of a specific gene for manic-depressive illness from studies of the Amish (Pennsylvania Dutch) sect. The Amish are used in this sort of research because they have a fairly high degree of inbreeding and a constant gene pool (outsiders do not marry in). A research team led by Janice Egeland located a dominant gene on chromosome 11 that appears to operate through its effects on the production of the hormone tyrosine hydroxylase (Egeland et al., 1987). All 19 of the individuals with bipolar disorder they studied showed the same genetic abnormality.

In sum, then, mood disorders can involve either unusual feelings of elation, or unusual feelings of sadness. Occasionally the two extremes combine in the same individual, although sadness often occurs without any accompanying manic episodes. It is important to point out that everyone experiences occasional depression and elation as a natural part of life. It is only when these feelings are extreme, persist for long periods, arise without explanation, and interfere with everyday functioning, that they are considered as psychological disorders.

ANXIETY DISORDERS

Anxiety is closely related to the emotion that most of us feel when our car suddenly spins out on an icy highway or when it is our turn to speak in front of the class. Anxiety is the term used for fearful emotional responses that occur in circumstances that do not seem to pose an objective threat to life or limb. Some people are petrified at the sight of a harmless household spider. Others cannot even identify a particular cause for their feelings of apprehension but nevertheless feel jumpy and nervous a good deal of the time. Anxiety is defined by cognitive, physiological, and behavioral components. Cognitively, anxiety takes the form of worry, fear, and mental images of potential harm. The sufferer is aware of a tightness in the chest, "butterflies in the stomach," and muscular tension. Physiologically, anxiety shows up as increased heart rate and blood pressure, changes in galvanic skin response (sweaty palms), dilation (widening) of the pupils, and biochemical changes in the bloodstream as adrenaline prepares the body for fight or flight. Behaviorally, it takes the form of such nervous symptoms as pacing, jumpiness, frequent urination, and muscular tension that may, in the extreme, result in shaking. It is normal to feel some amount of fear in threatening situations. The person with an **anxiety disorder,** however, feels that same emotion in situations that others would say pose no threat, and he or she feels it to a degree that interferes with everyday life.

GENERALIZED ANXIETY DISORDER

Someone who experiences the above symptoms for a prolonged period, with no specific cause, will be diagnosed as having a generalized anxiety disorder. Here is one woman's description of her symptoms:

> It was just like I was petrified with fear. . . . My heart was beating so hard and fast it would jump out and hit my hand. . . . My hands got icy, and my feet stung. There were horrible shooting pains in my forehead. . . . I couldn't breathe. I was short of breath. I literally get out of breath and pant just like I had run up and down the stairs. I felt like I had

run an eight-mile race. I couldn't do anything. I felt all in, weak, no strength. I can't even dial a telephone. Even then I can't be still when I'm like this. I am restless, and I pace up and down . . .
> *(from Laughlin, 1956)*

PHOBIAS ●

A phobia is a more specific fear. Instead of the vague dread associated with a generalized anxiety disorder, the phobic individual is fearful of some specific situation or event. One researcher classified the most common phobias into separation fears (for example, being lost in a crowd, traveling alone, being alone at home), animal fears (snakes, rats, insects), mutilation fears (blood, surgery), social fears (being watched while eating or working), and nature fears (the ocean, heights) (Torgerson, 1979). Women are more likely to have phobias (McNally, 1990), particularly agoraphobia (fear of open, crowded places) and animal phobias. (See Figure 15.3.) People with animal phobias and agoraphobias are often most afraid that they will panic when confronted with the situation that causes the fear (McNally, 1987). Given other evidence that women are more likely to experience general feelings of helplessness (Block, 1983), it may be that women are more likely to feel helpless when specifically faced with being lost in a crowd or confronted by an animal.

As we saw in the case of Little Hans (the boy afraid of horses and obsessed with "widdlers"), Freud believed that phobic disorders are caused by anxiety over unacceptable sexual and aggressive feelings. We also noted that behaviorists, such as Wolpe and Rachman, explained phobias as instances of classical conditioning. Early experimental psychologists believed that phobias could be conditioned to any neutral object, so it would be possible to have phobias about potential natural threats such as rats (if one were bitten), or of potential artificial threats such as kitchen pots (if one were burned). However, most actual phobias seem to involve such threats as crowds of strangers, heights, insects, and large animals, things that were once potentially dangerous to our ancestors (DeSilva, Rachman, and Seligman, 1977). And experimental studies indicate that it is more difficult to extinguish fear of these "naturally prepared" threats (spiders and snakes) than of such "unprepared" objects as houses or flowers (Ohman et al., 1976). Those studies seem to suggest that there are evolutionary constraints on the likelihood of learning fear of particular stimuli, although the evidence on this suggestion is not completely

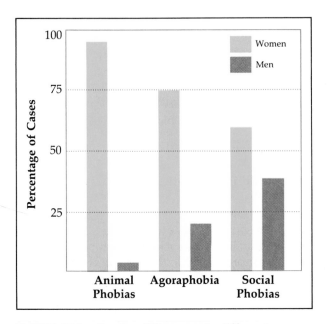

FIGURE 15.3 Gender differences in different categories of phobia. The sexes are most different in their fears of animals. Phobias seem to involve an interaction of a biological predisposition to fear certain kinds of threats and learning experiences that trigger that predisposition.

clear. It is possible that genetic predispositions make spiders and snakes unconditioned (or innate) fears for some people (McNally, 1987).

OBSESSIVE-COMPULSIVE DISORDER

Obsessive-compulsive disorder is an anxiety disorder that involves repetitious thoughts the person cannot get out of his or her mind—*obsessions*. These intrusive thoughts are frequently accompanied by *compulsions*, behavioral rituals that the person feels compelled to perform. Freud distinguished between anxiety from an external threat and anxiety from fear of losing control of one's own impulses. Obsessive thoughts often involve fears of the person's own sexual or aggressive impulses. One woman was obsessed with the idea that she might poison her husband, another with the fear she would reach out and choke one of the students in the kindergarten class she taught (Kisker, 1964). Compulsions may involve cleanliness rituals, as in the case of the girl who reported:

> In the morning when I got dressed, I was real afraid that there'd be germs all over my clothes and things, so I'd stand there and I'd shake them for half an hour. I'd wash before I did anything—like if I was gonna wash my face, I'd wash my hands first; if I was gonna brush my teeth, I'd wash my hands first; and

if I was gonna get dressed, I'd wash my hands first; and then it got even beyond that point. Washing my hands wasn't enough, and I started to use rubbing alcohol. It was wintertime and cold weather, and this really made my hands bleed.

(Spitzer et al., 1981)

In other cases, the individual carries out everyday tasks with extremely orderly routines. One man had a precise order for the way in which he dressed and undressed, brushed his teeth, and used the toilet. His concern that he might have done things out of order frequently led him to repeat the whole sequence, to be sure he had it right (Sarason and Sarason, 1987).

Although their rituals and thoughts may seem strange, obsessive-compulsive individuals do not usually appear to be out of touch with reality. However, they are unusually self-doubting and concerned about things that most of us would consider to be trivial. Many of them realize, on an intellectual level, that their rituals are not sensible. In fact, one study found that 78 percent of them viewed their rituals as silly or even absurd (Stern and Cobb, 1978). In these cases, however, intellectual understanding does not transfer to emotional understanding, and the person is unable to stop the obsessive thoughts.

DISSOCIATIVE DISORDERS

Have you ever wondered at the radical split between your waking and dreaming consciousness? What seems vivid and real during the dream seems ephemeral and distant when you wake up. You may have done things in the dream that you would never consider doing in real life—jumping off a cliff, punching someone, or undressing in public. In most cases, although your dream experiences may have been intense, you do not even remember them. Or perhaps you have been awed at the vague recollections of your completely uncharacteristic behavior when you got intoxicated one night. People who are diagnosed as having **dissociative disorders** experience these dramatic splits in consciousness, or dissociations, during their waking lives, even without the influence of drugs.

PSYCHOGENIC AMNESIA

The term **psychogenic amnesia** refers to a dramatic loss of memory that cannot be attributed to a physical trauma such as head injury. It is the most common dissociative disorder. Psychogenic amnesia is usually preceded by some emotionally upsetting episode, as in the case of a man who accidentally killed a pedestrian with his car. After speaking to the police and filling out an accident report (the police determined that the accident was not his fault) the man later began to wander around dazed, having forgotten his own name (Cameron, 1963). In some cases the person suddenly disappears after a traumatic event, and may not reappear for years, if at all. You may recall that in Chapter 7 we discussed this phenomenon, called *fugue state*, as an example of an unusual memory phenomenon. In a fugue state, the person appears to forget his or her name, identity, family, and friends, and takes on a new identity, all without forgetting such other types of factual knowledge as the name of the first president of the United States.

> Bernice L., a 42-year-old housewife . . . had disappeared from her home four years previously, and had recently been identified and returned from . . . a small town over a thousand miles away . . . She had at first appeared highly perturbed, anxious, and indecisive [on rejoining her family]. . . . Soon, however, she had begun to insist that she really had never seen them before, that her name was not Bernice L. but Rose P. and that it was all a case of mistaken identity. . . .
>
> *(Masserman, 1961)*

The case report goes on to say that, after years in a "loveless marriage with a man designated by her parents," and immediately after her younger and favorite child died, Bernice L. disappeared and returned to the town where she had gone to college. The name she used, Rose P., was the name of her best friend in college, who had left to marry a man who Bernice had secretly loved as well. As in the case of Bernice L., fugue states are generally precipitated by a traumatic emotional incident (Spitzer et al., 1981, among others).

MULTIPLE PERSONALITY

Muiltiple personality (discussed in Chapter 4 on consciousness) is a very rare but highly publicized form of dissociative disorder. In this disorder, the person actually shifts back and forth between two, three, or more distinct identities, in the fashion of Robert Louis Stevenson's "Strange Case of Dr. Jekyll and Mr. Hyde." A classic case described in 1943 involved a woman who would shift back and forth between two identities, "Sara" and "Maud." Sara was a conservative, intelligent woman who felt considerable guilt over her early liberal sexual behavior. However, she would switch into Maud, who was boisterous, flashy, guiltlessly promiscuous, a smoker, and used foul language. When given an IQ test as Maud, Sara dropped from her normally superior score of 128 to a score of 43 (Lipton, 1943). In shifting from one personality to another, multiple personalities seem to remember different early experiences, to change in personality test scores, and even to show differences on physiological measures such as the EEG (Lester, 1977).

Multiple personality. In the movie, *The Three Faces of Eve*, based on an actual case of multiple personality disorder, Joanne Woodward depicted the changes in behavior and mood that characterize this syndrome.

There are several predisposing factors for a multiple personality (Bliss, 1986). Multiple personalities generally begin following emotional crises before the age of six, commonly precipitated by extreme physical or sexual abuse. The multiple personality is usually not discovered until adulthood, when the person becomes curious about blackouts or periods that he or she cannot remember. Nine out of 10 cases are women (Kluft, 1987). The case of Truddi Chase (1987) is illustrative. Between the ages of two and 16, her stepfather sexually abused her and threatened her with harm if she told anyone. As an adult, she had great difficulty remembering any sexual experiences at all, despite the fact that she had been married and had a daughter. The psychologist who treated her claimed to have uncovered 92 separate "selves" (Chase, 1987). It seems that often abused children form an imaginary identity to handle situations or feelings (including anger and sexual arousal) that are overwhelming.

There is sometimes a question about whether a multiple personality is simply a dramatic put-on (Orne et al., 1984). For instance, forensic psychologist John Watkins hypnotized the "Hillside Strangler" Kenneth Bianchi and found evidence of a "hidden personality" whom Bianchi called "Steve." Orne and his colleagues point out that Bianchi was a chronic liar, and argue that he was faking a multiple personality to avoid responsibility for his crimes. You may recall from Chapter 4 that Orne also viewed hypnosis as a form of role-playing, rather than as a separate state of consciousness.

SOMATOFORM DISORDERS

Until recently, **somatoform disorders** were categorized together with anxiety disorders. As we discussed, an anxiety disorder often involves physical symptoms such as difficult breathing, pounding heart, headaches, and so on. People with somatoform disorders also experience physical symptoms, and many theorists believe that these symptoms arise from anxiety. Somatoform disorders differ from anxiety disorders, however, in that they involve chronic *physical* complaints usually associated with other illnesses, such as paralysis or pains in the abdomen. Unlike psychophysiological disorders such as ulcers (discussed in Chapter 14), which involve actual damage as a result of prolonged stress, somatoform disorders involve symptoms for which medical professionals are unable to find any actual physical cause. Of course, undiagnosable physical symptoms are not enough

to lead to a somatoform diagnosis. In addition, there must be "positive evidence, or a strong presumption, that the symptoms are linked to psychological factors or conflicts" (DSM III-R, 1987).

CONVERSION DISORDER

People suffering from a **conversion disorder** show a specific symptom with no obvious physical damage; their psychological disorder is converted into a physical ailment. Glove anesthesia, for example, is a form of paralysis that does not follow the known pathways of the nervous system (Davison and Neale, 1982). Instead, it follows the patient's ideas about the way the body is divided up. Without special surgery, for instance, it is not possible to have a completely paralyzed hand without any paralysis of the forearm.

As we mentioned earlier, this type of phenomenon fascinated Freud (Breuer and Freud, 1895/1966). Recall the case of Anna O., whose paralysis and headaches seemed to be the result of conflict over her father's illness. The fact that conversion symptoms could sometimes be removed by hypnosis convinced Freud that these physical symptoms were caused by psychological factors. In fact, the term "conversion" originated in Freudian theory, and refers to the transformation of energy from psychological conflict into a bodily symptom. In the last chapter we described the fascinating phenomenon of **group hysteria**, a peculiar form of conversion disorder in which a number of people all develop a similar illness through a process of social influence.

HYPOCHONDRIASIS

While a conversion disorder focuses on a very specific symptom, **hypochondriasis** is characterized by a general fear of physical illness. Hypochondriacs may complain of stomach troubles, back problems, headaches, and various other aches and pains, and diagnose themselves as having cancer, heart disease, tuberculosis, and so on. The diagnosis of hypochondria is used when medical doctors cannot find any evidence of physical disease. The hypochondriacal patient may not accept the negative medical diagnoses, will visit different doctors in search of prescriptions, and will stock the medicine cabinet with a wealth of nonprescription drugs. One study found that patients with such unfounded somatic complaints were significantly more likely to have unnecessary surgery (Woodruff et al., 1974). In fact, they were, compared with other similar patients, found to have had three times as much body tissue removed. The disorder often follows an experience with a true organic disease and/or a period of life stress (DSM III-R, 1987).

It is sometimes difficult to distinguish between those who really believe they are sick, and those who report symptoms that they know to be false. The DSM III-R uses the term **factitious disorder** for a physical complaint that is purposefully fabricated or greatly exaggerated by a patient. Although some patients do lie about their symptoms (factitious disorder), and others do imagine that they are sick when they are really healthy (hypochondriasis), these psychiatric labels have a high potential for misuse. Sometimes medical diagnosticians misapply a somatoform diagnosis when they are unable to detect real physical problems because of deficiencies in medical science. One follow-up study of patients diagnosed as having somatoform disorders revealed that, nine years later, the majority either had come down with a detectable physical illness or had died (Slater and Glithero, 1965). Diseases such as multiple sclerosis often begin with many vague complaints, for instance, and are sometimes misdiagnosed as somatoform disorders (DSM III-R, 1987).

ORGANIC MENTAL DISORDERS

The term somatoform disorder is reserved for physical symptoms that seem to exist only in the patient's mind and cannot be linked to bodily illness. In Chapter 14, we discussed physical problems that seem to begin with a psychological cause. **Organic disorders** involve another possible causal link between mind and body—they are psychological disorders caused by physical illness.

GENERAL PARESIS

Before the discovery of antibiotics as a treatment of syphilis, *general paresis* was a common form of mental illness. Although it is now rare, it provides a classic illustration of a mental disorder being caused by a physical disease. It is similar to schizophrenia. General paresis begins with irritability, depression, and impaired judgment, and later develops into emotional symptoms and sometimes bizarre delusions of grandeur. One man told the police officers who picked him up:

> I'm going to the wardens of the prisons in this state and all the other states and I'm going to buy the prisoners. I have an agreement with the wardens to take their prisoners and put them to work on farms, and I'll charge each prisoner $300 for doing it and for getting

him out of jail. I made $105,000 with prisoners just last week. . . ."

(Kolb, 1968)

This disorder was clearly linked to syphilis in 1897, when Richard Kraft-Ebing inoculated a group of paretic patients with syphilis bacteria, and none of them developed the usual early symptoms of the disease (Davison and Neale, 1982). If they had not previously had syphilis, they would have come down with the disease at that point. This procedure, though completely unacceptable by today's ethical standards, established that the paretic patients had already been infected with syphilis. In recent years, psychotic symptoms associated with syphilis are much more rare, since antibiotics have brought the disease under control (Dale, 1975).

SENILE DEMENTIA

Some older people begin to show the signs of disorganized thinking, loss of memory, and shifts of mood that we commonly call senility (DSM III-R uses the term **senile dementia**). A colleague of Kraeplin's at the University of Munich, Alois Alzheimer, examined the brain tissue of senile patients after they died. He found two types of microscopic abnormalities, which he called "senile plaques" and "neurofibrillary tangles." These are signs of extensive neuronal death, and they appear mostly in the area of the hippocampus. You may recall the case of H.M., discussed in Chapter 2, who suffered severe loss of long-term memory after part of his hippocampus was removed. It seems that senile patients suffer from naturally occurring lesions that are in some ways similar to H.M.'s, and that account for their loss of memory. (See Figure 15.4.) In Chapter 12 we discussed how symptoms of dementia similar to senility can be caused by Huntington's chorea. Other forms of dementia, including Korsakoff's syndrome, discussed in Chapter 7, can result from prolonged alcohol abuse.

Psychologists used to draw a sharp line between disorders caused by organic factors and those caused by psychological factors. Some biomedical theorists now believe that most serious psychological disturbances have some organic component (Andreasen, 1984, among others). Although not all psychologists agree, it is clear from the material we covered in the last chapter that the avenue between psychological events and the physical body runs in both directions. Psychological problems can produce actual physical damage, and physical damage from illness and disease

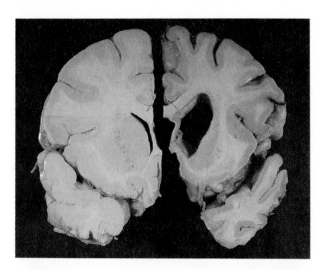

FIGURE 15.4   Cross-sections of a normal brain (left), and of the brain of a patient who had Huntington's chorea (right).   Note the two small cavities in the center (sulci) of the normal brain, and the extensive enlargement of the sulci and of the convolutions in the afflicted brain.

can lead indirectly to depression and anxiety, or, when the brain is damaged, directly to information processing deficits.

SCHIZOPHRENIC DISORDERS

Schizophrenia is generally regarded as the most severe form of psychological disorder. Thirty percent of all hospital beds in the United States are used by schizophrenics—this is greater than the number devoted to any other illness, mental or physical. This is not because schizophrenia is more prevalent than cancer or heart disease (less than one person in one hundred is schizophrenic) but because schizophrenics do not die of their illness, and are often either unwelcome at home or completely unable to live in the community. Schizophrenics are not usually prone to violence, but when they are it frequently takes a bizarre form that makes it newsworthy. David Berkowitz, "The Son of Sam," received nationwide news coverage during the 1970s when he murdered a number of young women in New York because he believed that he was receiving Satanic messages from his neighbor's dog.

Many schizophrenics, however, live out their lives in lonely obscurity, as the neighborhood eccentric or a patient on the "chronic ward" of the state hospital. Others, including Norma MacDonald, who wrote lucidly about her earlier schizophrenia (see beginning of this chapter), have long periods during which they can function normally.

SYMPTOMS OF SCHIZOPHRENIA

Schizophrenia is associated with a breakdown in the brain's normal processes (Gray et al., 1991). Consequently, schizophrenics' perceptions of reality are often fragmented and distorted. (Figure 15.5 illustrates the degree to which a distorted perception of reality has been reflected in a schizophrenic artist's renderings of a ghost who was his "other self.")

The most prominent defining characteristics of schizophrenia are disturbances of thought—delusions, hallucinations, incoherent thinking, marked social isolation or withdrawal, blunted or inappropriate emotions, and strange motor behaviors. Not all of these symptoms are found in every schizophrenic, but if two of them occur, they last for at least a week, they cannot be attributed to severe depression or organic damage, and the person has shown other signs of socially inappropriate behavior that have lasted for at least six months, then he or she meets the DSM III-R standards for a diagnosis of schizophrenia. Note that by these criteria, Rosenhan's pseudopatients today should not be defined as schizophrenic.

Delusions are faulty beliefs that have no basis in reality. David Berkowitz's belief that he was being controlled by Satan would be considered a delusion. **Hallucinations** are sensory experiences that have no basis in the external world. Mark Vonnegut, the son of novelist Kurt Vonnegut, described

FIGURE 15.5   A painting by a schizophrenic.   This painting demonstrates some of the perceptual confusions and thought disorder that characterize schizophrenia. The artist describes his own painting in the following way: "This was the 'ghost' I used to see all the time. It was my other self that I was always talking to. The deep eyes represent that mysteriousness of the self; and the background shows all the different kinds of thoughts a person experiences."

David Berkowitz ("The Son of Sam"). Berkowitz (right) suffered from delusions (false beliefs) that he was being controlled by the devil, which led him to murder several people.

his own experience with auditory hallucinations quite vividly:

> The Voices. Testing one, two, testing one. Checking out the circuits: "What hath God wrought. Yip di mina di zonda da boom di yaidi yoohoo.
>
> At first I'd had to strain to hear or understand them. They were soft and working with some pretty tricky codes. Snap-crackle-pops, the sound of the wind with blinking lights and horns for punctuations. I broke the code and somehow was able to internalize it to the point where it was just like hearing voices. In the beginning it seemed mostly nonsense, but as things went along they made more and more sense.
>
> *(Vonnegut, 1975)*

The *incoherent thinking* that is characteristic of schizophrenia shows up in rapid shifts of topic and loose associations. For instance, one schizophrenic patient wrote "I may be a 'Blue Baby' but 'Social' Baby not, but yet a blue heart baby could be in the Blue Book published before the war" (from Maher, 1966). These disorganized thoughts may be the result of an inability to control attention.

VARIETIES OR SUBTYPES OF SCHIZOPHRENIA

As we noted, not all schizophrenics show the same pattern of symptoms. Kraeplin described three different types that are still recognized today.

Paranoid Schizophrenia. Paranoid schizophrenia is the most common diagnosis in this group. The central symptoms of paranoid schizophrenia are *delusions of persecution* and *delusions of grandeur*. Paranoid people believe that others are plotting against them (delusions of persecution) and frequently attribute the plot to their own religious or political importance (delusions of grandeur). Just as Norma MacDonald believed that everyone on the street was trying to communicate with her through their glances, the paranoid individual may see personal relevance in newspaper headlines, radio announcements, and comments oveheard in the supermarket. The following conversation with a paranoid patient illustrates the central symptoms:

> DOCTOR: What are you doing here?
>
> PATIENT: Well, I've been sent here to thwart the Russians. I'm the only one in the world who knows how to deal with them. They got their spies all around here though to get me, but I'm smarter than any of them.
>
> DOCTOR: What are you doing to thwart the Russians?
>
> PATIENT: I'm organizing.
>
> DOCTOR: Whom are you going to organize?
>
> PATIENT: Everybody. I'm the only man in the world who can do that, but they're trying to get me. But I'm going to use my atomic bomb media to blow them up.
>
> DOCTOR: You must be a terribly important person then.
>
> PATIENT: Well, of course.
>
> DOCTOR: What do you call yourself?
>
> PATIENT: You used to know me as Franklin D. Roosevelt.
>
> DOCTOR: Isn't he dead?
>
> PATIENT: Sure he's dead, but I'm alive.
>
> DOCTOR: But you're Franklin D. Roosevelt?
>
> PATIENT: His spirit. He, God, and I figured this out. And now I'm going to make a race of healthy people. My agents are lining them up. Say, who are you?
>
> DOCTOR: I'm a doctor here.
>
> PATIENT: You don't look like a doctor. You look like a Russian to me.
>
> *(Coleman, 1972)*

It would be possible to meet a paranoid schizophrenic and not realize it, if you did not begin to discuss any topics that triggered his or her delusional beliefs. This might partly account for the fact that the normal behavior of Rosenhan and his colleagues did not immediately disqualify them as schizophrenics in the eyes of the hospital staff.

However, other schizophrenic syndromes result in behaviors that are almost impossible to miss, as we will describe next.

Disorganized Schizophrenia. Formerly known as *hebrephrenic schizophrenia*, this syndrome is characterized by very bizarre symptoms, including extreme delusions, hallucinations, and completely inappropriate patterns of speech, mood, and movement. You would immediately recognize something awry in the disorganized schizophrenic's childish giggling and strange style of dress, which might be combined with public urination, defecation, and obscene and babbling speech. One case was a 40-year-old man brought to the hospital by his mother. He was dressed in "a ragged overcoat, bedroom slippers, and a baseball cap and . . . several medals around his neck" (Spitzer et al., 1981). His mood shifted rapidly from anger at his mother—"She feeds me . . . what comes out of other people's rectums"—to giggling seductively at the interviewer. He was described as walking "with a mincing step and exaggerated hip movements," and speaking in an incoherent manner, making senseless rhymes and loose associations. For instance, when asked what he had been doing, he responded "eating wires and lighting fires."

Catatonic Schizophrenia. Catatonic schizophrenia is characterized by unusual motor symptoms—strange movements. A person in a catatonic state may remain stiff and immobile for hours, totally unresponsive to the outside world. At those times catatonic schizophrenics show what is called *waxy flexibility*, in which an arm or leg can be moved into any position without its owner even attempting to move it back into a normal posture. During these periods, the person moves very slowly if at all, will not talk or eat, and will urinate on his or her own clothing. At other times, the person may go to an opposite extreme, showing intense excitement, running about, tearing his or her clothes, talking and screaming incessantly, and becoming violent with anyone in his or her path.

IS SCHIZOPHRENIA AN ORGANIC DISORDER?

For a number of years, psychologists investigated the possibility that schizophrenia is a response to inappropriate communications from a child's parents (Wynne et al., 1977, among others). Although there is evidence that communication patterns in schizophrenic families are sometimes different from the norm, there is some question about whether this is a cause or an effect of the schizophrenia. For instance, it may be that a schizophrenic child, who is apt to behave in a bizarre fashion, disrupts normal family communications (Liem, 1974). Alternatively, a schizophrenic's parents may act inappropriately precisely because the parent and the schizophrenic child share some of the same genes. In fact, there is increasing evidence that schizophrenia is, at least in part, the result of a genetic predisposition. (See Table 15.3.)

Genetic Influences. Table 15.3 shows the results of recent studies of schizophrenics who had either an identical or a fraternal twin (from Gottesman et al., 1982). Two fraternal twins share a 14 percent **concordance rate,** which refers to the agreement in diagnosis. In other words, if one is schizophrenic, there is a 14 percent chance that the other will also be diagnosed as schizophrenic. For identical twins, the chance jumps to 46 percent. If there were no genetic component, the probability of the second twin's being schizophrenic, just by chance, would be less than one percent (the population probability). By the same reckoning, the probability of a set of quadruplets sharing a schizophrenic diagnosis is less than one in a million. For that reason, behavior geneticists were fascinated when all four of the "Genain" quadruplets were found to have schizophrenia.

As statistically improbable as it is to find all four of a set of quadruplets to be concordant for schizophrenia, it does not prove the genetic case, since

TABLE 15.3 Percentage of Twins Sharing a Diagnosis of Schizophrenia

	Identical Twins	Fraternal Twins
Investigator/Country		
Tienari/Finland	35*	13
Kringlen/Norway	45	15
Fischer/Denmark	56	27
Pollin et al./USA	43	9
Gottesman & Shields/U.K.	58	12
(Weighted average)	46	14

Note: The researchers began with a schizophrenic and then found his or her twin. The number indicates the percent of pairs in which the second twin was also schizophrenic. The term "concordant" simply refers to agreement between the diagnoses of the two twins. You would expect 100% concordance between identical twins for a highly penetrant gene, like eye color.

From Gottesman and Shields (1982).

The Genain quadruplets. These quads were genetically identical, and were all eventually diagnosed as schizophrenic. Chances of such coincidence for four siblings are less than three in 1000.

ly. In seven of the 12 cases both of the twins were schizophrenic, yielding a concordance rate of 58%, which is very close to the rate found for pairs of identical twins who are raised together (Gottesman et al., 1982). In general, children who are adopted and later grow up to become schizophrenic are found to have few schizophrenics in the adopted families who raised them, but many in their biological families, with whom they share only genes. This suggests that schizophrenia is more related to genes than to family environment.

Biochemical Influences. How would a genetic predisposition for schizophrenia have its effects? A likely possibility is that schizophrenics inherit a malfunction of normal brain biochemistry. In fact, there is evidence that at least some forms of schizophrenia may be related to an overabundance of dopamine in certain areas of the brain (Swerdlow and Koob, 1987). Several lines of evidence converge on this conclusion. First, antipsychotic medicines such as chlorpromazine seem to work by blocking the reabsorption of dopamine by neurons. Second, drugs that increase dopamine production, such as some stimulants, also worsen schizophrenic symptoms. Third, schizophrenics have been shown to have an unusually high number of dopamine receptors in their brains, particularly in the basal ganglia and the limbic system (Seeman et al., 1984).

The increased number of dopamine receptors in schizophrenics' brains also suggests a possible link between psychopathology and the structure of the brain. In recent years, it has been possible to study the structure of living brains using such brain-imaging techniques as CAT Scans and PET scans (short for Computerized Axial Tomography and Positron Emission Tomography, respectively). Brain-scan studies as well as post-mortem examinations indicate that schizophrenics sometimes have extensive atrophy (or wasting away) of brain tissue, particularly in the frontal portion of the cerebral cortex, which is involved in judgment and planning. The damage is more likely to appear in patients who have a long history of symptoms and a low likelihood of recovery (Andreasen et al., 1982).

the quadruplets were raised in the same home. It could be that their shared environment, not their shared genes, was responsible for the schizophrenia. The most stringent test for a behavior genetic model is to find identical twins reared apart; however, the chances of finding someone who is both schizophrenic, and an identical twin who was raised separately are very small. The probability of being schizophrenic (.0085), in combination with the probability of being an identical twin (.006), results in an expected probability of only 53 per million. Compound that already low figure with the very low probability that a pair of twins will be raised apart, and one would expect to find only a few cases in the world. Nevertheless, one team of researchers reports on 12 people who met all these criteria—each was schizophrenic, and had an identical twin who had been raised in a separate fami-

If schizophrenia were entirely the result of a genetic predisposition, the concordance rate for identical twins would be 100 percent. Since it is closer to 50 percent, some environmental factors must play a role in triggering the genetic predisposition. Those environmental factors may be related to parental behaviors, to stress, or even to other disease processes. As quoted at the beginning of the chapter, Norma MacDonald had a sickly childhood before the onset of her schizophrenia. Schizophrenics are more likely to be born in the late winter and early spring months, when viral infections are high, and they are more likely to have had viral infections throughout their lives (Andreason, 1984; Molner and Fava, 1987). This suggests that, given a genetic predisposition, the early disease process may trigger the adverse biochemical processes associated with schizophrenia. Psychologist Paul Meehl (1990) suggests that the predisposition for schizophrenia may not be triggered by anything as profound as an unloving father, a bad school, or a viral infection, but simply a series of unlucky small events that compound one another, such as failing at a sporting event and then being ridiculed as a "sissy" by another child. The normal child may quickly put this sort of event out of his mind, but the child with a predisposition towards schizophrenia may begin to ruminate about it, and then to begin avoiding other children, which in turn leads to more problems in relating to others.

PERSONALITY DISORDERS

Personality disorders are characteristic behavior patterns that have caused problems throughout a person's life, but that are neither totally debilitating nor socially bizarre in the way that schizophrenia, depression, and even anxiety disorders can be. In fact, an individual with a personality disorder will often be regarded as "normal," if sometimes somewhat socially irritating. Some believe that personality disorders precede more serious psychological disorders later in life (Sarason and Sarason, 1987). One category of personality disorders relates to odd or eccentric behaviors that are not serious enough to warrant a diagnosis of schizophrenia. For instance, the major defining characteristic for *paranoid personality disorder* is suspiciousness. Another category involves anxious or fearful behaviors, including *dependent personality disorder* (characterized by helpless and clinging interpersonal relationships). *Narcissistic personality disorder* is named for Narcissus, the Greek youth who saw his image in a pool and fell in love with himself. When psychologists say that someone is narcissistic, they mean that he or she is self-concerned to a degree that interferes with relationships with others.

ANTISOCIAL PERSONALITY

Among the personality disorders, by far the most research has been devoted to the **antisocial per-**

sonality. This disorder is the one that is most distinct from the categories we discussed earlier. In fact, the antisocial personality is best understood when contrasted with the anxious or depressed individual. While the anxious person is nervous about common everyday events, and the depressive feels guilt about trivial failings, the antisocial personality goes through life fairly devoid of anxiety and guilt, despite the fact that he or she exploits others to a degree that would shame a normal person. These cool, charming, frequently attractive individuals, sometimes called *psychopaths,* often come into conflict with the law because of their disregard for social rules, and their lack of any motivation to restrain their own impulses. Most criminals are not antisocial personalities, but some notorious "cold-blooded" murderers are. As the infamous murderer Gary Gilmore expressed it: "I almost never get blue. Though I've made a mess of my life, I never stew about the things I have done" (in Spitzer et al., 1983).

Most antisocial personalities are not murderers, although many commit crimes that show a disregard for the feelings and disapproval of others. Their crimes are likely to include con operations, passing bad checks, and bigamous marriages—without informing either wife, or even bothering to ask for a divorce. They are often successful in getting lenient treatment because of their charm, good looks, and ability to con authorities and juries. Many of them are successful enough without having to resort to street crimes. As psychopathy researcher Robert Hare said: "You find psychopaths in all professions. He's the shyster lawyer, the physican always on the verge of losing his license, the businessman with a string of deals where his partners always lose out" (Goleman, 1987). Hare found that psychopaths were four times more likely to violate parole than were nonpsychopathic prisoners. Psychopathy is a disorder of the young male; 80 percent of psychopaths are men, and the disorder decreases considerably by age 35 or 40. Such an overabundance of males is found for only one other category of disorder—paraphilias (deviant sexual preferences).

There is evidence that antisocial personality disorder may involve both a biological predisposition and some environmental triggers. Sarnoff Mednick (1985) notes that there are several biological markers of antisocial behavior, including slow brain-wave activity and an unresponsive autonomic nervous system that may make it difficult for antisocial people to learn from punishment. (Recall our discussion on personality in Chapter 13.) To investigate the relative contributions of genes and environments to psychopathy, Mednick and his colleagues have examined records for 14,427 adoptions in Denmark, and court records of 65,516 criminal arrests involving adoptees or their parents (Mednick, Gabrielli, and Hutchings, 1984). The results are shown in Figure 15.6. Of children who had neither an adopted nor a biological parent convicted, 13.5 percent went on to get arrested themselves. Having an adoptive parent with a criminal record had no appreciable effect on the antisocial behavior of children whose biological parents had never been arrested—14.7 percent of them went on to get arrested. Having a biological parent with an arrest record, however, increased

the arrest likelihood to 20 percent, suggesting some genetic component. The combination of genes from a criminal biological parent and being raised by a criminal adoptive parent was associated with the highest likelihood of committing a criminal act—24.5 percent. This suggests that the genetic predisposition made children particularly susceptible to learning antisocial behavior from criminal parents. Mednick found that poverty is another environmental factor that seems to trigger the genetic predisposition for antisocial behavior. It may be that the pressures of poverty provide an additional incentive for exploitative behaviors that are unnecessary for those in the upper and middle classes, who can more easily attain rewards within the bounds of convention.

FIGURE 15.6 The likelihood of criminal behavior in adoptees, as a function of criminal convictions in their biological and adoptive parents. As indicated, having only a criminal adoptive parent was not associated with substantial increases in criminal behavior in adoptees (beyond that found in children with neither a biological nor adoptive criminal parent). Having a criminal biological parent was, in itself, associated with a substantial increase. For children with a biological parent who was a criminal, a criminal adoptive parent was associated with further increases in criminal behavior. This pattern suggests that the biological predisposition interacts with experience.

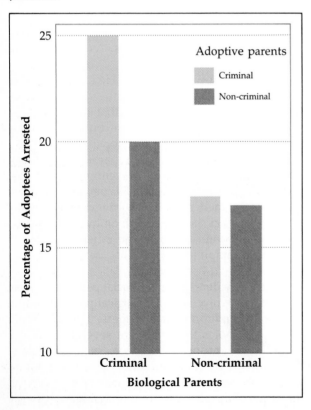

LINKING THE DIFFERENT PSYCHOLOGICAL DISORDERS

We have discussed many different types of psychological disorders in this chapter, and there are many others we have not had the space to mention. The DSM III-R lists approximately 300 different psychiatric diagnoses, and even that list could be lengthened, since several diagnostic labels are open-ended—"Other or unspecified psychoactive substance mood disorder." One goal of scientific theory is to simplify complexity, to organize unconnected facts into a coherent and understandable whole. As yet, there is no generally agreed-upon way to organize the complete miscellany of psychopathologies. However, there are several promising possibilities. We will consider three organizing questions in this section. First, are there common processes underlying different types of psychopathology? Second, might the familiar theoretical perspectives, including psychodynamic and social learning theories, each be used to explain and organize particular types of disorder? Third, how might the different theoretical processes interact with one another?

COMMON PROCESSES IN DIFFERENT PSYCHOLOGICAL DISORDERS

Charles Darwin, William McDougall, and Sigmund Freud all believed that we should study abnormal behavior if we want to understand the basis of normal human behavior. They believed that disorders were instructive because they revealed psychological processes in relative isolation and purity. These functions tended to be taken for granted in a healthy person.

Throughout this text we have noted how psychological disorder might be related to dysfunctions of such basic processes as learning, memory, emotion, and so on. Historically, different theorists have speculated that certain processes are particularly central to psychopathology.

ANXIETY

Freud's influential psychodynamic approach focused on motivational processes, viewing anxiety from repressed sexual and aggressive motives as the root of most nonorganic behavioral disorders. It goes without saying that anxiety is central to the anxiety disorders. We have also seen how Freud viewed conversion reactions as being the result of anxiety, as in Anna O's distressed feelings about her father. Multiple personality disorder also involves intense anxiety, often related to parental violence or sexual abuse. Antisocial disorders, on the other hand, stem from too little anxiety. Psychopathic prisoners have difficulty learning to avoid painful electric shocks unless they are given a boost of adrenaline (Latane and Schachter, 1962). It seems that a certain amount of fear of punishment helps in socializing us, while too much leads to disability.

SELF-ESTEEM

There has been some suggestion that a number of other disorders may be linked by a different process—they may all be attempts to ward off severe threats to self-esteem. As we saw in the chapter on personality, most normal individuals have a somewhat flattering view of themselves, seeing themselves as generally above average, and attributing their failures to factors outside themselves. However, this generalization does not hold for depressive individuals (Alloy, Abramson, and Viscusi, 1981), who are likely to have the opposite bias, and therefore see themselves in an overly derogatory way. At the opposite extreme, paranoid schizophrenics describe themselves in an inordinately positive light, sometimes claiming to be God. Psychologists Edward Zigler and Marion Glick (1988) suggest the possibility that paranoia may really be disguised depression, and paranoid's delusions thus a mask for deeply felt insecurities. These authors note the common observation that manic states, which often involve considerable self-aggrandizement, seem to be used as a defense against attacks of depression. It has been suggested that threats to self-esteem may lead directly to depressive disorder, or indirectly to mania, paranoia, or alcoholism (Zigler and Glick, 1988). In support of this point, recall the findings

that depression and alcoholism tend to run in the same families.) There is also evidence that people sometimes use alcohol to protect against threats to self-esteem (Berglas, 1985). Whether further evidence ultimately supports the suggested link between depression and paranoia, self-esteem threats are certainly an organizing theme for several disorders. And self-esteem that is too high, like anxiety levels that are too low, might also cause problems, as we saw in the case of narcissistic personality disorder.

BIOCHEMICAL LINKS

There are many other basic connections between different disorders. Recent physiological evidence has suggested the possibility that schizophrenia, mania, and psychotic depression may be linked by dopamine deficiencies in certain cortical and limbic areas of the brain (Swerdlow and Koob, 1987). To simplify a complex story, dopamine overactivity in the cortex may lead to schizophrenic symptoms, whereas dopamine underactivity may lead to depressive symptoms. Although the research evidence is far from conclusive on these issues, one thing is clear. An understanding of basic physiological and motivational processes can help us to understand diverse aspects of psychopathology.

DIFFERENT THEORIES FOR DIFFERENT DISORDERS?

As we noted in the historical section of this chapter, many of the same general theoretical perspectives used to organize normal personality have also been applied to disordered behavior. As with Freudian theory, these theories often began as explanations of disorder and were only later applied to normal personality. In this chapter, we have seen numerous examples of research drawn from the biomedical, psychodynamic, and social learning perspectives. At different times, each perspective has been advanced as the grand theory of all psychopathology. Although none has been completely successful, each has contributed to our understanding of particular disorders.

We have seen evidence for the biomedical perspective in connection with several disorders. There is evidence of genetic factors in schizophrenia, bipolar disorder, and antisocial personality. We also discussed evidence of biochemical imbalances and abnormal brain activity in several severe disorders. As we will see in some detail in Chapter 16, the biomedical model is further supported by evidence that drugs can successfully alleviate symptoms of some disorders, particularly schizophrenia and bipolar disorder. Physiological evidence has even suggested that schizophrenia might be better characterized by two more general syndromes (Crow, 1982). *Type I* schizophrenics show a predominance of "positive symptoms," such as hallucinations and delusions. Their strange symptoms often develop suddenly and respond well to medication. Autopsies reveal that the brains of Type I schizophrenics have super-abundant dopamine receptors (Swerdlow and Koob, 1987). *Type II* schizophrenics, on the other hand, show more "negative symptoms," including unemotionality and withdrawal. They show a gradual deterioration over their lives and respond poorly to drugs. Autopsies reveal an unusually *small* number of dopamine receptors in the brains of Type II schizophrenics.

Despite the usefulness of the biomedical approach, however, it has not adequately explained how it is that one member of a pair of identical twins can be schizophrenic, while the other one has about a 50 percent chance of being unafflicted. The biomedical perspective also fails to explain why some people can control, and even overcome, their symptoms by using therapeutic interventions based on learning and cognition. (This will be discussed in Chapter 16.) In fact, the usefulness of an unqualified medical approach has been under question ever since early researchers, including Breuer and Freud, showed that hysterical symptoms could be removed through hypnosis. This finding suggested that some physical symptoms were the result of psychological rather than physical dysfunction. Nevertheless, there is little question that the biomedical model provides a very useful framework for understanding several disorders, particularly schizophrenia and manic depression.

The psychodynamic perspective helps to organize our understanding of anxiety-related disorders and depression. We noted, for instance, that obsessive-compulsive disorder is commonly linked to sexual and aggressive impulses that the person fears he or she cannot control. We also noted that multiple personalities seem to derive from early overwhelming sexual or violent abuse. Though the psychodynamic approach is useful in explaining certain disorders, it has not generally provided a satisfying explanation of several others, especially schizophrenia.

As we saw in studies of phobic conditioning, psychologists working from the behavioral perspective have established that some pathological behaviors *can* be learned in the same way as normal behaviors. Learning theory also does a good job of explaining why there can be such great differences in the specific behaviors of two people who share the same diagnosis. In our society, for instance, a child is likely to get attention for claiming to hear the voice of the Virgin Mary, whereas in Tibet the same child might learn to interpret his voices as those of the Bodhisattva. The traditional behavioral perspective does not explain why only people with particular genetic predispositions develop schizophrenic symptoms, however, nor does it explain why phobic responses condition so much more readily to snakes than to artificial stimuli. Recently, learning theorists have begun to consider how our evolutionary history might have predisposed us to extinguish certain phobic responses, such as a fear of snakes, only with difficulty. This suggests that biological and environmental factors may interact in the development of psychopathology, and leads to our third question. How might the different theoretical processes interact with one another?

INTERACTIONS:
Connecting the Different Perspectives on Disorder

The causes of psychopathology are complex, and any attempt to explain these phenomena by focusing only on biology, or only on learning or cognition, will not be completely successful. In the case of the learning/biology interactions we just discussed, the processes described by each isolated model provide a partial, but incomplete, understanding. The insights of the general perspectives we have been discussing in this chapter each provides a part of an overall **interactionist perspective.** This perspective considers how the different processes highlighted by these different viewpoints might work together. Figure 15.7 is similar to one we presented in the opening chapter. It includes examples that help illustrate how the most ultimate or deeply-rooted influences on behavior and those which are more proximate or immediate can *interact* to produce or inhibit a disordered response.

Evolution

As we just noted, several researchers believe that humans are predisposed to develop phobic responses to natural threats because the avoidance of snakes, spiders, heights, and crowds of strangers was often adaptive for our ancestors. Since our

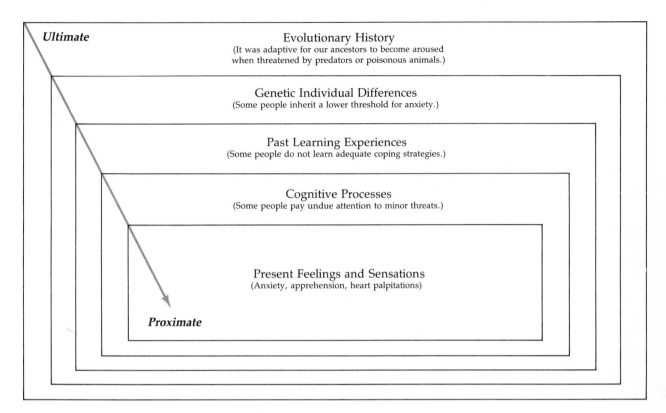

FIGURE 15.7 Interactions and psychological disorders. This figure demonstrates how various causes of anxiety interact with one another, but the same scheme could be applied to other disorders as well. At the ultimate level, all humans inherit a proneness to feel fear when they are threatened, because it was adaptive for their ancestors to mobilize in the face of threat. However, people differ in their inherited thresholds for feeling fear and anxiety. Those inherited dispositions interact with learning experiences—some people with a proneness to anxiety learn how to avoid threats, others do not. In turn, different life experiences may cause some people to devote undue attention to minor threats, or to magnify the significance of trivial events. The interactions of genetic predispositions, learning experiences, and cognitions lead, on a moment-to-moment basis, to differences between people in their feelings of anxiety and apprehension and to differences in psychological symptoms such as heart rate.

ancestors never encountered automobiles, electrical outlets, or hot stainless steel pots, however, there is no predisposition to avoid them even though they, too, can be dangerous. Though there are costs associated with excessive phobic behavior, the payoff for avoiding snakes and venomous insects was probably enough to incline our ancestors toward wariness toward them. Even something as seemingly maladaptive as depression could have an adaptive value under some circumstances (Bowlby, 1969; Kenrick et al., 1985; Schmale, 1970, among others). For instance, depression is related to a physiological *conservation–withdrawal response* that prompts rest and recuperation when we are physically or emotionally exhausted (Schmale, 1970).

Genetic Differences

At a slightly more proximate level, the results of natural selection are passed to modern generations on the genes studied by behavior geneticists. As we have seen, there are genes associated with several behavior disorders. One might wonder how a gene associated with schizophrenia could ever persist. At this point we do not know the answer to that question, but it may be associated with other tendencies that are useful. In a classic paper, Paul Meehl (1962) suggested that the genes that predispose a person towards schizophrenia might be associated with an adaptive tendency towards creative thinking. Edgar Allan Poe, James Joyce, and Kurt Vonnegut are prominent examples of creative writers who have had schizophrenic children. In combination with certain other genes, or with certain experiences, the otherwise useful genes might lead to maladaptive behavior.

Learning History

Genetic predispositions do not tell the whole story, however, since even identical twins differ in adult diagnoses (Downey and Coyne, 1990). The individual's learning history plays an important role in determining how the genotype will develop. As we saw, early traumatic experience seems to be involved in several disorders. Though Little Hans may have been somewhat predisposed to develop a fear of large threatening mammals, it was not until the boy was nearly crushed by a horse that he showed a phobic response.

Cognition

How we interpreted previous events will affect how we recall them, and how we experience new events. For instance, there is evidence that people with different disorders process information in different ways. Depressives tend to make self-defeating attributions for events ("It was my fault our relationship didn't work out"), and to think spontaneously about negative things (a relationship that didn't work out two years ago). Those with anxiety problems, on the other hand, tend to think spontaneously about threatening things ("I wonder if that overdue bill I sent in is going to get lost in the mail"), and to let thoughts about those potential threats distract them from the task at hand (Ingram et al, 1987). Other research on cognitive processes indicates that depressed as well as anxious individuals tend to hold irrational beliefs, such as "One must be perfectly competent, adequate, and achieving to consider oneself worthwhile" (Newmark et al., 1973; Vestre, 1983).

Norma MacDonald's experience nicely illustrates the connections between psychopathology and ongoing psychological processes on a moment-to-moment basis. She described how her schizophrenic episode brought changes in her mood ("pain and unutterable depression"), her

---

TABLE 15.4 Examples of Different Factors That Could Interact to Make a Particular Individual Become Depressed

ORGANISM ×	ENVIRONMENTAL CONDITIONS ×	COGNITIVE INTERPRETATION
Genetic Predispositions	**Personal Events**	**Ongoing Thoughts and Perceptions**
The person has a lower than usual threshold for a biochemical depression response.	Loss of a job Repeated failures in a relationship Loss of a loved one	Reminders of failures or loss of a loved one Paying attention to one's own failures or shortcomings Worrying about lack of social support or resources
Acute Biological Factors	**Ecological Conditions**	**Long-Term Thought Patterns**
Physical illness Physical exhaustion Stress-related biochemical changes from sources such as an inadequate diet or the use of drugs or alcohol	Resources (such as jobs and money) are unavailable or scarce. Climate is excessively cold. There are no relatives or other sources of social support nearby.	Person has a tendency to attribute failures to the self. Person chronically expects to fail even before beginning a task or a relationship.

Note: According to this framework, depression, like other disorders, results from interactions among 1) conditions of the person's biological organism, 2) events in the person's environment, and 3) the way the person thinks about those events. A value of zero for any of the three columns means that a person will not become depressed. This implies that biological predispositions, depressing environmental conditions, and self-defeating thoughts are all *necessary*, but none alone is *sufficient* to cause depression.

thinking (she found "overwhelming significance" in everyday events), and her perception ("I had very little ability to sort the relevant from the irrelevant . . . the filter had broken down"). We have already discussed research that connects the presence or absence of certain hormones and neurotransmitters to the symptoms of several disorders, like Ms. McDonald's schizophrenia.

Combining Different Ongoing Processes

Table 15.4 provides a way to think about how these different factors might interact to produce a serious episode of depression. Suppose you encounter a particular sort of *environmental event*— a serious argument with a spouse or someone you love. Not everyone who has an argument becomes clinically depressed. If you do not pay much attention to that unpleasant experience, it will not be a concern. On the other hand, if you mentally rehearse the argument, perhaps recalling other such arguments in previous disappointing relationships and interpret this as evidence that you will never be able to get along with others or they will always disappoint or mistreat you *(cognitive appraisal)*, then the event will be more likely to lead to depres-

sion. However, even this series of negative events may not lead to depression if you have a high physiological threshold for such a response *(organismic factors)*. Antisocial individuals can cause a great deal of harm without experiencing depression or remorse, while other individuals experience depression at the mere *thought* that they might have caused a problem. Furthermore, even individuals who are physiologically prone to depression may be able to weather negative events if they take drugs that block norepinephrine depletion in their bodies, or learn to think about potential threats in a more positive manner ("This argument brings out some issues that we could work on to develop a stronger long-term relationship").

H. L. Mencken once noted that for every complex problem there is usually a simple answer. He also noted that it is almost always wrong. The complex problem of psychopathology is no exception. However, our growing understanding of basic psychological processes and the various theoretical perspectives does promise to integrate the disparate fragments of this very elaborate puzzle. ∎

IN CONTEXT: PSYCHOLOGICAL DISORDERS

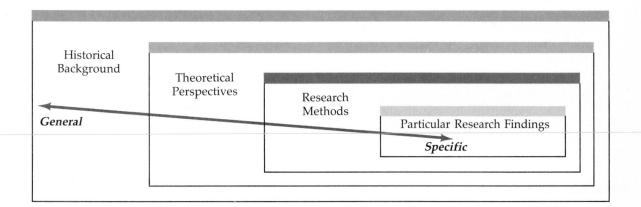

STUDY QUESTIONS

How can we best describe pathological behavior, and how is it different from normal behavior?

What relative roles do statistical abnormality, norm violation, personal distress, and harmful symptoms play in differentiating disordered and normal behavior?

What are the different categories of disorder?

How do biological causes, learning experiences, and ongoing thoughts combine to influence disordered behavior?

HISTORICAL BACKGROUND

1. The early Greeks believed that behavioral disorders could result from such bodily disorders as the imbalance of bodily fluids.

2. Scholars in the middle ages believed that behavioral disorders could result from demonic possession.

3. In the second half of the last century, Freud and his colleagues discovered that some physical symptoms appeared to be rooted in psychological conflict.

4. Early in this century, behaviorists found that such pathological behaviors as phobic fear could sometimes be learned.

5. During the 1950s, sociologically based research suggested that poverty and social class were related to behavioral disorder.

MODERN THEORETICAL PERSPECTIVES

1. The **biomedical** perspective views behavior disorder as a result of genetic anomaly or disease that affects the endocrine and nervous systems.

2. The **psychodynamic** perspective focuses on anxiety over sexual and aggressive conflicts that are rooted in childhood.

3. The **social learning** perspective views disordered behavior as resulting from normal learning principles, including conditioning and observational learning. Recent social learning theorists have focused on learned cognitive strategies.

4. The **interactionist** perspective views disordered behavior as a result of ultimate causes (genes selected by evolution) in combination with more proximate causes (learned information processing strategies, and ongoing physiological and environmental events).

RESEARCH METHODS

1. Researchers in the biomedical tradition use behavior genetic family and twin studies, brain-scanning techniques, biochemical assays, and brain autopsies to study disorders such as manic depression and schizophrenia (Gottesman et al., 1982; Swerdlow and Koob, 1987).

2. Psychodynamic researchers tend to use case studies, such as Breuer and Freud's (1895) work with Anna O., to understand the roots and dynamics of different disorders.

3. Experimental methods, as demonstrated by the research on phobic conditioning (Ohman et al., 1976), have been used to establish the role learning can play in abnormal behavior.

RESEARCH FINDINGS AND SUMMARY

1. Once a person is labelled as "insane," the label can lead others to interpret his or her normal behaviors as evidence of pathology.

2. **Mood disorders** include **depression** and **mania.** Depression is more common in women, and may result partly from learning to be helpless in the face of stressors. **Bipolar disorder** combines the extremes of mania and depression, and results from a genetic predisposition that affects brain biochemistry.

3. **Anxiety disorders** involve cognitive, physiological and behavioral symptoms similar to fear. **Phobias** are very specific fears, which generally involve an interaction of naturally prepared fears and conditioning experiences.

4. **Dissociative disorders** involve distinct splits in waking consciousness, and include **psychogenic amnesia** (following adult traumas) and **multiple personality** (related to childhood abuse).

5. **Somatoform disorders** involve physical symptoms for which there is no medical cause. Evidence suggests anxiety and previous medical problems as possible causes.

6. **Organic mental disorders** are physical diseases that affect the nervous system, and have behavioral consequences. Among the causes are syphilis and Alzheimer's disease.

7. **Schizophrenic disorders** involve major disruptions of thinking, perception, and social behavior. Research has established a genetic predisposition, which may involve the brain chemical dopamine.

8. **Personality disorders** are usually less extreme forms of disruptive behavior, including eccentric, fearful, dramatic, and antisocial patterns. Research suggests that antisocial personality disorder involves a genetic predisposition that reduces an individual's ability to learn from punishment, and that is exaggerated by poverty or criminal parents.

ADDITIONAL READINGS

Andreasen, N. C. 1984. *The broken brain: The biological revolution in psychiatry.* N.Y.: Harper & Row. A very readable account of the modern history of the medical approach to psychopathology.

Diagnostic and statistical manual of mental disorders: DSM III-R (1987). Washington, D.C.: American Psychiatric Association. A manual containing detailed descriptions of each of the various psychological disorders. It includes case studies and careful specifications of the criteria for diagnosing each disorder.

Endler, N. S. 1982. *Holiday of Darkness.* New York: Wiley-Interscience. A well known psychologist gives an insider's account of severe depression.

Gottesman, I. I. 1991. *Schizophrenia genesis: The origins of madness.* New York: Freeman. A discussion of the causes of schizophrenia, by one of the foremost behavior genetic researchers in the area.

Hollingshead, A. B., and Redlich, F. C. 1958. *Social class and mental illness: A community study.* New York: Wiley. A classic work in the field of community psychology.

Seligman, M. E. P. 1975. *Helplessness: On depression, development, and death.* San Francisco: W. H. Freeman. The main advocate of the "learned helplessness" model of depression covers findings from laboratory studies and the clinic.

CHAPTER
16

TREATMENT OF DISORDERED BEHAVIOR

P sychology has become something of a substitute for old belief systems. Different schools of therapy offer visions of the good life and how to live it, and those whose ancestors took comfort from the words of God and worshipped at the altars of Christ and Yahweh now take solace from and worship at the altars of Freud, Jung, Carl Rogers, Albert Ellis, Werner Ehrhard, and a host of similar authorities. . . . While it is overpromoted, overused, and overvalued, [psychotherapy] can be beneficial when used prudently, with clear understanding of its powers, limitations, and risks.

(Bernie Zilbergeld, 1983)

Chapter Outline

If you were asked to conjure up a mental image of psychotherapy, you might picture a quiet setting in which a person sits in an easy chair discussing his or her problems with a therapist who occasionally offers a bit of advice. Indeed, many forms of therapy follow just such a conversational model. Some treatments are even more benign, and have ranged from resting in hot baths to sitting in front of a bright fluorescent light. However, not all problems yield to such benign treatments, and people who suffer from debilitating psychopathological symptoms sometimes go to great extremes in their search for cures. One classic case involved a man who wanted to overcome his fetish (a socially inappropriate sexual attraction) for women's underwear. The therapy involved receiving electric shocks to his fingers while he was either engaging in fantasies or looking at photographs of women's undergarments (Kushner, 1965). This treatment, called **aversive counterconditioning,** involved only mild electric shocks, such as you might feel if you touched a frayed lamp cord. On the other hand, Professor Norman Endler (whose depressive episode we discussed in Chapter 15) submitted himself to a regimen of **electro-convulsive therapy** (ECT), a treatment for severe depression. For this treatment, he was given a tranquilizer, strapped to a table, and provided with a mouth guard to prevent him from biting his tongue. Then he was hooked up to a device that delivered an electrical current powerful enough to cause a convulsion equivalent to an epileptic seizure.

Most forms of treatment for psychological disorders do not involve physical treatments such as electrical shock. Instead, the predominant treatments involve **psychotherapy,** which involves psychological interventions based upon many of the principles we have discussed throughout this book. Treatment of disordered behavior is the main specialization of those with advanced degrees in psychology. Of the nearly 65,000 members of the American Psychological Association in 1986, 42,000 listed themselves as "health service providers" (based on Howard et al., 1986). In

addition, psychological treatment is a major specialty in medicine, nursing, and social work.

In 1955, only 1 percent of the American population had ever seen a mental health professional, by the 1980s the figure had reached 10 percent (Klerman, 1983). By that time, the total national bill for psychological treatment was estimated at $15 billion annually (Pines, 1982). There are reasons for Americans to pay great costs to alleviate psychological distress. As we noted in the last chapter, psychological problems can be very damaging, causing pain not only to those suffering from them, but also to their families and communities. This may explain why, despite the physical, psychological, and economic costs of therapy, most "consumers" of psychotherapy feel that it is worthwhile. One survey found that three-quarters of therapy clients were satisfied with their treatment, and half were "very satisfied" (Lebow, 1982). Many people feel that psychotherapy completely changed their lives, and proponents of electro-convulsive shock argue that every year a few short doses of electric shock could save thousands of depressed people from a much worse fate—death by suicide. With regard to the effects of the electro-shock treatment on his depression, Professor Endler felt: "A miracle had happened in two weeks" (Endler, 1982).

At face value, it is clear that Endler felt that he experienced a radical or "miraculous" change in his mood. On the other hand, some skeptical observers have raised questions about the extent to which psychological treatments affect miracle

A psychotherapy session. Treatments for disordered behavior have ranged from benign encounters such as lying on a couch discussing one's childhood, or sitting in front of a fluorescent light, to more rigorous regimens including imagining one's worst fears in gruesome detail or receiving electro-convulsive therapy.

cures. Given the evidence of life-long consistency in people's normal and abnormal behavior, (discussed in Chapters 13 and 15) many psychologists believe that radical changes in adult personality are rare. Skeptics thus question whether most psychotherapies are capable of producing dramatic effects (Zilbergeld, 1983). This is an important issue, because the majority of therapists practice outside the scientific realm of the research environment, and so it is difficult to adequately evaluate their treatments. One of the ways in which therapy has been evaluated is psychotherapy **outcome research,** which compares improvements in therapy clients with changes in other distressed people who have not been treated. On average, results of outcome studies are moderately positive. However, since you, your relatives, or your friends may one day consult a mental health professional, we want to stress the need for skepticism. Some therapy works, but some does not. Those therapies that work for one problem may not work for others. Finally, some people may actually be hurt by some forms of psychological or psychiatric treatment (Lambert et al., 1986).

To some extent, this chapter is an extension of the personality and psychopathology chapters. Several theories of normal and abnormal personality have their origins in the writings of such practicing clinicians as Sigmund Freud and Carl Rogers. The search for cures has been a major motivation for the study of behavior disorders, and so each of the different perspectives on psychopathology has given rise to a different type of treatment. After discussing these different types of treatment, we will consider some common benefits of different forms of psychotherapy, as well as which treatments work best with which behavioral disorders. Finally, we will show how a consideration of the interactions between people, their environments, and their cognitions can help determine which form of therapy will be most effective.

HISTORICAL BACKGROUND:
Changing Definitions of "Treatment"

How a psychologist treats a problem is, in large measure, determined by his or her theory about what caused it. Hippocrates, who held that psychopathology resulted from imbalances of bodily humors, believed that treatment should include rest, exercise, and retirement to a peaceful en-

vironment. This is an early version of the biomedical perspective, which holds that behavior disorders are physical imbalances to be treated with physical cures. Those who believed in supernatural causes of disorder in medieval Europe believed that pathology resulted from possession by evil spirits, and therefore should be treated by driving the malevolent forces from the body. In its more benign form, this meant treatment by an "exorcist," a specially trained priest whose holy influence simply made life miserable for the inner devils that caused disturbed behavior. Other supernatural treatments were much harsher: sometimes the body that was host to the offending spirit was tortured or burned at the stake.

One variant of the biomedical model which again became popular in the 1800s viewed psychopathology as due to "nervous exhaustion." The treatment for this proposed neurological fatigue was a direct descendant of the Hippocratic cure—a relaxing tour of the European natural baths (Drinka, 1984). Another biomedical theory popular among nineteenth-century physicians held that anxiety and depression followed from excessive masturbation. As explained in the *Home Encyclopedia of Health,* published in 1902 by medical professors from the University of Pennsylvania and Jefferson College, masturbation leads to anxiety

A depiction of the supernatural model. The supernatural model assumed that certain forms of psychopathology were due to possession of the body by satanic spirits. Treatment might involve exorcism, or, in the more extreme cases, burning the victim's body to dislodge the evil spirit.

and depression because "the secretion of the reproductive liquid . . . withdraws a very precious portion of the blood" (Richardson, Ford, and Vanderbeck, 1902). These medical experts recommended a treatment regimen of exercise, to divert "the superabundance of nervous power," and changes in diet because:

> In such cases, exciting and superabundant food is highly injurious. The diet should be chiefly or altogether vegetable, and no vinous or spiritous drinks should be permitted. The latter are indeed, of themselves, quite sufficient to produce, at any time, the worst habits. . . .
> *(Richardson and colleagues, 1902)*

Another recommended treatment at that time was circumcision (Paige, 1978). Though we might today disagree with this logic, we can, in each case, see a connection between the theory of cause and the theory of treatment, as well as the influence of the social values of the time.

Physical Symptoms and Psychological Causes

The psychodynamic perspective on pathology, which views behavior disorder as rooted in unconscious conflicts, suggests a different form of treatment. The roots of this approach to therapy can be seen in a case study of "devil possession" reported by French psychiatrist Pierre Janet in 1898. A man named Achille had begun to act strangely after returning from a business trip during the winter of 1890. He lost his energy, avoided his wife and children, and became preoccupied and uncommunicative. Medical experts first diagnosed his problem as diabetes, then as a heart condition. However, he suddenly began to show great energy, to shout blasphemies, and to claim that he was possessed by the devil. During this period, he attempted suicide several times. He was taken to the clinic at Salpetriere, where Janet hypnotized him. In the hypnotic state, the man confessed that he had had an affair during his business trip and was consumed with fear that he would slip and reveal it to his wife. Janet interpreted Achille's "possession by the devil" as serving two purposes. First, it gave the man an explanation of his own misbehaviors. Second, it was a form of self-punishment for those transgressions. Janet argued that: ". . . for those who were possessed, the devil is nothing for them but the incarnation of their regrets, their remorse, their terrors, or their vices. It is the remorse of Achille, it is the memory of his mistake which was the cause of his losing his mind" (Janet, 1898). After talking about his unacceptable impulsive behavior, Achille's symptoms disappeared, and had not resurfaced three years later when Janet wrote about the case.

Janet was a student of Jean-Martin Charcot. Charcot, a widely respected neurologist, had already identified and given name to multiple sclerosis when he became interested in hysterical conversion reactions (Martin, 1977). (As we discussed in the last chapter, conversion reactions are

Jean-Martin Charcot at his clinic at the Salpetriere Hospital in Paris. In clinical lectures like this, Charcot demonstrated how symptoms in hysterical patients could be induced and removed under hypnosis. These demonstrations influenced the young Sigmund Freud, who went to Paris to study under Charcot.

physical symptoms with psychological causes.) Charcot first thought that symptoms such as glove anesthesia resulted from damage to the central nervous system, but gradually changed his ideas when he found that he could remove those symptoms with hypnosis. Students from all over Europe came to study with Charcot, and one of these students was Sigmund Freud.

Freud's ideas were strongly influenced by the work of the French psychiatrists. Like Janet, Freud came to believe that pathological behaviors were symptoms of an inner conflict—some guilty or shameful memory or impulse. To this psychodynamic view, the goal of treatment was to bring that inner conflict to light, and to thereby take away the need for the symptom. Freud differed from Charcot and Janet in believing that hypnosis was not necessary for treatment. Instead, Freud favored a form of therapy developed by Josef Breuer, another Austrian physician who joined Freud to write *Studies in Hysteria* in 1895. During the 1880s, Breuer had successfully removed hysterical symptoms in a woman named Anna O. by simply having her remember and describe the circumstances under which the symptoms had first appeared. The patient called the treatment the "talking cure," a name that is still sometimes used to refer to psychodynamic treatment.

Around the same time that Freud, Janet, and Breuer were developing the psychodynamic approach to treatment, other European psychiatrists were seeking physical causes for behavioral symptoms. In the last chapter, we mentioned one form of psychosis, general paresis, that was traced directly to the effects of untreated syphilis. During the twentieth century, such links between psychological disorders and biological problems have been more widely explored than ever before. Biomedical research has led to some very unexpected treatments for mental illness. During the 1940s, a French surgeon named Henri Lavorit noticed that the antihistamine Phenothiazine made his patients less anxious and better able to withstand postoperative stress. This observation proved to have profound implications. Lavorit suggested that the drug might be useful in psychotherapy, so two other French physicians, Jean Delay and Pierre Deniker, tested a related compound called chlorpromazine on psychiatric patients. The drug not only had a relaxing effect on the patients but also seemed to alleviate schizophrenic hallucinations. Over the next several decades the use of chlorpromazine began a revolution in the treatment of schizophrenia, dramatically reducing the number of schizophrenics who required hospitalization (Andreasen, 1984).

The Rise of Behavior Therapy in America

Advocates of the biomedical and psychodynamic approaches considered psychopathology symptomatic of underlying psychic or physical disorders. While these models were being developed in Europe, American psychologists followed a different path. Influenced by developments in the study of learning and conditioning, John B. Watson and his followers made the assumption that psychopathology was learned just like any other behavior, and thus could be unlearned. These researchers began to develop a form of treatment later to be called **behavior modification**—the application of the principles of classical and operant conditioning to changing problem behaviors. Psychologist Mary Cover Jones reported a classic case in 1924. She described the case as a sequel to John Watson's demonstration of experimentally induced phobia of a white rat in Little Albert (discussed in Chapter 6). Her patient, a three-year-old named Peter, was "almost to be Albert grown a bit older." Peter was also "afraid of a white rat, and this fear extended to a rabbit, a fur coat, a feather, cotton, wool, etc." Since he was most afraid of rabbits, Jones selected three other children who were unafraid of rabbits to be playmates for Peter. In addition to giving Peter this opportunity to watch other children play fearlessly with a rabbit, the researcher gradually began putting Peter in situations requiring closer and closer contact with the animal. At first the boy showed fear with the rabbit anywhere in the room; later, he could tolerate it 12 feet away, then four feet away, and finally on his lap. The therapy suffered a setback when Peter was attacked by a dog, after which Jones began a program of classical conditioning. Whenever she introduced the rabbit, she simultaneously gave Peter some food he liked. Presumably, pairing the food with the rabbit would lead to conditioning of positive feeling from the food to the rabbit. At the end of this conditioning program, Peter had totally overcome his fear of rabbits. His reduced fear also generalized to other animals, including mice, rats, and frogs.

Although learning-based techniques were not widely used during the three decades following Jones's work, there was a resurgence of interest in behavior modification during the 1950s and 60s. The renewed interest followed an attack on psychodynamically based therapy by British psychologist Hans Eysenck (1952). Eysenck claimed that patients who entered psychoanalytic therapy showed no more improvement than patients who got no treatment at all. This coincided with three other historical events that, together, established a behaviorist revolution in treatment. First, B. F. Skinner published his book *Science and Human Behavior* (1953), in which he argued for the applicability of learning principles to a wide variety of topics, including psychotherapy. Second, Skinner and his student Ogden Lindsley used operant learning principles in an attempt to change behavior in schizophrenics (Matarazzo, 1985). Third, a South African psychologist named Joseph Wolpe published *Psychotherapy by Reciprocal Inhibition* (1958), in which he argued for the effectiveness of classical conditioning principles in treating anxiety disorders. As we will see, Wolpe's technique of **systematic desensitization** is basically an extension of Mary Cover Jones's treatment of young Peter.

Humanistic and Community Approaches to Therapy

Carl Rogers was another American psychologist who had a profound effect on modern approaches to treatment. Rogers worked mostly with adults and college students who had problems with low self-esteem and anxiety. He was opposed to psychiatric approaches that viewed patients as passive recipients of "treatment" by a doctor who supposedly knew more about their problems than the patients did, and he developed a humanistic form of treatment called *person-centered therapy* in which the therapist and client work on a much more equal basis to search for solutions to the client's problems. Rogers has been a staunch advocate of openness and honesty in the therapeutic process. In 1942 he published the first complete transcript of a therapy session. He was also a pioneer in the evaluation of therapy, using psychological tests, physiological measures, and ratings by family and friends to determine if therapy really worked. Rogers was aware that people often come to therapy when they are at their worst, and that therapists could be misled by spontaneous "improvement" in clients as the crisis passed. Therefore, he used control conditions in which some clients were placed on a waiting list for a short period of time while other similar clients received immediate treatment (Rogers and Dymond, 1954). As a result of his own studies, Rogers concluded that his person-centered psychotherapy was helpful for those with anxiety disorders, but not for schizophrenics.

Rogers's findings with schizophrenics were not atypical. During the 1950s, it became increasingly clear that verbal psychotherapies were not helpful to schizophrenics. Nor were there other optimistic alternatives. In fact, most schizophrenics were simply hospitalized, and given little treatment of any kind. Hospitalization was in many ways as much a problem as a solution. For instance, people hospitalized for behavioral disorders are labeled as "crazy," both by others and by themselves (Goffman, 1961). Some psychotherapists believed it inappropriate to single out people as "mentally ill" and send them off to mental hospitals when their problems involved interpersonal relations with family, friends, and co-workers (Szasz, 1960). Around this time of growing pessimism about traditional treatments for schizophrenics, several antipsychotic medications were discovered. These drugs, which often successfully alleviated the hallucinations and other extreme symptoms of schizophrenia, allowed many schizophrenics to be released from hospitals.

During the 1960s, the **community mental health** approach developed, in part in response to the problems of hospitalization. It involves treatment in the "real world" context: schools, homes, and neighborhoods. **Family systems therapy** has been a closely parallel development. Family systems therapists believe that behavioral problems stem from dysfunctional family interactions (Bateson, Jackson, Haley, and Weakland, 1956). Like community psychologists, family therapists have taken the view that the disturbed individual cannot be treated without treating his or her family environment.

The different schools of therapy have, to a certain extent, developed in different academic disciplines. Practitioners of the biomedical and psychodynamic models have, like Freud, often been trained in medicine. Practitioners of the behavior modification and person-centered therapy have more often been trained in psychology departments. Other treatment professionals have backgrounds in social work and counseling. Table 16.1 lists a number of different treatment practitioners, the type of degree they hold, and the predominant type of treatment techniques with which they have been associated.

Historically, there has been some association between the type of practitioner and the type of therapy he or she would be likely to use, as indicated in Table 16.1. For instance, psychiatrists would be more likely to adopt the biomedical or psychodynamic models, social workers the family and community models, and counseling psychologists the humanistic model. However, there is no rigid relationship between a practitioner's degree and the type of therapy he or she uses. There are clinical psychologists, for instance, who work

TABLE 16.1 Different Types of Therapists

Type of Therapist	Background/Training	Likely Treatment Approaches
Clinical Psychologist	Ph.D. psychologist with 4–5 years of graduate study in psychology, emphasizing outcome evaluation research, therapy techniques, and psychological testing. Also a one to two year internship in a clinical setting.	Behavioral, cognitive
Counseling Psychologist	M.A., Ph.D., or Ed.D. in counseling psychology with similar training to clinical psychology, though often with less emphasis on research.	Humanistic, behavioral
Psychiatrist	M.D. degrees, with an internship in which they have been supervised in the diagnosis of psychological disorders and the use of drugs, other biomedical treatments, and psychotherapy.	Biomedical, psychodynamic
Psychiatric Social Worker	M.S.W. (Masters in Social Work), which involves training in interviewing and therapy.	Family, community
Psychoanalyst	Predominantly M.D. degrees, but also practiced by those with Ph.D.s and M.S.W. All psychoanalysts have completed several years of training at a psychoanalytic institute where they both undergo psychoanalysis (a form of therapy, based on Freud's methods and theories, which is discussed later in this chapter) themselves as well as treating patients under the supervision of a training analyst.	Psychoanalysis

within the biomedical model, others who adopt the psychodynamic model, still others who practice family and community therapy, and so on. As we shall see, many practitioners today adopt an eclectic approach which includes elements of different approaches, sometimes designed to suit the particular client's problems. ▪

BIOLOGICALLY BASED TREATMENTS

Since the biomedical perspective views physiological problems as the source of psychopathology, it is no surprise that medical treatments are themselves physical in nature. These treatments fall into three main categories: psychoactive drugs, psychosurgery, and electro-convulsive therapy. The history of how these treatments were discovered and used tells us a great deal about the limits to our understanding of the biological bases of behavior. Each of these treatments was based upon accidental observations or erroneous

assumptions, and none are fully understood even today. Further, although there have been many benefits from medically based treatments, each one has some physical and psychological costs associated with it, and has therefore generated controversy about its use.

PSYCHOACTIVE DRUGS

Of all the medically based therapies available, **psychoactive drugs,** drugs which affect a person's thought processes and behavior, are by far the most commonly used. Since their development in the 1950s, they have relieved psychiatric hospitals of most of the need for physical restraints and have enabled some patients to live outside institutions. For the families of schizophrenics this has sometimes meant that a person formerly lost in his or her own world is now able to relate to them. More recently, other psychoactive drugs have been developed to provide relief to many people who suffer from anxiety or depression.

ANTIPSYCHOTIC MEDICATIONS

Henri Lavorit's serendipitous discovery that certain antihistamine compounds could alleviate the symptoms of schizophrenia ushered in three decades of intensive research, as biological investigators searched to find drug treatments for psychological ailments and to understand how those drugs work upon the brain and nervous system. Drugs that reduce psychotic symptoms such as the hallucinations and delusions of schizophrenia are called **antipsychotic medications.** Researchers have yet to find a more effective drug for schizophrenia than chlorpromazine, though it is not effective for all schizophrenics. A number of other drugs have similar primary effects, but different side effects (Tapia, 1983). For instance, some antipsychotic medications are better for patients with heart conditions, whereas others are suited to patients who also need sedation. All these drugs, including chlorpromazine, produce undesirable side effects. Common problems include an expressionless face, shuffling gait, stiff body posture, and tremors (called *pseudo-Parkinsonian symptoms* because of their resemblance to Parkinson's disease). Some patients also suffer from blurred vision, constipation, and dryness of the mouth. Over the long term, the drugs may lead to unpleasant symptoms like repetitive tongue thrusting and facial grimacing, a side effect called *tardive dyskinesia.* Despite these unfortunate side effects, antipsychotic medications are so effective in reducing the extreme symptoms of schizophrenic thought disorder and controlling aggressive and bizarre social behaviors that they have reduced the need for physical restraints (such as the legendary straight-jacket) and seclusion rooms. Some side effects can also be blocked with other drugs. For these reasons, most medical professionals believe that the benefits of taking the drugs far outweigh the costs.

It is still unclear exactly how chlorpromazine works to alleviate schizophrenic symptoms, but, as we mentioned in Chapter 2, the evidence suggests that it blocks the action of the neurotransmitter dopamine (Perontka and Snyder, 1980; Swerdlow and Koob, 1987). By blocking overactive neural transmission, antipsychotic drugs may suppress overactivity of the schizophrenic's nervous system, and thereby allow higher brain centers to process incoming information without being overwhelmed by irrelevant inputs.

ANTIDEPRESSANTS

After chlorpromazine was discovered, biochemical researchers began to test similar compounds in search of a more effective treatment for schizophrenia. Researchers noted that one compound with a chemical structure very similar to chlorpromazine was not an effective treatment for schizophrenia, but it did seem to put depressed schizophrenic patients into a better mood (Kuhn, 1958). This drug, *imipramine,* has since been commonly used to treat depression. Because depression is associated with reduced levels of amines (a group of neurotransmitters including norepinephrine and serotonin, discussed in Chapter 2) researchers believe imipramine may reduce depression by increasing the action of those amines (Tapia, 1983).

Another class of antidepressant medications is called *MAO inhibitors.* MAO (monamine oxidase) is a hormone that breaks down the energizing amines, and MAO inhibitors seem to block depression by hindering its action. Antidepressants also have undesirable side effects. For instance, MAO inhibitors lead to serious hypertension (high blood pressure) unless the patient avoids amine-rich foods such as ripe cheese, sour cream, wine, beer, chocolate, soy sauce, bananas, and raisins. Patients who use imipramine complain of a dry mouth and drowsiness. It may also lead to constipation and urinary difficulties and, in rare cases, to a specialized memory loss for common words (Tapia, 1983). Again, the costs of using these drugs must be weighed against their potential benefits in combating depression, with its increased risk of suicide.

ANTIANXIETY DRUGS

The most commonly prescribed psychoactive drugs are **antianxiety medications,** which, as their name suggests, are used to combat anxiety. Benzodiazepines such as Valium and Librium (formerly called "minor tranquilizers") also act on neural transmission. As we noted in Chapter 2, those drugs seem to reduce anxiety by their action on GABA receptors. (GABA is a neural transmitter that helps to control excessive neural excitation.) By acting on those receptors, antianxiety medications help to prevent "runaway" neural firing (which might contribute to the panic felt by someone suffering from anxiety). Although these drugs are potentially addictive and can cause death by overdose, they are much less dangerous than barbiturates, the tranquilizers most widely used a generation ago. (Barbiturates were implicated in many deaths, including Marilyn Monroe's.) Barbiturates have a more general depressing effect on neural activity, and by acting on the brainstem they can actually interfere with such basic life functions as breathing.

Finally, the drug *lithium carbonate* is used in the treatment of manic excitement. Lithium reduces the hyperactivity, insomnia, and grandiose speech associated with manic phases of bi-polar disorders, and can help control the depressive episodes as well. It can be difficult to determine the most effective dosages of lithium for each patient and to keep patients taking the drug faithfully. Some go off their medication because they miss the elation they may experience during manic episodes. Lithium produces some side effects, particularly muscle tremor.

PSYCHOSURGERY

As we noted in Chapter 2, psychosurgery began when Portuguese researchers observed that chimpanzees became less excitable after their brains' frontal cortexes were removed. This observation led to the development of the **prefrontal lobotomy,** in which an excitable or aggressive patient's frontal lobes are surgically severed from the rest of the brain. These operations were often quite crude. Surgeons would bore a hole in the thin bone of the temple or the eyesocket and then cut a wide and frequently rather imprecise swath with a long curved scalpel or a surgical needle. Since the frontal cortex can exaggerate emotional responses that begin in the limbic system the operation was designed to calm chronically agitated patients.

After tens of thousands of lobotomies were performed, and Antonio de Egas Moniz, who developed the procedure, was awarded a Nobel prize, researchers began to report a number of very harmful side effects, including stupor, seizures, and death (Barahal, 1958; Robbin, 1959). Some patients who received lobotomies were poorly diagnosed and did not benefit from the operation in the first place (Goodwin, 1980). When it was still in vogue, the operation was given to schizophrenics, depressives, and sometimes even to people with anxiety disorders (Davison and Neale, 1982). The use of crude lobotomies has been discontinued, although more specific surgery for severe depression and anxiety is still used. The modern techniques are much more precise than the earlier psychosurgery was. However, 5 to 10 percent of patients may still end up with disabling personality defects, even with the "improved" techniques (Tapia, 1983).

ELECTRO-CONVULSIVE THERAPY

Electro-convulsive therapy (ECT) was originally devised as a treatment for schizophrenia because a Hungarian physician named Von Meduna observed that epileptics were rarely schizophrenic. Today we know that Meduna's suggestion that epilepsy was "antagonistic" to schizophrenia was incorrect. It is true that schizophrenic adults are rarely epileptic, but neither are nonschizophrenic adults. Nevertheless, two Italian physicians named Ugo Cerletti and Lucio Bini developed a technique to produce epileptic seizures in humans. Their technique was to apply electrodes on each side of a patient's forehead and pass a current of 70 to 130 volts between them for a fraction of a second. As we described in the case of Professor Endler, this produces a reaction similar to an epileptic seizure. The seizure is followed by a period of electrical inactivity in the brain. After the treatment the patient is confused, and loses memory for the period preceding the operation and up to an hour after it.

Without adequate pretesting of the notion that ECT could in fact cure schizophrenia, the technique was widely applied to patients in psychiatric hospitals. Later controlled studies demonstrated that ECT did not help schizophrenics after all. However, the early indiscriminate application of the technique led to the discovery that ECT was

Electro-convulsive therapy. Electro-convulsive therapy (ECT) is a commonly used treatment for depression. It involves the administration of a powerful electric shock to the patient's head. The shock induces a seizure and loss of consciousness. The treatment was originally based on the mistaken notion that schizophrenia and epilepsy were incompatible. Research has indicated that ECT has no effect on schizophrenia symptoms, but widespread application led to the accidental finding that it does alleviate symptoms of severe depression. The exact mechanism for this effect is not yet known.

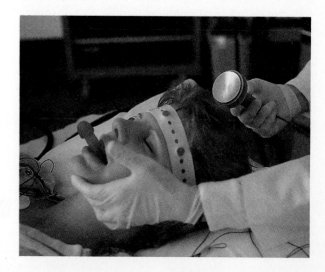

useful in alleviating severe depression. As one psychiatrist who suffered from depression noted:

> After the first treatment . . . I felt a blunting of the acute sadness of the depression. Whereas before treatment I became tearful with very little provocation, and felt intensely sad out of all proportion to the stimulus, after one single treatment I was no longer crushed by any chance sadness. The troublesome symptom of irritability also subsided early in the course of treatment. Before treatment, I was very easily irritated by trifles and expressed, on more than one occasion, an irrational belief that people were doing stupid things intentionally to annoy me.
>
> *(Anonymous, 1965)*

Patients remember no pain from the intense shock because the electrical current destroys their entire memory of the event. Like other medical treatments, ECT carries risks, including memory loss, neural damage, and occasional postoperative seizures. However, ECT works more quickly and sometimes more effectively than drug treatments for depression. Between 80,000 and 100,000 people receive ECT every year (Sackheim, 1985; Sobel, 1980). As we noted earlier in our discussion of biomedical treatments, it is important that the potential costs of ECT be weighed against its benefits: ECT may prevent a severely depressed person from committing suicide and may provide other chronically depressed patients with relief from the feelings of hopelessness and apathy that can plague them.

MILDER BIOMEDICAL TREATMENTS

Not all biomedical treatments are as radical as surgery, ECT, or psychoactive drugs. As we discussed, medical experts since Hippocrates have recommended treatments as simple as relaxation or exercise. In Chapter 14, we noted that exercise programs are often used to reduce work-related stress. There is evidence that a program of excercise can alleviate symptoms of depression, perhaps by changing the flow of such natural psychotropic biochemicals as endorphins and noradrenaline (McCann and Holmes, 1984; Martinsen, 1987). One biomedically based treatment is remarkably benign. It is called "phototherapy," and, as the name suggests, the treatment involves simply sitting in front of a light. As we indicated in Chapter 15, seasonal affective disorder (SAD) is a form of depression brought on by short winter days (Wurtman and Wurtman, 1989). Armed with

Phototherapy. Phototherapy for seasonal affective disorder (SAD) involves spending two hours a morning in front of a bright light. For patients whose depression is linked to short winter days, this treatment has been found to reduce depressive symptoms and the carbohydrate craving that often accompanies seasonal depression.

the developing knowledge about this disorder, Michael Terman (1988) had SAD patients sit in front of a bright light for two hours every morning. Half the patients experienced only a partial lifting of the depression, but for the other half, depression and the associated carbohydrate craving were completely gone within a few days.

EMOTIONAL INSIGHT THERAPIES

Pierre Janet's treatment of Achille was an early example of an emotional insight therapy. Janet believed that Achille was possessed not by the devil but by his inability to confront a part of himself about which he felt guilty—his memory of an extramarital affair. As Janet described it, once Achille could admit that unacceptable memory, he no longer needed his symptoms. **Insight therapies** share the assumption that many pathological behaviors would disappear if clients confronted unacceptable parts of themselves, and could thus develop self-understanding (or insight). Since they are aimed at psychological rather than physical causes of psychopathology, insight therapies are very unlike medical treatments. The main component of insight therapy is usually a series of conversations with the therapist, in which the client tries to recall and re-experience unpleasant memories or impulses. Although psychoanalysts and humanistic therapists differ about what it is that the client needs to confront, they share this verbal approach. Both approaches involve a form of conversation between therapist and client, with the ultimate goal of personal understanding by the client.

PSYCHOANALYSIS

As we discussed in Chapter 15, Sigmund Freud believed that unconscious conflicts about childhood aggression and sexuality are at the root of pathological behaviors. After studying with Pierre Janet and Jean-Martin Charcot in Paris and being impressed by their observations of the repressed traumatic memories revealed under hypnosis, Freud returned to his native Vienna. There he studied with Josef Breuer, who had discovered that one of his patients, Anna O., experienced relief from her hysterical symptoms by describing the events in her life that had led up to her hysteria (Matarazzo, 1985). Freud developed this method into the psychoanalytic approach. **Psychoanalysis** involves intensive discussions between patient and therapist, usually between three and four times a week. It involves techniques such as dream interpretation and free association, all aimed at uncovering the patient's unconscious conflicts. Often, the analyst remains relatively quiet while the patient uses **free association,** a technique in which the patient says whatever comes into his or her mind. This technique became one of the central tools of Freud's approach. Generally psychoanalysis takes place with the patient lying on a couch with the analyst seated.

Freud described the free association technique in his famous case report on the Rat Man (Freud, 1909; Gottlieb, 1989). This patient was obsessed with recurrent fears involving rats, as well as fears that harm would come to his father and a woman he admired. He also had irrational thoughts about cutting his own throat with a razor. In the case report, Freud characterized his instructions about free association: "I made him pledge himself to submit to the one and only condition of the treatment—namely, to say everything that came into his mind, even if it was *unpleasant* to him, or seemed unimportant or *irrelevant* or *senseless.*"

After agreeing to this, the Rat Man began to tell Freud about his early sexual experiences with his governess, and about his fears for his father (who, it turned out, was already dead). In a later session, he began telling Freud about his military experiences, and remembered an experience that made him very upset, at which time he begged Freud "to spare him the recital of the details." Freud described this impasse as a **resistance,** a point in therapy at which the person begins to approach a repressed conflict and tries to escape the confrontation. As it came out, the memory involved a story he had heard in the military about a torture:

". . . a pot was turned upside down on his buttocks . . . some rats were put into it . . . and they . . ."—he had again got up, and was showing every sign of horror and resistance—". . . bored their way in . . ."—"Into his anus," I helped him out

(Freud, 1909/1979)

As the case began to unfold Freud found out that the young man had seen a rat near his father's grave and had been struck with the macabre fear that the animal was gnawing on the corpse. The Rat Man later revealed that, as a youth, he once wished his father dead so that he could marry the young woman who, along with his father, occupied many of his obsessive thoughts.

An important part of psychoanalysis is the analyst's **interpretation,** a process of piecing together the twisted bits of unconscious logic that underlie the client's conflicts. Freud interpreted the Rat Man's case in the following manner:

1) the man had unconscious hostilities against his father, which caused tremendous guilt;

2) he and his father had quarreled about the woman, and he also felt guilt about that;

3) the obsessions about rats eating human bodies incorporated both the unconscious anger at his father and his guilt about that anger;

4) the suicidal impulses also stemmed from that unconscious guilt.

Note that Freudian interpretation often involves an assumption that a single symptom is determined by multiple causes. As in the case of Achille's possession, the Rat Man obsession was interpreted as the coalescence of several unconscious themes.

Dream analysis is another technique that psychoanalysts use to help uncover unconscious conflicts. Freud (1900) called dreams, "The royal road to the unconscious." He assumed that the energy from unconscious impulses had to go somewhere and that while some of that energy was expressed in the patient's symptom, some of it was expressed in his or her dreams. The Rat Man had dreams about Freud's daughter, and had fantasized about marrying her. Freud interpreted the dream as relating to his conflict about leaving the woman his father had rejected, and as indicating his unconscious confusion of Freud with his father.

Freud believed that patients in psychoanalysis commonly treat the therapist as the symbolic equivalent of the important figures in their lives, especially their parents. Freud called this process **transference.** By analyzing this transference, the analyst hopes to bring aspects of the patient's conflict to light. For example, in the dream described above, an analyst might say that the patient transferred to Freud both his desire to please his father and guilt about rejecting his beloved. As a result of free association, dream analysis, overcoming resistance, analyzing the transference, and interpretation by the therapist, Freud believed that the client achieves a series of **insights,** which involve a cognitive and emotional understanding of the roots of the conflict. Once the patient can rationally consider all of his irrational unconscious conflicts, the symptoms are no longer necessary. Freud concluded the case of the Ratman thus: "When we reached the solution that has been described above, the patient's rat delirium disappeared" (Freud, 1909/1979).

Later psychoanalysts differed with Freud on the importance of uncovering sexual and aggressive urges. Carl Jung (1933) believed that the analyst should search for unconscious symbols of primeval human conflicts, for instance, and Alfred Adler (1956) believed that people's problems were caused by repressed feelings of inferiority stemming from childhood inadequacies. However, most therapists of the analytic school continue to stress verbal conversation by the client and interpretation by the analyst.

THE HUMANISTIC APPROACH

Humanistic approaches to treatment stress individuals' own interpretations of events in their lives, and their free will to change negative self-images into positive ones. The best known humanistic approach was developed by Carl Rogers. In keeping with his humanistic philosophy, Rogers disagreed with Freud's emphasis on the negative, aggressive side of human nature:

One of the most revolutionary concepts to grow out of our clinical experience is the

growing recognition that the innermost core of man's nature, the deepest layers of his personality, the base of his "animal nature," is positive in nature—is basically socialized, forward-moving, rational, and realistic.

(Rogers, 1961)

As we noted earlier, Rogers's approach is called person-centered therapy. The person-centered therapist's goal is to help the client get in touch with his or her basically good inner core, and to pull together all the parts of the self the person had learned to suppress. In the person-centered approach, the therapist therefore tries to establish an atmosphere in which the client will feel completely accepted. Person-centered therapists also try to be *non-directive,* which is to say that they try not to lead the client in particular directions, or to insist that the client accept the therapist's interpretations about the client's life. Rogers assumes that the client knows his or her self better than the therapist does. Rather than directing the client towards certain issues, the person-centered therapist listens and tries simply to restate the client's feelings in more directly emotional terms. In discussing the case of Mrs. Oak, a housewife in her late thirties with difficulties in marital and family relationships, Rogers describes the major elements of his approach to uncovering repressed feelings. One essential element is *non-evaluative reflection*—restating the clients' feelings without making any evaluations about them:

> CLIENT: And then of course there's this damn bitterness that I want to get rid of. It's—it gets me into trouble. It's because it's a tricky thing. It tricks me. (Pause)
>
> THERAPIST: (You) feel as though that bitterness is something you'd like to be rid of because it doesn't do right by you.

Rogers assumed that if the therapist simply mirrored back the client's true feelings the client could come to accept those feelings that she had cut off from herself. In the case of Mrs. Oak, her feelings about herself were not only such negative ones as bitterness, but also positive ones:

> CLIENT: You know this is kind of goofy, but I've never told anyone this (nervous laugh) and it'll probably do me good. For years, oh, probably from early youth, from 17 on I, I have had what I have come to call to myself, told myself were "flashes of sanity." I've never told anyone this (another

Carl Rogers. Carl Rogers was the founder of client-centered therapy, and was also involved in popularizing encounter groups. Rogers's techniques are probably the most influential form of humanistic therapy. He was also an early pioneer in therapy outcome research.

embarrassed laugh), wherein, really I feel sane. And, and pretty much aware of life. And always with a terrific kind of concern and sadness of how far away, how far astray that we have actually gone. It's just a feeling once in a while of finding myself a whole kind of person in a terribly chaotic kind of world.

THERAPIST: It's been fleeting and it's been infrequent, but there have been times when it seems the whole you is functioning and feeling in the world, a very chaotic world to be sure—

CLIENT: That's right. . . .

In Chapter 13, we discussed the existentialist idea that people should search for "authenticity." This theme comes out very clearly in Rogers' approach, in which the goal is to have the client accept all the different parts of him or herself:

To take (an) example from Mrs. Oak: "I have thought that in some deep way I was bad, that the most basic elements in me must be dire and awful. I don't experience that badness, but rather a positive desire to live and let live. Perhaps I can be that person who is, at heart, positive.

(Rogers, 1961)

An essential component of successful therapy, according to Rogers, is the therapist's relationship with the client. Rogers felt the therapist must be *genuine, empathic,* and *respectful.* To be genuine means the therapist does not play a role with the client, but relates as one human being to another. To facilitate genuineness, Rogers eschewed the therapeutic couch and had the therapist and client sit face to face. To be empathic means that the therapist shares the feelings of the client, or tries to understand, on an emotional level, what the client is experiencing. To be respectful means the therapist is nonevaluative, accepting the client as he or she is without wishing to change his or her feelings and behaviors.

ENCOUNTER GROUPS

Encounter groups grew out of a series of leadership training workshops that took place during the 1950s at the National Training Laboratories in Bethel, Maine. They were later used extensively by humanistic psychologists. Typically, **encounter group** members share feelings and experiences with one another. The groups commonly involve a series of structured exercises, designed to overcome people's embarrassment about openly discussing their feelings. For instance, group members may take turns confessing some embarrassing fact about themselves, as well as something each is particularly proud of. Or members may pair off and discuss their first impressions with one another, with each sharing both a positive and a negative reaction they had to one another. Rogers (1970) described the process as involving some of the same elements as client-centered therapy, including expressing feelings about oneself, dropping facades, receiving feedback from others, and expressing negative and positive feelings about others. Participants learn that aspects of themselves that they had rejected—for example, anger at their children—are neither unusual nor hateful to others. As Rogers describes the process, "As the sessions proceed, an increasing feeling of warmth and group spirit and trust is built up, not out of positive attitudes only but out of a realness which includes both positive and negative feeling." Rogers thus notes that not all of the feelings expressed in encounter groups are positive, and offers two examples of the negative feelings that are expressed:

I took an instant dislike to you the first moment I saw you.

I don't have *any* respect for you, Alice. *None!*

(Rogers, 1970)

Rogers believed that the acceptance of both positive and negative feelings is part of the process of humanistic growth, and he felt that these negative feelings were not necessarily harmful. He also noted that most of the feelings expressed in the groups are positive ones. However, some observers were troubled by the potential harmful effects of the negative interactions that sometimes occur in such groups (Yalom & Lieberman, 1971, among others). Those concerns have been part of the larger general question about negative outcomes in therapy.

DYSFUNCTION:
Negative Outcomes in Psychotherapy

Like medical treatments, emotional insight therapies also involve some potential costs along with the chance for potential benefits. Some of the costs are short term—the result of emotional insight therapies delving into clients' unpleasant memories and negative feelings. As we just discussed, members of encounter groups sometimes say rather unpleasant things to one another, as in the case of the woman who frankly told another woman that she had taken an instant dislike for her. On rare occasions, the hostilities in such

groups have even escalated beyond verbal attacks—one psychologist interviewed a woman who had fought with another woman in an encounter group to the point of drawing blood (Zilbergeld, 1983). Such physical confrontations are quite rare, even in encounter groups, and can be prevented by an effective group leader. However, emotional confrontations are an integral part of many verbal therapies, as we saw in the case of Freud's Rat Man, who was asked to delve into his ambivalent feelings about his father as well as his grotesque memories about rats.

Like an exercise program, those short-term discomforts are endured in the interest of long-term growth and self-understanding. As we will discuss later, research on psychotherapy indicates that, in the long-run, psychotherapy leads to net benefits for people suffering from behavioral disorders. However, not every individual experiences a net benefit from psychotherapy, for several reasons. First, some people are not able to endure the short-term costs, in the same way that some people are not able to stick with an exercise program until they are physically fit. Second, some psychotherapists, like some surgeons, are not as adept as others. Third, some types of therapies are not well-matched to some types of problems. Rather than sweeping the potentially negative side-effects of psychotherapy under the rug, psychotherapy researchers have directly investigated them. It is hoped that a careful examination of the costs of psychotherapy will allow psychotherapists to minimize the costs while maximizing the benefits.

Consider one classic study which examined the possible negative outcomes of encounter groups. The researchers interviewed 170 undergraduate students who had previously participated in such a group. When questioned eight months later, the majority of the participants said that they had had positive experiences in the group and that the experience had made a positive impact on their lives. However, nearly 10 percent were judged by the researchers to have suffered significant psychological damage from the experience (Yalom and Lieberman, 1970). This sub-group showed increased depression or maladaptive feelings. To quote one of these students:

I was not in the mood for "encountering" and was almost forced to. I don't trust anyone in the group and felt threatened by it. I came away feeling insecure and having many self-doubts without being able to resolve them within the group. I overheard another member of the group describing my actions with his roommate, and he was reinforcing my own self-doubts about myself. I . . . was emotionally upset by the experience for several days afterward.

Because of their sometimes confrontative nature, encounter groups are not always ideal for especially sensitive individuals. The researchers found that negative experiences were most likely in those who were most disturbed to start out with, who had low self-esteem or poor social skills, or who had the greatest hope of fulfillment from the group (Lieberman, Yalom and Miles, 1973).

Individual psychotherapy also has its own potential costs. Some of these are inherent in confronting unpleasant experiences and perceived personal faults. Others stem from the special nature of the relationship between therapist and client. The very fact that the client shares his or her innermost thoughts and feelings with the therapist leads to feelings of intimacy between them. We described Freud's notion of transference, in which the patient transfers his or her feelings towards parents and lovers onto the therapist. The therapist is also human, and Freud felt it necessary to caution against **countertransference,** in which the therapist inappropriately transfers his or her feelings onto the client. Freud warned, in particular, that therapists should guard against acting on any sexual feelings towards the client. Recent research has demonstrated that therapists feel a range of positive feelings towards clients, from sexual attraction to love. Most therapists follow Freud's advice to avoid any sexual intimacy (Pope and Bouhoutsos, 1986). However, some therapists violate Freud's injunction against acting on those feelings, and the outcome can be harmful for the client.

It is important to distinguish negative effects due to unethical or incompetent techniques from those unpleasant effects arising in the standard course of therapy. There certainly can be negative outcomes from the normal course of verbal psychotherapy (Lambert et al., 1986). For example, large scale studies have found that about 10 percent of psychotherapy studies yield harmful results (Shapiro and Shapiro, 1982; Smith et al., 1980). And the percentage may really be even higher, since negative results are less likely to be published. After reviewing the research in this area, Michael Lambert and his colleagues concluded that negative outcomes are most likely with therapies that break down, challenge, or undermine the client's defenses, as opposed to more supportive therapies (Lambert, Shapiro, and Bergin, 1986). It appears that sometimes such therapies break down a patient's defenses without rebuilding a healthy approach in their place or providing an accepting, supportive atmosphere in which rebuilding can take place. Negative outcomes are also more likely with clients who were severely disturbed to begin with. These fragile individuals may be the least able to replace their psychological defenses with more adaptive coping mechanisms.

By learning about the potential negative outcomes in therapy, as we noted, it is hoped that therapists can learn to spot them and avoid them. For instance, a therapist might avoid confrontative techniques with a particularly sensitive client. As we shall discuss in a later section, many therapists now use a range of treatment techniques, attempting to match the appropriate approach to the particular client and his or her particular problems.

For the person considering undergoing psychological treatment, there are also some useful "consumer hints" in this research. If a client experiences negative feelings in therapy, there are several steps he or she should take in dealing with them. First, the feelings should be shared with the therapist. Insight therapists believe that learning to confront those very feelings can sometimes be the basis of greater self-understanding. If a client continues to feel what seem to be unduly negative feelings, the next step is to seek a second opinion. Another professional may be in a better position to distinguish negative feelings that are an integral part of self-growth from those that arise because of unethical or incompetent treatment, or from a poor match between client and therapist. In the same way that medical treatment often proceeds better with a change of prescription, psychological treatment often proceeds better with a change of therapy or therapist. Later in the chapter, we will return to the general issue of therapy outcome, and the specific issues of matching therapies with disorders as well as the features of a good therapist. ■

BEHAVIORAL APPROACHES

Behaviorists are fond of saying "you don't have to know where the fire started to put it out." For them, therapy does not involve delving into the forgotten thoughts and feelings of early childhood. Behavioral treatment aims directly at changing the problem behavior itself. Behavioral therapists assume that all behaviors, from normal behaviors such as reading detective novels to problems such as phobic fears, schizophrenic speech, and deviant sexual attractions, can be altered by changing their consequences, and can be replaced with more socially acceptable responses. Behavioral treatments can be divided into *classical conditioning* therapies and *operant conditioning* therapies.

CLASSICAL CONDITIONING THERAPIES

When Mary Cover Jones treated Peter's fear of rabbits, she used a technique based on classical conditioning principles. As shown in Figure 16.1, the approach assumed that Peter's fear stemmed from some earlier trauma, perhaps like the loud noise that Watson had used to produce a similar phobia in Little Albert. By associating the rabbit with tasty food and the companionship of his playmates, Jones was able to break the connection between the rabbit and the fear response, and establish a connection between the rabbit and pleasant feelings. During the 1950s, Joseph Wolpe refined this technique into a form of treatment known as **systematic desensitization.**

SYSTEMATIC DESENSITIZATION

In systematic desensitization, the goal is to gradually desensitize the client to the threatening stimulus. The treatment of "Roy" is a classic case of this form of treatment (Lazarus, 1965). Roy was a 33-year-old engineer. Though his therapist described him as talented and charming, Roy was nevertheless incapable of forming an acceptable relationship with a woman. He had been raised by an overpowering mother who zealously denounced promiscuity and preached the virtues of chastity. She expected him to adore her and his five sisters, but he was actually terrified of them. As an adult, he felt underlying hostilities towards women but was completely unassertive and passive in his face-to-face dealings with them. He was also incapable of attaining an erection with a woman, and had never been able to have intercourse. Although this case contains all the elements for a deep analysis of the man's childhood feelings of sexuality and aggression, his treatment was aimed simply and directly at decreasing his present anxieties. The therapist constructed several *anxiety hierarchies*, or graduated lists of situations that the client found threatening (Table 16.2).

In Roy's case, one hierarchy consisted of sexual intimacies progressing from embracing through kissing and fondling to intercourse. The other consisted of increasingly assertive discussions with women.

The other crucial component of desensitization is a *counterconditioning response*, something in-

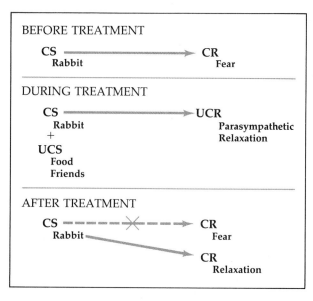

FIGURE 16.1 The process of systematic desensitization. Systematic desensitization uses the principles of classical conditioning in an attempt to undo a maladaptive fear response. Before Peter's treatment, the sight of a rabbit led to a conditioned fear response. During treatment, the rabbit was paired with pleasant stimuli, such as food and friends. After treatment, the association between the rabbit and fear was replaced with an association between the rabbit and relaxation.

Mary Cover Jones. In 1924, Mary Cover Jones developed a form of therapy that became the model for a behavioral treatment known as systematic desensitization, in which a person overcomes an irrational fear by gradually approaching the feared object in the presence of comforting stimuli.

TABLE 16.2 A Hypothetical Hierarchy for Systematic Desensitization

Least Threatening	Greeting an attractive woman on the street.
	Having a conversation with a woman at work.
	Inviting a woman to lunch.
	Asking a woman for a date.
	Talking with a woman on a date.
	Inviting a woman into his home.
	Holding a woman's hand.
	Kissing a woman.
	Caressing a woman.
	Undressing with a woman.
Most Threatening	Advanced foreplay.
	Intercourse.

compatible with anxiety. Usually, the client is taught deep muscle relaxation, an effective technique for removing tension and anxiety. Finally, the anxiety hierarchy is paired with the counter-conditioning response. Roy began gradually, while in a state of deep relaxation, to imagine becoming intimate with a woman, first kissing, then embracing, and so on. He would remain at each step in the imaginal hierarchy until he no longer felt anxiety associated with it. Then he would move to the next step. After several months, Roy had begun having successful sexual relations. The therapist closed the report by saying that Roy had gotten married and was the father of a two-month-old daughter.

AVERSIVE CONDITIONING

Systematic desensitization is designed to break the connection between a conditioned anxiety response and a situation that is either harmless or potentially pleasant—including being with someone on a date. It is well suited for people like Roy, who are not enjoying situations that are expected to be pleasurable. However, some people feel pleasurable responses to situations that the larger society finds unacceptable, such as excessive alcohol or drug use, or the sexual abuse of children. In these cases, the behavior therapist uses **aversive conditioning,** a classical conditioning procedure that establishes a connection between the undesirable situation and an aversive response.

Aversive conditioning has been used to treat undesirable problem behaviors such as smoking and sexual orientations that the client wishes to change (Feldman and MacCulloch, 1971). Because it is unpleasant, it raises a number of ethical questions (Davison and Neale, 1982). The treatment was described and caricatured in the novel (and movie) *A Clockwork Orange* which depicts an anti-social young man who takes pleasure in violent rape. After his arrest, he is shown films of rape while suffering from the effects of an emetic (a drug that causes nausea and vomiting). After therapy, he is tested by exposure to a beautiful, half-naked woman. He begins to run towards her, but stops several feet away, overcome with a fit of nausea. Although exaggerated in the movie, such treatments have actually been used. For instance, the drug *Antabuse* also works on aversive conditioning principles. As we noted in Chapter 5, when an alcoholic on Antabuse takes a drink of alcohol he becomes nauseous. After repeated use, the taste of alcohol alone elicits conditioned nausea. Although aversive treatments sound inhumane, they are usually only used with behaviors that have very serious long-term costs, such as alcoholism or illegal sexual behavior. In one study of alcoholics, a follow-up interview revealed a much higher-than-usual rate of abstinence among those treated with aversive procedures (Wiens and Menustik, 1983). Given the tremendous toll of continued alcoholism, the net benefits of the aversive procedure may be well worth the temporary unpleasantness.

As we noted in our earlier discussion of nausea conditioning, nausea is most easily conditioned to new tastes. Unfortunately, alcoholics have had numerous experiences drinking without nausea and so the nausea conditioning procedure does not always work. (Ironically, it would work better to prevent alcoholism in those who have never had a drink.) In recent years, the use of emetics or electric shock has been replaced with less extreme aversive stimuli. For instance, one treatment for rapists involves smelling ammonia during sexual fantasies (Freeman-Longo and Wall, 1986). As we shall see below, cognitive therapists have gone a step further, substituting imagined unpleasant stimuli for real ones.

OPERANT CONDITIONING THERAPIES

Classical conditioning treatments are designed to manipulate involuntary responses, such as anxiety and nausea. Operant treatments use reward, punishment, and shaping to influence voluntary behaviors. Reward is used to increase desirable behaviors. Thus, hospital staff may give attention, candy, or some other desirable reinforcer to a schizophrenic whenever he or she begins a normal conversation. Shaping is used to reinforce successively closer approximations to the desired end behavior. On the first day of treatment, the schizophrenic may only have to utter one sensible sentence to get a reward; after a month, he or she may be asked to converse normally for 20 minutes, without any bizarre comments throughout that whole time.

Punishment and extinction are used to decrease undesirable responses. We encountered the extinction technique in Chapter 6, when we described it as a treatment for a child's temper tantrums (Williams, 1959). In that case, parents who had previously reinforced a child with attention for screaming and raging at bedtime were able to stop these unpleasant behaviors by simply ignoring them, and thereby removing the rewards that maintained the behavior. Other researchers have used similar procedures with autistic children. These are children who are extremely socially withdrawn and inappropriate, and are often completely incapable of normal social interaction. Some of these children engage in bizarre tantrums, in which they may bang their heads to the point of causing concussions, or bite themselves until they bleed. Psychologist Ivar Lovaas and his colleagues (1965) used punishment to remove this self-destructive behavior. Lovaas followed any self-destructive act with an immediate and painful electric shock. Although such treatment sounds inhumane, the researchers argued that the immediate cost of adding a few moments of pain to the child's life is outweighed by removing behaviors that, in the long run, cause much more pain, and seriously damage the child's health.

As we mentioned earlier, punishment has other undesirable side effects. For instance, it leads a child to feel anxiety. And although punishment may remove behaviors, such as destructive temper tantrums, that have been rewarded with attention in the past, the punishment alone does not tell the child how to get rewards in an acceptable way. For these reasons, punishment is used only in extreme cases, and is usually combined with positive reinforcement for desirable behaviors. Returning to our discussion in the learning chapter, you should note the distinction between punishment and aversive conditioning. Punishment is used to alter voluntary behaviors, such as head-banging, in line with Edward L. Thorndike's Law of Effect. (As discussed in Chapter 6, this is the straightfor-

ward principle that behaviors that produce positive effects tend to be repeated, whereas those that produce negative effects tend not to be.) Aversive conditioning is used to alter involuntary reactions, such as pleasure at the taste of alcohol. Whenever punishment is used as an instrumental means of changing behavior, of course, some classically conditioned aversion reactions will also occur. For instance, a therapist who uses electric shock to change a child's head-banging may inadvertently teach the child fear at the sight of the therapist.

The first step in operant therapy is *functional analysis*, or a careful observation of the undesired behavior to determine which events precede and follow it. Such functional analyses often reveal how well-meaning friends and relatives inadvertently reward undesirable behaviors, while they simultaneously fail to reward alternative desirable behaviors. For instance, parents may say nothing when their child is sharing toys or drawing pictures, but give the child attention when he or she begins to whine, cry, or scream. Behavior therapists work to reverse these maladaptive reward patterns.

After a number of successful applications of operant principles to individuals, behavior therapists began to apply the principles to groups. These group operant programs are called token economies.

TOKEN ECONOMIES

In a **token economy,** groups of patients, inmates, or students are given tokens (usually poker chips or play money) that they can exchange for actual rewards. To earn the tokens people must either do something desirable—show up for an activity or a class—or refrain from doing something undesirable—throwing food or threatening the ward personnel. In 1968, psychologists John Atthowe and Leonard Krasner established one of the first token economies on a ward of chronic schizophrenic patients. Sixty percent of the patients were lethargic and required constant supervision. Patients were allowed to choose their own rewards, which included cigarettes, money, passes, watching TV, and even feeding kittens. To get the rewards, patients needed to earn tokens. Tokens were awarded for voluntarily participating in ward activities or for getting up on time and coming to breakfast without nursing assistance. As a result of the token system, the previously apathetic patients became much more active. About half of the formerly isolated patients began to leave the grounds on passes. As shown in Figure 16.2, there had been a weekly average of over 70 infractions in

A token economy. A token economy allows hospital inmates to earn reward tokens by getting up by themselves, grooming themselves, working, and so on. The tokens can be exchanged for a number of rewards, including a private bed, meals, and home visits.

FIGURE 16.2 Results of an operant treatment program. After reward tokens were introduced in a schizophrenic ward, the number of infractions (including refusing to get up or to participate in ward activities) dropped dramatically, and continued dropping over a two-month period.

carrying out morning routines (for example, resisting getting out of bed); six weeks after the tokens were introduced, the number had dropped to less than 10.

SOCIAL LEARNING APPROACHES

In recent years, learning-oriented therapists have applied principles of classical and operant conditioning to inner thoughts and feelings. An influential development was the publication of Albert Bandura's *Principles of Behavior Modification* in 1969. In his research on **modeling** Bandura demonstrated learning in subjects who simply observed another person but did not themselves perform any overt behavior nor receive any direct reinforcement. Bandura believed that the essential component of behavior change is a change in a person's *understanding* of the relationships between behavior and reward. For instance, Bandura and his colleagues showed that simply observing someone else approach a snake was as effective as systematic desensitization in reducing phobic behaviors (Bandura et al., 1969). Thus, it is sometimes possible to produce behavioral change by simply changing a person's cognitions.

Covert sensitization is a cognitive version of aversive conditioning. In covert sensitization the client is not actually exposed to shocks or other

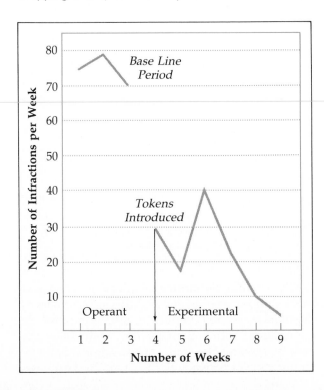

aversive stimuli, but is simply instructed to *think* of something unpleasant every time he or she feels an undesirable impulse. The following aversive scene was devised for the treatment of obesity:

I want you to imagine you've just had your main meal and you are about to eat your dessert, which is apple pie. As you are about to reach for the fork, you get a funny feeling in the pit of your stomach. You start to feel queasy, nauseous, and sick all over. As you touch the fork, you can feel food particles inching up into your throat. You're just about to vomit. As you put the fork into the pie, the food comes up into your mouth. You try to keep your mouth closed because you are afraid that you'll spit the food out all over the place. You bring the piece of pie to your mouth, you puke; you vomit all over your hands, the fork, over the pie. It goes all over the table, over other people's food. . . . Everybody is looking at you with a shocked expression.

(Cautela and Kearney, 1986)

Psychologist Joseph Cautela, who developed this technique, assumes that unpleasant feelings can be associated with a stimulus—for example, desserts, cigarettes, or liquor—simply by thinking about the two things together. If you found it unpleasant just to read the last paragraph, you can see how imagining something aversive might stimulate unpleasant feelings. Note that this approach is essentially the opposite of systematic desensitization. In systematic desensitization, a pleasant response is substituted for an unpleasant reaction. In covert sensitization, an unpleasant response replaces a pleasurable one. Obviously, the two procedures are used under different circumstances. Systematic desensitization is used when a person is avoiding some situation that should be pleasant (perhaps sex with a spouse) while covert sensitization is used when someone is enjoying some situation or state of affairs that should be avoided (smoking a cigarette, for example).

Covert conditioning may also involve positive thoughts to reward oneself for desirable behavior. For instance, a person trying to control his or her weight might imagine him or herself slender in a swimsuit after substituting an aerobic exercise class for drinking and snacking at a happy hour. One researcher reviewed over 100 studies of covert conditioning, and found that this form of treatment was, in the majority of cases, more effective than the other treatments to which it was compared (McCullogh, 1978).

Behavioral therapists originally dealt only with overt behaviors, but, in recent years, the dividing line between cognitive and behavioral therapies has become less distinct. In the next section, we discuss several combinations of cognitive and behavioral treatments in more detail.

COGNITIVE TREATMENTS

According to a strictly cognitive perspective it is not the actual events that happen to people that make them upset, but the way they view those events. All cognitive approaches attempt to teach people new tactics for viewing (or thinking about) events in their lives. Albert Ellis, the founder of an influential school of cognitive therapy, uses logical arguments, rather than punishment and reward principles, to modify a person's behavior. After discussing his approach to treatment, we will describe the cognitive approach to the treatment of depression.

RATIONAL-EMOTIVE THERAPY

Albert Ellis, the founder of an influential school of cognitive therapy, believes that psychopathology is caused by people's *irrational beliefs,* and that the therapist's mission is to teach people to think logically. Among the irrational beliefs Ellis lists "shoulds, oughts, and musts," or internal standards that people use to punish themselves. For instance:

A woman with severe emotional difficulties does not merely believe it is *undesirable* if her love partner is rejecting. She tends to believe, also, that (1) it is *awful;* (2) she *cannot stand* it; (3) she *should not, must not* be rejected; (4) she will *never* be accepted by any desirable partner; (5) she is a *worthless person* because one lover has rejected her; and (6) she *deserves to be damned* for being so worthless. Such common covert hypotheses are nonsensical and devoid of empirical referents. They can be easily elicited and demolished by any scientist worth his or her salt; and the rational-emotive therapist is exactly that; an exposing and nonsense-annihilating scientist.

(Ellis, 1979)

Ellis's **rational-emotive therapy** is, in some ways, opposite to that of Carl Rogers. Ellis believes the therapist should persuade, teach, and provide information, rather than let the client direct the flow of therapy. In some cases, rational-emotive therapists even argue with the client. In the following interview a new client has mentioned that she finds the therapist threatening:

CLIENT: Perhaps I would have followed your explanation a little better, if I hadn't been so threatened initially.

THERAPIST: But then, if I pat you on the head and hold back, et cetera, then you'll think for the rest of your life you have to be patted on the head! You're a bright woman!

CLIENT: All right. . . .

THERAPIST: That's another *should*. "He *should* pat me on the head and take it slowly—then (someone) like me can understand! But if he goes fast, and makes me think, oh my God I'll make an error—that is awful!" More horse ___ [expletive deleted]! You don't have to believe that horse ___! You're perfectly able to follow what I say—if you stop worrying about "I *should* do perfectly well!" For that's what you're basically thinking, sitting there. Well, why *should* you do perfectly well? Suppose we had to go over it 20 times before you got it?

CLIENT: I don't *like* to appear stupid!

THERAPIST: No. See. Now you're lying to yourself! Because you again said a sane thing—and then you added an insane thing. The sane thing was "I don't like to appear stupid, because *it's better* to appear bright." But then you immediately jumped over to the insane thing. "And it's *awful* if I appear stupid. . . ."

CLIENT: [laughs appreciatively, almost joyously]

THERAPIST: ". . . I *should* appear bright!" you see?

CLIENT: [with conviction] Yes.

THERAPIST: The same crap! It's always the same crap. Now if you would look at the crap—instead of "Oh, how stupid I am! He hates me! I think I'll kill myself!" then you'd get better right away.

CLIENT: You've been listening! [laughs]

THERAPIST: Listening to what?

CLIENT: [laughs] Those wild statements in my mind, like that, that I make.

(Ellis, 1979)

Ellis's techniques are very controversial, and not all clients are comfortable with this confrontational approach. It has even been suggested that there might be regional differences in the acceptance of Ellis's approach, with people from urban areas such as New York City making better

candidates than people from less confrontational areas, such as Willow Springs, Missouri (Kendall and Kriss, 1983). However, a number of more recent cognitive techniques are not so confrontational. Several approaches use more friendly interactions to teach people to record and modify what they think about when they are in unpleasant situations (Goldfried and Davison, 1976; Meichenbaum, 1977, among others). For instance, psychotherapist Donald Meichenbaum trains patients to alter how they "talk to themselves." A depressive college professor, for instance, might respond to a student leaving during her lecture with the thought "I must be boring them to tears." Meichenbaum would instruct her to catch those thoughts and replace them with more self-defensive ones, such as, "There I go again with those self-destructive ideas. Actually, the student probably has to run to study for a test next period. What a pity he will miss my brilliant lecture!"

COMBINING COGNITIVE AND LEARNING APPROACHES TO TREAT DEPRESSION

Cognitive learning theorists agree with Albert Ellis that irrational thinking contributes to maladaptive behavior (Lewinsohn, Hoberman, Teri, and Hautzinger, 1985). Instead of directly confronting the client's irrational thinking in the therapy session, however, a learning-oriented cognitive therapist would focus more on keeping careful records of specific real world incidents, and on having the client carry out behavioral "assignments" outside the therapy session. One well-known cognitive treatment that attempts to help clients learn new behaviors is psychologist Aaron Beck's approach to depression (Beck et al., 1979). Beck's procedure involves several important components:

- *Self-monitoring:* Clients are taught to record their moods as they go through their daily activities. A client might stop to record his or her moods every hour, and to note what went on during the preceding hour. This record could be used to make connections between particular events and moods that clients might not have noticed. For instance, a client might find out that his or her mood improves when working (Kendall and Kriss. 1983).

- *Recording Dysfunctional Thoughts:* Beck teaches depressed patients to record their upsetting thoughts when they occur. Along with the upsetting thoughts, clients describe the situation in which these thoughts occurred, and any feelings that accompany the thoughts. For instance, a client might note that every time her boyfriend is late for a date she begins to think that he doesn't really care about her, he wants to be free of her, and these thoughts might lead her to think about all the times she was rejected as a child.

■ *Collecting Data Relevant to Upsetting Thoughts:* Clients are asked three questions about their depressing thoughts: (1) What evidence do you have that your way of thinking is correct? (2) Is there another way of looking at it? (3) Even if it is true, is it as bad as it seems? After recording his or her depressing thoughts, the client discusses them with the therapist. Here is an example of a woman who becomes depressed when she begins to think that her social isolation is caused by her physical unattractiveness:

THERAPIST: Other than your subjective opinion, what evidence do you have that you are ugly?

CLIENT: Well, my sister always said I was ugly.

THERAPIST: Was she always right in these matters?

CLIENT: No. Actually, she had her own reasons for telling me this. But the *real reason* I know I'm ugly is that men don't ask me out. If I weren't ugly, I'd be dating now.

THERAPIST: That is a possible reason why you're not dating. But there's an alternative explanation. You told me that you work in an office by yourself all day and spend your nights alone at home. It doesn't seem like you're giving yourself opportunities to meet men.

CLIENT: I can see what you're saying, but still, if I weren't ugly, men would ask me out.

THERAPIST: I suggest we run an experiment: that is, for you to become more socially active, stop turning down parties and social events and see what happens.

■ *Scheduling Activities and Graded Task Assignments:* Often depressed people withdraw from the company of others. This in turn leads to fewer rewarding social interactions, and more depression. To break this cycle, Beck developed a strategy or schedule in which first the client is encouraged to participate in very low-cost, nonthreatening interactions—perhaps making an effort to say something to the grocery clerk, or going to a gathering at church. Using the behavioral principle of shaping (reinforcing successively more difficult performances), the schedule gradually adds more assertive activities. Later, when the client has become more comfortable initiating conversation, he or she may get an assignment to invite someone out. In this case, however, it is the client's perception of social interactions that is being shaped as much as his or her behavior.

■ *Self-reinforcement:* Beck also found that depressed people are often very hard on themselves, so his therapy emphasizes teaching people to reward themselves. Clients are taught to reward themselves both with actual reinforcers, such as a special dessert or a movie, and with cognitive reinforcers, such as self-praise after completing each graded task assignment. This self-reward serves a dual purpose: it increases the probability of repeating the desirable activity, and it also focuses attention on the individual's strengths. By paying attention to the positive things he or she does, a person is more likely to remember them, and to come to think of him or herself in more positive terms.

Beck's approach is characteristic of a number of treatment programs that integrate Ellis's rational approach with traditional behavior modification methods. In the last few years, researchers have started considering how to apply the most recent advances in cognitive psychology to clinical treatment. These researchers view maladaptive thinking in terms of the information processing metaphor we discussed in Chapter 7, and they are designing approaches to teach people new methods of attending to, storing, and remembering events in their lives (Ingram, 1986). For instance, if a person prone to depression gets into an argument with an abrasive shopclerk, he or she might begin to recollect other experiences of his or her own personal failures, thinking, "They have no respect for me. Even a clerk knows that I'm not worth bothering with." In this way, the depressive is forming additional associations between his or her self-concept and other unpleasant memories. As an alternative, he or she could interpret and categorize such an encounter as an example of "work stress," and recall instances of other pressured behaviors he or she has seen in people with difficult jobs. Over time, such directed categorization can block the tendency for new unpleasant encounters to "prime" a series of depressing thoughts. Modern cognitive therapists have thus begun to bridge the gaps between the humanistic trend toward increased client involvement, the learning principles from the animal laboratory, and the experimental research on human cognition.

SOCIAL SYSTEMS APPROACHES TO TREATMENT

From the sociological perspective, it makes no sense to define behavioral problems without reference to other people as we noted in the last chapter. The therapist who adopts this perspective considers how those problem behaviors fit into a family, peer group, school, or neighborhood. Most of this school's adherents would not label themselves as sociologists but they do adopt the sociological assumption that treatment should focus on social units larger than the individual. Family therapists treat family units as a whole; while community psychologists work at many levels, studying the psychological effects of schools, neighborhoods, or even government.

FAMILY THERAPY

Family therapy involves the treatment of whole families rather than single individuals. To some extent, the family therapy movement has its roots in the psychoanalytic school, with its emphasis on

relationships between children and their parents. However, the most important single event in the evolution of this approach occurred when anthropologist Gregory Bateson gathered a group of researchers to study disturbed family communication patterns. Anthropologists such as Bateson study how the different parts of a culture, including religion, politics, economy, and marriage customs, fit together into a cohesive system. To this *social systems* viewpoint, whenever one aspect of a culture changes it will change other aspects. For instance, the introduction of a money-based economy into a third world tribe will alter the entire interconnected system of religion, politics, marriage customs, and so on. Family therapists also view families as integrated systems, and assume that the family rules and the social roles played by each family member fit together into a coherent whole (Parkison, 1983). Stress in any one part of the family system will have ripple effects on the other parts. For instance, struggles for power between the father and the mother will necessarily influence the children. When a child develops a problem such as drug abuse or anorexia, it may appear to be solely maladaptive to someone outside the family system. However, family therapists assume that the troublesome behavior serves some useful purpose in maintaining family structure (Minuchin, 1974). For instance, a child may throw temper tantrums to reduce fighting between the

Family therapy. Advocates of the social systems approach to treatment believe that it is pointless to single out one individual as "disturbed" without treating the social environment that gave rise to the disordered behavior. Family therapy is one method of treatment that adopts a social systems perspective.

parents, who must unite to deal with the "problem."

Since the family therapist believes that symptoms can only be understood within the context of the whole family system, therapy must involve not only the person with the symptom but the rest of the family as well. During therapy, the family therapist observes how the family members communicate with one another, and notes whether they form power alliances in which several family members unite against one. Just as an anthropologist may try to join the tribe under study, the family therapist tries to enter the family unit by learning its special language and communication patterns. After gaining admittance, the therapist will try to change the family's interaction patterns so that the problem is no longer necessary or useful to it. An interesting technique developed by family therapists is called *paradoxical intervention* (Haley, 1963), in which the problem behavior is actually encouraged. For instance, the therapist may notice that a child throws temper tantrums when his parents exclude him from their attentions. After the tantrum starts, the parents may begin to pay attention to the child by pleading with him to stop. Rather than trying to block the temper tantrums, the family therapist might suggest that the child actually practice a temper tantrum in the therapy session. Then the therapist might give the child instructions about how to have even more effective tantrums. The parents may likewise be instructed to encourage the tantrums for the next week. Such a technique can serve to undermine the usefulness of the child's tantrums. It can also sensitize the parents to the need to pay attention to the child in a positive way. The intervention is called paradoxical because it begins as an attempt to increase, rather than decrease, the strength of the symptom. Evaluation studies have found that family therapy is as effective as traditional one-on-one therapy, and perhaps somewhat more effective in treating adolescent psychosomatic and drug problems (Parkison, 1983).

COMMUNITY PSYCHOLOGY

Community psychologists share an emphasis on social systems with family therapists. However, they go beyond the family and view the problem behavior in the context of the larger society. Community psychologists believe that treatments should be aimed at the societal conditions that cause behavior disorders, in the ultimate hope of preventing further problems. They also believe that treatments should be administered in the community, by community members, not in isolated medical settings.

The community movement gained momentum when Congress passed the Community Mental Health Centers Act in 1963. That law, made possible to a large degree by the discovery of psychoactive drugs, aimed for **deinstitutionalization,** or the release of patients from mental hospitals. In one of the earliest community programs, groups of hospitalized schizophrenics were moved out into neighborhood lodges (Fairweather et al., 1969). A few members of the hospital staff helped get them started. After the patients had set up their living arrangements, the nursing staff gradually phased itself out, and gave the patients increasing responsibility for their own lives. The patients set up their own janitorial business, and many of them eventually became completely self-supporting. Similar community programs are used with drug addicts, who have no problem going off drugs in a hospital but often return to them when they are back in their own environment. These **halfway houses** are treatment facilities that allow former addicts or mental patients to live partly in the community and partly in a treatment environment.

There have been some negative consequences of the deinstitutionalization policy. As budget cuts have closed many mental health halfway houses, some individuals who would previously have lived out their lives in state or county hospitals have joined the ranks of the homeless, and now wander the streets. Instead of being integrated back into the community, they remain outsiders. Many of these individuals are now in worse straits than they were in the institutions, and, as panhandlers and vagrants, they create new costs for the community. Observing the homeless in his city in 1986, former New York mayor Ed Koch called for a reconsideration of the policy of deinstitutionalization. Approximately one third of the 45,000 homeless people in New York suffer from psychological disorders, most commonly schizophrenia (Goleman, 1986). Similarly large percentages of disturbed people have been found among the homeless of other cities (Kahn et al., 1987). The goal of the community mental health act was not simply to discharge these patients with no additional supports. Community psychologists advocate *alternative* forms of treatment, as opposed to no treatment at all. When hospitalization has been compared to community-based treatment (as opposed to simply releasing patients onto the streets) the community approaches have shown clear advantages. One researcher examined the results of 10 separate studies in which severely disturbed individuals were randomly assigned to either traditional hospitalization or an alternative community program (Kiesler, 1982). The alternatives ranged from halfway houses to outpatient support groups. In nine of 10 comparisons, people assigned to community programs later showed better adjustment. They were also less likely to require future hospitalization. A further advantage to the community programs is that they were, on average, 40 percent less expensive than hospitalization. Thus, community treatments can be effective when there is actual treatment involved.

In addition to trying to place mental patients back into society, community psychologists reach out into the streets and neighborhoods. They try to get help to groups ignored by traditional approaches (Rappaport and Seidman, 1983). For instance, poor people, delinquents, and the unemployed are not only unable to afford traditional verbal psychotherapy, they are also uninterested in discussing their problems with someone from a very different background. A Ph.D. psychologist who wears tweed suits and drives a Volvo station wagon may have little credibility with a drug addict who belongs to a street gang. For this reason, community psychologists have focused on the training of **paraprofessionals.** A paraprofessional is someone without an advanced degree, who can offer psychological assistance and counseling when and where it is needed. They are also able to direct their clients to professional help if necessary. To this end, community psychologists have made use of former neighborhood drug abusers as drug counselors, and retired people as counselors for other elderly people. Research indicates that such programs benefit both the recipients and the counselors themselves (Gatz et al., 1982; Tefft and Kloba, 1981).

Community psychologists believe that the stresses of poverty and unemployment contribute to maladaptive behavior, so they also focus on the *prevention* of societal stress. Rather than waiting until someone is severely disturbed, community psychologists may target high-risk neighborhoods, schools, or families in an attempt to ward off problems before they begin (Cowen, 1982). For instance, one study set up social support groups and stress education classes for adults who were in the process of divorcing (Bloom, Hodges and Caldwell, 1982). These individuals showed fewer adjustment difficulties than expected during this typically stressful transition. Finally, many community psychologists believe that the best route to prevention is to change the underlying social conditions that lead to stress by fighting poverty, poor education, and unemployment. Some community psychologists go beyond the streets and neighborhoods, and aim to change the public policies that affect the lives of troubled groups (Cowen, 1983; Goodstein and Sandler, 1978). Instead of treating the psychological consequences of unemployment, an advocate of the community approach might work to set up a job training program that would make such treatment unnecessary in the future.

EVALUATING THE EFFECTIVENESS OF TREATMENT

In the area of treatment, where psychological principles are applied to people with serious problems, psychologists must be particularly careful to evaluate the validity of their ideas. Given that psychological treatment costs money, time, and effort, and may lead to unpleasant side-effects, we must ask three questions about it:

1) Does therapy really help alleviate psychological disorders?

2) Are some therapists better than others?

3) Are some therapies better suited for some problems?

Researchers have addressed each of these questions, and have found some reason to be wary of overly optimistic and overly generalized claims about psychotherapy.

OUTCOME RESEARCH: DOES THERAPY REALLY HELP?

In 1985, a Phoenix man was arrested and charged with fraud. He was earning thousands of dollars a week treating patients with "natural psychic healing." One of his specialties was "bloodless surgery." He claimed to remove cancerous growths without a single incision of the scalpel. During surgery, the patient would lie on a table while the "surgeon" focused his powers on the area of pain. Miraculously, a careful movement of his hand would remove a troublesome "tumor" every time. When a journalist investigated, she discovered that he kept a large supply of fresh chicken livers on hand, one of which would be deftly removed from beneath his belt during the surgery. The amazing thing about this charlatan's scam was that most of his patients were repeat visitors, and many of them swore that they had been helped. They were no doubt telling the truth. Years of research into the medical and psychological treatment process has taught one thing for certain: Almost any form of "treatment" that a person believes in leads to a perception of improvement in almost any kind of symptom. The technical term for this "faith healing" phenomenon is the **placebo** effect. Any research into therapy effectiveness must keep the placebo effect in mind. When doing outcome research or evaluating the results of a particular therapy, therefore, it is important that psychologists not take clients' perceptions at face value.

PLACEBO EFFECTS
AND SPONTANEOUS IMPROVEMENTS

Placebo effects are not bad in themselves. Jerome Frank (1961, 1983) compared psychotherapy to religious healing procedures and argued that placebo effects are a valid part of any therapy. In fact, the hope of cure that follows the administration of a placebo drug seems to lead our own bodies to release endorphins. These substances, as described in Chapters 2 and 10, are natural opiates that block pain. The drug nalaxone, which blocks endorphin action, may also block placebo effects (Levine et al., 1979). Placebo effects can be considered the common benefit of almost any form of therapy. Nevertheless, most therapists would not be satisifed to be doing nothing more than the village faith healer.

Earlier, we mentioned another problem in doing research on therapy effectiveness—spontaneous improvements. Given the normal fluctuations in life events, mood, and luck, most people's psychological state improves shortly after a crisis. As we noted, Hans Eysenck jarred the field with his 1952 finding that most patients improved over the time they would have been in therapy, even when they were left *untreated*. In fact, he claimed that the improvements found in untreated people, called **spontaneous improvements,** were at least as great as the improvements in those who were treated. Later researchers claimed he overestimated these spontaneous improvements. However, even Eysenck's critics found that the rate of spontaneous improvement was 43 percent (Bergin and Lambert, 1978).

Therapists sometimes quote glowing testimonials from former patients as proof of the effectiveness of their treatment. However, those testaments tell us nothing about whether the patient's improvement is due to a placebo effect, nor do they allow us to decide what would have happened with no treatment at all. Placebo effects and spontaneous improvements can be controlled for, but not without careful research methods. To be sure that spontaneous improvements are not mistakenly attributed to therapy, researchers must compare groups of patients who received treatment with control groups who received no treatment at all. If those comparisons show an effect we know that the therapy did something. However, even those comparisons still leave us uncertain as to whether that something was more than faith healing. A more adequate test of a therapy is to compare it to some form of placebo treatment.

TWO EXAMPLES OF OUTCOME RESEARCH

A classic study of systematic desensitization carefully considered possible placebo and spontaneous improvement effects. Psychotherapist Gordon Paul (1966) treated undergraduate students who suffered from public-speaking anxiety. The research used an experimental design in which a desensitization treatment group was compared to three control groups. One control group received no immediate treatment of any kind. Another was given an "attention-placebo" treatment—its members met with a therapist who showed interest and warmth. The therapist also administered a placebo "tranquilizer" while the subjects performed irrelevant tasks they were told would help their speaking anxieties. A final group was given insight-oriented therapy—they discussed the history of their public-speaking problem and delved into its relationship to their current interpersonal life. The results are shown in Figure 16.3.

The graph illustrates each of the issues we have been discussing. First, the untreated group showed some spontaneous improvement without any intervention. Second, the attention-placebo group showed more improvement than the untreated subjects, and as much as the insight group. Nevertheless, the desensitization group showed more improvement than any of the other groups. This unusually high success rate is probably due to the special match between public speaking anxiety and desensitization.

Not all problems yield so readily to all treatments—nonspectific anxieties or depression, for instance, are more difficult to treat than specific fears (Shapiro and Shapiro, 1982). Nevertheless, one study showed that 50 to 60 percent of depressed patients improved with either cognitive behavior therapy, insight therapy, or imipramine (a drug therapy), compared to less than 30 percent given placebos (Elkin, 1986). Other controlled outcome studies yield similar results (Robinson, Berman, and Neimeyer, 1990).

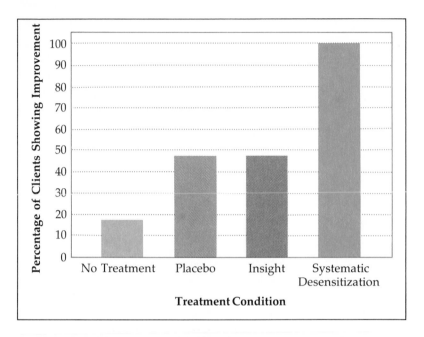

FIGURE 16.3 Results of a controlled therapy outcome study. Percentage of clients showing improvement in public speaking anxiety, as a function of different types of therapy. Note that untreated subjects showed some spontaneous improvement. Subjects given placebo therapy or verbal therapy improved somewhat more, but significantly less than those given systematic desensitization.

META-ANALYSIS

Since there have been hundreds and hundreds of psychotherapy studies performed, there is a danger that the results of any given study, though positive, are due simply to chance. Just as individual clinicians might be motivated to remember the glowing testimonials and forget their dissatisfied "customers," so might clinical researchers be motivated to report the studies that showed positive results and forget those that showed negative results or vice versa. Indeed, many studies show no effects of psychotherapy, and some studies even show negative effects, where the therapy made people worse. Although one might be tempted to throw up one's hands in confusion, there is a way to sort through these contradictory findings. Researchers have recently turned to a statistical technique called **meta-analysis** to organize findings in areas where there are many contradictory studies. A meta-analysis statistically combines a number of studies into one large analysis. To see how a meta-analysis might be used, imagine that 80 percent of all the people treated with psychotherapy improve, while 50 percent of those who receive no treatment also improve. In an ideal world, with no chance factors operating in any one study, every one of a sample of 10 studies would show 80 percent improvement in the treat-

ed clients, and 50 percent improvement in the untreated clients. As suggested in Table 16.3, chance factors alone add enough variation that few real studies would show exactly 80 versus 50 percent improvement rates. By chance, some studies will pick up little or no effects, and others will even show negative effects (indicated by a negative sign [–] as opposed to a positive sign [+] in the last column of Table 16.3). Over a large number of studies, however, the chance factors even themselves out. This underscores a point we made at the very beginning of this book and shows why researchers need to replicate their results. One can never place complete trust in the results of any single study.

Another advantage of meta-analysis is that it allows researchers to organize studies into groups so that, for example, all studies of behavior therapy can be compared with all studies of insight therapy (Figure 16.4).

The results of several meta-analyses indicate that overall, each of the different schools of therapy leads to more improvement than no treatment at all (Smith et al., 1980; Shapiro and Shapiro, 1982). Emotional insight psychotherapies have been found to be slightly better than placebo treatments, although researchers differ about whether those effects are meaningful (Dawes, 1983;

TABLE 16.3 Meta-Analysis: A Hypothetical Example of 10 Psychotherapy Studies (Numbers represent percent of clients improved)

RESULTS IF NO CHANCE FACTORS OPERATED		MORE TYPICAL RESULTS		
Treatment	Control	Treatment	Control	
80	50	51	91	−
80	50	59	59	
80	50	73	31	+
80	50	77	89	−
80	50	81	46	+
80	50	79	54	+
80	50	94	37	+
80	50	91	33	+
80	50	99	21	+
80	50	96	39	+
Mean 80	50	80	50	

Note: The figures on the left represent results that might be found if no chance factors operated—if no therapists had an unusually disturbed or an unusually healthy group of clients, if no therapists were better than the others, if all clients had the same number of other important events intervene during therapy, and so on. The findings at the right are more like results that are found in real studies. By considering average results across a large number of studies, meta-analysis helps correct for chance factors.

Prioleau, Murdock and Brody, 1983; Smith et al., 1983). Behavioral therapies, which tend to focus on more specific and manageable problems, are more successful than either no treatment, placebo-treatment, or emotional insight therapies (Shapiro and Shapiro, 1982). In sum, not everyone benefits from every therapy, but on average the results show that therapy is helpful, particularly behavioral therapy aimed at specific problems.

RESEARCH AND APPLICATION:
Evaluating Commercialized Self-Help Therapies

Take a trip to any local bookstore and find the section labelled "Psychology." If your bookstore is typical, you will find yourself confronting a wall full of volumes with titles promising to help you understand and improve yourself. Many of the books there were written by people with no special scientific credentials beyond a fervent belief in their own advice or the desire to make a few dollars. Others were written by therapy researchers who hope to apply their ideas more widely (and perhaps to make a few dollars as well). Gerald Rosen is an author of just such a book. His *Don't Be Afraid* (1976) claimed that "without the expense of professional counseling, and in the privacy of your own home," you could "learn to master those situations that now make you nervous or afraid" (Rosen, 1976). And all this could be accomplished "in as little as six to eight weeks."

Those claims are not unusual. In fact, Rosen found that magazines and newspapers often include advertisements making grand claims for various self-help programs. For example, one full page ad in a magazine promised "success, mindpower, winning, attractiveness, transformation, self-knowledge" and another advertisement promised a "Five Minute Phobia Cure." . . . (Rosen, 1987).

Very few of these self-help techniques have been subjected to the rigors of outcome research such as we have been describing. Rosen tested his own methods and found encouraging results for anxious subjects who worked with a therapist—all experienced some reduction in symptoms after a desensitization program. However, 50 percent of those who went it alone with a self-administered program failed to complete the therapy. A 50 percent drop-out rate is typical of self-administered behavior modification programs (Glasgow and Rosen, 1978). Rosen speculates that many authors of such texts may personally believe that they have good programs. However, even the best of ideas can go wrong in actual practice. In fact, when this researcher tried to improve his own self-treatment approach by including a self-reward component, things got worse. The number of clients who completed the "improved program" dropped from 50 to 0 percent! (Barrera and Rosen, 1977).

Helping 50 percent of clients with self-administered therapies might be better than nothing. However, Rosen (1987) reviews other research, showing that those who drop out of such programs might actually be hurt. For instance, one study found that family problems got worse after mothers tried unsuccessfully to control their children's behavior problems with a self-administered program (Matson and Ollendick, 1977). Likewise, people may feel even more helpless about their

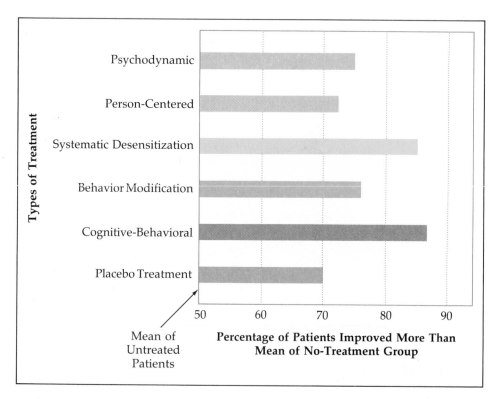

FIGURE 16.4 Meta-analysis of different therapies. Meta-analyses combine the results of many independent studies to make statistical comparisons of the effects of different therapies. Averaging across many studies, all of the major types of therapy discussed in this chapter produce some benefit beyond no treatment at all. A good part of that effect can be produced with a placebo treatment, as shown in the bottom column. Behavioral treatments are significantly more successful than either verbal therapies or placebo treatments in studies done thus far (Shapiro and Shapiro, 1982; Smith, Glass, and Miller, 1980).

problems after they have failed with a highly touted program, thinking "If even this program doesn't help, I must really have problems." It is also important to note that this research found problems with programs based on well-established behavioral treatments. From other outcome research, we know that these approaches are generally more successful than the others. Nonbehavioral self-cures may show even more discouraging results, and programs that promise increased psychic abilities are probably pure charlatanism, since well-controlled studies have never been able to convincingly demonstrate psychic abilities in anyone.

There are practical lessons in this line of research. Since some people are helped by the inexpensive self-administered therapies, they are worth considering. But people should not expect miracles from this type of program, nor be too disappointed if it does not work for them. Before spending any money, however, it is useful to

apply the general lesson of outcome research: be skeptical. The careful consumer will glance through a self-help book to see if the author reports data on how well the course works in actual self-application. If outcome data are provided, one must still ask whether the author included adequate control groups (people who received no treatment or a reasonable placebo treatment). The same lesson applies to any type of therapy, in fact. Before investing any money in a therapist or even in any series of self-help tapes, ask for exact statistics on how the treatment has been tested against controls. If you do not hear an adequate answer, look elsewhere. ■

WHAT MAKES SOME THERAPISTS BETTER THAN OTHERS?

We mentioned earlier that negative therapy outcomes are more likely with either uninvolved or challenging therapists (Lambert et al., 1986). Con-

Are some therapists better than others? Research indicates that therapists who show empathy with clients' problems are rated as more effective by clients. Unfortunately, clients' judgments about satisfaction with therapists are often unreliable indices of actual behavioral improvement.

versely, some types of therapists are likely to foster more positive outcomes. Clients respond better to therapists who were rated as genuine, warm, and accepting of the client. Female therapists are also rated as being somewhat more effective than males (Beutler et al., 1986). This may be explained by the research we discussed earlier on gender differences in personality traits. Females are generally higher in social skills, and may simply be better at expressing genuineness, warmth, and acceptingness, all key traits in a therapist. Females also score higher on measures of empathy (Eisenberg and Lennon, 1983), and it may be that female therapists are better at relating to and understanding a client's problems. The relationship between therapist and client also influences the outcome, and better outcomes are found when the client perceives the therapist as trustworthy and supportive. Unfortunately, it is not always easy to tease out cause and effect in these studies. Patients who report improvement in their symptoms also say nicer things about their therapists. As we have seen, the placebo effect may be at work in this finding. Is it that a good therapist–client relationship *leads to* positive changes in the client? Perhaps. But it may be due to the fact that positive changes in the client lead to better ratings of the therapist. Or it may be that some people tend to say nice things and others complain, regardless of the actual events in their lives. Complainers might actually improve as a result of therapy, but still

focus on their remaining problems, and complain about the therapist as well. Optimists might see the best side of their present life, and of their therapist, even though nothing has really changed. However, several studies have shown interesting findings that do not depend upon client rating biases. For instance, one of the most interesting findings in this area is that paraprofessionals who were trained in empathetic listening techniques appeared to be as effective as therapists with Ph.D.s or M.D.s (Hattie et al., 1984).

ARE SOME THERAPIES BETTER FOR SOME PROBLEMS?

Many therapists were once content to use the same technique for all patients. For instance, psychoanalysis was applied not only to cases of hysteric anxiety, but also to schizophrenics, psychopaths, and phobics. Although there are some common effects of all types of therapy (Frank, 1982; Strupp, 1986), outcome studies indicate that certain therapies are more effective with certain dysfunctions. For example, insight psychotherapy is somewhat effective with people who are predominantly well-functioning but suffer from general anxiety or depression. It has not been very effective with schizophrenics. On the other hand, schizophrenia does respond to drug treatment (Klerman, 1986).

We mentioned that systematic desensitization

may be more effective with specific fears. This is logical, since the treatment is designed to break the connection between a specific situation and a conditioned fear response. However, it would be inappropriate to use systematic desensitization to treat someone such as a rapist, who is suffering from an impulse control disorder. A rapist needs to learn an avoidance response, not to overcome one. The more common behavioral treatment used with sexual offenders or drug abusers is aversive conditioning. As we noted earlier, aversive conditioning has a goal exactly opposite in intention from desensitization—to produce a new conditioned fear.

Medical researchers, who view each different psychopathological "syndrome" as symptomatic of a different disease process, have been most attuned to matching the treatment to the problem. As a result of trying each of the different drugs on a wide range of patients, these researchers have found that antidepression, antianxiety, and antipsychotic medications each produce specific effects. Although each class of drugs may produce general relaxation and placebo effects, antidepressant drugs do not specifically help schizophrenic symptoms, and antipsychotic drugs do not help depressive symptoms. In some cases, the eclectic approach mentioned earlier, works best. Some researchers have studied how drugs combine with psychological therapies. For instance, severe depression seems to respond best to a combination of drug therapy and psychotherapy, which may itself be a mix of psychodynamic and cognitive techniques. In part, some psychological problems may respond better to a combination of different therapeutic techniques because those problems are themselves the result of the interaction of a number of factors (Klerman, 1986).

INTERACTIONS:
Changing the Person, the Environment, and the Person's Cognitions

As we noted in the last chapter, problem behavior can be viewed as the result of an interaction between the person, his or her environment, and his or her interpretation of events. According to this interactionist perspective, it is not useful to ask which is the one right treatment approach. It is pointless to argue whether it is better to treat the biological organism, the problem behavior, the environment, or the person's cognitions. Changing any one of these components will have some bearing on behavior, because they all influence one

another. In Table 16.4 we use the scheme from Chapter 15 to show which component of the interaction each of the different therapies focuses on. As this table explains, medical treatments aim to change the physical organism with surgery or drugs. Some operant treatments aim to change the organism by increasing the person's skill repertoire. Family/community approaches and some instrumental treatments aim to change the objective environment by working with family, school, neighborhood, or government. Cognitive and insight treatments are directed at changing the person's thoughts about the environment, while classical approaches aim to change very simple cognitive associations between perceived stimuli and emotional reactions. Changes in organism, environment, or cognition can all have beneficial effects. However, therapies that aim at the column that is the source of the problem should be most effective.

Medical treatments, such as drugs and surgery, aim to change the biological organism. Drugs and ECT alter the action of neural transmitters and surgery severs brain connections. Some behavioral techniques based on operant conditioning aim to make changes in the organism of a different sort by teaching new behavioral skills. Other behavioral techniques are aimed at altering reward contingencies in the person's environment. For instance, rather than trying to change a child's tantrums directly, a behavior or family therapist might train the child's parents to respond differently to those tantrums. Insight and cognitive therapies, on the other hand, work to alter cognitions. They try to train people to think differently about themselves and to look at the world in different ways. Classical conditioning therapies actually work on very simple cognitive associations between emotional responses (such as fear) and mental representations of environmental stimuli (for example, the thought of going on a date).

Since problematic behavior is a product of interactions among a person's environment, his or her cognitions, and his or her biological organism no one therapeutic approach has a monopoly as the "true" remedy for problem behavior. No matter how physiologically predisposed to depression a person is, that person may not become depressed if he or she can learn to avoid events in the environment that trigger the feelings of depression, such as people who are hostile and competitive. Or the person can use cognitions to avoid depression even in the face of an oppressive environment by reinterpreting unpleasant events (such as attributing other people's hurtful remarks

TABLE 16.4 Interactions and Psychotherapy

ORGANISM $\times$	OBJECTIVE ENVIRONMENT $\times$	COGNITION
Medical Treatments	**Behavioral–Operant**	**Behavioral–Classical**
Psychoactive drugs Brain surgery ECT	Alter reward contingencies used by parents and other authorities	Alter associations between feelings and environmental events
Behavioral–Operant	**Family/Community**	**Cognitive**
Teach person new response patterns	Reduce stresses in family, school, neighborhood, and work environment	Change a person's expectations and maladaptive interpretations
		Insight
		Teach the person to understand unconscious or unrealized feelings

to their insecurity, rather than assuming the blame personally).

Approaches that focus on any of the three categories (organism, environment, or cognition) will have some payoff, and this explains why all forms of therapy usually have some benefit beyond the placebo effect. However, it is a mistake to assume that any approach will have *equal* benefit for any problem. If a person's depression is largely attributable to a physiological imbalance, then drug treatment is likely to be most effective. On the other hand, if the person is not physiologically prone to a depressive response, but talks herself into a depressive state with incessant self-defeating interpretations, then cognitive therapy will do more good than drug treatment. Likewise, an environmental intervention makes sense when environmental factors are especially important in a person's depression. No amount of cognitive therapy or drug therapy may be as effective as finding a job for an unemployed man or woman or a new residence for the victim of a violent ex-spouse.

Eclectic Approaches to Therapy

Consistent with this interactionist perspective, most clinical psychologists no longer commit themselves faithfully to one school of treatment. Instead, over half of all therapists now combine elements of the different approaches in their treatment (Garfield and Bergin, 1986). We mentioned the trend toward combining cognitive and learning approaches. Other therapists combine psychoanalytic and learning approaches (Wachtel, 1977), or

even medical and behavioral interventions (Klerman, 1986).

Clinical Psychology and Basic Psychology

The material we discussed in this chapter is the application of many of the principles we have discussed up to this point. Basic neurophysiological processes are essential to understanding the operation of the drugs and surgery used by medically based practitioners. Research in animal learning and motivation has provided the basis of the behavioral approaches. Likewise, cognitive learning approaches have followed developments in the psychology of perception and cognition. Looking back to the most recent chapters, emotional insight therapies are based on concepts from the study of both normal and abnormal personality development. Looking ahead, the family and the community approaches are connected to the research on interpersonal and group processes we discuss in the book's upcoming chapters on social psychology.

By considering research on psychotherapy outcomes, we have also tried to stress another important point that arose in the first chapter. A basic understanding of research methodology is more than an academic requirement. If you or someone you know ever seeks psychological treatment, such an understanding can be a consumer tool. A basic knowledge of psychological research principles can therefore make us all better consumers of a commodity that chalks up a bill of $15 billion a year nationwide. ■

IN CONTEXT: TREATMENT OF DISORDERED BEHAVIOR

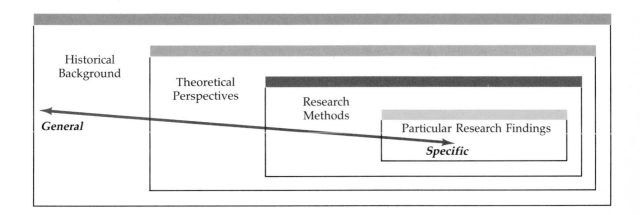

STUDY QUESTIONS

How can psychologists use knowledge about the causes of psychopathology to treat behavioral disorders?

How can we evaluate whether a therapeutic intervention really works?

Do some forms of treatment generally work better than others, or do some treatments work better with certain disorders?

HISTORICAL BACKGROUND

1. During the middle ages, proponents of **supernatural** models used exorcism and even torture to drive "evil spirits" from the body.

2. Medical doctors since the time of Hippocrates advocated rest, relaxation, and changes in diet as treatments for psychopathology.

3. During the last century, European physicians such as Charcot and Janet noted that some forms of psychological and physical disorder could be removed with hypnosis. These findings provided the basis for the psychoanalytic approach to treatment.

4. During the first half of this century, American psychologists applied concepts from the animal laboratory to treating disordered behavior.

MODERN THEORETICAL PERSPECTIVES

1. In attempting to treat the physical body, **biomedical** treatments use psychoactive drugs, psychosurgery, and electro-convulsive therapy (ECT).

2. **Insight** therapies use conversations with the therapist to understand unconscious roots of problem behaviors. Freudian **psychoanalysis** uses free association, dream analysis, interpretation, and analysis of transference to lead the client to an insightful understanding of repressed sexual and aggressive urges.

3. **Humanistic** approaches emphasize that people are basically positive and competent, and aim to improve people's self-perceptions and self-esteem. Carl Rogers's person-centered therapy involves a nondirective therapist who reflects back the client's feelings to get the person to accept negative and positive parts of the self. Encounter groups use honest feedback and expression of feelings to facilitate self-acceptance.

4. **Behavioral** approaches are based on principles of classical and operant conditioning. Systematic desensitization uses classical conditioning principles to gradually replace anxiety responses with relaxation. Aversive conditioning uses classical conditioning to produce an unpleasant response to an unacceptable stimulus, such as alcohol. Operant approaches use reward and shaping to train new desirable responses, and punishment and extinction to extinguish undesirable responses. Token economies apply operant principles to groups.

5. **Modelling** and **covert sensitization** techniques apply behavioral principles at the cognitive level, without direct reward or punishment to the client.

6. **Cognitive** treatments attempt to change people's maladaptive thought patterns. In **rational emotive therapy,** the therapist confronts the client's irrational beliefs with logical arguments. Recent cognitive learning approaches apply behavioral principles, such as self-reward, to change maladaptive thoughts.

7. **Social Systems** approaches to treatment focus on units larger than the single individual. **Family** therapists attempt to change family communication patterns, rules, and power alliances. **Community** therapists favor treatment outside of hospitals, in people's natural surroundings. Community approaches involve neighborhood crisis centers, training paraprofessionals, prevention programs, and working for social change to alleviate environmental causes of psychopathology.

8. The **interactionist** approach views psychopathology as the result of interactions between the environment, cognition, and organism. This view holds that no single approach to therapy has a monopoly on the "correct" treatment. Medical approaches focus on the organism, while cognitive, insight, and classical conditioning approaches focus on changing cognitive interpretations of the environment. Family and community treatments focus on changing problems in the objective environment itself. Finally, operant conditioning can focus either on changing the environment (by training parents or other reward agents) or changing the organism (by training the person in new skills).

RESEARCH METHODS

1. Much of the clinical literature has been based on **case studies** of individuals in therapy, such as Janet's (1898) treatment of Achille's "possession." Such cases are excellent ways to understand the processes used in different types of therapy, but are not too informative about possible beneficial outcomes of therapy. Any improvement in a particular case might be due to spontaneous improvements following other events in the client's life. Another problem in evaluating therapy is that almost any treatment will result in a **placebo** effect (an improvement due to faith in the therapy).

2. **Experimental** studies of the outcomes of therapy compare untreated controls or placebo-attention controls with people who have received actual treatment. An example is Gordon Paul's (1966) study of systematic desensitization.

3. **Meta-analysis** is a statistical technique for combining the results of several different studies (for instance, Shapiro and Shapiro, 1982). It helps researchers draw conclusions uncontaminated by the chance factors that might have influenced any single study.

RESEARCH FINDINGS AND SUMMARY

1. Researchers studying antihistamines during the 1940s accidentally discovered that certain drugs could alleviate schizophrenia. Another accidental finding indicated that severe depression could be alleviated with shock-induced seizures. Brain surgery can also change problem behaviors. Each of these medical approaches has costs associated with it. The costs must be weighed against potential benefits. Milder biomedical treatments include exercise and phototherapy (for seasonal affective disorder).

2. Encounter groups often have positive effects on participants, but sometimes lead to worsened symptoms in people who are already vulnerable. Verbal therapies also lead to occasional casualties, especially in people who are severely disturbed to begin with, and whose therapists are confrontive and challenging.

3. Experimental studies indicate that some form of treatment is better than none at all. Placebo effects account for much of the benefit.

4. Meta-analyses indicate that insight therapies are slightly better than placebo treatments, and significantly better than no treatment at all. Behavioral approaches are better than verbal therapies in studies done to date, though this may be due to the specific nature of problems they treat.

5. Some therapists are better than others. Characteristics of good therapists include genuineness, warmth, and the ability to inspire trust in the client.

6. Most treatments work better with some problems than with others. For instance, insight therapies work better with mildly anxious and depressed people than they do with schizophrenics.

ADDITIONAL READINGS

Corsini, R. J., 1984. ed. *Current psychotherapies,* 3rd ed. Itasca, IL: F. E. Peacock. A discussion of major current therapy techniques by prominent therapists from each school.

Endler, N. S. 1982. *Holiday of darkness: A psychologists's personal journey out of his depression.* New York: Praeger. A prominent psychology professor describes his personal experiences with depression and electroconvulsive therapy.

Frank, J. D. 1961. *Persuasion and healing: A comparative study of psychotherapy.* Baltimore, MD: Johns Hopkins Press. A classic volume, comparing psychological treatments to religious conversion.

Skinner, B. F. 1953. *Science and human behavior.* New York: MacMillan. A work that helped establish the behavioral approach to treatment. In it, Skinner describes how behavioral principles can be used to explain and modify behaviors in the normal and abnormal range.

Valenstein, E. S. 1986. *Great and desperate cures: The rise and decline of psychosurgery.* New York: Basic Books. A critical look at brain surgery.

Wedding, D., and Corsini, R. J., eds. 1979. *Great cases in psychotherapy.* Itasca, IL: F. E. Peacock. Includes a number of classic case studies; from Janet, Freud, and Mary Cover Jones through modern behavioral and family therapists.

Zilbergeld, B. 1983. *The shrinking of America: Myths of psychological change.* Boston: Little, Brown. A critical view of psychotherapy, in which the author argues against the prevalent notion that people with problems need to change themselves via therapy.

CHAPTER 17

ATTITUDES AND SOCIAL COGNITION

T
he human understanding when it has once adopted an opinion draws all things else to support and agree with it. And though there be a greater number and weight of instances to be found on the other side, yet these it either neglects and despises, or else by some distinction sets aside and rejects, in order that . . . its former conclusion may remain inviolate.

(Francis Bacon, 1620)

Turn to the "letters to the editor" column in almost any news periodical, on almost any day of the year, and you will observe a fascinating phenomenon. Different people can observe the actions of the same public figure or read the same account of a public event and come to opposite conclusions about what it all means. In 1987, the national news was buzzing with reports of a presidential aide's admissions that he had lied to the United States Congress. Colonel Oliver North had covered up a secret operation in which weapons were sold to Iran and the profits were used to finance a right wing counterrevolution in Nicaragua. After one national news magazine ran its report, several readers responded:

> How sad that we in the United States are so hard up for heroes that we have to make one out of Oliver North, a man who lied and deceived so that he could arm mercenaries who are killing civilians in Nicaragua. God help us. *(Sister Mary Rose Christy; Burlingame, California)*

> Colonel North stood up for his convictions and won't apologize. In this area of moral grayness and congressional vacillation, America needs more men like him. *(Steven Sullivan; Fairfax, Virginia)*

> *(Newsweek, August 10, 1987)*

In this instance, the same man's behavior is interpreted as proudly heroic by one person and viciously deceptive by another. The processes by which different people use the same evidence to come to such different conclusions, which fascinated Francis Bacon almost four centuries ago, have recently been the focus of research in the area of **social cognition** (Fiske and Taylor, 1991; Sherman, Judd, and Park, 1989; Wyer and Srull, 1986). Social cognition is the field of psychology that examines how we pay attention to, interpret, and remember social events such as Colonel North's congressional testimony, an encounter with someone of a different race, or a friend's passing remark about your outfit.

Bacon suggested that our interpretations of new evidence are biased to fit with our previously formed opinions. In reading the letters from Sister Mary Rose and Mr. Sullivan, one suspects that each of the letter writers had different political opinions even before reading about North's confessions. In fact, North's behavior polarized the political right and left. Patrick Buchanan, a conservative columnist, suggested that North's activities were part of a noble attempt to prevent "the enemies of the United States" from consolidating "a military beachhead on the mainland of North America," but that he was being victimized by Democrats in United States Congress who "wanted to slowly bleed Ronald Reagan of his popularity, to break his presidency" (Buchanan, 1987). Gore Vidal, a liberal novelist, saw the same events very differently:

Perhaps the most startling aspect of this whole affair has been the fact that no one seems particularly troubled. Congress is thrilled by the attention but its members refuse to lift the lid on anything important . . . Were arms flown by the agency to the contras in Nicaragua? And were those planes then filled with cocaine for the return journey? Of course only a communist would ask such a question. Meanwhile, Marines are casually sacrificed in Lebanon by a government with no morality and an officer corps with no sense; the President compulsively tells lies on television as he has done throughout his entire political career, and no one minds because he has such a nice smile.

(Vidal, 1987)

As did Bacon, social cognition researchers believe that our interpretations of social events are colored by pre-existing **attitudes** (Zimbardo and Leippe, 1991; Zanna and Rempel, 1988). An attitude is the tendency to respond in a particular way toward certain issues (abortion, military spending), people (George Bush; Saddam Hussein), objects (handguns; motorcycles), or events (St. Patrick's Day; the invasion of Kuwait). Attitudes are partly cognitions—the belief that Reagan was a compulsive liar, for instance—but they also involve emotions. Buchanan had positive feelings about North, while Vidal's feelings were negative. Attitudes are the stuff of the surveys commonly reported by the press. For instance, after North's admissions a Gallup poll found that 44 percent of a national sample of adults had very positive reactions to him. Those respondents felt that North was "a patriot and a hero." On the other hand, some people had a very negative reaction, and 20 percent thought that he should be indicted and tried on criminal charges (*Newsweek*, July 20, 1987), as he eventually was. Psychologists who study attitudes are interested not only in how our attitudes influence the way we think, but also in how those attitudes relate to the way we behave. For instance, can we guess from their attitudes whether Buchanan and Vidal voted for Republican George Bush or Democrat Michael Dukakis in the election that followed the debate over Colonel North?

One reason we devote so much attention to interpreting social events is that we want to understand what caused them. In this chapter we will also consider another aspect of social cognition—how we attribute responsibility for social events. The term **attribution** is used to describe the cognitive process of deciding who or what caused a particular event (Kelley and Michela, 1980; Ross and Fletcher, 1985). If we ask "Why did Oliver North lie to Congress?" we are searching for a cause to which we can attribute North's behavior. Was North responsible for his own illegal activities, or should they be blamed on his superiors, including George Bush and Ronald Reagan? After North's testimony, 81 percent of the public felt that he was still lying to Congress, even in his new "admissions." However, the public differed in their explanation of why he was lying. Fifteen percent believed that he was doing it to protect himself, while 53 percent believed that he was doing it to protect his superiors. As we will see, one important attributional question concerns this issue of personal responsibility.

In this chapter, then, we will discuss people's inner reactions to other people, including both cognitive and affective (emotional) reactions. After searching for the historical roots of the research on

Interpreting events. In 1987, when Colonel Oliver North admitted that he lied to the U.S. Congress about selling arms to Iran and using the money to finance an illegal war in Nicaragua, some interpreted his actions as inexcusable treason. Others, like this man, interpreted the same behavior as eminently patriotic. Social cognition researchers study how people's attitudes influence their interpretation of new information about people and social issues.

these inner reactions, we will examine social information processing, focusing on biases in the way we attend to, encode, and remember "the facts." Following this, we will discuss the complex cognitive processes involved in making causal attributions, and we will examine research on attitude formation and change. We will also consider how the "cold" cognitive and "hot" attitudinal processes interact with one another. Finally, we will show how these processes fit with other psychological processes as part of a whole human organism adapting to its environment.

HISTORICAL BACKGROUND:
Early Studies of Social Perception

Research on attitudes and social cognition is rooted in basic experimental psychology. As we described earlier, early structuralist psychologists tried to develop mental equivalents of the thermometer, using psychophysical methods to study sensations like warmth and cold. Around the turn of the century, other psychologists used similar techniques to study the components of intelligence. In the 1920s, intelligence researcher Louis Thurstone began using these mental measurement techniques in surveys of attitudes toward different ethnic groups (Jones, 1985). For

instance, Thurstone and Chave (1929) asked subjects to judge whether a number of statements about the Chinese were different from one another. The researchers used people's judgments to arrange the statements into a sort of thermometer for measuring attitudes towards the Chinese. As shown in Table 17.1, for instance, the statement "The Chinese are superior to all other races" had a scale value of .5 (highly positive), "The Chinese are different but not inferior" had a scale value of 5.2 (neutral), and the statement "I hate the Chinese" was rated as 11.5 (highly negative). Using these ratings, Thurstone and his colleagues could compare different people's attitudes towards the Chinese as we might compare temperatures that range from hot to lukewarm to cold.

TABLE 17.1 Some Items from a Thurstone Scale Measuring Attitudes Towards the Chinese

If you were a subject in Thurstone's research you would have been asked to indicate your agreement or disagreement with the following items, by marking a check mark (√) if you agreed with the statement, and a cross (x) if you disagreed. The scale value (left column) was not included with the original questionnaire. Low scale values mean that an item indicates positive attitudes, high scale values indicate negative attitudes.

.5	1. The Chinese are superior to all other races.
1.4	2. Chinese people have a refinement and depth of feeling that you don't find anywhere else.
2.8	3. The more I know the Chinese the better I like them.
3.5	4. I like the Chinese.
4.7	5. The Chinese are pretty decent.
5.2	6. The Chinese are different but not inferior.
6.5	7. I have no particular love nor hate for the Chinese.
7.7	8. Although I respect some of their qualities, I could never consider a Chinese person as my friend.
9.4	9. I don't see how anyone could ever like a Chinese person.
11.5	10. I hate the Chinese.

Based on Thurstone (1931).

The Gestalt school of perception research was also imported from experimental psychology to the study of social reactions (Rock, 1990). The Gestalt influence on social psychology had a strong influence on the study of **social perception,** or the processes by which we organize and interpret information about other people. As you may recall, Gestalt psychologists held that the brain exerts a strong influence on the perception of physical objects, organizing incomplete external stimuli into an aesthetically whole "good form." This top down approach to perception was brought to social psychology by Kurt Lewin, who came to the United States in 1933 as a refugee from Nazi Germany. He held that someone's response to a social situation depended more upon that person's phenomenological experience of that situation than on the actual objective situation. Whether you perceive a meal in a restaurant as a series of interactions with an unpleasant waiter, an interminable delay in getting your food, or a romantic interlude will depend on whether your present needs make unfriendliness, hunger, or flirtation most prominent.

Fritz Heider was another student of European Gestalt psychology who migrated to the United States. He brought with him two theories of social cognition that proved to be quite influential in this country. First, his **balance theory** addressed people's need to have consistency between their different attitudes (Heider, 1946; 1958). This idea was directly based on Gestalt notions of "good form," and assumed that the brain imposed balance on our attitudes because balance is more aesthically pleasing than imbalance. To Heider, the basic unit of social cognition was a triad involving a perceiver, (P); another person, (O); and some object about which they both hold attitudes, (X). As shown in Figure 17.1, P, O, and X are connected by lines with either a positive or a negative valence. A triad is balanced if all the signs multiply out to a positive sign. So, for instance, if you like

FIGURE 17.1 Fritz Heider's balance theory. Heider's theory postulated balance triads that included the perceiver (P), another person (O), and some attitude object (X). A structure was balanced if all three signs multiplied out to a positive sign, as shown in the second row. Imbalance (row 3) occurs when the signs come out negative, as when someone likes another person who disagrees with her about an important issue.

BASIC COGNITIVE STRUCTURE

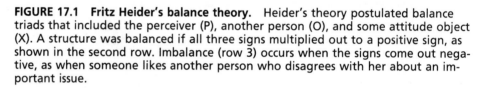

BALANCED STRUCTURES

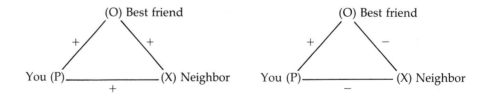

UNBALANCED STRUCTURES

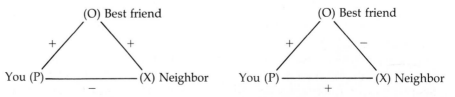

your next door neighbor, and she likes your best friend, the triad will be balanced. Likewise, if both you and your best friend dislike your neighbor the triad would still be balanced, since the two negatives would cancel to a positive valence. An example of an imbalanced triad would be if your best friend liked a neighbor whom you despised. You would then experience an unbalanced cognitive state. Balance could be restored by altering one of the relationships. For instance, you could convince your friend of the neighbor's despicable qualities. If the friend liked the neighbor too much, however, you might reconsider your judgment of one of them.

The other important theory that Heider developed was **attribution theory** (Heider, 1944), which deals with people's attributions about social events. When we see someone do something of social consequence, such as North's sale of arms to the Iranians, we ask whether the cause of that behavior was in the person (an internal attribution) or in the environment (an external attribution). Was North personally responsible for the controversial decision (internal attribution), or was he just carrying out orders from a superior (external attribution)? Even if we decide that someone is personally responsible, there are varying levels to which we will hold him or her accountable. For instance, if North just happened to be indirectly involved in actions carried out by his superiors he may be responsible by *association*. If he sold the arms, but did so because out of heart-felt empathy for the hostages rather than a desire to play "soldier of fortune," then his behavior may be seen as *justifiable*. These distinctions between levels of causality are very important in courts of law. For instance, a jury can agree that a defendant killed someone, but may recommend very different penalties depending on whether the surrounding evidence favors a verdict of self-defense, involuntary manslaughter, or first degree murder.

Social psychologist Solomon Asch brought to social psychology the Gestalt concept that the whole is more than the sum of its parts. Asch (1946) discovered that the exact same social description of a person will be interpreted very differently depending on the order in which it is presented. For instance, Asch asked subjects to form an impression of someone who was "intelligent, industrious, impulsive, critical, stubborn, and envious". Others read about someone who was "envious, stubborn, critical, impulsive, industrious, and intelligent". Although the second list contains the same information as the first list, people who read the list in the second order formed a substantially more negative impression. This is an example of a **primacy effect**—the tendency for our first impression of a person to bias how we interpret what he or she does later. Being critical may connote discernment and perception in someone who made a first impression as an intelligent and industrious person. In someone who first impressed us as being envious and stubborn, on the other hand, information that he or she is critical would be taken to mean cynical and nagging.

The behaviorists also had an influence on social psychology (Lott and Lott, 1985). Although they were more interested in such overt social behaviors as aggression (which we will discuss in the next chapter), some theorists did apply the learning model to the development of attitudes. In 1958, for instance, Arthur Staats and C. K. Staats did an experiment in which such unpleasant affective words as bitter or ugly were associated with the name of one nationality (either Dutch or Swedish), and such pleasant affective words as "happy" were presented along with the name of the other nationality. Staats and Staats found that subjects later rated the two nationalities in line with the affective quality of the associated words. They explained the result as being due to the operation of classical conditioning; that is, the nationality came to automatically elicit the feelings associated with the negative or positive words.

In recent years, many social psychologists have used information-processing models from cognitive psychology to explain attitudes and social cognition (for instance, Hummert, Crockett, and Kemper, 1990; Judd, Drake, Downing, and Krosnick, 1991). According to those who adopt the information-processing perspective, our social judgments are determined by the same limitations on attention, storage, and retrieval discussed in Chapter 7 (see for instance, Fiedler, 1991; Martin, Seta, and Crelia, 1990). Other researchers have been using the concepts born in experimental studies of categorization discussed in Chapter 7 to help understand how we think about social concepts ranging from personality traits (John, Hampson, and Goldberg, 1991) to love (Aron, Aron, Tudor, and Nelson, 1991; Fehr and Russell, 1991). As we will see, there is some controversy about whether people process information about people in the same way that they process information about objects or animals. Whatever the answer to specific questions such as this, we will see that the research on attitudes and social cognition clearly demonstrates an increasingly integrated understanding of the connections among different psychological processes, from psychophysiology to emotion to social interaction. ∎

SOCIAL INFORMATION PROCESSING

We are continuously confronted by a tremendous amount of social information—in the gossip we hear in the student union; in the facial expressions, dress styles, comments, and nonverbal behaviors of the people we talk to in the halls; in the news we hear on the radio; in the graffiti on the bathroom wall; and so on. Because of the limits of our brain's information-processing capacity, we can only pay attention to a small number of those social facts. Even when we have focused our attention on a particular bit of information, such as a smile on a door-to-door saleswoman, we have many memories with which to associate it—a friend who looked like the saleswoman, a memory of having bought something quite useless from a door-to-door salesperson just last week, and so on. We do not dwell on a single fact all day, but make only one or two selective associations to it. Which associations we make influence how we encode, or label, the information. For instance, the same smile can be encoded as a sign of friendliness or as a manipulative gesture. Finally, we do not remember every comment we hear. If the saleswoman tells you that she is from Appleton, Wisconsin, you might not remember that half an hour later. However, if your best friend happens to be from Appleton, you may remember the salewoman's hometown a week later when you next talk to your friend. Researchers who adopt an information-processing model (discussed in Chapter 7) have studied how various **selection biases** influence social cognition at three levels;

1. attention and information search,

2. encoding and storage, and

3. retrieval from memory.

We describe each of these processes in the sections that follow, and show how they can influence our social interactions.

ATTENDING TO AND SELECTING SOCIAL INFORMATION

How do we select from the flood of social information a manageable trickle to which we can devote our attention? To begin with, we devote inordinate attention to especially striking people. This attention to noticeable or striking people is called a **salience effect**. This extra attention results in the

Striking People

salient person's behavior being scrutinized more carefully and remembered better than those of most other people. For instance Shelley Taylor and her colleagues have found that people who have "solo status" in a group are seen as being more influential in that group (Taylor and Fiske, 1978). If a person is the only black in a group of whites, or the only woman in a group of men, other people tend to form more extreme opinions about his or her behavior. In a later section, we will discuss how this salience effect might contribute to prejudice.

We also search for social information in a way that favors our existing biases. For instance, if I suspect that someone is selfish or unfriendly I will look for behavioral evidence that I am right. Mark Snyder and William Swann studied this tendency in a series of experiments in which students were given the task of testing a hypothesis about a woman's personality. Half of the subjects were asked to find out whether she was a typical extravert, and were informed:

> Extraverts are typically outgoing, sociable, energetic, confident, talkative, and enthusiastic. Generally confident and relaxed in social situations, this type of person rarely has trouble making conversation with others. This type of person makes friends quickly and easily and is usually able to make a favorable impression on others.

Others were asked to find out whether the person was a typical introvert ("shy, timid, reserved, quiet, distant, and retiring"). Some were led to believe that the person was indeed an example of the type that had been described to them, while others were only told to check to see whether she fit the category. In all instances, even when there was no special reason to believe that she was a member of the category, people chose questions that would tend to confirm their original hypotheses. People testing the hypothesis that she was an extravert were more likely to choose such questions as "What would you do if you wanted to liven things up at a party?" while those testing the introvert hypothesis chose such questions as "What factors make it hard for you to really open up to people?" As Snyder and Swann (1978) point out, questions like these are likely to mistakenly confirm our initial biases. If you ask an introvert what she would do to liven up a party, she will not tell you about what she would do to avoid a party. Instead, she will answer your question, and tell you how she could liven up a party (without mentioning that she probably never *would*). Thus, you might mistakenly conclude that she was extraverted. Likewise, if you ask anyone a question about what makes it hard to relate to others, even an extravert will give you information that makes him or her look introverted. After all, almost everyone has had at least some difficulties relating to other people.

This tendency for our initial opinions to bias our future search for information is called the confirmation bias. Because people seek to confirm their initial beliefs, first impressions are particularly important. The confirmation bias can be particularly troublesome with negative impressions, which are especially resistant to change (Rothbart and John, 1985). On the other hand, people are not always biased in the way in which they collect information about other people (Skov and Sherman, 1986; Trope and Bassok, 1983). If we have no particularly strong ideas to begin with, if we make up our own questions, and if we are motivated to be accurate, we will be more likely to seek truly diagnostic information about another person (Dallas and Baron, 1985; Neuberg, 1989).

INTERPRETING SOCIAL INFORMATION

After you choose which aspects of another person on which to focus, you must interpret what you see. Even if two people may pay full attention to the exact same information, they may still respond

FIGURE 17.2 Is this man's expression a sinister smirk, or a kindly half-smile? Subjects in one study were shown a photo of a similar neutral-looking face. They judged the man to be smirking if they thought he was a Nazi, but to be smiling if they thought he was a member of the anti-Nazi underground who risked his life to save Jews from the concentration camps.

differently if they process the information differently. For instance, students at the University of Oregon were shown a picture of a man named Kurt Walden. When told that Walden was a Nazi Gestapo leader who conducted "experiments" on concentration camp inmates, the students interpreted his facial expression as cruel and frowning. However, other students looked at the same face but were told that Kurt Walden was a courageous leader of the anti-Nazi underground, who saved thousands of Jewish lives. Those students saw his expression not as cruel at all, but as warm and kindly (Rothbart and Birrell, 1977). (See Figure 17.2.)

In short, our beliefs about other people can influence how we mentally encode other aspects of their appearance. The same ambiguous facial expression will mean something completely different depending on what we are expecting to see. If we think the pretty, quiet young woman in our art history class is shy, we will interpret her gaze aversion differently than if we think she is a snob.

INTERPRETATIONS CONFIRM OUR INITIAL BIASES

When United States President George Bush gave his views on energy conservation, do you think he was being sincere or insincere? In addition to influencing our interpretations of simple facial expressions, our pre-existing views on a topic also influence how we interpret, or *encode,* more complex behaviors, such as a presidential speech. Of those who watched the first televised presidential debates between John Kennedy and Richard Nixon, 71 percent of those who originally favored Kennedy thought that Kennedy won. On the other hand, only 17 percent of viewers who started out in favor of Nixon gave the debate to Kennedy. That result was not peculiar to the Kennedy–Nixon debates (Kinder and Sears, 1985). During the 1988 Presidential election, a Gallup poll after a debate between Dukakis and Bush indicated that 80 percent of those who originally favored Dukakis thought he came out ahead. Bush supporters saw the same debate differently—73 percent of them said that they were *more* favorable towards Bush after they watched it (Newsweek poll, Oct. 3, 1988).

When a team of researchers at Stanford University systematically examined how students weighed the evidence about a social issue, they found a surprising lack of objectivity. Participants in the study were undergraduates at Stanford University who had previously completed a questionnaire that included several items about the death penalty. The researchers chose those students with the most favorable and least favorable initial opinions about capital punishment. These students were asked to read two studies of capital punishment, several criticisms of those studies, and responses to the criticisms by the study authors. (Such an interchange between researchers and critics is common in the scientific literature.) After reading the interchanges, the students were asked to use their "evaluative powers" in thinking about each study, what the critics had to say, and whether the research supported or opposed capital punishment. In all cases, they read one study that favored capital punishment and one that opposed it. For instance:

> PRO: Kroner and Phillips (1977) compared murder rates for the year before and the year after adoption of capital punishment in 14 states. In 11 of the 14 states, murder rates were *lower after* adoption of the death penalty. The research supports the deterrent effect of the death penalty.
> CON: Palmer and Crandall (1977) compared murder rates in 10 pairs of neighboring states with different capital punishment laws. In eight of the 10 pairs, murder rates were *higher* in the state *with* capital punishment. This research opposes the deterrent effect of the death penalty.

(Lord, Ross, and Lepper, 1979)

After reading each study, students heard criticisms of the research, and rebuttals of those criticisms from the authors. Given that the students had just heard evidence on *both* sides of the issue, they should have become less extreme in their opinions. However, just the opposite occurred. The students who originally opposed capital punishment became even more opposed, whereas those who had originally favored the death penalty now favored it even more. Why? It appears that students focused on the strengths of the evidence that supported their initial views, and on the weaknesses of the evidence that opposed them.

If someone has strong feelings about an issue he or she may view an objective opinion as biased in the opposite direction. When one team of researchers asked pro-Israeli students to watch several network news reports of the 1982 Beirut massacre, the vast majority thought that the news reports were biased against Israel. Pro-Arab students also thought that the reports were distorted, but in the opposite direction—the majority of these students thought that the reports were biased in favor of Israel (Vallone, Ross, and Lepper, 1985).

This tendency to bias interpretations of controversial information is even found among scientists, who have had years of training in the art of objectivity and open-mindedness. For instance, Michael Mahoney (1977) found that the editors of scientific journals were more likely to accept articles that supported their pet theories, and to find the methodological "flaws" in studies that opposed their viewpoint.

If scientists with years of training in objective and analytical thinking are subject to confirmation biases, is there any way to overcome them? In a replication of the capital punishment study, Lord and his colleagues found that an appeal by the experimenter to be "as objective and unbiased as possible" was to no avail. However, the researchers did find one technique for overcoming biased information processing. Some students were asked to consider what they would have said if the studies had come out in the opposite direction. Thus, if you read a study showing that capital punishment was effective, you would be asked to think about what you would have said if the study's results indicated instead that it was ineffective. Those students, who considered the opposite possibilities, were much more likely to evenly consider the evidence on both sides (Lord, Lepper, and Preston, 1984). This study contains a formula for increasing your open-mindedness: Before jumping to a conclusion, consider how you would feel about the evidence if it favored the opposite viewpoint. This is particularly important to do if the evidence goes against your original beliefs.

RECENT EVENTS PRIME PARTICULAR INTERPRETATIONS

The way we encode social information is not influenced only by our long-cherished opinions. How we respond to a new fact or a new person may simply be a function of what we have been thinking about recently (Higgins, 1989; Sherman, Mackie, and Driscoll, 1990; Wyer and Srull, 1986). The tendency for recent events to influence interpretation is called **priming.** As an example, students who are asked to make sentences out of lists such as "arm, leg, break, his," will later rate a stranger as hostile if sentences they read earlier "primed the pump" for thinking about hostility. Interestingly, some research suggests that this priming effect can even occur at an unconscious level. Students in one study were exposed to hostile words, but at a speed that was too fast to allow them to recognize the words. Nevertheless, students exposed to these subliminal stimuli later rated a stranger as more hostile than did subjects exposed to nonhostile words (Bargh and Pietromonaco, 1982). In another study, subliminal aggressive stimuli were found to increase competitive behavior among those students already inclined to be competitive (Neuberg, 1988). In sum, the way we encode new evidence about other people and social issues is biased by both our long-term attitudes and stimuli that prime us to pay special attention to one kind of evidence over another.

RETRIEVING SOCIAL INFORMATION

Imagine a world in which history is rewritten every time the state's policies change, as was the case in George Orwell's *1984*. Evidence from studies of how we retrieve our memories about ourselves and others suggest that all of us rewrite history a little (Ross, 1989). Even after two people have noticed the same event and interpreted it in the same way, they may nevertheless remember it differently in the light of new information. For instance, imagine that two roommates both meet the same friendly man at a picnic. One woman begins to date the man, but he later drops her to date and eventually marry the other. The first woman may think back to the meeting at the picnic, and clearly recall that the man seemed a little dishonest from the beginning. Her roommate, on the other hand, may remember only how sincere and sweet he seemed.

One study shows how this tendency to rewrite memory can reinforce stereotypes (Snyder and Uranowitz, 1978). Students read about a woman's dating history one week, and were asked to recall the details a week later. Before beginning the recall task, however, half the subjects "learned" that she had later become a lesbian and forsaken men completely, and the other half was informed that she later became happily married. The results showed that those who now believed that she was a lesbian remembered her as having less positive relationships with men in high school. On the other hand, those who later heard that she got married "remembered" her as dating more than did those who believed that she became a lesbian (Snyder and Uranowitz, 1978). Our changed impressions about people may lead us to remember their pasts differently then, and can sometimes strengthen stereotypes.

Our memories about ourselves can also be altered by new beliefs. Michael Ross and his colleagues (1981) induced a group of students to question the cultural truism that exercise is healthy. Students read a statement that the number of injuries and coronary complications from exercise far outweighed any benefits. One group was told that the statement was written by a "medical expert on exercise." Another group read the same statement, but was told that it came from a less credible source—the president of the local "fat is beautiful" club. As you might expect, students who heard the message from the medical expert were most convinced by the message. Afterwards, the students were asked to recall how much exercise they themselves had engaged in during the last month. Those who had been convinced that exercise was unhealthy rewrote their own histories to fit with their new beliefs: They recalled significantly less exercise than the comparison group. As we noted in the first chapter, this tendency for people to bias their memory searches sometimes causes problems for survey researchers. For instance, national health officials occasionally poll representative samples of the United States population about their smoking habits. When they ask people to estimate the number of cigarettes they smoke, it leads to an estimate of about 400 billion cigarettes smoked each year (Hall, 1985). However, the actual number sold is 600 million. People are either lying, or, perhaps more likely, they are biasing their memory search in the socially desirable direction.

Although we have discussed attention, encoding, and retrieval separately, they are not usually distinct processes (Hastie and Park, 1986; Wyer and Srull, 1986). If you do not pay much attention to the Presidential debates, then you will neither encode what the candidates are saying nor remember much about them. If you listen to a speech by your favorite candidate, focusing on the candidate is likely to jog memories of previous things he or she said, which may in turn influence how you interpret what you are hearing now. In the next section we will discuss the process of making social inferences, which often involves connections between attention, encoding, and long-term memory.

RESEARCH AND APPLICATION:
Prejudice and Stereotyping

The term **prejudice** literally means "prejudgment." In his classic work on *The Nature of Prejudice* (1954) Gordon Allport defined it as an unwarranted and inflexible generalization about a group or a particular member of that group. As we will discuss in the next two chapters, prejudiced opinions can stem from racist personality characteristics, or from direct competition between two groups. However, Allport believed that prejudices often stem from normal cognitive processes, including the ones we have been discussing in this chapter.

Psychologists became particularly interested in prejudice after World War II, when people began to realize the horrors of German treatment of the Jews. Writing in that period, Allport documented that prejudice was hardly limited to German Nazis, but seemed to be universal. He noted that Poles referred to the Germans as "swine," and to their Ukranian neighbors as "reptiles." During the second world war, says Allport, Englishmen said of Americans: "The only trouble with the Yanks is that they are overpaid, oversexed, and over here." Look around you, and you will see that modern-day Americans have their own prejudices. Some are based on racial distinctions—some whites see all blacks as lazy; some blacks see all whites as greedy and exploitive. Others are based on social class (white trash, rich snobs), ethnicity (heavy-drinking Irish, penny-pinching Scots), or even geographical roots (pushy New Yorkers, flaky Californians). Some prejudices divide people in the same families, such as the stereotypes based on gender (incompetent women drivers, testosterone-poisoned males). Like the Poles and Germans, many Americans also show strong prejudices against the citizens of other countries with which we are in conflict—from Japanese and Koreans to Cubans and Russians to Iranians and Iraquis over the last few decades. In Chapter 19, we will discuss how those inflexible generalizations can fuel further international hostilities.

Many modern researchers agree with Allport's claim that normal cognitive biases can lead to prejudice. In this section, we will consider how normal limitations on social information processing of the sort we have been discussing in the preceding pages can contribute to these occasionally dangerous prejudgments of the members of other groups.

Biased Attention to Unique People

As we noted earlier, unique individuals draw more attention than do the other members of groups. Because observers pay more attention to the outstanding individual, they make more extreme judgments about him or her (Taylor and Fiske, 1978). If a black man in a group of white women is pleasant and likeable, he will be praised more than if he were part of the group's majority. On the other hand, if the unique person is unpleasant or obnoxious, he or she will be disproportionately condemned. One study showed how this can interact with sex stereotypes. A lone man in a group of woman was perceived as prominent, and therefore a good leader, while a lone woman in a group of men was treated as an intruder (Crocker and McGraw, 1984).

One team of researchers examined how this uniqueness phenomenon applied to race relations. The interviewers asked suburban residents in predominantly white neighborhoods whether there had been any important changes in the neighborhood during the last year or so. If a black family had moved into the neighborhood in the last month, 80 percent of the respondents mentioned the new family. This might just indicate that any new family on the block is salient, though. In fact, 76 percent mentioned it if a new white family had moved in during the last month. On the other hand, if a new white family had moved in three months earlier, only 37 percent of the neighbors mentioned it. But 76 percent still mentioned a new black family three months later, indicating that they were still noticeable (Hamilton and Bishop, 1976). Simply labeling someone as a member of a deviant group such as the Ku Klux Klan leads people to notice things about him or her that they would otherwise have ignored (Langer and Imber, 1980).

Solo individuals are aware of their own unique status, and therefore particularly conscious of the group they are in and how they are performing in it (Frabel, Blackstone, and Scherbaum, 1990; Lord, Saenz, and Godfrey, 1987). One unfortunate consequence of this increased self-consciousness is that the unique individual has less cognitive workspace to devote to other tasks, and may therefore perform less adequately (Saenz and Lord, 1989). These findings have implications for "token" minorities on the job. If a token black woman in an office spends too much energy worrying about what her coworkers will think of her she will do less well on the job, and therefore inadvertently confirm the very prejudices she was hoping to disconfirm. This is one way in which a prejudiced expectation can become a **self-fulfilling prophecy**—a belief that was originally false but leads to behaviors that make it come true (Merton, 1957; Miller and Turnbull, 1986).

People pay attention not only to unique people but also to unique events. If we hear of someone stealing an old woman's purse, the story commands our attention. When the crime is committed by a member of a minority, we are especially likely to remember this doubly unique event. Several studies indicate that when members of small groups have a few deviant members, people perceive an **illusory correlation** between group membership and deviance (Hamilton and Gifford, 1976; Hamilton and Sherman, 1989). This means that they see the two things as going together even when they do not. Although heterosexuals may be just as likely to molest children as are homosexuals, an act of child molestation by a homosexual draws special attention, and observers may incorrectly come to see the two features (homosexuality and pedophilia) as going together. Such illusory correlations are not inevitable and are most likely to occur when the observer is uninvolved with the group he or she is observing, as in the case of a white suburbanite who reads about Cubans in the inner city (Schaller and Maass, 1989). It takes less effort to categorize someone with a group stereotype than to pay careful attention to his or her individuating characteristics, and the research indicates that we take the easy route unless we are motivated to do otherwise (Fiske and Neuberg, 1990)

Memory bias and stereotyping. Upon seeing a group of "low-riders" such as those pictured here, an Anglo-American with only occasional contact with Mexican-Americans may store a biased memory representation for Chicanos in general, and assume that they all drive flashy cars.

Effects of Interpretation and Memory Bias on Prejudice

People make fine distinctions about members of their own groups, but tend to clump the members of outgroups together (Linville, Salovey, and Fischer, 1986). To another Mexican American, fellow Chicanos are a diverse lot, some tough, some timid; some flashy dressers, some conservatively suited; some emotional, some apparently passionless. However, an Anglo-American may assume that all Chicanos are like the salient gang members he has seen driving their low-rider cars down the boulevards of West Los Angeles: tough, flashy, and passionate. People have particular difficulty in making distinctions between members of other racial groups. Psychologist Jack Brigham and his colleagues have done several studies showing how this can lead to unfair treatment of criminal suspects. In a line-up composed of white people, white witnesses do a reasonably good job of picking out the one they saw commit a crime. However, they are more likely to make mistakes in distinguishing between blacks in a line-up. This is not because blacks are less variable than whites. Black witnesses make fewer mistakes in distinguishing between blacks, but more mistakes in distinguishing between white suspects (Brigham and Malpass, 1985). To members of one group, then, the members of other groups tend to all look alike.

Even those people who try to be unprejudiced seem to have some of the same simplistic reactions to members of minority groups as do prejudiced people. The difference is that prejudiced people simply may not bother to suppress these reactions. If the stereotypes are triggered at a level too subtle for subjects to be aware of, both prejudiced and nonprejudiced whites give evidence of similar cognitive associations to blacks, as demonstrated in a study by Patricia Devine (1989). Subjects in those studies were exposed to either words related to blacks (such as "Negro," "Africa," "jazz," and "blues"), or to more neutral words (such as "water," "people," and "television"). Although the words were presented too rapidly to be recognized, subjects who had been exposed to words associated with blacks later judged a man in a story as being relatively more hostile than did control subjects. That nonconscious prejudicial effect held for both prejudiced and nonprejudiced people alike. The researcher suggests that it is important to distinguish between knowledge of stereotypes and acceptance of stereotypes. It is the acceptance of the stereotype, according to Devine, that defines prejudice.

People's prior beliefs can influence the way in which they interpret ambiguous evidence. If a white expects blacks to act aggressively, he may interpret a playful shove as hostile (Duncan, 1976; Sagar and Schofield, 1980). One researcher showed whites a film in which a white and a black had a heated discussion, and the black shoved the white. Other subjects watched similar interactions in which the race of the man being shoved and the man doing the shoving varied. A majority of the subjects viewed an act as hostile when a black man did it, but only a small percentage saw the same act as hostile if the perpetrator were white (Duncan, 1976). This research suggests that the same behavior may be interpreted very differently depending upon who is doing it.

In sum, four decades of research have confirmed Gordon Allport's argument that prejudice often stems from normal cognitive processes. Members of other groups stand out because they are unique, which emphasizes any small differences in behavior and can lead to self-fulfilling prophecies. In the interest of cognitive efficiency, we may take particular notice of behavior that fits our stereotypes, and thus have an easier time remembering events and people that fit those stereotypes.

Those cognitive biases may also contribute to biases in the process of making causal attributions. As we just discussed, observers impute a different underlying motive if a black and a white person make the same ambiguous gesture. When the white did the pushing, observers were more likely to interpret it as an attempt at humor. The question of how people go from observed behaviors to underlying motives is the topic of the next section, which deals with attributional processes. As we will see, the cognitive processing biases we have discussed work hand-in-hand with some of the biases in attribution. ■

ATTRIBUTIONAL PROCESSES

Instead of viewing humans as computers that process information more or less automatically, attribution researchers view us as amateur scientists who sort through the available information about behavior to answer the question "Why?" The most crucial distinction we make when we try to explain people's behavior is when we decide if this individual was personally responsible for what just happened (internal), or if the event was caused by something in the environment (external). Listen to a discussion about almost any controversial crime and you will hear people discussing these questions about intention. When the news about the involvement of Oliver North and Reagan's other aides in the Iran–Contra scandal broke, the Gallup pollsters asked people; "Who do you think is more at fault for the failures of the Iran–Contra affair, the President himself or his top advisors and aides?" Given the same events, incidentally, people differed in their attributions—36 percent thought Reagan most responsible, but 52

percent gave the bulk of blame to his advisors. (The remaining 12 percent were unsure where to ascribe responsibility.)

IS THE PERSON OR THE SITUATION RESPONSIBLE?

Situational pressures can either *augment* or *discount* internal attributions (Kelley, 1972). That is, situational pressures that favor a particular behavior—a salesperson, being friendly, for instance—will discount (or diminish) the importance that we assign to internal traits and motives (Hansen and Hall, 1985). When the insurance salesperson smiles and asks about our family, we assume her friendliness is due to the pressure to sell, rather than to a real liking for us. On the other hand, when situational pressures oppose a particular behavior (being jovial at a funeral, for example) they will augment or amplify the significance of internal traits and motives. When a waiter tells us that the day's fish is not very good and recommends a cheaper dish, we tend to assume that he really means it because the situational pressures go against it.

In a classic experiment demonstrating how behavior has more meaning when it goes against the situation, students were asked to evaluate the personality of someone who was applying for a job that required either an extravert or an introvert. Some subjects read about a man applying for a job on a submarine. The job description indicated that it would require working in cramped quarters with no privacy for long periods, and that an extravert would therefore be best suited for it. Other subjects read that the man was applying for a job as an astronaut, where he would have to spend long periods alone in a small space capsule. The astronaut's job description therefore called for an introvert. Half the time the man described his personality as fitting the job description. For instance, he said that he was an introvert when he was applying to be an astronaut. The other half of the subjects read about a man who claimed that his personality went against the job description. For instance, he said he was an introvert when he was applying for a job as a submariner. The researchers found that subjects believed the person's self-description most when it went against the job specifications (Jones, Davis, and Gergen, 1961). In short, when a person's behavior simply goes along with what is expected, it says less about that person than does a behavior that flies in the face of convention.

In making attributions, however, people sometimes ignore the power of situational pressures (Fleming, Darley, Hilton, and Kojetin, 1990; Gilbert and Jones, 1986; Fein, Hilton, and Miller, 1990). If you see the same librarian every day in the library you may assume that he is a naturally quiet person, whereas if you see his sister in her job as athletic director you may assume that she is naturally loud. However, even a loud person stays constrained in a library, and even a quiet person needs to speak up when coaching an athletic team. If they switched jobs, the brother would no doubt become quite a bit less quiet, the sister quite a bit more so.

Sometimes this tendency to ignore the role of the situation can lead to errors of judgment. Consider the case of a student who must prove her intellectual abilities during an oral examination for her doctorate in zoology. Her committee members can comfortably sit back and ask questions from any particular branch of the science they have studied (the mating behaviors of earthworms, perhaps, or the molecular structure of pheromones in ants) while she squirms in anxiety without the opportunity to quiz back. Small wonder that students in such examinations often seem less than brilliant in the eyes of their professors, who themselves come off looking like geniuses. (How amazing that he is so knowledgeable about the mating behaviors of invertebrates!) In an experiment examining just such a phenomenon, students were asked to judge the intelligence of other students who were randomly assigned to either answer or create difficult trivia questions (Ross, Amabile, and Steinmetz, 1977). One student was randomly assigned to the role of game show contestant, while the other was asked to play host. The host was to choose any area of knowledge that he or she wanted, so long as it was not actually impossible for the other person to know anything about it (it was not acceptable to ask the name of the host's aunt in northern Michigan, for instance). Since the host was free to choose any area from his or her lifetime store of general knowledge, he or she obviously had an easy task in coming up with obscure facts that only he or she would know. If you cannot answer "In what two ways was Charles Darwin related to the wealthy china producer Josiah Wedgewood?" it may only be because you have different interests from the second author of this textbook. (The answer is son-in-law and nephew—Darwin married his uncle Josiah's daughter.) Even though the student judges were aware that the questioner and answerer had been randomly assigned to the easy glamour and sure loser positions, they judged the general knowl-

edge of the questioners to be significantly above average, and saw the answerers as slightly below average. The actual contestants also disregarded their roles; questioners judged themselves as being above average, and answerers judged themselves to be below average in general knowledge.

People's tendency to ignore situational causes of behavior, and to favor internal explanations, has been called the "fundamental attribution error" (Ross, 1977; Ross and Nisbett, 1991). However, there is some disagreement about whether this bias is properly called an "error" (Cheng and Novick, 1990; Funder, 1987). For one thing, it may frequently make sense to ignore situational pressure, because people often choose the situations in their lives (Buss, 1987; Caspi and Herbener, 1990; Snyder and Ickes, 1985). Consider the case of the librarian and the athletic director again. It probably makes sense to assume that quiet people are more likely to choose jobs as librarians than as athletic directors, and vice versa. Further supporting people's ability to make accurate attributions, there is evidence that when the information from the situation is important, people will not, as a rule, ignore it (Trope, 1986). Finally, it may generally be a good rule of thumb to assume that people mean what they say. Most often, they probably do.

EXPLANATIONS FOR OUR OWN SUCCESSES AND FAILURES

When you find that you did not do as well on a test as you wanted to, what goes through your mind? Was it a lack of ability on your part? Were you not motivated to study that week? Or was it an impossibly difficult test? Whether we attribute our success or failure in a given situation, such as a math test, to internal or external causes can have profound effects both on how we see ourselves (as discussed in Chapter 13), and on how we approach similar situations in the future. We can attribute our performance in a given situation to ability, effort, task difficulty, or luck, as shown in Table 17.2 (Weiner, 1986; Weiner, Frieze, Kukla, Reed, Rest, and Rosenbaum, 1971).

Ability is an internal and stable attribution. That is, we tend to assume that people's abilities come from inside them rather from the situation they are in, and we assume that abilities do not change much from one day to the next. If you decide that your lackluster test performance is due to low ability, therefore, you will not expect to perform well in the future. On the other hand, if you attribute your performance to the external, unstable factor of luck, there is no particular reason for you to

TABLE 17.2 Attributions for Success or Failure

Locus of control	Internal	External
Stable	Ability ("I'm no good at math.")	Difficulty of task ("The course is a tough one.")
Unstable	Effort ("I didn't study.")	Luck ("I got a bad break with the particular questions on that test.")

When someone either does well or poorly on a test, their reaction depends on whether they interpret it as due to internal or external factors, and whether they see those factors as stable or unstable. An ability attribution is a stable internal cause; while luck is an unstable external cause. After failures, people try harder if they make internal unstable attributions.

From Weiner, Frieze, Kukla, Reed, Rest, and Rosenbaum (1971).

expect to fail in the future. Several researchers have used these attributional principles to design programs for academic success. For instance, college freshman who were concerned about failing college participated in an experimental treatment in which they were encouraged to attribute their poor grades to unstable factors such as effort and stress. They were also told to keep in mind that freshman grades are typically variable and thus poor predictors of later performance. Students also watched videotapes of advanced students who described how they had done poorly in their freshman year but then improved dramatically. Compared to a control group that did not receive the attributional intervention, these students got better grades in their sophomore year, and they were less likely to drop out of college (Wilson and Linville, 1982).

Another researcher took a similar approach with grammar-school children (Dweck, 1975). Students in the experimental group were given both success and failure experiences, and were encouraged to attribute the failures to a lack of effort. Those in the control group were given only success experiences, and were encouraged to attribute their success to high ability. Later, the children were all exposed to failure experiences. The children who had previously experienced failures they could attribute to low effort were more persistent

in the face of the failures, while the previously successful children gave up very quickly.

From all of these results, it appears that the most persistent students may not be those who have never experienced failure. In fact, some experience of failure is helpful, if it can be attributed to a lack of effort and then followed by success after hard work. These results relate to findings we discussed in the personality chapter (Chapter 13), where we noted that college students' success in school is related to their chronic attribution patterns. Those with an internal locus of control believe that they can exert control over their lives, and they do better in school than those who take the external view, seeing themselves as pawns in an uncontrollable world.

No one makes consistently external or internal attributions. When it comes to success and failure, there is a striking regularity with which people shift their attributions. Most people tend to attribute success to some stable internal aspect of themselves, such as their skills. On the other hand, most people tend to attribute failure to some feature of the situation, such as luck. For instance, students who do well on a test consider it a good measure of competence. Students who do poorly

Attributing responsibility. Someone observing a homeless person will regard him very differently if the observer attributes the homelessness to personal choice (an internal attribution) instead of to problems in society (an external attribution). Research discussed in the text indicates that as observers we are often unaware of the external causes of other people's behavior.

on the same test are likely to criticize the test's validity (Arkin and Maruyama, 1979; Davis and Stephan, 1980). Gamblers who win credit their own personal skill at picking the winners. If they lose, they blame it on bad luck or extraordinary circumstances (Gilovich, 1983). Some research even suggests that members of stigmatized groups can use the "discounting" principle to protect themselves from negative feedback. For instance, a woman or a black may attribute a poor performance appraisal to prejudice, and thus maintain a positive self-concept (Crocker, Voekl, Testa, and Major, 1991). All of the findings on attributions, then, suggest that people making causal attributions are indeed like scientists, but scientists wearing rose-colored glasses.

ATTITUDES

As we have seen, people do not always think about one another with the unemotional coolness of a computer or the uninvolved detachment of a scientist (Sorrentino and Higgins, 1986; Fiske and Taylor, 1991). When Sister Mary Rose concluded that Oliver North was responsible for the deaths of Nicaraguan citizens, or when conservative columnist Patrick Buchanan concluded that Oliver North was a crusader against communism and an un-American Congress, each felt either a negative or a positive reaction to North. And those thoughts and feelings prompted them to perform some behavior—to write down their opinions for the press. Our attitudes influence the way in which we process social information. In the following sections, we will discuss what an attitude is, and examine how it is related to behaviors and thought processes.

THE COMPONENTS OF AN ATTITUDE

What is an attitude? Attitudes can be divided into four components: cognition (beliefs, thoughts, or ideas), affect (feelings, emotional reactions), behavioral intention (decisions or resolutions to act in particular ways), and behavior (relevant actions). For instance, you may have an attitude favoring a pollution-free environment. That attitude would be likely to include cognitions (the belief that polluted air is unhealthy, for instance), feelings (a dislike for the sight of smog in the air), behavioral intentions (the resolution to vote for candidates who have supported pro-environmental bills), and behaviors (the use of mass transit instead of a car). Attitude researchers Philip Zimbardo and Michael Leippe (1991) refer to these

interconnected feelings, thoughts, intentions and behaviors as an **attitude system.** (See Figure 17.3.) In this system, the attitude is the summary of all the different components ("I favor a pollution-free environment.").

How do these different components of an attitude go together? Most of us like to think that we first form rational beliefs like an objective scientist, and that our feelings and behaviors follow directly from these rational beliefs. In fact, several decades of research suggest that people are motivated to maintain **cognitive consistency**—that is, congruence between what they do and what they believe (Festinger, 1957; Heider, 1958; Fiske and Taylor, 1991). Beyond the need for consistency, our attitudes are often central to how we define ourselves (Abelson and Prentice, 1989). However, social psychologists have found that people are not nearly as consistent as one might expect. For a variety of reasons, our behaviors do not always fall in line with our attitudes (Sherman and Fazio, 1983; Wicker, 1969).

Part of the inconsistency between attitudes and behaviors is due to situational pressures that can make people uncomfortable about freely expressing their attitudes. For instance, imagine a group of Catholic students discussing birth control. Imagine that Student A hears Students B and C make convincing arguments that birth control is now necessary to stem the population growth among Catholics in Central America. At the same time, he hears a majority of the group disagree. Research suggests that Student A is likely to go along with the majority in public, though he may change his private opinions to agree with the minority (Maass and Clark, 1984; Maass, West, and Cialdini, 1987; Moscovici, 1985). Likewise, you may have positive attitudes about premarital sex, and yet not express them in a conversation with your conservative aunt.

One of the most fascinating exceptions to the assumption that "attitudes lead to behavior" comes from findings that people sometimes make up their attitudes to justify their previous behaviors.

COGNITIVE DISSONANCE: WHEN BELIEFS ARE INCONSISTENT WITH BEHAVIORS

Sometimes we believe one thing and do another. The theory of **cognitive dissonance** describes the sometimes strange cognitive contortions that we use to keep our beliefs and our behaviors in line with one another. Leon Festinger, who advanced

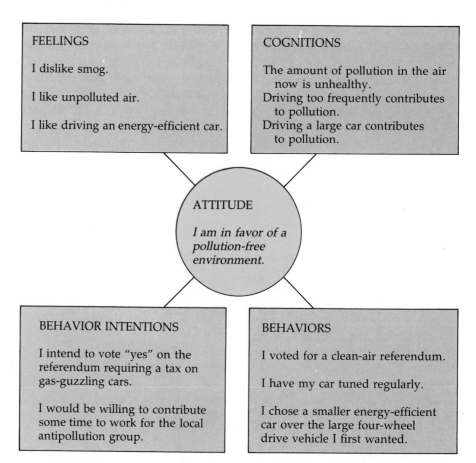

FEELINGS

I dislike smog.

I like unpolluted air.

I like driving an energy-efficient car.

COGNITIONS

The amount of pollution in the air
  now is unhealthy.
Driving too frequently contributes
  to pollution.
Driving a large car contributes
  to pollution.

ATTITUDE

I am in favor of a pollution-free environment.

BEHAVIOR INTENTIONS

I intend to vote "yes" on the
referendum requiring a tax on
gas-guzzling cars.

I would be willing to contribute
some time to work for the local
antipollution group.

BEHAVIORS

I voted for a clean-air referendum.

I have my car tuned regularly.

I chose a smaller energy-efficient
car over the large four-wheel
drive vehicle I first wanted.

FIGURE 17.3   An attitude system.   An attitude is composed of several components. The cognitive component consists of knowledge or beliefs that are relevant. The affective component consists of our feelings on the topic. Behavioral intentions are our expectations about what we will do in the future regarding the issue, and behaviors include the actual actions that we have taken that might be relevant.

this theory in 1957, postulated three possible relationships between beliefs and behaviors. Our behaviors and beliefs can be *irrelevant* to one another. For instance, you may have a strong belief in conserving a clean environment. That belief would have no consequences for your attendance at a modern art gallery; the two are thus irrelevant to one another. Sometimes our beliefs and behaviors are *consonant* (or consistent): if you favor a clean environment; that belief would be consistent with recycling your bottles, cans, and old newspapers. Festinger was most interested in what happens when behaviors and beliefs are *dissonant* (or inconsistent with one another). Suppose that despite your general preference for a clean environment, you have an old Toyota Land Cruiser that has no emission control system and gets 12 miles to the gallon. All of us are occasionally confronted with such discrepancies between our beliefs and our behaviors. How do we deal with them? Often we

simply avoid thinking about the inconsistencies. When we are forced to confront the discrepancies, however, Festinger believed that we experience an unpleasant state of cognitive dissonance, and we are motivated to reduce that state in one of several ways. One thing we can do is to change our behavior. If people are made aware of an inconsistency between their central values and their behavior, they will sometimes make an exaggerated gesture to reaffirm the original values (Sherman and Gorkin, 1980). For instance, most white people like to think of themselves as unprejudiced, and they will go well out of their way to avoid expressing their subtle feelings of prejudice against blacks (Gaertner and Dovidio, 1986). Whenever there are great costs, however, such as having to give up their own promotion for a member of a minority group, people are motivated to look for another alternative, and may change their beliefs. For instance, a person who is forced to compete for a job with a member of a minority group might actually come to see himself or herself as being more prejudiced.

Festinger and others have found a number of conditions in which people do bring their beliefs into line with their previous actions. In one classic experiment, Festinger and Merrill Carlsmith (1959) asked students to perform a very boring task. For a whole hour, the students simply rotated blocks mounted on pegs. When they had rotated all the blocks one turn, they were asked simply to begin again, then to do it again, and again, and again . . . for the whole hour. When the hour was up, the students were told that the experiment had been concerned with the effect of "mental set" on performance, and that they were in the control group. After the explanation, the experimenter said that the next student was scheduled to be told that the task was actually enjoyable. Each student was asked to help the experimenter by telling the next subject that he or she had really enjoyed what was really a hopelessly boring task. Some subjects were offered $1 for telling the lie, and others were offered $20. Festinger and Carlsmith reasoned that those who received $20 would have little dissonance. They had told a small lie, yes, but had been well compensated. Bear in mind that $20 in 1959 was worth a lot more than $20 today. To fully appreciate the subject's situation, imagine that you were offered $80 in the same situation. On the other hand, subjects offered $1 would have more dissonance. They would have to tell a lie with very little external justification. The researchers hypothesized that these subjects would reduce the dissonance by changing their beliefs about the task. By telling themselves that the task was not really so boring after all, they could decrease the discrepancy between their beliefs and their behavior. As shown in Figure 17.4, that is exactly what happened. Compared to those who had never been asked to lie at all (the control group) subjects in the $1 condition later rated the task as being significantly more interesting than they had right after having completed it. Subjects in the $20 condition, who should not be experiencing much dissonance, rated the task just like the control subjects did—as boring.

Festinger and Carlsmith's subjects probably experienced only a small amount of dissonance, telling a "little white lie" to help out in a scientific experiment. What sort of dissonance does a person experience after making a major commitment to a cause, perhaps devoting his or her life to a religious cult, only to confront later evidence that the commitment may have been unjustified?

When a group of social psychologists studied just such a question, they found strong support for the predictions of cognitive dissonance theory, as we discuss in the next section.

DISSONANCE AND SOCIAL DELUSIONS

Every few years, a new religious group predicts that the end of the world is at hand. So far, none of their predictions have come true. What happens to those groups when their cataclysmic public statements are disconfirmed? In 1956, Leon Festinger and his colleagues Henry Riecken and Stanley Schachter addressed this question in their book *When Prophecy Fails*. This book reports a case study of group behavior that provided fascinating support for Festinger's dissonance theory. Festinger and his colleagues became interested in the phenomenon when they read a local newspaper headline in September of 1954: "PROPHECY FROM PLANET CLARION. CALL TO CITY: FLEE THAT FLOOD." According to the newspaper report, Mrs. Marion Keech claimed that she had received messages from beings on the planet "Clarion." Those messages came to Mrs. Keech in the form of "automatic writing" that said the world would end in a great flood on December 21 of that year. Mrs. Keech and her followers were to be spared, since a flying saucer from Clarion would arrive at mid-

FIGURE 17.4 Ratings of positive feeling toward a boring task. Subjects who received only $1 rated the task most positively, presumably to reduce the cognitive discomfort of having lied for so little compensation. Subjects who received a larger compensation ($20) rated the task similarly to control subjects, who had told no lie.

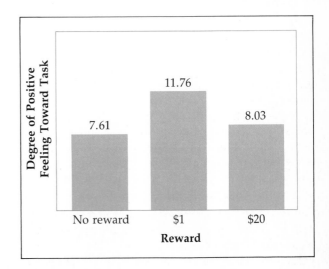

Parapsychic phenomenon or slight-of-hand? Research described in the text suggests that a belief in the existence of parapsychic phenomena will predispose the observer to the conclusion that the key being displayed by Uri Geller (right) was indeed bent out of shape by his extraordinary powers of psychokinesis.

night on December 20 to spirit them away. Mrs. Keech's believers had taken clear behavioral steps in line with this belief. Some had left college, some left their spouses, and some had begun to give away their earthly belongings. Festinger saw this as a perfect situation in which to investigate cognitive dissonance. When the end of the world did not come on December 21, 1954 (as Festinger was fairly certain it would not), all of the group's extreme behaviors would seem very irrational indeed, and the researchers could see how people deal with extreme personal inconsistencies. Thus, Festinger and his colleagues infiltrated the group, and reported on a very interesting series of events.

The group called itself the "Seekers," and had developed a set of beliefs supporting the idea that Mrs. Keech could receive messages from the heavens. During their meetings, the group members discussed various unusual "experiences" with ESP, reincarnation, mystical dreams, and the spirit world. Before the big event, they were shy about broadcasting their beliefs, and shunned publicity. On December 20, the eve of the predicted disaster, they gathered to await the arrival of their extraterrestrial saviors. While waiting, they removed all metallic items from their bodies. Watches, zippers, and the little clips on bra-straps were all discarded before midnight. At 12:00, no visitors had yet arrived, and the group members grew increasingly agitated. At 12:05, one of them noticed that another clock in the room said 11:55,

and they all agreed that that was the correct time. After the second clock struck midnight, the group sat silently for a long time. At 4:00 A.M., Mrs. Keech began to cry. At 4:45 A.M., Mrs. Keech suddenly went into a trance, and then received another message. The message said that the destruction of the world had been cancelled because of the valiant efforts of their little group. The next day, the group broke their secretive stance, and called the newspapers in the hopes that the publicity would spread their message to a broad audience. The effect of a direct disconfirmation of their beliefs was not to change those beliefs but to make them stronger. According to Festinger's dissonance theory, the extreme behaviors of the group members had made it too difficult for them to admit their mistakes.

This is not the only example of such a phenomenon (Zusne and Jones, 1982). One evangelical religious group of over 100 people confined themselves to a bomb shelter for over a month in the anticipation of a nuclear holocaust. When no holocaust transpired, they emerged from the bomb shelter more convinced than ever of the wisdom of their actions. Like Mrs. Keech's group, they proclaimed that their beliefs had saved the world (Hardyck and Braden, 1962).

Daniel Russell and Warren Jones (1980) studied the process of belief disconfirmation in a laboratory experiment. They found that cognitive dissonance can be related to biased information processing of the sort we discussed earlier. Russell and Jones asked students to read a description of research that showed either strong support or no support at all for the existence of ESP. They found that students who believed in ESP reported more unpleasant arousal when they read a study that disconfirmed its existence. On the other hand, skeptics became more unpleasantly aroused when they read a study that supported ESP. Those findings are consistent with the cognitive dissonance theory, which assumes that such discrepancies lead to a state of arousal (Croyle and Cooper, 1983; Kiesler and Pallak, 1976). The other interesting aspect of the study, however, was the measure of how the students recalled the research results. As shown in Figure 17.5, ESP believers had perfect memory for findings that supported their beliefs, but the majority of them misremembered a finding that disconfirmed their beliefs. Skeptics were more even in their memory; they remembered consistently about 90 percent of the time, whether the findings supported their original beliefs or not. Russell and Jones suggested that the existence of ESP may be more important to believers than to

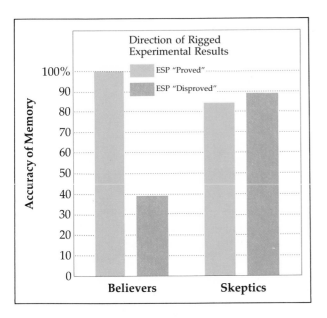

FIGURE 17.5 Selective remembering. Students who believed in the existence of ESP remembered the results of a research report perfectly if it supported their belief in ESP, but misremembered results that defied their beliefs. Skeptics were usually accurate regardless of the direction of the reported results. This study showed how cognitive dissonance can lead to biased information processing.

nonbelievers. Another possibility is that skeptics are generally more open-minded than "true believers."

HOW ATTRIBUTIONS AND INFORMATION PROCESSING AFFECT ATTITUDES

We have just seen how people's beliefs may change in order to justify their previous behaviors and thus reduce any unpleasant feelings of inconsistency. However, beliefs may follow behaviors even when there is no unpleasant state of dissonance to reduce. How do you feel about a proposition to create a new wilderness preserve in Nevada that will prevent logging in a 100-square-mile area? In a case like this, you may not even have thought through your attitudes until you were asked. Under these circumstances, you may consider your previous actions on related issues. Perhaps you have just signed a petition to prevent development of a logging area in your own state. Remembering that, you can quickly conclude that you have a favorable attitude toward the similar antilogging project in Nevada. To the extent that the issue is not very crucial for you, it is un-

necessary for you to feel any dissonance in order for past behaviors to influence present attitudes. For instance, students in one experiment were asked to read a personality description of someone whom they had never met. Later, they were asked to describe that person to a third party who, they were led to believe, knew and either liked or disliked the person being described. When the describers thought that they were talking to someone who disliked the target, they stressed his negative features. When they thought that the third party liked the target, on the other hand, they stressed his positive features. Like most of us do when we do not care about an issue, the describers tended to act agreeably by emphasizing what they thought the other person would want to hear (Higgins and McCann, 1984). Later, when asked to give their own opinions of the target, the describers liked him more if they had previously said positive things about him; but disliked him if they had said negative things. Although they had begun with no particular feelings about the target, they used their previous behaviors as information to answer the question about how they felt.

When we think back over our past for evidence about our attitudes, we may use attributional processes to decide whether our previous behaviors were motivated by the situation or our internal feelings. For instance, if you are asked about your attitudes toward the Sierra Club, you might use the same attributional principles you would use to decide about someone else's attitudes (Bem, 1972). You might weigh the evidence about the internal and external pressures on your previous behavior. If there are strong external pressures for you to say you oppose the Sierra Club (you are talking to an angry 200-pound logger who believes that the environmentalists are endangering his job) you may not attribute any internal beliefs to your statement. If you have gone against external pressures to make a stand (you tell the angry logger that you think forest conservation is, in the long run, more important than short-term profits for the logging industry) you may make an internal attribution.

All of these findings suggest that attitudes are complex and dynamic. Rather than having a simple and concrete attitude about "the environment" each of us has a complex set of beliefs, feelings, and past behaviors related to environmental issues. If asked about your attitude on a particular environmental issue, your response may differ depending upon which aspect of that complex attitude system you have recently been thinking about—your love for the old four-wheel gas-guzzler you are driving, or your feelings about the waste dump you just drove by (Cialdini, Reno, and Kallgren, 1990; Judd, Drake, Downing, and Krosnick, 1991).

CHANGING ATTITUDES: THOUGHTFUL VERSUS HEURISTIC APPROACHES

We have seen that people will sometimes go to great lengths to defend their existing beliefs—they avoid inconsistent information, bias their processing of inconsistencies they cannot avoid, and so on. Nevertheless, people do shift their attitudes. People change their musical preferences, their political affiliations, their spouses, and even their lifelong religious beliefs. There seem to be two different pathways to attitude change (Chaiken, Liberman, and Eagly, 1989; Petty and Cacioppo, 1986). When we do not have too many demands on our thinking time, or when a topic is very important to us, we will pay close and thoughtful attention to the issues. However, when an issue is not important to us, or when we are distracted and do not have much time to think about it, we will use simple **cognitive heuristics** to guide us. As we discussed in Chapter 8, a heuristic is simply a rule of thumb that has usually worked to solve a problem in the past.

If we have to make up our mind about an argument quickly, there are a number of simple heuristics that we often use as guides (Cialdini, 1988). For instance, an expert source is probably right more often than a nonexpert will be. As we mentioned earlier, people will be more likely to believe it when a medical researcher says that exercise is harmful than when the president of the "fat is beautiful" organization says the same thing. Another simple rule is to agree with the majority. If most of the members of a group seem to think that a new wilderness is a good idea, and the minority does not raise a consistent counterargument, people are likely to simply go along with the crowd (Latane and Wolf, 1981). Sometimes experts and majorities are wrong, but if the decision is of little consequence it makes sense to trust them and save our mental efforts for more weighty matters (Nemeth, 1986). Messages from outgroups may likewise be rejected without any careful processing of the information they offer (Mackie, Worth, and Asuncion, 1990).

On the other hand, you are not as likely to use a quick rule of thumb when an issue is very important to you (Petty and Cacioppo, 1979; 1990). If you make your living as an aerobic exercise instructor, you may question the statement that exercise is harmful, whether it comes from a medical expert or an advocate of obesity. If the medical expert uses sound, logical, two-sided arguments, however, you may be swayed. Richard Petty and John Cacioppo (1986) also point out that some people enjoy critical analytic thinking more than others, and those people are unlikely to use a simple rule of thumb in deciding on an issue. These researchers found such people are more likely to be convinced by logical arguments, in which both the pros and the cons are presented. When presented with a simplistic, one-sided message, critical thinkers tend to make up their own counterarguments. Consistently, one study found that people who scored low on a test of "need for cognition" (the desire to think critically) were strongly influenced by an audience's responses to a speech about probation for criminals. If the audience cheered enthusiastically and applauded loudly they were more convinced than they were if it was an unenthusiastic and jeering crowd. They thus took the simple heuristic solution—follow the crowd. However, those high in the need for cognition made up their own minds. They were more influenced by the quality of the arguments than by the response of the audience (Axsom, Yates, and Chaiken, 1987).

These findings show how attitudes relate to the research on social information processing discussed earlier in this chapter. It makes sense to assume that people devote little attention and thought to making social decisions of little importance, or when pressures require that we devote attention to more important matters. However, when another person or a controversial issue effects us directly, we switch into the scientist mode, giving careful thought to the matter at hand. Under those circumstances, we may even change an important opinion, but only if we are presented with strong logical arguments and different points of view and are not distracted from careful thought (Petty and Cacioppo, 1986).

AUTOMATIC SOCIAL PERCEPTION

As we just discussed, people sometimes respond to attitudinal arguments in a manner that is largely automatic or unthinking. Automatic processes also play a role in our perceptions of other people. Without being prompted, we may not notice the fabric of someone's clothes, whether she has a Boston accent, or whether she tugs at her hair while she speaks. However, there are several kinds of information about other people that we seem to process "automatically," including gender, status, friendliness, and current emotion. When we meet someone, we notice: "Is this a man or a woman?", "Is this person above or below my social status?", "Is this a friend or any enemy?", and "Is this person feeling an emotion now?" (Goldberg, 1981; Hastie and Park, 1986; Kenrick and Hogan, 1992).

Newborn babies can distinguish between male and female adults long before they have uttered their first words. When those babies grow older, gender becomes not only obvious but hard to ignore. As we noted in Chapter 5, subjects in dichotic listening experiments hear a different message in each ear but are asked to pay attention to only one. As those subjects try to concentrate on the message in one ear they are oblivious to most of the content of the message in the other. They will not notice if the unattended message changes from English into a foreign language, or even into a garbled string of nonsense syllables (Cherry, 1953). However, they will notice if the speaker changes from a man to a woman (or vice versa). In other research, subjects who read descriptions of another person's characteristics made a number of spontaneous guesses about what that person was like, regardless of the experimenter's instructions (Hastie and Park, 1986). At the top of the list of such automatic social codings was gender. Given even minimal information about another person, we begin to speculate about that person's gender (Brewer and Lui, 1989).

People who are given only minute amounts of information about another person also quickly begin to make spontaneous judgments about that person's social traits, especially his or her sociability (Hastie and Park, 1986; Winter and Uleman, 1984). In Chapter 13, we described a circumplex for personality traits that included two central dimensions: friendly–unfriendly and dominant–submissive (Wiggins and Broughton, 1985). As we noted, people in different cultures throughout the world use those dimensions to describe both themselves and the people around them (White, 1980). From the perspective of evolutionary theory, it makes survival sense to pay special attention to whether someone else is a friend or an enemy. It also makes sense to pay particular attention to another person's exact position above or below us in the dominance hierarchy, because groups with well-patterned dominance hierarchies have considerably less conflict (Baer and McEachron, 1982; Wilson, 1975). Paying attention to gender has important survival relevance, too. Gender is directly related to the central task of evolution: reproduc-

tion. Studies of dissonance and biased information processing sometimes give the impression that social cognition is a fault-ridden and even senseless process. However, more recent approaches have begun to focus on the overall efficiency and adaptive significance of the way we think about social information (Baron and Boudreau, 1990; McArthur and Baron, 1983). We do not spend all day creating a painstakingly accurate profile of every person we meet. Instead, we invest only as much energy as seems to be required to make an efficient decision, given our particular motivations at the time (Fiske and Neuberg, 1990). If we need to think carefully about another person, as when we are trying to choose a mate, we will. Otherwise, if we're trying to deal with a clerk in a supermarket, for instance, we will make a quick and efficient "automatic" impression based on one or two obvious characteristics, such as age, sex, or the presence of a smile.

Processing that seems automatic could stem from a great deal of practice doing something that previously required conscious effort (Glass and Holyoak, 1986). For instance, if you have driven home the same way hundreds of times, you will not have to think about where to turn. Likewise, thousands of experiences of discriminating between people of high and low status could allow one to make the distinction with little conscious effort. On the other hand, it could be that some of our responses to other people are based on perceptual abilities that, like the ability to use the rules of grammar, were never conscious in the first place (Hill and Lewicki, 1991). We turn next to the issue of "nonconscious" social information.

NONCONSCIOUS PROCESSING OF OTHER PEOPLE

Do people make social judgments at a level below consciousness? Several findings in social psychology suggest that they do. For instance, students asked to judge the faces in Figure 17.6 rated those in the center column as relatively most attractive and most intelligent (Hill and Lewicki, 1991). Actually, the faces in all three columns are the same, except that their lengths were altered slightly. Faces in the center are normal in proportion, while those on the left are slightly lengthened and those on the right are slightly shortened. Despite the fact that the length proportions had definite effects on their judgments, not a single subject was able to correctly identify the fact that this was the feature that had been manipulated. The students did come up with many explanations of why the

FIGURE 17.6 Nonconscious bases for judgments.
The faces on the left have been lengthened from normal proportions, while those on the right have been shortened. Students rated the faces in the center as more intelligent and attractive than those on the left or right. Despite the clear effects on judgments, students were not able to verbally describe why they rated the faces as they did. This research indicates the effect of nonconscious processes on social judgment.

ill-proportioned faces looked less intelligent and attractive, but their explanations were incorrect.

The findings of social judgments made below the level of consciousness have some interesting parallels in studies of brain-damage patients, which we discuss in the next section.

DYSFUNCTION:
Brain Damage and Social Recognition

Imagine what your social life would be like if you lost your ability to recognize other people's faces. Think of the difficulties it would pose if you went to the airport to pick up a group of relatives and could not tell whether the approaching person was your sister, your mother, an old friend, or a total stranger. People suffering from a rare form of brain damage experience just such a loss (Damasio, Damasio, and Van Hoesen, 1982). This inability to recognize faces is called **prosopagnosia** (based on the Greek words *gnosis* [knowledge], and *prosopon* [face]) (Carlson, 1988; Rosenzweig and Leiman, 1989).

An individual with prosopagnosia is not only unable to recognize the faces of friends and relatives, but is also unable to recognize his or her own face in the mirror. The loss of the ability to recognize faces is quite specific, and patients show normal intellectual functioning in most other respects.

For example, they can recognize friends and relatives from their voices, find emotional expressions in photographs, and even pick out facial features such as noses, lips, and eyes. In addition, patients can distinguish the sex and the age of the people they see. Thus, if you had this disorder you could look at your father, tell his age, point to his lips, and identify him as a man. You simply would be unable to say which older man's lips you were looking at, unless they spoke to you.

Researchers have identified a number of features of this disorder. For instance, it is caused by damage to the occipital-temporal region of the cerebral cortex (discussed in Chapter 2). The disorder is rare because the damage must be specific and bilateral (affecting both sides of the brain). Closer examination of the patients reveals that the disorder can involve some other interesting deficits. For instance, the patients can distinguish cars from trucks and buses, but they cannot distinguish particular cars from one another. One woman with the disorder had to read all the license plates of the cars in a parking lot to tell which one was hers (Damasio et al., 1982).

One study of this disorder revealed a fascinating dissociation between conscious and unconscious "recognition." Prosopagnosic patients were hooked up to electrophysiologic recording equipment while they observed photographs of familiar and unfamiliar people. As expected, they were not able to say which faces were familiar and which were unfamiliar. However, they did demonstrate marked changes in skin conductance in response to familiar faces (Tranel and Damasio, 1985). This study demonstrates that the patients are "recognizing" familiar faces at some level, but they are unable to connect that recognition to their verbal memories.

Other findings also indicate that the brain processes verbal information about other people differently from the way it processes nonverbal information. For instance, the split-brain patients described in Chapter 2 were completely unable to judge the physical attractiveness of a photograph shown only to the left (more verbally adept) hemisphere of the brain. On the other hand, they were able to accurately estimate how attractive a face appeared to a group of other raters when it was shown to the less verbally adept right hemisphere (Gazzaniga and Smylie, 1983). The findings from these neuropsychological case studies suggest that the brain processes we use to evaluate information about people are sometimes different from, and not always in touch with, those we use to talk about other people. ■

INFORMATION ABOUT PEOPLE IS PROCESSED DIFFERENTLY FROM OTHER KINDS OF INFORMATION

Patients with neurological disorders, as we just saw, sometimes show evidence that they can recognize a person at one level, yet be unable to put names to faces. Findings we discussed earlier suggest that even normal subjects sometimes are aware of social information that they are unable to put into words (such as the slight distortions of the faces in the Lewicki and Hill experiment). Even when we are dealing only with words, it seems that we organize them differently when they apply to people than when they apply to objects. Students in one study were asked to recall a list of adjectives that could be used to describe either people or objects (DeSoto, Hamilton, and Taylor, 1985). Half the time the words (such as warm, hard, sweet, and bright) were associated with a nonsense syllable, half the time with a person's name. When the students were later asked to remember the adjectives, they made a different pattern of errors in the two conditions. If the word "soft" had been associated with a person, for instance, students were likely to incorrectly remember "warm." If it had been associated with a nonsense syllable, on the other hand, they were likely to incorrectly remember "hard." This finding suggests that we store memories about people according to **implicit personality theories**—ideas about which characteristics go together in people (Schneider, 1973). Mistakenly remembering that a soft person is warm does not fit with language rules, which would lead to semantic errors such as replacing a word with one that has opposite meaning, but it does fit with implicit notions about which personality traits seem to fit together.

To summarize this section, people respond automatically to certain dimensions in others, gender, age, and status, for instance. Some of those automatic reactions are based on nonconscious information processing, and studies of brain-damaged patients suggest that our brains can process certain types of information about other people (such as their attractiveness and their emotional state) without any involvement of the areas that control conscious verbal thought-processes.

INTERACTIONS:
Emotion and Social Cognition

In this chapter, we have mentioned a number of biases that people often have when they think about others—stereotypes, prejudices, "confirmation biases," attribution errors, and so on. However, it is important to note that all of these biases stem from cognitive processes that are, under normal circumstances, not only efficient but also highly adaptive (Fiske and Taylor, 1991; Fiske and Neuberg, 1990; Funder, 1987; 1989). Cognitive processes such as attribution help us to deal with problems and opportunities that arise in the immediate environment, and to relate those problems to our past experiences. Is my roomate angry, or is he just in his usual depressed Monday mood? If he is angry, did I do anything that would make me responsible for his ire? Motivational processes prepare us for adaptive responses to the present environment. If I perceive an angry person who is waving a knife around, my fear response will get me aroused for a speedy flight to safety. Learning processes interact with cognition and emotion to store the results of our experiences for later reference. At the hint of a situation in which the neighborhood bully has become angry in the past, classical conditioning processes kick in a preparatory state of arousal. Underlying all of these processes are physiological mechanisms—hormones that trigger adaptive motivational states and brain structures that give special priority to important kinds of information. In the next section, we consider some findings that suggest an adaptive interconnection between social cognition and emotion.

Attunement to Other People's Emotions

Some interesting recent evidence suggests that we may be especially attentive to signs of anger in other people. Using a tachistoscope that allowed them to present photographic slides with precise control, Christine Hansen and Ranald Hansen (1988) showed students "crowds" of nine faces. In some cases, one person in a group showed a discrepant emotional expression. (See Figure 17.7.) For instance, some crowds included an angry face in a happy crowd; in others, a happy face was embedded in an angry crowd, and so on. Students most quickly identified an angry face in a happy or neutral crowd, and they were less likely to make an error if the discrepant face was angry than if it was happy. In another experiment, Hansen and Hansen varied the size of the crowds, and discovered an interesting relationship. If a happy face was embedded in an angry crowd, it became more difficult to notice as the size of the angry crowd increased. This makes sense, since a larger number of faces requires more cognitive "sorting out." However, if a single angry face was embedded in a

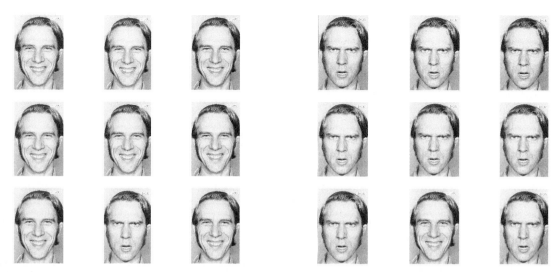

FIGURE 17.7 Pre-attentive processing. Students can pick an angry face from a happy crowd more rapidly and more accurately than they can pick a happy face from an angry crowd. The speed with which an angry face can be spotted, and the fact that a greater number of happy faces does not interfere with recognition of the angry face, suggest that angry faces are processed pre-attentively.

happy crowd, the size of the happy crowd made no difference. It was as if the angry face popped out of the stimulus array like a striped hornet on a white wall. Hansen and Hansen suggest that recognition of anger cues may occur pre-attentively, or without conscious processing. They speculate that their findings may fit with other research suggesting that recognition of facial cues for anger is innate. (See Chapter 10.) Thus, social perception seems to be linked to emotional responses that would have helped our ancestors adapt to living in social groups.

Once we have processed the information that another person is angry, or that someone is flirting with us, what is the next step? Social cognition seems to be directly linked to responses that help us adapt to our social environment (Baron and Boudreau, 1987). Recall from Chapter 10 that humans seem to have a number of motivational systems that link particular cognitive appraisals (such as the perception of a wild animal in our campsite) to special states of emotional arousal (fear) and to particular behaviors that will help us survive (running). An examination of the list of motivational/emotional systems reveals that most of them are linked to the appraisal of a social situation. Some of them, like anger, trust/acceptance, sexual arousal, and sadness, are almost exclusively tied to the perception of particular social situations. The others, such as fear and disgust, can be linked to nonsocial stimuli but are also commonly tied to social situations, such as seeing the neighborhood bully in an angry mood. Thus, social information

processing may be the main trigger for emotional experiences. Our ancestors evolved in groups of hunter-gatherers, and if they were to survive they had to get along with other people. Under those circumstances, a brain that is adept at analyzing and storing social information and is attuned to the emotional states of other people would have been quite important to our ancestor's adaptation.

Physiology and Social/Emotional Reactions

As we noted earlier, certain types of brain damage lead to a very specific inability to recognize faces. Prosopagnosic patients cannot recognize whose faces they are looking at, although they can recognize the emotion expressed in another person's facial expression. Other types of brain damage lead to specific disabilities in recognizing other people's emotional expressions or in expressing one's own emotions (Carlson, 1988). For instance, patients with certain kinds of damage to the right cerebral hemisphere are unable to recognize emotional expressions in other people's faces (Bowers and Heilman, 1981; DeKosky, Heilman, Bowers, and Valenstein, 1980). Other patients have difficulties recognizing emotion expressed in another person's tone of voice (Heilman, Scholes, and Watson, 1975). In one case, a man had just the opposite problem: He was fully able to recognize emotion in another person's tone of voice even though he was unable to comprehend the meaning of the words he was hearing (Heilman, Watson, and Bowers, 1983).

Related dissociations between emotional and verbal responses showed up in the split-brain patients we discussed in Chapter 2 (Gazzaniga, 1985). Brain researcher Michael Gazzaniga showed a fear-arousing film to one split-brain patient's right (less verbal) hemisphere. The left cortical hemisphere could not receive the information about the actual cause of the emotional response, but, since the lower brain centers were still connected, it was aware of the emotion. The patient proceeded to make up an explanation;

> PATIENT: I don't really know why but I'm kind of scared. I feel jumpy, I think maybe I don't like this room, or maybe it's you. You're getting me nervous. [The patient then turned to an assistant and said:] I know I like Dr. Gazzaniga, but right now I'm scared of him for some reason.
>
> *(Gazzaniga, 1985)*

Thus the patient's verbal brain area had made up an explanation of her feelings that was quite plausible but happened to be wrong. Gazzaniga suggests that the brain's "verbal interpreter" is also partly isolated, even in normal people whose brain hemispheres are connected.

Why might the human brain have special areas adept at storing and remembering information about other people and their emotions? David Sherry and Daniel Schacter (1987) argue that different memory systems could be the products of evolutionary pressures. From an evolutionary perspective it makes sense that humans would have specialized perceptual and memory systems for social information. Our ancestors evolved in groups, and the people in those groups depended upon one another for survival. Under those circumstances, it would be extremely useful to recognize signs of emotions such as anger or sexual arousal in other group members, or to recognize and remember evidence of personality traits such as dominance and unfriendliness. So it makes sense that the human brain would be designed to devote special attention to information about other people.

Social Thinking Works Hand in Hand with Other Psychological Processes

We have discussed how attitudes and social cognition fit into an adaptive system that connects physiology, emotion, and memory. Some of the ways in which we think about other people are linked to emotional systems in the brain in ways that would have helped our ancestors survive.

Acknowledging that there is some physiological basis for social cognition does not imply that we are wired up to respond to social situations as if we were robots, however. People are quite adept at learning and remembering new social categories (Mayer and Bower, 1986). Categories such as "yuppies," "hippies," "jocks," "punk rockers," "rednecks," and "college professors" would make little or no sense to most of our grandparents, much less to early homo sapiens living on the Plains of Northern Africa. Nevertheless, even the way in which we learn new social categories seems to interact with emotional systems in ways that make adaptive sense. For instance, people are significantly better at learning negative or positive prototypes than neutral ones (Mayer and Bower, 1986). It appears that the "friendly–unfriendly" dimension may have provided a basic framework that helped organize newer, more complex social categories. (See also Anderson and Klatzky, 1987.)

The importance of the "friendly–unfriendly" dimension highlights the connection between social cognition and personality. As we noted earlier in this chapter and in Chapter 13, there is evidence of a basic and universal cognitive system for thinking about how people differ from one another (the dominance–friendliness circumplex). In addition to these universals, there are also individual differences in the use of particular social schemas (Markus and Sentis, 1982). Some people are more likely to pay attention to information about a new acquaintance's intelligence, others process more for adjustment, and still others for social class. There is some evidence that we tend to be more prone to categorize others in terms of dimensions that are particularly important for our own self-images (Markus and Sentis, 1982). If you think of yourself as especially witty, you will be more attentive to the degree of wittiness versus dullness in the people you meet.

As we shall see in the next chapter, social thoughts are also connected to social behaviors. Whether we label someone as friend or enemy has implications for sexual attraction, aggression, and altruism. Whether we label someone as superior or inferior has implications for the amount of social influence that person will have on us. To some extent those labels may take on a life of their own when our behaviors cause people to act in line with our expectancies. In the final chapter, we will also see how the processes of social cognition can contribute to large-scale social problems. We will see that simple cognitive heuristics and biased information processing about out-groups may even contribute to international conflict. ■

IN CONTEXT: ATTITUDES AND SOCIAL COGNITION

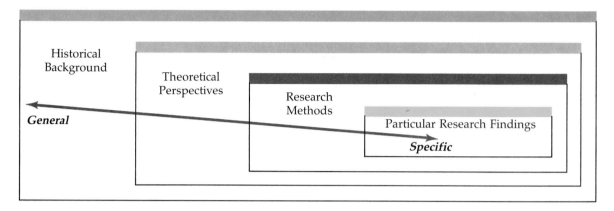

STUDY QUESTIONS

How do people process information about other people and social issues? What do we pay attention to and remember about others, and how do we retrieve that information?

How do we explain the causes of our own and other people's behaviors? What determines an attribution to internal (or personal) causes as opposed to external (or environmental) causes?

How are social attitudes formed and maintained, and how can they be changed?

HISTORICAL BACKGROUND

1. Early attitude researchers applied psychometric techniques from psychophysics and intelligence testing to the study of feelings about minority groups.

2. Lewin and Heider brought the gestalt perspective to attitude research, and studied how the brain imposed order on the social world. Asch's research on the primacy effect indicated that the same social description would be interpreted differently if positive information about a person were given before negative information.

MODERN THEORETICAL PERSPECTIVES

1. **Information processing** approaches consider how normal limitations on attention, encoding, and retrieval of information influence our reactions to other people.

2. **Attributional approaches** assume that people use logical inference processes in deciding about the causes for their own and other people's behavior. Social judgments can be divided into internal (person caused) and external (environmentally caused) categories.

3. **Cognitive consistency** theories begin with the assumption that people are motivated to maintain consistency between their attitudes and their behaviors. **Cognitive dissonance** is a feeling of discomfort that occurs when a person realizes that his or her beliefs and behaviors are not consistent with one another. It could theoretically be reduced by changing the beliefs, changing the behaviors, or distorting the relationship between the two.

4. The **interactionist** perspective views social cognition as part of an adaptive system that helped our ancestors survive in social groups.

RESEARCH METHODS

1. Researchers in this area have used mainly the **experimental** method. This has been particularly true of research done within the information processing model, such as Devine's (1989) research on prejudice.

2. Attitude researchers have often used **surveys.** Thurstone and Chave's (1929) scale for measuring attitudes towards the Chinese is an early example of such a survey. Scores on such a survey can be correlated with behaviors such as voting patterns.

3. Festinger and his colleagues (1956) applied the **case study** method to a group when they studied the "Seekers" who had predicted the end of the world.

RESEARCH FINDINGS AND SUMMARY

1. People pay more attention to others who are salient by virtue of being unusual in a group, and observers give salient people inordinate importance in judging social interactions. People also tend to search for information in such a way as to confirm their original beliefs about another person.

2. Even when people are presented with the same social information, there is a bias toward interpreting it to be consistent with earlier beliefs.

3. When people's beliefs change, they remember old information about themselves and others in line with the new beliefs.

4. Normal biases in cognitive processing may contribute to racial prejudice.

5. When a person does something in opposition to situational pressures, observers tend to attribute an internal cause by assuming that something about the person was responsible. When a person does something in line with situational pressures, observers tend to discount internal causes, although not as completely as logical analysis would lead us to expect.

6. Attributions can either be internal or external, and they can also be either stable or unstable. People who attribute their failures to an internal stable factor (ability) will try less in the future; those who attribute failures to an internal unstable factor (motivation) will try hardest.

7. Researchers have found that people sometimes deal with cognitive dissonance by changing their beliefs to fit behaviors to which they are publicly committed. Several studies have found that people in religious groups that have publicly predicted the end of world may increase their belief in the group after the prediction fails to come true.

8. Under some circumstances we may examine our past behavior to help us decide about our own opinions on a topic. If we have strong external pressure for acting in line with a certain belief we will attribute less of that belief to ourselves.

9. If a topic is unimportant to us, or if we cannot devote much attention to it, we may change our beliefs according to simple heuristic processing (uncritically accepting expert or majority opinion, for instance). If the topic is personally relevant, or if we tend to think carefully about issues, we are more likely to be influenced by carefully reasoned, two-sided appeals.

10. Evidence from split-brain and brain-injured patients indicates that some forms of social information may be processed in brain areas partially separated from verbal processing areas.

11. Complex information about faces can be processed at a nonconscious level. Social judges automatically code for signs of emotion in others, for gender, and for information about social traits.

ADDITIONAL READINGS

Festinger, L.; Riecken, H., and Schachter, S. 1956. *When prophecy fails.* Minneapolis: Univ. of Minnesota Press. The original account of Mrs. Keech's group, and their responses when the end of the world did not come as they predicted.

Fiske, S. T., and Taylor, S. E. 1991. *Social cognition.*, Second ed. New York: McGraw-Hill. A detailed treatment of the areas of research discussed in this chapter.

Gazzaniga, M. S. 1985. *The social brain.* New York: Basic Books. A stimulating account of the research on different brain "modules," with particular distinction between verbal and social/emotional processing areas.

Petty, R. E., and Cacioppo, J. T. 1981. *Attitudes and persuasion: Classic and contemporary approaches.* Dubuque, Iowa: W. C. Brown. A review of the research on attitude change, with a clear development of the distinction between thoughtful and heuristic processing.

Zimbardo, P. G., and Leippe, M. R. 1991. *The psychology of attitude change and social influence.* New York: McGraw-Hill. An engaging treatment of the research on attitudes, with applications to such topics as religious cult indoctrination, the "selling" of United States presidents, and the Jonestown mass suicide.

INTERPERSONAL RELATIONS

T o be alone is one of the greatest of evils for [man]. Solitary confinement is by many regarded as a mode of torture too cruel and
unnatural for civilized countries to adopt. To one long pent up on a
desert island the sight of a human footprint or a human form in the
distance would be the most tumultuously exciting of experiences.

(William James, 1890)

Chapter Outline

Up to now, we have focused on the psychology of
the *individual* human being. It makes sense to talk
about such processes as neuropsychology, perception, and cognition in this way because these
processes go on inside separate people's heads.
Even social cognition, discussed in the previous
chapter, is mainly concerned with interpretations
made inside the heads of individuals. In this
chapter, however, we shift our perspective somewhat. We are entering the realm where
psychology begins to overlap with sociology,
where it is meaningless to talk about one individual at a time. As William James noted at the turn
of the century, humans are naturally sociable
creatures. Some of the most fascinating human
behaviors involve *interactions between individuals*,
and in this chapter we discuss four major areas of
these interpersonal relations: attraction, aggression, altruism, and social influence.

Research on **attraction** examines how we form
and maintain friendships and intimate relationships. Human relationships based on love and
marriage are often powerful and long-lasting. Mol-
ly Weber and Lazarus Rowe were married for 86
years; another couple repeated their marriage
vows 40 times over as many years. Ninety-five
percent of American males and 94.6 percent of
American females will marry at least once. In 1986
alone, approximately 2,444,000 American couples
entered into wedlock (McFarlan, 1989). By definition, a mating relationship requires more than one
person.

In 1984, James Oliver Huberty left 21 dead after
a shooting spree in a McDonald's restaurant in
California. Had he been apprehended before his
gruesome act, it would have made little overall
difference in the United States murder statistics for
that year, during which 18,690 murders were re-

ported by the FBI (not to mention another 685,350 aggravated assaults). Psychologists who study **aggression** are concerned with behaviors that, like Huberty's, are intended to harm another person.

On the other hand, research on **altruism** examines behaviors intended to be helpful to others. For example, Everett Sanderson performed an especially altruistic act when he jumped into a train's path to save the life of a four-year-old girl who had fallen off a subway platform. With seconds remaining, he threw the girl to safety, but was unable to make it back up. At the last instant, the other bystanders pulled him out of the train's path (Young, 1976). As another example, successful musicians gave freely of their time to raise money for starving African children during the "Live Aid" concert. And altruism is not just an action performed by the heroic few. Hundreds of thousands of Americans dug into their pockets during that concert to donate a total of $70 million for the African children.

Not everyone who acts charitably does so for noble reasons. When someone agrees to donate money to a phone solicitor calling for the Little League, it may be to avoid social embarassment. Research on **social influence** examines the subtle pressures that lead people to give in to social pressure or go silently along with the crowd. Social influence can sometimes work in bizarre ways. The eighteenth-century German writer Goethe began his rise to fame with a book entitled *The Sufferings of Young Werther*, in which the hero

Altruistic behavior. Research on interpersonal relations examines positive behaviors such as altruism (pictured here in the 1986 "Hands Across America" demonstration of solidarity with starving people around the world) as well as negative behaviors such as aggression.

commits suicide. The book was widely banned in Europe because it led to an epidemic of imitative suicides. Two centuries later, on November 18, 1978, 910 members of the People's Temple joined the Reverend Jim Jones in his suicide. Survivors said that the first woman to drink from the vat of strawberry flavored poison also gave the drink to her baby. Like her, most of Jones's other followers went willingly to their deaths.

Psychologists interested in attraction, aggression, altruism, and social influence, therefore, consider processes that, by definition, require more than one individual. Since the field began, however, social psychologists have assumed that the elementary processes of individual psychology can help us understand these more complex social interactions.

HISTORICAL BACKGROUND: The Origins of Social Behavior

Why do we fall in love, raise our fists in anger, rush to help a fallen child, or strive to keep in fashion? Are these interpersonal behaviors controlled by hormones and brain structures? Are they, instead, the result of past rewards and punishments from our parents, teachers, and friends? Or could it be that these behaviors have nothing at all to do with mindless hormones and automatically conditioned responses, but are instead rationally calculated decisions? Questions like these are of more than academic interest when we try to understand a mass murderer such as James Oliver Huberty. If a judge and jury believe that a murder is based on a coolly calculated decision, they may rule differently than if they deem it to be the product of a biochemical imbalance or a bad home environment. And what we do to prevent the next Huberty from raising his gun may well depend on society's beliefs about the causes of violence. Should we try to reeducate violent people? Should we treat them with drugs? Should we hold them to blame or see them as victims of forces beyond their control? These are perennially controversial questions, and their answers depend on which theory we believe. It should come as no surprise, then, that the general theories of social behavior have, throughout history, arisen in the midst of controversy and continue to be hotly debated issues today.

When Charles Darwin published his classic *The Origin of Species* in 1859 he laid the groundwork for modern evolutionary theories of social behavior.

The evolutionary perspective was controversial in 1859, and it remains so today. What did Darwin say to provoke such a longstanding debate? At the most general level, he argued that social behaviors play an important role in survival. For example, he saw an important connection between sexual attraction and natural selection, arguing that what is fancied by one sex can influence the evolution of the other sex. Why do male peacocks look so very flamboyant? According to Darwin, it is because peahens for thousands of generations chose the most luxuriant males as mates (Darwin, 1859). Darwin believed this process of **sexual selection** also produced differences between men and women. One reason that men today have more muscular shoulders than women do could be that our female, but not our male, ancestors used muscles as a criterion for choosing mates. As we discussed in Chapter 10, Darwin (1872) also reasoned that facial expressions evolved to allow us to communicate with one another. For instance, the angry sneer can prevent unnecessary bloodshed by warning a potential combatant that the other intends to stand and fight. Recall the parallels between the snarling dog and the sneering woman depicted in Figure 10.3.

William McDougall was born in England in 1871, the year before Darwin published *Expression of Emotions*. A brilliant young scholar, McDougall went to the University of Manchester at the age of 14 to study biology, and from there on to Cambridge University. In late nineteenth-century Eng-

lish biological circles, Darwin's theory was still very big news, and when McDougall wrote *Social Psychology* in 1908, (the first psychology textbook devoted to this topic), he wrote from a Darwinian perspective.

McDougall accepted Darwin's idea that social behaviors evolved just like physical structures: adaptive mechanisms survived, maladaptive ones perished. He argued that there are seven basic human instincts—flight, repulsion, curiosity, pugnacity, self-abasement, self-assertion, and the parental instinct. When McDougall said that humans had "instincts," he did not mean that we are controlled by rigid genetic programs operating without any input from learning or intelligent thought. Instead, he viewed instincts as tendencies similar to hunger. According to McDougall, those tendencies cause us to: 1) *pay attention to certain events* in the environment, 2) *feel certain emotions* when we notice those important events happening, and 3) *act in particular ways* in response to those feelings. As an example, the pugnacity instinct is a predisposition to become angry and prepare to fight when someone obstructs the satisfaction of our needs. Although McDougall believed that we automatically become angry when others frustrate us, he also believed that we could learn to control and suppress that anger. As we discussed in Chapter 10, modern psychologists prefer the term "drive" to "instinct," because the word instinct is often taken to refer to genetic programs that are inflexible and unresponsive to experience.

McDougall's evolutionary perspective went out of vogue in the United States when behaviorism became the dominant psychological theory in the 1920s. However, the evolutionary approach to social behavior became the center of renewed controversy during the 1970s when Harvard biologist Edward O. Wilson (1975) argued that genes control such human social traits as aggression and altruism. Evolutionary theorists view attraction, aggression, altruism, and conformity as strategies for survival and reproduction, presuming that our ancestors survived by successfully attracting mates, defending resources, and cooperating with other group members. This perspective is still controversial among social psychologists, but evolutionary ideas have recently begun to generate a great deal of research on social behavior (Bell and Bell, 1989).

Although **behaviorists** differed with McDougall's evolutionary theory, they also stressed the *function*, or survival value, of social behavior. The crucial distinction between the behavioral and evo-

William McDougall. William McDougall developed an evolution based theory of social behavior. He saw instincts as tendencies to act in certain ways under certain circumstances, such as the tendency to anger when frustrated.

lutionary views is that early behaviorists had no interest in the evolutionary past, instead taking the view that each of us is born a "blank slate" whose characteristics are products of our life environment. John Watson was the early behaviorist famous for his claim that he could choose any child at random and raise him or her to be a "doctor, lawyer . . . beggarman, [or] thief" if he could simply control the child's environment. Using the same reasoning, he could have promised to raise mass-murderer James Oliver Huberty to be a gentle pacifist.

During the 1930s and 40s, John Dollard and Neal Miller led a team of researchers at Yale University who developed one of the more extensive behaviorist models of social behavior. In the 1939 book *Frustration and Aggression* they argued that we learn to be aggressive in order to get reinforcements. Like McDougall, Dollard and Miller thought that aggression occurred when an obstacle to our other needs got in our way. Two of the authors of *Frustration and Aggression,* for example, found more lynchings of blacks in the South during years when cotton prices were low, and interpreted this as supporting the **frustration–aggression hypothesis** (Mowrer and Sears, 1941). When the cotton price went lower, Southern whites faced increasing economic frustration, which they presumably vented as aggression towards blacks. You might think the frustration–aggression hypothesis sounds like McDougall's "instinct of pugnacity" wrapped in different words. However, there are important differences between the viewpoints. In particular, Dollard and Miller believed aggression was a learned response to frustration, not an automatic and innate reaction.

The view that social perceptions or cognitions guide much of our behavior provided the basis of much of the last chapter. It has also stimulated research on interpersonal processes. Those who adopt a **cognitive perspective** believe that our social actions follow our beliefs and attributions about other people. Recall that the phenomenologist Kurt Lewin had a major influence on the research in social cognition. Social psychologists who adopt Lewin's emphasis on phenomenology have focused on immediate situational determinants of behavior, often ignoring the person's history and the history of the species. Those who adopt the cognitive perspective have disagreed with the behaviorists about the importance of the "objective" environment. Instead, they emphasize the person's "subjective" world—the world as it is filtered through the person's interpretations and what he or she is paying attention to on a moment-to-moment basis. For instance, if someone had yelled "It's hopeless" just before Everett Sanderson jumped off the subway platform, he might not have tried to save the little girl's life. On the other hand, if another observer had just left an Indiana Jones movie, in which last-minute rescues are made to seem commonplace, Sanderson might have had company down on the tracks. In line with this approach some social interaction researchers examine how momentary perceptual biases influence how we interpret, and consequently react to, the behaviors of people around us.

Which theoretical perspective is right, then? Are our loving, fighting, sharing, and conforming behaviors programmed by our genes, conditioned by teachers and television idols, or based on immediate experience? Although the debates are far from over, the evidence seems to give a place to all these explanations. Moreover, it is important to keep in mind the interplay between biology, learning, and cognition. Ongoing thought processes do not just arise from the thin air of momentary perceptions, but from the rich soil of experiences in school, in the family, and on the streets. What we notice, what we care about, and what we remember from our innumerable experiences is in turn influenced by our biological heritage. The complex interaction of biology, learning, and cognition is particularly useful to keep in mind in the area of interpersonal relations. Because behaviors such as aggression, affiliation, and love are so important to society, political and cultural prejudices have often led psychologists and laypeople alike to adopt oversimplified views. ■

ATTRACTION AND LOVE

In *Annie Hall* and other movies, Woody Allen has made many of us relive our awkward attempts to make ourselves attractive to the opposite sex. Most of us can relate only too well to the bumbling attempts of Alvie Singer and Annie Hall to relate to one another. On the other hand, there are people like Giovanni Vigliotto, who not only had a way with women but managed to run a string of 104 bigamous marriages before being collared by the law. What makes someone like Giovanni Vigliotto attractive enough to convince over 100 women to marry him, when so many others, like Alvie Singer, have a hard time just getting a date for next Saturday night? Moving beyond the question of sexual attraction, what makes us like some people, dislike others, and take no interest at all in many others? To find an answer to these questions, we will first examine research on initial attraction, and then discuss research on relationship formation and love.

INITIAL ATTRACTION

Three general factors predict liking from the start: _physical attractiveness, similarity,_ and _proximity._ We are attracted to those who are good looking, who are like us, and who live or work nearby.

PHYSICAL ATTRACTIVENESS

In a now classic study conducted at the University of Minnesota, social psychologist Elaine Walster and her colleagues (1966) set up a "computer dance" and paired off 752 freshman students. Before the dance, they collected extensive data on each student's personality and intelligence, and secretly rated the students' looks when they arrived to collect their tickets. Midway through the dance, and again several months later, they asked the students how they liked their dates, and

The importance of physical attractiveness. Woody Allen's movies have often depicted the difficulties that a plain-looking person has in relating to attractive members of the opposite sex.

whether they planned to see one another again. The students' responses were intriguing. On the questionnaire filled out before the dance, the students had said that "personality" and "intelligence" were the most important considerations in their choice of dates. After they were paired, however, neither of these sterling attributes had any impact on students' actual responses to the people they had been matched with. Only one of the partners' characteristics predicted satisfaction with the date, and it also predicted attempts to see the person again. That characteristic was physical attractiveness. Later research has underscored the importance of physical attractiveness in predicting attraction for a date (Hatfield and Sprecher, 1986).

It may not surprise you that physical attractiveness is important in choosing a date. However, physical attractiveness has also been found to influence our liking for others in situations where it would not seem so important (Umberson and Hughes, 1987). For example, people are more likely to vote for the better looking political candidates (Efran and Patterson, 1974) and to hire the more attractive job applicants (Cash and Janda, 1984). Furthermore, cute school children are treated more favorably by teachers as compared to less attractive children. (Clifford and Walster, 1973; Dion, 1972).

Physical characteristics that make someone attractive vary across cultures as well as among individuals. A classic cross-cultural study found that although most societies value a bit of plumpness in a woman, thinness is valued in others (Ford and Beach, 1951). The extensive facial tattooing that makes for an attractive Maori man would probably not be an asset in an Iowa farm community. However, there are areas of cross-cultural agreement, as well. Ford and Beach found that deformity, signs of ill health, and bad grooming were universally unattractive across cultures in both sexes. American students shown photographs of beauty queens from other cultures agreed that the women were attractive. An analysis of the features that they found the most attractive suggested that people were most drawn to a combination of infantile characteristics, such as big eyes, and adult features, such as high cheekbones (Cunningham, 1986). Cross-cultural studies indicate that there is generally more emphasis on women's physical attractiveness than on men's. As you might guess, the features that make women attractive are not always attractive in males. For instance, mature features, such as a large jaw, increase a man's attractiveness, but not a woman's (Cunningham, 1990; Keating, Mazur, and Segall; 1981). Conversely, a small nose is attractive in a woman, but not in a man (Cunningham, 1986; Cunningham et al., 1990).

In short, there is agreement about what constitutes good looks within our society, and at least some evidence of agreement across cultures, especially about unattractive features. There is, nevertheless, enough difference of opinion within and across cultures so that most of us, even the Alvie Singers, can find someone who finds us attractive.

When we decide that someone is physically attractive, it is not an absolute judgment based on computer-like analysis of his or her physical features. Judgments about physical attractiveness are somewhat relative, and can be influenced, for example, by the looks of the other people to whom we have recently been exposed. Exposure to extremely attractive individuals seems to produce a **contrast effect** similar to that discussed in Chapter 3. If people have recently had their hands in buckets of ice-water, they will rate a bucket of lukewarm water as being hot by contrast. Applying this principle to attractiveness, several studies have found that average looking men and women were judged as relatively homelier if the judges had just been looking at photos of attractive models (Gutierres and Kenrick, 1979; Kenrick and Gutierres, 1980). Men were also more likely to rate their mates as less attractive if they had just been looking at beautiful women in magazine centerfolds (Kenrick, Gutierres, and Goldberg, 1989). Women were not so likely to downgrade their husbands and boyfriends after being exposed to attractive men, perhaps because women, compared to men, place relatively less value on physical attractiveness, and relatively more value on status and economic resources (Buss, 1989; Kenrick, Sadalla, Groth, and Trost, 1990). Thus, physical attractiveness depends not only on the features of the person being judged, but also on the gender of the judge and the comparative influence of the other people the judge has recently been looking at.

Although physical attractiveness is an obvious first cue for attractiveness, it is hardly the only consideration. Another important determinant of attraction is similarity.

SIMILARITY

Despite the adage that opposites attract, it appears that, in fact, we are more likely to be attracted by those with similar interests. In a classic study, Theodore Newcomb (1961) observed the formation of friendships in a dormitory at the University of Michigan. First friendships were generally formed between students living in the same or neighboring rooms (the subject of our next section), but later friendships were based upon shared attitudes and interests. For example, three conservative veterans formed one tight-knit group, while another clique included five politically progressive liberal arts majors. Later studies have replicated this finding of greatest attraction among "birds of a feather" (Byrne, 1971; Buss, 1985; Rushton, 1989). We tend to be most attracted to people who share our political views, religious beliefs, ethnic backgrounds, and even our drinking and social habits (Berscheid and Walster, 1978).

It may be that we befriend and marry similar others because we find their company rewarding. It feels good to be around someone who confirms our political beliefs, our religious preferences, and our style of dress. However, it could be that the motivation may actually be the converse of this. Some research suggests that we are not so much pleased by similarity in another person as we are repulsed by dissimilarity (Rosenberg, 1986). According to this analysis, punk rockers may go around together not because they think that all the other punkers are so beautiful, but because everyone else seems so unattractive to them. Whatever the ultimate explanation, the findings remain the same—we strongly prefer to see ourselves mirrored in our friends and lovers.

PROXIMITY

In the study of friendship formation in the Michigan dorms, the first predictor of liking was living in close quarters. This finding that we like the ones we're near has been replicated in numerous studies. Classroom friendships can even be predicted by the closeness of the students' last names (Segal, 1974). The students in Segal's research were seated alphabetically, and made friends with those closest to them. Similar findings emerged from a study of friendships in a student apartment complex at MIT (Festinger et al., 1950). Women residents were asked to name their best friends in the complex. Most frequently, they named the women living right next door. Another landmark study found that Philadelphians were much more likely to marry someone living on the same block than someone who lived only a block or two away (Bossard, 1932).

Why do we befriend and fall in love with our next door neighbors? For one thing, we interact more with those who live and work nearby. In the MIT apartment complex, people living near mailboxes, or at the bottom of a staircase, had more

Proximity and friendship. A number of studies of friendship formation have found that people are especially likely to make friends with their neighbors. Part of the reason is simply convenience: It is easy to interact with people we see on a daily basis. Another part of the reason is that we generally come to like the people (or things) we see frequently more than those we see less frequently.

friends because a greater number of potential friends regularly passed by these locations. In addition, there is the simple rule that exposure leads to liking. Research in which people are repeatedly exposed to faces, foreign words, or even nonsense syllables indicates that we come to feel positively towards anything that is familiar (Kunst-Wilson and Zajonc, 1980; Zajonc, 1968). In the same vein, we prefer reversed photographs of ourselves, but correct images of our friends (Mita et al., 1977). Why? We see ourselves, but not our friends, in the mirror.

There is an interesting exception to the proximity–attraction rule. Sociologist Joseph Shepher (1971) examined dating and marriage patterns in groups of Israeli kibbutz children raised with one another instead of in conventional families. Although these group-mates did grow very close and become lifelong friends, they were not sexually attracted to one another. Shepher found neither formal rules nor informal pressures against heterosexual contact between group-mates. Of fully 2,738 marriages involving people who had been raised in this group system, though, there was no case of marriage between two children raised together since birth. This is very unusual, given the strong tendency to become attracted to the girl or boy next door that we just discussed. Children of these kibbutz communes did show attraction for members of the group next door, but did not fall for the girl or boy who grew up in even closer than normal proximity. Why?

Animal studies have found that some animals become attracted to potential mates with features similar to those to which they are exposed early on in life. (This is a phenomenon called **sexual imprinting**). However, social animals also avoid the other animals with whom they were actually raised, in a process called negative imprinting. Since the other animals who share their nest are usually their siblings, Shepher argued that raising kibbutz children in continuous living contact accidentally triggered an innate negative imprinting mechanism. According to this argument, social animals evolved a negative imprinting mechanism to prevent excessive inbreeding. This avoidance prevents deformities due to recessive genes, which are more likely in sibling matings.

In sum, we prefer mates and friends who live or work in close proximity, probably due in part to our increased exposure to them. The limitation is that we do not prefer those who were raised under the same roof with us. The proximity effect on mate preference seems to stop at our front door.

FORMING RELATIONSHIPS

There is obviously more to a relationship than initial attraction. Each of the 2,444,000 couples who married last year went through a more complex process of courtship. First, they had to communicate their attraction for one another—many couples who seem to be well matched on paper pass in the night without even sharing a flirtatious look. Beyond their compatibility at first glance and the pleasure they take in flirting with each other, they must be able to work out a relationship that is mutually satisfying. If all goes extremely well, they may have to decide whether they feel "love" for one another. Let us consider some of the research on these processes.

FLIRTATION

Have you ever had the feeling that someone was attracted to you, but have been unable to say exactly why? It is rare for someone you hardly know to walk up and announce "I am attracted to you!" However, the message may be communicated nonverbally. Ethologist Irenaus Eibl-Eibesfeldt (1975) unobtrusively filmed flirting couples all around the world. When the film clips were examined in slow motion, he found fascinating evidence of a universal nonverbal language of courtship:

. . . we found agreement in the smallest detail in the flirting behavior of girls from

Samoa, Papua, France, Japan, Africa . . . and South American Indians. . . . The flirting girl at first smiles at her partner and lifts her eyebrows with a quick, jerky movement upward so that the eye slit is briefly enlarged. . . . Flirting men show the same movement of the eyebrow, which also can be observed during a friendly greeting between members of the same sex. After this initial, obvious turning toward the person, in the flirt there follows a turning away. The head is turned to the side, sometimes bent toward the ground, the gaze is lowered, and the eyelids are dropped [Figure 18.1]. Frequently, but not always, the girl may cover her face with a hand and she may laugh or smile in embarrassment. She continues to look at the partner out of the corners of her eyes and sometimes vacillates between that and an embarassed looking away.

(Eibl-Eibesfeldt, 1975)

This universal pattern seems unlikely to have been taught to young women in these widely sepa-

FIGURE 18.1   Cross-cultural signs of flirtation. Ethologist Irenaus Eibl-Eibesfeldt filmed flirtation gestures around the world, and found that women in Samoa, Papua, France, Japan, Africa, and South America all showed a similar sequence of movements. Here is a flirting Turkana woman from Kenya. Have you seen the same flirting gestures around campus?

rated cultures. Instead, Eibl-Eibesfeldt (1975) argues that the sequence is akin to courtship gestures in other animals. Just as peacocks and peahens can flirt without words, so can humans.

The above observations focused mostly on female flirtation. Rather than using coy gestures, psychobiologist G. D. Jensen (1973) suggested that male humans, like male chimps and baboons, use dominance gestures—swaggering, puffing the chest, and direct staring. Rasputin, the charismatic Russian monk and confidante of Czar Nicholas II's wife, Alexandra, was constantly surrounded by a group of female admirers. His approach featured a piercing stare and direct physical contact.

The direct stare, as opposed to the coy glance, is characteristic of dominance. A series of studies on nonverbal expressions of dominance found that dominance enhanced a man's attractiveness, but had no effect on ratings of a woman (Sadalla et al., 1987). This effect was very specific to dominance. Being aggressive or socially pushy was not attractive in either sex. In sum, then, humans communicate their early attraction through mutual glances and subtle movements that tell without speaking, and the form of these flirtation gestures seems to differ for males and females.

NEGOTIATION

There is obviously more to a relationship than flirtation. A couple must decide "Should we continue seeing one another?", and later "Should we move on to steady dating, or engagement, or even marriage?" How these questions are answered depends in part on our perception of the rewards and costs of the relationship (Rusbult, 1980). **Equity** refers to a state of affairs in which one feels that the benefits from the relationship, minus the costs of being in the relationship, are balanced with one's partner's costs and benefits (Hatfield, Traupmann, Sprecher, Utne, and May, 1985; Walster et al., 1978). At first, this decision may be based on such easily observable attributes as attractiveness or money. Later, each person can assess the partner's behaviors (Do I take out the garbage more than I should, considering that I wash the dishes?). Walster and her colleagues found that physically attractive people in their computer dance demanded more in a date than did the less attractive people. (Presumably, they saw their good looks as an asset that gave them more buying power in the social marketplace.)

One way to balance the cost–benefit sheet is to trade assets in one area for assets in another. During the 1970s, Richard Nixon's influential secretary of state, Henry Kissinger, dated some of the most beautiful women in Hollywood, and eventually married a woman much more physically attractive than himself. When a talk show host asked a guest what women saw in this rather plain-looking man, her answer was certain and quick: "Power." The February, 1987, issue of *People* magazine carried a question on its cover: "Does power make Lee Iacocca sexy?" Presumably, Kissinger and Chrysler Corporation's president Iacocca were able to trade their power for good looks. Researchers find evidence of this sort of cross-category trading in relationships. Women who are more attractive than the others in their high school yearbooks tend to marry wealthier men (Elder, 1969). In short, courting couples seem to "trade" assets in one category for assets in another.

All this may sound very unromantic, suggesting we act like calculating accountants in our love affairs. In fact, psychoanalyst Erich Fromm argued that just as the Germans had an "authoritarian" national character before World War II, so the Americans have a "marketing" national character. He reasoned that our capitalist economy influences our behaviors in other areas, including love relationships. Instead of looking for deep value in a partner, says Fromm, we look for a nice "package" so that we can impress others with what a great wheeler and dealer we are. And instead of caring about the other person's welfare, we are more concerned with whether we are getting a good "bargain." Fromm says that this selfish approach ultimately backfires, because selfish people end up being less lovable and less capable of truly relating to one another. Fromm's analysis was based upon his own observations, but those observations seem to fit with much of the data from more controlled studies (Walster et al., 1978). Certainly, it is worth thinking about. Do you take the "marketplace" approach to your relationships?

People may not always be quite as calculating as Fromm and the equity researchers would lead us to believe. Although people who expect superficial relationships do prefer an explicit accounting of the equity sort, those who expect long-term interactions move to a more **communal relationship** (Clark, Mills, and Powell, 1986; Mills and Clark, 1982). In a communal relationship partners share rewards and costs rather than emphasizing their own individual welfare. People in marriages or close friendships prefer to avoid the explicit tally sheet approach, although other research suggests that many of us still keep a rough record in our minds (Walster et al., 1978). In sum, we seem to look for an equitable balance of costs and benefits in relationships, but try not to make it too blatant if we expect the relationship to last.

LOVE

The powerful emotional bonds like those felt by Romeo and Juliet are common in humans, but most mammals do not form mating bonds. For some species, including the Ugandan kob (an African antelope), courtship takes only a minute or so. Females approach one of a few dominant males who have won a special courtship territory, exchange brief flirtations, are mounted by the male, and go on their way. The affair is over, and no love is lost. Most of our primate cousins, the other monkeys and apes, have polygamous mating arrangements. But humans are different. Even in this divorce-ridden country, the majority of us not only marry, but stay married for life. Even broken marriages last an average of eight years and are usually followed by another marriage (Brehm, 1985). It is obvious that we humans become very attached to our mates, and that attachment is facilitated by a peculiar set of feelings called love. But what is love?

Robert Sternberg (1986) is an intelligence researcher who attempted to answer this question. Studies of intelligence have asked whether the "IQ" consists of one general factor or a number of independent components. (See Chapter 9). Sternberg applied the same question to love: Does love consist of one component or many? Sternberg gave a number of different love and attraction questionnaires to students and asked them to rate lovers, relatives, and friends. He analyzed the data using the techniques of factor analysis (the statistical technique, discussed in Chapter 13, designed to find out which items in a test go together—like verbal and performance IQ). Three main components to love ratings emerged from this analysis, and he labeled them *passion*, *intimacy*, and *decision/commitment*. Intimacy is made up of such feelings as caring for the loved one's welfare, mutual understanding, and emotional support. Intimacy without passion and commitment characterizes friendships. The passion component is the most physiologically involving, composed of sexual desire, romantic feelings, and physical attraction. When unaccompanied by intimacy and commitment, passion characterizes infatuation, the heart-fluttering feeling of a high school crush. The final component, decision/commitment, is the more cognitive or rational side of love. In the short term, it has to do with whether you are willing to define yourself as "in love" with the other person, and in the long term with whether you are willing to commit yourself to a relationship with him or her. By itself, without intimacy or passion, decision/commitment characterizes the love of a couple that is "staying together for the kids."

Of the different components of love, passionate love has probably aroused the most curiosity not only in poets, but also in social psychologists. Ellen Berscheid and Elaine Walster (1971) applied Schachter and Singer's two-factor theory of emotion to passionate love. As you may recall from Chapter 10, this theory posits that all emotional states are physiologically the same. Thus, the first factor, general physiological arousal, is the same for anger, fear, joy, and love. We discriminate one emotion from another, according to this theory, by the second factor—our cognitive interpretation of the situation. If we find ourselves aroused and see a black widow spider on our bed, we surmise that we are afraid; if we find an attractive person there, we may surmise that we are in love.

The two-component theory of love was tested in a creative field experiment (Dutton and Aron, 1974). An attractive woman introduced herself to individual men walking alone across one of two bridges in a Canadian national park. One bridge was a shaky suspension span that shook in the wind 130 feet above the rocky canyon floor below. The other was wide, set a few feet above a gentle creek. Men who met the woman on the frightening suspension bridge later showed evidence of more attraction for her. In a laboratory study, these same researchers found that men who were threatened with electric shock also reported more attraction to a woman present in the lab. Why should a frightening situation increase romantic attraction? According to the two-factor theory, a fear situation leads to a general state of arousal that may be mistakenly attributed to a nearby attractive person. That is, the person notes his or her heart beating, sees the attractive other, and mistakenly assumes that the attractive other is causing the heartthrobs.

Not all social psychologists agree that we commonly mistake fear for love. It seems questionable whether people facing a clear threat of a deadly fall or a painful shock ignore the true cause of their arousal, and attribute it instead to sexual desire. But the fear–attraction results can be explained in another way. Perhaps people who share a stressful experience make no mistake about the true source of their arousal, but are instead consoled by the other person's presence (Kenrick and Cialdini, 1977). This fear–consolation explanation is supported by other findings. For one thing, people

Love? The two-factor theory of love assumes that we sometimes mistake other physiological states for passionate attraction.

seek out the company of others when they are under stress (Schachter, 1959). For another, the presence of other people actually serves to reduce the unpleasant arousal associated with fear (Bovard, 1959). Finally, unpleasant arousal increases attraction even between members of the same sex (Kenrick and Johnson, 1979, among others) even though same-sex people are less likely to attribute their arousal to one another. Sharing an unpleasant situation may promote attraction by increasing feelings of intimacy, not by leading to a mistaken attribution of passion. However, this issue is one that psychologists are still debating (Allen et al., 1989; White, Fishbein, and Rutstein, 1981).

Mistaken fear or no, passionate love seems to fade with time (Cimbalo et al., 1976; Driscoll et al., 1972, among others). This may seem lamentable, but there is some consolation. The other aspects of love, intimacy and commitment, seem to increase with time (Cimbalo et al., 1976; Sternberg, 1986). To summarize, love is composed of several different components—passion, intimacy, and commitment. Over time, the focus of a relationship tends to shift from passion to intimacy and commitment. Passion may be fueled by outside events that produce unpleasant arousal, but whether this is due to increasing intimacy or mislabeled arousal is still under debate.

AGGRESSION

In our tendency to form loving bonds, humans are special among mammals, many of whom mate without long-term relationships. Unfortunately, humans as a species are also adept at harming one another. As defined earlier, aggression refers to behavior intended to harm another person. The line between aggression and other forms of behavior is sometimes unclear. Not all aggression is physical—a hostile comment may be designed to hurt another's feelings. Some physically aggressive behavior is even playful, as when lovers pinch or poke one another without the intention to inflict any real harm (Gergen, 1990). Sometimes, however, playful aggression or verbal assaults escalate into physical violence (Wilson and Daly, 1985). As we noted, there are over 685,000 violent assaults and 18,000 killings in America each year. This darker side of human social behavior has inspired at least as much social psychological inquiry as has our loving side. The possible psychological explanations offered for aggression have included the influence of too much violence on television, high levels of male hormones in the perpetrators' bloodstreams, and even unpleasant weather. We will discuss evidence that each of these factors can play a role.

ENVIRONMENTAL FACTORS IN AGGRESSION

Aggression is sometimes fueled by factors completely outside the individuals involved. If you have ever been in a traffic jam on a hot and steamy August day, you may have found yourself becoming inordinately irritated at other drivers' minor discourtesies. One team of researchers observed drivers' reactions to a car that blocked their way at a green light in a suburb of Phoenix, Arizona, where summer temperatures commonly soar above 100 degrees Fahrenheit. Below 80 degrees, the majority of the frustrated drivers either did not honk or honked very briefly. Above 100, things changed—the majority of the drivers not only honked, they leaned on their horns for over half of the time that the light was green (Kenrick and MacFarlane, 1986). The same phenomenon applies to the more serious forms of interpersonal hostility. When the mercury rises, so does the number of murders, rapes, assaults, wife-batterings, and even political uprisings (Anderson, 1989). Those findings could be explained simply by the fact that more people, including criminals and potential vic-

tims, are out and around in hot weather. Yet if that were the explanation, then all sorts of crime would increase. This does not seem to be the case. Instead, hot weather increased the percentage of violent crimes in comparison to nonviolent crimes.

Environmental factors that lead to anonymity also increase aggressive behavior. One researcher examined the horrifying phenomenon of "suicide baiting," in which a crowd observing a potential suicide challenges the depressed person to jump to his or her death (Mann, 1981). Suicide baiting is unlikely when the individuals in the crowd are easily identifiable; for instance, when it is daylight or when the crowd is small. But as night falls and the crowd swells to the point that participants feel anonymous, they are likely to begin to shout "jump." The term **deindividuation** refers to a feeling that one will not be held responsible for his or her behavior. Deindividuation is increased by any factor that makes us feel anonymous, such as darkness, crowds, or even Halloween disguises (Zimbardo, 1970; Diener et al., 1976). So it seems as if the environment does have an impact on aggressiveness. Heat, darkness, and throngs of people can bring out the aggressive side of human behavior.

FRUSTRATION AND RETALIATION

Situations that cause frustration can also breed aggression. Think back to the overheated drivers whose way is blocked. In the historical background section, we noted that several early theorists postulated a relationship between frustration and aggression. Although aggression can occur even when a person is not frustrated (as when a bomber pilot follows orders to level a village below) and although frustration does not always lead to aggression, frustration can increase the likelihood of violence—especially if the frustration is caused by a person who appears to be frustrating us intentionally (Berkowitz, 1989; Kulik and Brown, 1979, among others).

Other people's intentional attempts to annoy us seem to be a most provocative sort of frustration. For instance, students who are rude or hostile to one another in an experiment are likely to lead other subjects to be hostile in return, thus beginning an escalating cycle of attack, retaliation, and counterretaliation (Goldstein et al., 1975). Margot Wilson and Martin Daly (1985) analyzed police reports for murders in Detroit and found that "retaliation for previous verbal or physical abuse" was the most frequently cited cause of a killing. Often the previous verbal or physical abuse is very minor, what police call a "trivial altercation," which then escalates as the participants try to better one another in front of witnesses. Here is one example:

> Case 121: Victim (male, age 19), offender (male, age 23) and others had been drinking together. Victim was a boxer and was talking about his fights. Offender showed off with his night stick by placing it between the victim's legs and lifting him in the air. Victim was embarrassed and asked offender to let him down. Victim accused offender of tearing his pants and told offender to pay for them. Offender and others were laughing at victim. Victim hit offender and both were told to leave. Victim left first, then stood on the porch. Offender says victim hit him again when he came out, so he shot him.

(Wilson and Daly, 1985)

These findings support the idea that it is the perceived intention behind the frustrating action that increases the likelihood that aggression will occur.

MEDIA VIOLENCE

By the time he or she reaches the age of 18, the average American child will have watched 200,000 acts of violence on television (Plagens, Miller, Foote, and Yoffe, 1991).

If you or your impressionable little brothers and sisters turn on your television during "prime time," when most people watch their favorite programs, you can watch people punching one another's noses, breaking chairs over one anothers' heads, brutally kicking each other's faces, stabbing one another, and blasting one another with automatic weapons. This gruesome spectacle is hard to avoid on television—fully eight out of ten programs include violence. What about children's programs on Saturday morning? These contain an average of 20 violent acts per hour! Social psychologists have done hundreds of studies to determine what all of this exposure to violence on TV does to people—especially children.

RESEARCH ON TELEVISION AND AGGRESSION

There is evidence that children, particularly boys, who watch a lot of violent television are quite a bit more aggressive than those who watch less (Belson, 1978; Friedrich-Cofer and Huston, 1986). As we have stressed before, a correlation between two variables such as watching violent TV and acting aggressively is not proof positive of cause and effect. Maybe violent TV causes the violent behavior, or maybe violent boys choose to watch more violent programs, or maybe some third factor (poverty, perhaps, or crowding) leads to both violence and violent program choice independently. (Perhaps poor people are more likely to watch violent television, but would be just as violent even without its influence.) One researcher was able to think of 22 possible "third factors" that could have produced the association, but when he measured and statistically removed their influence, the connection between violent TV and violent behavior remained (Belson, 1978).

In order to be certain that violent TV causes violent behavior, the researcher must experimentally control the amount of violent TV to which children are exposed, and then measure variations in their aggressiveness. Several psychologists have done just that, and they generally find that viewers of violent TV become more aggressive than those exposed to nonviolent TV (Leyens et al., 1975; Parke, 1977, among others). In any topic area where hundreds of studies have been done, there is an occasional study that shows a negative result. Although not all studies of violent TV and aggression produce exactly the same results, the vast majority of studies show that the two are positively related (Eron and Huesmann, 1985; Friedrich-Cofer and Huston, 1986). The safest conclusion at this point is that watching violent TV may increase violence in certain viewers who are predisposed to aggression. Although not everyone acts aggressively after watching violent TV, the effect across millions of viewers is worthy of national concern. The movie *Shaft* depicted a man being doused with gasoline and burned. Most adolescents who watched the movie did not go out and imitate this unusual act of cruelty, but several unconnected bands of youth across the country did—in one case burning a sleeping hobo, in another a woman walking home with her groceries. There are many other documented cases in which an unusual act of violence on television or in the movies has been followed by mimicry across the country (Brigham, 1986).

Some theorists have argued that watching violence can have the opposite effect, vicariously draining off violent tendencies in observers. For example, Freud's **catharsis** theory postulated that aggressive urges build up over time. Like hunger, they only get worse if the energy is not purged. ("Catharsis" is another term for purging.) Freud reasoned that we can satiate our aggressive appetite in several ways—we can immediately attack anyone who frustrates us (frowned on in civilized society); displace the anger in an indirect way (chop wood for a few minutes), or, most indirectly, vicariously identify with someone else's aggressive acts (watch a karate tournament). The overall evidence has not supported this theory. As we saw above, youngsters who watch more violent TV are more, not less, violent. Violent sports events such as hockey, football, and soccer are followed by increases in violence among viewers, not the decreases that catharsis theory would predict (Arms et al., 1979). Most alarmingly, Phillips (1985) found that the homicide rate goes up after a televised heavyweight boxing match.

PORNOGRAPHY AND VIOLENCE AGAINST WOMEN

Violence in the media is not limited to cops and robbers shooting at one another. Some pornographic films and magazines purposely mix violence and sexuality. Some critics of violent pornography point to findings that show that aggression is most likely to be imitated if the violent model is rewarded (Bandura, Ross, and Ross, 1961). They note that a common theme in rape films gives just such a message about sexual violence. In these films, the woman is commonly depicted as first

The controversy over violent pornography.
Research indicates that violent pornography can lead to violence towards women. Contrary to the claims of those who oppose all erotica, however, research by Edward Donnerstein and his colleagues (discussed in the text) suggests that it is the violence, rather than the sexuality, which is to blame. In this sense, prime-time television and popular movies often contain the same harmful ingredient as violent pornography—a message that violence can lead to positive outcomes.

resisting the rapist, but later enjoying herself and wanting more of the same treatment.

Let us consider the details of one study that tested the applicability of the vicarious reward principle to the area of pornography (Donnerstein and Berkowitz, 1981). In that research, undergraduate men at the University of Wisconsin arrived for an experiment that was supposedly intended to study "the effects of stress on learning and physiological responses." After being introduced to another participant (really a confederate of the experimenter), the students were asked to write an essay that the confederate was to evaluate. The confederate's "evaluation" was partly communicated through written comments. In addition, the confederate could also use electric shocks to express displeasure with the essay. In each case the confederate gave nearly the maximum allowable number of shocks, and made derogatory comments about the subject's essay. During the next phase of the experiment, the confederate was to study a list of words for his or her own stressful performance task. While the confederate presumably studied the list, the experimenter asked the student to rate a film to be used in "later research."

There were actually four films:

1) *Neutral:* A nonaggressive talk show clipping,

2) *Purely erotic:* A depiction of a couple engaged in sexual intercourse,

3) *Aggressive erotic–positive outcome:* A depiction of a woman who is tied up, slapped, and sexually attacked by her two male study partners, but who ends up smiling and in no way resisting, and

4) *Aggressive erotic–negative outcome:* Exactly like 3, except that the woman ends up suffering.

After watching one of the films, the students were given an opportunity to deliver shocks to the confederate who had insulted them earlier. The results are shown in Figure 18.2.

As you can see, the type of film viewed had little effect on the amount of shock given to a male confederate. However, the aggressive–erotic films increased the amount of shock that the male subjects gave to a female. Among these subjects, who were previously angered by the confederate, it did not make much difference whether the outcome of the film was positive or negative for the woman. A second experiment included subjects who were not made angry first, and found that only the positive outcome film increased attacks on the woman. These findings suggest that filmed de-

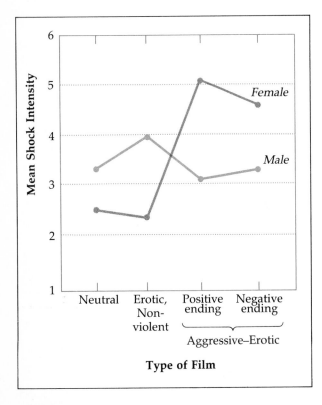

FIGURE 18.2 Violent erotica's effect on aggression. Men exposed to a film depicting violence against a woman were later more likely to act aggressively towards a female target. The type of film had no effect on aggression towards a male target. In this study, done with angered subjects, it did not make a significant difference whether the outcome of the film was positive or negative for the woman.

pictions of violence towards a woman can increase a man's tendency to violence towards another woman. If the outcome of that violence is positive, the depiction can increase aggression even in subjects who are not especially angry at the woman.

Note that an erotic film by itself has no effect (or, if anything, a slight inhibitory effect). In fact, earlier research using soft-core nonviolent erotica, such as Playboy centerfolds, has actually found decreased aggression following exposure (Baron, 1974). Research indicates that it is the violence, not the sex, that increases aggressiveness (Malamuth and Donnerstein, 1984). One general principle seems clear—depictions of violence, prevalent in everything from X-rated films to kiddie television programs, can increase aggressiveness in viewers.

HORMONES, GENDER, AND AGGRESSION

There is another, very different, sort of connection between sex and aggression. Numerous studies with animals have found that injections of the sex hormone **testosterone** can increase aggressive behavior (Rose et al., 1971, among others). Research with prison inmates found that testosterone levels in prisoners were unrelated to violence in prison, but were related to a history of violent crime in adolescence (Kreuz and Rose, 1972). Social psychologist James Dabbs and his colleagues (1987, 1988) found higher testosterone levels in the prison inmates convicted of violent as opposed to nonviolent crimes. Since women have lower testosterone levels than men, perhaps these hormonal effects are related to the much higher rates of violent behavior among males. How much more violent are males? Consider how many of the murders in the weekly news are committed by women. Every year, there are six John Oliver Hubertys for every one Lizzie Borden. As Figure 18.3 shows, men are, compared with women, nine times more likely to commit an arrest-worthy act of violence. Interestingly, it is the young males, who have the highest testosterone levels, who are the most likely to be violent (Wilson and Daly, 1985). As testosterone decreases with age, so does the tendency to commit violent crimes. Males and females in our society are exposed to very different expectancies about aggression, so the gender differences in violence could be explained partly or completely by cultural factors. Whether the cultural norms are the cause of sex differences in aggression, or simply another result of the same biological pressures, is a matter of some debate (Kenrick, 1987). Some evidence against a completely cultural argument comes from findings that gender differences in violent crime are not limited to our culture. In fact, they show up at least as strongly in other cultures (Daly and Wilson, 1988).

A note of caution is required here, however. The relationship between testosterone and aggression in humans is probably small (Kreuz and Rose, 1972). Most men with high testosterone levels do not commit violent crimes, and many violent criminals have normal testosterone levels. If testosterone does have an effect on aggressiveness, it seems more likely to operate by slightly increasing the likelihood that a person will act in a dominant manner, and not by inducing a state of uncontrollable rage. Across thousands of men, those slight increases in individual dominance behaviors could lead to an occasional violent altercation. Thus a high testosterone level would not lead directly to aggression, but might influence a person's responses to other factors in the situation. As in all of the behaviors we have discussed, it is important to keep in mind that biological states do not control people's behavior. Instead, those temporary states

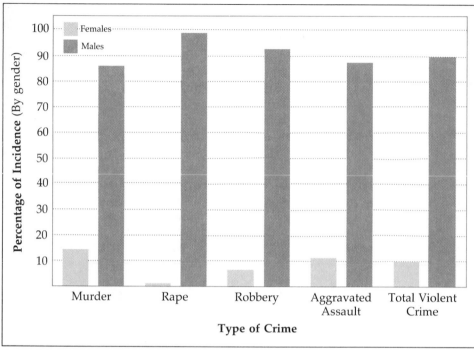

[handwritten note: Men are 9x more likely to commit violent acts]

FIGURE 18.3 Arrests for violent crimes as a function of the perpetrator's gender. Males commit six to 99 times more violent crimes than females, depending on the category.

interact with each individual's learning history and his or her interpretation of the current situation.

ALTRUISM

Sexual attraction and aggression are two domains in which behavior seems to be directly motivated by self-interest. But what about the selfless side of human behavior? Certainly there are plenty of instances of seemingly selfless action. Andrew Carnegie, the multimillionaire founder of U.S. Steel, is a case in point. Carnegie was no penny-pinching miser. He became a great philanthropist and, among other things, financed over 2,800 libraries. What motivates people such as Carnegie or the thousands of less noted philanthropists who gave to help the starving Africans during the Live Aid concert? What prompts someone like subway hero Everett Sanderson to risk his life for a total stranger? Ironically, the social psychological study of altruism began not with these helpful souls, but with a famous failure of human helpfulness.

At 3:30 A.M. on March 13, 1964, Kitty Genovese was returning to her Queens apartment after work. (She managed a bar.) Walking from her parking lot, she was grabbed by a man with a knife. According to neighbors' reports, she screamed "Oh, my God! He stabbed me. Please help me! Please help me!" Later inquiries revealed that 38 of her neighbors had heard her cries and went to their windows. One person shouted "Let that girl alone!" but the assailant returned to stab

her again. When a number of apartment lights went on, the assailant drove away, but returned again 10 minutes later. Ms. Genovese had crawled to the back of her building, but her pursuer found her there and stabbed her again. This went on for a half hour before someone finally called the police—after first calling a friend for advice. The police arrived in two minutes, but it was too late. Kitty Genovese was dead and the murderer had made a safe getaway. One man had begun to call before the last fatal attack, but was stopped by his wife, who said, "Thirty people have probably called by now."

BYSTANDER INTERVENTION (AND BYSTANDER APATHY)

The Genovese incident aroused the fascination of John Darley and Bibb Latane, two social psychologists who were in New York at the time. They began research to determine what could cause people to ignore emergencies such as this one. One factor they thought might be important in causing bystander apathy in a big city like New York is **diffusion of responsibility.** Diffusion of responsibility refers to the assumption that duty and accountability can be divided among the members of a group. When there are a number of potential helpers around, each may assume that the others will take responsibility. ("Thirty people have probably called by now.") To examine this dilution of personal accountability, they set up an experiment in which participants heard a fellow subject in a nearby room suddenly begin to have an epileptic seizure. Before dropping to the floor, he stammered out that he was going to die, and asked for help. Some subjects were led to believe that they were alone in the lab with the victim. These subjects all ran to help him very quickly. However, when subjects believed that they were in a group of five, only 62 percent did anything to help, and they did so only after a longer delay.

Latane and Darley hypothesized five steps a bystander must go through before helping someone in need. The steps are outlined in Figure 18.4. A bystander must first notice the event, then interpret it as an emergency. Some of Kitty Genovese's neighbors did not even hear the commotion, while others thought that it might be a lovers' quarrel and therefore not a "real" emergency. Even after deciding that a particular ruckus is an emergency, the observer must then decide whether he or she is the person responsible for helping. Some of Kitty Genovese's neighbors sensed that trouble was at hand, but expected that someone else would do something—this group includes the woman who assured her husband that someone else had called the police. After deciding to take responsible action, the onlooker must

choose which action to take. (Should I call the police? Rush out to help? Recruit other neighbors to rescue the victim?). Even the man who finally did call the police apparently had difficulty choosing an appropriate course of action, since he first called a friend for advice. Finally, the observer must carry out the plan. Normally this process does not require as much mental effort as it may sound. When the emergency is unmistakeable and the bystander's responsibility is clear, help normally comes within seconds (Clark and Word, 1972). Everett Sanderson jumped onto the tracks, saved the girl, and was himself saved by the other onlookers in the time it takes a subway train to roar into the station.

MOOD AND HELPING

How do our moods influence our charitability? Research shows that we are more inclined to show kindness if we are in an especially good or, sometimes, an especially low mood. The effects of pleasant experiences on helping are consistent and positive. For instance, people who have just been handed cookies or found change in a phone booth (Isen and Levin, 1972), heard good news on the

FIGURE 18.4 The bystander intervention process. A potential helper must go through several steps before coming to the rescue.

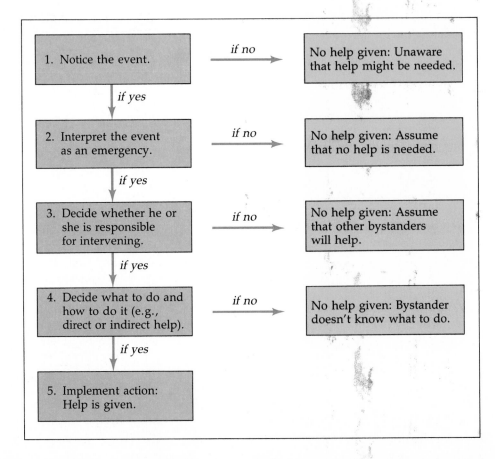

1. Notice the event. — *if no* → No help given: Unaware that help might be needed.

if yes

2. Interpret the event as an emergency. — *if no* → No help given: Assume that no help is needed.

if yes

3. Decide whether he or she is responsible for intervening. — *if no* → No help given: Assume that other bystanders will help.

if yes

4. Decide what to do and how to do it (e.g., direct or indirect help). — *if no* → No help given: Bystander doesn't know what to do.

if yes

5. Implement action: Help is given.

radio (Veitch et al., 1977), or remembered happy times (Manucia et al., 1984) are all more willing to show kindness to others. In the same vein, tips are more magnanimous on sunny days (Cunningham 1979). No doubt the uplifting music played during the Live Aid Concert helped to raise the $70 million in donations.

Bad mood has a less consistent effect on helping. In studies of children, bad mood seem to decrease helping (Isen et al., 1973, among others), but studies of adults often find that bad moods increase generosity (Cialdini et al., 1973). Perhaps the discrepancy can be explained by the lack of complete socialization in children. Why should this make a difference? Young children have not yet fully understood the value that society puts on kindness. They are basically selfish, and giving something away when they are in bad moods only makes them feel worse. Adults also want to feel better when they are in bad moods, but they have had years of being reinforced for sharing, and have thereby internalized the social reward value of charitableness. An adult can consequently pat herself on the back for altruism, and she knows that this is one way to make herself feel better when she is in a bad mood. Consistent with this reasoning, a number of studies show how altruism seems to change from a self-punishment to a self-reward as people grow older (Cialdini et al., 1981).

The issue underlies a major theoretical dispute about the roots of human kindness. Is there any behavior that can be called true altruism, or are there selfish hidden interests motivating even seemingly charitable actions? Daniel Batson and his colleagues argue that helping is often selfless, and point to their own findings on empathy and helping (Batson et al., 1988, among others). In some of these studies, students were confronted with a chance to help a fellow student named Katie. Students first listened to a taped radio program called "News from the Personal Side," which described how Katie's parents and sister have recently been killed in a car accident. As Katie describes in the interview, her parents did not have insurance, and she is desperately trying to support her younger brother and sister while she completes her last year in college. Before hearing the interview, some students were led to empathize with her by instructions to "try to imagine how the person who is being interviewed feels about what has happened." Others were instructed to "focus on the technical aspects of the broadcast." Later, students read a letter in which Katie asks for help from students who might be willing to pitch in with tasks such as babysitting, fixing things around the house, providing transportation, or stuffing envelopes for a fundraising project. Students who were led to feel empathy for her plight donated significantly more time to help her, even when they were given justification for not helping, and could easily have acted selfishly (Batson et al., 1988). Batson and his colleagues have even found that empathy can motivate students to volunteer to receive electric shocks in the place of another student.

Not everyone agrees with this view of empathic helping as being truly selfless. It may be that our responses to the pleas of others are better understood in terms of social influence, such as wanting others to think well of us, rather than altruism (Cialdini et al., 1987). Consider an example of an ostensibly altruistic behavior that was really only an example of social influence, which is the subject of our next section. One of the authors of this text was recently invited to a $50-a-plate fundraiser dinner for a local arts group. Someone had already paid $50 for the plate in question, but was unable to attend. I accepted out of totally selfish motivations, having no particular interest in the needs of the arts group, but happy to take a free meal. However, there was no free meal in this case. Several local celebrities had also volunteered to solicit additional donations during the event. Surrounded by wealthy businesspeople writing out checks, I dug out my own checkbook and made a donation for an amount substantially larger than college professors typically put aside for supper. No one ever explicitly asked for a donation, but I wrote the check to avoid the great sense of embarassment I would have felt had I not written it.

SOCIAL INFLUENCE

The presence of others can inspire us to donate more, to become more aggressive, or, as in the case of Kitty Genovese's neighbors, to do *less* than we might if we were acting alone. **Social influence** refers to changes people make in their behavior in response to real or imagined pressures from others. This section examines the basic forces by which social influence operates. These social pressures can range from direct orders to the unspoken rules of etiquette. Social influence researchers use the term **obedience** to refer to responses to orders and the term **compliance** to refer to responses to milder requests to persuade us to purchase something or donate to a cause. When a

Conformity with the members of the group is a cross-cultural phenomenon. On Pentecost Island (left), young males engage in a social ritual called the land dive, which involves jumping head first off a tower up to 100 feet high. London teenagers (right) achieve identity through outlandish dress.

person changes his or her behavior in response to actual or perceived social pressures, social influence researchers call it **conformity**.

We are very tuned to what sociologists call **social expectations,** our perceptions of how others expect us to behave. Most of the time, the influence of other people changes our behavior without any overt effort. Like the professor at the fundraiser, we respond to subtle unspoken rules. We look to see what others are doing, and feel uncomfortable if we do not "fit in." Parents, incredulous when their children eagerly conform to the latest fad, sometimes ask, "If your friends jumped off a cliff, would you follow them?" On Pentecost Island in the New Hebrides, the answer seems to be "Yes." There, young men join in an annual ritual called the "land dive." After building a wooden tower 100 feet up into the air, they jump off, head first. It's not completely crazy, they do tie a 90-foot vine to their legs that stretches just a little, so the diver's head snaps to rest a foot or two from the ground. If the vine tears, however, the land diver may die or be crippled from the impact. In the next section, we will discuss an even more dangerous form of social influence, involving the imitation of suicide.

DYSFUNCTION:
Suicide Imitation

On April 23, 1986, a UPI press release from Tokyo read:

> In what psychologists are calling a wave of suicides, at least 28 young people have killed themselves since a teen-age idol jumped to her death from a Tokyo building two weeks ago. . . . Teen-age singing star Yukiko Okada, 18, took her life April 8 by leaping from a seven-story building in downtown Tokyo in despair over a failed love affair. Local television stations spent hours showing interviews with Okada's friends and family. . . . The wave of suicides began two days later, with an average of one a day . . . most by falls from buildings.

This sort of mass suicide after the death of a famous person is nothing peculiar to Japanese culture. As we mentioned at the opening of this chapter, Goethe's novel about the suicidal young Werther led to an epidemic of suicides across Europe. And during August, 1962, the month after

Marilyn Monroe took her life, the number of suicides in the United States jumped by 200.

Sociologist David Phillips (1974; 1985) uncovered other fascinating data on imitative suicide. He reasoned that not everyone commiting suicide wants to be part of a public spectacle. To save their families and friends any additional grief, some people try to cover up their suicide by making their deaths appear to be unintentional. One way to do this is to hide among the many automobile fatalities by simply driving one's car off the road. When Phillips examined single-car accidents after a famous suicide, he found that the number of such "accidents" increased significantly. On average, there were several hundred extra traffic fatalities in the week after the famous suicide. Intriguingly, only single-car accidents increased, and, compared with normal months, the victims of single-car accidents during the postsuicide months died significantly more quickly. Those quick deaths are the signature of a suicide as opposed to a careless accident. In true accidents, drivers often attempt to save themselves by hitting the brakes at the last minute, reducing fatal injuries. A suicide just drives at full fatal speed into the nearest embankment.

Other evidence supports Phillips's "suicide epidemic" theory. A wave of accidents often is positively correlated with the amount of newspaper coverage of the event. Counting the number of column inches devoted to each suicide, Phillips found that the more inches, the more single-car crashes. Second, the accident victims tend to be similar to the famous person—older females if the famous person was an older female; younger males if it was a young male who took his life. This is consistent with other research on imitation, which finds similar models to have the most impact on observers' behavior. ■

An even more serious example of dysfunctional social influence was the conformity associated with Nazism, a massive movement that led not only to a tremendously chauvinistic military program, but also to the highly organized extermination of millions of Jews as well as gypsies, homosexuals, and others whom the Nazis judged to be "undesirable." The genocide that took place in Germany, Poland, and elsewhere in Eastern Europe prompted a number of psychologists, many of whom had fled to the United States to escape the Nazi movement, to examine the conditions under which such pathological conformity was likely to occur. What made so many people willing to obey orders to kill men, women and children?

THE AUTHORITARIAN PERSONALITY

Are some people especially susceptible to pathological conformity? During the 1940s, a team of researchers at Berkeley found evidence that the answer might be "yes" (Adorno et al., 1950). They developed the F (for Fascism) scale to measure the correlates of antisemitism. They found prejudice against Jews associated with a syndrome of other attitudes and personality traits, which they dubbed the **authoritarian personality.** People prejudiced against one minority group tend to be similarly prejudiced against any people not like themselves. Sociologists use the term **ethnocentric** for people like this, who see their own ethnic group as above the others. Authoritarians are extremely conventional in their behavior, rigid in their moral views, concerned with the propriety of other people's sexual behavior, and preoccupied with power and toughness. Another central characteristic of such individuals is their belief in the importance of a strong and powerful leader. The prototypical authoritarian is thus extremely politically conservative, conformist, and militaristic. According to Erich Fromm (1941), himself a refugee from Nazi Germany, German culture at the beginning of this century instilled these values in children and thus paved the way for the rise of Adolf Hitler and Nazism.

Beyond the general influence of culture, the F-scale researchers believed there was another key ingredient in the development of authoritarianism—threat to the ego. Their research indicated that authoritarians were raised by harsh disciplinarian parents, who were intolerant of any hostility or independence in the child. Presumably a child brought up by such parents would feel weak and helpless against authority, but, nevertheless, feel anger towards his parents. Since the hostile feelings cannot be directed against strict parents, it is redirected against safer targets—weak and unpopular outgroups. (In prewar Germany, these outgroups would have included Jews, gypsies, and homosexuals.) In the postwar United States, they have included blacks, Orientals, and most recently, Arabs.

There is some experimental support for the idea that people who are threatened become more identified with their own group and more prejudiced against outgroups. For instance, one study found

Authoritarianism. Authoritarian movements occur in our country as well as in Nazi Germany. Members of these groups tend to be prejudiced against anyone not like themselves. The original researchers believed that displaced hostility toward harsh parents contributed to authoritarianism.

that Arizona State University students whose self-esteem was lowered by false feedback about their performance were unusually likely to identify with the powerful Arizona State football team, and to say derogatory things about the school's traditional rival, the University of Arizona (Cialdini and Richardson, 1980).

OBEDIENCE TO AUTHORITY

Stanley Milgram was a social psychologist who was fascinated by the same question that intrigued Adorno and his colleagues. Rather than focusing on the personality of the overly conforming individual, though, Milgram examined the situational factors that might lead to behavior like that of the obedient guards in the concentration camps. This focus on situational pressures over individual personality has been characteristic of social psychology. From this vantage point, Milgram guessed that most Americans would have acted just like the obedient guards if faced with the same social pressures. Milgram believed that people faced with a powerful authority figure are loathe to question his directives. As the authority figure gets physically closer to us, his power over us becomes more overwhelming, and we become even more likely to obey without thinking. In Chapter 1, we examined some ethical questions about Milgram's research on obedience. We will now look in more detail at this study, one of the best known and most controversial in the history of psychology.

During the early 1960s, Milgram solicited adult men for a "learning experiment" at Yale University

(Milgram, 1974). (See Figure 18.5.) When each man arrived, he was introduced to "another subject," who was really an actor. The experimenter explained to both men that he was studying punishment and learning, and that one of them, as "learner," would receive a series of painful electric shocks. Those shocks would be administered by the other participant, who would be the "teacher." A supposedly random drawing was rigged so the real subject always got to be the teacher. The experimenter then took both men into the next room, where he strapped the unfortunate "learner" into what looked like an electric chair, complete with a large metal plate to deliver the shocks. As the experimenter applied electrode paste "to help prevent burns," the learner mentioned that he had a heart condition, and should perhaps discontinue. The experimenter "reassured" him that the shocks would cause "no permanent tissue damage."

Following this, the teacher-subject was taken into another room and shown an ominous-looking shock delivery machine with shock levers ranging from 15 to 450 volts. Groups of shock levers were labelled with progressively more frightening terms: "slight," "moderate," "strong," "very strong," "intense," and "extreme intensity." The levers from 375 to 420 were marked in red letters: "danger: severe electric shock," and, finally, the last three levers were marked with three red Xs! Before beginning, the teacher was given a painful "sample shock" and asked to estimate its strength. After most subjects estimated it to be strong or very strong, the experimenter told them that it was actually quite mild.

FIGURE 18.5 Milgram's obedience equipment.
(A) The shock machine used in the experiments.
(B) A "learner" is strapped into the chair prior to receiving shock. (C) A subject receives a sample shock from the generator.

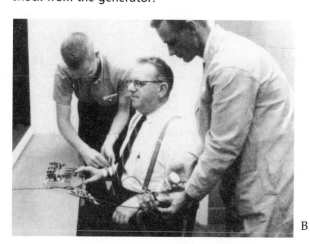

B

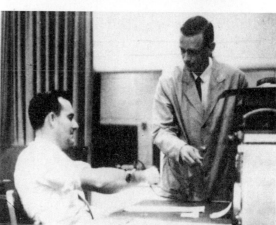

C

Once the learner-actor began his task, the subject was to give him a shock for every mistake, and increase the intensity one notch each time. The confederate made a preplanned series of mistakes, and responded to the shocks with a schedule of verbal responses. At first he just moaned "Ugh," then, at 120 v., he said "Hey, this really hurts." At 150 v. he shouted out:

That's all! Get me out of here. I told you I had heart trouble. My heart's starting to bother me now. Get me out of here, please. My heart's starting to bother me. I refuse to go on. Let me out.

If the real subject suggested that they should stop, the experimenter prodded him with "Please continue," "The experiment requires that you continue," "It is absolutely essential that you continue," and, finally "You have no other choice, you must go on." If the subject continued under the experimenter's prodding, the learner's cries became more and more agonized, until, at 330 volts, he screamed out:

Let me out of here. Let me out of here. My heart's bothering me. Let me out, I tell you. Let me out of here. Let me out of here. You

have no right to hold me here. Let me out! Let me out! Let me out! Let me out of here! Let me out! Let me out!

If a subject continued through this barrage of pleading, the learner suddenly became completely silent. The experimenter refused to check on him, but said to the subject: "Treat no response as a wrong response, and deliver the next highest level of shock." For the eight final shocks, each more intense than any that went before, the man who had been screaming so loudly now uttered not a sound.

How many men would follow orders to go all the way to 450 volts? When Milgram asked a group of psychiatrists to predict what would happen, they guessed that less than 1 percent of subjects would complete the shock series. What would you guess? Actually, the percentage was a bit higher than the psychiatrists had predicted. Fully 65 percent of subjects obeyed all the way to the bitter end. In later studies Milgram varied several aspects of the obedience situation to try to understand the elements that most contribute to conformity. (See Figure 18.6.) When the experimenter gave orders over the phone rather than in person, obedience dropped to 21 percent. In contrast, the nearer the victim was to the subject, the less the

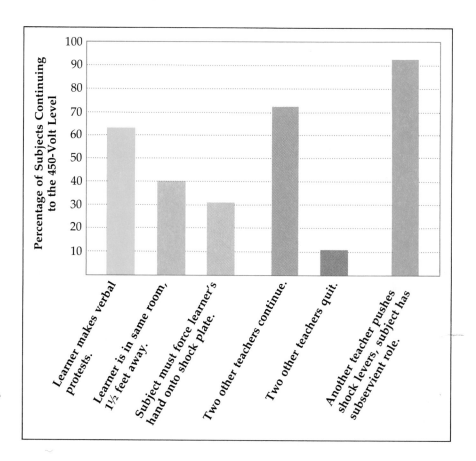

FIGURE 18.6   Results of Milgram's obedience experiment.   The graph at the right shows the percentage of subjects who completed the whole sequence of shocks as a function of variations in the situation.

obedience. If the suffering learner was in the same room, the obedience dropped to 40 percent. If the teacher had to force the learner's hand onto a shock plate, the number of obedient subjects again dropped. And if there were two confederates who refused to go on, as there was in a group version of the experiment, only 10 percent of the subjects obeyed orders to go on by themselves. In short, Milgram succeeded in showing that even pathological obedience to authority could be dramatically influenced by the pressures of a social situation.

Milgram's research is usually interpreted to show the important influence of situational pressures on people's behavior. Faced with a strange situation, we look to others to tell us what to do. If the nearest other is someone who is a local authority who acts confident and competent, people are likely to go along. If, on the other hand, the nearest other is the screaming victim or another research assistant who refuses to go along, subjects are more likely to stand against the experimenter (Milgram, 1974). But not everyone responded to the pressures of the situation, suggesting that personality factors may also have played a role. For instance, one study found that those with the authoritarian personality characteristics described earlier were most likely to obey, while those with

more democratic personality tendencies were most likely to defy the experimenter (Elms and Milgram, 1966). Once again, we can see the interaction of inner and outer determinants of behavior.

CONFORMITY: NORMATIVE AND INFORMATIONAL SOCIAL INFLUENCE

The subjects in Milgram's study faced strong pressure to go along with the experimenter's demands. Certainly, many situations arise in which people receive explicit orders about what they should and should not do. However, most social influence does not require such overt pressure. Executives wear dress suits to work and college students wear jeans to class without anyone ever even mentioning what the correct uniform is. Social psychologists distinguish between **normative social influence,** in which we comply with arbitrary social rules and conventions, and **informational social influence,** in which we conform to popular opinions about objective reality (Deutsch and Gerard, 1955). When we go home and change our jeans to fit into a party where everyone is dressed up, we are conforming to normative social influence—

"correct" party garb depends solely upon what other people have decided to wear. However, when we sleep in our car in Yellowstone Park because we see that no one else is camping out after last month's bear attack, we are conforming to informational social influence. We consider other people's judgments, then, in deciding about issues that have nothing to do with social convention.

It should come as no surprise to learn that when we are uncertain about an event we are likely to consult popular opinion to help us make up our minds (e.g., Sherif, 1935). But what would happen when a group of people expressed an obviously incorrect opinion about some unambiguous physical reality? Solomon Asch (1951) wanted to find out. He brought individual students into a room with five other people. Their task was to judge the lengths of various lines against a set of comparisons (Figure 18.7).

The discriminations were actually quite easy—subjects who were alone made mistakes on only 1 percent of the trials. In the group condition, however, the other subjects (really confederates of the experimenter) began to make incorrect judgments after the second trial. The real subjects often became visibly uncomfortable and strained their eyes to see whether they might be missing something. When their turn came, the actual subjects went against the visual evidence and voted with

the group on 37 percent of the trials. Some subjects never went along, and some went along all the time, but two-thirds of all subjects conformed with the incorrect group at least once. Asch showed that social norms can be important not only in matters of style but also in matters of hard physical reality. As we will see in the next section, our tendency to look to others to define social reality is sometimes exploited in business, politics, and organized religion.

RESEARCH AND APPLICATION:
The Tricks Influence Professionals Use

In this chapter and the last one, we have discussed a number of principles that apply to social influence. For instance, we look to authorities to give us useful information, and truly credible authorities serve us well more frequently than they serve us ill. If a physican tells you that a particular drug will help cure your infection, you follow a "rule of thumb" about medical authorities and trust the doctor, without doing a month of library research first. As we saw in Chapter 17, we do not apply all of our powers of reasoning to every new social situation we enter. That would be inefficient. If the new situation reminds us of other situations we have encountered in the past, we often function "mindlessly," using the rules that worked in previ-

FIGURE 18.7 Asch's conformity study. (A) An incredulous subject in Asch's conformity study looks more carefully after the other participants have just named the wrong comparison line as most similar to the standard. (B) Stimuli similar to those used in Asch's study. Subjects were asked to pick the comparison line that was closest in length to the standard line. After the first few trials, the other people in the room started agreeing about an incorrect answer. Asch found that the majority of subjects went against the evidence of their senses on at least one trial, and about one third of them went along with the incorrect group every time.

A

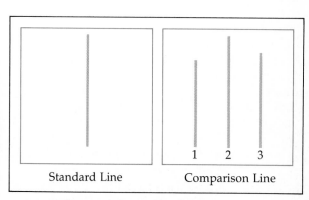

Standard Line   Comparison Line

B

ous situations. However, sometimes we function automatically when it would be better to think more deeply about what is actually going on. Social psychologist Robert Cialdini (1988) has examined how professionals in sales, politics, and profit-oriented religions exploit our mindless application of otherwise good rules.

Gaining Compliance

Cialdini observed the actions of compliance professionals at close hand by doing such things as training for employment in several door to door sales organizations and recording the soliciting strategies of religious groups at airports. He combined these field observations with laboratory and field experiments on compliance. There are several techniques frequently used on unwary people caught answering their doorbells, picking up their phones, or just out walking.

Reciprocation. If someone does us a favor, we are likely to want to return it. This **reciprocity norm** usually works well to promote mutual cooperation (Gouldner, 1960; Regan, 1971). You helped me when my car was stuck in the snow Monday, so I will help you lift a heavy box on Wednesday; neither of us could have functioned as well alone. Compliance artists know this social principle, and try to get us to apply it in an automatic, unthinking way. Over the years, members of such religious groups as the Hare Krishna Society and Reverend Moon's Unification Church have raised millions of dollars using just such a mechanism. The trick is to give you a "free" flower, funny button, or piece of candy. Cialdini noted that this makes the recipient uncomfortable, incurring an unexpected debt of reciprocity. The religious compliance pros know this, and immediately ask the newly indebted sucker for a "donation." Some doubly deceptive Krishnas dressed up as Santas and used "free" candy canes as their reciprocity hook. What Scrooge could turn down Santa, after all he has done for us?

Authority. As we have seen, people tend to defer to authority. People consult an engineer if they want to build a sound bridge, a dentist if they want to know how to care for their teeth, and a doctor if they want to make a decision about their health. Again, this appeal to authority is generally an efficient way to make decisions. Cialdini points out that compliance artists also understand this principle, and try to take unfair advantage of it. Advertisers use it when they hire an actor to play a physician speaking in favor of their product. One series of TV commercials used actor Robert Young to warn viewers about the physical dangers of

caffeine and recommend caffeine-free Sanka. Cialdini points out that the commercial was very successful at selling coffee, and was played for years. People were so willing to take an actor's word about the healthy consequences of decaffeinated coffee because, at the time, most of them knew Mr. Young not as an actor but as *Marcus Welby, M.D.*, a role he played in a very successful television series. Thus, the advertising agency had something better than a real medical authority—they had someone whom the public perceived and trusted as a medical authority. To the advertisers, it was irrelevant that the perception was erroneous, since, "as a practical matter, that man moved the Sanka" (Cialdini, 1988).

Consistency. You may recall from the last chapter that people are motivated to show consistency between their stated attitudes, their beliefs and their actions. Some health clubs use this principle on us when, before ever asking us to sign an agreement to pay hundreds of dollars for their exercise program, they first get us to make a public commitment to needing it. During the course of showing us around the spa, the salesperson will ask us whether or not we would like to be in better shape. The obvious answer, of course, is yes. Have we tried unsuccessfully to get ourselves in perfect shape in the past? Again, an undeniable yes. He

Exploiting the reciprocity norm. A member of the Hare Krishna group is arrested after pressuring customers to take candy canes as "gifts" during the Christmas season. Persuasion professionals often try to get us to use the reciprocity rule in an unthinking manner.

may also ask how much we spend on meals in restaurants every month. If we then refuse to sign up because we can not afford the exorbitant fees, he can use our public statements against us. "But you just said that you've been unsuccessful in getting yourself in shape. And you spend more money every month gorging at restaurants than you would spend getting into shape here!" The strategy is a successful one, and many people sign up on the spot. Most of those who commit to the program do not stay with it much longer than they stuck with their previous programs, incidentally, allowing the fitness hawkers to sell more memberships than their facility could otherwise handle. The salesperson's zeal in getting you to behave in a manner consistent with your fitness goal ends as soon as you sign your check.

Attraction. Advertisers also exploit the principle that people prefer to be associated with others who are physically attractive. You can see this principle at work by looking at the advertisements in almost any magazine. The physical attractiveness–liking rule is employed by political parties, too. It seems that a candidate's good looks is one of the best predictors of whether he or she will win election. Efran and Patterson (1974) found that physically attractive candidates in Canadian elections received more than twice as many votes as did less attractive candidates. Voters denied the influence of this factor on their voting, however, suggesting that people respond unthinkingly to good looks. Similarly, polls before the 1984 United States Presidential election showed that the public agreed more with Walter Mondale than with Ronald Reagan when it came to actual political issues such as military spending. But Reagan won by a landslide. Why? No doubt several factors were at work, but part of the explanation may be that the handsome actor's friendly smile and reassuring voice pushed the likeability button.

Conformity and Commitment. Advertisers also exploit our tendency to look to others to define what is appropriate. They use this principle when they tell us their product is the "fastest selling" or "largest selling." Bartenders salt their tip jars with a few dollar bills to simulate previous tips, and give customers the idea that tipping with bills, rather than coins, is the appropriate custom in their bar. One team of sociologists infiltrated a popular religious crusade, and found that these masters of conversion (and donation) may exploit this same principle (Altheide and Johnson, 1977). Before religious leaders come into a town, they sometimes send advance workers to orchestrate a "spontaneous mass outpouring of converts." Like

the pseudo-tips, this pseudo-mass conversion gets the rest of the crowd going.

Car salesmen often use a technique called "lowballing." When using the low ball, the salesman will offer a customer a very good buy on a car, designed to elicit a quick agreement. For instance, the salesman may offer to sell the car for $500 under the sticker price, and $200 under the price offered by a competing dealership. After the customer agrees to the sweet deal, the salesman goes to his manager to get "approval" for the sale. The salesman returns and tells the customer that his manager will not authorize the sale at that price, since the dealership would lose money. But, he says, the manager will allow the sale if the customer is willing to go up $250. Salesmen believe that once customers have committed to buying a particular car, and been relieved of the pressure of further shopping, they will go along with a deal they would never have accepted in the first place. Cialdini and his colleagues conducted a laboratory study in which they used the low-ball technique on students. When students were asked over the phone if they would be willing to participate in an experiment that began at 7:00 A.M., only 24 percent arrived. However, if they first agreed to participate, and were only later told that the experiment began at the crack of dawn, over 50 percent showed up (Cialdini et al., 1978). Further research has indicated that the low-ball technique works because people feel obligated to stick with their commitments (Burger and Petty, 1981).

To summarize, many of the social rules of thumb that we use to guide and simplify our social interactions can be turned against us. We use these principles without thinking carefully every time we reciprocate a favor, trust an authority or a friendly face, conform to group norms, or act consistently with our previously stated attitudes. Compliance professionals—and con artists—understand these principles, and try to get us to use them in an unthinking manner. Sometimes, this results in decisions that we might not have made if we had given them serious thought. Cialdini prescribes that, as consumers, we stop to think carefully before closing a deal that might cost us dearly. It is particularly important to go off automatic if we feel social pressure from a salesperson.

The discussion of compliance techniques offers a good example of the way in which social influence connects with the processes of social cognition. Sticking to our word with a salesman is really a form of cognitive consistency. Feeling we should reciprocate someone else's generosity without reflecting upon why that generosity is being extended (as in the case of airport solicitors who pin a flower on our lapel before asking us for money) is an example of automatic processing. Attraction and liking also play a role in how likely we are to be influenced. These studies of compliance are also a good illustration of the link between basic and applied research. In Cialdini's work researchers began by observing naturalistic (applied) interactions, such as those between car salesmen and their customers, then moved to the laboratory to test and expand the principles that appeared to be operating. Once these had been determined, the researchers moved back out to the field to apply those principles (for instance, by teaching consumers ways to avoid being duped). In the next section, we will consider how the research on social relations illustrates the general theoretical principles that thread throughout all of psychology.

INTERACTIONS:
From Genetic Structures to Ongoing Social Relations

In his 1908 *Social Psychology*, William McDougall argued that social behavior is rooted in basic physiological processes. He believed that those proximate physiological processes were based in evolutionary history, but were controlled by individual cognition and channeled by learning. In this chapter we have discussed research that runs the gamut from evolutionary or ultimate levels of explanation, as in the research on possible incest avoidance in the kibbutz; to more proximate or immediate cognitive influences such as the research suggesting that men might imitate filmed violence toward women. Social influence is also affected by still more proximate cognitive influences such as the "shaky bridge" research suggesting that our physiological state may affect our social perceptions.

It is useful to consider how these processes, from the ultimate effects of evolution to the proximate effects of physiological states, can affect one another. For instance, the findings of "incest avoidance" in the kibbutz suggest how a genetic mechanism from our evolutionary past might affect which people we will learn to be attracted to. Likewise, learning history plays a role in social cognition—young people who have never watched *Marcus Welby, M.D.* will not automatically pay attention to actor Robert Young's medical advice. Evolutionary history also plays a role in our ongoing physiological states. The release of adrenaline in the presence of a passionate lover demonstrates the general phenomenon of sympathetic arousal in response to events that relate to our survival and reproduction.

These links also highlight the very special role the behavior of other human beings plays at every phase of the proximate–ultimate continuum. Inputs from the social world link together our evolutionary past, our genetic predispositions, our individual learning histories, our ongoing cognitive processes, and the microscopic actions of hormones and neural transmitters. These processes mesh together within the individual, and they also link the individual into a world of other individuals. Consider several examples of the ways in which the social environment links together the processes we have discussed throughout this book.

Human Evolution is Evolution for Social Living. Human evolution was not simply a response to the physical environment. In addition to adapting to an upright bipedal posture, our ancestors had to adapt to life in social groups. As comparative anthropologists such as Jane Lancaster (1975) have pointed out, our hominid ancestors evolved in small close-knit groups that interacted on a daily basis. In such small groups, it would have been useful to remember who acted aggressively, who acted cooperatively, and who had leadership abilities. This could explain some of the findings we discussed in the personality chapter, which suggested that humans the world over characterize one another along dimensions of likeability versus unpleasantness and dominance versus submissiveness (White, 1980). Most other mammals do not form long-term mating bonds, and the intense attachments that form between lovers may be a product of the unique evolutionary history of humans (Mellen, 1980). Our special social history is almost certainly related to several special features of the human brain, such as the areas allocated to producing and understanding language, and other areas suited to recognizing human faces.

Important Genetic Differences Between People are Related to Social Relationships. Some of the genetically based differences between us seem to be linked to social behaviors that may have been important in our evolutionary past. For instance, several theorists have argued that higher levels of aggressiveness found in males across all human societies are linked to an evolutionary past in which males competed with one another for status (Daly and Wilson, 1988). To the extent that females were more likely to select high-status males, any genes linked to male aggressiveness would have increased in the population (Daly and Wilson,

1983). Another possible link between genes and the social environment is found in the research on temperament, discussed in the chapters on development and personality. Recall that children's temperament seems to be linked on the one hand to genetic predispositions and on the other to social behaviors such as extroversion and shyness. For example, reticent children grow up to be shy adults partly because of an innate tendency that leads them to avoid interacting with other people.

Most Human Learning is Social Learning. In the chapter on Learning (Chapter 6) we noted three basic types of learning: classical conditioning, operant conditioning, and observational learning. Each of those processes takes place in a social environment. As we noted earlier in this chapter, classical conditioning seems to play some role in determining who we like and who we dislike. Other people, such as our parents and friends, also introduce us to new foods, show us how to relax in threatening circumstances, and so on. Observational learning is learning from watching others. As Albert Bandura (1977) noted, most important human learning is acquired through observation. It would be almost absurd to think about learning a language if not for the presence of others. Other people also teach us how to play musical instruments, how to cook, and how to play chess. Learning how to drive a car or fly a plane by trial and error would be disastrous—most of us would not survive were it not for our ability to learn by observing others. In addition to their essential roles in vicarious learning, people play important roles in conditioning processes as well. Probably the most important rewards we work for,

for instance, come from our parents, teachers, friends, and lovers.

Much of Cognition is Concerned with Social Situations. As we discussed in the last chapter, a great deal of human thought involves other people. We give our attention to other people, who may easily distract us from whatever else we are trying to concentrate on; we remember other people's faces and personality characteristics; and we devote a lot of time to making attributions about what other people's behaviors mean about whether they love us, are angry at us, or are unaware of our existence.

From Individual Psychology to Group Sociology. The social behaviors we have discussed in this chapter, from love and altruism to aggression and conformity, are rooted in the basic psychological processes we discussed in the first sections of this book. As William McDougall suggested in 1908, then, each individual's development, learning, cognition, and psychophysiology all contribute to the ways he or she will relate to other individuals. In this text we have moved from the microscopic processes studied by biologists through the level of the complete individual, and now beyond the individual. In the next chapter we will consider processes that involve large groups of individuals, well into the common territory between psychology (which focuses on individual processes) and sociology (which focuses on processes involving groups of individuals). In the last chapter we consider the psychology of large scale social problems like crowding and the threat of nuclear war, and move further outward from the individual frame of reference. ■

IN CONTEXT: INTERPERSONAL RELATIONS

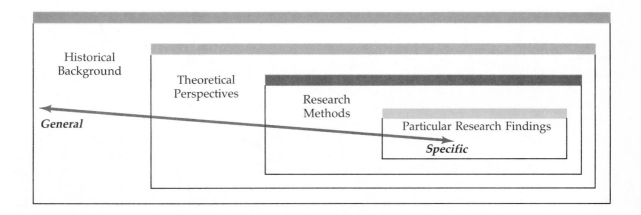

STUDY QUESTIONS

What factors influence behaviors that require *more than one individual?* More specifically, what causes people to act aggressively, to fall in love, or to act altruistically?

What are the processes by which people influence one another?

How do basic physiological, learning, and cognitive processes play a role in these complex social interactions?

HISTORICAL BACKGROUND

1. At the turn of this century, William McDougall applied evolutionary principles to social behavior. He postulated seven basic "instincts" or primary drives that underlie social behavior—flight, repulsion, curiosity, pugnacity, self-abasement, self-assertion, and the parental instinct.

2. During the 1930s and 40s, John Dollard, Neal Miller, and their colleagues developed a learning-based approach to social behavior. They explained social behaviors such as aggression in terms of rewards and punishments.

MODERN THEORETICAL PERSPECTIVES

1. The **evolutionary** perspective is based on the assumption that social relations evolved to promote survival. The research discussing cross-cultural universals in flirtation is an example of this approach.

2. **Social learning** theorists assume that social relationships develop according to the principles of classical and operant conditioning, and through observational learning. The studies discussing the role the media can play in modelling aggression are examples of this approach.

3. **Social cognition** theories are based on the principles discussed in the previous chapter. These approaches explain social interactions in terms of the way we process information and the kinds of attributions we make. The two-factor theory of love is an example of this approach.

4. Interpersonal relations can also be viewed as the combined outcome of biology, learning, and ongoing thought processes. The research showing sexual avoidance of kibbutz mates illustrates this **interactionist** approach.

RESEARCH METHODS

1. A variation of the *case study* method was illustrated in Cialdini's (1988) observations of compliance professionals such as airport "Moonies."

2. *Correlational* methods were used in several studies reported here. One example is research that shows a positive correlation between the amount of television violence one views and aggressive behavior (Belson, 1978).

3. *Experimental* methods are perhaps the most common method in this area. Milgram's (1974) research on obedience to authority, which systematically varied the proximity of the subject to the victim and the experimenter, is a good example of an experiment.

RESEARCH FINDINGS AND SUMMARY

1. Initial **attraction** is strongly influenced by physical attractiveness, similarity, and proximity. For sexual attraction, similarity and proximity effects seem to stop at the front door—people do not develop strong attractions for those with whom they are raised. Females focus relatively more on dominance and social status in a man, whereas men give relatively more weight to a woman's physical attractiveness.

2. Forming relationships involves a mutual interplay of behaviors at several levels. Flirtation gestures that begin courtship appear to be universal, and may be innate. Once a relationship begins, there is some negotiation for equitable distribution of costs and benefits, but permanent relationships tend to be more communal in orientation.

3. Feelings of **love** fall into three categories: passion, intimacy, and commitment. The two-factor theory of passionate love views this feeling as being physiologically identical to any other emotion, but distinguished by the information that it is caused by a sexually attractive person.

4. **Aggression,** or behavior intended to harm another person, is increased by several environmental factors, including heat, darkness, and crowds. Heat is associated with violent crime and the likelihood of riots. Darkness and crowds are believed to increase aggression

partly because they lead people to feel de-individuated, and therefore less responsible for their actions.

5. Frustration leads to aggression when it is caused by another person and appears to be intentional. Murders are commonly preceded by what police call "minor altercations" among young males, who may be responding to threats to their position in the social hierarchy.

6. Media violence shows a positive association with aggression in viewers. These findings lend support to a modelling theory as opposed to catharsis theory, which assumes aggressive energy can be drained off vicariously. Pornographic films dealing with rape commonly depict rewards for the rapist's aggressiveness. Evidence suggests that these films can increase aggression by males towards females, although the violence, rather than the sexual content of these films, is most crucial.

7. Men are several times more violent than women. This sex difference may be related to the hormone testosterone, which has been shown to increase aggressiveness in animals.

8. Onlookers to an emergency are less likely to help another person when there are a number of other people who could help, a phenomenon known as *diffusion of responsibility*. **Bystander intervention** seems to depend on a) noticing the event, b) interpreting it as an emergency, c) assuming responsibility, d) choosing a course of action, and e) carrying it out.

9. There is a debate about whether helping for others is motivated by selfless motives or by hidden selfish rewards. Some research indicates that empathy for a victim's plight can lead to selfless behavior, but other research suggests that even empathic helping is done for self-centered reasons.

10. **Social influence** is defined as a change in behavior in response to real or imagined pressures from others. It ranges from **conformity,** changes in behavior in response to unspoken social norms, through **compliance,** changes instigated by requests, to **obedience,** changes in behavior following explicit orders.

11. Psychologists have studied the personality characteristics associated with pathological deference to authority, such as those found in Nazi Germany. **Authoritarians** are rigid and overcontrolled individuals who show a wide range of prejudices and are oriented towards powerful others. The original researchers viewed authoritarian behavior in psychoanalytic terms, as due to displacement of hostile feelings.

12. Milgram studied situational factors associated with obedience to authority. Subjects were more likely to obey orders to shock another person when the authority was close, the victim was near, and there were no others who were willing to disobey.

13. **Normative social influence** occurs when we conform to other people's ideas about what is proper or appropriate behavior in a social situation. **Informational social influence** involves conformity to other people's ideas about physical reality. There is some evidence that people will occasionally ignore the evidence of their senses in favor of social opinion.

14. Persuasion professionals exploit our tendency to apply social rules without thinking. Some of the principles they exploit are reciprocity, credibility of authority, consistency, attraction, conformity, and commitment.

ADDITIONAL READINGS

Brehm, S. S. 1985. *Intimate relationships.* New York: Random House. An in-depth treatment of attraction and relationship formation.

Cialdini, R. B. 1988. *Influence: Science and practice,* (2nd ed.). Glenview, Ill.: Scott-Foresman. A highly readable account of the way that compliance professionals use rules of social influence to trick us.

Daly, M., and Wilson, M. 1983. *Sex, evolution and human behavior.* N. Scituate, MA.: Duxbury. A thorough account of the evidence for the evolutionary account of sexual attraction.

Daly, M., and Wilson, M. 1988. *Homicide.* Aldine de Gruyter. A well-written and thought provoking book which summarizes data on fatal violence from many cultures and historical periods.

Lumsden, C., and Wilson, E. O. 1983. *Promethean fire.* Cambridge, MA: Harvard Univ. Press. A readable account of how cognition, physiology, and cultural experience interact in producing social behavior.

Milgram, S. 1974. *Obedience to authority.* New York: Harper & Row. A fascinating account of Milgram's famous program of research on social influence.

Sternberg, R. J. and Barnes, M. L. (eds.) 1988. *The psychology of love.* New Haven, CT: Yale Univ. Press. A collection of articles by prominent researchers who adopt a range of theoretical perspectives on the causes of human love.

PSYCHOLOGY AND GLOBAL SOCIAL PROBLEMS

L ife on this planet depends on a delicate ecological balance. . . . Upset this equilibrium at any point, and monumental consequences ensue. . . . Only today, and slowly, are we coming to recognize that this great imperative of nature applies as much to us as to the creatures from whose study we have gained this knowledge. We can no longer blindly change the world about us, ignoring the consequences of change, without threatening our own survival as a species.

(Proshansky et al., 1976)

In 1854, when the total population of his home state of Washington was less than 5,000, Chief Seattle of the Susquamish tribe signed papers transferring his tribe's ancestral lands to the United States federal government. In a speech he gave on the occasion, the native American leader said that he signed the agreement out of fear that the white settlers would come with guns to take the land if the Indians refused the federal "offer." Besides his fear that white people would try to exterminate the Susquamish as they had other Indian tribes, Chief Seattle expressed some general concerns about the white American way of life:

(The white man's) appetite will devour the earth and leave behind only a desert. . . .
The sight of your cities pains the eyes of the red man. . . . There is no quiet place in the

white man's cities. No place to hear the unfurling of leaves in spring or the rustle of insects' wings. . . . The air is precious to the red man, for all things share the same breath—the beast, the tree, the man, they all share the same breath. The white man does not seem to notice the air he breathes. Like a man dying for many days, he is numb to the stench. This we know. The earth does not belong to man; man belongs to the earth. All things are connected. . . . Man did not weave the web of life; he is merely a strand in it. Whatever he does to the web, he does to himself.

(Chief Seattle, 1854)

The white settlers of 1854, many of whom regarded the Native Americans as a subordinate species, took little heed of the red man's ecological

FIGURE 19.1 Population of the state of Washington since 1850. In 1954, Chief Seattle gave his speech warning about the ecological dangers of our careless attitudes about population and the environment.

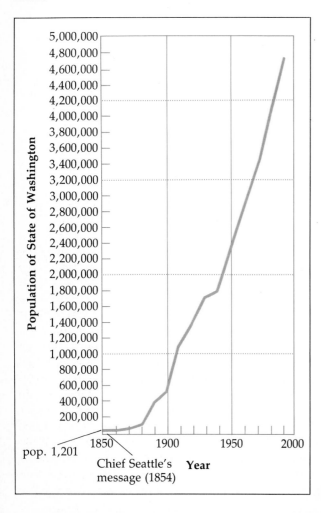

philosophy. Figure 19.1 shows the increase in population for the state of Washington in the years since Chief Seattle's speech. Today hundreds of thousands of cars cause smoggy traffic jams in the city that bears the old chief's name, and pollutants kill the fish in the local Duquamish river. The story of the conflict between white settlers and Native Americans, and of the noisy, polluted megalopolitan cities that replaced the quiet Indian villages, touches on each of the large-scale social problems we will discuss in this final chapter: overpopulation, environmental deterioration, and conflict between groups. As we will see, these social problems are interconnected with one another. We will also see that they have a special status within the field of psychology: Although they ultimately involve individual attitudes and behaviors, each of these problems must be considered at a level beyond the individual. Each necessarily involves large groups of individuals behaving in an interconnected fashion.

Global social problems are also studied by other academic disciplines, including sociology, political science, and ecology. Psychologists join in studying these problems for two reasons. First, group conflict, overpopulation, and environmental deterioration ultimately stem from behaviors at the individual level. Second, each of those global social problems has repercussions on the psychological states of individuals, increasing stress, lowering perceived life quality, and increasing individual psychopathology.

GLOBAL PROBLEMS RESULT FROM INDIVIDUAL BEHAVIORS

Consider the problem of overpopulation. Ultimately, that problem comes down to choices that individuals (or couples) make about reproduction. It may seem insignificant if one couple living in a rural area decides to have six children. Across a large number of individuals, however, this approach to reproduction has dramatic consequences in the modern world, where improved food distribution and health advances have greatly reduced mortality. Washington State's rate of growth is in no way unique. Figure 19.2 shows the similar curve for the United States as a whole. Some of the increase in United States population results from migration, which one could hope reflects a decrease elsewhere. Unfortunately, the rest of the world's population is growing at a considerably *higher* rate than that of the United States.

Environmental deterioration also depends, ultimately, upon the behaviors of individuals who

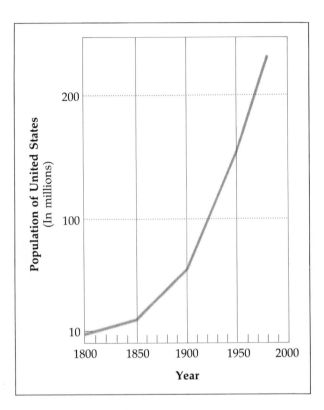

FIGURE 19.2 Population of the United States since 1800.

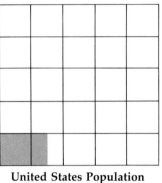

United States Population
As Percentage of World
Total

A

United States Energy Use
As Percentage of World
Total

B

FIGURE 19.3 American energy use. As demonstrated here, energy use in the United States is much higher than our population size justifies.

litter, pollute, or waste energy. Once again, it may seem of little consequence that one family keeps their home air conditioner set at a cool 72 degrees while they are out four-wheeling in their gas-inefficient pickup truck. However, that sort of behavior takes on enormous proportions when we look at the aggregate of all Americans. Every day, Americans use up the equivalent of about 38 million barrels of oil. One in nine barrels of petroleum used throughout the world goes into American automobiles, and three out of four Americans drive to work alone every day rather than take public transportation or a car pool (Zerega, 1981). Aside from transportation, most of the energy used by American households goes to keep our homes comfortable, and over half of that is wasted by inefficiency (Stern and Gardner, 1981; Stobaugh and Yergin, 1979). Americans use even more energy in the commercial sphere. (See Figure 19.3.) Petroleum waste will become more and more costly as world petroleum supplies dwindle over the next ten or twenty years, and it leads, in the meantime, to unsightly and unhealthy air pollution. (See Figure 19.4.) Nevertheless, given the ever-increasing population, the prospects for avoiding energy depletion and environmental pollution are dim unless people make radical changes in their

energy use and conservation behaviors, both at home and at work (Stobaugh and Yergin, 1979). Once again, the basis of the problem, as well as its potential solution, depends upon individual behaviors, in how we travel, insulate our homes, set our thermostats, and so on.

The problem of conflict between groups and nations also depends on attitudes, perceptions, and behavioral decisions made by individuals and small groups. In the United States, individual members of congress and cabinet advisors decide how to vote on weapons increases and foreign interventions. How politicians behave is determined in part by how individual citizens answer public opinion polls (Killeen, 1987; Nevin, 1985). Since World War II, the United States and the Soviet Union accumulated roughly 50,000 nuclear warheads, with a combined explosive power about 600,000 times as great as the bombs dropped on

A

B

FIGURE 19.4 Two views of Los Angeles. A dramatic contrast can be noted between the view on a clear day (A) and that of a day on which pollution has been trapped by an air inversion (B). Air pollution is one obvious example of environmental deterioration, made worse by careless energy consumption behaviors. Like the other global problems, air pollution stems from short-sighted behaviors, and results in long-term psychological consequences.

A nuclear explosion. The characteristic mushroom cloud rises moments after the atomic bomb was dropped on Nagasaki, Japan, on August 9, 1945.

scientific efforts from refining weapons technology to understanding the psychological triggers for group conflict, and to the development of effective principles of intergroup negotiation (Oskamp, 1985).

PSYCHOLOGICAL EFFECTS OF GLOBAL PROBLEMS ON INDIVIDUALS

Besides the fact that each of the three global problems is ultimately dependent upon individual attitudes and behaviors, those problems also have repercussions at the level of individual stress and psychopathology. Overpopulation leads indirectly to stressful consequences ranging from noise, traffic jams, and long lines in stores to food shortages and consequent starvation. In 1965, 25,000 Australians waited in line for 12,500 football tickets, and some stayed for over a week. Those queues were often accompanied by brawling and serious injury when people tried to cut into line (Mann, 1980). The population explosion has been accompanied by increasing urbanization, and city life has its own special stresses. For instance, the number of violent crimes—such as murder, rape, and aggravated assault—committed per capita is

Hiroshima and Nagasaki (Schell, 1982) (see Figure 19.5), and though the superpowers may be getting along this year, most of those hair-triggered weapons remain, and may soon be in the hands of several less pacific countries in the Middle East, such as Iraq. Unfortunately, the advances in weapons technology were not accompanied by scientific methods to control the primitive human tendency to distrust and compete with some "enemy" (Tajfel and Turner, 1986; Wilson, 1978). If the use of those weapons is to be avoided, many social scientists believe that we must now turn our

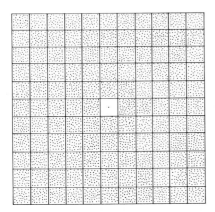

FIGURE 19.5 The current firepower of the world's nuclear armaments, expressed in comparison to the total firepower loosed in World War II. The center dot represents all the bombs dropped during all of World War II, including the nuclear bombs dropped on Nagasaki and Hiroshima. The other dots represent the world's nuclear arsenal in 1981. The current total is 6,000 times that used during World War II, but it could potentially be released in a single afternoon. The vast majority of existing nuclear weapons are American and Russian, although many other countries now have their own.

11 times greater in very large cities than in rural areas (Freedman, 1975; Statistical Abstract of the United States, 1988).

Environmental deterioration also has psychological costs. Pollution and energy shortages not only lower people's perceptions of the quality of their life, but can also be stressful in themselves (Evans and Jacobs, 1982). Likewise, the threat of nuclear war has stressful consequences. During several recent years of international tension in the 1980s, surveys indicated that most American high school and college students expected a nuclear war in their lifetimes, and did not expect to survive it (Doctor, et al., 1987; Goodman et al., 1983).

In this chapter we will consider three general questions. First, how do psychological processes contribute to each of the three global social problems? Second, what are the psychological consequences of each of these problems? Third, how might psychological principles help to solve each of these problems?

GLOBAL PROBLEMS AND THE INTEGRATIVE THEMES OF PSYCHOLOGY

In this book's opening chapter, we emphasized the importance of considering psychology as an integrated whole. At the end of this chapter, we will consider how we have moved from the microscop-

ic level of single neurons up to the level of groups of individuals affecting their global environment. Before beginning this final chapter, though, it is worth reconsidering the themes we have used to integrate the parts of the field, and emphasizing how they show up at this most macroscopic level, since the points in this chapter will tie back to each of the earlier chapters.

The most important integrative point to take away from this book is that specific research findings can best be understood in their more general context of method, theory, and historical background. This chapter will include findings from naturalistic observations of overcrowded animals, surveys of attitudes about nuclear fears, case studies of international leaders negotiating arms reductions, and laboratory experiments on group conflict. Again and again we've seen the limitations of these methods and the advantages of combining different methods—these will be evidenced here one more time. At a more general level, we will cover theoretical perspectives ranging from ultimate evolutionary analyses of overpopulation to proximate cognitive analyses of decisions to use birth control. Global problems nicely illustrate the interactionist themes that tie together different theoretical perspectives. Microscopic inner processes ranging from hormone flow to cognition combine to influence the behavior of the individual, and the individual's inner processes in turn interweave continuously with the behaviors of other people in the environment. As we shall see, those interactions between persons and environments are the joint products of past and present influences.

In this chapter, we shall see more than ever how the theoretical perspectives of psychology are influenced by historical developments in other areas of knowledge. For instance, the concern about global problems such as overpopulation and environmental deterioration can be attributed partly to recent advances in biology, especially the increasing emphasis on *ecology*, the study of relationships between animals and their environment.

We noted in the first chapter that psychologists have, from the start, been interested in applying scientific principles to understanding and changing problem behaviors. In this chapter, as in the others, we emphasize how dysfunctional consequences can stem from processes that are normally adaptive. In fact, overpopulation, environmental deterioration, and even international conflict may have grown out of psychological tendencies that, though harmful now, were useful to our ancestors.

Global problems demonstrate, perhaps more

than any of the other phenomena we have discussed, how an understanding of psychological principles can help us understand human nature. Most importantly, the study of global problems helps us see the connections between this discipline and the other branches of human knowledge, from biology to sociology and history. In the next section, in fact, we explore some of the common roots of psychology and sociology.

HISTORICAL BACKGROUND:
Mobs and Crowds

In 1908, the same year that psychologist William McDougall published his *Social Psychology*, another book of the same title was published by sociologist Edward Alsworth Ross. Instead of focusing on the social motivations within the individual, Ross was interested in groups of individuals acting together. He defined the field as the study of phenomena such as:

> The spread of the lynching spirit through a crowd in the presence of an atrocious criminal, the contagion of the panic in a beaten army, an epidemic of religious emotion. . . .
>
> *(Ross, 1908)*

The chapter titles in Ross's text include "The Crowd," "The Mob Mind," and "Public Opinion." He analyzed such historical incidents of group behavior as the 1799 "holy roller" revivalist movement in Kentucky; the Children's Crusade of 1212, in which thousands of children left their homes in search of the holy sepulchre; and the tulip bulb craze of 1634, in which the Dutch sold their houses and lands to speculate on flower roots that suddenly became worthless when the craze stopped. Ross held that people in mobs and crowds act on irrational emotions that overwhelm the normal reasoning abilities of individuals.

Ross was also interested in urbanization. He believed that the irrational mob is often paralleled in the impulsive and unreasoned behavior of city dwellers. He held that "these faults are due in part to the nervous strain of great cities. The bombardment of the senses by innumerable impressions tends to produce neurasthenia" (similar to *anxiety disorder*, in today's terminology).

Ross devoted one chapter to "prophylactics to mob mind," among which he included the study of psychology, sociology, and the classics, as well as sports, which train the individual to inhibit impulses. He also recommended country life, because he reasoned that people living in the city lose sight of "the unyielding laws of nature" that inspire more reasonable and cautious behavior.

Over the next few decades other psychologists examined social problems, using more sophisticated methods than Ross's observational and historical techniques. As we noted in Chapter 17, psychologists began to measure intergroup prejudice during the 1920s, when Thurstone did his work on attitudes toward the Chinese. And in the last chapter we mentioned that researchers interested in the Nazi phenomenon during the 1930s and 1940s began conducting experiments to study intergroup prejudice. As we noted, Neal Miller and his colleagues speculated that aggression is the result of frustration. These researchers speculated that intergroup prejudice might be a special example of this *frustration–aggression* relationship. In one of their experimental tests of this idea, boys in a summer camp were frustrated by being denied a movie that they were counting on. Then they were asked to rate Japanese and Mexicans. Compared with earlier ratings, the boys showed increased prejudice toward minority group members after they were frustrated (Miller and Bugelski, 1948).

Another classic series of studies of intergroup relations was conducted in a summer camp at Robbers' Cave state park in Oklahoma. Muzafer and Carolyn Sherif (1956) attempted to produce hostile relations between groups of boys, and then to determine which factors could reduce those intergroup conflicts. At the beginning of the summer of 1954, they divided campers into two groups. After a week, the groups had each adopted a name. The "Rattlers" and the "Eagles" put their names on their T-shirts and flags, and each group adopted a separate bunkhouse and a hide-out.

In an attempt to produce hostilities between the groups, the researchers arranged a tournament of athletic contests pitting one group against the other. Tensions started almost immediately, when the Eagles lost a tug of war to the Rattlers. In retaliation, the Eagles burned the Rattlers' flag. When the burned flag was discovered the next day, the groups began to scuffle and shout derogatory names at one another. Later, the Rattlers raided the Eagles' cabin, and the Eagles, in their turn, raided and ransacked the Rattlers' cabin.

At the end of the tournament, the researchers asked members of both groups to rate their own group as well as the outgroup. As shown in Figure 19.6, the groups made very favorable ratings of the members of their own group, but negative ratings of the other group. As we shall see later in this

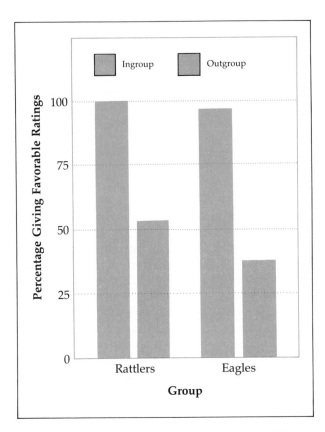

FIGURE 19.6 In-group prejudices. Ratings of in-group members were much more favorable than ratings of outgroup members after camp children had engaged in competitive games.

chapter, numerous researchers have since corroborated the finding that simply putting people into separate groups is enough to elicit conflict and group prejudice.

Following this phase, the researchers tried to reduce the intergroup hostilities. First they brought the groups together for noncompetitive social contacts. Given the existing hostile attitudes, this approach did not work. When the boys were brought together, they insulted and harassed one another. At meals, they began "garbage fights," in which the members of one group would throw leftovers, bottlecaps, and mashed potatoes at the members of the other group. The researchers finally managed to bring the groups into harmony by arranging a series of **superordinate tasks.** To succeed at a superordinate task, the two groups needed to pool their efforts. For instance, the researchers had someone vandalize the water system, and both groups worked together to find the source of the problem. In another case, both groups needed to tug a truck to get it started. At the end of the joint cooperation period, the boys again rated one another. At this time, the earlier

unfavorable ratings were replaced with favorable ratings. (See Figure 19.7.) At the end of the camp period, the boys voted to have a joint party, and to ride home on the same bus. Sherif and Sherif believed that several general principles apply here. Groups that compete come to dislike and distrust one another, and continued conflicts between the groups serve to reinforce their initial negative opinions. Groups that work together toward a common goal, however, can overcome their mutual hostilities.

Although research on intergroup conflict began early in the century, it was not until the 1960s that psychologists began research on the ecological imbalances of pollution and overcrowding that troubled Chief Seattle a century before. In 1968, the first program in **environmental psychology** was started at the City University of New York. The new environmental psychologists began to study the psychological aspects of *person–environment interactions,* including the effects of crowding, noise, and air pollution. Environmental psychology is

FIGURE 19.7 In-group prejudices reduced. After the camp children had been led to join their efforts in several superordinate tasks, the outgroup prejudices shown in Figure 19.6 were largely eradicated. New ratings of outgroup members were largely positive.

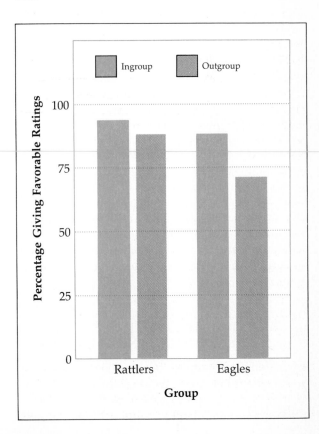

perhaps the most interdisciplinary branch of psychology, connecting psychology with areas as diverse as ecology, anthropology, architecture, political science, and urban planning (Altman and Chemers, 1980; Fisher, Bell, and Baum, 1985). As we will see, this new field has begun to yield some insights into the special social problems of the late twentieth century. ■

OVERPOPULATION: DENSITY AND CROWDING

The population explosion makes an indirect contribution to a legion of stressors. More and more people in the world will almost certainly mean that, as resources get scarcer, there will be more inflation, lowered standards of living, more starvation, and more pollution (Brown et al., 1976; Turk and Turk, 1984). What of the direct effects of high population density? Is it inherently stressful to live under crowded conditions? The answer is not as obvious as it might seem. Besides higher crime rates, traffic jams, and long supermarket lines, high density offers many benefits. A city the size of New York can support unique restaurants, specialty stores, museums, and theaters that would be impossible in a small town like Oskaloosa, Kansas. Even being part of the streaming crowds on a New York city street, diverse with foreign visitors, street musicians, finely-dressed urbanites, and bands of teenagers, may be more energizing and entertaining than stressful. Environmental psychologists often distinguish between **density** (the number of people in a given spatial area) and **crowding** (the psychological experience of spatial restrictions) (Holohan, 1982; Gifford, 1987). However, not all psychological researchers agree about the extent to which density has negative psychological consequences (Freedman, 1975; Galle and Gove, 1979; Milgram, 1970). All are agreed, however, that as the population increases, more and more people are, and will continue to be, living under high density conditions. We will discuss three areas of research on the effects of high density, and try to reconcile the differences of opinion.

BIOLOGICAL EFFECTS OF HIGH DENSITY ON ANIMALS

When four male and 21 female reindeer were introduced onto St. Paul Island off the coast of Alaska, the population increased exponentially. With no natural predators and abundant food, the rein-

deer population shot up to 2,000 in less than three decades. Then suddenly the population began to die off. In another fifteen years, there were only eight animals left (Krebs, 1972). Another herd of reindeer was introduced onto nearby St. George Island. The population of that herd also exploded in the first few years, but stabilized more quickly at about a dozen animals. This latter pattern is common among animals who have lived in an area for some time: the population finds a stable balance at some tolerable level. Population size is kept stable by a number of **density-dependent mortality factors** (mechanisms that act to kill more animals when population is high, and less when it is low). These include such external factors as predators—wolves also do better when the reindeer population in Siberia goes up, and more wolves bring the reindeer numbers down until the wolves start starving, and so on, in a well-balanced cycle. In addition, there are internal factors that keep animal populations under control, and these are most fascinating from a psychological standpoint.

When the density of an animal population goes up, the animals begin to show physiological changes similar to those brought on by stress. As you may recall from our discussion of Selye's General Adaptation Syndrome in Chapter 14, stress leads to a number of changes in the body's functioning. Some of those physiological changes seem to help the animal adapt to the stress of crowding. For instance, Ecologist J. J. Christian conducted a *naturalistic observation* of a group of Sika deer that were released onto an island off the coast of Maryland. Like the reindeer on St. Paul Island, these animals fared well. They reached a population of 300 by 1955, but then, despite the fact that they had abundant supplies of food, the population began to decline. Within a few years the deer population was down to 80. Christian examined the animals who died in the population crash after 1955, and found that their adrenal glands had grown to unusual proportions. The enlarged adrenal glands led to changes in behavior that helped limit the population. For instance, the animals became more aggressive and less inclined to reproduce. A number of other studies find that animals living under high density conditions go through physiological changes that lead them to become more defensive of territory and more inclined to limit their number of offspring (Wilson, 1975).

Probably the best-known research in this area is John Calhoun's work on population density and social pathology in rats. He observed that a group of rats placed in a quarter-acre outdoor pen limited their population to 150 despite having no predators and an unlimited food supply. The population was kept from growing larger by the fact that the animals organized into 13 separate colonies. The members of different colonies fought frequently, which interfered with rearing offspring and led to high infant mortality rates.

Next, Calhoun placed 32 adult rats in a 10' × 14' room divided into four separate pens. (See Figure 19.8.) Instead of stabilizing at four colonies of 12 animals, as expected, the number of rats went up to 80 in a year. At that point, Calhoun began removing surplus infants in order to observe the effects of a population density held at double what the animals would have endured in the outdoor pen.

Under these circumstances, two dominant males staked out territories in the end pens, where they maintained harems of eight to ten females. These arrangements were similar to the social arrangements that would have developed in the wild. However, the remaining 60 animals, crammed into the two central pens, developed a group syndrome that Calhoun (1962) dubbed the **behavioral sink**—a pattern of antisocial behaviors associated with high-density living. Any female in heat would be relentlessly harassed by packs of males. Some of the males would follow females into their nests, where they would occasionally find dead offspring. These males tended to become cannibalistic. The top ranking males would engage in frequent free-for-all fights, and less dominant males would occasionally go berserk and attack females and juveniles.

FIGURE 19.8   Calhoun's apparatus for subjecting rats to an overcrowded environment.   Rats in the two pens with only one entrance (top of figure) had fairly normal social arrangements. Those in other two suffered unusual levels of density, and developed hyperaggressive, antisocial, and deviant sexual behaviors.

Calhoun believed that the social pathology of the behavioral sink is a natural consequence of crowding. He also believed that those consequences held not only for rats, but for human beings, who likewise become hyperaggressive and sexually deviant under crowded conditions. To what extent is it justified to draw parallels between crowded rats and the modern residents of New York, Chicago, and Los Angeles? We now turn to the human research addressing that question.

EFFECTS OF CITY DENSITY ON HUMANS

As we indicated earlier, the rate of violent crimes in large metropolitan areas is eleven times greater than the crime rate in rural areas. Even in contrast to other, smaller, cities, the big cities have a five times higher crime rate (Freedman, 1975). For instance, for every 1000 people living in Los Angeles and New York City there were 20 violent crimes in 1986. This compares to 1.75 per 1000 in rural areas (Statistical Abstract of the United States, 1988). This difference suggests that something about high density living leads to antisocial behavior: Like crowded animals, crowded humans begin to compete when they are crowded in. When environmental psychologists use the term density, they mean the number of people living in a given area. Density can be distinguished from **city size,** defined as the total population of a city. Cities with large populations vary quite a bit in how densely their residents are packed into each square mile. For instance, metropolitan Los Angeles has a population of over three million, with a density of 6,380 people per square mile. With slightly over 1.6 million people, Philadelphia is only half as populous. However, Philadelphia is about twice the density of Los Angeles; there are 12,413 Philadelphians per square mile.

Some environmental psychologists have argued that density, in itself, has little effect on crime rates, or on other indices of stress and psychopathology. One team of researchers examined the crime rates for 117 large metropolitan areas, ranging in density from 40 to 13,000 people per square mile (Freedman, 1975; Freedman, Heshka, and Levy, 1975). Although city size was clearly associated with crime, density was only slightly associated with crime rate. Thus, a city like Los Angeles (which is a large-size, but low-density, city) has about the same crime rate as New York (which is a large size, high density, city). A city like Tulsa, Oklahoma, on the other hand, which has a density near that of Los Angeles, but which is much smaller in size, has a lower crime rate. What is more, even the slight relationship between city density and crime disappeared when other

City density and crime. Controversy exists among psychologists about whether life in the city directly contributes to antisocial behavior. City density does not have a simple relationship to antisocial behavior, but large cities do have more crime, possibly because people there are more anonymous.

variables, such as poverty, educational level, and ethnic background, were considered. It appeared that the small-density effect was attributable solely to the fact that the people living in the dense cities tend to be poor, less educated, and minorities. Some other researchers do find a relationship between density and antisocial behavior, even when other variables like education and socioeconomic status are considered (among them, Schmitt, 1966; Galle, Gove, and McPherson, 1972). While the relationship between city size and crime is clear, though, the relationship between city density and crime is generally weaker (Kirmeyer, 1978; Sadalla, 1978).

THE EFFECT OF ANONYMITY

Why is it that large cities are associated with antisocial behavior, regardless of how densely people are packed into them? One possibility is that people living in larger cities are more anonymous and deindivudated than those living in small towns (Sadalla, 1978). Thus, higher rates of crime in large cities might occur because city residents are less accountable for their behavior. You may recall from the last chapter that such conditions of anonymity lead to such antisocial behaviors as suicide baiting (Mann, 1981). Philip Zimbardo (1970) supported this conclusion in a field study in which he observed the same car parked in New York City and Palo Alto, California. The researcher first parked his car on a street in Palo Alto, leaving the windows down and the hood raised to make it appear that it was a vehicle in distress. He then watched from across the street, timing to see how long it would take for the first act of vandalism to occur. After waiting two days and seeing not a single act of vandalism, he was about to give up one rainy afternoon. At that point another vehicle pulled alongside the car, and the driver rushed over to the deserted vehicle. Instead of stealing something, however, the man rolled up the windows to protect the car's upholstery. After 64 hours of observation without a single act of vandalism, Zimbardo drove the car across the country and parked it on a street in the Bronx, again leaving the windows down and the hood up. Within ten minutes, the first visitors arrived. A man and his son emerged from their car with a set of tools and proceeded to remove the car radio. Over the next three days, Zimbardo observed 23 distinct acts of vandalism. Tires and other removable parts were stripped from the car. After this, the neighborhood boys came along, smashed the windows in, and then jumped up and down on the roof until it was flattened. Some of the vandals

appeared to be middle class, and included one well-dressed man who was pushing a baby carriage. Zimbardo argued that the cause of such extreme antisocial behavior in New York is that New Yorkers are just nameless faces in the crowd of 7 million strangers.

There is a problem of control with Zimbardo's field observations. There are many other differences between New York and Palo Alto besides anonymity. Different types of people live in the two cities, for instance—the people in the Bronx are more likely to be poor than those in Palo Alto. In more controlled laboratory studies, however, middle-class college students were more likely to deliver shocks to fellow subjects if their faces were covered so they could remain anonymous (Zimbardo, 1970). So anonymity, as found in large cities, *can* be responsible for antisocial behavior, even if it does not provide an airtight explanation of what happened to the car parked in the Bronx.

CROWDING IN INSTITUTIONAL ENVIRONMENTS

The reason that density in large cities is not necessarily stressful may be that people in cities, unlike animals on islands, have ways to escape from the madding crowd. The residents of Manhattan are not limited to grazing in Central Park, but can find solace behind the walls of their apartments. A poor apartment dweller in Albuquerque, New Mexico, probably has more private space than did an ancestor living in a tiny Pueblo village in the year 1000 A.D. (Sadalla, 1978). However, prison inmates face a situation similar to that faced by animals on an island. When the prison gets overcrowded, they are unable to retreat to the privacy of their apartments. Under those circumstances, there is evidence that density has a direct effect on stress and violence.

In one psychiatric prison the population rose from 450 to 630 between 1953 and 1961, then dropped to 369 over the next eight years. As shown in Figure 19.9, the death rate rose and fell along with the prison's population. When the prison population was below 400, less than one inmate per 100 died in any given year. When the prison population was at its peak, more than three inmates per 100 died every year. Death increases during the crowded years were the result of cancer and other illnesses, and not simply an increase in accidents or homicides. In a second study, the same researchers found that prison inmates also showed more psychiatric disturbances during

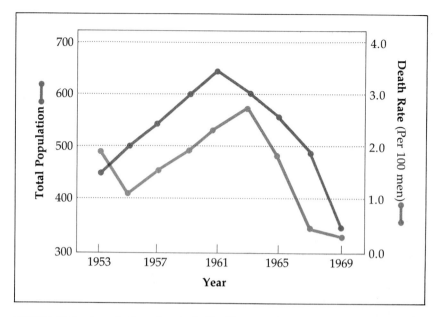

FIGURE 19.9 Population density's ill effects. The death rate in a prison rose and fell as a direct function of the total population in the prison studied by Paulus, McCain, and Cox. These researchers found other evidence that crowding in prisons leads to stress-related health problems.

years the prisons were crowded (Paulus, McCain, and Cox, 1982).

In line with research we discussed in Chapter 14, we might expect that such diseases as cancer might increase in crowded prisons because the inmates are experiencing stress. To examine this possibility directly, the researchers measured blood pressure in inmates living either two, three, or six to a cell. Consistent with the density–stress hypothesis, they found higher blood pressure in those living in the more crowded cells. Similarly, other researchers have found higher blood pressure in prisoners housed in multibed dormitories as opposed to one- or two-person units (D'Atri, 1975).

In a later study, the same researchers examined the relationship between prison density and violent assaults (Cox, Paulus, and McCain, 1984). When the number of inmates in one prison in Mississippi dropped 30 percent, the lowered density was accompanied by a 60 percent decrease in the number of assaults. When the density later increased by 19 percent, the assault rate went up 36 percent. Across a number of prisons, this pattern was found to be reliable. When prison population goes up or down, so goes the likelihood of assaults (Cox, Paulus, and McCain, 1984).

Although college dormitory living arrangements are not quite as dreadful as prisons, they are sometimes overcrowded in similar ways. Three college students are occasionally asked to live in rooms designed for two students. In other cases, students live along long open corridors, sharing common bath facilities with many other floor residents. Like prisoners, college roommates are usually not relatives, and often begin cohabitation as strangers to one another. College students living under those circumstances also show some adverse effects (Mullen and Felleman, 1990). In comparison with students living under less-crowded circumstances, for instance, they make more trips to the health center (Baron, Mandel, Adams, and Griffin, 1976), and they get poorer grades (Glassman, Burkhart, Grant, and Vallery, 1978). Students in crowded dorms also tend to become more socially withdrawn than less crowded students (Baum and Valins, 1977).

Thus, studies of humans living in crowded institutional settings show some parallels to the animal studies of crowding. It appears that when either human or nonhuman animals are living under conditions of crowding they cannot escape, they show adverse psychophysiological and behavioral effects. Studies of humans living in cities suggest it is not density per se, but city size that determines adverse psychological effects. Regardless of how thickly people are packed into a large city, they may be able to avoid the stress of the crowds by going inside their apartments. However, very large cities, regardless of the number of people on any given block, are more likely to involve anonymous, deindividuated interactions between strangers. It is this anonymity that may explain why crime rates are higher in large urban areas.

BIRTH CONTROL: APPLYING PSYCHOLOGICAL PRINCIPLES TO THE POPULATION PROBLEM

We have been discussing research on the psychological effects of overcrowding. Some psychologists have approached the problem from the other side, by asking: What psychological factors influence the likelihood of using birth control? This work focuses on birth control use in light of the literature on attitudes and attitude change (discussed in Chapter 17). These psychologists have considered how the likelihood of using birth control is related to people's relevant beliefs and feelings (among others, Jaccard, Helbig, Wan, Gutman, and Kritz-Silverstein, 1990).

Based on his own research in this area, sexuality researcher Donn Byrne (1983) outlined five cognitive and behavioral steps to contraception use. To avoid unwanted pregnancy, the sexually active person must:

- Learn accurate information about contraception.
- Acknowledge the likelihood that he or she might have sexual intercourse.
- Obtain the relevant contraceptive.
- Communicate with his or her sexual partner.
- Use the chosen method.

In order to use birth control effectively, a person must have adequate information. Many people throughout the world do not, as illustrated by the story of the family-planning worker demonstrating the use of condoms to a group of village men. "Discreetly he took a bamboo pole and put a condom over one end to show the men how it was to be done. All nodded understanding. On his next visit he found each hut magically protected against pregnancy by a bamboo pole stuck in the ground outside the door—each with a condom fitted over the end." (Pohlman, 1971)

Although college students would be unlikely to make such a mistake, there are other gaps in their knowledge about family planning issues. For instance, many college students are unaware that the risk of pregnancy is much higher midway between a woman's menstrual periods (Byrne, 1983).

OBSTACLES TO EFFECTIVE BIRTH CONTROL

Although family planning is impossible without information, knowledge about contraceptive methods does not, in itself, predict whether people use birth control (Munz et al., 1976). Beyond the simple knowledge that birth control is available, then, and some understanding of how to use it, it appears that information alone will not solve the population problem. People's emotional reactions to birth control, and their feelings about sexuality in general, also contribute to a person's decision to use birth control (Gerrard, 1987; Insko et al., 1970). Patients at an abortion clinic who feel guilt about sexuality, for instance, were likely to be using either no birth control, or such ineffective methods as rhythm or interrupted intercourse.

Another obstacle to effective birth control is the problem that sexual experiences for teenagers and college students are often unplanned, and many young people are unwilling to admit to themselves and others that they might have intercourse. People in established relationships are most likely to plan—young and inexperienced teens are least likely. Although most American teenagers now have premarital intercourse, Byrne (1983) notes research showing that the vast majority use no birth control at all the first time they "go all the way."

Despite the fact that a person has adequate information, and is willing to admit the possibility that he or she will have intercourse, there is some social embarrassment associated with actually getting the contraceptive devices. The person must go to a birth control clinic or the drug counter and publicly profess his or her intention to have sexual relations. In a field survey, Fisher, Fisher, and Byrne (1977) interviewed single male college students after they purchased condoms from a male pharmacist. Many of the young men found the simple purchase to be an emotionally unpleasant experience.

Some people, although adequately educated and armed with an effective method, nevertheless fail to use birth control during actual intercourse. Unless the woman is using birth control pills or an IUD, or the man has had a vasectomy, the moment comes when the partner must be told to hold on for a moment. Many college students, particularly those who are not in steady relationships, falter at the step of communicating with the partner (Byrne, 1983). Instead of stopping for a moment to take out a condom or a diaphragm, they simply proceed unprotected on the fear that they will spoil the mood.

The ease of using the chosen method plays an

important role. Some methods, including IUDs or vasectomies, require only a single decision. Byrne notes that 80 million couples now include one member who has been surgically sterilized. This fail-safe method is usually chosen by those who feel that they have had enough children. Unfortunately, young women who are most sexually active often have a false belief that they are especially invulnerable to pregnancy, and consequently use less effective methods such as rhythm, withdrawal, or no planning at all (Burger and Burns, 1990).

In an attempt to increase the effective use of contraceptives, one group of researchers first interviewed women who were using an ineffective method of contraception (Gerrard, McCann, and Fortini, 1983). Compared with women using the pill, a diaphragm, or an IUD, these women using ineffective methods had more negative attitudes and irrational fears about contraceptives. The researchers gave one group of these women information about the actual risks of, and the procedures for using, effective means of contraception. Another group was exposed to a *cognitive restructuring* treatment. Like the therapy techniques we described in Chapter 16, this treatment involved a rational and logical attack on the common negative attitudes and beliefs about contraception. A third (control) group was not treated. One month later, subjects in both the information and cognitive restructuring groups had increased their use of effective contraceptive techniques more than controls had. Three months later, however, only the cognitive restructuring group was still using significantly better contraceptive methods than the controls. In sum, some of the same psychological principles that were developed to treat psychopathological behavior and to change general attitudes have been applied to understanding and changing ineffective use of birth control.

ENVIRONMENTAL DETERIORATION

With overcrowding comes more waste, more pollution, and more need for energy. At first glance, these issues seem to pose only technological problems. Human ingenuity has allowed us to fly, to raise skyscrapers into the air, and to live beneath the sea or above the earth's atmosphere for weeks at a time. Many of us simply assume that same ingenuity will provide "technological fixes" for air pollution, for dwindling petroleum supplies, for acid rain, and for nuclear accidents like Chernobyl and Three Mile Island.

However, scientists are beginning to realize that better technology alone will not provide the answers to these problems. Whether or not the environment is damaged by energy sources will depend importantly upon the behavior of the people that use those energy sources. One economic analysis suggests that conservation is likely to be the principal source of additional energy as we approach the next century (Stobaugh and Yergin, 1979). In short, new technology alone cannot solve environmental problems unless people change their behaviors. Mass transportation, energy efficient cars, and solar heating devices are only useful to the extent that people are willing to use them.

Over ten years ago, energy experts estimated that Americans could cut their energy use by 40 to 50 percent without any new technologies (Stobaugh and Yergin, 1979). With a few simple steps, such as insulating our houses and factories, replacing our cars and other machines with maximally efficient models (but not until they wore out), and using mass transportation more frequently, we could have already drastically cut our dependence on petroleum, and cleaned up the skies over Los Angeles in the bargain. But we did not. Why? Part of the answer may stem from a very simple behavioral principle: The short-term consequences of performing a behavior (for example, the cost of buying and installing window shades today) exert greater control than the long-term consequences (the savings you would make on your summer air-conditioning bills if you kept the sun out with those shades). Even when the long-run costs are great, we will frequently persist in doing something that has only a small benefit in the short run. Some psychologists believe that this behavioral principle explains many large-scale social problems, particularly when the short-term benefits of destructive behaviors profit an individual while the long-term costs are shared by the group (Brechner, 1977; Platt, 1973). In the section that follows we consider these **social traps,** or situations in which the pursuit of short-term benefits leads to disastrous long-run consequences.

DYSFUNCTION:
Social Traps

In *The Wealth of Nations* (1776), British philosopher and economist Adam Smith made the definitive statement of individualistic capitalism. Each person freely allowed to seek his or her own self-interests would be "led by an invisible hand to promote . . . the public interest" (Smith, 1776). Smith reasoned that in a *laissez faire* world—a world in which there was no government interference)—the self-promoting interests of different groups would balance against one another. As Garrett Hardin (1968) pointed out in "The Tragedy of the Commons," however, the *laissez faire* approach does not work to protect the environment and its limited resources. To illustrate how individual selfishness can lead to ruinous consequences for the group, Hardin uses the example of the overgrazing of common pastures in New England. Those pastures were public areas where any sheepherder was free to graze his animals. On private pastures, herders would only graze as many animals as the land could support, aware that overgrazing quickly destroyed the grass and starved the whole herd. Herders showed no such restraint with the common areas, however, and the commons were frequently destroyed by overgrazing. It appeared that individual selfishness was the culprit (Hardin, 1968). For any individual herder, the benefit of adding a surplus animal was paid directly to him. However, the cost of the additional animal was shared by all the users of the commons. Thus, the most self-interested action an individual could take, in the short run, was to add an additional animal. When large numbers of herders followed that short-sighted strategy, however, the long-range cost was the destruction of the grazing area for the whole group.

Behavioral psychologist John Platt argues that most large-scale social problems today share some common features with the tragedy of the commons. Platt sees the commons dilemma as one of a set of social traps, or situations in which people start down a path that promises at first to be rewarding, but that later proves to be unpleasant and inescapable. According to Platt (1973), these social traps operate according to simple reinforcement principles. Traps occur when there are hidden costs for behavior. Those costs can be hidden for several reasons:

1. *Differences between short-term and long-term consequences*—when the short-term consequences of our behaviors are positive, while the long-term consequences are negative. For individual Americans, the benefits of driving to work alone are immediate and personal—you get to work as quickly as possible. The costs of shrinking petroleum resources become apparent many years later, and are not directly contingent on getting into the car today. In the opposite direction, the cost of spending an extra half hour on the bus are immediate and personal, while the benefits of cleaner city air and less congested roads are far removed.

2. *Ignorance of long-term consequences*. The designers of Russia's Chernobyl nuclear plant probably had no idea that their plant's meltdown would one day cover Europe with toxic radiation and the designers of the automobile did not foresee a war in which the United States battled over oil fields in the Middle East.

3. *Sliding reinforcers*—when a behavior leads to positive consequences unless it is repeated too often. When the first automobiles were introduced into Los Angeles, they provided convenience without much impact on air quality. It was only when several million of them were on the road that the machines turned the city's sunny skies into a cloud of grey smog.

Social psychologist Kevin Brechner (1977) was interested in simulating the social trap phenomenon in the laboratory. He offered groups of three students a chance to earn credit for a three-hour class requirement in one half hour, if they could succeed in winning 150 points in a game. To win the points, the students simply pressed a button that took a point from a common pool and put it into their own personal accounts. The common pool was displayed on a board with 24 lights. When any of the players took a point, one of the lights in the common pool went out. Like a field of grass for common grazing, the pool of points replenished itself. When the pool was near the top, it replenished rapidly—every two seconds. If it went below three-quarters full, it replenished more slowly—every four seconds; below half, it slowed the replacement rate to every six seconds; and if it was "grazed" down to one-fourth of its original size, it replaced points only every eight seconds. Once the last point was "grazed" the game was over, and the pool stopped replenishing completely. To succeed, students needed to cooperate in keeping the pool at a high level, so that it replenished at the maximal rate. When students were not allowed to communicate, they tended to do very poorly. In fact, most noncommunicating groups ran the pool dry in less than one minute. Those students earned an average of only 14 points each. When students were allowed to communicate with one another, they did quite a bit better, although they still usually failed to optimize, averaging about 70 points per person.

Other studies have found that subjects do better when the common pool is subdivided so that individuals each have a private portion (Cass and Edney, 1978).

Outside the laboratory, the principle of social traps applies to energy conservation. People who reside in master-metered buildings use 35 percent more energy than those who are held individually responsible for their own bills (Walker, 1979). These findings are reminiscent of the research on emergency helping (Latane and Darley, 1970), where, as we noted in the last chapter, people in crowds are apt to shirk their individual responsibility to help out. It seems that when people share responsibility for conserving a resource, they tend to look out for themselves, and leave it to "someone else" to conserve. Unfortunately, the other person is operating on the same self-serving principle, and everyone loses in the long run. ■

PSYCHOLOGICAL CONSEQUENCES OF ENVIRONMENTAL DETERIORATION

The human costs of environmental deterioration are usually measured in terms of health hazards, such as the 1952 "killer" smog in London, which cause 3,500 deaths (Nelson, 1970), or the risk of cancer from exposure to radiation from a nuclear generator (Gyorgy, 1979). Psychological costs are

less visible, but may affect even more people. Most of us can probably appreciate Chief Seattle's aversive reaction to crowded and polluted cities in contrast to the green and rolling countryside. Researchers have found that air that is bad-smelling or polluted with carbon monoxide can impair thought processes and interfere with job performance (Evans and Jacobs, 1982; Rotton, 1983). Other research suggests that air pollution levels in a city can also increase incidents of domestic violence and psychiatric disturbance (Rotton and Frey, 1984, 1985).

When nuclear reactors were introduced during the 1950s, they held out the promise of a technological solution to pollution: a source of clean and safe energy. However, nuclear reactors have added their own special psychological costs to the modern technological world—fears of the invisible radiation that spews out into the air, particularly when meltdowns occur. When asked to rank 30 risky activities or technologies, college students rated nuclear power as the most risky (Slovic et al., 1979). Although handguns and smoking each produce thousands of violent deaths each year, and nuclear power makes only a few indirect contributions to cancer death rates, students based their estimates on the "worst case scenario" of what they thought could happen in a particularly bad incident (Slovic et al., 1981). Nuclear power, when

The great London smog of 1952. An example of air pollution at its worst, the smog resulted from sulfur dioxide fumes caused by burning coal and oil, and was responsible for some 3,500 deaths.

it does go wrong, was seen as particularly uncontrollable and catastrophic.

If a cross-section of college students is seriously worried about the risks of nuclear power, one might imagine that the concerns would take on very stressful levels in those living near the site of a nuclear catastrophe. Three Mile Island (TMI) is a nuclear plant near Harrisburg, Pennsylvania. (See Figure 19.10.) During the spring of 1979 the reactor cooling system failed and the nuclear core began to melt down, releasing a radioactive cloud into the air. The governor of Pennsylvania issued an evacuation advisory for pregnant women and small children living within a five-mile radius of the plant. Even after the meltdown was over, highly radioactive gases and contaminated waste remained. Nearby residents suffered continuing concerns about the utility company's plan to vent the remaining gases directly into the atmosphere.

There were numerous indications that residents living near TMI found the experience particularly stressful. Though no formal evacuation order was ever actually given, 30 to 65 percent of those living nearby nevertheless evacuated shortly after the accident. A study of young mothers in the area indicated evidence of heightened depression and anxiety (Bromet, 1980b). Residents also experienced increased psychophysiological disorders, such as headaches and gastrointestinal problems, and increased use of alcohol and tranquilizers

(Houts et al., 1980). Nine months after the accident, stress levels in TMI neighbors were still higher than those in people living 40 miles away (Houts et al., 1980). One study found a number of classical signs of post-traumatic stress disorders in nearby residents: increased physical symptoms, depression, difficulty in concentrating, and heightened levels of urinary adrenaline and noradrenaline (Baum et al., 1982).

Not all of the consequences of energy technology need to be negative. Some experts predict that as petroleum supplies run down, and people become increasingly skeptical about accumulating nondisposable nuclear waste, we will come to rely more on safer and cleaner solar energy. We will also need to change the social environment in some pleasant ways, dispersing into smaller, less mobile groups whose members live and work close to energy sources rather than relying heavily on automobiles (Stern and Gardner, 1981). Instead of continually buying new products designed for quick replacement, we may begin to emphasize high-quality, long-lasting goods, and to recycle rather than just to discard. There may also be more personal and small-group control of the basic influences on our social lives, like workplaces. Further, we might begin to expand our awareness of the "role of humanity as part of a larger ecosystem and the responsibility of people to maintain its functioning" (Stern and Gardner, 1981). If these

FIGURE 19.10 The nuclear reactor at Three Mile Island. Researchers have found signs of severe stress in residents living near this reactor, which released a cloud of radioactive gases after a partial meltdown in 1979.

predictions hold, we may all finally be forced by our own technology to listen to Chief Seattle's advice.

ENERGY CONSERVATION: APPLYING PSYCHOLOGICAL PRINCIPLES TO ENVIRONMENTAL PROBLEMS

Environmental deterioration will not stop unless people replace their current patterns of buying, traveling, and living with conservation-conscious ones. In short, a large part of the solution to the environmental crisis lies in changing people's behavior. But if energy waste is maintained by social traps—by powerful short-term reinforcements that override long-term consequences—is there any hope? Simply raising people's awareness of the long-term consequences with persuasive appeals does not seem to be enough (Edney, 1980). In fact, if people become aware that a resource is getting scarcer, they may simply rush to take a bigger share of it (Linder, 1982). However, John Platt suggested that there are ways to escape the entrapping grip of immediate reinforcement over behavior:

1) *Move the future negative consequences into the present.* This approach is used when a cigarette smoker keeps a picture of a lung-cancer operation attached to each pack of cigarettes, bringing the future punishments into the present where they can compete with the immediate reinforcement of a cigarette. To change energy-wasting behaviors, thermostats in houses and odometers in cars could be attached to a bright digital calculator that flashed a running tally of the dollar cost of fuel for the last month. In fact, researchers have found that simply giving people frequent feedback about their energy consumption reduces energy use by 10 to 20 percent (Stern and Gardner, 1981).

2) *Reinforce more desirable environmental behaviors.* In some cities, traffic control agencies have set up special conveniences for those who ride in car pools or on buses. Vehicles that have more than one passenger are allowed to drive in special faster lanes, while cars with single occupants are relegated to more congested regular lanes. One study found a five-fold increase in bus riding after it was made more convenient by increasing the number of peak-period buses, and then allowing them to drive in special fast lanes (Rose and Hinds, 1976).

3) *Change the nature of the long-term consequences.* This is the "technological fix"—changing the technology so that people can continue to behave as they always have, without having to pay the price. By using more solar energy, insulating our homes, covering our windows, and tuning our furnaces, we could save more than 75 percent of the energy used in house heating, for instance (Yates and Aronson, 1983). Well-tuned four-cylinder automobiles can now get 40 to 50 miles to the gallon, in contrast to 10 or 15 for a poorly tuned eight-cylinder model. As we noted earlier, however, improved technology is useless if people do not change their behaviors to take advantage of it. People need to adopt the technological innovations for them to work. Nevertheless, Stern and Gardner (1981) note that it is easier for people to make "one-shot" changes. Once someone buys an efficient small car, he or she will save gas for years. Tuning engines and filling tires also reduce gas costs, but they require repeated behaviors.

4) *Use social pressures* to keep people honest in their attempts to break out of social traps. It is much harder to break a diet if you have made a public pronouncement of your intention to lose several pounds than if you make a secret resolution. One team of social psychological researchers increased conservation behaviors by using the commitment–consistency principle discussed in Chapter 18. Those participants in a field experiment who were induced to make a highly public commitment to save energy did a significantly better job of conservation that the others, who were led to make a similar but nonpublic commitment. The researchers asked the public commitment group to sign their permission to have their names and commitments published in the newspaper. Even though the names were not actually published, the initial expectation that they might be led to more concerted conservation efforts, which still persisted when the researchers returned a year later (Pallak, Cook, and Sullivan, 1980).

In sum, there is some evidence that we can be induced to conserve energy when (1) the long-term costs of consumption are moved closer to our actual consumption behaviors; (2) we are given immediate rewards for environmentally positive alternatives; (3) we make one-shot adoptions of more efficient technologies; and (4) we publicly commit ourselves to reducing our wastefulness.

There will be costs associated with improving

the quality of the environment. If we are to stop destroying and depleting our environment, argued Garrett Hardin (1968) in his discussion of the "tragedy of the commons," then our basic selfish tendencies will need to be curbed by "mutual coercion, mutually agreed upon." Taxes and laws that make it difficult for individuals to exploit the common air, water, and energy supplies are probably inevitable. Hardin argued that in a crowded world with finite resources, the individual right to waste at leisure (and to breed to one's heart's content) must go the way of the right to take other people's money from the bank. To the extent that we can discover ways to make this "mutual coercion" take the form of positive incentives instead of punishments, it will be experienced as less unpleasant (Skinner, 1972). Some psychologists disagree with Hardin's pessimistic view of human nature, and hold that it is a mistake to view people as responding to egoistic motivations (among others, Caporael, Dawes, and Orbell, 1989; Lynn and Oldenquist, 1986). In line with the more optimistic view, there is some research to indicate that people will act less selfishly if they are simply made aware that they are part of a larger group (Kramer and Brewer, 1984).

It is probably a safe assumption that most people's attitudes favor a cleaner environment, and that few people go out of their way to pollute and waste energy. However, there are a number of reasons why people's pro-environmental attitudes might not translate into behaviors. At the simplest level, people often do not perceive their behaviors as wasteful. Several social psychologists have begun to apply research and theory on attitude–behavior relationships (discussed in Chapter 17) to reducing the gap between environmental attitudes and conservation behaviors (Costanzo, Archer, Aronson, and Pettigrew, 1986). In this way, research findings from several other areas of psychology, ranging from learning to social cognition, are being applied to the problem of environmental deterioration.

INTERNATIONAL CONFLICT

The threat of nuclear war is different from the threats of overpopulation and environmental depletion. We are fairly certain about the likely effects of continuing overpopulation and pollution, but we are uncertain about how close we are to a nuclear war. The very uncertainty surrounding modern military technology is part of what has made it a psychological problem. In addition to the threat of nuclear war is the continuing reality of conventional war. There have been millions of casualities from international conflicts in the decades since World War II. So common are these conflicts that we are not even surprised by weekly stories of battles, bombings, assassinations and massacres in Latin America, Africa, Asia, and the Middle East. As this text was being written in 1991, the United States was dropping thousands of bombs on Iraq, and Iraq was retaliating by bombing residential areas in Israel. In this section, we explore the basic psychological processes that contribute to escalating and de-escalating conflict at the individual and at the group level.

THE INGROUP/OUTGROUP DISTINCTION

All around the world, people seem to regard the members of their own group as more talented, attractive, intelligent, and even more "human" than the members of other groups (LeVine and Campbell, 1972). The American settlers from Europe were not alone in viewing Chief Seattle and the other Native Americans as a lesser subspecies. All human groups have tended to view themselves as having a special connection to the gods (Wilson, 1978). One facet of this phenomenon is "geocentrism," or the tendency to view one's own country or locale as the center of the world (Whittaker and Whittaker, 1972). When asked to judge the desirability of different countries, people tend to place their own at the top of the list. Gould and White (1974) asked people from Europe and Africa to rank the countries of the world in terms of preferred living conditions. Swedes ranked Sweden at the top, followed by the other Scandinavian countries and England. Germans had nothing against Sweden, but they thought that Germany and the other German-speaking countries topped the list. Italians, on the other hand, put Italy out in front, and also favored other Catholic and Latin countries like Spain and France.

When students in one of our psychology classes were asked to draw a map of the world, a very interesting thing happened. Most of the students put the United States at the center of the map, and made it much larger than it actually should have been. Whole continents, like Africa and South America, were often viewed as smaller than the U.S.A. One student in the class was from Iran, however, and she drew a very different map. The United States was tiny and squashed down into the corner of the map, while Iran loomed large in the center. These students' tendencies to see their own countries as the center of the world are consistent with research done in very different cultures. (See Figure 19.11.)

The preference for the lay of the local land is part of a more general cognitive tendency. Part of the attraction of Italy to Italians is that the people there are, in their opinion, so much more amiable, sophisticated, intelligent, and creative than Germans, Englishmen, or Americans. In the words of one Italian "Italians have discovered America for the Americans; taught poetry, statesmanship, and the ruses of trade to the English; military art to the Germans; cuisine to the French; acting and ballet to the Russians; and music to everybody" (Barzini, 1964).

Americans, Englishmen, Germans, Frenchmen, and Russians see things somewhat differently, and all can wax eloquent about their own contributions to world culture. Sociologist William Sumner (1906) used the term **ethnocentrism** to describe what he believed was a universal human tendency to view one's own ingroup as better than outer outgroups, or to view "us" as better than "them." Research has indicated that the tendency is not quite universal—although many cultural groups do view themselves as being better than others, underprivileged minorities may not (Tajfel, 1982). Two things do appear to be universal, however. All groups seem to view themselves in more positive terms than they are viewed by outsiders, and people everywhere divide themselves into ingroups and outgroups (Tajfel, 1982; LeVine and Campbell, 1972). There is always some other group to look down on, and to blame for the general problems of the world. Ingroups and outgroups can be based on a wide array of distinctions—ethnic background (Chicanos, Irish,

Jews, . . .), place of birth (New Yorkers, Californians, North Dakotans . . .), and even sports alliances (Raider fans, Bronco fans, and so on).

THE PREVALENCE OF OUTGROUP PREJUDICES

One explanation of such outgroup prejudices comes from Marxist economics—the prejudices stem from competition for scarce resources. In the last chapter, we mentioned findings that prejudice against blacks increased when the Southern economy was doing poorly (Hovland and Sears, 1940; Hepworth and West, 1988). A poor economy means less resources to go around, and more need to fight with any other group that has a claim on these limited resources. However, later research has shown that actual competition between groups is unnecessary for the outgroup bias to begin. In fact, people seem predisposed to dislike members of outgroups that are based on minimal distinctions indeed. For instance, one study found that subjects divided into "blue" and "green" teams simply for the purposes of a laboratory experiment quickly began to discriminate against one another (Rabbie and Horwitz, 1969). European psychologist Henri Tajfel (1982) has found that almost any distinction between two groups is sufficient to begin the process of ingroup favoritism and outgroup discrimination. In some of his studies, Tajfel has asked students to give their preferences between several works of abstract art. Some are told that their choices indicate that they prefer works by Paul Klee, while others are told that they favor Wassily Kandinsky. When subjects are later asked to divide rewards among the other group members, they favor the others whom they believe

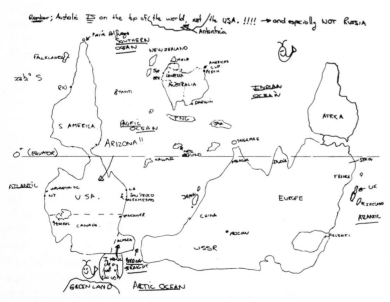

FIGURE 19.11 Geocentrism. People's tendency to see their own country as the center of the world (geocentrism) is graphically illustrated by this map drawn by an Australian. Note that it places Australia in the top center, and, from our perspective, "flips" the world over.

to have similar art preferences. Klees give more to other Klees, and cheat the Kandinskys, and vice versa. The irony is that subjects in Tajfel's research are actually randomly assigned to the different groups. Although there are really no differences between Klees and Kandinskys, the students quickly become convinced that there are.

Distinctions between "blues" and "greens" and between Klee and Kandinsky afficionados are not of great concern outside the social psychology laboratory. However, the fact that people are so quick to be divisive should give us pause the next time that we rightously condemn some group other than ours. Outgroup prejudices have been used as a justification for warfare throughout human history (Wilson, 1978). In a world with 50,000 nuclear warheads set to launch, it becomes especially important to re-examine our own prejudgments about the other people of the earth. For the four decades following World War II, Russians were a favorite "outgroup" for Americans. For instance, in 1980 former United States president Richard Nixon said of the Russians:

> It may seem melodramatic to say that the U.S. and Russia represent Good and Evil, Light and Darkness, God and the Devil. But if we think of it that way, it helps to clarify our perspective of the world struggle.
>
> *(quoted in Ford et al., 1982)*

During his own presidency, Ronald Reagan echoed Nixon's anti-Russian sentiments:

> They are the focus of evil in the modern world. [It is a mistake] to ignore the facts of history and the aggressive impulses of an evil empire, to simply call the arms race a giant misunderstanding and thereby remove yourself from the struggle between right and wrong, good and evil.
>
> *(quoted in Plous and Zimbardo, 1984)*

This sort of sentiment contributed to the situation in which the United States government, during the late 1980s, spent approximately 300 billion dollars a year on military expenditures (Union of Concerned Scientists, 1988). The Cold War between Russia and the United States is of particular interest for several reasons. It involved two modern "civilized" countries who were allies just before the conflict began. It illustrates some of the classic principles of conflict escalation, reaching a point where many Americans, like the high school students we described earlier, believed that it would almost certainly lead to their deaths. It

seems, at present, to have a reconciliation that illustrates some of the principles of successful conflict management. In the next sections, we will examine some of these basic psychological processes that increase and decrease intergroup conflict.

SOCIAL TRAPS REVISITED: HOW GROUP CONFLICT CAN SPIRAL

Many psychologists believe that the Soviet–American arms race illustrated basic psychological processes of conflict and cooperation that apply to all levels of human social interaction (for example, Deutsch, 1986). One explanation of nuclear escalation uses the concept of a **conflict spiral** (Deutsch, 1973). A conflict spiral is a competitive situation that feeds itself, so that what begins as a fairly mild difference grows ever larger and less rational. Conflict spirals can involve individuals, groups, or nations. They often follow the pattern of social traps—each side begins because it expects a quick and easy reward, but gets entrapped in a situation that becomes more and more aversive for all concerned. One researcher studied these entrapment processes in a laboratory study of the "dollar game" (Teger, 1980). In the dollar game, a group of people are allowed to bid for a dollar. The experimenter agrees to give the dollar to the highest bidder, even if the highest bid is only five cents. There is one special rule in the dollar auction, however: The second highest bidder must also pay, but receives nothing. So if one person bids 10 cents, and another bids 15, the experimenter gets 25 cents for his or her dollar. When one of the authors conducts this game in his classes, people begin playing in good spirits, with initial hopes of getting a decent bargain on the dollar. Someone almost always begins with a minimal bid, like a nickel, and is then outbid by another person willing to chance a dime on the hopes of an easy dollar. Another student may then kick in a 15-cent bid, and so on. The bidding quickly escalates to 50 cents, and the students realize that the instructor is about to make over a dollar back. However, the person who bid 45 usually goes up to 55 rather than totally lose his or her bid. At that point, the bidders are usually reduced to two people, each of whom now stands to lose at least half a dollar if he or she does not come out on top. There is usually some hesitation when the bid reaches $1, as the bidders realize that this is now a "no-win" situation—either break even, or lose 90 cents. However, the bidding usually crosses what at first seems an absurd threshold, and the number two bidder shouts out "A dollar and five cents!" as a bid on the dollar. Now the game is different, as each bidder pushes on in hopes of minimizing losses. In one class, the bidding went up to $8 before the instructor stopped the game (and, of course, let the bidders off the hook). In a study in which a number of groups bid for a dollar under these same circumstances, one group went up to $20! Entrapped bidders could not understand why their opponents kept bidding. (In one of our classes, a student who bid $8 said of his opponent, "That guy must have been crazy!"). When asked why they themselves continued beyond the $1 "no-win" level, bidders often reported that their motivations had changed. No longer motivated by the lure of easy money, they become concerned with saving face; they want to win the game so that they do not appear weak (Teger, 1980).

The build-up of nuclear weapons demonstrated all the features of this sort of social entrapment. When the first nuclear weapons were invented, some United States military and political leaders believed that they might have a positive side, allowing us to enforce "a lasting peace" (Air Force General Carl Spatz, 1948, quoted in Ford et al., 1982). It was perhaps for this reason, suggested Colorado Senator Edwin Johnson in 1947, that "God almighty in his infinite wisdom dropped the A-Bomb in our lap." However, nuclear weapons seemed less of a godsend when the Russians blessed the earth with their own in 1949. The United States went on to develop the more powerful hydrogen bomb in 1952, but the lead did not last long; Russia had the H-bomb by 1953. During the later 1950s, the United States military became concerned that the Russians had more nuclear bombers than they did, so they feverishly began building B-52 bombers. By 1961, the United States had 600 nuclear bombers to the Russians' 190. However, by this time the Russians had developed the rocket technology to launch *Sputnik*, the first satellite, and American leaders became fearful that the United States would fall behind in the space race, which at that time consisted of rocket-launched missiles. By 1961, America had built 200 intercontinental ballistic missiles, and the Russians had an arsenal of 50. When the numbers rose to 800 and 200 in 1964, American president Lyndon Johnson proposed a freeze, but the Russians rejected it because the United States had more nuclear weapons than they did. Five years later the Russians had 1300 nuclear weapons, but the United States now had 4200, including a new missile that could launch multiple warheads at differ-

ent targets. During the 1970s, American President Ford and Soviet General Secretary Brezhnev tried to "limit" each side to 2400 launchers, many of which were capable of sending off multiple warheads. By this time, people no longer argued that the weapons were a divine gift of peace, but Henry Kissinger and others did argue that atomic bombs kept us safe because of "Mutually Assured Destruction" (MAD)—since both sides had many more nuclear weapons than were necessary to retaliate and destroy all major targets in the other country, if either side used the weapons, it was quite certain that all of us would be destroyed.

Although the awareness of mutual destruction sounds like a bizarre enough way to end the game, it did not stop there. After the 1970s, there were more escalations still, including very small "cruise" missiles designed to evade radar detection, and such giant, deadly accurate missiles as the MX. To keep the threat value of nuclear weapons alive after both sides realized the implications of Mutually Assured Destruction, leaders began to talk about actually using the weapons as part of a "winnable nuclear war." For instance, then Vice President George Bush stated during the early 1980s that you could have a "winner" in a nuclear war if you could inflict "more damage on the opposition than it can inflict upon you . . . if everybody fired everything he had, you'd have more than [5 percent of the population] survive." To help our side "win" in that type of nuclear war, the United States government further increased military spending as it cut back on domestic programs during the late 1980s. Compared to the costs of the cold war between Russia and the United States, the student who bid $20 for a single dollar does not seem to have gotten off so badly. As Carl Sagan noted, Russia and America during the 1980s seemed like two men standing waist deep in a great tank of gasoline, arguing about who has more matches.

CONFLICT IN THE LABORATORY: THE PRISONER'S DILEMMA

In an attempt to understand the basic psychological processes that increase and decrease conflict spirals, researchers have observed laboratory subjects faced with a dilemma between cooperation and conflict. These subjects often play a game called the **prisoner's dilemma** (Rapaport, 1960). The game takes its name from the problem faced by two prisoners who are suspected of a crime.

Each prisoner faces a choice dilemma with four possible outcomes:

1) *The prisoner confesses the crime, and the partner does not.* Under these circumstances, the prisoner will get off more lightly, but will provide stronger evidence to be used against the partner.

2) *The prisoner keeps silent, but the partner confesses.* This is the worst state of affairs for the prisoner. The partner will get off, but there will now be strong evidence against the prisoner.

3) *Both confess.* Under these circumstances, they both will get moderate sentences.

4) *Neither confesses.* This cooperative choice is the best state of affairs for the prisoner, since both of them will either get off or be booked on a much lesser offense.

In a simulation of this dilemma, students are presented with a "payoff matrix" resembling the one in Figure 19.12. The best payoff for any individual comes if he "defects," but the best payoff for the pair comes if they "cooperate."

In most variations of the prisoner's dilemma game, the students do not simply face the dilemma once, but interact over repeated trials. In this way, the researchers can investigate what follows when one player cooperates or defects over a series of trials. By using confederates who play a prearranged strategy, experimenters can also study which strategies are most successful in invoking cooperation, and which strategies tend to escalate selfish competition (Oskamp, 1971). Three general findings emerge from this research: (1) conflict quickly escalates when either player refuses to cooperate; (2) completely cooperative players are often exploited by their opponents, who defect and gain additional points for themselves; and (3) a "tit for tat" strategy, in which a player only defects after the opponent's defections, then returns to cooperating, seems to work best to induce cooperation in a reluctant partner.

Morton Deutsch (1986) described the results of several studies in which he used a slightly more complex prisoner's dilemma situation. In Deutsch's experiment players were given the choice of five types of strategies they could play on any given trial:

- *Noncooperative self-interest.* The subject got a small money reward regardless of her opponent's play.

- *Supercooperative.* The strategy rewarded the opponent, gave no payoff to the subject.

- *Cooperative.* The strategy provided a large reward if both players used it, but only a very small reward if only one of them did.

- *Competitive.* This approach took away a reward from the opponent, and gave it to the subject.

- *Noncooperative defense.* If an opponent made a competitive attack, this strategy would neutralize the attack.

Unbeknownst to the real subjects, their partners were actually confederates of the experimenter. Deutsch's experimental confederates tried out several different strategies for inducing cooperation from a partner. One of these was a *punitive deterrent* strategy, in which the accomplice used the cooperative reward strategy on the first trial, and responded with an attack if the real player used either the noncooperative self-interest, the noncooperative defense, or the competitive strategy. When the accomplice used the punitive deterrent strategy, the subject suffered if he or she did anything except cooperate. Another strategy was the *nonpunitive deterrent* strategy. In this case, the accomplice matched the partner's previous trial unless the subject chose an attack or a defense. Nonpunitive accomplices followed an attack with a defense, and followed the partner's defense by cooperating. Finally, some accomplices used a *turn the other cheek* strategy. In this case, the accomplice started out playing cooperatively, and kept cooperating. If attacked by the opponent, he would follow the attack with a supercooperative

FIGURE 19.12 The prisoner's dilemma. The payoff matrix in a prisoner's dillemma game demonstrates that subjects receive most joint rewards for cooperation (upper left cell), but most individual rewards for one-sided defection.

Player B's Choices

		Cooperate	Defect
Player A's Choices	Cooperate	Both gain 5 points	B gains 10 points / A loses 5 points
	Defect	A gains 10 points / B loses 5 points	Both gain 1 point

response. The results of a typical experiment are presented in Figure 19.13. Note that the most successful strategy was the nonpunitive deterrence approach. The least successful was the totally cooperative turning of the other cheek. The punitive deterrence strategy started out somewhat successfully, but dropped over time. Deutsch explained that "the subject [confronted with punitive deterrence] usually responded with anger and with counterattacks to this attempt to dominate his behavior."

Deutsch has argued that the principles of conflict and cooperation found in these laboratory dilemmas apply to interactions between groups, and even between nations. When one nation uses coercive pressure on another, as when the United States escalated the war in Vietnam with antipersonnel bombs and defoliation, it is prone to lead to anger and counterhostility. When one nation "turns its other cheek" to another nation's aggressions, as when the Allies "appeased" Hitler when he first began invading his neighbors, it is likely to lead to exploitation.

FIGURE 19.13 The results of a typical laboratory competition study. Subjects who "turn the other cheek" to an opponent tend to be exploited. Those who use a punitive deterrent strategy tend to elicit increasing retaliation as the game goes on. Those who use a nonpunitive deterrent strategy do best overall.

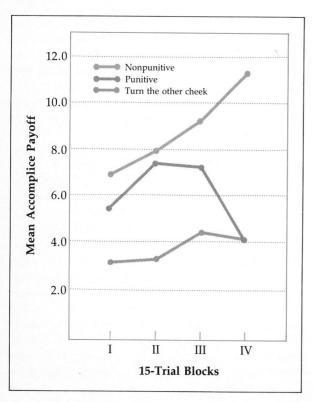

PERCEPTUAL DILEMMAS: WHEN CONFLICT SPIRALS MEET OUTGROUP PREJUDICES

During the 1980s, a political psychologist, Scott Plous, found evidence that American and Soviet leaders both wanted mutual disarmament but perceived the other side as wanting nuclear superiority. He argued that this **perceptual dilemma** led to competitive behaviors reminiscent of those found in laboratory prisoner's dilemma games—even though both sides preferred mutual disarmament to any other outcome (Plous, 1985). In contrast to a prisoner's dilemma, a perceptual dilemma is based on mistaken beliefs about what the other side wants. In the case of the United States and the Soviet Union, self-serving ingroup biases led each side to imagine that the other had diabolical intentions. American leaders believed that the Soviets were striving for nuclear superiority, while Soviet leaders believed that it was the Americans who were seeking superiority.

To test the idea that Russian and American leaders during the 1980s suffered from a perceptual dilemma in their estimations of the other side's desires, Plous sent questionnaires to the members of the United States Senate, asking the Senators to rate the desirability of America's continued arming or disarming if the Russians either armed or disarmed. The senators were also asked to estimate what the Russians would prefer. The desirabilities were rated on a scale from "–10" (worst possible outcome) to "+10" (best outcome imaginable). The results are depicted in Figure 19.14. The senators clearly felt that it would be best for America if both sides disarmed. America's continuing to arm while Russia disarmed was only a distant second choice for the senators. They strongly disfavored either continued escalation or a situation in which the United States disarmed while Russia continued to arm. Note, however, the great discrepancy in the way that the senators thought Soviet leaders viewed things. The United States senators thought that the Soviet Union's first choice was not joint peace, but to continue arming while the United States disarmed. Under those circumstances, the United States would be left with no alternative but to reluctantly keep building arms. A survey of Soviet leaders, however, showed that the Soviets saw things as just the reverse (Guroff and Grant, 1981). The Soviets themselves viewed arms control as "imperative," but found it "difficult to interpret proposed massive new arms expenditures in the United States as other than attempts to, first, gain military superiority and, second, drive the Soviet

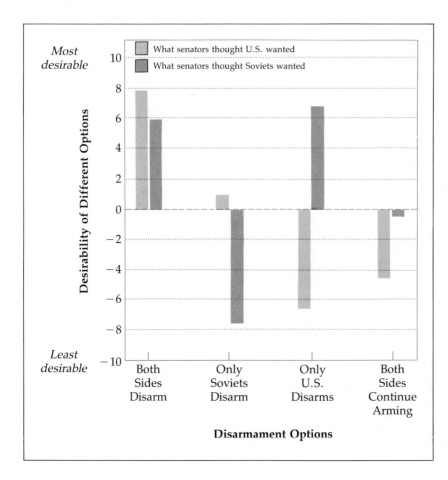

FIGURE 19.14 Perceptual dilemma? United States senators during the 1980s were asked to evaluate the desirability of four different disarmament options as they thought Americans and Soviets viewed them. Note that they believed that the United States viewed mutual disarmament as most desirable, whereas they believed the Soviets had a preference to see only the United States disarm while the Soviet Union continued to arm. On the other hand, the senators did not think that it would be particularly desirable to have the United States continue to arm while the Soviets disarmed. Note also that the senators thought that Americans were more opposed to a continuation of the arms race.

economy to bankruptcy." Finally, Plous analyzed the public statements of top American and Soviet leaders and found that the statements made by each side indeed suggested a perceptual dilemma (see Table 19.1).

One consolation of these findings is that they suggested that neither the Soviets nor the Americans had purely aggressive intentions in stockpiling nuclear weapons. Instead, they were mainly trying to communicate their threat potential to the other side. Unfortunately, coercive threats take on a life of their own. Threats have been found to escalate conflict not only in simulated conflicts in the laboratory (Deutsch, 1986), but also in "real-world" international conflicts. One analysis of 99 serious international disputes involving troop movements, port blockades, withdrawn ambassadors, and other such incidents found that only four percent of them led to war if they had not been preceded by an arms race. Of those that were preceded by an arms race, on the other hand, fully 82 percent resulted in war (Wallace, 1979). As we enter the 1990s, the Soviet Union and the United States have taken important steps toward limiting the escalation of their nuclear weapons. Nevertheless, as we noted earlier, most of the weapons still

exist. Because they are so abundant and set for such hair-trigger automatic response, there is a remaining danger of an accidental nuclear war (Blair and Kendall, 1990). In addition, several other countries now have their own stockpiles. Given that modern science has enabled us to create the problems of nuclear weapons, can it help us develop the effective techniques of international negotiation that are now essential to our future?

RESEARCH AND APPLICATION:
Increasing Intergroup Cooperation

We have discussed a number of obstacles to intergroup cooperation, obstacles that would seem to bode poorly for the future of a world with such advanced military technology. People seem to naturally divide themselves into beloved ingroups and despised outgroups (Tajfel, 1982). Once conflicts begin in the lab, they tend to escalate (Deutsch, 1986). Once arms races begin between nations, they tend to end up in wars (Wallace, 1979). However, the upward spiral of conflict is not inevitable, and it can be reversed. Recall

TABLE 19.1 Statements About Disarmament By American and Soviet Leaders

STATEMENT BY UNITED STATES PRESIDENT	STATEMENT BY THE SOVIET GENERAL SECRETARY
Assumption 1: Our side prefers that both sides disarm together	
"We want more than anything else to join them in reducing the number of weapons" (Reagan, *The New York Times*, 6/15/84)	"We have been and remain convinced advocates of halting the arms race and reversing it" (Chernenko, *Pravda*, 4/9/84)
Assumption 2: We do not want to disarm while the other side builds more weapons	
"We refuse to become weaker while potential adversaries remain committed to their imperialist adventures" (Reagan, *The New York Times*, 6/18/82)	"Our country does not seek (nuclear) superiority, but it also will not allow superiority to be gained over it" (Chernenko, *Pravda*, 4/9/84).
Assumption 3: The other side would prefer that only our side disarms	
"For the Soviet leaders peace is not the real issue; rather, the issue is the attempt to spread their dominance using military power" (Reagan, *The New York Times*, 6/28/84)	"The main obstacle—and the entire course of the Geneva talks is persuasive evidence of this—is the attempts by the U.S. and its allies to achieve military superiority" (Andropov, *Pravda*, 1/13/84).

From Plous (1985).

Sherif's research with the warring summer campers. Once the "Rattlers" and "Eagles" were induced to *work together toward common goals,* the boys dropped their negative perceptions of the other group and put their conflicts aside. That finding suggests that the United States and the Soviet Union could further buttress the present peace by working together towards some mutually beneficial end. For instance, all human beings do share the same enemy in viruses and cancer-producing agents. The billions that have been spent on weapons designed to fight other humans, including the work done on germ warfare, might be turned towards fighting our mutual biological enemies.

The obstacle to that sort of international cooperation has been each side's distrust of the other's motives, and fear of being exploited. American and Soviet leaders' statements during the cold war indicated that they commonly held a "deterrence" view of international conflict (Tetlock, 1983). According to this cognitive image of conflict, any sign of weakness on "our side" will be exploited by the opponent. In fact, laboratory studies find support for the idea that unconditional cooperation will be exploited (Deutsch, 1986). As a way out of the two-sided dilemma of increasing threat versus exploited appeasement, psychologist Charles Osgood (1962) suggested the use of what he called the **GRIT** strategy. This strategy, the "Graduated and Reciprocated Initiatives in Tension Reduction," calls for one side of the conflict to begin with some small step toward a unilateral peaceful initiative. In order to avoid the appearance of weakness, or to chance an imbalance of power, that first step should be a small one. The initiative should be accompanied with the public pronouncement of more gradual reductions in conflict that will follow if the other side follows suit with peaceful initiatives of its own. By reciprocating gradually larger reductions in armaments, both sides can thereby avoid ever being in a highly disadvantaged position. And, instead of challenging one another towards increasing competition, the opponents involved in GRIT are challenging one another towards increased cooperation.

Osgood's GRIT strategy has been tested in laboratory conflict situations and found effective in producing cooperation, even after conflict escalated to high levels. The strategy works best when the person who initiates the conciliations is in a position of power equal or superior to that of the opponent. Laboratory competitors in a very superior position do not readily yield their advantage (Lindskold and Aronoff, 1980).

Does the GRIT strategy work in the real world of international relations? It can be argued that John F. Kennedy used just such a strategy to slow down the escalating conflict with the Soviet Union after the Cuban Missile Crisis (during which Kennedy and Soviet Premier Nikita Khruschev went head to head over the Soviet Union's placement of missiles in Cuba). Eight months after the crisis Kennedy made a conciliatory speech called "A Strategy for Peace," in which he called for an end to the crisis between the United States and the Soviet Union. Kennedy also proposed a unilateral act of disarmament by the United States. He said that the United States would stop open-air testing of nuclear weapons and would not resume it until another country did. In this way, he offered the Soviet Union the chance to follow his lead. Kennedy's speech was published in the Soviet newspapers and played on the radio there. Five days later Khruschev followed with a speech welcoming Kennedy's proposal, and calling for an end to the stockpiling of nuclear weapons. Khruschev not only agreed to stop atmospheric testing, but also offered a psychological gesture by his own by halting the production of strategic bombers. A month later, the two countries entered into negotiations, and they signed a nuclear weapons treaty that summer. Although many of these gestures were more symbolic than meaningful, they did serve to reduce the escalating tensions, and to change the psychological climate between the two superpowers (Etzioni, 1986).

In recent years, it appears that Soviet Premier Mikail Gorbachev may have used a very similar strategy in bringing United States President Ronald Reagan to the bargaining table. Gorbachev first proposed a one-sided weapons test ban in the Soviet Union and offered to extend it if the United States would reciprocate. When our government did not reciprocate, Gorbachev showed his resolve by beginning weapons tests again, after the moratorium deadline. However, his first gesture did produce a positive reaction in American public opinion and he tried again the following year by

offering important concessions at the Geneva accords, including the permission to have American inspectors verify Russian arms reductions. This time he was successful, and President Reagan agreed to a treaty that required some reductions in nuclear armaments on both sides. Gorbachev's policy of reciprocal concessions has indeed led to a happy outcome. Although there are still pressures towards militarism in both countries, the progress in reducing mutual hostilities had gone far enough by 1989 that *Newsweek* magazine could declare, "the cold war is over" (Barry, Warner, and Thomas, 1989). Unfortunately, that does not mean the end of world conflict. Two years later, Soviet troops were marching into Lithuania, and the United States was spending billions of dollars a day to fight a new enemy in the Middle East.

INTERACTIONS:
Avoiding Primitive Solutions to Modern Problems

Throughout this book, we have used the interactionist perspective to show the connections

Gorbachev confers with Reagan and Bush. Soviet President Mikail Gorbachev used a strategy similar to GRIT in his attempts to bring United States President Ronald Reagan to the nuclear bargaining table. Gorbachev first made a small unilateral (one-sided) cooperative move, agreeing to stop testing nuclear arms for a limited time. He promised to do more if the United States would reciprocate. When there was no reciprocation, Gorbachev began nuclear tests again, but later made additional cooperative overtures in the form of arms control concessions and one-sided reductions in arms.

among different findings and theoretical perspectives within psychology. That connection can be extended from individual psychological tendencies to global social problems. Let us summarize the three general interactionist principles:

1) *Microscopic* parts combine into a *macroscopic* whole.

2) The *person* and the *environment* are in continuous interplay.

3) *Proximate* influences (or causes in the immediate present) are best understood in light of *ultimate* (or background) causes.

These general principles can help us understand how global social problems reflect the different psychological influences we have discussed throughout the book.

The Ultimate Background of Modern Global Problems

Global social problems may be especially troublesome because our natural cognitive and biological processes do not fit with the demands of the modern technological world. Our characteristically human ways of thinking and feeling served our ancestors well, enabling them to "conquer the elements," to prosper and multiply, and to cover most of the surface of the earth. It is a basic tenet of Darwin's (1876) evolutionary theory that animals that reproduce more effectively, or exploit their environment more selfishly, will survive at the expense of those that are chaster or less self-concerned. Perhaps the plight of Chief Seattle's ecologically oriented tribe is a good recent example of this harsh process. Of course, human beings did not survive just by exploiting other human groups. Our ancestors evolved a large brain that helped them to understand and solve novel problems posed by the environment, and helped them to remember the best solutions for future reference. The paradox is that those same characteristically human ways of thinking and feeling could lead to our downfall in the crowded, new technological world we have so ingeniously constructed.

Consider how each of the global social problems represents a conflict posed by old human motivations in combination with new technologies. New agricultural and medical technologies removed some of the limits to population growth, but old human motivations kept us reproducing so fast that the world population now exceeds the total number of human beings born in the million years before the year 1860. Although we now realize the extent of the global problem, most of the people of the world seem to be expecting everyone else to stop reproducing, not them. Sexual behaviors are still as powerfully motivating as when the world was less crowded. Engineering breakthroughs have given us powerful and marvelous machines to meet the needs of the five billion new people, but those machines need tremendous amounts of energy from forests, petroleum fields, or new nuclear machines to run, so they quicken the pace at which the massive new population exhausts its natural resources and pollutes the air, land, and sea. Motivated by the old selfish responses to immediate personal reward, we have great difficulty slowing down the process even when we can see its destructive results around us. The third global social problem—the threat of nuclear war—also results from a combination of new technology and an age-old human tendency. The new technology is the atomic weaponry invented during the 1940s. The old human tendency that makes that technology so dangerous is the tendency to feel ethnocentric distaste towards people outside our "ingroup" (Barash and Lipton, 1985; Wilson, 1978).

Global Social Problems and Ongoing Person/Environment Interactions

At a more proximate level, we can think about global social problems, and their potential solutions, in light of the Organism × Environment × Cognition interactionist scheme (Table 19.2).

As you can see in Table 19.2, social problems result from an interaction of selfish organismic tendencies with inappropriate environmental contingencies and inappropriate cognitions. The biological organism contributes to social problems with sexual hormones that keep us reproducing, homeostatic mechanisms of the limbic system that impel us to seek personal comfort, and hormones that contribute to aggressive responses. The environment contributes to social problems with such rewards as tax incentives for having children, energy rates that favor heavy users, and social status and approval for big houses and cars.

Interventions at any of the three levels could be used to change the behaviors that contribute to each of the problems. However, various factors gravitate against the likelihood of intervention. Our leaders, who are in a position to change those reward structures by changing the legal supports for the social problems, face pressures from military lobbyists, powerful polluting industries,

TABLE 19.2 The Interactionist Model Applied to Social Problems

ORGANISM	×	ENVIRONMENT	×	COGNITION
Ultimate Factors		**Citizen's Environment**		**Attitudes About:**
Ingroup/outgroup kin favoritism Resource seeking		***Incorrect Payoffs*** Tax incentives for children Social status of big cars/houses/ possessions ***Costs*** Of conservation technology		Birth control/overpopulation Environmental issues Military vs. cooperation Religious ideas about Armegeddon, birth control, etc.
Proximate Factors		**Leader's Environment**		**Interpretations**
Homeostatic/comfort-seeking drives Sexual hormones Hormones related to aggression		Pressures of polluting industries, military lobby, religious groups (that oppose birth-control)		Selective attention to historical events (e.g., WW II vs. Vietnam) Misjudgments of other country's desires for peace vs. war

religious groups that oppose birth control, and so on. Cognitively, negative attitudes about birth control, conservation, and pacifism contribute to each of these problems. Religious leaders and the mass media sometimes contribute to regressive attitudes of large groups of people.

Cognitive variables that influence attention, interpretation, and memory can also contribute to the problems. For instance, Gilovich (1981) conducted a laboratory study in which some students were "primed" to think about Hitler and World War II by being summoned to an experiment in Winston Churchill Hall, where they met in a geography classroom with a map of wartime Europe on the wall, while others were similarly primed to think about Vietnam. Students reminded of World War II recommended more aggressive military responses to an international incident than did people given subtle reminders of Vietnam.

The interactionist perspective suggests that interventions to solve global problems might operate at any of those three levels. Birth control pills and sterilization programs operate at the biological level to interfere with the overpopulating consequences of sexual behaviors. Biological interventions for environmentally destructive behaviors seem less likely. Few would be likely to advocate brain surgery on five billion individuals, or reprogramming the genes of their ten billion offspring, to make them more peaceful. However, by understanding the triggers that underlie warlike hostility toward other groups, we might be able to trick those mechanisms, or use them to help reduce harmful ethnocentrism (Wilson, 1978). One possible way to make the thought of nuclear war less acceptable would be to have military and political leaders of powerful nations send their children and grandchildren on long-term live-in exchange programs in the countries of potential adversaries. In that way, people's nepotistic tendency to favor their own group members might be used to dampen the very hostilities it sometimes fuels.

Environmental interventions would include changes in the laws that make it profitable to pollute, overpopulate, and build weapons. For instance, instead of giving unlimited tax exemptions for children the laws could give very favorable supports for small families—perhaps lowered taxes and scholarships for the first one or two children—but remove the rewards for over-reproducing. These sorts of government incentive programs have already been used successfully in several overpopulated nations (Cone and Hays, 1980). Singapore, for instance, has increasing hospital fees, higher taxes, less educational funds, lower priority for housing support, and no maternity leave for any children after the second. That approach evidently worked to reduce the birth rate by over 50 percent since the late 1950s (Fook-Kee and Swee-Hock, 1975). In India, the government set up "vasectomy camps" where tens of thousands of men participated in exchange for cash rewards, gifts, and lottery coupons.

At a cognitive level, educational programs could be used to change people's attitudes about large cars, big families, and military aggression. For instance, large overpowered cars could be associated with laziness and obesity instead of the sexy exciting people now shown in the advertisements. Young children could be taught to think of the citizens of other nations not as dangerous enemies, but in the same way that Americans now think of the residents of other states. Instead of learning to think of other nationalities as inferior, they could be taught to think of wasteful and warlike people in their own society as the "outgroup."

From Microscopic Neurons to Macroscopic Global Behaviors

We began our study of psychological processes at the simplest level, by studying the single neural cell. Since that time, we have moved to higher and higher levels of analysis, considering how neurons and biochemicals interact to carry messages to and from the brain, and then how special groups of neurons connect the brain to the sights, sounds, and smells of the outside world. In later chapters, we described how our brains remember and learn from those experiences, and then go on to solve new problems posed by our environments. In recent chapters, we considered psychological processes at another level, discussing how we think about and respond to what other thinking and feeling human beings do around us. In this chapter, we considered special problems that only arise at the level of large groups of people thinking, feeling, and behaving in ways that lead them all towards potential disaster.

These global social problems bring us into the territory of sociology and the other social sciences, but that turf should not be an alien land to psychology. Our ancestors evolved not as separate individuals thinking thoughts of their own, but as social beings thinking about how to get along with the other people in their lives. The brain and behavior of *homo sapiens* evolved to deal with environmental problems that were largely social in nature. Even the way we learn is commonly social, as shown in the research on modeling discussed in Chapter 6. Our amazing ability to communicate with other people is made possible by the special adaptations of the brain that allow us to absorb language easily. As discussed in the chapters on emotion and social cognition, our emotional reactions are designed to deal with problems that are often social ones, and those very reactions include facial expressions that are themselves communications to other human beings.

As we have discussed in this last chapter, the social problems of overpopulation, environmental deterioration, and the threat of nuclear war grow out of individual human behaviors. We noted how selfish biological motivations combine with an environment structured to reward socially harmful behaviors, and with maladaptive cognitive tendencies, to lead us further along these socially entrapping pathways. Some biological theorists even argue that our large brain is itself an adaptation to the problems posed by warlike conflict with other intelligent hominids (Baer and McEachron, 1982). However, the human brain may be capable of solving these problems as we have solved earlier ones. Just as the individual child learns to delay immediate gratification in hopes of long-term rewards, so whole human groups may be able to forego immediate selfishness and outgroup hostility in the interest of the long-term preservation of our species' global ecological niche. The solutions to these problems must include an awareness of economics and political science. Changing individual attitudes and behaviors, one at a time, is inefficient when all five and a half billion members of human society must change. Nevertheless, if economic and political policies are to be effective they must take account of the individual cognitive and motivational biases of the citizens and social leaders affected by them. In closing, then, we echo the sentiments of the pioneering social psychologist William McDougall, who argued in 1908 that social policies based on faulty assumptions about individual human motivation and cognition are doomed to failure. For this reason, psychology is:

the essential common foundation on which all the social sciences—ethics, economics, political science, philosophy of history, sociology, and cultural anthropology— . . . must be built up.

(McDougall, 1908) ■

IN CONTEXT: GLOBAL SOCIAL PROBLEMS

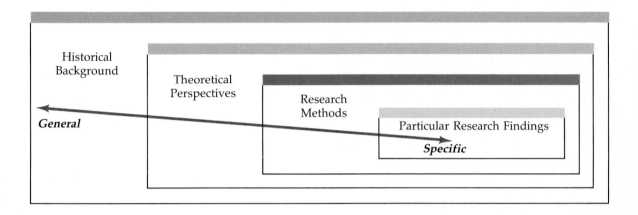

STUDY QUESTIONS

How do individual behaviors, feelings, and cognitions contribute to the global-scale problems of overpopulation, environmental deterioration, and international conflict?

How can understanding basic psychological processes such as psychobiology, learning, and cognition contribute to the solution of those global social problems?

HISTORICAL BACKGROUND

1. Early research on group problems involved historical analyses of mobs, crazes, and panics, as described by E. O. Ross.

2. Researchers during the 1930s and 1940s, including Sherif and Sherif, experimentally manipulated prejudice and group conflict.

3. During the 1960s, a new field of **environmental psychology** was started to study person-environment interactions, including the effects of crowding, noise, and air pollution.

MODERN THEORETICAL PERSPECTIVES

1. A **Biological perspective** is represented in several theoretical approaches in this chapter. Theories that humans evolved from warlike hominids who were selected for selfish reproductive patterns take an ultimate perspective. At a more proximate level, Calhoun and Christian's work on crowding in animals assumes that physiological responses are linked to changes in the social and physical environment.

2. The **Behaviorist approach** views global problems as outgrowths of maladaptive reward contingencies. This approach is represented in the early studies of prejudice and frustration.

Platt's **social traps** analysis also took a behaviorist perspective, assuming that destructive group behaviors are maintained by short-term individual rewards that outweigh long-term group punishments.

3. A **cognitive perspective** focuses on the contribution of information processing to social problems. The view of Soviet–U.S. cold war relations as a perceptual dilemma represents this approach.

4. An **interactionist perspective** considers how biology, learning history, and cognition interact in contributing to social problems. The view that international conflict results from cognitive categorizations that tap into a basic human bias against outgroups is an example of this approach.

RESEARCH METHODS

1. The **experimental approach** is demonstrated in studies of the "prisoner's dilemma," in which subjects are randomly assigned to play against either cooperative or competitive opponents in a laboratory game (Deutsch, 1986).

2. The **correlational approach** is shown in the research that looked at the association between

city size, density, and crime statistics (Freedman, Heschka, and Levy, 1975).

3. The study of American senators' attitudes toward disarmament is an example of the **survey** method (Plous, 1985).

4. The method of **naturalistic observation** was used in the study of deer living on a crowded island (Krebs, 1972).

RESEARCH FINDINGS AND SUMMARY

1. Research with nonhuman species has indicated that overcrowding leads to unpleasant physiological and behavioral reactions that generally serve to limit population growth. Overcrowded rats were found to become hyperaggressive, sexually deviant, and cannibalistic.

2. Studies of humans living in crowded cities do not show such a clear relationship. Although crime is much higher in large cities, the relationship does not seem to depend upon density—people per square mile—but upon the absolute size of the city.

3. Some research suggests that the anonymity of living in a large city can contribute to the higher level of antisocial behavior there.

4. Density in a city may be bearable because people can escape into their private dwellings. Crowding in prisons indicates results more in line with the animal studies: Crowded prisoners show health problems and increased violence. Students living in crowded dorms also show signs of stressful reactions.

5. To control population, individuals and couples need to change their birth control behaviors. Contraception use involves five steps: (1) acquiring information, (2) acknowledging the likelihood of intercourse, (3) obtaining the contraceptive device, (4) communicating with one's sexual partner, and (5) using the chosen method. Cognitive and behavioral techniques used in individual psychotherapy have been used to change ineffective birth control behaviors.

6. Americans could cut energy use by 40 to 50 percent by changing their conservation behaviors, but social traps provide an important obstacle. Social traps are situations in which immediate rewards lead individuals or groups into behavioral patterns that are harmful in the long run. They can result from (1) short-term rewards exercising more control than long-term negative consequences, (2) ignorance of long-term consequences, and (3) sliding reinforcers that change from rewarding to punishing with overuse.

7. Research on residents living near the faulty Three Mile Island nuclear reactor indicated signs of traumatic stress disorder after the accident there.

8. Environmentally destructive behaviors could be changed by making long-term consequences immediate, reinforcing alternative desirable behaviors, changing the nature of the long-term consequences, and using social pressures to induce less selfishness.

9. International conflict is fueled by a basic distinction that people make between ingroups and outgroups. People tend to regard their own geographic region and ethnic group as better than others, and even to prefer people who have meaningless similarities to them.

10. In a special form of social trap, students bidding for a dollar can be easily led into a situation where they bid several dollars for one to avoid potential losses. The U.S.S.R.–U.S. arms race showed features of this sort of trap, in which initial potential rewards are replaced with a willingness to pay dearly to avoid losing face.

11. Laboratory studies of conflict and cooperation indicate that neither punitive deterrence nor "turning the other cheek" are effective strategies against an adversarial opponent. A "tit for tat" or nonpunitive deterrent strategy is more effective.

12. Research indicates that both Soviet and American leaders during the 1980s were involved in a perceptual dilemma, in which each side saw itself as seeking peace, but saw the other as seeking domination.

13. Ongoing conflict can be reduced by working toward common goals, and by the use of a series of graduated initiatives in tension-reduction that challenge the opponent towards cooperation instead of conflict.

14. The study of social problems brings us to the threshold of the other social sciences. As McDougall pointed out almost a century ago, potential solutions involving economics, political science, and sociology are not likely to be effective unless they take account of individual psychological processes.

ADDITIONAL READINGS

Barash, D. P., and Lipton, J. E. 1985. *The caveman and the bomb: Human nature, evolution, and nuclear war*. New York: McGraw-Hill. An evolutionary perspective on the roots of warfare, with suggestions for how we can overcome our "Neanderthal mentality."

Cone, J. D., and Hayes, S. C. 1980. *Environmental problems/behavioral solutions*. Monterey, CA: Brooks/Cole. A behaviorally based analysis of the causes and potential solutions for problems of overpopulation and environmental deterioration. Includes chapters on recycling, energy conservation, litter reduction, population control, and several others. Also discusses experimental social reform.

Earth Works Group. 1989. *Fifty simple things you can do to save the earth*. Berkeley, CA: Earthworks Press. For those interested in making their own personal contribution to slowing environmental deterioration, this book gives a number of useful hints, from toting your own cloth shopping bag to using your own coffee cup instead of the styrofoam at the office.

Fisher, J. D., Bell, P. A., and Baum, A. S. 1984. *Environmental psychology*, 2nd ed. New York: Holt, Rinehart, and Winston. A general text covering the research and theory on crowding and pollution, as well as other topics in person/environment interactions.

Insel, P. M. and Lindgren, H. C. 1978. *Too close for comfort*. Englewood Cliffs, NJ: Prentice Hall/Spectrum. A highly readable account of much of the classic research on the effects of overcrowding.

White, R. K. 1986. *Psychology and the prevention of nuclear war*. New York: NYU Press. A book of readings that includes original articles by leading researchers in the area of international conflict and negotiation.

THE USE OF STATISTICS IN PSYCHOLOGY

L oose phrases such as "miles away," "poles apart," "a giant's stride," "minute," "pinpoint," "in a nutshell," though picturesque, are notably inaccurate. Though this is unimportant in conversational or literary activity, . . . when transferred to the fields of serious thought, where important and far-reaching decisions are being made, . . . vague impressions will not do. Accurate measurement and comparison, and estimation in a scientific form, are vital.

(Vesselo, 1965)

Chapter Outline

Statistics is often perceived as "dull," "boring," or "mathematically complex." Little wonder then that the thought of studying statistics is likely to unnerve even the most dedicated student. Yet, even if you do not intend to become a psychology major—much less a working psychologist—you still need an understanding of statistics to see why it is vital to psychology. **Statistics** is the branch of mathematics that deals with the collection and interpretation of numerical data. It is used as a research tool in virtually every field of psychology. For example, a neuropsychologist would use statistics to describe measurements of an animal's behavior before and after a brain operation. A developmental psychologist would use statistics to interpret patterns in the speech of young children. And a clinical psychologist would use statistics to assess the effectiveness of different forms of psychotherapy on patients with a psychological disorder. In each instance, numerical data are collected and interpreted with the aid of statistics.

In this brief overview, only a few formulas and mathematical derivations are used. Our aim is not to provide you with a set of procedures for making statistical calculations. Rather, our goal is to provide you with an introductory acquaintance so that you will understand how psychologists use statistics to organize and make decisions about data. Statistics provides the means for making systematic and objective decisions about numbers.

ORGANIZATION AND DESCRIPTION OF DATA

NUMERICAL OBSERVATIONS

STATISTICAL DATA

Much of the research that psychologists do results in the collection of **statistical data.** Data consists of a group of numbers that represent measurements of a particular property or phenomenon. In psychology, the numbers could represent IQ scores from an intelligence test given to a group of students, the number of items recognized by subjects in an experiment on recognition memory, or the number of aggressive acts committed by a child during an hour on the playground. Intelligence, memory, and aggression are but a few of the phenomena whose measurement results in numerical data.

Suppose, for example, that you are interested in exploring the quality of life at your school. To determine how satisfied fellow students are with the quality of their lives at college, you decide to conduct a survey. You could ask students to make a judgment about their quality of life by selecting a number on a scale from 0 to 10, where 0 equals "very dissatisfied" and 10 is "very satisfied." After sending your survey to each student on campus, you would gather the completed surveys and attempt to see what you found. For the sake of simplicity, let us assume that your data, as shown in Table A.1, consists of ratings from only 30 students.

Looking at the individual raw scores in the table reveals a bewildering array of numbers—some low, some high, and many in between. What did your survey find about the quality of life at your institution? Glancing at just the raw numbers (in reality you might have hundreds, if not thou-

sands, of ratings), in fact, reveals very little. To get a total picture of the student ratings it is necessary to organize your data.

FREQUENCY DISTRIBUTIONS

One of the easiest ways to begin organizing your data is to make a **frequency distribution.** A frequency distribution is made by placing the survey ratings in numerical sequence and noting by tally marks how often each rating was selected. According to custom, the highest ratings go at the top of the distribution and the lowest ratings go at the bottom. Table A.2 shows the same data arranged in a frequency distribution. Looking at this table, you can see how the frequency distribution gets its name. Each rating is listed once, along with its frequency of selection. Checking these data with those of Table A.1, we see that there was no rating of 10, two ratings of 9, four ratings of 8, and so on. Moreover, we can see how the frequency of ratings were distributed. The most frequently selected rating was a 7; the least frequently selected ratings were 0, 1, 3, and 10.

Even more useful for visualizing the results of your study is to convert your tally marks for each rating into a **frequency histogram.** A histogram is a bar graph representation of a frequency distribution. To construct a histogram, each rating is represented as an interval along the base of a graph and

TABLE A.1 Hypothetical Quality of Life Data from 30 Students

2	9	6	5	4
7	8	9	5	7
6	7	5	7	2
7	6	7	7	7
4	7	8	6	7
8	5	6	6	8

Note: Scores are individual student ratings on a scale from 0 to 10.

TABLE A.2 A Frequency Distribution of Quality of Life Ratings from 30 Students

Rating	Tally	Frequency
10		0
9	11	2
8	1111	4
7	1111111111	10
6	111111	6
5	11111	5
4	11	2
3		0
2	1	1
1		0
0		0
		N = 30

a bar is drawn for each interval to a height that is determined by the rating's frequency. Figure A.1 shows how our present data would appear in the form of a histogram.

As an alternative to a histogram, the same data could be graphically portrayed in the form of a **frequency polygon.** In this case, ratings are again presented as intervals along the base of a graph, but now frequency is plotted as a point directly above each rating. By connecting the data points, as was done with our data in Figure A.2, a frequency polygon emerges. This method of data organization takes its name from the many-sided figure that is displayed in the graph.

Each of these methods of data organization—frequency distribution, histogram, and frequency polygon—rearranges and groups the individual scores to make patterns in the data more apparent. In each instance we can see that the students in our survey tended to rate their quality of life as being more positive than negative, and that few people scored at either extreme.

MEASURES OF CENTRAL TENDENCY

Merely saying that students tended to rate their quality of life as positive is not a terribly precise way of describing the data. Now that we have

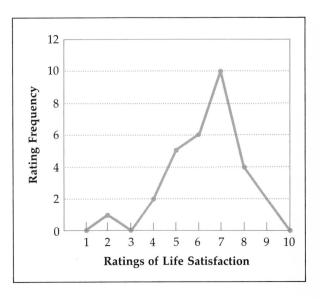

FIGURE A.2   A frequency polygon of the data shown in Figure A.1 and Table A.2. Instead of bars, frequency is plotted along the ordinate as a point at the center of each rating interval. The points are connected to form a frequency polygon.

organized the ratings into a frequency distribution we need a way to summarize the entire distribution more succinctly. What is the "typical" rating? In statistics, typical is defined as a **measure of central tendency,** the central point or points in a frequency distribution around which other ratings or scores are scattered. Three different measures of central tendency are used. They are the **mean,** the **median,** and the **mode.**

THE MEAN

The mean is the most sensitive measure of central tendency, because it takes each individual score into account. Although it is commonly referred to as the "average" this term is not very satisfactory, since the word "average" is occasionally used for any measure of central tendency. The mean is obtained by adding all of the scores together and dividing this sum by the total number of scores. It is expressed by the formula

$$\bar{X} = (\text{Sum of X})/N$$

In our example, the mean is obtained by adding all the scores together and then dividing this sum (Sum of X = 191) by the number of ratings (N = 30). The result is a mean quality of life rating of 6.37. Compared to our earlier generalization of the results obtained from the frequency distribution, that students rated their quality of life as being more positive than negative, the mean represents the results of the survey with considerable precision and succinctness.

FIGURE A.1   A histogram of the data from the frequency distribution shown in Table A.2. Each rating is represented by an interval along the base or abscissa of the graph, while frequency is represented by a bar above each interval. The height of each bar is determined by the rating's frequency of occurrence and is measured along the side, or ordinate, of the graph.

THE MEDIAN

The median represents the midpoint of all of the data. To obtain the median, arrange all of the scores in numerical order from lowest to highest. The median is the score in the middle of the order. In our example, arranging the ratings from lowest to highest yields a median of 7. Unlike the mean whose value is determined by each rating in the distribution, the value of the median is determined only by the number of scores on either side of it.

In most instances, the mean is a better measure of central tendency than the median because it is sensitive to all scores in the distribution. However, under special circumstances, such as when there are a few divergent scores, the median is a better measure of central tendency because it does not take the value of extreme scores into account. In our example, if three students had rated their quality of life as 0 instead of 7, the median would drop slightly to 6.5, while the mean would fall to 5.67, much closer to the "neutral" section of the rating scale. In this case, only the median would reflect the fact that the majority of students rated their quality of life as positive. Consequently, the median is preferred when there are a few divergent scores that make the mean a distorted measure of central tendency. For example, surveys of household income report median rather than mean income because a small number of wealthy individuals would elevate the mean greatly out of proportion to their number.

THE MODE

The easiest measure of central tendency to determine, the mode is the most frequently occurring score. In our example, the mode was 7 because this was the most frequently selected individual rating. The mode is less informative than either the mean or the median because it tells us nothing about the value of other scores or the mode's position in the frequency distribution. It merely tells which rating was selected most frequently. When there are ties in rating frequency, a distribution is said to be **bimodal** (two ratings share the highest frequency) or **multimodal** (more than two ratings share the highest frequency).

To summarize the three measures of central tendency:

- The mean is the average of all numerical observations in a frequency distribution.

- The median is the midpoint in a frequency distribution below which—and above which —half of the numerical observations lie.

- The mode is the most frequently occurring numerical observation (or observations) in a frequency distribution.

MEASURES OF VARIABILITY

Measures of central tendency help to describe the data, but they provide us with only a part of the information we need to summarize a distribution of scores. For example, knowing that the mean of our quality of life survey was 6.37 tells us nothing about the **variability** of scores in our distribution. Were most of the individual ratings similar to the mean in value or were the ratings so widely distributed that the average represented by the mean was unlike any of the individual ratings? For example, a mean of approximately 6.3 could be obtained from a set of very similar ratings (for example, 6, 6, 7) or a set of very dissimilar ratings (perhaps 1, 8, 10). In the case of similar or *low variability* scores, the mean is a more accurate indicator of individual student ratings than in the case of dissimilar or *high variability* scores. In other words, a measure of variability can tell us how representative a measure of central tendency is. Therefore, to describe our data more completely, we need both a measure of central tendency (to tell us what is typical of scores in a distribution) and a measure of variability (to tell us how the scores are distributed). Two different measures of variability are the *range* and the *standard deviation*.

THE RANGE

The **range** is a crude measure of variability; it is the difference between the highest and lowest scores in a frequency distribution. In our example, the highest and lowest ratings were 9 and 2. Consequently, our range was 7.

Knowing the range as a measure of variability is a lot like knowing the median or mode as a measure of central tendency. Each of these measures ignores the numerical value of much of the data. While the range tells us about the spread of variability, it says very little about how individual scores are distributed. For example, two sets of ratings can have the same range (for example, 2, 4, 7, 9 and 2, 9, 9, 9 both have a range of 7), yet each set can differ in its distribution of scores. We need a measure of variability that, like the mean as a measure of central tendency, is calculated by taking the specific value of each score into account. That measure is the standard deviation.

THE STANDARD DEVIATION

The most frequently used measure of variability is the **standard deviation.** It is defined as the average distance of each score in a distribution from the mean of that distribution. Although the standard deviation is harder to calculate than the range, it is a more sensitive measure of variability because it is calculated on the basis of every score in the distribution, not just the two most extreme scores.

To calculate the standard deviation, subtract the mean of a distribution from each score in the distribution. Square each of these differences, add all of these squared differences together, and divide this sum by the number of scores minus one (a correction factor). Finally, find the square root of this value. The standard deviation is expressed by the formula

$$SD = \sqrt{\text{Sum of } d^2/(N-1)}$$

where d stands for the difference between a score and the mean. As shown in Table A.3, the standard deviation for our quality of life survey was 1.72. This means that, on the average, the ratings in our suvery of 30 students were 1.72 units away from the mean. Keep in mind that the smaller the standard deviation, the lower the variability of scores in our distribution, and the closer each score is, on the average, to our mean. The closer each score is to the mean, the better the mean is at summarizing the distribution of scores. This is why we said earlier that a measure of variability tells us how representative our measure of central tendency is. In our example, the mean has been shown to be an accurate and representative measure.

DISTRIBUTIONS AND CURVES

You might think that, after calculating a measure of central tendency and a measure of variability, you have completed the description of your data. In fact, there is more to do. Distributions can be described not only by measures of typicality and variability, but also in terms of their shape. After considering a number of differently shaped distributions, we will return to our discussion of the standard deviation. To fully understand the importance of this statistical measure to psychology, we need to consider some of the different ways in which data may be distributed before we examine an important theoretical distribution known as the normal distribution.

TABLE A.3 Calculation of the Standard Deviation

Student	Rating	Mean	Difference	Difference Squared
1	2	6.37	−4.37	19.10
2	7	6.37	.63	.40
3	6	6.37	− .37	.14
4	7	6.37	.63	.40
5	4	6.37	−2.37	5.62
6	8	6.37	1.63	2.66
7	9	6.37	2.63	6.92
8	8	6.37	1.63	2.66
9	7	6.37	.63	.40
10	6	6.37	− .37	.14
11	7	6.37	.63	.40
12	5	6.37	−1.37	1.88
13	6	6.37	− .37	.14
14	9	6.37	2.63	6.92
15	5	6.37	−1.37	1.88
16	7	6.37	.63	.40
17	8	6.37	1.63	2.66
18	6	6.37	− .37	.14
19	5	6.37	−1.37	1.88
20	5	6.37	−1.37	1.88
21	7	6.37	.63	.40
22	7	6.37	.63	.40
23	6	6.37	− .37	.14
24	6	6.37	− .37	.14
25	4	6.37	−2.37	5.62
26	7	6.37	.63	.40
27	2	6.37	−4.37	19.10
28	7	6.37	.63	.40
29	7	6.37	.63	.40
30	8	6.37	1.63	1.88

Sum of d^2 = 85.50

$SD = \sqrt{(\text{Sum of } d^2)/(N-1)}$

$SD = \sqrt{85.50/29}$

$SD = \sqrt{2.95}$

$SD = 1.72$

SKEWED DISTRIBUTIONS

When frequency distributions are plotted as frequency polygons, the data that are plotted in the graph can form a variety of shapes. For example, if a professor gave a test to a large class of introductory psychology students, the distribution of test scores might look like that shown in Figure A.3. This graph is similar in general shape to that shown previously for our quality of life survey. (Look back to Figure A.2.) It differs, however, in one important respect. Due to the large number of test scores in Figure A.3, the bumps and irregularities have been smoothed over. This turns a frequency polygon (an irregular, many-sided figure) into a smooth curve called a **distribution curve.**

Figure A.3 is a graphic representation of a frequency distribution that is constructed in the same manner as a frequency polygon. Possible test scores are listed along the horizontal axis of the graph—the *abscissa*—and the frequency of each score on the test is listed on the vertical axis—the *ordinate*. If the majority of test scores are either high or low, the distribution is said to be asymmetrical, or **skewed.** In this particular example the curve is said to be *negatively skewed*, as the "tail" or longest end of the curve tapers off to the left in the direction of the lower test scores.

Conversely, if the professor had made the test extremely difficult, a different distribution curve would result, more like the curve shown in Figure A.4. In this example, the majority of students did very poorly. Since the tail of this distribution

FIGURE A.3   A negatively skewed distribution curve. When the majority of scores in a distribution are high, the distribution is asymmetrical or skewed. It is negatively skewed because the tail or longest end of the distribution points in the direction of the lower test scores. In this example, a class of students did only moderately well on a psychology exam.

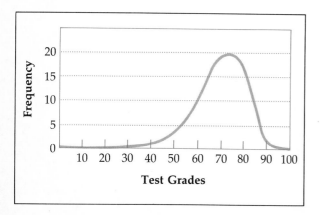

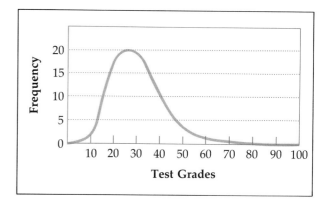

FIGURE A.4   A positively skewed distribution curve. When the majority of scores in a distribution are low, the distribution is once more asymmetrical, or skewed. It is positively skewed because the tail or longest end of the distribution points in the direction of the higher test scores. In this example, a class of students did very poorly on a psychology test.

points to the right in the direction of the higher test scores, this curve is described as *positively skewed*.

THE NORMAL DISTRIBUTION

As we have noted, distributions come in many different shapes and sizes. Yet for a great many psychological phenomena the data are distributed in the form of a symmetrical, bell-shaped curve known as the **normal curve.** Figure A.5 represents a normal curve as a theoretical distribution; a curve, devoid of specific scores or frequencies, as it might apply to a wide variety of data. However, like all frequency distributions, scores would be listed along the abscissa and frequency along the ordinate.

Among the important features of the normal

FIGURE A.5   The normal distribution or normal curve. In this theoretical distribution of scores, which represents scores from many different psychological measures, the distribution is symmetrical and bell-shaped, with the mean, median, and mode all having the same value.

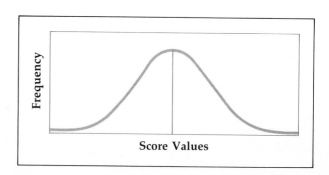

The Use of Statistics in Psychology

distribution is the fact that its curve is symmetrical. The distribution of scores is exactly the same on each side of the distribution's midpoint. Second, the majority of scores occur around the midpoint of the distribution, and there are progressively fewer scores in the direction of either tail. Finally, the mean, median, and mode all have the same numerical value. Unlike our earlier example of a negatively skewed distribution (Figure A.2) where measures of central tendency can differ, in a normal distribution the mean is located at the midpoint of the distribution and is the most frequently occurring score.

The standard deviation is related to the normal distribution in a particularly useful way. As shown in Figure A.6, for data that are normally distributed, 68.26 percent of all scores fall between the mean and one standard deviation above and below the mean. (Recall that since a normal curve is symmetrical, 34.13 percent are located one standard deviation below the mean and 34.13 percent are located one standard deviation above the mean.) Similarly, 95.44 percent of all scores fall within two standard deviations of the mean, and 99.74 percent of all data are located within three standard deviations. These statistical properties are true of all normal curves.

Knowing these properties allows psychologists to interpret individual scores if the mean and standard deviation of a normal distribution are available. For example, IQ scores follow a normal curve with a mean of 100 and a standard deviation of 15 (Figure A.7). Since we know from Figure A.6 how standard deviation units are related to areas under the normal curve, we can take these percentages and use them to determine a person's position relative to an entire group. Assume, for example, that a person received a score of 130 on an IQ test. From Figure A.7, we can see that this score is two standard deviation units above the mean of 100. By looking back to Figure A.6, we can see that someone with a score of two standard deviation units above the mean surpassed 97.72 percent of all people who took the test (the sum of all percentages to the left of two standard deviations above the mean). Alternatively, someone who received a score of 85 (one standard deviation below the mean) did better than only 15.87 percent of all people.

The important point of these examples is that if we assume that the data are normally distributed, and we know the mean and standard deviation, then we can calculate the percentage of scores lying above or below any value. By the same token,

FIGURE A.6 The relationship between the standard deviation and the normal curve. With the mean at the midpoint, the majority of all scores (68.26 percent) fall within plus or minus one standard deviation of the mean. Virtually all scores (99.74 percent) fall within plus or minus three standard deviations of the mean.

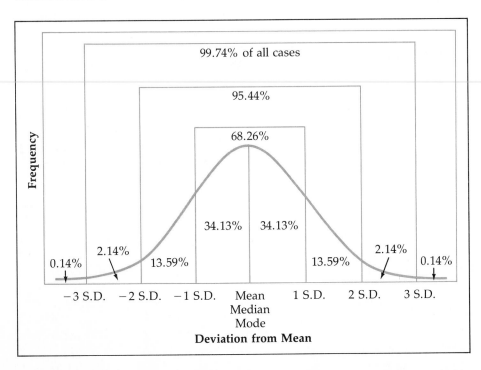

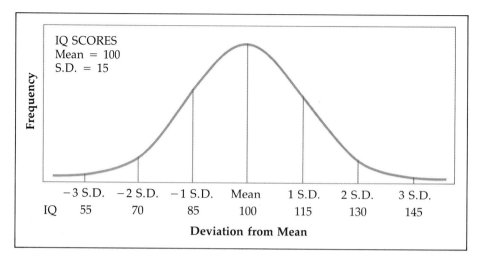

FIGURE A.7 A normal distribution of IQ scores with a mean of 100 and standard deviation of 15 units. With a normal distribution and a known mean and standard deviation, it is possible to calculate the percentage of scores lying above or below any value. From Figure A.6, we see that a person with an IQ score of 115 must have scored higher than 84.13 percent of all other people.

given a normal distribution of data with a known mean and standard deviation, we can use the percentages shown in Figure A.6 to determine the probability of selecting a person at random with a score above or below any particular value. For these reasons, describing a set of data in terms of central tendency, variability, and the shape of its distribution are important.

CORRELATION

Until now, we have considered sets of data in which each person contributes a single score, as in our quality of life survey. Sometimes, however, we have scores on two different phenomena for each person and we might like to know how these scores are related. For example, we could have information from a group of students about their college SAT scores and their subsequent grades in college. To what extent are SAT scores and college grades related? Or we might have cross-cultural data on income and life satisfaction from different countries. In keeping with our earlier example of a quality of life survey on a college campus, let us look at some actual data comparing the quality of life for people from different countries with their annual per capita (per person) income (Table A.4). How is life satisfaction related to income in different countries of the world? Do countries with the highest per capita income show the highest levels of life satisfaction? To answer these types of questions involving relationships between two different measures, we turn to different forms of data

analysis—the *scattergram* and the *method of correlation*.

THE SCATTERGRAM

Political scientist Ronald Inglehart and opinion researcher Jacques-Rene Rabier (1985) examined 10 years of public opinion surveys to find out how satisfied people were with their lives in each of the countries listed. In Table A.4, life satisfaction scores are expressed as a mean based on an average of numerous ratings. Per capita income was obtained by dividing each country's gross national product by its number of residents for the year 1979, approximately the middle of the ten-year period of study. It, too, represents an average.

Since plotting our earlier data was helpful in detecting an overall trend (see Figures A.1 and A.2) we will repeat this process. Now, however, instead of plotting a frequency polygon, we will construct a **scattergram** by putting the life satisfaction ratings and income data together into a single graph. In a scattergram, where data points are "scattered" throughout the graph, one data set is presented on the abscissa and the other is presented on the ordinate.

In our example, shown in Figure A.8, each pair of scores for a country is represented by a single point on the graph. For example, to find the data point for Denmark, find its approximate life satisfaction rating on the abscissa (8.03) and its approximate per capita income on the ordinate ($8,470). Look *up* from the point on the abscissa (8.03) and to the *right* of the point on the ordinate (about

TABLE A.4 Life Satisfaction and Per Capita Income in 19 Countries*

Country	Average Satisfaction**	Gross National Product Per Capita (1979)
Denmark	8.03	$ 8,470
Sweden	8.02	10,071
Switzerland	7.98	9,439
Norway	7.90	8,762
Netherlands	7.77	7,057
N. Ireland	7.77	3,560
Iceland	7.76	3,533
Finland	7.73	5,814
Luxembourg	7.64	7,754
U.S.A.	7.57	10,765
Britain	7.52	4,972
Belgium	7.33	7,978
W. Germany	7.23	9,507
Austria	7.14	6,311
France	6.63	8,619
Spain	6.60	2,830
Italy	6.58	4,191
Japan	6.39	7,244
Greece	5.58	2,881

*Data obtained between 1974 and 1983.

**Satisfaction based on a rating scale where 0 = very dissatisfied and 10 = very satisfied.

From Inglehart and Rabier (1985).

halfway between $8,000 and $9,000) to where imaginary lines from each of these points intersect. At this intersection, the data point for Denmark is located. Data points for each of the other countries were placed in the same way.

Looking at the data in the scattergram, we see that despite a wide range of per capita income, there is not a great deal of variation in the life satisfaction ratings. While there are specific countries which show relatively low or high life satisfaction and income scores (for example, Greece is relatively low on both, while Sweden is relatively high on both), over all life satisfaction is generally positive (a mean of 7.34 for all countries) and not strongly related to per capita income. The researchers who conducted this study suggested that people in different countries had different ideas about life satisfaction and judged their lives according to their particular culture's criteria. In the main, based on the countries surveyed, income had only a moderate bearing on this judgment (Inglehart and Rabier, 1985).

THE CORRELATION COEFFICIENT

Suppose, however, the data were different from those actually observed. In fact, let us assume that a variety of scattergrams are possible. Figure A.9, for example, shows five different hypothetical scattergrams constructed in the same manner as before, yet each showing a different relationship between life satisfaction and income level. Moreover, let us assume that each scattergram contains data on each of fifty different countries. What do the various scattergrams show? To an-

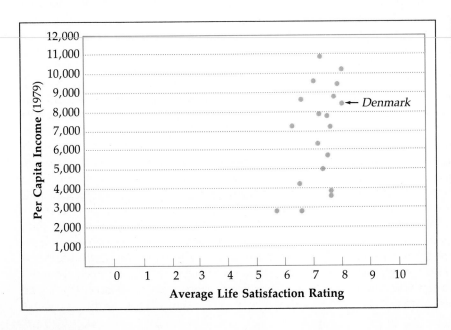

FIGURE A.8 A scattergram of life satisfaction ratings and per capita income for 19 different countries. Each point represents the pair of scores for each country shown in Table A.4. This scattergram indicates fairly wide variation in per capita income among countries, but only moderate variation among life satisfaction ratings. According to these data, life satisfaction and per capita income are not strongly related.

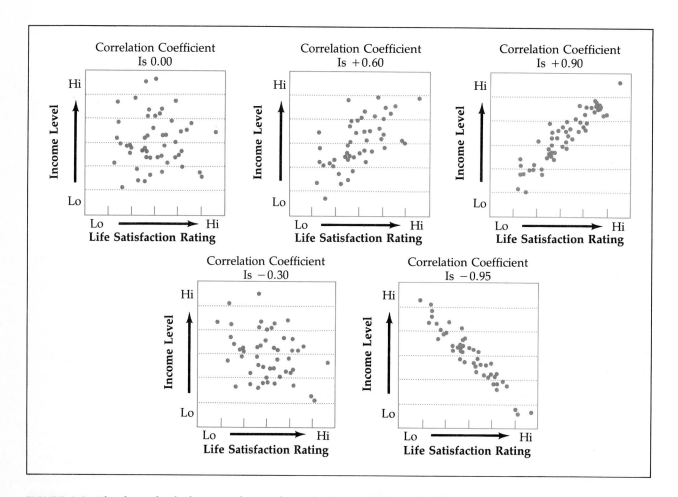

FIGURE A.9   Five hypothetical scatterplots and correlation coefficients for life satisfaction ratings and per capita income levels for 50 countries.   A zero correlation in A indicates no relationship between life satisfaction and income as the data points are widely dispersed in the graph. Positive correlations are indicated in B and C as the data points tend to group themselves in a line running from the lower left to the upper right corner of each graph. In these instances, increases in life satisfaction tend to correspond to increases in income. Finally, negative correlations are shown in D and E as the data cluster in a line running from the upper left to the lower right corner of each graph. In these instances, increases in life satisfaction tend to correspond to decreases in income. The more closely the data resemble a diagonal line (C and E), the stronger the relationship between the two sets of data and the stronger the correlation coefficient.

swer this question precisely we need to turn to a statistical procedure that we outlined initially in the first chapter of this text.

To determine the mathematical relationship between two sets of numerical data we calculate a statistic called the **correlation coefficient.** Rather than deal with the extensive computations that are involved in calculating a correlation, we will remind you from Chapter 1 that a correlation yields a score that can range in value from –1.00 to 0 to +1.00. If two sets of data are completely unrelated such that one measure (for example, adult shoe size) has absolutely no bearing on the other (per-

haps adult vocabulary size), the measures will yield a *zero correlation.* If, however, an increase in scores in one data set (say IQ scores) is accompanied by an increase in scores in the other data set (for example, grades in high school), a *positive correlation* will be obtained. Positive correlations can vary from zero to +1.00, where +1.00 is a perfect positive correlation. Alternatively, if an increase in scores in one data set (perhaps alcohol consumption) is accompanied by a decrease in scores in the other set (say driving performance), a *negative correlation* will be obtained. As with positive correlations, a negative correlation can range in value from zero to –1.00, with –1.00 a perfect negative correlation. Perfect correlations, whether positive or negative, are extremely rare.

Returning to the scattergrams of Figure A.9, we can see different relationships in the data in each graph, along with the numerical value of each correlation coefficient. When two measures such as life satisfaction and income have no relationship to each other (Graph A), the correlation is zero. As the two measures become increasingly related, such that increases in one measure correspond to increases in the other measure, the correlation becomes increasingly positive (Graphs B and C). But if the two measures are related in the opposite fashion, such that increases in life satisfaction tend to be associated with decreases in per capita income, the correlation becomes increasingly negative (Graphs D and E).

In each instance, as the data points in Figure A.9 move in the direction of a diagonal line the resulting correlation betweern the two measures becomes stronger. In this way, psychologists can often get a rough idea about the degree of relationship between two sets of data, as we did earlier in Figure A.8, by merely observing their relationship in a scattergram. However, by calculating the correlation coefficient, a researcher provides a precise mathematical index of this relationship.

CORRELATION, PREDICTION, AND CAUSALITY

How are correlation coefficients useful to psychologists? To the extent that different measures may be correlated, either in a positive or negative manner, correlations are useful for making predictions. For example, we noted in Chapter 1 (Table 1.2) that the correlation between identical twins in general scholastic ability was +.86. On the basis of this relationship, if we knew the school grades of one twin and we wanted to predict the performance of the other twin, we would base our prediction on the strong positive correlation. If one twin were an outstanding student, it is likely that the other twin would also be outstanding. By the same token, if one twin were only a mediocre student, the other twin would likely be mediocre as well.

Negative correlations also allow researchers to make predictions. Regardless of the direction of the correlation, the greater the strength of the correlation, the greater the accuracy of the prediction. The strength of the correlation is not determined by whether the correlation is positive or negative (+.86 and –.86 are equally strong correla-tions). Strength and, therefore, predictive accuracy are determined by how closely a correlation is to being perfect—whether it is positive or negative.

In psychology, correlations greater than .60 are considered strong, correlations between .20 and .60 are moderate, and correlations less than .20 are weak. As an example of a moderate correlation, a correlation of +.44 was obtained for the life satisfaction and per capita income data shown in Table A.4. Strong and moderate correlations have theoretical value and can be useful in making predictions, while weak correlations indicate tenuous relationships and are therefore only minimally useful in making predictions. Two areas in which psychologists use correlations for making predictions involve academic achievement and job performance. For instance, if a test score correlated +.70 with job performance, a psychologist could make fairly confident predictions about how someone with a particular score would perform on the job. If the correlation were +.15, the psychologist could not predict much better than chance.

Given a strong correlation between two different measures, it is tempting to believe that changes in one measure are responsible for changes in the other, and that this causal relationship is the basis for the strong correlation. But, as we said earlier in Chapter 1, correlation does not imply causality. When two factors are highly correlated, we might suspect that the factors have some causal agent in common, but we cannot conclude this from the correlation. For example, if we found that life satisfaction was strongly and positively correlated with income, what could we conclude? Maybe high income causes high life satisfaction, maybe high life satisfaction causes high income (perhaps happy people work harder and earn more), or maybe high life satisfaction and higher income are the result of a combination of other factors such as a quality education and a rewarding career. Nothing in the correlation itself determines which of these interpretations might be correct. Of course, correlations are sometimes based on causal relationships, and a search for these suspected sources can provide leads to promising avenues of research designed to make causal inferences. This is another way in which correlations are useful to psychologists.

STATISTICAL INFERENCE

To this point we have been concerned with organizing and describing data. What is the typical score in a distribution, how much variability is associated with that score, and how are two sets of data related? Answering such fundamental questions is a necessary first step in data analysis. Psychologists must often do more, however. For example, rather than merely describe two sets of data, psychologists often wish to know if the two sets of data are different. An educational psychologist might want to assess the effectiveness of two different reading programs on children of grammar school age. After dividing a class of children into two comparable groups and exposing each group to a different reading program, the psychologist would measure the reading ability of each child. Did one group perform better than the other, and, more importantly, can the results be applied to other children? The psychologist's goal is to reveal general relationships that are true of a population (here, all grammar school children) based on observations of a sample (the particular children who were studied). This process of making judgments about populations based on observations of samples is called **statistical inference.**

POPULATIONS AND SAMPLES

SAMPLING ERROR

In Chapter 1, we drew a distinction between a **population** and a **sample.** A population, we said, is defined as all of the people about whom an investigator wishes to draw a conclusion, while a sample is a part or subset of the population. Researchers almost never make observations on all of the people in a population. Educational psychologists do not study all students, developmental psychologists do not study all children, and clinical psychologists do not study all people suffering from schizophrenia or depression. All of any category of people is simply too large a group to study. Instead, psychologists study samples of populations and try to generalize their findings to all people in the relevant populations.

Studying samples and generalizing to populations is chancy, however. How do we know that the measures we obtain from a sample accurately reflect the true values of a population? Consider the following example. For the sake of simplicity, assume that our population consists of 100 grammar school children and our data consists of their scores on a reading test. These scores are listed in Table A.5. Assume also that you wish to learn about this population by observing a more limited sample. You randomly select five children to make up your sample. Their scores—49, 85, 60, 36, 65—yield a mean of 59.0 and a standard devia-

| TABLE A.5 | Hypothetical Reading Scores for a Population of 100 Elementary School Children |

64	81	49	70
50	59	75	73
72	70	68	65
66	67	56	55
60	64	60	49
67	58	58	38
55	46	81	49
75	61	75	69
65	65	67	68
70	80	63	70
59	74	70	78
71	65	68	58
60	58	65	60
64	74	59	54
61	85	55	65
73	60	72	88
80	59	62	74
58	62	47	62
58	68	80	64
68	71	58	55
65	91	74	49
70	36	63	81
68	70	69	64
60	81	66	50
82	65	56	73

tion of 18.32. Do these sample measures of central tendency and variability accurately reflect those values of the population? What if you obtained another sample of five children—70, 64, 88, 91, 80—and obtained a mean of 68.8 and a standard deviation of 17.74?

It is a statistical fact that when different children are sampled, the mean and standard deviation are almost always different from the previous sample. Which sample provides the best estimates of the population's measures? We can never be sure because of **sampling error,** the discrepancy between the actual values of a population and the estimates of the population's values obtained from a sample. While in our limited population of 100 students the mean of 65.08 and the standard deviation of 10.12

can be readily calculated from Table A.5, in reality population values are unknown as all people in a population are never tested. Hence, sampling error is always present in varying degrees. By means of advanced statistical techniques, the size of this sampling error can be estimated to determine how accurately the sample values approximate those of the population.

SAMPLE SIZE

One way to obtain better estimates of population values is to obtain a larger sample of scores. Instead of selecting five children from a population of 100, we could randomly select 50. Scores for these children (the first two columns of Table A.5) yield a mean of 66.22 and a standard deviation of 9.91. Notice that these values are closer to the true population values than either of the two samples of five. In general, the larger the randomly selected sample, the more accurate the sample estimates of the population in question. This is why we place greater faith in surveys involving large numbers of people than in more limited studies.

STATISTICAL TESTS

Given the presence of sampling error and the fact that psychologists normally do not know the true values of a population, how do psychologists know if two sets of data come from the same or different populations? In terms of our earlier example on the effectiveness of two reading programs, how would the educational psychologist know if the scores of each group were different? Remember, different samples invariably lead to different measures of central tendency and variability, even when the samples are obtained from the same population. Would a difference in reading scores reflect just sampling error and thereby imply that the two reading programs are not really different? Or is the difference in scores due to different reading programs producing two different populations of readers?

To answer such questions, researchers use mathematical procedures based on probability theory. These procedures, known as **statistical tests,** determine if two samples of scores come from the same population or from two different populations. In general, the greater the difference between the means of each sample and the smaller the standard deviations, the more likely it is that a difference in sample scores reflects a difference in populations. This is how the educational psychologist would determine if one reading program was better than the other. By calculating the mean and

standard deviation for each group of children and applying the appropriate statistical test to the data, the psychologist could decide if the particular scores obtained from each group came from one population or two. By convention, psychologists say that a difference between two means is "statistically significant" if the difference is likely to be obtained by chance alone less than five times in 100 ($p < .05$).

As an example of the use of a statistical test, assume that Table A.6 contains the reading achievement scores of two groups of grammar school children. The only difference between the groups was their reading instruction. One group took part in a new experimental reading program, while the other group received traditional instruction. As shown by the difference in means, it looks like the experimental group did better than the traditional group, but how can we know for sure? Merely repeating this study with different samples of children would likely produce different scores.

To find out if the difference between the means is due to the reading programs or just sampling error we need to use a statistical test. We must calculate a *critical ratio*—the ratio of the observed differences between the two means and an estimate of the variability of this difference (called

TABLE A.6 Hypothetical Reading Scores for Two Groups of Elementary School Children

	Experimental Program	Traditional Program
	64	53
	81	72
	93	61
	75	48
	88	67
	90	50
	84	78
	89	65
	79	81
	92	74
Mean	83.50	64.90
Standard Deviation	9.03	11.70
Standard Error of the Mean	2.86	3.70

the standard error of the difference between the means):

$$\text{Critical ratio} = D_m/\sigma_{D_M}$$

If the critical ratio is 2.0 or larger, we will conclude that the difference between the means is statistically significant. To understand why a ratio of 2.0 is used as the limit, think of 2.0 as two standard deviation units. Looking back to Figure A.6, you can see that the likelihood of getting a score (in this case a difference score) more than two standard deviations from the mean in either direction is only 4.56 percent (100 percent minus 95.44 percent), or about five times out of 100. Thus, if the critical ratio is 2.0 or larger, we would make fewer than five errors in 100 in concluding, on the basis of our samples, that there is a significant difference between the means when none really exists.

From the data in Table A.6, we can calculate the critical ratio. The first step is to find the standard error of the difference between the means. It is provided by the following formula:

$$= \sqrt{(\sigma_{M_1})^2 + (\sigma_{M_2})^2}, \text{ where } \sigma_M = \sigma/\sqrt{N}$$
$$= \sqrt{(2.86)^2 + (3.70)^2}$$
$$= 4.68$$

The critical ratio is

$$D_m/\sigma_{D_M} = \frac{83.5 - 64.9}{4.68} = 3.97$$

Because the ratio is larger than 2.0, we conclude that the difference between the means is significant at the 5 percent level. This indicates that the difference between the two groups was due to the reading programs and not due to sampling error.

In summary, statistical tests allow psychologists to make probabilistic statements about numerical data and thereby make inferences from sample observations about population values.

CONCLUSION

In this brief overview, we have seen that statistics are useful to psychologists in two different, but related, ways. First, statistics are used to organize and describe data. In this sense, statistics offer a way to conveniently and accurately summarize a large body of numbers. Second, statistics are used to make inferences or draw conclusions about data. In this sense, statistics offer a way to generalize from particular instances. Each of these uses of statistics is necessary for the analysis and interpretation of psychological data.

SUMMARY

1. Statistics is the branch of mathematics that deals with the collection and interpretation of numerical data. Psychologists use statistics to organize and describe data and to make inferences about data.

2. Frequency distributions and their related graphic representations—histograms and frequency polygons—organize data according to how frequently each numerical observation occurred. By grouping individual scores, patterns in the data become apparent.

3. The three measures of central tendency are the mean, the median, and the mode. The mean is the arithmetic average of all scores, the median is the middle score, and the mode is the most frequently occurring score in a frequency distribution.

4. Measures of variability provide information on the degree of change of scores in a distribution. The range is the difference between the highest and lowest score, while the standard deviation is the average distance of each score from the mean in a distribution.

5. In most instances, the mean provides the best measure of central tendency and the standard deviation provides the best measure of variability, since each measure is based on each score in a distribution.

6. Frequency distributions come in many different shapes and sizes. When a large data set is graphed, it forms a distribution curve. If the majority of its scores are high or low the curve may be asymmetrical, or skewed. Skewness is either positive or negative depending on the direction of the curve's tail.

7. If a distribution curve is symmetrical and bell-shaped, it is called a normal curve. In this curve, the majority of scores occur around the midpoint of the distribution with progressively fewer scores in the direction of either tail. Because the curve is symmetrical, the mean, median, and mode have the same value.

8. If a set of data is normally distributed and its mean and standard deviation are known, then it is possible to calculate the percentage of scores lying above or below any individual score. Alternatively, for data that are normally distributed with a known mean and standard deviation, it is possible to use the percentages associated with the normal curve to determine the probability of selecting a person at random with a score above or below any particular value.

9. Scattergrams are graphs that show how two sets of data are related. A correlation coefficient is a statistic that measures the mathematical relationship between two sets of data. Correlations, which can range in value from –1.00 to 0 to +1.00, are useful for making predictions when data are related in a positive or negative manner. Correlations do not imply causality.

10. Statistical inference is the process of making judgments about populations based on observations of samples. Different samples, however, vary in their measures of central tendency and variability due to sampling error, the discrepancy between the actual values of a population and those estimated from a sample. Sampling error can be reduced by increasing sample size.

11. Statistical tests are used to determine if different samples come from the same or different populations. The greater the difference between sample means and the smaller the sample standard deviations, the more likely the difference between means is statistically significant. Statistical tests produce probabilistic statements about numerical data and thereby allow inferences to be made from samples about populations.

ADDITIONAL READINGS

Elzey, F. F. 1967. *A first reader in statistics*. Belmont, CA: Brooks/Cole. A tiny but effective book, that provides an introduction to the rationale and fundamental concepts in statistics in a nontechnical and nonmathematical way.

Kimble, G. 1978. *How to use (and mis-use) statistics*. Englewood Cliffs, NJ: Spectrum Books. A book for people with limited knowledge in mathematics about the use and misuse of statistics in a variety of practical areas.

Myers, A. 1987. *Experimental psychology*, 2nd ed. Monterey, CA: Brooks/Cole. An introduction to experimental design and research methods in psychology. It explains key principles clearly within the context of concrete examples.

Walker, J. T. 1985. *Understanding statistics for psychological research*. New York: Holt, Rinehart, and Winston. One of many fine books on quantitative methods in psychology. This text provides a good introduction to the basic principles of statistics as applied to behavioral research.

GLOSSARY

A

Absolute threshold The weakest level of stimulus intensity that is capable of producing a sensation 50 percent of the time.

Accommodation The process of revising a person's cognitive structure to meet environmental demands and make it more congruent with experience. (*See also* Assimilation)

Achievement test An instrument designed to measure a person's present abilities.

Acquisition In classical or instrumental conditioning, the name of the process by which a response is learned.

Action potential The rapid change in electrical charge that flows along a neuron, caused by a change in the permeability of the cell membrane.

Adaptation The process of changing behavior to fit environmental conditions.

Adaptation level theory A theory that shows how prior stimulation can influence present sensory experience. Sensory adaptation provides a frame of reference so that changes in stimulation are more noticeable than unchanging inputs.

Additive color mixture When lights of different wavelengths simultaneously stimulate the eye, their combined or additive effect is a new color determined by the positions of the wavelengths on the color circle. (*See also* Subtractive color mixture)

Adolescence The transitional period between puberty and adulthood, roughly ages 13 to 20.

Adolescent growth spurt Rapid increase in a person's height and weight during the early teenage years.

Adoption studies Research comparing children adopted at birth used to determine the relative impact of genes and the environment on development.

Adrenal glands Two glands located above the kidney that secrete hormones that influence our mood and our ability to cope with stress.

Afterimage The sensory experience that occurs following the withdrawal of a prolonged stimulation. Staring at the color red, for example, will produce an afterimage of green when the red is replaced by a blank white field.

Opponent-process theory provides an explanation of afterimage.

Aggression Behaviors that are intended to do harm.

Alcohol The most commonly used depressant often mistaken for a stimulant because it affects the brain regions that normally inhibit behavior.

Alcohol-aversion therapy A treatment for alcoholism that involves the simultaneous ingestion of alcohol with the administration of Antabuse, a drug that induces vomiting. The alcoholic gradually develops an aversion to alcohol as an association is built up between the sight, smell, and taste of alcohol and the unpleasant sensation of nausea.

Algorithm A step-by-step procedure that produces a solution to a problem because it considers all possible solutions.

All-or-none law The principle that a neuron responds completely (that is, fires its action potential) or not at all. Thus, the impulse in a single neuron is independent of the strength of the stimulation.

Altered state of consciousness A change in mental experience from that of normal waking consciousness. (*See also* Consciousness.)

Altruism Behaviors that are intended to be helpful to others.

Alzheimer's disease A neurological disorder that attacks the brain and causes severe cognitive impairment.

American Sign Language (ASL) A method of communication used by deaf people, which utilizes hand gestures to represent units of speech.

Amnesia A form of memory loss that can be caused by physical trauma or psychological distress. Memory loss for events after a traumatic event is called anterograde amnesia; memory loss for events before a traumatic event is called retrograde amnesia.

Amplitude The magnitude of a sound or light wave; the main determinants of loudness or brilliance.

Amygdala A small limbic structure that plays an important role in regulating emotions and storing memories.

Anal stage The second stage in Freud's theory of personality development,

when a child's erotic feelings according to the theory, center on the anus and elimination.

Analogy A heuristic strategy in which the solution to one problem is used to guide solutions to another.

Androgynous Possessing a balanced combination of characteristics formerly thought to be appropriate for only one gender or the other.

Animal cognition A term that refers to the animal's use of an internal representation as the basis for action.

Anterograde amnesia Following the onset of amnesia, the inability to learn or retain new information. (*See also* Amnesia; Retrograde amnesia)

Antianxiety medications Psychoactive drugs that are prescribed to combat anxiety.

Antipsychotic medications Drugs that reduce psychotic symptoms such as hallucinations and delusions of grandeur.

Antisocial personality A person who goes through life without anxiety or guilt, despite the fact that he or she exploits others to a degree that would shame a normal person.

Anxiety The term used for fearful emotional responses that occur in situations that do not seem to pose threat to life or limb.

Anxiety disorder Disorders in which anxiety is a characteristic feature or the avoidance of anxiety seems to motivate abnormal behavior.

Apparent movement The perception of movement where there is none.

Applied research Research that is directed toward solving specific individual or social problems with psychological knowledge. (*See also* Basic research)

Aptitude tests Tests designed to predict what a person could potentially accomplish.

Archetypes According to Carl Jung, inherited tendencies to perceive and feel in certain ways about certain objects.

Artificial intelligence The use of computer programs to perform tasks normally done by the human mind.

Assimilation According to Piaget, the process by which a person perceives and modifies information from the external world in accordance with his or her cognitive structure. (*See also* Accommodation)

Association areas The areas of the cerebral cortex that integrate sensory information and appear to be involved in learning and thinking.

Associative bias A form of preparedness in which a learner is biologically predisposed to learn relationships between certain stimuli more easily than others.

Associative learning Learning of a relation or contingency between events in the world.

Atmospheric perspective A monocular depth cue based on the fact that the farther away an object is from an observer, the less sharp its retinal image and the less clearly the object is seen.

Attachment The development of specific behaviors whereby infants seek to be close to certain people, usually their parents or primary caregivers.

Attention The focusing of perception on a limited number of stimuli, resulting in heightened awareness.

Attitude system The interconnected feelings, thoughts, intentions, and behaviors that are the components of an attitude.

Attitudes The tendency to respond in a particular way toward certain issues, people, objects, or events.

Attribution theory A theory concerned with rules poeple use to infer the causes of behavior they observe in others.

Auditory canal One of two structures that make up the outer ear. (*See also* Pinna)

Authoritarian personality Individuals who are extremely conventional in their behavior, rigid in their moral views, concerned with the propriety of others' behavior, and preoccupied with power and toughness.

Autism A form of abnormal behavior that primarily affects young children, thought to be caused by some type of neurological disorder. It is characterized by unresponsiveness, repetitive movements, and self-mutilation.

Autobiographical memory A record of the past that is filtered by one's personality and current beliefs.

Autokinetic movement An illusion of movement when a stationary point of light is perceived to move when viewed against a dark homogeneous background.

Automaticity The ability to perform a task with little or no demand on attentional capacity. Reduced attentional demand is achieved after considerable practice.

Autonomic nervous system A division of the peripheral nervous system that connects the brain and spinal cord to vital organs such as the stomach and heart. This system consists of the sympathetic and parasympathetic divisions. (*See also* Parasympathetic division; Peripheral nervous system; Sympathetic division)

Autoshaping In instrumental conditioning, the self-shaping of a conditioned response through the process of classical conditioning. (*See also* Shaping)

Availability heuristic A rule of thumb by which we estimate the frequency or likelihood of an event on the basis of how easily such examples come to mind.

Aversive conditioning A classical conditioning procedure that establishes a connection between an unpleasant stimulus and an undesired response.

Aversive punishment A form of punishment that takes the form of an unpleasant stimulus.

Avoidance conditioning A process through which an appropriate response avoids exposure to an aversive stimulus. (*See also* Escape conditioning)

Axon The single strand or fiber that emerges from the cell body of a neuron that is used to transmit neural impulses to other cells. (*See also* Dendrite; Neuron)

B

Baby biographies Day-to-day accounts of individual development, first used by Darwin to record his son's perceptual and motor development.

Backward conditioning The classical conditioning procedure in which the unconditioned stimulus briefly precedes the presentation of the conditioned stimulus. (*See also* Delayed, Trace, and Simultaneous conditioning)

Balance theory A theory of social relations that postulates a need to have consistency between one's different attitudes.

Basic anxiety According to Karen Horney, the childhood feeling of being isolated and helpless in a potentially hostile world.

Basic research Studies of psychological phenomena aimed at establishing fundamental principles of behavior without regard to the immediate application of the results. (*See also* Applied research)

Basilar membrane Vibrating membrane in the cochlea of the inner ear that contains sense receptors for sound.

Behavior genetics A field that poses questions about the extent to which the differences between people are affected by the genes they inherit from their parents, their environments, and the interaction of genes and environmental factors.

Behavior modification The application of the principles of classical and operant conditioning to changing problem behaviors.

Behavioral medicine A new field in psychology that seeks to integrate knowledge and techniques from psychology and medical science.

Behavioral neuroscience The field of study that examines the biological roots of behavior. This interdisciplinary approach includes the study of genetic factors, hormonal factors, neuroanatomy, drugs, developmental factors, and environmental factors to learn about brain–behavior relations.

Behavioral perspective The idea that psychology should focus only on observable behaviors and their relationship to events that can be objectively measured.

Behavioral sink A pattern of antisocial behaviors in animals associated with high-density living.

Binocular disparity A binocular depth cue based on the fact that an object projects slightly different images to each retina due to the slightly different positions of the two eyes.

Biofeedback The use of instrumental conditioning procedures with electronic equipment to allow people to monitor and change physiological responses formerly thought to be involuntary.

Biomedical model Assumes that abnormal behavior is like other forms of illness, caused by bodily disturbances from outside infections or internal malfunctions.

Bipolar affective disorder A behavioral disorder that combines the extremes of mania and depression.

Blind spot The point where blood vessels and neurons enter and exit the eye.

Blocking The failure to learn about a second stimulus that has been presented in compound with a conditioned stimulus.

Bodily feedback theory The idea that bodily changes come before our conscious experience of an emotion and help us to decide which emotion we are feeling.

Bottom-up processing The view that perception is guided by the passage of information from the sensory receptors to the different areas of the brain. (*See also* Top-down processing)

Brainstem The central core structure of the brain that provides a transition from the end of the spinal cord to the base of the brain. This structure controls the most fundamental aspects of behavior.

Brief sensory store A large capacity memory register that holds unprocessed sensory signals to allow time for pattern recognition processes to translate the information into a more meaningful form.

Brightness constancy Objects seem to stay the same brightness regardless of changes in illumination.

Broca's area A portion of the frontal lobe of the left hemisphere of the brain that is involved in the production of speech. People with brain damage in this area have difficulty enunciating words and speak in a halting, labored manner. (*See also* Wernicke's area)

C

Case Study A narrative description of a person's life or a detailed description of a particular period in a person's life.

CAT scan A series of X-ray measurements made from different orientations around a person's head.

Catatonic schizophrenia A type of schizophrenia in which disturbed motor behaviors (including long periods of complete immobility) are prominent.

Catharsis The purging of aggressive impulses. Freud theorized that aggressive urges build up over time and get worse if they are not purged.

Central fissure The large convolution that runs from the top of the brain down each side and separates the frontal and parietal lobes.

Central nervous system The portion of the nervous system that receives sensory information and guides coordinated movement.

Cerebellum The lobed portion at the rear of the brain that receives sensory information and guides coordinated movement.

Cerebral cortex The outer surface of the brain that is responsible for intelligent behavior.

Cerebral hemispheres Two large halves of the brain, separated by a deep tissue, but connected by a thick bundle of nerve fibers called the corpus callosum. (*See also* Left hemisphere; Right hemisphere)

Chromosomes Rodlike structures that are found in pairs in all body cells. They carry the genes that are trans-

mitted by parents and determine the hereditary makeup of their offspring. A human cell has 46 chromosomes arranged in 23 pairs. (*See also* Genes)

Chunk A unit of information that functions as a single stimulus. The capacity of short-term storage is seven plus or minus two chunks. (*See also* Short-term memory store)

Circadian rhythm The daily pattern of changes in waking and sleeping, body temperature, and blood pressure that are tied to the 24-hour cycle of light and dark.

City size The total population of a city. (*See also* Density)

Classical conditioning An elementary form of associative learning that enables us to make connections between events in the environment. In Pavlovian terms, the repeated pairing of a previously neutral conditioned stimulus with an unconditioned stimulus so that the conditioned stimulus comes to produce a conditioned response. (*See also* Instrumental conditioning)

Client-centered therapy Developed by Carl Rogers, the goal of this technique is to help the client get in touch with his or her inner feelings and to pull together all the parts of the self the person had learned to suppress.

Codes Memory representations of the appearance, sound, and meaning of stimuli.

Cognition The mental operations involved in the acquisition and use of knowledge. These mental operations include perception, memory, language, and thought.

Cognitive bias The tendency to use inappropriate information or an inappropriate strategy in making a decision.

Cognitive consistency The motivation to maintain congruence between what one does and what one believes.

Cognitive dissonance According to Festinger's theory, an unpleasant state of arousal that occurs when our beliefs and our behaviors are in line with one another.

Cognitive heuristics Rules of thumb that have usually worked to solve a problem in the past.

Cognitive learning A form of learning that involves forming internal representations of events in the world.

Cognitive maps A mental representation of a spatial layout that an animal or person stores in memory.

Cognitive model of depression The view that maladaptive ways of thinking contribute to depression.

Cognitive needs According to Maslow, those needs that involve the use of higher intelligence.

Cognitive perspective The study of mental processes such as perceiving, remembering, and thinking.

Cognitive psychology The study of how people acquire and use knowledge.

Cognitive structure A set of behavior patterns or rules that determines how a child comes to understand the world.

Cognitive style A characteristic way in which a person approaches a cognitive task and the manner of thinking that constitutes a part of an individual's personality. (*See also* Field dependence; Field independence)

Cognitive-social learning perspective An extension of the behavioral perspective which adds an emphasis on such cognitive factors as expectancies in human learning.

Collective unconscious According to Jung, a universal set of ideas inherited from our ancestors.

Color agnosia The inability to distinguish different colors or name colors that are associated with particular objects.

Color blindness Partial or total inability to perceive variations in color.

Color constancy The tendency to see objects as having the same color, even under very different conditions of illumination.

Color mixture The color produced when two or more different wavelengths of light combine.

Communal relationship A situation in which partners share rewards and costs rather than emphasize their own individual welfare.

Communication network Billions of individual neurons in the nervous system that link widely separated parts of the body.

Community therapy Treatment outside of hospitals in the patient's natural surroundings.

Complementary color Colors opposite each other on the color circle that when mixed together produce a neutral gray.

Compliance Changes in behavior that are instigated by requests from another person or a group.

Concordance rate The degree of similarity between two individuals on a measure of a psychological variable, usually indicated by a correlation coefficient.

Concrete operation period In Piaget's third period of cognitive development, children between the ages of 7 and 12 become capable of logical thought and achieve understanding of the general principles of conservation. (*See also* Conservation)

Concurrent validity The degree of agreement between different types of measures given at the same time.

Conditioned reinforcers In instrumental conditioning, stimuli that become reinforcing through their association with a primary reinforcer. (*See also* Primary reinforcers)

Conditioned response In classical conditioning, the response that is elicited by a conditioned stimulus by virtue of its prior pairing with an unconditioned stimulus. (*See also* Conditioned stimulus; Unconditioned response; Unconditioned stimulus)

Conditioned stimulus In classical conditioning, a previously neutral stimulus that, after being paired with an unconditioned stimulus, elicits a conditioned response. (*See also* Conditioned response; Unconditioned response; Unconditioned stimulus)

Conditioning The process by which conditioned responses are learned. (*See also* Classical conditioning; Instrumental conditioning)

Conduction deafness Hearing loss caused by problems in the middle ear. Typically, the stapes becomes calcified and less able to transmit vibrations to the inner ear. Hearing aids can often correct the problem by amplifying the vibrations and forcing the stapes to transfer them to the inner ear. (*See also* Nerve deafness)

Cones Light sensitive cells in the retina of the eye that provide a high degree of visual acuity and the ability to distinguish different colors. (*See also* Rods)

Confirmation bias A tendency to seek information that is consistent with our existing beliefs.

Conflict spiral A competitive situation that feeds itself, so that what begins as a fairly mild difference grows more and more intense.

Conformity A person's tendency to pattern his or her behavior after that of a larger social group to which he or she belongs.

Connectionism An approach used to study memory that uses the neural processes of the brain as a model for memory processes.

Consciousness Our awareness of body sensations, perception, emotions thoughts, and recollections at a particular moment in time.

Conservation Piaget's term for the ability to recognize that certain properties of objects, such as their volume or mass, do not change despite changes in an object's appearance. (*See also* Preoperational period)

Construct validity The extent to which a test measures the particular psychological process it is designed to measure.

Contiguity The formation of mental associations between ideas.

Contrast effect A shift in the judgment of one stimulus away from a previously judged extreme along the same dimension. For instance, an average-looking face will be judged more attractive following a series of unattractive faces.

Contrast threshold The just-barely detectable difference in brightness between light and dark stripes in gratings. Gratings show how the visual system is designed to detect spatial and temporal changes in stimulation.

Control group A group that is treated identically to an experimental group, except that it is not exposed to the crucial experimental manipulation.

Convergent thinking A type of thinking that proceeds toward a single solution to a problem.

Conversion disorder A disorder characterized by an apparent physical ailment, but believed to be rooted in psychological distress.

Convolutions The characteristic wrinkles of the brain that result from the vast evolutionary development of the cortex.

Coping Cognitive and behavioral attempts to bring stress under control.

Cornea The transparent covering at the front of the eye that provides protection and support.

Corpus callosum A thick bundle of nerve fibers that connect the left and right cerebral hemispheres.

Correlation coefficient A mathematical index of the direction and extent of a relationship between two sets of data. Correlations can be positive, negative, or zero, and range in value from -1.00 to 0 to +1.00.

Correlational method A means of looking for a relationship between two observed variables by examining the extent to which the variables occur together.

Cortical lobes The major areas of the cortex, including the frontal (front), parietal (top), temporal (sides), and occipital (back) lobes.

Countertransference The inappropriate transfer of a therapist's feelings onto his or her client.

Covert sensitization A form of therapy in which the client is instructed to think of something unpleasant every time he or she feels an undesirable impulse.

Creativity The ability to produce original and appropriate ideas.

Cross-cultural research A research technique that compares subjects from different cultural groups. For example, a comparison of children from the United States and China.

Cross-sectional research A research technique that compares the performance of subjects of different age groups at the same time. For example, a study of three groups of children, aged 6, 8, and 10.

Crowding The psychological experience of spatial restrictions.

Crystalized intelligence The factual knowledge that a person has acquired which increases over the age span. (*See also* Fluid intelligence)

Cue-dependent forgetting A type of forgetting in which information that may be available is inaccessible without the right cue to guide the search for the information.

Cumulative recorder A device for measuring an animal's rate of response in an operant chamber.

D

Dark adaptation An increase in sensitivity when illumination is considerably reduced.

Daydream A shift of attention away from an ongoing physical or mental task toward a response to an internally generated stimulus.

Decay For memory the process of forgetting when information that is not rehearsed fades away with the passage of time.

Deductive reasoning The use of general rules to draw conclusions about particular instances. (*See also* Inductive reasoning)

Defense mechanism Cognitive strategies that people use to cope with anxiety-provoking thoughts and impulses.

Deindividuation Refers to the feeling that one will not be held responsible for his or her behavior.

Deinstitutionalization The release of patients from mental hospitals.

Delayed conditioning The classical conditioning procedure in which the conditioned stimulus comes on briefly before the unconditioned stimulus and remains on until a response is made. (*See also* Backward, Simultaneous, *and* Trace conditioning)

Delirium tremens (DTs) A dangerous withdrawal syndrome that occurs when a person who has been drinking excessively for a long time suddenly stops. Symptoms include tremors, disorientation hallucinations, and acute sense of panic.

Delusions Faulty beliefs that have no basis in reality.

Demographics The statistical study of the size and distribution of human populations.

Dendrite The neuron's major receptive surface (together with the cell body), this tree-like structure receives neural impulses from other neurons. (*See also* Axon; Neuron)

Density The number of people in a given spatial area.

Density-dependent mortality factors Mechanims that act to kill more animals when population is high and less when it is low.

Dependent variable In an experiment, the behavior that is measured. Changes in this variable are attributed to the influence of the independent variable. (*See also* Independent variable)

Depressants A class of drugs that calm the user by slowing the heartbeat and relaxing the muscles or that induce sleep. Common depressants are sedatives, tranquilizers, and narcotics such as heroin, morphine, and opium.

Depression A mood disorder whose symptoms include an unhappy mood and the loss of interest and pleasure in life. This state is commonly associated with insomnia, loss of appetite, fatigue, feelings of guilt, and thoughts of suicide and death.

Deprivation theory According to this theory, any activity can function as a reinforcer if the subject is restricted from performing this activity as often as it would otherwise be performed.

Descriptive methods Research techniques that provide different ways to describe behavior, without any attempt to interfere with the behavior under study. These methods provide useful information about how different events and behaviors are related to each other.

Developmental behavioral genetics The field of study within biology and psychology that seeks to relate changes in behavioral characteristics that occur over the life span to changes in heredity.

Developmental psychology The field of psychology that seeks to describe and explain changes in physical, cognitive, and social development that occur over the life span.

Dichotic listening task A procedure used to study attention whereby a person is simultaneously presented with different messages to each ear.

Difference threshold The smallest change in stimulus intensity that is capable of being detected 50 percent of the time. (*See also* Just-noticeable difference (JND))

Differentiation The process through which infants learn to differentiate people from inanimate objects, familiar people from strangers, and themselves from others.

Diffusion of responsibility Refers to the assumption that duty and accountability can be divided among the members of a group. When there are a number of potential helpers around, each may assume that the others will help.

Dishabituation An increase in responsiveness to new stimulation. (*See also* Habituation)

Disorganized schizophrenia This syndrome is characterized by very bizarre symptoms, including extreme delusions, hallucinations, and completely inappropriate patterns of speech, mood, and movements.

Discrimination Differential responding to stimuli on the basis of prior associations (*See also* Generalization)

Discrimination training In instrumental conditioning, the process of learning that reinforcers are related to some stimuli but not to others.

Discriminative stimulus In instrumental conditioning, the stimulus that signals that reinforcement is available.

Dissociative disorders Behavioral problems involving distinct splits in waking consciousness including psychogenic amnesia and multiple personalities.

Distal stimuli Objects in the physical environment that produce proximal stimulation that can be received by the sense organs. (*See also* Proximal stimuli)

Divergent thinking A type of thinking that involves moving outward from a problem in many different directions.

Dizygotic twins Twins developed from separate eggs. They are no more genetically alike than ordinary brothers and sisters. (*See also* Monozygotic twins)

Dominant gene Member of a gene pair that controls the appearance of a certain trait.

Down's syndrome A form of chromosomal abnormality associated with various physical defects and moderate to severe mental retardation. In the most common form of this disorder, children have an extra or third chromosome in their twenty-first pair. (*See also* Chromosomes)

Dream analysis A technique used by psychoanalysts to help uncover unconscious conflicts.

Dreaming An altered state of consciousness that occurs during sleep, appears to be real and immediate, and transcends rational thoughts.

Drive reduction The assumption that humans are motivated by a desire to turn off the physiological states associated with hunger, thirst, and other drives.

Drives Sources of physiological arousal that originate inside the body.

Drug Any substance other than food that when ingested can stimulate or depress mental and/or physical functioning by acting on the nervous system.

Drug dependence Continued use of a drug with or without addiction. Physical dependence is an addiction; psychological dependence, while not an addiction, results in a strong craving when the drug is not available. (*See also* Drug tolerance)

Drug tolerance With continued use of a drug, larger doses become necessary to produce the desired effect. (*See also* Drug dependence)

Dual coding theory This theory says that pictures are remembered better than words because our probability of recalling either a pictoral or verbal code is higher than our probability of recalling only a verbal code.

E

Eardrum Transmits sound through its auditory passage by vibrating.

Echo A brief auditory memory trace that occurs following the presentation of an auditory stimulus. (*See also* Sensory memory stores)

Ectomorphs According to William Sheldon, one of three body types, characterized as thin and delicate, with the largest brains in proportion to their body size. Ectomorphs were hypothesized to be sensitive, self-conscious, private, and intellectual.

Effector cells A neural structure in our muscles or glands that generates movements or chemical secretions.

Ego According to Freud's theory of personality, the more sensible part of our personality that acts to get things done in an efficient and socially acceptable manner.

Egocentrism According to Piaget, the inability of a person to take the perspective of someone else during early childhood. During adolescence, it is a form of self-preoccupation that reflects a person's search for identity, according to Erikson.

Eidetic imagery The ability to retain visual information in an accurate and highly detailed visual image. Only a minority of people tested suggest evidence of eidetic imagery. (*See also* Mental imagery)

Elaborative rehearsal A form of thinking about information in short-term storage that, through alterations or additions, results in the establishment of strong traces in long-term storage. (*See also* Long-term memory store; Maintenance rehearsal)

Electrical stimulation A procedure for studying the effects of brain stimulation on an animal's behavior. Electrical current is passed directly to a particular brain structure by a thin wire called a micro-electrode inserted into the brain.

Electroconvulsive therapy (ECT) A treatment for severe depression in which an electrical current is passed through the brain, producing convulsions equivalent to an epileptic seizure.

Electroencephalogram (EEG) A brain wave record produced by a machine called an electroencephalograph.

Embryo The developing organism during its early differentiation of physical structures, a period lasting six to eight weeks after conception. (*See also* Fetus; Zygote)

Emotion-focused coping strategies Used in situations seen as unchangeable, these strategies are aimed at regulating distressing emotional responses.

Encoding One of three memory processes in which we transform information into a representation that can be placed in memory. (*See also* Retrieval and Storage)

Encounter groups A technique used extensively by humanistic psychologists, in which group members share feelings and experiences with one another.

Endocrine glands Glands of the endocrine system that release hormones into the bloodstream.

Endocrine system A set of glands such as the pituitary and kidneys that influence behavior and internal states by secreting hormones directly into the bloodstream. The hormones serve to integrate bodily activity. (*See also* Hormones)

Endomorphs According to William Sheldon, one of three body types, characterized by a heavy-set build, and a tendency to love physical comfort, socializing, and eating.

Environmental psychology The study of person–environment interactions, including the effects of crowding, noise, and air pollution.

Epilepsy A neurological disorder of the brain produced by the uncontrolled firing of neurons. Two of the most common types of epilepsy are *petit mal* and *grand mal* epilepsy.

Epinephrine Hormone secreted by the adrenal gland during stressful situations. It constricts the blood vessels in the stomach and intestines and increases the heart rate.

Episodic memory A form of memory that represents knowledge of personally experienced events and their order of occurrence. (*See also* Procedural memory; Semantic memory)

Equipotentiality theory According to this view, there are few, if any, specialized regions of the brain. Instead, different areas of the brain are seen as equivalent to one another.

Equity The perception that the benefits of a relationship, minus the costs of being in the relationship, are balanced with one's partner's costs and benefits.

Escape conditioning A process through which an appropriate response terminates an aversive stimulus. (*See also* Avoidance conditioning)

Ethnocentric A term used to describe people who see their own ethnic group as superior to others.

Ethological approach The study of animal behavior in its natural habitat with a focus on how innate behaviors are used to adapt to the environment.

Evolutionary perspective An approach to behavior that emphasizes the differences and similarities in behavior across different animal species, with a focus on the adaptive significance of inherited behavioral tendencies.

Excitatory influences Stimulation of the neuron that increases the likelihood of firing.

Expectancy The anticipation of a future stimulus based on past experience and current stimuli.

Experiment A research method involving the systematic manipulation of one or more independent variables in order to observe an effect on one or more dependent variables. (*See also* Dependent variables; Independent variables)

Experimental group A group for whom the experimenter alters some feature of the environment.

Experimental method (*See* Experiment)

Experimental psychology The study of psychological phenomena by means of the experimental method. (*See also* Experiment)

Expertise The ability to use a broad and highly organized body of knowledge systematically.

Expressive aphasia An inability to use speech normally. People suffering from expressive aphasia can understand speech, but have difficulty pronouncing words correctly.

Extinction In classical conditioning, the elimination of a conditioned response due to the withholding of the unconditioned stimulus. In instrumental conditioning, the elimination of a response due to the removal of the reinforcement.

Extrasensory perception (ESP) The belief that sensory information can be acquired in ways that are not dependent on any known form of sensory stimulation. Telepathy and clairvoyance are two types of extrasensory perception.

Extraversion A major factor emerging in trait research; composed of characteristics such as talkative, sociable, and adventurous.

Extrinsic motives Instigations of behavior that stem from outside forces, such as the desire for reward, rather than internal forces such as curiosity.

F

Factitious disorder A physical complaint that is purposefully fabricated or greatly exaggerated by a patient.

Factor analysis A sophisticated method of data analysis used in test construction and in the interpretation of test scores. The method computes the least number of factors needed to account for the correlations of test scores in a battery of tests.

Family systems therapy Based on the belief that behavioral problems stem from dysfunctional family interactions, family therapists treat the disturbed individual and his or her family environment.

Farsighted An improper functioning of the lens. A farsighted person can only focus clearly on objects that are far away.

Feature anaysis In pattern recognition, analysis consists of features extraction, specifying the features that make up a stimulus, and features interpretation, matching those features to feature sets that define particular stimuli.

Feature detection The translation of different patterns of retinal stimulation into particular types of brain stimulation that enables us to see different features.

Feature extraction An aspect of pattern recognition that involves specifying the particular details that make up a stimulus.

Feature interpretation An aspect of pattern recognition that consists of matching those details to feature sets that define different possible stimuli.

Fechner's law A psychophysical relationship in which ever-greater increases in stimulus intensity are needed to produce a constant increase in sensory experience.

Fetal alcohol syndrome A developmental malformation that affects infants born to alcoholic mothers.

Fetus The name of the developing organism in the womb from about two months after conception until birth. (*See also* Embryo; Zygote)

Field dependence A type of cognitive style that has difficulty ignoring extraneous cues from a surrounding perceptual field.

Field independence A type of cognitive style that involves maintaining spatial orientation and ignoring irrelevant perceptual cues.

Figure-ground The perception of a form or pattern as the foreground (figure) against a background (ground). The figure is perceived as closer than the surround.

Fixed action patterns Behavioral configurations that appear in the same form in all members of a species, such as tail-wagging in a dog.

Fixed interval schedule In instrumental conditioning, reinforcement follows the first response made after a specified period of time. (*See also* Fixed ratio, Variable interval, *and* Variable ratio schedules)

Fixed ratio schedule In instrumental conditioning, an animal is reinforced after it emits a fixed number of responses. (*See also* Fixed interval, Variable interval, *and* Variable ratio schedules)

Fluid intelligence The ability, which declines with age, to deal with new problems. (*See also* Crystalized intelligence)

Forgetting curve According to Ebbinghaus, the relation between savings—number of trials needed to relearn information—and the time between learning and relearning.

Formal operations thinking The level of cognitive development in which a person can form hypotheses, reason abstractly, and think in a systematic way. Although not found in all people and not used all the time, formal operations thinking occurs during adolescence and adulthood. It is the highest level of cognitive development, according to Piaget.

Fovea A small indentation in the retina that is the center of the visual field.

Fraternal twins (*See* Dizygotic twins)

Free association A method developed for psychoanalysis in which a person says whatever comes to mind.

Free recall task A procedure in which a subject studies a list of words and then recalls the words in any order possible.

Frequency The number of expansion and compression cycles per second in a sound wave; the primary determinant of pitch.

Frequency distribution A list of the number of scores that occur in each equal size interval over the entire range of scores.

Frequency theory Theory that pitch is determined by the rate of the brain cell's response.

Frontal lobes The largest of the association areas that make an important contribution to intelligent behavior.

Frustration-aggression hypothesis A view that aggression occurs when an obstacle prevents a person from reaching a goal.

Fugue state A condition in which a person runs away from a traumatic situation and suffers a memory loss for all personally identifying information.

Functional fixedness The inability to see a new or unique use for a common object.

G

Galvanic skin respone (GSR) Changes in the electrical conductivity of the skin, detected by a galvanometer. The GSR is commonly used as a physiological indicator of emotionality.

Gate control theory A theory of pain that holds that the brain or spinal cord can cut off receptivity to pain if there is stimulation in other areas of the body.

Gender conservation A child's realization, between ages five and seven, that he or she will always be male or female.

Gender roles Behavior that is considered culturally appropriate for a person because of the person's sex. Also called sex roles, these differences in characteristic ways of acting masculine and feminine are the result of differences in biology and socialization. (*See also* Sex roles; Socialization)

Genes The fundamental units of heredity, located in the chromosomes. Typically occurring in pairs, genes have one member of the pair provided by the father and the other member provided by the mother. Each chromosome contains numerous genes. (*See also* Chromosome)

General adaptation syndrome According to Hans Selye, physiological response to any stressor follows a three-stage pattern: alarm, resistance, and exhaustion.

General intelligence (g) That aspect of intelligence, according to Spearman, that is constant across a variety of intelligence tests. (*See also* Intelligence)

General paresis A form of mental illness caused by syphilis. Symptoms include irritability, depression, and impaired judgment.

Generalization When a conditioned response has been acquired, stimuli that are similar to the conditioned stimulus will also evoke that response.

Genital stage The final stage in Freud's theory of psychosexual development, during which sexual feelings presumably re-emerge in the adolescent.

Genotype The genetic characteristics that a person has inherited and will transmit to descendants, whether or not the person manifests these different characteristics. (*See also* Genetics; Phenotype)

Gerontology The study of aging and the problems of the aged.

Gestalt psychology A psychological theory of perception that is concerned with the organization of stimulus elements into perceptual forms.

Gifted retardates Term used to describe the very small minority of intellectually handicapped people who display skills that would be extraordinary even for people of normal intelligence.

Glial cells Nerve cells that support and protect the neurons.

Gonadotropins Hormones that produce a series of changes in other endocrine glands. They stimulate the production of sex hormones, which eventually make a person capable of sexual reproduction.

Gonads The reproductive glands, testes in the male and ovaries in the female.

Graceful degradation The process by which the brain loses large numbers of neurons and their interconnections in the normal course of ageing, leaving the memory functional.

GRIT strategy A strategy suggested for resolving international conflict that calls for one side of the conflict to begin with some small step toward increased cooperation, followed by gradually increasing and reciprocal reductions of tensions.

GSR (*See* Galvanic skin response)

H

Habituation   A decrease in responsiveness to unchanging stimulation. (*See also* Dishabituation)

Halfway houses   Treatment facilities that allow former addicts or mental patients to live partly in the community and partly in a treatment environment.

Hallucinations   Sensory experiences that have no basis in the external world.

Hallucinogenics   A class of drugs that modify personal consciousness by affecting a person's sensation, perception, thinking, self-awareness, and emotion.

Haptic perception   The perception of objects by touch.

Hardiness   A set of personal characteristics that relate to stress resistance.

Health psychology   That field of psychology concerned with the role of psychological factors in preventing illness and maintaining good health.

Heritability   A statistical estimate of the relative influence of genes on a trait, given a particular range of environmental stimulation.

Heuristics   Mental short-cuts or rules of thumb that suggest possible solutions to a problem.

Higher-order conditioning   A variation of classical conditioning in which a new stimulus precedes a conditioned stimulus to elicit a conditioned response. (*See also* Classical conditioning)

Hippocampus   A part of the limbic system that has an important role in normal memory functioning.

Histrogram   A bar graph representation of a frequency distribution.

Homeostasis   An ideal balanced state in the body's internal environment.

Hormones   The chemical secretions of the endocrine glands that are distributed by the bloodstream throughout the body. (*See also* Endocrine system)

Hue   The perception of color that is determined by the light's wavelength.

Humanistic approach   A view of behavior that stresses individuals' own interpretation of events in their lives and their free will to change themselves and their relationship to their environment.

Hypermnesia   Improved recall of previously forgotten events with the passage of time.

Hypersomnia   A sleeping disorder characterized by excessive sleepiness and many periods of microsleep at inappropriate times during the day (*See also* Insomnia)

Hyperstimulation   The relief of pain in one area of the body by irritation of another area.

Hypnosis   A state of consciousness characterized by increased suggestibility and imagination, along with reduced initiative and reality-testing. Some psychologists consider hypnosis an altered state, while others believe it to be a form of role-enactment.

Hypnotic age regression   The idea that hypnotized subjects are able to relive earlier episodes of their lives.

Hypochondriasis   A disorder characterized by exaggerated concerns about physical illness.

Hypothesis   A tentative and testable assumption, an "educated guess."

Hypothalamus   Located under the thalamus, this small structure is involved in many different aspects of behavior, including eating, sleeping, sexual behavior, and maintaining the proper balance of essential bodily conditions.

Hypothetico-deductive reasoning   A manner of thinking or problem-solving in which hypotheses are formed and tested by logical systematic procedures. This form of thinking is first manifested during adolescence.

I

Icon   A brief visual memory trace that occurs following the presentation of a visual stimulus. (*See also* Sensory memory stores)

Id   According to Freud's theory of personality, the basic structural foundation for personality, composed of a common set of drives for self-preservation and reproduction. (*See also* Pleasure principle)

Identical twins   (*See* Monozygotic twins)

Identification   The process by which children copy, partly unconsciously, the social roles of important adults in their lives. (*See also* Gender roles)

Identity   A unified, consistent personality embodying diverse values and beliefs. A sense of identity emerges during adolescence as a person changes from a child to an adult.

Identity foreclosure   Selection of identity too early in adolescence before other alternatives have been considered. (*See also* Psychosocial moratorium)

Illusion   A perceptual experience that does not corresond to reality. Visual illusions are studied in perception to learn about accurate perception.

Illusory correlation   The mistaken perception that two features go together,

sometimes found when members of small groups have a few deviant members, and observers attribute those characteristics to all members.

Imaginative thinking   The ability to see things in new ways, to recognize relations, and to make new connections.

Immune system   The body's wall of defense against illness, including cells in the skin and bloodstream that detect and destroy potentially harmful bacteria and viruses.

Implicit theory   A set of beliefs that we use to form opinions about the intelligence of the people we know.

Impossible figure   Representation of three-dimentional figures that could not possibly exist in the world.

Incentives   External stimuli, such as the smell of a pie baking, that excite drives.

Incubation effect   The process through which the passage of time and a refocusing of attention reduce an inappropriate mental set and allow us to consider new strategies to solve a problem.

Incus   One of three small bones, which, together with the malleus and the stapes, make up the middle ear and through which vibration from the eardrum is transmitted.

Independent variable   In an experiment, the factor that is manipulated to observe its effect on behavior. (*See also* Dependent variable)

Induced movement   An illusion in which a small, stationary object appears to move when viewed against a larger, moving background.

Inductive reasoning   The discovery of general rules from specific experiences. (*See also* Deductive reasoning)

Infancy   A period that extends through the second year of life.

Information processing   A conceptual approach to memory that is concerned with the mental operations that intervene between a stimulus and a response.

Informational social influence   Conforming to popular opinions about reality.

Inhibitory influences   Stimulations of the neuron that slow it down.

Insight   In psychoanalysis, a cognitive and emotional understanding of the roots of a conflict.

Insight therapies   Based on the assumption that many pathological behaviors would disappear if clients confronted unacceptable parts of themselves, these treatments usually involve a conversation between therapist and client, with the ultimate goal being personal understanding by the client.

Insomnia A sleep disorder characterized by an inability to get sufficient sleep. (*See also* Hypersomnia)

Instinct An inherited tendency to act in a certain way in response to a particular set of environmental and internal cues.

Integrative network A function of the nervous system to organize information it receives from both inside and outside of the body.

Intelligence The ability to learn from experience, to think effectively, and adapt to changing environmental conditions. (*See also* Intelligence quotient)

Intelligence quotient (IQ) A scale unit that is used for reporting intelligence test scores, determined by dividing a person's mental age by chronological age and multiplying by 100. (*See also* Mental age)

Interactionist perspective A modern view of psychology that links the various theoretical perspectives to understand the whole human being. According to this view, ongoing cognitive and behavioral responses to environmental inputs are constrained by past learning, which is in turn constrained by individual differences and evolved genetic constraints.

Interference The process of forgetting when information is dislodged from memory by the arrival of new information.

Intermittent reinforcement schedule A schedule of reinforcement in which only some of the responses are reinforced or reinforcement is available for only specified periods of time. (*See also* Schedules of reinforcement)

Internal representation The form in which information is held in memory.

Interneurons Nerve cells that transmit stimulation back and forth between different parts of the brain and the spinal cord. (*See also* Motor neurons; Sensory neurons)

Interposition (*See* Overlap)

Interpretation A psychoanalytic technique in which the analyst attempts to piece together the unconscious logic underlying a patient's conflicts.

Instrumental conditioning A form of learning, first studied by Thorndike, that allows us to learn the consequences of our behavior. In instrumental conditioning, reinforcement is contingent upon a particular response being made. (*See also* Classical conditioning; Reinforcement)

Intrinsic motivation The inclination to perform some behavior for the pure joy of it rather than for some external reward.

Introspection A process of analyzing a conscious experience by reporting the sensory qualities of the stimuli that are experienced, without the intrusion of meanings or interpretations.

Ions Electrically charged molecules located in the cell's protoplasm and in the liquid surrounding the cell.

Iris A richly pigmented, muscular structure that determines the size of the pupil and gives the eyes their color.

Irreversibility The inability to rearrange objects mentally.

J

Just-noticeable difference (JND) The smallest change in stimulus intensity that is capable of being detected 50 percent of the time. Each JND produces a new sensory experience (*See also* Difference threshold)

K

Kinesthesis A proprioceptive sense in which sensory reception in the muscles, tendons, and joints provides information about body position and limb movements.

Korsakoff's syndrome A disorder that is characterized by profound memory impairment due to extensive brain damage associated with chronic alcohol consumption.

L

Language A system of gestures, sounds, or written symbols that is used for communication.

Latency stage The fourth hypothesized stage of Freud's theory of personality development, during which a child's sexual urges are presumably suppressed until puberty.

Latent content According to Freud, the hidden content of dreams, which contains the underlying motives that would disturb a sleeping person if they were consciously expressed. (*See also* Manifest content)

Latent learning Learning that is not immediately shown in performance. Latent learning is demonstrated when motivation to perform is enhanced by the availability of reinforcement.

Lateralization A difference or asymmetry of function for each of the cerebral hemispheres. (*See also* Left hemisphere; Right hemisphere)

Law of effect A principle of learning, stated by Thorndike, that responses followed by satisfaction (reinforce-

ment) will tend to increase in strength or frequency. (*See also* Instrumental conditioning; Reinforcement)

Laws of organization According to Gestalt psychologists, patterns of perceptual grouping—proximity, similarity, good continuation, closure, and common fate—that capture various elements and determine how we see them.

Learned helplessness The tendency to give up without trying to overcome a stressor, presumably acquired as a result of failed attempts to control stressors in the past; believed to be a component of depression.

Learning A relatively permanent change in behavior or behavior potentiality that results from experience.

Left hemisphere The left cerebral hemisphere is specialized for language, analyzing information, and sequential tasks. It controls the right side of the body. (*See also* Right hemisphere)

Lens A transparent structure in the eye that focuses light. (*See also* Retina)

Lesion procedure A brain operation to determine how damage to a particular area or structure affects an animal's behavior.

Level of processing The progression of stimulus analysis from analysis of physical features to the analysis of meaning.

Life transition Events or nonevents that alter our roles, relationships, and beliefs.

Lifespan psychology The study of the description, explanation, and optimalization of developmental processes that occur during human life between conception and death. Much life-span research focuses on developmental changes during adulthood and ageing.

Light adaptation A reduction in sensitivity when illumination changes from dim to very bright.

Limbic system A set of interrelated structures between the brain-stem and the cerebral cortex of the brain that coordinates information transmission, regulates emotional responses, and monitors motivated behaviors essential for survival.

Linear perspective A monocular depth cue based on the fact that as objects become more distant they appear to recede and converge on a distant point.

Linguistic relativity hypothesis Holds that the language of any culture determines how the people in that culture perceive and understand their world.

Linguistics The study of natural languages and their grammatical rules.

Localization theory   The view that specific psychological functions are associated with specific areas or locations of the brain.

Locus of control   A scale that measures individual differences in beliefs about whether we can control the rewards and punishments we receive.

Long-term memory store   The relatively permanent component of the memory system that is the repository of all the things we know. (*See also* Sensory memory stores; Short-term memory store)

Long-term potentiation (LTP)   The increase in synaptic response strength when a neural pathway is stimulated. LTP also occurs when two converging neural pathways are stimulated at the same time. LTP is believed to be an important memory mechanism.

Longitudinal research   A research technique that examines the performance of the same subjects at different periods of development; for example, a comparison of the performance of the same people at ages 12, 20, and 40.

M

Maintenance rehearsal   A form of mental repetition that serves mainly to hold information in short-term storage. (*See also* Elaborative rehearsal; Short-term memory store)

Malleus   One of three small bones, which, together with the incus and the stapes, make up the middle ear and through which vibration from the eardrum is transmitted.

Mania   A mood disorder characterized by extreme upswings of mood. Individuals in a manic state often lose control of themselves in their excitement and begin to act in inappropriate and self-destructive ways.

Manifest content   According to Freud, the obvious content of dreams, which comes from a person's memory, daily events, and bodily sensations during the night. (*See also* Latent content)

Mass psychogenic illness   A phenomenon in which a group of people suddenly come down with symptoms that seem to have no organic basis.

Maturation   Growth processes that result in orderly changes in behavior. The timing and pattern of these processes are independent of experience given a normal environment.

Mean   The numerical average of a frequency distribution of scores obtained by adding the scores together and dividing the sum by the total number of scores.

Means-end analysis   A type of heuristic in which a problem is divided into a number of subproblems or components to reduce the difference between the original state and the goal state.

Median   The middle score in a frequency distribution. The median is used when the distribution is skewed. (*See also* Skewness)

Meditation   A set of primarily mental exercises designed to produce concentration, awareness, and a sense of tranquility and equilibrium.

Medulla   The lowest part of the brain, the medulla regulates vital body functions such as heart rate, blood pressure, respiration, and digestion. (*See also* Pons)

Meiosis   The process through which mature sex cells of each parent split to form separate cells.

Memorists   People who demonstrate superior memory.

Memory span   The maximum number of stimuli that can be recalled in perfect order 50 percent of the time. The memory span has an upper limit of seven plus or minus two chunks. (*See also* Chunk)

Memory structures   The parts of the memory system that are permanent. These include the sensory memory store, the short-term memory store, and the long-term memory store.

Memory trace   A physical change in the nervous system that is produced by all of our experiences.

Menarche   The first menstrual period, a sign of sexual maturity in a girl.

Mental age   In a test such as the Stanford-Binet, the age level associated with the last task (or series of tasks) a child could complete successfully.

Mental imagery   The process of constructing mental pictures that bear a resemblance to physical reality. Mental imagery is used as an aid to memory. Note that mental imagery is different from eidetic imagery. (*See also* Eidetic imagery; Mnemonics)

Mental operations   According to Piaget, a process children use to transform and manipulate what they see or hear according to logical rules.

Mental rehearsal   A process for maintaining information placed in the short-term store by repeating the information over and over.

Mental retardation   Subnormal mental functioning (IQ below 70) and impairment in adaptive behavior.

Mental set   In pattern recognition, the context for how a stimulus should be received.

Mentally gifted   People who score above 130 on an intelligence test.

Mesmerism   The precursor of hypnosis developed by Fredrich Mesmer.

Mesomorphs   According to William Sheldon, one of three body types, characterized as predominantly bone and muscle. Mesomorphs are hypothesized to love adventure, risk, and competition.

Meta-analysis   Statistical technique used to organize findings in areas where there are many, often-contradictory, studies.

Meta-components of intelligence   High-order processes that we use to analyze a problem and to pick a strategy for solving it.

Metamemory   Awareness of one's own memory and mental ability.

Method of constant stimuli   A procedure used for calculating the absolute threshold of a sensory stimulus. Stimuli of different intensities are presented in a random order until the absolute threshold is established. (*See also* Method of limits)

Method of limits   A procedure used for calculating the absolute threshold of a sensory stimulus. The energy level is changed in an ascending to descending manner until the stimulus passes its absolute threshold. (*See also* Method of constant stimuli)

Method of magnitude estimation   A direct measure of sensitivity in which observers provide a psychophysical scale by making judgments of sensory stimuli of different magnitudes in comparison to a standard.

Method of successive approximation   The procedure of shaping a desired behavior by carefully reinforcing and strengthening each small step toward a target response.

Mid-life crisis   A term, originated by Jung, that describes developmental changes at mid-life.

Mnemonics   Techniques or strategies used to enhance memory. Mnemonics work because they organize information, ensure a deep level of processing, and provide a plan for remembering.

Mode   The most frequently occurring score in a frequency distribution.

Modeling   A process of learning in subjects who simply observe another person but do not themselves perform any overt behavior nor receive any direct reinforcement.

Monozygotic twins   Twins developed from the same egg. They are always of the same sex and often similar in appearance. (*See also* Dizygotic twins)

Moral reasoning   The process by which children come to adopt their society's standards of right and wrong.

Morphemes The smallest language unit that possesses meaning.

Motherese Simplified speech characterized by a special tone of voice, slow rate of talking, high pitch, and exaggerated intonations, used by adults in talking to an infant.

Motor cortex A thin strip of cortex, located directly in front of the central tissue in the frontal lobe, that governs motor movements. (*See also* Somatosensory cortex)

Motor neurons Nerve cells that transmit stimulation from the brain and spinal cord to the effector cells in the muscles and glands. (*See also* Interneurons; Sensory neurons)

Movement aftereffect An illusion of movement that follows prolonged perception of movement in a particular direction. When a stationary field is viewed, movement in the direction opposite the initial perception is observed.

Movement parallax In perception, a depth cue in which nearby objects move across the field of vision faster than more distant objects.

Multiple personality A form of dissociative disorder in which a person shifts back and forth between two or more distinct identities.

Myelin sheath A fatty, insulating material that surrounds certain axons. Axons with myelin insulation transmit impulses faster than those without such insulation. (*See also* Axon)

N

Narcolepsy A disorder in which one is chronically sleepy and suffers irresistible attacks of sleepiness at inappropriate times of the day.

Naturalistic observation A method of research that involves observing and recording the behavior of people or animals in their natural environments.

Nearsightedness An improper functioning of the lens which only focuses clearly on objects that are near.

Need for achievement The need to compete with some standard of excellence.

Negative contrast effect In instrumental conditioning, a decrease in the effectiveness of a reinforcer that occurs when the reinforcer is presented later than expected.

Negative identity According to Erikson, a form of acting out through delinquency, drug abuse, or suicide that results from a failure to achieve a positive sense of identity during adolescence.

Negative imprinting An aversion to forming a sexual attraction based on experience, occurs when social animals avoid other animals with whom they were raised.

Negative reinforcement In instrumental conditioning, stimuli whose termination or removal increase the likelihood of a response. (*See also* Punishment)

Neonatal period The first month after birth.

Nerve A group of elongated axons composed of hundreds or even thousands of neurons. (*See also* Axon; Neuron)

Nerve cell (*See* Neuron)

Nerve deafness Hearing loss caused by problems with the inner ear. (*See also* Conduction deafness)

Neural impulse The wave of electrical activity that travels down the axon of a neuron when the cell's firing threshold is reached. Synonymous with action potential.

Neural noise Spontaneous neural activity that can make near-threshold sensory stimuli more difficult to detect. In signal detection theory, observers must distinguish sensory signals from background neural noise.

Neurologists Physicians who treat patients with diseased or damaged nervous systems.

Neuron The nerve cell; the functional unit of the nervous system. Neurons receive and transmit signals to all parts of the body. (*See also* Neurotransmitter; Synapse)

Neuropsychology The field of psychology that seeks to understand the role of the nervous system in behavior.

Neuropsychological perspective A general approach to psychology, involving the examination of how behavior and mental processes relate to changes in the brain and nervous system.

Neurotransmitter A chemical substance used in the transmission of neural impulses across a synaptic junction from one neuron to another. (*See also* Neuron; Synapse)

NMDA receptor A molecule that is believed to turn on certain biochemical reactions that lead to the encoding of memories.

NMR scan Provides an image of the brain's interior structure.

Nonspecificity hypothesis The assumption that any type of stress will lead to a general pattern of physical deterioration.

Norepinephrine Hormone secreted by the adrenal gland that causes blood pressure to rise. It can also function as a neurotransmitter when released by a presynaptic neuron.

Norm The average or typical performance of individuals under specific conditions. Norms can provide standards of average growth and performance on intellectual tasks. In another sense, norms can be standards of conduct by which people are expected to act.

Normal curve The standard symmetrical bell-shaped frequency distribution.

Normal Distribution A symmetrical, bell-shaped frequency distribution that describes scores on many different physical and psychological variables. In a normal distribution, the mean, median, and mode are identical. (*See also* Normal curve)

Normative social influence Compliance with arbitrary social rules and conventions.

O

Obedience A change of behavior in response to a command from another person, typically an authority figure.

Object permanence Piaget's term for the realization that objects continue to exist even if they are hidden from view. This reality is the principle achievement of the sensorimotor period of cognitive development. (*See also* Sensorimotor period)

Observational learning Learning that occurs from watching the behavior of others and observing the consequences of their actions.

Obsessive-compulsive disorder A disorder that involves repetitious behaviors and thoughts a person cannot get out of his or her mind.

Occipital lobe Part of the cerebral cortex that is involved in integrating visual information.

Olfaction The sense of smell, dependent on odor molecules stimulating the receptors at the top of the nose. Stimulation may result from chemical or physical stimuli.

Operant conditioning The form of behavioral conditioning studied by B. F. Skinner. (*See also* Instrumental conditioning; Reinforcement)

Opponent process model of motivation The idea that every physiological state of arousal automatically leads to an opposing state, used to explain phenomena such as drug tolerance.

Opponent-process theory of vision Theory of color vision that proposes that three sets of color receptors respond in an either/or fashion to determine the color you experience.

Optical rearrangement The alteration of the normal relationship between distal stimuli and their retinal images by the use of special lenses worn over the eye.

Oral stage According to Freud's theory of personality development, the first year of life, when breast feeding and weaning usually occur.

Oral-aggressive personality According to Freud, a syndrome of adult personality that may develop when a mother is too harsh when weaning a child from the breast. It is supposedly characterized by pessimism, suspiciousness, sarcasm, and argumentativeness.

Oral-receptive personality According to Freud, a syndrome of adult personality that may develop if a mother is too indulgent. It is supposedly characterized by dependency, gullibility, and a fondness for sweets and smoking, as well as an obsession with oral sex.

Organ of Corti Transmits neural impulse to nerve fibers in the auditory nerve.

Organic disorders Psychological disorders caused by physical illness. (*See also* General paresis; Senile dementia)

Organization In perception, the strong tendency to group stimulus elements on the basis of their similarity, proximity, continuation, and simplicity.

Outcome research A method of comparing improvements in therapy clients with changes in other distressed people who have not been treated, or who have received alternative therapies.

Overlap A monocular depth cue in which objects that are partially obscured by other objects are perceived as farther away.

P

Paradoxical intervention A technique used by family therapists in which the problem behavior is actually encouraged.

Paranoid schizophrenia A behavioral disorder characterized by a belief that others are plotting against one and commonly by accompanying attributions about one's own religious or political importance.

Paraprofessional Someone without an advanced degree who can provide treatment. An important component of the community approach to treatment.

Parasympathetic division A division of the autonomic nervous system that is active during relaxed or quiescent states. (*See also* Sympathetic division)

Parathyroid glands Four tiny glands embedded in the thyroid that maintain the level of calcium in the blood.

Parietal lobes Part of the cerebral cortex that is particularly important for directing attention to changes in the environment and developing expectations of what is likely to happen next.

Partial reinforcement (*See* Intermittent reinforcement)

Pattern recognition In perception, the meaningful interpretation of form. Pattern recognition entails feature extraction and feature interpretation. (*See also* Feature analysis)

Pegword mnemonic A type of mnemonic that relies on the use of visual imagery to form strong associations to organize information in memory.

Perception The processes of organizing and interpreting sensory information. (*See also* Distal stimulus; Proximal stimulus)

Perceptual dilemma A situation that contributes to intergroup conflict, characterized by mistaken negative beliefs about what the other side wants, and exaggerated views of the innocence of motivation on one's own side.

Perceptual invariant An unchanging aspect of a stimulus that can be used as a cue for accurate perception. Texture gradients, for example, provide invariant information on depth. (*See also* Texture gradient)

Peripheral nervous system The portion of the nervous system, outside of the brain and spinal cord, that includes the autonomic and somatic nervous systems. (*See also* Automatic nervous system; Somatic nervous system)

Personal constructs According to George Kelly, individuals' personal theories about themselves and their world.

Personality traits Recurring patterns of behavior such as friendliness, social dominance, conventionality, emotional adjustment, and aesthetic inclination.

PET Scan Measures the amount of glucose—a form of sugar that is the brain's primary source of energy—being consumed in numerous brain locations.

Phallic stage In Freud's theory of personality development, the stage occurring during the third to fifth years when a child often becomes obsessed with genitalia.

Phantom limb pain Pain in a part of the body that no longer exists. Phantom limb pain is fairly common in amputees.

Phenomenological perspective A view of behavior that focuses on a person's subjective, conscious experience.

Phenotype The genetic characteristics that are displayed by a person such as eye color or height. *See also* Genetics; Genotype)

Pheromones Chemicals released by different organisms to elicit specific reactions by other members of the same species. Lower organisms use pheromones as a primitive method of communication.

Phobia A persistent fear reaction that is greatly out of proportion to the reality of danger.

Phonemes A limited number of distinct speech sounds which are used to distinguish one word from another.

Phrenology The nineteenth-century belief that character analysis could be determined by examining the bumps on a person's head.

Pinna One of two structures that make up the outer ear. (*See also* Auditory canal)

Pituitary gland Located at the base of the brain, the pituitary gland produces many different hormones that exert control over the other endocrine glands.

Place theory States that sound waves of different frequencies cause different portions of the basilar membrane to vibrate.

Placebo effect An improvement in symptoms that follows any form of treatment that a person believes in, even if the treatment has no therapeutic substance, such as an inert sugar pill.

Pleasure principle According to Freud, the way in which the id seeks immediate gratification for an impulse.

Pons The large bulge in the brainstem involved in alertness, attention, and movement. (*See also* Medulla)

Population All the members of a group from which a sample may be drawn. In survey research, a randomly drawn sample permits an investigator to draw conclusions about a population. (*See also* Sample)

Postsynaptic neuron The cell that receives stimulation from the electrical impulses that travel through the presynaptic neuron. (*See also* Neurotransmitter; Presynaptic neuron)

Practical intelligence Intelligence that operates in the real world and is shown by a person's ability to adapt to or change an environment. (*See also* Intelligence)

Predictive validity The extent to which a test score predicts future behaviors, as when an IQ test predicts later academic success.

Prefrontal lobotomy The surgical removal of an excitable or aggressive patient's frontal lobes from the rest of the brain.

Prejudice An unwarranted generalization about a group or a particular member of that group.

Premack principle A view that any behavior with a high frequency of occurrence could be used to reinforce any other behavior that has a lower frequency of occurrence.

Preoperational period   In Piaget's second period of cognitive development, children between the ages of two and seven can think symbolically, but their thinking is egocentric and dominated by their perceptual experience. They do not understand the principles of conservation. (*See also* Conservation; Egocentrism)

Preparedness   (*See* Associative bias)

Presynaptic neuron   The transmitting cell through which electrical impulses travel to stimulate another neuron across the synaptic junction. (*See also* Neurotransmitter; Postsynaptic neuron)

Primary drives   Unlearned physiologically-based motivations, such as hunger, that is not learned.

Primacy effect   The tendency for our first impression of a person to bias how we interpret what he or she does later.

Primary reinforcers   Stimuli in instrumental conditioning, such as food or warmth, that are essential for an animal's survival. (*See also* Conditioned reinforcers)

Primary sex characteristics   The physiological characteristics that enable an organism to sexually reproduce. During puberty females show development of their ovaries, uterus and vagina and begin menstruation, while males show growth in their scrotum, testes, and penis and begin to produce sperm.

Priming   The tendency for recent events to influence current interpretations.

Proactive interference   The forgetting of new material due to the disruptive effects of previously learned material.

Problem-focused coping strategies   Used in situations seen as changeable, these strategies are aimed at doing something to change the problem causing distress.

Procedural memory   A form of memory that enables people to remember how to perform various acts. (*See also* Episodic memory; Semantic memory)

Projection   A defense mechanism in which a person deals with a threatening impulse by attributing it to others.

Projective test   A test with ambiguous items for which there are no objectively "correct" answers. It is designed to allow subjects to "project" their own needs and desires into their responses.

Propositional thinking   The ability during adolescence to reason about abstractions and verbal statements.

Proprioception   The sense of bodily feedback.

Prosopagnosia   A brain damage syndrome characterized by the inability to recognize faces.

Provocative motion   A form of body motion in which there is a mismatch between sensory cues and information about gravity. The result is dizziness and nausea.

Proximal stimuli   Patterns of physical energy that strike sensory receptors and cause them to generate neural impulses. (*See also* Distal stimuli)

Proximate   Explanations that focus on the short-term or immediate causes of behavior.

Psychoactive drugs   Drugs which affect a person's thought processes and behavior.

Psychoactive substances   Drugs that affect sensation, perception, thinking, self-awareness, and emotion. They include such drugs as LSD, mescaline, PCP, and marijuana. (*See also* Drug dependence; Drug tolerance)

Psychoanalysis   An approach to therapy, popularized by Freud, that seeks to reveal the unconscious motives that underlie behavior through intensive discussions between patient and therapist.

Psychoanalytic perspective   The general viewpoint developed by Freud and his followers. According to this view, much of what we think and do is motivated by thoughts that may exist completely outside of our conscious awareness.

Psychogenic amnesia   Refers to a dramatic loss of memory that cannot be attributed to a physical trauma such as head injury.

Psycholinguistics   A branch of psychology that examines language as an aspect of behavior.

Psychology   The science of behavior and mental processes.

Psychometric approach   Involves analyzing the results of intelligence tests to determine the structure of human intelligence and whether intelligence consists of one general factor or a variety of factors.

Psychopath   (*See* Antisocial personality)

Psychopathology   Translated from its Greek roots into "mental illness," this term is used to describe disordered behavior.

Psychophysical scale   The relationship between a quantifiable physical stimulus and a subjective measure of its sensory experience.

Psychophysics   The study of the relationship between physical stimulation and sensory experience.

Psychosocial moratorium   During adolescence, a time for education and personal development before selecting an adult role and assuming the responsibilities of family and work. (*See also* Identity foreclosure)

Psychosomatic disorders   Physical disorders that seem to result from prolonged psychological conflict.

Psychosurgery   The destruction of brain tissue to alleviate emotional and behavioral disorders, usually reserved for severe and otherwise untreatable problems.

Psychotherapy   Use of psychological interventions to treat disordered behaviors.

Puberty   The sexual maturation of the child, demonstrated by menstruation in girls and the production of sperm in boys.

Punishment   In instrumental conditioning, the use of an aversive stimulus to decrease the likelihood of a particular response. (*See also* Negative reinforcement)

Pupil   The opening or black spot that appears in the center of the iris. The size of the pupil controls the amount of light that enters the eye. (*See also* Iris; Lens; Retina)

R

Range   A crude measure of variability that is obtained by subtracting the lowest from the highest score in a frequency distribution.

Rapid eye movements (REM)   Rapid movements of the eyes during sleep that are associated with periods of dreaming.

Rational-emotive therapy   A form of psychotherapy in which the therapist persuades, teaches, and provides information, in an attempt to break down the client's irrational and self-defeating ideas.

Rationalization   A defense mechanism that involves making excuses for one's failures or transgressions.

Receptive aphasia   The inability to comprehend speech.

Receptive field   The area in the visual field in which a stimulus will produce a response.

Receptor cell   A neural structure in our sense organs—for example, the eyes or ears—that receives environmental stimulation.

Recessive gene   Member of a gene pair that can control the appearance of a certain trait only if it is paired with another recessive gene.

Reciprocity norm The social convention that if someone does us a favor, we ought to return it.

Reflexes Involuntary responses to particular stimuli that are based on existing connections in the nervous system.

Reinforcement A stimulus in instrumental conditioning that increases the likelihood of the behavior it follows.

Relative height A monocular cue for depth. For objects above the visual horizon, the higher the object, the closer it appears; for objects before the horizon, the higher the object, the farther away the object appears.

Relative size A monocular depth cue based on the fact that as objects become more distant, their retinal image grows smaller in size.

Reliability The consistency with which a test measures whatever it is intended to measure.

Replication The ability to reproduce the results of any given study in a different setting and under the same or slightly different conditions.

Representativeness heuristic A decision-making process in which the likelihood of an event is determined by noting the similarity between the evidence and the possible outcomes.

Repression An unconscious defense mechanism designed to protect a person by preventing unpleasant memories from reaching conscious awareness.

Resistance A point in therapy at which the person presumably begins to approach a repressed conflict and tries to escape the confrontation.

Response chaining In instrumental conditioning, linking or tying together a series of instrumentally-conditioned responses.

Response cost In punishment, the removal of positive reinforcement.

Reticular formation A network of neural pathways in the brainstem that relays sensory information and controls arousal and sleep.

Retina A paper-thin lining at the rear of the eye that is composed of millions of light-sensitive receptors.

Retrieval One of three memory processes in which the representation of information is recovered through the act of remembering. (*See also* Encoding; Storage)

Retroactive interference The forgetting of previously learned material due to the disruptive effect of new learning.

Retrograde amnesia The inability to remember events that were immediately followed by a traumatic event. (*See*

also Amnesia; Anterograde amnesia)

Right hemisphere The right cerebral hemisphere is specialized for spatial abilities and synthesizing information; it controls the left side of the body. (*See also* Left hemisphere)

Rods Light sensitive cells in the eye that distinguish black, white, and shades of gray. The rods provide for night vision and peripheral vision, the sensitivity to visual stimuli away from the center of focus. (*See also* Cones)

Role confusion Uncertainty over one's role in life brought on by a failure to develop a sense of identity during adolescence.

Role-taking Child's ability to comprehend what another person sees, feels, and thinks.

Rooting reflex A reflex in newborn infants that causes them to turn their heads and mouths in the direction of stimulation to their cheeks.

S

Saccades Voluntary eye movements that occur between one and five times a second.

Salience effect The human tendency to devote extra attention to noticeable or striking people.

Sample In survey research, a subset that is randomly drawn from a population. (*See also* Population)

Sampling Error The discrepancy between the true values of a population and the estimates of those values obtained from a sample.

Scattergram A graph that shows how two different data sets are related. The shape of the cluster of data points indicates the type and degree of relationship.

Schedules of reinforcement In instrumental conditioning, a relationship or contingency that exists between a response and a reinforcer. (*See also* Fixed interval, Fixed ratio, Variable interval, *and* Variable ratio schedules)

Schema A memory structure that is an abstract representation of objects or events in the real world.

Schizophrenia A disorder characterized by delusions, hallucinations, incoherent thinking, social isolation or withdrawal, inappropriate emotions, and strange motor behaviors.

Script A generalized sequence of actions that describes a well-learned routine.

Secondary drives Specific preferences that are learned through classical conditioning.

Secondary reinforcers (*See also* Conditioned reinforcers)

Secondary sex characteristics The physical characteristics that distinguish a sexually mature male from a sexually mature female.

Self-actualized personalities People who develop to the highest reaches of their potential.

Self-awareness The state of becoming conscious of ourselves as distinct from the environment.

Self-concept One's knowledge of, and beliefs about, oneself.

Self-efficacy beliefs The belief that one will succeed in the future. (*See also* Learned helplessness)

Self-esteem How we evaluate ourselves.

Self-fulfilling prophecy A belief that was originally false but leads to behavior that makes it come true.

Self-reinforcement Rewarding oneself with actual reinforcers, such as a movie, or with cognitive reinforcers such as self-praise.

Self-serving bias A tendency to compare ourselves to others in such a way that we flatter ourselves.

Semantic memory A form of memory that represents knowledge of words, symbols, and concepts, including their meaning and rules for manipulation. (*See also* Episodic memory; Procedural memory)

Semicircular canals Three ring-like structures that extend from the cochlea and help provide our sense of balance.

Senile dementia Commonly called senility, this disorder affecting older people is characterized by signs of disorganized thinking, loss of recent memory, and shifts of mood.

Sensation The process of obtaining environmental information from the sensory channels and the consious experience associated with that stimulation.

Sensorimotor period Piaget's first period of cognitive development in which an infant learns through its senses and motor behavior. (*See also* Object permanence)

Sensory adaptation The reduction in sensitivity that occurs as a result of prolonged, continuous stimulation.

Sensory memory store The part of the memory system that maintains sensory information very briefly after a stimulus is presented. (*See also* Long-term *and* Short-term memory store)

Sensory neurons Nerve cells that receive stimulation from the receptor cells in the sense organs and transmit it to the brain and spinal cord. (*See also* Motor neurons)

Sensory preconditioning A procedure through which one stimulus becomes associated with another stimulus before either is related to an unconditioned stimulus.

Set point A body's target weight maintained by increases or decreases in metabolism and hunger.

Sex roles Characteristic ways of acting masculine or feminine. (*See also* Gender roles)

Sex-typed behavior Behavior that is held to be appropriate for only members of one sex. (*See also* Gender roles; Socialization)

Sexual imprinting A process in which some animals are attracted to potential mates whose features are similar to those to which they were exposed early on in life.

Shape constancy The tendency to see a familiar object as the same shape regardless of the change in retinal image caused by changes in viewing angle or distance.

Shaping In instrumental conditioning, the process of reinforcing behaviors that are increasingly similar to the desired behavior until that behavior is produced. (*See also* Reinforcement)

Short-term memory store A limited capacity component of the memory system that can retain information in conscious awareness for a brief period of time. (*See also* Long-term memory; Sensory memory store)

Signal detection theory A theory of sensitivity that separates an observer's sensitivity from factors such as motivation and expectations that can influence sensory judgments.

Simultaneous conditioning The classical conditioning procedure in which the conditioned and unconditioned stimuli are presented at the same time. (*See also* Backward, Delayed, *and* Trace conditioning)

Size constancy The tendency to see a familiar object according to its actual size regardless of the changes in the retinal image due to changes in object distance.

Skewness A term used to describe an asymmetrical frequency distribution where the majority of scores are either high (negatively skewed) or low (positively skewed).

Sleep apnea Difficulty in breathing while asleep.

Social cognition A field of psychology that examines how we pay attention to, interpret, and remember social events.

Social expectation Perceptions of how others expect us to behave.

Social facilitation A change in performance due to the presence of observers.

Social influence Changes people make in their behavior in response to real or imagined pressures from others.

Social motives Motivations related to interactions with other people, such as the need to affiliate with others and the need to achieve.

Social perception The processes by which we organize and interpret information about other people.

Social support Consists of emotional, informational, and material aid from others that assists in coping with stress.

Social traps Situations in which the pursuit of short-term benefits leads to disastrous long-run consequences.

Socialization The process by which children acquire the attitudes, beliefs, and customs of their family and culture. (*See also* Identification)

Sociological perspective on disorder A model in which disordered behavior is viewed as being rooted in the wider society rather than in the individual.

Somatic nervous system A division of the peripheral nervous system that connects the brain and spinal cord to the muscles and sensory receptors. (*See also* Peripheral nervous system)

Somatoform disorders Disorders involving symptoms of chronic physical complaints for which medical professionals are unable to find any actual physical cause.

Somatosensory cortex A narrow strip of the parietal lobe, just behind the central fissure, where the sense of touch is localized on the surface of the brain. (*See also* Motor cortex)

Sound localization The ability to locate the source of a sound.

Sound waves Air pressure fluctuations that stimulate the receptor cells of the ear. People are normally sensitive to sound waves with frequencies between 20 and 20,000 Hz.

Span of attention The number of stimuli that can simultaneously be perceived and reported.

Specificity hypothesis The hypothesis that assumes that specific conflicts are associated with specific illnesses.

Speech perception The identification of auditory linguistic stimuli.

Spontaneous recovery The return of a classically- or instrumentally-conditioned response after extinction following a period of rest. (*See also* Extinction)

Standard deviation The most frequently used measure of variability, it is the average distance of each score in a frequency distribution from the mean of the distribution.

Standardization The requirement that tests be given acording to standard instructions, be scored objectively, and that a representative sample of people be used to interpret relative test performance.

Stapes One of three small bones that make up the middle ear and through which vibration from the eardrum is transmitted.

Statistical data A group of numbers that represents measurements of some property or phenomenon.

Statistical inference The process of making judgments about population values based on observations of samples.

Statistics The branch of mathematics that deals with the collection and interpretation of numerical data. Psychologists use both decriptive and inferential statistics.

Stimulants A class of drugs that reduce fatigue when administered in small amounts, and increase energy and excitement when given in large amounts.

Storage One of three memory processes in which the representation of information is retained in the memory susten. (*See also* Encoding; Retrieval)

Stress The physical and psychological response to perceived environmental threat.

Stroboscopic movement An illusion of movement that results from the successive presentation of individual stimuli arranged in a sequence.

Structuralism An early approach to the study of consciousness that sought to understand how basic elements were structured by the mind to produce different conscious experiences.

Subjective contour A type of illusion in which there is a perception of a well-defined form where there really is none.

Subliminal perception The perception of objects and events below the threshold of awareness.

Subtractive color mixture Mixing paints together causes certain wavelengths to be absorbed or subtracted from a painted surface so that a new color is reflected when light shines on the surface. (*See also* Additive color mixture)

Superego According to Freudian theory, an internalized representation of parents' value system.

Suppression A defense mechanism which involves a person becoming aware of an unpleasant memory or impulse, but consciously trying not to think about it.

Survey A large-scale questionnaire or interview method of research which yields summaries of the opinions, beliefs, and behaviors of a group of people.

Sympathetic division A division of the autonomic nervous system that is active during excitement and stress. (*See also* Parasympathetic division)

Synapse The tiny gap that separates an axon from one neuron from the receiving portion of another cell. (*See also* Neuron; Neurotransmitter)

Syntax Grammatical rules for combining words into phrases and sentences.

Systematic desensitization A classical conditioning therapy for anxiety which involves a patient gradually confronting threatening stimulus under non-threatening circumstances.

T

Taste aversion The association of food and physical illness, which results in avoidance of the particular food in the future.

Taste buds Receptors for the sense of taste, located primarily on the tongue and responsive to the qualities of sweet, sour, salty, and bitter.

Templates In perception, forms or memory representations used to produce pattern recognition through the matching of stimulus features.

Temporal lobes Part of the cerebral cortex that is important for the processing of auditory and, to a lesser extent, visual information.

Terminals Small structures at the end of the axon that transmit neural signals to the dendrites or cell body of an adjacent cell.

Testosterone The hormone produced in adrenal glands and the male's testes that appears to be a primary determinant of the sex drive in men and women, and which has also been found to lead to increases in aggressive behavior in animals.

Thalamus Located above the brainstem, the thalamus relays sensory information from the different sensory systems, including eyes, ears, and skin, to higher centers in the brain.

Thematic Apperception Test (TAT) A projective test used to uncover motivations such as the need for achievement.

Theory A set of assumptions that helps us organize a complicated set of findings and that helps a scientist decide where to look for new evidence.

Thought The mental manipulation of symbols that stand for objects, events, or ideas in memory.

Threshold level The level of stimulation a neuron must receive to generate an impulse.

Thyroid gland Endocrine gland located below the voice box.

T-maze A t-shaped runway used to study instrumental conditioning of choice behavior.

Token economy The use of tokens (usually poker chips or play money) that patients, inmates, or students can earn by doing something desirable or by refraining from doing something undesirable. The tokens can then be exchanged for actual rewards.

Top-down processing The view that perception is guided by mental processes such as set or expectancy. (*See also* Bottom-up processing)

Trace conditioning The classical conditioning procedure in which the conditioned stimulus comes on and goes off briefly before the unconditioned stimulus is presented. (*See also* Backward, Delayed, *and* Simultaneous conditioning)

Trait approach A systematic effort to describe and classify the behavioral characteristics that differentiate people from one another.

Transduction The conversion of physical energy, by sensory receptors, into neural impulses that are transmitted to the different sensory areas of the brain.

Transference In psychoanalysis, the idea that patients view the therapist as the symbolic equivalent of the important figures in their lives, especially their parents.

Trephining The ancient practice of chipping a hole in the skull of a disturbed person to rid the brain of the evil forces believed to cause abnormal behavior.

Trial-and-error learning The use of one problem-solving strategy after another until one is successful.

Triangulation The process of observing a phenomenon using two (or more) different methods to determine whether similar findings appear from different vantage points.

Triarchic theory A theory of intelligence involving componential, experiential, and contextual aspects of intelligence.

Trichromatic theory The view that perceived color is based on the output of three color receptors in the retina (usually red, green, and blue receptors).

Twin studies Research carried out with fraternal and identical twins who have been separated at birth and raised in separate environments to determine the relative impact of genes and the environment on behavior and development.

Type A syndrome A pattern of behavior characterized by hostility and time urgency and believed to increase susceptibility to stress-related illnesses.

U

Unconditioned response A response in classical conditioning that is elicited automatically by an unconditioned stimulus. (*See also* Conditioned response; Conditioned stimulus; Unconditioned response)

Unconditioned stimulus A stimulus in classical conditioning that automatically and reflexively elicits an unconditioned response. (*See also* Conditioned response; Conditioned stimulus; Unconditioned response)

Ultimate explanations Explanations of behavior that take a relatively long-range view, focusing on previous learning history, genes, or the evolutionary history of the human species.

V

Validity The requirement that a test measures what it purports to measure.

Variable interval schedule In instrumental conditioning, reinforcement occurs after the first response that is made after a specified period of time that varies from one reinforcement to the next. (*See also* Fixed interval, Fixed ratio, *and* Variable ratio schedules)

Variable ratio schedule In instrumental conditioning, an animal is reinforced after a specified number of responses have been emitted, but this number varies from one reinforcement to the next. (*See also* Fixed interval, Fixed ratio, *and* Variable interval schedules)

Ventricles The fluid-filled cavities of the brain.

Vestibular sacs Sacs in the inner ear that are filled with a jelly-like substance and that serve as a mechanism of balance.

Vestibular sense Our sense of balance is achieved by receptors located in the inner ear.

Visual acuity The ability to see fine detail clearly.

Visual object agnosia The inability to name a familiar object, show how it is used, or recall ever having seen it before. (*See also* Color agnosia; Prosopagnosia)

Visual spectrum The portion of the electromagnetic energy spectrum that is visible to the eye, the visual spectrum consists of a narrow band of wavelengths from 390 to 760 nanometers.

W

Wavelength Because electromagnetic energy travels in waves, this energy spectrum is scaled in terms of wavelengths which are the distance from the crest of one wave to the crest of the next.

Weber's Law A psychophysical relationship that states a just-noticeable difference is always proportional to the magnitude or intensity of a stimulus. (*See also* Just-noticeable difference (JND))

Wechsler Adult Intelligence Scale (WAIS) An intelligence test used to measure IQ in children aged seven to 16.

Wernicke's area The portion of the temporal lobe of the left hemisphere of the brain that is involved in understanding language. People with brain damage in this area have difficulty comprehending speech. (*See also* Broca's area)

Working backward A heuristic strategy in which we begin knowing the desired outcome or goal state and work back to the original state.

Working memory A form of short-term store that is used to manipulate information in consciousness.

Y

Yerkes-Dodson Law The hypothesized principle that arousal, whether due to stress, exercise, or a cup of coffee, will lead to an improvement in performance up to a point but hurt performance beyond that point.

Z

Zygote A fertilized ovum or egg. (*See also* Embryo; Fetus)

REFERENCES

Abel, Z.L. 1980. Fetal alcohol syndrome: Behavior teratology. *Psychological Bulletin* 87: 29–50.

Abelson, R.P., and Prentice, D.A. 1989. Beliefs as possessions: A functional perspective. In *Attitude structure and function*, A.R. Pratkanis, S.J. Breckler, and A.G. Greenwald, eds. Hillsdale, NJ: Erlbaum.

Abramson, L.Y., Seligman, M.E.P., and Teasdale, J.D. 1978. Learned helplessness in humans: Critique and reformulation. *Journal of Abnormal Psychology* 87: 49–74.

Ackerman, B.P. 1987. Selective attention and distraction in context interactive situations in children and adults. *Journal of Experimental Child Psychology* 44: 126–46.

Ackerman, P.L. 1987. Individual differences in skill learning: An integration of psychometric and information processing perspectives. *Psychological Bulletin* 102: 3–27.

Adams, J.L. 1979. *Conceptual blockbusting*. New York: Norton.

Adelson, J., and Doehrman, M.J. 1980. The psychodynamic approach to adolescence. In *Handbook of the psychology of adolescence*, J. Adelson, ed. New York: Wiley.

Ader, R., and Cohen, N. 1985. CNS–immune system interaction: Conditioning phenomena. *Behavioral and Brain Sciences* 8: 379–94.

Adler, A. 1930. Individual psychology. In C. Murchison (Ed.), *Psychologies of 1930*. 395–405. Worcester, MA: Clark University Press.

———. 1956. *The individual psychology of Alfred Adler*, H.L. Ansbacher and R.R. Ansbacher, eds. and trans. New York: Harper and Row.

Adorno, T., Frenkel-Brunswik, E., Levinson, D., and Sanford, R.N. 1950. *The authoritarian personality*. New York: Harper.

Aganthanos, H., and Stathakpolou, N. 1983. Life events and child abuse: A controlled study. In *Child abuse and neglect: Research and innovations in NATO countries*, J. Leavitt, ed. Netherlands: Kluwer.

Ainsworth, M.D. 1973. The development of infant-mother attachment. In *Review of child development research*, vol. 3, B. Caldwell and H. Ricciuti, eds. Chicago: University of Chicago Press.

Ainsworth, M.D., Blehar, M., Waters, E., and Wall, S. 1978. *Patterns of attachment*. Hillsdale, NJ: Erlbaum.

Alcock, J. 1989. *Animal behavior: An evolutionary approach*, 4th ed. Sunderland, MA: Sinauer Associates.

Alexander, F. 1934. The influence of psychologic factors upon gastro-intestinal disturbances: A symposium. *Psychoanalytic Quarterly* 3: 501–39.

Alexander, R.D. 1987. *The biology of moral systems*. Hawthorne, NY: Aldine de Gruyter.

Allen, G.W. 1967. *William James: A biography*. New York: Viking.

Allen, J.B., Kenrick, D.T., Linder, D.E., and

McCall, M.A. 1989. Arousal and attraction: A response facilitation alternative to misattribution and negative reinforcement models. *Journal of Personality and Social Psychology* 57: 261–270.

Allen, M.G. 1976. Twin studies of affective illness. *Archives of General Psychiatry* 33: 1476–78.

Allison, J., Miller, M., and Wozny, M. 1979. Conservation in behavior. *Journal of Experimental Psychology: General* 108: 4–34.

Allman, L.R., and Jaffe, D.T. 1982. Preface. In *Readings in adult psychology*, 2nd ed, L.R. Allman and D.T. Jaffe, eds. New York: Harper and Row.

Alloy, L.B., and Abramson, L.Y. 1979. Judgment of contingency in depressed and nondepressed students: Sadder but wiser? *Journal of Experimental Psychology: General* 108: 441–85.

Alloy, L.B., Abramson, L.Y., and Viscusi, Z. 1981. Induced mood and the illusion of control. *Journal of Personality and Social Psychology* 41: 1129–40.

Allport, G.W. 1954. *The Nature of Prejudice*. Reading, MA: Addison-Wesley.

Allport, G.W. 1966. Traits revisited. *American Psychologist* 21: 1–10.

Allport, G.W. and Odert, H.S. 1936. Trait names: A psycho-lexical study. *Psychological monographs* 47 (1, Whole No. 211).

Altheide, D.L., and Johnson, J.M. 1977. Counting Souls: A Study of Counseling at Evangelical Crusades. *Pacific Sociological Review* 20: 323–48.

Altman, I., and Chemers, M. 1980. *Culture and environment*. Monterey, CA: Brooks/Cole Publishing Co.

Altman, L.K. 1988. Cocaine's many dangers: The evidence mounts. *New York Times*, January 26.

Amabile, T.M. 1983. *The social psychology of creativity*. New York: Springer-Verlag.

———. 1985. Motivation and creativity: Effects of motivational orientation on creative writers. *Journal of Personality and Social Psychology* 48: 393–99.

———. 1987. The motivation to be creative. In *Frontiers in creativity: Beyond the basics*, S. Isaksen ed. Buffalo, NY: Bearly Limited.

Amabile, T.M., and Kabat, L.G. 1982. When self-description contradicts behavior: Actions do speak louder than words. *Social Cognition* 1: 311–35.

Amelang, M., and Borkenau, P. 1986. The trait concept: Current theoretical considerations, empirical facts, and implications for Personality Inventory Contraction. In *Personality assessment via questionnaire*, A. Angleitner and J.S. Wiggins, eds. London: Plenum Press.

American Psychological Association. 1981. Ethical principles of psychologists. *American Psychologist* 36: 633–38.

Amoore, J.E. 1969. A plan to identify most of the primary odors. In *Olfaction and taste*, vol. 3, C. Pfaffman, ed. New York: Rockefeller University Press.

Amsel, A. 1958. The role of frustrative nonreward in continuous reward situations. *Psychological Bulletin* 55: 102–19.

Anastasi, A. 1982. Psychological testing, 5th ed. New York: Macmillan.

Andersen, S.M., and Klatzky, R.L. 1987. Traits and social stereotypes: Levels of categorization in person perception. *Journal of Personality and Social Psychology* 53: 235–46.

Anderson, C.A. 1989. Temperature and aggression: The ubiquitous effects of heat on the occurrence of human violence. *Psychological Bulletin* 106: 74–96.

Anderson, C.A., and Anderson, D.C. 1984. Ambient temperature and violent crime: Tests of the linear and curvilinear hypotheses. *Journal of Personality and Social Psychology* 46: 91–97.

Anderson, E.R., Hetherington, E.M., and Clingempeel, W.G. 1986. Pubertal status and its influence on the adaptation to remarriage. Paper presented at the Society for Research on Adolescence. Madison, WI.

Anderson, J.R. 1990. *Cognitive psychology and its implications*, 3rd ed. New York: Freeman.

Anderson, J.R., and Ross, B.H. 1980. Evidence against a semantic-episodic distinction. *Journal of Experimental Psychology: Human Learning and Memory* 6: 441–66.

Anderson, K.J. 1990. Arousal and the inverted-U Hypothesis: A critique of Neiss's "reconceptualizing arousal." *Psychological Bulletin* 107: 96–100.

Anderson, R.C., and Pichert, J.W. 1978. Recall of previously unrecallable information following a shift in perspective. *Journal of Verbal Learning and Verbal Behavior* 17: 1–12.

Andreason, N.A. 1984. *The Broken Brain: The Biological Revolution in Psychiatry*. New York: Harper and Row.

Andreasen, N.C., Olson, S.A., Dennert, J.W., and Smith, M.R. 1982. Ventricular enlargement in schizophrenia: Relationship to positive and negative symptoms. *American Journal of Psychiatry* 136: 944–47.

Andrews, J.D.W. 1967. The achievement motive in two types of organizations. *Journal of Personality and Social Psychology* 6: 163–68.

Andriole, S.J., ed. 1985. *Applications in artificial intelligence*. Princeton, NJ: Petrocelli Books.

Angier, N. 1990. Cheating on sleep: Modern life turns America into the land of the drowsy. *The New York Times*, May 15 C1, C8.

Anonymous 1965. A practicing psychiatrist: The experience of electroconvulsive therapy. *British Journal of Psychiatry* 111: 365–67.

Antrobus, J. 1987. Cortical hemisphere asymmetry and sleep mentation. *Psychological Review* 94: 359–68.

Antrobus, J.S., and Singer, J.L. 1964. Visual signal detection as a function of sequential variability of simultaneous speech. *Journal of Experimental Psychology* 68: 603–10.

APA Monitor, January, 1987. Psychology luring more students. p. 36.

Argyle, M., and Little, B.R. 1972. Do personality traits apply to social behavior? *Journal for the Theory of Social Behavior*, 2: 1–35.

Arizona Republic (Jan. 10, 1989). Class of '92 supports drug, AIDS testing. P. A1, A4.

Arkin, R.M., and Maruyama, G.M. 1979. Attribution, affect, and college exam performance. *Journal of Educational Psychology* 71: 85–93.

Arms, R.L., Russell, G.W., and Sandilands, M.L. 1979. Effects on the hostility of spectators of viewing aggressive sports. *Social Psychology Quarterly* 42: 275–79.

Arndt, R., and Chapman, L. 1984. *Preventing illness and injury in the workplace.* Washington, DC: Office of Technology Assessment.

Aron, A., Aron, E.N., Tudor, M., and Nelson, G. 1991. Close relationships as including other in the self. *Journal of Personality and Social Psychology*, 60: 241–53.

Asch, S.E. 1946. Forming impressions of personality. *Journal of Abnormal and Social Psychology* 41: 258–90.

———. 1951. Effects of group pressure upon the modification and distortion of judgment. In *Groups, leadership, and men*, M. Guetzkow, ed. Pittsburgh: Carnegie.

Aserinsky, E., and Kleitman, N. 1953. Regularly occurring periods of eye motility, and concomitant phenomena during sleep. *Science* 118: 273.

Ashcraft, M.H. 1989. *Human memory and cognition.* Glenview, IL: Scott, Foresman.

Ashmead, D.H., Clifton, R.K., and Perris, E.E. 1987. Precision of auditory localization in human infants. *Developmental Psychology* 23: 641–47.

Astin, A.W., Green, K.C., and Korn, W.S. 1987. *The American freshman: Twenty year trends.* Los Angeles: American Council on Education and UCLA.

Atkinson, K., MacWhinney, B., and Stoel, C. 1970. An experiment on recognition of babbling. *Papers and reports on child language development.* Stanford, CA: Stanford University Press.

Atthowe, J.M., and Krasner, L. 1968. Preliminary report on the application of contingent reinforcement procedures (token economy) on a "chronic" psychiatric ward. *Journal of Abnormal Psychology* 73: 37–43.

Awaya, S., Miyake, Y., Imayuni, Y., Shiose, Y., Kanda, T., and Komuro, K. 1973. Amblyopia in man, suggestive of stimulus deprivation amblyopia. *Japanese Journal of Ophthalmology* 17: 69–82.

Axsom, D., Yates, S., and Chaiken, S. 1987. Audience response as a heuristic cue in persuasion. *Journal of Personality and Social Psychology* 53: 30–40.

Ayllon, T., and Azrin, N.H. 1968. *The token economy: A motivational system for therapy and rehabilitation.* New York: Appleton-Century-Crofts.

Ayllon, T., Haughton, E., and Hughes, H.B. 1965. Interpretation of symptoms: Fact or fiction? *Behavior Research and Therapy* 3: 1–8.

Bachman, J.G., and O'Malley, P.M. 1977. Self-esteem in young men: A longitudinal analysis of the impact of educational and occupational attainment. *Journal of Personality and Social Psychology* 35: 365–80.

Bachman, L. 1991. Recognition memory across the adult life span: The role of prior knowledge. *Memory and Cognition* 19: 63–71.

Bachrach, A.J. 1970. Diving behavior. In *Human performance and SCUBA diving: Proceedings of the symposium on underwater physiology.* Chicago: The Athletic Institute.

Bachrach, A.J., Erwin, W.J., and Mohr, J.P. 1965. The control of eating behavior in an anorexic by operant conditioning techniques. In *Case studies in behavior modification*, L. Ullmann and L.P. Krasner, eds. New York: Holt, Rinehart and Winston.

Bach-y-Rita, P. 1972. *Brain mechanisms in sensory substitution.* New York: Academic Press.

Bacon, F. 1620/1960. The New Organon and Related Writings. New York: Liberal Arts Press.

Baddeley, A.D. 1979. Working memory and reading. In *Processing of Visible Language*: I, P.A. Kolers, M.E. Wrolstad, and H. Bouma, Eds. New York: Plenum.

Baddeley, A.D. 1986. *Working memory.* Oxford, UK: Clarendon Press.

———. 1990. *Human memory.* Boston: Allyn and Bacon.

Baer, D., and McEachron, D.L. 1982. A review of selected sociobiological principles: Application to hominid evolution I. The development of group social structure. *Journal of Social and Biological Structures* 5: 69–90.

Bagar, R., and Biancolli, L. 1947. *The concert companion.* New York: McGraw-Hill.

Baggett, P. 1975. Memory for explicit and implicit information in picture stories. *Journal of Verbal Learning and Verbal Behavior* 14: 538–48.

Baillargeon, R., and Graber, M. 1988. Evidence of location memory in 8-month-old infants in a nonsearch AB task. *Developmental Psychology* 24: 502–11.

Baltes, P.B., Reese, H.W., and Lipsitt, L.P. 1980. Life-span developmental psychology. *Annual Review of Psychology* 31: 65–110.

Bancroft, J. 1978. The relationship between hormones and sexual behavior in humans. In *Biological determinants of sexual behavior*, J.B. Hutchinson, ed. New York: Wiley.

———. 1986. Low sexual desire. In *Hormones and Behaviour*, L. Dennerstein and I. Fraser, eds. Amsterdam: Excerpta Medica.

Bandura, A. 1965. Vicarious processes: A case of no-trial learning. In *Advances in experimental social psychology*, vol. 2, L. Berkowitz, ed. New York: Academic Press.

———. 1969. *Principles of Behavior Modification.* New York: Holt, Rinehart and Winston.

Bandura, A. 1977. *Social learning theory.* Englewood Cliffs, NJ: Prentice Hall.

———. 1977. Self-efficacy: Toward a unifying theory of behavioral change. *Psychological Review* 84: 191–215.

———. 1986. *Social foundations of thought and action: A social–cognitive theory.* Englewood Cliffs, NJ: Prentice Hall.

Bandura, A., Blanchard, E.B., and Ritter, B. 1969. Relative efficacy of desensitization and modelling approaches for inducing behavioral, affective, and attitudinal changes. *Journal of Personality and Social Psychology* 13: 173–79.

Bandura, A., Ross, P., and Ross, S.A. 1961. Transmission of aggression through imitation of aggressive models. *Journal of Abnormal and Social Psychology* 63: 575–82.

Bandura, A., and Walters, R.H. 1963. *Social learning and personality development.* New York: Holt, Rinehart and Winston.

Barahal, H.S. 1958. 1000 prefrontal lobotomies: Five-to-ten year follow-up study. *Psychiatric Quarterly* 32: 653–78.

Barash, D.P., and Lipton, J.E. 1985. *The caveman and the bomb: Human nature, evolution, and nuclear war.* New York: McGraw-Hill.

Barber, T.X. 1975. Responding to "hypnotic" suggestions: An introspective report. *American Journal of Clinical Hypnosis* 18: 6–22.

Barber, T.X., and Calverley, D.S. 1964. Experimental studies in "hypnotic" behavior: Suggested deafness evaluated by delayed auditory feedback. *British Journal of Psychology* 55: 439–46.

Barchas, J.D., Berger, P.A., Ciaranello, R.D., and Elliot, G.R. 1977. *Psychopharmacology: From theory to practice.* New York: Oxford University Press.

Barclay, C.R., and Wellman, H.M. 1986. Accuracies and inaccuracies in autobiographical memories. *Journal of memory and language* 25: 93–103.

Bard, P., and Mountcastle, V.B. 1948. Some forebrain mechanisms involved in expression of angry behavior. *Association for Research in Nervous Diseases Proceedings* 27: 326–404.

Bargh, J.A., and Pietromonaco, P. 1982. Automatic information processing and social perception: The influence of trait information presented outside of conscious awareness on impression formation. *Journal of Personality and Social Psychology* 43: 437–49.

Barlow, H.B. 1982. Physiology of the retina. In *The senses*, H.B. Barlow and J.D. Mollon, eds. Cambridge, England: Cambridge University Press.

Barlow, H.B., and Mollon, J.D., eds. 1982. *The senses.* Cambridge, England: Cambridge University Press.

Barling, J., and Rosenbaum, A. 1986. Work stressors and wife abuse. *Journal of Applied Psychology* 71: 346–48.

Barnett, P.A., and Gotlib, I.H. 1988. Psychosocial functioning and depression: Distinguishing among antecedents, concomitants, and consequences. *Psychological Bulletin* 104: 97–126.

Baron, J., Badgio, P.C., and Gaskins, I.W. 1986. Cognitive style and its improvement: A normative approach. In *Advances in the psychology of human intelligence*, vol. 3, R.J. Sternberg, ed. Hillsdale, NJ: Erlbaum.

Baron, R.A. 1974. The aggression-inhibiting influence of heightened sexual arousal. *Journal of Personality and Social Psychology* 30: 318–22.

Baron, R.M., and Boudreau, L.A. 1987. An ecological perspective on integrating personality and social psychology. *Journal of Personality and Social Psychology* 53: 1222–28.

Baron, R.M., Mandel, D.R., Adams, C.A., and Griffin, L.M. 1976. Effects of social density in university residential environments. *Journal of Personality and Social Psychology* 34: 434–46.

Barr, H.M., Streissguth, A.P., Darby, B.L., and Sampson, P.D. 1990. Prenatal exposure to alcohol, caffeine, tobacco, and aspirin: Effects of fine and gross motor performance in 4-year-old children. *Developmental Psychology* 26: 339–48.

Barrera, M. 1981. Social support in the adjustment of pregnant adolescents Assessment issues, In *Social support in the adjustment of pregnant adolescents*, ed. B.H. Gottlieb, 69–96. Beverly Hills, CA: Sage.

Barrera, M., Jr. 1986. Distinctions between social support concepts, measures, and models. *American Journal of Community Psychology* 14: 413–46.

Barrera, M., Jr., and Rosen, G.M. 1977. Detrimental effects of a self-reward contracting program on subjects' involvement in self-administered desensitization. *Journal of Consulting and Clinical Psychology* 45: 1180–81.

Barron, F., Jarvik, M., and Bunnel, S., Jr. 1964. The hallucinogenic drugs. *Scientific American* 210: 29–37.

Barron, F.H. 1963. *Creativity and psychological health: Origins of personality and creative freedom.* Princeton, NJ: Van Nostrand.

Barron, F.H., and Harrington, D.M. 1981. Creativity, intelligence, and personality. *Annual Review of Psychology* 32: 439–76.

Barry, H., III, Child, I.L., and Bacon, M.K. 1959. Relation of child training to subsistence economy. *American Anthropologist* 61: 51–63.

Barry, J.W., Warner, M.G., and Thomas, E. 1989. After the cold war. *Newsweek*, June 29, p. 22.

Bartlett, F.C. 1932. *Remembering: A study in experimental and social psychology.* London: Cambridge University Press.

Bartlett, J., Bridges, P., and Kelly, D. 1981. Contemporary indications for psychosurgery. *British Journal of Psychiatry* 138: 507–11.

Bartoshuk, L.M., Cain, W.S., and Pfaffman, C. 1985. Taste and olfaction. In *Topics in the history of psychology*, vol. 1, G.A. Kimble and K. Schlesinger, eds. Hillsdale, NJ: Erlbaum.

Bartrop, R.W., Lazarus, L., Luckhurst, E., Kiloh, L.G., and Penny, R. 1977. Depressed lymphocyte function after bereavement. *Lancet* 1: 834–36.

Baruch, G., and Barnett, R. 1983. *Lifeprints: New patterns of love and work for today's woman.* New York: New American Library.

Barzini, L. 1964. *The Italians.* New York: Atheneum.

Bassis, M.S., Gelles, R.J., and Levine, A. 1982. *Social problems.* New York: Harcourt Brace Jovanovich.

Bates, E., Beeghley-Smith, M., Bretherton, I., and McNew, S. 1982. Social basis of language development: A reassessment. In *Advances in child development and behavior*, vol. 16, H. Reese and L. Lipsett, eds. New York: Academic Press.

Bates, E., Thal, D., and Marchman, V. 1989. Symbols and syntax: A Darwinian approach to language development. In *The biological foundations of language development*, N. Kransnegor, D. Rumbaugh, M. Studdert-Kennedy, and R. Schiefelbusch, eds. New York: Oxford University Press.

Batson, C.D., Dyck, J.L., Brandt, J.R., Batson, J.G., Powell, A.L., McMaster, M.R., and Griffitt, C. 1988. Five studies testing two new egoistic alternatives to the empathy-altruism hypothesis. *Journal of Personality & Social Psychology*, 55: 52–77

Bateson, G., Jackson, D., Haley, J., and Weakland, J. 1956. Towards a theory of schizophrenia. *Behavioral Science* 1: 251–64.

Bauer, R.M., and Rubens, A.B. 1985. Agnosia. In *Clinical neuropsychology*, 2nd ed., K.M. Heilman and E. Valenstein, eds. New York: Oxford University Press.

Baum, A., Fleming, R., and Singer, J.E. 1982. Stress at Three Mile Island: Applying psychological impact analysis. In *Applied Social Psychology Annual 3*, L. Bickman, ed. Beverly Hills, CA: Sage. pp. 217–248.

Baum, A., and Valins, S. 1977. *Architecture and social behavior.* Hillsdale, NJ: Erlbaum.

Baumeister, R. 1986. *Identity.* New York: Oxford University Press.

———. 1991. Self-concept and identity. In *Personality Contemporary theory and research*, V.J. Derlega, B.A. Winstead, and W.H. Jones, eds. Chicago: Nelson-Hall.

Baumeister, R.F., and Scher, S.J. 1988. Self-defeating behavior patterns among normal individuals: Review and analysis of common self-destructive tendencies. *Psychological Bulletin* 104: 3–22.

Baumrind, D. 1967. Child care practices anteceding three patterns of preschool behavior. *Genetic Psychology Monographs* 75: 43–88.

———. 1977. Socialization determinants of personal agency. Paper presented at the biennial meetings of the Society for Research in Child Development. New Orleans. (Cited in Maccoby, E.E. *Social Development.* 1980. New York: Harcourt Brace Jovanovich.)

Bayley, N. 1970. Development of mental abilities. In P. Mussen, ed. *Carmichael's Manual of Child Psychology*, vol. 1. New York: Wiley.

Baxt, N. 1871. Cited in Murray, D.J. 1976. Research on human memory in the nineteenth century. *Canadian Journal of Psychology* 30: 201–20.

Beatty, W.W., and Shavalia, D.A. 1980. Spatial memory in rats: Time course of working memory and effects of anesthetics. *Behavioral and Neural Biology* 28: 454–62.

Beaumont, J.G. 1983. *Introduction to neuropsychology.* New York: Guilford.

Beck, A.T. 1982. *Depression: Clinical, experimental, and theoretical aspects.* New York: Harper and Row.

Beck, A.T., Kovacs, M., and Weissman, A. 1975. Hopelessness and suicidal behavior: An overview. *Journal of the American Medical Association* 234: 1146–49.

Beck, A.T., Rush, A.J., Shaw, B.F., and Emery, G.D. 1979. *Cognitive therapy of depression.* New York: Guilford Press.

Beck, R. 1986. *Applying psychology*, 2nd ed. Englewood Cliffs, NJ: Prentice Hall.

Beecher, H.K. 1959. *Measurement of subjective responses.* New York: Oxford University Press.

Bekesy, G. von 1960. *Experiments in hearing.* New York: McGraw-Hill.

———. 1966. Taste theories and the chemical stimulation of single papillae. *Journal of Applied Physiology* 21: 1–9.

Bell, R.Q., and Harper, L.V. 1977. *Child effects on adults.* Hillsdale, NJ: Erlbaum.

Bell, R.W., & Bell, N.J. 1989 *Sociobiology and the social sciences.* Lubbock, TX: Texas Tech University Press.

Bellezza, F.S. 1981. Mnemonic devices: Classification, characteristics, and criteria. *Review of Educational Research* 51, 247–75.

Belsky, J.K. 1990. *The psychology of aging: Theory, research and practice*, 2nd ed. Monterey, CA: Brooks/Cole.

Belson, W.A. 1978. *Television violence and the adolescent boy.* Westmead, UK: Saxon House, Teakfield Ltd.

Bem, D.J. 1972. Self-perception theory. In *Advances in experimental social psychology*, vol. 6, L. Berkowitz, ed. New York: Academic Press.

Bem, D.J., and Funder, D.C. 1978. Predicting more of the people more of the time: Assessing the personality of situations. *Psychological Review* 85: 485–501.

Bem, S.L. 1976. Probing the promise of androgyny. In *Beyond sex-role stereotypes: Readings toward a psychology of androgyny*, A.G. Kaplan and J.P. Bean, eds. Boston: Little, Brown.

Benedict, R. 1934. *Patterns of culture.* Boston: Houghton Mifflin.

Benson, A.J. 1982. The vestibular sensory system. In *The senses*, H.B. Barlow and J.D. Mollon, eds. Cambridge, England: Cambridge University Press.

Benson, H. 1975. *The relaxation response.* New York: Morrow.

Benson, H., and Friedman, R. 1985. A rebuttal to the conclusions of David S. Holmes' article: "Meditation and somatic arousal reduction." *American Psychologist* 40: 725–28.

Bentler, P.M., and Newcomb, M.D. 1978. Longitudinal study of marital success and failure. *Journal of Consulting and Clinical Psychology* 46: 1053–70.

Bentz, V.J. 1985. Research findings from Personality Assessment of executives. In *Personality Assessment in organizations*, H.J. Bernardin and D.A. Bownas, eds. New York: Praeger.

Bergin, A.E., and Lambert, M.J. 1978. The evaluation of therapeutic outcomes. In *Handbook of psychotherapy and behavior change: An empirical analysis* 2nd ed., S.L. Garfield and A.E. Bergin, eds. New York: Wiley.

Berglas, S. 1985. Self-handicapping and self-handicappers: A cognitive/attributional model of interpersonal self-protective behavior. In *Perspectives in Personality*, vol. I, R. Hogan and W.H. Jones, eds. Greenwich, CT: JAI Press.

Berkeley, G. 1709/1950. *A new theory of vision.* London: Dent.

Berkowitz, L. 1971 The "weapons effect," demand characteristics and the myth of the complaint subject, *Journal of Personality and Social Psychology* 20: 332–38.

Berkowitz, L. 1989. Frustration-aggression hypothesis: Examination and reformulation. *Psychological Bulletin* 106: 59–73.

Berkun, M.M., Kessen, M.L., and Miller, N.E. 1952. Hunger-reducing effects of food by stomach fistula versus food by mouth measured by a consummatory response. *Journal of Comparative and Physiological Psychology* 45: 550–54.

Berlyne, D.E. 1963. Motivational problems raised by exploratory and epistemic behavior. In *Psychology: A study of a science*, vol. 5, S. Koch, ed. New York: McGraw-Hill.

Bernacki, E.J., and Baun, W.B. 1984. The relationship of job performance to exercise adherence in a corporate fitness program. *Journal of Occupational Medicine* 26: 529–531.

Berndt, T.J. 1979. Developmental changes in conformity to peers and parents. *Developmental Psychology* 15: 608–16.

Berndt, T.J., and Perry, T.B. 1990. Distinctive

features and effects of early adolescent friendships. In *From childhood to adolescence: A transitional period?*, R. Montemayor, G.R. Adams, and T.P. Gullotta, eds. Newbury Park, CA: Sage.

Bernstein, I.L. 1985. Learned food aversions in the progression of cancer and its treatment. In *Experimental assessments and clinical application of conditioned food aversions*, N.S. Braverman and P. Bernstein, eds. *Annals of the New York Academy of Sciences*, Vol. 443.

Berrueta-Clement, J., Schweinhart, L.J., Barnett, W.S., Epstein, A.S., and Weikart, D.P. 1984. *Changed lives: Effects of the Perry Preschool Program on youths through age 19.* Ypsilanti, MI: High/Scope Press.

Berscheid, E.K. and Walster, E.H. 1971. A little bit about love. In T.L. Huston, Ed. *Foundations of interpersonal attraction.* New York: Academic Press.

———. 1978. Interpersonal attraction, 2nd ed. Reading, MA: Addison-Wesley.

Bersh, P.J. 1951. The influence of two variables upon the establishment of a secondary reinforcer for operant responses. *Journal of Experimental Psychology* 41: 62–73.

Bertenthal, B.I., Proffitt, D.R., and Cutting, J.E. 1984. Infant sensitivity to figural coherence in biomechanical motions. *Journal of Experimental Child Psychology* 37: 213–30.

Beutler, L.E., Crago, M., and Arizmendi, T.G. 1986. Therapist variables in psychotherapy process and outcome. In *Handbook of psychotherapy and behavior change*, 3rd ed., S.L. Garfield and A.E. Bergin, eds. New York: Wiley.

Bexton, W.H., Heron, W., and Scott, T.H. 1954. Effects of decreased variation in the sensory environment. *Canadian Journal of Psychology* 8: 70–76.

Biederman, I. 1972. Perceiving real-world scenes. *Science* 177: 77–80.

———. 1981. On the semantics of a glance at a scene. In *Perceptual organization*, M. Kubovy and J. Pomerantz, eds. Hillsdale, NJ: Erlbaum.

———. 1987. Recognition-by-components: A theory of human image understanding. *Psychological Review* 94: 115–47.

———. 1990. Higher-level vision. In *Visual cognition and action*, vol. 2, D.N. Osherson, S.M. Kosslyn, and J.M. Hollerbach, eds. Cambridge, MA: MIT Press.

Bijou, S. 1976. *Child development: The basic stage of early childhood.* Englewood Cliffs, NJ: Prentice Hall.

Billings, A.G., and Moos, R.H. 1982. Social support and functioning among community and clinical groups: A panel study. *Journal of Behavioral Medicine* 5: 295–311.

Binet, A. 1911. *Les idees modernes sur les enfants.* Paris: Flammarion.

Binet, A., and Simon, T. 1905. New methods for the diagnosis of the intellectual level of subnormals. *Annals of Psychology* 11: 191–244.

Birren, J., Cunningham, W., and Yamamoto, K. 1983. Psychology of adult development and aging. *Annual Review of Psychology* 34: 543–76.

Birren, J.E., and Schaie, W.K., eds. 1985. *Handbook of the psychology of aging*, 2nd ed. New York: Van Nostrand Reinhold.

Bjork, E.L., and Cummings, E.M. 1984. Infant search errors: Stage of concept development or stage of memory development. *Memory and Cognition* 12: 1–19.

Bjork, R.A., and Jongeward, R.H., Jr. 1975. Rehearsal and mere rehearsal. Cited in Bjork, R. A. Short-term storage: The ordered output of a central processor. In *Cognitive theory*, Vol. 1., F. Restle, R.M. Shiffrin, N.J. Castellan, H.R. Lindman, and D.B. Pisoni, eds. New York: Wiley.

Blackburn, R.T., Pellino, G.R., Boberg, A., and O'Connell, C. 1980. Are instructional improvement programs off target? *Current Issues in Higher Education* 1: 32–48.

Blair, B.G., and Kendall, H.W. 1990. Accidental nuclear war. *Scientific American* 263: 53–59.

Blakemore, C. 1977. *Mechanics of the mind.* Cambridge, England: Cambridge University Press.

Blakemore, C., and Cooper, G.F. 1970. Development of the brain depends on the visual environment. *Nature* 228: 477–78.

Blakeslee, T.R. 1980. *The right brain.* New York: PBJ Books.

Bliss, E.L. 1986. *Multiple personality, allied disorders, and hypnosis.* New York: Oxford University Press.

Block, J.H. 1980. Another look at sex differentiation in the socialization behavior of mothers and fathers. In *Psychology of women: Future directions of research*, F. Denmark and J. Sherman, eds. New York: Psychological Dimensions.

———. 1983. Differential premises arising from differential socialization of the sexes: Some conjectures. *Child Development* 54: 1335–54.

Bloom, B., Hodges, W., and Caldwell, R. 1982. A preventative program for the newly separated: Initial evaluation. *American Journal of Community Psychology* 10: 251–264.

Bloom, B.L., Asher, S.J., and White, S.W. 1978. Marital disruption as a stressor: A review and analysis. *Psychological Bulletin* 85: 867–94.

Bloom, B.S. 1964. Stability and change in human characteristics. New York: Wiley.

Boden, M.A. 1977. *Artificial intelligence and natural man.* New York: Basic Books.

Bohannon, J.N., III, and Stanowicz, L. 1988. The issue of negative evidence: Adult responses to children's language errors. *Developmental Psychology* 24: 684–89.

Bolles, R.C., and Fanselow, M.S. 1982. Endorphins and behavior. *Annual Review of Psychology* 33: 87–102.

Boring, E.G. 1950. *A history of experimental psychology*, 2nd ed. New York: Appleton-Century Crofts.

Bornstein, M.H., and Lamb, M.E., eds. 1988. *Developmental psychology: An advanced textbook*, 2nd ed. Hillsdale, NJ: Erlbaum.

Bornstein, R.F., Leone, D.R., and Galley, D.J. 1987. The generalizability of subliminal mere exposure effects: Influence of stimuli perceived without awareness on social behavior. *Journal of Personality and Social Psychology* 53: 1070–79.

Bornstein, M.H., and Sigman, M.D. 1986. Continuity in mental development from infancy. *Child Development* 57: 251–74.

Bossard, J.H.S. 1932. Residential propinquity as a factor in mate selection. *American Journal of Sociobiology* 38: 219–24.

Bouchard, T.J., and McGue, M. 1981. Familial studies of intelligence: A review. *Science* 212: 1055–58.

Bouchard, T.J., and McGue, M. 1990. Genetic and rearing environmental influences on personality: An analysis of adopted twins reared apart. *Journal of Personality* 58: 263–92.

Bovard, E. 1959. The effects of social stimuli on the response to stress. *Psychological Review* 66: 267–77.

Bower, G.H. 1972. Mental imagery and associative learning. In *Cognition in learning and memory*, L.W. Gregg, ed. New York: Wiley.

———. 1981. Mood and memory. *American psychologist* 36: 129–48.

Bower, G.H., Clark, M.C., Lesgold, A.M., and Winzenz, D. 1969. Hierarchical retrieval schemes in recall of categorized word lists. *Journal of Verbal Learning and Verbal Behavior*, 8, 323–43.

Bower, G.H., Black, J.B., and Turner, T.J. 1979. Scripts in memory for text. *Cognitive Psychology* 11: 177–220.

Bower, T.G.R. 1979. *Human development.* San Francisco: Freeman.

Bower, T.G.R., Broughton, J.M., and Moore, M.K. 1970. Infant responses to approaching objects: An indicator of response to distal variables. *Perception and Psychophysics* 9: 193–96.

Bowerman, M. 1974. Learning the structure of causative verbs. *Papers and reports on child language development.* Stanford, CA: Stanford University Press.

Bowers, D., and Heilman, K.M. 1981. A dissociation between the processing of affective and nonaffective faces. Paper presented at the meeting of the International Neuropsychological Society, Atlanta.

Bowers, K.S. 1983. *Hypnosis for the seriously curious.* New York: Norton.

Bowman, M.L. 1989. Testing individual differences in ancient China. *American Psychologist* 44: 576–78.

Bowlby, J. 1969. *Attachment.* New York: Basic Books.

———. 1973. *Separation and loss.* New York: Basic Books.

Boyd, J.H., and Weissman, M.M. 1981. Epidemiology of affective disorders. *Archives of General Psychiatry* 38: 1039–46.

Boynton, R.M. 1988. Color vision. *Annual Review of Psychology* 39: 69–100.

Bradley, D.R., Dumais, S.T., and Petry, H.M. 1976. Reply to Cavonis. *Nature* 261: 77–78.

Brady, J.V. 1961. Motivational-emotional factors and intracranial self-stimulation. In *Electrical stimulation of the brain*, D.E. Sheer, ed. Austin: University of Texas Press.

Bransford, J.D., and Johnson, M.K. 1973. Considerations of some problems of comprehension. In *Visual information processing*, W.G. Chase, ed. New York: Academic Press.

Bransford, J.D., Sherwood, R.D., and Sturdevant, T. 1987. Teaching thinking and problem solving. In *Teaching thinking skills*, J.B. Baron and R.J. Sternberg, eds. New York: Freeman.

Bransford, J.D., and Stein, B.S. 1984. The IDEAL problem solver: A guide for improving thinking, learning, and creativity. New York: Freeman.

Braun, J.J., and Nowlis, G.H. 1989. Neurological foundation of learned appetitive aversions. *Nutrition* 5: 121–27.

Bray, G.A. 1969. Effect of caloric restriction on energy expenditure in obese patients. *Lancet* 2: 397–98.

Brazelton, T.B., and Yogman, M.W. Eds. 1986. *Affective development in infancy.* Norwood, NJ: Ablex.

Brechner, K.C. 1977. An experimental analysis of social traps. *Journal of Experimental Social Psychology* 13: 552–64.

Bregman, E.O. 1934. An attempt to modify the emotional attitudes of infants by the conditioned response technique. *Journal of Genetic Psychology* 45, 169–98.

Brehm, S.S. 1985. *Intimate relationships.* New York: Random House.

Bremer, J. 1959. *Assexualisation: A Follow-up of 244 Cases.* New York: Macmillan.

Brett, J.M. 1980. The effect of job transfer on employees and their families. In *Current concerns in occupational stress,* C.L. Cooper and R. Payne, eds. New York: Wiley.

Breuer, J., and Freud, S. [1895] 1950. *Studies in hysteria.* A.A. Brill, trans. New York: Nervous and Mental Disorders Publishing Co.

Brewer, M.B., and Lui, L.N. 1989. The primacy of age and sex in the structure of person categories. *Social Cognition* 7: 262–72.

Brierley, J.B. 1977. The neuropathology of amnesia states. In *Amnesia,* 2nd ed., C.W.M. Whitty and O.L. Zangwill, eds. New York: Appleton-Century-Crofts.

Bridges, K.M.B. 1932. Emotional development in early infancy. *Child Development* 3: 324–41.

Briggs, S.R. 1991. Personality measurement. In *Personality: Contemporary theory and research,* V.J. Derlega, B.A. Winstead, and W.H. Jones, eds. Chicago: Nelson-Hall.

Briggs, S.R., Cheek, J.M., and Jones, W.H. 1986. Introduction. In *Shyness: Perspectives on research and treatment,* W.H. Jones, J.M. Cheek, and S.R. Briggs, eds. New York: Plenum Press.

Brigham, J.C. 1986. *Social psychology.* Boston: Little, Brown, and Co.

Brigham, J.C., and Malpass, R.S. 1985. The role of experience and contact in the recognition of faces of own- and other-race persons. *Journal of Social Issues* 41: 139–56.

Brindley, G.S. 1988. Blindness, neural prosthesis. In *Sensory systems I: Readings from the encyclopedia of neuroscience.* Boston: Birkhauser.

Britt, S.H. 1958. Subliminal advertising: Psychologist questions experimental design. *Advertising Agency* 51: 14–16.

Broad, W.J. 1985. March 12. Subtle analogies found at the core of Edison's genius. *The New York Times.*

Broadbent, D. 1982. Task combination and selective intake of information. *Acta Psychologica* 50: 253–90.

Brody, E.B., and Brody, N. 1976. *Intelligence: Nature, determinants, and consequences.* New York: Academic Press.

Brody, J.E. 1990. Personal health: An internal hearing aid. *The New York Times,* September 20.

Brody, N. 1983. *Human Motivation: Commentary on goal-directed action.* New York: Academic Press.

Brogden, W.J. 1939. Sensory preconditioning. *Journal of Experimental Psychology* 25: 323–32.

Bromet, E. 1980. *Three Mile Island: Mental health findings.* Pittsburgh: Western Psychiatric Institute and Clinic and the University of Pittsburgh.

Bronfenbrenner, U. 1975. Is early intervention

effective? In *The family as educator,* H.J. Leichter, ed. New York: Teachers College Press.

Brooks-Gunn, J., Petersen, A.C., and Eichorn, D. 1985. Time of maturation and psychosocial functioning in adolescence. *Journal of Youth and Adolescence* 14: 3–4.

Browman, C.P., Sampson, M.G., Gujavarty, K.S., and Mitler, M.M. 1982. The drowsy crowd. *Psychology Today,* August, 35–38.

Brown, A.L., Campione, J.C., and Barclay, C.R. 1979. Training self-checking routines for estimating test readiness: Generalization from list learning to prose recall. *Child Development* 50: 501–12.

Brown, E.L., and Deffenbacher, K. 1979. *Perception and the senses.* New York: Oxford.

Brown, J. 1977. *Mind-brain and consciousness.* New York: Academic Press.

Brown, J.K. 1969. Adolescent initiation rites among preliterate people. In *Studies in adolescence,* 2nd ed., R.E. Grinder, ed. New York: Macmillan.

Brown, L.R., McGrath, P.L., and Stokes, B. 1976. The population problem in 22 dimensions. *The Futurist,* October, pp. 238–245.

Brown, P., Salazar, A.M., Gibbs, C.J., Jr., and Gajdusek, D.C. 1982. Alzheimer's disease and transmissible virus dementia (Crentzfeldt-Jakob disease). *Annals of the New York Academy of Sciences* 396: 131–43.

Brown, R. 1958. *Words and things.* New York: Free Press.

———. 1973. *A first language: The early stages.* Cambridge: Harvard University Press.

Brown, R., and Hanlon, C. 1970. Derivational complexity and order of acquisition in child's speech. In *Cognition and the development of language,* J.R. Hayes, ed. New York: Wiley.

Brown, R., and Kulik, J. 1971. Flashbulb memories. *Cognition* 5: 73–99.

Brown, R.W., and McNeill, D. 1966. The tip-of-the-tongue phenomenon. *Journal of Verbal Learning and Verbal Behavior* 5: 325–37.

Browne, M.W. 1988. Methematicians turn to prose in an effort to remember pi. *New York Times,* July 5.

Bruce, V., and Green, P.R. 1990. *Visual perception: Physiology, psychology, and ecology.* Hove and London, UK: Erlbaum.

Brudny, J., Grynbaum, B.B., and Korein, J. 1974. Spasmodic torticollis: Treatment by biofeedback of the EMG. *Archives of Physical and Medical Rehabilitation* 55: 403–8.

Bryden, M.P. 1981. *Laterality: Functional asymmetry in the intact brain.* New York: Academic Press.

Buchanan, P.J. 1987. Whom will history indict? *Newsweek,* July 13, p. 21.

Buchsbaum, M.S., and Haier, R.J. 1983. Psychopathology: Biological approaches. *Annual Review of Psychology* 34: 401–30.

Buckhout, R. 1974. Eyewitness testimony. *Scientific American* 231: 23–31.

Buckwald, S., Zoren, W.A., and Egan, E.A. 1984. Mortality and follow-up data for neonates weighing 500 to 800 g at birth. *American Journal of Diseases of Children* 138: 779–82.

Budzynski, T.H., Stoyva, J.M., Adler, C.S., and Mullaney, D.J. 1974. EMG biofeedback and tension headaches #19. In *Biofeedback and self-control 1973,* N.E. Miller, T.X. Barber, L.V. DiCara, J. Kamiya, D. Shapiro, and J. Stoyva, eds. Chicago: Aldine.

Bugliosi, V. (with Gentry, C.). 1974. *Helter skelter.* New York: Bantam.

Burger, J.M., and Burns, L. 1990. The illusion of unique invulnerability and the use of effective contraception. *Personality and Social Psychology Bulletin* 14, 264–70.

Burger, J.M., and Petty, R.E. 1981. The low-ball compliance technique: Task or person commitment? *Journal of Personality and Social Psychology* 40: 492–500.

Busch, C.M., Schroeder, D.H., and Biersner, R.J. 1982. Personality attributes associated with personal and social adjustment in small, isolated groups. Paper presented at the 53rd annual convention of the Eastern Psychological Association, Baltimore.

Bushnell, E.W., Shaw, L., and Strauss, D. 1985. Relationship between visual and tactual exploration by 6-month-olds. *Developmental Psychology* 21: 591–600.

Buss, A.M., and Plomin, R. 1975. *A temperamental theory of personality development.* New York: Wiley-Interscience.

Buss, D.M. 1985. Human mate selection. *American Scientist* 73: 47–51.

———. 1987. Selection, evocation and manipulation. *Journal of Personality and Social Psychology* 53: 1214–1221.

———. 1989. Sex differences in human mate preference: Evolutionary hypothesis tested in 37 cultures. *Behavioral and Brain Sciences.* 12: 1–49.

———. 1989. Conflict between the sexes: Strategic interference and the evocation of anger and upset. *Journal of Personality and Social Psychology* 56: 735–47.

———. 1990. Toward a biologically informed psychology of personality. *Journal of Personality* 58: 1–16.

Buswell, G.T. 1922. Fundamental reading habits: A study of their development. *Supplementary Educational Monographs,* No. 21.

Butler, R.A., and Harlow, H.F. 1954. Persistence of visual exploration in monkeys. *Journal of Comparative and Physiological Psychology* 47: 258–63.

Butterfield, E.C., Nelson, T.O., and Peck, V. 1988. Developmental aspects of the feeling of knowing. *Developmental Psychology* 24: 654–63.

Byrne, D. 1971. *The attraction paradigm.* NY: Academic Press.

Byrne, D. 1983. Sex without contraception. In *Adolescents, sex, and contraception,* D. Byrne and W.A. Fisher, eds. Hillsdale, NJ.: Erlbaum.

Cagas, C.R., and Riley, H.D., Jr. 1970. Age of menarche in girls in a west-south-central community. *American Journal of Diseases of Children* 120: 303–8.

Cain, W.S. 1982. Odor identification by males and females: Predictions vs. performance. *Chemical Senses* 7: 129–42.

———. 1988. Olfaction. In *Steven's handbook of experimental psychology,* vol. 1, R.C. Atkinson, R.J. Herrnstein, G. Lindzey, and R.D. Luce, eds. New York: Wiley.

Calhoun, J.B. 1962. Population density and social pathology. *Scientific American* 206: 139–48.

Cameron, N. 1963. *Personality development and psychopathology: A dynamic approach.* Boston: Houghton Mifflin.

Campbell, D., Sanderson, R.E., and Laverty, S.G. 1964. Characteristics of a conditioned response in human subjects during extinction trials following a single traumatic conditioning trial. *Journal of Abnormal and Social Psychology* 68: 627–39.

Campbell, F.W., and Wurtz, R. 1978. Saccadic omission: Why we do not see a grey-out during a saccadic eye movement *Vision Research* 18: 1297–1303.

Campbell, H. 1896. Morbid shyness. *The British Medical Journal* 2: 805–7.

Campbell, J.I.D., and Charness, N. 1990. Age-related declines in working-memory skills: Evidence from a complex calculation task. *Developmental Psychology* 26: 879–88.

Campione, J.C., Brown, A.L., and Ferrara, R.A. 1982. Mental retardation and intelligence. In *Handbook of human intelligence*, R.J. Sternberg, ed. Cambridge: Cambridge University Press.

Campos, J.J., Hiatt, S., Ramsay, D., Henderson, C., and Svejda, M. 1978. The emergence of fear on the visual cliff. In *The development of affect*, M. Lewis and L.A. Rosenblum, eds. New York: Plenum.

Cerella, J., and Fozard, J.L. 1984. Lexical access and age. *Developmental Psychology* 20: 235–43.

Cannon, W.B. 1927. The James-Lange theory of emotions: A critical examination and the alternative theory. *American Journal of Psychology* 39: 106–24.

Cannon, W.B. 1929. *Bodily changes in pain, hunger, fear, and rage.* New York: Branford.

———. 1942. "Voodoo" death. *American Anthropologist* 44: 169–81.

Cannon, W.B., and Washburn, A.L. 1912. An explanation of hunger. *American Journal of Physiology* 29: 441–54.

Cantor, N., and Kihlstrom, K. 1987. *Personality and social intelligence.* New York: Prentice Hall.

Cantril, H. 1940. *The invasion from Mars.* Princeton, NJ: Princeton University Press.

Capaldi, E.J., and Miller, D.J. 1988. Counting in rats: Its functional significance and the independent cognitive processes that constitute it. *Journal of Experimental Psychology: Animal Behavior Processes* 14: 3–17.

Caparulo, B., and Zigler, E. 1983. The effects of mainstreaming on success and expectancy and imitation in mildly retarded children. *Peabody Journal of Education* 60: 85–98.

Caplan, P.J., MacPherson, G.M., and Tobin, P. 1985. Do sex-related differences in spatial abilities exist? A multilevel critique with new data. *American Psychologist* 40: 786–99.

Caporael, L.R. 1989. Selfishness examined: Cooperation in the absence of egotistic incentives. *Behavioral and Brain Sciences* 12: 683–705.

Carlson, N.R. 1988. *Foundations of physiological psychology.* Boston: Allyn & Bacon.

Carlson, R. 1984. What's social about social psychology? Where's the person in personality research? *Journal of Personality and Social Psychology* 35: 1055–74.

Carpenter, G. 1975. Mother's face and the newborn. In *Child alive*, R. Lewin, ed. London: Temple Smith.

Carpenter, P.A., and Just, M.A. 1983. What your eyes do while your mind is reading. In *Eye movements in reading*, K. Rayner, ed. New York: Academic Press.

Carpenter, P.A., and Just, M.A. 1986. Spatial ability: An information processing approach

to psychometrics. In *Advances in the psychology of human intelligence*, vol. 3, R.J. Sternberg, ed. Hillsdale, NJ: Erlbaum.

Carr, D.B., Bullen, B.A., Skrinar, G.S., Arnold, M.A., Rosenblatt, M., Beitins, I.Z., Martin, J.B., and McArthur, J.W. 1981. Physical conditioning facilitates the exercise-induced secretion of beta-endorphin and beta-lipotropin. *The New England Journal of Medicine* 305: 560–62.

Carr, K.D., and Coons, E.E. 1982. Rats self-administered nonrewarding brain stimulation to ameliorate aversion. *Science* 215: 1516–17.

Carroll, D.W. 1986. *Psychology of language.* Monterey, CA: Brooks/Cole.

Carroll, J.B. 1982. The measurement of intelligence. In *Handbook of human intelligence*, R.J. Sternberg, ed. Cambridge: Cambridge University Press.

Carrington, P., Collins, G.H., Benson, H., Robinson, H., Wood, L.W., Lehrer, P.M., Woolfolk, R.L., and Cole, J.W. 1980. The use of meditation-relaxation techniques for the management of stress in a working population. *Journal of Occupational Medicine* 22: 221–31.

Cartarette, E.C., and Friedman, M.P., eds. 1974–1978. *Handbook of perception*, vols. 2, 4, 5, 6a. New York: Academic Press.

Carver, C.S., and Scheier, M.F. 1981. *Attention and self-regulation: A control-theory approach to human behavior.* New York: Springer-Verlag.

Carver, C.S., and Scheier, M.F. 1988. *Perspectives in Personality.* Boston, MA: Allyn and Bacon.

Carver, R.P. 1987. *Reading comprehension and reading theory.* Springfield, IL: Charles C. Thomas.

Cautela, J.R., and Kearney, A.J. 1986. *The covert conditioning handbook.* New York: Springer.

Cazden, C. 1965. Environmental assistance to the child's acquisition of grammar. Unpublished doctoral dissertation, Graduate School of Education, Harvard University.

Cash, T.F. and Janda, L.H. 1984. The eye of the beholder. *Psychology Today*, December, 46–52.

Caspi, A., Bem, D.J., and Elder, G.H., Jr. 1989. Continuities and consequences of interactional styles across the life course. *Journal of Personality* 57: 375–406.

Caspi, A., and Herbener, E.S. 1990. Continuity and change: Assortative marriage and the consistency of personality in adulthood. *Journal of Personality and Social Psychology* 58: 250–58.

Cass, R.C., and Edney, J.J. 1978. The commons dilemma: A simulation testing the effects of resource visibility and territorial division. *Human Ecology* 6: 387–95.

Cattell, R.B. 1956. Validation and interpretation of the 16 P.F. questionnaire. *Journal of Clinical Psychology* 12: 205–14.

Cattell, R.B. 1965. *The scientific analysis of personality.* Baltimore, MD: Penguin.

Chaiken, S., Liberman, A., and Eagly, A.H. 1989. Heuristic and systematic information processing within and beyond the persuasion context. In *Unintended thought*, J.S. Uleman and J.A. Bargh, eds. New York: Guilford Press.

Chapman, L.J., and Chapman, J.P. 1973. *Disordered thought in schizophrenia.* New York: Appleton-Century-Crofts.

Chase, M.H. 1981. The dreamer's paralysis. *Psychology Today*, November, 108.

Chase, M.H., and Morales, F.R. 1990. The atonia and myoclonia of active (REM) sleep. *Annual Review of Psychology* 41: 557–84.

Chase, T. 1987. *When Rabbit Howls.* New York: E. P. Dutton.

Chase, W.G. 1983. Spatial representations of taxi drivers. In *Acquisition of symbolic skills*, D.R. Rogers and J.H. Slobada, eds. New York: Plenum.

Chase, W.G., and Ericsson, K.A. 1982. Skill and working memory. In *The psychology of learning and motivation*, vol. 16, G. Bower, ed. New York: Academic Press.

Chase, W.G., and Simon, H.A. 1973. The mind's eye in chess. In *Visual information processing*, W.G. Chase, ed. New York: Academic Press.

ChaZanna, M.P., and Rempel, J.K. 1988. Attitudes: A new look at an old concept. In *The Social Psychology of Knowledge*, D. Bar-Tal and A.W. Kruglanski, eds. New York: Cambridge University Press.

Cheek, J.M. 1982. Aggregation, moderator variables, and the validity of personality tests: A peer-rating study. *Journal of Personality and Social Psychology* 43: 1254–69.

Cheng, P.W., and Novick, L.R. 1990. A probabilistic contrast model of causal induction. *Journal of Personality and Social Psychology* 58: 545–68.

Cherry, E.C. 1953. Some experiments on the recognition of speech with one and with two ears. *Journal of the Acoustical Society of America* 25: 975–79.

Chi, M.T.H. 1987. Representing knowledge and metaknowledge: Implications for interpreting metamemory research. In *Metacognition, motivation and understanding*, F.E. Weinert and R.H. Kluwe, eds. Hillsdale, NJ: Erlbaum.

Chi, M.T.H., Feltovich, P.J., and Glasser, R. 1981. Categorization and representation of physics problems by experts and novices. *Cognitive Science* 5: 121–25.

Chief Seattle. 1854/1977. Chief Seattle's Message. In Cooney, R. and Michalowski, H. *The power of the people: Active nonviolence in the United States.* Culver City, CA: Peace Press.

Child, I.L. 1950. The relation of somatotype to self-rating on Sheldon's temperamental traits. *Journal of Personality* 18: 440–53.

Chodoff, P. 1970. The German concentration camp as a psychological stress. *Archives of General Psychiatry* 22: 78–87.

Chollar, S. 1989. Conversations with the dolphins. *Psychology Today*, April, pp. 52–57.

Chomsky, N. 1959. A review of B.F. Skinner's *Verbal Behavior. Language* 35: 26–58.

———. 1972. *Language and mind*, 2nd ed. New York: Harcourt Brace Jovanovich.

Chorover, S.L. 1979. *From genesis to genocide.* Cambridge, MA: The MIT Press.

Christian, J.J. 1963. Endocrine adaptive mechanisms and the physiologic regulation of population growth. In *Physiological memmalogy, 1*, M.V. Meyer and R. vanGelder, eds. New York: Academic Press.

Christianson, S.A. 1989. Flashbulb memories: Special, but not so special. *Memory & Cognition* 17: 435–43.

Christman, R.J. 1979. *Sensory experience*, 2nd ed. New York: Harper and Row.

Churchland, P.M. 1990. Cognitive activity in artificial neural networks. In *Thinking: An invitation to cognitive science*, D.N. Osherson and E.E. Smith, eds. Cambridge, MA: MIT Press.

Cialdini, R.B. 1988. *Influence: Science and practice*, 2nd ed. Glenview, IL.: Scott, Foresman/ Little, Brown.

Cialdini, R.B., Baumann, D.J., and Kenrick, D.T. 1981. Insights from sadness: A three-step model of the development of altruism as hedonism. *Developmental Review* 1: 207–23.

Cialdini, R.B., Cacioppo, J.T., Bassett, R., and Miller, J.A. 1978. Lowball procedure for producing compliance: Commitment then cost. *Journal of Personality and Social Psychology* 36: 463–76.

Cialdini, R.B., Darby, B.L., and Vincent, J.E. 1973. Transgression and altruism: A case of hedonism. *Journal of Experimental Social Psychology* 9: 502–16.

Cialdini, R.B., Reno, R.R., and Kallgren, C.A. 1990. A focus theory of normative conduct: Recycling the concept of norms to reduce littering in public places. *Journal of Personality and Social Psychology* 58: 1015–26.

Cialdini, R.B., and Richardson, K.D. 1980. Two indirect tactics of image management: Basking and blasting. *Journal of Personality and Social Psychology* 39: 406–15.

Cialdini, R.B., Schaller, M., Houlihan, D., Arps, K., Fultz, J., and Beaman, A.L. 1987. Empathy-based helping: Is it selflessly or selfishly motivated? *Journal of Personality and Social Psychology* 52: 749–58.

Cimbalo, R.S., Faling, V., and Mousaw, R. 1976. The course of love: A cross-sectional design. *Psychological Reports* 38: 1292–94.

Claparède, E. 1911. Recognition et moiite. *Archives de Psychologie Geneve* 11: 79–90.

Clark, E.V. 1977. From gesture to word: On the natural history of deixis in language acquisition. In *Human growth and development*, J.S. Bruner and A. Garton, eds. Oxford, UK: Oxford University Press.

Clark, H.H., and Clark, E.V. 1977. *Psychology and language*. New York: Harcourt Brace Jovanovich.

Clark, L.A., and Watson, D. 1988. Mood and the mundane: Relations between daily life events and self-reported mood. *Journal of Personality and Social Psychology* 54: 296–308.

Clark, M.S., Mills, J., and Powell, M.C. 1986. Keeping track of needs in communal and exchange relationships. *Journal of Personality and Social Psychology* 51: 333–38.

Clark, R.D. III, and Word, L.E. 1972. Why don't bystanders help? Because of ambiguity? *Journal of Personality and Social Psychology* 23: 392–400.

Clarke, A.M., and Clarke, A.D.B. 1976. The formative years? In *Early experience: Myth and evidence*, A.M. Clarke and A.D.B. Clarke, eds. New York: Free Press.

Clarke-Stewart, K.A. 1978. And daddy makes three: The father's impact on mother and young child. *Child Development* 49: 466–78.

Clayton, K.N. 1964. T-maze choice: Learning as a joint function of the reward magnitudes of the alternatives. *Journal of Comparative and Physiological Psychology* 58: 333–38.

Clifford, M.M. and Walster, E.H. 1973. The effect of physical attractiveness on teacher expectation. *Sociology of Education* 46: 248–58.

Cofer, F., and Huston, A.C. 1986. Television violence and aggression: The debate continues. *Psychological Bulletin* 100: 364–71.

Cogan, R., Cogan, D., Waltz, W., and McCue, M. *Journal of Behavioral Medicine* 10: 139–44.

Cohn, J.F., and Tvonick, E.Z. 1987. Mother–infant face-to-face interaction. *Developmental Psychology* 23: 63–77.

Cohen, L.B., DeLoache, J.S., and Strauss, M.S. 1978. Infant visual perception. In *Handbook of infancy*, J. Osofsky, ed. New York: Wiley.

Cohen, N.J., and Corkin, S. *The amnesic patient H.M.: Learning and retention of a cognitive skill*. Paper presented at the Society for Neuroscience Convention, Los Angeles, May 1981.

Cohen, N.J., and Squire, L.R. 1980. Preserved learning and retention of pattern-analyzing skill in amnesia: Dissociation of knowing how and knowing that. *Science* 210: 207–10.

Cohen, R. 1987. Suddenly I'm the adult? *Psychology Today*, May, pp. 70–71.

Cohen, S. 1980. Coca paste and freebase: New fashions in cocaine use. *Drug Abuse and Alcoholism Newsletter* 9: 3.

Cohen, S., Evans, G.W., Krantz, D.S., Stokols, D., and Kelly, S. 1981. Aircraft noise and children: Longitudinal and cross-sectional evidence on adaptation to noise and the effectiveness of noise abatement. *Journal of Personality and Social Psychology* 40: 331–45.

Cohen, S., Glass, D.C., and Singer, J.E. 1973. Apartment noise, auditory discrimination, and reading ability in children. *Journal of Experimental Social Psychology* 9: 407–22.

Cohen, S., and Hoberman, H. 1983. Positive events and social supports as buffers of life change stress. *Journal of Applied Social Psychology* 13: 99–125.

Cohen, S., and Wills, T.A. 1985. Stress, social support, and the buffeting hypothesis. *Psychological Bulletin* 98: 310–57.

Colby, K.M., Weber, S., and Hilf, F.D. 1971. Artificial paranoia. *Artificial Intelligence* 2: 1–25.

Cole, M., and Cole, S.R. 1989. *The development of children*. New York: Scientific American Books.

Cole, R.A., and Jakimik, J. 1980. A model of speech perception. In *Perception and production of fluent speech*, R.A. Cole, ed. Hillsdale, NJ: Erlbaum.

Coleman, J.C. 1972. *Abnormal Psychology and Modern Life*, 4th ed. Glenview, IL: Scott, Foresman.

Coles, R., and Stokes, G. 1985. *Sex and the American teenager*. New York: Harper and Row.

Collins, E. 1987. Eyeing myopia: Research suggests how reading could lead to nearsightedness. *Scientific American* 257: 36.

Collins, W.A. 1990. Parent-child relationships in the transition to adolescence. In *From childhood to adolescence: A transitional period?*, R. Montemayor, G.R. Adams, and T.P. Gullotta, eds. Newbury Park, CA: Sage.

Coltheart, M. 1980. Iconic memory and visual persistence. *Perception and Psychophysics* 27: 183–228.

Colwill, R.M., and Rescorla, R.A. 1985. Postconditioning devaluation of a reinforcer affects instrumental responding. *Journal of Experimental Psychology: Animal Behavior Processes* 11: 120–32.

Cone, J.D., and Hayes, S.C. 1980. *Environmental problems/ Behavioral solutions*. Monterey, CA: Brooks/Cole.

Condon, R.G. 1987. *Inuit youth*. New Brunswick, NJ: Rutgers University Press.

Conger, J.J. 1977. *Adolescence and youth: Psychological development in a changing world*. New York: Harper and Row.

Conley, J.J. 1985. Longitudinal stability of personality traits: a multitrait-multimethod-multioccasion analysis. *Journal of Personality and Social Psychology* 49: 1266–82.

Cook, M., and Mineka, S. 1990. Selective associations in the observational conditioning of fear in Rhesus monkeys. *Journal of Experimental Psychology: Animal Behavior Processes* 16: 372–89.

Cooley, C.H. 1902. *Human nature and the social order*. New York: Scribner's.

Cooper, J.R., Bloom, F.E., and Roth, R.H. 1978. *The biochemical basis of neuropathology*. New York: Oxford University Press.

Cooper, L.A., and Shepard, R.N. 1984. Turning something over in the mind. *Scientific American* 251, December, 106–14.

Cooper, M.J., and Aygen, M.M. 1979. A relaxation technique in the management of hypercholesterolemia. *Journal of Human Stress* 5: 24–27.

Cooper, W.E. 1983. The perception of fluent speech. *Annals of the New York Academy of Sciences* 405: 48–63.

Corballis, M.C. 1980. Laterality and myth. *American Psychologist* 35: 284–95.

Corkin, S. 1980. A prospective study of cingulotomy. In *The psychosurgery debate*, E.S. Valenstein, ed. San Francisco: Freeman.

Corkin, S., Sullivan, E.V., Twitchell, T.E., and Grove, E. *The amnesic patient H.M.: Clinical observations and test performance 28 years after operation*. Paper presented at the Society for Neuroscience Convention, Los Angeles, May, 1981.

Coren, S. 1972. Subjective contours and apparent depth. *Psychological Review* 79: 359–67.

Coren, S., and Ward, L.M. 1989. *Sensation & Perception*, 3rd ed. San Diego: Harcourt Brace Jovanovich.

Cornell, J. 1984. Science vs. the paranormal. *Psychology Today*, March, 28–34.

Costa, P.T., Jr., and McCrae, R.R. 1988. Personality in adulthood: A six-year longitudinal study of self-reports and spouse ratings on the NEO Personality Inventory. *Journal of Personality and Social Psychology* 54: 853–63.

Costanzo, M., Archer, D., Aronson, E., and Pettigrew, T. 1986. Energy conservation behavior: The difficult path from information to action. *American Psychologist* 41: 521–28.

Cotman, C.W., and Iverson, L.L. 1987. Excitatory amino acids in the brain—focus on NMDA receptors. *Trends in Neuroscience* 10: 263–65.

Cowan, N. 1988. Evolving conceptions of memory storage, selective attention, and their mutual constraints within the human information-processing systems. *Psychological Bulletin* 104: 163–91.

Cowen, E.L., ed. 1982. Research in primary prevention in mental health. *American Journal of Community Psychology* 10: 3. (Special issue.)

Cowen, E.L. 1983. Primary prevention in mental health: Past, present, and future. In *Preventive psychology: Theory, research, and practice*, R.D. Felner, L.A. Jason, J.N. Moritsugu, and S.S. Farber, eds. New York: Pergamon Press.

Cowart, B.J. 1981. Development of taste perception in humans: Sensitivity and preference throughout the life span. *Psychological Bulletin* 90: 43–73.

Cox, V.D., Paulus, P.B., and McCain, G. 1984. Prison crowding research: The relevance of prison housing standards and a general approach regarding crowding phenomena. *American Psychologist* 39: 1148–60.

Coyne, J.C. 1976. Depression and the response of others. *Journal of Abnormal Psychology* 85: 186–93.

Craik, F.I.M., and Lockhart, R.S. 1972. Levels of processing: A framework for memory research. *Journal of Verbal Learning and Verbal Behavior* 11: 671–84.

Craik, F.I.M., and McDowd, J.M. 1987. Age differences in recall and recognition. *Journal of Experimental Psychology: Learning, Memory, and Cognition* 13: 474–79.

Craik, F.I.M., and Tulving, E. 1975. Depth of processing and the retention of words in episodic memory. *Journal of Experimental Psychology: General* 104: 269–94.

Craik, F.I.M., and Rabinowitz, J.C. 1984. Age differences in the acquisition and use of verbal information. In *Attention and performance,* vol. 10, J. Long and A. Baddeley, eds. Hillsdale, NJ: Erlbaum.

Craik, F.I.M., and Watkins, M.J. 1973. The role of rehearsal in short-term memory. *Journal of Verbal Learning and Verbal Behavior* 12: 599–607.

Crain, W.C. 1985. *Theories of development: Concepts and applications.* Englewood Cliffs, NJ: Prentice Hall.

Cramer, P. 1991. Anger and the use of defense mechanisms in college students. *Journal of Personality* 59: 39–55.

Crawford, L. 1987. Healthy denial. *Psychology Today,* October, p. 24.

Crespi, L.P. 1942. Quantitative variations of incentive and performance in the white rat. *American Journal of Psychology* 55: 467–517.

Crick, F., and Mitchison, G. 1983. The function of dream sleep. *Nature* 304: 111–14.

Crocker, J., and McGraw, K.M. 1984. What's good for the goose is not good for the gander: Solo status as an obstacle to occupational achievement for males and females. *American Behavioral Scientist* 27: 357–69.

Crocker, J., Voeckl, K., Testa, M., and Major, B. 1991. Social stigma: The affective consequences of attributional ambiguity. *Journal of Personality and Social Psychology* 60: 218–28.

Crockett, L.J., and Petersen, A.C. 1987. Pubertal status and psychosocial development: Findings from the Early Adolescence Study. In *Biological-psychosocial interactions in early adolescence: A life-span perspective,* R.M. Lerner & T.T. Foch, eds. Hillsdale, NJ: Erlbaum.

Cronbach, L.J. 1984. *Essentials of psychological testing,* 4th ed. New York: Harper and Row.

Cronin-Golomb, A. 1986. Subcortical transfer of cognitive information in subjects with complete forebrain commissurotomy. *Cortex* 22: 499–519.

Croyle, R.T., and Cooper, J. 1983. Dissonance arousal: Physiological evidence. *Journal of Personality and Social Psychology* 45: 782–91.

Crow, T.J. 1982. Two syndromes in schizophrenia? *Trends in Neurosciences* 5: 351–54.

Cunningham, M.R. 1979. Weather, mood, and helping behavior: Quasi-experiments with the sunshine Samaritan. *Journal of Personality and Social Psychology* 37, 1947–56.

———. 1986. Measuring the physical in physical attractiveness: Quasi-experiments on the sociobiology of female facial beauty. *Journal of Personality and Social Psychology* 50: 925–35.

Cunningham, M.R., Barbee, A.P., and Pike, C.L. 1990. what do women want? Facialmetric assessment of multiple motives in the perception of male facial physical attractiveness. *Journal of Personality and Social Psychology* 59: 61–72.

Curtis, P. 1979. Animals that care for people. *New York Times Magazine,* May 20, 110–13.

Curtiss, S. 1977. *Genie: A linguistic study of a modern-day "wild child."* New York: Academic Press.

———. 1980. *The critical period and feral children.* Paper presented at the First Annual Conference: Language/Reading: Comprehension and Products, San Diego State University.

Cutting, J.E. 1986. *Perception with an eye for motion.* Cambridge, MA: MIT Press.

Cutting, J.E., and Proffitt, D.R. 1981. Gait perception as an example of how we may perceive events. In *Perception and perceptual development,* vol. 2, H. Pick and R. Walk, eds. New York: Plenum.

———. 1982. The minimum principle and the perception of absolute, common, and relative motions. *Cognitive Psychology* 14: 211–46.

Cytryn, L., and Lourie, R.S. 1975. Mental retardation. In *Comprehensive textbook of psychiatry-II,* vol. 1, A.M. Freedman, H.I. Kaplan, and B.J. Sadock, eds. Baltimore: Williams and Williams.

Dabbs, J.M., Jr., Frady, R.L., Carr, T.S., and Besch, N.F. 1987. Saliva testosterone and criminal violence in young adult prison inmates. *Psychosomatic Medicine* 49: 174–82.

Dabbs, J.M., Jr., Ruback, R.B., Frady, R.L., Hopper, C.H. and Sgoutas, D.S. 1988. Saliva testosterone and criminal violence among women. *Personality and Individual Differences.* 9: 269–75.

Dacey, J.S. 1982. *Adolescents today,* 2nd ed. Glenview, IL: Scott, Foresman.

Dahlstrom, W.G., Welsh, G.S., and Dahlstrom, L.E. 1975. *An MMPI Handbook, Vol. II. Research developments and applications.* Minneapolis: University of Minnesota Press.

Dakof, G.A., and Taylor, S.E. 1990. Victim's perceptions of social support: What is helpful from whom? *Journal of Personality and Social Psychology* 58: 80–89.

Dale, A.J.D. 1975. Organic brain syndromes associated with infections. In *Comprehensive textbook of psychiatry—II,* vol. 1, A.M. Freedman, H.I. Kaplan, and B.J. Sadock, eds. Baltimore: Williams and Wilkins.

Dallas, M.E.W., and Baron, R.S. 1985. Do psychotherapists use a confirmatory strategy during interviewing? *Journal of Social and Clinical Psychology* 3: 106–22.

Daly, M., and Wilson, M. 1983. *Sex, evolution, and behavior.* N. Scituate, MA: Duxbury.

———. 1988. Evolutionary social psychology and family homicide. *Science* 242: 519–24.

———. 1988. *Homicide.* New York: Aldine deGruyter.

Damasio, A.R. 1985. Prosopagnosia. *Trends in Neuroscience* 8: 132–35.

Damasio, A.R., Damasio, H., and Van Hoesen, G. W. 1982. Prosopagnosia: Anatomic basis and behavioral mechanisms. *Neurology* 32: 331–41.

Damon, W., and Hart, D. 1982. The development of self understanding from infancy through adolescence. *Child Development* 53: 841–64.

Damrad-Frye, R., and Laird, J.D. 1989. The experience of boredom: The role of the self-perception of attention. *Journal of Personality and Social Psychology* 57: 315–24.

Darley, J.M., and Latane, B. 1968. Bystander intervention in emergencies: Diffusion of responsibility. *Journal of Personality and Social Psychology* 8: 377–83.

Darley, J.M., and Shultz, T.R. 1990. Moral rules: Their content and acquisition. *Annual Review of Psychology* 41: 525–56.

Darwin, C. [1839] 1909. *Voyage of the Beagle.* New York: P.F. Collier and Son.

Darwin, C. 1859. *The origin of species.* London: Murray.

———. 1871. *Descent of man.* London: Murray.

———. 1872. *The expression of emotions in man and animals.* London: Murray.

Darwin, C.J., Turvey, M.T., and Crowder, R.G. 1972. An auditory analogue of the Sperling partial report procedure: Evidence for brief auditory storage. *Cognitive Psychology* 3: 255–67.

Datan, N., Rodeheaver, D., & Hughes, F. 1987. Adult development and aging. *Annual Review of Psychology* 38: 153–80.

D'Atri, D.A. 1975. Psychophysiological responses to crowding. *Environment and behavior* 7: 237–51.

Davidson, J.M., Smith, E.R., Rodgers, C.H., and Bloch, G.J. 1968. relative thresholds of behavioral and somatic responses to estrogen. *Physiology and Behavior,* 227–29.

Davidson, R.J. 1991. Biological approaches to the study of personality. In *Personality: Contemporary theory and research,* V.J. Derlega, D.A. Winstead, and W.H. Jones, eds. Chicago: Nelson-Hall.

Davidson, R.J., and Fox, N.A. 1982. Asymmetrical brain activity discriminates between positive versus negative affective stimuli in human infants. *Science* 218: 1235–37.

Davis, M.H., and Franzoi, S.L. 1991. Self-awareness and self-consciousness. In *Personality: Contemporary theory and research,* V.J. Derlega, B.A. Winstead, and W.H. Jones, eds. Chicago: Nelson-Hall.

Davis, M.H., and Stephan, W.G. 1980. Attributions for exam performance. *Journal of Applied Social Psychology* 10: 235–48.

Davis, P.H., and Osherson, A. 1977. The current treatment of a multiple-personality woman and her son. *American Journal of Psychotherapy* 31: 504–15.

Davison, G.C., and Neale, J.M. 1982. *Abnormal Psychology,* 3rd ed. New York: Wiley.

Dawes, R.M. 1983. Trends based on cotton candy correlations. *Behavioral and Brain Sciences* 6: 287–88.

Dawkins, R. 1986. *The blind watchmaker.* New York: Norton.

Dean, L.M., Willis, F.N., and Hewitt, J. 1975. Initial interaction distance among individuals equal and unequal in military rank. *Journal of Personality & Social Psychology* 32: 294–99.

DeAraujo, G., van Arsdel, P.P., Holmes,

T.H., and Dudley, D.L. 1973. Life change, coping ability, and chronic intrinsic asthma. *Journal of Psychosomatic Research* 17: 359–63.

Deci, E.L. 1975. *Intrinsic motivation.* New York: Plenum.

DeFries, J.C., Kuse, A.R., and Vandenberg, S.G. 1979. Genetic correlations, environmental correlations and behavior. In *Theoretical advances in behavior genetics,* J.R. Royce, ed. Alphen aan den Rijn, Netherlands: Sijhoff Noordhoff International.

DeFries, J.C., Johnson, R.C., Kuse, A.R., McClearn, G.E., Polvina, J., Vandenberg, S.G., and Wilson, J.R. 1979. Familial resemblance for specific cognitive abilities. *Behavior Genetics* 9: 23–43.

DeGroot, A.D. 1966. Perception and memory versus thinking. In *Problem solving,* B. Kleinmuntz, ed. New York: Wiley.

DeKosky, S., Heilman, K.M., Bowers, D., and Valenstein, E. 1980. Recognition and discrimination of emotional faces and pictures. *Brain and Language* 9: 206–14.

Delgado, J.M.R. 1969. *Physical control of the mind: Toward a psychocivilized society.* New York: Harper and Row.

DeLongis, A., Coyne, J.C., Dakof, G., Folkman, S., and Lazarus, R.S. 1982. Relationship of daily hassles, uplifts, and major life events to health status. *Health psychology* 1: 119–36.

DeLongis, A., Folkman, S., and Lazarus, R.S. 1987. The impact of daily stress on health and mood: Psychological and social resources as mediators. *Journal of Personality and Social Psychology* 54: 486–95.

Dember, W.N., and Bagwell, M. 1985. A history of perception. In *Topics in the history of psychology,* vol. I, G.A. Kimble and K. Schlesinger, eds. Hillsdale, NJ: Erlbaum.

Dement, W.C. 1960. The effect of dream deprivation. *Science* 131: 1705–7.

———. 1976. Daytime sleepiness and sleep "attacks." In *Narcolepsy,* C. Guilleminault, W.C. Dement, and P. Passouant, eds. New York: Spectrum.

———. 1978. *Some must watch while some must sleep.* New York: Norton.

Demetras, M., Post, K., and Snow, C. 1986. Feedback to first language learners: The role of repetitions and clarification questions. *Journal of Child Language* 13: 275–92.

Denney, N.W. 1982. Aging and cognitive change. In *Handbook of developmental psychology,* B.B. Wolman, ed. Englewood Cliffs, NJ: Prentice Hall.

Denny, M.R. 1980. *Comparative psychology: An evolutionary analysis of animal behavior.* New York: John Wiley and Sons.

DeSilva, P., Rachman, S., and Seligman, M.E.P. 1977. Prepared phobias and obsessions: Therapeutic outcome. *Behaviour Research and Therapy* 15: 65–77.

DeSoto, C.B., Hamilton, M.M., and Taylor, R.B. 1985. Words, people, and implicit personality theory. *Social Cognition* 3: 369–82.

Deutsch, J.A., ed. 1983. *The physiological basis of memory,* 2nd ed. Orlando, FL: Academic Press.

Deutsch, J.A., Puerto, A., and Wang, M.L. 1978. The stomach signals satiety. *Science* 201: 165–67.

Deutsch, M. 1973. *The resolution of conflict.* New Haven, CT: Yale University Press.

———. 1986. Strategies for inducing cooperation. In *Psychology and the prevention of nuclear*

war, R.K. White, ed. New York: New York University Press.

Deutsch, M., and Gerard, M. B. 1955. A study of normative and social influences upon individual judgment. *Journal of Abnormal and Social Psychology* 51: 629–36.

DeValois, R.L., and DeValois, K.K. 1975. Neural coding of color. In *Handbook of perception,* vol. 5., E.C. Carterette and M.P. Friedman, eds. New York: Academic Press.

Devine, P.G. 1989. Stereotypes and prejudice: Their automatic and controlled components. *Journal of Personality and Social Psychology* 56: 5–18.

deVries, H.G., and Adams, G.M. 1972. Electromyographic comparison of single doses of exercise and meprobamate as to effects on muscular relation. *American Journal of Physical Medicine* 51: 130–41.

DeVries, R. 1969. Constancy of generic identity in the years three to six. *Society for Research in Child Development Monographs* 34 (3, Serial No. 127).

Dewsbury, D.A. 1981. Effects of novelty on copulatory behavior: The Coolidge effect and related phenomena. *Psychological Bulletin* 89: 464–82.

Deyo, R. Diehl, A., and Rosenthal, M. 1986. How many days of bed rest for acute low back pain? *New England Journal of Medicine* 315: 1064–70.

Diaconis, P. 1978. Statistical problems in ESP research. *Science* 201; 131–36.

Diener, E., Fraser, S.C., Beaman, A.L., and Kelem, R. 1976. Effects of deindividuation variables on stealing among Halloween trick-or-treaters. *Journal of Personality and Social Psychology* 33: 178–83.

Dinolfo, J. 1984. The lesson of Ed Duffy. *The Hartford Courant, Northeast Magazine,* November 25.

Dion, K.K. 1972. Physial attractiveness and evaluations of children's transgressions. *Journal of Personality and Social Psychology* 24: 207–13.

Dixon, N.F. 1981. *Preconscious processing.* New York: Wiley.

Dobelle, W.H. 1977. Current status of research on providing sight to the blind by electrical stimulation of the brain. *Journal of Visual Impairment and Blindness* 71: 290–97.

Dobelle, W.H., Mladejovsky, M.J., Evans, J.R., Roberts, T.S., and Girvin, J.P. 1976. "Braille" reading by a blind volunteer by visual cortex stimulation. *Nature* 259: 111–12.

Doctor, R.M., Goldenring, J.M., and Powell, A. 1987. Adolescents' attitudes about nuclear war. *Psychological Reports* 60: 599–614.

Dollard, J., Doob, L., Miller, N., Mowrer, O.H., and Sears, R.R. 1939. *Frustration and aggression.* New Haven, CT: Yale University Press.

Dollard J., and Miller, N. 1950. *Personality and psychotherapy: An analysis in terms of learning, thinking, and culture.* New York: McGraw-Hill.

Domjan, M. 1980. Ingestional aversion learning: Unique and general processes. *Advances in the study of behavior,* Vol. 11 New York: Academic Press.

———. 1981. Ingestional aversion learning: Unique and general processes. In *Advances in the study of behavior,* vol. 11, J.S. Rosenblatt, R.A. Hinde, C. Beer, & M. Busnel, eds. New York: Academic Press.

———. 1987. Animal learning comes of age. *American Psychologist* 42: 556–64.

Domjan, M., and Burkhard, B. 1986. *The principles of learning and behavior,* 2nd ed. Monterey, CA: Brooks/Cole.

Donnelly, J. 1978. The incidence of psychosurgery in the United States, 1971–1973. *American Journal of Psychiatry* 135: 1476–80.

Donnerstein, E., and Berkowitz, L. 1981. Victim reactions to aggressive erotic films as a factor in violence against women. *Journal of Personality and Social Psychology* 41: 710–24.

Dornbusch, S.M., Ritter, P.L., Leiderman, P.H., Roberts, D.F., and Fraleigh, M.J. 1987. The relation of parenting style to adolescent school performance. *Child Development* 58: 1244–57.

Downey, G., and Coyne, J.C. 1990. Children of depressed parents: An integrative review. *Psychological Bulletin* 108: 50–76.

Drachman, D.A., 1978. Central cholinergic system and memory. In *Psychopharmacology: A generation of progress* M.A. Lipton, A. DiMascio, and K.F. Killam, eds. New York: Raven Press.

Draper, P.A. 1947. Prefrontal lobotomy: A new type of brain surgery. *Psychology Digest,* June, 3–7.

Drinka, G.F. 1984. *The myth of neurosis: Myth, malady, and the Victorians.* New York: Simon & Schuster.

Driscoll, R., Davis, K.E., and Lipetz, M.E. 1972. Parental interference and romantic love: The Romeo and Juliet effect. *Journal of Personality and Social Psychology* 24: 1–10.

Droscher, V.B. 1971. *The magic of the senses: New discoveries in animal perception.* New York: Harper.

DSM-III-R (Diagnostic and Statistical Manual of Mental Disorders). 1987. Washington, DC: American Psychiatric Association.

Dubois, P.H. 1970. *A history of psychological testing.* Boston: Allyn and Bacon.

Duncan, B.L. 1976. Differential social perception and attributions of interracial violence: Testing the lower limits of stereotyping of blacks. *Journal of Personality and Social Psychology* 34: 590–98.

Duncker, K. 1938. Induced motion. In *A source book of Gestalt psychology,* W.D. Ellis, ed. New York: Harcourt, Brace.

———. 1945. On problem-solving. *Psychological Monographs* 58, Whole No. 270.

Dunn, J.P., and Cobb, S. 1962. Frequency of peptic ulcer among executives, craftsmen, and foremen. *Journal of Occupational Medicine* 4: 343–48.

Dunphy, D.C. 1963. The social structure of urban adolescent peer groups. *Sociometry* 26: 230–46.

Dutton, A., and Aron, A. 1974. Some evidence for heightened sexual attraction under conditions of high anxiety. *Journal of Personality and Social Psychology* 30: 510–17.

Duyme, M. 1988. School success and social class: An adoption study. *Developmental Psychology* 24: 203–9.

Dweck, C.S. 1975. The role of expectations and attributions in the alleviation of learned helplessness. *Journal of Personality and Social Psychology* 31: 674–85.

Dworkin, B.R. 1979. *Behavioral principles in the treatment of disease.* Paper presented at Annual Meeting of the American Psychological Association, New York.

Earle, J.R., and Parricone, P.T. 1986. Premarital sexuality: A ten-year study of attitudes and behavior on a small university campus. *Journal of Sex Research* 22: 304–10.

Easterbrooks, M.A., and Goldberg, W.A. 1985. Effects of early maternal employment on toddlers, mothers, and fathers. *Developmental Psychology* 21: 774–83.

Ebbinghaus, H. [1885] 1964. *Memory.* Reprint. New York: Dover.

Eckholm, E. 1985. Kanzi the chimp: A life in science. *New York Times*, June 25.

Edgerton, R.B. 1979. *Mental retardation.* Cambridge, MA: Harvard University Press.

Edney, J.J. 1980. The commons problem: Alternative perspectives. *American Psychologist* 35: 131–50.

Edwards, A.E., and Acker, L.E. 1962. A demonstration of the long-term retention of a conditioned galvanic skin response. *Psychosomatic Medicine* 24: 459–63.

Edwards, B. 1986. *Drawing on the artist within.* New York: Simon and Shuster.

Edwards, G., Duckitt, A., Oppenheimer, E., Sheehan, M., and Taylor, C. 1983. What happens to alcoholics? *The Lancet*, July, 269–71.

Eells, K., Davis, A., Havighurst, R.J., Herrick, V.E., and Tyler, R.W. 1951. *Intelligence and cultural differences.* Chicago: University of Chicago Press.

Efran, M.G., and Patterson, E.W. 1974. Voters vote beautiful: The effect of physical appearance on a national election. *Canadian Journal of Behavioral Science* 6: 352–56.

Egan, K.J., Kogan, H.N., Garber, A., and Jarrett, M. 1983. The impact of psychological distress on the control of hypertension. *Journal of Human Stress* 9: 4–10.

Egeland, J., Gerhard, D.S., Pauls, D.L., Sussex, J.N., Kidd, K.K., Allen, C.R., Hostetter, A.M., and Housman, D.E. 1987 Bipolar affective disorders linked to DNA markers on chromosome 11. *Nature* 325: 783–87.

Ehrhardt, A.A., and Meyer-Bahlburg, H.F.L. 1981. Effects of prenatal sex hormones on gender-related behavior. *Science* 2ll: 1312–18.

Ehrlichman, H., Antrobus, J.S., and Weiner, M. 1985. EEG asymmetry and sleep mentation during REM and NREM sleep. *Brain and Cognition* 4: 477–85.

Eibl-Eibesfeldt, I. 1973. The expressive behavior of the deaf-and-blind-born. In *Social communication and movements,* M. von Cranach and I. Vine, eds. New York: Academic Press.

———. 1975. *Ethology: The biology of behavior,* 2nd ed. New York: Holt, Rinehart and Winston.

———. 1980. Strategies of social interaction, In *Emotion: Theory, research, and experience,* vol. 1, R. Plutchik, and H. Kellerman, eds. New York: Academic Press.

Eimas, P., Siqueland, E.R., Jusczyk, P., and Vigorito, J. 1971. Speech perception in infants. *Science* 171: 303–6.

Eisenberg, N., and Lennon, R. 1983. Sex differences in empathy and related abilities. *Psychological Bulletin* 94: 100–31.

Ekman, P. 1973. Cross-cultural studies of facial expression. In *Darwin and Facial Expression,* P. Ekman, ed. New York: Academic Press.

Ekman, P. 1985. *Telling lies.* New York: Norton.

Ekman, P., and Friesen, W.V. 1971. Constants across cultures in the face and emotion. *Journal of Personality and Social Psychology* 17: 124–29.

Ekman, P., and Friesen, W.V. 1974. Constants across cultures in the face and emotion. *Journal of Personality and Social Psychology* 17: 124–29.

———. 1975. *Unmasking the face.* Englewood Cliffs, NJ: Prentice Hall.

Ekman, P., Friesen, W.V., O'Sullivan, M., Chan, A., Diacoyanni-Tarlatzis, I., Heider, K., Krause, R. LeCompte, W.A., Pitcairn, T., Ricci-Bitti, P.E., Scherer, K., Tomita, M., and Tzavaras, A. 1987. Universals and cultural differences in the judgments of facial expressions of emotion. *Journal of Personality and Social Psychology* 53: 712–17.

Ekman, P., Levenson, R.W., and Friesen, W.V. 1983. Emotions differ in autonomic nervous system acitivty. *Science* 221: 1208–10.

Elder, G.H. 1969. Appearance and education in marriage mobility. *American Sociological Review* 34: 519–33.

Elkind, D. 1970. Erik Erikson's eight ages of man. *New York Times Magazine,* April 5.

———. 1984. *All grown up and no place to go.* Reading, MA: Addison-Wesley.

Elkin, I. 1986. Outcome findings and therapist performance. Paper presented at American Psychological Association convention.

Elliot, C.H. 1983. Behavioral medicine: Background and implications. In *Handbook of clinical psychology: Theory, research, and practice,* C.E. Walker, ed. Homewood, IL.: Dow Jones–Irwin.

Ellis, A. 1979. Rational-emotive therapy. In *Current psychotherapies,* 2nd ed., R.J. Corsini, ed. Itasca, IL: Peacock.

Ellison, J. 1984. The seven frames of mind— A conversation with Howard Gardner. *Psychology Today* June, pp. 20–26.

Elmadjian, F.J., Hope, J., and Lamson, E.T. 1957. Excretion of epinephrine and norepinephrine in various emotional states. *Journal of Clinical Endocrinology* 17: 608–20.

Elms, A.C., and Milgram, S. 1966. Personality characteristics associated with obedience and defiance toward authoritative command. *Journal of Experimental Research in Personality,* 2: 272–89.

Endler, N.S. 1982. *Holiday of Darkness.* New York: Wiley-Interscience.

Endler, N.S., Hunt, J. McV., and Rosenstein, A.J. 1962. An S-R inventory of anxiousness. *Psychological Monographs* 76, (17, Whole No. 536).

Endler, N.S., and Magnusson, D. 1976. *Interactional psychology and personality.* Washington, DC: Hemisphere.

Endler, N.S., and Parker, J.D.A. 1990. Multidimensional assessment of coping: A critical evaluation. *Journal of Personality and Social Psychology* 58: 844–54.

Engen, T. 1982. *The perception of odors.* New York: Academic Press.

Epstein, A.N., Fitzsimons, J.T., and Rolls, B.J. 1970. Drinking induced by injections of angiotensin into the brain of the rat. *Journal of Physiology* 210: 457–74.

Epstein, S. 1980. The stability of behavior: II. Implications for psychological research. *American Psychologist* 35: 790–806.

Epstein, S., and O'Brien, E.J. 1985. The person-situation debate in historical and current perspective. *Psychological Bulletin* 98: 513–37.

Epstein, S., and Roupenian, A. 1970. Heart rate and skin conductance during experimentally induced anxiety: The effect of

uncertainty about receiving a noxious stimulus. *Journal of Personality and Social Psychology* 16: 20–28.

Erdelyi, M.H. 1985. Psychoanalysis: Freud's cognitive psychology. New York: Freeman.

Ericsson, K.H., Chase, W.G., and Faloon, S. 1980. Acquisition of a memory skill. *Science* 208: 1181–82.

Ericsson, K.A., and Polson, P.G. 1988. An experimental analysis of the mechanisms of a memory skill. *Journal of Experimental Psychology: Learning, Memory, and Cognition* 14: 305–16.

Eriksen, C.W., and St. James, J.D. 1986. Visual attention within and around the field of focal attention: A zoom lens model. *Perception and Psychophysics* 40: 225–40.

Erikson, E.H. 1963. *Childhood and society.* New York: Norton.

———. 1968. *Identity: Youth and crisis.* New York: Norton.

Erikson, E.H., Erikson, J.M., and Kivnick, H.Q. 1986. *Vital involvement in old age.* New York: Norton.

Eron, L.D., and Huesmann, L.R. 1985. The role of television in the development of prosocial and antisocial behavior. In *Development of antisocial and prosocial behavior,* D. Olweus, M. Radke-Yarrow, and J. Block, eds. Orlando, FL: Academic Press.

Estes, W.K. 1980. Is human memory obsolete? *American Scientist* 68: 62–69.

Etzioni, A. 1986. The Kennedy experiment: Unilateral initiatives. In *Psychology and the prevention of nuclear war,* R.K. White, ed. New York: New York University Press.

Evans, C. 1984. *Landscapes of the night: How and why we dream.* New York: Viking Pres.

Evans, E.G. 1982. Functional anatomy of the auditory system. In *The senses,* H.B. Barlow and J.D. Mollon, eds. Cambridge, England: Cambridge University Press.

Evans, G.W. Environmental cognition. *Psychological Bulletin* 88: 259–87.

Evans, G.W., and Jacobs, S.V. 1982. Air pollution and human behavior. In *Environmental stress,* G.W. Evans, ed. New York: Cambridge University Press.

Evans, G.W., Marrero, D., and Butler, P. 1981. Environmental learning and cognitive mapping. *Environmental Behavior* 13: 83–104.

Everly, B.S., Jr., and Rosenfeld, R. 1981. *The nature and treatment of the stress response: A practical guide for clinicians.* New York: Plenum, Press.

Eyferth, K. 1961. Leistungen verschiedner Gruppen von Besaltzungskindern in Hamburg-Wechsler Intelligenztest fur Kinder (HAWIK). *Archiv dur die gesamte Psychologie* 113: 222–241.

Eysenck, H.J. 1952. The effects of psychotherapy: An evaluation. *Journal of Consulting Psychology* 16: 319–24.

———. 1953. The biological basis of personality. *Nature* 199: 1031–34.

———. 1970. *The structure of human personality.* London: Methuen.

———. 1981. *A model for personality.* Berlin: Springer-Verlag.

———. 1987. The several meanings of intelligence. *The Behavioral and Brain Sciences* 10: 663.

Eysenck, H.J., and Kamin, L.J. 1981. *The intelligence controversy.* New York: Wiley.

Fabricius, W.V., and Hagen, J.W. 1984. Use of causal attributions about recall performance to assess metamemory and predict strategic memory behavior in young children. *Developmental Psychology* 20: 975–87.

Fairweather, G.W., Sanders, D.H., Cressler, D.L., and Maynard, H. 1969 *Community life for the mentally ill: An alternative to institutional care.* Hawthorne, N.Y.: Aldine.

Fagan, J.F. 1984. The intelligent infant: Theoretical implications. *Intelligence* 8: 1–9.

Fagan, J.F., and Singer, L.T. 1983. Infant recognition memory as a measure of intelligence. In *Advances in infancy research,* vol. 2, L.P. Lipsett, ed. Norwood, NJ: Ablex.

Fagot, B.I. 1977. Consequences of moderate cross-gender behavior in children. *Child Development* 48: 902–7.

Falkenberg, L.E. 1987. Employee fitness programs: Their impact on the employee and the organization. *Academy of Management Review* 12: 511–22.

Fant, L.G. 1972. *Ameslan: An introduction to American Sign Language.* Silver Spring, MD: National Association of the Deaf.

Farah, M.J. 1990. *Visual agnosia: Disorders of object recognition and what they tell us about normal vision.* Cambridge, MA: MIT PRess.

Farah, M.J., Hammond, K.M., Levine, D.N., and Calvanio, R. 1988. Visual and spatial mental imagery: Dissociable systems of representation. *Cognitive Psychology* 20: 439–62.

Faraone, S.V., Kremen, W.S., and Tsuang, M.T. 1990. Genetic transmission of major affective disorders: Quantitative models and linkage analysis. *Psychological Bulletin* 108: 109–27.

Farber, I.E. 1964. A framework for the study of personality as a behavioral science. In *Personality change,* P. Worchel and D. Byrne eds. New York: Wiley.

Farrell, M.P., and Rosenberg, S.D. 1981. *Man at midlife.* Dover, MA: Auburn House.

Feather, B.W., Chapman, C.R., and Fisher, S.B. 1972. The effect of a placebo on the perception of painful radiant heat stimuli. *Psychosomatic Medicine* 34: 290.

Fehr, B., and Russell, J.A. 1991. The concept of love viewed from a prototype perspective. *Journal of Personality and Social Psychology* 60: 425–38.

Fein, S., Hilton, J.L., and Miller, D.T. 1990. Suspicion of ulterior motivation and the correspondence bias. *Journal of Personality and Social Psychology* 58: 753–64.

Feingold, A. 1988. Cognitive gender differences are disappearing. *American Psychologist* 43: 95–103.

Feldman, M.P. 1966. Aversion therapy for sexual deviations: A critical review. *Psychological Bulletin* 65: 65–69.

Feldman, M.P., and MacCulloch, M.J. 1971. *Homosexual behavior: Therapy and assessment.* Oxford, UK: Pergamon Press.

Felton, B. and Kahana, E. 1974. Adjustment and situationally bound locus of control among institutionalized aged. *Journal of Gerontology* 29: 295–301.

Fenigstein, A. 1984. Self-consciousness and the overperception of self as a target. *Journal of Personality and Social Psychology* 47; 860–70.

Fenz, W.D. 1988. Learning to anticipate stressful events. *Journal of Sport and Exercise Physiology* 10: 223–28.

Fenz, W.D., and Epstein, S. 1967. Gradients of physiological arousal, skin conductance, heart rate, and respiration rate as function of experience. *Psychosomatic Medicine* 29: 33–51.

Fernald, A. and Kuhl, P. 1987. Acoustic determinants of infant preference for motherese speech. *Infant Behavior and Development* 10: 279–93.

Festinger, L. 1954. A theory of social comparison processes. *Human Relations* 7: 117–40.

———. 1957. *A theory of cognitive dissonance.* Evanston, IL: Row, Peterson.

Festinger, L., and Carlsmith, J.M. 1959. Cognitive consequences of forced compliance. *Journal of Abnormal and Social Psychology* 58: 203–10.

Festinger, L., Riecken, H.W., and Schachter, S. 1956. *When prophecy fails.* Minneapolis: University of Minnesota Press.

Festinger, L., Schachter, S., & Beck, K. 1950. *Social pressures in informal groups: A study of human factors in housing.* New York: Harper and Bros.

Fieldler, K. 1991. The tricky nature of skewed frequency tables: An information loss account of distinctiveness-based illusory correlations. *Journal of Personality and Social Psychology* 60: 24–36.

Finke, R. 1990. *Creative imagery: Discoveries and inventions in visualization.* Hillsdale, NJ: Erlbaum.

Fisher, J.D., Bell, P.A., and Baum, A. 1984. *Environmental psychology,* 2nd ed. New York: Holt, Rinehart and Winston.

Fisher, W.A., Fisher, J.D., and Bryne, D. 1977. Consumer reactions to contraceptive purchasing. *Personality and Social Psychology Bulletin* 3: 293–96.

Fiske, S.T., and Neuberg, S.L. 1990. A continuum of impression formation, from category-based to individuating processes: Influences of information and motivation on attention and interpretation. In *Advances in experimental social psychology* vol. 23, M.P. Zanna, ed. New York: Academic Press.

Fiske, S.T., and Taylor, S.E. 1991. *Social cognition,* 2nd ed. New York: McGraw-Hill.

Flaherty, C.F., Uzwiak, A.J., Levine, J., Smith, M., Hall, P., and Schuler, R. 1980. Apparent hyperglycemic and hypoglycemic conditional reponses with exogenuous insulin as the unconditioned stimulus. *Animal Learning and Behavior* 8: 382–86.

Flavell, J.H. 1985. *Cognitive development,* 2nd ed. Englewood Cliffs, NJ: Prentice Hall.

Flavell, J.H., Beach, D.R., and Chinsky, J.M. 1966. Spontaneous verbal rehearsal in a memory task as a function of age. *Child Development* 37: 283–99.

Flavell, J.H., Flavell, E.K., and Green, F.L. 1987. Young children's knowledge about the apparent–real and pretend–real distinctions. *Developmental Psychology* 23: 816–22.

Fleming, J.H., Darley, J.M., Hilton, J.L., and Kojetin, B.A. 1990. Multiple audience problem: A strategic communication perspective on social perception. *Journal of Personality and Social Psychology* 58: 593–609.

Fletcher, C.R. 1986. Strategies for the allocation of short-term memory during comprehension. *Journal of Memory and Language* 25: 43–58.

Flynn, J.R. 1984. The mean IQ of Americans: Massive gains 1932 to 1978. *Psychological Bulletin* 95: 29–51.

———. 1987. Massive IQ gains in 14 nations: What IQ tests really measure. *Psychological Bulletin* 101: 171–91.

Folkins, C.H., and Sime, W. 1981. Physical fitness training and mental health. *American Psychologist* 36: 373–89.

Folkman S., and Lazarus, R. S. 1985. If it changes it must be a process: Study of emotion and coping during three stages of a college examination. *Journal of Personality and Social Psychology* 48: 150–70.

Fook-Kee, W., and Swee-Hock, S. 1975. Knowledge, attitudes, and practice of family planning in Singapore. *Studies in Family Planning* 6: 109–112.

Ford, C.S., and Beach, F.A. 1951. *Patterns of sexual behavior.* New York: Harper and Row.

Ford, C.W., and Beach, F.A. 1951. *Patterns of sexual behavior.* New York: Harper and Row.

Ford, D., Kendall, H., and Nadis, S. 1982. *Beyond the freeze: The road to nuclear sanity.* Boston: Beacon Press.

Fordyce, W., Brockway, J., Bergman, J., and Spengler, D. 1986. A control group comparison of behavioral vs. traditional management methods in acute low back pain. *Journal of Behavioral Medicine* 5: 127–40.

Fordyce, W.E. 1988. Pain and suffering: A reappraisal. *American Psychologist* 43: 276–83.

Forgas, J.P., Bower, G. H. and Krantz, S. E. 1984. The influence of mood on perceptions of social interactions. *Journal of Experimental Social Psychology* 20: 497–513.

Foulkes, D. 1985. *Dreaming: A cognitive psychological analysis.* Hillsdale, NJ: Erlbaum.

Fountain, S.B. 1990. Rule abstraction, item memory, and chunking in rat serial-pattern tracking. *Journal of Experimental Psychology: Animal Behavior Processes* 16: 96-105.

Fouts, R.S., Hirsch, A.D., and Fouts, D.H. 1982. Cultural transmission of human language in a chimpanzee mother/infant relationship. In *Psychological perspectives: Child Nurturance series,* vol. 4, H.E. Fitzgerald, J.A. Mullins, and P. Page, eds. New York: Plenum.

Fox, H.E., Steinbrecher, M., Pessel, D., Inglis, J., Medvid, L., and Angel, E. 1978. Maternal ethenol ingestion and the occurrence of human fetal breathing movements. *American Journal of Obstetrics and Gynecology* 132: 354–58.

Fox, N.A., and Davidson, R.J. 1988. Patterns of brain electrical activity during facial signs of emotion in 10-month-old infants. *Developmental Psychology* 24: 230–36.

Frable, D.S., Blackstone, T., and Scherbaum, C. 1990. Marginal and mindful: Deviants in social interactions. *Journal of Personality and Social Psychology,* 59: 140–49.

Frank, J.D. 1961. *Persuasion and Healing: A comparative study of psychotherapy.* Baltimore: John Hopkins Press.

———. The placebo is psychotherapy. *Behavioral and Brain Sciences,* 6: 291–92.

———. Therapeutic components shared by all psychotherapies. In *The master lecture series: Volume 1. Psychotherapy research and behavior change,* J.M. Harvey and M.A. Parks, eds. Washington, DC: American Psychological Association.

Franz, C.E., McClelland, D.C., and Weinberger, J. 1991 Childhood antecedents of conventional social accomplishment in midlife adults: A 36-year prospective study. *Journal of Personality and Social Psychology* 60: 586–95.

Freedman, J.L. 1975. *Crowding and behavior.* San Francisco: Freeman.

Freedman, J.L., Heshka, S., and Levy, A. 1975. Population density and pathology: Is there a relationship? *Journal of Experimental Social Psychology* 11: 539–52.

Freeman, E.W. 1980. Adolescent contraceptive use: Comparisons of male and female attitudes and information. *American Journal of Public Health* 70: 790–97.

Freeman-Longo, R.E., and Wall, R.V. 1986. Changing a lifetime of sexual crime. *Psychology Today.* March, pp. 58–64.

French, J.R.P. 1968. The conceptualization and the mreasurement of mental health in terms of self-identity theory. In *The definition and measurement of mental health,* S.B. Sells, ed. Washington, DC: Department of Health, Education, and Welfare.

Frerichs, R.R., Aneshensel, C.S., and Clark, V.A. 1981. Prevalence of depression in Los Angeles County. *American Journal of Epidemiology* 113: 333–40.

Freud, S. 1900/1953. *The interpretation of dreams. The standard edition of the complete psychological works of Sigmund Freud,* vols. 4 & 5. London: The Hogarth Press.

———. [1901] 1965. *The psychopathology of everyday life.* Translated by A. Tyson. Reprint New York: Norton.

———. 1908/1952. *Creative writers and daydreaming. The standard edition of the complete psychological works of Sigmund Freud,* vol. 9. London: The Hogarth Press.

———. [1909] 1979. A case of obsessional neurosis. In *Great cases in psychotherapy,* D. Wedding and R.J. Corsini eds. Itasca, IL: Peacock.

———. [1915] 1950. Instincts and their vicissitudes. In Sigmund Freud, M.D., L.L.D., collected papers. London: Hogarth.

———. 1924/1952. *A general introduction to psychoanalysis.* New York: Washington Square Press.

Freud, S. 1933. *New introductory lectures on psychoanalysis.* New York: Norton.

Frey, W.H., and Langseth, M. 1986. *Crying: The mystery of tears.* Minneapolis: Winston Press.

Friedman, H.S., and Booth-Kewley, S. 1987. The "disease-prone personality:" A meta-analytic view of the construct. *American Psychologist* 42: 539–55.

Friedman, M., and Rosenman, R.H. 1974. *Type A behavior and your heart.* New York: Knopf.

Friedrich-Cofer, L., and Huston, A. 1986. Television violence and aggression: The debate continues. *Psychological Bulletin* 100: 364–71.

Frieze, I.M., Parsons, J.E., Johnson, P.B., Ruble, D.N., and Zellman, G.L. 1978. *Women and sex roles: A social psychological perspective.* New York: Norton.

Frisch, R.E. 1988, Fatness and fertility. *Scientific American* 258: 88–95.

Frisk, V., and Milner, B. 1990. The role of the left hippocampal region in the acquisition and retention of story context. *Neuropsychologia* 28: 349–59.

Fromm, E. 1941. *Escape from freedom.* New York: Farrar and Rinehart.

Fromm, E. 1947. *Man for himself.* Greenwich, CT: Fawcett.

———. 1956. *The Art of Loving.* New York: Harper.

———. 1962, *Escape from Freedom.* New York: Harper and Row.

Funder, D.C. 1987. Errors and mistakes: Evaluating the accuracy of social judgment. *Psychological Bulletin* 101: 75–90.

Funder, D.C. 1989. Accuracy in personality judgment and the dancing bear. In *Personality psychology: Recent trends and emerging directions,* D.M. Buss and N. Cantor, eds. New York: Springer-Verlag.

Funder, D.C., and Colvin, C.R. 1988. Friends and strangers: Acquaintanceship, agreement, and the accuracy of personality judgment. *Journal of Personality and Social Psychology.* In press.

Funder, D.C., and Dobroth, J.M. 1987. Differences between traits: Properties associated with inter-judge agreement. *Journal of Personality and Social Psychology* 52: 409–18.

Gangestad, S.W., and Simpson, J.A. 1990. Toward an evolutionary history of female sociosexual variation. *Journal of Personality* 58: 69–96.

Funkenstein, D.H. 1955. The physiology of fear and anger. *Scientific American* 192: 74–80.

Furman, W., Rahe, D., and Hartup, W.W. 1979. Rehabilitation of socially withdrawn preschool children through mixed-age and same-age socialization. *Child Development* 50: 915–22.

Furstenberg, F.F., Jr., Brooks-Gunn, J., and Morgan, S.P. 1987. *Adolescent mothers in later life.* Cambridge, UK: Cambridge University Press.

Gaertner, S.L., and Dovidio, J.F. 1986 The aversive form of racism. In *Prejudice, discrimination, and racism,* J.F. Dovidio and S. L. Gaertner, eds. San Diego: Academic Press.

Gallagher, J.T. 1983. Gifted and talented students. In *Science and public policy seminars.* Washington, DC: Frederation of Behavioral, Psychological, and Cognitive Sciences.

Galanter, E. 1962. Contemporary psychophysics. In *New directions in psychology,* R. Brown, E. Galanter, E.H. Hess, and G. Mandler, eds. New York: Holt, Rinehart and Winston.

Galle, O.R., and Gove, W.R. 1979. Crowding and behavior in Chicago, 1940–1970. In *Residential crowding and design,* J.R. Aiello and A. Baum, eds. New York: Plenum.

Galle, O.R., Gove, W.R., and McPherson, J.M. 1972. Population density and pathology: What are the relationships of man? *Science* 172: 23–30.

Gallup, G., Jr. 1986. Gallup Youth Survey (August–October 1985). Princeton, NJ: The Gallup Organization.

Ganellen, R.J., and Blaney, P.H. 1984. Hardiness and social support as moderators of the effects of life stress. *Journal of Personality & Social Psychology* 47: 156–63.

Garcia, J., and Koelling, R.A. 1966. Relation of cue to consequence in avoidance learning. *Psychonomic Science* 4: 123–24.

Garcia, J., McGown, B.K., and Green, K.F. 1972. Biological constraints on conditioning. In *Classical conditioning II: Current theory and research,* A.H. Black and W.F. Prokasy, eds. New York: Appleton-Century-Crofts.

Gardner, B.T., and Gardner, R.A. 1969. Teaching sign language to a chimpanzee. *Science* 165: 664–72.

———. 1972. Two-way communication with an infant chimpanzee. In *Behavior of nonhuman primates,* A.M. Schrier and F. Stollnitz, eds. New York: Academic Press.

Gardner, H. 1975. *The shattered mind: The person after brain damage.* New York: Knopf.

———. 1982. *Developmental psychology,* 2nd ed. Boston: Little, Brown.

———. 1983. *Frames of mind: The theory of multiple intelligences.* New York: Basic Books.

———. 1985. *The mind's new science: A history of the cognitive revolution.* New York: Basic Books.

Gardner, R.A., and Gardner, B.T. 1978. Comparative psychology and language acquisition. *Annals of the New York Academy of Science* 309: 37–76.

Garfield, S.L. and Bergin, A.E. 1986. Introduction and historical overview. In *Handbook of psychotherapy and behavior change,* 3rd ed., S.L. Garfield and A.E. Bergin, eds. New York: Wiley.

Garling, T., Book, A., and Lindberg, E. 1984. Cognitive mapping of large-scale environments. *Environment and Behavior* 16: 3–34.

Garretson, H.B., Fein, D., and Waterhouse, L. 1990. Sustained attention in children with autism. *Journal of Autism and Development Disorders* 20: 101–14.

Gatchel, R.J., Baum, A., and Krantz, D. 1989. *An introduction to health psychology,* 2nd ed. New York: Random House.

Gatz, M., Barbarin, O.A., Tyler, F.B., Hurley, D.J., Mitchell, R.B., Moran, J.A., Wirbicki, P.J., Drawford, J., and Engelmann, A. 1982. Enhancement of individual and community competence: The older adult as community worker. *American Journal of Community Psychology* 10: 291–304.

Gazzangia, M.S. 1967. The split brain in man. *Scientific American* 217: 24–29.

———. 1972. One brain—two minds? *American Scientist* 60: 311–17.

———. 1985. *The social brain: Discovering the networks of the mind.* New York: Basic Books.

———. 1987. Perceptual and attentional processes following callosal section in humans. *Neuropsychologia* 25: 119–33.

———. 1988. Brain modularity: Towards a philosophy of conscious experience. In *Consciousness in contemporary science.* A.J. Marcel and E. Bisiach, eds. Oxford, UK: Oxford University Press.

Gazzaniga, M.S., and LeDoux, J.E. 1978. *The integrated mind.* New York: Plenum Press.

Gazzaniga, M.S., and Smylie, C.S. 1983. Facial recognition and brain asymmetries: Clues to underlying mechanisms. *Annals of Neurology,* 13: 536–40.

Geer, J.H., Davison, G.C., and Gatchel, R.I. 1970. Reduction of stress in humans through nonveridical perceived control of aversive stimulation. *Journal of Personality and Social Psychology* 16: 731–38.

Gelman, R. 1978. Cognitive development. *Annual Review of Psychology* 29: 297–332.

Gelman, R., Spelke, E.S., and Meck, E. 1983. What preschoolers know about animate and inanimate objects. In *The acquisition of symbolic skills,* D. Rogers and J.A. Sloboda, eds. New York: Plenum.

General Mills American Family Report 1977. *Raising children in a changing society.* Minneapolis: General Mills.

Gentner, D.R., and Norman, D.A. 1984. The typist's touch. *Psychology Today*, March, 66–72.

Gergen, M. 1990. Beyond the evil empire: Horseplay and aggression. *Aggressive behavior* 16: 381–87.

Gerrard, M. 1987. Emotional and cognitive barriers to effective contraception: Are males and females really different? In *Females, males, and sexuality: Theories and research*, K. Kelley, ed. Albany: State University of New York Press.

Gerrard, M., McCann, I.L., and Fortini, M. 1983. Prevention of unwanted pregnancy. *American Journal of Community Psychology* 11: 153–68.

Gerwirtz, J.L. 1965. The course of infant smiling in four child rearing environments in Israel. In *Determinants of infant behavior*, vol. 3, B.M. Foss, ed. New York: Wiley.

Gescheider, G.A. 1979. *Psychophysics: Method and theory*. Hillsdale, NJ: Erlbaum.

Geschwind, N. 1979. Specialization of the human brain. *Scientific American* 241: 180–99.

Gibbons, F.X. 1978. Sexual standards and reactions to pornography: Enhancing behavioral consistency through self-focused attention. *Journal of Personality and Social Psychology* 36: 976–87.

Gibbons, F.X. and McCoy, S.B. 1991. Self-esteem, similarity, and reactions to active versus passive downward comparison. *Journal of Personality and Social Psychology* 60: 414–24.

Gibson, E.J., and Walk, R.D. 1960. The "visual cliff." *Scientific American* 202: 64–71.

Gibson, K.R., and Petersen, A.C., eds. 1991. *Brain maturation and cognitive development: Comparative and cross-cultural perspectives*. Hawthorne, NY: Aldine de Gruyter.

Gibson, J.J. 1966. *The senses considered as perceptual systems*. Boston: Houghton Mifflin.

———. 1979. *The ecological approach to visual perception*. Boston: Houghton Mifflin.

Gick, M.L., and Holyoak, K.J. 1980. Analogical problem solving. *Cognitive Psychology* 12: 306–55.

Gifford, R. 1987. *Environmental Psychology: Principles and Practice*. Boston: Allyn and Bacon.

Gifford-Jones, W. 1977. *What every woman should know about hysterectomy*. New York: Funk and Wagnalls.

Gilbert, D.T., and Jones, E.E. 1986. Perceiver-induced constraint: Interpretations of self-generated reality. *Journal of Personality and Social Psychology*, 50: 269–80.

Gilinsky, A.S. 1984. *Mind and brain*. New York: Praeger.

Gilligan, C. 1977. In a different voice: Women's conception of self and morality. *Harvard Educational Review*, 47: 481–517.

Gilligan C. 1982. *In a different voice: Psychological theory and women's development*. Cambridge, MA: Harvard University Press.

Gilovich, T. 1981. Seeing the past in the present: The effect of associations to familiar events on judgments and decisions. *Journal of Personality and Social Psychology* 40: 797–803.

———. 1983. Biased evaluation and persistence in gambling. *Journal of Personality and Social Psychology* 44: 1110–26.

Ginsburg, H.P., and Opper, S. 1988. *Piaget's theory of intellectual development*, 3rd ed. Englewood Cliffs, NJ: Prentice Hall.

Glanzer, M., and Cunitz, A.R. 1966. Two storage mechanisms in free recall. *Journal of Verbal Learning and Verbal Behavior* 5: 351–60.

Glaser, R., and Chi, M.T.H. 1988. Overview. In *The nature of expertise*, M.T.H. Chi, R. Glaser, and M.J. Farr, eds. Hillsdale, NJ: Erlbaum.

Glasgow, R.E., and Rosen, G.M. 1978. Behavioral bibliotherapy: A review of self-help behavior therapy manuals. *Psychological Bulletin* 85: 1–23.

Glass, A.L., and Holyoak, K.J. 1986. *Cognition*, 2nd ed. New York: Random House.

Glassman, J.B., Burkhart, B.R., Grant, R.D., & Vallery, G.G. 1978. Density, expectation, and extended task performance: An experiment in the natural environment. *Environment and Behavior* 10: 299–316.

Gleser, G.C., Green, B.L., and Winget, C. 1981. *Prolonged psychosocial effects of disaster: A study of Buffalo Creek*. New York: Academic Press.

Gleason, J.B. 1985. *The development of language*. Columbus, OH: Merrill.

Glucksberg, S., and Danks, J.H. 1975. *Experimental psycholinguistics: An introduction*. Hillsdale, NJ: Erlbaum.

Glucksberg, S., and King, L.J. 1967. Motivated forgetting mediated by implicit verbal chaining: A laboratory analog of repression. *Science*, October 27, pp. 517–19.

Glueck, S. and Glueck, E. 1956. *Physique and delinquency*. New York: Harper and Row.

Goddard, H.H. 1917. Mental tests and the immigrant. *Journal of Delinquency* 2: 243–77.

Goethe, J.W. 1962. *Sufferings of young Werther*. New York: Bantam Books.

Goffman, E. 1961. *Asylums*. New York: Anchor.

Gold, R.M. 1973. Hypothalamic obesity: The myth of the ventromedial nucleus. *Science* 182: 488–90.

Goldberg, L.R. 1981. Language and individual differences: The search for universals in personality lexicons. In *Review of Personality and Social Psychology*, L. Wheeler, ed. Beverly Hills, CA: Sage.

Goldberg, L.R., and Werts, C.E. 1966. The reliability of clinician's judgments: A multitrait-multimethod approach. *Journal of Consulting Psychology* 30: 199–206.

Goldiamond, I. 1965. Stuttering and fluency as manipulatable operant response classes. In *Research in behavior modification*, L. Krasner and L.P. Ullmann, eds. New York: Holt, Rinehart and Winston.

Goldman-Eisler, F. 1956. Breast-feeding and character formation. In *Personality in nature, society, and culture*, C. Kluckhohn, H.A. Murray, and D.M. Schneider, eds. New York: Knopf.

Goldman, W. and Lewis, P. 1977. Beautiful is good: Evidence that the physically attractive are more socially skillful. *Journal of Experimental Social Psychology* 13: 125–30.

Goldfried, M.R., and Davison, G.C. 1976. *Clinical behavior therapy*. New York: Holt, Rinehart and Winston.

Goldstein, A. 1978. Opiate receptors and opiod peptides: A ten year overview. In *Psychopharmacology: A generation of progress*, M.A. Lipton, A. DiMascio, and K.F. Killam, eds. New York: Raven.

Goldstein, E.B. 1981. The ecology of Gibson's perception. *Leonardo* 14: 191–95.

———. 1984. *Sensation and perception*, 2nd ed. Belmont, CA: Wadsworth.

Goldstein, J.H., Davis, R.W., and Herman, D. 1975. Escalation of aggression: Experimental studies. *Journal of Personality and Social Psychology* 31: 162–70.

Goleman, O. 1980. 1,528 little geniuses and how they grew. *Psychology Today*, February, pp. 28–53.

Goleman, D. 1986. To expert eyes, city streets are open mental wards. *The New York Times*, Nov. 11, pp. C1, C3.

———. 1987. Teen-age risk-taking. *New York Times*, November 24.

———. 1987. Brain defect tied to utter amorality of the psychopath. *New York Times*, July 7, C1–C2.

———. 1988. Probing the enigma of multiple personality. *New York Times*, June 28.

———. 1989. Study defines major sources of conflict between sexes. *The New York Times*, June 13, p. C1.

———. 1990. Compassion and comfort in middle age. *The New York Times*, February 6, pp. C1, C14.

Goleman, D., and Davidson, R.J., eds. 1979. *Consciousness: Brain, states of awareness, and mysticism*. New York: Harper and Row.

Goodman, I.J., and Brown, J.L. 1966. Stimulation of positively and negatively reinforcing sites in the avian brain. *Life Sciences* 5:693–704.

Goodman, L.A., Mack, J.E., Beardslee, W.R., and Snow, R.M. 1983. The threat of nuclear war and the nuclear arms race: Adolescents experience and perceptions. *Political Psychology* 4: 501–30.

Goodstein, L.D., and Sandler, I.N. 1978. Using psychology to promote human welfare: A conceptual analysis of the role of community psychology. *American Psychologist* 33: 882–92.

Goodwin, D.W. 1980. Biological psychiatry. In *New Perspectives in abnormal psychology*, A.E. Kazdin, A.S. Bellack, and M. Hersen, eds. New York: Oxford University Press.

Goodwin, D.W. 1989. Alcoholism and heredity: A review and hypothesis. *Archives of General Psychiatry* 36: 57–61.

Gormezano, I., Prokasy, W.F., and Thompson, R.F., eds. 1987. *Classical conditioning*, 3rd ed. Hillsdale, NJ: Erlbaum.

Gotlib, I.H., and Robinson, L.A. 1982. Responses to depressed individuals: Discrepancies between self-report and observer rated behavior. *Journal of Abnormal Psychology* 91: 231–40.

Gottesman, I.I. 1962. Differential inheritance of the psychoneuroses. *Eugenics Quarterly* 9: 223–27.

Gottesman, I.I., Shields, J., and Hanson, D.R. 1982. *Schizophrenia: The epigenetic puzzle*. Cambridge, UK: Cambridge University Press.

Gottlieb, J., ed. 1980. *Educating mentally retarded persons in the mainstream*. Baltimore: University Park Press.

Gottlieb, R.M. 1989. Technique and countertransference in Freud's analysis of the Rat Man. *Psychoanalytic Quarterly*, 58: 29–62.

Gough, H.G., and Thorne, A. 1986. Positive, negative, and balanced shyness: Self-definitions and the reactions of others. In *Shyness*, W.H. Jones, J.M. Cheek, and S.R. Briggs, eds. New York: Plenum Press.

Gould, C.G. 1983. Out of the mouths of beasts. *Science 83*, April, pp. 69–72.

Gould, P.R., and White, R. 1974. *Mental maps*. New York: Penguin books.

Gouldner, A. 1960. The norm of reciprocity: A preliminary statement. *American Sociological Review* 20: 161–78.

Graf, P., Squire, L.R., and Mandler, G. 1984. The information that amnesic patients do not forget. *Journal of Experimental Psychology: Learning, Memory, and Cognition* 10: 164–78.

Gray, C.R., and Gummerman, K. 1975. The enigmatic eidetic image: A critical examination of methods, data, and theories. *Psychological Bulletin* 82: 383–407.

Gray, J.A., Feldon, J., Rawlins, J.N.P., Hemsley, D.R., and Smith, A.D. 1991. The neuropsychology of schizophrenia. *Behavioral and Brain Sciences* 14: 1–84.

Graziano, W.G., Feldesman, A.B., and Rahe, D.F. 1985. Extraversion, social cognition, and the salience of aversiveness in social encounters. *Journal of Personality and Social Psychology* 49: 971–80.

Greenberg, M.S., and Farah, M.J. 1986. The laterality of dreaming. *Brain and Cognition* 5: 307–21.

Greene, K.J., Desor, J.A., and Maller, O. 1975. Heredity and experience: Their relative importance in the development of taste preference in man. *Journal of Comparative and Physiological Psychology*, 89: 279–84.

Greeno, J.G. 1977. Process of understanding in problem solving. In *Cognitive theory*, vol. 2, N.J. Castellan, Jr., D.B. Pisoni, and G.R. Potts, eds. Hillsdale, NJ: Erlbaum.

Greenough, W.T. 1984. Possible structural substrate of plastic neural phenomena. In *Neurobiology of learning and memory*, G. Lynch, J.L. McGaugh, and N.M. Weinberger, eds. New York: Guilford Press.

Greenough, W.T., Wood, W.E., and Madden, T.C. 1972. Possible memory storage differences among mice reared in environments varying in complexity. *Behavior and Biology* 7: 17–22.

Greenwald, A.G., and Breckler, S.J. 1985. To whom is the self presented? In *The self and social life*, B.R. Schlenker, ed. New York: McGraw-Hill.

Gregory, R.L. 1978. *Eye and brain*, 3rd ed. New York: McGraw-Hill.

Gregory, W.L., Chartier, G.M., and Wright, M.H. 1979. Learned helplessness and learned effectiveness: Effects of explicit response cues on individuals differing in personal control expectancies. *Journal of Personality and Social Psychology* 37: 1982–92.

Grice, G.R. 1948. The relation of secondary reinforcement to delayed reward in visual discrimination learning. *Journal of Experimental Psychology* 38: 1–16.

Grossman, F.K., Pollack, W.S., and Golding, E. 1988. Fathers and children: Predicting the quality and quantity of fathering. *Developmental Psychology* 24: 82–91.

Grossman, H.J., ed. 1982. *Manual on terminology and classification in mental retardation*, 3rd rev. Washington, DC: American Association of Mental Deficiency.

Guilford, J.P. 1982. Cognitive psychology's ambiguities: Some suggested remedies. *Psychological Review* 89: 48–49.

Guroff, G., and Grant, S. 1981. *Soviet elites: World view and perceptions of the U.S.* (USICA Report No. R-18-81). Washington, DC: Office of Research, United States International Communication Agency.

Gustafson, G.E., and Harris, K.L. 1990. Women's responses to young infants' cries. *Developmental Psychology* 26: 144–52.

Gutierres, S.E., and Kenrick, D.T. 1979. Effects of physical attractiveness of stimulus photos on own self esteem. Paper presented at the Western Psychological Association meeting.

Gyorgy, A. 1979. *No nukes: Everyone's guide to nuclear power*. Boston: South End Press.

Haan, N. 1975. Hypothetical and actual moral reasoning in a situation of civil disobedience. *Journal of Personality and Social Psychology* 32: 255–70.

Haber, R.N. 1969. Eidetic images. *Scientific American* 220: 36–44.

———. 1979. Twenty years of haunting eidetic imagery: Where's the ghost? *The Behavioral and Brain Sciences* 2: 583–629.

———. 1983. The impending demise of the icon. *The Behavior and Brain Sciences* 6: 1–11.

Haber, R.N., and Haber, L.R. 1981. The shape of a word can specify its meaning. *Reading Research Quarterly* 13: 334–45.

Hale, G.A., Miller, L.K., and Stevenson, H.W. 1968. Incidental learning in film content: A developmental study. *Child Development* 39: 69–77.

Haley, J. 1963. *Strategies of psychotherapy*. New York: Grune and Stratton.

Hall, C.G., and Van de Castle, R.L. 1966. *The content and analysis of dreams*. New York: Appleton-Century-Crofts.

Hall, C.S., & Lindzey, G. 1957. *Theories of personality*. New York: Wiley.

Hall, G.S. 1904. *Adolescence*. New York: Appleton.

———. 1922. *Senescence*. New York: Appleton.

Hall, T. 1985. The unconverted: Smoking of cigarettes seems to be becoming a lower-class habit. *The Wall Street Journal*, June 25, pp. 1, 17.

Hall, W.G., and Oppenheim, R.W. 1987. Developmental psychobiology: Prenatal, perinatal, and early postnatal aspects of behavioral development. *Annual Review of Psychology* 38: 91–128.

Halpern, D.F. 1989. *Thought and knowledge: An introduction to critical thinking*. Hillsdale, NJ: Erlbaum.

Hamilton, D.L., and Bishop, G.D. 1976. Attitudinal and behavioral effects of initial integration of white suburban neighborhoods. *Journal of Social Issues* 32: 47–67.

Hamilton, D.L., and Gifford, R.K. 1976. Illusory correlation in interpersonal perception: A cognitive basis of stereotypic judgments. *Journal of Experimental Social Psychology*, 12: 392–407.

Hamilton, D.L., and Sherman, S.J. 1989. Illusory correlations: Implications for stereotype theory and research. In *Stereotypes and prejudice: Changing conceptions*, D. Bar-Tal, C.F. Graumann, A.W. Kruglanski, and W. Stroebe, eds. New York: Springer-Verlag.

Hamilton, W.D. 1964. The genetical evolution of social behavior. *Journal of Theoretical Biology* 7: 1–52.

Hampson, E., and Kimura, D. 1988. Reciprocal effects of hormonal fluctuations on human motor and perceptual-spatial skills. *Behavioral Neuroscience* 102: 456–59.

Han, P.W., and Liu, A.C. 1966. Obesity and impaired growth of rats force fed 40 days after hypthalamic lesions. *American Journal of Physiology* 211: 229–31.

Hansel, C.E.M. 1966. *ESP: A scientific evaluation*. New York: Scribner's Sons.

———. 1980. *ESP and parapsychology: A critical reevaluation*. Buffalo, NY: Prometheus Books.

Hansen, C.H., and Hansen, R.D. 1988. Finding faces in the crowd: An anger superiority effect. *Journal of Personality and Social Psychology*. 54: 917–24.

Hansen, R.D., and Hall, C.A. 1985. Discounting and augmenting facilitative and inhibitory forces: The winner takes almost all. *Journal of Personality and Social Psychology* 49: 1482–93.

Hanson, J.W., Streissguth, A.P., and Smith, D.W. 1978. The effects of moderate alcohol consumption during pregnancy on fetal growth and morphogenesis. *Journal of Pediatrics* 92: 457–60.

Hanusa, B.A., and Schulz, R. 1977. Attributional mediation of learned helplessness. *Journal of Personality and Social Psychology* 35: 602–11.

Hardin, G. 1968. The tragedy of the commons. *Science* 162: 1243–48.

Hardyck, J., and Braden, H. 1962. Prophecy fails again: A report of a failure to replicate. *Journal of Abnormal and Social Psychology* 65: 136–41.

Harlow, H.F. 1949. The formation of learning sets. *Psychological Review* 56: 51–65.

———. 1971. *Learning to love*. San Francisco: Albion.

Harlow, H.F., Harlow, M.K., and Meyer, D.R. 1950. Learning motivated by a manipulation drive. *Journal of Experimental Psychology* 40: 228–34.

Harrell, T.W., and Harrell, M.S. 1945. Army General Classification Test scores for civilian occupations. *Educational Psychological Measurement* 5: 229–39.

Harrington, A. 1967. A visit to inner space. In *LSD: The consciousness-expanding drug*, D. Solomon, ed. New York: Putnam.

Harris, C.S. 1980. Insight or out of sight?: Two examples of perceptual plasticity in the human adult. In *Visual coding and adaptability*, C.S. Harris, ed. Hillsdale, NJ: Erlbaum.

Harsch, N., and Neisser, U. 1989. Substantial and irreversible errors in flashbulb memories of the Challenger explosion. Paper presented at the Psychonomic Society Meeting, in November, Atlanta, GA.

Hartline, H.K. 1938. The response of single optic nerve fibers of the vertibrate eye to illumination of the retina. *American Journal of Physiology* 121: 400–15.

Hass, A. 1979. *Teenage sexuality: A survey of teenage sexual behavior*. New York: Macmillan.

Hastie, R., and Park, B. 1986. The relationship between memory and judgment depends on whether the judgment task is memory based or on-line. *Psychological Review* 93: 258–68.

Hatfield, E., and Sprecher, S. 1986. *Mirror, mirror: The importance of looks in everyday life*. Albany: SUNY Press.

Hatfield, E., Traupmann, J., Sprecher, S., Utne, M., and Hay, J. 1985. Equity and intimate relations: Recent research. In *Compatible and incompatible relationships*, W. Ickes, ed. New York: Springer-Verlag.

Hattie, J.A., Sharpley, C.F., and Rogers, H.J. 1984. Comparative effectiveness of professional and paraprofessional helpers. *Psychological Bulletin* 95: 534–41.

Haviland, J.M., and Lelwica, M. 1987. The induced affect response. *Developmental Psychology* 23: 97–104.

Hayes, C. 1952. *The ape in our house*. London: Gollacz.

Haynes, S., and Feinleib, M. 1980. Women, work, and coronary heart disease: Prospective findings form the Framingham heart study. *American Journal of Public Health* 70: 133–41.

Healy, D., and Williams, J.M.G. 1988. Dysrhythmia, dysphoria, and depression: The interaction of learned helplessness and circadian dysrhythmia in the pathogenesis of depression. *Psychological Bulletin* 103: 163–78.

Heath, R.G. 1964. Pleasure response of human subjects to direct stimulation of the brain: Physiologic and psychodynamic considerations. In *The role of pleasure in behavior*, R.G. Heath, ed. New York: Harper and Row.

Heather, N., and Robertson, I. 1983. *Controlled drinking*. London: Methuen.

Hebb, D.O. 1972. *Textbook of psychology*, 3rd ed. Philadelphia: Saunders.

Hecaen, H., and Albert, M.L. 1978. *Human neuropsychology*. New York: Wiley.

Heidbrder, E. 1947. The attainment of concepts: II. The process. *Journal of Psychology* 24: 93–108.

Heider, E.R., and Oliver, D. 1972. The structure of the color space in naming and memory for two languages. *Cognitive Psychology* 3: 337–54.

Heider, F. 1944. Social perception and phenomenal causality. *Psychological Review* 51: 358–74.

————. 1946. Attitudes and cognitive organization. *Journal of Psychology* 21: 107–12.

————. 1958. *The psychology of interpersonal relations*. New York: Wiley.

Heilman, K.M., Scholes, R., and Watson, R.T. 1975. Auditory affective agnosia: Disturbed comprehension of affective speech. *Journal of Neurology, Neurosurgery, and Psychiatry* 58: 69–72.

Heilman, K.M., Watson, R.T., and Bowers, P. 1983. Affective disorders associated with hemisphere disease. In *Neuropsychology of human emotion*, K.M. Heilman and P. Satz, eds. New York: Guilford.

Heller, M.A. 1983. Haptic dominance in form perception with blurred vision. *Perception* 12: 607–13.

Hellige, J.B. 1990. Hemispheric asymmetry. *Annual Review of Psychology* 41: 55–80.

Helson, H. 1964. *Adaptation-level theory*. New York: Harper and Row.

Helson, R., Mitchell, V., and Moane, G. 1984. Personality and patterns of adherence and nonadherence to the social clock. *Journal of Personality and Social Psychology* 46: 1079–97.

Henderson, N.D. 1982. Human behavior genetics. *Annual Review of Psychology* 33: 403–40.

Hendrick, S., Hendrick, C., Slapion-Foote, M., and Foote, F. 1985. Gender differences in sexual attitudes. *Journal of Personality and Social Psychology* 48: 1630–42.

Henke, P.G. 1988. Electrophysiological activity in the central nucleus of the amygdala: Emotionality and stress ulcers in rats. *Behavioral Neuroscience* 102: 77–83.

Hepworth, J.T., and West, S.G. 1988. Lynchings and the economy: A time series reanalysis of Hovland and Sears (1940). *Journal of Personality and Social Psychology* 55: 239–47.

Hergenhahn, B.R. 1982. *An introduction to theories of learning*, 2nd ed. Englewood Cliffs, NJ: Prentice Hall.

Herman, C.P., and Mack, D. 1975. Restrained and unrestrained eating. *Journal of Personality* 43: 647–60.

Hess, E. H. 1965. Attitude and pupil size. *Scientific American* 212: 46–54.

Hetherington, E.M. 1979. Divorce: A child's perspective. *American Psychologist* 34: 851–58.

————. 1989. Coping with family transitions: Winners, losers, and survivors. *Child Development* 60: 1–14.

Hetherington, E.M., and Parke, R.D. 1986. *Child psychology*. New York: McGraw-Hill.

Hewitt, P., and Massey, J.O. 1969. *Clinical clues from the WISC*. Palo Alto, CA: Consulting Psychologists Press.

Higgins, E.T. 1989. Knowledge accessibility and activation: Subjectivity and suffering from conscious sources. In *Unintended thought*, J.S. Uleman and J.A. Bargh, eds. New York: Guilford.

Higgins, E.T., and McCann, C.D. 1984. Social encoding and subsequent attitudes, impressions and memory: "Context-driven" and motivational aspects of processing. *Journal of Personality and Social Psychology* 47: 26–39.

Higgins, E.T., Strauman, T., and Klein, R. 1986. Standards and the process of self-evaluation: Multiple affects from multiple stages. In *Handbook of motivation and cognition*, R.M. Sorrentino and E.T. Higgins, eds. New York: Guilford Press.

Hilgard, E.R. 1977. *Divided consciousness: Multiple controls in human thought and action*. New York: Wiley.

————. 1980. Consciousness in contemporary psychology. *Annual Review of Psychology* 31: 1–26.

————. 1986. A study in hypnosis. *Psychology Today*, January, 23–27.

————. 1987. *Psychology in America: A historical survey*. New York: Harcourt Brace Jovanovich.

————. 1974. Imaginative involvement: Some characteristics of the highly hypnotizable and the non-hypnotizable. *International Journal of Clinical and Experimental Hypnosis* 22: 138–56.

Hill, A.L. 1975. Investigation of calendar calculating by an idiot savant. *American Journal of Psychiatry* 132: 557–59.

Hill, T., and Lewicki, P. 1991. The unconscious. In *Personality: Contemporary theory and research*, V.J. Derlega, B.A. Winstead, and W.H. Jones, eds. Chicago: Nelson-Hall.

Hillyard, S.A., and Kutas, M. 1983. Electrophysiology of cognitive processing. *Annual Review of Psychology* 34: 33–62.

Hinde, R.A. 1984. Why do the sexes behave differently in close relationships? *Journal of Social and Personal Relationships* 1: 471–501.

Hirst, W., Johnson, M.K., Phelps, E.A., and Volpe, B.T. 1988. More on recognition and recall in amnesics. *Journal of Experimental Psychology: Learning, Memory, and Cognition* 14: 758–62.

Hirst, W., and Kalmar, D. 1987. Characterizing attentional resources. *Journal of Experimental Psychology: General* 116: 68–81.

Hirsh-Pasek, K., Treiman, R., and Schneiderman, M. 1984. Brown and Hanlon revisited: Mother's sensitivity to ungrammatical forms. *Journal of Child Language* 11: 81–88.

Hobsen, J.A. 1989a. Sleep, functional theories of. In *States of brain and mind*, J.A. Hobson, ed. Readings from the *Encyclopedia of neuroscience*. Boston: Birkhauser.

————. 1989b. Dreaming. In *States of brain and mind*, J.A. Hobson, ed. Readings from the *Encyclopedia of neuroscience*. Boston: Birkhauser.

Hobson, J.A., and McCarley, R.W. 1977. The brain as a dream state generator: An activation-synthesis hypothesis of the dream process. *American Journal of Psychiatry* 134: 1335–48.

Hochberg, J. 1970. Attention, organization, and consciousness. In *Attention: Contemporary theory and analysis*, D.I. Mostofsky, ed. New York: Appleton-Century-Crofts.

Hochberg, J. 1988. Visual perception. In *Stevens' Handbook of experimental psychology*, R.C. Atkinson, R.J. Herrnstein, G. Lindzey, and R.D. Luce, eds. New York: Wiley.

Hockett, C.D. 1960. The origin of speech. *Scientific American* 203: 88–96.

Hoffman, D.D. 1983. The interpretation of visual illusions. *Scientific American* Dec. Reprinted in *Readings from Scientific American: The mind's eye*. 1986. New York: Freeman.

Hoffman, L.W. 1984. Maternal employment and the young child. In *Parent-child interactions and parent-child relations in child development*, M. Permutter, ed. Minnesota Symposia on Child Psychology, vol. 17. Hillsdale, NJ: Erlbaum.

Hofling, C.K., Brotzman, E., Dalrymple, S., Graves, N., and Pierce, C.M. 1966. An experimental study in nurse–physician relationships. *Journal of Nervous and Mental Disease* 143: 171–80.

Hogan, R. 1976. *Personality theory: The personological tradition*. Englewood Cliffs, NJ: Prentice Hall.

Hogan, R. 1982. A socioanalytic theory of personality. *Nebraska Symposium on Motivation, 1981*. Lincoln: University of Nebraska Press.

Hogan, R. 1992. Personality and personality measurement. In *Handbook of Industrial/ Organizational Psychology*, M. Dunnette and L. Hough, eds. In press.

Hogan, R., Carpenter, B.N., Briggs, S. R., and Hansson, R.O. 1985. Personality assessment and personnel selection. In *Personality assessment in organizations*, H.J. Bernardin and D.A. Bownas, eds. New York: Praeger.

Hohmann, G.W. 1966. Some effects of spinal cord lesions on experienced emotional feelings, *Psychophysiology* 143–56.

Holahan, C.J. 1982. *Environmental psychology*. New York: Random House.

Holahan, C.J., and Moos, R.H. 1990. Life stressors, resistance factors, and improved psychological functioning: An extension of the stress resistance paradigm. *Journal of Personality and Social Psychology* 58: 909–17.

Holland, J. 1966. *The psychology of vocational choice*. Waltham, MA: Blaisdell.

Hollingshead, A.B., and Redlich, F.C. 1958. *Social class and mental illness: A community study*. New York: Wiley.

Holmes, D.S. 1980. Meditation and somatic arousal reduction: A review of the experimental evidence. *American Psychologist* 39: 1–10.

Holmes, D.S. 1987. The influence of meditation versus rest on physiological arousal: A second examination. In *The psychology of meditation*, M.A. West, ed. New York: Oxford University Press.

Holmes, T.H., and Rahe, R.H. 1967. The social readjustment rating scale. *Journal of Psychosomatic Research* 11: 213–18.

Holmes, T.H., and Masuda, M. 1974. Life change and illness susceptibility. In *Stressful life events: Their nature and effects*, B.S. Dohrenwend and B.P. Dohrenwend, eds. New York: Wiley.

Holstein, C. 1976. Development of moral judgment: A longitudinal study of males and females. *Child Development* 47: 51–61.

Holyoak, K.J. 1990. Problem solving. In *Thinking: An invitation to cognitive science*, D.N. Osherson and E.E. Smith, eds. Cambridge, MA: MIT Press.

Homa, D. 1983. An assessment of two extraordinary speed-readers. *Bulletin of the Psychonomic Society* 21: 123–26.

Honey, R.C. 1990. Stimulus generalization as a function of stimulus novelty and familiarity in rats. *Journal of Experimental Psychology: Animal Behavior Processes* 16: 178–84.

Hopson, J.L. 1986. The unraveling of insomnia. *Psychology Today*, June, 43–49.

Horn, J.L. 1970. Organization of data on life-span development of human abilities. In *Life-span developmental psychology: Research and theory*, L.R. Goulet and P.B. Baltes, eds. New York: Academic Press.

Horn, J.L. 1976. Human abilities: A review of research and theory in the early 1970s. *Annual Review of Psychology* 27: 437–85.

———. 1978. The nature and development of intellectual abilities. In *Human variation*, R.T. Osborne, C.E. Noble, and N. Weyl, eds. New York: Academic Press.

Horn, J.L., and Donaldson, G. 1980. Cognitive development in adulthood. In *Constancy and change in human development*, O. Brim & J. Kagan, eds. Cambridge, MA: Harvard University Press.

———. 1983. The Texas adoption project: Adopted children and their intellectual resemblance to biological and adoptive parents. *Child Development* 54: 268–75.

Horn, J.M., Loehlin, J.C., and Willerman, L. 1979. Intellectual resemblance among adoptive and biological relatives: The Texas adoption project. *Behavior Genetics* 9: 177–207.

Horne, J. 1988. *Why we sleep*. Oxford, UK: Oxford University Press.

Horney, K.D. 1945. *Our inner conflicts*. New York: Norton.

Hothersall, D. 1990. *History of psychology*, 2nd ed. New York: McGraw-Hill.

House, J.S. 1981. *Work stress and social support*. Reading, MA: Addison Wesley.

House, J.S., Robbins, C., and Metzner, H.L. 1982. The association of social relationships with mortality: Prospective evidence from the Tecumseh Community Health Study. *American Journal of Epidemiology* 116: 123–40.

Houston, J.P. 1991. Fundamentals of learning and memory, 4th ed. San Diego: Harcourt Brace Jovanovich.

Houts, P.S., Miller, R.W., Tokuhata, G.K., and Ham, K.S. 1980. Health-related behavioral impact of the Three Mile Island nuclear accident. Report submitted to the TMI Advisory Panel on Health Research Studies

of the Pennsylvania Department of Health, Hershey, PA, April.

Hovland, C.J., and Sears, R.R. 1940. Minor studies in aggression: Correlation of lynchings with economic indices. *Journal of Psychology* 9: 301–10.

Howard, A., Pion, G.M., Gottfredson, G.D., Flattau, P.E., Oskamp, S., Pfafflin, S.M., Bray, D.W., and Burstein, A.G. 1986. The changing face of American psychology: A report from the committee on employment and human resources. *American Psychologist* 41: 1311–27.

Howard, J. 1984. *Margaret Mead: A Life*. New York: Simon and Schuster.

Hubel, D.H. 1988. *Eye, brain, and vision*. New York: Scientific American Library.

Hubel, D.H., and Wiesel, T.N. 1959. Receptive fields of single neurons in the cat's striate cortex. *Journal of Physiology* 148: 574–91.

———. 1962. Receptive fields, binocular interaction and functional architecture in the cat's visual cortex. *Journal of Physiology* 160: 106–54.

———. 1963. Receptive fields of cells in striate cortex of very young visually inexperienced kittens. *Journal of Neurophysiology* 26: 994–1002.

———. 1979. Brain mechanisms in vision. *Scientific American* 241: 250–63.

Hudson, J.A. 1990. Constructive processing in children's event memory. *Developmental Psychology* 26: 180–87.

Huey, E.B. 1908. *The psychology and pedagogy of reading*. New York: Macmillan. Reprinted 1968, Cambridge, MA: MIT Press.

Hughes, J., Smith, T.W., Kosterlitz, H.W., Fothergill, L.A., Morgan, B.A., and Morris, H.R. 1975. Identification of two related pentapeptides from the brain with potent opiate agonist activity. *Nature* 258: 577–79.

Hull, C.L. 1943. *Principles of Behavior*. New York: Appleton-Century-Crofts.

Hull, J.G., Van Treuren, R.R., and Virnelli, S. Hardiness and health: A critique and alternative approach. *Journal of Personality and Social Psychology* 53: 518–30.

Hume, D. 1739/1949. *A treatise on human nature*. Oxford: Clarendon Press.

Hummert, M.L., Crockett, W.H., and Kemper, S. 1990. Processing mechanisms underlying use of the balance schema. *Journal of Personality and Social Psychology* 58: 5–21.

Humphreys, L.G. 1979. The construct of general intelligence. *Intelligence* 3: 105–20.

Hunt, E. 1980. Intelligence as an information processing concept. *British Journal of Psychology* 71: 449–74.

———. 1985. Verbal ability. In *Human abilities; An information-processing approach*, R.S. Sternberg, ed. New York: Freeman.

———. 1989. Cognitive science: Definition, status, and questions. *Annual Review of Psychology* 40: 603–29.

Hunt, J. McV. 1961. *Intelligence and experience*. New York: Ronald Press.

Hunter, F.T. 1985. Adolescent's perception of discussions with parents and friends. *Developmental Psychology* 21: 433–40.

Hunter, I.M.L. 1978. The role of memory in expert mental calculations. In *Practical aspects of memory*, M.M. Gruneberg, P.E. Morris, and R.N. Sykes, eds. London: Academic Press.

Hurvitz, L.M. 1978. Two decades of op-

ponent processes. In *Color 77*, F.W. Bilmeyer and G. Wyszecki, eds. Bristol, England: Adam Hilger.

Huston, A. 1983. Sex-typing. In *Handbook of Child Psychology*, vol. IV, 4th ed., E.M. Hetherington, ed. New York: Wiley.

Hyde, J.S. 1981. How large are cognitive gender differences? *American Psychologist* 36: 892–901.

———. 1985. *Half the human experience*, 3rd ed. Lexington, MA: D.C. Heath.

Hyde, J.S., Fennema, E., and Lamon, S.J. 1990. Gender differences in mathematics performance: A meta-analysis. *Psychological Bulletin* 107: 139–55.

Hyde, J.S., and Linn, M.C. 1988. Gender difference in verbal abilities: A meta-analysis. *Psychological Bulletin* 104: 53–69.

Hyde, T.S., and Jenkins, J.J. 1969. Differential effects of incidental tasks on the organization of recall of a list of highly associated words. *Journal of Experimental Psychology* 82: 472–81.

Hyman, B.T., Van Hoesen, G.W., Damasio, A.R., and Barnes, C.L. 1984. Alzheimer's disease: Cell-specific pathology isolates the hippocampal formation. *Science* 225: 1168–70.

Hyman, R. 1977. The case against parapsychology. *The Humanist* 37: 47–49.

Iggo, A. 1982. Cutaneous sensory mechanisms. In *The senses*, H.B. Barlow and J.D. Mollon, eds. Cambridge, England: Cambridge University Press.

Ingalls, R.P. 1978. *Mental retardation: The changing outlook*. New York: Wiley.

Ingles, J., Campbell, D., and Donald, M.W. 1976. Electromyographic biofeedback and neuromuscular rehabilitation. *Canadian Journal of Behavioral Science* 8: 299–323.

Ingram, R., ed. 1986. *Information processing approaches to clinical psychology*. Orlando, FL: Academic Press.

Ingram, R.E. 1990. Self-focused attention in clinical disorders: Review and conceptual model. *Psychological Bulletin* 107: 156–76.

Ingram, R.E., Kendall, P.C., Smith, T.W., Donnell, C., and Ronan, K. 1987. Cognitive specificity in emotional distress. *Journal of Personality and Social Psychology* 53: 734–42.

Inhelder, B., and Piaget, J. 1958. *The growth of logical thinking from childhood to adolescence*. New York: Basic Books.

Inouye, E. 1965. Similar and dissimilar manifestations of obsessive-compulsive neuroses in monozygotic twins. *American Journal of Psychology* 121: 1171–75.

Insko, C.A., Blake, R.R., Cialdini, R.B., and Mulaik, S. 1970. Attitudes toward birth control and cognitive consistency: Theoretical and practical implications of survey data. *Journal of Personality and Social Psychology* 16: 228–37.

Intons-Peterson, M.J., and Smyth, M.M. 1987. The anatomy of repertory memory. *Journal of Experimental Psychology: Learning, Memory, and Cognition* 13: 490–500.

Irvine, S.H. 1969. The factor analysis of African abilities and attainments: Constructs across cultures. *Psychological Bulletin* 71: 20–32.

———. 1970. Affect and construct—a cross-cultural check on theories of intelligence. *Journal of Social Psychology* 80: 23–30.

Isen, A.M., Horn, N., and Rosenhan, D.L. 1973. Effects of success and failure on children's generosity. *Journal of Personality and Social Psychology* 27: 239–47.

Isen, A.M. and Levin, P.F. 1972. Effect of feeling good on helping: Cookies and kindness. *Journal of Personality and Social Psychology* 21: 384–88.

Itard, J.-M.-G. 1804/1962. The wild boy of Aveyron. Englewood Cliffs, NJ: Prentice Hall.

Ittelson, W.H. 1951. Size as a cue to distance: Static localization. *American Journal of Psychology* 64: 54–67.

———. 1952. *The Ames demonstrations in perception*. Princeton, NJ: Princeton University Press.

Izard, C.E. 1971. *The Face of Emotion*. New York: Appleton-Century-Crofts.

Izard, C.E., and Buechler, S. 1980. Aspects of consciousness and personality in terms of differential emotions theory. In *Emotion: Theory, research, and experience*, vol. 1, R. Plutchik, and H. Kellerman, eds. New York: Academic Press.

Izquierdo, I., Dias, R.D., Perry, M.L., Souza, D.O., Elisaretsky, E., and Carrascao, M.A. 1982. A physiological amnestic mechanism mediated by endogenous opiod peptides, and its poosible role in learning. In *Neuronal plasticity and memory formation*, C. Ajmone Marson and H. Mathies, eds. New York: Raven.

Jaccard, J., Helbig, D.W., Wan, C.K., Gutman, M.A., and Kritz-Silverstein, D.C. 1990. Individual differences in attitude-behavior consistency: The prediction of contraceptive behavior. *Journal of Applied Social Psychology* 20: 575–67.

Jacobs, J. 1887. Experiments on 'prehension.' *Mind* 12: 75–79.

Jacobson, E. 1932. The electrophysiology of mental activities. *American Journal of Psychology* 44: 677–94.

Jacobson, G. 1983. *The multiple crises of marital separation and divorce*. New York: Grune and Stratton.

Jackson, S.E., and Schuler, R.S. 1985. A metal-analysis and conceptual critique of role ambiguity and role conflict in work settings. *Organizational Behavior and Human Decision Processes* 36: 16–78.

James, W. 1890. *The principles of psychology*. New York: Holt.

———. 1907. *Pragmatism*. New York: Longmans, Green.

Janet, P. [1898] 1979. A case of possession and modern exorcism. In *Great cases in psychotherapy*, D. Wedding and R.J. Corsini, eds. Itasca, IL: F.E. Peacock.

Janowitz, H.D., and Hollander, F. 1953. Effect of prolonged intragastric feeding on oral ingestion. *Federation Proceedings* 12: 72.

Jellinek, E.M. 1960. *The disease concept of alcoholism*. New Brunswick, NJ: Hillhouse Press.

Jemmott, J.B., and Locke, S.E. 1984. Psychosocial factors, immunological mediation, and human susceptibility to infectious diseases: How much do we know? *Psychological Bulletin* 95: 78–108.

Jenkins, J.G., and Dallenbach, K.M. 1924. Oblivescence during sleep and waking. *American Journal of Psychology* 35: 605–12.

Jensen, A.R. 1969. How much can we boost IQ and scholastic achievement? *Harvard Educational Review* 39: 1–123.

———. 1980. *Bias in mental testing*. New York: Free Press.

———. 1984. Political ideologies and educational research. *Phi Delta Kappan*, March, 460–62.

———. 1985. The nature of the black-white difference on various psychometric tests: Spearman's hypothesis. *Behavioral and Brain Sciences* 8: 193–219.

Jensen, G.D. 1973. Human sexual behavior in primate perspective. In *Contemporary Sexual Behavior: Critical Issues in the 1970s*, J. Zubin and J. Money, eds. Baltimore: Johns Hopkins University Press.

Jessor, S., and Jessor, R. 1975. Transition from virginity to nonvirginity among youth: A social-psychological study over time. *Developmental Psychology* 11: 473–84.

Johansson, G. 1977. *Case report on female catecholamine excretion in response to examination stress* (Department of Psychology Report No. 515.) Stockholm: University of Stockholm.

John, O.P. 1990. The "Big Five" factor taxonomy: Dimensions of personality in the natural language and in questionnaires. In *Handbook of personality theory and research*, L. Pervin, ed. New York: Guilford Press.

John, O.P., Hampson, S.E., and Goldberg, L.R. 1991. The basic level in personality-trait hierarchies: Studies of trait use and accessibility in different contexts. *Journal of Personality and Social Psychology* 60: 348–61.

Johnson, D., and Drenick, E.J. 1977. Therapeutic fasting in morbid obesity: Long term follow-up. *Archives of Internal Medicine* 137: 1381–82.

Johnson, J.S., and Newport, E.L. 1989. Critical period effects in second language learning: The influence of maturational state on the acquisition of English as a second language. *Cognitive Psychology* 21: 60–99.

Johnson, O., Dailey, V., Reed, A. Jr., Bruno, W.E., and Lyons, D.M. 1989. *The 1989 Information Please Almanac*. Boston: Houghton Mifflin.

Johnson, S. 1984. Male-female longevity gap widening. *New York Times*, May 22.

Johnston, L.D., Bachman, J.G., and O'Malley, V.M. 1982. *Student drug use, attitudes, and beliefs: National trends 1975–1982*. Rockville, MD: National Institute on Drug Abuse, U.S. Government Printing Office.

Johnston, L.D., O'Malley, P.M., and Bachman, J.G. 1989. *Illicit drug use, smoking, and drinking by America's high school students, college students, and young adults, 1975–1987*. Rockville, MD: National Institute on Drug Abuse.

Johnston, W.A., and Dark, V.J. 1986. Selective attention. *Annual Review of Psychology* 37: 43–76.

Jones, E.E. 1985. History of social psychology. In *Topics in the history of psychology*, vol. 2, G.A. Kimble and K. Schlesinger, eds. Hillsdale, NJ: Erlbaum.

Jones, E.E., and Davis, K.E. 1965. From acts to dispositions: The attribution process in person perception. In *Advances in experimental social psychology*, vol. 2, L. Berkowitz, ed. New York: Academic Press.

Jones, E.E., Davis, K.E., and Gergen, K.J. 1961. Role playing variations and their informational value for person perception. *Journal of Abnormal and Social Psychology* 63: 302–10.

Jones, E.E., and Harris, V.A. 1967. The attribution of attitudes. *Journal of Experimental Social Psychology* 3: 1–24.

Jones, E.E., and Nisbett, R.E. 1971. *The actor and the observer: Divergent perceptions of the causes of behavior*. Morristown, NJ: General Learning Press.

Jones, E.E., Rock, L., Shaver, K.G., Goethals, G.R., and Ward, L.M. 1968. Pattern of performance and ability attribution: An unexpected primacy effect. *Journal of Personality and Social Psychology* 10: 317–40.

Jones, E.F., Forrest, J.D., Goldman, N., Henshaw, S.K., Lincoln, R., Rosoff, J.I., Wostoff, C.F., Wulf, W., and Wulf, D. 1985. Teenage pregnancy in developed countries: Determinants and policy implications. *Family Planning Perspectives* 17: 53–63.

Jones, H.C., and Lovinger, P.W. 1985. *The marijuana question and science's search for an answer*. New York: Dodd, Mead.

Jones, K.L., Smith, D.W., Ulleland, C.V., and Streissguth, A.P. 1973. Pattern of malformation in offspring of chronic alcoholic mothers. *Lancet* 1: 1267–71.

Jones, M.C. 1924. The elimination of children's fears. *Journal of Experimental Psychology* 7: 382–90.

———. 1924. A laboratory study of fear: The case of Peter. *Pedagogical Seminary* 31: 308–15.

Jones, M.C., and Mussen, P.H. 1958. Self-conceptions, motivations, and interpersonal attitudes of early- and late-maturing girls. *Child Development* 29: 491–501.

Jones, R.T. 1980. Human effects: An overview. In *Marijuana research findings: 1980*, R.C. Petersen, ed. NIDA Research Monograph No. 31, DHHS Publication No. ADM 80-1001. Washington, DC: U.S. Government Printing Office.

Jones, W.H., Cheek, J.M., and Briggs, S.R. 1986. *Shyness: Perspectives on research and treatment*. New York: Plenum Press.

Jordan, T.G., Grallo, R., Deutch, M., and Deutch, C.P. 1985. Long-term effects of enrichment: A 20-year perspective on persistence and change. *American Journal of Community Psychology* 13: 393–414.

Jouvet, H.C. 1973. Serotonin and sleep in the cat. In *Serotonin and behavior*, J. Barchus and E. Usdin, eds. New York: Academic Press.

Judd, C.M., Drake, R.A., Downing, J.W., and Krosnick, J.A. 1991. Some dynamic properties of attitude structures: Context-induced response facilitation and polarization. *Journal of Personality and Social Psychology* 60: 193–202.

Julian, J., and Kornblum, W. 1983. *Social problems*, 4th ed. Englewood Cliffs, NJ: Prentice Hall.

Jung, C.G. [1921] 1971. *Psychological types*. Princeton, NJ: Princeton University Press.

———. 1933. *Modern man in search of a soul*. New York: Harcourt.

———. 1936. *The collected works of C.J. Jung*. Princeton, NJ: Princeton University Press.

Jusczyk, P.W., and Derrah, C. 1987. Representation of speech sounds by young infants. *Developmental Psychology* 23: 648–54.

Just, M.A., and Carpenter, P.A. 1980. A theory of reading: From eye fixations to comprehension. *Psychological Review* 87: 329–54.

———. 1987. *The psychology of reading and language comprehension*. Boston: Allyn & Bacon.

Kagan, J., and Reznick, J.S. 1986. Shyness and temperament. In *Shyness*, W.H. Jones, J.M. Cheek, and S.R. Briggs, eds. New York: Plenum Press.

Kagan, J., Reznick, J.S., & Snidman, N. 1988. Biological bases of childhood shyness. *Science* 240: 167–71.

Kahn, M.W., Hannah, M., Hinkin, C., Montgomery, C., and Pitz, D. 1987. Psychopathology on the streets: Psychological assessment of the homeless. *Professional Psychology* 18: 580–86.

Kahneman, D. 1973. *Attention and effort.* Englewood Cliffs, NJ: Prentice Hall.

Kahneman, D., and Chajczyk, D. 1983. Tests of the automaticity of reading: Dilution of Stroop effects by color-irrelevant stimuli. *Journal of Experimental Psychology: Human Perception and Performance* 9: 497–509.

Kahneman, D., and Tversky, A. 1971. Subjective probability: A judgment of representativeness. *Cognitive Psychology* 3: 430–54.

Kail, R. 1979. *The development of memory in children.* San Francisco: Freeman.

Kail, R., and Pellegrino, J.W. 1985. *Human intelligence: Perspectives and propects.* New York: Freeman.

Kalat, J.W. 1988. *Biological psychology,* 3rd ed. Belmont, CA: Wadsworth.

Kalish, H.I. 1981. *From behavioral science to behavior modification.* New York: McGraw-Hill.

Kallgren, C.A., and Kenrick, D.T. 1989. *Ethical judgments of nonhuman research subjects: The effects of phylogenetic closeness and affective valence.* Paper presented at meetings of Eastern Psychological Association, Boston, MA.

Kamin, L.J. 1969. Predictability, surprise, attention, and conditioning. In *Punishment and aversive behavior,* B.A. Campbell and R.M. Church, eds. New York: Appleton-Century-Crofts.

Kandel, D.B. 1981. Peer influences in adolescence. *Annual Meeting of the Society for Research in Child Development.* Boston (April).

Kanizsa, G. 1976. Subjective contours. *Scientific American* 234: 48–52.

————. 1979. *Organization in vision.* New York: Praeger.

Kanner, A.D., Coyne, J.C., Schaefer, C., and Lazarus, R.S. 1981. Comparison of two modes of stress measurement: Daily hassles and uplifts versus major life events. *Journal of Behavioral Medicine* 4: 1–39.

Kaprio, J., Koskenvuo, M., and Rita, H. 1987. Mortality after bereavement: A prospective study of 95,647 widowed persons. *American Journal of Public Health* 77: 283–87.

Kasden, A.E. 1989. *Behavior modification in applied settings,* 4th ed. Pacific Grove, CA: Brooks/Cole.

Kastenbaum, R. 1981. *Death, society, and human experience,* 2nd ed. St. Louis: Mosby.

Kaufman, A.S., and Doppelt, J.E. 1976. Analysis of WISC-R standardization data to terms of the stratification variables. *Child Development* 47: 165–71.

Kaufman, L., and Rock, I. 1962. The moon illusion. *Scientific American* 207: 120–32.

Keating, C.F. 1985. Gender and the physiognomy of dominance and attractiveness. *Social Psychology Quarterly* 48: 61–70.

Keats, D.M. 1982. Cultural bases of concepts of intelligence: A Chinese versus Australian comparison. *Proceedings: Second Asian Workshop on Child and Adolescent Development,* pp. 67–75.

Kelley, H.H. 1972. Causal schemata and the attribution process. In *Attribution: Perceiving the causes of behavior,* E. Jones, D. Kanouse, H. Kelley, R. Nisbett, S. Valins, and B. Weiner, eds. Morristown, NJ: General Learning Press.

————. 1973. The process of causal attribution. *American Psychologist* 28: 107–28.

Kelley, H.H., and Michela, J.L. 1980. Attribution theory and research. *Annual Review of Psychology,* 31: 457–501.

Kelley, K. 1986. *His way: The unauthorized biography of Frank Sinatra.* New York: Bantam Books.

Kellogg, W.N., and Kellogg, L.A. [1933] 1967. *The ape and the child: A study of environmental influence upon early behavior.* New York: Hafner.

Kelly, G. 1955. *The psychology of personal constructs.* New York: Norton.

Kemler Nelson, D.G., Hirsh-Pasek, K., Jusczyk, P.W., and Cassidy, K.W. 1989. How the prosodic cues in motherese might assist language learning. *Journal of Child Language* 16: 55–68.

Kenrick, D.T. 1987. Gender, genes, and the social environment: A biosocial interactionist perspective. In *Review of personality and social psychology,* vol. 7, P.C. Shaver and C. Hendrick, eds. Newbury Park, CA: Sage.

Kenrick, D.T., and Cialdini, R.B. 1977. Romantic attraction: Misattribution vs. reinforcement explanations. *Journal of Personality and Social Psychology* 35: 381–91.

Kenrick, D.T., and Dantchik, A. 1983. Interactionism, idiographics, and the social psychological invasion of personality. *Journal of Personality* 51: 286–307.

Kenrick, D.T., Dantchik, A., and MacFarlane, S. 1983. Personality, environment, and criminal behavior: An evolutionary perspective. In *Personality theory, moral development, and criminal behavior,* W.S. Laufer and J.M. Day, eds. Lexington, MA.: Heath.

Kenrick, D.T., and Funder, D.C. 1988. Profiting from controversy: Lessons of the personal-situation debate. *American Psychologist* 43: 23–34.

————. 1991. Do personality traits really exist? In *Personality: Contemporary research and theory,* V. Derlega, B. Winstead, and W.H. Jones, eds. Chicago: Nelson-Hall.

Kenrick, D.T., and Gutierres, S.E. 1980. Contrast effects and judgments of physical attractiveness: When beauty becomes a social problem. *Journal of Personality and Social Psychology,* 38: 131–40.

Kenrick, D.T., Gutierres, S.E., and Goldberg, L. 1989. Influence of erotica on judgments of strangers and mates. *Journal of Experimental Social Psychology.* 25: 159–167.

Kenrick, D.T., and Hogan, R. 1992. Cognition. In *The sociobiological imagination.* M. Maxwell, ed. Albany: SUNY Press.

Kenrick, D. T., and Johnson, G.A. 1979. Interpersonal attraction in aversive environments: A problem for the classical conditioning paradigm? *Journal of Personality and Social Psychology* 37: 572–79.

Kenrick, D.T., and Keefe, R.C. 1992. Age preferences in mates reflect sex differences in reproductive strategies. *Behavioral and Brain Sciences* 14. In press.

Kenrick, D.T. and MacFarlane, S.W. 1986. Ambient temperature and horn-honking: A field study of the heat/aggression relationship. *Environment and Behavior* 18: 179–191.

Kenrick, D.T., McCreath, H.E., Govern, J., King, R., and Bordin, J. 1990. Person-environment intersections: Everyday settings and common trait dimensions. *Journal of Personality and Social Psychology* 58: 685–98.

Kenrick, D.T., Montello, D., and MacFarlane, S. 1985. Personality: Social learning, social cognition, or sociobiology? In *Perspectives in personality,* vol. 1, R. Hogan and W. Jones, eds. Greenwich, CT: JAI press.

Kenrick, D.T., Sadalla, E.K., Groth, G., and Trost, M.R. 1990. Evolution, traits, and the stages of human courtship: Qualifying the parental investment model. *Journal of Personality* 58: 97–117.

Kenrick, D.T., and Stringfield, D.O. 1980. Personality traits and the eye of the beholder: Crossing some traditional philosophical boundaries in the search for consistency in all of the people. *Psychological Review* 87: 88–104.

Kenrick, D.T., Stringfield, D.O., Wagenhals, W., Dahl, R., and Ransdell, H. 1980. Sex differences, androgyny, and approach responses to erotica: A new variation on the old volunteer problem. *Journal of Personality and Social Psychology* 38: 517–24.

Kenrick, D.T., and Trost, M.R. 1987. A biosocial model of heterosexual relationships. In *Males, females, and sexuality: Research and theory,* K. Kelly, ed. Albany: SUNY Press.

————. 1989. A reproductive exchange model of heterosexual relationships: Putting proximate economics in ultimate perspective. In *Review of Personality & Social Psychology,* vol. 10. C. Hendrick, ed. Newbury Park, CA: Sage.

Kendall, P.C. 1978. Anxiety: States, traits—situations? *Journal of Consulting and Clinical Psychology* 46: 280–87.

Kendall, P.C., and Kriss, M.R. 1983. Cognitive-behavioral interventions. In *Handbook of clinical psychology,* C.E. Walker, ed. Homewood, IL: Dow Jones—Irwin.

Keniston, K. 1970. Youth: As a stage of life. *American Scholar* 39: 631–54.

Kennedy, J.M. 1982. Haptic pictures. In *Tactile perception,* W. Schiff and E. Foulke, eds. Cambridge, UK: Cambridge University Press.

Kenny, D.A., and LaVoie, L. 1984. The social relations model. In *Advances in experimental social psychology,* vol. 18, L. Berkowitz, ed. Orlando, FL: Academic Press.

Keon, T.L., and McDonald, B. 1982. Job satisfaction and life satisfaction: An empirical evaluation of their interrelationship. *Human Relations* 35: 167–80.

Keppel, G.A. 1967. A reconsideration of the extinction-recovery theory. *Journal of Verbal Learning and Verbal Behavior* 6: 476–86.

Kety, S.S. 1974. From rationalization to reason. *American Journal of Psychiatry* 131: 957–63.

Keverne, E.B. 1982. Chemical senses: Taste. In *The senses,* H.B. Barlow & J.D. Mollon, eds. Cambridge, England: Cambridge University Press.

Keys, A., Brozek, J., Henschel, A., Mickelson, O. and Taylor, H.L. 1950. *The biology of human starvation.* Minneapolis: University of Minnesota Press.

Khan, A.U. 1986. *Clinical disorders of memory.* New York: Plenum.

Kiecolt-Glaser, J., Garner, W., Spreicher, C., Penn, G., Holliday, J., and Glaser, R. 1985. Psychosocial modifiers of immunocompetence in medical students. *Psychosomatic Medicine* 46: 7–14.

Kiecolt-Glaser, J.K., and Glaser, R. 1988. Psychological influences on immunity: Implications for AIDS. *American Psychologist* 43: 892–98.

Kienan, G. 1987. Decision making under stress: Scanning of alternatives under controllable and uncontrollable threats. *Journal of Personality and Social Psychology* 52: 639–44.

Kiesler, C.A. 1982. Mental hospitals and alternative care: Noninstitutionalization as potential public policy for mental patients. *American Psychologist* 37: 1323–39.

Kiesler, C.A., and Pallak, M.S. 1976. Arousal properties of dissonance manipulations. *Psychological Bulletin* 83: 1014–25.

Kihlstrom, J.F. 1985. Hypnosis. *Annual Review of Psychology* 36: 385–418.

Kihlstrom, J.F., Schacter, D.L., Cork, R.C., Hurt, C.A., and Behr, S.E. 1990. Implicit and explicit memory following surgical anesthesia. *Psychological Science* 1: 303–6.

Killeen, P.R. 1987. Peace and consequences. Paper presented at the Association for Behavior Analysis. Nashville, TN, May.

Kimble, G.A. 1961. *Hilgard and Marquis' conditioning and learning*, 2nd ed. Englewood Cliffs, NJ: Prentice Hall.

———. 1985. Conditioning and learning. In *Topics in the history of psychology*, vol. 1, G.A. Kimble and K. Schlesinger, eds. Hillsdale, NJ: Erlbaum.

Kimmel, D.C. 1974. *Adulthood and aging*. New York: Wiley.

Kimmel, D.C., Price, K.F., and Walker, J.W. 1978. Retirement choice and retirement satisfaction. *Journal of Gerontology* 33: 575–85.

Kimmel, H.D. 1974. Instrumental conditioning of automatically mediated responses in human beings. *American Psychologist* 29: 325–35.

Kimura, D. 1983. Sex differences in cerebral organization for speech and praxic functions. *Canadian Journal of Psychology* 37: 19–35.

———. 1985. Male brain, female brain: The hidden difference. *Psychology Today*, Nov., 50–58.

Kinder, D.R., and Sears, D.O. 1985. Public opinion and political action. In *The handbook of social psychology*, 3rd ed., G. Lindzey and E. Aronson, eds. New York: Random House.

Kinloch, G.C. 1970. Parent-youth conflict at home: An investigation among university freshmen. *American Journal of Orthopsychiatry* 40: 658–64.

Kinsey, A.C., Pomeroy, W.B., and Martin, C.E. 1948. *Sexual behavior in the human male*. Philadelphia: Saunders.

Kinsey, A.C., Pomeroy, W.B., Martin, C.E., & Gebhard, P.H. 1953. *Sexual behavior in the human female*. Philadelphia: Saunders.

Kirmeyer, S.L. 1978. Urban density and pathology. *Environment and Behavior*, 10: 247–69.

Kisker, G.W. 1964. *The disorganized personality*. New York: McGraw-Hill.

Kitterle, F., ed. 1989. *Cerebral laterality: Theory and research*. Hillsdale, NJ: Erlbaum.

Klahr, D., and Kotovsky, K., eds. 1989. Complex formation processing: The impact of Herbert A. Simon. Hillsdale, NJ: Erlbaum.

Klein, N., Hack, M., Gallagher, J., and Fanaroff, A.A. 1985. Preschool performance of children with normal intelligence who

were very low-birth-weight infants. *Pediatrics* 75: 531–37.

Klein, S.B. 1982. *Motivation: Biosocial Approaches*. New York: McGraw-Hill.

Klerman, G.L. 1983. The efficacy of psychotherapy as the basis for public policy. *American Psychologist* 38: 929–34.

———. 1986. Drugs and psychotherapy. In *Handbook of Psychotherapy and Behavior Change*, 3rd ed., S.L. Garfield and A.E. Bergin, eds. New York: Wiley.

Klerman, G.L., and Izen, J.E. 1977. The effects of bereavement and grief on physical health and general well-being. *Advances in Psychosomatic Medicine* 9: 63–104.

Klima, E., and Bellugi, U.; with Battison, R., Boyes-Braem, P., Fischer, S., Frishberg, N., Lane, H., Lentz, E.M., Newkirk, D., Newport, E., Pedersen, C., & Siple, P. 1979. *The signs of language*. Cambridge, MA: Harvard University Press.

Kling, A.S., Lancaster, J., and Benitone, J. 1970. Amygdalectomy in the free ranging vervet (Cercopithecus althiops). *Journal of Psychiatric Research* 7: 191–99.

Kling, A.S., Lloyd, R.L., and Perryman, K.M. 1987. Slow wave changes in amygdala to visual, auditory, and social stimuli following lesions of the inferior temporal cortex in squirrel monkey (Saimiri sciureus). *Behavioral and Neural Biology* 47: 54–72.

Klinger, E. 1987. The power of daydreams. *Psychology Today*, October, 37–39, 42–44.

Kluft, R.P. 1987. An update on multiple personality disorder. *Hospital and Community Psychiatry* 38: 363–73.

Kobasa, S.C. 1979. Stressful life events, personality, and health: An inquiry into hardiness. *Journal of Personality and Social Psychology* 37: 1–11.

———. 1984. How much stress can you survive? *American Health Magazine*. September, pp. 64–77.

Koestler, A. 1964. *The act of creation*. London: Hutchinson.

Kohlberg, L. 1963. Development of children's orientation toward a moral order. 1. Sequence in the development of moral thoughts. *Vita Humana* 6: 11–36.

———. 1966. A cognitive-developmental analysis of children's sex-role concepts and attitudes. In *The development of sex differences*, E.E. Maccoby, ed. Stanford, CA: Stanford University Press.

———. 1969. Stage and sequence: The cognitive-developmental approach to socialization. In *Handbook of socialization theory and research*, D.A. Goslin, ed. Chicago: Rand McNally.

———. 1981. *The philosophy of moral development*. New York: Harper and Row.

Kohn, A. 1987. It's hard to get left out of a pair. *Psychology Today*, October, pp. 53–57.

Kohn, M.L. 1979. The effects of social class on parental values and practices. In *The American family: Dying or developing*, D. Reiss and H.H. Hoffman, eds. New York: Plenum Press.

Kohut, H. 1977. *The restoration of the self*. New York: International Universities Press.

Kolb, B., and Whishaw, I.Q. 1990. *Fundamentals of human neuropsychology*, 3rd ed. New York: Freeman.

Kolb, L.C. 1968. *Noyes' modern clinical psychiatry*, 7th ed. Philadelphia: Saunders.

Kopp, C.B. 1983. Risk factors in development. In M.H. Haith & J.J. Campos, Eds., *P.H. Mussen's Handbook of child psychology*, Vol. 2. New York: Wiley.

Kosslyn, S.M. 1975. Information representation in visual images. *Cognitive Psychology* 7: 341–70.

———. 1987. Seeing and imaging in the cerebral hemispheres: A computational approach. *Psychological Review* 94: 148–75.

———. 1988. Aspects of a cognitive neuroscience of mental imagery. *Science* 240: 1621–26.

———. 1990. Mental imagery. In *Visual cognition and action: An invitation to cognitive science*, D.N. Osherson, S.M. Kosslyn, and J.M. Hollerbach, eds. Cambridge, MA: MIT Press.

Kraft, C. 1978. A psychophysical approach to air safety. In *Psychology: From research to practice*, H.L. Pick, H.W. Leibowitz, J.E. Singer, A. Steinschneider, and H.W. Stevenson, eds. New York: Plenum Press.

Kramer, R.M., and Brewer, M.B. 1984. Effects of group identity on resource use in a simulated commons dilemma. *Journal of Personality and Social Psychology* 46: 1044–57.

Krantz, D.S., Baum, A., and Singer, J.E., eds. 1983. *Handbook of psychology and health: Vol. 3. Cardiovascular disorders and behavior*. Hillsdale, NJ: Erlbaum.

Krebs, C.J. 1972. *Ecology*. New York: Harper & Row.

Krebs, R.L. 1967. *Some relationships between moral judgement, attention, and resistance to temptation*. Unpublished doctoral dissertation, University of Chicago.

Kreuz, L.E., and Rose, R. M. 1972. Assessment of aggressive behavior and plasma testosterone in a young criminal population. *Psychosomatic Medicine* 34: 321–32.

Kripke, D.F., and Simons, R.N. 1976. Average sleep, insomnia, and sleeping pill use. *Sleep Research* 5: 110.

Kroll, N.E.A., Schepeler, E.M., and Angin, K.T. 1986. Bizzare imagery: The misremembered mnemonic. *Journal of Experimental Psychology: Learning, Memory, and Cognition* 12: 42–53.

Krueger, L.E. 1989. Reconciling Fechner and Stevens: Toward a unified psychosocial law. *Behavioral and Brain Sciences* 12: 251–320.

Kubler-Ross, E. 1969. *On death and dying*. New York: Macmillan.

Kuhn, D., Nash, S.C., and Brucken, L. Sex role concepts of two- and three-year-olds. *Child Development* 49: 445–51.

Kuhn, R. 1958. The treatment of depressive states with G22355 (imipramine hydrochloride). *American Journal of Psychiatry* 115: 459–64.

Kulik, J.A., Baugert-Drowns, R.L., and Kulik, C-L.C. 1984. Effectiveness of coaching for aptitude tests. *Psychological Bulletin* 95: 179–88.

Kulik, J.A. and Brown, R. Frustration, attribution of blame, and aggression. *Journal of Experimental Social Psychology* 15: 183–194.

Kunst-Wilson, W.R., and Zajonc, R.B. 1980. Affective discrimination of stimuli that cannot be recognized. *Science* 207: 557–58.

Kupfer, D.J., Ulrich, R.F., Coble, P.A., Jarrett, D.B., Grochocinski, V.J., Doman, J., Matthews, G., and Borbely, A.A. 1985. Electroencephalographic sleep of younger depressives. *Archives of General Psychiatry* 42: 806–10.

Kurtines, W.H., and Gewirtz, J.L., eds. 1984. *Morality, moral behavior, and moral development.* New York: Wiley.

Kurtines, W.H., and Grief, E.B. 1974. The development of moral thought: Review and evaluation of Kohlberg's approach. *Psychological Bulletin* 81: 453–70.

Kushner, M. 1965. The reduction of a long-standing fetish by means of aversive conditioning. In *Case studies in behavior modification*, L.P. Ullmann and L. Krasner, eds. New York: Holt, Rinehart and Winston.

Labov, W. 1973. The boundaries of words and their meanings. In *New ways of analyzing variations in English*, C.J.N. Bailey and R.W. Shuy, eds. Washington, DC: Georgetown University Press.

Laidlaw, J., and Rickens, A., eds. 1976. *A textbook of epilepsy.* Edinburgh: Churchill and Livingstone.

Laird, J.D. 1974. Self-attribution of emotion: The effects of expressive behavior on the quality of emotional experience. *Journal of Personality and Social Psychology* 29: 475–86.

———. 1984. The real role of facial expression in the experience of emotion: A reply to Tourangeau and Ellsworth and others. *Journal of Personality and Social Psychology* 47: 909–17.

Lamb, M.E. 1977. Father-infant and mother-infant interaction in the first year of life. *Child Development* 48: 167–81.

Lambert, M.J., Shapiro, D.A., and Bergin, A.E. 1986. the effectiveness of psychotherapy. In *Handbook of psychotherapy and behavior change*, 3rd ed., S.L. Garfield and A.E. Bergin, eds. New York: Wiley.

Lamiell, J.T. 1981. Toward an idiothetic psychology of personality. *American Psychologist* 36: 276–89.

Lancaster, J.B. 1975. *Primative behavior and the emergence of human culture.* New York: Holt, Rinehart and Winston.

Langer, E.J., and Imber, L. 1980. The role of mindlessness in the perception of deviance. *Journal of Personality and Social Psychology*, 39: 360–67.

Lansdell, H. 1962. A sex difference in effect of temporal lobe neurosurgery on design preference. *Nature* 194: 852–54.

Larkin, J., McDermott, J., Simon, D.P., and Simon, H.A. 1980. Expert and novice performance in solving physics problems. *Science* 208: 1335–42.

LaRoche, C., Cheifetz, P., Lester, E.P., Shibur, L.D., Tommaso, E., and Engelsmann, F. 1985. Psychopathology in the offspring of parents with bipolar affective disorders. *Canadian Journal of Psychiatry* 30: 337–43.

Lashley, K.S. 1929. *Brain mechanisms and intelligence.* Chicago: University of Chicago Press.

Latane, B., and Darley, J.M. 1970. *The unresponsive bystander: Why doesn't he help?* New York: Appleton-Century-Crofts.

Latane, B., and Schachter, S. 1962. Adrenaline and avoidance learning. *Journal of Comparative and Physiological Psychology*, 55: 369–72.

Latane, G., and Wolf, S. 1981. The social impact of majorities and minorities. *Psychological Review* 88: 438–53.

Lau, S., Lew, W.J.F., Hau, K.-T., Cheung, P.C., and Berndt, T.J. 1990. Relations among perceived parental control, warmth, indulgence, and family harmony in Chinese mainland China. *Developmental Psychology* 26: 674–77.

Lauer, J., and Lauer, R. 1985. Marriages made to last. *Psychology Today*, June. pp. 22–26.

Laughlin, H.T. 1956. *The neuroses in clinical practice.* Philadelphia: Saunders.

Lawson, C. 1989. Toys: Girls still apply makeup, boys fight wars. *The New York Times*, June 15. p. C1.

Lazar, I., and Darlington, R. 1982. Lasting effects of early education: A report from the Consortium for Longitudinal Studies. *Monographs of the Society for Research in Child Development* 47(2–3), Serial No. 195.

Lazarus, A.A. 1965. The treatment of a sexually inadequate man. In *Case studies in behavior modification*, L.P. Ullman and L. Krasner, eds. New York: Holt, Rinehart and Winston.

Lazarus, R.S., and Folkman, S. 1984. *Stress, appraisal, and coping.* New York: Springer.

Lazarus, R.S., Kanner, A.D., and Folkman, S. 1980. Emotions: A cognitive-phenomenological analysis. In *Emotion: Theory, research, and experience*, vol. 1, R. Plutchik, and H. Kellerman, eds. New York: Academic Press.

Leahey, T.H. 1988. William James, Heroic metaphysician. *Contemporary Psychology* 33: 199–202.

Leahey, T.H., and Harris, R.J. 1989. *Human learning.* Englewood Cliffs, NJ: Prentice Hall.

Leak, G.K. and Christopher, S.B. 1982. Freudian psychoanalysis and sociobiology. *American Psychologist* 37: 313–22.

Leask, J., Haber, R.N., and Haber, R.B. 1969. Eidetic imagery in children: II. Longitudinal and experimental results. *Psychonomic Monograph Supplements* 3. Whole No. 35.

Lebow, J. 1982. Consumer satisfaction with mental health treatment. *Psychological Bulletin* 91: 244–59.

Ledwidge, R. 1980. Run for your mind: Aerobic exercise as a means of alleviating anxiety and depression. *Canadian Journal of Behavioral Science* 12: 126–40.

Lee, V.E., Brooks-Gunn, J., and Schnur, E. 1988. Does Head Start work? A 1-year follow-up comparison of disadvantaged children attending Head Start, no preschool, and other preschool programs. *Developmental Psychology* 24: 210–22.

Leeper, 1970. The motivational and perceptual properties of emotions as indicating their fundamental character and role. In *Feelings and emotions: The Loyola symposium*, M.B. Arnold, ed. New York: Academic Press.

Lehrman, D.S. 1966. The reproductive behavior of ring doves. In *Frontiers of Psychological Research*, S. Coopersmith, ed. San Francisco: W.H. Freeman and Co.

Leib, S., Benfield, G., and Guidubaldi, J. 1980. Effects of early intervention and stimulation on the preterm infant. *Pediatrics* 66: 83–90.

Lejeune, J., Turpin, R., and Gautier, M. 1959. Le mongolisme, premier example d'abberation autosemique humaine. *Annales Genetique* 2: 41–48.

Lempers, J., Flavell, E.L., and Flavell, J.H. 1977. The development in very young children of tacit knowledge concerning visual perception. *Genetic Psychology Monographs* 95: 3–53.

Lenneberg, E.H. 1967. *Biological foundations of language.* New York: Wiley.

Lepper, M.R., Greene, D., and Nisbett, R.E. 1973. Undermining children's intrinsic interest with extrinsic rewards: A test of the "overjustification" hypothesis. *Journal of Personality and Social Psychology* 28: 129–37.

Lerner, A.B. 1973. *Einstein and Newton.* Minneapolis: Lerner Publications.

Lerner, R.M. 1984. *On the nature of human plasticity.* New York: Cambridge University Press.

Lester, B.M., Garcia-Coll, C., Valcarcel, M., Hoffman, J., and Brazelton, T.B. 1986. Effects of atypical patterns of fetal growth on newborn (NBAS) behavior. *Child Development* 57: 11–19.

Lester, D. 1977. Multiple personality: A review. *Psychology* 14: 54–59.

Lettieri, D.J., and Ludford, J.P., eds. 1981. Drug abuse and the American adolescent. *National Institute on Drug Abuse Research Review.* Washington, DC: U.S. Department of Health and Human Services.

Lettvin, J.Y., Maturana, H.R., McCulloch, W.S., and Pitts, W.H. 1959. What the frog's eye tells the frog's brain. *Proceedings of the Institute of radio Engineers* 47: 1940–51.

Leuba, C., Birch, L., and Appleton, J. 1968. Human problem-solving during complete paralysis of the voluntary musculature. *Psychological Reports* 22: 849–55.

Levine, J.D., Gordon, N.C., and Fields, H.L. 1979. The role of endorphins in placebo analgesia. In *Advances in Pain Research and Therapy*, vol. 3, J.J. Bonica, J.C. Liebesking, and D. Albe-Fessard, eds. New York: Raven.

Levine, M. 1988. *Effective problem solving.* Englewood Cliffs, NJ: Prentice Hall.

LeVine, R.A., and Campbell, D.T. 1972. *Ethnocentrism: Theories of conflict, ethnic attitudes, and group behavior.* New York: Wiley.

Levinson, D.J., with Darrow, C.N., Klein, E.B., Levinson, M.H., and McKee, B. 1978. *The seasons of a man's life.* New York: Knopf.

Levinson, S.E., and Liberman, M.V. 1981. Speech recognition by computer. *Scientific American* 244, April. 64–76.

Levinthal, C.F. 1990. *Introduction to physiological psychology*, 3rd ed. Englewood Cliffs, NJ: Prentice Hall.

Lewis, M., and Brooks, J. 1975. Infants' reaction to people. In *The origin of fear*, M. Lewis and L. Rosenblum, eds. New York: Wiley.

———. 1978. Self-knowledge and emotional development. In *The development of affect*, M. Lewis and L.A. Rosenblum, eds. New York: Plenum Press.

Lewinsohn, P.M., Hoberman, H., Teri, L., and Hautzinger, M. 1985. An integrative theory of depression. In *Theoretical issues in behavior therapy*, S. Reiss and R. Bootzin, eds. New York: Academic Press.

Lewontin, R. 1976. Race and intelligence. In *The IQ controversy: Critical readings*, N.J. Block and G. Dworkin, eds. New York: Pantheon.

Leyens, J.P., Camino, L., Parke, R.D. and Berkowitz, L. 1975. Effects of movie violence on aggression in a field setting as a function of group dominance and cohesion. *Journal of Personality and Social Psychology* 32: 346–60.

Leyland, C.M., and Mackintosh, N.J. 1978. Blocking of first and second-order autoshaping in pigeons. *Animal Learning and Behavior* 6: 391–94.

Liberman, A.M., Mattingly, I.G., and Turvey, M.T. 1972. Language codes and memory codes. In *Coding processes in human memory*, A.W. Melton and E. Martin, eds. Washington, DC: Winston.

Lichtman, S., and Poser, E.G. 1983. The effects of exercises on mood and cognitive functioning. *Journal of Psychosomatic Research* 27:43–52.

Lieberman, M.A., Yalom, I.D., and Miles, M.B. 1973. *Encounter groups: First facts.* New York: Basic Books.

Liem, J.H. 1974. Effect of verbal communication of parents and children: A comparison of normal and schizophrenic families. *Journal of Consulting and Clinical Psychology*, 42: 438–50.

LIFE: The first 50 years. 1986. New York: Time, Inc.

Lifton, R.J. 1982. *Death in Life: Survivors of Hiroshima.* New York: Basic Books.

Liggett, J. 1974. *The human face.* New York: Stein and Day.

Light, L.L. 1990. Memory and aging: Four hypotheses in search of data. *Annual Review of Psychology* 42: 333–76.

Light, L.L., and Burke, D.M., eds. 1988. *Language, memory and aging.* New York: Cambridge University Press.

Light, K.C., Koepke, J.P., Obrist, P.A., and Willis, P.W., Jr. 1983. Psychological stress induces sodium and fluid retention in men at high risk for hypertension. *Science* 220: 429–31.

Linden, W., ed. 1988. *Biological barriers in behavioral medicine.* New York: Plenum.

Linder, D.E. 1982. Social trap analogs: The tragedy of the commons in the laboratory. In *Cooperation and helping behavior: Theories and research*, V. Derlega and J. Grzelak, eds. New York: Academic Press.

Lindsay, P.H., and Norman, D.A. 1977. *Human information processing*, 2nd ed. New York: Academic Press.

Lindskold, S., and Aronoff, J.R. 1980. Conciliatory strategies and relative power. *Journal of Experimental Social Psychology* 16: 187–97.

Lindzey, G. 1965. Morphology and behavior. In *Theories of Personality: Primary sources and research*, G. Lindzey and C.S. Hall, eds. New York: Wiley.

Lingjaerde, O. 1983. The biochemistry of depression. *Acta Psychiatrica Scandinavica Supplementum* 69: 36–51.

Linn, R.L. 1982. Ability testing: Individual differences, prediction, and differential prediction. In *Ability testing: Uses, consequences, and controversies*, A. Wigdor and W. Gardner, eds. Washington, DC: National Academy Press.

Linville, P.W., Salovey, P., and Fischer, G.W. 1986. Stereotyping and perceived distributions of social characteristics. In J.F. Dovidio and S.L. Gaertner, Eds. *Prejudice, discrimination, and racism* (pp. 165–208). Orlando, FL: Academic Press.

Lipsitt, L. 1979. Perinatal and neonatal factors. *International Journal of Behavior Development* 2: 23–42.

Lipton, S. 1943. Dissociated personality: A case report. *Psychiatric Quarterly* 17: 35–36.

Livingstone, M.S., and Hubel, D.H. 1984. Anatomy and physiology of a color system in the primate visual cortex. *Journal of Neuroscience* 4: 309–56.

Loehlin, J.C. 1987. Twin studies, environmental differences, age changes. *Behavioral and Brain Sciences* 10: 30–31..

Loehlin, J.C., Willerman, L., and Horn, J.M. 1988. Human behavior genetics. *Annual Review of Psychology* 39: 101–34.

Loftus, E.F., Donders, K., Hoffman, H.G., and Schooler, J.W. 1989. Creating new memories that are quickly accessed and confidently held. *Memory & Cognition* 17: 607–16.

Loftus, E.F., and Loftus, G.R. 1980. On the permanence of stored information in the human brain. *American Psychologist* 35: 409–20.

Loftus, E.F., and Palmer, J.C. 1974. Reconstruction of automobile destruction: An example of the interaction between language and memory. *Journal of Verbal Learning and Verbal Behavior* 13: 585–89.

LoLordo, V.M. 1979. Selective associations. In *Mechanisms of learning and motivation.* A. Dickenson and R.A. Boakes, eds. Hillsdale, NJ: Erlbaum.

Lord, C.G., Lepper, M.R., and Preson, E. 1984. Considering the opposite: A corrective strategy for social judgment. *Journal of Personality and Social Psychology* 47: 1231–41.

Lord, C.G., Ross, L., and Lepper, M.R. 1979. Biased assimilation and attitude polarization: The effects of prior theories on subsequently considered evidence, *Journal of Personality and Social Psychology* 37: 2098–109.

Lord, C.G., Saenz, D.S., and Godfrey, D.K. 1987. Effects of perceived scrutiny on participant memory for social interactions. *Journal of Experimental Social Psychology* 23: 498–517.

Lord, W. 1955. *A night to remember.* New York: Holt.

Lorenz, K.Z. 1963. *On aggression.* New York: Harcourt, Brace and World.

Lott, B., and Lott, A.J. 1985. Learning theory in contemporary social psychology. In *Handbook of social psychology*, 3rd ed., G. Lindzey & E. Aronson, eds. New York: Random House.

Lovaas, I. 1967. A behavior therapy approach to the treatment of childhood schizophrenia. In *Minnesota symposia on child development*, vol. 1, J.P. Hill, ed. Minneapolis: University of Minnesota Press.

Lovaas, O.I., Freitag, G., Gold, V.J., and Kassorla, I.C. 1965. Experimental studies in childhood schizophrenia: Analysis of self-destructive behavior. *Journal of Experimental Child Psychology* 2: 67–84.

Lovaas, O.I., Koegal, R., Simmons, J.Q., and Long, J.S. 1973. Some generalization and follow-up measures on autistic children in behavior therapy. *Journal of Applied Behavioral Analysis* 6: 131–65.

Lucas, G.A., Timberlake, W., Gawley, D.J., and Drew, J. 1990. Anticipation of future food: Suppression and facilitation of saccharin intake depending on the delay and type of future food. *Journal of Experimental Psychology: Animal Behavior Processes* 16: 169–77.

Luce, G.G., and Segal, J. 1966. *Sleep.* New York: Coward-McCann.

Luchins, A.S. 1942. Mechanization in problem solving. *Psychological Monographs* 54, No. 248.

Ludemann, P.M., and Nelson, C.H. 1988. Categorical representation of facial expressions by 7-month-old infants. *Developmental Psychology* 24: 492–501.

Ludwig, A.M., Brandsma, J.M., Wilbur, C.B., Bendfeldt, F., and Jameson, D.H. 1972. The objective study of a multiple personality. *Archives of General Psychiatry* 26: 298–310.

Lummis, M., and Stevenson, H.W. 1990. Gender differences in beliefs and achievement: A cross-cultural study. *Developmental Psychology* 26: 254–63.

Lumsden, D.P. 1975. Toward a systems model of stress: Feedback from an anthropological study of the impact of Ghana's Volta River Project. In *Stress and anxiety*, Vol. 2, I.G. Sarason and C.D. Spielberger, eds. Washington, DC: Hemisphere.

Lumsden, C.J., and Wilson, E.O. 1981. *Genes, mind, and culture: The coevolutionary process.* Cambridge, MA: Harvard University Press.

Luria, A.R. 1968. *The mind of a mnemonist.* New York: Basic Books.

———. 1973a. *The man with a shattered world.* London: Cape.

———. 1973b. *The working brain.* New York: Penguin.

———. 1980. *Higher cortical functions in man*, 2nd ed. New York: Basic Books.

Lynch, G. 1984. A magical memory tour. *Psychology Today*, April, pp. 70–76.

Lynch, G., and Baudry, M. 1984. The biochemistry of memory: A new and specific hypothesis. *Science* 224: 1057–63.

Lynch, K. 1960. *The image of the city.* Cambridge, MA: MIT press.

Lynn, M., and Oldenquist, A. 1986. Egoistic and nonegoistic motives in social dilemmas. *American Psychologist* 41: 529–34.

Maass, A., and Clark, R.D. 1984. Hidden impact of minorities: Fifteen years of minority influence. *Psychological Bulletin* 95: 428–50.

Maass, A., West, S.G., and Cialdini, R.B. 1987. Minority influence and conversion. In *Review of personality and social psychology*, vol. 8, C. Hendrick, ed. Newbury Park, CA: Sage.

Maccoby, E.E. 1980. *Social development.* New York: Harcourt Brace and Jovanovich.

Maccoby, E.E., and Jacklin, C.N. 1974. *The psychology of sex differences.* Stanford, CA: Stanford University Press.

———. 1980. Sex differences in aggression: A rejoinder and reprise. *Child Development* 51: 964–80.

MacDonald, N. 1960. The other side: Living with schizophrenia. *Canadian Medical Association Journal* 82: 218–21.

Mace, W.M. 1977. James J. Gibson's strategy for perceiving: Ask not what's inside your head, but what your head's inside of. In *Perceiving, acting and knowing: Toward an ecological psychology*, R. Shaw and J. Bransford, eds. Hillsdale, NJ: Erlbaum.

Mack, S. 1981. Novel help for the handicapped. *Science* 212: 26–27.

MacKay, W.A., and Crammond, D.J. 1987. Neuronal correlates in posterior parietal lobe of the expectation of events. *Behavioral Brain Research* 24: 167–79.

Mackenzie, B. 1984. Explaining race differences in IQ: The logic, the methodology, and the evidence. *American Psychologist* 39: 1214–33.

Mackie, D.M., Worth, L.T., and Asuncion, A.G. 1990. Processing of persuasive in-group messages. *Journal of Personality and Social Psychology* 58: 812–22.

MacKinnon, D.W., and Hall, W.B. 1972. Intelligence and creativity. *Proceedings, XVIIth*

International Congress of Applied Psychology, vol. 2, 1883–88.

Macnamara, J. 1972. Cognitive basis of language learning in infants. *Psychological Review* 79: 1–13.

Maddi, S.R., Bartone, P.T., and Puccetti, M.C. 1987. Stressful events are indeed a factor in physical illness: Reply to Schroeder and Costa. *Journal of Personality and Social Psychology* 52: 833–43.

Maher, B.A. 1966. *Principles of psychopathology: An experimental approach.* New York: McGraw-Hill.

Mahoney, M.J. 1977. Publication prejudices: An experimental study of confirmatory bias in the peer review system. *Cognitive Therapy and Research* 1: 161–65.

Maier, N.R.F. 1931. Reasoning in humans II: The solution of a problem and its appearance in consciousness. *Journal of Comparative Psychology* 12: 181–94.

Malamuth, N., and Donnerstein, E. 1984. *Pornography and sexual aggression.* Orlando, FL: Academic Press.

Mandler, G. 1980. The generation of emotion: A psychological theory. In *Emotion: Theory, research, and experience.* vol. 1, R. Plutchik, and H. Kellerman, eds. New York: Academic Press.

Mandler, G. 1985. *Cognitive psychology: An essay in cognitive science.* Hillsdale, NJ: Erlbaum.

Mann, L. 1981. The baiting crowd in episodes of threatened suicide. *Journal of Personality and Social Psychology* 41: 703–9.

Mann, L. 1980. Queue culture: The waiting line as a social system. In *Sociology Full Circle: Contemporary readings on society,* 3rd ed, W. Feigelman, ed. New York: Holt, Rinehart and Winston.

Mäntylä, T. 1986. Optimizing cue effectiveness: Recall of 500 and 600 incidentally learned words. *Journal of Experimental Psychology: Learning, Memory, and Cognition* 12: 66–71.

Mäntylä, T., and Nilsson, L.-G. 1988. Cue distinctiveness and forgetting: Effectiveness of self-generated retrieval cues in delayed recall. *Journal of Experimental Psychology: Learning, Memory, and Cognition* 14: 502–09.

Manucia, G.K., Baumann, D.J., and Cialdini, R.B. 1984. Mood influences on helping: Direct effects or side effects? *Journal of Personality and Social Psychology* 46: 357–64.

Maranon, G. 1924. Contribution a l'etude de l'action emotive de l'adrenaline. *Revue Francaise d'Endocrinologie* 2: 301–25.

Marcel, A.J. 1983. Conscious and unconscious perception: Experiments on visual masking and word recognition. *Cognitive Psychology* 15: 197–237.

Marek, G.R. 1975. *Toscanni.* London: Vision Press.

Markman, H.J., Floyd, F.J., Stanley, S.M., and Storaasli, R.D. 1988. Prevention of marital distress: A longitudinal investigation. *Journal of Consulting and Clinical Psychology* 56: 210–17.

Marks, I.M. 1969. *Fears and phobias.* New York: Academic Press.

Markus, H., and Nurius, P. 1986. Possible selves. *American Psychologist* 41: 954–69.

Markus, H., and Sentis, K. 1982. The self in information processing. In *Psychological perspectives on the self,* vol. 1, J. Suls, ed. Hillsdale, NJ: LEA.

Marlatt, G.A., Demming, B., and Reid, J.B. 1973. Loss of control drinking in alcoholics: An experimental analogue. *Journal of Abnormal Psychology* 81: 233–41.

Marlatt, G.A., and Rose, F. 1980. Addictive disorders. In *New perspectives in abnormal psychology,* A.E. Kazdin, A.S. Bellack, and M. Hersen, eds. New York: Oxford University Press.

Marshall, D.S. 1971. Sexual behavior on Mangaia. In *Human Sexual Behavior: Variations in the Ethnographic Spectrum,* D.S. Marshall and R.G. Suggs, eds. New York: Basic Books.

Marshall, G.D., and Zimbardo, P.G. 1979. Affective consequences of inadequately explained physiological arousal. *Journal of Personality and Social Psychology* 37: 970–88.

Martin, B. 1977. *Abnormal Psychology.* New York: Holt, Rinehart and Winston.

Martin, L.L., Seta, J.J., and Crelia, R.A. 1990. Assimilation and contrast as a function of people's willingness and ability to expend effort in forming an impression. *Journal of Personality and Social Psychology* 59: 27–37.

Martin, R.A., and Lefcourt, H.M. 1984. Sense of humor as a moderator of the relations between stressors and moods. *Journal of Personality & Social Psychology* 45: 1313–24.

Martindale, C. 1991. *Cognitive psychology: A neural-network approach.* Pacific Grove, CA: Brooks/Cole.

Martinsen, E.W. 1987. The role of aerobic exercise in the treatment of depression. *Stress Medicine* 3: 93–100.

Martorano, S.C. 1977. A developmental analysis of performance on Piaget's formal operations tasks. *Developmental Psychology* 13: 666–72.

Maslow, A. 1954. *Motivation and Personality.* New York: Harper and Row.

Massaro, D.W. 1970. Preperceptual auditory images. *Journal of Experimental Psychology* 85: 411–17.

Masserman, J.H. 1961. *Principles of dynamic psychiatry,* 2nd ed. Philadelphia: Saunders.

Massey, C.M., and Gelman, R. 1988. Preschooler's ability to decide whether a photographed unfamiliar object can move itself. *Developmental Psychology* 24: 307–17.

Masters, W.H., Johnson, V.E., and Kolodny, R.C. 1982. *Human sexuality.* Boston: Little, Brown.

Matarazzo, J.D. 1980. Behavioral health and behavioral medicine: Frontiers for a new health psychology. *American Psychologist* 35: 807–17.

———. 1982. Behavioral health's challenge to academic, scientific, and professional psychology. *American Psychologist* 37: 1–14.

———. 1985. Psychotherapy. In *Topics in the history of psychology,* G.A. Kimble and K. Schlesinger, eds. Hillsdale, NJ: Erlbaum.

Mateer, C.A. 1983. Motor and perceptual functions of the left hemisphere and their interaction. In *Language functions and brain organizations,* S.J. Segalowitz, ed. New York: Academic Press.

Matlin, M.W. 1983. *Cognition.* New York: Holt, Rinehart and Winston.

———. 1987. *The psychology of women.* New York: Holt, Rinehart and Winston.

———. 1988. *Sensation and perception,* 2nd ed. Boston: Allyn and Bacon.

Matson, J.L., and Ollendick, T.H. 1977.

Issues in toilet training normal children. *Behavior Therapy* 8: 549–53.

Matthews, K.A., Scheier, M.F., Brunson, B.I., and Carducci, B. 1980. Attention, unpredictability, and reports of physical symptoms: Eliminating the benefits of predictability. *Journal of Personality and Social Psychology* 38: 525–37.

Matthies, H. 1989. Neurobiological aspects of learning and memory. *Annual Review of Psychology* 40: 381–404.

Mayer, D.J., Price, D.D., Barber, J., and Rafii, A. 1976. Acupuncture analgesia: Evidence for activation of a pain inhibitory system as a mechanism of action. In *Advances in pain research and therapy,* vol. 1, J.J. Bonica and D. Albe-Fessard, eds. New York: Raven Press.

Mayer, J.D., and Bower, G.H. 1986. Learning and memory for personality prototypes. *Journal of Personality & Social Psychology* 51: 473–92.

Mayer, R.E. 1983. *Thinking, problem solving, cognition.* New York: Freeman.

Mays, V.M., and Cochran, S.D. 1988. Issues in the perception of AIDS risk and risk reduction activities by Black and Hispanic/Latina women. *American Psychologist* 43: 949–57.

McArthur, L.Z., and Baron, R. 1983. Toward an ecological theory of social perception. *Psychological Review* 86: 287–330.

McCall, R.B., Appelbaum, M.I., and Hogarty, P.S. 1973. Developmental changes in mental performance. *Monographs of the Society for Research in Child Development* 38 (Serial No. 150), 1–84.

McCann, I.L., and Holmes, D.S. 1984. Influence of aerobic exercise on depression. *Journal of Personality and Social Psychology* 46: 1142–47.

McCarthy, R.A., and Warrington, E.K. 1990. *Cognitive neuropsychology: A clinical introduction.* San Diego: Academic Press.

McClelland, D.C. 1951. Measuring motivation in fantasy: The achievement motive. In *Groups, leadership, and men,* H. Guertkow, ed. Pittsburgh: Carnegie Press.

———. 1961. *The Achieving Society.* Princeton, NJ: Van Nostrand.

———. 1985. *Human Motivation.* Glenview, IL: Scott, Foresman.

McClelland, D.C., and Atkinson, J.W. 1948. The projective expression of needs. I: The effects of different intensities of the hunger drive on perception. *Journal of Psychology* 25: 205–22.

McClelland, D.C., and Winter, D.G. 1971. *Motivating economic achievement.* New York: The Free Press. (Afterward to paperback edition.)

McClelland, J.L. 1981. Retrieving general and specific knowledge from stored knowledge of specifics. *Proceedings of the Third Annual Conference of the Cognitive Science Society.* Berkeley, CA.

McClelland, J.L., and Rummelhart, D.E. 1981. An interactive model of context effects in letter perception. *Psychological Review* 88, 375–407.

McClelland, J.L., Rumelhart, D.E., and The PDP Research Group. 1986. *Parallel distributed processing: Explorations in the microstructure of cognition. Vol. 2: Psychological and biological models.* Cambridge, MA: Bradford Books.

McCloskey, M., Wible, C.G., and Cohen, N.J. 1988. Is there a special flashbulb-memory mechanism? *Journal of Experimental Psychology: General* 117: 171–81.

McCloskey, M., and Zaragoza, M. 1985. Misleading postevent information and memory for events: Arguments and evidence against memory impairment hypotheses. *Journal of Experimental Psychology: General* 114: 1–16.

McConkie, G.W. 1983. Eye movements and perception during reading. In *Eye movements in reading*, K. Rayner, ed. New York: Academic Press.

McCormick, D.A., and Thompson, R.F. 1984. Cerebellum: Essential involvement in the classically conditioned eyelid response. *Science* 223: 296–99.

McCormick, E., and Ilgen, D. 1985. *Industrial and organizational psychology*. Englewood Cliffs, NJ: Prentice Hal.

McCrae, R.R. 1982. Consensual validation of personality traits: Evidence from self-reports and ratings. *Journal of Personality and Social Psychology* 43: 293–303.

McCullogh, L. 1978. The efficacy of covert conditioning. Paper presented at the meeting of the Association for Advancement of Behavior Therapy. Chicago, November.

McDaniel, M.A., and Pressley, M. 1987. *Imagery and related mnemonic processes*. New York: Springer-Verlag.

McDougall, W. 1908. *Social psychology: An introduction*. London: Methuen.

McFie, J., and Zangwill, O.L. 1960. Visual-constructive disabilities associated with lesions of the left cerebral hemisphere. *Brain* 83: 243–60.

McGhee, P.E. 1976. Children's appreciation of humor: A test of the cognitive congruence principle. *Child Development* 47: 420–26.

McGhie, A., and Chapman, J. 1961. Disorders of attention and perception in early schizophrenia. *British Journal of Medical Psychology* 34: 103–16.

McGlone, J. 1978. Sex differences in functional brain assymetry. *Cortex* 14: 122–28.

McGrath, J.E. 1982. Dilemmatics. In *Judgment calls in research* eds. J.E. McGrath, J. Martin, and R.A. Kukla. Beverly Hills, CA: Sage Publications.

McGuire, W.J., and McGuire, C.V. 1988. Content and process in the experience of self. In *Advances in experimental social psychology*, vol. 21, L. Berkowitz, ed. San Diego: Academic Press.

McHose, J.H., and Tauber, L. 1972. Changes in delay of reinforcement in simple instrumental conditioning. *Psychonomic Science* 27: 291–92.

McKeithen, K.B., Reitman, J.S., Rueter, H.H., and Hirtle, S.C. 1981. Knowledge organization and skill differences in computer programmers. *Cognitive Psychology* 13: 307–25.

McKirnan, D.J., and Johnson, T. 1986. Alcohol and drug use among "street" adolescents. *Addictive Behaviors* 11: 201–205.

McKoon, G., Ratcliff, R., and Dell, G.S. 1986. A critical evaluation of the semantic-episodic distinction. *Journal of Experimental Psychology: Learning, Memory, and Cognition* 12: 295–306.

McNally, R.J. 1987. Preparedness and phobias: A review. *Psychological Bulletin* 101: 282–303.

———. 1990. Psychological approaches to panic disorder: A review. *Psychological Bulletin* 108: 403–19.

McNeill, D. 1966. Developmental psycholinguistics. In *The genesis of language: A psycholinguistics approach*, F.L. Smith and G.A. Miller, eds. Cambridge: MIT Press.

McQuade, D., Atwan, R., Banta, M., Kaplan, J., Minter, D., Tichi, C., and Vendler, M.L. 1987. *Harper American Literature*. New York: Harper and Row.

Mechanic, D. 1962. *Students under stress*. New York: Free Press.

Medin, D.L., and Wattenmaker, W.D. 1987. Family resemblance, conceptual cohesiveness, and category construction. *Cognitive Psychology* 19: 242–79.

Mednick, S.A. 1985. Crime in the family tree. *Psychology Today*, March, pp. 58–61.

Mednick, S.A., Gabrielli, W.F., and Hutchings, B. 1984. Genetic influences in criminal convictions: Evidence from an adoption cohort. *Science* 224: 891–94.

Meehl, P.E. 1962. Schizotaxia, schizotypy, schizophrenia. *American Psychologist* 17: 827–38.

———. 1990. Schizotaxia as an open concept. In *Studying persons and lives*, A.I. Rabin, R.A. Zucker, R.A. Emmons, and S. Frank, eds. New York: Springer.

Mehrabian, A., and Russell, J.A. 1968. *An approach to environmental psychology*. Cambridge, MA: M.I.T. Press.

Mehrabian, A., and Russell, J.A. 1974. *An approach to environmental psychology*. Cambridge, MA: MIT Press.

Meichenbaum, D.H. 1977. *Cognitive behavior modification: An integrative approach*. New York: Plenum Press.

Mellen, S.L.W. 1981. *The evolution of love*. Oxford, England: W.H. Freeman and Co.

Meltzer, H.Y., and Stahl, S.M. 1976. The dopamine hypothesis of schizophrenia. *Schizophrenia Bulletin*, 2: 19–76.

Meltzoff, A.N. 1988. Imitation of televised models by infants. *Child Development* 59: 1221–29.

Meltzoff, A.N., and Moore, M.K. 1983. Newborn infants imitate adult facial gestures. *Child Development* 54: 702–709.

Melzack, R. 1973. *The puzzle of pain*. New York: Basic Books.

Melzack, R., and Dennis, S.G. 1978. Neurophysiological foundations of pain. In *The psychology of pain*, R.A. Sternbach, ed. New York: Raven Press.

Melzack, R., and Wall, P.D. 1965. Pain mechanisms: A new theory. *Science* 150: 971–79.

Menyuk, P. 1983. Language development and reading. In *Pragmatic assessment and intervention issues in language*, T.M. Gallagher and C.A. Prutting, eds. San Diego: College-Hill Press.

Menzel, E.M. 1978. Cognitive mapping in chimpanzees. In *Cognitive processes in animal behavior*, S.H. Hulse, H. Fowler, and W.K. Honig, eds. Hillsdale, NJ: Erlbaum.

Merton, R.K. 1957. *Social theory and social structure*. New York: Free Press.

Messenger, J. 1971. Sexual repression in an Irish folk community. In *Human sexual behavior*, D. Marshall and R. Suggs, eds. New York: Basic Books.

Messick, S. 1980. *The effectiveness of coaching for the SAT*. Princeton, NJ: Educational Testing Service.

Messick, S., and Jungeblut, A. 1981. Time and method of coaching for the SAT. *Psychological Bulletin* 89: 191–216.

Metcalfe, J., and Wiebe, D. 1987. Intuition in insight and noninsight problem solving. *Memory and Cognition* 15: 238–46.

Meyer, J.S., Ishikawa, Y., Hata, T., and Karacan, I. 1987. Cerebral blood flow in normal and abnormal sleep and dreaming. *Brain and Cognition* 6: 266–94.

Meyers, C.E., MacMillan, D.L., and Yoshida, R.K. 1980. Regular class placement of EHR students—From efficacy to mainstreaming. In *Educating mentally retarded persons in the mainstream*, J. Gottlieb, ed. Baltimore: University Park Press.

Midkiff, E.E., and Bernstein, I.L. 1985. Targets of learned food aversions in humans. *Physiology and Behavior*, 34: 839–41.

Milgram, S. 1963. Behavioral study of obedience. *Journal of Abnormal and Social Psychology* 67: 371–78.

———. 1970. The experience of living in cities. *Science* 167: 1461–68.

———. 1974. *Obedience to authority*. New York: Harper and Row.

Mill, J. 1829/1912. *Analysis of the phenomena of the human mind*. Boston: Houghton Mifflin.

Mills, J., and Clark, M.S. 1982. Exchange and communal relationships. In *Review of Personality and Social Psychology*, vol. 3, L. Wheeler, ed. Beverly Hills, CA: Sage.

Millar, S. 1985. The perception of complex patterns by touch. *Perception* 14: 293–303.

Miller, A. 1988. "Stress on the Job." *Newsweek*, April 25, pp. 40–45.

Miller, D.T., and Turnbull, W. 1986. Expectancies and interpersonal processes. In *Annual review of psychology*, vol. 37, M.R. Rosenzweig and L.W. Porter, eds. Palo Alto, CA: Annual Reviews.

Miller, F.T., Bentz, W.K., Aponte, J.F., and Brogan, D.R. 1974. Perception of life crisis events: A comparative study of rural and urban samples. In *Stressful life events: Their nature and effects*, B.S. Dohrenwend and B.P. Dohrenwend, eds. New York: Wiley.

Miller, G.A. 1956. The magical number seven, plus or minus two: Some limits on our capacity for processing information. *Psychological Review* 63: 81–97.

———. 1984. The test. *Science 84*, November, pp. 55–57.

Miller, G.A., Galanter, E., and Pribram, K.H. 1960. *Plans and the structure of behavior*. New York: Holt, Rinehart and Winston.

Miller, J.L., Aibel, I.L., and Green, K. 1984. On the nature of rate-dependent processing during phonetic perception. *Perception and Psychophysics* 35: 5–15.

Miller, N.E. 1983. Behavioral medicine: Symbiosis between laboratory and clinic. *Annual Review of Psychology* 34: 1–33.

Miller, N.E. 1985. Rx: Biofeedback. *Psychology Today*, February, 54–59.

Miller, N.E., and Brucker, B.S. 1979. Learned large increased in blood pressure apparently independent of skeletal responses in patients paralyzed by spinal lesions. In *Biofeedback and self-regulation*, N. Birbaumer & H.D. Kimmel, eds. Hillsdale, NJ: Erlbaum.

Miller, N.E., and Bugelski, R. 1948. Minor studies of aggression: II. The influence of frustrations imposed by the in-group on attitudes expressed toward out-groups. *Journal of Psychology* 25: 437–42.

Miller, R.R., and Spear, N.E., eds. 1985. *Information processing in animals: Conditioned inhibition.* Hillsdale, NJ: Erlbaum.

Miller, S.A. 1986. Certainty and necessity in the understanding of Piagetian concepts. *Development Psychology* 22: 3–18.

Milner, B. 1970. Memory and the medial temporal regions of the brain. In *Biology of memory,* K.H. Pribram and D.E. Broadbent, eds. New York: Academic Press.

Milner, B., Corkin, S., and Teuber, H.-L. 1968. Further analysis of the hippocampal amnesic syndrome: 14-year follow-up study of H.M. *Neuropsychologia* 6: 215–34.

Mineka, S., Davidson, M., Cook, M., and Keir, R. 1984. Observational conditioning of snake fear in rhesus monkeys. *Journal of Abnormal Psychology* 93: 355–72.

Minor, C.A., and Neel, R.G. 1958. The relationship between achievement motive and occupational preference. *Journal of Counseling Psychology* 5: 39–43.

Minuchin, S. 1974. *Families and family therapy.* Cambridge, MA: Harvard University Press.

Mirin, S.M. 1989. Substance abuse. In *Abnormal states of brain and mind,* J.A. Hobson, ed. Readings from the *Encyclopedia of neuroscience.* Boston: Birkhauser.

Mischel, W. 1970. Sex-typing and socialization. In *Carmichael's manual of child development,* vol. 1, P.H. Mussen, ed. New York: Wiley.

Mischel, W. 1979. On the interface of cognition and personality: Beyond the person-situation debate. *American Psychologist* 34: 740–54.

Mita, T.H., Dermer, M., and Knight, J. 1977. Reversed facial images and the mere-exposure hypothesis. *Journal of Personality and Social Psychology* 35: 597–601.

Mitchell, D.B., and Perlmutter, M. 1986. Semantic activation and episodic memory: Age similarities and differences. *Developmental Psychology* 22: 86–94.

Modigliani, V., and Hedges, D.G. 1987. Distributed rehearsals and the primacy effect in single-trial free recall. *Journal of Experimental Psychology: Learning, Memory, and Cognition* 13: 426–36.

Mohler, H., and Okada, T. 1977. Bezodiazepine receptor: Demonstration in the central nervous system. *Science* 198: 849–51.

Molnar, G., and Fava, G.A. 1987. Intercurrent medical illness in the schizophrenic patient. In *Principles of medical psychiatry,* A. Stoudemire and B.S. Fogel, eds. Orlando, FL: Grune and Stratton.

Moncrief, R.W. 1949. *The chemical senses.* London: Hill.

Monmaney, R. 1987. Are we led by the nose? *Discover,* September, 48–56.

Montemayor, R., Adams, G.R., and Gullotta, T.P., eds. 1990. *From childhood to adolescence: A transitional period?* Newbury Park, CA: Sage.

Montgomery, G. 1988. Color perception: Seeing with the brain. *Discover,* December, pp. 52–59.

Moos, R.L., and Lunde, D.T. 1969. Fluctuations in symptoms and moods during the menstrual cycle. *Journal of Psychosomatic Research* 13: 37–44.

Morishima, A. 1975. His spirit raises the ante for retardates. *Psychology Today,* June, pp. 72–73.

Morris, D. 1958. The reproductive behavior of the ten spined stickleback (Pygosteus pungitius L.) *Behavior,* suppl. 6.

Morris, R.G., and Kopelman, M.D. 1986. The memory deficits in Alzheimer-type dementia: A review. *The Quarterly Journal of Experimental Psychology* 38A: 575–602.

Morrongiello, B.A., Fenwick, K.D., and Chace, G. 1990. Sound localization acuity in very young infants: An observer-based testing procedure. *Developmental Psychology* 25: 75–84.

Moscovici, S. 1985. Social influence and conformity. In *Handbook of social psychology,* 3rd ed. G. Lindzey and E. Aronson, eds. Hillsdale, NJ: Erlbaum.

Moscovitch, M. 1982. Multiple dissociations of function in amnesia. In *Human memory and amnesia,* L.S. Cermak, ed. Hillsdale, NJ: Erlbaum.

Moskowitz, D.S. 1982. Coherence and cross-situational generality in personality: A new analysis of old problems. *Journal of Personality and Social Psychology* 43: 754–68.

Moulton, D.G. 1977. Minimum odorant concentrations detectable by the dog and their implications for olfactory receptivity. In *Chemical signals in vertebrates,* D. Miller-Schwarze and M.M. Mozell, eds. New York: Plenum.

Mountjoy, C.Q., Rossor, M.N., Iversen, L.L., and Roth, M. 1984. Correlation of cortical cholinergic and GABA deficits with quantitative neuropathological findings in senile dementia. *Brain* 107: 507–18.

Movshon, J.A., and Van Sluyters, R.C. 1981. Visual neural development. *Annual Review of Psychology* 32: 477–522.

Mukherjee, A.M., and Hodgen, G.D. 1982. Maternal ethenol exposure induces transient impairment of umbilical circulation and fetal hypoxia in monkeys. *Science* 218: 700–2.

Mullen, B., and Felleman, V. 1990. Tripling in dorms: A meta-analytic integration. *Basic and Applied Social Psychology* 11: 33–44.

Müller, E., Hollien, H., and Murry, T. 1974. Perceptual responses to infant crying: Identification of cry types. *Journal of Child Language* 1: 89–95.

Munz, D., Carsons, S., Brock, B., Bell, L., Kleinman, I., Robert, M., and Simon, J. 1976. Contraceptive knowledge and practice among undergraduates at a Canadian university. *American Journal of Obstetrics and Gynecology* 24: 499–505.

Murdock, B.B., Jr. 1962. The serial position effect in free recall. *Journal of Experimental Psychology* 64: 482–88.

Murray, D.J. 1976. Research on human memory in the nineteenth century. *Canadian Journal of Psychology* 30: 201–20.

Murphy, G.E. 1983. The problems in studying suicide. *Psychiatric Developments* 4: 339–50.

Murphy, T.N. 1982. Pain: Its assessment and management. In *Handbook of psychology and health. Vol. 1: Clinical psychology and behavioral medicine,* R.J. Gatchel, A. Baum, and J.E. Singer, eds. Hillsdale, NJ: Erlbaum.

Musen, G., Shimamura, A.P., and Squire, L.P. 1990. Intact text-specific reading skill in amnesia. *Journal of Experimental Psychology: Learning, Memory, and Cognition* 16: 1068–76.

Mussen, P.H., Jones, M.C. 1957. Self-conceptions, motivations, and interpersonal attitudes of late- and early-maturing boys. *Child Development* 28: 243–46.

Muter, P. 1980. Very rapid forgetting. *Memory & Cognition* 8: 174–79.

Myers, D.G. 1987. *Social psychology.* New York: McGraw-Hill.

Naditch, M.P. 1985. STAYWELL: Evolution of a behavioral medicine program in industry. In *Behavior medicine in industry,* M.F. Cataldo and T. Coates, eds. Orlando, FL: Academic Press.

Nash, M. 1987. What, if anything, is regressed about hypnotic age regression? A review of the empirical literature. *Psychological Bulletin* 102: 42–52.

Nathans, J. 1989. The genes for color vision. *Scientific American* 260: 42–49.

Natsoulas, T. 1978. Consciousness. *American Psychologist* 33: 906–14.

———. 1983. Addendum to "Consciousness." *American Psychologist* 38: 121–22.

Nauta, W.J.H., and Feirtag, M. 1986. *Fundamental neuroanatomyy.* New York: Freeman.

Neimark, E.D. 1975. Longitudinal development of formal operations thought. *Genetic Psychology Monographs* 91: 171–225.

Neiss, R. 1988. Reconceptualizing arousal: Psychobiological states in motor performance. *Psychological Bulletin* 103: 345–66.

———. 1990. Ending arousal's reign of terror: A reply to Anderson. *Psychological Bulletin* 107: 101–5.

Neisser, U. 1967. *Cognitive psychology.* New York: Appleton-Century-Crofts.

———, ed. 1982. *Memory observed: Remembering in natural contexts.* San Francisco: Freeman.

———. 1968. The processes of vision. *Scientific American* 219: 204–14.

———. 1979. The concept of intelligence. In *Human intelligence: Perspective on its theory and measurement,* R.J. Sternberg and D.K. Detterman, eds. Norwood, NJ: Ablex.

———. 1983. The rise and fall of the sensory register. *The Behavioral and Brain Sciences* 6: 35.

Neisser, U., and Winograd, E. 1988. *Remembering reconsidered: Ecological and traditional approaches to the study of memory.* Cambridge, UK: Cambridge University Press.

Nelson, C.A., and Nugent, K.M. 1990. Recognition memory and resource allocation as revealed by children's event-related potential responses to happy and angry faces. *Developmental Psychology* 26: 171–79.

Nelson, D.L. 1979. Remembering pictures and words: Appearance, significance, and name. In *Levels of processing in human memory,* L.S. Cermak and F.I.M. Craik, eds. Hillsdale, NJ: Erlbaum.

Nelson, J. 1970. Pollution and a concerned public. *Current History* 59: 31–35.

Nelson, K.E. 1973. Structure and strategy in learning to talk. *Monographs of the Society for Research in Child Development* 38. (1–2, Ser. No. 149).

Nelson, K.E., Denninger, M.M., Bonvillian, J.D., Kaplan, B.J., and Baker, N. 1983. Maternal input adjustments and nonadjustments as related to children's linguistic advances and to language acquisition theories. In *The development of oral and written languages,* A.D. Pellegrini and T.D. Yawkey, eds. Norwood, NJ: Ablex.

Nemeth, C. 1986. Differential contributions of majority and minority influence. *Psychological Review* 93: 23–32.

Neuberg, S.L. 1988. Behavioral implications of information presented outside of conscious awareness. *Social Cognition* 6: 207–30.

———. 1989. The goal of forming accurate impressions during social interactions: Attenuating the impact of negative experiences. *Journal of Personality and Social Psychology* 56: 374–86.

Neugarten, B.L. 1980. Acting one's age: New rules for old. *Psychology Today*, April, pp. 66–80.

Neugarten, B.L., and Neugarten, D.A. 1986. Age in the aging society. *Daedalus* 115: 31–49.

Nevin, J.A. 1985. Behavioral analysis, the nuclear arms race, and the peace movement. In *Applied social psychology annual*, vol. 6, S. Oskamp, ed. Beverly Hills, CA.: Sage.

Newcomb, T.M. 1961. *The acquaintance process*. New York: Holt, Rinehart and Winston.

Newell, A., Shaw, J.C., and Simon, H.A. 1958. Elements of a theory of human problem solving. *Psychological Review* 65: 151–66.

Newmark, C.S., Frerking, R.A., Cook, L., and Newmark, L. 1973. Endorsement of Ellis' irrational beliefs as a function of psychopathology. *Journal of Clinical Psychology* 29: 300–2.

Newport, E.L. 1977. Motherese: The speech of mothers to young children. In *Cognitive theory*, vol. 2, N.J. Castellan, D.B. Pisoni, and G.R. Potts, eds. Hillsdale, NJ: Erlbaum.

Newport, E.L. 1984. Constraints on learning: Studies in the acquisition of American Sign Language. *Papers on child language development*, 23. Stanford, CA: Stanford University Press.

Newton, N., and Modahl, C. 1978. Pregnancy: The closest human relationship. *Human Nature* 1: 40–56.

Newsweek. 1987. My turn: The mail. *Newsweek Magazine*, Aug. 10, p. 8.

Newsweek. 1988. The *Newsweek* poll: sizing up the impact. *Newsweek*, Oct. 3, p. 25.

Newsweek. 1989. A rather sad figure. *Newsweek* June 29. p. 22.

Nisbett, R.E. 1968. Taste, deprivation, and weight determinants of eating behavior. *Journal of Personality & Social Psychology* 10: 107–16.

———. 1972. Eating behavior and obesity in man and animals. *Advances in Psychosomatic Medicine* 7: 173–93.

Nisbett, R.E., and Schachter, S. 1966. Cognitive manipulation of pain. *Journal of Experimental Social Psychology* 2: 227–36.

Nisbett, R.E., and Wilson, T. 1977. Telling more than we know: Verbal reports on mental processes. *Psychological Review* 84: 231–59.

Nissen, M.J., Ross, J.L., Willingham, D.B., Mackenzie, T.B., and Schacter, D.L. 1988. Memory and awareness in a patient with multiple personality disorder. *Brain and Cognition* 8: 117–34.

Nolen-Hoeksema, S. 1987. Sex differences in unipolar depression: evidence and theory. *Psychological Bulletin* 101: 259–82.

Norman, D.A. 1981. Twelve issues for cognitive science. In *Perspectives on cognitive science*, D.A. Norman, ed. Hillsdale, NJ: Erlbaum.

Norman, D.A., and Bobrow, D.G. 1975. On data-limited and resource-limited processes. *Cognitive Psychology* 7: 44–64.

Norman, W.T., and Goldberg, L.R. 1966. Raters, ratees, and randomness in personality structure. *Journal of Personality and Social Psychology* 4: 681–91.

Norem, J. 1989. Cognitive strategies as personality: Effectiveness, specificity, flexibility, and change. In *Personality psychology: Recent trends and emerging directions*, D.M. Buss and N. Cantor, eds. New York: Springer-Verlag.

O'Brien, M., and Huston, A.C. 1985. Development of sex-typed play behavior in toddlers. *Developmental Psychology* 21: 866–71.

Obrist, P.A., Sutterer, J.R., and Howard, J.L. 1972. Preparatory cardiac changes: A psychobiological approach. In *Classical conditioning II. Current theory and research*, A.H. Black and W.F. Prokasy, eds. New York: Appleton-Century-Crofts.

Ochs, E. 1980. *Talking to children in western Samoa*. Unpublished paper. University of Southern California.

O'Connor, E.J., Peters, L.H., Rudolf, C.J., and Pooyan, A. 1982. Situational constraints and employee affective reactions: A partial field replication. *Group and Organizational Studies* 7: 418–28.

Oden, M.H. 1968. The fulfillment of promise: 40-year follow-up of Terman gifted group. *Genetic Psychology Monographs* 77: 3–93.

Ohman, A., Fredrikson, M., Hugdahl, K., and Rimmo, P. 1976. the premise of equipotentiality in human classical conditioning: Conditioned electrodermal responses to potentially phobic stimuli. *Journal of Experimental Psychology—General* 105: 313–37.

O'Leary, A. 1990. Stress, emotion, and human immune function. *Psychological Bulletin* 108: 363–82.

O'Leary, K.D., and Smith, D.A. 1991. Marital interactions. *Annual Review of Psychology* 42: 191–212.

Olds, J.M. 1958. Self-stimulation of the brain. *Science* 127: 315–24.

Olds, J.M., and Milner, P.M. 1954. Positive reinforcement produced by electrical stimulation of the septal area and other areas of the rat brain. *Journal of Comparative and Physiological Psychology* 47: 419–27.

Olds, M.E., and Fobes, J.L. 1981. The central basis of motivation: Intracranial self-stimulation studies. *Annual Review of Psychology* 32: 523–74.

Olson, R.A., and Elliott, C.H. 1983. Behavioral medicine: Assessment, patient management, and treatment interventions. In *Handbook of clinical psychology: Theory, research, and prediction*, C.E. Walker, ed. Homewood, IL: Dow-Jones/Irwin.

Olton, D.S. 1979. Mazes, maps, and memory. *American Psychologist* 34: 583–96.

Olton, D.S., and Samuelson, R.J. 1976. Remembrance of places passed: Spatial memory in rats. *Journal of Experimental Psychology: Animal Behavior Processes* 2: 97–116.

O'Neill, C., and Zeichner, A. 1984. Working women: A study of relationships between stress, coping, and health. Paper presented at the meetings of *The Society of Behavioral Medicine*. Philadelphia: May.

Oomura, Y., Ono, T., Oogama, H., and Wagner, M.J. 1969. Glucose and osmosensitive neurons of the rat hypothalamus. *Nature* 222: 282–284.

Oppenheim, D., Sagi, A., and Lamb, M.E. 1988. Infant-adult attachments on the Kibbutz and their relation to socioemotional development 4 years later.. *Developmental Psychology* 24: 427–33.

Orford, J., and Keddie, A. 1986. Abstinence or controlled drinking in clinical practice: Indications of initial assessment. *Addictive Behaviors* 11: 71–86.

Orford, J., Oppenheimer, E., and Edwards, G. 1976. Abstinence or control: The outcome for excessive drinkers two years after consultation. *Behavior Research and Therapy* 14: 409–18.

Orne, M.T. 1977. The construct of hypnosis: Implications of definition for research and practice. In *Conceptual and investigative approaches to hypnosis and hynotic phenomena*, W.E. Edmonston, Jr. ed. *Annals of the New York Academy of Sciences* 296: 14–33.

Orne, M.T., and Dinges, D.F. 1989. Hypnosis. In *States of brain and mind*, J.A. Hobson, ed. Readings from the *Encyclopedia of neuroscience*. Boston: Birkhauser.

Orne, M.T., Dinges, D.F., and Orne, E.C. 1984. On the differential diagnosis of multiple personality in the forensic context. *International Journal of Clinical and Experimental Hypnosis* 32: 118–69.

Ornitz, E.M., Atwell, C.W., Kaplan, A.R., and Westlake, J.R. 1985. Brain-stem dysfunction in autism. *Archives of General Psychiatry* 42: 1018–25.

Ornstein, P.A., Medlin, K.G., Stone, B.P., and Naus, M.J. 1985. Retrieving for rehearsal: An analysis of active rehearsal in children's memory. *Developmental Psychology* 21: 633–41.

Ornstein, R., and Sobel, D. 1987. *The Healing Brain: A new perspective on the brain and health*. New York: Simon and Schuster.

Orwell, G. 1949. *Nineteen eighty-four*. New York: Harcourt, Brace.

Osgood, C.E. 1962. *An alternative to war or surrender*. Urbana, IL: University of Illinois Press.

Osherson, D.N., and Lasnik, H. eds. 1990. *Language: An invitation to cognitive science*, vol. 1. Cambridge, MA: The MIT Press.

Osherson, D.N., and Markman, E.M. 1975. Language and the ability to evaluate contradictions and tautologies. *Cognition* 2: 213–26.

Oskamp, S. 1971. Effects of programmed strategies on cooperation in the prisoner's dilemma and other mixed-motive games. *Journal of Conflict Resolution* 15: 225–29.

Oskamp, S. 1985. Introduction. In *Applied Social Psychology Annual 6: International conflict and national public policy issues*, S. Oskamp, ed. Beverly Hills, CA: Sage.

Paige, K. 1978. The ritual of circumcision. *Human Nature* 1 (May), 40–49.

Paivio, A. 1971. *Imagery and verbal processes*. New York: Holt, Rinehart and Winston.

Pallak, M.S., Cook, D.A., and Sullivan, J.J. 1980. Commitment and energy conservation. In *Applied social psychology annual*, vol. 1, L. Bickman, ed. Beverly Hills, CA: Sage.

Palmer, T., and Tzeng, O.J.L. 1990. Cerebral asymmetry in visual attention. *Brain and Cognition* 13: 46–58.

Panksepp, J. 1982. Toward a general psychobiological theory of emotions. *Behavioral and Brain Sciences* 5: 407–67.

Parke, R.D., Berkowitz, L. Leyens, J.P., West, S.G., and Sebastian, J. 1977. Some effects of violent and nonviolent movies on the behavior of juvenile delinquents. In L. Berkowitz, Ed., *Advances in experimental social psychology* (Vol. 10). New York: Academic Press.

Parkson, S.C. 1983. Family therapy. In *Handbook of clinical psychology*, vol. 2, C.E. Walker, ed. Homewood, IL: Dow Jones–Irwin.

Parks, T.E. 1965. Post-retinal visual storage. *American Journal of Psychology* 78: 145–47.

———. 1987. On the relative frequency of depth effects in real versus illusory figures. *Perception and Psychophysics* 42: 333–36.

Partridge, F.M., Knight, R.G., and Feehan, M. 1990. Direct and indirect memory performance in patients with senile dementia. *Psychological Medicine* 20: 111–18.

Partridge, L., and Harvey, P.H. 1988. The ecological context of life history evolution. *Science* 241: 1449–55.

Passini, F.T., and Norman, W.T. 1966. A universal conception of personality structure? *Journal of Personality and Social Psychology* 4: 44–49.

Patrusky, B. 1982. What causes aging? *Science 82*, January/February, p. 112.

Patsiokas, A.T., Clum, G.A., and Luscomb, R.L. 1979. Cognitive characteristics of suicide attempters. *Journal of Consulting and Clinical Psychology* 47: 478–84.

Patterson, F.G. 1978. The gestures of a gorilla: Language acquisition in another pongid. *Brain and Language* 5: 72–97.

Paul, G.L. 1966. *Insight versus desensitization in psychotherapy*. Stanford, CA: Stanford University Press.

Paulus, P.B., McCain, G., and Cox, V.C. 1982. Death rates, psychiatric commitments, blood pressure, and perceived crowding as a function of institutional crowding. In *Experimenting in society: Issues and examples in applied social psychology*, J.W. Reich, ed. Glenview, IL: Scott, Foresman.

Pavlov, I.P. 1927. *Conditioned reflexes.*, tr. G.V. Anrep. London: Oxford University Press.

Paykel, E.S. 1985. Life-events, social support, and psychiatric disorder. In *Social support: Theory, research, and applications*, I.G. Sarason and B.R. Sarason, eds. The Hague: Martinus Nijhiff.

Pearce, J.M. 1987. A model for stimulus generalization in Pavlovian conditioning. *Psychological Review* 94: 61–73.

Pearce, J.M., and Hall, G. 1980. A model for Pavlovian learning: Variations in the effectiveness of conditioned but not of unconditioned stimuli. *Psychological Review* 87: 532–52.

Pellegrino, J.W. 1985. Anatomy of analogy. *Psychology Today*, October, pp. 49–54.

Pendery, M.L., Maltzman, I.M., and West, L.J. 1982. controlled drinking by alcoholics? New findings and a reevaluation of a major affirmative study. *Science* 217: 169–75.

Penfield, W. 1947. Some observations on the cerebral cortex of man. *Proceedings of the Royal Society* 134: 349.

———. 1952. Memory mechanisms. *American Medical Association Archives of Neurology and Psychiatry* 67: 178–91.

———. 1975. *The mystery of the mind*. Princeton, NJ: Princeton University Press.

Penfield, W., and Rasmussen, T. 1950. *The cerebral cortex of man*. New York: Macmillan.

Pennebaker, J.W. 1982. *The psychology of physical symptoms*. New York: Springer-Verlag.

Pennebaker, J.W., and Lightner, J.M. 1980. Competition of internal and external information in an exercise setting. *Journal of Personality and Social Psychology* 39: 165–74.

Perl, E.R. 1984. Characterization of nociceptors and their activation of neurons in the superficial dorsal horn—first steps for the sensation of pain. In *Neural mechanisms of pain: Advances in pain research and therapy*, L. Kruger and J.C. Liebeskind, eds. New York: Raven Press.

Perontka, S.J., and Snyder, S.H. 1980. Relationship of neuroleptic-drug effects at brain dopamine, serotonin, a-adrenergic, and histamine receptors to clinical potency. *American Journal of Psychiatry* 137: 1518–22.

Perry, B.P. 1935. *The thought and character of William James*. Boston: Little, Brown, and Co.

Persky, H. 1987. *Psychoendocrinology of human sexual behavior*. New York: Praeger.

Pert, C.B., and Snyder, S.H. 1973. Opiate receptor: Demonstration in nervous tissue. *Science* 179: 1011–14.

———. 1987. Those gangly years. *Psychology Today*, September, pp. 28–34.

———. 1988. Adolescent development. *Annual Review of Psychology*, 39: 583–608.

Petersen, A.C., and Crockett, L.J. 1985. Pubertal timing and grade effects on adjustment. *Journal of Youth and Adolescence* 14: 191–206.

Peterson, L.R., and Peterson, M.J. 1959. Short-term retention of individual verbal items. *Journal of Experimental Psychology* 58: 193–98.

Peterson, R. 1978. Review of the Rorschach. In *The eighth mental measurement yearbook*, vol. 1, O.K. Buros, ed. Highland Park, NJ: Gryphon Press.

Peterson, R.C. 1989. Marijuana. In *Abnormal states of brain and mind*, J.A. Hobson, ed. Readings from the *Encyclopedia of neuroscience*. Boston: Birkhauser.

Petri, H.L. 1981. *Motivation: Theory and research*. Belmont, CA: Wadsworth.

Petty, R.E., and Cacioppo, J.T. 1979. Issue involvement can increase or decrease persuasion by enhancing message-relevant cognitive responses. *Journal of Personality and Social Psychology* 37: 1915–26.

———. 1986. The elaboration likelihood model of persuasion. In *Advances in experimental social psychology*, vol. 19, L. Berkowitz, ed. New York: Academic Press.

Petty, R.E., and Cacioppo, J.T. 1990. Involvement and persuasion: Tradition versus integration. *Psychological Bulletin* 107: 367–74.

Pezdek, K., Maki, R., Valencia-Laver, D., Whetstone, T., Stoeckert, J., and Dougherty, T. 1988. Picture memory: Recognizing added and deleted details. *Journal of Experimental Psychology: Learning, Memory, and Cognition* 14: 468–76.

Phares, E.J. 1976. *Locus of control in personality*. Morristown, NJ: General Learning Press.

———. 1979. *Locus of control in personality*. Morristown, NJ: General Learning Press.

Phillis, D.E., and Gromko, M.H. 1985. Sex differences in sexual activity: Reality or illusion? *Journal of Sex Research* 21: 437–48.

Phillips, D.P. 1974. The influence of suggestion on suicide: Substantive and theoretical implications of the Werther effect. *American Sociological Review* 39: 340–54.

———. 1985. Natural experiments on the effects of mass media violence on fatal aggression: Strengths and weaknesses of a new approach. In *Advances in experimental social psychology*, vol. 19, L. Berkowitz, ed. Orlando, FL: Academic Press.

Phillips, J.L. 1969. *The origins of intellect: Piaget's theory*. San Francisco: Freeman.

Phoenix, C.H., Goy, R.W., Gerall, A.A., and Young, W.C. 1959. Organizing action of prenatally administered testosterone proprionate on the tissues mediating mating behavior in the female guinea pig. *Endocrinology* 65: 369–82.

Piaget, J. 1926. *Judgement and reasoning in the child* trans. M. Worden. New York: Harcourt, Brace and World.

———. 1954. *The construction of reality in the child*. New York: Basic Books.

———. 1965. *The child's conception of the world*. Totowa, NJ: Littlefield, Adams.

———. 1970. Piaget's theory. In *Carmichael's manual of child psychology*, vol. 1, P.H. Mussen, ed. New York: Wiley.

Piaget, J., and Inhelder, B. 1969. *The psychology of the child*. New York: Basic Books.

Piedmont, R.L., McCrae, R.R., and Costa, P.T. Jr. 1991. Adjective check list scales and the five-factor model. *Journal of Personality and Social Psychology* 60: 630–37.

Pillemer, D.B., Goldsmith, L.R., Panter, A.T., and White, S.H. 1988. Very long-term memories of the first year in college. *Journal of Experimental Psychology: Learning, Memory, and Cognition* 14: 709–15.

Pinker, S. 1990. Language acquisition. In *Language: An invitation to cognitive science*, vol. 4, D.N. Osherson and H. Lasnik, eds. Cambridge, MA: MIT Press.

Pinker, S., and Bloom, P. 1990. Natural language and natural selection. *Behavioral and Brain Sciences* 13: 707–84.

Pinel, J.P.J. 1990. *Biopsychology*. Needham Heights, MA: Allyn & Bacon.

Pines, M. 1982. Movement grows to create guidelines for mental therapy. *New York Times*, May 4, p. C1.

Place, E.J.S., and Gilmore, G.C. 1980. Perceptual organization in schizophrenia. *Journal of Abnormal Psychology* 89: 409–18.

Plagens, P., Miller, M., Foote, D., and Yoffe, E. 1991. Violence in our culture. *Newsweek*, April 1, pp. 46–52.

Platt, J. 1973. Social traps. *American Psychologist* 28: 641–51.

Plomin, R. 1986. Behavior genetic methods. *Journal of Personality* 54: 226–61.

———. 1988. The nature and nurture of cognitive abilities. In *Advances in the psychology of human intelligence*, vol. 4, R.J. Sternberg, ed. Hillsdale, NJ: Erlbaum.

Plomin, R., and Daniels, D. 1986. Genetics and shyness. In *Shyness: Perspectives in research and treatment*, W.H. Jones, J.M. Cheek, and S.R. Briggs, eds. New York: Plenum Press.

———. 1987. Why are children in the same family so different from one another? *Behavioral and Brain Sciences* 10: 1–60.

Plomin, R., and DeFries, J.C. 1985. *Origins of individual differences in infancy: The Colorado Adoption Project*. Orlando, FL: Academic Press.

Plomin, R., DeFries, J.C., and Loehlin, J.C. 1977. Genotype–environment interaction and correlation in the analysis of human behavior. *Psychological Bulletin* 84: 309–22.

Plomin, R., DeFries, J.C., and McClearn, G.E. 1990. *Behavioral genetics,* 2nd Ed. New York: W.H. Freeman and Co.

Plomin, R., Willerman, L., and Loehlin, J.C. 1976. Resemblance in appearance and the equal environments assumption in twin studies of personality. *Behavior Genetics* 6: 43–52.

Plous, S. 1985. Perceptual illusions and military realities: A social-psychological analysis of the nuclear arms race. *Journal of Conflict Resolution* 29: 363–89.

Plous, S., and Zimbardo, P.G. 1984. The looking glass war. *Psychology Today,* November, pp. 48–59.

Plutchik, R. 1980. A general psychoevolutionary theory of emotion. In *Emotion: Theory, research, and experience,* vol. 1, Plutchik, R. and Kellerman, H., eds. New York: Academic Press.

———. 1984. Emotions: A general psychoevolutionary theory. In *Approaches to Emotion,* K.B. Scherer and P. Ekman, eds. Hillsdale, NJ: Erlbaum Press.

Pohlman, E. 1971. *How to kill population.* Philadelphia: Westminster Press.

Pollack, I., and Pickett, J.M. 1964. Intelligibility of excerpts from fluent spech. *Journal of Verbal Learning and Verbal Behavior* 3: 79–84.

Pollio, H.R. 1982. *Behavior and existence.* Monterey, CA: Brooks/Cole.

Polson, M.C., and Richardson, J.J., eds. 1988. *Foundations of intelligent tutoring systems.* Hillsdale, NJ: Erlbaum.

Poon, L.W., Fozard, J.L., Cermak, L.S., Arenberg, D., and Thompson, L.W. 1980. *New directions in memory and aging.* Hillsdale, NJ: Erlbaum.

Poon, L., Fozard, J., Paulschock, D., and Thomas, J. 1979. A questionnaire assessment of age differences in retention of recent and remote events. *Experimental Aging Research* 5: 401–11.

Pope, K.S., and Bahatsos, J.C. 1986. *Sexual intimacy between therapists and patients.* New York: Praeger.

Porter, R.H., Cernoch, J.M., and McLaughlin, F.J. 1983. Maternal recognition of neonates through olfactory cues. *Physiology and Behavior* 30: 151–54.

Porter, R.H., and Moore, J.D. 1981. Human kin recognition by olfactory cues. *Physiology and Behavior* 27: 493–95.

Posner, M.I., Nissen, M.J., and Klein, R.M. 1976. Visual dominance: An information-processing account of its origins and significance. *Psychological Review* 83: 157–71.

Posner, M.I., Snyder, C.R.P., and Davidson, B.J. 1980. Attention and the detection of signals. *Journal of Experimental Psychology: General* 109: 160–74.

Posner, M.I., Walker, J.A., Friedrich, F.A., and Rafal, R.D. 1987. How do the parietal lobes direct covert attention? *Neuropsychologia* 25: 135–45.

Postman, L. 1961. The present status of interference theory. In *Verbal learning and verbal behavior,* C.N. Cofer, ed. New York: McGraw-Hill.

———. 1975. Verbal learning and memory. *Annual Review of Psychology* 26: 291–335.

———. 1985. Human learning and memory. In G.A. Kimble and K. Schlesinger (Eds.) *Topics in the history of psychology,* Vol. 1. Hillsdale, NJ: Erlbaum.

Potkay, C.R., and Allen, B.P. 1986. *Personality: Theory, research, and applications.* Monterey, CA: Brooks/Cole.

Power, R.P. 1981. The dominance of touch by vision: Occurs with familiar objects. *Perception* 10: 29–33.

Power, T.G., and Parke, R.D. 1982. Play as a context for early learning: Lab and home analyses. In *The family as a learning environment,* L.M. Laosa and I.E. Sigel, eds. New York: Plenum.

Powley, T.L., and Keesey, R.E. 1970. Relationship of body weight to the lateral hypothalamic feeding syndrome. *Journal of comparative and Physiological Psychology* 70: 25–36.

Premack, D. 1965. Reinforcement theory. In *Nebraska symposium on motivation,* D. Levine, ed. Lincoln: University of Nebraska Press.

———. 1971. Language in chimpanzees. *Science* 172: 808–22.

———. 1983. Animal cognition. *Annual Review of Psychology* 34: 351–62.

———. 1985. "Gavagai!" or the future history of the animal language controversy. *Cognition* 19: 207–96.

Premack, D., and Premack, A.J. 1985. *The mind of an ape.* New York: Norton.

Price, R.H., and Bouffard, D.L. 1974. Behavioral appropriateness and situational constraint as dimensions of social behavior. *Journal of Personality and Social Psychology* 30: 579–86.

Prioleau, L., Murdock, M., and Brody, N. 1983. An analysis of psychotherapy versus placebo studies. *Behavioral and Brain Sciences* 6: 275–310.

Proshansky, H.M., Ittelson, W.H., and Rivlin, L.G. 1976. *Environmental psychology: People and their physical settings,* 2nd ed. New York: Holt, Rinehart and Winston.

Provence, S., & Lipton, R.C. 1962. *Infants in institutions.* New York: International Universities Press.

Proust, M. 1934. *Remembrance of things past.* New York: Random House.

Pulkkinen, L. 1982. Self-control and continuity from childhood to adolescence. In *Lifespan development and behavior,* vol. 4, P.B. Baltes and D.G. Brim, eds. New York: Academic Press.

Putnam, F.W. 1982. Traces of Eve's faces. *Psychology Today,* October, 88.

Putnam, F.W., Guroff, J.J., Silberman, E.K., Barban, L., and Post, R.M. 1985. The clinical phenomenology of multiple personality disorder: 100 recent cases. *Journal of Clinical Psychiatry* 47: 285–93.

Rabbie, J.M., and Horwitz, M. 1969. Arousal of ingroup–outgroup bias by a chance win or loss. *Journal of Personality and Social Psychology* 13: 269–77.

Rahula, W. 1959. *What the Buddha taught.* New York: Grove Press.

Ramachandran, V.S. 1986. What does the brain do with illusory contours? *Perception and Psychophysics* 39: 216.

Randi, J. 1982. *Flim-flam!.* Buffalo, NY: Prometheus Books.

Rapaport, A. 1960. *Fights, games, and debates.* Ann Arbor: University of Michigan Press.

Rappaport, J., and Seidman, E. 1983. Social and community interventions. In *Handbook of clinical psychology,* vol. 2, C.E. Walker, ed. Homewood, IL: Dow Jones–Irwin.

Ratcliff, G., and Newcombe, F. 1982. Object recognition: Some deductions from the clinical evidence. In *Normality and pathology in cognitive functions,* A. Ellis, ed. London: Academic Press.

Ratner, H.H., Schell, D.A., Crimmins, A., Mittelman, D., & Baldinelli, L. 1987. Changes in adults' prose recall: Aging or cognitive demands. *Developmental Psychology* 23: 521–25.

Rausch, M.L. 1977. Paradox, levels, and junctures in person-situation systems. In *Personality at the crossroads,* D. Magnusson and N.S. Endler, eds. Hillsdale, NJ. Lawrence Erlbaum Associates.

Raps, C.S., Peterson, C., Reinhard, K.E., and Abramson, L.Y. 1982. Attributional style among depressed patients. *Journal of Abnormal Psychology* 91: 102–8.

Ray, O. 1983. *Drugs, society, and human behaviors,* 3rd ed. St. Louis: Mosley.

Ray, W.J., and Ravizza, R. 1985. *Methods toward a science of behavior and experience,* 2nd ed. Belmont, CA: Wadsworth.

Rayner, K. 1983. The perceptual span and eye movement control during reading. In *Eye movements in reading,* K. Rayner, ed. New York: Academic Press.

———. 1986. Eye movements and the perceptual span in beginning and skilled readers. *Journal of Experimental Child Psychology* 41: 211–36.

Rayner, K., and Pollatsek, A. 1989. *The psychology of reading.* Englewood Cliffs, NJ: Prentice Hall.

Raynor, J.O. 1970. Relationships between achievement-related motivation and future orientation on level of performance. *Journal of Personality and Social Psychology* 17: 36–41.

Raz, N., Willerman, L., and Yama, M. 1987. On sense and senses: Intelligence and auditory information processing. *Personality and Individual Differences* 8: 201–10.

Rebok, G.W. 1987. *Life-span cognitive development.* New York: Holt, Rinehart and Winston.

Reder, L.M., and Anderson, J.R. 1980. A comparison of texts and their summaries: Memorial consequences. *Journal of Verbal Learning and Verbal Behavior* 19: 121–34.

Regan, J.W. 1971. Guilt, perceived injustice, and altruistic behavior. *Journal of Personality and Social Psychology* 18: 124–32.

Register, P.A., and Kihlstrom, J.F. 1987. Hypnotic effects on hypermnesia. *The International Journal of Clinical and Experimental Hypnosis* 35: 155–69.

Reich, J.W., and Zautra, A. 1981. Life events and personal causation: Some relationships with satisfaction and distress. *Journal of Personality and Social Psychology* 41: 1002–12.

Reinke, B.J., Ellicott, A.M., Harris, R.L., and Hancock, E. 1985. Timing of psychosocial changes in women's lives. *Human Development* 28: 259–80.

Reisenzein, R. 1983. The Schachter theory of emotion: Two decades later. *Psychological Bulletin* 94: 239–64.

Reisman, J.M. 1976. *A history of clinical psychology.* New York: Irvington.

Reitman, J.S. 1974. Without surreptitious rehearsal, information in short-term memory decays. *Journal of Verbal Learning and Verbal Behavior* 13: 365–77.

Renken, B., Egeland, B., Marvinney, D., Mangelsdorf, S., and Sroufe, L.A. 1989. Early childhood antecedents of aggression and passive-withdrawal in early elementary school. *Journal of Personality* 57: 257–81.

Renninger, K.A., and Wozniak, R.H. 1985. Effect of interest on attentional shift, recognition, and recall in young children. *Developmental Psychology* 21: 624–32.

Rescorla, R.A. 1967. Pavlovian conditioning and its proper control procedures. *Psychological Review* 74: 71–80.

———. 1987. A Pavlovian analysis of goal-directed behavior. *American Psychologist* 42: 119–29.

———. 1990. The role of information about the response-outcome relation in instrumental discrimination learning. *Journal of Experimental Psychology: Animal Behavior Processes* 16: 262–70.

Rescorla, R.A., and Wagner, A.R. 1972. A theory of Pavlovian conditioning. Variation in the effectiveness of reinforcement and non-reinforcement. In *Classical conditioning II*, A.H. Black and W.F. Prokasy, eds. New York: Appleton-Century-Crofts.

Rest, J.R., and Thoma, S.J. 1985. Relation of moral judgment development to formal education. *Developmental Psychology* 21: 709–14.

Restak, R.M. 1988. *The mind*. Toronto: Bantam Books.

Reynolds, R.I. 1985. No role of object-hypotheses in the organization of fragmented figures. *Perception* 14: 49–52.

Rheingold, H.L., and Cook, K.V. 1975. The contents of boys' and girls' rooms as an index of parents' behavior. *Child Development* 46: 459–63.

Richardson, J.G., Ford, W.H., and Vanderbeck, C.C. 1902. *Medicology: or Home encyclopedia of health*. New York: University Medical College.

Richter, C.P. 1957. On the phenomenon of sudden death in animals and man. *Psychosomatic Medicine* 19: 191–98.

Ricks, D.M. 1975. Vocal communication in preverbal normal and autistic children. In *Language, cognitive deficits, and retardation*, N. O'Connor, ed. London: Butterworth.

Riesen, A.H. 1947. The development of visual perception in man and chimpanzee. *Science* 106: 107–8.

———. 1965. Effects of early deprivation of photic stimulation. In *The biosocial bases of mental retardation*, S. Osler and R. Cooke, eds. Baltimore: Johns Hopkins University Press.

Riggs, L.A. 1985. Sensory processes: Vision. In *Topics in the history of psychology*, vol. I, G.A. Kimble and K. Schlesinger, eds. Hillsdale, NJ: Erlbaum.

Rips, L.J. 1990. Reasoning. *Annual Review of Psychology* 41: 321–53.

Robbin, A.A. 1959. The value of leucotomy in relation to diagnosis. *Journal of Neurology, Neurosurgery, and Psychiatry* 22: 132–36.

Roberts, W.A., and Van Veldhuizen, N. 1985. Spatial memory in pigeons on the radial maze. *Journal of Experimental Psychology: Animal Behavior Processes* 11: 241–60.

Robins, L.N., Schoenberg, S.P., Holmes, S.J., Ratcliff, K.S., Benham, A., and Works, J. 1985. Early home environment: A test of concordance between siblings with and without psychiatric disorders. *American Journal of Orthopsychiatry* 55: 27–41.

Robinson, L.A., Berman, J.S., and Neimeyer, R.A. 1990. Psychotherapy for depression: A comprehensive review of controlled outcome research. *Psychological Bulletin*, 108: 30–49.

Roche, A.F. 1979. Secular changes in size and maturity: Causes and effects. *Monographs of the Society of Research in Child Development*. 44 (No. 179), 59–120.

Rock, I. 1975. *An introduction to perception*. New York: Macmillan.

———. 1985. Perception and knowledge. *Acta Psychologica* 59: 1–20.

Rock, I., and Harris, C.S. 1967. Vision and touch. *Scientific American* 216: 96–104.

Rock, I., and Palmer, S. 1990. The legacy of Gestalt psychology. *Scientific American* December, pp. 84–90.

Rodin, J. 1981. Current status of the internal-external hypothesis for obesity: What went wrong? *American Psychologist* 36: 361–72.

———. 1982. Obesity: Why the losing battle? In *Psychological Aspects of Obesity*, B.B. Wolman, ed. New York: Van Nostrand Reinhold Company.

———. 1985. Insulin levels, hunger and food intake: An example of feedback loops in body weight regulation. *Health Psychology* 4: 1–18.

Rodin, J., and Langer, E.J. 1977. Long-term effects of a control-relevant intervention with the institutionalized aged. *Journal of Personality and Social Psychology* 35: 897–902.

Roebuck, J.B., and Spray, S.L. 1967. The cocktail lounge: A study of heterosexual relations in a public organization. *American Journal of Sociology* 72: 386–96.

Rogers, C.R. 1942. *Counseling and psychotherapy*. Boston: Houghton Mifflin.

———. 1961. *On becoming a person*. Boston: Houghton Mifflin.

———. 1964. Toward a science of the person. In *Behaviorism and Phenomenology*, T.W. Wann, ed., 109–33. Chicago: University of Chicago Press.

———. 1970. *On encounter groups*. New York: Harper and Row.

Rogers, C.R., and Dymond, R.F., eds. 1954. *Psychotherapy and personality change*. Chicago: University of Chicago Press.

Rogers, J., and Morrison, J.H. 1985. Quantitative morphology and regional and laminar distributions of senile plaques in Alzheimer's disease. *Journal of Neuroscience* 5: 2801–8.

Roitblat, H.L. 1987. *Introduction to comparative cognition*. New York: Freeman.

Rollins, B.C., and Feldman, H.J. 1970. Marital satisfaction over the life cycle. *Journal of Marriage and the Family* 32: 20–28.

Rolls, B.J., Wood, R.J., and Rolls, E.T. 1980. Thirst: The initiation, maintenance, and termination of drinking. In *Progress in psychobiology and physiological psychology*, vol. 9, J.M. Sprague and A.N. Epstein, eds. New York: Academic Press.

Roopnarine, J.L., Talukder, E., Jain, D., Joshi, P., and Srivastav, P. 1990. Characteristics of holding, patterns of play, and social behaviors between parents and infants in New Delhi, India. *Developmental Psychology* 26: 667–73.

Roos, P.E., and Cohen, L.H. 1987. Sex roles and social support as moderators of life stress adjustment. *Journal of Personality and Social Psychology* 52: 576–85.

Rosch, E. 1973. On the internal structure of perceptual and semantic categories. In *Cognitive development and the acquisition of language*, T.E. Moore, ed. New York: Academic Press.

———. 1974. Linguistic relativity. In *Human communication: Theoretical perspectives*, A. Silverstein, ed. New York: Halsted Press.

———. 1978. Human categorization. In *Studies in cross-cultural psychology*, N. Warren, ed. New York: Academic Press.

Rosch, E.R., Mervis, C.B., Gray, W., Johnson, D.M., Boyes-Braem, P. 1976. Basic objects in natural categories. *Cognitive Psychology* 8: 382–439.

Rose, H.S., and Hinds, D.H. 1976. South Dixie Highway contraflow bus and car-pool lane demonstration project. *Transportation Research Record* 606: 18–22.

Rose, R.M., Holaday, J.W., and Bernstein, I. 1971. Plasma testosterone, dominance rank, and aggressive behavior in male rhesus monkeys. *Nature* 231: 366–68.

Rosen, C.M. 1987. The eerie world of reunited twins. *Discover* September, pp. 36–46.

Rosen, G.M. 1976. *Don't be afraid*. Englewood Cliffs, NJ: Prentice Hall.

———. 1987. Self-help treatment books and the commercialization of psychotherapy. *American Psychologist* 42: 46–51.

Rosenbaum, M.E. 1986. The repulsion hypothesis: On the nondevelopment of relationships. *Journal of Personality and Social Psychology* 61: 1156–66.

Rosenblatt, J.S., and Aronson, L.R. 1958. The decline in sexual behavior in male cats after castration with special reference to the role of prior sexual experience. *Behaviour* 12: 285–338.

Rosenhan, D.L. 1973. On being sane in insane places. *Science* 179: 250–58.

Rosenhan, D.L., and Seligman, M.E.P. 1984. *Abnormal Psychology*. New York: Norton.

Rosenstein, M.J., and Milazzo-Sayre, C. 1981. *Characteristics of admissions to selected mental-health facilities*. Rockville, MD: U.S. Dept. of Health and Human Services.

Rosenthal, D. 1963. *The Genain Quadruplets*. New York: Basic Books.

———. 1970. *Genetic theory and abnormal behavior*. New York: McGraw-Hill.

Rosenzweig, M.R. 1984. Experience, memory, and the brain. *American Psychologist* 39: 365–76.

Rosenzweig, M.R., and Bennett, E.L. 1978. Experiential influences on brain anatomy and brain chemistry in rodents. In *Studies on the development of behavior and the nervous system*, vol. 4, G. Gottlieb, ed. New York: Academic Press.

Rosenzweig, M.R., Bennett, E.L., and Diamond, M.C. 1972. Brain changes in response to experience. *Scientific American* 226: 22–29.

Rosenzweig, M.R., and Lieman, A.L. 1989. *Physiological psychology*, 2nd ed. New York: Random House.

Rosett, H.L., and Weiner, L. 1985. *Alcohol and the fetus: A clinical perspective*. New York: Oxford University Press.

Ross, E.A. 1908. *Social Psychology*. New York: Macmillan.

Ross, B.H., and Kennedy, P.T. 1990. Generalizing from the use of earlier examples in problem solving. *Journal of Experimental Psychology: Learning, Memory, and Cognition* 16: 42–55.

Ross, L.D. 1977. The intuitive psychologist and his shortcomings: Distortions in the attribution process. In *Advances in Experimental Social Psychology* Vol. 10, L. Berkowitz, ed. New York: Academic Press.

Ross, L. 1988. Situationist perspectives on the obedience experiments. *Contemporary psychology*, 33: 101–4.

Ross, L.D., Amabile, T.M., and Steinmetz, J.L. 1977. Social roles, social control, and biases in social-perception processes. *Journal of Personality and Social Psychology* 35: 485–94.

Ross, L., and Nisbett, R.E. 1991. *The person and the situation*. New York: McGraw-Hill.

Ross, M. 1989. Relation of implicit theories to the construction of personal histories. *Psychological Review* 96: 341–57.

Ross, M., and Fletcher, G.J.O. 1985. Attribution and social perception. In *The handbook of social psychology* 3rd ed., G. Lindzey and A. Aronson, eds. Reading, MA: Addison-Wesley.

Ross, M., McFarland, C., and Fletcher, G.J.O. 1981. The effect of attitude on the recall of personal histories. *Journal of Personality and Social Psychology*, 40: 627–34.

Rothbart, M., and Birrell, P. 1977. Attitude and the perception of faces. *Journal of Research in Personality* 11: 209–15.

Rothbart, M., and John, O.P. 1985. Social categorization and behavioral episodes: A cognitive analysis of the effects of intergroup contact. *Journal of Social Issues* 41: 81–104.

Rotter, J. 1966. Generalized expectancies for internal versus external control of reinforcement. *Psychological Monographs* 80: 1–28.

Rotter, J.B. 1972. *Applications of a social learning theory of personality*. New York: Holt, Rinehart and Winston.

Rotton, J. 1983. Affective and cognitive consequences of malodorous pollution. *Basic and Applied Social Psychology* 4: 171–91.

Rotton, J., and Frey, J. 1984. Psychological costs of air pollution: Atmospheric conditions, seasonal trends, and psychiatric emergencies. *Population and Environment* 7: 3–16.

———. 1985. Air pollution, weather, and violent crimes: Concomitant times-series analysis of archival data. *Journal of Personality and Social Psychology* 49: 1207–20.

Routh, D.K. 1982. *Learning, speech, and the complex effects of punishment*. New York: Plenum.

Rowe, D.C. 1991. Heredity. In *Personality: Contemporary theory and research*, V.J. Derlega, B.A. Winstead, and W.H. Jones, eds. Chicago: Nelson-Hall.

Rozin, P., and Kalat, I.W. 1971. Specific hungers and poison avoidance as adaptive specializations of learning. *Psychological Review* 79: 259–76.

Rubenstein, J., and Howes, C. 1976. The effects of peers on toddler interaction with mother and toys. *Child Development* 47: 597–605.

Rubin, D.C. 1977. Very long-term memory for prose and verse. *Journal of Verbal Learning and Verbal Behavior* 16: 611–21.

———, ed. 1986. *Autobiographical memory*. Cambridge, UK: Cambridge University Press.

Rubin, J.L., Provenzano, F.J., and Luria, Z. 1974. The eye of the beholder: Parents' views on sex of newborns. *American Journal of Orthopsychiatry* 43: 720–31.

Ruff, H. 1986. Components of attention during infants' manipulative exploration. *Child Development* 57: 105–114.

Ruhlman, L.S., West, S.G., and Pasahow, R.J. 1985. Depression and evaluative schemata. *Journal of Personality* 53: 46–92.

Rumbaugh, D.M. 1977. *Language learning by a chimpanzee: The Lana project*. New York: Academic Press.

Rumelhart, D.E. 1977. Toward an interactive model of reading. In *Attention and performance*, Vol. 6, S. Dornic, ed. Hillsdale, NJ: Erlbaum.

Rumelhart, D.E., McClelland, J.L., and the PDP Research Group. 1986. *Parallel distributed processing: Explorations in the microstructure of cognition*. Vol. 1: *Foundations*. Cambridge, MA: MIT Press/Bradford Books.

Rundus, D. 1971. Analysis of rehearsal processes in free recall. *Journal of Experimental Psychology* 89: 63–77.

Runyan, W.M. 1981. Why did Van Gogh cut off his ear? The problem of alternative explanations in psychobiography. *Journal of Personality and Social Psychology* 40: 1070–77.

Rusbult, C.E. 1980. Commitment and satisfaction in romantic associations: A test of the investment model. *Journal of Experimental Social Psychology* 16: 172–86.

Rushton, J.P. 1989. Genetic similarity, human altruism, and group selection. *Behavioral and Brain Sciences* 12: 503–45.

Russek, M. 1971. Hepatic receptors and the neurophysiological mechanisms controlling feeding behavior. In *Neurosciences Research* vol. 4, S. Ehrenpreis, ed. New York: Academic Press.

Russell, D., and Jones, W.H. 1980. When superstition fails: Reactions to disconfirmation of paranormal beliefs. *Personality and Social Psychology Bulletin* 6: 83–86.

Russell, J.A., and Mehrabian, A. 1978. Approach-avoidance and affiliation as functions of the emotion-eliciting quality of an environment. *Environment and Behavior* 10: 355–87.

Russell, M.J., Dark, K.H., Cummins, R.W., Ellman, G., Callaway, E., and Peeke, H.V.S. 1984. Learned histamine release. *Science* 225: 733–34.

Rutter, D.R., and Durkin, K. 1987. Turn-taking in mother-infant interaction. *Developmental Psychology* 23: 54–61.

Rutter, M., and Schopler, E. 1987. Autism and pervasive developmental disorders: Concepts and diagnostic issues. *Journal of Autism and Developmental Disorders* 17: 159–86.

Saarinen, T.F. 1973. Student views of the world. In *Image and environment: Cognitive mapping and spatial behavior*, R.M. Downs and D. Stea, eds. Chicago: Aldine.

Sachs, J.S. 1967. Recognition memory for syntactic and semantic aspects of connected discourse. *Perception and Psychophysics* 2: 437–42.

Sachs, J.S., and Johnson, M. 1976. Language development in a hearing child of deaf parents. In *Baby talk and infant speech*, W. von Raffler Engel and Y. LeBrun, eds. Amsterdam: Swets and Zeitlinger.

Sackheim, J.A. 1985. The case for ECT. *Psychology Today*. June, pp. 36–40.

Sacks, O. 1985. *The man who mistook his wife for a hat*. New York: Summit.

Sadalla, E.K. 1978. Population size, structural differentiation, and human behavior. *Environment and Behavior* 10: 271–91.

Sadalla, E.K., Kenrick, D.T., and Vershure, B. 1987. Dominance and heterosexual attraction. *Journal of Personality and Social Psychology* 52: 730–738.

Saenz, C.G., and Lord, C.G. 1989. Reversing roles: A cognitive strategy for undoing memory deficits associated with token status. *Journal of Personality and Social Psychology* 56: 698–708.

Sagar, H.A., and Schofield, J.W. 1980. Racial and behavioral cues in black and white children's perceptions of ambiguously aggressive acts. *Journal of Personality and Social Psychology* 39: 590–98.

Saghir, M.T., and Robins, E. 1973. *Male and female homosexuality: A comprehensive investigation*. Baltimore: Williams and Wilkins.

Salkind, N.J. 1983. The effectiveness of early intervention. In *Early childhood education*, E.M. Goetz and K.E. Allen, eds. Gaithersburg, MD: Aspen Systems Corporation.

Salmon, D.P., Zola-Morgan, S., and Squire, L.R. 1987. Retrograde amnesia following combined hippocampus-amygdala lesions in monkeys. *Psychobiology* 15: 37–47.

Sampson, H.A., and Jolie, P.L. 1984. Increased plasma histamine concentrations after food challenges in children with atropic dermatitis. *The New England Journal of Medicine* 311: 372–76.

Sanders, R.J. 1985. Teaching apes to ape language: Explaining the imitative and nonimitative signing of a chimpanzee (Pan troglodytes). *Journal of Comparative Psychology* 99: 197–210.

Sapolsky, R.M. 1990. Why you feel crummy when you're sick. *Discover*, July, pp. 66–70.

Sarason, I.G., Johnson, J.H., and Siegel, J.M. 1978. Assessing the impact of life changes: Development of the Life Experiences Survey. *Journal of Consulting and Clinical Psychology* 46: 932–46.

Sarason, I.G., Levine, H.M., and Sarason, B.R. 1982. Assessing the impact of life changes. In *Handbook of clinical health psychology*, T. Millon, C. Green, and R. Meagher, eds. New York: Plenum.

Sarason, I.G., and Sarason, B.R. 1987. *Abnormal psychology*, 5th ed. Englewood Cliffs, NJ: Prentice Hall.

Sarbin, T.R., and Coe, W.C. 1972. *Hypnosis: A social psychological analysis of influence communication*. New York: Holt, Rinehart and Winston.

Sargent, S.S., and Stafford, K.R. 1965. *Basic teachings of the great psychologists*. Garden City, NY: Dolphin Books.

Savage-Rumbaugh, S., McDonald, K., Sevcik, R.A., Hopkins, W.D., and Rubert, E. 1986. Spontaneous symbol acquisition and communicative use by pygmy chimpanzees (Pan paniscus). *Journal of Experimental Psychology: General* 115: 211–35.

Savin-Williams, R.C., and Small, S.A. 1986. The timing of puberty and its relationship to adolescent and parent perceptions of family interactions. *Developmental Psychology* 22: 342–47.

Scales, P., and Gordon, S. 1978. The effects of sex education. In *The sexual adolescent*, S. Gordon and P. Scales, eds. North Scituate, MA: Duxbury.

Scarr, S. 1981. The transmission of authoritarianism in families: Genetic resemblance in social-political attitudes? In *Race, social class, and individual differences in IQ,* S. Scarr, ed. Hillsdale, NJ: Erlbaum.

Scarr, S., and Carter-Saltzman, L. 1982. Genetics and intelligence. In *Handbook of human intelligence,* R.J. Sternberg, ed. Cambridge, UK: Cambridge University Press.

Scarr, S., and Weinberg, R.A. 1976. IQ test performance of black children adopted by white families. *American Psychologist* 31: 726–39.

———. 1983. The Minnesota adoption studies: Genetic differences and malleability. *Child Development* 54: 260–67.

Schachter, S. 1959. *The psychology of affiliation.* Stanford, CA: Stanford University Press.

———. 1971. *Emotion, obesity, and crime.* New York: Academic Press.

———. 1982. Don't sell habit-breakers short. *Psychology Today,* August, pp. 27–33.

Schachter, S., and Rodin, J., eds. 1974. *Obese humans and rats.* Washington, DC: Erlbaum.

Schachter, S., and Singer, J.E. 1962. Cognitive, social, and physiological determinants of emotional state. *Psychological Review* 69: 379–99.

Schacter, D.L. 1987. Implicit memory: History and current status. *Journal of Experimental Psychology: Learning, Memory, and Cognition* 13: 501–18.

Schaeffer, J., Andrysiak, T., and Ungerleider, J.T. 1981. Cognition and long-term use of ganja (cannabis). *Science* 213: 456–66.

Schaie, K.W., and Willis, S.L. 1986. Can decline in adult intellectual functioning be reversed? *Developmental Psychology* 22: 223–32.

Schaller, M., and Maass, A. 1989. Illusory correlation and social categorization: Toward an integration of motivational and cognitive factors in stereotype formation. *Journal of Personality & Social Psychology* 56: 709–21.

Scheier, M.F., Weintraub, J.K., and Carver, C.S. 1986. Coping with stress: Diverging strategies of optimists and pessimists. *Journal of Personality and Social Psychology* 51: 1257–64.

Schell, J. 1982. *The fate of the earth.* New York: Knopf.

Schieffelin, B.B., and Eisenberg, A.R. 1981. Cultural variation in children's conversations. In *Early language acquisition and intervention,* R.L. Schiefelbusch and D.D. Bricker, eds. Baltimore: University Park Press.

Schiffman, H.R. 1976. *Sensation and perception: An integrated approach.* New York: Wiley.

Schleifer, S.J., Keller, S.E., Siris, S.G., Davis, K.L., and Stein, M. 1985. Depression and immunity. *Archives of General Psychiatry* 42: 129–33.

Schlenker, B.R., and Miller, R.S. 1985. Egotism in group members: Public and private attributions of responsibility for group performance. *Social Psychology Quarterly* 48: 85–89.

Schlesinger, A.M. 1978. *Robert Kennedy and his times.* New York: Ballantyne Books.

Schlesinger, K. 1985. A brief introduction to a history of psychology. In *Topics in the history of psychology,* vol. 1, G.A. Kimble and K. Schlesinger, eds. Hillsdale, NJ: Erlbaum.

———. 1985. Behavior genetics and the nature-nurture question. In *Topics in the history of psychology,* vol. 2, G.A. Kimble and K. Schlesinger, eds. Hillsdale, NJ: Erlbaum.

Schlossberg, N.K. 1987. Taking the mystery out of change. *Psychology Today,* May, pp. 74–75.

Schmale, A.H. 1970. Adaptive role of depression in health and disease. In *Separation and depression,* J.P. Scott and E.C. Senay, eds. Washington, DC: American Association for the Advancement of Science Publication.

Schmeck, H.M., Jr. 1984. Implant brings sound to deaf. *New York Times,* March 27.

Schmidt, W.E. 1983. Gifted retardates: The search for clues to mysterious talent. *New York Times,* July 12.

Schmitt, M. 1973. Influences of hepatic portal receptors on hypothalamic feeding and satiety centers. *American Journal of Physiology* 225: 1089–95.

Schmitt, R.C. 1966. Density, health and social disorganization. *Journal of the American Institute of Planners* 32: 38–40.

Schneider, D.J. 1973 Implicit personality theory: A review. *Psychological Bulletin* 79: 294–309.

Schneiderman, N., Weiss, S.M., and Kaufmann, P.G., eds. *Handbook of research methods in cardiovascular behavioral medicine.* New York: Plenum.

Schnier, J. 1950. The blazing sun: A psychoanalytic approach to Van Gogh. *American Imago* 7: 143–62.

Schreiner-Engel, P., Schiavi, R.C., White, D., and Ghizzani. 1989. Low sexual desire in women: The role of reproductive hormones. *Hormones and Behavior* 23: 221–34.

Schroeder, D.H., and Costa, P.T. 1984. Influence of life event stress on physical illness: Substantive effects or methodological flaws? *Journal of Personality and Social Psychology* 46: 853–63.

Schuckit, M.A. 1983. The genetics of alcoholism. In *Medical and social aspects of alcohol use,* B. Tabakoff, P.B. Sutker, & C.L. Randall, eds. New York: Plenum.

———. 1989. *Drug and alcohol abuse,* 3rd ed. New York: Plenum.

Schulz, R. 1976. Effects of control and predictability on the physical and psychological well-being of the institutionalized aged. *Journal of Personality and Social Psychology* 33: 563–73.

Schulz, R., and Brenner, G. 1977. Relocation of the aged: A review and theoretical analysis. *Journal of Gerontology* 32: 323–33.

Schulz, R., and Hanusa, B.H. 1978. Long-term effects of control and predictability-enhancing inventions: Findings and ethical issues. *Journal of Personality and Social Psychology* 36: 1194–1201.

Schustack, M.W., Ehrlich, S.F., and Rayner, K. 1987. Local and global sources of contextual facilitation in reading. *Journal of Memory and Language* 26: 322–40.

Schwartz, B. 1989. *Psychology of learning and behavior,* 3rd ed. New York: Norton.

Scott, J.P. 1980. The function of emotions in behavioral systems: A systems theory analysis. In *Emotion: Theory, research, and experience,* vol. 1, R. Plutchik and H. Kellerman, eds. New York: Academic Press.

Seamon, J.G. 1976. Effects of generative processes on probe identification time. *Memory and Cognition* 4: 759–62.

———. 1978. Rehearsal, generative processes, and the activation of underlying stimulus

representations. *Perception and Psychophysics* 23: 381–90.

———. 1980. *Memory & cognition: An introduction.* New York: Oxford University Press.

——— 1980. *Human memory: Contemporary readings.* New York: Oxford University Press.

Seamon, J.G., Brody, N., and Kauff, D.M. 1983. Affective discrimination of stimuli that are not recognized: Effects of shadowing, masking, and cerebral laterality. *Journal of Experimental psychology: Learning, Memory, and Cognition* 9: 544–55.

Seamon, J.G., Marsh, R.L., and Brody, N. 1984. Critical importance of exposure duration for affective discrimination of stimuli that are not recognized. *Journal of Experimental Psychology: Learning, Memory, and Cognition* 10: 465–69.

Seamon, J.G., and Murray, P. 1976. Depth of processing in recall and recognition memory: Differential effects of stimulus meaningfulness and serial position. *Journal of Experimental Psychology: Human Learning and Memory* 2: 680–87.

Seamon, J.G., and Virostek, S. 1978. Memory performance and subject-defined depth of processing. *Memory of Cognition* 6: 283–87.

Seamon, J.G., and Wright, C.E. 1976. Generative processes in character classification: Evidence for a probe encoding set. *Memory and Cognition* 4: 96–102.

Sears, P.S., and Barbee, A.H. 1977. Career and life satisfactions among Terman's gifted women. In *The gifted and the creative: Fifty-year perspective,* J.C. Stanley, W.C. George, and C.H. Solano, eds. Baltimore: Johns Hopkins University Press.

Sears, R.R. 1977. Sources of life satisfaction of the Terman gifted man. *American Psychologist* 32: 119–28.

Sebrechts, M.M., Marsh, R.L., and Seamon, J.G. 1989. Secondary memory in very rapid forgetting. *Memory and Cognition* 17: 693–700.

Seeman, P., Ulpian, C., Bergeron, C., Riederer, P., Jellinger, K. Gabriel, E., Reynolds, G.P., and Tourtellotte, W.W. 1984. Bimodal distribution of dopamine receptor densities in brains of schizophrenics. *Science* 225: 728–31.

Segal, M.W. 1974. Alphabet and attraction: An unobtrusive measure of the effect of propinquity in a field setting. *Journal of Personality and Social Psychology* 30: 654–57.

Sejnowski, T.J., and Rosenberg, C.R. 1987. Parallel networks that learn to pronounce English text. *Complex Systems* 1: 145–68.

Sekuler, R., and Blake, R. 1985. *Perception.* New York: Knopf.

Selfridge, O.G., (1959). Pandemonium: A paradigm for learning. In *Symposium on the mechanization of thought processes.* London: H.M. Stationery Office.

Seliger, S. 1982. Stress can be good for you. *New York.* August 2.

Seligman, C., Fazio, R.H., and Zanna, M.P. 1980. Effects of salience of extrinsic rewards on liking and loving. *Journal of Personality and Social Psychology* 38: 453–60.

Seligman, M.E.P. 1970. On the generality of the laws of learning. *Psychological Review* 77: 406–18.

———. 1972. Phobias and preparedness. In *Biological boundaries of learning,* M.E.P. Seligman and J.L. Hager, eds. New York: Appleton-Century-Crofts.

———. 1975. *Helplessness: On depression, development, and death.* San Francisco: Freeman.

Seligman, M.E.P., and Schulman, P. 1986. Explanatory style as a predictor of productivity and quitting among life insurance sales agents. *Journal of Personality and Social Psychology* 50: 832–38.

Selman, R.L. 1980. *The growth of interpersonal understanding.* New York: Academic Press.

Selman, R. L., and Byrne, D.F. 1974. A structural-developmental analysis of levels of role taking in middle childhood. *Child Development* 45: 803–6.

Selye, H. 1936. A syndrome produced by diverse nocuous agents. *Nature* 138: 32.

———. 1976. *The stress of life.* New York: McGraw-Hill.

Shaffer, J.W., Graves-Pirrko, L., Swank, R. and Pearson, T.A. 1987. Clustering of personality traits in youth and the subsequent development of cancer among physicians. *Journal of Behavioral Medicine* 10: 441–47.

Shaffer, L.H. 1975. Multiple attention in continuous verbal tasks. In *Attention and performance V,* P.M.A. Rabbitt and S. Dornic, eds. New York: Academic Press.

Shank, J.C. 1983. Disease incidence and prevalence. In *Family medicine: Principles and practice,* R.B. Taylor, ed. New York: Springer-Verlag.

Shapiro, D.A., and Shapiro, D. 1982. Meta-analysis of comparative therapy outcome studies: A replication and refinement. *Psychological Bulletin* 92: 581–604.

Shapiro, D.H. 1985. Clinical use of meditation as a self-regulation strategy. *American Psychologist* 40: 719–22.

Shaughnessy, J.J. 1981. Memory monitoring accuracy and modification of rehearsal strategies. *Journal of Verbal Learning and Verbal Behavior* 20: 216–30.

Sheehy, G. 1976. *Passages.* New York: Dutton.

Sheldon, W.H. 1944. Constitutional factors in personality. In *Personality and the behavior disorders,* J. McV. Hunt, ed. New York: Ronald Press.

Shepard, R.N. 1967. Recognition memory for words, sentences, and pictures. *Journal of Verbal Learning and Verbal Behavior* 6: 156–63.

———. 1988. The imagination of the scientist. In *Imagination and education,* K. Egan and D. Nadaner, eds. New York: Teachers College Press.

Shepard, R.N., and Metzler, J. 1971. Mental rotation of three-dimensional objects. *Science* 171: 701–3.

Shepher, J. 1971. Mate selection among second generation kibbutz adolescents and adults: Incest avoidance and negative imprinting. *Archives of Sexual Behavior* 1: 293–307.

Shepher, J. & Reisman, J.R. 1985. Pornography: A sociobiological attempt at understanding. *Ethology and Sociobiology* 6: 103–114.

Sherif, M. 1937. A study of some social factors in perception. *Archives of Psychology* 27: 1–60.

Sherif, M., and Sherif, C.W. 1956. *An outline of social psychology.* New York: Harper & Row.

Sherman, J.A. 1978. *Sex-related cognitive differences.* Springfield, IL: Charles C. Thomas.

Sherman, S.J., and Fazio, R.H. 1983. Parallels between attitudes and traits as predictors of behavior. *Journal of Personality* 51: 308–45.

Sherman, S.J., and Gorkin, L. 1980. Attitude bolstering when behavior is inconsistent with central attitudes. *Journal of Experimental Social Psychology* 16: 388–403.

Sherman, S.J., Judd, C.M., and Park, B. 1989. Social sognition. In *Annual review of psychology,* vol. 40, M.R. Rosenzweig and L.W. Porter, eds. Palo Alto, CA: Annual Reviews.

Sherman, S.J., Mackie, D.M., and Driscoll, D.M. 1990. Priming and the differential use of dimensions in evaluation. *Personality and Social Psychology Bulletin* 16: 405–18.

Sherry, D.F., and Schacter, D.L. 1987. The evolution of multiple memory systems. *Psychological Review* 94: 439–54.

Sherwin, R., and Corbitt, S. 1985. Campus sexual norms and dating relationships: A trend analysis. *Journal of Sex Research* 21: 258–74.

Shiels, M., Agrest, S., and Sciolino, E. 1975. A wealthy beggar. *Newsweek,* Sep. 29, p. 21.

Shiffrin, R.M. 1985. Attention. In *Stevens' handbook of experimental psychology,* R.C. Atkinson, R.J. Herrnstein, G. Lindsey, and R.D. Luce, eds. New York: Wiley.

Shiffrin, R.M., and Cook, J.R. 1978. Short-term forgetting of item and order information. *Journal of Verbal Learning and Verbal Behavior,* 17: 189–218.

Shiffrin, R.M., and Schneider, W. 1977. Controlled and automatic human information processing: II. Perceptual learning, automatic attending, and a general theory. *Psychological Review* 84: 127–90.

Shneiderman, E.S. 1976. Death work and stages of dying. In *Death: Current perspectives,* E.S. Shneiderman, ed. Palo Alto, CA: Mayfield.

Shorey, H.H. 1977. Pheromones. In *How animals communicate,* T.A. Sebeck, ed. Bloomington: Indiana University Press.

Shortliffe, E.H. 1983. Medical consultation systems: Designing for doctors. In *Designing for human computer communication,* M.E. Sime and M.J. Coombs, eds. New York: Academic Press.

Shortliffe, E.H., Axline, S.G., Buchanan, B.G., Merigan, T.C., and Cohen, N.S. 1973. An artificial intelligence program to advise physicians regarding antimicrobial therapy. *Computers and Biomedical Research* 6: 544–60.

Siegal, S. 1977. Morphine tolerance acquisition as an association process. *Journal of Experimental Psychology: Animal Behavior Processes* 3: 1–13.

Siegler, R.S. 1991. *Children's thinking,* 2nd ed. Englewood Cliffs, NJ: Prentice Hall.

Siegler, R.S., and Richards, D.D. 1982. The development of intelligence. In *Handbook of human intelligence,* R.J. Sternberg, ed. Cambridge, UK: Cambridge University Press.

Simon, H.A. 1974. How big is a chunk? *Science* 183: 482–88.

———. 1982. Unity of the arts and sciences: The psychology of thought and discovery. *Bulletin of the American Academy of Arts and Sciences* 35: 26–53.

Simon, H.A., and Newell, A. 1971. Human problem solving: The state of the theory in 1970. *American Psychologist* 26: 145–59.

Simon, W., and Gagnon, J. 1977. Psychosexual development. In *Exploring human sexuality,* D. Byrne and L.A. Byrne. New York: Thomas Y. Crowell.

Simmons, R.G., and Blyth, D.A. 1987. *Moving into adolescence: The impact of pubertal change and school context.* New York: Aldine.

Simonton, D.K. 1984. *Genius, creativity, and leadership: Historiometric inquiries.* Cambridge, MA: Harvard Univ. Press.

Sims, E.A. 1974. Studies in human hyperphagia. In *Treatment and management of obesity,* G. Bray and J. Bethune, eds. New York: Harper and Row.

Singer, J.L., and McCraven, V. J. 1961. Some characteristics of adult daydreaming. *Journal of Psychology* 51: 151–64.

Sitaram, N., Weingartner, H., Caine, E.D., and Gillin, J.C. 1978. Choline: Selective enhancement of serial learning and encoding of low imagery words in man. *Life Sciences* 22: 1535–60.

Skinner, B.F. 1938. *The behavior of organisms: An experimental analysis.* Englewood Cliffs, NJ: Prentice Hall.

———. 1953. *Science and human behavior.* New York: Free Press.

———. 1957. *Verbal behavior.* New York: Appleton-Century-Crofts.

———. 1972. *Beyond freedom and dignity.* New York: Bantam Books.

———. 1975. The steep and thorny way to a science of behavior. *American Psychologist* 30: 42–49.

———. 1987. Whatever happened to psychology as the science of behavior. *American Psychologist* 42: 780–86.

———. 1990. Can psychology be a science of mind? *American Psychologist* 45: 1206–10.

Sklar, L.S., and Anisman, H. 1981. Stress and Cancer. *Psychological Bulletin* 89: 369–406.

Sklar, R.B., and Sherman, S.J. 1986. Information-gathering processes: Diagnosticity, Hypothesis-confirmatory strategies, and perceived hypothesis confirmation. *Journal of Experimental Social Psychology* 36: 1202–12.

Slater, A., II., and Morison, V. 1985. Shape constancy and slant perception of birth. *Perception* 14: 337–44.

Slater, E., and Glithero, E. 1965. A follow-up of patients diagnosed as suffering from a hysteria. *Journal of Psychosomatic Research* 9: 9–13.

Slovic, P., Fischoff, B., & Lichtenstein, S. 1979. Facts and fears. *Environment* 21: 14–39.

———. 1981. Perception and acceptability of risk from energy systems. In *Advances in environmental psychology* vol. 3, A. Baum and J.E. Singer, eds. Hillsdale, NJ: Erlbaum.

Small, G.W., and Nicholi, A.M. 1982. Mass hysteria among school children. *Archives of General Psychiatry* 39: 89–90.

Smith, A. 1776/1976. *The wealth of nations.* Oxford, England: Clarendon Press.

Smith, E.A., Udry, J.R., and Morris, N.M. 1985. Pubertal development and friends: A biosocial explanation of adolescent sexual behavior. *Journal of Health and Social Behavior* 26: 183–92.

Smith, J. 1989. *Senses and sensibilities.* New York: Wiley.

Smith, M.C., Coleman, S.R., and Gormezano, I. 1969. Classical conditioning of the rabbits' nictitating membrane response. *Journal of Comparative and Physiological Psychology* 69: 226–31.

Smith, M.L., Glass, G.V., and Miller, T.I. 1980. *The benefits of psychotherapy*. Baltimore: Johns Hopkins Press.

———. 1983. Placebo effects in psychotherapy outcome research. *Behavioral and Brain Sciences* 6: 293–94.

Smith, R.E., Sarason, I.G., and Sarason, B.R. 1986. *Psychology: The frontiers of behavior*, 3rd ed. New York: Harper and Row.

Smith, S.M., Brown, H.O., Toman, J.E.P., and Goodman, L.S. 1947. The lack of cerebral effects of d-tubocurarine. *Anaesthesiology* 8: 1–14.

Smith, W.J. 1985. *Dying in the human life cycle*. New York: Holt, Rinehart and Winston.

Smolensky, P. 1988. On the proper treatment of connectionism. *The Behavioral and Brain Sciences* 11: 1–74.

Smythies, J.R., and Ireland, C.B. 1989. Hallucinogenic drugs. In *Abnormal states of brain and mind*, J.A. Hobson, ed. Readings from the *Encyclopedia of neuroscience*. Boston: Birkhauser.

Snow, C.E. 1981. The uses of imitation. *Journal of Child Language* 8: 205–12.

Snow, C.P. 1966. *Variety of men*. New York: Scribner's.

Snyder, F. 1970. The phenomenology of dreaming. In *The psychodynamic implication of the physiological studies on dreams*, L. Madow and L.H. Snow, eds. Springfield, IL: Thomas.

Snyder, F.W., and Pronko, N.H. 1952. *Vision with spatial inversion*. Witchita: Univ. of Kansas Press.

Snyder, M. 1979. Self-monitoring processes. In *Advances in experimental social psychology*, vol. 12, L. Berkowitz, ed. New York: Academic Press.

———. 1983. The influence of individuals on situations. *Journal of Personality* 51: 497–516.

———. 1984. When belief creates reality. In *Advances in experimental social psychology*, vol. 18, L. Berkowitz, ed. New York: Academic Press.

Snyder, M., and Ickes, W. 1985. Personality and social behavior. In *Handbook of social psychology*, 3rd ed., vol. II, G. Lindzey and E. Aronson, eds. Reading, MA: Addison-Wesley.

Snyder, M., and Swann, W.B. 1978. Hypothesis-testing processes in social interaction. *Journal of Personality and Social Psychology* 36: 1202–12.

Snyder, M., Tanke, E.D., and Berscheid, E. 1977. Social perception and interpersonal behavior: On the self-fulfilling nature of social stereotypes. *Journal of Personality and Social Psychology* 35: 656–66.

Snyder, M., and Uranowitz, S.W. 1978. Reconstructing the past: Some cognitive consequences of person perception. *Journal of Personality and Social Psychology* 36: 941–50.

Sobel, D. 1980. Freud's fragmented legacy. *The New York Times Magazine*, October 26, pp. 28ff.

Sobell, M.B., and Sobell, L.C. 1973. Individualized behavior therapy for alcoholics. *Behavior Therapy* 4: 49–72.

———. 1978. *Behavior treatment of alcohol problems: Individualized therapy and controlled drinking*. New York: Plenum.

Solomon, R.L. 1980. The opponent-process theory of acquired motivation: The costs of pleasure and the benefits of pain. *American Psychologist* 35: 691–712.

Solomon, R.L., and Corbit, J.D. 1974. An opponent-process theory of motivation. *Psychological Review* 81: 119–45.

Solso, R.L. 1991. *Cognitive psychology*, 3rd ed. Boston: Allyn and Bacon.

Sontag, C.W., Baker, C.T., and Nelson, V.L. 1958. Mental growth and personality development: A longitudinal study. *Monographs of the Society of Research in Child Development* 23 (Serial No. 68).

Sorrentino, R.M., and Higgins, E.T. 1986. *The handbook of motivation and cognition*. New York: Guilford Press.

Sosa, R., Kennell, J., Klaus, M., Robertson, I., and Urrutia, J. 1980. The effect of a supportive companion on perinatal problems, length of labor, and mother–infant interaction. *New England Journal of Medicine* 303: 597–600.

Spanos, N.P. 1986. Hypnotic behavior: A social-psychological interpretation of amnesia, analgesia, and "trance logic." *The Behavioral and Brain Sciences* 9: 449–502.

Spanos, N.P., and Hewitt, E.C. 1980. The hidden observer in hypnotic analgesia: Discovery of experimental creation? *Journal of Personality and Social Psychology* 39: 1201–14.

Spanos, N.P., and Radtke-Bodorik, H.L. 1980. Integrating hypnotic phenomena with cognitive psychology: An illustration using suggested amnesia. *Bulletin of the British Society for Experimental and Clinical Hypnosis* 3: 4–7.

Spearman, C. 1927. *The abilities of man*. London: Macmillan.

Spector, P.E., Dwyer, D.J., and Jex, S.M. 1988. Relation of job stressors to affective, health, and performance outcomes: A comparison of multiple data sources. *Journal of Applied Psychology* 73: 11–19.

Speisman, J.C., Lazarus, R.S., Mordkoff, A.M., and Davison, L. 1964. Experimental reduction of stress based on ego-defense theory. *Journal of Abnormal and Social Psychology* 68: 367–80.

Spelke, E.S. 1979. Perceiving bimodally specified events in infancy. *Developmental Psychology* 15: 626–36.

Spelke, E.S., Hirst, W., and Neisser, U. 1976. Skills of divided attention. *Cognition* 4: 215–30.

Sperling, G. 1960. The information available in brief visual presentations. *Psychological Monographs* 74 Whole No. 498.

Sperry, R.W. 1968. Hemisphere deconnection and unity in conscious experience. *American Psychologist* 23: 723–33.

———. 1976. Changing concepts of consciousness and free will. *Perspectives in Biology and Medicine* 20: 9–19.

———. 1987. Structure and significance of the consciousness revolution. *The Journal of Mind and Behavior* 8: 37–66.

Spielberger, C.D., Johnson, E.H., Russell, S.F., Crane, R.J., Jacobs, G.A., and Worden, T.J. 1985. The experience and expression of anger. In *Anger and hostility in behavioral medicine*, M.A. Chesney, S.E. Goldston, and R.H. Rosenman, eds. New York: Hemisphere/McGraw Hill.

Spiegel, D., Bierre, P., and Rottenberg, J. 1989. Hypnotic alteration of somatosensory perception. *American Journal of Psychiatry* 146: 749–54.

Spitzer, R.L. 1975. On pseudoscience in *Science*, logic in remission, and psychiatric diagnosis: A critique of Rosenhan's "On Being Sane in Insane Places." *Journal of Abnormal Psychology* 84: 442–52.

Spitzer, R.L., Endicott, J., Robins, E., Kuriansky, J., and Gurland, B. 1976. Preliminary report of the reliability of research diagnostic criteria applied to psychiatric records. In *Prediction in psychopharmacology*, A. Sudilofsky, B. Beer, and S. Gershon, eds. New York: Raven Press.

Spitzer, R.L., Forman, J.B., and Nee, J. 1979. DSM-II field trials: I. Initial inter-rater diagnostic reliability. *American Journal of Psychiatry* 136: 818–20.

Spitzer, R.L., Skodal, A.E., Gibbon, M., and Williams, J.B.W. 1981. *DSM-III Case book*. Washington, DC: American Psychiatric Association.

———. 1983. *Psychopathology: A casebook*. New York: McGraw-Hill.

Spring, D.R. 1974. *Effects of maternal speech on infant's selection of vocal reinforcement*. Unpublished paper. University of Washington.

Springer, S.P., and Deutsch, G. 1989. *Left brain, right brain*, 3rd ed. New York: Freeman.

Squire, L.R. 1987. *Memory and brain*. New York: Oxford University Press.

Sroufe, L.A. 1978. Attachment and the roots of competence. *Human Nature* 1: 50–57.

Staats, A.W., and Staats, C.K. 1958. Attitudes established by classical conditioning. *Journal of Abnormal and Social Psychology* 57: 37–40.

Stapley, J.C., and Haviland, J.M. 1989. Beyond depression: Gender differences in normal adolescents' emotional experiences. *Sex Roles* 20: 295–308.

Stanley, J.C. 1976. Concern for intellectually talented youths: How it originated and fluctuated. *Journal of Clinical Child Psychology* 5: 38–42.

Stanley, J.C., and Benbow, C.P. 1983. SMPY's first decade: Ten years of posing problems and solving them. *Journal of Special Education* 17: 11–25.

Stanton, M., Mintz, J., and Franklin, R.M. 1976. Drug flashbacks. *International Journal of Addictions* 11: 53–59.

Statistical Abstract of the United States. 1988. Washington, DC: United States Department of the Census.

Stein, N., and Sanfilipo, M. 1985. Depression and the wish to be held. *Journal of Clinical Psychology* 41: 3–9.

Steinberg, L. 1987. Impact of puberty on family relations: Effects of pubertal status and pubertal timing. *Developmental Psychology* 23: 451–60.

———. 1987. Bound to bicker. *Psychology Today*, September, pp. 36–39.

Steiner, J.E. 1977. Facial expressions of the neonate infant indicating the hedonics of food-related chemical stimuli. In *Taste and development: The genesis of sweet preference*, J.M. Weiffenbach, ed. DHEW Publication No. NIH 77–1068. Washington, DC: Government Printing Office, pp. 173–88.

Steklis, H.D., and Kling, A. 1985. Neurobiology of affiliative behavior in non-human primates. In *The psychobiology of attachment and separation*, M. Reife and T. Field, eds. New York: Academic Press.

Stelmack, R.M. 1990. Biological bases of extraversion: Psychophysiological evidence. *Journal of Personality* 58: 293–311.

Stephen, R., and Sweigenhaft, R.L. 1985. The effect on tipping of a waitress touching male and female customers. *Journal of Social Psychology* 126: 141–42.

Stern, L. 1985. *The structure and strategies of human memory.* Homewood, IL: Dorsey.

Stern, P.C., and Gardner, G.T. 1981. Psychological research and energy policy. *American Psychologist* 36: 329–42.

Stern, R.S., and Cobb, J.P. 1978. Phenomenology of obsessive compulsive neuroses. *British Journal of Psychiatry* 182: 233–39.

Sternberg, R.J. 1977. *Intelligence, information processing and analogical reasoning: The componential analysis of human abilities.* Hillsdale, NJ: Erlbaum.

———. 1982. Reasoning, problem solving, and intelligence. In *Handbook of human intelligence,* R.J. Sternberg, ed. Cambridge, UK: Cambridge University Press.

———. 1985. *Beyond IQ: A triarchic theory of human intelligence.* Cambridge, UK: Cambridge University Press.

———. 1986. *Intelligence applied: Understanding and increasing your intellectual skills.* New York: Harcourt Brace Jovanovich.

———. 1986. A triangular theory of love. *Psychological Review* 93: 119–35.

———. 1990. *Metaphors of mind.* Cambridge, UK: Cambridge University Press.

Sternberg, R.J., Conway, B.E., Ketron, J.L., and Bernstein, M. 1981. People's conceptions of intelligence. *Journal of Personality and Social Psychology* 41: 37–55.

Sternberg, R.J., and Davidson, J.E. 1982. The mind of the puzzler. *Psychology Today,* June, pp. 37–44.

Sternberg, R.J., and Smith, C. 1985. Social intelligence and decoding skills in nonverbal communication. *Social Cognition* 2: 168–92.

Stevens, K.A. 1983. Evidence relating subjective contours and interpretations involving interposition. *Perception* 12: 491–500.

Stevens, J.C., and Cain, W.S. 1986. Smelling via the mouth: Effect of aging. *Perception and Psychophysics* 40: 142–46.

Stevens, S.S. 1957. On the psychophysical law. *Psychological Review* 64: 153–81.

———. 1962. The surprising simplicity of sensory metrics. *American Psychologist* 17: 29–39.

———. 1975. *Psychophysics: An introduction to its perceptual, neural, and social prospects.* New York: Wiley.

Stevenson, R.L. 1883/1923. *Treasure Island.* New York: Scribner's Sons.

Steward, A.L., and Lupfer, M. 1987. Touching as teaching: The effect of touch on students' perceptions and performance. *Journal of Applied Social Psychology* 17: 800–9.

Stewart, J., de Wit, H., and Eikelboom, R. 1984. Role of unconditioned and conditioned drug effects in the self-administration of opiates and stimulants. *Psychological Review* 91: 251–68.

St. George-Hyslop, P.H., Tanzi, R.E., Polinsky, R.J., Haines, J.L., Nee, L., Watkins, P.C., Myers, R.H., Feldman, R.G., Pollen, D., Drachman, D., Growdon, J., Bruni, A., Foncin, J.F., Salmon, D., Frommelt, P., Amaducci, L., Sorbi, S., Piacentini, S., Stewart, G.D., Hobbs, W.J., Conneally, M., and Gusella, J.F. 1987. The genetic defect causing familial Alzheimer's disease maps on chromosome 21. *Science* 235: 885–90.

Stich, S.P. 1990. Rationality. In *Thinking: An invitation to cognitive science,* D.N. Osherson and E.E. Smith, eds. Cambridge, MA: MIT Press.

Stipek, D.J., Gralinski, J.H., and Kopp, C.B. 1990. Self-concept development in the toddler years. *Developmental Psychology* 26: 972–77.

Strack, F., Martin, L., and Stepper, S. 1988. Inhibiting and facilitating conditions of the human smile: A nonobtrusive test of the facial feedback hypothesis. *Journal of Personality and Social Psychology* 54: 768–77.

Strack, S., and Coyne, J.C. 1983. Social confirmation of dysphoria: Shared and private reactions to depression. *Journal of Personality and Social Psychology* 44: 798–806.

Strauss, M.A., and Gelles, R.J. 1980. *Behind closed doors: Violence in the American family.* New York: Anchor/Doubleday.

Streissguth, A.P., Barr, H.M., and Martin, D.C. 1983. Maternal alcohol use and neonatal habituation assessed with the Brazelton Scale. *Child Development* 54: 1109–18.

———. 1984. Intrauterine alcohol and nicotine exposure. *Developmental Psychology* 20: 533–41.

"Stress on the job." *Newsweek,* April 25, pp. 40–45.

Strupp, H.H. 1986. Psychotherapy: Research, practice, and public policy (How to avoid dead ends). *American Psychologist* 41: 120–30.

Stobaugh, R., and Yergin, D. 1979. *Energy future: Report of the energy project at the Harvard Business School.* New York: Random House.

Stone, A.A., Cox, D.S., Valdimarsdottir, H., Jandorf, L., and Neale, J.M. 1987. Evidence that secretory IgA antibody is associated with daily mood. *Journal of Personality and Social Psychology* 52: 988–93.

Stone, A.A., Reed, B.R., and Neale, J.M. 1987. Changes in daily event frequency precede episodes of physical symptoms. *Journal of Human Stress* 13: 70–74.

Stone, L.J., and Church, J. 1968. *Childhood and adolescence.* New York: Random House.

Stumpf, S.E. 1966. *Socrates to Sartre: A history of philosophy.* New York: McGraw-Hill.

Stunkard, A.J. 1968. Environment and obesity: Recent advances in our understanding of regulation of food intake in man. *Federation Proceedings* 27: 1369.

Stunkard, A.J., Sorenson, T., Honis, C., Teasdale, T.W., Chakraborty, R., Schull, W.J., and Schulsinger, F. 1986. An adoption study of human obesity. *New England Journal of Medicine* 314: 193–98.

Suga, N. 1990. Biosonar and neural computation in bats. *Scientific American* June, 60–68.

Sulik, K.K., Johnston, M.C., and Webb, M.A. 1981. Fetal alcohol syndrome. *Science* 214: 936–38.

Sullivan, H.S. 1953. *The interpersonal theory of psychiatry.* New York: W.W. Norton.

Sumner, W.G. 1906. *Folkways.* New York: Ginn.

Suomi, S.J., Harlow, H.F., and McKinney, W.T. 1972. Monkey psychiatrist. *American Journal of Psychiatry* 128: 41–46.

Sussman, K., and Lewandowski, L. 1990. Left-hemisphere dysfunction in autism: What are we measuring? *Archives of Clinical Neuropsychology* 5: 137–46.

Svare, B., and Kinsley, C.H. 1987. Hormones and sex-related behavior: A comparative analysis. In *Males, females, and sexuality: Theory and research,* K. Kelley, ed. Albany: State University of New York Press.

Swerdlow, N.R., and Koob, G.F. 1987. Dopamine, schizophrenia, mania, and depression: Toward a unified hypothesis of cortico-striato-pallido-thalamic function. *Behavioral and Brain Sciences* 10: 197–245.

Symonds, D. 1979. *The evolution of human sexuality.* New York: Oxford University Press.

Szasz, T.S. 1960. The myth of mental illness. *American Psychologist* 15: 113–18.

——— ed. 1974. *The age of madness: The history of involuntary hospitalization.* Northvale, NJ: Jason Aronson.

Tagatz, C.E. 1976. *Child development and individually guided education.* Reading, MA: Addison-Wesley.

Tajfel, H. 1982. Social psychology of intergroup relations. *Annual Review of Psychology* 33: 1–39.

Tajfel, H., and Turner, J.C. 1986. The Social identity theory of intergroup behavior. In S. Worchel and W.G. Austin, eds. *The psychology of intergroup relations.* Chicago: Nelson Hall.

Takano, Y. 1989. Perception of rotated forms: A theory of information types. *Cognitive Psychology* 21: 1–59.

Talland, G.A. 1969. *The pathology of memory.* New York: Academic Press.

Tanabe, T., Iino, M., and Takagi, S.F. 1975. Discrimination of odors in olfactory bulb, pyriform-amygdaloid areas and orbito-frontal cortex of the monkey. *Journal of Neurophysiology* 38: 1284–96.

Tanner, J.M. 1978. *Foetus into man: Physical growth from conception to maturity.* Cambridge, MA: Harvard University Press.

Tanner, J.M., Whitehouse, R.H., and Takaishi, M. 1966. Standards from birth to maturity for height, weight, height-velocity, and weight velocity: British children, 1965. Part 1. *Archives of Disease in Childhood* 41: 454–71.

Tapia, F. 1983. Current status of psychopharmacology and organic treatments. In *Handbook of clinical psychology,* vol. 2, C.E. Walker, ed. Homewood, IL: Dow Jones–Irwin.

Taskin, D.P., Coulson, A., Clark, V., and collaborators. 1985. Respiratory symptoms and lung function in heavy habitual smokers of marijuana alone and with tobacco, smokers of tobacco alone and nonsmokers. *American Review of Respiratory Disease* 131: A198.

Taylor, S.E. 1986. *Health psychology.* New York: Random House.

Taylor, S.E., and Fiske, S.T. 1978. Salience, attention, and attribution: Top of the head phenomena. In *Advances in experimental social psychology,* vol. 11, L. Berkowitz, ed. New York: Academic Press.

Taylor, S., and Fiske, S. 1984. *Social cognition.* New York: Random House.

Teevan, R.C., and McGhee, P.E. 1972. Childhood development of fear of failure motivation. *Journal of Personality and Social Psychology* 21: 345–48.

Tefft, B.M., and Kloba, J.A. 1981. Underachieving high school students as mental health aides with maladapting primary grade children. *American Journal of Community Psychology* 9: 303–20.

Teger, A. 1980. *Too much invested to quit.* New York: Pergamon Press.

Teitlebaum, P. 1961. Disturbances in feeding and drinking behavior after hypothalamic lesions. In *Nebraska Symposium on Motivation,* M.R. Jones, ed. Lincoln: University of Nebraska Press, pp. 39–65.

Teitlebaum, P., and Epstein, A.N. 1962. The lateral hypothalamic syndrome: Recovery of feeding and drinking after lateral hypothalamic lesions. *Psychological Review* 69: 74–90.

Temerlin, M.K. 1970. Diagnostic bias in community mental health. *Community Mental health* 6: 110–17.

Terman, L.M. 1954. The discovery and encouragement of exceptional talent. *American Psychologist* 9: 221–30.

Terman, L.M., and Merrill, M.A. 1972. *Stanford-Binet intelligence scale—manual for the third revision, Form L-M.* Boston: Houghton Mifflin.

Terman, M. 1988. On the question of mechanism in phototherapy for seasonal affective disorder: Considerations of clinical efficacy and epidemiology. *Journal of Biological Rhythms* 3: 155–72.

Termine, N.T., and Izard, C.E. 1988. Infants' responses to their mothers' expressions of joy and sadness. *Developmental Psychology* 24: 223–29.

Terrace, H., Petitto, L., and Bever, T. 1976. Project Nim: Progress reports I and II. Distributed by Columbia University Psychology Department.

Terrace, H.S., Petitto, L.A., Sanders, R.J., and Bever, T.G. 1980. On the grammatical capacity of apes. In *Children's Language,* vol. 2, K.E. Nelson, ed. New York: Gardner.

Tervoort, B.T. 1961. Esoteric symbolism in the communication behavior of young deaf children. *American Annals of the Deaf* 106: 436–80.

Tesser, A. 1988. Toward a self-evaluation maintenance model of social behavior. In L. Berkowitz (Ed.), *Advances in experimental social psychology,* Vol. 21, San Diego: Academic Press.

Tesser, A. and Campbell, J. 1983. Self-definition and self-evaluation maintenance. In *Psychological perspectives on the self,* vol. 2, J. Suls and A.G. Greenwald, eds. Hillsdale, NJ: Erlbaum.

Testa, T.J. 1975. Effects of similarity and temporal intensity pattern of conditioned and unconditioned stimuli on the acquisition of conditioned suppression in rats. *Journal of Experimental Psychology: Animal Behavior Processes* 104: 114–21.

Tetlock, P.E. 1983. Policy makers' images of international conflict. *Journal of Social Issues* 39: 67–86.

Thayer, S. 1988. Close encounters. *Psychology Today,* March, 31–36.

Thomas, A., and Chess, S. 1977. *Temperament and development.* New York: Bruner/Mazel.

Thompson, J.K., Jarvie, G.J., Lahey, B.B., and Cureton, K.J. 1982. Exercise and obesity: Etiology, physiology, and intervention. *Psychological Bulletin* 91: 55–79.

Thompson, P. 1980. Margaret Thatcher: A new illusion. *Perception* 9: 483–84.

Thompson, R.F. 1983. Neuronal substitutes of simple associative learning: Classical conditioning. *Trends in Neuroscience* 6: 270–75.

———. 1985. *The brain.* New York: Freeman.

———. 1986. The neurobiology of learning and memory. *Science* 233: 941–47.

Thorndike, E.L. 1898. Animal intelligence: An experimental study of the associative processes in animals. *Psychological Review Monograph Supplement* 2: No. 8.

———. 1911. *Animal intelligence.* New York: Macmillan.

Thorndike, R.L., Hagen, E.P., and Sattler, J.M. 1986. *Stanford-Binet intelligence scale: Guide for administering and scoring the fourth edition.* Chicago: Riverside.

Thornhill, R., and Thornhill, N.W. 1989. The evolution of psychological pain. In *Sociobiology and the Social Sciences,* R.W. Bell and N.J. Bell, eds. Lubbock, TX: Texas Tech University Press.

Thurber, J. 1942. The secret life of Walter Mitty. In J. Thurber, *My world and welcome to it.* New York: Harcourt.

Thurstone, L.L. 1938. Primary mental abilities. *Psychometric Monographs,* No. 1. Chicago: University of Chicago Press.

Thurstone, L.L., and Chave, E.J. 1929. *The measurement of attitude.* Chicago: University of Chicago Press.

Tienari, P., Sorri, A., Lahti, I., Naarala, M., Wahlberg, K.E., Konkko, T., Pohjola, J., and Moring, J. 1985. The Finnish adoptive family study of schizophrenia. *The Yale Journal of Biology and Medicine* 58: 227–37.

Timberlake, W., and Allison, J. 1974. Response deprivation: An empirical approach to instrumental performance. *Psychological Review* 81: 146–64.

Tims, F.M., and Leukefield, C.G., eds. 1986. Relapse and recovery in drug abuse. *National Institute on Drug Abuse Research Monograph Series,* Vol. 72. Rockville, MD.

Tinbergen, N. 1951. *The study of instinct.* Oxford, UK: Oxford University Press.

Tinklepaugh, O.L. 1928. An experimental study of representative factors in monkeys. *Journal of Comparative Psychology* 8: 197–236.

Toch, H. 1979. *Psychology of crime and criminal justice.* New York: Holt, Rinehart and Winston.

Tolman, E.C., and Honzik, C.H. 1930. Introduction and removal of reward, and maze performance in rats. *University of California Publications in Psychology* 4: 257–75.

Tomkins, S.S. 1970. Affect as a primary motivational system. In *Feelings and emotions: The Loyola symposium,* M.B. Arnold, ed. New York: Academic Press.

———. 1980. Affect as amplification: Some modifications in theory. In *Emotion: Theory, research, and experience,* vol. 1, R. Plutchik and H. Kellerman, eds. New York: Academic Press.

———. 1981. The quest for primary motives: Biography and autobiography of an idea. *Journal of Personality and social Psychology* 41: 306–29.

Tooby, J., and Cosmides, L. 1989. Evolutionary psychology and the generation of culture, 1: Theoretical considerations. *Ethology and Sociobiology* 10: 29–50.

Torgerson, S. 1979. The nature and origin of common phobic fears. *British Journal of Psychiatry* 134: 343–51.

Townsend, J.M., & Levy, G.D. 1990. Effects of potential partner's costume and physical attractiveness on sexuality and partner selection: Sex differences in reported preferences of university students. *Journal of Psychology* 124, 371–76.

Tranel, D., and Damasio, A.R. 1985. Knowledge without awareness: An autonomic index of facial recognition by prosopagnosics. *Science* 228: 1453–54.

Traupmann, J., and Hatfield, E. 1981. Love and its effects on mental and physical health. In *Aging: Stability and change in the family,* R.W. Fogel, E. Hatfield, S.B. Kiesler, and E. Shanas, eds. New York: Academic Press.

Treiman, R.A., and Hirsh-Pasek, K. 1983. Silent reading: Insights from second generation deaf readers. *Cognitive Psychology* 15: 39–65.

Treisman, A.M. 1964. Verbal cues, language and meaning in selective attention. *American Journal of Psychology* 77: 215–16.

Treisman, A.M., and Souther, J. 1986. Illusory words: The roles of attention and of top-down constraints in conjoining letters to form words. *Journal of Experimental Psychology: Human Perception and Performance* 12: 3–17.

Trickett, P.K., and Susman, E.J. 1988. Parental perceptions of child-rearing practices in physically abusive families. *Developmental Psychology* 24: 270–76.

Trivers, R.L. 1972. Parental investment and sexual selection. In *Sexual selection and the descent of man,* B. Campbell, ed. Chicago: Aldine.

Trivers, R. 1985. *Social evolution.* Menlo Park, CA: Benjamin/Cummings.

Trope, Y. 1975. Seeking information about one's own ability as a determinant of choice among tasks. *Journal of Personality and Social Psychology* 32: 1004–13.

———. 1986. Identification and inferential processes in dispositional attribution. *Psychological Review* 93: 239–57.

Trope, Y. and Bassok, M. 1982. Confirmatory and diagnosing strategies in social information gathering. *Journal of Personality and Social Psychology* 43: 22–34.

Trotter, R.J. 1986. Three heads are better than one. *Psychology Today,* August, pp. 56–62.

Tsang, Y.C. 1938. Hunger motivation in gastectomized rats. *Journal of Comparative Psychology* 26: 1–17.

Turiel, E. 1974. Conflict and transition in adolescent moral development. *Child Development* 45: 14–29.

———. 1983. *The development of social knowledge: Morality and convention.* New York: Cambridge University Press.

Turvey, M.T., and Shaw, R.E. 1979. The primacy of perceiving: An ecological reformulation of perception for understanding memory. In *Perspectives on memory research,* L.G. Nilsson, ed. Hillsdale, NJ: Erlbaum.

Tulving, E. 1983. *Elements of episodic memory.* New York: Oxford University Press.

———. 1986. What kind of a hypothesis is the distinction between episodic and semantic memory? *Journal of Experimental Psychology: Learning, Memory, and Cognition* 12: 307–11.

Tulving, E., and Pearlstone, Z. 1966. Availability versus accessibility of information in memory for words. *Journal of Verbal Learning and Verbal Behavior* 5: 381–91.

Turk, J., and Turk, A. 1984. *Environmental Science.* Philadelphia: Saunders.

Turnbull, C. 1962. *The forest people.* New York: Simon & Shuster.

Tversky, A., & Kahneman, D. 1973. Availability: A heuristic for judging frequency and probability. *Cognitive Psychology* 5: 207–32.

Twain, Mark. 1884/1983. *The adventures of Huckleberry Finn*. New York: New American Library.

Udry, J.R., and Morris, N.M. 1968. Distribution of coitus in the menstrual cycle. *Nature* 220: 503–96.

Umberson, D., and Hughes, M. 1987. The impact of physical attractiveness on achievement and psychological well-being. *Social Psychology Quarterly* 50: 227–36.

Underwood, B.J. 1957. Interference and forgetting. *Psychological Review* 64: 49–60.

Underwood, B.J., Boruch, R.F., and Malmi, R.A. 1978. Composition of episodic memory. *Journal of Experimental Psychology: General* 107: 393–419.

Ungerleider, L.G., and Mishkin, M. 1982. Two cortical visual systems. In *Analysis of visual behavior*, D.J. Ingle, M.A. Goodale, and R.J.W. Mansfield, eds. Cambridge, MA: MIT Press.

Union of Concerned Scientists. 1988. *Voter Information Kit*. Cambridge, MA: Union of Concerned Scientists.

United Press International. 1984. Foot tickles put suspect in a pickle. *Phoenix Gazette*, June 26, p. A7.

Uretsky, N.J. 1989. Amphetamines. In *Abnormal states of brain and mind*, J.A. Hobson, ed. Readings from the *Encyclopedia of neuroscience*. Boston: Birkhauser.

U.S. Office of Strategic Services. 1948. *Assessment of men: Selection of personnel for the office of strategic services*. New York: Rinehart.

Uttal, W.R. 1973. *The psychobiology of sensory coding*. New York: Harper and Row.

———. 1983. Don't exterminate perceptual fruit flies! *The Behavioral and Brain Sciences* 6: 39–40.

———. 1981. *A taxonomy of visual processes*. Hillsdale, NJ: Erlbaum.

Valentine, C.W. 1930. The innate bases of fear. *Journal of Genetic Psychology* 37: 394–419.

Valenstein, E.S., ed. 1980. *The psychosurgery debate*. San Francisco: Freeman.

———. 1980a. Historical perspective. In *The psychosurgery debate*, E.S. Valenstein, ed. San Francisco: Freeman.

———. 1980b. Rationale and surgical procedures. In *The psychosurgery debate*, E.S. Valenstein, ed. San Francisco: Freeman.

Vallone, R.P., Ross, L., and Lepper, M.R. 1985. The hostile media phenomenon: Biased perception and perceptions of media bias in coverage of the Beirut massacre. *Journal of Personality and Social Psychology*. 49: 577–85.

Van Biema, D. 1987. Teen sex. *People*, April 13, 111–21.

Van de Castle, R.L. 1971. *The psychology of dreaming*. Morristown, NJ: General Learning Press.

Vandenberg, S.G. 1967. Hereditary factors in normal personality traits (as measured by inventories). In *Recent advances in biological psychiatry*, vol. 9, J. Wortes, ed. New York: Plenum.

Vane, J. 1973. Intelligence and achievement test results of kindergarten children in England, Ireland and the United States. *Journal of Clinical Psychology* 29: 191–93.

Veitch, R., DeWood, R., and Bosko, K. 1977.

Radio news broadcasts: Their effects on interpersonal helping. *Sociometry* 40: 383–86.

Vestre, N.D. 1983. Irrational beliefs and self-reported depressed mood. 93: 239–41.

Victor, M., Adams, R.D., and Collins, G.H. 1971. *The Wernicke-Korsakoff syndrome*. Philadelphia: Davis.

Vidal, G. 1987. The con-man as Peck's bad boy. *Newsweek*, July 13, p. 20.

Vinter, A. 1986. The role of movement on eliciting early imitations. *Child Development* 57: 66–71.

von Frisch, K. 1974. Decoding the language of the bee. *Science* 185: 663–68.

Vonnegut, M. 1975. *The Eden express: A personal account of schizophrenia*. New York: Praeger.

von Senden, M. 1960. *Space and sight*. P. Heath, trans. New York: Free Press.

Vurpillot, E., and Ball, W.A. 1979. The concept of identity and children's selective attention. In *Attention and cognitive development*, G. Hale and M. Lewis, eds. New York: Plenum Press.

Vygotsky, L. 1967. Play and the role of mental development in the child. *Soviet Psychology* 5: 6–18.

Wachtel, P.L. 1977. *Psychoanalysis and behavior therapy: Toward an integration*. New York: Basic Books.

Wagner, A.R., and Rescorla, R.A. 1972. Inhibition in Pavlovian conditioning: Application of a theory. In *Inhibition and learning*, R.A. Boakes and M.S. Halliday, eds. New York: Academic Press.

Wagner, D.A. 1982. Ontogeny in the study of culture and cognition. In *Cultural perspectives on child development*, D.A. Wagner and H.W. Stevenson, eds. San Francisco: Freeman.

Wald, G. 1964. The receptors of human color vision. *Science* 145: 1007–17.

Walker, J.M. 1979. Energy demand behavior in a master-metered apartment complex: An experimental analysis. *Journal of Applied Psychology* 64: 190–96.

Walker, J.T., and Shank, M.D. 1987. The Bourdon illusion in subjective contours. *Perception and Psychophysics* 42: 15–24.

Walker, L.J., de Vries, B., and Bichard, S.L. 1984. The hierarchical nature of stages of moral development. *Developmental Psychology* 20: 960–66.

Wallace, M.D. 1979. Arms races and escalations: Some new evidence. In *Explaining war: Selected papers from the correlates of war project*, J.D. Singer, ed. Beverly Hills, CA: Sage.

Wallace, R. 1969. *The world of Van Gogh (1853–1890)*. Alexandria, VA: Time-Life Books.

Wallace, R.A. 1978. *The ecology and evolution of animal behavior*, 2nd ed. Santa Monica, CA: Goodyear.

Walster, E.H., Walster, G.W., and Berscheid, E. 1978. *Equity: Theory and research*. Boston: Allyn and Bacon.

Walster, E.H., Aronson, V., Abrahams, D., and Rottmann, L. 1966. Importance of physical attractiveness in dating behavior. *Journal of Personality and Social Psychology* 4: 508–16.

Walster, E.H., Traupmann, J., and Walster, G. 1978. Equity and premarital sex. *Journal of Personality and Social Psychology* 7: 127–41.

Walters, G.C., and Grusec, J.E. 1977. *Punishment*. San Francisco: Freeman.

Walters, J.H., and Gardner, H. 1986. The theory of multiple intelligences: Some issues and answers. In *Practical intelligence: Nature and origins of competence in the everyday world.*, R.J. Sternberg and R.K. Wagner, eds. Cambridge, UK: Cambridge University Press.

Wapner, W., Judd, T., and Gardner, H. 1978. Visual agnosia in an artist. *Cortex* 14: 343–64.

Warga, C. 1987. Pain's gatekeeper. *Psychology Today*, August, 51–56.

Warner, R.R. 1984. Mating behavior and hermaphroditism in coral reef fishes. *American Scientist* 72: 128–34.

Wason, P.C., and Johnson-Laird, P.N. 1972. *Psychology of reasoning: Structure and content*. London: Batsford.

Waters, E., and Sroufe, L.A. 1983. Social competence as a developmental construct. *Developmental Review* 3: 79–97.

Watson, J.B. 1913. Psychology as a behaviorist views it. *Psychological Review* 20: 158–77.

———. 1925. *Behaviorism*. New York: Norton.

———. 1928. *Psychological care of infant and child*. New York: Norton.

Watson, J.B., and Morgan, J.J.B. 1917. Emotional reactions and psychological experimentation. *American Journal of Psychology* 28: 163–79.

Watson, J.B., and Rayner, R. 1920. Conditioned emotional reactions. *Journal of Experimental Psychology* 3: 1–14.

Watson, R.I. 1978. *The great psychologists from Aristotle to Freud*, 4th ed. Philadelphia: Lippincott.

Waxenberg, S. E., Drellick, M.G., and Sutherland, A.M. 1959. The role of hormones in human behavior. I: Changes in female sexuality after adrenalectomy. *Journal of Clinical Endocrinology* 19: 193–202.

Webb, W.B. 1985. Sleep and dreaming. In *Topics in the history of psychology*, vol. 2, G.S. Kimble and K. Schlesinger, eds. Hillsdale, NJ: Erlbaum.

Webb, W.B., and Bonnet, M.H. 1979. Sleep and dreams. In *Foundations of contemporary psychology*, M.E. Meyer, ed. New York: Oxford University Press.

Webb, W.B., and Cartwright, R.D. 1978. Sleep and dreams. *Annual Review of Psychology* 29: 223–52.

Weber, R.A., Levitt, M.J., and Clark, M.C. 1986. Individual variation in attachment security and strong situation behavior: The role of maternal and infant temperament. *Child Development* 57: 56–65.

Wegner, D.M., Schneider, D.J., Carter, S.R., and White, T.L. 1987. Paradoxical effects of thought suppression. *Journal of Personality and Social Psychology* 53: 5–13.

Weikart, D.P. 1982. Preschool education for disadvantaged children. In *Learning from experience: Evaluating early childhood demonstration programs*, J.R. Travers and R.J. Light, eds. Washington, DC: National Academy Press.

Weinberg, J., and Levine, S. 1980. Psychobiology of coping in animals: The effects of predictability. In *Coping and health*, S. Levine and H. Ursin, eds. New York: Plenum.

Weiner, B. 1986. *An attributional theory of motivation and emotion*. New York: Springer-Verlag.

Weiner, B., Frieze, I., Kukla, A., Reed, L., Rest, B., and Rosenbaum, R.M. 1971. Perceiving the causes of success and failure. In *Attribution: Perceiving the causes of behavior*, E.E. Jones, D.E. Kanouse, H.H. Kelley, R.E. Nisbett, S. Valins, and B. Weiner, eds. Morristown, NJ: General Learning Press.

Weisenberg, M. 1977. Pain and pain control. *Psychological Bulletin* 84: 1008–44.

Weiss, J.M. 1968. Effects of coping response on stress. *Journal of Comparative and Physiological Psychology* 65: 251–61.

———. 1971. Effects of coping behavior in different warning signal conditions on stress pathology in rats. *Journal of Comparative and Physiological Psychology* 77: 1–13.

———. 1977. Psychological and behavioral influences on gastrointestinal lesions in animal models. In *Psychopathology: Experimental models*, J.D. Maier and M.E.P. Seligman, eds. San Francisco: Freeman.

Weiss, R.D. 1989. Cocaine. In *Abnormal states of brain and mind*, J.A. Hobson, ed. Readings from the *Encyclopedia of neuroscience*. Boston: Birkhauser.

Weissman, M.M., Myers, J.K., and Thompson, W.D. 1981. Depression and its treatment in a U.S. urban community, 1975–1976. *Archives of General Psychiatry* 38: 417–24.

Welker, W.I., Johnson, J.I., and Pubols, B.H. 1964. Some morphological and physiological characteristics of the somatic sensory system in raccoons. *American Zoologist* 4: 75–94.

Wells, B.W.P. 1983. *Body and personality*. Essex, UK: Longman.

Wertheimer, M. 1961. Psychomotor coordination of auditory-visual space at birth. *Science* 134: 1692.

West, M.A., ed. 1987. *The psychology of meditation*. New York: Oxford University Press.

West, S.G., and Graziano, W.G. 1989. Longterm stability and change in personality: An introduction. *Journal of Personality* 57: 175–93.

Wetzel, J.R. 1987. *American youth: A statistical report*. The William T. Grant Foundation.

Wever, E.G. 1949. *Theories of hearing*. New York: Wiley.

White, G.L., Fishbein, S., and Rutstein, J. 1981. Passionate love and misattribution of arousal. *Journal of Personality and Social Psychology* 41: 56–62.

White, G.M. 1980. Conceptual universals in inerpersonal language. *American Anthropologist* 82: 759–81.

———. 1980. Conceptual universals in inerpersonal language. *American Anthropologist* 82: 759–81.

Whitehurst, G.J., Falco, F.L., Lonigan, C.J., Fischel, J.E., DeBaryshe, B.D., Valdez-Menchaca, M.C., and Caulfield, M. 1988. Accelerating language development through picture book reading. *Developmental Psychology* 24: 552–59.

Whitfield, I.C. 1978. The neural code. In *Handbook of perception*, vol. 4, E.C. Carterette and M.P. Friedman, eds. New York: Academic Press.

Whittaker, J.O., and Whittaker, S.J. 1972. A cross-cultural study of geocentrism. *Journal of Cross-Cultural Psychology* 3: 417–21.

Whorf, B.L. 1956. Science and linguistics. In *Language, thought, and reality: Selected writings of Benjamin Lee Whorf*, Cambridge. MA: MIT press.

Wickelgren, W.A. 1979. *Cognitive psychology*. Englewood Cliffs, NJ: Prentice Hall.

Wicker, A.W. 1969. Attitudes versus actions: The relationship of verbal and overt behavioral responses to attitude objects. *Journal of Social Issues* 25: 41–78.

Wicklund, R.A., and Frey, D. 1980. Self-awareness theory: When the self makes a difference. In *The self in social psychology*, D.M. Wegner and R.R. Vallacher, eds. New York: Oxford University Press.

Wietgrefe, S., Zupancic, M., Haase, A., Chesebro, B., Race, R., Frey, W. II, Rustan, T., and Friedman, R.L. 1985. Cloning of a gene whose expression is increased in scrapie and in senile plaques in human brain. *Science* 230: 1177–79.

Wiens, A.N., and Menustik, C.E. 1983. Treatment outcome and patient characteristics in an aversion therapy program for alcoholism. *American Psychologist* 38: 1089–96.

Wildenstein, D., and Cogniat, R. 1971. *Gaugin*. Milan, Italy: Gruppo Editoriale Fabbri.

Wiggins, J.S., and Broughton, R. 1985. the interpersonal circle: A structural model for the integration of personality research. In *Perspectives in personality*, vol. 1, R. Hogan and W.H. Jones, eds. Greenwich, CT: JAI Press.

Wiggins, J.S., Wiggins, N., and Conger, J.C. 1977. Social correlates of heterosexual somatic preference. *Journal of Experimental Social Psychology* 13: 253–68.

Wikler, A., and Pescor, F.T. 1967. Classical conditioning of a morphine abstinence phenomenon, reinforcement of opioid-drinking behavior and "relapse" in morphine-addicted rats. *Psychopharmacologia* 10: 255–84.

Wilbur, R. 1986. A drug to fight cocaine. *Science 86*, March, 42–46.

Wilcoxon, H., Dragoin, E., and Kral, P. 1972. Illness-induced aversion in rats and quail. In *Biological boundaries of learning*, M.E.P. Seligman and J.L. Hager, eds. New York: Appleton-Century-Crofts.

Willerman, L. 1979. *The psychology of individual and group differences*. San Francisco: Freeman.

Williams, C.D. 1959. The elimination of tantrum behavior by extinction procedures. *Journal of Abnormal and Social Psychology* 59: 269.

Williams, R.B., Jr. 1984. An untrusting heart. *The Sciences*, September/October, pp. 30–36.

Willis, S.L., and Nesselroade, C.S. 1990. Long-term effects of fluid ability training in old-old age. *Developmental Psychology* 26: 905–10.

Wilson, E.O. 1963. Pheromones. *Scientific American* 108: 100–14.

———. 1975. *Sociobiology: The new synthesis*. Cambridge, MA: Harvard University Press.

———. 1978. *On human nature*. Cambridge, MA: Harvard University Press.

Wilson, G.T., and Abrams, D.B. 1977. Effects of alcohol on social anxiety and physiological arousal: Cognitive versus pharmacological processes. *Cognitive Therapy and Research* 1: 195–210.

Wilson, J.R. 1964. *The mind*. New York: Time-Life Books.

Wilson, M., and Daly, M. 1985. Competitiveness, risk taking, and violence: The young male syndrome. *Ethology and Sociobiology* 6: 59–73.

Wilson, R.S. 1985. Risk and resilience in early mental development. *Developmental Psychology* 21: 795–805.

Wilson, T.D., and Linville, P.W. 1982. Improving the academic performance of college freshman. Attribution therapy revisited. *Journal of Personality and Social Psychology* 42: 367–76.

Winograd, E., and Soloway, R.M. 1986. On forgetting the locations of things stored in special places. *Journal of Experimental Psychology: General* 115: 366–72.

Winston, P.H. 1984. *Artificial intelligence*, 2nd ed. Reading, MA: Addison-Wesley.

Winter, L., and Uleman, J.S. 1984. When are social judgments made? Evidence for the spontaneousness of trait inferences. *Journal of Personality and Social Psychology* 47: 237–52.

Wise, R.A. 1984. Neural mechanisms of the reinforcing action of cocaine. In *Cocaine: Pharmacology, effects and treatment of abuse*, J. Grabowski, ed. NIDA Research Monograph 50. National Institute on Drug Abuse.

———. 1988. The neurobiology of craving: Implications for the understanding and treatment of addiction. *Journal of Abnormal Psychology* 97: 118–32.

Wise, R.A., and Rompre, P.-P. 1989. Brain dopamine and reward. *Annual Review of Psychology* 40: 191–225.

Witelson, S.F. 1976. Sex and the single hemisphere: Specialization of the right hemisphere for spatial processing. *Science* 193: 425–27.

———. 1989. Brain asymmetry, Functional aspects. In *Speech and Language, Readings from the Encyclopedia of Neuroscience*, D. Kimura, ed. Boston: Birkhauser.

Wittgenstein, L. 1953. *Philosophical investigations*. Oxford, UK: Blackwell.

Wober, M. 1974. Towards an understanding of the Kiganda concept of intelligence. In *Culture and cognition: Readings in cross-cultural psychology*, J.W. Berry and P.R. Dasen, eds. London: Metheun.

Wolfe, H.K. 1886. Cited in Murray, D.J. 1976. Research on human memory in the nineteenth century. *Canadian Journal of Psychology* 30: 201–20.

Wollen, K.A., Weber, A., and Lowry, D. 1972. Bizarreness versus interaction of mental images as determinants of learning. *Cognitive Psychology* 3: 518–23.

Wollman, M., and Antrobus, J. 1984. Visuospatial abilities of right hemisphere. In *Functions of the right cerebral hemisphere*, A.W. Young, ed. New York: Academic Press.

Wolpe, J. 1958. *Psychotherapy by Reciprocal Inhibition*. Stanford, CA: Stanford University Press.

Wolpe, J., and Rachman, S. 1960. Psychoanalytic "evidence," a critique based on Freud's case of Little Hans. *Journal of Nervous and Mental Disease* 131: 135–47.

Woodruff, R.A., Goodwin, D.W., and Guze, S.B. 1974. *Psychiatric diagnosis*. New York: Oxford University Press.

Woodworth, R.S. 1939. *Experimental psychology*. New York: Henry Holt and Co.

Woody, C.D. 1986. Understanding the cellular basis of memory and learning. *Annual Review of Psychology* 37: 433–94.

Woolfolk, R.L., Carr-Kaffashan, K., and Lehrer, P.M. 1976. Meditation training as a treatment for insomnia. *Behavior Therapy* 7: 359–65.

Wortman, C.B., and Conway, T.L. 1985. The role of social support in adaptation and recovery from physical illness. *Social support and health*. New York: Academic Press.

Wundt, W. 1873. *Principles of physiological psychology*. Leipzig: Englemann.

Wurtman, R.J., and Wurtman, J.J. 1989. Carbohydrates and depression. *Scientific American*, January, pp. 68–75.

Wyer, R.S., and Srull, T.K. 1986. Human cognition in its social context. *Psychological Review* 93: 322–59.

Wylie, R.C. 1978. *The self concept*, vol. 2 Lincoln: University of Nebraska Press.

Wynne, L.D., Singer, M.T., Bartko, J.J., and Tookey, M.L. 1977. Schizophrenics and their families: Research on parental communication. In *Developments in psychiatric research*, J.M. Tanner, ed. London: Hodder and Stoughton.

Yalom, I.D., and Lieberman, M.A. 1971. A study of encounter group casualties. *Archives of General Psychiatry* 25: 16–30.

Yankelovich, D. 1981. *New rules*. New York: Random House.

Yates, S.M., and Aronson, E. 1983. A social psychological perspective on energy conservation in residential buildings. *American Psychologist* 20: 435–44.

Yesavage, J.A., Leier, V.O., DeNari, M., and Hollister, L.E. 1985. Carry-over effect of marijuana intoxication on aircraft pilot performance: A preliminary report. *American Journal of Psychiatry* 142: 1325–30.

Young, W.R. 1977. There's a girl on the tracks! *Reader's Digest*, February, pp. 91–95.

Young, W.S., III, and Kuhar, M.J. 1980. Radiohistochemical location of benzodiazepine receptors in rat brain. *Journal of Pharmacological Experimental Therapy* 212: 337–46.

Youniss, J. 1980. *Parents and peers in social development: A Sullivan-Piaget perspective*. Chicago: University of Chicago Press.

Yuille, A.L., and Ullman, S. 1990. Computational theories of low-level vision. In *Visual cognition and action: An invitation to cognitive science*, D.N. Osherson, S.M. Kosslyn, and J.M. Hollderbach, eds. Cambridge, MA: MIT Press.

Yuille, J.C., and McEwan, N.H. 1985. Use of hypnosis as an aid to eyewitness memory. *Journal of Applied Psychology* 70: 389–400.

Yussen, S.R., and Kane, P.T. 1985. Children's conception of intelligence. In *The growth of reflection in children*, S.R. Yussen, ed. New York: Academic Press.

Zajonc, R.B. 1965. Social facilitation. *Science* 149: 269–74.

———. 1968. Attitudinal effects of mere exposure. *Journal of Personality and Social Psychology Monograph Supplement* 9: 1–27.

———. 1980. Feeling and thinking: Preferences need no inferences. *American Psychologist* 35: 151–75.

———. 1985. Emotion and facial efference: A theory reclaimed. *Science* 228: 15–21.

Zajonc, R.B., Murphy, S.T., and Inglehart, M. 1989. Feeling and facial efference: Implications of the vascular theory of emotion. *Psychological Review* 96: 395–416.

Zakia, R. 1975. *Perception and photography*. Englewood Cliffs, NJ: Prentice Hall.

Zanna, M., and Rempel, J.K. 1988. Attitudes: A new look at an old concept. In D.Bar-Tal and A.W. Kruglanski (Eds.) *The social psychology of knowledge*, pp. 315–34. Cambridge, England: Cambridge University Press.

Zaragoza, M.S., and Koshmider, J.W., III. 1989. Misled subjects may know more than their performance implies. *Journal of Experimental Psychology: Learning, Memory, and Cognition* 15: 246–55.

Zelazo, P.R., Kearsley, R.B., and Ungerer, J.A. 1984. *Learning to speak: A manual for parents*. Hillsdale, NJ: Erlbaum.

Zepelin, H., and Rechtschaffen, A. 1974. Mammalian sleep, longevity, and energy metabolism. *Brain, Behavior, and Evolution* 10: 425–70.

Zerega, A.M. 1981. Transportation energy conservation policy: Implications for social science research. *Journal of Social Issues* 37: 31–50.

Zeskind, P.S., and Iacino, R. 1984. Effects of maternal visitation to preterm infants in the neonatal intensive care unit. *Child Development* 55: 1887–93.

Zigler, E.F. 1973. Project Head Start: Success or failure? *Learning* 1: 43–47.

Zigler, E.F., and Berman, W. 1983. Discerning the future of early childhood intervention. *American Psychologist* 38: 894–906.

Zigler, E.F., and Cascione, R. 1984. Mental retardation: An overview. In *Malformations of development: Biological and psychological sources and consequences*, E.S. Gollin, ed. New York: Academic Press.

Zigler, E.F., and Finn-Stevenson, M. 1987. *Children: Development and social issues*. Lexington, MA: Heath.

Zigler, E.F., and Glick, M. 1988. Is paranoid schizophrenia really camouflaged depression? *American Psychologist* 43: 284–90.

Zigler, E.F., Lamb, M.E., and Child, I.L. 1982. *Socialization and personality development*, 2nd ed. New York: Oxford University Press.

Zigler, E.F., and Seitz, V. 1982. Social policy and intelligence. In *Handbook of human intelligence*, R.J. Sternberg, ed. Cambridge, UK: Cambridge University Press.

Zigler, M.J. 1932. Pressure adaptation time: A function of intensity and extensity. *American Journal of Psychology* 44: 709–20.

Zilbergeld, B. 1983. *The shrinking of America: Myths of psychological change*. Boston: Little, Brown.

Zill, N. 1985. *Happy, healthy and insecure: A portrait of middle childhood in the United States*. New York: Cambridge University Press.

Zimbardo, P.G. 1970. The human choice: Individuation, reason, and order versus deindividuation, impulse, and chaos. In W.J. Arnold and D. Levine, Eds. *Nebraska symposium on motivation, 1969*. Lincoln: University of Nebraska Press.

Zimbardo, P.G. 1986. The Stanford Shyness Project. In *Shyness: Perspectives on research and treatment*, W.H. Jones, J.M. Cheek, and S.R. Briggs, eds. NY: Plenum Press.

Zimbardo, P.G., and Leippe, M.R. 1991. *The psychology of attitude change and social influence*. New York: McGraw-Hill.

Zuckerman, M. 1978. The search for high sensation. *Psychology Today* February, pp. 38–46.

———. 1979. *Sensation-seeking: Beyond the optimal level of arousal*. Hillsdale, N.J.: Erlbaum.

———. 1984. Sensation-seeking: A comparative approach to a human trait. *Behavioral and Brain Sciences* 7: 413–71.

———. 1990. The psychophysiology of sensation seeking. *Journal of Personality* 58: 313–45.

Zuckerman, M., Bernieri, F., Koestner, R., and Rosenthal, R. 1989. To predict some of the people some of the time: In search of moderators. *Journal of Personality and Social Psychology* 57: 279–93.

Zukier, H., and Pepitone, A. 1984. Social roles and strategies in prediction: Some determinants of the use of base-rate information. *Journal of Personality and Social Psychology* 47: 349–60.

Zusne, L., and Jones, W.H. 1982. *Anomalistic psychology: A study of extraordinary phenomena of behavior and experience*. Hillsdale, NJ.: LEA.

ACKNOWLEDGMENTS

PHOTOGRAPHS

Chapter 1: xxvi Alexander Lowry/Photo Researchers • **2** *William James* Gay Wilson Allen, New York: Viking Press, 1967 • **5** Leif Skoogfors/ Woodfin Camp and Associates • **6** The Bettman Archive • **8** Marvin Newman/Woodfin Camp and Associates • **10** Elizabeth Cross/The Image Works • **11** Culver Pictures • **12** Hanson Carroll/Peter Arnold • **15** Dick Rowan/Photo Researchers • **18** Mike Yamashita/Woodfin Camp and Associates • **20** (*bottom, left*) Richard Hutchins/Photo Researchers; (*bottom, right*) Richard Dasley/Stock, Boston • **27** Patrick J. Watson/The Image Works • **29** C. Vergara/Photo Researchers • **30** UPI/Bettmann • **31** Roger Clark/Photo Researchers

Chapter 2: 34 Jean-Claude Lejeune/Stock, Boston • **37** Jean-Loup Charmet, Paris • **38** Emory University Yerkes Primate Research Center • **39** (*left and center*) Howard Sochurek/Woodfin Camp and Associates; (*right*) Science Photo Library/Photo Researchers • **43** J. and L. Weber/Peter Arnold • **48** Courtesy John Heuser, Washington University School of Medicine • **51** Dr. William Greenoough • **57** Lester V. Bergman • **59** A. Glauberman/Photo Researchers • **62** Prof. Francois Lhermitte • **63** Dr. M. Raichle/Peter Arnold

Chapter 3: 76 Jack Spratt/The Image Works • **79** The Bettmann Archive • **88** (*bottom*) Lennart Nilsson photo from *Behold Man*, published by Little, Brown, and Co. • **89** PAR/NYC, Inc./Bryan Stephens • **93** Lauros-Giraudon/Art Resource • **94** University of Utah Medical Center • **96** (*bottom*) Fritz Goro/LIFE • **97** The Art Institute of Chicago, Helen Birch Bartlett Memorial Collection • **105** Merlin B. Tuttle/Photo Researchers

Chapter 4: 116 H. Armstrong Roberts • **118** Roxby Press Ltd., London • **119** William Carter/Photo Researchers • **121** Art Resource • **122** (*top*) Evelyn Scolney/Monkmeyer; (*bottom*) Felicia Martinez/Photo Edit • **123** Ron James • **124** Kaiser Porcelain, Ltd. • **126** (*top*) The Art Institute of Chicago; (*bottom*) Dr. Peter Thompson • **128, 147** (*bottom*) From *Mind Sights* © 1990 Roger N. Shepard, W.H. Freeman Co., New York, N.Y. • **129** (*left*) © 1988 M.C. Escher Heirs/Cordon Art/DeBaarn/ Holland; (*right*) from *Man-Machine Engineering* by A. Chapanis, © 1965 Wadsworth, Inc. Reprinted by permission of Brooks/Cole Publishing Co., Pacific Grove, CA • **133** I. Biederman, "Recognition by Components: A Theory of Human Image Understanding," *Psychological Review*, 1987, *94*, 115–47 • **135** Audrey Gottlieb/Monkmeyer (based on a study by I. Biederman) • **141** (*top, left*) Chris Caswell/Photo Researchers; (*top, right*) Susan McCartney/Photo Researchers; (*bottom, left*) William Wright/ Monkmeyer; (*bottom, right*) Ron Karten/OPC • **142** Lee Boltin • **143** National Gallery of Art, Washington, D.C./Art Resource • **145** Science Museum of Virginia, Richmond • **147** (*top*) from *Perception* by Irvin Rock © 1984 Scientific American books. *Visual Illusions* by Richard L. Gregory © 1968 Scientific American, Inc. All rights reserved • **154** Edwin Land

Chapter 5: 158 Bonnie Freer/Photo Researchers • **160** Dr. Ronald Siegel • **162** Historical Pictures Service • **169** Richard Hutchings/Photo Researchers • **174** Ted Spagna/Photo Researchers • **177** The Bettmann Archive • **185** Terry Qing/FPG • **188** Yoav Levy/Phototake • **189** Alan Carey/Image Works

Chapter 6: 194 Superstock • **197** Culver Pictures • **198** Teachers College, Columbia University • **199** *Journal of the History of the Behavioral Sciences*, Volume VIII, Number 1, January 1972. Copyright 1972, Clinical Psychology Publishing Company, Inc. • **202** Larry Stessin/Photo Researchers • **205** Dr. Benjamin Harris • **209** Nudar Alexanian/Stock, Boston • **210** Will Rapport, courtesy B.F. Skinner • **211** (*top*) Historical Pictures Service; (*bottom*) Mimi Forsyth/Monkmeyer • **212** Yerkes Regional Primate Center, Atlanta • **217** From *Case Studies in Behavior Modification* by Leonard P. Ullmann and Leonard Krasner (Holt, Rinehart and Winston, Inc., New York) • **224** Hank Morgan/Rainbow

Chapter 7: 230 Chester Higgins, Jr./Photo Researchers • **234** (*top*) The Bettmann Archive; (*bottom*) The Library, St. John's College, Cambridge, England • **239** Anne Hubbard/Photo Researchers • **242** Charles Gupton/ Stock, Boston • **249** Random House • **255** NASA

Chapter 8: 266 Gordon Rapp • **269** David Redfern/Retna Ltd. • **270** Sloan Foundation Science Series/Basic Books • **272** Norman R. Lightfoot/Photo Researchers • **279** Jonathan Perry • **283** *The New York Times* • **300** Jerry Jacka Photography

Chapter 9: 304 Charles Gatewood/Stock, Boston • **307** Scala Art Resource • **308** Historical Pictures Service• **314** Blair Seitz/Photo Researchers • **318** Richard Hutchings • **321** Jeffry Dunn • **324** Laura Dwight/Peter Arnold, Inc. • **327** Paul Conklin/Monkmeyer Press • **331** Arthur Tress/Photo Researchers • **332** Dr. Sternberg/Yale University

Chapter 10: 340 R.M. Collins/The Image Works • **342** Wide World Photos • **343** Charles Darwin, "Expression of Emotion in Man and Animals" (1872) • **345** Oxford Scientific Films/Animals, Animals • **347** I. Eibl-Eibesfeldt, from "Human Ethology" • **349** Julius Steiner • **355** Harlow Primate Laboratory, University of Wisconsin • **362 363** Paul Ekman/Human Interaction Lab/UCSF • **367** Robert Zajonic

Chapter 11: 376 Rosa A. Castillo • **378** Herb Snitzer/Stock, Boston • **381** Wayne Behling/Ypsilanti Press • **383** E. Beranger/Photo Researchers • **385** Children's Hospital, Boston • **386** Matthew McVay/ SABA • **387** Ansell Horn/Phototake • **389** Nancy Rader • **390** Doug Goodman/Monkmeyer • **391** A.N. Meltzoff • **393** U. Markus-Ganssen/ Photo Researchers • **395** Harlow Primate Laboratory, University of Wisconsin • **398** Marcia Weinstein • **400** Mark Seamon • **404** George Goodwin/Monkmeyer

Chapter 12: 412 Randy Matusow/Monkmeyer Press • **414** Berenholtz/ The Stock Market • **415, 416** Historical Pictures Service • **418** Bill Gillette • **421** Shirley Zeiberg • **423** Will McIntyre/Photo Researchers • **428** Addison Geary/Stock, Boston • **432** Gabe Palmer/The Stock Market • **438** Joseph Nettis/Photo Researchers • **442** Jacques Chenet/Woodfin Camp and Associates

Chapter 13: 448 Photography Collections, University of Maryland, Baltimore County • **450** (*left*) Art Resource/Musée D'Orsay; (*right*) Art Resource/National Gallery of Art, Washington, D.C. • **455** Jon Feingersh/ Stock, Boston • **461** G. Zimbel/Monkmeyer • **467** Roswell Angier/Stock, Boston • **468** Arnold Zann/Black Star • **474** Bob Daemmrich/Image Works • **478** "You are fair . . ." by Mankoff • **481** The Baltimore Museum of Art: The Cone Collection, formed by Dr. Claribel Cone and Miss Etta Cone of Baltimore, Maryland

Chapter 14: 486 Arthur Tress/Photo Researchers • **489** Elliott Errwitt/ Magnum • **490** © Karsh/Ottawa/Woodfin Camp and Associates • **496** Frank Siteman/Monkmeyer • **505** Robert French/TSW/Click Chicago • **506** AP Wide World Photos • **512** *Syracuse Herald Tribune*/Sygma

Chapter 15: 518 Jerry Cooke/Photo Researchers • **521** (*right*) The Granger Collection • **522** *St. Anthony Tormented by Demons* (engraving) by Martin Schongauer (ca. 1480) The Metropolitan Museum of Art, Jacob S. Rogers Fund • **524** Chie Nishio/Omni • **528** Hank Morgan/Rainbow • **536** Culver Pictures • **539** (*top*) Dr. Andrew J. Dwork; (*bottom*) Mark Blumenthal, *Schizophrenia Bulletin* • **540** UPI/Bettman

Chapter 16: 552 Randy Matusow • **554** Richard Hutchings • **555, 556** The Granger Collection • **561** Will McIntyre/Photo Researchers • **562** S. Varnedoe • **565** Michael Rougier/*Life* Magazine © Time Warner, Inc. • **568** G. Paul Bishop • **571** David Gonzales/Camarillo State Hospital • **575** Joseph Nettis/Photo Researchers • **582** Glyn Cloud

Chapter 17: 588 Will McIntyre/Photo Researchers • **591** Jacques Chenet/ Woodfin Camp and Associates • **595** H. Armstrong Roberts • **599** Richard DeLoach • **602** Photo Researchers • **606** Wide World Photos • **610** L. Lewicki • **612** Paul Elman/Human Interaction Lab (UCSF)

Chapter 18: 616 Gordon Rapp • **618** Scott A. Fischer/FPG • **619** Wide World Photos • **621** *Movie Star News* • **624** © I. Eibl-Eibesfeldt/Photo by Hans Hass • **626** Flying Fish, L.A. • **629** M. Austin/Photo Researchers • **634** (*left*) Karl Muller/Woodfin Camp and Associates; (*right*) Cheuva/Photo Researchers • **636** (*left*) Wide World Photos; (*right*) Bill Daemmrich/Stock, Boston • **637** Courtesy of Alexandra Milgram • **639** William Vandivert • **640** Wide World Photos

Chapter 19: 646 Sebastiao Salgado/Magnum • **650** (*left*) South Coast Air Quality Management District; (*right*) Wide World Photos • **656** Ray Pfortner/Peter Arnold • **662** Liverpool Daily Post and Echo, Ltd • **663** Bill Pierce/Woodfin Camp and Associates • **673** John Fich/Woodfin Camp and Associates

FIGURES

Chapter 1: *Scientific American* Nov. 1988

Chapter 2: Fig. 2.3 From Bruce, R.L., *Fundamentals of Physiological Psychology*, New York: Holt, Rinehart, and Winston, 1977, p. 77. © 1977 by Holt, Rinehart, and Winston, Inc., reproduced by permission of the publisher • **Fig. 2.4** From *Fundamentals of Human Neuropsychology, 2E*, by Bryan Kolb and Ian Q. Whishaw. Copyright © 1980, 1985 by. W.H. Freeman and Company. Reprinted with permission • **Fig. 2.6** Adapted from Penfield and Jasper, 1954. © 1954 by Little, Brown. Adapted with permission • **Fig. 2.7** From Morgan et al., *Introduction to Psychology 6/E*. Copyright © by McGraw-Hill, Inc. Reprinted by permission of McGraw-Hill, Inc. • **Fig. 2.11 B** From *The Cerebral Cortex of Man* by Wilder Penfield and Theodore Rasmussen. Copyright 1950 Macmillan Publishing Company. Copyright renewed © 1978 Theodore Rasmussen. Reprinted by permission of Macmillan Publishing Company • **Fig. 2.15** From *The Working Brain* by A.R. Luria, translated by Basil Haigh (Penguin Books, 1973). Copyright © by Penguin Books Ltd. • **Fig. 2.17** Modified from Gazzaniga (1967) • **Fig. 2.18** From "The Split Brain in Man," by Michael S. Gazzaniga. Copyright © 1967 by *Scientific American, Inc* • **Fig. 2.19** From "The Split Brain in Man," by M. Gazzaniga. Reprinted by permission of the author • **Fig. 2.20** Reprinted with permission from *Annals of Neurology*, 1977, 2, 417–421.

Chapter 3: Fig. 3.1 From *Sensation and Perception 1/E* by E. Bruce Goldstein, © 1980 by Wadsworth, Inc. Reprinted by permission of the publisher • **Fig. 3.2** Adapted Figure 4.2 from *Introduction to Psychology 8/E* by Rita L. Atkinson, Richard C. Atkinson, and Ernest R. Hilgard. Copyright © 1983 by Harcourt Brace Jovanovich, Inc. Reprinted by permission of the publisher • **Fig. 3.3** The American Psychological Association • **Fig. 3.4** Fig. 4.8 from *Introduction to Psychology 8/E* by Rita L. Atkinson, Richard C. Atkinson, and Ernest R. Hilgard. Copyright © 1983 by Harcourt Brace Jovanovich, Inc. Reprinted by permission of the publisher • **Fig. 3.7** From *Psychology* by Henry L. Roediger III et al. Copyright © 1984 by Henry L. Roediger III, J. Philippe Rushton, Elizabeth D. Capaldi, and Scott G. Paris. Reprinted by permission of Harper Collins Publishers • **Fig. 3.9** From *Psychology Today 5/E* by Bootzin et al. Published by McGraw-Hill, Inc. Reprinted by permission of McGraw-Hill, Inc. • **Fig. 3.18** From *Sensation and Perception 1/E* by E. Bruce Goldstein © 1980 by Wadsworth, Inc. Reprinted by permission of the publisher • **Fig. 3.19** Carol Donner • **Fig. 3.21** From *Human Anatomy and Physiology* by Anthony J. Gaudin and Kenneth C. Jones. Copyright © 1989 by Holt, Rinehart, and Winston, Inc. Reprinted by permission of the publisher • **Fig. 3.23** Carol Donner

Chapter 4: Fig. 4.2 From Brown and Deffenbacher, *Perception and the Senses*, Oxford University Press, 1979 • **Fig. 4.3** D. Hoffman, "Visual Illusions," reprinted from *Scientific American*, Dec. 1983 • **Fig. 4.8** From M. Matlin, *Sensation and Perception 2/E*. Copyright © 1988. Reprinted by permission of Allyn and Bacon, Inc. • **Fig. 4.11 A,B** From "Subjective Contours," by Gaetano Kaniza. Copyright © 1976 by *Scientific American, Inc*. All rights reserved • **Fig. 4.11 C** Reprinted by permission from *Nature*, Vol. 261, pp. 77–78. Copyright © 1976 Macmillan Magazines Ltd. • **Fig. 4.12** From L.S. Penrose and R. Penrose, "Impossible Objects: A Special Type of Visual Illusion." *British Journal of Psychology* (1958) 49, 31–33 • **Fig. 4.15** From John G. Seamon, *Memory and Cognition*, Oxford University Press, 1980 • **Fig. 4.16** also **Fig. 4.17** Adapted from *Introduction to Psychology 10/E* by Rita L. Atkinson, Richard C. Atkinson, and Ernest R. Hilgard. Copyright © 1990 by Harcourt Brace Jovanovich, Inc. Reprinted by permission of the publisher • **Fig. 4.19** W. Wapner et al. • **Fig. 4.21 A,B** From *Sensation and Perception 2/E* by E. Bruce Goldstein. Copyright © 1984 by Wadsworth, Inc. Reprinted by permission of the publisher • **Fig. 4.21 C,D** From D.E. Rumelhart, Toward an Interactive Model of Reading. In *Attention and Performance*, S. Domic (ed.), Hillsdale, NJ: Lawrence Erlbaum, 1977, Copyright © 1977 by the American Psychological Association. Reprinted by permission • **Fig. 4.22** Just and Carpenter, "A Theory of Reading," *Psychological Review*, 1980, 87, 329–54. Copyright © by the American Psychological Association. Reprinted by permission • **Fig. 4.23** From J.L. McClelland and D.E. Rumelhart, "An Interactive Model of Context Effects in Letter Perception," *Psychological Review*, 1981, 88, 375–407. Copyright © 1981 by the American

Psychological Association. Reprinted by permission • **Fig. 4.28** Figure 10.3 from *Sensation and Perception 3/E* by Stanley Coren and Lawrence M. Ward. Copyright © 1989 by Harcourt Brace Jovanovich, Inc. Reprinted by permission of the publisher • **Fig. 4.29** From *Psychology 3/E* by Andrew B. Crider et al. Copyright © 1989 by Andrew B. Crider, George R. Geothals, Robert D. Kavanaugh, and Paul R. Solomon. Reprinted by permission of Harper Collins Publishers • **Fig. 4.32B** From *Mind Sights* by Roger N. Shepard. Copyright © 1990 by Roger N. Shepard. Reprinted with permission of W.H. Freeman and Company • **Fig. 4.33** From *Sensation and Perception 2/E* by E. Bruce Goldstein. Copyright © 1984 by Wadsworth, Inc. Reprinted by permission of the publisher • **Fig. 4.34** From "Haptic Pictures," by John M. Kennedy, *Tactical Perception* (ed. W. Schift and E. Foulke), Cambridge University Press, 1982

Chapter 5: Fig. 5.2 From *Psychology* by Henry L. Roediger III et al. Copyright © 1984 by Henry L. Roediger III, J. Philippe Rushton, Elizabeth D. Capaldi, and Scott G. Paris. Reprinted by permission of Harper Collins Publishers • **Fig. 5.3** From *Cognition* by Glass et al. Copyright © 1979 and published by McGraw-Hill, Inc. Reprinted by permission of McGraw-Hill, Inc. • **Fig. 5.5** From *Sleep* by Gay Gaer Luce and Julius Segal. Copyright 1966 by Gay Gaer Luce and Julius Segal. Reprinted by permission of Bill Berger Associates • **Fig. 5.6** From J.A. Hobson (ed.), *States of Brain and Mind*, Readings from the *Encyclopedia of Neuroscience*. Reprinted by permission of Birkäuser Boston, Inc. • **Fig. 5.7** Adapted from *The Human Body* (U.S. News Books) • **Fig. 5.8** From Hilgard and Hilgard, *Hypnosis in the Relief of Pain*, Los Altos, CA: William Kaufman, Inc., 1975 • **Fig. 5.9** From *Triangle, Sandoz Journal of Medical Science*, 1955, 2, 119–23

Chapter 6: Fig. 6.1B From E. L. Thorndike (1898) • **Fig. 6.2** From Yerkes and Morgulis (1909) • **Fig. 6.5** From *Psychology* by Andrew B. Crider et al. Copyright © 1983 by Scott, Foresman and Company. Reprinted by permission of Harper Collins Publishers • **Fig. 6.12** From *Theories of Motivation*, p. 293 after Crespi, 1942, by R.C. Bolles, 1975, New York: Harper and Row. Copyright 1967, 1975 by R.C. Bolles. Reprinted by permission of Harper and Row, Publishers, Inc. • **Fig. 6.13** From *The Principles of Learning and Behavior* by Domjan and Burkhard. Copyright © 1982 by Wadsworth, Inc. Used with permission of Brooks/Cole Publishing Company, Pacific Grove, CA 93950 • **Fig. 6.15** From Birbaumer and Kimmel (eds.), *Biofeedback and Self-Regulation*, Hillsdale, N.J.: Erlbaum Associates, 1979. Copyright by the American Psychological Association. Reprinted by permission • **Fig. 6.16** Modified from Hilgard et al., *Psychology 7/E*, copyright © Harcourt Brace Jovanovich • **Fig. 6.17** From E.C. Tolman and C.H. Honzik, "Introduction and Removal of Reward, and Maze Performance in Rats," *University of California Publications in Psychology*, 1930, 4, 257–75

Chapter 7: Fig. 7.1 Modified from N. Cowan, "Evolving Conceptions of Memory Storage, Selective Attention, and Their Mutual Constraints Within the Human Information-Processing System, *Psychological Bulletin* 104, 163–91. Copyright © 1988 by the American Psychological Association. Adapted by permission • **Fig. 7.3** F.C. Bartlett, *Remembering*, Cambridge, 1932 • **Fig. 7.4** Modified from *Post-Retinal Visual Storage* by T.E. Parks. Published by the University of Illinois Press • **Fig. 7.5** The American Psychological Association • **Fig. 7.6** The American Psychological Association • **Fig. 7.7** Modified from D. Rundus and R. C. Atkinson, 1970 in the *Journal of Verbal Learning and Verbal Behavior, 9*, 99–105. By permission of Academic Press • **Fig. 7.8** Modified from J.G. Seamon, *Memory and Cognition*, New York: Oxford University Press, 1980 • **Fig. 7.9** Modified from Bower et al., 1969 in the *Journal of Verbal Learning and Verbal Behavior, 8*, 323–43. By permission of Academic Press • **Fig. 7.11** Modified from H.C. Ellis and R.R. Hunt, *Fundamentals of Human Memory and Cognition*, Dubuque: W.C. Brown, 1983 • **Fig. 7.12** From G.R. Loftus and E.F. Loftus, *Human Memory*, Hillsdale, N.J.: Lawrence Erlbaum Associates, 1976. Copyright the American Psychological Association. Reprinted by permission • **Fig. 7.13** From Jenkins and Dallenback, "Oblivescence During Sleeping and Waking," *American Journal of Psychology*, 35, 605–12 • **Fig. 7.14** Adapted from figure by Robert Pasternak in "Scientists Identify 'Gate' in Brain as Crucial to Memory," by George Johnson, *The New York Times*, May 10, 1988. Copyright © 1988 by The New York Times Company. Reprinted by permission • **Fig. 7.15** Copyright, Cognitive Science Society, Incorporated. Used by permission.

Chapter 8: Fig. 8.2 From *Language and Speech* by George A. Miller. Copyright © 1981 by W.H. Freeman and Company. Reprinted with permission • **Fig. 8.4** After Liberman, Mattingly, and Turvery, *Language Codes and Memory Codes* (1972) • **Fig. 8.5** From Pollak and Pickett: "Intelligibility of Excerpts from Fluent Speech." In the *Journal of Verbal Learning and Verbal Behavior*, 1964, 3, 79–84 • **Fig. 8.6** Modified from E. Lenneberg, *Biological Foundations of Language*, New York: John Wiley, 1967 • **Fig. 8.7** From Shepard and Metzler, "Mental Rotation of Three-Dimensional Objects," in *Science*, Vol. 171, pages 701–3, February 19, 1971. Reprinted by permission • **Fig. 8.8** From *Conceptual Blockbusting: A Guide to Better Ideas* by James L. Adams. Copyright James L. Adams and the Stanford Alumni Association, Stanford, CA • **Fig. 8.9** From *Cognitive Psychology and Its Implications 2/E* by John R. Anderson. Copyright © 1980, 1985 by W.H. Freeman and Company. Reprinted with permission • **Fig. 8.11** From W. Labov, "The Boundaries of Words and Their Meanings." In C. Bailey and R. Shuy (eds.), *New Ways of Analysing Variations in English.* Washington, D.C.: Georgetown University Press, 1973 • **Fig. 8.12** From Heidbreder, "The Attainment of Concepts: III. The Process, "*Journal of Psychology,* 1947, 24, 93–108 • **Fig. 8.13** From J. Pellegrino, "Anatomy of Analogy," *Psychology Today,* (Oct., 1985)

Chapter 9: Fig. 9.1 From Douglas A. Bernstein, Edward J. Roy, Thomas K. Skrull, and Christopher D. Wickens, *Psychology 2/E.* Copyright © 1991 by Houghton Mifflin Company. Used with permission • **Fig. 9.2** From Bernstein et al., *Psychology* • **Fig. 9.3** From Jensen, *Bias in Mental Testing,* New York: Free Press, 1980 • **Fig. 9.6** From Goleman, *Psychology Today,* 1980 • **Fig. 9.7** From T.W. Harrell and M.S. Harrell, "Army General Classification Test Scores for Civilian Occupations." *Educational and Psychological Measurement, 5,* 229–39

Chapter 10: Fig. 10.4 W.B. Cannon, 1929. In M.C. Muchison (ed.). *Foundations of Experimental Psychology,* Worcester, MA: Clark University Press • **Figs. 10.15, 10.16** From R. Plutchik and H. Kellerman (eds.), *Emotion: Theory, Research, and Experience,* Vol. 1, 1980. Reprinted by permission of Academic Press • **Fig. 10.17** Based on A. Mehrabian and J.A. Russell, *An Approach to Environmental Psychology,* published by the MIT Press. Copyright © 1974 by The MIT Press. Reprinted with permission • **Fig. 10.18** R.L. Solomon and J.D. Corbit, 1974. "An Opponent-Process Theory of Motivation," *Psychological Review, 81,* 119–45. Copyright © 1974 by the American Psychological Association. Reprinted by permission

Chapter 11: Fig. 11.3 Modified from P.D. Eimas et al., "Speech Perception in Infants," Vol. 171, pp. 303–6, Jan. 22, 1971. Copyright © 1971 by the AAAS • **Fig. 11.11** Modified from *Happy, Healthy, and Insecure: A Portrait of Middle Childhood in the U.S.* by N. Zill, 1985. Reprinted by permission of Cambridge University Press

Chapter 12: Fig. 12.1 From *Developmental Psychology 2/E* by Howard Gardner. Copyright © 1982 by Howard Gardner. Reprinted by permission of Harper Collins Publishers • **Fig. 12.2** From Tanner, Whitehouse and Takaishi (1966) • **Fig. 12.3** From M. Levine, *Effective Problem Solving,* Englewood Cliffs, N.J.: Prentice-Hall, 1988 • **Fig. 12.4** From L. Kohlberg (1969). "Stage and Sequence: The Cognitive-Developmental Approach to Socialization." In D.A. Goslin (ed.) *Handbook of Socialization Theory and Research.* Reprinted by permission of D.A. Goslin • **Fig. 12.5** From D.C. Dunphy, "The Social Structure of Adolescent Peer Groups, *Sociometry,* 1963, 26, 230–46 • **Fig. 12.6** From Kenrick and Trost (1987) • **Fig. 12.7** From Atkinson, Atkinson, and Hilgard, (1983) • **Fig. 12.8** From Astin et al. (1987) • **Fig. 12.9** Copyright © 1984 by the New York Times Company. Reprinted by permission

Chapter 13: Fig. 13.1 From H.J. Eysenck and S. Rachman, *The Causes and Cures of Neurosis,* San Diego, CA: EDITS Robert A. Knapp, 1965 • **Fig. 13.3** From J.S. Wiggins and R. Broughton, "The Interpersonal Circle: A Structural Model for the Integration of Personality Research," *Perspectives in Personality,* edited by R. Hogan and W.H. Jones. Published by JAI Press, Inc., 1985 • **Fig. 13.4** Reproduced by special permission of the Agent, Consulting Psychologists Press, Inc., Palo Alto, CA 94303. From *Manual for the Strong Interest Inventory, Form T325, Fourth Edition by Jo-Ida C. Hansen and David P. Campbell Strong Interest Inventory of the Strong Vocational Interest Blanks, Form T325 Copyright 1933, 1938, 1945, 1946, 1966, 1968, 1974, 1981, 1985* by The Board of Trustees of the Leland Stanford Junior University. All rights reserved. Further reproduction is prohibited without the Agent's written consent • **Fig. 13.5** Reprinted from 1982 Nebraska Symposium on Motivation, by permission of University of Nebraska Press © 1982. • **Fig. 13.6** The *Minnesota Multiphasic Personality Inventory.* Copyright © 1976 by the University of Minnesota Press. From Hathaway and McKinley (1982) • **Fig. 13.7** Based on Geoffrey White (1980)

Chapter 14: Fig. 14.1 From W. Weiten (1986). *Psychology Applied to Modern Life: Adjustment in the 80s 2/E.* Reprinted by permission of Brooks/Cole Publishing Company • **Fig. 14.2** From Fenz and Epstein (1967) • **Fig. 14.3** From Johansson (1977) • **Fig. 14.4** From H.S. Friedman and S. Booth-Kewley, 1987. "The 'Disease-Prone Personality': A Meta-Analytic View of the Construct," *American Psychologist, 42,* 539–55. Copyright © 1987 by the American Psychological Association. Reprinted by permission • **Fig. 14.5** Based on Melzack and Walsh (1965) and Melzack (1973) • **Fig. 14.7** *American Health Magazine.* Copyright © 1984 by H. Kobasa

Chapter 15: Fig. 15.2 From R.J. Wurtman and J.J. Wurtman, "Carbohydrates and Depression," *Scientific American,* Jan. 1989 • **Fig. 15.3** Based on I.M. Marks, *Fears and Phobias,* 1969, Academic Press. Reprinted by permission of the author • **Fig. 15.6** Based on Mednick (1985)

Chapter 16: Fig. 16.1 Based on M.C. Jones (1924) • **Fig. 16.2** From J.M. Atthowe and L. Krasner, 1968. "Preliminary Report on the Application of Contingent Reinforcement Procedures (Token Economy) on a 'Chronic' Psychiatric Ward," *Journal of Abnormal and Social Psychology, 73,* 37–43. Copyright © by the American Psychological Association. Adapted by permission • **Fig. 16.3** From G.L. Paul (1966). *Insight versus Desensitization in Psychotherapy* (Table 7, p. 37). By permission of Stanford University Press • **Fig. 16.4** Based on Shapiro and Shapiro (1982) and Smith, Glass, and Miller (1980)

Chapter 17: Fig. 17.1 Based on Fritz Heider, *The Psychology of Interpersonal Relations* (1958). Reprinted with permission of Grace M. Heider • **Fig. 17.3** Based on P.G. Zimbardo and M.B. Leippe, *The Psychology of Attitude and Social Influence.* Copyright © 1991 and published by McGraw-Hill, Inc. Reprinted by permission of McGraw-Hill, Inc. • **Fig. 17.4** From Festinger and Carlsmith (1959) • **Fig. 17.5** From Russell and Jones (1980)

Chapter 18: Fig. 18.2 From E. Donnerstein and L. Berkowitz (1981). "Victim Reactions to Aggressive Erotic Films as a Factor in Violence Against Women," *Journal of Personality and Social Psychology, 41,* 710–24. Copyright © 1981 by the American Psychological Association. Reprinted by permission • **Fig. 18.4** Based on B. Latane and J.M. Darley (1969), "Bystander Apathy," *American Scientist, 57,* 224–68; B. Latane and J.M. Darley (1970), *The Unresponsive Bystander: Why Doesn't He Help?* New York: Appleton-Century-Crofts • **Fig. 18.6** Brigham (1986)

Chapter 19: Fig. 19.3 Based on R.G. Ridker and W.D. Watson, Jr. (1980). *To Choose a Future: Resources and Environmental Problems of the United States,* Baltimore, MD: Johns Hopkins University Press • **Fig. 19.5** From *Hope: Facing the Music on Nuclear War and the 1984 Elections* by the editors of Ground Zero Fund, Inc. and Roger Molander. Copyright © 1983 by Ground Zero Fund, Inc. Reprinted by permission of Long Shadow Books, a division of Simon and Schuster • **Fig. 19.8** Adapted from *Population Density and Social Pathology* by John B. Calhoun (1962) Copyright © 1962 by Scientific American, Inc. All rights reserved • **Fig. 19.9** From J.W. Reich (ed.) *Experimenting in Society: Issues and Examples in Applied Social Psychology,* Scott, Foresman, 1982 • **Fig. 19.11** Courtesy, National Geographic Society • **Fig. 19.12** Figure adapted from L. Ofshe and R. Ofshe, *Utility and Choice in Social Interaction.* Copyright © 1970. Reprinted by permission of Prentice-Hall, Inc., Englewood Cliffs, N.J. 07632 • **Fig. 19.13** From *The Resolution of Conflict* by Morton Deutsch. Copyright © 1973 by Yale University. Reprinted by permission of Yale University Press

Appendix: Figs. A.3, A.4, A.5, A.6, A.7 From *A First Reader in Statistics* by Elzey. Copyright © 1967 by Wadsworth, Inc. Used with permission of Brooks/Cole Publishing Company, Pacific Grove, CA 93950 • **Fig. A.8** Reprinted with permission of the American Enterprise Institute for Public Research, Washington, D.C. • **Fig. A.9** From *Psychology* by Henry L. Roediger III et al., Copyright © 1984 by Henry L. Roediger III, J. Philippe Rushton, Elizabeth D. Capaldi, and Scott G. Paris. Reprinted with permission of Harper Collins Publishers

TABLES

3.1 E. Galanter, "Contemporary Psychophysics" in *New Directions in Psychology,* Holt, Rinehart, and Winston, 1962 • **7.1** F.C. Bartlett, *Remembering: A Study in Experimental and Social Psychology,* London: Cambridge University Press • **7.2** From A.R. Luria, *The Mind of a Mnemonist.* Reprinted with permission of Michael Cole • **7.4** Copyright, Cognitive Science Society Incorporated. Used by permission • **8.1** From *Psycholinguistics 2/E* by Dan Isaac Slobin. Copyright © 1979, 1974 by Scott, Foresman and Company. Reprinted by permission of Harper Collins Publishers • **8.2** A.S. Luchins, 1942, "Mechanization in Problem Solving," *Psychological Monographs, 54,* No. 248 • **9.2** From Nietzel et al., *Introduction to Clinical Psychology,* Englewood Cliffs, N.J.: Prentice-Hall, Inc. • **9.3** The Psychological Corporation • **9.5** Adapted from a survey of 111 studies compiled by Bouchard and McCue. In *Science,* Vol. 212, pp. 1055–59, May 29, 1981. Copyright © 1981 by the American Association for the Advancement of Science • **9.6, 9.7** From *Intelligence Applied: Understanding and Increasing Your Intellectual Skills,* by Robert J. Sternberg. Copyright © 1986 by Harcourt Brace Jovanovich, Inc. Reprinted by permission of the publisher • **9.9** R. Plomin, J. DeFries, and J.C. Loehlin, 1977, "Genotype-Environment Interaction and Correlation in the Analysis of Human Behavior," *Psychological Bulletin 84,* 309–22. Copyright © 1977 by the American Psychological Association. Adapted by permission • **10.1** S. Schachter, *American Psychologist,* Copyright © by the American Psychological Association. Reprinted by permission • **10.3** From R. Plutchik and M. Kellerman (eds.), *Emotion: Theory, Research, and Experience* (Vol. 1), 1980. Reprinted by permission of Academic Press • **10.2** Reprinted with permission from *Psychology Today* Magazine. Copyright © 1978 by Sussex Publishers, Inc. • **12.1** Adapted from *Childhood and Society 2/E*, by Erik H. Erikson. Copyright 1950, © 1973 by W.E. Norton and Company, Inc. Copyright renewed 1978 by Erik H. Erikson. Reprinted by permission of W.W. Norton and Company, Inc. • **13.4** R.H. Price and D.L. Bouffard, 1974, "Behavioral Appropriateness and Situational Constraint as Dimensions of Social Behavior," *Journal of Personality and Social Psychology*, 30, 579–86. Copyright © 1974 by the American Psychological Association. Reprinted by permission • **14.2** A.D. Kanner et al., 1981, "Comparison of Two Models of Stress Management: Daily Hassles and Uplifts Versus Major Life Events," *Journal of Behavioral Medicine*, 4, 1–39 • **4.4** Based on R.S. Lazarus and S. Folkman, *Stress, Appraisal, and Coping*. Copyright © 1984 Springer Publishing Company, Inc. New York. 10012. Used by permission of the pub-

lisher • **15.2** American Psychiatric Association, *Diagnostic and Statistical Manual of Mental Disorders 3/E, Revised*, Washington, D.C., American Psychiatric Association, 1987 • **15.3** I.I. Gottesman et al, 1982, *Schizophrenia: The Epigenetic Puzzle*, Cambridge: Cambridge University Press • **17.1** E.E. Jones, 1985, "History of Social Psychology," in *Topics in the History of Psychology* Vol. 2, G.A. Kimble and K. Schlesinger (eds.), Hillsdale, N.J.: Erlbaum. Copyright © 1985 by the American Psychological Association. Reprinted by permission • **17.2** From *Perceiving the Causes of Success and Failure* by Bernard Weiner, Irene Frieze, Andy Kukla, Stanley Rest, and Robert M. Rosenbaum. Reprinted by permission of Silver Burdett and Ginn, Inc. All rights reserved • **A.4** Reprinted with permission of the American Enterprise Institute for Public Policy Research, Washington, D.C.

AUTHOR INDEX

AUTHOR INDEX

SUBJECT INDEX